The James and Mary Murray Murdoch
Family History

The James and Mary Murray Murdoch Family History

The James and Mary Murray Murdoch Family Organization

WAKING LION PRESS

Cover border: The Murdoch tartan.

The views expressed in this book are the responsibility of the authors and do not necessarily represent the position of the publisher. The reader alone is responsible for the use of any ideas or information provided by this book.

ISBN (paperback) 978-1-4341-0234-8.

Published by Waking Lion Press, an imprint of The Editorium.

Waking Lion Press™, the Waking Lion Press logo, and The Editorium™ are trademarks of The Editorium, LLC.

The Editorium, LLC
West Valley City, UT 84128-3917
wakinglionpress.com
wakinglion@editorium.com

This record of James and Mary Murdoch and their family is affectionately dedicated to their descendants of this and future generations. May the story of our noble ancestors—truth seekers, pioneers, community builders, and lovable people—ever spur us on to useful and honorable effort and service. May their memory help us surrender to the unchanging truths that impelled them to walk righteously, to meet sacrifice with a smile, to tame the mountains and deserts with sturdy wills, and to toil gladly for the common good. May we, as they did, strive to leave behind us imperishable, worthy, living monuments of our labors on earth.

Dallas Earl Murdoch, President 1977–1981

To know nothing of our ancestry or from whence we came, to have no reverence for the precious memories of the past, is to ignore the elements and influences that have made us what we are. And who so dead to sympathy and affection, to kindred and country, that would not preserve the records of his ancestors, the place of his birth, the home of his childhood and the sacred spot where repose the loved ones of earth?

Author unknown

Contents

Preface   ix

Acknowledgments   xi

The Murdoch Name   xii

Map of Scotland   xiii

Map of Gaswater-Auchinleck Area   xiv

Historical Sketch of Scotland, 560–1850   1

A Brief History of the Children and Grandchildren of James and Mary Murray Murdoch   6

Sketch of Heber City, Utah, 1850–1920   8

Murdochs in Idaho   16

Statistics of the Murdoch Family, 1982   18

Murdoch Family Reunions   19

Recent Events of Significance to the Murdoch Family   35

Biographies of the James and Mary Murray Murdoch Family   **41**

James and Mary Murray Murdoch   43

    Janet Murdoch Smith   49

       Alexander Smith   51

    James Murdoch   56

    Veronica Murdoch Caldow Giles   62

    Mary Murdoch, Allan Mair, and Daniel McMillan   69

       John Mair and Katherine Connoly   81

       James M. Mair and Mary Ann Pengelly   83

       Allan Foulds Mair and Jean Ronald   86

       Mary Mair and William Lindsay   95

       Andrew Mair and Mary Ann Thompson   126

       Alexander Mair and Eliza Thompson   154

    John Murray Murdoch, Anne Steel, and Isabella Crawford   179

Mary Murray Murdoch, James Duke, and William Ryan   217

Ann Murdoch, William M. Giles, and Rachel Howarth Fortie Giles   237

Janett Osborne Murdoch and Henry Lufkin McMullin   284

Sarah Jane Murdoch, Thomas Heber Rasband, and William Lindsay   304

Jacobina Wells Osborne Murdoch and William Jonathan Clegg   327

Thomas Todd Murdoch and Sarah Ingeborg Hansen   348

Joseph "A" Murdoch and Martha Ellen Fortie   358

David Steel Murdoch and Mary Emily Van Wagenen   375

Millicent Sophia Murdoch and Edward Teancum Murdock   392

Margaret Ann Murdoch and Lewis Joshua Hawkes   405

Catherine Campbell Murdoch and David William Hicken   418

James Crawford Murdoch and Sarah Elizabeth Giles   434

Brigham Murdoch, Blanche Alexander, and Louannie Hammon   449

Robert Murdoch   482

John Murray Murdoch Jr., Minnie Marie Miller, and Cora Leona Vail Bigler 483

Isabella Crawford Murdoch and Hyrum Chase Nicol   497

William Murdoch, Janet Lennox, and Mary Reid Lindsay   515

   Elizabeth Murdoch   524

   James "D" Murdoch, Lizzie Lindsay, and Eliza Thackeray   525

   David Lennox Murdoch and Elizabeth Pinkerton Thyne   543

   Janet Murdoch and William Baird   567

   Margaret Murdoch and John Adamson   579

   William Louis Murdoch and Elizabeth Ivie   595

   Mary Murray Murdoch   600

   Lizziebell Murdoch and Hugh J. Davis   602

Writings Of David Lennox Murdoch on the James Murdoch Family   609

The Passing of the Pot   623

Biographical Sketches of Current Officers of the James and Mary Murray Murdoch Family Organization   624

Message from the Family Ancestral Genealogist   641

Bibliography   669

Preface

The principal purpose of this book is to record for posterity a general history of the James and Mary Murray Murdoch ("Wee Granny") family up to and including the third generation. The fourth and succeeding generations are given showing the line of descent of each of the family lines.

In writing and publishing the history and stories of the James and Mary Murray Murdoch family and their descendants, much effort has been made to give a complete and accurate account of them and their posterity. Much of the history is taken from the genealogical records of The Church of Jesus Christ of Latter-day Saints. These records have, in most part, been verified and are therefore quite accurate. Other stories have been handed down from generation to generation through diaries, journals, and minutes taken from family records. The stories are given authenticity through repetition, many family members telling the same story, and through personal experiences of the compilers.

As much as anything else, the book has brought together family members; each contributor has learned a little bit more of his ancestors—some of their trials and hardships, their hopes and ambitions, their convictions and testimonies. The family representatives have tried to bring each family into focus by writing, in their own way, the history of James and Mary and their children. They tell in a special way how a father and his two wives were happy and contented and taught their children and grandchildren their purposes and feelings of life.

The Murdoch family members are very zealous in their love one for another. Through their united efforts, the family has become united and blessed. There are on record more than six thousand names of members of the family. Many are sealed for time and all eternity through the marriage covenant in the temple.

Others are included in the family as in-laws or as adopted children, and receive the great blessing of being members of the Murdoch Family.

Because the children of James and Mary were always very close in their relationship to one another, this love and friendship has continued in the lives of their descendants down to the writing of this history. This is shown by the desire of the family to gather together as often as possible to renew acquaintances and to share their love and devotion.

The famous Murdoch reunions have brought together, each year, family members from all parts of the United States as well as other countries. They have rejoiced together, wept together, and have learned to love one another very deeply. The gathering has also been a fun time. The bonfire programs, the dress-up parades, the camping, and the delicious meals and games for the young and old brought much joy and happiness to all. The Murdochs were a patriotic family and contributed to every call of the government. Many gave their lives that we might enjoy the freedoms we now have. For many years the Sunday reunions were blessed through church activities. Because many members of the family were members of The Church of Jesus Christ of Latter-day Saints, this was a sacred day, and Sunday services included priesthood meeting, sacrament meeting, and Sunday School. The sacrament was served to all who attended the sacrament services.

This book is full of hope, courage, love, admonition, sadness, sickness, sorrow, and sometimes death; yet through it all there is a feeling of, and an assurance of, a life after death when there will be another gathering, and peace and happiness will once again be restored.

It is hoped that through the publication of the history of the James and Mary Murray Murdoch family, the descendants will write their own histories and, perhaps, publish their own books and enrich the lives of many who will follow the traditions and family footsteps that will lead to eternal life and happiness. Thus, this history consists of the following thirty-eight family biographies:

(1) James and Mary Murray Murdoch.

(2) Six of their children and their spouses.

(3) Thirty of their grandchildren and their spouses, if they were married.

Many family members have been involved in gathering the information contained in this book. Most of the information that is biographical or genealogical in nature has been published in the "Murdoch Messenger" and members of each branch of the family have had opportunities to make corrections and deletions.

Therefore, the officers of the James and Mary Murray Murdoch family organization make no claim that the information contained herein is totally accurate except in those instances where documentation of the record is included.

John Murray Nicol

Acknowledgments

The Murdoch Family Organization has been in effect informally since the early 1900s. In recent years it has been formalized as it now exists, with a legal organization, officers, and a sophisticated organization to help keep in touch with all its members.

Most family members are unaware of the great efforts that have been expended by current and past officers and their committees. This book is a culmination of their efforts. It has been talked and dreamed about for years. It has been the driving force of our president, Dallas E. Murdoch, whose vision and execution have brought this publication to fruition. We owe him much gratitude, as this book will bless our lives and posterity for generations to come.

This book contains a detailed biography of the first two generations of the Murdoch Family—James and Mary Murray (Wee Granny) Murdoch and their children. It also contains less-detailed biographies of the third generation (grandchildren). It is hoped that the third-generation family organizations will work toward having their own books published. Those will be much more complete biographies of the grandchildren of James and Mary and their descendants than is contained in this volume. They can thus honor their progenitors and posterity, leaving an important history.

It is difficult to give credit to everyone deserving, as some will surely be overlooked. Current family officers who have played a major role in compiling the necessary information are John Nicol, managing editor; Oscar Hunter, descendant genealogist; Janet O. Gill, ancestral genealogist; Ruth Schulz, editor of the *Murdoch Messenger;* Jack Lyon and his wife Anne, who have done the typing, editing, and proofreading; Bill Mair, president-elect and Mair family representative; Mark Cram, formerly descendant genealogist and presently John Murray and Ann Steel Murdoch family representative; Guy Murdoch, John Murray and Isabella Crawford Murdoch family representative; James M. Hunter, William Murdoch family representative, Jeanette S. Boggan, Janet Murdoch Smith family representative; Virginia H. Davis, secretary; Cuthbert (Bert) F. Murdoch, bulk mailing chairman, and Joan M. Maxwell, historian.

Another important area is that of finance. Mary Ellen Ladle as family treasurer has done an excellent job. Several members were asked to contribute substantial funds to help get the book printed. We acknowledge with thanks the Gordon and Janet Gill family; the Seth and Elaine Oberg family; the Kathryn Gauchay family; the Afton Warner family; the Bob and Barbara Patterson family; the Herman and Virginia Zobrist family and their children's families; and the Phil and Donna Rasmussen family. Without their unselfish help, this book may not have been published.

While the purpose of this book is to honor our forebears and maintain a record that future generations can appreciate, it is hoped that it will help us live better lives because of their examples. How grateful we should be for their sacrifice in leaving their native Scotland and coming to this great land that we might enjoy the freedom and opportunity it affords us. Through them we have been greatly blessed, both materially and spiritually. We have been blessed with the gospel of Jesus Christ, for which they gave their all, including their lives. Because of their efforts, we can accomplish the earthly ordinances that will bind us together as families and allow us to dwell eternally with them and our Father in Heaven and his Son Jesus Christ. These are the greatest blessings we could possibly hope to attain. I therefore challenge each of you to remain worthy of these blessings, and to instill in your families this same desire. In this way we will show our gratitude for our great Murdoch heritage.

R. Phillip Rasmussen, Immediate Past President, Murdoch Family Organization

MURCHISON, Murcheson, Murchieson. An Englishing of G. *MacMhurchaidh,* 'son of Murchadh,' Englished Murdoch. Fowill Morthoison was burgess of Inverness, 1452 (*Invernessiana,* p. 122). John Murchosone was witness in Peebles, 1473 (*Peebles,* 21). Findlay Murquhasson and Neill Murquhason or Murquhessoun were tenants in Tiree, 1541 (ER., xvii, p. 614, 647). Alexander Murquhosonn and John, his son, were cruelly slain in Caithness, 1566 (RPC., i, p. 447). Johnne Murchosoun was reidare at Kintail, 1574 (BMR.) and in 1582 Donald Murchesoun was presented to the same church on the demission of John (OPS., ii, p. 391). Ewander Murchieson of Octerteir took the Test in Rossshire, 1685 (RPC., 3. ser. xi, p. 417). Duncan Murchison in Achtatoralan and Donald Murchieson in Auchtertite appear in 1726 (HP., ii, p. 324, 326).

MURDIE. A rare surname in Sutherland, perhaps connected with Murchison or Murdieson. William Murdie, M.A., M.B., of Stronchrubie, Assynt, died 1941. Perhaps from Murdoch through (Mac)Murdo, q.v.

MURDOCH, Murdock. Two Gaelic names, *Muireach* and *Murchadh,* of different origin, both coalesce and are hopelessly confused in this name. (1) *Muireach* in MC. *Muiredhaigh* (gen., M'Vurich), *Murreich* (Dean of Lismore), *Muireadhaigh* (1467 MS.), Ir. *Muircadhach,* Elr. *Muiredach* (for *Muirfedach*), Ir. Lat. *Muirethac-us,* and in Adamnan (V. C., i, 12) *Muiredachus,* 'belonging to the sea, a mariner.' From this comes Macvurich (*MacMhuirich*), q.v. (2) *Murchadh,* Elr. *Murchad,* from * *mori-catus,* 'sea warrior.' From this comes Murchie, Macmurchie, Murchison, and Murphy (formerly in Arran). Murdac and Murdoc are found in DB. as names of landowners in Yorkshire, Sussex, and Oxfordshire. They were either Gaels or Norsemen of Irish descent. Murdac was dean of Appleby, Westmoreland, 1175. Walter Murdac, Morthaich, or Murdoch was a person of prominence in the reign of William the Lion and figures as witness in several charters, and other Murthaes or Murdaks are mentioned about the same time and in the following century. Murdoch, second duke of Albany, executed in 1425, is referred to in English records (in *Bain,* iv) as: Mordac, Mordake, Mordik, Mordoc, Mordok, Mordyk, Moreduc, Mourdac, and Murthak. William Murdoch (1754–1839), inventor of gas-lighting, was proclaimed a deity by Nassred-din, Shah of Persia, who believed him to be a re-incarnation of Merodach or Marduk, 'god of light.' Murdock is a less common spelling of the name.

MURDOCHSON, Murdoson, 'son of Murdoch,' q.v. Gilbert filius Mordaci (Latin gen.) was tenant of the earl of Douglas in the vill of Prestonn, 1376 (RHM., i, p. lxi), and John Muroksone or Murosison appears in the Douglas rental of Kilbochoke (Kilbucho) in the same year (ibid., i, p. xlvii, xlviii; ii, p. 16). John filius Murthaci had charter of a tenement in Carale, c. 1380 (*Neubotle,* p. 236). In 1421 mention is made of the land of Gilbert Murdaci (RAA., i, 56), and in 1456 and in 1472 Thomas Murdaci appears as chaplain and presbyter of Brechin (REB., i, 182; ii, 276). Malcolm Murthosoun had sasine of the lands of Camlongan-Murthosoun in 1468 (*Gallovidian*). The widow of Finlay Murthawsone was tenant of Auchinbard in 1480 (ER., ix, p. 592), and three years later Patrick Murdachsone was half tenant of the same lands (ibid., p. 595; RMS., ii, 1623). Another Patrick Murdesone was burgess of Perth, 1539. Donald Murdowsone, a follower of Murdow McCloyd, was one of those who took part in the attack on the galley of the laird of Balcomie in 1600 (RPC., xiv, p. cxviii). John Murthesoun in Otterswick, Shetland, witness, 1624 (OSS., i, 64). Murdosone 1546, Murthoson 1483, Murthosoum 1468, Murdachsone 1484, Murdachsoun 1500.

MURDOSTOUN. Katherine Mordourstoun recorded in Quodquen in 1624 (*Lanark*) most probably derived her surname from Murdostoun near Newmains, Lanarkshire.

MURDY. Andrew Murdy, servitor to the miller of Stitchill, 1694 (*Stitchill,* p. 114). Margaret Murdy in Chirnside, 1754 (BNCH). Cf. Murdie.

MURE. *See under* MUIR.

MUREHALL. Local, perhaps from Muirhall, Carnwath, Lanarkshire. Henrie Muirhall or Murehall in Leith accepted the king's coronation, 1567 (RPC., i, p. 563).

MURGANE. James Murgane in Drumtuthill, 1637 (*Pitfirrane,* 560). Arthur Murgane took the oath, 1689 (RPC., 3. ser. xiv, p. 618). Cf. Morgan.

MURIE, Muiry. Local, from Murie in the parish of Errol, Perthshire. John Murie and Andrew Murie from Glendevon, exiled Covenanters, were drowned off Orkney, 1679 (*Hanna,* ii, p. 253). John Muirie of Path of Struichill, 1757 (*Dunkeld*).

MURIEL. Ir. *Muirgheal,* earlier *Muirgel,* 'seawhite.' A favorite name for women in the twelfth and thirteenth centuries. (1) Muriel, spouse of Robert de Landeles, a. 1174 (*Kelso,*

The Surnames of Scotland: Their Origin and Meaning

By George F. Black Ph.D.

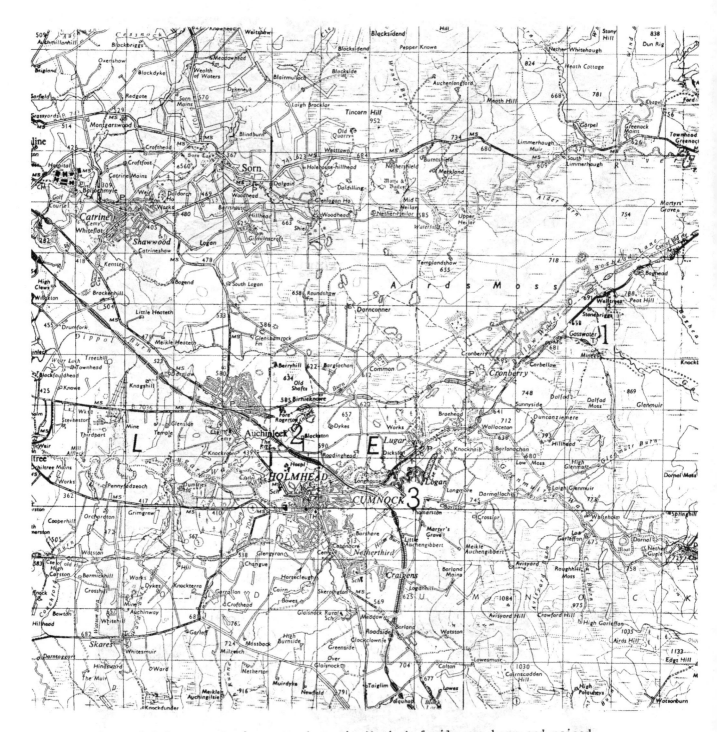

Vicinity map showing area where the Murdoch family was born and raised.

Scale: 1 inch = 1 mile

1. Gaswater
2. Auchinleck
3. Cumnock

Historical Sketch of Scotland, 560–1850

This is my country
The Land that begat me;
These windy spaces
Are surely my own.

Like our forebears of yesteryear, we in our day are pioneers. As they of long ago, we are building our world for a better tomorrow. From old letters, journals, poems, and pictures our ancestors' experiences and feelings suddenly become an exciting, stimulating fact of the present. Echoes from their past teach us lessons for the present and help us better appreciate how the memorable incidents which molded their lives have reached out and affected us for good.

With these things in mind, it seems reasonable that they would he happy if we would learn and appreciate something of the origin of the Scottish people, our ancestors, and the country they lived in. Surely that history and environment had much to do with the courage, independence, and strength they so unselfishly displayed and shared throughout their lives.

The first Scots were Irishmen, members of a tribe called the Scots who lived in Ireland. About 1,500 years ago they moved into a part of Scotland now known as Argyll. When the Scots arrived, they found other people already living in the country. These were a strange forest people who painted themselves blue to frighten their enemies. The Romans called them Picts from their Latin word "pictor" meaning painter. The Romans had tried unsuccessfully to conquer these fierce, mysterious Celts, but in A.D. 563 the Scots, led by a warrior-prince-missionary named Columba, landed on the tiny Scottish island of Iona, and eventually converted Brude, king of the Picts, to Christianity.

Sometimes the Picts and Scots fought with each other or among themselves, but finally in A.D. 844 a Scottish prince with some Pictish blood in his veins united the two peoples. He was Kenneth McAlpin, the first king of Scotland. He was a great leader and warrior who was determined to protect his people from their enemies—and there was no shortage of enemies.

To the southwest were Britons, to the southeast were the Angles, and all around the coasts the Vikings—Danes and Norsemen—were attacking. In the long struggle that followed, neither the Britons, Angles, nor Vikings won complete victory or met utter defeat. The blood of all three was stirred into the people of Scotland—the people we now call Scots.

Scotland today is joined to England, Wales, and North Ireland in a nation known as the United Kingdom of Great Britain and Northern Ireland, or sometimes simply Britain, so we could wonder what the fighting was all about. The answer is found in the remarkable Declaration of Arbroath: "We fight not for glory, nor for wealth nor honor, but for freedom alone, which a good man gives up only with his life." It was signed by King Robert the Bruce himself in the Abbey at Arbroath on Scotland's east coast. What makes this declaration so unusual is that it also said that Robert was king by the consent of his subjects and that if he failed to defend their laws and customs they would choose another king. The Scots had established a basic principle of democracy and gained their independence more than 450 years before the United States declared her independence from another king of England.

Scotland is about the same size as South Carolina, which ranks fortieth in area among our fifty states. The greatest length of the mainland from northeast to southwest is only 288 miles, but much farther by road because of the mountains. The width from the Atlantic Ocean to the-North Sea varies from 25 to 146 miles, but you would seldom be more than 40 miles from salt water. Packed into this comparatively small area are many kinds of land and people. Every few miles the landscape changes, sometimes gradually, but often suddenly and dramatically. In a few minutes you can drive from the center of Glasgow, a crowded city of more than a million people, to Loch Lomond, one of the most beautiful lakes in the world. In less than an hour you can be riding a pony across wild, lonely mountains or swimming at a sandy beach.

Many people think of Scotland as consisting of the Highlands in the north and Lowlands in the south; however, the geography is more complex than that. Not every place in the Highlands is really high, nor is all of the Lowlands really low. The mountain ranges run diagonally across Scotland from southwest to northwest and are separated by narrow valleys called glens and wider ones known as straths. The peaks are usually called bens. The highest peak, Ben Nevis, rises 4,406 feet above the sea and is the highest point in all the British Isles. Two fault lines run in the same diagonal direction. The fault which is the furthest north runs generally from Helensburg on the west coast to Stonehaven on the east coast. This is the Highland Boundary Fault that divides the Highlands from the Lowlands. South of the Firths of Clyde and Forth another fault line, the Southern Boundary Fault, runs from Girvan to Dunbar. Between these two geographical boundaries is the fertile plain called the Lowlands. Its area makes up only one tenth of the whole country, but two-thirds of Scotland's 5.2 million people live there. Within this relatively narrow strip most of Scotland's mineral wealth is found. Here also is Ayrshire, the county so full of meaning to our families. All of the Lowlands is not commercialized. As you turn away from the mines, factories, and related industries you find that agriculture is also a major Lowland industry. Fields are tilled, grain is sown and reaped, and the fruits of the earth are gathered. Cattle and sheep graze, and nearly everywhere are signs of good husbandry. Around the coasts are the ports of Clyde and Forth, Dundee and Aberdeen, where many ships, great and small, come and go; and fishing villages tell of daily bread earned at sea. Ayr is a secondary seaport.

South of the Lowlands are two other regions—the Borders and the Southern Uplands. The latter holds particular interest for us because some of our kin spent part of their lives in this area. If we placed the point of a compass at the city of Ayr and scribed a fifty-mile arc from North to South we would encompass or touch those shires (counties) that contained the villages and towns that James and Mary Murray Murdoch and their kin called home. Commondyke, Fogston, Ochiltree, Boghead, Muirhead, Glencairn, Dumfries, Sanquahar, Lanark, Kilmarnock, Wanlockhead, and Kirkconnell were found within this relatively small area.

The total population of Scotland was estimated in 1755 to be 1,265,380; by 1801 (the first official census) it had grown to 1,608,420, and by 1821 the figure had risen to 2,091,521. Each of Scotland's thirty-three shires had shown an increase over the entire period.

However, the contrast in population growth in the four fastest-growing shires (Ayr, Edinburgh, Lanark, and Renfrew) is sharp, for each of them more than doubled its inhabitants during the period. These counties were deeply involved in the early phase of the Industrial Revolution. The following figures typify the growth in those shires and their parishes.

Ayrshire's population in 1755 was 59,009; in 1801 it was 84,207; in 1821 it had risen to 127,229. Comparable figures for the parish of Ayr indicate that the population in 1755 was 2,914; by 1801 it was 5,492, and by 1821 it had increased to 7,455.

The slow-growing shires were mainly concerned with farming, and were as yet little touched by the new industries, and had no large towns. Economic causes accounted for the differences. In the fast-growing counties the cotton trade was flourishing and the rising coal industry had taken root. These counties contained Scotland's three largest towns. Overall, new life was being infused into decaying hamlets by the adoption of linen spinning and weaving, coal and ironstone mining, and cotton and woolen manufacturing. The new industries created a new demand for laborers, all sorts of "marginal" workers such as blacksmiths, wheelrights, joiners, masons, slaters, ditchers, and dikers. We can appreciate how these skills were used as Scottish Saints helped establish Zion in America. The rises in wages that accompanied the increased production benefited most members of the communities.

On comparing Scotland at the beginning of the eighteenth century with what it was at the close, the contrast is startling—a change from social stagnation to general energy, from abject poverty to wide-spread prosperity. People increasing in comfort and busy with industry acquired a new independence of manner and thought. Villages had grown into towns, towns had developed into centers of industry. Perhaps we can better visualize the transformation that was taking place by learning that by the end of the century the revenue had increased fifty-one times since its beginning, while the population had only increased from 1.1 million to 1.6 million. Students at universities were drawn from every class—noblemen, farmers, ministers, lairds, school masters, and mechanics, and from the hard-working tenants. Belief has been long and strong in Scotland that poverty should not prevent a good student from attending a university. Outstanding doctors, engineers, theologians, and scientists have enabled Scots to accomplish far more in every corner of the world than could be expected from such a small nation.

A new appreciation for cultural things was steadily growing. It has been said that "Scottish ballads cannot anywhere be equalled for simplicity, intensity—a stark sincerity and beauty of expression that shines in them like a flower growing in a cleft of rock." Our lives have been made more enjoyable from the influence that great Scottish writers and poets such as Walter Scott, Robert Burns, and James Hogg had on our Scottish ancestors.

Religion has played a big part in what Scots believe make their nation different. Nearly all Scots are members of a church, but most seldom attend except at special holiday services. Most Scots are Protestants, belonging to the Church of Scotland. The second largest number are Roman Catholic. And so it was when the first missionaries arrived in Great Britain to preach the restored gospel of Jesus Christ. From the Scottish Mission in Edinburgh we received the following Church history information:

"Great Britain is a cradle of modern Israel. It is almost as if the Lord has held Great Britain in His hands. In an otherwise darkened world, He prepared its people to receive the Gospel; and when liberty and industry and religious reformation had been established here, He whispered to His prophet, 'Let my servant Heber go to England and proclaim my gospel and open the door of salvation to that nation.'"

The man the Lord had called was Heber C. Kimball, an apostle. Penniless, he came with Orson Hyde, Willard Richards, Joseph Fielding, and three other missionaries to England. It was July 22, 1837 when they went to Preston, Lanarkshire. (The stories of great missionary experiences at Preston, Liverpool, John Benbow's farm, the Isle of Man, and Ireland have thrilled Saints throughout the Church ever since.)

S. James Mulliner and Alexander Wright introduced the gospel to Scotland in the middle of winter in 1839. Each had joined the Church and emigrated to America, where they were called to return to Scotland. Elder Mulliner stopped in Edinburgh to see his parents and begin systematic proselyting.

Elder Wright went further north to where his family lived, in a memorable episode of courage. No boats operated in that season, so he, poorly fed and clothed, walked all the way, sleeping some of the nights in the icy open. He was repeatedly troubled by an illness that a chemist diagnosed. He had smallpox. And, strangely, when he arrived at his former home, he was completely well!

Elder Mulliner baptized the first Scottish family on January 14, 1840, and five days later, at the confirmation service, received the gift of tongues—divine approbation of the gospel beginnings in Scotland.

By the time Orson Pratt arrived in May, Scotland had eighty Latter-day Saints. The morning after he first saw Edinburgh he did a remarkable thing: he climbed a jutting hill not far away—some still remember it as "Pratt's Hill"—and importuned the Lord to give him 200 souls in baptism. Then he worked. When, six months later, he attended the mission conference in Manchester, he reported over 250 Church members in the Edinburgh-Glasgow area.

What great beginnings! Perhaps now we should join those who loved Scotland and left it for the gospel in looking back to say, "Goodbye, and thank you for all the good and kindly things, for friendship, for courage and traditions, for humor and beauty."

Guy G. Murdoch

The main street in Auchinleck, Ayrshire, Scotland. Auchinleck is the town where the parish, cemetery, and municipal offices are located for the smaller communities such as Gaswater. Gaswater is located about five miles southeast of Auchinleck. Photo taken in 1975.

Where the town of Gaswater once stood, the Cairnhill Coal Mine now stands. Gaswater, Ayrshire, Scotland, is where James and Mary Murdoch resided. Also a number of their descendants were born and raised in Gaswater. Gaswater was located about three miles east of Cumnock. Photo taken in 1975.

The main thoroughfare in Cumnock, Ayrshire, Scotland. Cumnock is the more prominent town in the vicinity of Gaswater. A number of Murdoch descendants presently reside in this town. Cumnock is located about three miles west of the old town of Gaswater. Photo taken in 1975.

The remains of the old Auchinleck Parish. It was replaced by a newer facility in the early 1900's. This building was constructed in the 1400's and remodeled several times. This undoubtedly is where many Murdochs attended church and married. Photo taken in 1975.

A Brief History of the Children and Grandchildren of James and Mary Murray Murdoch

James and Mary Murray were blessed with a family of eight children. Two of these, Mary, who was born in 1813, and Margaret, who was born in 1822, both died in their childhood. The remaining six children all married and had descendants. In fact, James and Mary had a total of seventy-two grandchildren.

The oldest daughter, Janet, married Alexander Smith, and they had twelve children. Three of them died in childhood, and the rest of their children remained in Scotland except for two sons, William and Alexander. They immigrated to America and eventually settled in Washington State. Two of Alexander's grandchildren, Jeanette Smith Boggan and her sister Pauline Smith McDonald Mercer, joined with the family in reunions in 1977 and 1978. They were delightful people, and everyone enjoyed meeting them.

James married Margaret McCall, and to them came nine children. Two of them died in childhood. One son, William, came to America and lived for a time in Heber City and Park City. He died in Salt Lake City on November 2, 1899, and was buried in the City Cemetery. When David Lennox Murdoch was in Scotland on a mission from 1905 to 1907, he advertised in the paper for any of their family but received no response.

Veronica married George Caldow, and to them were born eleven children. Veronica came to Utah in 1878 with her brother William. Apparently all of her children remained in Scotland. In 1906 David Lennox found the three oldest sons alive. George was unmarried and living with his brother-in-law, a Mr. Baird, who had married George's older sister Mary, who had passed away. James lived in Mauchline and John in Burubank, Scotland. This information was given to David Lennox by a granddaughter of Veronica, a Mrs. Nichol, who was then living in Cumnock, Scotland. No record had been found of the other children. According to available temple records, Veronica had seven of her children, who were dead, sealed to Thomas Giles in 1890.

Mary Murdoch and Allan Mair were the parents of nine children. Three of them died in childhood, and one son, Allan Foulds, remained in Scotland. The two oldest sons, John and James, left Scotland first and eventually resided in the states of Kansas and Maryland. They left no posterity. The three younger children, Mary, Andrew, and Alexander, all came to Utah with their mother and settled in Heber City. They have left a very numerous posterity. The father, Allan Mair, lived in Scotland with his son Allan Foulds until he died. Allan Foulds has many descendants in Scotland today.

John Murray had fifteen children by his first wife, Ann Steel, and seven children by Isabella Crawford. Seven of these children died very young, and the remaining fifteen married and had posterity. All of these children except the first two were born in America. Only one of his children by Ann Steel left Utah. This was Thomas Todd, who moved to Idaho. Two of Isabella's children moved to Idaho, Margaret Hawkes and Brigham Murdoch. The rest remained in Utah.

William had six children in Scotland by his first wife, Janet Lennox, and three children in Utah by Mary Reid Lindsay. Three of these died before marriage, and of the others, four immigrated from Scotland to Utah and two were born in Utah. Two daughters, Janet and Margaret moved to Idaho in 1898.

A total of twenty-four grandchildren were members of the Church of Jesus Christ of Latter-day Saints, and married, and had posterity. It is the history of the latter group that forms the bulk of the material in this volume. However, it should be recognized that there are many descendants of James and Mary who also should be included in this volume but whose histories are unknown. It is the firm desire of the family members involved in the publication of this book that someday their record also may be recorded.

The following is a summary of these seventy-two grandchildren of James and Mary Murray Murdoch:

A. Births

1. Forty-nine were born in Scotland.

2. One was born on the plains near Kansas City 3. Twenty-two were born in Utah.

B. Immigration

1. Thirty-five remained in Scotland.

2. Fourteen immigrated to America. (a) Six settled in Utah. (b) Two moved to Washington. (c) Two moved to Idaho. (d) One lived in Maryland. (e) One lived in Kansas. (f) Two died en route to Utah.

C. Posterity

1. Nineteen died without posterity.

2. Thirty-three married and had posterity.

3. Twenty have not had sufficient research to know if they married or had children.

Sketch of Heber City, Utah, 1850–1920

Nestled high in the Wasatch Mountains is a lovely valley, protected by a circle of friendly hills, with majestic Timpanogos rising high as a sentinel. Lush green meadows border the banks of the Provo River that runs through the center of this bowl-like paradise.

Perhaps the first white men to view this beautiful valley were Catholic priests. In 1776 Father Dominguez and Father Escalante are believed to have traveled along the Strawberry, through Diamond Fork into Spanish Fork Canyon and then to the shores of Utah Lake. Between this visit and the beginning of settlements in 1858, only hunters and trappers frequented the area in search of beaver and mink. Often they followed the paths and trails made by the Indians. The area was also explored in 1852 by men looking for timber, and they found it was plentiful in the upper valleys of the Provo and the Weber Rivers.

One summer morning in 1857, a group of workmen at a sawmill in Big Cottonwood Canyon decided to spend the day at the rumored "paradise land" in the tops of the Wasatch Mountains. The men hiked to the summit of the range, then came over the ridge to Snake Creek and followed the river down into the valley. They brought back glowing reports of a desirable agricultural valley.

Regardless of rumors that there was frost every month of the year in the valley of the Provo, many people were anxious to settle there.

The first steps toward settlement came in July, 1858, when a party of men, with a surveyor, J. W. Snow of Provo, went up to the valley and laid out a section of ground just north of the present site of Heber City. Here twenty-acre tracts were surveyed, and each man in the party selected his farm.

The construction of the Provo Canyon road was the initial step in the settling of Provo Valley. As early as 1852 William Gardner said, "Provo Canyon is the best canyon for a road that I have seen, having fine narrow valleys, with rich soil and good pastures."

By the summer of 1858, timber was badly needed, so the building of the road began. The river had to be bridged at the mouth of the canyon. This crude road that twisted its way up the canyon from Provo City to the grass-covered valley some twenty-five miles away was significant in the settlement of Wasatch County.

Interest in the valley was divided between groups.

The abundance of grass and water seemed ideal for stock raising, but as an agricultural venture, some felt the climate was too cold and the growing season was too short, but many were willing to experiment with farming in the valley. The cattle raisers made the first attempt at settlement. In the summer of 1858 three men, George Bean, Aaron Daniels, and William Wall, drove stock up the canyon to feed on the meadow grass along the Provo River.

On April 29, 1859, a group of ten men, serious about settling, came to Provo Valley and were surprised to find three men from Juab County, William Davidson, Robert Broadhead, and James Davis, plowing a strip of ground.

The company from Provo moved their wagons to a spring which they had discovered on the east side of the valley. Here they built a wickiup of poles covered with willows, wheat grass, and dirt. It was large enough to hold thirty men. The spring was called "London Spring" as many of the men had come originally from Great Britain. The shelter was shared with the groups that soon followed and became known as the "London Wickiup." The spring still bears the name.

The first order of business was for each man to claim his section of land, either twenty or forty acres, and as quickly as possible to prepare the ground for planting.

Much of the earth was covered with sagebrush, which was very thick and hard to clear. But they cleared away the brush and planted the seeds—the seeds of crops and the seeds of a new home for themselves and their loved ones.

The men started building log houses. They decided to build close together in a fort, so they could protect themselves from the Indians if necessary. The houses were built of green cottonwood logs that were cut on the river bottoms. They had dirt floors and dirt roofs, with mud packed between the logs. By winter many of the men decided to return to Provo for the winter months, but eighteen families were established in the fort, and they resolved to stay the winter.

During the first summer some one thousand bushels of grain were raised in the valley. Because there was no grist mill, the settlers ground the wheat in small hand mills or boiled the wheat and ate it whole with milk.

To feed the cattle for the winter, it was necessary to cut meadow hay and swamp grass. It proved to be a very hard task, as they had to cut it by hand with a scythe.

For those who remained in the valley, the first winter was a long and dreary one. In November the snow came early, and in December the weather turned intensely cold. For nearly four months they were without communication from the rest of the world. During Christmas week a group of young people from Provo braved the weather and came through the canyon by sleigh and spent the holidays with families in the valley. They enjoyed a gay round of dancing and amusement until New Year's Day. Then they returned home. From then until March there were no visitors and no mail, only bitter cold weather. But this did not mean the settlers sat twiddling their thumbs or had long faces— quite the opposite. Meeting in the various homes, they held church meetings on the Sabbath Day and during the week gathered for dancing, singing, and dramatics.

By the end of March the snow was still deep and there was no sign of spring. Some began to get discouraged. So it was decided to hold a fast meeting at the home of Thomas Rasband to seek the help of the Lord. They prayed sincerely and earnestly that the Lord would cause the snow to melt and spring to come so that their famished oxen and cows might get grass to eat, and that they could plant their crops and be in touch with friends in the lower valleys. Before the meeting was dismissed there was water dripping from the eaves of the house, and spring was born in the valley.

When spring, 1860, came to Provo Valley, as the newly settled area was called because of the Provo River, an influx of new settlers came from all the surrounding territory. News that grain had matured encouraged many to come. They were anxious to secure homes and water rights while good land was still available. They came for several reasons, but each one had a desire for freedom from want and freedom to worship God and live as he chose.

In the early summer William W. Wall was appointed Presiding Elder, with John M. Murdoch and James Laird as his counselors.

About this time the Saints began planning a July Twenty-fourth celebration and some suggested a bowery should be built for the occasion. Brother John M. Murdoch said with just a little more effort a meetinghouse could be built that could serve as a church, school, dance hall, theater, and so on. Enthusiastically, everyone approved the idea, and logs were brought from the hills, stone was quarried for the two fireplaces and chimneys that stood at each end of the building, and the structure was completed and used for the Pioneer Day celebration. It was twenty feet by forty feet and was erected inside the fort string of houses. Even though it had only a dirt floor and hand-hewn furniture, the people rejoiced and gave thanks for it.

It was the duty of the deacons to make the fires for the church house. They were to furnish the wood, kindle the fires, and keep them fueled. It took nearly one-half cord of wood each Sunday to keep the fires going.

The new little town was named Heber, after Heber C. Kimball, a counselor to Brigham Young.

Along with building homes, the people began building barns and stables and other shelters for their oxen and cattle.

Because the animals grazed in open range lands during the summer, it was necessary to build fences to protect precious crops. The most common type of fence was the worm or zigzag fence. It was made of poles, but required no nails or wire to build.

For the harvest in 1860, a threshing machine was brought into the valley. It was run with horses as the source of power and threshed very slowly.

The prospects of winter looked better, as the people were now more adequately prepared. To help pass the time, a dramatic group was organized. They looked forward to regular church services and a choir was formed. Schools were conducted through the winter for the education of the people.

More than sixty families spent the winter of 1860–61 in the fort. There were such family names as Carlile, Crook, Rasband, Giles, Duke, Boren, Davie, Broadhead, Oaks, Johnson, Rooker, Damaron, Lamon, Lee, Sessions, Jones, Thomas, Cummings, Walton, Carroll, Sprouse, Hicken, Thompson, Jacobs, Moulton, Forman, Muir, Murdoch, Todd, Henry, Clotworthy, Palmer,

Burns, McDonald, Hamilton, Clyde, Witt, and Jordan. Many of these names are still prominent in the valley.

By 1861 the Church leaders organized Heber into a ward and sent Joseph S. Murdock from American Fork to be the bishop. His counselors were John W. Witt and Thomas Rasband.

Another bridge was built over the Provo River, this one six miles north of Heber on the road to Salt Lake City. A good wagon road was made through Provo Canyon with toll being charged for the use of the road, so transportation was improved.

John M. Murdoch organized a cooperative sheep herd in 1860 and cared for the sheep during the summer months himself. He was able to take the sheep far enough south to winter that they did not need special supplies of hay. This method of caring for the sheep enabled nearly everyone to have a few sheep to furnish wool for spinning and weaving into a cloth called "jean." Practically everyone wore clothing made from this type of cloth. Wool was also used to knit stockings.

Many of the settlers built two-room log houses. Everyone was busy; there was work for all. From the beef fat, tallow candles were made. The fat was also used in soap making. The settlers' menu included wheat, dried service berries, ground cherries, and squash. The cows provided milk from which butter and cheese were produced.

Wasatch County was created in 1862. It was bound on the west by the summit of the Wasatch Range, on the north by Summit County, on the east by the territorial line between Utah and Colorado, and on the south by Sanpete County. Heber was named the county seat.

In 1862 the property value in the valley was assessed at $48,350.

When Johnston's Army was summoned to return to the east, the troops passed through the valley on their way. They sold some of their wagons and supplies very cheaply to the settlers of Provo Valley rather than carry them back. The settlers traded vegetables and grain to the troops for old wagon covers and seamless sacks. In John Crook's journal he says, "The material we got in this way furnished us with about all the common wearing apparel we could get in those days, and men thought themselves well dressed when they had canvas suits consisting of pants and jumper made from an old wagon sheet"

Shoes were equally scarce. Many went without shoes. When leather soles wore out, the uppers were nailed to wooden soles.

William Lindsay tells of winters with four feet of snow on the ground. He says, "We had no overcoats, overshoes, or underwear, and how we were able to stand the cold going to the canyons for wood with our ox teams and sleds in the deep snow is hard to understand, unless we acknowledge that the hand of the Lord was over us."

By 1877 the area had grown sufficiently that the Wasatch Stake was organized, with former bishop Abram Hatch called as the first stake president, and Heber was divided into two wards. Ten years after the stake was formed the stake tabernacle was built at a cost of over $30,000.

The members of the Church built churches in the various settlements—churches where they could worship God.

The Relief Society was first established in the Heber Ward in 1869.

The first Sunday School meetings held in the valley were at the homes of the members, and as wards were organized they included the Sunday School. The Y.L.M.I.A. was organized in 1872 and in 1879 Y.L.M.I.A.s were carried out in some of the wards. The Primary was organized in 1879. The priesthood quorums were set up at the time of the organization of the stake.

The Church has always been an important phase in the lives of the people of this valley.

Small schools were soon developed in each of the communities of the valley. Children of all ages met together in one room where they were taught the three Rs. There were not many trained teachers in the area, so young men and women who had attended school taught in the various classrooms.

In 1866 it became necessary for Wasatch County to organize infantry and cavalry companies, that they might better protect themselves from the Indians. The men had to furnish their own guns and ammunition. The Indians made seven raids on this county and nearly always got away with valuable stock. Two hundred and seventy-five men were enrolled to protect the valley in this Blackhawk War. John M. Murdoch was a Captain of an infantry company. Peace was made in the spring of 1867.

The first few years in the valley several different men started merchandising businesses, but their attempts were fruitless. No one had any money, and the stock of goods in the log cabin stores was small and had to be hauled many miles to Heber. The event that was to change this picture was the stagecoach contract. In 1862 Ben Holliday took over the stagecoach route and government mail contract between St. Joseph, Missouri, and Sacramento, California. Salt Lake City was the center of the route and the hub for the branch lines that extended to towns and mining camps in Southern Utah, Idaho, Nevada, and Montana.

Every ten or twelve miles along the route were stations where hay and grain were kept to supply the horses and mules for the stagecoach.

In 1863 John W. Witt of Heber was given a contract to supply oats to the stations as far east as Green River. Under this contract, men and teams and wagons periodically set out from Heber to the supply stations. There was work for everyone who owned a wagon. John Crook said, "This was the beginning of good times for Heber. Plenty of money rolled in. Grain kept raising until oats sold for $3.00 a bushel and wheat for $5.00. Merchandise was high, also. Stoves were $150.00 to $200.00 each. Sugar and nails were $1.00 per pound. Factory and prints cost 50c to $1.00 per yard. A good wagon cost $300.00."

Two of the early successful business enterprises in Heber were Abram Hatch's store and Mark Jeffs' store. The Hatch store later became the Heber Exchange, and Mark Jeffs' store was incorporated into the Heber Mercantile. These stores ran competition to each other for many years.

Of all the phases of pioneer life which were to test the ingenuity, resourcefulness, and cooperative spirit of the people, irrigation was foremost. Water was precious to those who hoped to farm the semi-arid Wasatch valleys. At times there was fierce competition among the settlers.

The Provo River winds through the center of the valley, and there were several large creeks such as Lake Creek, Center Creek, Daniels Creek, Snake Creek, and Round Valley Creek, along with several springs from which the people irrigated. They also dug canals by hand. Two prominent ones were the Timpanogos Canal and the Wasatch Canal, also called the "Big Ditch."

In 1878 reservoirs to conserve the water were started east of Heber in Center Creek Canyon. It took many years to complete them, but they were some of the first water storage projects in Utah.

Many fine sandstone buildings and homes were erected in the area because of the availability of the sandrock at the quarry east of Heber.

In 1905 Heber installed a water system and by 1909 the Heber Power Plant was built, so electric power came to the valley.

Within a few decades after the first settlers, Heber Valley became a flourishing, growing group of communities. It was a desirable place to live, and offered future development. The cultivated lands had turned into beautiful, thriving farms. Businesses of most kinds lined the main street.

It was in this beautiful, tranquil valley that the Murdochs from Scotland cast their lots. John M. Murdoch arrived here in 1860; Mary Murdoch Mair came in 1866; and in 1878 William Murdoch and Veronica Murdoch Caldow joined their brother and sister. From this valley they received protection, freedom, opportunity, and challenge. They in turn met the challenge, and in return for a peaceful, secure, beautiful home they gave allegiance, hard work, leadership, devotion, their talents, faith, and love. They are a part of the valley, as the valley is a part of them.

Today the valley is known as "Beautiful Heber Valley, Paradise of the Rockies." (Information from *How Beautiful upon the Mountains* and *Under Wasatch Skies*.)

The Timpanogos Valley

Of all the vales of Utah there's one I love the best
Watered by Timpanogos stream and near the Wasatch crest.
Though high up in the mountains and covered oft with snow
I love its rugged canyons and the peaceful vale below.
I love these grand old mountains that round this valley stand
The cold and sparkling fountains that cool the thirsty land
The rich and fertile valley, its crops of grain and hay
The green grass on the hillsides in April and in May.
I came here in my boyhood, my age was then fifteen
Like others I had crossed the plains with plodding slow ox teams
To gather up to Zion, the dear land of the free.
For sixty years I've lived here and led a happy life

'Twas here I grew to manhood; 'twas here I won my wife
It was here we raised our family, our dearest girls and boys.
It was here I've made my dearest friends and had my greatest joys.
It is here my dear old mother lies, my dearest Mary too;
Three of my own dear children and many friends I knew.
And when my time on earth is done, it's here I want to rest
Beneath these grand old mountains near those I love the best.

—*William Lindsay January 18, 1923*

(Put together by Phyllis Van Wagoner and Virginia Christensen.)

The old Wasatch Stake House. Later was used as a Pioneer Playhouse. Located on Main Street between Center Street and 100 North.

The Sleepy Hollow School, one of Heber's early school buildings.

Heber City Central Grade School, where a majority of the greatgrandchildren attended.

Wasatch High School and seminary building where a majority of the grandchildren and great grandchildren attended school. Older portion constructed in 1904. Building razed in 1977.

The old Heber City Third Ward chapel, situated on the southeast corner of 400 South and Main Street.

The old courthouse, located on Main Street where the County Building now stands. Building razed in 1958.

Murdochs in Idaho

From among those twenty-four grandchildren who were raised in Utah, a total of seven migrated to Idaho. Four of these were William's children and three were John Murray's. The honor of being the first belongs to William's daughters, Janet and Margaret.

Margaret married John Adamson on January 16, 1879. Janet married William Baird on February 5, 1880. William and Janet farmed near Heber City while John and Margaret lived in Park City, where John worked in the mines.

In 1897 the mines in Park City stopped operating because of an economic depression. Because John was out of work and since their boys were getting old enough to work in the mines, he and Margaret felt this might be a good time to move elsewhere. At the time, William and Janet wanted some land with more irrigation water than they could obtain in Heber City, so they too were ready for a move. After much investigation, consideration, and advice, and with some financial assistance from Janet's and Margaret's brother, James "D," they bought the Hot Springs Ranch in Carey, Idaho.

In April 1898 they left Utah. They made the trip to Idaho by train. Each family took personal belongings, farm animals and equipment, and other miscellaneous items. They settled in log houses on the property.

William and Janet had a baby girl born to them five months after their arrival. Three days later, on September 23, 1898, Janet passed away from complications of childbirth. William later married Isabella Sneddon in 1902.

In 1902 John sold his share of the ranch to William.

He bought an interest in the general store, which was named Blaine Co-op. Both families grew to maturity in Carey.

They were loved and admired as industrious, hardworking people, honest in their dealings and faithful to their testimonies of the gospel.

The next member of the family to migrate to Idaho was Margaret Ann, the daughter of John Murray and Isabella Crawford Murdoch. She married Lewis J. Hawkes on November 7, 1889. Ile worked for several years for the railroad and in the mines at Park City. In September of 1899 they moved to a farm in Teton, Fremont County, Idaho. The hard work and harsh winters took their toll on Margaret and affected her health. Lewis built a small house for his family with two rooms and a small storage shed. On March 5, 1904, their sixth child was born. Margaret was unable to regain her health and passed away on March 11, 1904. Lewis remained in Idaho and eventually moved to St. Anthony in 1936. He died April 23, 1943, and was buried next to Margaret in Teton County.

The next Murdochs to migrate to Idaho were Thomas Todd, son of John Murray and Ann Steel, and Brigham, a son of John Murray and Isabella Crawford. Although raised with a farming background, they too had become involved in the mines at Park City. Since they preferred farming and livestock to mining, they were attracted to the undeveloped land available in Idaho. They moved in the spring of 1901 with livestock and machinery by railroad to the end of the line at Rexburg, Idaho. After a brief stay with their sister Margaret Ann Hawkes, they moved to their homesteads at Farnum, a community south of Ashton.

Brig bought 107 acres of a partly "proved up" interest of a settler, while Tom homesteaded on 160 acres south of Brig's farm. A Danish immigrant, Hans Neilsen, homesteaded west of Tom. The three bachelors lived together in a home on Brig's farm. At first they dry-farmed, but later they watered the land from a canal. Brig married Martha Louannie Hammon, and to them were born ten children. Rue, Brig's son by his earlier marriage to Mary Blanche Alexander, also came to live with them. Tom married Sarah Hansen and to them were born seven children.

The two brothers were inseparable in their pioneering and homesteading and in their later years as their families came along. They worked together in civic and religious activities and were leaders in their community. Each man served as the bishop of the Farnum Ward.

The last of the third generation Murdochs to leave Utah were William's children, William Louis and Lizziebell They were both children of William's wife, Mary Reid Lindsay.

Lizziebell married Hugh Davis on October 26, 1912. He worked at a variety of jobs for several months. He was a good barber but had not been to school. Since Idaho did not require a license to practice, they moved to Lorenzo, where Hugh barbered. A year later he went to Thornton, three miles to the north to barber. They also purchased a store in Thornton. Later they sold the store and bought a ranch in Chester. Although they had little experience in ranching, they learned a lot. Lizziebell loved ranch life, though it was a struggle. She worked along with her husband,

helping where she could. They had one son, whom they named William.

William Louis Murdoch and his wife Elizabeth Ivie came to Idaho in 1917, about four years after their marriage.

They farmed in Lorenzo for one year and then moved three miles north to Thornton, where they farmed until William's death in 1937. To William and Elizabeth were born six children.

William and Lizziebell's mother, Mary Reid Lindsay Murdoch, came to live in Lorenzo in 1919 in order to be near her family. She passed away on June 22, 1929. Following her mother's death, Hugh and Lizziebelle felt an urge to return to Utah. They were able to dispose of their property and purchase a merchandise store in Vineyard.

Statistics of the Murdoch Family, 1982

Since these early years, the Murdoch family has increased greatly. The latest computer figures show there are about six thousand descendants of James and Mary Murray Murdoch. The twelfth edition of the Murdoch Messenger was sent to 1,350 families. It was mailed in February of 1982 and was sent to thirty-four states and Washington, D.C. Copies were also sent to Germany, Scotland, West Africa, and Puerto Rico. Three copies were sent to APO addresses in New York City. The ten top states receiving copies are as follows:

Utah, 798
Wyoming, 34
California, 130
Arizona, 25
Idaho, 126
Oregon, 17
Nevada, 46
Colorado, 14
Washington, 45
Montana, 14

The towns in Utah receiving the most copies are as follows:

Salt Lake City, 187
Springville, 33
Heber City, 117
Ogden, 33
Provo, 60
American Fork, 29
Orem, 46
Murray, 20
Sandy, 40

The towns in Idaho receiving the most copies are as follows:

Idaho Falls, 19
Carey, 11
Ashton, 11
Boise, 10
Pocatello, 9
St. Anthony, 8

Murdoch Family Reunions

It seems Murdoch reunions have always been in existence. Most of us grew up with the idea the three-day family reunion was the thing not to be missed. Those of us who had farms made arrangements for irrigation turns, harvesting to be done, and cows to be milked by neighbors while the three-day reunion was in progress. The reunions started long before annual vacations became a must. The most important activity of the summer was the meeting together of families. Transportation was not a problem. You either rode the train, drove a horse and buggy or packed up the wagon. Few cars were around, but to be there was a must! It was a grand time for socializing. The families just met together. In 1923, someone started making a list of those attending, even though it was not the first reunion. It was important that we become acquainted with our cousins, uncles, and aunts. How we loved to sing the old songs and listen to stories of our ancestors.

Little by little traditions began setting in. Sitting around an evening bonfire turned into expected tidbits of family fun. Aunt Em and Uncle Dave Murdoch's family started with "Miss Clarinola's Ball," 'til it became an annual song. Then, as families increased in size, individual participation had to become a family group number; then it became important to see which aunt or uncle had the greatest number of family members attending. Soon it became important to recognize great-grandchildren; then when they became too numerous for individual recognition, it turned into the oldest person attending and the youngest child there, the newest bride and groom, and as years accumulated, the ones who had traveled the farthest to attend.

Vivian Park, in Provo Canyon, became the meeting place for the reunions. There was a river to swim in, cold as it was, and a huge boulder to either sun on or dive from. It was a challenge for many of us to swim across the river and reach that rock. Oh, what an accomplishment when you could battle the current and be among the big kids. There was the stream for fishing, and mountains for climbing. Some cabins were available in case it rained, but the grove of trees provided plenty of tent space and an area for the animals to be hobbled and wagons parked. Beds were in wagon beds and on the ground. Meals were served outside and because it was August, corn on the cob, tomatoes, and garden vegetables were plentiful. Chicken was the main meal course along with fresh fish from the river. Pitching horseshoes and fishing were in close competition.

It was always a special treat when the aunts and uncles from Idaho could attend. It wasn't too many years before Aunt Sarah's recitation of "The Family Pot" became another tradition. She was Uncle Tom's wife, and they came clear from Farnum, Idaho, along with Uncle Brig and Aunt Louannie and some of the girl and boy cousins.

Joy O. Clegg, Aunt Jake and Uncle Will's boy soon became the official official of the bonfire program. He served willingly for so many years and was such a superb group leader. He had an uncanny ability in getting group participation. It wasn't long until one of Uncle Dave Murdochs sons-in-law became family famous for his interpretation of a funeral sermon. That, too, became another family tradition.

For a number of years the single young men and women added to the reunions with their singing from the cliff above the boat lake. Their young, clear voices blending in beautiful harmony in the early dusk, echoing over the camp grounds, became part of the looked-forward-to activities of the reunion. It was the secret desire of many of us to hurry and grow up so we, too, could join them in harmony, singing from the cliff. The musical heritage of all the Murdochs passed on by our ancestors is a great blessing to be honored by our striving towards perfection.

As the Murdoch posterity increased there was need for more activity for the youngsters. Whether it came as a brilliant brainstorm or as a spontaneous gesture, the annual parade was born. This was fun participation for everyone! Aunt Sarah and Bessie Dawson and Maybell and Annie became unofficial officials in leading the parade. Articles at hand and the ingenuity of Murdoch minds united to create the most outlandish outfits beheld by a fun-loving people. As soon as some became senior citizens and derived their pleasure from observing rather than participating, someone was always there to step in and fill any vacancies. Some of our cousins came with beautiful costumes and hats and different jewelry that made us think they were the most beautiful and stylishly dressed individuals around. Their arrival in the parade was looked forward to with much anticipation.

It wasn't too many years until Dutch Rasmussen and LeIsle and their young family won everyone's heart singing "Rootin'-Ti'-Tootin'-Ti'-Too." He accompanied them on the guitar. This song, with everyone singing, became another family tradition.

Family reunion attendance became so large, we could hold our own sacred services on Sunday. The family organization purchased our own sacrament trays and there were always enough Aaronic Priesthood in attendance to take care of this sacred ordinance, supervised by the Melchizedek Priesthood. Later, on recommendation of our Church authorities, Sunday reunions had to be discontinued so our home ward could be benefited and Sunday wouldn't become a holiday or a day of recreation. The Murdochs having the religious beginnings we had showed no hesitation in following our church leaders.

When community populations increased and employment recreation became more desirable and Vivian Park could no longer be used for our family reunions because of public demand, we tried Upper Falls resort in Provo Canyon until it became extinct due to highway changes. When Deer Creek reservoir came into existence, the campground at the base of the dam was tried, but it was unsatisfactory because of lack of accommodations.

During the years of World War II, with restrictions and rationing prevalent, one-day reunions were tried. These were held in Charleston, Wasatch County, and we even tried having one at a Heber City motel. During this time a memorial reunion was held for all of our kin serving our country and a special booklet was printed listing all their names.

When the affairs of state settled down somewhat, and recreation vehicles became prevalent again, reunions became important. It was decided to try three-day reunions again, and every third year the annual Murdoch reunion was to be held in Idaho, with a one-day reunion in Utah. Oh, it was so much fun to camp at Warm River campgrounds, near Ashton, Idaho. It was almost a complete new set of cousins attending since the older generations were getting older or had passed away and the younger generations were anxious to carry on the family traditions. Idaho reunions were held at Warm River, Uncle Tom's cabin at Drummond, Idaho, and at the girls' camp near Big Mesa Falls.

The Utah reunions were held at the Wasatch State Park, Charleston, Alma Nicol's ranch in Midway, and Daniels Canyon in Wasatch County.

On August 11, 1973, the James and Mary Murray Murdoch Family Organization was organized with a constitution and bylaws. The reunions have pretty well followed these regulations and rules and each year we are more appreciative of the superb leadership we have had through our duly-elected officers.

On August 14, 1976, it was decided to hold the 1978 reunion in Idaho. In August of 1978, the family reunion was held in Rigby, Idaho. We met at the East Rigby Stake Chapel. At the business meeting held in the Relief Society room it was voted upon and passed by those attending to change the James and Mary Murray Murdoch annual reunions to annual business meetings, the third generations branching into their own social family reunions.

This was advisable since the population of each of the third generation branches was much larger than the original Murdoch branch. There was no place that could accommodate such a crowd and accomplish all the things the family desired. A Murdoch organization was formed with representatives chosen from each of the third generation branches, the objective of the organization being better genealogical work, and to arrange and send out a family *Murdoch Messenger* to enable us all to keep in contact with one another and to work towards publishing a Murdoch Family book. When the book is ready, we will again have a grand and glorious Murdoch reunion to distribute our family book and renew our cousinly bond one with another.

James and Mary Murdoch Family Reunion Highlights

Reunion dances: While the famous "Murdoch Bonfire Program" continued to be the highlight of the Murdoch reunions, other outstanding events also took place which, in the beginning, contributed to the enjoyment of the family members.

On the Saturday evening, after the bonfire program was concluded and most of the young children were asleep, the Uncle Dave and Aunt "Em" Murdoch family would furnish the music and the family members would do the dancing, mostly to the tune of "Turkey in the Straw." There would be rounds and squares and many of the old and young alike would enjoy the fox trot or the old-time waltz. The music was played with fun and enthusiasm. Everybody danced and no one was ever left on the sideline.

> Twirling, whirling, fun and laughter,
> A memory to keep forever after.
> Sliding and gliding around the hall,
> The Murdoch family is having a ball.

Maybell and Annie do their thing: For many years during the high times of the Murdoch family reunions, after most everyone, except the oldest of the clan, had gone to bed, many of us would wend our way to the cabin or tent of Maybell Moulton and Annie Rasband to visit and watch them as they did the traditional "Highland Fling." After a short visit the real show would begin. Out would come Annie and Maybell dressed in their outlandish Highland uniforms and do their thing. They would start slow and easy, then increase in tempo until they became so tired that they, and all present, began to laugh at the way they would cavort and interpret the way the "Highland Fling" should be danced.

Sometimes we would laugh so hard that the tears would flow. They danced so hard that within ten minutes they would be so tired that they would have to stop. After another short visit we would take off for our own quarters to wait until another time when we would enjoy another evening of visiting with our loved ones.

What great joy it was to visit with these lovely daughters of our Heavenly Father and to feel of their special spirit. Their spirit of love and devotion always kept the reunions something special to remember.

Togetherness: The Murdoch family really enjoyed being together as much as possible. We remember when the reunions first began that most everyone would sleep in the same tent. Uncle Tom and Aunt Sarah, Uncle Brigham and Aunt Louannie, Uncle Jim and Aunt Sarah, Uncle Dave and Aunt Kate Hicken, Uncle Dave and Aunt "Em" Murdoch, and Hyrum and Tress Nicol, along with their children and sometimes other members of the family would set up one large tent, cover the floor with straw, and make a common bed; the children would sleep at the bottom and the other relatives at the top. It was great fun when we could all

be together and visit with one another. Because of the closeness of the family, they all had lots to talk about. We young ones would lay awake for hours listening to stories of many happy and exciting times of a great family who had not seen one another for sometimes many years. Because many of the brothers and sisters had come many miles for this special occasion, they had much to talk about. Many of the old songs, familiar to most, were sung over and over, again and again. We would thrill as they would sing such songs as "We're Tenting Tonight on the Old Camp Grounds," I Will Take You Home Again Kathleen," "Down by the Old Mill Stream," "There's a Long, Long Trail A-winding," and many others which seemed to have some special meaning to the members of the family.

Sometimes there were some sad and emotional stories or family happenings which brought tears to our eyes. Then there were the happy stories and the stories remembered that would bring much joy and laughter and sometimes a heartache, but they all understood.

> This is a happy Murdoch family,
> A joy to be a part.
> The love they shared with one another,
> Came from a loving and caring heart.

The great fish fry: For one solid year, from the end of one to the beginning of another, the Murdoch planning committee was kept busy evaluating and working toward making the next reunion more valuable and exciting than the one before.

We will always remember the year of the great fish fry. The Murdochs from Idaho went fishing. They caught and saved the biggest and best fish, which they planned to cook and serve at the next Murdoch family gathering at-Warm River in Idaho. There never was anything like that fish fry. They took the fish to one of the local restaurants and had them deep fry them. They were done to perfection. There was enough fish to feed all of the relatives who came for the big event. They came from near and far and were royally dined. With the fish cooked to a perfection, a good bed, and the company of the members of a great family, we indeed felt we had a beautiful blessing.

The "Burdoch Tramp": How well we remember the day the "Burdoch Tramp" invaded the Murdoch reunion at Warm River, Idaho. The daylight was just beginning to turn into dark and the annual Murdoch bonfire was beginning to light up the sky. Joy O. Clegg, the official master of ceremonies, was just beginning the family program when an unwanted freight train blew a screeching whistle and began to slow down just as it began to pass through the Warm River resort. As the train passed by the bonfire, out of the darkness came the most bedraggled man any of us had ever seen. His clothes were in tatters. He had a big bushy beard and on the top of his head was an ill-fitting skull cap and he was as dirty as any person could ever be. His first words were, "Where do I find the Burdoch clan?" He came up to the fire without an invitation and began to tell of how he had traveled hundreds of weary miles on freight trains, camels, horses, and afoot through desert, prairie, mountains, and swamplands to find his long lost relatives, the "Burdochs." As he concluded his story we all gathered a little closer to the fire, completely fascinated. Who was this great story teller? Why was he stopping here?

How did he know where to get off? Indeed, there was some slight resemblance to someone we had known from somewhere. Who was this tramp who had come to find his long-lost relatives? Surely it couldn't be but it was. You guessed it. It was our own Oscar Hunter—the "Burdoch Tramp."

Wrestling, Indian-style: Who has ever heard of a woman wrestling all comers Indian-style? There was only one—Clara Murdoch. Clara, a quiet, laughing, modest, and unassuming daughter of Uncle Tom and Aunt Sara Murdoch and weighing a modest number of pounds, desired to demonstrate her technique of Indian-style wrestling. While at the annual Murdoch family reunion at Warm River, Idaho, she issued her challenge to engage all or anyone in the Murdoch tribe to wrestle her for the Murdoch championship.

At first there were few challengers. A man wrestling a woman any style, especially Indian-style, was not heard of. However, curiosity got the best of some of the most adventurous men. Gradually more and more came to try and teach Clara a lesson. Each time they were disappointed, but stayed around to watch Clara do her thing.

Clara quickly disposed of challengers, no matter what size. We watched fascinated as the champion and the challenger laid down on the ground in opposite directions; then locked their arms, and at the count of three would raise one leg and lock them together behind the knees, and try to tip the opponent over his own head and onto his back. Clara is still and always will be the undefeated champion of the Murdochs.

Patriotism: "My country 'tis of thee, land of the noble free, of thee we sing."

No people on earth are more proud of their country than are the descendants of James and Mary Murdoch. Many have given their lives in defense of the land of their choice There is something special, even sacred, as they arise each day to see the sun as it rises over the tops of the eastern hills and at the same time pay their respects to their beloved country.

It's a thrilling, exciting, and humbling experience to stand as a member of the family and participate in the traditional flag-raising ceremony. It's something special to stand and watch as the flag is raised and special tributes are given. Then to sing the national anthem with gratitude and praise gives one a special feeling of love and thanksgiving. Many stand and give special thanks and then, as they slowly walk away, they remember freedom, love, honor, charity, and independence.

"The land of the free and the home of the brave."

The flag waves its stars and stripes over many of our homes. Along with the official flag of the United States may be seen smaller ones that indicate the honor and respect we all have for those who gave their lives that we might enjoy the freedoms we now have. What a blessing it is to be free!

What a blessing it is to be free,
To choose our life and what we'll be,
To stand for all that is good and true,
The stars and stripes, red, white and blue.
The music that swells our hearts with pride.
Gives courage to the weak as we march side by
    side.
Our thoughts never turn to what might have been;
We're thankful to our God for the country we're in.
The United States of America,
May her flag always wave
O'er the land of the free,
And the home of the brave.

By John Nicol & Joan M. Maxwell

Ready for the grand parade, Murdoch reunion 1932

Murdoch reunion, Warm River, 1960

Katie Murdoch Lyon, 1960

Dressed for the grand parade, 1960

Parade with Sarah Hansen Murdoch in the lead, 1960

MURDOCH REUNION AUGUST 10, 1940
Descendants are marked *
In-laws are marked +
Friends are marked –

Back Row—left to right:
Albert A. Holdaway+, Sylvan Rasband+, Legrand Holland+, Jennie W. Murdoch and Lecia Rael, Elroy Murdoch*, Alvin Harding*, William Wells*, Darrell Clegg*, Janet Ruth Clegg*, Cleo Harding–, Elden Harding*, Lewis Clegg*, Arch Davis+, William Clegg*, Floyd Clegg*, Bud Rasmussen*, Von Murdoch*, Merlene W. Bailey–, Verna Harding*, Donavieve Nicol*, Phyllis Van Wagoner*, Paul Van Wagoner+.

Second Row—standing left to right:
Joy O. Clegg*, Malicent C. Wells*, George F. Wells+, Jens V. Holland*, Baby Lee Holland*, Victor Cram+, Emma Murdoch+, Emmet Murdoch*, Embell Cram*, Henry Moulton+, Maybell Moulton*, Oriel Clegg+, Annie Rasband*, Earl Loyd+, Afton Warner*, Nora Harding*, Aretha Lloyd*, Bina Clegg*, Clara Murdoch*, Leland Wells*, Deon Lloyd*, Lola Gammon–, Janette Rasband*, Reva Clegg+, Gilbert Murdoch*, Malinda Clegg+, Shirley Squires–, Cathryn Davis+, Betty Murdoch*, Billy Davis*, Earline Lloyd*, Marilyn Rasmussen*, Mary Lou Harding*, Wilda Wells*, Jean Clegg*, Virginia Rasmussen*, Tom Moulton*, Joy Cram*, Baby*, Mary McMullin+, Dale Cram*, Jennie Davis+.

Seated—left to right:
Dutch Rasmussen+, LeIsle Rasmussen*, D. S. Murdoch*, Anabel Clegg*, Carol Jean Murdoch*, Emily Murdoch*, Sarah E. Murdoch+, James C. Murdoch*, Janet McMullin*, Joseph A. Murdoch*, Martha E. Murdoch+, Hyrum Nicol+, Sarah H. Murdoch+, Thomas T. Murdoch*, Lizziebelle M. Davis*, Hugh J. Davis+, Udel Clegg*, John M. Nicol*, John Nicol Jr.*, Dale Harding*, Margaret N. Nicol+, Baby Rue Nicol*, Alma Nicol*, Nadine Lloyd*, Boyd Moulton*, Dale Rasband*.

Children—left to right:
Ray Lloyd*, Neil Rasmussen*, Von Clegg*, Lloyd Boy*, Morris Clegg*, Billie Clegg*, Norma Clegg*, Teddy Starley*, Carol Moulton*, Neilsen boy–, Hal Holland*, Miss Miller–, Richard Gammon–, Friend–, Miss Miller–, Lin Murdoch*, Studebaker–, Donna Rasmussen*, Carma Rasband*, Louanna Clegg*, Gail and Ruth Gammon–, Philip Van Wagoner*, Ann Rasband*, Larry Stewart–.

The reunion picture was taken in 1940 at the Upper Falls Resort in Provo Canyon. The information above was supplied by Joan M. Maxwell.

Murdoch reunion parade, 1945

Murdoch reunion parade, 1950. Paul VanWagoner, Grant Bailey

Murdoch reunion, 1945

Murdoch reunion parade, 1950. Oscar Hunter

Thomas Todd and James Crawford Murdoch

LuAnn Hammon Murdoch, Helen and Ronald Hall and Stephanie

Isabell Bratt and Maybell Moulton Reunion 1960 Warm River, Idaho

Children of John Murray Murdoch and Ann Steel and Isabella Crawford. From left to right: James Crawford Murdoch, Brigham Murdoch, David Steel Murdoch, Thomas Todd Murdoch, Joseph A. Murdoch, Tressa Murdoch Nicol, Catherine Murdoch Hicken, Janett Osborne Murdoch.

From left to right: Sarah Murdoch Rasband Lindsay, Jacobina Murdoch Clegg, Isabella (Tressa) Murdoch Nicol, Catherine Murdoch Hicken, Janett Murdoch McMullin.

A TRIBUTE TO OUR MURDOCHS
IN THE ARMED SERVICE

★

Dear relatives, though you may be in the four corners of the earth and on battle fields fighting, may you have the same undaunted courage that typified your great progenitor, James Murdoch, who went down into the bottom of a gas filled coal mine to rescue a fellow worker, knowing that he too may be overcome and whose life was lost in so doing. We are sure that the same courage and love for mankind, he manifest, fills your hearts wherever you may be.

We Murdochs assembled today appreciate what you are doing for us and our country and we feel there are no finer soldiers in all the world, because by your noble examples your buddies will honor you. Be of good cheer for there is a kind heavenly Father who has promised his faithful ones joy in this world and exaltation in the eternities.

We at home honor and love every one of you and will be glad when the glorious day comes when you will all come marching home, knowing full well that you have done your part in the world's greatest conflict. And so today we assembled in this reunion send our love to you in far away Siapan, Iceland, China, England, France, Australia, the States, on the land, in the air, or on the sea -- wherever you are; and in humility pray for your safe return. We love you and miss you, and in our hearts is gratitude untold for those brave Murdochs who left their native land in far away Scotland to bring us here to the Valley of the Mountains, where we are permitted to enjoy the peace and quiet that is ours. So as our songs, laughter and tears are mingled together, we renew our love for each other and our hearts are filled with pride for the fine type of manhood and womanhood that represents us throughout the world. God bless you all and our desire is to keep the home front bright and cheery for that happy home coming.

★

GREETINGS to our loved ones in the armed forces from the James Murdoch family members assembled in the twenty-third annual reunion at Upper Falls Resort, Provo Canyon, August 18-19-20, 1944.

★

JAMES MURDOCH HONOR ROLL
Descendants of Mary Murdoch Mair

Lt. Mary V. Hunter
S 2/c Dick Mair
Cpl. Alex Mair
Pvt. Dean Mair
Pvt. Willie Mair
F 1/c Jimmie Mair
Pfc. Victor A. Mair
Pfc. Lynn M. Mair
S 2/c Rex Mair
Pvt. Ralph W. Mair
Pvt. Daniel A. Mair
Pfc. William L. Mair
Pvt. George L. Mason
Sgt. Lamar Simmons
Alex Simmons
S 2/c Elmo Simmons
Ralph Simmons
S 1/c William L. Hunter
Cpl. Allan Lindsay
Pvt. Joseph Lindsay
T/Sgt. Boyde Clyde
S 2/c Doyle Clyde
Dale Lindsay
A/S Marvis Lindsay
F 2/c Rex Lindsay
Lt. Jay W. Rasband
S 2/c John A. Lindsay
A.A.M. 3/c Keith Lindsay
S 1/c Robert L. Roach

Clifford L. Roach
Ernest L. Prather
A.R.M. 2/c Bert Lindsay
Pvt. John Andres Dreitzler
Pvt. Tommy Davis
Pvt. Leo Farrer
Thomas Farrer
George Richardson. Jr.
Pvt. Carl Farrer
*Gold Star

INLAWS

Ralph Ingles
Cpl. Milo L. Killian
Sgt. Wilson B. Cox
S 1/c Joseph Hilton
Cpl. Elroy Widdison
Lt. Gorden Jensen
Angel Gongales
Capt. Wallace Parkinson
Capt. Adolph Neilson
Sgt. J. Russel Wall
Sgt. Harris Parcel
Ezra Van Wagner
Lt. Carl Clark
Pfc. William J. Christensen
Pvt. Dwight E. Lenzi
Pvt. Thomas E. K. Haslam

Descendants of John Murry Murdoch

Sgt. Roe Duke
Hal Duke
Milton Giles
Sgt. Doyle Giles
Rex Giles
Pvt. Lawrence Giles
Cpl. Dee Clayburn
Pvt. Theo Clayburn
S 2/c Thomas Clayburn
S 2/c Theron Clayburn
T. Sgt. Clarence Galli
T. Sgt. Melvin Galli
Pvt. Francis W. W. Byrne
Pvt. James R. Sharp
Leo A. Dean
S 2/c Cloud C. Dean
Sgt. Basil McMullin
Sgt. Curtis McMullin
Maj. Asael Moulton
Sgt. James Heber Moulton
Pvt. Boyd L. Moulton
Thomas D. Moulton
Pvt. Neil L. Davis
Lt. Col. Theran M. Davis
Capt. Floyd A. Davis
Lt. Victor Davis
Newell P. Davis
Merrill Rasband
Wayne Rasband
Mark Cram
S 1/c Joy Cram
S 1/c Raymond R. Rassmussen
Cpl. Keith Clegg
Sgt. Wallace Eugene Clegg
Lt. La Vere W. Clegg
*Gold Star
A/S Howard Clegg
Lt. Lewis F. Wells
A/S Eldon R. Harding
Capt. Richard Murdoch
Emmett Murdoch
Sgt. Joe Lloyd

Kenneth Lloyd
Pvt. Bliss Bushman
Sgt. Alma R. Murdoch
Pfc. Roy Murdoch
Pfc. Jay Montgomery
Pvt. Ralph Murdoch
Ensign Ward Hicken
Sgt. Russell Hicken
Dee Christensen
Cpl. Ray Parks
Pfc. Wallace P. Murdoch
Pvt. James Howard Murdoch
Pvt. Lynn T. Reiman
S. Sgt. Hazen Emery Hawkes
*Gold Star
Pvt. Harold Bratt
Pfc. Alva M. Nicol
Sgt. Grant B. Murdoch
Pfc. T. Verd Murdoch

INLAWS

Lt. Glen Reese
Harold Christensen
Don Charpivick
S. Sgt. Frank D. Roberts
Don Christensen
Ralph A. Findley
Walter O. Bostwick
Paul Dixon
S 1/c Herman A. Zolrist
Lt. Gale C. Loveless
Pfc. Richard K. Miner
Major T. C. Montgomery
Capt. Grant W. Turner
Ensign Ken Jensen
Sgt. Chester Aiken
William Wilson
Pvt. Darrell Brown
S 2/c Ralph R. Godfrey
Pvt. Marion E. Tighe

Descendants of William Murdoch

WAC Bonnie Murdoch
WAC Jean Adamson
Maj. James M. Hunter
Pvt. Oscar M. Hunter
Pvt. Robert G. Murdoch
Lt. Jack Adamson
Pvt. John B. Hooper
Mary Rawson
Reed Rawson

Lenord Baird
Y 3/c Joseph Warner
Phm. 2/c David Warner
Charles Clark

INLAWS

Lt. Phillip R. Gauchat
Lt. Wally Omo

Additional Members

MY PRAYER FOR ALL LOVED ONES AWAY
★

Please, God, bless all our loved ones
　　At home or wherever they be,
Out in that big open somewhere,
　　In the air, on land or the sea.

Send them our heart throbs of faith
　　And give them our hand clasps of grit,
Bless them with health and strength;
　　We know they are doing their bit.

Let them know we are loving them still
　　And waft them this grandmother's prayer,
We humbly pray again and again
　　In the dear name of Jesus, Amen.

Janet McMullin
Oldest living descendant
Heber City

Murdocks Home From Reunion

Two hundred members of the James Murdock family returned to their respective homes Sunday night, following a delightful three-day reunion, an annual event, held at Upper Falls resort in Provo canyon.

A bonfire program was featured Friday evening, with Joy O. Clegg in charge. Saturday, children's sports and an amateur program were held and in the evening, with Victor Cram, of Salt Lake City, as master of ceremonies, a bonfire program was furnished.

The Sunday morning sacred program was in charge of Mrs. Annie Rasband, and was centered around the theme, "Our Heritage." A duet was sung by Joy O. Clegg and Mrs. Maybell Moulton; short talks by Mrs. Virginia Christensen, Mrs. Ruby Hooper of Anabelle and Ascel Moulton of Heber City; solo, Verna Harding, accompanied by Mrs. Leah Rowley.

A genealogical meeting and a family dinner followed.

Family members were present from Idaho, Wyoming, and all parts of Utah.

Next year's officers include: Mr. and Mrs. Victor Cram of Salt Lake City; Mrs. Crissie Duke of Heber, John Nicol of Provo, and Mrs. Afton Warner of Salt Lake.

Reunion 1940

Murdock Family To Hold Big Reunion

The James Murdock family members will hold their twenty-fourth annual reunion at Upper Falls resort Aug. 10, 11 and 12, and all descendants and close friends are urged to join in the three-day outing.

A bonfire program is scheduled for Friday night and a dance for Saturday night. Saturday is children's day and Mrs. Jena V. Holland is in charge of events. Sunday morning, a sacred program will be held.

Included on the committee are Mrs. Nora Harding of Vineyard, Mrs. Annie Clyde of Salt Lake City, Merrill Murdock of Heber City, and William Davis of Provo.

Camping facilities are available, the committee reports.

August 1945

Murdoch Family Reunion Proves Delightful Event

After a delightful three-day outing at Upper Falls resort members of the James Murdock family returned to their homes Sunday night. Two-hundred descendants from Idaho, Wyoming and all parts of Utah, joined in the merriment.

Friday evening, Joy Clegg had charge of the bonfire program, and Mrs. Jena V. Holland directed the children's day activities which were featured Saturday with a hike, treasure-hunt and "talent show. Saturday evening, a jolly time was spent at the bonfire program, highlighted with a torch-lighting ceremony, under the direction of Harold Bailey. A representative of each of the seven generations of the family present participated. Many prizes were awarded. A weiner roast and dancing rounded out the day's events. Joy Clegg and Mrs. Annie K. Rasband, Heber City, were in charge.

A sacred program was presented Sunday morning, under the direction of Mrs. Annie Lindsay of Salt Lake City. El Ray Murdoch led in singing and T. T. Murdoch of Idaho Falls, opened with prayer. There was a duet by Mrs. Vera Muir and daughter of Heber; tribute to poets of the family, Mrs. Ruby Hooper of Anabelle; talk, Lennox Adamson, Salt Lake; solo, Doris Murdoch, Heber; tribute to the 130 descendants now in the armed forces, Miss Fay Henrie, Heber City; talk, Lawrence Moss, Salt Lake; tribute to Janet McMullen of Heber, 88, the oldest member of the family, Mrs. George Wells; song, descendants of Patriarch John M. Murdoch; benediction, Bert Murdoch, Salt Lake.

Officers for next year were elected as follows: J. Wallace Clegg, Springville; John Nicol, Grandview; William Davis, Provo and Annie Lindsay, Salt Lake City.

Mrs. Nora Harding of Vineyard was chairman this year, with Mrs. Ruby Hooper, genealogist, and Mrs. Annie Rasband, treasurer.

* * *

August 1945

Silver Jubilee Reunion Held By Murdochs

More than 250 family members participated in the Murdoch family reunion held at Vivian park over the week-end, representatives being present from Idaho, New Mexico, Nevada, Oregon, Wyoming and California.

This year was the silver jubilee reunion and as a highlight event, more than 150 men of the family who served in the armed forces were honored at the bonfire program and the sacred program Sunday morning.

Joy O. Clegg was master of ceremonies at the bonfire party and, as a special feature for Saturday evening, David Barclay of Salt Lake City, attired in colorful highland tartan of the Scotch clan, and with bagpipes, entertained with old-fashioned Scotch aires.

The sacred program Sunday morning was in charge of John Nicol, and Dr. Wesley P. Lloyd was the guest speaker.

J. Wallace Clegg of Springville, was general chairman.

Out-of-town family members enjoying the annual event were Mr. and Mrs. Reed Murdoch and son, Katie Murdoch, Mrs. Blanche Reiman and daughter Helen, of Ashton, Idaho, Mr. and Mrs. T. T. Murdoch, Mr. and Mrs. Vaughn Murdoch, Mrs. Leora Lords, of Idaho Falls, Mrs. Jean Blanchard of Chester, Mr. and Mrs. Montell Wickham, Mrs. Tressa Garret of St. Anthony, Mr. and Mrs. Bliss Bushman and family of Albuquerqe, New Mexico, Mr. and Mrs. Grant Turner and children of Elko, Nev., Mrs. Rhea Steffensen and family of Anaheim, Calif.

Attending from Provo were Mr. and Mrs. Hugh Davis, Mr. and Mrs. William Davis and children, Mr. and Mrs. John Nicol and family, Miss Donna V. Nichol, Mr. and Mrs. Lynn Starley and son, Mr. and Mrs. George Thomas and son Michael, Mrs. Velda Long and son William, W. F. Clegg, D. S. Murdoch, Dr. and Mrs. Wesley P. Lloyd, Mr. and Mrs. Emmett Murdoch and children, Mr. and Mrs. Ray Murdoch and children, Mrs. Paul Salisbury and children, Mr. and Mrs. George Stewart and son, Mrs. Ethel Wilson and children, Mr. and Mrs. Chester Aiken and children and Mr. and Mrs. Harold Bailey and children.

August 1946

Murdoch Family At Three-Day Gathering

Descendants of James Murdoch held their annual family reunion at Deer Creek resort Friday, Saturday and Sunday. Over 350 persons attended, coming from Idaho, Oregon, Wyoming and all parts of Utah.

The program Friday evening, held at the site of a large bonfire, was under the direction of Heber Moulton of Salt Lake City. Children's games and sports were directed Saturday by ElRoy Murdoch of Genola and Vida Fillmore of Salt Lake City. Joy O. Clegg, of Vineyard, was in charge of the Saturday evening program, which featured community singing, contests and a program.

Many prizes were awarded during the outing for such distinctions as oldest, youngest, heaviest and those claiming the largest number of children. Prizes were awarded to B. F. Murdoch, Bishop Thomas Murdoch of Ashton, Ida.; Ione Mallett, Salt Lake City; Nan and Nett Holdaway of Vineyard; David Hicken, Heber; Mr. and Mrs. Bob Merrill, Provo; Mrs. Victoria Dixon, Salt Lake City; T. T. Murdoch, Idaho Falls; John T. Giles, Heber and Mrs. Ruby Hooper of Annabella, Utah.

Sunday school was held in the amusement hall, which was decorated with pictures and flowers. Oscar Hunter of Salt Lake City presided.

A family dinner, Sunday concluded the three day meet.

Mrs. Janette McMullen of Heber, who is past 90 years of age, was crowned family centennial queen by Mrs. Wilda Wells Larsen of Vineyard.

Officers for next year, when the reunion will be held in Ashton, Ida., include: Thomas Murdoch, ElRoy Murdoch, Oscar Hunter, V. Christensen, Annie Rasband and Ruby Hooper.

August 1947

Murdoch Family Reunion Marks Centennial

A reunion of the James Murdoch family, held Saturday and Sunday at the girls canyon home in Provo Canyon, commemorated the centennial anniversary of the arrival of John Murray Murdoch, his wife and daughter in Salt Lake Valley.

Highlights of the Saturday program of events were a picnic dinner, games directed by Mrs. Leora Harding and Elroy Murdoch, and a parade headed by Afton Warner. During the evening each family participated in an impromptu program.

A special souvenir for each person at the reunion was a booklet containing a history of the family, compiled by Mrs. George F. Wells. Favorite songs of family members have been printed in booklet form and were also distributed at the reunion.

Bishop Mark Cram presided at the Sunday morning sacred services. Elroy Murdoch directed the singing and tributes to her grandparents were given by Jane Ann Sharp. Books were presented to J. C. Murdoch, 82, and Thomas Murdoch, 86, the only living members of the original family. A tribute to Mrs. Lizzabelle Davis was given by Afton Warner and Ann Dawson paid tribute to the William Murdoch family. Nettie Bonner sang a solo, Karen and Mary Murdoch sang a duet and the D. S. Murdoch family sang a song composed by John M. Murdoch when he left Scotland. Other songs were sung by the W. J. Clegg family and by Hal Duke. A talk was given by Darrel Clegg and Virginia Davis read a letter written by grandfather Murdoch. The program was arranged by Maybell Moulton.

Elected during a business meeting were the following officers who will be in charge of next year's reunion: D. L. Rasmussen, James and Oscar Hunter, Mrs. Zoa Christensen, Mrs. Zola Park, Mrs. Maybell Moulton, Mrs. Nettie Bonner, secretary, Ruby Hooper, genealogist, and Mr. and Mrs. Joy O. Clegg. Thomas Murdoch, oldest family member, is honorary president.

James Murdoch Family Reunion Set

Descendants of James Murdoch will hold their annual reunion on August 19, 20 and at Vivian Park in Provo canyon.

A bonfire program will presented on Friday evening. On Saturday sports of all kinds will be featured and a talent show will be conducted for the children. A bonfire program on Saturday evening will be followed by a dance. A recording will be made of the sacred program to be held on Sunday morning.

Officers in charge of the activities are Elroy Murdoch of Goshen, Bishop Thomas Murdoch of Ashton, Idaho, Mrs. Kathryn Hooper Gauchay of Provo and Mrs. Virginia Christensen and Mrs. Annie Rasband of Heber City.

Cabins and camping grounds will be available for those who wish to stay at the park during the reunion. About 250 family members are expected from Idaho, California, Wyoming and all parts of Utah.

August 1949

Murdoch Reunion At Canyon Glen

Crowding all their activities into one day this year, the James Murdoch family members celebrated one of the most delightful of reunions, at Canyon Glen.

One-hundred and fifty members were in attendance for the big family dinner, horse-shoe pitching, ballgame, program and other entertainment. Mrs. Aritha Lloyd of Strawberry, was chairman.

Joseph A. Murdoch led out in community singing, with Mrs. Donna Montgomery of Heber City, as accompanist. Dr. Wesley P. Lloyd offered the invocation, and more songs were sung, with Joy O. Clegg in charge. A report of the family boys in the service proved interesting.

Mr. and Mrs. W. L. Holland and family received a prize for being the first family on the grounds, and the W. J. Clegg family for having the largest number of members (72 in attendance.

Bert Lindsay of Heber City, was named chairman for next year, and Merrill Murdoch of Heber City, Mrs. Nora Harding of Vineyard and Mrs. Ruby Hooper of Annabelle, as assistants.

* * *

Murdoch Clan Returns From Family Meet

Concluding one of the most successful family get-to-gethers, descendants of Joseph Murdoch returned to their homes Monday after spending three days together in Provo canyon.

Highlighting the first evening's program was a talk by Joseph Warner of Midvale who recently returned from three years of study at the Royal Academy of Dramatic Art in London. Mr. Warner has also studied in Switzerland and France. He recently visited the birthplace of the family founder, Joseph Murdoch in Scotland.

Saturday featured a dress-up parade which caused much merriment and an amateur hour program in which Cherie Harding with a dance number and Arnel Winters with a reading were awarded the prizes.

Two hundred and fifty persons were served a hot southern fried chicken and roasting ears supper. This was followed by a bonfire gathering at which some 300 persons participated. Alma Murdoch was master of ceremonies and various program numbers were highlighted with a song by David Hicken who is 89 years old. Square dancing followed the program.

A sacred meeting was conducted Sunday by Dr. and Mrs. Wesley P. Lloyd and during the day a baby was christened; Steven Ted Nicol, infant son of Mr. and Mrs. Alva Nicol. Tributes were paid to all the living descendants.

A substantial funds was collected to be donated to the BYU fieldhouse and presented to Dr. Lloyd for this purpose.

Out-of-town visitors who attended the reunion included Mr. and Mrs. T. F. Murdoch, Idaho Falls; Mrs. Bessie Dawson, daughter Ann and son John, of Idaho Falls; Bishop and Mrs. Thomas Murdoch and family; Mr. and Mrs. Angus Blanchard and family; Mrs. Luanna Murdoch o Ashton, Ida.; Mr. and Mrs. Frank Davis and children of Seattle Mrs. Verna Loveless and chil,. Iren of Menlo Park and Mrs. Jea Webster of Parker, Ariz.

Committees for next year include Bessie Dawson, Alma Murloch, Ward Hicken, Hazen Hawkes, Maude Phillip Rasmussen, Ruby Davis, Margaret Murloch Young and Lizabelle M. Davis. Mrs. Catherine Gauchay headed the committee for this year. Harold Bandley headed the field house drive and Mrs. Vida Fillmore had charge of the amateur hour.

Reunion 1950

100 Utahns Return From Three-Day Murdoch Reunion

One hundred Utahns went to Warm River, Ida., last weekend to join in the James Murdoch family three-day encampment held there.

Friday, the Idaho Murdochs were hosts at a fish fry and bonfire program with Bishop Thomas M. Murdoch in charge. On Saturday, games, races and treats preceded a dress-up parade held 4 p.m. The same evening th group gathered around a bonfi for program and chuck wagc supper served by the Idal branch. Mrs. Annie Rasband Heber supervised the program.

An especially impressive Sui day morning sacred service w held on a side hill with 146 a tending. Speakers included Jc O. Clegg, Provo, and Bishop Pa Van Wagenen of Salt Lake Ci and J. Wallace Clegg of Sprin ville.

A committee to arrange ne: year's reunion was selected a business session. The gatherir will commemorate 100 years sinc the entrance into the Salt Lak valley of John Murray Murdoc and his wife Anne Steele in 1852 Joy O. Clegg, Provo, was unani mous choice as chairman witl Mrs. Maybelle Moulton and Jame and Oscar Hunter, Salt Lak City; Alma Nicol, Provo an Ward Hicken, Heber, as com mittee members. Mrs. Nettie Bon ner of Midway is family organi zation secretary; Mrs. Ruby Hoor er, Anabella, family genealogis Mrs. Bessie Dawson, Idaho Fall was general chairman for th reunion just concluded with th entire program being arranged b the Idaho family branches.

Reunion 1951

Utah county residents attending the James Murdock reunion at Warm River resort in Idaho Friday, Saturday and today include the Joy Cleggs, Lewis Cleggs and Joseph C. Cleggs and their families; Mr. and Mrs. Leland J. Wells and daughter; Dr and Mrs. Desmond O. Larsen and children; Mrs. Harold Bailey and son David; Mr. and Mrs. Clement Daley, Mr. and Mrs. Roland Harding, Bina Clegg and the George F. Wells family.

1951

Murdoch Family Attends Reunion

With memories of a delightful three-day reunion spent at Vivian park, descendants of the James Murdoch family returned Sunday night to their homes throughout the state and in neighboring states.

Approximately 175 persons attended the outing, and movies were taken of the entire camp and the different groups down to the seventh generation.

An interesting part on the sacred program Sunday morning was the reading of the honor list of 23 boys of the family who are in the armed services. Also, nine service men who are married to Murdoch girls, and seven missionaries now out in the various fields.

The Salt Lake group, with Mrs. Afton Warner as chairman, had charge of Friday night's bonfire program, and Saturday's events included a dress-up parade, also, games, and stunts for the children, with prizes in charge of Mrs. Jena V. Holland. The bonfire program Saturday night was in charge of Joy O. Clegg, and a weiner roast was followed by motion pictures of California and Arizona, shown by Lewis Wells. The day ended with dancing.

Murdoch Clan Returns From Family Meet

Concluding one of the most successful family get-to-gethers, descendants of Joseph Murdoch returned to their homes Monday after spending three days together in Provo canyon.

Highlighting the first evening's program was a talk by Joseph Warner of Midvale who recently returned from three years of study at the Royal Academy of Dramatic Art in London. Mr. Warner has also studied in Switzerland and France. He recently visited the birthplace of the family founder, Joseph Murdoch in Scotland.

Saturday featured a dress-up parade which caused much merriment and an amateur hour program in which Cherie Harding with a dance number and Arnel Winters with a reading were awarded the prizes.

Two hundred and fifty persons were served a hot southern fried chicken and roasting ears supper. This was followed by a bonfire gathering at which some 300 persons participated. Alma Murdoch was master of ceremonies and various program numbers were highlighted with a song by David Hicken who is 89 years old. Square dancing followed the program.

A sacred meeting was conducted Sunday by Dr. and Mrs. Wesley P. Lloyd and during the day a baby was christened; Steven Ted Nicol, infant son of Mr. and Mrs. Alva Nicol. Tributes were paid to all the living descendants.

A substantial funds was collected to be donated to the BYU fieldhouse and presented to Dr. Lloyd for this purpose.

Out-of-town visitors who attended the reunion included Mr. and Mrs. T. F. Murdoch, Idaho Falls; Mrs. Bessie Dawson, daughter Ann and son John, of Idaho Falls; Bishop and Mrs. Thomas Murdoch and family; Mr. and Mrs. Angus Blanchard and family; Mrs. Luanna Murdoch of Ashton, Ida.; Mr. and Mrs. Frank Davis and children of Seattle; Mrs. Verna Loveless and children of Menlo Park and Mrs. Jean Webster of Parker, Ariz.

Committees for next year include Bessie Dawson, Alma Murdoch, Ward Hicken, Hazen Hawkes, Maude Phillip Rasmussen, Ruby Davis, Margaret Murdoch Young and Lizabelle M. Davis. Mrs. Catherine Gauchay headed the committee for this year. Harold Bandley headed the field house drive and Mrs. Vida Fillmore had charge of the amateur hour.

• • •

James Murdock Reunion Held Over Weekend

The James Murdoch family met for its annual reunion Saturday and Sunday at a Midway resort.

Saturday was devoted to general visiting, a dress-up parade and swimming. In the evening a lovely community supper was prepared and served to the 200 family members from Utah, Idaho, California and Texas, and two guests from Kansas City, Mo. by the Heber relatives.

A splendid program followed under the direction of Joy O. Clegg whose daughter Mrs. Janet Sundbloom accompanied all the musical numbers. Each family was called on for a part on the program.

Sunday the group met in the afternoon for a sacred meeting conducted by Paul Van Wagoner. Special tribute was paid to Mrs. Mary Murray Murdoch, the grandmother of the family, who was called "Wee Granny." Wee Granny was a member of the ill-fated Martin Handcart Company. As this is the Centennial year, the program followed the theme of the Handcart crossing.

Afton M. Warner recited a poem, Phyllis Van Wagener sang a solo, Annie Rasband read items of family happenings since the last reunion, Ruby M. Hooper gave the family genealogy report and Virginia Christensen gave the history of Wee Granny. ElRoy Murdoch conducted community singing of Scotch songs with Donna Montgomery at the piano.

Announcement was made that the next reunion will be held in Idaho at the Warm River Resort June 28-29-30, 1957.

July 21-22 1956

200 Attend Reunion at Heber City

Two hundred members of the James Murdoch family met for a three-day reunion at the El Rancho motel in Heber City. Swimming and an amateur program followed dinner at Luke's in Midway Saturday, with games, singing and children's prizes entertaining the group. Mr. and Mrs. William M. Davis were in charge of Saturday's program.

A dress-up parade and a bonfire program were enjoyed Saturday evening with Joy O. Clegg in charge. Oscar Hunter gave humorous skits; Doyle, Mary Jean and Kathleen Davis sang songs dressed in Scotch attire. Prizes were awarded to James C. Murdoch as the oldest family member; Effie M. Hunter, oldest member of the William Murdoch family; Dennis James, son of Mr. and Mrs. David Hooper, youngest baby; Mrs. Gail C. Loveless of Whippney, N.J., having traveled the longest distance to attend.

A sacred program was held Sunday afternoon at the Memorial hall. Preliminary music was played by Mrs. Clayton Montgomery who played a series of old Scotch airs at the organ. David Warner was in charge of the program which included a solo, Doris Mohoney; tribute to William Murdoch and family, James C. Murdoch song, a recording made several years ago of "Scotland, Oh, My Scotland;" reading "The House Where I Was Born," by David C. Murdoch, read by Mrs. Joseph Warner. A tribute was paid to Mrs. Lizzebelle M. Davis, only remaining child of William Murdoch and she read the history of her father. A report was given by Mrs. Ruby Hooper, family genealogist.

The William Murdoch family was in charge of this year's reunion with Mrs. Davis acting as chairman.

• • •

Recent Events of Significance to the Murdoch Family

One of the most exciting chapters in the history of the Murdoch family is the one relating to the recent past. It is during this period that the family officially became organized with constitution and by-laws, the *Murdoch Messenger* became a reality, a computerized file of all family members was initiated, and the publication of this book was completed. The purpose of this chapter is to record for posterity that story and to give recognition to dedicated family members who sacrificed incredible time, talent, and financial resources to make this all a reality.

Over the years there were many family members who saw the need to record the history of the family. One such individual was Joseph A. Murdoch, son of Ann Steel and John Murray Murdoch. In the late 1930's, he collected many biographies of the descendants of James and "Wee Granny" T-Murdoch. A copy of these early biographies is found in the Church genealogical library. Later R. Phillip Rasmussen collected a series of biographies on the lives of James and Mary Murray Murdoch and their children and printed a number of these in a small edition. This edition was widely distributed at family reunions for a number of years and served as the primary source of information for hundreds of family members about our early progenitors.

It is perhaps to Phil Rasmussen more than any other individual that the family owes a debt of gratitude for catching a vision of things that needed to be done in our family organization and seeing that they were accomplished. Phil is the son of LeIsle and Lorin "Dutch" Rasmussen, and is a sixth generation descendant of Ann Steel and John Murray Murdoch through their daughter Sarah Jane. He attended many of the Murdoch reunions in his growing years and developed a strong love for his progenitors and the family members he associated with at the reunions.

In 1969, the annual reunion was held at Bear Gulch, north of Ashton, Idaho. In attendance at that reunion was Dallas E. Murdoch, son of Brigham Dallas Murdoch and Winona Lee. He came to the reunion because of a desire he had to become better acquainted with his Murdoch relatives. At the conclusion of this reunion he was placed in charge of the next reunion which was to be held in Idaho in three years.

The reunion of 1972 was held at Warm River, just north of Ashton. This had been a traditional place for Murdoch reunions in years past and being there evoked memories of earlier times by those present. One highlight of this reunion was a report given by B. Dallas Murdoch on the "History of the Murdoch Family in Idaho." This report was later enlarged and refined and is a chapter in this book. Following this reunion, Dallas was again designated to be in charge of the next reunion to be held in Idaho in the year of 1975.

The reunion which was held in Heber Valley in August, 1973 was one that held special significance in terms of the future direction of the Murdoch family. Under the direction of Phil Rasmussen, a constitution and by-laws were adopted by the family. It provided for a definite slate of officers, outlined their duties and terms of office, and defined the purpose and goals of the family organization. It stated that in 1974 there would be an election of officers, with their terms of office to extend for three years.

The reunion of 1974 was again held in Heber Valley, and at that time a -group of officers were formally elected. Phil Rasmussen was chosen as president, John Nicol as first vice-president and Dallas E. Murdoch as second vice-president. The secretary-treasurer was Phyllis VanWagner. She had already served in this capacity for many years. Evan Murdoch was designated as historian.

The year 1975 was again the year for the Murdoch's in Idaho to host the reunion. It was held between the Ashton City Park and the auditorium of an adjacent Ashton school. Reed Murdoch, the custodian of the school, was very helpful in arranging the facility.

Since our nation was approaching its two-hundredth

birthday, Dallas E. Murdoch felt impressed that the family should have a program that would emphasize its rich cultural history. He asked his sister, Ruth Murdoch Schulz, to write a play that could be presented in the auditorium. She wrote a play which she entitled "The Good Shepherd Calls to Zion." She utilized a readers theater type approach in which actors representing the various progenitors told of their story in being converted to the Church, of coming to Zion, and of the many trials they faced in so doing. During the presentation of the play she arranged for actual descendants of the various individuals portrayed to play the part of their ancestor.

The result was a very moving story of struggle, hardship, sorrow, and accomplishment. Many tears were shed as family members received a personal witness of what their ancestors had gone through to enable them to receive the blessings they enjoyed.

Following this reunion, Janet Gill was designated as the family genealogist. Janet is a fifth generation descendant of William Murdoch through his son James. She possesses a deep-felt desire to see the Murdoch family members more united in their cultural and spiritual roots. Also Jim Baird, a fifth generation descendant of William Murdoch, was designated to be in charge of the next reunion to be held in Idaho. The next two years were ones of struggle for the officers of the family organization. Now that the family was organized, they needed to define their goals, the scope of their activity, and what they hoped to achieve as a family organization. At the suggestion of President Phil Rasmussen, a series of meetings were held at which time the various officers were able to discuss the needs of the Murdoch family as an ancestral organization, and what were worthwhile objectives.

Reunions were attracting upwards of 150 people each summer, but there were thousands of Murdochs who were out of touch with the family organization. An inadequate mailing list made it difficult to keep everyone informed as to what was happening. Since the release of Ruby Hooper as family genealogist, there had been little done by the family organization in genealogical research. As the executive committee of the family organization met and prayerfully considered the problems and challenges they faced, they reached the following conclusions:

1. The Murdoch family was rapidly growing larger, was becoming more and more scattered, and the annual reunions were not reaching the vast majority of them.

2. Children were growing up without an apprecia-

tion of the rich cultural heritage they should be aware of as members of the Murdoch family.

3. Since most members of the family were members of The Church of Jesus Christ of Latter-day Saints, it would be well to follow Church guidelines in the direction the family organization followed.

With these thoughts in mind the executive committee came to the following conclusions as to the course of action they intended to follow:

1. A computerized list of all the descendants of James and Mary Murray Murdoch would be gathered. From this list of names a program could be developed to mail information to all members of the family included in the file.

2. A family newsletter would be published as the primary vehicle to keep the entire family in touch with one another and for genealogical purposes.

3. Eventually the main Murdoch reunion would become a correlating reunion with individual grandchildren (third generation) families encouraged to hold their own social reunions.

On March 12, 1977, a meeting of all officers of the family organization was held in Salt Lake City, Utah, under the direction of President Phil Rasmussen. Mark Cram, a fifth generation descendant of John Murray Murdoch and Ann Steel through their daughter Sarah Jane, was asked to serve as descendant genealogist in charge of developing a computerized mailing list. With advice and counsel from Heber Moulton, the son of Maybell and Thomas Moulton, Mark accomplished a marvelous task. He spent countless hours setting up the file and compiling the several thousand names that were turned in by family members. This responsibility was later assumed by Oscar Hunter.

At this meeting it was decided to send out a family periodical that was named the *Murdoch Messenger.* Ruth Murdoch Schulz, who had made such a contribution to family literature in writing the play for the reunion of 1975, was asked to serve as the editor. Bert Murdoch, a fourth generation son of Joseph A. Murdoch, was designated as mailing chairman. The first edition was to be printed and mailed during April, 1977. All those present at the meeting felt a great rejoicing and realized that family history was being made.

Another important event for the family occurred on May 1, 1977. Under the direction of President Phil Rasmussen, the James and Mary Murray Murdoch Family Charitable Trust was officially and legally formed. As a result of this action, the family organization legally became a non-profit entity and all donations to it were tax-exempt. It also qualified for a non-profit mailing permit allowing issues of the *Murdoch Messenger* to be sent at a greatly reduced cost.

The annual Murdoch family reunion for 1977 was held at Midway, Utah, on August 12 and 13. Dallas E. Murdoch was sustained as president of the family organization. During the annual business meeting he submitted a list of goals to the family members present. They were unanimously approved by all present. The following is a list of those goals as printed in the October 1977 issue of the *Murdoch Messenger*:

1. Continue publishing the *Messenger* in its present format until all third generation biographical data has been accumulated. It is assumed the *Messenger* will continue to be published, but it will become more of a current events, genealogical correlation, and items of interest type of publication.

2. Publish a book on the James and Mary Murray Murdoch family history. It will include biographical and genealogical material published in the *Messenger* down to the third generation level, plus other pertinent information about each branch of the family.

3. Establish long-term objectives for genealogical research, correlation, family filing system, and printing and distribution of the information.

4. Continue holding the annual reunion of the James and Mary Murray Murdoch family (the ancestral family). This reunion will serve primarily to correlate the accumulation of genealogical and biographical material with individual family members and the various branches of the family.

5. Organize the various third generation branches of the family and encourage each family member to attend the reunion of that branch of the family of which they are a member.

At that time the organizational structure of the family organization was changed to a 'president and a board of directors. Each second generation family member was entitled to one member on the board of directors, except John Murray Murdoch who, because of his large posterity was given two members; one representing the descendants of Ann Steel and one representing the descendants of Isabella Crawford. Those chosen to serve on the board of directors were as follows:

William (Bill) Mair: Mary Murdoch Mair
Mark Cram: John M. Murdoch and Ann Steel
Guy Murdoch: John M. Murdoch and Isabella Crawford
James Baird: William Murdoch

Jeanette Boggan: Janet Murdoch Smith
(Veronica Murdoch Caldow Giles and James Murdoch both have descendants, but they are not known to the Murdoch family organization at this time.)

Officers sustained at this time were as follows: Mary Ellen Maxwell Ladle: Secretary-treasurer Janet Oberg Gill Family genealogist

Janet Oberg Gill: Family genealogist

Ruth Murdoch Schulz: Editor of the *Murdoch Messenger*

Cuthbert Fortie (Bert) Murdoch: Bulk mailing chairman

In November, 1977, a meeting was held in Salt Lake City of all the officers of the family organization. At that time Oscar Hunter was asked to serve as a descendant genealogist. He assumed the work began by Mark Cram in developing a computerized list of all members of the Murdoch family. Janet Gill was designated as the ancestral genealogist. Virginia Davis was sustained as secretary, and Mary Ellen Ladle, who had been serving both as secretary and treasurer, became the family treasurer.

The annual reunion of the family in 1978 was held in Rigby, Idaho, on August 10, 11, and 12. At that time Joan Maxwell, a daughter of Joseph A. Murdoch, was sustained as family historian. President Dallas E. Murdoch proposed, and it was accepted by those present, to discontinue holding the annual social reunion in the summer of each year. Instead an annual meeting would be held in the spring of each year to correlate the activity between the various branches of the family. This change would allow the third and fourth generation families to hold a social-type reunion each summer and not create a conflict with the ancestral family.

At the close of the meeting, Jim Baird, who was in charge of the reunion in Rigby, was released as the member of the board of directors over the William Murdoch branch of the family. He was replaced by William Murdoch, Jr., a fifth generation son of William Murdoch. William was later called to serve a mission for the Church and this position is presently filled by James Murdoch Hunter.

The years from 1977–1982 were filled with much activity in terms of gathering biographical material and publishing it in the *Messenger*. Two members of the family organization in particular stood out for the tremendous effort they made in behalf of family members. One of these was Ruth Murdoch Schulz. Ruth and her husband, Alan, live in Salt Lake City, and are the parents of two children, Rebecca and Mark. During this time Alan was a bishop and Ruth was stake Primary president She devoted countless hours of effort in gathering material that appeared in the *Messenger.* Assisting her were her mother-in-law, Mary E. Schultz, and a niece, Stephanie Hall. During this time a total of twelve editions of the *Messenger* have been published. They have included biographies, family group sheets, pictures, and other material on the lives of James and Mary Murdoch, their children, and all grandchildren for which a record could be obtained. A total of over fifty biographies were printed. This material is the foundation for the contents of this book and so to a great extent the existence of this book is a tribute to the dedicated efforts of Ruth and her staff.

From the beginning, the *Messenger* has been sent to every household on the computerized list of family members. The first mailing went to 776 households and the last mailings went to more than 1400 families. Each family was asked to pay $10.00 per year in dues. Interesting enough, although the budget was extremely close, when it was time to mail a new edition of the *Messenger,* there was always enough money in the bank to pay for it.

The other individual who played a key role in the success of this endeavor was Oscar Murdoch Hunter. Oscar is a fifth generation descendant of William Murdoch. He and his wife Orpha are the parents of five children and live in Salt Lake City. He has long been a supporter of Murdoch reunions and would often come to a reunion dressed as a "Wandering Jew" or some other unusual character. For years at reunion-time, he would keep track of his Murdoch relatives in a loose-leaf folder. When he was asked to take Mark Cram's place as the descendant genealogist and update the computerized mailing list, it was as if he had been asked to fulfill a role that he had been foreordained to in the pre-existence. He literally took six months from his work to complete and update the file. Because of his efforts we now have approximately 6,000 names of descendants of James and Mary in our file. It is because of dedicated efforts of family members like Ruth and Oscar that this book has become a reality.

During the summer of 1979, after much thought and prayer, President Dallas E. Murdoch and past president Phillip Rasmussen journeyed to Orem and asked John Nicol to serve the family as the editor of this book. John is the son of Isabella Crawford Murdoch and Hyrum Chase Nicol. He is a retired school principal and he and his wife Margaret are the parents of seven children. They had just recently returned home from serving a mission in Florida. Prior to his mission call he had been involved in printing a book on the history of Orem. John accepted the call very graciously and with his usual enthusiasm rolled up his sleeves and went to work. His assignment included overall responsibility for the contents of the book, working with the publisher and the typist, and in general being the sparkplug for the whole operation. He has worked very closely with Joan Maxwell, the family historian.

Joan was given the assignment to oversee the collection of that section of this book that is historical in nature. Joan and her husband Glen live in Rigby, Idaho, and are the parents of four children. She came by this assignment naturally, since her own father, Joseph, had served the family as a historian and genealogist for a number of years. She is another dedicated family member who has put in many hours to see this work become a reality.

Early in 1980, as the time drew nearer for the actual assembly and printing of the book, Phil Rasmussen was asked to accept a very important assignment as the finance chairman for the book. After some consideration he decided that in order to raise enough money to make the down payment, he would ask various members of the family for a donation of upwards of $1,000.00. Family members responded to this request, and their contributions provided a great help in financing this book and making it possible for family members to obtain it at the lowest cost possible. There is a page elsewhere in this book to honor these wonderful family members. The balance of the book was financed by sending an order to all family members in the computerized mailing list and asking them to order as many books as they desired with a $10.00 payment in advance for each book ordered.

At the annual meeting on April 19, 1980, at the Church's genealogical building in Salt Lake City, a motion was made and approved by family members present to engage Community Press of Provo to print 2,500 copies of this book to be known as *The James and Mary Murray Murdoch Family History.* The knowledge that this work was soon to be accomplished brought a feeling of jubilation to all who had worked so hard to make it a reality.

During the summer and fall of 1980, there was a concentrated effort by family members to complete their assignments for the material contained within this book so that it could then be edited, proofread, and typed into its final book form and sent to the publisher for publication. Family officers were very desirous of finding someone in the family who was professionally qualified to accept this difficult assignment. The Lord blessed them through the selection of Jack M. Lyon to accomplish this difficult task. Jack is the son of Glade and Katie Lyon and was born and raised in Ashton, Idaho. His wife is the former Cecilia Anne Williams, and she typed the book. They are the parents of four children and are presently living in Magna, Utah. He graduated from Brigham Young University and is the associate editor of Deseret Book Company in Salt Lake City. Through Jack's professional skill and personal concern this book has become a literary accomplishment that each member of the Murdoch family can be proud of.

All members of the family who have been involved in this work have felt the spirit of the Lord and sensed the importance of this work being completed. The influence of this book on future generations will be endless as they obtain from it an appreciation of their rich heritage and of the blessings they presently enjoy because of the faith and sacrifice of a noble ancestry.

It is the desire of the family officers that this book will be a springboard for many more books to follow. Each third generation family should write a book about their third generation ancestor that will be a sequel to this book. It should be a much more complete biography of the third generation family than is contained in this volume.

May we as members of this great Murdoch family organization accept this challenge to perpetuate the memories of our glorious ancestors, that the "Hearts of the children will turn to the fathers and the hearts of the fathers will turn to the children," that we may have a family record worthy of all acceptation when that great and dreadful day of the Lord will come.

Dallas E. Murdoch

Biographies of the James and Mary Murray Murdoch Family

James and Mary Murray Murdoch

James and Mary were married in Auchinleck, Ayrshire, Scotland, January 10, 1811. We have little recorded history of James except that he was born about 1786, at Commondyke, Ayrshire, Scotland. His father was James Murdoch and his mother Janet Osborne. He was said to be a second cousin of William Murdoch, the inventor of gas lighting. He was employed at the Lime Works in Gaswater, Ayrshire, and on October 20, 1831, lost his life trying to rescue a man who had fallen a victim of foul air in the bottom of a new mine shaft they were sinking. Both were overcome by the gas and died.

Mary, or Wee Granny, as she was called, was born October 13, 1782, at Glencairn, Dumfries, Scotland. Her father was John Murray, and Margaret McCall was her mother. We know very little of Mary until 1811, when on January 10, she married James Murdoch.

They were the parents of eight children; they were: Janet, who married Alexander Smith; Mary, who died in childhood; James, who married Margaret McCall (the same name as Mary Murdoch's mother); Veronica, who married George Caldow; Mary, who married Allan Mair; John Murray, who married Ann Steel and Isabella Crawford; Margaret, who died in childhood; and William, who married Janet Lennox and Mary Reid Lindsay.

Mary was a hard worker and was a thrifty, frugal wife, and a kind and loving mother to her children. She knew how to control them and still retain their love and respect. She was four feet seven inches tall, weighing a little over ninety pounds, with blue-gray eyes and with a medium complexion.

The sudden death of her husband caused Mary much grief and sorrow, yet she had a brave and courageous spirit, and she was always able to prove herself equal to her task, as she did in the trial of losing her husband.

Wee Granny, as we affectionately know her, was left with six children, and an orphaned niece, Margaret Murray, who was about four years of age. The four oldest children, Janet, James, Veronica, and Mary, were old enough to work and do for themselves. John was ten years of age and William was six. Wee Granny found work for herself as well as the older children, and they were able to provide the necessities of life.

A few years after her husband's death, she was able, with the help of her sons, to build a little thatched-roof stone cottage which they could call their own. Much love and happiness was crowded into its four walls.

In 1907 William Lindsay visited Ayrshire and saw the ruins of Wee Granny's cottage. He also saw the spot where James Murdoch lost his life. The shaft in which he died was just a new one and was about twenty-five feet deep, but after the tragedy it was never sunk any deeper, but was allowed to cave in and fill up. The depression was about five feet deep and had wild daisies growing in it.

In 1850 the Mormon elders came to Scotland preaching the restored gospel. John, who was married, readily accepted it. Wee Granny and Mary, her daughter, made a careful and prayerful investigation of the new doctrine and they were also convinced of its truth. They were baptized by those who held the priesthood and could officiate in this ordinance. Wee Granny was sixty-seven years old at this time. Later Veronica and William were baptized. These four, John, Mary, Veronica, and William were the children who came to Utah.

In 1852, John, his wife, and two children immigrated to Utah, and in 1856 he sent his mother the money that she might come to Zion. Wee Granny was almost seventy-four years of age when she started on the long, wearisome 6,000-mile journey, alone as far as her family was concerned, but in the company with John's brother-in-law, James Steel, and his wife and two children, George and James. She had a determined will to accomplish what she deemed was right. She loved the gospel, and her desire was to be with her son and Saints in Zion. When she arrived at Iowa City, she was assigned to the Martin Handcart Company.

There were five companies to leave in the summer of 1856. The first three arrived safely with little difficulty, but the Martin and Willie companies met with tragedy. Because wagons and oxen were very expensive, these groups used handcarts that they could pull themselves. They could actually walk faster than the slow, plodding oxen. Because the handcarts and tents were not ready, the Martin and Willie companies were forced to wait until late July. They were advised not to make the trek so late in the season, but it was their desire to go.

The Martin Company was the last to leave. This group was made up largely of immigrants from England, Scotland, and Scandinavia. Many of them were women, children, and aged. They left Iowa City on July 28, and it was a month later that they left Florence, Nebraska, the last settlement for hundreds of miles. Their hastily constructed handcarts were made of unseasoned wood, and they fell to pieces in the hot prairie sun. It took precious time to repair them. The Cheyennes were on the warpath, and word came to the suffering pioneers of massacres by the red man. A.W. Babbitt, secretary of Utah Territory, and some of his party had been killed. Their food was very scarce, and they were weakened by the lack of nourishment. They were improperly clad for the inclement weather. An early and severe winter had set in. By September there were heavy frosts. Of the 575 members of the company, almost one fourth of them died before they reached Utah. They were buried in shallow graves, usually wrapped only in a sheet. Sometimes a common grave was dug and all who died that day were buried together. Some poor souls were buried in a bank of snow. Much has been written of the handcart pioneers, and their history is Wee Granny's history. Wee Granny trudged bravely on as far as Chimney Rock, Nebraska. Here she succumbed to fatigue, exposure, and the hardships of the journey on October 3, 1856. Her weary, worn-out body was buried in a shallow grave, without a coffin, by the side of the wagon trail. Just before passing, she said to her friends gathered around her, "Tell John I died with my face toward Zion."

No word of murmur or complaint ever passed her lips. Who shall say she is not entitled to a martyr's crown in the mansions of glory?

To us Wee Granny is a symbol of fineness, bravery, nobleness, of a true Latter-day Saint—she stands for everything that is good and sweet. She is a living symbol—while in the flesh she personalized these fine qualities, now her living and progressing spirit is gaining exaltation by these same attributes. May we ever appreciate Wee Granny, and may we and our children never forget her.

Temple work has been completed as follows in the Manti Temple:

James was baptized September 16, 1890. He was endowed September 18, 1890.

Mary (Wee Granny) was baptized December 22, 1851. She was endowed September 17, 1890.

She was sealed to James November 19, 1902, in the Salt Lake Temple. All eight children were sealed to their parents in the Salt Lake Temple.

James Steel (Picture taken at Kilmarnock, Scotland)

Elizabeth Wyllie

James Steel

Elizabeth Wyllie introduced James Steel to the gospel. James introduced John Murray and Anne Steel to the gospel. Crossing the plains James died shortly after Wee Granny. Elizabeth and their two sons completed the trek to Salt Lake Valley.

A Tribute to "Wee Granny" Mary Murray Murdoch who died in 1856 at Chimney Rock

On the broad plains of Nebraska stands a lonely sentinel—
Majestic Chimney Rock! What stories it could tell.
If only it could speak, I'd say, "Old rock, do you recall
The Mormon handcart pioneers who came late in the fall
Of eighteen hundred and fifty-six? One of the Martin band
Was my little Scottish Grandma, en route to the Promised Land.
On the purple heathered highland she had spent her childhood days,
There she won a fine Scotch laddie with her sweet and winning ways.
Eight wee bairns blessed their humble home, and the cup of happiness they quaffed.
When the brave kind husband tried to save a dying man from a gas filled shaft,
Both lost their lives. Then my Wee Granny raised her family alone.
She taught them thrift and work, and love of truth, and kin, and home.
In a rough-stone, thatch-roofed cottage she watched her family grow,
And saw them choose mates of their own and from her fireside go.
In 1850, the elders came from Christ's Church of latter-days
The gospel in its fulness swelled her soul with joy and praise
That she could know salvation's plan while still she lived on earth,
And with some of her children be baptized and have new birth.
As time passed, she longed for Zion, where her son had found a home.
For the first time in seventy-three years, Wee Granny began to roam.
She bade farewell to loved ones, looked last at the bonnie braes,

A lone but happy pilgrim, she set out upon her way.
Across the wide Atlantic in sailing vessel tossed,
From New York on to Iowa, but she counted not the cost
On her frail and aging body, for her spirit was so strong.
And she felt so close to Utah, she could travel right along.
With the Martin handcart company, the last to leave, her unhappy lot was cast.
Their handcarts broke, their food was scarce, they felt the chilling blast
Of a hard and early winter, but bravely they went along,
In their hearts a prayer to God, and on their lips a song.
Perhaps old Chimney Rock would speak with the voice of the sighing wind:
"I saw that last brave handcart band, and my stone heart wept within.
Scores of women, children, aged, from a mild and gentle land,
Combatting hunger, fear, and weariness, 'twas more than the strong could stand
At my side these brave souls huddled, sick and dying, cold and weak,
But no complaining word or grumble did I ever hear them speak.
I longed to reach my rough arms out and lift them as they fell,
But they sang as they buried their many dead, 'All is well—all is well.'
I lift my head with pride and reverence. My Wee Granny's buried at your feet.
How she longed to enter Utah, the Saints and her son to meet.
She was never known to murmur. She did her tasks both large and small.
With her life she loved the gospel, and for it she gave her all.
When her weary life was ebbing, with her eyes turned to the west:
'Tell my son John I faced Zion when I died; he'll know the rest.'
She truly was a Saint. Chimney Rock, you're the monument to show
The hallowed ground wherein she lies; you're the sign to make us know
How much we owe Wee Granny for the blessed gospel light."
Oh may we never fail her, but keep her ideals bright.

Written by Virginia D. Christensen for the 1956 reunion—100 years after Wee Granny passed away.

Sunrise at Chimney Rock

What solemn thoughts pervade the soul
As on this scene we meditate,
This resting place for wearied Saints
Tired, travel stained, and desolate.
This scene portrays in vivid ways
A spot made dear on journey drear
By handcart means in early days,
A halfway place on journey here.
Impelled by faith and filled with hope
That soon they'd reach the appointed place
In wed to toil, with trials cope,
To Utah's vales they set their face.
But some along this dreary road
Worn out and faint, oft fell asleep
Ere they could reach the cherished spot
The Valley dear and friends to greet.
Brave honest souls at early morn
As pilgrims in a holy cause

Who dared to face a world of scorn
To obey God's call and keep his laws.
Somewhere around the stopping place
As years go by—'tis fifty-seven—
Wee Granny died. There is no trace
Of earth's abode; her soul's in Heaven.
"Tell John," she said as she lay down
Her worn-out frame in this lone place,
"That I died here, but with my face
Turned Zionwards, the cherished place."
Blest be their names with fondest love.
We'll cherish aye their mem'ries dear,
Soon we may meet with them above
And greet them in their higher sphere.

David L. Murdoch, December 24, 1913

HUSBAND	James Murdoch
Birth	About 1786
Place	Commondyke, Ayrshire, Scotland
Married	10 January 1811
Place	Auchinleck, Ayrshire, Scotland
Death	20 October 1831
Place	Auchinleck, Ayrshire, Scotland
Burial	Gaswater, Ayrshire, Scotland
Father	James Murdoch
Mother	Janet Osborne

WIFE	Mary Murray
Birth	13 October 1782
Place	Glencairn, Dumfriesshire, Scotland
Death	3 October 1856
Burial	Chimney Rock, Scottsbluff, Nebraska
Father	John Murray
Mother	Margaret McCall
Where information obtained	Ruby E. Murdoch Hooper
	Janet Oberg Gill

1ST CHILD Janet Murdoch Smith

Birth	8 December 1811
Place	Boghead, Ayrshire, Scotland
Married	Alexander Smith
Date	20 December 1833
Place	Auchinleck, Ayrshire, Scotland
Died	28 June 1866
Place	Scotland

2ND CHILD Mary Murdoch

Birth	16 June 1813
Place	Boghead, Ayrshire, Scotland
Died	As a child
Place	Ayrshire, Scotland

3RD CHILD James Murdoch

Birth	29 July 1814
Place	Gaswater, Ayrshire, Scotland
Married	Margaret McCall
Date	24 November 1841
Place	Leadhills, Lanark, Scotland
Died	12 September 1884
Place	Glasgow, Lanark, Scotland

4TH CHILD Veronica Murdoch Caldow Giles

Birth	16 June 1816	
Place	Gaswater, Ayrshire, Scotland	
Married	George Caldau	Thomas Giles
Date	15 Feb 1839	3 July 1879
Place	Scotland	S.L.C., Utah
Died	4 October 1908	
Place	Heber City, Wasatch, Utah	

5TH CHILD Mary Murdoch Mair McMillan

Birth	3 October 1818	
Place	Gaswater, Ayrshire, Scotland	
Married	Allan Mair	Daniel McMillan
Date	4 June 1841	26 June 1871
Place	Scotland	S.L.C., Utah
Died	5 December 1900	
Place	Heber City, Wasatch, Utah	

6TH CHILD John Murray Murdoch

Birth	28 December 1820	
Place	Gaswater, Ayrshire, Scotland	
Married	Ann Steel	Isabella Crawford
Date	25 Feb 1848	9 Aug 1862
Place	Scotland	S.L.C., Utah
Died	6 May 1910	
Place	Heber City, Wasatch, Utah	

7TH CHILD Margaret Murdoch

Birth	30 December 1822
Place	Gaswater, Ayrshire, Scotland
Died	As a child
Place	Ayrshire, Scotland

8TH CHILD William Murdoch

Birth	3 July 1825	
Place	Gaswater, Ayrshire, Scotland	
Married	Janet Lennox	Mary Reid Lindsay
Date	23 June 1846	26 Nov 1887
Place	Scotland	Heber City, Utah
Died	12 March 1913	
Place	Heber City, Wasatch, Utah	

JAMES AND MARY MURRAY MURDOCH
(Three Generations)

DESCENDANTS

<pre>
                                                        S James   SMITH   1834-1865??
                                                        A William   "   1836-1905MC
                                                        S John   "   1838-1863??
                         S Alexander Smith   S Robert   "   1840-1871M?
                            About 1808-1876   S James   "   1842-1865??
                            Married 20 Dec 1833   S John   "   1845-?1936?
                         S JANET MURDOCH   S Mary   "   1846-1864 D
                            1811-1866   S Stewart   "   1848-ChildD
                                                        S Stewart   "   1850-1877??
                                                        S Agnes   "   1852-?1890M?
                         S MARY MURDOCH   S Janet Osborne "   1854-1859 D
                            1813-Died as Child   A Alexander   "   1856-1936MC

                                                        S James   MURDOCH 1841- ? ??
                                                        S Alexander   "   1843-1861 D
                         S JAMES MURDOCH   S John   "   1846- ? ??
                            1814-1884   S William   "   1848-1854 D
                            Married 24 Nov 1841   S Robert   "   1851-1873??
                         S Margaret McCall   S Thomas   "   1853-1879??
                            About 1820-1880   U William   "   1856-1899??
                                                        S George   "   1859- ? ??
                                                        S Andrew   "   1861-1862 D

                                                        S Mary   CALDOW 1839- ? MC
                                                        S George   "   1841- ? ?
                         S George Caldow   S James   "   abt. 1844??
                            About 1812-before 1878   S John   "   abt. 1847MC
                            Married 15 Feb 1839   S Alexander   "   abt. 1849??
                         U VERONICA MURDOCH   S William   "   1851-1855
                            1816-1908   S Thomas   "   abt. 1853??
                            Married 3 July 1879   S Joseph   "   abt. 1855??
                            U Thomas Giles   S David   "   abt. 1857??
                                                        S Brigham   "   abt. 1859??
                                                        S Nephi   "   abt. 1861??

                         S Allan Mair   A John   MAIR   1841-1872MC
                            1815-1897   A James   "   1843-1915M
                            Married 4 Jun 1841   S Allan Foulds   "   1845-1907MC
                         U MARY MURDOCH   S Matthew   "   1848-ChildD
                            1818-1900   S William   "   1850-ChildD
                            Married 1 Dec 1866   U Mary   "   1852-1916MC
                            U Thomas Todd (divorced)   S Janet   "   1854-1855 D
                            Married 26 June 1871   U Andrew   "   1856-1924MC
                            U Daniel McMillan   U Alexander   "   1859-1936MC

                                                        A Elizabeth   MURDOCH 1848-1852 D
                                                        A James   "   1850-1852 D
                                                        U Mary M.   "   1852-1917MC
                         U JOHN MURRAY MURDOCH   U Ann   "   1854-1890MC
                            1820-1910   U Janet Osborne "   1856-1949MC
                            Married 25 Feb 1848   U Sarah Jane   "   1859-1933MC
                         U Ann Steel   U JacobinaWellsOsborne 1860-1933MC
                            1829-1909   U John M.   "   1863-1863 D
                                                        U Isabella Lovina "   1864-1870 D
                                                        U John William   "   1864-1864 D
                                                        U Thomas   "   1866-1953MC
                                                        U Lucy Veronica "   1867-1873 D
                                                        U Joseph A.   "   1870-1943MC
                                                        U David Steel   "   1872-1950MC
                                                        U Millicent Sophia "   1874-1916MC

                            Married 9 Aug 1862
                         U Isabella Crawford   U Margararet Ann "   1863-1904MC
                            1836-1916   U Catherine Campbell   1864-1945MC
                                                        U James Crawford "   1869-1959MC
                                                        U Brigham   "   1870-1947MC
                         S MARGARET MURDOCH   U Robert   "   1872-1893
                            1822-Died as Child   U John Murray   "   1874-1928MC
                                                        U Isabella Crawford   1876-1940MC

                         U WILLIAM MURDOCH   S Elizabeth   MURDOCH 1847-1864 D
                            1825-1913   U James D.   "   1850-1924MC
                            Married 23 June 1846   U David Lennox   "   1852-1928MC
                         S Janet Lennox   S Mary   "   1854-1854 D
                            1821-1877   U Janet Lennox   "   1855-1898MC
                            Married 29 June 1882   U Margaret   "   1858-1915MC
                            U Christina Graham (div)
                            Married 26 Nov 1887   U William Louis "   1888-1937MC
                         U Mary Reid Lindsay   U Mary Murray   "   1891-1918
                            1851-1929   U Lizziebelle   "   1894-   MC
</pre>

JAMES MURDOCH
Born   About 1786
Where Commondyke,Ayr,Sctl.
Died   20 Oct 1831 (45 years)
Where Gaswater,Ayr,Scotland

Married 10 Jan 1811

MARY MURRAY
Born   13 Oct 1782
Where Glencairn,Dmfrs,Sctl.
Died   3 Oct 1856 (73 years)
Where Chimney Rock,
        Scottsbluff,Nebraska

S-Remained in Scotland
A-Came to U.S.A.
U-Immigrated to or born Utah
M-Married
C-Had Children
D-Died under 20

Janet Murdoch Smith

Janet Murdoch Smith was the first child of James and Mary Murray Murdoch and was born December 8, 1811, in Boghead, Ayrshire, Scotland. She was probably named after her grandmother Janet Osborne Murdoch, the wife of James Murdoch, her father's father.

Being the oldest, much was expected of Janet in helping the family in the meager times they lived in. She helped in the care of seven other children born to the family. She was probably sent out to work on nearby farms as soon as she was old enough to do so, as were her younger brothers and sisters James, Veronica, Mary, John Murray Murdoch, and William.

Her father, James, being a miner, died in a mine shaft on October 20, 1831,when trying to rescue a young man who had gone down into the pit and was overcome by foul gas "black damp."

Two years later, on December 20, 1833, Janet, at about the age of twenty-two, married an Alexander Smith who is listed as a coalminer in the 1851 and 1861 Scottish census. Janet was listed as a handsewer. Our present records say they were the parents of twelve children. Two children died under age eight and five more under the age of thirty-one. Janet died on June 28, 1866, of heart disease at only fifty-four years of age. Her youngest child would have been ten at this time. Alexander, her husband, died in about 1876 in Glasgow, Lanark, Scotland.

David Lennox Murdoch, son of William Murdoch, said the following concerning the family: "Aunt Jennie, the oldest, married Alex Smith, lived in Birnieknowe about three miles from Grasswater. She had quite a family and was in rather poor circumstances the most of her life. Her husband—a good man,—but rather delicate and asthmatical. A son William whom I knew in Glasgow, immigrated to the state of Washington some number of years after we came. He and his wife are now gone, but they have left up there several sons and at least one daughter." (From his Writings about Murdochs.)

June 1, 1906: "I then called upon Mrs. MacFarlane, 42 Minard Road, Crossmyloaf, who is eldest daughter of my cousin William Smith who died last fall in the State of Washington, U.S.A. She has five sons I think. Her eldest son 17 years of age went out there in the month of March last. She resembles the Murdoch's very much. A good deal like Aunt Veronica." (David Lennox Murdoch, Missionary Journal.)

August 27,1906: "Called on Mrs. Agnes Johnston at Kilmaurs and read the account of Kirsty Lindsay's death to her—an old time friend." October 24, 1906: "Went out to Kilmaurs saw Mrs. Johnston." (Perhaps this is Agnes Smith Johnston, who was a daughter of Janet Murdoch Smith.)

From Genealogical Society Library film #103–651 A-B and Film #103–799 A dated 1851 and 1862 respectively, we have a record of the children of Alexander Smith and Janet Smith listed as Robert—son 10, James—son 8, John—son 6, Mary—daughter 4, and on the 1861 census we find listed besides Alexander Smith and wife Janet, Mary—daughter 14, Stewart—son 10, and Alexander—son 5.

Agnes Smith (Johnston)

Janet Murdoch Smith

Alexander Smith

Alexander Smith was born January 24, 1856 at Birnieknowe, Auchinleck Parish, in Ayrshire Scotland. He was the youngest child in the family of twelve children of Alexander and Janet Murdoch Smith.

His mother was in bad health from the time he was born; she died of heart disease June 28, 1866.

Alexander was ten years of age at his mother's death so was reared by his sister Agnes who was just four years older than he. He grew up in the hill country where he learned to care for sheep and cattle on his father's ranch. (In the 1851 and 1861 Scottish census his father's occupation is listed as coalminer.) When he was a young man he learned to survey and worked for several years at that trade before coming to the United States in 1882.

He came to Iowa, where he stayed with relatives named Johnson, and worked at surveying around Cherokee. In 1888 he moved further west to Endicott in Whitman County, Washington. He purchased land in the southern end of Whitman County and had quite a prosperous sheep ranch with headquarters not far from the Snake River near Riporia, Washington.

In 1902 he married Margaret Boyd Scott who had come to Endicott from Glasgow, Scotland with his brother William's family. They lived on the sheep ranch until 1915 when he sold the ranch and moved to Clarkston, Washington where they built a house and had a fruit orchard for the next five years. In 1920 they moved to a wheat ranch in southern Asotin County where they lived for two years, moving into the small town of Anatone when his eyesight began to fail.

He was a deeply religious man who wrote poetry and did a great deal of reading until he lost his sight. His children remember him as a quiet, kind, gentle person who loved all children and animals. He and his wife were the parents of five children who are all living at the present time. He died at Anatone in 1936 and is buried at Endicott, Washington in the family plot.

His children are Agnes Mabel Smith Bacon of Brewster, Washington; Margaret Jeanette Boggan of Clarkston, Washington; Pauline Smith McDonald Mercer of Spokane, Washington; and Andrew Glen Smith. He has eleven grandchildren and fourteen great-grandchildren that we are aware of at this time.

Alexander Smith

William Smith and Alexander Smith

Alexander Smith and Margaret B. Scott

Descendants of Janet Murdoch and Alexander Smith

1 Murdoch James 1786-1831
1 Murdoch Mary Murray 1782-1856

   2 Smith Janet Murdoch 1811-1866 M-20 Dec 1833
   2 Smith Alexander 1808-1876, Spouse

      3 Smith James 1834-

      3 Smith William 1836-1905
      3 Smith Jane Farquhar Gray, Spouse

         4 McFarland Mary Smith
         4 McFarland Alex, Spouse killed World War I

            5 McFarland Alfred
            5 McFarland Thomas D-about 1916
            5 3 other sons perhaps ?

         4 Smith Alexander D-1954
         4 Smith Mary Lauder Scott, Spouse D-1940

            5 Smith Donald B. B-1901
            5 Smith Mary Irene Cole, Spouse B-1900

               6 Smith James B-1937
               6 Smith Claudia Wilson, Spouse

                  7 Smith Glenda
                  7 Smith Cheryl

               6 McKinley Carol Donna Smith B-1940
               6 McKinley Judson, Spouse

                  7 McKinley Christy
                  7 McKinley Kimberly

            5 Smith Alexander 1899-1954 (unmarried)

         4 Fields Jeanie Smith
         4 Fields Vernon, Spouse

         4 Smith William
         4 Smith Mary McPherson, Spouse

         4 Smith David Gray
         4 Smith Sarah Johnson, Spouse

3   Smith John 1838-

3   Smith Robert 1840-1871
3   Smith Catherine, Spouse

3   Smith James 1842-1865

3   Smith John 1845-1863

3   Smith Mary 1846-1864

3   Smith Stewart 1848-

3   Smith Stewart 1850-1877

3   Johnston Agnes Smith 1852-1890?
3   Johnston James, Spouse

3   Smith Janet Osborne 1854-1859

3   Smith Alexander 1856-1936
3   Smith Margaret Boyd Scott, Spouse 1878-1964
                              M-13 Apr 1902

    4   Bacon Agnes Mabel Smith B-9/20/1906
    4   Bacon George Thomas, Spouse B-10/27/1905
                                    M-4/14/1928

        5   Sheets Alice Corrine Bacon B-2/3/1929
        5   Sheets Robert Franklin, Spouse D-1978

            6   Sheets Lonnie R.
            6   Sheets Robert Thomas
            6   Sheets Harold Boyd
            6   Sheets Rion Bonson
            6   Sheets Melody Lynn

        5   Bacon Harold Glenn 5/23/31-6/30/1975

        5   McKenzie Margaret B (Peggy) B-5/5/1932
        5   McKenzie Orville Theodore (Ted), Spouse

            6   McKenzie Thomas Orville
            6   McKenzie Dana Lynn
            6   McKenzie Daniel Jessie

    4   Smith Robert Alexander B-3/10/1910
    4   Smith Bonnie Sterling, Spouse M-7/20/1969

    4   Boggan Margaret Jeanette Smith B-6/9/1915
                                        M-4/12/1934
    4   Boggan Carroll Stephen, Spouse B-7/4/1903
                                        D-5/5/1978

```
5   Boggan Jerry Carrol   B-6/21/1935
5   Boggan Nancy Jordan, Spouse   M-8/29/1929

    6   Boggan Scott Lee   B-9/15/1959
    6   Boggan Mark Steven   B-4/20/61

5   Boggan Walter Clyde   B-11/10/1938

5   Botts Janice Clairene Boggan   B-8/1/1941
5   Botts Norman Dwight, Spouse   B-5/28/1929
                                  M-6/25/1960

    6   Botts Tracie Lynne   B-12/12/1960
    6   Botts Keven Dwight   B-10/1/1963
    6   Botts Melanie Jean   B-1/27/1970

5   Runquist Toni Jean Boggan   B-3/2/1955
5   Runquist Randall, Spouse   B-8/16/1955
                               M-5/28/1977

4   Mercer Pauline Smith M.   B-10/22/1917
4   McDonald Earl Augustus, Spouse   M-12/24/1943
4   Mercer Ray, Spouse   M-10/21/1958

    5   McDonald Michael Earl   B-10-14-1944

    5   McDonald Ronald Boyd   B-8/12/1946
    5   McDonald Jane Elizabeth Kelley, Spouse   M-1969

    5   Dewey Carole Gayle McDonald   B-12/19/1950
    5   Dewey Hary Maxwell, Spouse   M-1969

        6   Dewey Michael James

4   Smith Andrew Glen   B-5/17/1920 or 21
4   Smith Alberta Rape   M-1948 now divorced

    5   Smith Darlene   B-1949
```

B-Born
D-Died
M-Married
1,2,3,4,5,6-Generation #

James Murdoch

James Murdoch was the third child of eight children born to James and Mary Murray Murdoch. His date of birth is July 29, 1814, in Gaswater, Ayrshire, Scotland. He no doubt was named after his father and grandfather, being the first son in the family. He was seventeen years old when his father lost his life on October 20, 1831, in a mine pit trying to rescue a young man who had gone into it and was overcome with foul gas. James then had two younger sisters and two younger brothers to assist his mother (Wee Granny). Being the eldest son he became man of the family. He had probably already been working for some years by now to earn his own keep and assist the family in the meager times they lived in. John Murray Murdoch in his own history mentions James helping them to build a cottage for Mary Murray Murdoch (Wee Granny) and the rest of the family to live in following their father's death. He also said that he worked for his brother James doing repairs on a mine at Lugar in 1851. (Murdoch Messenger, #3, pp. 11–12.)

James did not get married until he was twenty-seven years of age. His sisters Janet, Veronica, and Mary all preceded him in marriage. He married Margaret McCall on November 24, 1841, at Leadhills, Dumfriesshire, Scotland. Margaret is said also to have been born there about 1820.

Before November 7,1853, James had moved his family to Glasgow, Lanark, Scotland. This was the date of his son Thomas's birth in Glasgow. Here on August 26, 1854, he and Margaret were to experience the death of their six-year-old William. This was only the beginning of sorrow for them, as four other sons were also to die soon under the age of twenty-seven and preceding James in death, as did his wife also. They were parents to nine sons.

David Lennox Murdoch said about James: "James married Margaret McCall. They had a large family and lived in Glasgow. I think they all must be gone now as I could get no trace of any of them while over there 1905–06–07 altho I even advertised in the paper for them. A son William (second) came here and lived for a time in Heber City and Park City. He died in this city and was buried in the City Cemetery." William died in Salt Lake City.

Margaret McCall is said to have died about 1880 in Scotland, and James September 12, 1884,at seventy years of age in Glasgow, Lanarkshire, Scotland. From the letter printed from James to his nephew David Lennox Murdoch written on December 16, 1878 we sense a loneliness. "I hope you are all in good health and that it is not trouble or want of time that some of you are not minding old Jamie that you have left behind with a bit letter at a time to cheer up his cast down spirits, you don't know how glad I am in a morning when my Laird comes up to my door with a letter in his hand saying its an American." James was now alone except for nieces and nephews from the Smith family and his sons, perhaps James, John, Thomas, William, and George, for whom we do not have death dates. His mother and his only living sisters and brothers and their families had all gone to America.

Perhaps there are some of his descendants today in Scotland from the sons mentioned above that we do not know about as a family organization. If anyone in the family has more information concerning this family, your family officers would appreciate knowing of it. Neither James nor any of his sons ever joined the Church as his mother, two sisters, and two brothers did. All temple work has been done for this family.

These were among David Lennox Murdoch's pictures that were taken at J.C. Burne Photographer Court House Square, Glasgow, Scotland. David Labeled them thus:

Mrs. James Murdoch   John Murdoch

1851 Scottish Census   Village of Auchinleck   #24   June 27,1851   Film # 103-651   A-B

Place or Street	Residents	Relation to head	Married Unwed	Age	Occupation	Place of Birth
#13	James Murdoch	Head	M	36	Grocer	Ayr., Auchinleck
	Margaret	Wife	M	31		Dumfries, Sanquhar
	James	Son	U	9	Schl	Lenark, Crawford
	Alexander	Son	U	7	"	Ayr., Auchinleck
	John	Son	U	5	"	Ayr., Old Cumnock
	William	Son	U	2	"	Ayr., Auchinleck
	Ann McCall	Sister-in-law	U	22	Muslin Sewer	Lanark, Crawford

James Murdock
Bowmans Court
21 Nicholson St
Glasgow. S.S

Monday Night 10 Oclock
Bells Ringing — Hard Frost
very Cold, pipes frozen up
no water in my place since
Friday it is a very severe
Storm

Dear Nephew I have read your invitation
with much interest, I have read nearly the
same several times over I find no fault with
what you have said — When you & I have a
Chat now it is a great differ the pen instead
of the tongue. Still give us a few days we
can know that each other are alive yet

31st Oct was the last I have got from you
I was glad to see it as I thought you had
Taken the huff & was not going to mind me
but let me stand like Something forgotten
as you did your tobacco & pipes never
To be mended — I gave William Smith
the pipes not long ago but the tobacco & paper
was into a rotten mass with damp through the
wall — I do not wish to fill up my space with
much of what you have said at same time I
want you to understand that I have read it
4p or 5 times over — William Smith is the
only one has seen it, he was over one night
with a walking Stick For me it is a long
promise I was to have it for my journey to
South I went rather sooner than he expected
But I have it now & it is a good one

I intend before long to go to Townhead
and call upon my Friends in that quarter
and learn how they are getting through this
Hard winter & have all my Mormon letters
gathered home, I have put none of them
to their proper place Since I left 222

and now I have a goodly number do not Slack we will have Mormon Books yet

Davie I did not intend to write in this manner, neither did I intend to trouble you with much of any kind at this time But I cannot think on Standing Behind — Their are many things I could let you know & would if I was beside you an hour or two — Their are one thing I am the Same man as you left me & in the Same place — it Stands thus, they know where I am when they want me — your answer was Thats it — It Stands So — what I have Said makes you understand a great deal more —

I have to remove at whitsunday for alterations — I am not desided what I may do, My Laird wishes me to remain But I will have to shift for a time & return again that is a hard job for me — If I See a place convenient before that time I will try and make one Shift do — I hope you are all in good health & that it is not trouble or want of time that Some — of you are not minding old Jamie that you have left behind with a bit letter at a time to Cheer up his cast down Spirits, you dont know how glad I am in a morning when my Laird comes up to my door with a Letter in his hand Saying its an american I See from the Stamp that is on it — 6000 500 miles I Said this morning — I begin to think I put a wee bit to it but we will let that stand at present as I dont think my pen did it Knowingly — I hope you will find time — Shortly to give me a few lines to satisfy my craving desire

Glasgow Dec 16th/78 yours Jas. Murdoch

Copy.

Given Names and Dates ...

[handwritten genealogical record, partially legible]

... Murdoch ... the third ... Grandfather
Communitie Auchinleck, Ayrshire, the first, and James Murdoch
Pearlwater was my father, the second. And ... James Murdoch was in
Glasgow on the third and Father of this family.

James Murdoch ... Margaret McCall was married at ... November 24, 1841

James Murdoch was born July 26, 1841
... Murdoch was born May 30, 1843 died at Brigham Feb 2, 1861
John Murdoch was born Feby 11, 1846
William Murdoch was born July 1, 1848 died in Glasgow Aug 26, 1854
Robert Murdoch was born May 15, 1851 died in Glasgow June 28, 1873
Thomas Murdoch was born Novr 7, 1853 died in Glasgow Oct 25, 1879
William Murdoch second was born Apl 5, 1856 died in Salt Lake City 2 Novr 1899
George Murdoch was born Feby 23, 1859
Andrew Murdoch was born Jany 25, 1861 died in Glasgow Oct 6, 1862

Copied by Robert Dixon Paton, Glasgow, 6th Feby 1885.

Written in David Lenox Murdoch's handwriting
in his copy of John Murray Murdoch's
and temple record book.

Veronica Murdoch Caldow Giles

Veronica Murdoch, daughter of James and Mary Murray Murdoch, was born June 16, 1816, at Gaswater, Ayrshire, Scotland, the fourth child in a family of eight. She was christened June 30, 1816, at Auchinleck Parish Church.

Her father was employed in the coal mines at Gaswater and in 1831 lost his life trying to save a young man who had fallen into a mine shaft and was overcome by poisonous gas, or black damp, as it was called. The children who were old enough to work had to help in every way possible to assist their widowed mother. Veronica adapted herself to all kinds of hard work. She was not able to attend school regularly but took advantage of every opportunity to learn. She was a constant reader and retained well what she read.

She was married to George Caldow February 15, 1839. She was the mother of eleven children, Mary, George, James, John, Alexander, William, Thomas, Joseph, David, Brigham, and Nephi. She was left a widow and worked diligently to raise her family and provide for their needs.

Her brother, John M., was the first of her family to join the Mormon Church, and he was able to convert and baptize his mother, Mary Murray Murdoch, Veronica, and Janet Lennox Murdoch, wife of his brother, William.

John M. and family were the first to come to Utah, in January 1852. Veronica's mother attempted to come with the Mormon Handcart Company and died at Chimney Rock, Nebraska, October 3, 1856. Veronica's sister, Mary Mair, came next in 1866.

In 1878, her brother William and his family made plans to come to Utah, and arrangements were made for her to come with him, he being responsible for her and paying her way. Her family was agreeable to her coming, thinking it best for her to be with her brothers and sister in Utah and with the body of the church she had joined. None of her family joined the Church. She was in straitened circumstances and at the age of sixty-two, suitable work was hard to find in Scotland.

I am sure that she had thought that at some future time at least part of her family would join her, but this was not to be.

Preparations were made as soon as possible for their departure. Sturdy boxes were made for their possessions, one each for their personal belongings and several large ones for general storage. Each box was labeled with their name and destination. I can well remember Aunt Vachey's, labeled Veronica M. Caldow, Utah, U.S.A. They were painted a steel gray with black lettering. Several years later, Auntie's was painted red. Crissie Lindsay Duke is the proud owner of Aunt Vachey's box. Brother David L. kept a day-by-day diary of their trip. He says: "May 24, 1878, busy getting luggage on board. Steam_ tender lying at #4 bridge landing stage for the ship 'Nevada,' a good company of over 300 souls. Danes, English, Scotch, and Irish all busy looking after their luggage and beds. A great many strangers looking on, evidently wondering at so many going to Utah, U.S.A. Left the landing at 7 o'clock for our ship 'Nevada' lying in mid river. Arriving in just a very short time, 30 minutes or so, women and children were hurried on board. The luggage was slung over on board and very roughly handled. It is our hope that it will reach its destination something like safety."

David L. and his wife Lizzie traveled first class while William, his two daughters, Margaret and Janet, and Aunt Vachey and John Adamson were down in the steerage along with many Saints and others in route to America.

David says of the first night on ship: "I arose early, May 26 and went down to inquire of the kin in the steerage quarters. All were ailing. Father and Auntie vexed about the noise of people playing musical instruments and singing most of the night. Father said, 'There is no fool like those of the latter days.' Of course the Scotch Saints would be the best behaved. All felt better by breakfast."

"Sunday morning, May 26, we are off the coast of

Ireland and rain is failing fast. Soon we enter the harbor of Cook, here 30 passengers were taken on board. With field glasses we are able to view the beautiful scenery. 11:45 A.M. Leaving Queenstown and shortly will have the last sight of land for several days. From here on we saw nothing but the great expanse of the mighty deep as far as the eye could see.

"We were given advice as to our habits etc., while on the ship. Brother Ball in charge spoke very plainly to the saints as to using plenty of soap and keeping clean. The voyage was very rough at times and most of the passengers were too ill to be up at all. Father and Auntie were neither one very ill."

David goes into detail about the meals each day. All of the meetings were held in the steerage. Each family cooked its own meals. It was Tuesday, June 5, at about 11:00 A.M., that land was sighted. Steerage passengers hurriedly threw their beds overboard along with unneeded cooking utensils. All were checked by a doctor and found to be in good health. They steamed up the Hudson River to the union pier where brother James D. met them. He had left work in Pittsburgh to greet his loved ones on their arrival from Scotland.

On the night of June 6 they started their railway journey, arriving in Pittsburgh about 2:00 A.M. Here they bade James D. goodbye and changed trains. Traveling across Nebraska and the balance of the trip was much more tiresome than all the trip this far. All the way they were thinking of Wee Granny traveling on foot and pushing a handcart. Even though they thought their trip was hard, they could see how easy it was compared to the trek of the handcart pioneers. They reached Cheyenne, Wyoming, June 11 at about 4:00 P.M. They reached Salt Lake June 13 at 9:00 P.M. a day early and no one was there to meet them. They stayed overnight at the Valley House and early the next morning went back to the depot to claim their baggage. Soon Uncle John M. arrived along with William Giles and William Lindsay, each with a wagon to take them all to Heber. A wonderful welcome was awaiting them in Heber, and soon they were busy making their own adjustment in their new location. Their journey was made in nineteen days—eleven days on the sea, one day and night in New York, and seven days by rail across the continent of America. Their luggage was all intact, no loss of any kind. All those people were housed in a small home rented from a Mr. Thomas Giles. It was located on the northwest corner of second north and third west. The house faced the south. It consisted of one large log room with a lean-to on the north, a front porch the entire length of the south of

the house, and a root cellar and woodshed on the west. They managed well for a time, and David and Lizzie found a home to themselves. Father and the girls and John Adamson moved to Lake Creek, where Father had bought a farm. John Adamson and Margaret had been married by this time, and later on Janet was married to William Baird.

Auntie Vachey was married to Thomas Giles on July 3, 1879, and continued to live in the little home they had rented from Mr. Giles. Her life with him was a pleasant one. They had many friends and were invited to all socials and entertainments. He provided well for her, and when he died several years later he left moderate means to take care of her needs. She had a pleasant disposition and with her bit of humor and Scotch brogue fit in to all occasions. After she was again left a widow she lived alone for several years.

Her neighbors, other than relatives, were Katie and Mary Forman, Mary Montgomery, Ann Howarth, Harriet Luke, and Esther Hoagland. Harriet and Esther were sisters and lived side by side in the block west of Auntie. Esther kept a cow and each day she herded it along the streets or in the lot by the old rock schoolhouse about second west and third north. I have gone with Auntie many times to find her friend Esther, and while they chatted I would herd the cow. Esther also sold sulfur matches, and mother would sometimes send me to buy a box. She would tell me to stop in at Auntie's and fill up her wee match holder on the mantel. The old rock schoolhouse was the first one to be built in Heber. It was near the fort. It served church meetings and all socials and dramatics. It was in this schoolhouse that David L. was a teacher. His Scotch brogue amused his students and at times they made it rough for him.

Aunt Vachey did some knitting but her main pastime was sewing carpet rags for people. She always kept busy.

She loved pets and had one large yellow dog called Charley. She would give a low whistle and call "Chairly," and he would come on the run to be fed or petted. She also kept a multitude of cats, much to the dislike of her visitors, but they were company for Auntie and that was all that mattered. Even with all the cats, there were still mice to be troublesome. Auntie liked to tell jokes on herself. I remember her telling of going to the doctor. She had been bothered with a chest pain and went to have an examination. She told the doctor how miserable the pain was and also said, "I feel like there is something living about me." When she unbuttoned the tight quilted basque she was wearing, a poor little mouse jumped out. She and the doctor had a good laugh. He said, "'Sure enough Auntie, there was something living about you."

She looked good in her clothes. She always liked pretty hats. I remember one time when she came to show us a new hat she had bought at Louvie Alexander's Hat Shop. Another time while she was staying with cousin Mary and William Lindsay she got a new bonnet-style hat and a new dress and small cape. I thought no one ever had a prettier auntie.

She was kind to all of us children, always bringing us a bit of candy or a cookie. What a treat when she would open her box and give us a peppermint or a pink musk candy, and we could smell the orange peel. They were her perfume.

Father and Uncle John M. kept a watchful eye on her. They arranged to have my brother Louis or cousin Rue, who was living with his grandmother Bella at that time, take turns going each morning to see if she was up and to start her fire for her. They, along with other sons of relatives, kept Auntie in kindling wood and other fuel.

Every Christmas Eve and also New Year's Eve Auntie would hang her stocking on her outside door knowing that it would be filled. New Year's was "Hogmany" and I was lead to believe on that eve the Scotch Santa came all the way from Scotland to fill the stockings.

The time came now that Auntie was no longer able to live alone, so she spent a few months at a time with all her kin. It must have been hard for her to give up her little home but she didn't object, and all enjoyed having her.

I have some pleasant memories of her visits at our house. One time she had a close call to being hurt when she fell in a trench. During the time that the water lines were being put in Heber, she slipped off the boardwalk across the trench on Main Street. It was about dark, and she walked back and forth calling for help. Finally a friend and neighbor heard her and helped her to climb out. She must have been near eighty years but she laughed about it and paid no attention to the bruises. I think if she were telling this story she would say, "It was thru the help o a guid frien and neighbor that she wan oot."

One time when she was living with cousin Mary and William in Lake Creek, she came to visit us while they were away shopping. She said to Father, "Noo, Willie, when I lived wi you I voted Democrate, noo I'm wi William and Mary I've voted Republican." Crissie told me that Auntie entered into their childish games and enjoyed them. One night while her mother and

father were away to a party, they began some childish pranks. They were kneeling over and Auntie tried it too. She couldn't quite make it so Dave gave her a push. Over she went and to cause a laugh she said, "Oh, oh, you've broke my neck."

I like to think of the story she told of putting tea leaves "oot to dry thinking they'll doe to lend." She "couldna keep secrets very week" so if a surprise party was to be given she was late in hearing about it. One time when a party was to be held for Aunt Mary, Auntie rushed in ahead of the others and said, "Mary, a wheen folk are coming bu dinna let on."

The dear old soul must have had many hours of loneliness thinking of the family in Scotland. I am sure that in the beginning she had hopes that they too would come to Zion. Now her only hope was to meet them in their eternal home. She was not one to burden others with her heartaches and woes. She went on about each day's duties keeping silent on any unpleasant thought.

To know her was to love her. Her last days were with her nephew Andrew Mair and his good wife Mary Ann. She passed away at their home October 4, 1908. Her funeral service was held in the Wasatch Stake House. Burial was in the Heber City Cemetery.

She was baptized September, 1852, and was rebaptized July 28, 1878.

She was endowed July 3, 1879, in the Endowment House. She was sealed to Thomas Giles July 3, 1879.

Written by Lizziebell Murdoch Davis, a niece.

Editors Note: Veronica was supposedly the mother of eleven children, namely Mary, George, James, John, Alexander, William, Thomas, Joseph, David, Brigham, and Nephi. (Genealogical sheets done by Ruby Hooper) David Lennox Murdoch said the following about her family in his writings about Murdochs and Missionary Journal 1905–6–7, in Scotland. "Aunt Veronica was another member of that family from Grasswater and the Mother of a large family by her husband George Caldow in Scotland. She saw hard times, trials, and difficulties and poverty being a widow alone, her family having all married but one. He was old enough to be almost a Grandfather, she was immigrated and came with us in 1878." "Sept. 10, 1906: While in Cumnock I hunted up where Cusin Mary Caldow Baird used to live and found a daughter, a Mrs. Nichol living not far from there. I had a talk with her. Her father is living, her Uncle George, unmarried, lives with him. Her Uncle John lives at Burubank,

a widower with a family. Her Uncle James lives at   Mauchline. She promised to write to her Grannie, Aunt
Vachey, in Heber City and to let her know all about
her relatives."

Veronica is found in the 1841 Scottish census records
as follows: Genealogical Library of The Church of Jesus
Christ of Latter-day Saints, Salt Lake City, Utah, film
#101-820 M-N 604-610 Muirkirk (II Part) #1:

Street or Road	Names	Age	Sex	Occupation	Born in Scotland
Small Burn	George Caldow	25	M	Drainer	Yes
	Veronica Murdoch	20	F		Yes
	Mary Caldow	1	F		Yes
	Hugh Caldow	20	M	Drainer	

Scottish Census 1851 Genealogical Library Salt Lake City, Utah Film #103-657-M-N

Village of Muirkirk #33

Street or Road	Names	Relation to head	Age	Occupation	Place of Birth
#155	George Caldow	H	36	Lab.	Ayr. Auchinleck
	Veronica	W	34		"
	Mary	D	11		"
	George	S	9	Scholar	"
	James	S	7	"	"
	John	S	4		"

James Caldow (probably). Picture taken at Nobel & Son, 81 Quarry St. Hamilton. The woman next to the old man looks a lot like Veronica. Picture left in Veronica's possessions.

Veronica Murdoch Caldow Giles

Thomas Giles

Thomas and Veronica Giles

Mary Caldow Baird

Mary Caldow Baird's children

DESCENDANTS OF VERONICA MURDOCH CALDOW GILES

```
1 MURDOCH, James           1786-1831                    B-Born
1 MURDOCH, Mary MURRAY, Sp. 1782-1856                   M-Married
                                                        D-Died

  2 GILES, Veronica MURDOCH Caldow B-16 Jun 1816 D-4 Oct 1908
  2 CALDOW, George, Sp. B-About 1812 M-15 Feb 1839 D-before 1 Aug 1855
 +2 GILES, Thomas, Sp. (2) B-3 Oct 1804 M-3 July 1879 D-1 Jul 1887

     3 BAIRD, Mary CALDOW B-28 Jul 1839 D-  ?
     3 BAIRD,          Sp. B-         M-          D-alive 1906*

          4 NICHOL, Mrs      BAIRD B-        M-         D-alive 1906*
          4 NICHOL,          Sp. B-

               5 ?

          4 BAIRD, Male      B-         M-         D-        (Picture)

          4 BAIRD, Male      B-         M-         D-        (Picture)

     3 CALDOW, George B-17 June 1841 Unmarried 1906 living with brother-in-law Mr. Baird*

     3 CALDOW, James  B- 7 Jan 1844 M- ?     D-alive 1906 living  in Mauchline, Scotland*

     3 CALDOW, John   B-About 1847 M-yes?     D-alive 1906 living in Burubank, Scotland a
                                                        widower with a family*
          4

     3 CALDOW, Alexander B-About 1849
```

```
     3 CALDOW, William   B-About 1851 D-1 Aug 1855    Last seven children were listed as
                                                      dead on 19 September 1890 and sealed
     3 CALDOW, Thomas     B-About 1853                by Veronica to herself and Thomas
                                                      Giles who was also dead at this time.
     3 CALDOW, Joseph     B-About 1855                Father, George, listed dead on death
                                                      registration of William 1 Aug 1855?
     3 CALDOW, David      B-About 1857      *David Lennox Murdoch's   "Scottish Missionary
                                                                      Journal"
     3 CALDOW, Brigham    B-About 1859

     3 CALDOW, Nephi      B-About 1861
```

```
 +  GILES, Thomas B-3 Oct 1804 D-1 Jul 1887
    GILES, Maria KIRKHAM, Sp. (1) B-15 Apr 1807 M-30 May 1832 D-1 Mar 1887

       GILES, Thomas Jr. B-21 Jan 1833 D-at sea 1862

       GILES, Elizabeth  B-25 Dec 1834 D-as a child

       GILES, George "M" B- 9 Mar 1840 M-4 Jul 1867 to Mary Elizabeth Mayoh D-7 May 1908

       GILES, Elizabeth  B-10 Sep 1842 M-           to John GILES D-

       GILES, William "M" B- 3 Sep 1846 M-5 Jun 1871 to Ann MURDOCH D-30 Apr 1926

       (One history says oldest sister stayed in England)
```

Mary Murdoch, Allan Mair, and Daniel McMillan

Mary Murdoch Mair McMillan was the fourth daughter and fifth child of James and Mary Murray Murdoch. She was born at Gaswater, Ayrshire, Scotland, October 3, 1818. Her father having died when she was very young, she was compelled to go out to work for other people to help earn her living. They were living in an area where most of the people were farmers and stock raisers and she, of course, went to work in homes of that type of people and learned to do all kinds of work that women and girls did around farms. In those days in Scotland the women usually milked the cows and fed them, made the butter and cheese, and also had to help rake the hay and harvest the grain. There was no machinery used in the harvest fields in those days; all the hay was cut by hand with scythes, and the grain was cut with sickles and bound by hand. It was very hard work and a very slow process. The fields were surrounded by hills that were covered with the bonnie bloomin' heather, which is really beautiful along in July and August when it is in full bloom. It is also the chief supply of food for the sheep and cattle which graze on the hills most of the year.

Mary helped knit the family's stockings. During the winter she attended school. She and her sister Veronica were in the same room. One day when Mary was coughing, the teacher told her she must stop coughing or leave the room. Veronica went to her and whispered in her ear, "Mary, ye dinna ha to." She did not attend school very long but did learn to read, write, spell, and count. Thus she grew to be a strong and healthy young woman, quite efficient in all kinds of women's work and as such, with a cheerful disposition, she attracted the attention of the young men in that neighborhood. When about twenty-two years of age she was married to a very steady young man named Allan Mair who grew up with her in the little village.

This was a strictly religious community where practically everybody attended church, and the Sabbath day was very strictly observed by all. Allan, being a very steady, industrious young man and a willing worker,

and Mary being of a frugal, saving disposition, they were soon comfortably settled down in a little cottage with simple furnishings and happy and contented with their lot in life. This was about 1840. In 1841 their oldest child, a son named John, was born and in a very few years they had quite a little family to provide for. They had a total of nine children. They were both hardworking and saved what means came into their hands, and of course got along very well and seemed to be prospering nicely. In 1850 the Mormon elders came preaching the restored gospel of Jesus Christ in their vicinity, and not long after, Mary's brother, John Murray, and his wife, Ann Steel, became interested in their doctrines and after due consideration were baptized. Mary, having recently lost two of her children, Matthew and William, in infancy, readily accepted their doctrine of the plan of salvation and life after death. She tried hard to convince her husband of the truth of Mormonism too, but he could not see the need of making a change in his religion. Mary went ahead and was baptized on June 4, 1851, by William Aird, and was confirmed by John Drennan on the same date. Her mother, Mary Murray, her sister, Veronica, and brother William's wife, Janet Lennox, also joined the Church within the next two years.

Because of Mary's affiliation with this new religion, some contention began to develop that disrupted the harmony in their home. She had received a strong testimony of the gospel, and it caused her much sorrow when she could not convince her husband of its truthfulness, and her children could not be brought up in this new faith as she so much desired they should. There also arose a spirit of persecution by former friends and neighbors against those who had joined the Mormon Church. The words of the Savior were literally fulfilled in Mary's case, as he said his doctrines would "set a man at variance against his father, and the daughter against her mother, and the daughter-in-law against her mother-in-law. And a man's foes shall be they of his own household. He that loveth father or mother more than me is not worthy of me: and he that loveth son or daughter more than me is not worthy of me. And he that taketh not his cross and followeth after me, is not worthy of me." (Matthew 10:35–38.) Mary desired to be worthy and bore her cross patiently for fourteen years.

Mary's brother John and his wife came to Utah in 1852, and in 1856 he sent for their mother, Wee Granny, and she too started for Utah. However, like so many others who started to cross the plains with handcarts in that year, she perished by the wayside at Chimney Rock, Nebraska. Thus, Mary felt quite alone as far as discussing the gospel with her family, except that once in a while she had occasion to talk with her brother William's wife, Janet, who, like she had joined the Church without her husband yet joining. They had long confidential talks together and perhaps Veronica also joined them in their conversations.

About 1865, at the close of the war between the northern and southern states, Mary's two oldest sons left home and came to Maryland, USA, hoping to better their condition financially, and her third son was making preparations to be married. She still had three children left at home, Mary, thirteen; Andrew, ten; and Alexander, six; three children having by now died in infancy. She became desperate to think that her children were growing up in ignorance of the truths of the gospel, which she could not even teach in her own home. She finally made up her mind if Mary, who was thirteen, would help her carry out her plan, she would leave her husband and home and go to Utah, where her younger children could be taught the gospel, and they could make their home among the Saints in Zion.

Daughter Mary readily took hold of the proposition, and together they began to make preparation for leaving as soon as all arrangements could be made for their trip to Liverpool John Aird, a member of the Church, acted as agent for them, making all necessary arrangements. He forwarded their baggage that had been sent to him in small parcels that Mary had carried to the station. They had also sent him money to secure their passage across the ocean. He notified them just when the ship would sail from Liverpool so they could leave home at the right time. She gave her husband to understand they were just going on a short visit and in this way left him and started for Utah. Andrew, not knowing that he would not be back home in a few days, asked his father to feed his rabbits till he came back. This was in the month of May, 1866. They boarded the *Saint Mark,* a sailing ship bound for New York with a company of Mormon emigrants.

They sailed from Liverpool, England, June 6, 1866, with a Mr. A. Stevens in charge. Their voyage was a fairly good one, and they arrived in New York on the twenty-sixth of June.

The father learned of this and had a cablegram sent to his sons in Maryland asking them to go to New York and at least prevent the children from coming to Utah to live among the Mormons. His sons got the message and came to New York but they were too late, the company having left just a few days before. They then gave up the chase and returned to Maryland.

Mary and the family reached the Missouri River after the usual trials and hardships incident to such a journey, and were assigned to Captain Andrew Scott's ox train. Here they were to cross the dreary plains of some thousand miles where everybody had to walk the distance traveled by the oxen each day. This journey took two months, as the teams traveled very slowly. They traveled some fifteen to twenty miles each day, often lying over on Sunday.

They walked in the heat and dust all day and cooked their food by a smoky fire, sometimes with no wood and poor water. They slept in tents outdoors on the hard ground with ten to twelve persons to a tent. They got along fairly well, however, until they came to the Black Hills or mountain country, where young Mary became ill with mountain fever. She was very sick and had to be carried in the wagon the rest of the way. However, her condition was much improved when they arrived at Uncle John Murray Murdoch's in Heber about the last of September, 1866.

It was a very happy meeting. It had been fourteen years since Mary had last seen her brother, John, and everyone had passed through many trying times since they bade each other goodbye in their native land. Now that they were all safe in Zion they had cause to rejoice. They had many sorrowful tales to tell each other, and especially in speaking of their dear mother's death on the plains while she was trying to reach her son, John. There was also the sad fate of James Steel, who died on the plains, leaving a wife and two small children. James Steel was a brother of Ann Steel, wife of John Murray Murdoch. They talked of how they had pinched and saved to be able to send money to pay the fare of his mother and brother-in-law, both of whom died on the way.

Not long after their arrival Thomas Todd, who had known Mary in Scotland, came to visit her, and after a few visits he asked her to become his plural wife. She accepted his offer, and they went to the Endowment House in Salt Lake City and were married. They went to their new home, where Alex and Mary recuperated from their illness and began to work for different families. Andrew got a job feeding stock and doing chores for his board and lodging. Their marriage did not prove entirely satisfactory, and in less than four years they separated. He gave to her a lot with a log cabin on it and wood and flour to last her a year as required by Bishop Hatch. He did this, as he considered she was entitled to some consideration on account of the treatment she had received. In this way their matrimonial partnership ended. In December 1868 daughter Mary, at sixteen years of age, married William Lindsay. They later became the parents of eleven children.

About 1871 Daniel McMillan, the village blacksmith and a widower with a grown family, asked Mary to marry him, and she accepted his offer. She had been properly divorced from Thomas Todd. They were duly married in the Endowment House on June 26, 1871, and Mary went to his home and took up her abode. It was a log cabin and not very well furnished, but he was kind and gentle to her in his own way. He was quite an intelligent man too, but had contracted the habit of drinking liquor, which caused Aunt Mary trouble and anxiety all the rest of her life. However, he was an honest and hard-working man and earned good wages, but had not been able to save much. So, of course, Aunt Mary did all she could to change this condition, as through her whole life she had practiced thrift and economy. In her quiet Scotch way she had saved every cent that she possibly could and began making improvements in their home and surroundings. In a very few years, through her strict economy and saving, she managed to save enough to build quite a respectable stone house in which to live, and furnished it so that they were very comfortable. They also bought some land and had several cows, pigs, and chickens to help make their living. Through her thrift and economy with his earnings, he became wealthy compared with his financial condition before Mary became his wife. Mary's son Andrew married Mary Ann Thompson in 1879, and Alexander married Eliza Thompson in 1883. Andrew later had eleven children and Alexander ten.

While Mary was able to work she not only took care of her husband's earnings, but she earned means in every way possible herself. She acted as a midwife for some years and did a great deal of needlework for others. Always busy, she was a splendid example of industry. She was never more happy than when talking over the beauties of the gospel plan or listening to some of the discourses of the leaders of the Church.

She never felt to murmur or complain, and she earnestly desired that her children would become active workers in the Church and show that they appreciated what she had done for them in bringing them to Zion.

One day a woman with three children came along and asked if they could stay in the old house for a few weeks, and of course she was given permission. After being there a few days she asked if Mary would take care of her two little girls, four and six years of age, as she had to make a short visit to Park City. This was also granted and the woman left and never came back. Mary cared for them just as if they had been her own and supplied all their wants and sent them to school. In later years Mary had an attack of rheumatism in her back and was unable to walk. The girls by this time were old enough to attend to the housework and wait on her when necessary, and they both proved true and faithful to Mary and waited on her just as if she had been their real mother. She could give the girls direction with the housework, and even while lying in that condition she did a great amount of knitting for others. She just could not be idle. The girls' name was Olsen, Elva and Nettie. They both married well and raised good families. Elva married Joseph Howarth and Nettie married James Reid Lindsay. So the little girls left in her care actually proved a blessing to her in her later years.

In March 1869, Mary's oldest son came and had a few days' visit. He seemed to be quite favorably impressed with what he saw. In fact, he said that perhaps it was better for the younger children that they came to Utah. He had come west with a group of bridge builders for the Union Pacific Railway, all the way from Omaha. They were paying good wages and he wanted to come west to see his mother, brothers, and sister. He could only stay two days as he had to go back to his work. When the railroad was completed he went to his home in North Lawrence, Kansas, and died there in 1872, leaving a wife and two children, Allan and Mary. (These two grandchildren never married or had children.)

In 1898 Mary's other son, James Mair, came to Heber and stayed two or three weeks, visiting his mother and all the relatives. He too seemed to enjoy his visit very much and formed a very good opinion of the Mormon people and their way of living. He admitted before he returned home that the Mormons were a much better people than he had had any idea of. He had some long talks with his dear mother and felt to forgive her for leaving her husband in the way she did. He also felt that the children were much better off in every way than they would have been with their father in Scotland. He married in Maryland in October, 1868, to a very good woman named Mary Ann Pengelly from Cornwall, England. She was a very neat and tidy woman. They were unable to have children. He returned to his home in Maryland and reported conditions in Utah as he found them to his wife. She became quite interested and expressed a desire to visit his Utah relatives and the Mormon people. Some three years later he and his wife came and spent a month visiting all the relations in their homes and attending various Church services. They were taken to see all the sights of interest in the valley as well as Park City and Salt Lake City, where a few of the Murdoch families were. They were treated royally by all. They fully appreciated the kindness shown and expressed a desire to come again. They had long talks with John Murray and William, Mary's brothers, on religion and other topics, and also with William Lindsay, with whom they stayed most of the time. James and his wife returned in 1912 and had another four weeks'

visit, which they thoroughly enjoyed. They seemed hesitant to leave their Mormon friends. However, they returned to Eckhart, Maryland, where James Mair died in April, 1915; his wife died there in October, 1922. They were good, honest, and kind-hearted people and very much respected in their community. Mary, James's sister, visited them in Eckhart in 1907 and was royally treated by them for some three weeks.

Mary Murdoch Mair McMillan died on December 5, 1900, at the age of eighty-one years. She was loved and respected by all who knew her, and never lost her faith in God or in the gospel for which she had suffered so much. Although very thrifty, she was generous and kind to the poor, sick, and afflicted. While able, she was always willing to lend a helping hand. She set a worthy example for children and friends to follow of faith, patience, and loyalty to God. She was indeed a humble and faithful member of The Church of Jesus Christ of Latter-day Saints. (Family histories by Phil Rasmussen and others.)

Daniel McMillan, shown here in the entrance of his shop, was one Heber's early blacksmiths, Andrew Mair, Sr., is in photo shoeing the horse.

Allan Mair

Allan Mair, the son of John Mair and Mary Foulds, was born April 23, 1815 in Mauchline, Ayrshire, Scotland. He came from a family of thirteen children, having nine brothers and three sisters. His father at one time was a servant in the small village of Killoch, a short distance north of Mauchline. When Allan was just a boy, his family moved to a small town called Gaswater, where ironstone mining was the prime industry.

Allan spent a good portion of his growing-up years in Gaswater and was employed at the mines. On June 4, 1841 he married Mary Murdoch, a girl whom he had known since childhood. They made their home in a small settlement known as High Gaswater which is situated 300 yards up the hill from the main village of Gaswater. They were able to own a small but comfortable home. Allan and Mary also lived in other areas known as the Stables and on the Carbellow Farm which are both within one mile of Gaswater.

Allan and Mary were blessed with nine children, seven boys and two girls. One girl and two of the boys died in infancy.

Allan was a hard worker and a good provider for his family. Besides being employed as an ironstone miner, he did some farming while living in Carbellow. His occupation was listed as "retired watchman" in the 1891 Auchinleck Parrish Census. He was probably employed at the mine or at the Stables.

Allan and his wife had a fine home and a wonderful family; however, there was some discontentment concerning religion. Mary had joined the Mormon Church on June 4, 1851, and Allan did not want anything to do with it. Mary's brother, John Murray, had also joined this church, left Scotland for the United States, and settled in Heber City, Utah. Also her mother, Mary Murray Murdoch, left Scotland to join her son, John Murray, in Utah but died en route at Chimney Rock, Nebraska.

Mary, having a great desire to have her family raised up in the Mormon Church, secretly left her husband, taking her three youngest children to Utah, arriving in 1866. These children were Mary, Andrew, and Alexander. Two older sons, John and James, had previously left Scotland and settled in the eastern part of the United States. This left Allan and his son, Allan Foulds, who was twenty-one years of age, alone in Scotland. They were both very lonely for a long time, hoping that some day Mary would return. In 1870 the son, Allan Foulds, married Jane Ronald of Muirkirk and was eventually blessed with eleven children. Allan was very close to his family and had great comfort in their companionship. He spent some of the later years of his life living in their home. He also lived with his granddaughter Mary Mair Moffat. Allan Mair died on May 2, 1897 at the age of eighty-two and was buried in the Auchinleck Cemetery.

Annie Lindsay Clyde of Heber City, Utah, corresponded for some time with Mary Mair Moffat in Scotland. A direct quotation from a letter written by this granddaughter dated February 5, 1933 describes Allan Mair as follows: "I am just going to talk plain truth, no use going around about way, well, Dear Old Grandfather was a very standoffish man and we never heard him mention much of his life. I know he was very much put out when my Grandmother left for Salt Lake. She had wanted him to go out there, but he said no of course she went out there herself and we never heard him mention her name others ways than she was a good wife, of course you must understand it left a bitter feeling with him. He was a very strict man and he ruled us with a rod of iron indeed we always clung to him."

Grave site of Allan Mair in the Auchinleck cemetery. These pictures were taken by Bill Mair, who found that the upper portion of the gravestone had fallen off.

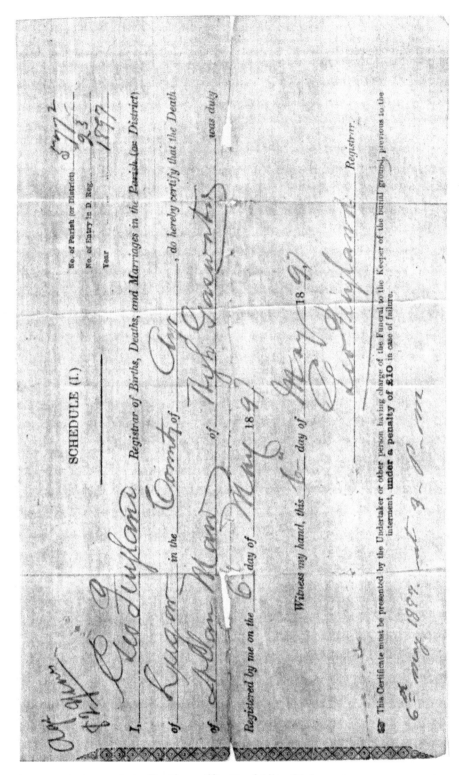

Death certificate of Allan Mair.

Twenty-nine years after Mary Murdoch Mair McMillan came to Utah,
she received this letter from her son Allan Foulds Mair. She had left
him and her husband Allan Mair in Scotland. She and three children;
Mary, Andrew, and Alexander came to Utah for the gospel.

Gasawater november the 7: 1897

My dear "Mother" I sit down to write you
a few lines in answer to your welcom letter
and we weare all verry happy to sea that you
were in your would helths and I mus thanke
youll verry kindelly for your present
for it showes the respect you had for father
and Dear mother you want to now the kind
of felling we had when you went away
for my father I think he always thought
you would com backagin for he woul never
alou the dour to be bared at nigt and he
allways wondered how the cheldren would
be getting along and for my self I fell
verry lonaly for a long time and Dear
mother I have sarched the scriptuers a god
deall and I dont see it makes much which one
one may be living in for the serves of our
lord and savour for he says that wharever
to or three is met in my name their will I be
in the midst of them and you say we ar to love all
and follow our lord and your wright to but is
scotland not as near to heaven as amarica
for their is as much wickednes the one place as the
other but we have the life of our lord and savour
while on this erth for our guid for you now
that of ourr selves we can donothing unles our
lord inclines our harts toward him but moth
er if I was near you we would have a sweet
talk over it but if we dont meat in this wo
uld I hop Dear mother to meat in the one to com
and Dear mother yo wanted to now about father
brothers and sisters births and their father
and mothers births but I could not get them

The Different Ages Of

John Mair Jane Killoch

Allan Mair
Father

Born June 14 - 1809 John Mair
" January 10 - 1811 Mattew Mair
" Janry 19 - 1813 Wm Mair
" April 28 - 1815 Allan Mair
" May 18 - 1817 Jannitt Mair
May 27 - 1819 Andrew Mair
June 4 - 1821 Alexander Mair
Feb 21 - 1823 James Mair
April 1 - 1825 Elen Mair
feb 21 - 1827 David Mair
March 6 - 1829 Jean Mair
Nov 2 - 1831 Christpher Mair
Augt 4 - 1833 Thomas Mair

but this is his brathers and sisters births
and the ar all ded but Christopher and his
wife is ded to and he has one daug her maried
and uncel williams is living yet wife is
Living and John is carriaing on the busnes and
the tw daughters is married to farmers and
marry has now famely but Jane hase twelv
e of a famaly eleven suns and one daughter
and James had four one died other three
maried and aunt Jane died September the
14 last and she was up hear seaing us
a fortnight before in good helth and
asking verry kindly for yow and we were
togithir best respects and Christpher the sam
and Dear mother I mus draw to a close hoping
this will find yowall as it leaves us in good helth
thank god for his grate blesings to us all
yowr san Allan Foulds Mair +++

Daniel McMillan

"Daniel McMillan was born at Dumbarton, Scotland, on March 2, 1819. When a lad of fifteen he moved with his parents to England, where he served several years' apprenticeship as a blacksmith. In 1845 he married Janet Davis.

Born and reared a Catholic and remaining devout to this religion nearly thirty years, he studied Mormon literature and listened to the missionaries. Finally the family joined the Church as converts of George Q. Cannon. They were baptized into The Church of Jesus Christ of Latter-day Saints in the year 1849, emigrating to America in 1863, crossing the sea in an old-style sailing ship driven hither and thither by the winds and waves. They crossed the plains with ox teams in the heat, dust, and wind, sharing all the hardships and inconveniences of the two months' travel on that 1,000 mile journey. They reached Heber in 1865, where Daniel began plying his trade as blacksmith and, with the aid of his loving wife, began to clear what was then a wilderness and make for themselves a happy home. Before their hopes were realized, however, the cruel hand of death visited his home and snatched away the loving wife and mother. In 1871 he married Mary Mair Murdoch, who died in 1900. No children were had from the second marriage, but by his first wife he was the father of four: Ephraim, Phebe Hanna, Mary Ellen, and William. He had three stepchildren, Mary, Andrew, and Alexander Mair. Elva and Annette Olsen, two little girls, were left in Mary's and his care for a few days by their mother, but she never returned. Daniel and Mary adopted them and reared them until they were married.

Daniel McMillan was known as 'Uncle Dan' to everyone who knew him. Heber was his home for over a quarter of a century. Being generous to a fault and without any enemy in town, his friends were as numerous as his acquaintances. During his long residence in Heber he established for himself a record as a man of integrity and uprightness. He died at the home of his son William, peacefully, as the blotting out of the sun's rays by a passing cloud, on April 29, 1902."

HUSBAND Allan MAIR

Birth	28 April 1815
Place	Killoch, Mauchline, Ayrshire Scotland
Chr.	
Married	4 June 1841
Place	Cronberry, Auchinleck, Ayrshire, Scotland
Death	2 May 1897 Gaswater, Ayrshire, Scotland
Burial	Auchinleck Cemetery, Ayrshire, Scotland
Father	John MAIR
Mother*	Mary FOULDS
Other Wives (if any)	

WIFE Mary MURDOCH

Birth	3 October 1818
Place	Gaswater, Auchinleck, Ayrshire, Scotland
Chr.	8 November 1818 Old Cumnock, Ayrshire, Scotland
Death	5 December 1900 Heber, Wasatch, Utah
Burial	8 December 1900 Heber City Cemetery, Utah
Father	James MURDOCH
Mother*	Mary MURRAY
Other Has (if any)	Thomas TODD-2 Daniel McMILLAN-3

Where was information obtained?

*List complete maiden name for all females.

1st Child John MAIR
- Birth: 6 September 1841
- Place: Carbellow, Ayrshire, Scotland
- Married to: Catherine CONNOLY
- Married: 1867 United States
- Died: 27 May 1872 N. Lawrence Kansas

2nd Child James MAIR
- Birth: 17 December 1843
- Place: Carbellow, Ayrshire, Scotland
- Married to: Mary Ann PENGELLY
- Married: 4 October 1868 Lonaconing, Maryland
- Died: 27 April 1915 Eckhart, Maryland

3rd Child Allan Foulds MAIR
- Birth: 25 December 1845
- Place: Carbellow, Ayrshire, Scotland
- Married to: Jane RONALD
- Married: 10 June 1870 Auchinleck,Ayr,Scotland
- Died: 14 June 1907

4th Child Matthew MAIR
- Birth: 17 January 1848
- Place: Carbellow, Ayrshire, Scotland
- Married to:
- Married:
- Died: As a child Scotland

5th Child William MAIR
- Birth: 3 May 1850
- Place: Carbellow, Ayrshire, Scotland
- Married to:
- Married: As a Child Scotland
- Died:

6th Child Mary MAIR
- Birth: 1 August 1852
- Place: Carbellow, Ayrshire, Scotland
- Married to: William LINDSAY
- Married: 15 December 1868 Salt Lake City,Utah
- Died: 3 June 1916 Heber, Wasatch, Utah

7th Child Janet MAIR
- Birth: 4 November 1854
- Place: Carbellow, Ayrshire, Scotland
- Married to:
- Married:
- Died: 17 March 1855 Scotland

8th Child Andrew MAIR
- Birth: 17 February 1856
- Place: Carbellow, Ayrshire, Scotland
- Married to: Mary Ann THOMPSON
- Married: 24 July 1879 Heber, Wasatch, Utah
- Died: 6 July 1924 Heber, Wasatch, Utah

9th Child Alexander MAIR
- Birth: 18 February 1859
- Place: Gaswater, Stables, Ayrshire, Scotland
- Married to: Eliza THOMPSON
- Married: 15 February 1883 Heber,Wasatch,Utah
- Died: 11 April 1936 Heber, Wasatch, Utah

10th Child
- Birth:
- Place:
- Married to:
- Place:

Place Picture of Child in Left Blank

Place Picture of Wife or Husband in Right Blank

Or Wedding Picture To Cover Both Blanks

Bookcraft Inc. S.L.C. (Wilson Form)

ALLAN AND MARY MURDOCH MAIR
(Three Generations)

DESCENDANTS

A JOHN MAIR 1841-1872 Married 1867 A Catherine Connoly	A Allan MAIR 1869-1946 A Mary " 1870-1966	

A JAMES M. MAIR 1843-1915 Married 4 Oct 1868 A Mary Ann Pengelly	No Children

S ALLAN FOULDS MAIR 1845-1907 Married 10 June 1870 S Jane Ronald	S Jean	MAIR	1866-1904
	S Mary	"	1869- ? MC
	S Nellie	"	1871- ? MC
	S Allan Foulds	"	1873-1908MC
	S John	"	1875- ? MC
	S Thomas	"	1877- ? MC
	S Jessie	"	1879 ? MC
	S James	"	1882-1968MC
	S Margaret	"	1884- ? MC
	S Andrew	"	1886- ? MC
	S Marion	"	1890- ? MC

S MATTHEW MAIR
1848-Died as Child

S WILLIAM MAIR
1850-Died as Child

S ALLAN MAIR
Born 28 April 1815
Where Mauchline,Ayrshire,Sctl.
Died 2 May 1897
Where Gaswater,Ayrshire,Sctl.

Married About 1838-1840

U MARY MURDOCH
Born 3 October 1818
Where Gaswater,Ayrshire,Sctl.
Died 5 December 1900
Where Heber,Wasatch,Utah

U William Lindsay 1847-1932 Married 15 Dec 1868 **U MARY MAIR** 1852-1916	U Mary M.	LINDSAY	1869-1948MC
	U William Howie	"	1871-1939MC
	U James Lyon	"	1873-1932MC
	U John Allan	"	1875-1958MC
	U Daniel McMillan	"	1877-1887 D
	U Andrew Alexander	"	1879-1947MC
	U Samual	"	1881-1882 D
	U Christina Veronica	"	1886-1974MC
	U David Pryde	"	1888-1926MC
	U Baby Girl	"	1890-1890 D
	U Annie Murdoch	"	1892-1978MC

S JANET MAIR
1854- 1855

U ANDREW MAIR 1856-1924 Married 24 July 1879 U Mary Ann Thompson 1863-1953	U William Allen MAIR		1880-1931MC
	U Mary Elizabeth	"	1882-1961MC
	U Sarah Jane	"	1884-1966MC
	U Esther Isabell	"	1886-1946MC
	U Andrew	"	1889-1962MC
	U John M.	"	1891-1921MC
	U Franklin Alexander		1893-1893 D
	U Martha Ann	"	1895-1926MC
	U Nellie	"	1899-1975MC
	U Mable Veronica	"	1901-1979MC
	U Emma	"	1905-1969MC

U ALEXANDER MAIR 1859-1936 Married 15 Feb 1883 U Eliza Thompson 1865-1959	U George A.	MAIR	1884-1956MC
	U Allan Fowles	"	1886- MC
	U John William	"	1889-1973MC
	U Daniel	"	1892-1964MC
	U Nettie	"	1894- MC
	U Mary M.	"	1896- MC
	U Thomas	"	1898- MC
	U James	"	1901- MC
	U Andrew	"	1903-1975MC
	U Lindsay	"	1907 MC

S-Remained in Scotland
A-Came to U.S.A.
U-Immigrated to or born Utah
M-Married
C-Had Children
D-Died as Child

John Mair and Katherine Connoly

John Mair was the oldest of the nine children of Mary Murdoch Mair and Allan Mair. He was born in Auchinleck, Ayrshire, Scotland, on September 6, 1841. His boyhood days were spent at Carbellow Farms, where his father was employed. When he reached young manhood he and his brother, James, came to America to seek their fortune. They found work in Pennsylvania and were making their home there in 1866 when they received word from their father in Scotland that their mother had left Scotland with her three youngest children, Mary, Andrew, and Alexander, and was bound for Utah. The father requested his sons to meet the ship in New York and send his family back to him. John and James arrived in New York too late to stop their mother from going to Zion.

In the year 1867, John married Katherine Connoly, and they lived in Lawrence, Kansas. A son, Allan, was born to John and Katherine Connoly Mair in 1869, and then on March 26, 1870, they were blessed with a baby girl, whom they named Mary.

John Mair was a carpenter and helped to build the bridges of the Union Pacific Railroad. He worked on the railroad bridges from Omaha to Utah in 1868 and 1869. While working on the railroad in Utah John visited his mother, brothers, and sister in Heber City in March 1869 for a couple of days. The railroad from the east met the one from the west on May 10, 186q at Promontory, Utah, and was then completed. John returned to North Lawrence, Kansas, and on May 27, 1872, his life ended. He was only thirty-one years old when death took him from his wife and two little children.

Some years later, his wife and children moved to Kansas City, Kansas. Some of their relatives from Heber City went to Kansas throughout the years and visited with them and found them very hospitable and gracious.

The son, Allan, was very kind and gentle. He spent his life on the police force. Mary was a very lovely lady, and she was a bookkeeper. Neither Allan nor Mary ever married, so there are no living descendents of John Mair.

Katherine Connoly Mair died February 16, 1926, at the age of eighty-four. Allan passed away February 1, 1946. About a year later Mary came to Utah and spent a month at the home of her cousin Crissie L. Duke. She became acquainted with all her cousins and kinfolk. All who met her loved her. She visited points of interest concerning her family. Mary was a Baptist, and felt she had been "saved," so she saw no need for another religion. Mary died in Kansas City, November 27, 1966, the last of the John Mair family.

John Mair

Katherine Connoly Mair

Allan Mair, Katherine Connoly Mair, Mary Mair

James M. Mair and Mary Ann Pengelly

James M. Mair, the second son of Allan and Mary Murdoch Mair, was born in Carbellow, Auchinleck, Ayrshire Scotland, December 17, 1843. He spent his youth at Carbellow farms. When he was a young man, he and his older brother John came to America. They worked in the mines in Pennsylvania for a time. In 1866 they received a wire from their father in Scotland telling them that their mother had left home with the three younger children Mary, Andrew, and Alexander (Alec) and was on her way to Utah. He wanted James and John to go to New York and try to persuade them to return, but they were too late. Mary Murdoch Mair and family were on their way west to Zion.

James went to Maryland where he met Mary Ann Pengelly, a young woman who had been born in England September 2, 1847. Their friendship ripened into love and they were married October 4, 1868 at Lonaconing, near Frostberg, Maryland, where James worked at the trade of carpet weaver. He also became a Baptist minister and was intelligent and very well read. Before his death he became a "Millennial Dawner." He also served as a member of congress from Maryland for one term. In politics he was Republican. James and Mary Ann were gentle and refined people and were greatly loved and respected by the people of that area.

James often thought about his mother living out west among the Mormons, and he wondered about his brothers and sister. What were the conditions under which they lived? Were they poor and downtrodden, or what? So in 1899 he wrote to his sister Mary, saying he would like to come and visit his family in Utah if it was all right with them. By return mail an invitation was sent to him and his wife to come and spend some time with Mary and her husband William Lindsay, so he could visit his mother and brothers and their families.

James, or "Uncle Jimmy," as we called him, arrived in Utah in June 1899, but he came alone, perhaps to see just what living conditions were in a Mormon community. It was indeed a happy reunion, the first time mother and son had seen each other for over thirty years. His mother was bedfast, suffering from rheumatism. One outstanding event was a family gathering at his mother's home, where all his kinsmen met to renew acquaintance and to show off the next generation. His mother, Mary Murdoch Mair McMillan, passed away the following year.

In 1902, James came again and brought his wife with him this time. Also, again in 1912, the Mairs from Maryland came to enjoy the companionship of their dear ones in Utah.

On both visits, they were entertained at dinners in Heber and Park City. Excursions to Luke's Hot Pots in Midway proved to be lots of fun with many family members joining in. By horse and buggy they visited all points of interest in the Heber Valley. There was much happiness and laughter as they visited their fellow Scotsmen. Uncle Jimmy helped in the fields and became acquainted with the life of a farmer. On September 2, 1902, a surprise dinner party was held for Auntie (Mary Ann Mair) and sixty-three guests called at the Lindsay farm three miles east of Heber and partook of one of Mary M. Lindsay's delicious banquets. It was a happy day for the visitors from the East.

They also visited with Andrew and Alec and their families.

Uncle Jimmy attended church when he was in Heber, and occasionally a religious discussion followed. Often at the Lindsay home where they were staying, religion was the topic of conversation and sometimes it became a little heated.

When he was here on his first visit, his brother-in-law, William Lindsay, gave him copies of the Book of Mormon and *A Voice of Warning*. After his return home, Uncle Jimmy wrote back and said he had read both books and formed a good opinion of both. He also enjoyed and used other LDS books.

Each time the Mairs returned to Maryland they carried home gifts and good wishes from their loved ones in Utah. And they were impressed by the Mormon people and their relatives in Heber.

In 1907, James's sister Mary and William Lindsay went to Maryland to pay them a visit, and they were treated royally by the Mairs. One Sunday, Uncle Jimmy put a white vest on William and took him to church. He introduced him as Dr. Lindsay from Utah and called on him to speak. "Dr." Lindsay took advantage of the situation and preached a good gospel sermon. He also found Reverend James Mair was preaching a lot of Mormonism, himself.

Clipping from a Maryland newspaper dated Friday October 18, 1907:

RECEPTION AT ECKHART

"Mr. and Mrs. James M. Mair entertain visitors."

Mr. and Mrs. James M. Mair of Eckhart gave a reception at their home 'fountain View" on Thursday evening in honor of their guests, Mr. and Mrs. William Lindsay of Heber, Utah.

The house was tastefully decorated with flowers and an air of good feeling spread over all. The host acted as toastmaster. Everyone enjoyed his address on "My Maryland." The following gentlemen responded in a hearty manner: Rev. R.D. Stephenson, James Bannatyne, James Weston and Prof. A.D. Boyle. Dr. Lindsay then made an address, saying, while this was a very beautiful and prosperous country, the West is not to be forgotten, the words of Horace Greely: "go west young man and grow up with the country." At 10:30

the doors leading to the dining room were thrown open. There was to be found many good things that proved pleasing to the palate.

Those present were Mr. and Mrs. William Lindsay, Utah; Rev. and Mrs. R.D. Stephenson; Mr. and Mrs. James Weston, Miss Rena Weston, Mr. and Mrs. Conrad Lapp, all of Frostberg; Mr. and Mrs. James Bannatyne, Mr. and Mrs. Albert Bender, Mr. and Mrs. Thomas Eckhart. Mrs. Fred Crowe, Miss Maglie Crowe, Mrs. Katherine Simons, Misses May and Emma Simons, Mr. and Mrs. William B. Griffith, Mr. and Mrs. Alex G. Close, and Miss Kate Walters, all of Eckhart.

James and Mary Ann never had any children, but they did raise a girl whose name was Annie and she later married a Mr. Griffith.

On their visits to Utah, James tried to convert his sister Mary to the Baptist faith—and Mary tried to convince him of the truth of Mormonism. So before leaving for home the last time, he said, "Mary, how could I become a Mormon, and then go back to Maryland and face my congregation? But when I die, I'd like you to do for me what your church does for the dead."

James Mair died April 27, 1915, in Eckhart Mines, Maryland. His wife died there also on October 21, 1922.

In 1925 their temple work was done by relatives in Utah.

James M. Mair

Mary Ann Pengelly Mair

Home of James M. Mair in Eckhart, Maryland

Allan Foulds Mair and Jean Ronald

Allan Foulds Mair was the third child of Allan Mair and Mary Murdoch, born December 25, 1845 at Carbellow, Ayrshire, Scotland. Carbellow is a small mining community located about two miles east of the more prominent towns of Cumnock and Auchinleck. Foulds was raised in a humble home along with five other brothers and sisters. About 1865 his older brothers John and James left their home in Scotland and immigrated to the United States. His mother, who had joined the Mormon Church, sister Mary, and younger brothers Andrew and Alexander left home during May 1866 and also immigrated to the United States. Because of contention in their home concerning religion, they left without Foulds and his father knowing of their plans. This left Foulds very lonely for a long time. Foulds was the only child to remain in Scotland. His brothers John and James made their homes in the states of Kansas and Maryland respectively. His mother, sister Mary, and brothers Andrew and Alexander settled in Heber City, Utah.

Foulds soon married a young lady from the neighboring town of Muirkirk. Her name was Jean Ronald. They were married on June 10, 1870. They made their home in Gaswater with Foulds assuming the same occupation as his father by working in the mines. Foulds and Jean had a large family consisting of eleven children, six girls and five boys. Foulds, Jean, and their sons and daughters all remained in Scotland. The 1881 and 1892 Auchinleck Parish Census Records indicate their family lived in a two-room house and also that Foulds's father lived with them for a short time. The birth records of their sons John and Allan Foulds, Jr., indicate the family had lived in an area about one mile from Gaswater known as the Stables.

In 1897, just after his father died, he corresponded with his mother in Utah. He expressed his thoughts about how lonely he and his father were after his mother left.

He related that his father would never lock the door at night hoping that someday she would return. He also stated he had studied the scriptures a good deal and it didn't matter which country one lived in—that they could still worship the Savior.

In 1905, William Lindsay, the husband of Foulds's sister Mary, who was a Mormon missionary laboring in England, took the opportunity of visiting his brother-in-law in Scotland. He found that Foulds was in poor health and had not been able to work for the past three years. He became acquainted with all the children of Foulds and Jean. At this particular time four children had married and six were still single. James, a grown son dressed in kilts, played the bagpipes for his special benefit. William Lindsay describes Foulds as five feet nine inches tall, 170 pounds, with blue-gray eyes and light-colored hair. Foulds was especially interested in pets, such as birds and rabbits. He worked in the coal mines for fifty years. He was the father of a large family of stalwart sons and daughters, all hardworking, honest, and respectable members of the community in which they lived. Foulds seemed to be a very nice,_ mild-tempered man, very kindly disposed to all around him, and was respected by his neighbors.

David Lennox Murdoch, a cousin of Foulds, served a mission in Scotland for The Church of Jesus Christ of Latter-day Saints also. While there he visited Foulds and stated the following about the visit in his journal: "September 3, 1906. Took 8:10 train for Cronberry. Walked up to High Gaswater to see cousin Foulds Mair. He lives a little below where Grannie (Mary Murray Murdoch) used to live. It is a little row running north and south with perhaps four or five houses in it. Foulds and his family uses two of the places—the rest used for store rooms or byres or the likes. All that remains now where Grannie lived is the gable and walls. It is evidently long roofless. Foulds is getting white and old looking and is much troubled with his breathing. He showed me around the place and pointed out the hole in the ground that represented the pit where Grandfather (James Murdoch) lost his life in attempting to save others who had gone down and were overcome with fire damp or rather black damp. I pulled some heather not far from where Grannie lived and will send it home to friends. They have ten children living—one being dead. The only ones I saw were Mary who lives in Barters row and is a Mrs. Moffat and has five of a family and Marion who is at home and is about seventeen years old. Two sons are also at home, but they were off working. I did not see them. One son is a policeman in Paisley and another is a policeman in Glasgow. One daughter is in service about Sanquahar and another is in service about West Kilbride. One son lives in Lugar and a daughter Mrs. Walls lives (Glentagart, Douglas), I forget just where. Mrs. Mair looks pretty well but is somewhat troubled with one of her legs which makes her a little lame. She is a Ronald of Muirkirk.

"I forgot to mention that Foulds has Grannies cupboard and sugar bowl. The cupboard has been a fancy article in its day. It has Chinese designs on the outside and inside. There are a number of little drawers and pigeon holes of which one is kept the sugar bowl."

Allan Foulds Mair died of asthma on June 14, 1907, and was buried by his father, Allan Mair, in the Auchinleck Cemetery behind the Parish.

Children of Allan Foulds Mair and Jean Ronald

Jean Mair died at age thirty-eight and never married. Mary Mair married John Moffat, who was a farm worker and lived in Gaswater.

Nellie Mair married John Walls, a shepherd.

Allan Foulds Mair, Jr., married Euphamia Wilson and was a coal miner.

John Mair married Mary McNaughton and was a police sergeant in Paisley.

Thomas Mair married Jane Smith. He was a policeman in Glasgow.

Jessie Mair married Tom Kirk, a shepherd.

James Mair married Christina Love and was a coal miner. Margaret Mair married Robert Clark, who was

a farmer. Andrew Mair married Kate McLean. He was a Campdoffie worker in Glasgow.

Marion Mair married John Adam, owner of Aerated Waterworks in Port Glasgow.

Four generations: Jean Ronald Mair, her daughter Mary Mair Moffat, and her daughter Jane Moffat Boyle and son James Boyle

Allan Foulds Mair Jr. with wife Euphamia Wilson Mair and children Jean, Allan, Nellie and Margaret. Older woman believed to be the mother-in-law.

Thomas Mair with wife Jane Smith Mair and children Margaret, Allan, and Archie.

Marion Mair Adams with husband John Adams and children Allan and Janet.

Four grandchildren of Allan Foulds Mair, who are all sisters and the daughters of James Mair and Christina Love Mair. They are presently living in or near Cumnock, Ayrshire, Scotland. They are from left to right: Jessie, Kirsty, Bessie, and Jean. Photo recently taken at Kirsty's silver wedding anniversary.

HUSBAND   Allan Foulds MAIR

Birth   25 Dec 1845
Place   Carbellow Ayrshire, Scotland
Chr.
Married   10 June 1870
Place   Scotland
Death   14 June 1907
Burial   Auchinleck Parish, Ayrshire, Scotland
Father   Allan MAIR
Mother*   Mary MURDOCH

(1ST CHILD) Jean MAIR–Photo not available B-1866 Scot
Not Married   Died July 1904 Scot

WIFE   Jane RONALD

Birth   1843
Place   Muirkirk, Aryshire, Scotland
Chr.
Death
Burial
Father
Mother*
Other Hus (if any)
Where was information obtained?   William Dale Mair
*List complete maiden name for all females.

2ND Child   Mary MAIR
Birth   1869
Place   Gaswater, Ayrshire, Scotland
Married to   John Moffat
Married
Place

3RD Child   Nellie MAIR
Birth   1871
Place   Gaswater, Ayrshire, Scotland
Married to   John WALLS
Married
Place

4TH Child   Allan Foulds MAIR
Birth   1 January 1873   Died 1908
Place   Gaswater, Ayrshire, Scotland
Married to   Euphamia Wilson
Married
Place

5TH Child   John MAIR
Birth   11 February 1875
Place   Gaswater, Ayrshire, Scotland
Married to   Mary McNAUGHTON
Married
Place   Paisley

6TH Child   Thomas MAIR
Birth   1877
Place   Gaswater, Ayrshire, Scotland
Married to   Jane SMITH
Married
Place   Cronberry, Ayrshire, Scotland

7TH Child   Jessie MAIR
Birth   1879
Place   Gaswater, Ayrshire, Scotland
Married to   Thomas KIRK
Married   16 March 1908
Place   Gaswater, Ayrshire, Scotland

8TH Child   James MAIR
Birth   16 January 1882   Died 1968
Place   Gaswater, Ayrshire, Scotland
Married to   Christina LOVE
Married   3 February 1911
Place   Lomark, Ayrshire, Scotland

9TH Child   Margaret MAIR
Birth   1884
Place   Gaswater, Ayrshire, Scotland
Married to   Robert CLARK
Married   4 December 1907
Place   Gaswater. Ayrshire, Scotland

10TH Child   Andrew MAIR
Birth   1886
Place   Gaswater, Ayrshire, Scotland
Married to   Kate McLEAN
Married   1920
Place   Isle of Skye

11TH Child   Marion MAIR
Birth   1890
Place   Gaswater, Ayrshire, Scotland
Married to   John ADAMS
Married   1914
Place   Gaswater, Ayrshire, Scotland

```
1 MURDOCH, James 1786-1831              2 MAIR, Mary MURDOCH 1817-1900
1 MURDOCH, Mary MURRAY, Sp. 1782-1856   2 MAIR, Allen, Sp. 1815-1897

                                 3 MAIR, ALLAN FOULDS 1845-1907
         DESCENDANTS OF---------
                                 3 MAIR, JEAN RONALD 1843-

   4 MAIR, Jean B-        1866 D-        1904

   4 MOFFAT, Mary MAIR B-          1869 D-
   4 MOFFAT, John, Sp. B-              M-           D-

          5 MOFFAT, John B-
          5 MOFFAT, Elizabeth BROWN, Sp. B-            M-

          5 BOYLE, Jean MOFFAT B-
          5 BOYLE, William, Sp. B-              M-

                 6 BOYLE, James        B-

                 6 BOYLE, Jean         B-

                 6 BOYLE, Mary M.      B-

                 6 BOYLE, John Moffat B-

                 6 BOYLE, Allan M.     B-

                 6 BOYLE, Winifred     B-

                 6 BOYLE, Elizabeth    B-

          5 MOFFAT, Allan B-

          5 MOFFAT, David B-

          5 MOFFAT, Thomas B-             D-         1979

          5 GIBSON, Mary MOFFAT B-
          5 GIBSON, Hugh, Sp. B-

                 6 JONES, Maureen GIBSON B-
                 6 JONES, Harry, Sp. B-            M-

                        7 JONES, Colin           B-

                        7 JONES, Belinda         B-

                 6 GUTHRIE, Irene GIBSON B-
                 6 GUTHRIE, Sam, Sp. B-            M-

                        7 GUTHRIE, Jacqueline    B-

                        7 GUTHRIE, Kenneth       B-

                 6 GIBSON, John MOFFAT B-
                 6 GIBSON, Ruth PYPER, Sp. B-         M-

                        7 GIBSON, Caroline       B-

                        7 CIBSON, Alistair       B-

                 6 GIBSON, William     B-

                 6 GIBSON, David       B-

          5 MOFFAT, Jessie B-

   4 WALLS, Nellie MAIR B-        1871 D-
   4 WALLS, John, Sp. B-              M-           D-

          5 PRINGLE, Jean R. WALLS B-
          5 PRINGLE, William, Sp. B-              M-
```

```
            6 PRINGLE, Adam B-
            6 PRINGLE, Jean          Sp. B-              M-

                    7 PRINGLE, James                    B-

                    7 PRINGLE, Jean                     B-

      5 WALLS, John B-              D        1914

      5 WALLS, Allan B-

      5 CRAIG, Agnes WALLS B-
      5 CRAIG, John, Sp. B-              M-              D-

            6 CRAIG, William B-
            6 CRAIG, Sarah LAIRD, Sp. B-           M-

                    7 CRAIG, Linda                      B-

                    7 CRAIG, William                    B-

                    7 CRAIG, Jacqueline                 B-

            6 CRAIG, James B-
            6 CRAIG, Agnes WHITEFORD, Sp. B-               M-

                    7 CRAIG, John                       B-

                    7 CRAIG, Morag                      B-

            6 CRAIG, Ian B-
            6 CRAIG, Roberta COLWELL, Sp. B-               M-

                    7 CRAIG, Pauline                    B-

            6 CRAIG, Ronald B-
            6 CRAIG, Jane WYTE, Sp. B-            M-

                    7 CRAIG, Tracy                      B-

                    7 CRAIG, Allan                      B-

            6 GRAHAM, Elizabeth CRAIG B-
            6 GRAHAM, William, Sp. B-             M-

                    7 GRAHAM, Una                       B-

                    7 GRAHAM, Kristy                    B-

                    7 GRAHAM, Zaura                     B-

            6 CRAIG, Agnes B-

4 MAIR, Allan Foulds B-1 Jan 1873 D-
4 MAIR, Euphamia WILSON, Sp. B-              M-              D-

      5 MAIR, Margaret          B-

      5 MAIR, Allan             B-

      5 MAIR, Jean              B-

      5 MAIR, Nellie            B-

      5 MAIR, Andrew            B-

      5 MAIR, John              B-

4 MAIR, John B-11 Feb 1875 D-
4 MAIR, Mary McNAUGHTON, Sp. B-              M-
```

```
        5 MAIR, Allan          B-

        5 MAIR, Andrew         B-

        5 MAIR, John           B-

        5 MAIR, Margaret       B-

        5 MAIR, Jean           B-

4 MAIR, Thomas B-      1877 D-
4 MAIR, Jane SMITH, Sp. B-              M-              D-

        5 MAIR, Allan F. B-
        5 MAIR, Molly       Sp. B-              M-

        5 McNAB, Margaret W. MAIR B-
        5 McNAB, John, Sp. B-              M-

                6 McNAB, Tom           B-

                6 McNAB, John          B-

                6 McNAB, Sherna S.     B-

        5 MAIR, Archie S. B-
        5 MAIR, Catherine McGREGOR, Sp. B-              M-

                6 MAIR, Tom            B-

        5 MAIR, Thomas         B-

4 KIRK, Jessie MAIR B-      1879 D-
4 KIRK, Thomas, Sp. B-              M-16 Mar 1908 D-

        5 KIRK, Jean           B-

        5 KIRK, Jessie         B-

4 MAIR, James B-16 Jan 1882 D-
4 MAIR, Christina LOVE, Sp. B-      1886 M-3 Feb 1911  D-

        5 MAIR, Elizabeth (Bessie) B-          1911

        5 BANNATYNE, Jean MAIR B-          1913
        5 BANNATYNE, Alex, Sp. B-              M-

                6 BANNATYNE, Hugh R. B-
                6 BANNATYNE, Margaret GIBSON, Sp. B-              M-

                        7 BANNATYNE, Douglas A.      B-      1965

                        7 BANNATYNE, Hazel M.        B-      1967

        5 MAIR, Allan Foulds B-          1918 D-      1935

        5 ROBERTSON, Jessie MAIR B-          1920
        5 ROBERTSON, John, Sp. B-              M-

        5 HARKNESS, Christina MAIR B-          1924
        5 HARKNESS, Alexander, Sp. B-              M-

                6 HAINEY, Christina HARKNESS B-
                6 HAINEY, Martin, Sp. B-              M-

                        7 HAINEY, Allan M.           B-

                6 HARKNESS, Aileen    B-
```

4 CLARK, Margaret MAIR B-   1884 D-
4 CLARK, Robert, Sp. B-   M- 4 Dec 1907 D-

        5 CLARK, John B-
        5 CLARK, Elizabeth Patterson, Sp. B-   M-

                6 CLARK, Jean   B-

        5 CLARK, Allan F. B-
        5 CLARK, Janet Howat, Sp. B-   M-

                6 CLARK, Jessie   B-

                6 CLARK, Robert   B-

        5 CLARK, Robert B-
        5 CLARK, Barbara, Sp. B-   M-

                6 CLARK, Carol Anne B-

                6 CLARK, Elizabeth   B-

                6 CLARK, Barbara   B-

                6 CLARK, Margaret   B-

                6 CLARK, Robert   B-

        5 THOM, Jean R. CLARK B-
        5 THOM, John, Sp. B-   M-

                6 THOM, Ian Clark   B-

                6 THOM, Jean R. B-
                6 THOM, David, Sp. B-   M-

                6 CUNNINGHAM, Margaret THOM B-
                6 CUNNINGHAM, Ronald, Sp. B-   M-

                        7 CUNNINGHAM, Joyce   B-

                        7 CUNNINGHAM, John   B-

                6 JACKSON, Millis THOM B-
                6 JACKSON, William, Sp. B-   M-

4 MAIR, Andrew B-   1886 D-
4 MAIR, Kate McLEAN, Sp. B-   M-   1920 D-

        5 GORDON, Margaret Vicky MAIR B-
        5 GORDON, Charles, Sp. B-   M-

        5 MAIR, Andrew B-
        5 MAIR, Sylvia, Sp. B-   M-

4 ADAM, Marion MAIR B-   1890 D-
4 ADAM, John, Sp. B-   M-   1914 D-

        5 ADAM, Janet   B-

        5 ADAM, Allan   B-

        5 ADAM, Alexander   B-

Mary Mair and William Lindsay

Mary Mair Lindsay, the daughter of Mary Murdoch and Allan Mair, was born at Carbellow near Lugar in Auchinleck Parish, Ayrshire, Scotland on August 1, 1852. Her father was a farmhand, or shepherd, and was mostly employed herding sheep on the bonny heather hills. Her mother was an industrious woman, having worked out for people in her youth to help her mother sustain the family after her father lost his life trying to save the life of another.

Mary was the only girl in the family; she had five brothers, three older than herself and two younger. The two oldest, John and James, came to America when they became of age, and went to Maryland, one working as a carpenter and the other as a coal miner. One girl and two boys died as children.

Allan Mair and Mary Murdoch were married in June 1841, and they seemed to get along nicely until about 1850 when the Mormon elders came to that part of Scotland preaching an entirely different doctrine than what was taught by the ministers of the churches. Allan Mair, Mary's father, like many others could not see any need of a new religion. The church and religion of his fathers was good enough for him. Her mother, on the other hand, became very interested in the new religion, and she was baptized on June 4, 1851, by a missionary, William Aird. Wee Grannie and William Murdoch's wife and Veronica Murdoch Caldow also became baptized.

She tried to convert her husband, but he refused to hear the gospel or have anything to do with it. And now in a home where there had been peace and harmony, there was friction. So there came a time when Mary's mother decided to leave her husband and home, and if possible to bring her three youngest children to Utah, where they would enjoy the blessings of the gospel. This was in the year 1866. To do this, it was necessary to get Mary's cooperation, which she did. Mary was then thirteen years of age, Andrew was ten, and Alex seven. An older brother, Foulds, was

soon to be married, and his mother felt that he would look after his father.

It took some time making the arrangements and getting everything ready for leaving without her father suspecting that something was going on. Mary's mother would fix bundle after bundle of clothing of all kinds, and Mary would carry these to the station and mail them to a friend who would keep them until the time they would start for Utah. This friend, John Aird, had to keep them posted as to when to leave home just in time to get on the ship taking Mormon emigrants, as delays would have been dangerous. John Aird had secured them passage on the *St. Mark,* a sailing vessel.

Everything worked out just right, and the mother and children left home with the understanding that they were only going on a short visit. Andrew asked his father to care for his rabbits until he got back. Of course, when Allan, the father, found out that his wife and three children were actually gone on a ship, the *St. Mark,* bound for New York, he sent a telegram to his sons in Maryland asking them to at least prevent the children from going to Utah. His sons came to New York, but were just a little too late. So of course, the mother and children went on.

This was the last time Mary was to see her father and brother, Foulds. Some thirty-one years later on May 2, 1897, her father, Allan Mair, died, and in November of that year Foulds answered a letter he had received from Mary Murdoch Mair, his mother. In part the letter from Foulds says: "Dear Mother, You want to know the kind of feeling we had when you went away; for my father, I think he always thought you would come back again, for he would never allow the door to be barred at night and he always wondered how the children would be getting along. And for myself, I felt very lonely for a long time. And Dear Mother, I have searched the scriptures a good deal, and I don't see it makes any difference which country you may be living in, for the service of our Lord and Savior. . . . You say we are to leave and follow our Lord, and are right too, but is Scotland not as near to heaven as America. . . . If I was near you we would have a sweet talk over it. But if we don't meet in this world, Dear Mother, I hope we'll meet in the one to come. . . ."

What wonderful faith and courage Mary's mother manifested to leave her husband and home under such circumstances, and to undertake such a journey, knowing too that her dear old mother had perished on the way crossing the plains, and that her brother John and wife saw their two children die on the way to Utah, some years before. But knowing all this, she still had faith and courage enough to undertake the long and wearisome journey across the ocean and across the dreary plains.

They felt the hand of the Lord helped them across the mighty deep. It took them ten days to go from New York to Florence, Nebraska, on the Missouri River. It was a hard journey for emigrants, as there were many changes to make from steamboats to railroads and back again several times. There was no direct line from the East to the West at that time. But Mormon emigrants always had some person in charge whose business it was to look after all the rest and see that they and their baggage were properly cared for.

They were assigned to cross the plains in Captain Andrew Scott's ox train. This of course, wa8 another new and strange experience for them, and one that was very trying for everyone. The teamsters with their oxen and wagons had come all the way from Utah for the purpose of hauling the sick and infirmed and the baggage and food supplies necessary to sustain them on their long and tedious journey. The teamsters were usually rather rough-looking young men, many of them less than eighteen years old, dressed mostly in homespun or buckskin, armed with heavy long whips, and calling loudly "whoa," "ha," and "gee." This was the means they used to guide the oxen. Of course all this shouting at the oxen, who were slow and stupid, and the cracking of the long whips was new to the emigrants. The sleeping in tents, cooking over fires in skillets and frying pans in the smoke, traveling in wind, and dust and rain was rather trying. Flour and bacon were practically all that was provided in the way of food, and many did not know how to make bread or fry their bacon over a campfire. Everyone had to walk that possibly could, and they were warned to keep near the wagons even if it was dusty and uncomfortable. Of course, prayers were attended to night and morning in the corral formed by the wagons for protection from Indians and also where the oxen could

be easily yoked up. Thus they traveled from day to day for two months.

As they came into the mountains, Mary was taken ill with mountain fever, which was similar to typhoid. This, of course, was the cause of great anxiety to her mother, but through the blessings of the Lord in answer to prayer, and through her mother's kind care, she was spared. They arrived safely at Uncle John Murdoch's in Heber about the eighth of October, 1866. Thirty persons had died on this dreary journey. Thousands have laid their wearied bodies down by the wayside, trying to reach the gathering place of the Saints. Mary's mother and her family all reached the valley and found good, kind friends in her brother John Murdoch and family, who took them into their home and supplied their wants until they were able to provide for themselves.

Mary, though still weak and pale from her illness, soon recovered and was baptized November 25, 1866 by Thomas Todd. She could not be baptized while in Scotland, as her father would not consent to it. Her mother was married to Thomas Todd as a plural wife, and he began to provide for the needs of the family. But Mary began to work out for other families and in that way earned her own living.

Soon after her arrival in Heber, she became acquainted with a young man named William Lindsay, and an attachment sprang up between them as the years went by. William had come to Heber from Scotland four years before.

The following is William Lindsay's description of Mary when he first met her: "Mary was then fourteen years of age, and she attracted my attention more than any other girl I had seen, and I visited her quite often. She had been ill crossing the plains, but soon got well and strong and was a very fine looking girl. Her cheeks were red, her eyes blue gray, and her hair was a very light yellow. And above all, she had a smiling face and a kindly sociable disposition, and a winning way that won my heart, and I seemed to win hers. There were two or three suitors who tried to win her affection, but they gave it up as they saw I was her choice. We were very happy in each other's company always, which in time, was very frequent; at meetings, Sunday School, dances, concerts and theaters. She had to work at different homes to earn her living and I used to visit her there at times. We never had any lover's quarrels as some do Of course, I had to go off at times to work here and there, but I always got a welcome home from Mary."

William Lindsay, the man in Mary Mair's life, was

born near Ardie, Lanarkshire, Scotland, on February 11, 1847. He was the second son in a family of nine children, born to William and Christina Howie Lindsay. When he was about fifteen months old he lost the sight of his right eye by being struck with a sharp piece of a broken dish. His parents were members of the LDS Church at this time. He screamed and cried with the severe pain of his injured eye, so they had the elders lay their hands on his head and give him a blessing. He stopped crying and the pain left him. This special blessing strengthened the Lindsay's faith in the gospel they had recently embraced a month or so before.

His father was a coal miner, and wages were less than a dollar a day. For various reasons they had to move quite often, so William did not get much chance to go to school—one year was all, but he had a very good teacher and made rapid progress, being in fourth grade when he was nine years old. At that age he went into the coal mine with his brother, Robert, to work with their father. The boys pushed the little cars of coal from where their father mined it to the bottom of the shaft, where it was taken to the surface and most of it loaded onto ships and sent to other countries.

There was a law in Scotland that boys under ten years of age could not work in the mines unless they could read and write. One day the mine inspector was inspecting the mine in company with the mine owner. The inspector noticed William, who was only nine years old, and small for his age. The inspector asked his age and then said, "Read for me," and he drew a book from his pocket. William passed the test; then he was asked to spell "Carmelbank," which he did successfully. As a reward, the inspector gave him a shilling, the first shilling William had ever had. He felt very rich indeed, but went straight to his father and gave it to him.

Soon after his father was baptized, he was ordained an elder and presided over the Ayr Branch of the Church. Every Sunday they walked three miles to church and three miles back, and the mother often carried a little child fastened on her back with a shawl. William Lindsay, Sr., had a great desire to raise his family properly, and to bring them to Utah to help build Zion.

On October 17, 1861, William and his brother, James were working in the mine with their father. They were moving the coal that their father dug in little coal cars. When they returned with the cars, they found him dead under a large stone. It was indeed a sad day. Besides losing their dear father, it seemed all their hopes of coming to Utah were blasted. The brave little mother called her children around her and said, "Never mind, we'll go to Zion on the first boat in the spring." And her words proved true. Their father was buried in Saint Andrew's Kirkyard in the town of Kilmarnock. The boys had to go back to the mine to support the family.

In April 1862, the Lindsay family received word from the Church office in Liverpool that arrangements had been made for Christina and all her family to cross the Atlantic with a company of 700 Saints. There was great rejoicing in their home. Christina sold everything she would not need for the journey, and on the morning of April 18 they left Bonnie Scotland. When they reached Liverpool they boarded the sailing ship *John J. Boyd* to go to America. They stood the voyage all right, and arrived in New York after two weeks on the ocean. They went by train to Saint Joseph on the Missouri and then went by steamboat to Florence. Here they were met by old Robert McKnight, with a basket full of scones and a bucket of milk, which were very much appreciated after their rations. He arranged for the Lindsay family to live in a small log cabin while waiting at Florence to cross the plains.

The ox teams arrived about the twentieth of July, and the Lindsay family was assigned to John Turner's wagon from Heber, Utah. They were in the Homer Duncan Company, and were the first Church train to leave Florence for Utah that year. About the third day out they reached the Platte River, and a dance was held on a sandy place in honor of the twenty-fourth of July, the day Brigham Young and his pioneer band reached Salt Lake City fifteen years before. This company had the same trials, hardships, and experiences as other similar groups, and many nights they gathered around the campfire and sang songs together. The Lindsay family traveled without sickness or serious trouble. At Silver Creek they were met by John and George Muir, who urged the Lindsays to come to Heber, which was just being settled and where land was cheap and water was plentiful. And being in a Heber wagon, they went straight to Heber.

Christina Lindsay and her children, Robert, William, James, Samuel, Andrew, Jean, Elizabeth, and Isabell were glad to settle down after five months of traveling.

William said, "I liked the looks of the little valley the first time I saw it, which was on the 21st of September 1862. I hoped to make my future home here, and help subdue the wilderness." William was then fifteen years old.

The family arrived in Heber on Friday and on Sunday it was arranged for William to go to work for

George Carlile on Monday. His wages were to be $100.00 for a year's work to be paid in wheat at $2.00 a bushel. The grain was just being harvested, and his job was raking the bundles of wheat. As George Carlile cut the wheat with a cradle, his poor old mother bound it in bundles as William raked them into shape. He soon got so he could rake the bundles and help to bind them too. His brother Robert also hired out, and this way their mother could get wheat for herself and her children. William attended Sunday School in the log meetinghouse, and he was made a deacon and helped to chop the wood and carry it into the meetinghouse to keep the two fireplaces going in the winter.

Later William was able to buy a cow so his mother and brothers and sisters could have milk and butter on their bread. He began working as a farmhand; he fed stock, hauled poles for fences, and hauled sand rock to build houses. He was finally able to get a yoke of steers, and he and his brother invested in a wagon. He then hauled wood and coal to Salt Lake to sell. He took one load of wood to President Brigham Young's woolen factory at the mouth of Parley's Canyon to trade for some certain kinds of cloth his mother needed. The man in charge there needed the wood and had the kinds of cloth William wanted, but he said he could not dispense any cloth without an order signed by President Young. So William, in his dirty, rough clothes, went into Salt Lake to Brigham Young's, and President Young signed the order.

On the twenty-sixth of May, 1866, William enrolled in the territorial militia and joined John M. Murdoch's Company of Infantry. This was because of the Indians under Black Hawk causing trouble.

In the fall of 1867, William was called to haul rock from the Little Cottonwood Quarry to the Salt Lake Temple which was then under construction. When spring came in 1868, he was to bring emigrants back to Utah. But before he left he got a promise from his dear girl, Mary Mair, that she would marry him when he returned.

The trip east was not an easy one. They had high rivers to cross and sometimes had to build bridges and had trouble getting across some rivers where they had to swim. They traveled through Indian country and had to be on the lookout all of the time. They waited on the North Platte for the emigrants to arrive by train. His emigrants were Scandinavians and of course they had a little trouble communicating. But they soon learned to understand each other. They returned to Salt Lake the last of September.

As soon as William reached Heber, he found that many of the local men were up at Echo Canyon, working on the grade of the Union Pacific Railroad. He was anxious to earn some money before winter set in as he and Mary were planning to get married before the year was out, so he set out for Echo Canyon. There he found about twenty-two men from Heber working, but they were badly in need of cooks and dishes.

The men were living in dugouts on the side of the hill. They agreed to build an extra dugout for William and the cooks if William would get someone. Immediately William returned to Heber and got his mother to say she would go with him and bring her stove and dishes. Then he saw his best girl, Mary, and got her consent to come along, so she got her mother's permission. So early the next morning, the three of them started on the two-day journey to Echo. Everything was ready for the women when they arrived, so they went right to work preparing and serving the food. They got along fine and gave excellent satisfaction. They stayed there for two months, each woman receiving $45.00 per month for her services. The men with teams got $10.00 a day.

As soon as they arrived home on December 3, they began making wedding preparations for the middle of December.

William and Mary

The story of William and Mary from here on is one story, and here it is in William's own words:

"We were planning to go to the Endowment House to be married so my brother, Robert, and his girl, Sarah Murdock, decided to go with us. Sarah was 15 years old and Robert was 23. Mary was 16 and I was 21 years of age. On the 12th of December 1868, we started out with two yoke of oxen and a wagon. Mother went with us and also Ann Richardson and her two children. The first night we camped in the camp house at Kimball's in Parley's Park. It was a very cold night. The next morning we started out very early, but the roads were frozen and very slippery, so we traveled very slowly as the oxen kept falling down. It got dark while we were still up in Parley's Canyon. Some men with a horse team tried to pass us and their horses fell down and one was floundering under the wagon tongue. It was very dark and Robert and I went to help. One of the men said: 'You boys stand back, you might get hurt.' Mother quickly spoke up in her Scottish brogue and said, 'They are nae boys, they are on their way to get married!'

"We finally reached N.C. Murdoch's house in Salt Lake, where we all stayed. The next day was Sunday and we attended church. On Monday we went to the Endowment House, but there were so many ahead of us, we had to wait until the next day. So we went and had our pictures taken and bought wedding rings for our bonnie brides. In the evening we attended the Salt Lake Theater and saw some very good actors present 'Romeo and Juliet.' (Mary had a sage green dress with white dots for this special occasion. She had an engagement ring with a green stone, and the wedding rings that were purchased were made of black guterperchie buttons. Aunt Sarah says the girls felt like queens at the theater and they were very proud of their grooms in their homemade clothes.)

"On December 15, 1868, we were united in marriage in the Endowment House, by Daniel H. Wells, for time and all eternity. Of course, we had our endowments and sealings. I received one of the greatest blessings any man can receive in this life, a good, true, faithful, loving wife.

"The next day we bought a hundred pounds of flour at $10.00, two common chairs and a rocking chair, a gallon of molasses, and a brass kettle. I had bought some plates and other articles while I was back after emigrants. We stayed that night at the home of John Muir. Robert and Sarah stayed in Salt Lake a week more. The next day we started our journey home, Mother, Mary and me. One ox was lame, so I chained him and his mate behind the wagon, and I gave Mary a long stick to switch the oxen to make them walk up and not hold back. I drove the other yoke of oxen that were hitched to the wagon. Mary walked most of the way. I guess we presented a rather strange picture of a bridal tour. But I can say that there was no complaining and we all were quite happy. This was the start of our honeymoon, and I am sure with it all we enjoyed ourselves as well or better than some do in their fine cars. From this day on Mary Mair was Mary Lindsay.

"My brother, Robert, had a large log house in Heber, and we had made arrangements to live with him and Sarah that winter, so when we arrived in Heber, we moved our few articles in and started housekeeping. We lived with Robert and Sarah that first winter. Some long winter evenings were spent reenacting 'Romeo and Juliet.'

"I owned a lot on 3rd East and 1st North and before our marriage I had dug a cellar 12 feet square, and walled it up. I also had logs on the ground all ready to build a house over the cellar in the spring. As soon as it was possible, I built my log cabin and we moved into it and felt quite proud of our own little home. I had a chimney and a fireplace in one end and a nice stone flag for a hearthstone. A trap door and a stairway went down into our fine cellar. I walled up a well. Later I built a lean-to for a summer kitchen and put shingles on the roof of our little log cabin. I farmed on shares and quarried rock to sell, and also hauled wood to sell.

"In our little log cabin, our first child was born, October 20, 1869. We named her Mary Murdoch, after Grandma, and called her Mamie. My Mary got along very nicely. She proved to be a thrifty, tidy housekeeper, and a cheerful, loving companion throughout her whole life of service to others. Not only in her own home and to her own family, but wherever anybody needed help, she would find some way to help them, and make them happy if possible. On the 24th of October, 1871, our son, William Howie, was born, and again all went well. We had to depend on midwives as there were no doctors.

"In 1871 I helped John Galligher teach school and was able to buy myself a yoke of steers and a wagon. I felt almost like I was rich. I made a claim on land up on Lake Creek with my brothers, Robert and James.

"I went to Evanston the winter of 1872 and worked in the coal mine and got our first stove—a charter oak—and Mary was very proud of it. As soon as I could, I got her a sewing machine as she did all the sewing for the family and made her own clothes, and she often helped others with their sewing too. Although she worked hard and for long hours, she was always good natured and happy.

"In 1876 I walked to Salt Lake City and got my citizenship papers and entered a quarter section of land on Lake Creek. In 1878 we left our little home in Heber. By this time we had two more children, James L. and John Allan. The year before that, I had built a log cabin up Lake Creek and we were increasing in property, and had three cows and some young cattle.

"We all worked very hard on our homestead; the sagebrush was tall and thick and hard to clear off the land. We had to build stables and sheds for the cows and oxen, we made ditches and canals and put up fences. The boys were still too small to help much. They had to herd cows on the hills when they were not in school. We called this place Lindsay's Dell. (It is now called Lindsay's Hill.)

"We had three more boys; Daniel McMillan, Andrew Alexander, and Samuel. Then there came a time when Mary's health failed, and for about five years she was barely able to move about. At times it looked like she could not live long. That was from 1881 to 1886. Crissie was born on July 15, 1886, and Mary had suffered severe pain with sciatic rheumatism all that summer and was very weak. I took care of the baby and fed her with a bottle for two weeks. Mary gradually got stronger and finally was well again. She had several severe illnesses, but had a great deal of faith and was healed a number of times by the power of God and the administration of the Elders.

"Our little boy, Samuel, died of whooping cough when ten months old in 1882; and our fine boy, Daniel, died when nearly 10 years of age in 1887. The doctor said he had ulceration of the stomach, but he was kicked in the stomach by a boy.

"We were regular in attending our meetings and Sunday School even though we had three miles to go. We would hitch the oxen on the wagon and all of us got in and off we would go. It took an hour to get there, so we had to start early and we were seldom late.

"We built a very nice house of hewn logs and covered it with rustic lumber outside, and plastered the inside. We had four good sized rooms and a pantry downstairs and three bedrooms upstairs. It was finished about 1885. The dining room was large and in it we had many dinners and dances for our friends who came often with surprise parties. They were always made so happy and so welcome that they wanted to come again. No one ever went away from Mary's home hungry. The first question she asked her visitors was, "Are you hungry?"

"In 1872 she received a patriarchal blessing from John Smith and among other things he said to her, 'Your table shall be spread with the bounties of the earth and you shall impart to many.' She was a splendid cook and served much delicious food. She always served her food in the best way possible and with cheerfulness. Mary prepared many banquets and wedding dinners, and topped them off with a beautifully decorated cake.

"We had visits occasionally from the Indians, but we treated them kindly and got along very well. However, Mary got frightened one day when we were all away from the house excepting herself. She saw a strange man coming toward the house and as he came nearer she could see he was Negro. She asked him what he wanted and he said he was hungry and wanted food. Mary said, 'All right, I will get food for you, but you must stay outside.' She gave him a liberal supply and he went away. We found out that he was a soldier and had deserted from Fort Duchesne.

"In December of 1893, I was called to take a Sunday School course at Provo, and I had to walk part of the way down. I attended classes at the Academy and boarded at Hannah Galligher's. In March, I came home and walked most of the way again, the snow was still very deep. In 1895, I was set apart as the Superintendent of the Heber Sunday School. We then met in the Stake House and there were 400 or more attended. I was a Sunday School teacher for many years before. I was a ward teacher from the time I was 17 years old. I was set apart to the High Council of the stake on February 4, 1890.

"Mary was a counselor to Alice Lambert in the Heber First Ward Relief Society for several years. The poor and the sick were made happy from her visits as she had a great sympathy for the ill and unfortunate. She was also an officer in the Sunday School. Her office was that of 'Welcomer.' That was a very fitting position for her as she gave all a very cheerful smile and a hearty handshake as they entered the church on the Sabbath day.

"Mary was 40 years of age and one day over when our youngest was born. The birth dates of our eleven children are as follows: Mary Murdoch (Mamie), Oct. 20, 1869; William Howie, Oct. 24, 1871; James Lyon, Sept. 21, 1873; John Allan (Jack), Sept. 15, 1875; Daniel McMillan, Aug. 15, 1877; Andrew Alexander, Oct. 23, 1879; Samuel, Dec. 3, 1881; Christina Veronica (Crissie), July 15, 1886; David Pryde, Aug. 16, 1888; stillborn female baby, Jan. 20, 1891; Annie Murdoch, Aug. 1, 1892. Quite a family (parish records show Mary's birth Aug, 1. 1852).

"After we got into our new house, about 1885, there was a raid made on the Polygamists and we kept Joseph Moulton's two wives and their children some six weeks. Later we kept Nephi Thayne's plural wife about six weeks, so that the Mormon haters did not get them.

"For years Mary baked bread nearly every day, and used 50 pounds of flour every week. We were nearly always well supplied with plenty of vegetables. Then there was the sewing, the washing and ironing, churning the butter, sweeping, making the beds and supplying all of our wants. These were busy days for her, but she was happy and cheerful all the day long.

"In 1905 I was called on a mission to Great Britain. This I am sure was a greater trial to Mary than to me. I made some trades and sold some animals to raise money and got my son Andrew to look after the farm for a year. I had bought a lot in Heber some two years before and there was a three room log house on it.

Mary, Crissie, Dave, and Annie moved down into the little house. I was 58 years old when I left.

"Mary never said a word to discourage me from going. We had a little meeting at my son Will's home the day I was to leave, about the 20th of March. Every member of my family was there, and of course all were feeling rather downcast and each one was shedding tears. After I had spoken a short time advising them to be kind to each other and especially to their dear Mother, Mary stood up and spoke and said she knew the mission call was from the Lord. She asked the children to take my advice and help her all they could, and the Lord would bless us and all would be well.

"We went to the train depot and all tried to make the parting as easy as possible. Just as I got on the cars, my youngest son David got hold of me and would not let go. I had all I could do to get him off the train without him getting hurt.

"Mary had gone out different times to help women who had given birth to children, and while I was gone she did this a great deal and earned all she could to help support the family. Whenever she waited on anyone they always wanted her again, so she became very popular in this kind of work. She was a kind, efficient nurse, and prepared good food for the family and cleaned the house.

"After arriving in England I was assigned to the Birmingham Conference and I enjoyed my missionary labors. I got the credit of distributing more tracts and having more conversations than any Elder in the conference, but I did not hold as many street meetings as some. During the Bank Holidays in 1905, I visited my wife's brother, Foulds Mair, and his family in Scotland. I found them well except Foulds who had not been able to work for three years because of his asthma. They were glad to see me and treated me very well and did all they could to entertain me. They were not interested in the gospel, but had no fault to find with the doctrines I explained to them. They had a fine stalwart family of grown sons and daughters.

"I visited the house where my dear Mary lived until she came to Utah, and plucked branches of the bonnie bloomin' heather from the bushes she had plucked it from when she was a bonnie wee lassie, runnin' bare footed at the house called The Stables, near the burn that is called Gaswater. Of course, in a couple of days I returned to my missionary work, but had a warm invitation to visit the Mairs again.

"I want to say that I was greatly blessed all the time I was gone and was able to keep my mind on my missionary work and enjoyed it very much. I had the spirit of my mission for one thing. My family at home wrote regularly once each week and the letters were always cheerful and encouraging and never complaining or wishing I would come home until I was honorably released. All these things helped me to be contented and happy with my lot.

"In March 1907 I was given an honorable release so I could visit for three weeks in Scotland before my ship would sail to America.

"In Scotland I visited Foulds Mair, my wife's brother, and his family again. They treated my royally. I spent five days in Edinburgh and spent most of the time in the Registrar's office looking for names and dates. I spent a few days in Glasgow with D.L. Murdoch and other elders. I went to Kilmarnock and spoke at a street meeting at Kilmarnock Cross where I had stood as a boy and heard my father preach the same Gospel nearly 50 years earlier. I went to Ayr and from there went on foot to Craighall, Burnbrae, St. Quivax. I went back to see Foulds before I left Scotland and got my clothes that they had washed and ironed. They gave me a little broom and some playthings that were Mary's when she was a child. I went back to England and was soon on my way to my dear home. Before I left I bought some white silk for Crissie's wedding dress.

"Mary and the family were blessed with good health while I was gone. With the help of the children I was supplied with all the money I required while on my mission. I was blessed with good health and had fair success in my missionary labors.

"I arrived home on April 30, 1907. As I came up Provo Canyon on the trail I said like William Tell: 'Ye crags and peaks, I am with you once again!' I was met at the Heber Depot by my dearest family, friends and neighbors. Mary had invited my brothers and their wives to eat dinner with us, and she had set tables out on the lawn in front of our little log house. We ate and talked and enjoyed each other's company for hours. It seemed like a real taste of heaven on earth. The only drawback to our complete happiness was that my dear old faithful mother had died while I was gone. During her illness Mary had nursed her and done all in her power to ease the pain and to make her comfortable. Mary had gone out nursing and Crissie taught school to earn means to support themselves and me.

"I took my place on the High Council when I returned and visited the wards reporting my labors in the mission field and bearing my testimony. I soon found work for the city fixing roads and bridges and laying stone walks at street crossings.

"Mary and I decided to make a visit to Maryland to see her brother, James Mair. He had visited her twice at our farm home. We left Sept. 1907 on the D.&R.G. Railroad. We went to Washington, D.C., and stayed one night. The next morning we went down the Potomac River and passed Mount Vernon on a steamboat. We passed the Chesapeake Bay and arrived at Norfolk, Virginia, after dark. While there, we visited the Jamestown Exposition and saw many wonderful things. We saw a picture show for the first time and saw many things of interest. We spent the night in Norfolk and the next morning we took a steamboat back to Washington, D.C. We got there after dark as it is 196 miles. Mary stood the boat ride very well. We found a lodging house for the night. We spent the next day visiting the White House, the Halls of Congress, the Library, the Smithsonian Institute, the Treasury Building, and finally went up the Washington Monument some 500 feet on an elevator. Washington is a fine looking city with wide, straight streets. We took the train for Cumberland and then went on the electric car to Eckhart, Maryland, where our brother, James, and his wife, Mary Ann, were waiting for us. They had made every preparation to entertain us and make us comfortable and happy while we stayed for two weeks. They took us to other towns and arranged visits with their friends and relatives. We visited their churches and public entertainments.

"They invited their minister, school teacher, and other prominent citizens to a party at their home and we were the guests of honor. We had a jolly time. We had some talks on religious topics and although we didn't see eye to eye, at least they were kindly and friendly discussions. Jammie had sent me $20.00 while I was in England and had thus far helped to preach Mormonism. They are both kind-hearted, honest people, but he, like many more could not see the truth and beauty of the Gospel. After a pleasant fortnight with them and their friends, we left for our mountain home. We went by way of Pittsburg, Chicago and Kansas City where we stopped to visit with John Mair's widow and two children. They also received us kindly. We went to Independence to see the site of the great temple that is to be built there, according to Joseph Smith's words. The gate was locked so we could not get inside the lot. Mary, however, pushed her feet as far as possible under the gate so she could say her feet had stood on the sacred spot. When our train reached Heber, we found our children at the depot to welcome us home.

"Mary got somewhat dizzy on the train and got tired trying to take in all the sights. She did enjoy her trip very much, but was glad to get home. This was the only pleasure trip that either of us had ever taken and it gave us something to tell about for a long time.

"In 1908 I sold our farm to my son, Will, for $3500.00 and built a nice brick home on our lot in Heber at 1st N. and 4th E. It was built as nearly as possible to suit Mary's plan to be convenient for her. She did not want an upstairs in it. She was proud of her new home and fully appreciated it after living three years in the small log house. We moved into our new home Dec. 15, 1908, just forty years from our wedding day. We had a grand dinner and had all of our living children in the new home to celebrate the 40th anniversary of our marriage. We felt quite proud of our nice new home with all the modern conveniences: running hot and cold water, electricity, and a bathroom. The children bought us a fine new heating stove and put it in the dining room, and Mary looked as happy and as cheerful as she did forty years before. Then there were two of us, and now there were ten and all the grandchildren.

"We began having prayers night and morning in our home when we got married and we very seldom missed a day in all the years after.

"In July 1912, Mary's brother, James Mair, and his wife came from Maryland and spent three happy weeks with us Mary had a way of making visitors feel very welcome at our home.

"In October our dear little Annie had to have a goiter operation which was a great worry for Mary and all of us.

"Early in 1914 Mary had a stroke of paralysis. She had been to a funeral and being sympathetic and feeling very bad she started home, but fell by the way and had to be carried home. Her whole right side was affected and she could not talk to be understood. I cannot describe my feelings when I saw my dear Mary lying there helpless and speechless. She who had been so kind, so faithful, so true to me and the children. She who had worked for and waited on us so willingly all these many years. The elders administered to her several times. And in a week she showed improvement, but she was never able to dress herself without help for over two years. When she felt better, she asked me to go to town and get some extra wide silk ribbon and with her left hand she crocheted and was able to make nice little bags for her daughters and daughters-in-law, nieces, and friends. She still had the desire to serve others. Even in this condition, Mary was cheerful and tried to be happy in her home, but she could not stand to go out in a crowd where they were enjoying themselves. I took her out a few times in a wheel chair but I had to bring her home.

"On the 9th of June, 1915, Annie was married. Poor Mary had a good cry to think her youngest child had left our happy home and gone to make a nest of her own. When her body was strong, she rejoiced to see her children get married, knowing that was the proper thing for them to do. Her two eldest sons were married on the same day, and she worked hard for days to give them a grand reception. Mamie had been living with us for some time and she helped to see that Annie had a grand reception in Amusement Hall. Mary was taken in an automobile and held up quite well. However, it was a sad change for her, at all her other children's weddings she had been the chief actor, but now she was almost helpless. But she never murmured or complained. She did her very best to keep up that cheerful smile that was so natural to her.

"Mary was not only kind and loving to her children and her husband, but her sympathy went out to every person that stood in need of assistance. Many a person outside of her own family had cause to remember her for her deeds of kindness in times of sickness or trouble, and she was never known to boast of the good she did.

"On the 3rd of June, 1916, I was working on the street north of my home, and Mary asked me to help her to the corner of the boardwalk and to place a chair for her to sit underneath the little box elder tree. It was warm and she sat and watched me work until noon. I helped her in the house and she ate dinner all right, but as she finished she was stricken and passed away without uttering a word. My dear Mary, who was so full of faith, so loving and kind and true, was dead. It was a dreadful shock to all of us, even though we knew that in her condition she could not live very long. She was 63 years old.

"The funeral was in the Stake House with Bishop Robert Duke in charge. The house was filled with mourners. Speakers were J.C. Jensen, Joseph Moulton, G. Frank Ryan, and Bishop Duke. A quartette consisting of Frank Epperson, Alva Coleman, Alice Wood, and Marilla Murdock sang 'Come, Come Ye Saints,' 'Sister Thou wast Mild and Lovely,' and 'Who Are These Arrayed in White.' George Smith and William H. Harvey offered the prayers. Many carriages filled with her friends and admirers went to the cemetery.

"May we all fill our earthly mission as well and faithfully as she did here, and be worthy to enjoy her society in that place where sorrow and parting are unknown, is my humble prayer."

—*William Lindsay*

His daughter, Mamie Fisher, lived with William for a while. He served as tithing clerk for the three wards of Heber from 1917 to 1925. In 1918 he married a widow, Sarah Murdoch Rasband. They got along well and were happy to be independent and not have to live with their children. William enjoyed good health which he attributed to his strict observance of the Word of Wisdom and engaging in hard work. He never went in debt for anything. He was a ward teacher for over sixty years and answered every call made to him by the leaders of the Church. He was proud of his children and especially rejoiced when they were good Latter-day Saints and active in the Church. His two sons James L. and David filled missions.

William was interested in research and temple work, and spent time and money in searching out his ancestors. He wrote many histories of his own family and also of friends. The records that he kept have proved very valuable to many of us. He loved poetry and anything in rhyme, and he composed many poems during his lifetime. He watched Heber Valley grow from a sagebrush-covered land to a modern settlement, and he did his share to make it a lovely, livable place.

He was never afraid of work, and up to the end of his days he kept a cow and had a lovely, productive garden. In his latter years he was bailiff of the court and fireman for the Bank of Heber City and Heber Merc. He served as timekeeper on several building projects.

William Lindsay held many positions in the Church and filled them all faithfully. More than once he walked to Wallsburg and other wards of the valley, in very deep snow, to fill high council assignments. He was a man of humility and faith, and many, many people requested him to administer to them or perform ordinances for them. Their faith and trust in "Uncle William," as he was affectionately called, was great. He was loved sincerely by his children and grandchildren, and they all felt him near to perfection.

He always had a pocket full of peppermints and all the children on his street had their hands ready for a treat when they saw him coming. He was truly a sweet and gentle man and a good example for us all to follow.

He said of himself: "Now after all is said and done I feel that I have been a very ordinary individual and have had many faults and failings to contend with. But I feel that I have been very much blessed of the Lord and he has been merciful to me all through my life."

The winter of 1932 he had a stroke. His daughter, Mamie Fisher, took him to her home and cared for him until he passed away on May 14, 1932, at the age of 85. A wonderful man gone.

Mary Mair and William Lindsay were progenitors of whom we are very proud, and whose lives we should emulate. They loved the Gospel of Jesus Christ and truly lived it to the end of their lives. They truly endured to the end.

Compiled by Virginia D. Christensen; taken from the writings of William Lindsay

Mary Mair and William Lindsay, wedding picture, December 15, 1868

Mary Mair and William Lindsay at the farm house.

Mary Mair and William Lindsay, 1913

This home was located at Lindsay's Dell, near Heber City, Wasatch, Utah

WILLIAM LINDSAY HOME LOCATED IN HEBER CITY, Utah

Lines written on the fortyeighth Anniversary
of our marriage which occured Dec.15th 1868

Written by William Lindsay

Today my mind has wandered back unto the happy day
When Mary Dear & I were wed, but it seems quite far away
So many scenes have passed since then & some sad changes too
But Mary Dear though you are gone I oft times think of you
I think of all you did for me & for our children dear
How true & faithful you have been through all the passing year
We had no wealth of lands or gold but our hearts were good & true
I felt that I was blest indeed when I had health & you
For forty seven years & more we labored side by side
And at the end I loved you more than when you were my bride
Because through all life's trials of which you had your share
You always did your duty well with patient love & care
Eleven times you risked your life to give your children birth
May those who live all honor you while they remain on earth
You sure have earned a good reward for noble deeds done here
And now you're mingling with the just in a high & holy sphere
But I'm sure your thoughts will oft times turn to those you loved so well
For whom you sacrificed so much yea more than tongue can tell
We know you cant come back to us but we will come to you
To dwell with you eternally if we prove faithful too
This thought brings comfort to my heart more than all else in life
That I will yet in Heaven meet my Dear Beloved Wife.

HUSBAND WILLIAM LINDSAY

Birth _11 February 1847_
Place _near Ardrie, Lanarkshire, Scotland_
Chr. _____
Married _15 December 1868_
Place _Salt Lake City, Salt Lake, Utah_
Death _14 May 1932 Heber City, Wasatch, Utah_
Burial _17 May 1932 Heber City, Wasatch, Utah_
Father _William LINDSAY_
Mother* _Christina HOWIE_
Other Wives (if any) _Sarah Murdoch RASBAND M-6 Sep 1918_

WIFE MARY MAIR

Birth _1 August 1852_
Place _Carbellow, Ayrshire, Scotland_
Chr. _____
Death _3 June 1916 Heber City, Wasatch, Utah_
Burial _5 June 1916 Heber City, Wasatch, Utah_
Father _Allan MAIR_
Mother* _Mary MURDOCH_
Other Hus (if any) _____
Where was information obtained? _Virginia Christensen_
*List complete maiden name for all females.

1st Child Mary Murdoch LINDSAY
Birth _20 October 1869_
Place _Heber City, Wasatch, Utah_
Married to _James FISHER_
Married _7 December 1892_
Place _Logan, Cache, Utah_
Death _7 December 1948_

2nd Child William Howie LINDSAY
Birth _24 October 1871_
Place _Heber City, Wasatch, Utah_
Married to _Margaret Elinor THOMAS_
Married _31 July 1895_
Place _Salt Lake City, Salt Lake, Utah_
Death _27 June 1939_

3rd Child James Lyon LINDSAY
Birth _21 September 1873_
Place _Heber City, Wasatch, Utah_
Married to _Elizabeth JONES_
Married _31 July 1895_
Place _Salt Lake City, Salt Lake, Utah_
Death _15 October 1932_

4th Child John Allan LINDSAY
Birth _15 September 1875_
Place _Heber City, Wasatch, Utah_
Married to _Ella Minerva BUNNELL_
Married _19 April 1900_
Place _Center Creek, Wasatch, Utah_
Death _20 June 1958_

5th Child Daniel McMillan LINDSAY
Birth _15 August 1877 Death 6 March 1887_
Place _near Heber City, Wasatch, Utah_

6th Child Andrew Alexander LINDSAY
Birth _23 October 1879_
Place _near Heber City, Wasatch, Utah_
Married to _Martha Agnes SULSER_
Married _9 December 1899_
Place _Park City, Summit, Utah_
Death _4 December 1947_

7th Child Samuel LINDSAY
Birth _3 December 1881_
Place _near Heber City, Wasatch, Utah_
Married to _____
Married _____
Place _____
Death _4 October 1882_

8th Child Christina Veronica (Crissie) LINDSAY
Birth _15 July 1886_
Place _near Heber City, Wasatch, Utah_
Married to _Adolphia R. DUKE_
Married _12 June 1907_
Place _Salt Lake City, Salt Lake, Utah_
Death _15 July 1974_

9th Child David Pryde LINDSAY
Birth _16 August 1888_
Place _near Heber City, Wasatch, Utah_
Married to _Leah BUNNELL_
Married _12 June 1917_
Place _Heber City, Wasatch, Utah_
Death _24 February 1926_

10th Child Daughter LINDSAY
Birth _20 January 1890 Death 20 Jan 1890_
Place _near Heber City, Wasatch, Utah_

11th Child Annie Murdoch LINDSAY
Birth _1 August 1892_
Place _near Heber City, Wasatch, Utah_
Married to _Edward Delbert CLYDE_
Married _9 June 1915_
Place _Salt Lake City, Salt Lake, Utah_
Death _21 April 1978_

1 MURDOCH, James 1786-1831
1 MURDOCH, Mary MURRAY, Sp. 1782-1856

2 MAIR, Mary MURDOCH 1817-1900
2 MAIR, Allan, Sp. 1815-1897

DESCENDANTS OF------------3 MAIR, Mary 1852-1916
3 LINDSAY, William, Sp. 1847-1932

B-Birth
M-Marriage
D-Death
Sp-Spouse
Div. Divorced
Numbers-Generation

4 FISHER, Mary Murdoch LINDSAY B-20 Oct 1869 M-7 Dec 1892 D-7 Dec 1948
4 FISHER, James, Sp. B-21 Sep 1866 D-3 Dec 1955

    5 HUNTER, Mary Lindsay FISHER B-27 Mar 1895 M-16 Dec 1919
    5 HUNTER, Albert Mendosa, Sp. B-14 Mar 1898 D-8 May 1975

        6 HUNTER, James Albert B-26 Jul 1920 M-10 Mar 1942
        6 HUNTER, Mamie Luceil SMOUT, Sp. B-27 Aug 1920

            7 HUNTER, Thomas Albert B-10 Jun 1945 M-3 Jun 1966
            7 HUNTER, Janet BENSON, Sp. B-14 Feb 1946

                8 HUNTER, Nicole   B- 1 Aug 1971
                8 HUNTER, Leslie Nyree B-23 Jul 1973

            7 HUNTER, Richard James B-21 Jul 1950 M-20 June 1969
            7 HUNTER, Ann BALLIF, Sp. B-31 Aug 1950

                8 HUNTER, Jeffrey Richard B-20 Jul 1969
                8 HUNTER, Amy   B-12 Jul 1970

        6 WHITE, Mary Victoria HUNTER B-8 Nov 1921 M-20 Aug 1947
        6 WHITE, Lynn Thornley, Sp. B-28 Feb 1922

            7 WINN, Mary Victoria WHITE B-7 Jan 1949 M-11 Jun 1968
            7 WINN, Stephen Morris, Sp. B-23 Mar 1945

                8 WINN, Bryan Steven   B-19 May 1969
                8 WINN, Holly Marie   B-18 May 1971
                8 WINN, Greg Lindsay   B- 8 May 1974

            7 WHITE, James Lynn B-14 Jan 1950 M-23 Aug 1976
            7 WHITE, Donna STOKES, Sp. B-

                8 WHITE, Lori   B-22 Mar 1978

            7 WHITE, Helen Denet   B-14 Nov 1951
            7 WHITE, Ann Christine   B- 2 May 1954
            7 WHITE, Patricia Vilate B-18 Jul 1963

        6 HUNTER, Keith B-19 Nov 1923 M- Not   D-25 Dec 1932

        6 HUNTER, William Lindsay B-21 Jun 1925 M-20 Mar 1946
        6 HUNTER, Evelyn PACKARD, Sp. B-8 Feb 1925

            7 MILLER, Susan HUNTER Bailey B-3 Feb 1947
            7 BAILEY, Richard, Sp. (1) B-   M-14 Dec 1968 Div.
            7 MILLER, Lawrence, Sp. (2) B-   M-1 Apr 1972

            7 HUNTER, William Paul B-31 Jan 1949 M-17 Dec 1971
            7 HUNTER, Judy WORTHEN, Sp. B-12 Dec 1950

                8 HUNTER, Gregory James B-13 Jan 1973
                8 HUNTER, Dianna   B-21 Sep 1975
                8 HUNTER, Meshelle   B- 8 Jun 1977
                8 HUNTER, Benjamin Paul B-27 May 1979

            7 FLOYD, Becky Ann HUNTER Ayre B-22 Oct 1951
            7 AYRE, Rick, Sp. (1) B-   M-11 Nov 1973 Div.
            7 FLOYD, James, Sp. (2) B-   M-4 Jul 1976

                8 FLOYD, Robert J   B-4 Jan 1977

        6 FARMER, Ruth Ann HUNTER B-22 Feb 1928 M-20 Jun 1952
        6 FARMER, William James, Sp. B-21 Aug 1916
         FARMER, LaPriel MONSON, Sp. (1) B-   M-26 Jun 1944 Div.
            7 HARPER, Frankie FARMER B-2 Jun 1953 M-31 May 1974
            7 HARPER, Dennis Louis, Sp. B-

```
                 8 HARPER, Nathan Lewis      B- 6 Mar 1975
                 8 HARPER, Maizie            B-18 Nov 1977


         7 FARMER, Michael Mendosa B-17 Nov 1958 M-

6 WANGSGARD, Theone HUNTER Mc Laughlin, B-17 Jun 1929
6 MC LAUGHLIN, Bertram Clark, Sp. (1) B-18 Jan 1923 M-15 Oct 1954 D-23 Sep-
6 WANGSGARD, Lynwood, Sp. (2) B-          M-20 Aug 1976              1963


         7 COWDEN, Linda MC LAUGHLIN B-23 Ma  1955 M-17 Jul 1975
         7 COWDEN, Douglas Kermit, Sp. B-8 Jan 1951


                 8 COWDEN, Douglas Kermit    B- 4 May 1971
                 8 COWDEN, Gabriel Neil      B- 5 Oct 1976
                 8 COWDEN, Morgan Bertram    B-17 Oct 1977 D-21 Nov 1977
                 8 COWDEN, Tanner Lynnwood   B- 6 Oct 1978


         7 MC LAUGHLIN, Scott  B-5 May 1956 M-

6 HUNTER, Kenneth Duke  B-18 Dec 1930 M-2 Sep 1955
6 HUNTER, LaPriel GAILEY, Sp. B-5 Jul 1930


         7 HUNTER, Kenneth "M"      B-11 Jun 1956
         7 HUNTER, Keri             B-30 Nov 1957
         7 HUNTER, Kelli            B-14 Jan 1959
         7 HUNTER, Kyle             B-18 Sep 1961
         7 HUNTER, Kristopher "D"   B-21 Jul 1963


6 HUNTER, John David  B-16 Mar 1932 M-23 Aug 1955
6 HUNTER, Yvonne Janis DINSDALE, Sp. B-4 Apr 1933


         7 HUNTER, David Keith      B-26 Apr 1957 D-27 Apr 1957

         7 STEWART, Natalie HUNTER  B-10 May 1958 M-5 Aug 1977
         7 STEWART, Scott Clark, Sp. B-2 Nov 1954

                 8 STEWART, Erika           B- 7 Dec 1978

         7 HUNTER, Jana             B-17 Aug 1959
         7 HUNTER, Jolene           B-20 Nov 1962
         7 HUNTER, Jonnett          B- 2 Jul 1968
         7 HUNTER, Jill             B- 2 Dec 1969


6 TANNER, Virginia HUNTER B-31 Oct 1933 M-6 May 1955
6 TANNER, Delmar LaMont, Sp. B-27 Jul 1935 D-


         7 TANNER, Lindsay LaMont B-29 Feb 1956 M-29 Sep 1977
         7 TANNER, Gwen NIELSON, Sp. B-3 Jun 1959

         7 STANGER, Teri TANNER B-13 Dec 1957 M-13 Jan 1977
         7 STANGER, Jerry Dale, Sp. B-28 Sep 1952

         7 TANNER, Kathryn          B-28 Feb 1962
         7 TANNER, Tim Valison      B-16 Jun 1963
         7 TANNER, Jennybeth        B-23 Mar 1970


6 TUCKER, Jeannette HUNTER B-8 Jun 1937 M-20 Nov 1959
6 TUCKER, Larry Emmitte, Sp. B-15 Jul 1936


         7 TUCKER, Keith Lawrence   B- 6 Jan 1961
         7 TUCKER, Ann              B- 3 Aug 1962
         7 TUCKER, Robert Lee       B- 2 Jul 1964


6 TAYLOR, Cathrynn HUNTER B-23 Feb 1939 M-29 Oct 1965
6 TAYLOR, Hugh Alvin, Sp. B-7 Mar 1942


         7 TAYLOR, Heidi            B-24 Aug 1966
         7 TAYLOR, Marysia          B-10 Feb 1968
         7 TAYLOR, Tiffany Ruth     B- 2 May 1970
         7 TAYLOR, Audra            B-17 Jun 1973
         7 TAYLOR, Dandy Hugh       B-20 Oct 1974
         7 TAYLOR, Trulee           B-26 Aug 1976
         7 TAYLOR, Everett Wayne    B-28 Dec 1977


5 FISHER, Martha Ann B-4 Jul 1901 D-4 Jul 1901

5 FISHER, James Glade B-21 Jan 1904 D-23 Apr 1904
```

5 FISHER, Daryl James B-7 Feb 1908 M-20 May 1930
5 FISHER, Larena PRICE, Sp. B-6 Jul 1911

     6 TAYLOR, Nevada Deon FISHER B-20 Jan 1931 M-3 Dec 1952
     6 TAYLOR, Gale Everett, Sp. B-   D   1966

        7 TAYLOR, Steven B-10 Jul 1953 M-
        7 TAYLOR, Lily J ARCHULETA, Sp. B-

     6 FISHER, Mason James B- 20 Mar 1933 M-14 Nov 1954
     6 FISHER, Rebecca MURRAY, Sp. B-

        7 FISHER, Michael James   B-26 Jul 1955
        7 FISHER, Linda Day Ann   B-13 Aug 1958

4 LINDSAY, William Howie B-24 Oct 1871 M-31 Jul 1895 D-26 Jun 1939
4 LINDSAY, Margaret Elenor THOMAS, Sp. B-9 Jan 1877 D-5 May 1958

    5 LINDSAY, Martin Steven B-30 Mar 1896 D-2 Nov 1959
    5 LINDSAY, Maggie BYRNE, Sp. (1) B-   M-19 Feb 1919 Div.

      6 LINDSAY, William Byrne B-   Jan 1920 M-   ?

    5 LINDSAY, Lora McAFFEE, Sp. (2) B-25 Apr 1909 M-18 Oct 1924 Div.

      6 NORTHCUTT, Clara LINDSAY Widdison Thompson, B-17 Feb 1926
      6 WIDDISON, Elvoy, Sp. (1) B-   M-
      6 THOMPSON, Bill, Sp. (2) B-   M-
      6 NORTHCUTT,   Sp. (3) B-   M-

        7 WILLIAMS, Linda Rae WIDDISON B-   M-
        7 WILLIAMS,   Sp.

        7 ROBINSON, Carroll Ann WIDDISON B-   M-
        7 ROBINSON,   Sp.

        7 WIDDISON, Steven Elvoy   B-
        7 WIDDISON, Clarence William   B-

      6 MORRELL, Betty Joe LINDSAY B-27 Apr 1927
      6 BURGENER, J B, Sp. (1) B-   M-4 Jul 1941 Div. 29 Oct 1945
      6 MORRELL, Paul Vincent, Sp. (2) B-15 Sep 1923 M-26 Jan 1946

        7 MORRELL, Priscilla Ann, B-7 Dec 1946 M-

        7 DURRANT, Vikie Lynn MORRELL Johnson B-23 Apr 1948
        7 JOHNSON, Wayne E., Sp. (1) B-   M-8 Apr 1967
        7 DURRANT, Jack LeRoy, Sp. (2) B-   M-

        7 WOOD, Marie Elaine MORRELL B-23 Aug 1949 M-31 May 1967
        7 WOOD, Cary F., Sp. B-

        7 MORRELL, Philip Martin B-17 Apr 1955 (Stillborn)

        7 COLE, Lora Lee MORRELL Bishop B-14 Apr 1956
        7 BISHOP, Ronald Lee, Sp. (1) B-   M-13 Nov 1974
        7 COLE, Don Ross, Sp. (2) B-   M-

        7 MORRELL, David Paul B-26 Nov 1957 M-6 Dec 1974
        7 MORRELL, Karen LOWE, Sp. B-

        7 MORRELL, Richard Dean B-30 Dec 1959 M-

    5 LINDSAY, Ellen RASMUSSEN, Sp. (3) B-   M-

    5 LINDSAY, Dawson B-25 Feb 1898 M-3 Apr 1925 D-
    5 LINDSAY, Helen MESERVY, Sp. B-1 Sep 1901 D-11 May 1972

      6 JENSEN, Helen Joyce LINDSAY B-29 Oct 1926 M-5 Nov 1943
      6 JENSEN, Arthur Gordon, Sp. B-27 Oct 1921

        7 BERRETT, Judy Gay JENSEN B-17 Oct 1944 M-20 Sep 1963
        7 BERRETT, Allen Peterson, Sp. B-14 Dec 1943

          8 BERRETT, Bobbi Lyn   B-6 Apr 1964
          8 BERRETT, Pamela   B-

```
              8 BERRETT, Rozanne           B-
              8 BERRETT, Annette           B-


        7 JENSEN, Scott Arthur B-    Apr 1946 D-    Apr 1946


        7 CAMPBELL, Michelle L. JENSEN B-24 Jul 1952 M-
        7 CAMPBELL, Lawrence, Sp. B-


        7 JENSEN, Darla B-           M-
    6 JOHNSON, Evelyn Dawn LINDSAY B-8 Jun 1928 M-19 Mar 1947
    6 JOHNSON, H Arthur Jr., Sp. B-25 Jul 1927


          7 STEELE, Dawn Marie JOHNSON B-22 Jan 1949 M-8 Dec 1972
          7 STEELE, Jesse Lynn, Sp. B-10 Oct 1949


                  8 STEELE, Josie Dawn      B-25 Nov 1974
                  8 STEELE, Thad Jesse      B- 8 Jun 1976
                  8 STEELE, Jacob Lynn      B-19 Jun 1977


          7 JOHNSON, David Arthur B-22 Mar 1950 M-28 Jun 1972
          7 JOHNSON, Katherine LAW, Sp. B-13 Feb 1951


                  8 JOHNSON, Kimberly       B-11 Jul 1973
                  8 JOHNSON, Brenda         B-25 May 1975
                  8 JOHNSON, Teresa         B- 1 Nov 1976
                  8 JOHNSON, Aaron          B-18 Jun 1978


          7 JOHNSON, Robert H B-20 Nov 1951 M- 13 Dec 1974
          7 JOHNSON, Willa Ann MILGATE, Sp. B-3 Mar 1953


                  8 JOHNSON, Holli Ann      B-19 Aug 1976
                  8 JOHNSON, Mandie         B-10 Jul 1979


          7 LAWRENCE, Patricia JOHNSON B-29 Jul 1953 M-19 Oct 1977
          7 LAWRENCE, Michael Kean, Sp. B-8 Oct 1951


                  8 LAWRENCE, Dustin Kean     B-24 May 1978


          7 ANDERSON, Susan JOHNSON B-15 Aug 1954 M-13 Sep 1974
          7 ANDERSON, Michael Edward, Sp. B-12 Mar 1955


                  8 ANDERSON, Rebecca       B-18 Aug 1975
                  8 ANDERSON, Mark Edward   B-23 Jul 1977
                  8 ANDERSON, Wendy         B-10 Aug 1979


          7 HART, Karen JOHNSON B-8 Aug 1956 M-18 Nov 1977
          7 HART, Neal, Sp. B-25 Jan 1955


                  8 HART, HEATHER           B-    Feb 1979


          7 WEEKS, Jamie JOHNSON B-31 May 1959 M-17 Aug 1979
          7 WEEKS, Jeff, Sp. B-


          7 JOHNSON, James Lindsay B-4 Feb 1961 M-8 Jun 1979
          7 JOHNSON, Catherine PAGE, Sp. B-7 Mar 1962


          7 JOHNSON, Catherine      B-11 Feb 1964
          7 JOHNSON, Christina      B- 6 Dec 1965


    6 LINDSAY, David Vernon B- 3 Aug 1932 D- 9 Feb 1935


    6 LINDSAY, Robert Lynn B-23 Apr 1936 M-16 Mar 1957
    6 LINDSAY, Lorelee Estelle GOODREAU, Sp. B-4 Feb 1941


          7 LINDSAY, Tamera Lynne     B-11 Oct 1959
          7 LINDSAY, David Vernon     B- 5 Feb 1961
          7 LINDSAY, Shaun Thomas     B- 4 Sep 1963
          7 LINDSAY, Zane             B-

5 TATUM, Sarah Elizabeth LINDSAY Clyde Miller B- 19 Jun 1900 D-10 Aug 1962
5 CLYDE, Lyndon, Sp. (1) B-10 Aug 1895 M-1 Jun 1918 D-          1930
5 MILLER, Alma C., Sp. (2) B-           M-6 Aug 1934
5 TATUM, Ralph, Sp. (3) B-             M-13 Oct 1935


      6 GONZALES, Phyllis Carol CLYDE B-25 Dec 1918 M-14 Sep 1942 D-14 Jan 1965
      6 GONZALES, Angel Herman, Sp. B-1 July        D-
```

7 SCHERMERHORN, Christine Eloise GONZALES B-12 Sep 1947 (Adopted)
7 SCHERMERHORN, Michael Robert, Sp. B-   M-20 Jun 1964

7 GONZALES, Jerry Dean B-21 May 1952 M-   ?   (Adopted)

6 CLYDE, Lyndon Boyd B-25 Aug 1919 M-   D-
6 CLYDE, Betty Drietzler, Sp. B-   D-

    7 BRERTON, Gloria Jean CLYDE B-   M-
    7 BRERTON,   Sp. B-

    7 CLYDE, Lynn B-   M-

    7 PARKER, Betty Lou B-   M-
    7 PARKER,   Sp. B-

6 CLYDE, Doyle Allen B-4 Apr 1925 M-

6 CLYDE, Mickey Joe B-30 Jun 1929 M-18 Dec 1948
6 CLYDE, Colleen Cummings, Sp. B-1 May 1931

    7 CLYDE, Michael Joe, B-14 Dec 1949 M-2 Nov 1968
    7 CLYDE, Conceitia GUTIERREZ, Sp. B-   May

        8 CLYDE, Joe Dee   B-17 Nov 1970
        8 CLYDE, Cristopher Wade   B-28 Feb 1974
        8 CLYDE, Jami   B-17 Aug 1977

    7 CLYDE, Craig Lynn B-24 Feb 1952 M-
    7 CLYDE, Gail Ann HESS, Sp. B-3 Aug 1954

        8 CLYDE, Jason Lynn   B-12 Apr 1975
        8 CLYDE, Cari Loree   B-15 Aug 1976
        8 CLYDE, Ryan Keith   B- 3 Sep 1977

    7 PANNELL, Jacquelyn CLYDE B-4 Feb 1955
    7 ROBERTS, Thomas, Sp. (1) B-   M-17 Feb 1973 Div. 19Oct1977
    7 PANNELL, Larry, Sp. (2) B-   M-   Nov 1978

        8 Roberts, Brandy   19 Sep 1973
        8 Roberts, Nathan   24 Apr 1975

    7 CLYDE, Thomas Lindsay   B-9 Jan 1969

5 LINDSAY, William Harold B-13 Mar 1903 D-
5 LINDSAY, Hilda McDonald, Sp. (1) B-21 Jan 1907 M-24 Apr 1925 D-8 Apr 1945
5 LINDSAY, Nancy Almira BARNEY Liston Beams, Sp. (2) B-12 Dec 1903 M-11 Mar 1946

    6 LINDSAY, Rex William B-20 Feb 1926 M-10 Oct 1946
    6 LINDSAY, Beatrice STANLEY, Sp. B-9 Dec 1929

    7 LINDSAY, Richard William B-4 Jul 1947 M-
    7 LINDSAY, Larea POWELL, Sp. (1) B-   M-14 Mar 1969
    7 LINDSAY, Jane Carrie CASE, Sp. (2) B-30 Jul 1951 M-17 Dec 1973

        8 LINDSAY Rex William   B-19 Jul 1974
        8 LINDSAY, Amanda Dee   B-28 Sep 1977

    7 CROSS, Terry Ann LINDSAY Williams B-25 Jan 1949
    7 WILLIAM, Michael, Sp. (1) B-9 Apr 1948 M-10   1966
    7 CROSS, Paul, Sp. (2) B-21 Sep 1947 M-21 Jun 1969
        8 WILLIAMS, Angela L.   B-21 Apr 1967
        8 CROSS, Amber   B-23 Jan 1973

    7 LARSEN, Hilda Rae LINDSAY B-16 Mar 1951 M-19 Jun 1970
    7 LARSEN, Gregory Gene, Sp. B-6 Dec 1950

        8 LARSEN, Kirt   B-15 Jan 1971
        8 LARSEN, Veronica   B-25 Apr 1974

    7 MERCER, Robyn Diane LINDSAY Sornson B-7 Jun 1953
    7 SORNSON, Craig, Sp. (1) B-   M-   Aug 197
    7 MERCER, David, Sp. (2) B-3 Jul 1953 M-   Aug 1974

        8 SORNSON, Jamie   B-28 Jan 1973
        8 MERCER, Robert   B-27 Mar 1976

7 ANDERSON, Shelly Virginia LINDSAY B-23 Jun 1952 M-18 May 1974
7 ANDERSON, Bradford Allen, Sp. B-31 Aug 1947

        8 ANDERSON, Clinton Lindsay B-8 Nov 1976

7 LINDSAY, Jack Scott B-20 Nov 1953

6 LINDSAY, Virginia Rae B-13 Sep 1933 D-19 Dec 1935

6 LINDSAY, Laurence Duane B-14 Jun 1935
6 LINDSAY, Afton SOOM, Sp. (1) B-   M-   Sep 1953 Div.
6 LINDSAY, Shirley Ann LEE, Sp. (2) B-22 Oct 1935 M-2 Aug 1957

    7 LINDSAY, Stanley Duane   B-9 Jul 1964

6 LINDSAY, Madelyn B-28 Mar 1937

5 FRISBY, Blanche Austin LINDSAY B-23 Nov 1906 M-6 Apr 1925
5 FRISBY, Clifford, Sp. B-18 Sep 1905

6 RISNER, Reve' L FRISBY Hilton B-7 Jan 1926
6 HILTON, Joseph Laurence, Sp. (1) B-   M-8 Mar 1944 Div.
6 RISNER, William Stanley, Sp. (2) B-8 Feb 924 M-12 Dec 1948

    7 REVILL, Renita Fay Hilton RISNER B-17 May 1948 (Adopt. 14 Sep
    7 REVILL, John Charles, Sp. B-Oct 5 1946 M-24 Oct 1967   1959)

        8 REVILL, Amy   B-14 May 1969
        8 REVILL, Wendy   B- 5 Feb 1971
        8 REVILL, John Charles   B-10 Feb 1973
        8 REVILL, Cydnee   B-26 Oct 1977

    7 LATHAM, Janis Lynn RISNER Warner B-1 Mar 1950
    7 WARNER, Kenneth Charles, Sp. (1) B-   M-14 Feb 1968 Div.
    7 LATHAM, Terry Deloy (Boone), Sp. B-16 Jul 1944 M-28 Nov 1972

        8 LATHAM, William D Warner B-15 Sep 1968
        8 LATHAM, Joseph R   B-20 Jul 1973
        8 LATHAM, Daniel E.   B-11 May 1978

    7 BLUFF, Peggy Rae RISNER B-5 Mar 1955 M-20 Mar 1976
    7 BLUFF, Richard, Sp. B-5 Jul 1951

        8 BLUFF, Adreann   B-18 Apr 1977
        8 BLUFF, Maxie Rae   B-14 Mar 1979

    7 RISNER, William George B- 6 Sep 1957 D-27 Dec 1958
    7 RISNER, Jack E   B-21 Jan 1960
    7 RISNER, Geni   B-21 Sep 1964
6 FRISBY, Baby   (Stillborn) B-24 Sep 1929
6 FRISBY, Clifford Larry B-13 Nov 1930 M-8 Jun 1949 D-20 Sep 1968
6 FRISBY, Morjorie Ann Cummings, Sp. B-24 Dec 1932

    7 FRISBY, Clifford Patrick B-22 Nov 1949 M-3 Oct 1975
    7 FRISBY, Tamera MARBLE, Sp. B-31 Jul 19

    7 FRISBY, Bradley Larry B-31 Aug 1952 M-   Sep
    7 FRISBY, Sandra MARBLE, Sp. B-

        8 FRISBY, Dustina   B- 2 Oct 1975
        8 FRISBY, Larry Wayne   B-19 Sep 1978

    7 WILLIAMS, Diane FRISBY Smith B-4 Apr 1953
    7 SMITH, Vaughan, Sp. (1) B-   M- Aug 1969 (Div. 1970)
    7 WILLIAMS, Jerry, Sp. (2) B-   M-   1976

        8 SMITH, Austin Beau   B- 6 Apr 1970
        8 WILLIAMS, Lacy   B-23 Aug 1975

    7 COOPER, Brenda FRISBY Hatley B-6 Sep 1954
    7 HATLEY, Thomas, Sp. (1) B-   M-   Div.
    7 COOPER, Peter, Sp. (2) B-   M-   Div. 1979
        8 COOPER, Courtney   B-14 Oct 1978

    7 MONICO, Lana FRISBY B-26 Dec 1955
    7 MONICO, Terry, Sp. B-   M-

                        8 MONICO, Louis   B-4 Sep 1978

            7 FRISBY, J. Lee   B-11 May 1958
            7 FRISBY, Alan Wade   B-11 Apr 1960

    6 FRISBY, Thomas Bruce B-13 Jun 1941
    6 FRISBY, Irene EICKER, Sp. (1) B-14 Nov 1945 M-24 Oct 1964 Div.
      Donmeese, Terry, Sp. to Irene
            7 FRISBY, Tonya Lynn   B-27 Oct 1966
            7 FRISBY, Tod Bruce   B-25 May 1967

    6 FRISBY, Vicky GRIENBRING, Sp. (2) B-   M-   Oct 1972 Div.

            7 FRISBY, Travis Bruce   B-25 May 1972
            7 FRISBY, Thomas Brent   B-30 Aug 1973

    6 FRISBY, William Joseph B-1 Jun 1945 M-2 Nov 1968
    6 FRISBY, Peggy Jowinn TUCKER, Sp. B-6 May 19

            7 FRISBY, Mindy   B-15 Aug 1969
            7 FRISBY, Jenifer   B-30 Oct 1970
            7 FRISBY, Dawnelle   B-26 Mar 1972
            7 FRISBY, William Tyler   B-26 Oct 1973
            7 FRISBY, Joseph Scott   B- 8 May 1975
            7 FRISBY, Brinton   B-24 Feb 1977
            7 FRISBY, Ayrn   B-11 Apr 1979

    6 FRISBY, George Robert B-9 Jun 1952 M-25 Apr 1970
    6 FRISBY, Josie Ann REID, Sp. B-25 Sep 1951

            7 FRISBY, James Robert   B- 9 Aug 1974
            7 FRISBY, Lindsay Jo   B-24 Mar 1977

5 LINDSAY, Harold Thomas B-9 May 1909 D-12 Nov 1969
5 LINDSAY, Doris PROVOST, Sp. (1) B-   M-10 Sep 1935 Div.

        6 COX, Judy LINDSAY B-   M-
        6 COX, Eugene, Sp. B-

        6 FARRER, Diane LINDSAY B-   M-
        6 FARRER, Grant, Sp. B-

5 LINDSAY, Dortha DAVIS Stewart, Sp. (2) B-1 Feb 1916 M-8 Aug 1953 D-24 Apr 1970
  Stewart, Glen E. Sp. (1) B-   M-   1935

        6 LINDSAY, Valoris (Val) B-1 May 1942 M-18 Feb 1966
        6 LINDSAY, Sharon ALLEN, Sp. B-

            7 LINDSAY, Jeffrey Allen   B-
            7 LINDSAY, Pamela Ann   B-
            7 LINDSAY, Mark David   B-
            7 LINDSAY, Danny   B-

        6 PETERSON, Ranae LINDSAY B-   M-
        6 PETERSON, Bruce, Sp. B-

            7 PETERSON, Steven Bruce   B-
            7 PETERSON, Brent Ronald   B-
            7 PETERSON, Kent Harold   B-

5 LINDSAY, Allan Washinton B-22 Feb 1911 M-20 Sep 1940 D-13 May 1967
5 LINDSAY, Helen BONNER, Sp. B-

5 BAIRD, Dorothy May LINDSAY B- 14 Mar 1913 M-27 Dec 1934
5 BAIRD, George "R", Sp. B-18 Mar 1912 D-22 Aug 1978

        6 BAIRD, Alan George B-18 Feb 1938 M-22 Jun 1968
        6 BAIRD, Dayle SESSIONS, Sp. B- Apr

            7 BAIRD, Michael Alan   B-10 Jan 1970
            7 BAIRD, Scott Dean   B-22 Dec 1970
            7 BAIRD, Michelle   B-22 Jul 1975
            7 BAIRD, Jenfer   B-17 Dec 1978

```
        6 JASPERSON, Margaret Jill BAIRD B-7 Apr 1943 M-26 Oct 1962
        6 JASPERSON, Donald Max, Sp. B-30 Sep 1942

                7 JASPERSON, Bruce Max      B-29 Apr 1963
                7 JASPERSON, Amy            B-14 Aug 1966
                7 JASPERSON, Heidi          B-30 Apr 1971


        6 BAIRD, Dan "E" B-8 Apr 1948 M-28 Jan 1972
        6 BAIRD, Norma Gail ELY, Sp. B-23 May 1950

                7 BAIRD, Shane Christofer   B-25 Nov 1975

5 JEFFS, Nellie LINDSAY B-21 Oct 1915 M-17 Jun 1933
5 JEFFS, Harry Mayho, Sp. B-23 Sep 1912

        6 JEFFS, William Hal B-10 Feb 1934 M-21 Jan 1955
        6 JEFFS, LaRae SWEAT, Sp. B-17 Sep 1934

                7 JEFFS, Steven O.          B-10 Oct 1956
                7 JEFFS, William H.         B-26 Dec 1957
                7 JEFFS, Julie              B-30 Jan 1960
                7 JEFFS, Clark Alan         B-16 Apr 1964
                7 JEFFS, Lewis Ray          B-14 Oct 1968


        6 JEFFS, Mark Dee B-14 Mar 1936 M-24 Jun 1960
        6 JEFFS, Rura LaRue WOODALL, Sp. B-6 Oct 1930

                7 JEFFS, JoLene             B- 8 May 1961
                7 JEFFS, Mark Troy          B-27 Jun 1963
                7 JEFFS, Philip Dee         B-15 Sep 1965
                7 JEFFS, Paula Michelle     B-10 Nov 1971


        6 KENDALL, Phyllis Kaye JEFFS B-19 Nov 1937 M-23 Sep 1953
        6 KENDALL, Don George, Sp. B-29 Aug 1933

                7 KENDALL, Jeffery Don B-9 May 1954 M-23 Mar 1978
                7 KENDALL, Laurie LUNDGREEN, Sp. B-

                7 KENDALL, Lynn C. B-3 Jul 1957 M-19 Aug 1977
                7 KENDALL, Christine WORTHINGTON, Sp. B-

                7 CUMMINGS, Karen KENDALL B-17 Oct 1958 M-29 Apr 1977
                7 CUMMINGS, Micheal William, Sp. B-

                7 KENDALL, Marie            B-17 Apr 1963
                7 KENDALL, Paul Thomas      B-18 May 1975


        6 HARDMAN, Ruth JEFFS B-26 Jul 1939 M-30 Jan 1958
        6 HARDMAN, Elwood, Sp. B-15 Aug 1938

                7 HARDMAN, Von              B-17 Jan 1959 D-17 Jan 1959
                7 HARDMAN, Jill             B- 2 Feb 1960
                7 HARDMAN, James Elwood     B-28 Oct 1961
                7 HARDMAN, Bryan Jeffs      B-11 Oct 1966
                7 HARDMAN, Jerald T.        B- 9 Mar 1962 (adopted)


        6 JEFFS, Harry Lindsay B-11 Mar 1941 M-28 Aug 1962
        6 JEFFS, Barbara Esther WILSON, Sp. B-27 Apr 1943

                7 JEFFS, Terry Miller       B-30 Dec 1964
                7 JEFFS, John Wilson        B-30 Oct 1967
                7 JEFFS, Richard Mayho      B-13 Jun 1970
                7 JEFFS, Jay Lindsay        B-26 Apr 1972
                7 JEFFS, Janelle            B- 9 May 1975
                7 JEFFS, Kimberly           B- 3 Feb 1978


        6 JEFFS, Joseph Dean B-19 Apr 1957

5 LINDSAY, Joseph Athol B-6 Aug 1918 M-19 Apr 1940
5 LINDSAY, Mildred June LEE, Sp. B-23 June 1920
```

6 LINDSAY, William Scott B-11 Feb 1969

4 LINDSAY, James Lyon B-21 Sep 1873 M-31 Jul 1895 D-15 Oct 1932
4 LINDSAY, Elizabeth JONES. Sp. B-3 Sep 1877 D-11 Jun 1945

    5 RASBAND, Elvira LINDSAY B-31 Mar 1896 M-3 Oct 1917 D-22 Jul 1974
    5 RASBAND, Walter Jeffs, Sp. B-13 Apr 1897 D-22 Jan 1978

        6 JIACOLLETI, Fae RASBAND Van Wagoner B-24 Feb 1918
        6 VAN WAGONER, Ezra Earl, Sp. B-   M-19 Nov 1937
        6 JIACOLLETI, Raymond N. Sp. B-   M-

            7 SABEY, Patricia VAN WAOGONER B-   M-
            7 SABEY, Dee, Sp. B-

                8 SABEY, Scott   B-
                8 SABEY, Susan   B-
                8 SABEY, Shelly   B-

            7 VAN WAGONER, Michael E. B-   M-
            7 VAN WAGONER, Christine HILLER, Sp. B-

                8 VAN WAGONER, HILLERY   B-
                8 VAN WAGONER, Ryan Michael B-
                8 VAN WAGONER, Jared Michael B-

            7 PINTER, Jane VAN WAGONER B-   M-
            7 PINTER, Victor Joseph Jr. Sp. B-

                8 PINTER, Vicki Jo   B-
                8 PINTER, AMY   B-
                8 PINTER, Van   B-

            7 VAN WAGONER, Tim E. B-   M-
            7 VAN WAGONER, Mary Ann McDONALD, Sp. B-

        6 PIMENTAL, Elizabeth RASBAND B-25 Feb 1920 M-26 Jun 1947
        6 PIMENTAL, James H., Sp. B-

            7 PIMENTAL, Jeff   B-

        6 RASBAND, Jay Walter B-   M-31 Oct 1942
        6 RASBAND, Myrl MADSEN, Sp. B-

            7 RASBAND, Ron Jay B-   M-
            7 RASBAND, Susan McDONALD, Sp. B-

                8 RASBAND, Stephen Jay   B-
                8 RASBAND, Scot Wayne   B-

            7 RASBAND, Rick Walter   B-
            7 RASBAND, Tami   B-

        6 PARCELL, Phyllis RASBAND B-6 May 1924   M-5 Apr 1944
        6 PARCELL, Harris, Sp.

            7 GILES, Dixie Ann PARCELL B-   M-
            7 GILES, Paul, Sp. B-

                8 GILES, July Ann   B-
                8 GILES, Paul Le Roy   B-

            7 KNUDSEN, Karen PARCELL B-   M-
            7 KNUDSEN, Andy, Sp. B-

            7 PARCELL, Joyce Lee   B-
            7 PARCELL, Walter Harris B-
            7 PARCELL, Jill   B-

        6 BIGLER, Darlene RASBAND B-26 Mar 1930 M-10 Sep 1954
        6 BIGLER, Adelbert H. Sp. B-

            7 BIGLER, Christine Susan B-
            7 BIGLER, Steven A.   B-
            7 BIGLER, Alan James   B-

6 RASBAND, Jospeh "R" B-30 May 1931 M-14 Sep 1950
6 RASBAND, Vera Maria THACKER, Sp. B-

      7 RASBAND, Paul Joseph B-   M-
      7 RASBAND, Jenifer Louise EDWARDS, Sp. B-

         8 RASBAND, Kara Lynn   B-
         8 RASBAND, Jenifer Rae   B-

      7 RASBAND, Carol   B-
      7 RASBAND, Ray   B-
      7 RASBAND, Richard   B-
      7 RASBAND, Philip   B-
      7 RASBAND, Kirk   B-

6 WRIGHT, Mary Vee RASBAND B-20 May 1934 M-2 Oct 1962
6 WRIGHT, Joe F. Sp. B-

      7 WRIGHT, Don   B-
      7 WRIGHT, Gary   B-
      7 WRIGHT, Sue   B-
      7 WRIGHT, Diane   B-
      7 WRIGHT, Lynn
      7 WRIGHT, Mark   B-
      7 WRIGHT, Coleen   B-

5 PARKINSON, Agnes LINDSAY B-15 Mar 1898 M-2 Jun 1925 D-25 Dec 1954
5 PARKINSON, Wallace Benson, Sp. B-

    6 GARST, Janet PARKINSON B-10 May 1935 M-
    6 GARST, William, Sp. B-

5 NELSON, Mary "J" LINDSAY B-18 May 1900 M-28 Feb 1928
5 NELSON, Kenneth Henry, Sp. B-7 Jan 1898

    6 NELSON, Lindsay H. B-   M-
    6 NELSON, Elsie STOKER, Sp. B-

      7 NELSON, Lindsay   B-
      7 NELSON, Debbie   B-
      7 NELSON, Kenneth   B-

5 OSTLUND, Mamie Della LINDSAY B-6 Nov 1902 M-3 Aug 1927
5 OSTLUND, Clarence, Sp. B-12 Jun 1887 D-19 Aug 1946

    6 OSTLUND, James Jonas B-14 Feb 1935 M-7 Jun 1955
    6 OSTLUND, Eulala Darlene BUTTERS, Sp. B-11 Jun 1934

      7 SMITH, Kym OSTLUND B-3 May 1956 M-2 Apr 1975
      7 SMITH, Ernest Phillip, Sp. B-23 Apr 1948

         8 SMITH, Melissa   B-30 Jul 1976
         8 SMITH, Amanda   B-28 Jul 1978
         8 SMITH, Melanie   B-11 May 1980
      7 OSTLUND, Stillborn baby B- Jun 1957
      7 OSTLUND, James Butters B- 4 Apr 1959
      7 OSTLUND, Cindy   B-10 Apr 1962
      7 OSTLUND, Jamie   B-21 Oct 1965
      7 OSTLUND, Julie   B-28 Jan 1969

    6 PETERSON, Clare OSTLUND B-13 May 1940 M-11 Sep 1964
    6 PETERSON, John Carl, Sp. B-26 Jul 1942

      7 PETERSON, Lisa Marie   B-17 Dec 1965
      7 PETERSON, John Lindsay B-21 May 1967
      7 PETERSON, Clark Ostlund B-14 Dec 1968
      7 PETERSON, Carla Sue   B-24 Jan 1972
      7 PETERSON, Katie Jo   B-12 Jun 1975
      7 PETERSON, Keli Ann   D-28 Mar 1978

5 LINDSAY, Richard Jones B-26 Oct 1905 M-16 Dec 1924 D-16 Dec 1937
5 LINDSAY, Arvilla DUKE, Sp. B-22 Oct 1906

    6 LINDSAY, James Lyon B-25 Apr 1928 or 9 M-
    6 LINDSAY, Louise HULMES, Sp. B-

      7 LINDSAY, Stephen B-   M-

```
              7 LINDSAY, Scott          B-
              7 LINDSAY, David          B-
              7 LINDSAY, Jason          B-

  5 LANE, Edna LINDSAY Carlisle B-24 May 1909 D-8 Sep 1963
  5 CARLISLE, William Alan, Sp. (1) B-'8 Sep 1899 M-29 Jan 1936 D-19 Jun 1946
  5 LANE, Dick, Sp. (2) B-

  5 NIELSEN, Bertha Elizabeth LINDSAY B-10 Mar 1912 M-23 Sep 1938
  5 NIELSEN, Adolph Martin, Sp. B-7 Jan 1911

          6 NIELSEN, Richard LINDSAY B-8 Oct 1941
          6 NIELSEN, Rebekah CLINGER, Sp. (1) B-          M-18 Mar 1966 Div.
          6 NIELSEN, Kathleen PORTER, Sp. (2) B-31 Aug 1942 M-9 Apr 1977

          6 CARLQUIST, Elizabeth Lynne NIELSEN B-25 Sep 1944 M-15 Jun 1966
          6 CARLQUIST, David Alma, Sp. B-7 May 1944

                  7 CARLQUIST, Sara Elizabeth B-26 Oct 1970
                  7 CARLQUIST, John David     B-13 Jan 1973

          6 NIELSEN, Heidi Kay B-2 Apr 1950

          6 KIMBALL, Kristine Joan NIELSEN B-18 Feb 1952 M-30 Aug 1974
          6 KIMBALL, Briant Ashby, Sp. B-19 Feb 1952

                  7 KIMBALL, Jedediah Clayton B-21 Nov 1975
                  7 KIMBALL, Daniel Martin    B-18 Apr 1978

  5 MOSS, Jennie Merle LINDSAY B-29 Aug 1915 M-10 Jan 1936
  5 MOSS, Stephen Lawrence, Sp. B-13 Jan 1905

          6 BALL, LaRae MOSS B-           M-
          6 BALL, Alfred Vernon, Sp. B-

                  7 BALL, Julie          B-
                  7 BALL, Jeffrey Vernon B-
                  7 BALL, Annette        B-
                  7 BALL, William        B-
                  7 BALL, David Lawrence B-

          6 MOSS, Stephen Lawrence Jr. B-        M-
          6 MOSS, Rosalie Ball, Sp. B-

                  7 MOSS, Stephen Lance  B-
                  7 MOSS, Kathryn        B-
                  7 MOSS, Ronald         B-

          6 BROADBENT, Susan Jane MOSS B-              ,-
          6 BROADBENT, Ray Siddoway, Sp. B-

                  7 BROADBENT, Jospeh Laurence B-
                  7 BROADBENT, Emily Jane (Twin) B-
                  7 BROADBENT, Jennifer Sue (Twin) B-

          6 MOSS, Thomas J. B-           M-
          6 MOSS, Sherri McQUARRY, Sp. B-

          6 MOSS, James William B-           M-
          6 MOSS, Virginia Dale MORGAN Sp. B-

                  7 MOSS, Shantell H       B-

          6 BELNAP, Elizabeth Ann Moss B-           M-
          6 BELNAP, Paul Manning, Sp. B-

                  7 BELNAP, Jamiee Beth     B-

  5 LENZI, LaRae LINDSAY B-1 Oct 1916 D-9 Feb 1958
  5 TURNER, Bert "M", Sp. (1) B-           M-
  5 LENZI, Wilson Roy, Sp. (2) B-7 Feb 1910 M-14 Jan 1942

          6 LENZI, Gary W. B-24 Dec 1942
          6 LENZI, Mary Jane SHELTON, Sp. B-24 Jul 1945 M-16 May 1968

                  7 LENZI, Jennifer         B- 9 Apr 1970
                  7 LENZI, James Shelton    B- 9 Mar 1972
                  7 LENZI, Christopher Shelton B-24 Nov 1974
                  7 LENZI, Daniel Shelton   B-31 May 1977
                  7 LENZI, Jacob Shelton    B-13 Jan 1980
```

```
                6 LENZI, Roy B-                    M-
                6 LENZI, Sue STRINGHAM, Sp. B-

                        7 LENZI, Tina            B-
                        7 LENZI, Tony            B-
                        7 LENZI, Ty              B-

        5 WALL, Vilate LINDSAY B-19 Jul 1918 M-30 Jan 1941 D       1974
        5 WALL, James Russell, Sp. B-16 Jul 1918

                6 WALL, James Russell Jr. B-9 Aug 1943 M-7 Mar 1968
                6 WALL, Pamela Kay HUNTSINGER, Sp. B-5 Feb 1948

                6 WALL, William "D" B-4 Sep 1944 M-25 Jul 1963 D-21 Feb 1978
                6 WALL, Karolyn KOHLER, Sp. B-5 Oct 1946

                        7 WALL, Troy K.          B-24 Dec 1963
                        7 WALL, William Todd     B-20 Nov 1967
                        7 WALL, Chad Arnold      B- 5 Apr 1972

                6 WALL, Jamie Beth B-23 May 1953 D-25 May 1953

                6 SULLIVAN, Shirla WALL B-10 May 1955 M-6 Jun 1975
                6 SULLIVAN, Paul Orman, Sp. B-28 Nov 1952

                        7 SULLIVAN, Jaimie       B- 9 Sep 1976

                6 WALL, Fred "M" B-16 Aug 1958

    4 LINDSAY, John Allan  B-15 Sep 1875 D-20 Jun 1958
    4 LINDSAY, Ella Minerva Bunnell, Sp. B-15 Jul 1883 M-19 Apr 1900 D- 4 Apr 1932
    4 LINDSAY, Rose SNYDER Workman, Sp. (2) B-23 Sep 1883 M-26 Oct 1933 D-16 Sep 1970
      Workman, Dee Ovitt, Sp. to Rose M-30 Mar 1904
            5 ROACH, Mary Fisher LINDSAY B-8 Jun 1901 M-30 Jun 1920 D-31 Jan 1945
            5 ROACH, Robert Leslie, Sp. B-17 Apr 1891

                6 ROACH, Robert Leslie II. B-10 Sep 1921 M-1 Jun 1957
                6 ROACH, Jane Ellen CULLEN, Sp. B-6 Jun 1934

                        7 ROACH, Robert Leslie III B-17 Jul 1958
                        7 ROACH, Thomas Patrick     B-21 Jan 1960

                6 POLYCHRONIS, Jessie Minerva B-23 Aug 1923 M-31 May 1953
                6 POLYCHRONIS, George Ernest, Sp. B-14 Jun 1927

                        7 POLYCHRONIS, Jeff T     B- 1 Jul 1954
                        7 POLYCHRONIS, Tim T.     B- 6 Apr 1959

                6 ROACH, Clifford Lindsay B-28 Jun 1925
                6 ROACH, Barbara Kaye KIDDER, Sp. (1) B-2 Apr 1932 M-16 Apr 1952 D-7Dec1968

                        7 ROACH, Mary Jean        B-20 Jun 1954
                        7 ROACH, Paula Kaye       B-15 Jul 1956
                        7 ROACH, Randy Cliff      B-23 Dec 1957 D-25 Dec 1957
                        7 ROACH, Kelly L. stillbornB- 8 Oct 1961
                        7 ROACH, Mickie Lynn      B- 4 Aug 1962
                        7 ROACH, Leslie Ann       B-11 Jul 1964

                6 ROACH, Betty FARNSWORTH, Sp (2) B-27 Apr 1931 M-28 Apr 1970

                        7 ROACH, Janella         B- 1 Feb 1971
                        7 ROACH, Rachelle        B-16 Jan 1972

                6 ELLIOTT, Bonnie Jean B-30 Jan 1927 M-28 Mar 1953
                6 ELLIOTT, Donald Elburn, Sp. B-28 Nov 1928

                        7 ELLIOTT, Sandy          B-17 Mar 1954
                        7 ELLIOTT, Steven         B-11 Jun 1955
                        7 ELLIOTT, Dawn           B-23 Jun 1957

                6 ROACH, James Larry B-25 Mar 1942 M-1 Jun 1970
                6 ROACH, Pamela Jean NORRIS, Sp. B-

                        7 ROACH, Jamie Lucille    B-
                        7 ROACH, Daniel Norris    B-
                        7 ROACH, David Lindsay    B-
```

```
            6 ROACH, John Gary B-25 Mar 1942 M-28 Oct 1966
            6 ROACH, Joan MILES, Sp. B-

                    7 ROACH, Julie Chris        B-
                    7 ROACH, Jennifer Mary      B-
                    7 ROACH, John Miles         B-
                    7 ROACH, Jill Noel          B-
                    7 ROACH, Jeana Marie        B-

     5 PRATHER, Gwendolyn LINDSAY B-3 Feb 1903 M-27 Feb 1923
     5 PRATHER, Ernest Henry, Sp. B-7 Oct 1903 D-29 Jul 1941

            6 PRATHER, Ernest Lindsay B-22 Aug 1923 M-22 Jun 1946
            6 PRATHER, Jean LEFLER, Sp. B-

                    7 PRATHER, Ernie J.          B-24 Jul 1948

            6 LEFLER, Ella Juanita PRATHER B-18 May 1926 M-8 Feb 1945
            6 LEFLER, John Arthur, Sp. B-22 Jan 1924

                    7 LEFLER, Curtis Arthur      B- 8 Jul 1946
                    7 LEFLER, Cathy Jo           B-25 Jul 1948
                    7 LEFLER, Denise             B- 6 Mar 1955

            6 PRATHER, Ray Dean B-23 Aug 1929 M-26 Feb 1955
            6 PRATHER, Joyce HOLT, Sp. B-9 Jan 1935

                    7 PRATHER, Debbie Jo         B-31 Dec 1955

            6 OFFRET, Betty Jean B-2 Apr 1932 M-12 Jan 1952
            6 OFFRET, Ralph E., Sp. B-6 Oct 1927

                    7 OFFRET, Cindy Kay          B-18 Apr 1953
                    7 OFFRET, Linda Ray          B-18 Apr 1953
                    7 OFFRET, Steven R.          B- 5 Oct 1955

     5 KOFFORD, Grace LINDSAY B-25 Dec 1904 M-15 Jun 1927
     5 KOFFORD, Myrel A., Sp. B-24 Feb 1890 D-16 Aug 1966

            6 KOFFORD, Dick Lindsay B-18 May 1930 M-2 Nov 1949
            6 KOFFORD, Donna Rose PETERSON, Sp. B-5 Apr 1931

                    7 ALMEDA, Sherrie Lynn KOFFORD B-27 May 1950 M-1 Apr 1972
                    7 ALMEDA, Manuel Jarmin, Sp. B-8 Nov 1951

                    7 KOFFORD, Glenna Elaine     B-16 Mar 1952
                    7 KOFFORD, Nancy Lee         B-30 Apr 1958

            6 KOFFORD, Glen Allen B-10 Dec 1932 M-12 Apr 1958 D-28 Dec 1960
            6 KOFFORD, Annette Layne, Sp. B-12 Mar 1937

                    7 KOFFORD, Peggy Ann         B-19 Apr 1959
                    7 KOFFORD, Lynda             B-28 Dec 1960

            6 KOFFORD, Paul Myrel B-28 Nov 1938
            6 KOFFORD, Patricia Karen SPROULE, Sp. B-          M-28 May 1960
            6 KOFFORD, Lorraine STREET, Sp. (2) B-5 Aug 1948 M-3 Nov 1967

                    7 KOFFORD, Mariam Diane      B- 3 Aug 1968
                    7 KOFFORD, Michele           B-26 Nov 1969

     5 GARNES, Avilda LINDSAY B-25 Jun 1913 M-5 Mar 1934
     5 GARNES, Paul, Sp. B-19 Nov 1912

            6 GARNES, Paula Carol  B-24 Dec 1942
            6 GARNES, Jerry        B-24 Jun 1950
            6 GARNES, George Allen B-28 Sep 19

     5 WINN, Crissie Marie LINDSAY B-16 Feb 1915 M-30 Sep 1933 D-15 Jan 1969
     5 WINN, Harold Delmar, Sp. B-25 Jul 1910

            6 WINN, Ann Doreene     B-10 Sep 1939 D-10 Sep 1939
            6 WINN, Connie Lorreene B-12 Apr 1943
            6 WINN, Harold Gregory  B-29 Sep 1951
            6 WINN, Delsa Lee       B- 1 May 1955
```

5 LINDSAY, Daniel B. B-24 Jul 1918 D-1 Dec 1918

5 LINDSAY, John Allen Jr. B-8 Jan 1921 M-26 Jun 1948
5 LINDSAY, Lela Beverly HIMES, Sp. B-25 Feb 1928

      6 LINDSAY, James Allen B-8 Aug 1950
      6 LINDSAY, Diana SATHERS, Sp. B-

          7 LINDSAY, Julie   B-3 Jan 1979

      6 EVANS, Susan Kay LINDSAY B-28 Feb 1952 M-
      6 EVANS, Lloyd, Sp. B-

          7 EVANS, Danielle   B-26 Oct 1974
          7 EVANS, Melissa Sue   B-29 Jan 1977
          7 EVANS, Heather   B- 2 Jan 1979

      6 LINDSAY, William David B-24 Nov 1955
      6 LINDSAY, Richard Mark B-28 Jan 1959

5 LINDSAY, Keith H. B-2 Apr 1923 M-14 Feb 1948
5 LINDSAY, Thelma S. FRANTZ, Sp. B-7 Nov 1928

4 LINDSAY, Daniel McMILLAN B-15 Aug 1877 D-6 Mar 1887

4 LINDSAY, Andrew Alexander B-23 Oct 1879 M-9 Dec 1899 D-4 Dec 1947
4 LINDSAY, Martha Agnes SULZER, Sp. B-22 Nov 1880 D-9 Oct 1930

      5 LINDSAY, Willard Sulser B-2 May 1900 M-23 Dec 1922 D-12 Apr 1946
      5 LINDSAY, Minerva REYNOLDS, Sp. B-3 Aug 1906

          6 LINDSAY, Willard Burt B-14 Aug 1923 M-22 Dec 1944
          6 LINDSAY, Lucy Fay HOLCOMB, Sp. B-15 Oct 1924

              7 LINDSAY, Robert Wayne B-4 Oct 1945 M-21 Aug 1971
              7 LINDSAY, Cheryl Lynn HALE, Sp. B-28 May 1949

                  8 LINDSAY, Christopher   B-25 Aug 1975
                  8 LINDSAY, Laura Jeanetta B- 4 Jan 1978
              7 SHAW, Teresa Kay LINDSAY B-8 Apr 1949 M-15 Aug 1969
              7 SHAW, Jerry Fred, Sp. B-

          6 GOMEZ, Theda Vernell LINDSAY B-20 Dec 1926 M-2 Feb 1952
          6 GOMEZ, Albert, Sp. B-29 Jun 1918

              7 GOMEZ, Albert W.   B-13 Feb 1954
              7 GOMEZ, Mark R.   B 1 Jun 1956
              7 GOMEZ, Joan   B-15 Sep 1958
              7 GOMEZ, Bryan Andrew   B- 4 Nov 1960

5 LINDSAY, Bert M B-7 Nov 1901 M-16 Jun 1930 D-4 Jun 1971
5 LINDSAY, Frances LeOra OHLWILER, Sp. B-16 Jun 1907

      6 LINDSAY, Stanley Wendell B-2 Dec 1935 M-3 Nov 1960
      6 LINDSAY, Nelda Marie GIBSON, B-26 Jun 1938

          7 LINDSAY, Stanley Brian   B- 8 Oct 1961
          7 LINDSAY, Carolyn Marie   B- 7 Feb 1964

      6 LINDSAY, Richard Bert B-9 Jul 1944 M-
      6 LINDSAY, Clyda ALLEN, Sp. B-

          7 LINDSAY, Brett Allen   B-
          7 LINDSAY, Gregg Richard   B-

5 LINDSAY, Hope B-23 Jun 1903 D-4 Nov 1916

5 MURDOCK, Millie LINDSAY B-19 Dec 1904 M-7 Jul 1921 D-26 Jan 1978
5 MURDOCK. Thomas Calvin, Sp. B-7 Jan 1902 D-4 Aug 1959

      6 CLARK, Hope Lindsay MURDOCK B-29 Oct 1921 M-8 May 1941
      6 CLARK, Carl Donald, Sp. B-28 Jan 1918

          7 CLARK, Calvin Lester B-11 Nov 1944
          7 CLARK, Penelope Carol COMPTON, Sp. (1) B-11May1945 M-27Nov1965
           Skauge, Richard, Sp. (2) M-16 Oct 1976 to Penelope

```
                    8 CLARK, Mia-Jane Nancy      B-10 Jun 1966

          7 CLARK, Carolyn Jane MAJORS, Sp. (2) B-          M-14 Jul 1972

                    8 CLARK, Amy Marie         B-17 May 1976
                    8 CLARK, Jesse Samuel      B- 9 Jul 1978

          7 CLARK, Jed Allen B-9 Dec 1948 M-4 Jun 1971
          7 CLARK, Christine SWENSEN, Sp. B-23 May 1950

                    8 CLARK, Aaron Jed         B-18 Apr 1977

          7 CLARK, Carl Benton B-4 May 1952 M-24 Apr 1974
          7 CLARK, Kari Ellen TAYLOR, Sp. B-7 Aug 1956

                    8 CLARK, Carl Dustin       B-13 Jul 1975
                    8 CLARK, Kira Michelle     B- 5 Aug 1977

          7 CLARK, Jon Eric B-31 Dec 1954 M-6 Aug 1975
          7 CLARK, Maureen Lyn RECORD, Sp. B-2 Aug 1956

                    8 CLARK, Jennifer Ohlin    B-21 Jun 1976

          7 CLARK, Dan Wilford        B- 9 Feb 1959
          7 CLARK, Joel Glen          B-23 Sep 1960

    6 MAHONEY, Doris Elaine MURDOCK B-23 Apr 1925 M-19 Aug 1946
    6 MAHONEY, Neil Kenneth, Sp. B-25 Jul 1922

          7 ABPLANALP, Virginia B-31 May 1947 M-14 Aug 1964
          7 ABPLANALP, Larry Floyd, Sp. B-6 Nov 1944

                    8 ABPLANALP, Alawna         B-26 Feb 1965
                    8 ABPLANALP, Lynn Ivon      B-26 Feb 1969
                    8 ABPLANALP, Gregory Floyd B-26 Nov 1973
                    8 ABPLANALP, Ryan Neil      B-18 Feb 1979

          7 ANDERSON, Claudia Ann MAHONEY B-4 Jun 1950 M-10 Jul 1970
          7 ANDERSON, Steven Anders, Sp. B-26 Feb 1949

                    8 ANDERSON, Angela Lyn     B- 9 Mar 1971
                    8 ANDERSON, Alisha Ann     B- 4 Jul 1972
                    8 ANDERSON, Blake Steven   B- 9 Sep 1975
                    8 ANDERSON, Blair Kenneth  B-28 Aug 1976
                    8 ANDERSON, Colby Daren    B-20 Mar 1978

          7 MAHONEY, Kent Neil        B-26 Sep 1956
          7 MAHONEY, Roger Allen      B- 3 May 1961

    6 MURDOCK, Calvin J. B-21 Mar 1927 D-23 Sep 1933

    6 MURDOCK, Vernon LeRoy  B-9 Sep 1928 M-20 Aug 1958
    6 MURDOCK, Elizabeth Joan VANCE, Sp. B-3 Dec 1933

          7 MURDOCK, Eric Vernon      B- 3 Aug 1963
          7 MURDOCK, Shaun Carlos     B-12 Dec 1966
          7 MURDOCK, Amy              B-21 Feb 1970
          7 MURDOCK, Alisa            B-14 Sep 1976

    6 MURDOCK, Thomas Jarald B-19 Jun 1930 M-22 Dec 1961
    6 MURDOCK, Lois Jean SCOTT, Sp. B-9 Apr 1935

          7 MURDOCK, Valerie          B- 6 Oct 1962
          7 MURDOCK, Cheri Kaye       B-20 Oct 1963
          7 MURDOCK, Terrie           B-24 Nov 1964
          7 MURDOCK, McRay Scott      B- 6 Jan 1967

    6 CAMPBELL, Kathleen Martha B-13 July 1932 M-28 Jul 1955
    6 CAMPBELL, Ohlan "M", Sp. B-19 Nov 1930

          7 CAMPBELL, Lindsay "M"     B- 3 Mar 1957
          7 CAMPBELL, Ohleen Merie    B-13 Feb 1959
          7 CAMPBELL, Louis Michael   B-30 Sep 1960

    6 MURDOCK, Baby son (Stillborn) B-1 May 1937

    6 MURDOCK, Lee Stewart B-4 Oct 1940 M-2 Feb 1961
    6 MURDOCK, Barbara Jean HANSEN, B-7 Feb 1940
```

```
                7 MURDOCK, Launa Lee        B-19 Oct 1961
                7 MURDOCK, Douglas Calvin   B- 5 May 1963
                7 MURDOCK, Carolyn Kaye      B-27 Oct 1966
                7 MURDOCK, Patricia Jean     B-13 Jan 1971

5 AGLE, Martha Mae Lindsay B-6 Feb 1907 M-3 Jun 1927
5 AGLE, Roy or Rolf, Sp. B-3 Nov 1906 D-      1973

        6 AGLE, Barbara Dawn B-9 Dec 1928 D-14 Dec 1928

        6 AGLE, Roy Lindsay B-23 Jan 1931 M-23 Apr 1955
        6 AGLE, Sally Ann HOWE, Sp. B-31 Aug 1936

                7 AGLE, Jeffrey Lynn        B- 2 Sep 1958
                7 AGLE, Bradley Roy         B- 5 Aug 1961
                7 AGLE, Brian Elmer         B-20 Oct 1962

        6 AGLE, Norman Larry B-5 Jul 1933
        6 AGLE, Mabel Elouise VAN METRE, Sp. (1) B-14 Jun 1936 M-17 Jul 1954 Div.

                7 AGLE, Martha Ann          B-11 Jun 1955

        6 AGLE, Mary Elizabeth SUMAN, Sp. (2) B-27 Sep 1940 M-3 Jun 1960

                7 AGLE, Travis Lindsay      B-31 Aug 1962
                7 AGLE, Joshua Suman        B-31 Aug 1962
                7 AGLE, Matthew Crippen     B- 4 Jun 1965
                7 AGLE, Susan               B-13 Oct 1966
                7 AGLE, Andrew Andersen     B-26 Feb 1969
                7 AGLE, Peter Martin        B-13 Aug 1971
                7 AGLE, Amy                 B-21 Apr 1974
                7 AGLE, Wendy               B- 7 Feb 1976
                7 AGLE, Daniel Sulser       B-13 Aug 1977

        6 AGLE, Andrew Nils B-16 Nov 1937
        6 AGLE, Judith Jean SPINKS, Sp. (1) B-26 Sep 1941 M-18 Jun 1960

                7 AGLE, Dawn  Diane         B- 8 May 1961
                7 AGLE, David Richard       B-11 Dec 1963

        6 AGLE, Gerlinda (Laura) EHRLICHER, Sp. (2) B-10 Feb 1944 M-

                7 AGLE, Alexander Paul      B- 2 Oct 1974
                7 AGLE, Nicholas Preston    B-26 May 1977

        6 AGLE, Diane   B-9 Apr 1946 D-11 Apr 1946

5 GROSS, Anna Elenore B-29 Feb 1912
5 BOSHARD, Max C., Sp. (1) B-15 Sep 1908 M-10 Jan 1929 Div.1929
5 GROSS, Robert, Sp. (2) B-      1914 M- 9 Feb 1939   D-      1953

        6 BOSHARD, Jay Lindsay B-5 Jun 1929  M-
        6 BOSHARD, Ramona CLYDE, Sp. B-

                7 JOHNER, Clara Ann BOSHARD B-           M-
                7 JOHNER,            Sp. B-

                7 BOSHARD, Andrew Jay B-

        6 GROSS, George Robert B-5 Jan 1940
        6 GROSS, Judith BURNS, Sp. (1) B-      1941 M-          Div. 1975
        6 GROSS, Patti LESTER, Sp. (2) B-17 Oct 1953 M-22 Sep 1975

                7 GROSS, Stephanie Ann      B-15 Feb 1960
                7 GROSS, Troy Earl          B-16 Jan 1962
                7 GROSS, Jennifer           B-18 Jun 1969
                7 GROSS, Jonathan Lester    B-21 Jul 1980

        6 GROSS, Jackson Joe B-7 Aug 1975

5 LINDSAY, baby son (Stillborn) B-30 Sep 1913 D-30 Sep 1913

5 LINDSAY, Andrew Jr. B-15 Jun 1917 D-25 Nov 1918

5 HUISH, Areva LINDSAY B-7 Sep 1918 M-26 Dec 1940
5 HUISH, Robert David, Sp. B-
```

4 LINDSAY, Samuel B-3 Dec 1881 D-4 Oct 1882

4 DUKE, Christina Veronica B-15 Jul 1886 M-12 Jun 1907 D-15 Jul 1974
4 DUKE, Adolphia "R", Sp. B-16 Nov 1882 D-22 May 1958

     5 CHRISTENSEN, Virginia DUKE B-7 Oct 1908 M-31 Jul 1929
     5 CHRISTENSEN, William Gorden, Sp. B-12 Nov 1906

          6 TONTI, Luanne CHRISTENSEN B-9 Aug 1934 M-21 Apr 1963
          6 TONTI, Anthony Gene, Sp. B-15 Feb 1938

7 TONTI, Lisa Maria	B-22 Feb 1964	
7 TONTI, Marc Anthony	B-13 Sep 1966	
7 TONTI, Gina Christina	B- 9 Aug 1977	

          6 CHRISTENSEN, Carolyn CHRISTENSEN B-24 Oct 1941 M-30 Jun 1959
          6 CHRISTENSEN, Jerry LaMar, Sp. B-29 Jan 1941

7 CHRISTENSEN, Kym	B- 9 May 1960	
7 CHRISTENSEN, Karri Lyn	B- 2 Jan 1963	
7 CHRISTENSEN, Mark Jerry	B- 4 Feb 1965	
7 CHRISTENSEN, Michelle	B-19 Oct 1968	
7 CHRISTENSEN, Malinda	B- 4 Oct 1971	

     5 DUKE, Kenneth Lindsay B-22 Feb 1912 M-21 Sep 1934
     5 DUKE, Lucretia BURGESS, Sp. B-8 Feb 1914

          6 DUKE, Barbara Ann B-19 Oct 1935

          6 DUKE, Kenneth Miles B-21 Aug 1943 M-29 May 1968
          6 DUKE, Diane GLEASON, Sp. B-2 Sep 1948

7 DUKE, Jennifer Ann	B-14 Sep 1971	
7 DUKE, Jonathan Lindsay	B-30 Aug 1973	
7 DUKE, Jessica Carey	B-16 Feb 1975	
7 DUKE, James	B- 1977	

          6 DUGGAN, Lucretia DUKE Veasey B-30 Jun 1946
          6 VEASEY, Aubrey Dee, Sp. (1) B- M-2 May 1969 Div.
          6 DUGGIN, George Michael, Sp. (2) B- M- 1974

7 VEASEY, Adam Christopher B-10 Mar 1970		
7 DUGGIN, George Miles	B-14 May 1978	

     5 HILLER, Lucile DUKE B-14 Apr 1915 M-1 Jan 1935
     5 HILLER, Rudolph William B-2 Oct 1909

          6 HILLER, William Dee B-1 Feb 1936 D-13 Nov 1936

          6 HILLER, Kenneth Rudolph B-18 Jan 1938 M-21 Mar 1957
          6 HILLER, Klea Louise DIXION, Sp. B-1 Jul 1938

7 HILLER, Jani	B-15 Sep 1958	
7 HILLER, Lynette	B-18 May 1960	
7 HILLER, Kendra Sue	B-12 Jul 1962	
7 HILLER, Krisan	B-23 Dec 1964	
7 HILLER, Rebecca	B-11 Feb 1970	
7 HILLER, Amy Kay	B-20 Oct 1972	

          6 DEAKINS, Linda Lue HILLER B-28 Mar 1940
          6 KYRIOPOULOS, Thomas LeRoy Jr., Sp. (1) B-13 Nov 1935 M-12 Jun 1957 Div.
          6 DEAKINS, Darwin Harold, Sp. (2) B-10 Jul 1933 M-16 Feb 1969
            Mitchell, Barbara, Sp. to Darwin Div.

7 DEAKINS, Chelsea Anna	B-21 May 1973 (adopted)	
7 DEAKINS, Scott	B-	
7 DEAKINS, Lisa	B-	

          6 PETERSON, Jeannette HILLER B-15 Mar 1945 M-21 May 1964
          6 PETERSON, Ronald Grant, Sp. B-23 Jun 1938

7 PETERSON, Erik Ronald	B- 1 Nov 1967	
7 PETERSON, Candace Lydia	B-17 Dec 1969	
7 PETERSON, Emily Anne	B-15 Apr 1974	
7 PETERSON, Jeffery Brian	B- 4 May 1975	
7 PETERSON, Matthew David	D-30 Nov 1976	

```
                6 VAN WAGONER, Christine HILLER B-4 Oct 1950 M-2 Apr 1970
                6 VAN WAGONER, Michael E., Sp. B-18 Jul 1946

                        7 VAN WAGONER, Hillery        B-16 Jul 1971
                        7 VAN WAGONER, Ryan Michael   B- 7 May 1974
                        7 VAN WAGONER, Jared Michael  B- 4 Nov 1976

                6 HILLER, David Kim B-1 Nov 1952 M-23 May 1974
                6 HILLER, Jennifer Sally BOOTH, Sp. B-8 Mar 1951

                        7 HILLER, JENIFER             B-15 May 1975
                        7 HILLER, David Joseph        B-14 Jan 1977
                        7 HILLER, Sarrah Jane         B-13 Jan 1979

        5 RYAN, Maryan DUKE B-3 May 1922 M-19 Sep 1941
        5 RYAN, Ray Lowell, Sp. B-17 Apr 1917

                6 RYAN, Kay Lowell B-11 Dec 1942 M-11 Dec 1964
                6 RYAN, Arlene Vey CURTIS, B-11 Sep 1942

                        7 RYAN, Kristy Kaye           B-16 Dec 1965
                        7 RYAN, Julie Dawn            B- 8 Dec 1966
                        7 RYAN, Robert Charles        B-29 Nov 1968
                        7 RYAN, William Lowell        B-12 May 1971
                        7 RYAN, Rebecca Ann           B-14 Oct 1973

                6 RYAN, Vaun D. B-17 Aug 1945 M-20 Mar 1970
                6 RYAN, Joan SULLIVAN, Sp. B-5 Sep 1948

                        7 RYAN, Matthew Vaun          B-10 Oct 1971
                        7 RYAN, Katherine             B-30 Mar 1974
                        7 RYAN, David Lowell          B-21 Jul 1979

                6 RYAN, Richard William B-2 Oct 1948
                6 RYAN, Sharon Audrey BOWDEN, Sp. (1) B-20 Nov 1947 M-19 Sep 1969 Div.
                6 RYAN, Sandra HOWELLS, Sp. (2) B-            M-17 Apr 1976

                6 SWEAT, Janalee RYAN B-19 Sep 1955 M-19 Apr 1974
                6 SWEAT, Allen Howard, Sp. B-17 Sep 1953

                        7 SWEAT. Chelsea Lindsay    B- 7 Dec 1978

                6 RYAN, Gary Russell B-8 Nov 1956 M-22 Nov 1978
                6 RYAN, Claudia Marcella FUCCI, Sp. B-16 Oct 1957

4 LINDSAY, David Pryde, B-16 Aug 1888 M-12 Jun 1917 D-24 Feb 1926
4 LINDSAY, Leah BUNNELL, Sp. B-27 Aug 1896 D-29 Sep 1921

        5 LENZI, Melba LINDSAY B-27 Dec 1917 M-10 Jan 1938
        5 LENZI, Dwight Earl, Sp B-13 Aug 1916 D-4 Jul 1978

                6 LENZI, William DWight B-19 Feb 1939 M-21 Jun 1960
                6 LENZI, Beverly Ann OVERSON, Sp. B-20 Oct 1941

                        7 LENZI, David Dwight         B- 7 Apr 1962
                        7 LENZI, Loren Dean           B-31 Dec 1963
                        7 LENZI, Timmy Michael        B-16 Apr 1966
                        7 LENZI, Carol Ann            B-12 Jul 1971

                6 HELLER, Kathleen LENZI B-23 Nov 1942 M-11 Jun 1963
                6 HELLER, Dean Walter, Sp. B-28 Apr 1934

                        7 HELLER, Eric Teru           B-27 Jul 1965
                        7 HELLER, Heide Suzann        B-18 Nov 1969

                6 PERDUE, Peggy Ann LENZI B-26 Aug 1951 M-29 May 1970
                6 PERDUE, Ronnie Lewis, Sp. B-8 Dec 1943
                        7 PERDUE, Ronnie L. III       B-23 Nov 1970
        5 LINDSAY, Leah B-6 Apr 1920

4 LINDSAY, Daughter baby B-20 Jan 1890 D-20 Jan 1890

4 CLYDE, Annie Murdoch LINDSAY B-1 Aug 1892 M-9 Jun 1915 D-21 Apr 1978
4 CLYDE, Edward Delbert, Sp. B-30 Sep 1891 D-4 Sep 1964
```

Andrew Mair and Mary Ann Thompson

Andrew Mair was born at Carbellow, Ayrshire, Scotland, February 17, 1856, to Allan and Mary Murdoch Mair. He was the eighth child and the sixth son of a family of nine children. His brothers and sisters were John, James, Allan Foulds, Matthew, William, Mary, Janet, and Alexander.

Andrew's parents had a comfortable home, and although its furnishings were plain and simple, the family was happy and contented in it. His father was a hard worker and a good provider.

Mary, Andrew, and Alexander were good children. They, being the youngest of the family, were often off having fun on the heather-covered hills of old Scotland. Andrew helped his father somewhat on the farm. He had some rabbits of which he was very fond, and he took very good care of them.

Andrew was ten years old when his father and mother were having problems over religion. In 1851, five years before Andrew was born, his mother, Mary Murdoch Mair had joined the Mormon Church with the consent of her husband. Her mother, Wee Grannie, also accepted the Gospel and was baptized the same year. For awhile, they got along pretty well, but Allan would not have anything to do with this new religion and wouldn't allow the children to be taught its principles. Allan was a good man, but very set in his ways.

Mary had a strong testimony of The Church of Jesus Christ of Latter-day Saints, and she so much wanted her children to know what a wonderful gospel it was. But Allan forbade her teaching them. In 1865, John and James, the two oldest boys, had left Scotland to come to America. Allan Foulds, another brother who was twenty-one years old, was planning on getting married soon. Matthew, William, and Jessie had died in infancy, so just Mary, Andrew, and Alexander were left at home. Andrew's mother kept coaxing Allan to let the children learn of the gospel but still he refused. He told her she could go to America, but she would have to leave the children at home. He became very bitter.

Mary became desperate to think her children were growing up in ignorance of the truths of the gospel, and in the year 1866 she made up her mind—she would leave her husband and come to America, bringing Mary who was now thirteen Andrew, now ten, and Alexander, seven. She made plans and confided in her daughter that they would come to America and then go on to Utah.

Mary told Allan they were going to visit some relatives, and Allan had given his consent. Andrew, not knowing he would never return to his home, asked his father to care for his bunnies.

A friend, John Aird, had secured passage for Mary and her children on the sailing vessel *Saint Mark*. They reached Liverpool, England, in safety and then boarded the ship in company with other LDS emigrants and were bound for New York City in America. They had a fairly good voyage crossing the great Atlantic Ocean. This took four weeks. A few days after the departure, the father learned about their real whereabouts and sent a cablegram to his sons in Maryland asking them to meet the ship and see if they could persuade their mother to return, and if not to at least prevent the children from going to Utah. The boys went to New York only to find the emigrants had started their westward journey to Utah a few days previous.

The family crossed the plains in Andrew Scott's ox train company and passed through all the trying experiences of pioneers making that dreary, tiresome journey of one thousand miles. They reached their destination in October 1866. They went to the home of her brother, John M. Murdoch, whom she had not seen for fourteen years; here they were royally welcomed. Both Mary and John had passed through many trying experiences and had many sorrowful as well as pleasant tales to tell.

After a few years living in Heber City, Utah, Andrew's mother married Daniel McMillan. He was a kind man and was good to Mary and her three children. Andrew learned the blacksmith occupation and did well at it. Some of his other occupations were herding sheep and farming.

On July 24, 1879, Andrew married Mary Ann Thompson. She was a very pretty girl with black hair and pretty brown eyes and fair skin. In November of 1879, Andrew and Mary Ann were sealed to one another for time and eternity in the Salt Lake City LDS Endowment House. They made their home in Heber City, and lived there all their married life.

Andrew and Mary Ann had a family of eleven children, ten of whom lived to maturity, married, and had families of their own. One died shortly after birth.

Andrew kept a cow, chickens, and a pig or so to help with the family living. He also kept a few hives of honey bees. One day when he was trying to get some of the bees that were swarming into the hive, he was stung many times, and this made him so sick that he almost died.

Andrew stayed with the blacksmith and horseshoeing business, but he had to do it the hard way, using bellows pumped by hand to fan the fire in the forge so it would heat the steel and horseshoes so he could mold them in shapes to be used. After the steel was red-hot he would pound it on the anvil with a sledgehammer, or hammer it into the shape he wanted it, then put the finished product into a tub of cold water to cool it. He did some outstanding work. A masterpiece of his work was the steel and iron braces he made that are in the walls and ceiling in the old Heber LDS Second Ward meetinghouse built in 1915, now owned by the Catholic Church. Andrew's motto was always "If a task is once begun, never leave it till it's done. Whether great or small, do it well or not at all."

Andrew's love and devotion to the young people were outstanding. Bishop Grant Broadbent and Patriarch Ralph Giles and others have told about when they were small boys and that if they ever had a broken wagon or toy that needed mending, all they thought they had to do was take it to Uncle Andrew (as he was called) and he would fix it for them free of charge; and many things he did fix.

Andrew was very kind to the widows and fatherless children and to all who were unfortunate. In cases of sickness, such as epidemics of scarlet fever, diphtheria, smallpox, and typhoid fever, which were prevalent in his day, or a burnout, Andrew was one of the first to give a helping hand and was always willing to give more than his share to help lighten a burden.

He owned one of the first surreys (a two-seated buggy with a top on it) in the town. They were very popular to ride in. He loved to go fishing, and many times he drove a horse hitched to a buggy and went out to Strawberry Valley, which is about twenty-five miles east of Heber, and caught fish from the Strawberry River. He always caught his share. He also loved to play checkers with his uncles John M. and William Murdoch.

Andrew and his good wife were always good to their children and grandchildren. It was a pleasure and treat to go to their home. On July 6, 1924. Andrew died at his home of cancer. He was buried July 7, 1924, in Heber City Cemetery. He held the office of High Priest in the LDS Church.

Mary Ann Thompson Mair was born to William and Sarah Fenn Thompson, October 6, 1863, at Provo, Utah. The family later moved to Heber City. She was the fourth child of a family of fifteen children. Needless to say, she learned how to work while very young. Her mother would send her to gather hops used in making yeast. She would also gather wheat straw, which her mother used in making very attractive hats for the ladies.

Mary Ann cultivated an art for cleanliness. She always kept a spotlessly clean house, and it was said she was one who could make a palace out of a hut. She was under sixteen years old when she married Andrew Mair, but together they lived in love and happiness.

Mary Ann was an angel of mercy in cases of sickness and death. She was a practical nurse; many a mile she has traveled on foot in the darkness as well as daylight and at the wee hours of the morning to aid a mother in childbirth or to comfort a family where someone was ill or had passed away. Many a corpse she has washed and laid out when an undertaker was hardly heard of.

When Mary Ann went to aid the sick, many times she would carry a kettle of soup or a loaf of homemade bread, a bottle of jam, or a cake or cookies to help out with the family meal. No one was ever turned away hungry from the home of Andrew and Mary Ann Mair, and many times someone more unfortunate than they was given money to help them on their way.

Mary Ann loved to do temple work. She did endowments for many of her kindred dead and kept accurate and interesting records. She died October 10, 1953, at the age of ninety years and was buried in Heber City, Utah.

When Andrew and Mary Ann Mair died neither left gold, silver, or great stores of material wealth behind, but each had stored great treasures in heaven. They left memories of their honesty, love, kindness, and charity on this earth.

Five generations: 1st Mary Ann Thompson Mair, 2nd Mary Mair Giles, 3rd Ruth Giles Davis Sweat, 4th Faye Davis Henrie, 5th Thomas D Henrie.

Andrew Mair's blacksmith shop was located on Fourth West Street between First and Second South, Heber, Utah. Photo taken about 1922. L. to R. Alexander Mair (brother) shoeing the mule, Fred Clegg (local truant officer), Andrew Mair, Kunie Gertch, Sheldown Horrocks, and Glen Horrocks (grandsons).

George Giles, son of Ann Murdoch
Giles and his wife Mary Elizabeth
Mair Giles, daughter of Andrew Mair

Jacobina Murdoch Clegg, Andrew
Mair and Tennie Smithers

Thomas Horrocks and his wife, Sarah Mair Horrocks, daughter of Andrew Mair

1 MURDOCH, James 1786-1831   2 MAIR, Mary MURDOCH 1818-1900
1 MURDOCH, Mary Murray, Sp. 1782-1856 2 MAIR, Allan, Sp. 1815-1897

DESCENDANTS OF------ 3 MAIR, ANDREW 1856-1924
       3 MAIR, MARY ANN THOMPSON, Sp. 1863-1953

4 MAIR, William Allen B-19 Oct 1880 M-31 Jan 1902 D-30 Sep 1931
4 MAIR, Isabella McIntosh BURT, Sp. B-28 Nov 1881 D-2 Nov 1957

  5 MAIR, William Allen Jr. B-12 Apr 1903 M-14 Jun 1926 D-4 Apr 1979
  5 MAIR, Nellie LaVora GILES, Sp. B-28 Feb 1904

    6 DAVIS, Shirley Lavora MAIR B-18 Apr 1929 M-26 Jun 1946
    6 DAVIS, Barton W. Sp. B-6 Jan 1923

      7 SMITH, Linda Dianne DAVIS B-3 Oct 1948 M-
      7 SMITH, George Albert, Sp. B-

        8 SMITH, Jennifer Lyn   B- 5 Jun 1972

        8 SMITH, Jami   B-16 Jul 1976

        8 SMITH, Bart   B- 8 Nov 1979

      7 Davis, Dennis Bruce   B- 7 May 1952

      7 DAVIS, Carol Ann   B-5 Dec 1964

    6 VANWAGONER, Marjorie Helen MAIR B-26 Apr 1931 M-1 Sep 1949
    6 VANWAGONER, Joseph Alfred, Sp. B-18 Jun 1924

      7 VANWAGONER, Patrick Read B-20 Jun 1948 M-
      7 VANWAGONER, Annette TRIMBLE, Sp. B-24 Jan 1948

        8 VANWAGONER, James Read B-27 Sep 1968

        8 VANWAGONER, Tricia   B-24 Oct 1970

        8 VANWAGONER, Joquel   B-16 Jun 1975

        8 VANWAGONER, Lisha   B-15 Sep 1978

      7 VANWAGONER, William J. B-27 Feb 1951 M-
      7 VANWAGONER, Joyce WRIGHT, Sp. B-23 Aug 1951

        8 VANWAGONER, Kristi   B-25 Apr 1970

        8 VANWAGONER, Sean J.   B-26 May 1973

      7 VANWAGONER, Scott M. B-1 Aug 1955 M-
      7 VANWAGONER, Kay ERCANBRACK, Sp. B-9 Oct 1951

        8 VANWAGONER, Amy Jo   B-26 Mar 1975

        8 VANWAGONER, Bradley   B-15 Jul 1978

      7 VANWAGONER, Joan   B-21 Jul 1960

  5 MAIR, John B. B-19 Nov 1904 M-25 Nov 1933
  5 MAIR, Nina SESSIONS, B-10 Mar 1914

    6 MAIR, William Dale B-15 Oct 1934 M-1 Mar 1963
    6 MAIR, Susann HUNTSMAN, Sp. B-4 Mar 1940

      7 MAIR, Beverly   B-22 Jul 1964

      7 MAIR, Brent William B-31 Dec 1966

      7 MAIR, James Dale   B- 8 Aug 1970

      7 MAIR, Paul Jeffery B-28 Mar 1972

6 MAIR, John Keith B-11 Sep 1936 M-7 May 1959
6 MAIR, LaVon DYE, Sp. B-13 Jan 1935

    7 MAIR, Bruce Keith   B-22 Apr 1961

    7 MAIR, Brian John   B-24 May 1962

    7 MAIR, Launa   B-10 Jul 1964

    7 MAIR, Keri   B-20 Sep 1967

    7 MAIR, Todd Gardiner   B- 6 Aug 1966

    7 MAIR, Dean Gardiner   B- 8 Oct 1970

6 NYE, Nina Kay B-16 Feb 1942 M-11 Jul 1958
6 NYE, Allen E. Sp. B-22 Dec 1938

    7 LARSON, Valerie Kaye NYE   B-10 Feb 1960
    7 LARSON, Tracy, Sp. B-6 Oct 1959 M-24 Apr 1981
    7 NYE, Gary Allen   B-24 Feb 1962

    7 NYE, Troy Jay   B- 2 Oct 1965

5 FINNEGAN, Mary Isabella MAIR B-25 May 1906 M-26 Jan 1928
5 FINNEGAN, Thomas Henry, Sp. B-27 Feb 1905 D-10 Apr 1947

5 RICHARDSON, Blanche MAIR B-1 Aug 1907 M-3 May 1926
5 RICHARDSON, George Henry, Sp. B-1 Apr 1906 D-30 Dec 1963

    6 RICHARDSON, George Jr. B-31 Dec 1926 M-1 Jun 1947
    6 RICHARDSON, Anita Mae BROADHEAD, Sp. B-10 Mar 1928

        7 RICHARDSON, Keith Allen B-20 Mar 1948 M-28 Aug 1970
        7 RICHARDSON, Patsy Wauneta PARKER, Sp. B-29 Dec 1947

            8 RICHARDSON, Dusty Allan   B-29 Jun 1980

        7 DAVIS, Vicki Anita RICHARDSON B-27 Aug 1950 M-25 Jul 1970
        7 DAVIS, Stan J., Sp. B-14 Jul 1945

            8 DAVIS, Quinn J.   B- 2 Feb 1971

            8 DAVIS, Kevin R.   B- 9 Jul 1973

            8 DAVIS, Curt W.   B-17 Jan 1976

            8 DAVIS, Corey   B-12 Mar 1977

    6 RICHARDSON, John Leslie B-6 Nov 1928 M-6 Mar 1953
    6 RICHARDSON, Edna MITCHELL, Sp. B-28 Sep 1932

        7 RICHARDSON, Michael J B-29 May 1954 M- 9 Mar 1973
        7 RICHARDSON, Diane MAIR, Sp. B-17 Dec 1956

            8 RICHARDSON, Tracie Lynn   B-30 Mar 1973

            8 RICHARDSON, Jason Michael   B- 9 Dec 1975

        7 RICHARDSON, Leslie John B-6 Jun 1956
        7 RICHARDSON, Lois DUFFY, Sp. B-8 Oct 1957 M-31 Dec 1976

            8 DUFFY, Lois L.   B-

            8 DUFFY, James Smith   B-12 Sep

        7 REPPOND, Susanne Ann RICHARDSON B-2 Jan 1959
        7 REPPOND, Daniel, Sp. B-20 Jan 1957 M-9 Oct 1976

            8 REPPOND, Brandy Dawn   B-8 May 1977

            8 REPPOND, Jennifer Ann   B-23 Sep 1979

        7 RICHARDSON, Ricky   B-24 May 1960

6 BOWMAN, Joyce RICHARDSON B-10 Sep 1931 M-3 Jul 1948
6 BOWMAN, Roland Henry, Sp. B-8 Apr 1925

    7 TODD, Linda BOWMAN Farrer B-28 Jun 1950
    7 FARRER, Glenn Grant, Sp. B-   M-5 Feb 1971 Div.
    7 TODD, Robert Waters, Sp. B-30 Mar 1955 M-16 Feb 1979

        8 FARRER, Phillip R.   B- Jan

        8 FARRER, Kevin Grant   B- Nov

    7 BOWMAN, Roland Jay B-11 Feb 1953
    7 BOWMAN, Christine PETERSON, Sp. B-4 Oct 1954

        8 BOWMAN, Heather Cherise   B-18 Jul 1972

        8 BOWMAN, Tressa Ann   B- 6 Feb 1974

        8 BOWMAN, Jolynn   B-30 Dec 1976

        8 BOWMAN, Travis   B-11 Mar 1979

    7 BOWMAN, William Lee B-17 Dec 1955 M-19 Jan 1980
    7 BOWMAN, Debbie Jean MONTAGUE, Sp. B-23 Apr 1961

    7 BOWMAN, Ada Ann   B-26 Jul 1957 D-   1957

    7 BOWMAN, Kathy Ann   B-15 Nov 1959

5 MAIR, Grace B-2 Jan 1910 D-11 Jan 1910

5 GEORGIO, LeOra MAIR B-13 Mar 1912 M-28 Nov 1932 D-   1981
5 GEORGIO, John Albert, Sp. B-11 Apr 1906 D-   1981

    6 HUGHES, LeOra Geraldine GEORGIO B-20 Jun 1933 M-
    6 HUGHES, Charles LeRoy, Sp. B-13 Jan

    7 HUGHES, Gail Lynn   B- 8 Sep 1951

    7 PISCITELLI, Mary Serene HUGHES B-12 Oct 1959
    7 PISCITELLI, Robert Thomas, Sp. B-   M-24 May 1980

    7 HUGHES, Charles Kim   B-13 Feb 1956 D-15 Jun 1961

    7 HUGHES, Gregory A.   B-23 Oct 1962

6 GONZALES, Betty Alberta GEORGIO B-2 Aug 1935
6 GONZALES, Larry, Sp. B-   M-   Div.

    7 GONZALES, Michael Allen B-5 Apr 1958
    7 GONZALES, Linda COOK, Sp. B-   M-21 Jun 1980

    7 GONZALES, Victoria Annette   B-4 Nov 1959

6 GEORGIO, John W. B-20 Oct 1938
6 GEORGIO, Julie Ann KINSEY, Sp. B-14 Jan 1940 M-13 Nov 1959 D-29 May 1980

    7 STEFFENSEN, Cindy Lou B-5 Apr 1959
    7 STEFFENSEN, Theodore, Sp. B-   M-

        8 STEFFENSEN, Jeremey   B-   1977

        8 STEFFENSEN, Todd   B-   1979

    7 GEORGIO, John K.   B-11 Jul 1960

    7 GEORGIO, Lee   B- 7 Dec 1961

    7 GRIFFES, Tracy Ann GEORGIO B-16 Jun 1963
    7 GRIFFES, Michael Scott, Sp. B-   M-2 Aug 1980

    7 GEORGIO, Jeffery Scott   B-24 Feb 1968

6 GEORGIO, Paul Howard B-3 Jan 1944
6 GEORGIO, Betty JoAnn HENNING, Sp. B-14 Apr 1945 M-26 Apr 1962

      7 GEORGIO, Paul Jeffrey   B-10 Jul 1963 D-11 Jul 1963

      7 GEORGIO, Vaughn Allan   B-14 Jan 1965

      7 GEORGIO, Anita Marie   B-25 Jul 1968

5 MAIR, Floyd B-2 Mar 1915 M-26 Nov 1934 D-20 Jan 1974
5 MAIR, Theressa McDONALD, Sp. B-17 Feb 1915

    6 WINTERROSE, Audrey Mae Mair B-11 Dec 1935
    6 WINTERROSE, John Dean, Sp. B-9 Nov 1926 M-5 Jul 1957

      7 WORLEY, Christine MAIR B-4 Jun 1953
      7 WORLEY, Collins Bryan, Sp. B-8 Nov 1952 M-4 Sep 1971

        8 WORLEY, Micah Scott   B-19 Feb 1976

        8 WORLEY, Jeremy Collins   B-19 Jan 1979

      7 WINTERROSE, John M.   B-20 Nov 1960

      7 WINTERROSE, Jeffrey   B-14 Oct 1963

      7 WINTERROSE, Kathy   B- 1 Aug 1965

    6 MAIR, Floyd LeRoy B-28 Jul 1938
    6 MAIR, Karlyn CROOK, Sp. B-15 Jun 1940

      7 MAIR, Diane   B- 1 Jul 1959

      7 MAIR, Steven L   B-14 May 1961

      7 MAIR, Wayne C   B- 4 Mar 1965

      7 MAIR, Julie   B-19 Mar 1970

    6 MAIR, Steve B. B-31 Jul 1944 M-25 Oct 1963
    6 MAIR, Betty HUMES, Sp. B-27 Feb 1946

      7 MAIR, Laine S.   B-28 May 1964

      7 MAIR, Eric S.   B-14 Dec 1966

      7 MAIR, Trent   B- 9 Oct 1972

      7 MAIR, Lisha   B-29 Jun 1978

5 MAIR, Burt B-2 May 1917
5 MAIR, Leah GORDON, Sp. B-19 Sep 1921 M-30 Jan 1941

    6 MAIR, Gordon Burt B-15 Oct 1941
    6 MAIR, Dixie Rae HATCH, Sp. B-27 Jul 1944

      7 MAIR, Randall G. B-18 Mar 1961
      7 MAIR, Lori BRISK, Sp. B-12 Feb 1964 M-18 Jul 1980

      7 MAIR, Leon Burt   B-18 Mar 1961 D-18 Mar 1961

      7 MAIR, Richard D   B-30 Mar 1963

      7 MAIR, Kristina   B- 8 Mar 1967

      7 MAIR, Ronald Ray   B-26 Dec 1969

      7 MAIR, Susan   B-25 Oct 1972

    6 MAIR, Larry J B-15 Jan 1943
    6 MAIR, Jinny Lyn CARTER, Sp. B-2 Jan 1944 M-25 Apr 1963

```
              7 MAIR, Gina Rae              B-25 Jun 1964

              7 MAIR, Jill                  B-20 Aug 1965

              7 MAIR, Brad                  B-18 Oct 1968

              7 MAIR, Brett James           B-14 Mar 1972

      6 MAIR, Janice B-8 May 1944

      6 MAIR, Dennis William B-19 Jul 1952
      6 MAIR, Lanette SULSER, Sp. B-20 Dec 1952 M-8 Aug 1969

              7 MAIR, Kerry D.              B-7 Mar 1970

      6 MAIR, Bryan B-23 Sep 1957

5 INGELS, Afton MAIR B-18 May 1920
5 INGELS, Ralph Armond, Sp. B-4 Apr 1921 M-2 May 1941

      6 BONNER, Carol INGELS B-12 Jul 1939
      6 BONNER, Gary Earl, Sp. B-8 Apr 1933 M-8 Jul 1961

              7 BONNER, Gary Lynn           B-23 Dec 1962

              7 BUDD, Kristine BONNER B-1 May 1963
              7 BUDD, Teddy, Sp. B-9 Sep 1960 M-   Feb 1979

                      8 BUDD, Tristie Lynn          B-20 Jul 1980

              7 BONNER, Thomas William      B-2 Apr 1969

              7 BONNER, Brandon Ralph       B-14 Nov 1973

      6 INGELS, Thomas Allen B-25 Apr 1942
      6 INGELS, Launie HAIR, Sp. B-          M-14 Dec 1962 Div.
      6 INGELS, Delores Marie HAKALA, Sp. B-9 Dec 1935 M-22 Mar 1969

              7 INGELS, Taunie              B-22 May 1964

              7 INGELS, Trudie              B-24 Jul 1966

              7 INGELS, Tim Allen           B-20 Jun 1967

              7 INGELS, Stephanie Darleen   B- 1 Feb 1970

              7 INGELS, Brenda Dee          B-17 Aug 1973

      6 NEWBERRY, Bonnie INGELS Parker B-24 Mar 1953
      6 PARKER, Dale Edward, Sp. B-          M-24 Oct 1969 Div.
      6 NEWBERRY, Jerry, Sp. B-3 Nov 1945 M-10 Aug 1976

              7 PARKER, James E.            B-25 Apr 1970

      6 HORTIN, Connie INGELS B-24 Mar 1953
      6 HORTIN, Donald Deforest, Sp. B-25 Jan 1947 M-4 Jun 1971

              7 HORTIN, Shellie Dawn        B-11 Aug 1973

              7 HORTIN, Wesley I.           B-12 Oct 1977

              7 HORTIN, Russell Arlen       B-27 Aug 1980

5 PINTER, Phyllis MAIR Lylle B-29 Feb 1924
5 LYLLE, William Joseph, Sp. B-          M-11 Jun 1941 Div.
5 PINTER, Victor Joseph, Sp. B-          B-24 Dec 1943 Div.

      6 PINTER, William Phillip B-9 Mar 1942
      6 PINTER, Faye GIVENS, Sp. B-          M-
```

```
                7 PINTER, Ricky              B-

                7 PINTER, Tressa            B-

                7 PINTER, Jeannie           B-

        6 PINTER, Victor Joseph Jr. B-4 Mar 1945
        6 PINTER, Jane VAN WAGONER, Sp. B-         M-

                7 PINTER, Vicki Jo          B-

                7 PINTER, Amy               B-

                7 PINTER, Van               B-

        6 PINTER, Mary Jean B-18 May 1946

    5 McRAY, Lucille MAIR B-6 May 1926 M-26 Sep 1947
    5 McRAY, John Francis, Sp. B-28 Jun 1920

        6 McRAE, Frank John B-24 May 1954
        6 McRAE, Tamara HUNLEY, Sp. B-            M-          Div.
        6 McRAE, Anita Jean WILSON, Sp. B-14 Feb 1948 M-26 Sep 1977

                7 MASSA, Brian              B-13 Jul 1968

                7 MASSA, Brenda Kay         B-30 Jun 1970

                7 McRAE, Tressa             B-13 Jul 1972

                7 McRAE, John Frank         B- 8 May 1979

        6 ROBERTS, Patrica McRAE B-2 Jul 1956
        6 ROBERTS, John Franklin, Sp. B-14 Aug 1948

                7 ROBERTS, Kevin Franklin   B-26 Dec 1974

                7 ROBERTS, Carrie Patricia  B-5 Feb 1978

        6 McRAE, Kelly Burt B-13 Sep 1960
        6 McRAE, Judy YOUNG, Sp. B-            M-15 Jul 1981
4 GILES, Mary Elizabeth MAIR B-15 Aug 1882 D-17 May 1961
4 GILES, George David, Sp. B-11 Jan 1879 M-25 Dec 1899 D-21 Mar 1946

    5 FORRER, Mary Ann GILES B-22 Dec 1900 D-26 Jul 1973
    5 FORRER, Karl William, Sp. B-19 Jun 1899 M-20 Sep 1920 D-        1974

        6 PATTERSON, Phyllis Mary FORRER B-29 Dec 1922 M-28 Sep 1945 D-25 Jul 1951
        6 PATTERSON, Frank David, Sp. B-
        6 PATTERSON, Marie KREBS, Sp. (2) B-          M-

                7 KELSEY, Carol PATTERSON B-15 Feb 1947
                7 KELSEY, Martin, Sp. B-22 Aug 1949 M-2 Jun 1972

                        8 KELSEY, Christopher       B-9 Sep 1973

                        8 KELSEY, Kathryn           B-16 Nov 1976

                        8 KELSEY, Kimball Franklin  B-27 Mar 1979

                7 BAKER, Cheryl PATTERSON B-15 Feb 1947
                7 BAKER, Timonthy, Sp. B-14 Feb 1946 M-10 Aug 1973

                        8 BAKER, Amy Elizabeth      B-11 Sep 1975

                        8 BAKER, Amber Marie        B- 9 Mar 1977

                        8 BAKER, Joel Alan          B-15 Apr 1979

                7 ADAMS, Cindy Ann PATTERSON B-22 Apr 1951
                7 ADAMS, Gregory, Sp. B-            M-3 Mar 1972
```

```
                8 ADAMS, Gregory              B-10 Nov 1972 D-12 Dec 1972

                8 ADAMS, Melanie Ann          B- 5 Nov 1973

                8 ADAMS, Melissa Ann          B- 5 Jun 1977

    6 PICO, Lois Ann Forrer Bronson Thorpe B-19 Oct 1924
    6 BRONSON, LaZelle, Sp. B-         M-15 Apr 1942 Div.
    6 THORPE, Peter Emil, Sp. (2) B-        M-19 Oct 1946 Div.
    6 PICO, Joseph Mervin, Sp. (3) B-       M-3 Dec 1951

        7 TRUJILLO, Lynda Ann BRONSON Rose B-
        7 ROSE, James Arnold, Sp. (1) B-          M-
        7 TRUJILLO,         Sp. (2) B-          M-

                8 ROSE, Mary Ann              B-

                8 ROSE, James Arnold II       B-

        7 HUGHES, Barbara THORPE B-
        7 HUGHES, George, Sp. B-          M-

                8 HUGHES, Debra Ralene        B-

                8 HUGHES, Jeana Christina     B-

        7 EPPERSON, Sharon THORPE Grace B-
        7 GRACE, Robert, Sp. (1) B-          !-
        7 EPPERSON, Michael Irving, Sp. (2) B-          M-

                8 GRACE, Stephen Robert       B-

                8 GRACE, Michael Ivan         B-

        7 COPLIN, Karon THORPE B-
        7 COPLIN, David, Sp. B-          M-

                8 COPLIN, Douglas Allen       B-

                8 COPLIN, Latisha Renee       B-

    6 FORRER, Ada B-23 Dec 1927 D-11 Jan 1928

    6 FORRER, George Grant B-7 Aug 1933
    6 FORRER, Diane STEWART, Sp. B-8 Mar 1936 M-2 Feb 1951

        7 FORRER, Glen Grant B-24 Feb 1953
        7 FORRER, Linda BOWMAN, Sp. B-          M-          Div.

                8 FORRER, Phillip             B-

                8 FORRER, Kevin               B-

        7 FORRER, William Kay B-11 Jun 1954
        7 FORRER, JOAN DUNLAP, Sp. B-          M-

        7 BROWN, Sandra Lynn FORRER Sabey B-8 Apr 1956
        7 SABEY, Lynn, Sp. (1) B-          M-
        7 BROWN, Larry, Sp. (2) B-          M-

                8 SABEY, Gregory              B-

                8 BROWN, John Douglas         B-

        7 FORRER, Paul Allen          B-22 Nov 1957

        7 FORRER, Clyde Brent         B-29 Oct 1960

5 SWEAT, Ruth GILES Davis B-2 Mar 1903
5 DAVIS, Orval, Sp. (1) B-26 Nov 1898 M-13 Apr 1925 D-23 Nov 1962
5 SWEAT, Orvel, Sp. (2) B-          M-23 Jul 1974
```

6 HENRIE, Faye DAVIS B-26 Jan 1947 M-10 Jun 1943
6 HENRIE, Thomas "A", Sp. B-6 Feb 1923

    7 HENRIE, Thomas Dale B-28 Jan 1947
    7 HENRIE, Alicia Antonia MACIEL, Sp. B-15 Jan 1954 M-25 Oct 1975 Div.

        8 HENRIE, Olivia Josine   B- 6 Feb 1976

    7 HENSON, Myrna Joy HENRIE B-29 Aug 1948
    7 WARREN, Paul W. Sp. B-22 Dec 1949 M-18 Oct 1968 Div. Jun 1975
    7 HENSON, Donald Dale, Sp. (2) B-7 Nov 1942 M-12 Oct 1975

        8 WARREN, Stephanie Kim   B-5 Jul 1972
        8 HENSON, Laurie   B-
    7 HENRIE, Robert "A" B-19 Mar 1951
    7 HENRIE, Patricia HANSEN, Sp. B-17 Apr 1955 M-26 Jun 1976

        8 HENRIE, Kinsi Ann   B-10 Jul 1977

        8 HENRIE, Brittany Faye   B-22 Aug 1979

    7 SCOTT, Jane HENRIE B-11 Mar 1955
    7 SCOTT, Lawrence Richard, Sp. B-25 Jan 1951 M-8 Aug 1975

        8 SCOTT, Julie Marie   B-11 Mar 1955
        8 SCOTT, Jennifer Lynn   B- 1 Oct 1979

    7 ROBINSON, Janice HENRIE B-11 Mar 1955
    7 ROBINSON, Gary Russell, Sp. B-10 Jan 1951 M-2 Jan 1975

        8 ROBINSON, Lisa Bree   B-29 Sep 1975

        8 ROBINSON, David Thomas   B-27 May 1977

        8 ROBINSON, LeAnn   B- 8 Jan 1979

        8 ROBINSON, Lindsey Elaine B-12 May 1981

    7 HENRIE, David William   B-13 Sep 1957

5 GILES, Verna B-20 Feb 1910 D-21 Mar 1932

5 GILES, Ray B-1 Jul 1913 D-13 Jan 1977
5 GILES, Therma Mae BALL, Sp. B-8 Apr 1917 M-3 Dec 1936

    6 GILES, Gary William B-11 Feb 1938
    6 GILES, Rava Annie CLARK, Sp. B-10 Jan 1939 M-30 Jul 1957

        7 GILES, Gary Ray   B-25 Sep 1959

        7 GILES, Albert Troy   B-26 Oct 1960

        7 GILES, Keyo Lyn   B-16 Aug 1963

        7 GILES, Dirk Frank   B- 8 Nov 1973

        7 GILES, Chi LeAnn   B- 2 Jul 1975

    6 GILES, George David B-25 Jul 1939
    6 GILES, Nelida Beatriz ZANOTTA, Sp. B-6 May 1941 M-10 Aug 1964

        7 GILES, Nellie Gaye   B-16 May 1966

        7 GILES, Marcia Kay   B- 2 Jan 1969

        7 GILES, Cindy Lou   B-22 Jun 1971

        7 GILES, Shelly Ann   B-25 Jul 1973

        7 GILES, Mary Elena   B- 3 Aug 1977

6 SWENA, Velda Kaye GILES B-23 Aug 1941
6 SWENA, Marvin, Sp. B-8 Jan 1938 M-11 May 1959
6 SWENA, Colleen DAVIS Knecht, Sp. (1) B-   M-

        7 SWENA, William K   B-14 Sep 1959

        7 SWENA, Lloyd Brent   B-20 Sep 1960

        7 SWENA, Mark G   B-31 Mar 1968

6 JOHNSON, Ruth Lou Ann GILES B-19 Nov 1942
6 JOHNSON, Richard, Sp. B-26 Apr 1940 M-31 Aug 1962

      7 JOHNSON, Elizabeth Gwendolyn B-16 Jun 1963

      7 JOHNSON, Richard Blake   B- 9 Jul 1964

      7 JOHNSON, Susan Rae   B- 5 Nov 1965

      7 JOHNSON, Heidi Ann   B- 3 Oct 1970

      7 JOHNSON, Danni Marie   B- 4 Apr 1975

6 NELSON, May Rae GILES B-12 Apr 1954
6 NELSON, Donald Gene, Sp. B-18 Dec 1950 M-8 Oct 1971

      7 NELSON, Donald Gene Jr.   B-30 Dec 1972

      7 NELSON, David Ray   B-14 Jul 1975

      7 NELSON, Matthew Giles   B-11 Aug 1976

  5 GILES, Helen B-3 Jun 1919 D-4 Jun 1919

  5 GILES, Phyllis B-26 Aug 1921 D-28 Aug 1921

4 HORROCKS, Sara Jane MAIR B-14 Oct 1884 D-19 Jan 1966
4 HORROCKS, Thomas, Sp. B-17 Apr 1878 M-6 Dec 1902 D-20 Mar 1975

    5 SARKISIAN, Rachel HORROCKS Murray B-10 Jun 1903 D-6 Sep 1969
    5 MURRAY, Arthur, Sp. (1) B-   M-17 May 1923
    5 SARKISIAN, Arthur, Sp. (2) B-   M-

    5 BROWN, Ruth HORROCKS Farrer B-10 Jun 1903 D-12 Jul 1976
    5 FARRER, Henry Helman, Sp. (1) B-   M-20 Nov 1920 Div.
    5 BROWN, Walter Russell, Sp. (2) B-   M-5 Jul 1933

      6 DRISCOLL, Lillian Virginia FARRER B-
      6 DRISCOLL, Coy Samuel, Sp. B-   M-

      6 FARRER, Thomas Le Roy B-
      6 FARRER, Gladys NORTH, Sp. B-   M-

        7 FARRER, Vance B-
        7 FARRER, Peggy WADE, Sp. B-   M-

          8 FARRER, Shalayne   B-

          8 FARRER, Kerri Lynn   B-

          8 FARRER, Marsha   B-

          8 FARRER, Wade   B-

          8 FARRER, Justin   B-

        7 JACOBSEN, Janice FARRER B-
        7 JACOBSEN, Bernard, Sp. B-   M-

          8 JACOBSEN, Roger   B-

          8 JACOBSEN, Bryan   B-

          8 JACOBSEN, Janine   B-

          8 JACOBSEN, Matthew   B-

        7 FARLEY, Gladys Arlene FARRER B-
        7 FARLEY, Joseph, Sp. B-   M-

          8 FARLEY, Justin   B-

```
              8 FARLEY, Brandon                    B-

              8 FARLEY, Sara                       B-

       7 FARRER, Wayne B-
       7 FARRER, Lori STRICKER, Sp. B-                    M-

              8 FARRER, Kimberly                   B-

              8 FARRER, Nancee                     B-

  6 CLARK, Helen Dean FARRER Runnels B-
  6 RUNNELS, Audie Morris, Sp. (1) B-              M-
  6 CLARK, Joseph Arthur, Sp. (2) B-              M-

       7 RUNNELS, James Craig B-
       7 RUNNELS, Bonnie Jean WILLIAMS, Sp. B-                    M-

              8 RUNNELS, Kenneth Craig            B-

              8 RUNNELS, Peggy Sue                B-

              8 RUNNELS, Brian David              B-

       7 RUNNELS, Mary Ruth B-        1943 D-        1943

       7 JENSON, Barbara Jeanne RUNNELS B-
       7 JENSON, LaVerne, Sp. B-               M-

              8 JENSON, Shelly Kay               B-

              8 JENSON, Christopher LaVerne      B-

       7 RUNNELS, Jay Dee B-
       7 RUNNELS, Linda Rae CHURCH, Sp. B-                    M-

              8 RUNNELS, Cody Jay                B-

              8 RUNNELS, Jody Lee                B-

       7 RUNNELS, Cathy Jayne B-            M-

5 HORROCKS, Thomas Russell B-1 May 1906
5 HORROCKS, Mary Verllian BROADHEAD, Sp. B-              M-12 Feb 1926

       6 IVES, Margie HORROCKS Marsili B-
       6 MARSILI, Joseph, Sp. (1) B-           M-
       6 IVES, Stanley P. Sp. B-           M-

              7 MARSILI, Steven Russell B-
              7 MARSILI, Mary        Sp. B-              M-

                     8 MARSILI, Amy              B-

                     8 MARSILI, Stephen          B-

              7 AMOROSE, Linda Susan MARSILI B-
              7 AMOROSE, Robert, Sp. B-              M-

       6 HORROCKS, Kenneth R. B-
       6 HORROCKS, Marian Casper, Sp. (1) B-              M-
       6 HORROCKS, Alice, Sp. (2) B-           M-
       6 HORROCKS, Pearl STARLING, Sp. (3) B-              M-

              7 JACOBSON, Melaney Ann HORROCKS Lopez B-
              7 LOPEZ, Ben, Sp. (1) B-           M-
              7 JACOBSON, Jerry, Sp. (2) B-              M-

                     8 JACOBSON, Hidie           B-

                     8 JACOBSON, Michelle        B-
```

```
            7 ANDERSON, Debbie HORROCKS B-
            7 ANDERSON, James, Sp. B-                        M-

                    8 ANDERSON, Gary                    B-

            7 HORROCKS, Cathy Lynn              B-                D-

            7 HORROCKS, Kimberly Kay            B-

    6 GILES, Barbara Jean HORROCKS Johnson B-
    6 JOHNSON, Dale, Sp. (1) B-              M-
    6 GILES, James R., Sp. (2) B-           M-

            7 STEELE, Dale Lynn JOHNSON Young B-
            7 YOUNG, Robert, Sp. (1) B-              M-
            7 STEELE, Michael, Sp. (2) B-              M-

                    8 YOUNG, Monique                B-

                    8 YOUNG, Russell                B-

                    8 STEELE, Jospeh                B-

            7 PETTIT, Geniel L. JOHNSON B-
            7 PETTIT, Ricahrd, Sp. B-              M-

                    8 PETTIT, Jarad                 B-

            7 SWENA, Carolyn JOHNSON B-
            7 SWENA, David, Sp. B-              M-

                    8 SWENA, Tracey                 B-

                    8 SWENA, Steven                 B-

            7 TITCOMB, Susan JOHNSON B-
            7 TITCOMB, Ronald, Sp. B-              M-

            7 GILES, Jamie                    B-

    6 HORROCKS, Dennis Lee B-
    6 HORROCKS, Debra Lee ESKELSON, Sp. B-              M-

            7 HORROCKS, Denise Evonne        B-

            7 HORROCKS, Peggy Lee            B-

            7 HORROCKS, Barbara Jean         B-

5 MAYNARD, Florence HORROCKS B-5 Aug 1908
5 MAYNARD, Archie, Sp. B-              M-3 May 1926

    6 SWEATFIELD, Norma LaRae MAYNARD B-
    6 SWEATFIELD, Melvin, Sp. B-              M-

            7 SWEATFIELD, Bobbie B-
            7 SWEATFIELD, Lynn DOLTON, Sp. B-              M-

                    8 SWEATFIELD, Bobbie Lee        B-

                    8 SWEATFIELD, Lora Lynn

            7 SWEATFIELD, Billey B-
            7 SWEATFIELD, Becky SMITH, Sp. B-              M-

                    8 SWEATFIELD, Melvin            B-

            7 SWEATFIELD, William            B-

    6 JOHNSON, Wilma MAYNARD Jordan B-
    6 JORDAN, Glade, Sp. (1) B-              M-
    6 JOHNSON, Lloyd Dean, Sp. (2) B-              M-
```

```
       7 JORDAN, Valorie              B-

       7 JORDAN, Paul                 B-

   6 OKEEFE, Clara Dean MAYNARD Watkins B-
   6 WATKINS, Wayne, Sp. (1) B-            M-
   6 OKEEFE, Wendle, Sp. (2) B-           M-

       7 WATKIN, Sharrie             B-

       7 WATKIN, Ross                B-

   6 MAYNARD, Kenneth Lee B-
   6 MAYNARD, Mayvon WEBB, Sp. B-         M-

       7 MAYNARD, Leslie             B-

       7 MAYNARD, Janet              B-

       7 MAYNARD, Buddy              B-

       7 MAYNARD, Rickey             B-

   6 MAYNARD, Clyde B-

5 HORROCKS, William Glen B-12 Nov 1910
5 HORROCKS, Leah Luella GILES, Sp. B-25 Oct 1914 M-29 May 1933

   6 AZLIN, Glenna HORROCKS B-23 Apr 1934
   6 AZLIN, Bob CARL, Sp. B-          M-4 Aug 1954

       7 MOULTON, Kathleen AZLIN B-
       7 MOULTON, Kent L., Sp. B-             M-

           8 MOULTON, Kurt L.           B-

           8 MOULTON, Kevin Duane       B-

       7 AZLIN, Carolyn Y.           B-

       7 AZLIN, Connie R.            B-

   6 HORROCKS, Thomas H. B-
   6 HORROCKS, Jean Sweat, Sp. (1) B-       M-4 Jun 1958 Div.
   6 HORROCKS, Elma Rae KOHLER, Sp. (2) B-       M-

       7 HORROCKS, David B-
       7 HORROCKS, Cathy McKENZIE, Sp. B-              M-

           8 HORROCKS, David Scott      B-

       7 BURKS, Patricia HORROCKS B-
       7 BURKS, Clay, Sp. B-           M-

       7 HORROCKS, Tamra             B-

       7 HORROCKS, Valorie           B-

       7 HORROCKS, Amy               B-

       7 HORROCKS, Michael C.        B-

5 HORROCKS, George Sheldon B-12 Apr 1912
5 HORROCKS, Helen Marie ARCHIBALD, Sp. B-29 Nov 1912 M-19 May 1931

   6 HORROCKS, Sheldon Glen B-22 Sep 1932
   6 HORROCKS, Alene Phillips, Sp. B-          M-10 Sep 1952

       7 HORROCKS, Sheldon Glen Jr.   B-

       7 HORROCKS, James Phillip B-
       7 HORROCKS, Koreen BURKE, Sp. B-              M-
```

```
                        8 HORROCKS, James Phillip        B-

        7 BURT, Tawna Jean HORROCKS B-
        7 BURT, Timothy, Sp. B-                  M-

                        8 BURT, Bradley                  B-

                        8 BURT, Mandy Lynn               B-

        7 HORROCKS, Tamara                B-

        7 HORROCKS, Joel Scott B-
        7 HORROCKS, Tamara Rae KELSEY, Sp. B-                    M-

                        8 HORROCKS, Bart                 B-

                        8 HORROCKS, Tina Shantre         B-

6 GINES, Yuletta Marie HORROCKS B- 13 Apr 1934
6 GINES, Ken, Sp. B-            M-25 Jul 1953

        7 GINES, Stephen B-
        7 GINES, Dawn Kirkman, Sp. B-             M-

                        8 GINES, Mindy Rae               B-

        7 SABEY, Shelley GINES Christensen B-
        7 CHRISTENSEN, Brent, Sp. B-              M-
        7 SABEY, Phil, Sp. (2) B-                 M-   (

                        8 CHRISTENSEN, Sheldon Ken       B-

                        8 CHRISTENSEN, Branden           B-

                        8 SABEY, Shannon Lee             B-

        7 GINES, Val K. B-
        7 GINES, Jan CHRISTENSEN, Sp. B-                  M-

                        8 GINES, Allen                   B-

                        8 GINES, Valarie                 B-

        7 BARNES, Salley Jane Gines B-
        7 BARNES, Lamar, Sp. B-                 M-

                        8 BARNES, Samatha Marie          B-

        7 Gines, Kendra Lee              B-

6 MARCELLIN, Audrey Jean HORROCKS B-19 Sep 1936
6 MARCELLIN, James, Sp. B-            M-16 Jul 1955

        7 McKENNA, Helen Marie MARCELLIN B-
        7 McKENNA, George, Sp. B-                M-

        7 MARCELLIN, Marrianne

                        8 MARCELLIN, Eche Jean           B-

        7 MARCELLIN, James               B-

        7 MARCELLIN, Madlyn              B-

6 HORROCKS, James Roger B-14 Jun 1941
6 HORROCKS, Shriley BALLARD, Sp. B-              M-4 Feb 1960

        7 GREEN, Mary Ellen HORROCKS B-
        7 GREEN, William, Sp. B-               M-

                        8 GREEN, Leslie                  B-

                        8 GREEN, Lynn                    B-
```

```
              7 HORROCKS, Roger James        B-        1962 D-      1975

              7 HORROCKS, Teresa             B-

     6 HORROCKS, Terry Allen B-1 Nov 1944
     6 HORROCKS, Margie Lou RICHARDSON, Sp. B-         M-8 Jul 1963

              7 HORROCKS, Terrie Sue         B-

              7 HORROCKS, Randy Allen        B-

              7 HORROCKS, Rhonda Lou         B-

5 HORROCKS, Harold (Tobe) B-20 May 1915 D-30 Jun 1972
5 HORROCKS, Evelyn Liddie BROADHEAD, B-13 Dec 1914 M-26 Sep 1932

     6 HORROCKS, Harold Le Roy B-1 Jan 1933
     6 HORROCKS, Arlene BEREN, Sp. B-          M-11 Apr 1952

              7 HORROCKS, Kent B-6 Oct 1953
              7 HORROCKS, Patricia ORGILL, Sp. B-         M-

                     8 HORROCKS, Dianna       B-

                     8 HORROCKS, Kirk         B-

              7 HORROCKS, Tim  B-24 Apr 1955
              7 HORROCKS, Melinda KUPPER, Sp. B-         M-

                     8 HORROCKS, Shan         B-

              7 HORROCKS, Dwane B-14 May 1956
              7 HORROCKS, LaReta BUNDY, Sp. B-          M-

                     8 HORROCKS, Brandon      B-

              7 HORROCKS, Ronnie B-23 Oct 1957
              7 HORROCKS, Ellen YOUNG, Sp. B-           M-

                     8 HORROCKS, Jared        B-

              7 HORROCKS, Mark B-14 Feb 1959
              7 HORROCKS, Salley SHEPHERD, Sp. B-        M-

              7 HORROCKS, Bruce         B-28 Sep 1961

              7 HORROCKS, Blaine        B-26 May 1963

     6 BAKER, Edith JoAnn HORROCKS B-19 Jun 1936
     6 BAKER, Alvin, Sp. B-        M-12 Oct 1959

              7 BAKER, Kenny            B-

              7 BAKER, Keven            B-

              7 BAKER, Wendy            B-

     6 AYRES, Karen LaRae HORROCKS B-26 Sep 1942
     6 AYRES, Larry, Sp. B-        M-9 Aug 1963

              7 AYRES, Bobby            B-

              7 AYRES, David            B-

              7 AYRES, Lee Ann          B-

              7 AYRES, Kristy           B-

              7 AYRES, Jennifer         B-
```

```
      6 HORROCKS, Brent LaVar B-19 Sep 1952
      6 HORROCKS, Charlene SIMMONS, Sp. B-                    M-


            7 HORROCKS, Lesley Ann              B-

            7 HORROCKS, Amey Lynn               B-

   5 RHOADES, Pearl HORROCKS Beckendorf B-5 Jan 1918
   5 BECKENDORF, William, Sp. B-        1910 M-26 Jun 1934 D-        1951
   5 RHOADES, Stanley Selin, Sp. (2) B-15 May 1921 M-16 Apr 1952

         6 BECKENDORF, Joan B-8 Feb 1943

         6 FILLMORE, Helen Jane BECKENDORF B-14 Apr 1949
         6 FILLMORE, Melvin Vern, Sp. B-          M-

            7 FILLMORE, Valorie Jane            B-

            7 FILLMORE, Michelle Marie          B-

            7 FILLMORE, Tammy Jean              B-

         6 BECKENDORF, William Fredrick B-23 Feb 1951
         6 BECKENDORF, Jane CLYDE, Sp. B-           M-

            7 BECKENDORF, William Thomas        B-

            7 BECKENDORF, Susan                 B-

   5 HORROCKS, Arthur Billie B-14 Apr 1929
   5 HORROCKS, Verna Jane WRIGHT, Sp. (1) B-          M-24 Jan 1952
   5 HORROCKS, Sharlene GATES, Sp. (2) B-           M-

         6 HORROCKS, Jeffrey            B-

         6 HORROCKS, Lisa               B-

         6 HORROCKS, Dian               B-

         6 HORROCKS, Steven Charles  B-

4 DAVIS, Esther Isabel MAIR B-18 Dec 1886 D-7 Dec 1946
4 DAVIS, Thomas Goddard, Sp. B-7 Oct 1871 M-1 Dec 1903 D-8 Feb 1954

      5 HICKS, Florence DAVIS B-14 Mar 1904
      5 HICKS, John, Sp. B-              M-18 May 1922

         6 NEWMANN, Norma Fay HICKS B-
         6 NEWMANN, Earl Walter, Sp. B-                    M-

            7 CHAMERLAIN, Carol Ann NEWMANN B-

         6 HENDERSON, Helen HICKS B-
         6 HENDERSON, John Victor, Sp. B-                  M-

            7 FOSTER, Linda Rae HENDERSON B-
            7 FOSTER,            Sp. B-                    M-

            7 HENDERSON, James V.               B-

            7 HENDERSON, Pamela Noreen          B-

         6 HICKS, James William B-
         6 HICKS, Eileen MICKELSON, Sp. B-                 M-

            7 HICKS, James William Jr.         B-

            7 HICKS, Tawny Lynn                 B-

            7 HICKS, Tina Louise               B-

            7 HICKS, Tanna Lee                  B-

            7 HICKS, Jack Michael              B-
```

5 PERRY, Mary DAVIS B-10 Jun 1909
5 PERRY, Clyde, Sp. B-   M-3 Nov 1927

     6 MACANA, LaRae PERRY B-
     6 MACANA,   , Sp. B-   M-

     6 PERRY, Roy   B-

5 DAVIS, William Bert B-22 Sep 1911
5 DAVIS, Marjorie ARCHIBALD, Sp. B-17 Nov 1915 M-28 Jul 1933

     6 DAVIS, Glen B-15 Feb 1934 D-15 Feb 1934

     6 ATKINSON, LaDene DAVIS B-22 Aug 1935
     6 ATKINSON, Duane T. Sp. B-25 Aug 1935 M-10 Oct 1953

          7 ATKINSON, Kim   B-29 Jul 1954

          7 ATKINSON, Kevin D   B-15 Oct 1955

          7 ATKINSON, Rodney D   B-15 Sep 1957

          7 ATKINSON, Christine   B-27 Sep

     6 DAVIS, William Richard B-24 Apr 1938
     6 DAVIS, Karen Marie MORRISON, Sp. B-   M-9 Jan 1959

          7 DAVIS, Debra   B-

          7 DAVIS, Scot   B-

          7 DAVIS, Diane   B-

          7 DAVIS, Gina   B-

          7 DAVIS, Jill   B-

          7 DAVIS, Ricky   B-

     6 KIRKHAM, Shirley Mae DAVIS B-20 Dec 1939
     6 KIRKHAM, Fay, Sp. B-   M-9 Jun 1959

          7 KIRKHAM, Robert   B-

          7 TAYLOR, Teri Sue KIRKHAM B-
          7 TAYLOR,   Sp.B-   M-

          7 KIRKHAM, Jim   B-

     6 DAVIS, Thomas Bert B-9 Oct 1942
     6 DAVIS, Donna SMITHIES, Sp. B-   M-

          7 DAVIS, Bret   B-

          7 DAVIS, April   B-

     6 DAVIS, Joe Robert B-12 Nov 1944
     6 DAVIS, Carol Gardner, Sp. B-   M-27 Oct 1962
     6 DAVIS, Kathy Lee, Sp. (2) B-

          7 DAVIS, Carrie Jo   B-

          7 DAVIS, Kelly Daun   B-

          7 DAVIS, Brandy   B-

5 ULLAND, Grace DAVIS B-10 Apr 1916
5 ULLAND, Alvin, Sp. B-   M-15 Mar 1939

     6 ULLAND, Kevin   B-

     6 ULLAND, Keith   B-

5 DAVIS, Dean G. B-25 Aug 1920 D-18 Apr 1942

5 DAVIS, Jack T. B-9 Mar 1923 D-16 Jan 1949
5 DAVIS, Dorma CURTAIN, Sp. B-   M-17 Sep 1945

      6 DAVIS, Jerry G   B-

      6 DAVIS, Linda   B-

5 DAVIS, Thomas R. B-9 Apr 1925
5 DAVIS, Dorma CURTIAN, Sp. B-   M-17 Jun 1950

      6 DAVIS, Alan   B-

      6 DAVIS, Robert   B-

5 DAVIS, June B-5 Jun 1928

4 MAIR, Andrew Jr. B-14 Apr 1889 D-7 Feb 1962
4 MAIR, Myrtle YOUNG, Sp. B-25 Jan 1893 M-19 Oct 1909 D-   1981

      5 MAIR, Marlowe B-4 Aug 1910 M-29 May 1932 D-14 Jun 1946
      5 CASSIDY LaPreal MASON Mair Mecham, Sp. B-7 Dec 1914
         MECHAM, Herald, Sp. (2) B-   M-   Div.
         CASSIDY, Ross, Sp. (3) B-   M-

            6 MAIR, Jerald   B-17 Jan 1934
            6 MAIR, Nada OLMSTEAD, Sp. B-   M-

                 7 SMITH, Cindy Lee MAIR B-
                 7 SMITH, Steve, Sp. B-   M-

                     8 SMITH, Steven Adrian   B-

                 7 MAIR, Jerry G.   B-

                 7 MAIR, Lynn Andrew   B-

                 7 MAIR, Steven Allen   B-

            6 MAIR, Howard Marlow B-18 Feb 1935
            6 MAIR, Leah JONES, Sp. B-   M-

                 7 MAIR, Debra Ann   B-

                 7 MAIR, Howard Marlow Jr.   B-

                 7 WILSON, Brenda Lee MAIR B-
                 7 WILSON, David, Sp. B-   M-

                 7 MAIR, Colleen Kay   B-

            6 BARGER, Darlene Marie MAIR B-6 Mar 1938
            6 BARGER, Robert Byron, Sp. B-   M-

                 7 BARGER, Bruce Lynn   B-

                 7 BARGER, Brent Byron   B-

                 7 BARGER, Mark   B-

            6 MAIR, Wayne Jay B-3 Mar 1943
            6 MAIR, Diane FRANCE, Sp. B-   M-

                 7 MAIR, Bonnie Lee   B-

                 7 MAIR, Becky Lynn   B-

            6 KEELE, Marlene MAIR B-20 Jul 1946
            6 KEELE, Bobby, Sp. B-   M-

7 KEELE, Tamera Ann   B-

7 KEELE, Ricky Lynn   B-

7 KEELE, Treasa Lee   B-

7 KEELE, Sandra Marie   B-

7 KEELE, Eric Jay   B-

JOHNSTON, Ranae MECHAM Breeze B-
BREEZE, Mike, Sp. B-   M-   Div.
JOHNSTON, Johnny, Sp. B-   M-   Div.

     BREEZE, Mike   B-

     BREEZE, Lisa Marie   B-

     BREEZE, Tom L.   B-

CASSIDY, Ross Woodrow B-
CASSIDY, Shriley Archuleta, Sp. B-   M-

     CASSIDY, David Joseph   B-

     CASSIDY, Daniel Roger   B-

     CASSIDY, Tammera Marie B-

     CASSIDY, Donald Ross   B-

     CASSIDY, Tonya Jean   B-

5 MAIR, Ernest B-4 Mar 1912 D-6 Oct 1967
5 MAIR, Matilda KNIGHT, Sp. B-26 Nov 1915 M-11 Oct 1932

     6 MAIR, Raymond Dale B-25 Aug 1933
     6 MAIR, Karole Lee HATCH, Sp. B-   M-12 Jun 1957

          7 MAIR, David Ray   B-

          7 MAIR, Dale Lee   B-11 Dec 1958 D-11 Dec 1958

          7 MAIR, Brent C.   B-

          7 WEBB, Marla Dee MAIR B-
          7 WEBB, Jimmy Wayne, Sp. B-   M-

               8 WEBB, Ashlee Lynn   B-

          7 MAIR, Wendy   B-

          7 MAIR, Kraig   B-

     6 GIBSON, Donna Ray MAIR B-9 Nov 1935 M-6 Jun 1953 (1) Div.
     6 GIBSON, Angus Gene, Sp. B-17 Aug 1931
       GIBSON, Carma COLENE, Sp. (2) B-   M-10 Nov 1961 Annulled
       GIBSON, Linda LEWIS Kelson, Sp. (3) B-13 Apr 1923 M-31 Jan 1964
       Kelson, Rex Albert, Sp. (1) to Linda Lewis B-   M-20 Feb 1954 Div.

          7 GIBSON, Michael Ray   B- 7 Mar 1954

          7 GIBSON, Carla Jean   B-14 Feb 1955

          7 GIBSON, Mary Anne   B-23 Mar 1956

          7 GIBSON, Adele   B-29 Apr 1956

          7 GIBSON, Terry Lynn   B-11 Jul 1957

     6 MAIR, David Jay B-19 Feb 1941 D-3 Nov 1956

```
       6 MAIR, Stanley Ernest B-16 Jun 1946
       6 MAIR, Edith GLAZIER, Sp. B-            M-

              7 MAIR, Lisa Marie              B-        1969

              7 MAIR, Pamela Jean            B-        1971

              7 MAIR, Michelle Lyn           B-        1973

              7 MAIR, James Stanle           B-        1978

       6 MAIR, Andrew Gale B-16 Apr 1952
       6 MAIR, Debbie PRICE, Sp. B-          M-

       6 WOOTON, Sandra Fay MAIR B-10 Jul 1954
       6 WOOTON, Kimm, Sp. B-          M-           Div.

5 MAIR, Loren B-24 Nov 1914 D-12 Mar 1970
5 MAIR, Zella HOWARTH, Sp. B-13 Jan 1920 M-25 Nov 1933

       6 MAIR, Clinton B-4 Feb 1942
       6 MAIR, Judy WEBSTER, Sp. B-          M-22 Nov 1963

              7 MAIR, Connie Lynne           B-

              7 MAIR, Karen Kaye             B-

              7 MAIR, Marc L                 B-

              7 MAIR, Mont C                 B-

       6 MAIR, Alma Ray B-1 Oct 1944

5 MARTINEZ, Mabel Elaine MAIR B-11 Apr 1917
5 MARTINEZ, Alphonzo, Sp. B-          M-25 Nov 1933

       6 MARTINEZ, Richard Alfonzo B-28 Jan 1935
       6 MARTINEZ, Rhea Leona Hall, Sp. B-17 Oct 1934 M-3 Jul 1953

              7 WELCH, Deanna Lynn MARTINEZ B-30 Jan 1955
              7 WELCH, Arlen Kent, Sp. B-19 Jun 1953 M-22 Aug 1974

                     8 WELCH, Kodi Kent         B- 6 Apr 1976

              7 GROSE, Jana Rae MARTINEZ B-18 Aug 1956
              7 GROSE, Thomas Rex, Sp. B-23 Feb 1954 M-15 Nov 1972

                     8 GROSE, Jami Rae          B- 8 Jun 1973

                     8 GROSE, Thomas Rory       B-15 Nov 1977

              7 MARTINEZ, Richard Hall B-11 Oct 1957
              7 MARTINEZ, Carol Lee NIELSON, Sp. B-17 Mar 1957 M-6 May 1976

                     8 MARTINEZ, Leslee Dawn     B- 3 Jul 1977

              7 MARTINEZ, Vicent Clark      B-26 Aug 1958

              7 MARTINEZ, Barney Crae       B-19 Sep 1960

              7 MARTINEZ, Robyn Lee         B-26 Mar 1963

              7 MARTINEZ, Cori Ann          B-13 May 1968

              7 MARTINEZ, Trent Alfonzo     B-22 Dec 1970

              7 MARTINEZ, Holly Elaine      B- 1 Dec 1972

5 MAIR, Darrel (Buck) B-25 Sep 1920 D-
5 MAIR, June SWEATFIELD, Sp. B-          M-28 Nov 1942
```

```
        6 MAIR, Darrell Jr. B-        1943
        6 MAIR, Carol Lee Brant, Sp. B-              M-

                7 MAIR, Jason Darrell           B-        1970

                7 MAIR, Zendia Lee              B-        1972

                7 MAIR, Bodie John              B-        1974

                7 MAIR, Aaron Scott             B-        1975

        6 CHATWIN, Rozella MAIR B-        1946
        6 CHATWIN, Jerry Clifton, Sp. B-              M-

                7 CHATWIN, Margaret June        B-        1971

                7 CHATWIN, Tammy Ann            B-        1973

                7 CHATWIN, Emily Jean           B-        1975

                7 CHATWIN, Laura Marie          B-        1977

        6 MAIR, Leanna MAIR B-        1954
        6 MAIR, Joseph, Sp. B-              M-

                7 MAIR, Curtis Joe              B-        1970

                7 MAIR, Julieann               B-        1974

    5 CURTIS, Daphine MAIR B-25 Aug 1923   D-
    5 CURTIS, Charles Elijah, Sp. B-22 May 1920 M-12 Feb 1940

        6 RYAN, Arlene Vey CURTIS B-11 Sep 1942
        6 RYAN, Kay Lowell, Sp. B-11 Dec 1942 M-12 Dec 1964

                7 RYAN, Kristy Kaye            B-16 Dec 1965

                7 RYAN, Julie Dawn             B- 8 Dec 1966

                7 RYAN, Robert Charles         B-29 Nov 1968

                7 RYAN, William Lowell         B-12 May 1971

                7 RYAN, Rebecca Ann            B-

        6 DONALDSON, Lora Jean CURTIS B-13 Feb 1947
        6 DONALDSON, Daniel F., Sp. B-              M-

                7 DONALDSON, Amy               B-

                7 DONALDSON, Richlyn           B-

                7 DONALDSON, Fred Leon         B-

4 MAIR, John M  B-28 Aug 1891 D-7 Mar 1921
4 MAIR, Alma Florence HARCOURT, Sp. B-10 Nov 1893 M-8 Mar 1911

    5 THOMAS, Ruby MAIR B-23 Feb 1912
    5 THOMAS, Thomas David, Sp. B-              M-

        6 THOMAS, David Elwin B-
        6 THOMAS, Lena Mae NELSON, Sp. B-              M-

                7 THOMAS, Elwin Dee B-
                7 THOMAS, Christina Hazel WORKMAN, Sp. B-              M-

                        8 THOMAS, Brian Dee            B-

                        8 THOMAS, Mark David           B-

                7 COFFIN, Kaye LeAnn THOMAS B-
                7 COFFIN, Robert Tristrum, Sp. B-              M-
```

```
        7 SCOTT, Terri Lynn THOMAS B-
        7 SCOTT, Curtis T., Sp. B-              M-

              8 SCOTT, Curtis Patrick          B-

        7 THOMAS, Vicky Marie              B-

  6 THOMAS, Darwin J. B-            D-

5 MAIR, Coral Andrew B-19 May 1914 D-23 Apr 1979
5 MAIR, Virl Olive MINCHEY, Sp. B-2 Jun 1913 M-15 Jul 1938

  6 PAYNE, Mary LaRue MAIR Bell B-13 Jul 1939
  6 BELL, Gordon Stanley, Sp. B-              M-22 Jul 1958 Div.
  6 PAYNE, Gilbert, Sp. B-            M-17 Jul 1966

        7 MAIR, Gilbert              B-

  6 CAMP, Ruby Delila MAIR Baker B-17 Jul 1941
  6 BAKER, John, Sp. B-            M-14 Feb 1959 Div.
  6 CAMP, Thomas, Sp. B-            M-

        7 BAKER, Sonja              B-

        7 BAKER, Cherrie              B-

        7 BAKER, Naomi              B-

        7 BAKER, Michael              B-

        7 BAKER, Ida Marie              B-

  6 STOKER, Virl Florence MAIR B-10 Aug 1946
  6 STOKER, John, Sp. B- 14 Oct 1942 M-20 Feb 1964

        7 STOKER, Shaunna              B- 4 Oct 1964

  6 MAIR, Coral John B-26 Nov 1948
  6 MAIR, Gaye READ, Sp. B-25 Nov 1949 M-23 Sep 1971

        7 MAIR, Timothy Coral          B-17 Aug 1973

        7 MAIR, Andrew Jason          B- 6 Oct 1974

        7 MAIR, Garrett Don          B- 1 Apr 1977

  6 KENDALL, Mabel Alma MAIR B-26 Apr 1952
  6 KENDALL, Charles, Sp. B-          M-   Jun 1974

        7 MAIR, Melonie              B-

        7 MAIR, Jodel              B-

        7 MAIR, Virlann              B-

        7 KENDALL, Wendy              B-

  6 MAIR, Harold Edgar B-20 Apr 1953 D-20 Apr 1953
  6 MAIR, Ester Janet B-26 Feb 1960 D- 6 Feb 1961

5 THOMAS, Mary Alma MAIR B-23 Apr 1917
5 THOMAS, Elmer, Sp. B-          M-

  6 THOMAS, Gary B-
  6 THOMAS, Gloria, Sp. B-          M-

        7 THOMAS, Duane              B-

        7 THOMAS, Debra              B-

        7 THOMAS, Bruce              B-
```

5 MAIR, Genieva B-11 Jul 1919 D-11 Jul 1919

5 MAIR, John Kenneth B-18 Jun 1920 D-10 Mar 1922

4 MAIR, Franklin Alexander B-1 Sep 1893 D-1 Sep 1893

4 FORRER, Martha Ann MAIR Mann B-17 Jun 1895 D-3 Feb 1926
4 MANN, HENRY Memory, Sp. B-12 Aug 1891 M-17 Sep 1915 D-30 Oct 1919
4 FORRER, John Frederick, Sp. (2) B-22 Jul 1892 M-21 May 1920 D-28 Jul 1962

    5 MANN, Edith B-19 Jun 1916 D-13 Aug 1958

    5 FORRER, Thelma B-1 Aug 1921 D-19 Nov 1921

    5 FORRER, Clyde Frederick B-3 Oct 1922
    5 FORRER, Norma CARTER, Sp. B-   M-3 Oct 1942

    5 FORRER, Kenneth B-30 Nov 1924 D-2 Dec 1924

    5 FORRER, Leo John B-31 Jan 1926 M-22 Dec 1945 D-11 Oct 1949
    5 FORRER, Kathryn JONES, Sp. B-

        6 FORRER, Clyde Leo B-31 Jul 1946

4 JOHNSON, Nellie MAIR McKenzie Dreitzler B-15 Sep 1899 D-4 Mar 1975
4 McKENZIE, Harold Hunter, Sp. (1) B-   M-14 Oct 1918
4 DRIETZLER, Glen Austin, Sp. (2) B-   M-18 Nov 1920
4 JOHNSON, Willard, Sp. B-   M-23 Oct 1951

    5 KILLIAN, Gladys Larraine DRIETZLER B-8 Dec 1922
    5 KILLIAN, Milo, Sp. B-   M-

        6 MAYO, Glenna KILLIAN White B-
        6 WHITE,   Sp. (1) B-   M-   Div.
        6 MAYO, Leslie, Sp. (2) B-   M-

            7 WHITE, Regina   B-

            7 WHITE, Milo   B-

            7 WHITE, Timothy   B-

        6 LEE, Jolene KILLIAN B-
        6 LEE, Darin, Sp. B-   M-

            7 KILLIAN, Sharie   B-

            7 KILLIAN, Sandie   B-

            7 LEE, Christy   B-

        6 WALL, Julie KILLIAN Allison B-
        6 ALLISON, Sidney, Sp. B-   M-   Div.
        6 WALL, Guy, Sp. B-   M-

            7 ALLISON, Shane   B-

            7 ALLISON, Kim   B-

        6 MONDREGEN, Joan KILLIAN B-
        6 MONDREGEN, Fred, Sp. B-   M-

    5 DREITZLER, John Andrew B-21 Oct 1925
    5 DREITZLER, Evelynn HERRON, Sp. B-   M-18 Dec 1946

        6 DREITZLER, Ronald John B-19 Mar 1948
        6 DREITZLER, Debbie SCHINDLER, Sp. B-   M-1 Nov 1975

        6 DREITZLER, Larry Steven B-18 Apr 1951
        6 DREITZLER, Debbie KIRK, Sp. B-   M-20 Nov 1971

            7 DREITZLER, Camille Ann   B- 5 Jul 1974

        6 DREITZLER, James Allen   B-29 Jul 1956

        6 DREITZLER, Debbie Alice   B-21 Jul 1961

5 CLYDE, Betty Jean DRIETZLER B-20 Jul 1927
5 CLYDE, Boyd, Sp. B-   M-

        6 BRERETON, Gloria Jean CLYDE B-14 Sep 1946
        6 BRERETON, William H, Sp. B-   M-

                7 BRERETON, William Boyd   B-31 Oct 1965

                7 BRERETON, G'Anelle   B-22 Jan 1972

        6 CLYDE, Lynn B. B-3 Oct 1947
        6 CLYDE, Diane MURDOCK, Sp. B-   M-   Div.
        6 CLYDE, Kathy SORENSON, Sp. (2) B-

                7 CLYDE, Lynnae   B-13 Mar 1970

                7 CLYDE, Lorianne   B-31 Dec 1972

        6 PARKER, Betty Lou B-12 Feb 1952
        6 PARKER, Glen Charles, Sp. B-   M-

5 JACOBS, June DRIETZLER McNiel B-8 Jun 1929
5 McNIEL, Martin, Sp. B-   M-   Div.
5 JACOBS, Raymond, Sp. B-   M-

        6 JACOBS, Marlene   B-

        6 JACOBS, Karen   B-

        6 JACOBS, Glen   B-

        6 JACOBS, Thayne   B-

        6 JACOBS, Allison   B-

        6 JACOBS, Lesa   B-

4 WALL, Mabel Veronica MAIR Olofson B-24 Sep 1901 D-   1979
4 OLOFSON, Clarence Edward, Sp. B-22 Jan 1898 M-14 May 1922 D-18 Mar 1925
4 WALL, Cecil Isaac, Sp. B-14 Sep 1884 M-15 Apr 1926 D-   1947

        5 RIDING, Evelyn OLOFSON Greer B-14 Mar 1922 D-16 May 1976
        5 GREER, William James Sp. B-   M-30 Aug 1931
        5 RIDING, Robert G., Sp. (2) B-   M-

                6 GREER, William Randy B-4 Sep 1954
                6 GREER, Nancy, BOWMAN, Sp. (1) B-   M-
                6 GREER, Karole KOFEOD, Sp. (2) B-   M-

                        7 GREER, Elizabeth Ann   B-

                        7 GREER, Sharon M   B-

                6 DOMAN, Terrie GREER Channel B-17 Aug 1955
                6 CHANNEL, Tim, Sp. (1) B-   M-
                6 DOMAN, Ted D., Sp. (2) B-   M-

                        7 CHANNEL, Jason Andrew   B-

                        7 DOMAN, Jamie Evelynn   B-

                6 GREER, Robert James B-
                6 GREER, Dawn WOODLAND, Sp. B-   M-

                        7 GREER, Robert Benton   B-

                6 GREER, Michael Howard   B-30 Dec 1957

5 GILLETTE, Viola OLOFSON Cox B-8 May 1923
5 COX, Wilson B., Sp. (1) B-   M-19 Jan 1943
5 GILLETTE, John Kenneth, Sp. (2) B-   M-

      6 CONNELLY, Charlene COX B-13 Mar 1944
      6 CONNELLY, Tom, Sp. B-   M-

           7 CONNELLY, Christy Ann   B-

           7 CONNELLY, Camie Ann   B-

      6 GILLETTE, Kenneth Scott B-

      6 GILLETTE, Meloney   B-

      6 GILLETTE, Jeffery John B- 9 Mar 1958

5 SEARS, Maxine WALL B-24 Dec 1927
5 SEARS, Ambrose K., Sp. B-   M-

      6 ROBINSON, Karla Kay SEARS B-
      6 ROBINSON, Robert Michael, Sp. B-   M-

           7 ROBINSON, Randi Kay   B-

           7 ROBINSON, Ryan Michael   B-

5 WALL, Howard Elden B-19 Dec 1929
5 WALL, Delores Kathryn BLUMKE, Sp. B-   M-

      6 WALL, Edward Howard B-20 Feb 1951
      6 WALL, Phyllis   , Sp. B-   M-

           7 WALL, Emily Ann   B-

      6 WALL, David Erwin   B- 9 Apr 1959
      6 WALL, Julie M. CARRINGTON, Sp. B-   M-1 May 1981
5 WALL, Richard Cecil B-   1932
5 WALL, Nellie Rose LARSEN, Sp. B-   M-

      6 WALL, Cecil Isaac B-
      6 WALL, Tammie GRETIS, Sp. B-   M-

      6 WALL, Richard Allen B-
      6 WALL, Susan MAIR, Sp. B-   M-

      6 WALL, Deborah Lee   B-

      6 WALL, Tina Marie   B-

      6 WALL, Harold Lynn   B-

      6 WALL, Warren Guy   B-

5 MUHLESTEIN, Dee Ann WALL B-12 May 1939
5 MUHLESTEIN, John Clark, Sp. B-   M-

      6 MUHLESTEIN, Bryan Clark B-13 Feb 1967

      6 MUHLESTEIN, Brett John B-19 Jan 1969

4 CARLISLE, Emma MAIR Street B-6 Nov 1905
4 STREET, George Arthur, Sp. B-14 Jun 1903 M-19 Sep 1923 D-16 Jun 1969
4 CARLISLE, Eric Clarence, Sp. (2) B-   M-

    5 STREET, George Arthur B-   1930 D-   1930

Alexander Mair and Eliza Thompson

Alexander Mair was the youngest child of Allan Mair and Mary Murdoch. He was born in Gaswater, Ayrshire, Scotland, on February 18, 1859. He came from a large family having six brothers and two sisters. His brothers and sisters were as follows: John the oldest, James M., Allen Foulds, Matthew, William, Mary, Janet, and Andrew. Matthew, William, and Janet died in infancy. All others grew to maturity and had families of their own.

The Mair family lived comfortably; however, they did not have many luxuries. His father was a hard worker and did the best he could to provide for his family. Problems between his parents developed when his mother joined The Church of Jesus Christ of Latter-day Saints. His dad was a stubborn man when it came to the church and refused to be part of it. His mother wanted to go to America so that she could join the saints going West, but again his father refused to even consider the possibility. Without his father's knowledge, his mother took the three youngest children and left for America. Alexander was only seven years old and the journey to Utah was the beginning of his growth from a child to a man.

Alexander was educated in Scotland until the age of seven when he joined his mother, his sister Mary and his brother Andrew on their voyage to America. His next education came in a different manner. He learned

what he could sailing across the Atlantic Ocean and while walking fifteen to twenty miles a day across the plains to cover the one thousand miles to Heber City, Utah. It was a long journey and many hardships had to be endured, going across the plains was the toughest. Even the young were made to walk so as to lighten the already heavy loads of the oxen. Only the sick were allowed to ride in the wagons. Finally on October 1, 1866, the small family arrived in Heber City, Utah, tired and glad their lives had been spared. A home was established and once again, Alexander attended school; only this time in America.

His education was short because his able body was needed to help support the family. Alexander learned at an early age the value of hard work. As a young boy, Alexander, along with his friends Mark Jeffs, Johnny Fortie and Bill Murdoch, would herd cattle from Heber to Midway. They only had one pair of shoes between them so they would take turns wearing them so their feet wouldn't get too sore. For most of his life Alexander was a sheepherder by trade. Each winter he would take his sheep all the way from Heber to Delta, Utah. This, however, was not always enough, so to supplement his income he also ran a farm for President Abraham Hatch, hauled sand stone from the red ledges to Heber so it could be used to build stores and houses in Heber and also worked with his brother Andrew in a blacksmith shop.

Alexander married a pretty girl by the name of Eliza Thompson on February 15, 1883 in Heber, Wasatch, Utah. Together they had ten children. They are: George Allen, Allen Fowles, John William, Daniel, Nettie, Mary M., Thomas Todd Murdoch, James M., Andrew A., and Lindsay. By saving their money together, Alexander and Eliza bought their own home, for approximately $200.00 to $300.00, where they spent the rest of their lives together.

Eliza Thompson was the daughter of William Thompson and Sarah Fenn. She was born November 14, 1865 in Heber City, Utah. She came from a family of fifteen children. She had eight sisters and six brothers. Four of her brothers and sisters died as children. The brothers and sisters that remained each had large families of their own. Eliza's older sister Mary Ann married Alexander's brother Andrew.

Alexander loved his family and was a good provider. He was quiet and inoffensive, honorable and especially honest in all his dealings with his fellowman. He always gave an honest days work for the pay he received. He was bashful and of a retiring disposition. He belonged to The Church of Jesus Christ of Latter-day Saints and raised his children in the church although he wasn't very active himself. He always believed in the gospel.

Alexander was five feet, ten inches tall, of medium build and weighed approximately one hundred and eighty pounds. He always wore a mustache and as a young man went prematurely gray.

He was a stern but fair father. When he told you to do something, he wanted it done now. He might tell you two or three times, but if you weren't moving by the third request, he'd help you along with the toe of his shoe. He taught his children to speak kindly of everyone and set the example by never saying anything bad about anyone. He didn't associate much with other people but spent his time mostly with his family. He believed in the commandment "Thou shalt not steal," and taught his children to obey it. If they took something that didn't belong to them, Alexander would make them take it back with an apology. Once someone came into his yard and stole some sheep.

When his children questioned him as to what he was going to do about it, he told them nothing and then explained that the thief must have needed them more than they did.

Alexander liked to read. 'He spent much of his free time with a book or paper in his hand, just relaxing and getting what enjoyment he could out of them. He also liked to play cards, especially a game called sluff. Many hours passed with his fishing pole down by some lake, river or stream trying to catch whatever he could to take home to his large family. When it came to fishing, he was a pro. He taught his sons some of his trade secrets which enabled them to enjoy the sport as much as he did.

In his later life, Alexander suffered greatly from rheumatism in his feet, the pain was considerable, due to the fact that the disease was so pronounced. Then to make matters worse, he went blind which made it hard to get around. On Wednesday, April 8, he became ill with what was thought to be another cold. By Saturday, April 11, 1936, Alexander Mair had died at the age of seventy-seven from plural pneumonia.

Alexander and Eliza have left a family of over three hundred descendants in three generations. He was a man to respect, love and honor. His trials and tribulations are a tribute to the type of man he was. He never faltered in what he believed, even in the smallest things. He gave his descendants a code of honor to live by. During World War II, they had seventeen grandsons in the service. Two gave their lives in the service of their country. Many others since have served their country or gone on missions for the church that he loved. Some have even gone back to Gaswater, Ayrshire, Scotland, where this story began.

Compiled by Lyndon A. Mair Written by William (Bill) Mair.

Sincere thanks and appreciation go to the following people for furnishing the information needed to compile this history. Without their help this genealogy of Alexander Mair might never have been completed. Thanks go to Aunt Nettie Mair Mason, Uncle Allen Fowles Mair, Delores Mair Evans (first cousin), and my father Lindsay Mair.

Allen F. Mair, son of Alexander Mair, and his wife Robena Burt Mair
and their thirteen children.

Mary Ann Thompson Mair, Eliza Thompson Mair, Isabella Burt Mair
and Robena Burt Mair. Mary Ann and Eliza were sisters who
married brothers, Andrew and Alexander Mair.

HUSBAND ALEXANDER MAIR

Birth: 18 February 1857
Place: Gaswater, Ayrshire, Scotland
Chr:
Married: 15 February 1883
Place: Heber, Wasatch, Utah
Death: 11 April 1936 Heber, Wasatch, Utah
Burial: 14 April 1936 Heber, Wasatch, Utah
Father: Allan MAIR
Mother: Mary MURDOCH
Other Wives (if any):

WIFE ELIZA THOMPSON

Birth: 14 November 1865
Place: Heber, Wasatch, Utah
Chr:
Death: 19 November 1959 Heber, Wasatch, Utah
Burial: 23 November 1959 Heber, Wasatch, Utah
Father: William THOMPSON
Mother: Sarah FENN
Other Hus. (if any):
Where was information obtained? Family Records
*List complete maiden name for all females.

1st Child	George Allen MAIR	
Birth	7 June 1884	
Place	Heber, Wasatch, Utah	
Married to	Annie Bennette BARNES	
Married	15 April 1914	
Place	Heber, Wasatch, Utah	
Death	1 September 1956 Talmage, Duchesne, Ut.	
2nd Child	Allen Fowles MAIR	
Birth	11 September 1886	
Place	Heber, Wasatch, Utah	
Married to	Robena BURT	
Married	30 July 1909	
Place	Heber, Wasatch, Utah	
Death		
3rd Child	John William MAIR	
Birth	17 April 1889	
Place	Heber, Wasatch, Utah	
Married to	Hazel IVIE	
Married	18 October 1921	
Place		
Death	18 July 1973 West Jordan, S.L. Utah	
4th Child	Daniel MAIR	
Birth	14 March 1892	
Place	Heber, Wasatch, Utah	
Married to	Ellen Pearl HAMILTON	
Married	25 June 1913	
Place	Heber, Wasatch, Utah	
Death	16 February 1964 Heber, Wasatch, Utah	
5th Child	Nettie MAIR	
Birth	22 July 1894	
Place	Heber, Wasatch, Utah	
Married to	Lynn Wells MASON	
Married	16 Dec 1913	
Place	Springville, Utah, Utah	

6th Child	Mary M. MAIR	
Birth	20 October 1896	
Place	Heber, Wasatch, Utah	
Married to	Willis A. SIMMONS	
Married	13 July 1914	
Place	Heber, Wasatch, Utah	
Death		
7th Child	Thomas Todd Murdoch MAIR	
Birth	14 October 1898	
Place	Heber, Wasatch, Utah	
Married to	Violet Ann DAWSON	
Married	7 February 1946	
Place	Heber, Wasatch, Utah	
Death		
8th Child	James M. MAIR	
Birth	13 March 1901	
Place	Heber, Wasatch, Utah	
Married to	Thelma Vienna LINDSAY	
Married	18 April 1925	
Place	Provo, Utah, Utah	
Death		
9th Child	Andrew A. MAIR	
Birth	29 June 1903	
Place	Heber, Wasatch, Utah	
Married to	Vera Merle IVIE	
Married	15 May 1929	
Place	Coalville, Summit, Utah	
Death	15 December 1975 Toole,Toole,Utah	
10th Child	Lindsay MAIR	
Birth	24 February 1907	
Place	Heber, Wasatch, Utah	
Married to	Edna Mae HAMILTON	
Married	17 September 1928	
Place	Provo, Utah, Utah	
Death		

1 MURDOCH, James 1786-1831   2 MAIR, Mary MURDOCH 1817-1900
1 MURDOCH, Mary MURRAY, Sp. 1782-1856   2 MAIR, Allen, Sp. 1815-1897

                              3 MAIR, ALEXANDER 1857-1936   B-Birth
        DESCENDANTS OF   M-Married
                              3 MAIR, ELIZA THOMPSON, Sp. 1865-1959   D-Died
                                                                 Div.-Divorced

4 MAIR, George Allen B-7 Jun 1884 M-15 Apr 1914 D-1 Sep 1956
4 MAIR, Annie Bennette BARNES, Sp. B-20 Mar 1894 D-18 Nov 1936

    5 FORD, Madie, M. MAIR Gilbert B-19 Apr 1915 D-23 Aug 1971 D-17 Jun 1954
    5 GILBERT, James Austin, Sp. B-24 Jan 1888 M-2 Jun 1942
    5 FORD, Robert Roy, Sp. B-   M-   D-

        6 GILBERT, Stanley Duane B-24 Jul 1933 M-11 Jul 1952
        6 GILBERT, Sarah Arlene MIFFLIN, Sp. B-

        6 HUNSAKER, Helen Francis GILBERT B-24 Nov 1938 M-22 Nov 1957
        6 HUNSAKER, Grant Kay, Sp. B-

        6 GILBERT, Jock Austin B-16 Oct 1939 M-4 Dec 1959
        6 GILBERT, Sharon Mortensen, Sp. B-

        6 GILBERT, Alex. Bernell B-3 Sep 1940
        6 GILBERT, Janet BERGAN, Sp. B-   M-21 Aug 1962
        6 GILBERT, Diane Gay BLOOMQUIST Anderson, Sp. B-   M-

        6 GILBERT, Rhoton James B-3 Jan 1942 M-27 Feb 1962
        6 GILBERT, Shanna Lenore Sp. B-

        6 CHRISTENSON, Susan GILBERT Keene B-12 Mar 1945
        6 KEENE, Moscoe Walter, Sp. B-   M-5 Sep 1961
        6 CHRISTENSON, Frank Allen B-   M-

        6 GILBERT, Dean Lindsay B-10 Jun 1946 M-19 Oct 1964
        6 GILBERT, Rolayne Ann JOHNSON, Sp. B-

        6 GILBERT, Billie Allen B-17 Mar 1948 D-3 Nov 1963

        6 GILBERT, Jimmie B-12 May 1950 M-3 Feb 1969
        6 GILBERT, Brenda Kay BILLS, Sp. B-

        6 SHURTZ, Virginia Lucille GILBERT B-21 Apr 1951 M-19 Aug 1970
        6 SHURTZ, Victor Ellis, Sp. B-

    5 MAIR, John Allen B-2 Dec 1916 M-16 Jun 1938 D-17 Jul 1971
    5 MAIR, Charlotte JACKSON, Sp. B-

        6 MAIR, Steven A. B-

        6 PEARSON, Charlene MAIR B-   M-
        6 PEARSON, David, Sp. B-

        6 NICHOLS, Annette MAIR B-   M-
        6 NICHOLS, Gerold, Sp. B-

        6 JACKSON, Laurel MAIR B-   M-
        6 JACKSON, Edward K., Sp. B-

    5 MAIR, Alexander B-22 Feb 1918 M-   D-3 Apr 1972
    5 MAIR, Marie Olsen Greer Sp. B-

    5 MAIR, Dean Lindsay B-2 Jun 1919 D-30 Mar 1945
    5 MAIR, Katherine PIRRAGLIO, Sp. B-   M-30 Jun 1940

        6 MAIR, Fay   B-

        6 MAIR, Ruth Ann B-

    5 BATES, Janet MAIR B-10 Oct 1920 M-7 Jun 1937
    5 BATES, Lawrence Aurther, Sp. B-22 Apr 1912 D-24 Jan 1980

        6 BATES, George Lawrence B-21 Jul 1938 M- 2 Jul 1959
        6 BATES, Barbara Sweat, Sp. B-

        6 THOMAS, Janet Deann BATES B-27 May 1942 M-
        6 THOMAS, George Arnold, Sp. B-

        6 BATES, Willis Gayle B-28 Oct 1943 M-
        6 BATES, Pat PETERSON, Sp. B-

    5 MAIR, Dorothy B-8 Jun 1922 D-24 Sep 1922

    5 MAIR, Allan B-16 Aug 1923 M-24 Dec 1942
    5 MAIR, Mary UGARTE, Sp. B-30 Jun 1926

        6 WOOLMAN, Juanita MAIR B-8 Apr 1944
        6 WOOLMAN, James, Sp. B-   M-   Sep1962

        6 MAIR, Allan Leon B-12 Mar 1945 D-31 Mar 1968

        6 WELCH, Connie MAIR B-9 Nov 1949 M- 18 Apr 1969
        6 WELCH, Leon, Sp. B-

    5 MAIR, Willis B-19 Dec 1924
    5 MAIR, Norma Schear, Sp. B-15 Feb 1931 M- 5 Nov 1947 D-12 Aug 1974
    5 MAIR, Edna May Roberts Gibert, Sp. B-18 Nov   M-14 Jul 1978
        6 MAIR, Linda Lue B-6 Mar 1949 D-6 Mar 1949

        6 RYAN, Ronda MAIR B-2 Oct 1950 M-11 Jun 1971
        6 RYAN, Brad, Sp. B-

        6 MAIR, Stewart B-23 May 1953 M-12 Jul 1974
        6 MAIR, Maxine MARCHANTE, Sp. B-

        6 MAIR, Rusty B-21 Apr 1958 M-
        6 MAIR, Latischa COOPER, Sp. B-

    5 MAIR, Jimmie B-15 Jun 1926 D-5 Jun 1949

    5 MAIR, Richard B-22 Jul 1927 M-20 Jul 1945 D-24 Apr 1977
    5 MAIR, Barbara Jean MURRAY, Sp. B-

        6 MAIR, Richard B-

        6 MAIR, Patricia Ann B-

    5 MAIR, Billie Joe B-5 Jan 1930
    5 MAIR, Marjorie BIRD, Sp. (1) B-   M-
    5 MAIR, Ada PERKINS, Sp. (2) B-9 Jul 1933 M-15 Aug 1955

        6 MAIR, Billie Shane B-2 Apr 1953
        6 MAIR, LeAnn PHILLIPS, Sp. B-7 Jul 1959 M-14 Nov 1979

        6 MAIR, Terry Lee B-27 Jun 1956

        6 MAIR, Larry Lynn B-10 Dec 1957

    5 MAIR, Georgia B-3 May 1932 D-12 Apr 1935

4 MAIR, Allen Fowles B-11 Sep 1886 M-30 Jul 1909
4 MAIR, Robena BURT, Sp. B-30 Apr 1892 D-   1971

    5 EVANS, Delores MAIR B-28 Jul 1910 M-27 Mar 1929
    5 EVANS. John Henry Sp. B-11 Jul 1902 D-7 Apr 1958

        6 EVANS, Jack Allen B-10 May 1930
        6 EVANS, DeVora Jean HIGGINS, Sp. (1) B-   M-14 Jan 1953 Div.
        6 EVANS, Mickey Geneva JENSEN, Sp. (2) B-20 Jan 1936 M-5 Nov 1954

            7 HYMAS, Karla Ann EVANS Loneman B-15 Nov 1958
            7 LONEMAN,   Sp. (1) B-   M-
            7 HYMAN,   Sp. (2) B-   M-

                8 LONEMAN, Kori Ann   B-3 Sep 1975

                8 LONEMAN, Kody Jean   B-26 Apr 1980

7 WEBB, Jackie Lynn EVANS B-20 Aug 1955 M-6 Oct 1973
7 WEBB, Lance Glade, Sp. B-

     8 WEBB, Dustin Wade   B- 4 Sep 1974

     8 WEBB, Brandy Lynn   B-17 Feb 1977

     8 WEBB, Bryon Lance   B- 7 Dec 1979

  7 EVANS, Layne J.   B-5 May 1958

  7 EVANS, Larry Allen B-16 Sep 1963

6 EVANS, Wilma Mae B-28 Oct 1931 D-28 Apr 1934

6 JENSEN, Ada Jean EVANS B-21 Apr 1933 M-30 Sep 1950
6 JENSEN, Clarence Donald, Sp. B-

  7 HOBLEY, Leslie Dawn JENSEN Hewlett B-9 Aug 1951
  7 HEWLETT, Terry Lee, Sp. (1) B-   M-12 May 1969 Div.
  7 HOBLEY, George Addison, Sp. (2) B-29 Nov 1948 M-12 Apr 1975

     8 HEWLETT, David Don   B-31 Aug 1971

     8 HOBLEY, Kimberlee Jean   B-31 Mar 1979

  7 JENSEN, Michael Wayne B-25 Apr 1953 M-28 Apr 1973
  7 JENSEN, Barbara Loraine BENSON, Sp. B-18 Jun 1954

     8 BENSON, Angela Lynn   B-1 Nov 1972

  7 JENSEN, Chris Evan B-18 Sep 1955
  7 JENSEN, Yevonne ZEATHANASUS, Sp. B-

     8 ZEATHANASUS, Diamonda   B-13 Oct 1977

     8 ZEATHANASUS, Angela Lee   B-17 Feb 1978

     8 JENSON, Christi Evan   B-29 Aug 1979

  7 JENSEN, Paul Anthony   B- 2 June 1957

  6 EVANS, Ella Kay B-22 Feb 1941

5 FINNEGAN, Eliza Bernice B-18 May 1912 M- 1 Mar 1930
5 FINNEGAN, William John, Sp. B-27 Jan 1907 D-   1972

  6 BECK, Ardith Marie FINNEGIN B-4 Jul 1931 M-14 Aug 1948
  6 BECK, Carl Clifton, Sp. B-

     7 BECK, William Carl B-1949
     7 BECK, Charlene BUELL, Sp. (1) B-   1949 M-   Div.
     7 BECK, Renee Allen, Sp. (2) B-   1943 M-1 Dec 1978

        8 BECK, Brandon Kent   B-   1970

        8 BECK, Jason Wade   B-   1972

     7 BECK, Robert Ray B-   1953 M-14 Jan 1974
     7 BECK, Susan PINKNEY, Sp. B-   1955

        8 BECK, Isacc Robert   B-   1974

     7 BECK, Karla Jeanine   B-   1963

  6 FINNEGAN, John William B-7 Jun 1934
  6 FINNEGAN, Wanda Marie Paulsen, Sp. (1) B-   M-
  6 FINNEGAN, Val Jean HENRY, Sp. (2) B-   M-

     7 FINNEGAN, John   B-

     7 FINNEGAN, Shauna Marie   B-

     7 FINNEGAN, Lawrence   B-

     7 FINNEGAN, Kelly Patrick   B-

```
        7 FINNEGAN, Kathleeen            B-

        7 FINNEGAN, Karrie               B-

    6 FINNEGAN, Lawrence Dee B-8 Aug 1937 M- 25 Aug 1961
    6 FINNEGAN, Carolyn, Sp. B-

        7 MECHAM, McKell Marie FINNEGAN B-       1962 M-       1976
        7 MECHAM, Dean Sp. B-

            8 MECHAM, Owen                   B-

        7 FINNEGAN, Lisa Ann         B-        1963

        7 FINNEGAN, Brian Spencer    B-

    6 FINNEGAN, Michael Bruce    B-22 Sep 1944

    6 FINNEGAN, Thomas Lynn      B-25 Oct 1945

    6 MACKAY, Sharon Bernice FINNEGAN B-30 Oct 1949
    6 MACKAY, Brent Everett B-      1946

        7 MACKAY, Justin Thomas      B-        1969

        7 MACKAY, Nathan Samuel      B-        1974

5 McDONALD, Reva Marie MAIR B-7 Sep 1914 M- 7 Oct 1932
5 McDONALD, Eldon H., Sp. B-2 May 1910

    6 McDONALD, Reta B-19 Jun 1933 D-19 Jun 1933

    6 McDONALD, James Allen B-30 Jul 1936 M- 10 Sep 1962
    6 McDONALD, Shari Marlene PEDERSEN, Sp. B-9 Sep 1945

        7 McDonald, Raymond Monroe   B-13 Feb 1962

        7 McDONALD, Jody Kay          B-22 May 1963

        7 McDONALD, Gaylene Ann       B-23 Apr 1965

        7 McDONALD, Tammara Marie     B-21 Dec 1968

    6 McDONALD, Marvin Eldon B-9 Feb 1939 M-1 Apr 1961
    6 McDONALD, Norma Jean GROSE, Sp. B-14 Aug 1942

        7 McDONALD, Micheil Sheldon   B- 2 Sep 1962

        7 McDONALD, Tracy LeAnn       B-16 Nov 1965

    6 COCHRAN, Dixie Lyn McDONALD B-9 Mar 1945 M-22 Jun 1967
    6 COCHRAN, Marshall Kent, Sp. B-9 Jul 1944

        7 COCHRAN, BRYAN Kent         B-11 Jun 1970

        7 COCHRAN, DeLyn              B-7 Aug 1972

        7 COCHRAN, Amy Kaye           B-21 Feb 1975

    6 McDONALD, Karl Ray  B-28 Jun 1948 M-
    6 McDONALD, Welma Rose Pederson, Sp. B-14 May 1953

        7 McDONALD, Anthony Karl      B-16 Sep 1968

        7 McDONALD, Jennifer Lynn     B- 8 Nov 1971

        7 McDONALD, Shanna Marie      B-28 Apr 1973

        7 McDONALD, Krista Jolyn      B- 3 Dec 1975

5 REYNOLDS, Erma Alberta MAIR Sproule B-17 Feb 1917
5 SPROULE, Emmett George, Sp. (1) B-2 Sep 1905 M-23 Dec 1933 D-24 Apr 1961
5 REYNOLDS, Boyd Pollock, Sp. (2) B-13 Apr 1916 M-       D-20 May 1977

    6 LAKE, Mildred Mureta SPROULE  B-8 Nov 1934 M-
    6 LAKE, Leo, Sp. B-
```

7 PEAREY, Wanda Darlene LAKE B-23 Oct 1955 M-31 May 1975
7 PEAREY, Alden Dennis, Sp. B-

        8 PEAREY, MerRita Darlene   B-13 Sep 1977

    7 LAKE, Richard Emmett   B-21 May 1957

    7 ELLSWORTH, Janice Alberta LAKE B-8 Dec 1958 M-2 Sep 1978
    7 ELLSWORTH, Kelly Ken, Sp. B-

    7 LAKE, David Leo   B-10 Feb 1960

6 SPROULE, George Allan B-24 Dec 1935 D-3 Sep 1936

6 BARNES, Viola Joan SPROULE B-14 Jul 1937 M-17 Mar 1956
6 BARNES, Joseph North, Sp. B-

    7 BARNES, Thomas LaMar B-1 Jan 1957 M-5 Dec 1975
    7 BARNES, Sally Jane GINES, Sp. B-

        8 BARNES, Samantha Marie   B-16 Jun 1976

    7 PHILLIPS, LuWanna Jean B-25 Feb 1958 M-28 Feb 1975
    7 PHILLIPS, Rulan Dennis, Sp. B-

        8 PHILLIPS, Daniel J.   B-26 Jan 1980

    7 BARNES, Joeseph Michael B-7 Apr 1959 M-28 Jul 1978
    7 BARNES, Peggy BAKER, Sp. B-

    7 LAWRENCE, Jennifer Ann BARNES B-27 Apr 1961 M-16 Jun 1979
    7 LAWRENCE, Glenn, Sp. B-

6 SPROULE, Emmett LaMar   B-15 Jul 1938 D-14 Feb 1955

6 SPROULE, Daniel Gary B-7 Jul 1939 M-
6 SPROULE, Deon MITCHEL, Sp. B-

    7 SPROULE, Tressa Lynn   B-11 Nov 1962

    7 SPROULE, Sandra Ramona   B- 3 Jan 1967

    7 SPROULE, Daniel Dean   B- 3 Feb 1969

6 SPROULE, Thomas Neal B-25 Aug 1940 M-
6 SPROULE, Naomi Summerall, Sp. B-

    7 SPROULE, Thomas Neal   B-14 Dec 1962

    7 SPROULE, Terrie Jean   B- 9 Oct 1964

    7 SPROULE, Shelly Lynn   B- 2 Mar 1966

    7 SPROULE, Becky Ann   B-30 Aug 1969

6 SPROULE, Howard Arther   B-20 Oct 1941 D-1 Nov 1941

6 ETCHEPARE, Patricia Karen SPROULE Kofford Johnson Fox B-10 Oct 1942
6 KOFFORD, Paul, Sp. (1) B-   M-   Div.
6 JOHNSON, Gerold, Sp. (2) B-   M-   Div.
6 FOX, Jerry, Sp. (3) B-   M-   Div.
6 ETCHEPARE, Isislore Domonique, Sp. (4) B-   M-

        7   DeWayne D.   B-15 Apr 1968

5 MAIR, Victor Allen B-26 May 1918
5 MAIR, Francis Daw PENNINGTON, Sp. B-   M- 1 Oct 1948   Div.

    6 MAIR, Vicky Marie   B- 4 Dec 1949

    6 MAIR, Shauna Diane   B- 6 Aug 1951

    6 MAIR, Ramona Lee   B- 6 Dec 1952

    6 MAIR, Bruce Wayne   B-28 Apr 1954

```
        6 MAIR, Lonnie Ray      B-27 May 1955

        6 MAIR, Roberta Sue     B-19 Jul 1956

5 BROADHEAD, Mildred MAIR B-27 May 1920 M-5 Mar 1938
5 BROADHEAD, Lynn, Sp. B-5 Jul 1956

        6 BECK, Shirley BROADHEAD B-21 Sep 1938 M-22 Sep 1957
        6 BECK, Waldo Ray, Sp. B- 10 Jun 1924

                7 BECK, Bonnie Rae          B-26 Jun 1958

                7 BECK, Carolee             B-26 Jun 1959

                7 BECK, Margie Marie        B- 5 Dec 1960

                7 BECK, Charlene Rose       B-18 May 1964

                7 BECK, Darrell Lynn        B-5 Jul 1968

        6 BROADHEAD, Larry Tex B-31 Dec 1939 M-13 Oct 1957
        6 BROADHEAD, Nancy Morie Burgener, Sp. B-14 Mar 1939

                7 BROADHEAD, Ray Lynn       B- 9 Dec 1958

                7 MARTINEZ, Cindy Marie BROADHEAD B-11 Mar 1961 M-23 Feb 1979
                7 MARTINEZ, Vincent Clark, Sp. B-26 Aug 1958

                        8 MARTINEZ, Elisha Marie    B-30 Jul 1979

                7 WARD, Debbie Ann BROADHEAD B-3 Apr 1962
                7 WARD, Robin, Sp. B-17 Aug 1949

        6 RICHARDSON, Patricia Lyn BROADHEAD Huggard B-27 Aug 1944
        6 HUGGARD, Keith, Sp. (1) B-15 Mar 1941 M-            Div.
        6 RICHARDSON, Joseph Earl, Sp. (2) B-15 May 1936 M-

                7 HUGGARD, Christine Patricia B-5 Aug 1966

                7 HUGGARD, Craig            B-29 Aug 1962

                7 WOODARD, Brenda Lee HUGGARD B-6 Aug 1963 M-
                7 WOODARD, James Curtis, Sp. B-17 Nov 1958

                        8 HUGGARD, Justin Lynn B-12 Dec 1977

                7 HUGGARD, Pauline Marie    B-29 Aug 1966

                7 RICHARDSON, Jodie Lynn    B- 3 Mar 1970

        6 BROADHEAD, Randy Lee B-18 Nov 1955 M-
        6 BROADHEAD, Darlene Elaine HANSEN, Sp. B-12 Mar 1955

                7 BROADHEAD, Cassie Lynn    B-16 Jan 1977

                7 BROADHEAD, Daniel Lee     B-13 Jan 1978

5 MAIR, Lynn Mason B-11 Feb 1922 D-25 Jun 1967
5 MAIR, Lois Mae BIRD, Sp. (1) B-       1929 M-12 Feb 1949 D-      1957
5 MAIR, Anna LeNora FISHER, Sp. (2) B-           M-

        6 NELSON, Linda Diane MAIR Stolz B-      1949
        6 STOLZ, Joe      , Sp. (1) B-          M-            Div.
        6 NELSON, Kenneth, Sp. (2) B-           M-

        6 MAIR, Becky        B-      1957 D-      1957

        6 MAIR, Marie Ann    B- 7 Aug 1960

        6 MAIR, David Lynn   B-18 Jul 1962

5 MAIR, Ralph Wallace B-12 Nov 1923 D-13 Mar 1950
5 MAIR, Birdie Mae SWEAT Bird, Sp. (1) B-9 May 1909 M-11 Feb 1947
  Bird, Reaves Alexander, Sp. (1) B-           M-
5 MAIR, Rex Wayne, Sp.(3) B-28 Jul 1926 M-
```

        6 MAIR, Judy Ann   B-21 Sep 1948
        6 MAIR, Gay Lynn   B-19 Oct 1949

5 MAIR, Rex Wayne B-28 Jul 1926
5 MAIR, Ella Lucille DUNN, Sp. (1) B-23 Mar 1928 M-13 Feb 1948 D-2 Jul 1949
5 MAIR, Birdie Mae SWEAT Bird Mair, Sp. (2) B-9 May 1909 M-
5 MAIR, Ralph Wallace, Sp. (1) B-12 Nov 1923 M-11 Feb 1947 D-13 Mar 1950

5 MAIR, Leslie Darwin B-21 Jul 1928 M-29 Sep 1950
5 MAIR, Nona Verlene DRAPER Baker, Sp. B-9 Jul 1925
   Baker, Richard Dale, Sp. (1) B-   M-
        6 MAIR, Ralph Allen B-17 May 1951 M-22 Jul 1971
        6 MAIR, Ann Marie SLATER, Sp. B-21 Jan

            7 MAIR, Sheri Joan   B-17 Aug 1972

            7 MAIR, Michael Allen   B-21 May 1974

            7 MAIR, Charles Byron   B-22 Nov 1977

        6 MAIR, Jessie Darwin B-20 Nov 1952 M-
        6 MAIR, Sheri FORMAN, Sp. B-9 Jun

            7 MAIR, Scotty Lee   B-29 Jul 1975

            7 MAIR, Travis   B-

            7 MAIR, Mellissa   B- 2 Mar 1979

        6 NELSON, Dora Ann MAIR B-31 May 1954 M-
        6 NELSON, Bobby LeRoy, Sp. B-22 Nov

            7 NELSON, Julie Ann   B-27 Jan 1973

            7 NELSON, Lisa   B-25 Nov 1975

            7 NELSON, Chrystal Rae Nae B-21 Apr 1978

        6 RICHARDSON, Leslie Diane MAIR B-17 Dec 1956 M-
        6 RICHARDSON, Michael Joseph, Sp. B-29 May 1954

            7 RICHARDSON, Tracy Lynn   B-30 Mar 1973

            7 RICHARDSON, Jason Michael B- 9 Dec 1975

5 MAIR, Robert Reed B-11 Jun 1930
5 MAIR, Annette KIDDY, Sp. B-28 Sep 1943

        6 MAIR, Tammy Marie   B-17 Nov 1967

5 MAIR, John Douglas B-26 Feb 1932
5 MAIR, Edna Belle RAPHIEL, Sp. (1) B-10 Oct 1932   M-17 Oct 1952 Div.
5 MAIR, Josephine PINEDA, Sp. (2) B-   M-

        6 MAIR, Philman Paphiel B-11 Aug 1953 M-
        6 MAIR, Connie Ranae STREETS, Sp. B-26 Sep 1951

            7 MAIR, Misty Ranae   B-28 Dec 1977

        6 MAIR, Mark Douglas B-6 Jan 1955 M-
        6 MAIR, Charlene TURNBOW, Sp. B-1 Apr 1954

            7 MAIR, Aaron Leon   B-30 Nov 1972

            7 MAIR, Christy Lynn   B-21 Jun 1974

        6 MAIR, Suzanne B-2 Apr 1959

            7 MAIR, John Allen   B-   Mar 1979

        6 MAIR, Travis B-

5 MAIR, Eldon Dee B-15 Jun 1933
5 MAIR, Wanda Margaret BRISSE, Sp. B-15 Dec 1942 M-   Div.

    6 McKINLEY, Debbie MAIR B-20 Mar 1960 M-
    6 McKINLEY, Ronald Malcom, Sp. B-20 Mar 1957

        7 McKINLEY, Jinnifer Lyn   B-20 Mar 1977

        7 McKINLEY, Mindy Ann   B-28 Jun 1979

    6 MAIR, Randy Lee   B-11 Jun 1961

    6 MAIR, Allen Edwin   B-11 Mar 1963

    6 MAIR, Jack LeRoy   B-18 Oct 1965

    6 MAIR, Lori Ann   B- 8 Jul 1972

    6 MAIR, Mary Anne   B- 6 Mar 1975

4 MAIR, John William B-17 Apr 1889 M-18 Oct 1921 D-18 Jul 1973
4 MAIR, Hazel IVIE, Sp. B-23 Feb 1902 D-29 Mar 1960

    5 MAIR, Arnold B-13 Jul 1922 M-   D-   1968
    5 MAIR, Hilda BATES, Sp. B-6 Apr 1925

        6 MAIR, MarvinA.B-17 Jun 1943 M-30 Nov 1963
        6 MAIR, Beverly Jean CARTER, Sp. B-

        6 MAIR, Dennis James B- 8 Oct 1943 M-   D-   1969
        6 MAIR, Frankie Ann BOND, Sp. B-
        6 MAIR, Ronnie A.   B-12 Jun 1951

        6 MAIR, Brent   B-24 Jun 1956

    5 MAIR, Vernal James B-13 Mar 1925 M-
    5 MAIR, Wanda Mae ORIGILL, Sp. B-1 May 1927

        6 HENDERSON, LaWanna MAIR B-31 May 1946 M-12 Jul 1968
        6 HENDERSON, Sebron Edgar, Sp. B-

        6 HANSON, Shirley Ann MAIR B-6 Nov 1949 M-9 Feb 1968
        6 HANSON, Victor Raymond, Sp. B-

        6 MAIR, Kent James B-2 May 1951 M-10 Oct 1970
        6 MAIR, Jacklyn FOULGER, Sp. B-

        6 MAIR, Randy Vernal B-16 Sep 1955 M-17 Mar 1978
        6 MAIR, Sheila Kay SIEBURT, Sp. B-

    5 MAIR, Donald Dwaine B-5 Apr 1933 M-16 Feb 1957
    5 MAIR, Anna Charlene MICHELSEN, Sp. B-12 Jun 1939

        6 MAIR, Blake D.   B- 6 Sep 1957

        6 MAIR, Dianna   B-24 Apr 1959

        6 MAIR, Dwaine M.   B- 5 Aug 1960

        6 MAIR, Bradley J.   B- 4 Oct 1966

        6 MAIR, Scott Read   B-

4 MAIR, Daniel B-14 Mar 1892 M-25 Jun 1913 D-16 Feb 1964
4 MAIR, Pearl HAMILTON, Sp. B-5 Jan 1890 D-10 Mar 1966

    5 MAIR, Edna Mae Hamilton MAIR B-25 Jan 1911 M-17 Sep 1928 D- 4 May 1977
    5 MAIR, Lindsay, Sp. B-24 Feb 1907

        6 MAIR, Arvila Mae   B-16 Feb 1930 D-12 Dec 1930

6 BROZOVICH, Patsy Juanita MAIR Ramsey B-17 Mar 1932
6 RAMSEY, John Jr., Sp. (1) B-   1928   M-7 Jul 1949 D-   1958
6 BROZOVICH, Nick George, Sp. (2) B-   M-

    7 KUNTZ Carla Jean RAMSEY Birman B-
    7 BIRMAN, James Michael, Sp. (1) B-   M-
    7 KUNTZ, Charles, Sp. B-   M-

        8 BIRMAN, James Michael Jr.   B-

        8 BIRMAN, Timothy Allen   B-

        8 BIRMAN, Brandi Chantell   B-

        8 KUNTZ, Trevor Charles   B-

    7 RAMSEY, Claude Lee B-   M-
    7 RAMSEY, Cynthia Jane SCHWAHN, Sp. B-

    7 BROADHEAD, Elizabeth Ann RAMSEY B-   M-
    7 BROADHEAD, Derrell, Sp. B-

        8 BROADHEAD, Chiedy Marie RAMSEY B-

    7 RAMSEY, Johnny Lynn   B-

6 MAIR, Darwin Lindsay B-22 Sep 1934 M-12 Sep 1956
6 MAIR, Beth Elaine SUTTON, Sp. B-

    7 MAIR, Darwin Lee   B-

    7 MAIR, Connie Jean   B-

    7 MAIR, Carolee   B-

    7 MAIR, Elaine   B-

    7 MAIR, Christine   B-

    7 MAIR, Trudy Lyn   B-

    7 MAIR, Shirley Ann   B-

6 BELCHER, Barbara Jean MAIR B-10 Mar 1937 M- 7 Sep 1953
6 BELCHER, Floyd, Jr. Sp. B-

    7 BELCHER, Billy Ray   B-

    7 RYAN, Jackie Lynn BELCHER B-
    7 RYAN, John, Sp. B-

    7 DYKE, Doris Jean BELCHER   B-   M-
    7 DYKE, Thomas, Sp. B-

    7 BELCHER, Barbara Louise   B-

    7 BELCHER, Jimmy Dean   B-

6 MAIR, Lyndon A. B-14 Nov 1945 M-17 Apr 1970
6 MAIR, Linda J PARKIN, Sp. B-

    7 MAIR, Lyndon Shane   B-

    7 MAIR, Tammy Raquel   B-

    7 MAIR, Brock Lindsay   B-

    7 MAIR, Jarom Alexander   B-

5 COX, Eliza Lavaun MAIR B-2 May 1914 M-15 Oct 1934
5 COX, Loren Elijah, Sp. B-13 Sep 1906

    6 COX, Gene Williard B-30 Sep 1935 M-
    6 COX,   Sp. B-

6 SEEVERS, Ellen Roberta COX B-18 Nov 1937 M-4 Sep 1954
6 SEEVERS, James Edward, Sp. B-

6 TITCOMB, Linda Carol COX B-18 Dec 1939 M-9 Apr 1955
6 TITCOMB, John Preston, Sp. B-

6 WORTHINGTON, Doris Patricia B-24 Mar 1942 M-13 Mar 1959
6 WORTHINGTON, Larry Dee, Sp. B-

6 COX, Daniel David B-10 Mar 1944 M-28 Jul 1967
6 COX, Mary Dee PITT, Sp. B-

6 COX, Ronald Arlen B-2 Sep 1946 M-11 Oct 1975
6 COX, Collen Faith LONG, Sp. B-

6 SCHEAR, Vanita Dorene B-13 Apr 1949 M-2 Nov 1965
6 SCHEAR, Ricky, Sp. B-

6 GALE, Janice Vivian B-8 May 1952 M-2 Nov 1965
6 GALE, DelRay, Sp. B-

6 FAWLER, Velda Carlene B-9 Oct 1956 M-17 Aug 1973
6 FAWLER, Franklin Henry, Sp. B-

6 COX, Laurita Sue B-29 Jan 1961

5 MAIR, Lola Pearl B-9 Dec 1915 D-16 Sep 1916

5 MAIR, Daniel Alexander B-14 Oct 1917 M-30 Jun 1947
5 MAIR, Virginia MATSON, Sp. B-

6 MAIR, Marvin Dee B-4 Dec 1950 M-21 Apr 1972
6 MAIR, Arlene MEDINA, Sp. B-

6 BAKER, Claudia Ann MAIR B-27 Sep 1952 M-3 Sep 1971
6 BAKER, Kent, Sp. B-

7 BAKER, Alicia Joy   B-

6 WALL, Suzann MAIR B-12 Feb 1956 M-19 Nov 1976
6 WALL, Richard Allen, Sp. B-

6 MAIR, Dana Lea   B-27 Aug 1958

6 MAIR, Karen Yvonne B-30 Aug 1960

6 MAIR, Jeffrey Lynn B-11 Jul 1969

5 BROADHEAD, Verda MAIR B-30 Jul 1919 M-8 Jan 1936
5 BROADHEAD, Dean, Sp. B-

6 BROADHEAD, Carolee B- 5 Sep 1937 D-23 Jun 1952

6 BROADHEAD, Neil B-18 Jan 1940 M-2 Mar 1961
6 BROADHEAD, Patricia Ann LEE, Sp. B-

6 BROADHEAD, Baby Boy B-26 Oct 1950 D-27 Oct 1950

5 MAIR, William LaVar B-24 Sep 1921 M-20 Nov 1951
5 MAIR, Joan GLADDEN, Sp. B-11 Aug 1936

6 MAIR, Michael La Var B- 7 Aug 1958 M-

6 MAIR, William Edward B-12 Oct 1962

6 MAIR, Margaret Pearl B-25 Sep 1967

5 DAVIS, Viola Maud MAIR, B-20 Sep 1924 M-20 Apr 1943
5 DAVIS, Edgar Eli, Sp. B-22 Jul 1921

6 CARLSON, Carolyn DAVIS B-7 Aug 1943 M-18 Jul 1961
6 CARLSON, Donald Oscar, Sp. B-

7 CARLSON, Donald Eric   B-

```
        6 DAVIS, RAY E. B-7 May 1946 M-1 Feb 1969
        6 DAVIS, Margaret Ellen     , Sp. B-

        6 DAVIS, Dean    B-16 Feb 1948

        6 DAVIS, Gary Lee B-2 Nov 1952 M-16 Jan 1972
        6 DAVIS, Marlene Sydney MILLWARD, Sp. B-

            7 DAVIS, Shane Lee          B-

            7 DAVIS, Jason Niel          B-

        6 DAVIS, Ricky   B-26 Jun 1959

        6 DAVIS, Vicky   B-26 Jun 1959

5 MILLS, Evelyn Irene MAIR B-20 Jan 1926 M-22 Jan 1942
5 MILLS, Dee, Sp. B-30 Jun 1922

        6 HARDING, Sherrie Ann MILLS B-2 Feb 1943 M- 24 Jan 1961
        6 HARDING, Jack Royal, Sp. B-

        6 MILLS, Steven Dee B-16 Nov 1944 M-20 Dec 1968
        6 MILLS, Bonnie SMITH, Sp. B-

        6 MILLS, Wendi   B-22 Mar 1967

5 MAIR, Melvin B-9 Apr 1928 M-20 Jun 1948
5 MAIR, Margaret MATSON, Sp. B-10 Feb 1932

        6 RYDALCH, Deborah Myrlene MAIR B-6 Jul 1952 M-24 Sep 1971
        6 RYDALCH, John Dee, Sp. B-

            7 RYDALCH, Randee Kae        B-

            7 RYDALCH, Ryan John         B-

        6 MAIR, Melvin Dennis B-2 Jul 1954 M-27 Feb 1976
        6 MAIR, Ernestine MEDINA, Sp. B-

        6 MAIR, Steven Richard B-31 Jan 1957 M-6 Dec 1975
        6 MAIR, Shonie Aleen JONES, Sp. B-

            7 MAIR, Jeremiah, B-

        6 MAIR, Robert Allen     B-23 Mar 1961

        6 MAIR, Christopher Jon  B-13 May 1970

5 .BETHEA, Bonita Jean MAIR Jarvis B-10 May 1930
5 JARVIS, James W. Jr., Sp. B-13 Oct 1926 M-2 Jan 1948
5 BETHEA,         Sp. (2) B-         M-
        6 JARRELL, Bonnie Gayle JARVIS B-22 Dec 1948 M-21 Aug 1967
        6 JARRELL, Carl Eugene, Sp. B-

        6 JARVIS, Jimmy Wayne  B-18 Oct 1950

        6 ACAIN, Betty Jean JARVIS B-28 Feb 1952 M-21 Dec 1975
        6 ACAIN, Fred, Sp. B-

        6 JARVIS, Michael Eugene B- 9 Jul 1954

        6 JARVIS, Barbara Ellen   B-25 Apr 1956

4 MASON, Nettie MAIR B-22 Jul 1894 M-16 Dec 1913
4 MASON, Lynn Wells, Sp. B-13 Dec 1894 D-6 Dec 1956

    5 CASSIDY, Lapreal MASON Mair Mecham B-7 Dec 1914
    5 MAIR, Marlow, Sp. B-4 Aug 1910 M-29 May 1932 D-14 Jun 1946
    5 MECHAM, Harold, Sp. B-         M-         Div.
    5 CASSIDY, Ross, Sp. B-      1907 M-         D-      1972
```

6 MAIR, Gerald B-17 Jan 1934 M-26 Jan 1959
6 MAIR, Nada OLMSTEAD, Sp. B-

    7 SMITH, Cindy Lee MAIR B-   M-
    7 SMITH, Steve, Sp. B-

        8 SMITH, Steven Adriean   B-

    7 MAIR, Jerry G.   B-

    7 MAIR, Lynn Andrew   B-

    7 MAIR, Steven Allen   B-

6 MAIR, Howard Marlow B-18 Feb 1935 M-18 Jan 1956
6 MAIR, Leah JONES, Sp. B-

    7 MAIR, Debra Ann   B-

    7 MAIR, Howard Marlow Jr.   B-

    7 WILSON, Brenda Lee MAIR   B-   M-
    7 WILSON, David, Sp. B-

    7 MAIR, Colleen Kay   B-

6 BARGER, Darlene Marie MAIR B-6 Mar 1938 M-12 Nov 1959
6 BARGER, Robert Byron, Sp. B-

    7 BARGER, Bruce Lynn   B-

    7 BARGER, Brent Byron   B-

    7 BARGER, Mark   B-

6 MAIR, Wayne Jay B-3 Mar 1943 M-12 Oct 1963
6 MAIR, Diane FRANCE, Sp. B-

    7 MAIR, Bonnie Lee   B-

    7 MAIR, Becky Lynn   B-

6 KEELE, Marlene MAIR B-20 Jul 1946 M-2 Aug 1968
6 KEELE, Bobby, Sp. B-

    7 KEELE, Tamera Ann   B-

    7 KEELE, Ricky Lynn   B-

    7 KEELE, Treasa Lee   B-

    7 KEELE, Sandra Marie   B-

    7 KEELE, Eric Jay   B-

6 JOHNSTON,Ranae MECHAM Breeze B-4 Jan 1949
6 BREEZE, Mike, Sp. B-   M-   Div.
6 JOHNSTON,Johnny, Sp. B-   M-   Div.

    7 BREEZE, Mike   B-

    7 BREEZE, Lisa Marie   B-

    7 BREEZE, Tom L.   B-

6 CASSIDY, Ross Woodrow B-25 Dec 1954 M-
6 CASSIDY, Shirley ARCHULETA, Sp. B-

    7 CASSIDY, David Joseph   B-

    7 CASSIDY, Daniel Roger   B-

    7 CASSIDY, Tammera Marie B-

```
            7 CASSIDY, Donald Ross        B-

            7 CASSIDY, Tonya Jean         B-

5 McDONALD, Marie MASON Christensen B-26 Aug 1916
5 CHRISTENSEN, Heber Dee, Sp. (1) B-              M-23 Mar 1933 D-27 Apr 1972
5 McDONALD, Ronald James, Sp. (2) B-31 Dec 1907 M-16 Jul 1973

      6 CHRISTENSEN, Junior Dee  B-26 Apr 1934 M-24 Jun 1955
      6 CHRISTENSEN, Myrl WARDELL, Sp. B-

            7 PETERSEN, Carrie Marie CHRISTENSEN B-              M-
            7 PETERSEN, Dean, Sp. B-

            7 CHRISTENSEN, Vern Dee B-             M-
            7 CHRISTENSEN, Leslie EMERSON, Sp. B-

                  8 CHRISTENSEN, Shawn        B-

                  8 CHRISTENSEN, Clifton Roy  B-

            7 CHRISTENSEN, Tony Lynn       B-

            7 CHRISTENSEN, Laura LeNore  B-

      6 CHRISTENSEN, Kent Lynn B-22 Jul 1944 M-10 Jan 1964
      6 CHRISTENSEN, Janice Lee CLYDE, Sp. B-

            7 CHRISTENSEN, Gary           B-

            7 CHRISTENSEN, Chad           B-

            7 CHRISTENSEN, Shawn H.       B-

      6 CLARK, Jean CHRISTENSEN B-22 Jan 1947
      6 CLARK, Roger Dean, Sp. B-              M-15 Feb 1964 Div.

            7 CLARK, Terry Dean          B-

            7 CLARK, Christopher Justin  B-

            7 CLARK, Dawn Marie          B-

5 RUKAVINA, Maude MASON B-12 Nov 1918 M-12 Jan 1935
5 RUKAVINA, Jack, Sp. B-6 Jun 1912

      6 LAFERRE, Shirley Marie RUKAVINA Kummer B-30 Oct 1935
      6 Kummer, Thomas W., Sp. (1) B-      1927 M-31 Oct 1953 D-      1976
      6 LAFERRE, Sterling, Sp. (2) B-          M-

            7 KUMMER, Thomas  B-
            7 KUMMER, Becky HILL, Sp. B-              M-

                  8 KUMMER, Jennie      B-

                  8 KUMMER, April       B-

            7 HENRY, Cherl Kummer Sargent B-
            7 SARGENT, Mark, Sp. (1) B-              M-              Div.
            7 HENRY, Billie, Sp. (2) B-              M-

                  8 SARGENT, Nora              B-

                  8 SARGENT, Kyle              B-

                  8 SARGENT, Chad              B-

                  8 SARGENT, Irene             B-

      6 RUKAVINA, Jack L. B-13 Jun 1942 M-23 Nov 1966
      6 RUKAVINA, Arlette Andree' GRAMME, Sp. B-

            7 RUKAVINA, Lesley Ann       B-

            7 RUKAVINA, Carrie Andree'   B-
```

5 MASON, George Lynn B-23 Oct 1922
5 MASON, Maxine SESSIONS, Sp. (1) B-18 Mar   M-26 Feb 1941 Div.
5 MASON, Jacqueline RASMUSSEN, Sp. (2) B-   M-

        6 MASON, Gerold George B-1 Mar 1942 M-2 Mar 1961
        6 MASON, Cheryl SPEARIN, Sp. B-

                7 KEEL, Terrie Lee MASON B-   1961 M-
                7 KEEL, Scott, Sp. B-

                        8 KEEL, Jamie Lee   B-   1978

                7 MASON, Scott   B-   1964

                7 MASON, Shane Michael   B-   1970

                7 MASON, Brian Kirk   B-   1972

        6 MASON, Edward Lynn B-1 Jun 1947 M-21 Dec 1967
        6 MASON, Deanna LUKE, Sp. B-

                7 MASON, Deana Lizette   B-

                7 MASON, Lynn Edward   B-

                7 MASON, Brandon   B-

        6 STRATTON, Deanna MASON B-21 Dec 1949 M-11 Oct 1968
        6 STRATTON, Kenneth Lynn, Sp. B-

                7 STRATTON, Kelle Lynn   B-

                7 STRATTON, Ricky James   B-

4 SIMMONS, Mary M. MAIR B-20 Oct 1896 M-13 Jul 1914
4 SIMMONS, Willis A, Sp. B-18 Oct 1889 D-7 May 1936

        5 SIMMONS, Willis Alexander B-9 May 1915 M-26 Jun 1937
        5 SIMMONS, Edna BLANEY, Sp. B-17 Mar 1916

                6 BRIMHALL, Dorene Marie SIMMONS B-   M-
                6 BRIMHALL, Larry D., Sp. B-

                        7 BLANCHARD, Laurie Ann BRIMHALL B-   M-
                        7 BLANCHARD, Michael, Sp. B-

                                8 BLANCHARD, Brandon   B-

                                8 BLANCHARD, Brandon   B-

                        7 WATTS, Peggi BRIMHALL B-   M-
                        7 WATTS, James, Sp. B-

                                8 WATTS, Janica Linn   B-

                        7 McHENRY, Jackalyn BRIMHALL B-   M-
                        7 McHENRY, Brent, Sp. B-

                                8 McHenry, Mandy   B-

                        7 BRIMHALL, Angela   B-

                6 VANCE, Edna Beth SIMMONS B-   M-
                6 VANCE, Richard L., Sp. B-

                        7 CARTER, Kelly VANCE B-·   M-
                        7 CARTER,   Sp. B-

                                8 HANSEN, Justin   B-

                        7 VANCE, Shauna   B-

                6 PETERSON, Connie Lou SIMMONS B-   M-
                6 PETERSON, Albert Ernest, Sp. B-

```
        7 PETERSON, Janalee           B-

        7 PETERSON, Peggi             B-

        7 PETERSON, Lesli             B-

    6 SIMMONS, Willis Alex B-
    6 SIMMONS, Dian Valynn CHILDS, Sp. (1) B-        M-           Div.
    6 SIMMONS, Jeanine HUNTER, Sp. (2) B-            M-

        7 SIMMONS, Valynn             B-

        7 SIMMONS, Sherry             B-

        7 SIMMONS, Rachelle           B-

    6 WOLF, Alexis Ann SIMMONS B-           M-
    6 WOLF, Thomas Allen, Sp. B-

        7 WOLF, Shanie                B-

        7 WOLF, Jason                 B-

5 SIMMONS, LaMar B-
5 SIMMONS, Marion Elizabeth MOSER, SP. (1) B-22 Aug 1924   M-12 Sep 1947 D-10 Mar 1963
5 SIMMONS, Leona M. CAIN Wallace, Sp. (2) B-            M-

    6 SIMMONS, Jerald B-9 May 1948 M-
    6 SIMMONS, Diane LEWIS, Sp. B-

    6 POWEL, Karen SIMMONS B-5 Jun 1950      M-
    6 POWEL, Ivan Lynn, Sp. B-

        7 POWEL, Gregory              B-
    6 SIMMONS, Marion B-22 May 1961
5 PEDERSON, Elaine SIMMONS B-25 Jan 1919
5 PEDERSON, Jessie Oliver, Sp. B-2 Jun 1916  M-30 Mar 1935

    6 PEDERSON, Karl Neilson B-13 Feb 1936  M-28 Jun 1958
    6 PEDERSON, Sherolyn Marie MECHAM, Sp. B-

        7 MALMROSE, Julie Ann PEDERSON B-          M-
        7 MALMROSE, Cary, Sp. B-

            8 MALMROSE, Michael           B-

        7 PEDERSON, Joni Kay          B-

        7 PEDERSON, Patricia Marie    B-

        7 PEDERSON, Alice Elaine      B-

    6 WINN, KATHRYN Janeen PEDERSON    B-7 Aug 1937
    6 WINN, Thomas Eden, Sp. B-        M-8 Jan 1956

        7 WINN, David Lloyd           B-

        7 WINN, Brian                 B-

        7 WINN, Janet                 B-

        7 WINN, Mark Eden             B-

5 CHRISTENSEN, Eliza Bernice SIMMONS Pedersen B-27 Jul 1920
5 PEDERSEN, Clifford Wayne, Sp. (1) B-4 May 1913 M-12 Mar 1936 D-14 Jul 1948
5 CHRISTENSEN, Neel Leslie, Sp. (2) B-16 Mar 1925 M-18 Jun 1949

    6 PEDERSON, Clifford Harold B-3 Oct 1936
    6 PEDERSON, Sandra JOHNSON, Sp. (1) B-25 Apr 1936 M-          D-24 Aug 1968
    6 PEDERSON, Helen Kaye MECHAM Schoenfeld, Sp. (2) B-23 Apr 1940 M-28 May 1969

        7 PEDERSON, Kevin Wayne       B-26 Dec 1957

        7 PEDERSON, Clifford Neel     B-21 Feb 1958
```

7 PEDERSEN, Kristen Marie   B-15 May 1964

7 PEDERSON, Karen Diane   B- Stilborn

7 PEDERSON, Karma   B- 3 May 1968

7 PEDERSON, Rachel Ann   B-30 Jun 1971

7 PEDERSEN, Randal Franz SCHOENFELD B-23 Apr 1958

7 PARKER, Heidi SCHOENFELD PEDERSON B-15 Feb 1960
7 STEWART, Gilbert, Sp. (1) B-   M-5 Mar 1976 Div. 1981
7 PARKER, Thomas, Sp. (2) B-   M-1 Aug 1981

        8 STEWART, Heather Marie   B- 8 Oct 1976

        8 STEWART, April Lynn   B-15 Apr 1978

7 LORDS, Kim SCHOENFELD PEDERSEN B-12 Sep 1962
7 LORDS, Steven J., Sp. (1) B-   M- Nov 1979 Div.

7 PEDERSEN, Sonja Marie SCHOENFELD B-19 Jul 1963

6 PEDERSEN, Dianna Marie B-15 Nov 1937 D   Jan 1938

6 PEDERSEN, Thomas Lamar B- 2 Feb 1945
6 PEDERSEN, Linda Lee WELCH, Sp. (1) B-7 Oct 1947 M-20 Sep 1947 Div.-20 Sep 1974
6 PEDERSEN, Jorja Lynn GARDNER (Vorhees) Hunter Sp. (2) B-31 Jul 1947 M-20 Feb 1976

        7 PEDERSEN, Jason David   B-5 May 1967

6 ROGERS, Nancy Lois Christensen B-6 Jun 1950
6 ROGERS, Dale Lewis, Sp. (1) B-25 Sep   M-20 Dec 1968 Div.

        7 ROGERS, Ryan Mark   B-14 Nov 1970

5 PEDERSON, Luella Mae SIMMONS Haslen B-7 Jul 1922
5 HASLEN, Thomas Elden, Sp. (1) B-   M-30 Sep 1939   Div.
5 PEDERSON, Wilbur DeVore, Sp. (2) B-   M-4 Oct 1946

    6 PEDERSON, Wilbur Dee B- 11 Nov 1945 M-
    6 PEDERSON, Peggy Marie MARTIN, Sp. B-

        7 PEDERSON, Wilbur Dee Jr   B-

        7 PEDERSON, Joey Lee   B-

        7 PEDERSON, Chritopher Robin B-

    6 MATHYS, Mary Lou PEDERSON B- 7 Oct 1949
    6 MATHYS, Alan David, Sp. B-

        7 MATHYS, Stephan Craig   B-

        7 MATHYS, Scott Alan   B-

5 SIMMONS, Elmo B-18 Nov 1925 M-
5 SIMMONS, Deon SPENCER, Sp. B- 19 Oct 1928

    6 SIMMONS, Steven B- 29 May 1947   M-
    6 SIMMONS, Maurene BECKSTEAD, Sp. B-

        7 SIMMONS, Stevie   B-

        7 SIMMONS, Brent   B-

        7 SIMMONS, Sandy   B-

        7 SIMMONS, Tammy   B-

6 BURBANK, Gail SIMMONS B- 5 Sep 1948   M-
6 BURBANK, Brian, Sp. B-

        7 BURBANK, Heather   B-

6 SIMONS, Richard B- 15 Apr 1954
6 SIMMONS, Chynell BETHEL, Sp. B-   M-   Div.
6 SIMMONS, Judy ALLBRIGHT, Sp. B-   M-

        7 SIMMONS, Brick   B-

        7 SIMMONS, Doug   B-

        7 SIMMONS, Cassey   B-

    6 SIMMONS, Ellen Marie   B-2 Oct 1957

    6 SIMMONS, Gregory   B-8 Feb 1961

5 SIMMONS, James Ralph B-14 Mar 1927 M-25 Apr 1946
5 SIMMONS, Dorothy Loranne CHANDLER, Sp. B-

    6 SIMMONS, James R. B-4 Oct 1946   M-
    6 SIMMONS, Martina MAYENBURG, Sp. B-

        7 SIMMONS, Jonny R.   B-

    6 SIMMONS, John Randall B-9 Dec 1950
    6 SIMMONS, Marsha HANSEN, Sp. B-   M-   Div.
    6 SIMMONS, Christina Lynn SEKIERRING, Sp. B-   M-

        7 SIMMONS, Scott James   B-

    6 STRICKLAND, Chynthia SIMMONS B-9 May 1954
    6 WHILE, Richard, Sp. B-   M-   Div.
    6 STRICKLAND, Mathew, Sp. B-   M-

        7 WHILE, Richard J.   B-

        7 WHILE, Crystal Ann   B-

        7 Strickland, Chynthia Michelle B-

    6 CUMMINGS, Julie Ann SIMMONS B-17 Jun 1958   M-
    6 CUMMINGS, Bennie Frank, Sp. B-

        7 CUMMINGS, Justin James   B-

    6 FRANCON, Carol SIMMONS B-14 Sep 1960   M-
    6 FRANCON, Douglas, Sp. B-

        7 FRANCON, Caron Ann   B-

        7 FRANCON, Donald James   B-

5 SIMMONS, Dean B-2 Mar 1929 M-
5 SIMMONS, Mary Louise DYKMAN, Sp. B-28 May 1933

    6   , Deana Marie SIMMONS B-17 Apr 1955   M-
    6   ' Lynn, Sp. B-

        7   B-

        7   B-

        7   B-

        7   B-

        7   B-

    6 SIMMONS, Ronnie Paul   B-10 Jan 1956

    6 SIMMONS, Kirk Robert   B-16 Nov 1957

    6 SIMMONS, Dean Allen   B-12 Jan 1959

    6 SIMMONS, Richard Scott   B-28 May 1962

    6 SIMMONS, Daniel Lee   B-31 Jan 1967

    6 SIMMONS, Ted Aaron   B-14 Feb 1969

    6 SIMMONS, Bruce Edward   B-20 Aug 1970

5 SIMMONS, Pierce B-23 Jan 1931 M-
5 SIMMONS, Estella OROZCO, Sp. B-4 Mar 1932

    6 LAWSON, Anita Valentine SIMMONS B-14 Mar 1954   M-
    6 LAWSON, Thomas G., Sp. B-

        7 LAWSON, Tamara Genette   B-

    6 McCULLOUGH, Micheal SIMMONS B- 28 Jun1958   M-
    6 McCULLOUGH, Phyllip, Sp. B-

5 VASELLEOU, Nellie Louise SIMMONS B- 17 Feb 1933   M-
5 VASELLEOU, Chriss, Sp. B-11 Jan 1931

    6 VASELLEOU, Michael Angelo B- 29 Apr 1963
    6 VASELLEOU, Sandy WRIGHT, Sp.   B-   M-   Div.
    6 VASELLEOU, Jan Louise CREARY, Sp. B-   M-

        7 VASELLEOU, Nicoles Angelo B-

    6 VASELLEOU, Douglas Chriss B-1 Dec 1956   M-
    6 VASELLEOU, Sally Christina NAY, B-

5 ALLEN, Shirlene SIMMONS Rogers B-31 Jan 1935
5 ROGERS, Robert Ivan, Sp. B-5 Oct 1936 M-23 Dec 1951 Div. 1953
5 ALLEN, Roger Duane, Sp. (2) B-21 Apr 1945 M-6 Nov 1964 T.M.-18 Nov 1978

    6 COHEN, Debra Lin ROGERS B-10 Oct 1952 M-11 Aug 1979
    6 COHEN, Amir, Sp. B- 5 May 1954

    6 ALLEN, Brandee Lea   B-22 Sep 1967

    6 ALLEN, Troy Duane   B-24 Jun 1969

    6 ALLEN, Tanya Louise   B-24 Jun 1969

4 MAIR, Thomas Todd Murdoch B-14 Oct 1898 M-7 Feb 1946 D-
4 MAIR, Violet Ann DAWSON, Sp. B-25 Sep 1915 M-7 Feb 1946

    5 CROWDER, Judy Ann MAIR Rhodes Miller B-10 Nov 1946 D-
    5 RHODES, Lancel Edwin, Sp. (1) B-   M-25 Jan 1964 Div.
    5 MILLER, Frank, Sp. (2) B-   M-   Div.
    5 CROWDER, Melvin D., Sp. (3) B-   M-

        6 RHODES, Lance   B-10 Jul 1965

        6 RHODES, Tracie Thomas   B-16 Jan 1967

        6 Miller, Albert Frank   B-   D-

        6 CROWDER, Stephanie Renae   B-14 Oct 1976

        6 CROWDER, Jeramie Douglas   B-15 May 1978

    5 MAIR, Thomas Arthur B-2 Apr 1948
    5 MAIR, Vickie Lee SMITH, Sp. B-   M-19 Mar 1969 Div,

```
        6 MAIR, April Marie    B-16 Apr 1971

    5 McNEIL, Shiela MAIR, Webb B-27 Apr 1953
    5 WEBB, Donny William, Sp. B-25 May 1952 M-10 Sep 1971
    5 McNEIL, Glen Alvin, Sp. (2) B-26 Feb 1952 M-22 Jul 1977

        6 WEBB, Emily Ann          B- 5 Apr 1972

        6 WEBB, Jamie Marie        B-13 Dec 1976

    5 MAIR, Timothy Alexander B-28 Aug 1954 M-8 Oct 1971 D-15 Jan 1972
    5 MAIR, Kathy CARRICK, Sp. B-

4 MAIR, James M.  B-13 Mar 1901 M-18 Apr 1925
4 MAIR, Thelma Vienna LINDSAY, Sp. B-6 Aug 1907

    5 MAIR, Clyde  B-5 Jan 1926 D-1 Nov 1934

    5 MAIR, Kenneth  B-18 Jul 1928 D-

    5 MAIR, Joe B-1 Feb 1930 M-19 Jul 1951
    5 MAIR, Eleanor Marie KILASKE, Sp. B-

        6 MAIR, Joe Reed  B-6 Jul
        6 MAIR, Leann        Sp. B-

    5 WEBB, Wanda MAIR B-27 Jan 1933 M-31 Aug 1949
    5 WEBB, William Hal, Sp. B-

        6 WEBB, Gary Lee           B-      1951 D-      1951

        6 WEBB, Baby Girl          B-      1954 D-      1954

        6 WEBB, Rickey B           B-

        6 WEBB, Jimmie Wayne       B-

        6 WEBB, Vickie Lynn        B-

    5 MAIR, Doyle  B-27 Apr 1937

    5 MURDOCK, Dorthy MAIR B-15 Nov 1940 M-
    5 MURDOCK, Joseph Royal, Sp. B-

        6 COVER, Wendy Jo MURDOCK B-5 Dec 1962 M-29 Dec 1977
        6 COVER, Jerry Wayne, Sp. B-

        6 MURDOCK, Vince           B- 6 Aug 1965

        6 MURDOCK, Kelly           B-28 May 1970

    5 MAIR, Sharon  B-4 Jul 1942 D-30 May 1943

4 MAIR, Andrew A. B-29 Jun 1903 M-15 May 1929 D-15 Dec 1975
4 MAIR, Vera Murl IVIE, Sp. B-18 Apr 1912 D-6 May 1974

    5 BUZIANIS, Norma Carol MAIR Clegg B-25 Dec 1930
    5 CLEGG, Daniel, Sp. (1) B-           M-1 Sep 1948
    5 BUZIANIS, James, Sp (2) B-          M-19 Jan 1957

        6 SWAIN, Gloria Jean CLEGG Allison B-18 Jun 1949
        6 ALLISON, Ted, Sp. (1) B-           M-
        6 SWAIN, Mark, Sp. (2) B-            M-

            7 ALLISON, Troy Dan        B-

            7 ALLISON, Toni Lynn       B-

            7 ALLISON, Tiffiny Jean    B-
```

        6 CLEGG, Daniel Merlin Jr. B-24 Jun 1954
        6 CLEGG, Janis TABOR, Sp. B-   M-24 Jun 1974

        6 BUZIANIS, James Gus Jr.   B-21 Nov 1957

        6 BUZIANIS, Pamela Kay   B-24 Aug 1959

    5 MAIR, Arthur Jay B-29 Feb 1932
    5 MAIR, Dorthy DIPO, Sp. B-12 Jul 1934 M-20 Jan 1951

        6 MAIR, Michael Jay   B-31 Aug 1952

        6 MAIR, Tresa Kay   B-15 Oct 1954

    5 TAYLOR, Wilma Murl MAIR B-12 May 1936 M-13 Jun 1953
    5 TAYLOR, Kent G., Sp. B-15 Feb 1935

        6 BEAGLEY, Su Ann TAYLOR B-22 Mar 1955 M-
        6 BEAGLEY, Richard, Sp. B-

        6 TAYLOR, Allen C. B-14 Mar 1956 M-
        6 TAYLOR, Lynell MANN, Sp. B-

        6 TAYLOR, Bryan Wayne   B-24 Mar 1958

        6 TAYLOR, Dennis K.   B-11 Mar 1959

        6 TAYLOR, Gaye Lyn   B-19 Jun 1962

4 MAIR, Lindsay B-24 Feb 1907 M-17 Sep 1928
4 MAIR, Edna Mae HAMILTON, Sp. B-25 Jan 1911 D-4 May 1977

    5 MAIR, Arvilla Mae   B-16 Feb 1930 D-12 Dec 1931

    5 BROZOVICH, Patsy Juanita MAIR Ramsey B-17 Mar 1932
    5 RAMSEY, John Jr., Sp. (1) B-8 Mar 1929 M-7 Jul 1949 D-2 Nov 1958
    5 BROZOVICH, Nick George, Sp. B-   M-

        6 KUNTZ, Carla Jean RAMSEY Birman B-31 May 1950
        6 BIRMAN, James Michael, Sp. (1) B-   M-19 Apr 1966
        6 KUNTZ, Charles, Sp. (2) B-   M-

            7 BIRMAN, James Michael Jr. B-

            7 BIRMAN, Timothy Allen   B-

            7 BIRMAN, Brandi Chantell   B-

            7 BIRMAN, Trebor Charles   B-

        6 RAMSEY, Claude Lee B-28 Jan 1953
        6 RAMSEY, Cynthia Jane SCHWAHN, Sp. B-   M-10 Nov 1973

        6 BROADHEAD, Elizabeth Ann RAMSEY B-
        6 BROADHEAD, Derrell, Sp. B-   M-15 Nov 1957

            7 BROADHEAD, Chiedy Marie Ramsey B-

        6 RAMSEY, Johnny Lyn   B-12 Jan 1959

    5 MAIR, Darwin Lindsay B-22 Sep 1934
    5 MAIR, Beth Elaine SUTTON, Sp. B-11 Jun 1938 M-12 Sep 1956

        6 MAIR, Darwin Lee   B-20 Aug 1957

        6 WOODS, Connie Jean MAIR B-21 Feb 1960
        6 WOODS, Michael Val, Sp. B-   M-26 May 1978

        6 MAIR, Carolee,   B-12 Nov 1961

        6 MAIR, Elaine   B-13 Jan 1963 D-16 Jan 1963

        6 MAIR, Christine   B- 4 Dec 1964

        6 MAIR, Trudy Lyn   B-29 Jul 1966

        6 MAIR, Shirley Ann   B-24 May 1970

5 BELCHER, Barbara Jean MAIR B-10 Mar 1937
5 BELCHER, Floyd Jr., Sp. B-19 Jan 1934 M-7 Sep 1953

        6 BELCHER, Billy Ray B-25 Oct 1954
        6 BELCHER, Nancy JOHNSON, Sp. B-   M-22 Nov 1974

        6 RYAN, Jacke Lynn BELCHER B-24 Oct 1956
        6 RYAN, John, Sp. B-   M-27 Apr 1974

        6 DYKE, Doris Jean BELCHER B-6 Mar 1958
        6 DYKE, Thomas, Sp. B-   M-12 Apr 1974

        6 MATHEWS, Barbara Louise BELCHER B-9 Oct 1959
        6 MATHEWS,   Sp. B-   M-

        6 BELCHER, Jimmy Dean   B-21 Sep 1961

5 MAIR, Lyndon A.   B-14 Nov 1945
5 MAIR, Linda J. PARKIN, Sp. B-6 Oct 1951 M-17 Apr 1970

        6 MAIR, Lyndon Shane   B- 2 Jun 1972

        6 MAIR, Tammy Raquel   B-12 Jul 1973

        6 MAIR, Brock Lindsay   B- 7 Aug 1975

        6 MAIR, Jaron Alexander   B- 3 Nov 1976

John Murray Murdoch, Anne Steel, and Isabella Crawford

John Murray Murdoch was born December 28, 1820, at Gaswater, Auchinleck, Ayrshire, Scotland, the sixth child of James and Mary Murray Murdoch. He was reared in the wild heathery hills of Scotland. In his youth he was a shepherd. His opportunities for education were very limited inasmuch as he lived quite a distance from the nearest school. His father had lost his life trying to rescue a young man who had fallen a victim to foul air in the bottom of a new shaft they were sinking in a mine. This left Mary a poor widow with seven children. John was just ten years of age at this time. The family was living in a rented house belonging to the limeworks where James had been working prior to his death. John's mother remained a widow and through her industry was able to support herself and her youngest child William, who was then five, and her niece Margaret Murray, an orphan, who was about four. John's brother James and his sisters Janet, Veronica, and Mary were old enough to care for themselves. Before this time he had been herding sheep but came home that winter and went to school. They lived very humbly as their mother had to earn their living. Their diet at that time consisted mainly of potatoes and salt. In the spring John went herding again and from that time forth supported himself as well as others. He continued to herd until he was about nineteen years old. By this time his mother, with the help of her family and a few kind neighbors, had built a home of her own. John went to work in the coal mines and boarded with his mother until he was twenty-seven years old. Wages were good, and he was able to save a little money. He was the last child to leave his mother's home.

On February 25, 1848, John married Ann Steel and went to Kirkconnell where her parents lived on a small farm. He remained there but still worked in the mines. On November 21, 1848, their first child, Elizabeth, was born. Their second child, James, was born in June of 1850.

It was about this time he first heard of the people called Latter-day Saints. A young man named James Steel, his wife's brother, had been in England for some time and had been converted to that faith by a young woman, Elizabeth Wyllie, whom he later married. He visited with John and Ann in Kirkconnell and preached the gospel to them. John found, to his surprise, that his teachings were far in advance of the religious teachings of the day, and that he had gained such a wonderful knowledge of the scriptures in the short time he had been gone. "He left his testimony with us which we never forgot, and returned to England." At this time John was a member of two different churches and was acquainted more or less with the creeds of the Catholic and Protestant churches. These were so different from the gospel as taught by Jesus and his apostles as recorded in the New Testament. In fact, because of the confusion, he had become disgusted with the whole lot and would have become infidel to all religion if not for the testimony of that young man.

John felt quite lonely after James returned to England, and night and day pondered over the things he had told them. This was the first he had heard of the gospel, as there were no Saints in that part of the country. John had a dream, and in his dream he thought he went out into the garden and saw a very pretty little tree that his brother-in-law had planted a few days before. It looked green and thrifty, and he caught hold of it and to his surprise found that it had already taken root and was firmly in the ground.

On November 29, 1850, John and his wife were baptized by Thomas Hittley. A branch of the Church was organized and met in their home from then until they left for Utah. During that time he had ample proof of the interpretation of his dream. The gospel had taken root, and John was the firstfruits in that part of the country.

Being a new member of the Church, John was anxious to gain and build a strong testimony. He had heard some speak in tongues and others interpret. He had heard some prophesy. These outward signs did not come to him, and after reading the scriptures and pondering over the marvelous things that happened to the Saints anciently, he felt that he was not worthy of these greater gifts. He prayed for the gift of being able to write poetry. Branch meetings were still being held at his home, and the following is what John received, which was in the form of an invitation to a dear friend whom he was anxious to convert to the gospel.

Dear Thomas my friend, these few lines I send,
I truly abhor strife and schism.
But I humbly pray, that you make no delay,
Till you taste the sweet fruits of baptism.

We know from the work that three bear record
'Mongst the glorious armies of heaven.
So likewise on earth, we receive the new birth
And the same three-fold record is given.

So, next Sunday noon I invite you to come
Where the truth it will shine bright as day
And the laws of the Lord as revealed in His word
Shall be open for you to obey.

Dear Thomas, my friend, to these few lines attend
And the truth for yourself you shall know.
Like the eunuch of old, as we plainly are told,
On your way you rejoicing will go.

About this time he moved away to another coal mine where he was pleased to find a few Saints. These folks met regularly at his home, and in a short time several were baptized. John was soon ordained a priest. Soon two traveling elders were sent to that part of the country, and a good branch was soon prospering. Most of these Saints were poor, as times were very difficult. John had an opportunity to get steadier work some six miles away where wages were also much better. Now came a great trial. If he were to leave, what would become of the little branch that he had been partly feeding and clothing? Some of the Saints came quite a distance on Saturday to meet with them on Sundays, and it was John and his family who would take care of them. Because of this and the times being as hard as they were, John barely had the means to care for his family.

He inquired of the elders as to what he should do, and they advised that they could not counsel, but the Lord would direct him. He was working for his brother James at the time, doing repairs in the mine, and while thinking of his problem he felt impressed to ask

the Lord for wisdom in making his decision. He had prayed many times before that he might have the gift of tongues, but he never had sufficient faith to exercise it. After he had finished praying he began speaking in tongues. Although he realized he was speaking in tongues he did not understand what he was saying. He reasoned, however, that if the Lord had given him the one gift that He would surely give him the other. Soon it came to him that he should get up and leave the place, for in less than six months there would not be a blowing furnace in Lugar. This seemed almost impossible and very unlikely, as it would cost the company so much money to close down and then to start up again. It would also mean the closing down of all the coal mines in that vicinity.

He immediately left the place, trusting in the Lord and not knowing what would happen to the little branch.

It turned out all right however, as the Saints continued to come to John's new home and hold their meetings. Some of the folks had to travel as far as fifteen miles to attend, and John still provided for them. This was not nearly so difficult now, as he was working steadily and making better wages. A few more Saints were baptized while here, and an additional traveling elder was sent from Glasgow. The three elders with them were William Aird, John Drennan, and Andrew Ferguson, all good and faithful brethren.

John had now been in the Church a little over a year, and by this time thousands had been baptized and many hundreds had emigrated to America. It was about this time that the Perpetual Emigration Fund was started. Thousands of the poor Saints who had been members long before John were looking forward to their deliverance. This made him realize that his deliverance was still a long way off and many years of hard work and poverty were to be his lot. The Lord thought differently, as soon a call came from Franklin D. Richards, president of the British Mission, for two Scotch sheepherders and their dogs to go to Utah and herd sheep for President Brigham Young. John was about the only one of the members who was qualified to do this, and he was instructed to prepare to go to Utah. He was to sell all his belongings and put what money he could into the Emigration Fund. This he did and sent what he could to Liverpool.

Then a letter came from Brother Calvin, the second man selected, saying that he had bargained for the dogs but had no money to pay for them. They were to cost three sovereigns ($14.67), and he asked John to send him the money. This he did, but it was difficult in view of his limited funds. A party was given in their honor by Brother Gallacher, one of John's converts, some six miles distant at New Cummock. A pleasant time was had by all with many hearty handshakes, farewells, and heartfelt blessings showered upon them. Everyone was expected to perform in some way. His wife, Ann, sang a beautiful number from the LDS hymnbook:

Yes my native land, I love thee
All thy scenes I love them well;
Friends, connections, happy country
Can I bid you all farewell?
Can I leave thee
Far in distant lands to dwell?

Then John sang the following song, which he composed for the occasion, sung to the tune of "Flow Gently, Sweet Afton":

Oh Scotland my country, my dear native home,
Thou land of the brave and the theme of my song.
Oh why should I leave thee and cross the deep sea,
To a strange land far distant, lovely Scotland, from thee?

How pleasant to view are thy mountains and hills,
Thy sweet blooming heather and far famed bluebells.
Thy scenes of my childhood where in youth I have strayed,
With my faithful companions, my dog, crook, and plaid.

Oh, Scotland, my country and land of my birth,
In fondness I'll ever remember thy worth.
For wrapped in thy bosom my forefathers sleep,
Why then should I leave thee and cross the wild deep?

But why should I linger or wish for to stay?
The voice of the Prophet is "Haste, flee away.
Lest judgements o'er take you and lay Scotland low."
To the prophets in Zion, Oh, then let me go!

Farewell then my kindred, my home and my all
When duty requires it we bow to the call.
We brave every danger and conquer each foe,
To the words of the Prophet, Oh, then let me bow.

Farewell then, dear Scotland, one last fond adieu,
Farewell my dear brethren so faithful and true.
May angels watch o'er you till warfares are o'er,
And in safety we all meet on Zion's fair shore.

He then bade farewell to all his kindred and friends in Gaswater, where he was born and raised. He then took his wife and two children back to Kirkconnell, where her mother and stepfather and brothers and sisters lived. Her mother and stepfather were the only ones belonging to the Church. Brother and Sister Thomas Todd were also living there, and the four of them were the only Latter-day Saints in the town. They bade them farewell.

At this time the people in the area were bitterly opposed to the Church, and a strong spirit of persecution was with them. They were so bitter that they gathered at times to discuss the best way of doing away with the Mormons. They preached that if left alone that the Church would spread and destroy the morals of the whole country. Although most of the people were prejudiced and bitter, the family still had a few good friends. Some of their well-meaning friends did not want them to leave and devised a plan where they would hide their children, as they were sure they would not leave without them. They didn't carry it out though. This final party was held December 31, 1851. The next morning was New Year's Day, and they boarded the train, hard though it was to break away from their loved ones.

Five of the six months given by interpretation of tongues were now past and soon they would be at sea and John would probably never know if it would be fulfilled. Later, however, when William Aird came to Utah, some one year afterward, and John had confided in him as to his manifestation, he revealed that practically to the day, the furnaces were all "blown out." In his heart he thanked God for his mindfulness of his poor servant. When his brother William came many years afterward, he testified as to its fulfillment as well.

They arrived in Glasgow that same day and first met his sheepherder companion who was to travel with them. The Saints in Glasgow took them in and had another party for them. They all envied their going to Zion and wished they had been sheepherders to warrant their going. They stayed that night and the next day with an old friend and were treated wonderfully. John had loaned this man nine sovereigns ($44.01) some years before, and he repaid him one ($4.89), which helped very much.

That night they boarded a steamer bound for Liverpool. The night was stormy and the winds so strong that they blew the smokestack down. They arrived in Liverpool safely but were detained there some ten days. Ann at this time was three to four months pregnant, and Elizabeth was three and a half and James about one and a half. Soon they boarded the ship *Kennebec* and started their voyage across the stormy sea. John described the crew as a motley crew. They left January 10, 1852, with John S. Higbee in charge of the Saints. There were about one hundred Irish immigrants of the very lowest grade on board, and they were partitioned off in the forepart of the ship. The Saints were all on deck and all had to cook on the same big stove or "galley" as it was called. The passage was rather rough, taking some nine weeks from Liverpool to New Orleans. At the mouth of the Mississippi the ship became stuck on a sandbar for some ten days. The captain had supplied the Irish immigrants with oatmeal only, but being at sea longer than expected had to draw from the stores of the Saints. Many of the passengers suffered from lack of food and water. Small boats came alongside the ship to sell food, but only those with money could buy. As for John, he got along nicely with the oatmeal and brackish river water. Unfortunately, it was not sufficient for their small children, and both were taken ill. It was evident to John that there were ample stores of food on the ship but the proper care was not taken in handling.

Finally they were transferred to a steamboat and started up the Mississippi River for Saint Louis. They had no food except what they could beg from the person in charge, John S. Higbee. He did not seem to be as thoughtful of others as he might have been. Just before reaching land a terrific wind came up, and the mighty waves rocked and tossed the ship until many of the passengers became panic stricken. Whether the captain and his crew were alarmed was not known, but one purporting to be an officer went among the passengers and warned them that unless they lightened the load the ship would sink. He asked all to prepare part of their belongings to be thrown overboard. All complied with the request. As the storm subsided and they went further up the river, they came to a little clearing and to their astonishment saw hanging on a clothesline many of the articles that were supposed to have been thrown overboard. Among them were some beautiful Scotch plaids and other things which they treasured very much.

The steamboat was very crowded, and it was some time before all were given berths or even places where they could be sheltered from the sun and rain. Sometimes it was quite cold. John got permission to rig pieces of wood to make a bed under a steampipe where he hoped his wife and sick children could be reasonably comfortable and out of the rain. Efforts were made to make them move, but finally they were allowed to stay. Their children were getting weaker by the day, as the only food they had to give them was some of the oatmeal from the Kennebec. Although the parents were able to get along, the children just couldn't get by, and it affected their bowels terribly. They begged the person in charge of their group for some nourishing food for the children, but he said he had not money to provide for them. John's wife, Ann, begged with tears in her eyes for a small piece of pie for her sick boy, but was advised it was medicine and not pie that the boy needed, and he said he would get her some. Neither the medicine nor the pie ever came. John felt bad that they received this type of treatment when they so needed help.

It was a heart-rending experience for John to look on the wasted body of his little boy crying for food and none to give him. John had always been independent, and rather than bow down and beg for things he felt he would rather die. His son's condition humbled him, however, and he went to a single man aboard ship, not a member of the Church. He told him his boy was dying and needed food, to which the man said he did not believe it. John ran from his presence and hid himself behind the paddlewheel of the boat. He was then about thirty years of age, and had not shed a tear since being a boy of twelve or thirteen. He had thought his days of crying were past, but not so. If he had not given vent to his feelings in a flood of tears, he felt his heart would burst. He had to unbutton his vest and pants to allow for the surging of his wounded heart. As soon as he could compose himself, he hurried back to the place where he had left his little boy with his grief-stricken wife. She was calm, and a pleasant smile on her careworn face told him that the boy had received some bread. John was grateful to the stranger who gave them the bread for him, but it was to be the last bread he would ever eat. He died on the twentieth of March. They buried him in a woodyard on the banks of the Mississippi River twelve miles from Columbia. Shortly he met the man that he had begged bread from only to be turned away, and he told him he had a little sago in the hold of the boat and offered some for his little boy. John advised him he had no need for it now as his boy was dead. He apologized for his actions and told John that the people had run all over him for his food to where he scarcely had enough for himself. John forgave him, for he felt he was telling the truth.

They landed in Saint Louis, and were promptly put under the direction of Abraham O. Smoot from Utah, who had charge of the emigration that year. Their little girl was still extremely sick, and despite the loving care she was given, she too passed away. She was buried in this strange land among strange people. The people of Saint Louis seemed very kind to them, but they soon found this to be incorrect. After their little girl's body was prepared for burial and placed in a substantial box, a stranger came along and seemed to sympathize with John in his bereavement. He told him of a cemetery a short distance away and that he would send his wagon to convey the casket to the cemetery free of charge. He gladly accepted his kind offer. When all was ready he pointed to a large building and advised that the wagon had to take a road around it and that it was closer for him to follow a small trail on a more direct route. He asked him to take that route so he would be at the cemetery when the wagon arrived. The wagon came and the box was deposited in the grave. John carefully covered it over with earth. Being extremely sad he began walking back, and he went by way of the road where the wagon traveled. When he approached the large building, he became inquisitive and went inside. He saw a large vat of boiling water, and as he stood there a human form came to the surface. It was almost more than he could bear when he saw that it was the head and body of his own little girl. He saw her curly yellow hair rise to the surface and then disappear. John was horror-stricken, and it was all he could do to return to camp under his own power. (John never told this experience to anyone until he wrote his history in the later years of his life. He found out that the large building was a dissecting and fertilizer plant.)

They remained in Saint Louis for another month waiting for another shipload of Saints that left Liverpool after they did. When they arrived they again boarded ship and went up the Missouri River to what is now Kansas City. It was here that they got their outfit for crossing the plains. Here cholera broke out, so they immediately went nine miles west on the plains. Quite a few Saints died from it, and were buried with split rails for coffins. John was relieved from all camp duties to nurse the sick and to bury the dead. (John's little boy was just one year and eight months old when he died. Their little girl died April 4 when just three years and eight months of age. This left them childless in this strange land, with no means or money, but not without friends.)

On the twentieth of May, 1852, a baby girl was born to them. It was a stormy night in the midst of a terrific thunderstorm, and the birth presented many problems considering they were living in a tent. She was given the name of Mary Murray Murdoch, after her grandmother.

In a few days they started on their long and wearisome journey. Captain Smoot was in charge, with Christopher Layton as his assistant. They also had a captain of every ten wagons. There were two yoke of oxen and a yoke of cows on each wagon. Each person was allowed 100 pounds of luggage, including bedding and cooking utensils. Everything over 100 pounds was not allowed. The cholera that had taken so many lives was now entirely cleared up, and the general health of the company was very good. Captain Smoot warned everyone not to eat too much. John's wife, Ann, was able to walk, and carried her baby almost every foot of the way to Zion. The baby was about eight days old at this point. After a few days John had quite an experience trying to locate one of their cows that had strayed away. He located it only to have it get away again (possibly with help of an Indian), and finally after three days he gave up. Even though he was lost most of the time he was searching for the cow, he found his way back to camp, hungry and very tired. His wife and friends had nearly given up hope of seeing him again.

Captain Smoot took ill, and John was appointed a nurse unto him and spent several days nursing him back to health. They constructed sort of a carriage for him to ride in. As he was still quite weak, each time the train stopped they lifted him out of the wagon and laid him on a bed on the ground. Once in John's haste to make a bed for him, he put it on an ant bed without noticing it. When Captain Smoot saw what had happened, he said, "Brother John, never mind; I am glad to get laid down, and if the ants will leave me alone, I will leave them alone." John and Captain Smoot soon became very close friends, and soon he was calling John his little Scotch Johnnie. John was very diligent in administering to his every need, and he soon nursed him back to health. Later in their journey, in the Black Hills area, John was taken ill with mountain fever and became very sick. Captain Smoot insisted on being his nurse in gratitude for the service he had rendered to him. He could not have treated John better if he had been his own son.

On the third day of September, 1852, they reached

Salt Lake City, safe but very weary. This was the first company that had come to Utah aided by the Perpetual Emigration Fund. They camped on the public square. President Brigham Young came and gave them a hearty welcome and words of encouragement. All were introduced to President Young by Captain Smoot, and of course the two shepherds and their dogs were given a special introduction. President Young said he had no sheep at present, as most had been lost, and the few that were left were rented out to his brother Lorenzo for five years. Under those conditions shepherds would not be needed, but he told them to rest and stay in camp and there would soon be work available. Before the close of the second day, everyone had left except the two shepherds and their families. A man named Dalton came from Farmington and hired them to work for one month. He took them into his home and was very kind to them. John's companion was troubled with a sore foot and had to return to Salt Lake. John stayed on for the month, received his pay, and journeyed to Salt Lake, where he divided his pay with his lame companion. Then President Young hired him to dig his potatoes. John dug one-and-one-half acres, all with a spade. He felt blessed to work for a prophet of the Lord and received much joy in his labors. While doing this work a few dissatisfied men came around and told John that they had worked for Brigham and that he had not paid them as he ought to have, and led John to believe that he would not receive his pay. They asked what share he was to receive for his hard work, and John replied that he had made no bargain but was sure that President Young would do right by him. They turned away laughing, saying that he would soon learn better. John kept right on working, and when he had finished, President Young's dealings were entirely satisfactory. John and his family had quite a struggle to keep in food and shelter. President Young gave John a blessing and told him he would live to have houses and lands and would prosper.

On March 28, 1856, John and Ann received their endowments and were sealed as husband and wife for eternity. By this time they had acquired a yoke of oxen and used them for all types of work. They also had a cow. John worked hard mowing hay to feed the animals during the coming winter. In the fall he turned the oxen into a big field, thinking they could feed there until winter came. Then he could bring them home and feed them the hay. When winter came he spent days looking for them, but no one seemed to have seen them. Of course he felt bad after working so hard to get the hay to feed them. After everything else failed, John sought the Lord in prayer and asked that he would assist him in finding them. As he prayed, a voice said, "You will find your oxen." Still no word came of his oxen. Feed was scarce that year, and after John was offered a good price for it he decided to sell. He still had faith that he would find the oxen. Next spring he was notified by Apostle F. D. Richards that a large herd of cattle was being brought to a certain corral in the city, and John thought he could buy a yoke of oxen from that herd. He went to look at the cattle and behold, he saw his own oxen there. He informed the men in charge that two of the oxen belonged to him, and they said it was impossible. He immediately went to Apostle Richards, and together they returned to the corral. The man in charge was not satisfied, as there were no marks or brands on the oxen. He asked if there were any others besides himself who could identify them. John said, "Yes, every man, woman and child in the Third Ward. We will not need them, however. If I call the oxen they will come to me, and if they will not own me, I will not own them." "All right, try it," they said. He got off the fence and went to a place where the oxen could see and hear him and held out his hat and said, "Come, Bob." The ox came right up to him. He put his right arm over his neck and called, "Come under, Bright." The other ox came right up and stood as if under the yoke. The two men clapped their hands and said, "These are his oxen, and no one can dispute that kind of evidence." He then selected a well-matched yoke of young oxen and bought them, thus making two yoke.

In 1854 the grasshoppers destroyed most of the crops, and many of the people had but very little to eat. Ann, along with others, went to the hills and dug sego and thistle roots to help appease their hunger. John soon bought a city lot in the Third Ward and built a small house where they lived for some years. He was ordained a high priest by Presiding Bishop Hunter, and set apart as a counselor to Jacob Weiler, bishop of the Third Ward in Salt Lake City. He held this position as long as he lived in the ward. On the fourteenth of September, 1854, Ann gave birth to another baby girl, who was named Ann after her mother. After they had settled down and began gathering a little property, their thoughts turned to their dear friends back in the old country. They knew they were desirous of coming to Zion, and of course John was desirous of helping his dear old mother to come so he could care for her in her old age. His wife was equally anxious to help her brother James Steel and his family to come. To accomplish this they both agreed to save every cent possible. It was 1856 before they had saved enough. They sent their savings to Scotland, and it was gratefully accepted. His mother, though nearly seventy-four years of age, bravely started the journey, knowing full well that most of the Saints were to cross the plains in handcarts that year.

They sailed from Liverpool May 25, 1856, on the ship *Horizon.* Edward Martin was in charge of the company. They landed in Boston and journeyed to Iowa City by rail, arriving July 8. They were detained until August 25, waiting for the handcarts to be made. On this day, they left Florence, Nebraska, starting on their long and dreary journey over mountains and plains. Because they were getting started so late in the season, they traveled just as far as they could each day, walking every inch of the way. John's dear mother came down with cholera, which was so common on the trail, and about seven hundred miles along the way, near Chimney Rock, Nebraska, she passed away. This was October 3, 1856. Just before she died she said, "Tell John I died with my face turned towards Zion." She was a martyr for the gospel's sake.

James Steel and his family, with whom John's mother had been traveling, continued on and suffered greatly from cold and hunger. They were caught by snow soon after leaving the Platte River. Their provisions were very short, and with all these hardships, it is no wonder that so many perished. James Steel succumbed to the cold and hunger along the way. His wife and two little boys survived the ordeal and came on to relate the terrible experiences that they had witnessed. Had not relief been sent from Utah, they would all have perished back on the Sweetwater. Even with all their sore trials they did not complain, but rather felt to acknowledge the hand of the Lord even in their bereavement. James's wife and two boys stayed in John's home until they found a place of their own.

On the twentieth of December, 1856, Ann gave birth to another daughter, and she was given the name of Janett Osborne As usual, all went well with mother and baby.

In the fall of 1857 John was one of the noble band that went to Echo Canyon to prevent Johnston's Army from coming into Utah. He was made a captain of fifty under Major Daniel McArthur. They were there some eight weeks and prevented the army from coming in. They were forced to make their winter quarters at Fort Bridger, where times were so difficult that they actually had to live on mule meat without salt for part of the winter. When the army came into Utah the

next spring, they were under orders not to make a permanent camp within thirty-five miles of Salt Lake City. The army really proved a blessing financially to the people of Utah, although it had not intended to. When arrangements had been made for the army to come to Utah in the spring of 1858, President Young advised all his people to move south at least as far as Provo. They were also advised to make preparations to burn their homes in the event the army showed signs of hostility. John's family followed the admonition, of course, and loaded their wagons with their belongings. With their two yoke of oxen, they journeyed south as far as Goshen.

They spent the summer there, and in the fall everyone was advised to return to their homes.

John and his family lived in Salt Lake until the spring of 1860. It had been reported that a few families had gone into the Provo Valley, a new settlement, in 1859, and had proved that wheat could be matured there. It was also learned that land could be bought for merely paying the surveyor's fees, and irrigation water was plentiful. John decided to go and get some land where he could make a permanent home and settle down and raise his family. He also wanted to help settle and build a new town as the original pioneers had. On January 15, 1859, while still in Salt Lake, still another daughter blessed their home, and she was named Sarah Jane.

Early in the spring of 1860 John disposed of his property in Salt Lake, and in company with William Foreman and others loaded all of their belongings into their wagons and started for Provo valley. It took about three days to drive with their oxen. Soon after their arrival, they secured some land and also a place in the fort, where John made a dugout for his family to live in until he could put in his crops. He succeeded in getting a small crop of wheat, oats, and potatoes, and began making preparations to build a log house. There were a good number of cottonwood trees over on the river that were straight and good for building houses and buildings for cattle. They brought a cow, pig, and a few sheep and chickens from Salt Lake. The fort where they were living was given the name of Heber, named in honor of Heber C. Kimball, first counselor to Brigham Young. The few people who were there in 1860 had no meetinghouse, and they wanted to celebrate the twenty-fourth of July. It was suggested that they build a bowery in which to hold the celebration. In his wisdom, however, John suggested they build a meetinghouse while they were at it. He reasoned it would not take much longer to build, and then they would have a place where they could meet in the winter and that could be used for dances, plays, and so on. His proposition was accepted, and everyone went to work in earnest. The meetinghouse was made from logs and was twenty-four feet by eighteen feet wide. It was used for the above-mentioned purposes for about six years.

About this time William M. Wall had been appointed as branch president, and he chose John M. Murdoch and James Laird as his counselors. In 1861 Joseph S. Murdock was ordained a bishop and sent to Heber by President Young. A ward was organized, and John was given charge of the high priests. About two years later a high priests quorum was organized, and John was chosen as president. He held this position until within a few years of his death. There were many inconveniences the Saints had to put up with the first few years. Because there was no mill in the valley for the first two years, they could not grind their wheat into flour, so much of it was eaten whole with milk. In 1861 a chopper was installed to chop the wheat. Although this was a big improvement over what they had had, it was still run by horsepower. There was a grist mill in Provo, but the road was bad, and with an ox team it took three days to complete the round trip. Inasmuch as the seasons where shorter in this high valley, which was some fifteen hundred feet higher than Salt Lake, everyone worked long and hard during the productive season. A great many roads had to be constructed in the canyons to get poles so the fields could be fenced. This was necessary to keep the cattle from destroying the growing crops. Likewise the poles were needed to build houses, sheds, and corrals. One of John's most difficult jobs during the first few years was to provide feed for their oxen and cows through the long winter months. All of the hay had to be mown by hand, and it took at least four tons of hay in addition to straw and chaff to feed a yoke of oxen through the winter.

There were no stoves to be had for many years, and likewise no coal, but merely an open fireplace where wood could be burned and bake skillets were used to cook the bread. A few pots and pans were also used. People generally made all of their own soap for washing, and candles to give them light. It is evident that the women were kept as busy as the men. People were generally healthy and happy, but all were alike inasmuch as they were all poor. There was a good brotherly feeling that existed for each other.

Wasatch County was organized in January 1862, and John was made county treasurer. He organized the first cooperative sheep herd, which he had charge

of for a number of years. He was always able to pay a dividend to the owners. When this was dissolved he still ran a herd of his own. He wintered them in the south and brought them back in the summer months. This way special supplies of hay were not needed for them, and it enabled nearly everyone to have a few sheep to furnish wool for spinning and weaving into a cloth called "jean." Practically everyone wore clothing made from this type of cloth.

On August 8, 1862, in obedience to the LDS teachings at the time, John took as his plural wife a beautiful dark-eyed Scotch lass by the name of Isabella Crawford, a native of Blantyre, Scotland. As a young woman she emigrated to America and worked in the cotton mills at Holyoke, Massachusetts, to get money to come to Utah. She too had left loved ones and her all for the gospel's sake. She never saw or heard of her family again after being driven from her home when she joined the Church. She was twenty-six years old at the time of their marriage and a very fine young woman. She proved to be a good and loving wife to John as long as he lived. She became the mother of 7 children by him. John's first wife, Ann, bore him 15 children. In all, John had 22 sons and daughters and 137 grandchildren. After marrying Aunt Bella, as she came to be called, he built a large frame house with six or seven rooms in order to accommodate his large family. Fifteen of those 22 children grew to maturity in the Heber valley, the other 7 dying very young. John, both wives, and all the children lived together under one roof for many years in peace and harmony. John later took up a ranch about six miles north of Heber where he could keep his sheep during the summer months. He built another home there for part of his family.

In 1866 when the Blackhawk Indian War first broke out, John was made a captain in the infantry in the Utah Militia. There were fifty men under his jurisdiction. This lasted almost two years, and he did his share in bringing peace once more unto the land.

One winter John went south with his sheep, intending to winter them as usual. It was an extra hard winter, and his health failed him. Therefore he leased his sheep to a man who lived nearby and returned home where he could receive the proper care. The man either lost or sold the sheep, but John never saw them again nor did he receive anything for them. This was very unfortunate, as he had spent years in building up the herd. Inasmuch as the man had no other property, John merely dropped the matter.

In June of 1869, Bishop Abram Hatch established

a Relief Society in the Heber Ward, and Ann was chosen as a counselor to the president Margaret Muir. Mary McMullin was the other counselor. Forty members were enrolled in that first group. In September of 1879, Eliza R. Snow and Emmeline B. Wells organized a Stake Relief Society; ward Primaries were also formed. In 1883 Ann was called to be the first Wasatch Stake Primary president. She served in this capacity for twelve years. Isabella served in the Heber West Ward Relief Society presidency from 1879 to 1895 as a counselor.

In 1878 John's brother William and his family came to Utah from Scotland. This group included William's son, David L., and his wife Elizabeth, his daughters Janet and Margaret, and his sister Veronica. John, William M. Giles, and William Lindsay met them in Salt Lake with two horse teams so they could transport them to Heber. After being separated some twenty-six years, it was an extremely happy meeting for the two brothers. They arrived the following day at John's ranch and the following day went on into Heber. Ann was overjoyed to see them.

About 1887 to 1891 the federal officials in Utah started a crusade against polygamists. They sent deputy marshalls into all parts of the state to make arrests. On Tuesday, April 21, 1891, John was arrested and taken before Judge Blackburn in Provo. He was sentenced to one month in the penitentiary. John politely told the Judge that his home was in Heber and he had not brought a change of underclothing. Inasmuch as he had not anticipated being sent to prison, he asked for the privilege of returning home to get his clothing. He promised to go right to the penitentiary without an officer or without extra expenses to the government. The judge agreed to let him go. According to his promise John went home, got his clothing, and promptly presented himself at the penitentiary for admittance. The warden asked for his commitment papers, but John had none. For a time the warden refused to admit him, but John insisted and served his time. He was in the company of criminals. However, a good portion of the inmates were like himself, serving time for "unlawful cohabitation." He was discharged May 21, 1891, after serving for one month.

In 1890, John was ordained a patriarch by Apostle Francis L. Lyman. He gave many wonderful patriarchal blessings to the members of the stake. The Lord blessed him with the spirit of his calling, and he took a great deal of joy and interest in pronouncing blessings upon the people.

On the twenty-fourth of February, 1898, John and Ann Steel celebrated their golden wedding anniversary in Turner's Hall. Nearly all of the older folks in Heber were invited to come and partake of the anniversary feast. Some 400 people were in attendance, and all had a good time. All of John and Ann's living children and grandchildren were present to show their honor and respect. James "D" Murdoch, a nephew, made the presentation speech and presented John with a gold-headed cane and each of his wives with a diamond ring. These articles were purchased by the close relatives as a token of their love and respect for them. A picture was taken at this time of John and Ann and John and Isabella. At this time they all were enjoying good health and did considerably well after the trials and tribulations that had come into their lives.

Through his thrift and hard work and assisted by his two good wives John managed to gather around him considerable profit. Inasmuch as it was against the law to live or sleep with his plural wife, he built still another nice home where she and her children lived comfortably for many years. At a later date when all of the children were married and gone except Thomas, he sold his larger homes and built still another smaller one especially suited for the convenience of his two faithful wives. They all lived under one roof, but each wife had her own bedroom and kitchen separated by a bath in-between, accessible to each family. This house was built near the meetinghouse, which made it convenient for them to attend their meetings. It was also close to their daughter Nettie's (Janett) house where she could watch over them. This she and her good husband did for many years. They were comfortable and contented in their new home and enjoyed its conveniences for a few years.

Finally Ann became very feeble, and on the fifteenth of December, 1909, she passed away. For over sixty years she had been a true and faithful wife. Her married life was a very eventful one, and she was always ready to do her part. She had been an active Church worker from the time she was baptized to within a few years of her death. For years she was stake Primary president, which necessitated a great deal of travel by wagon and carriage to visit the different towns in Wasatch Stake. No woman could have been more faithful and diligent than Ann in attending to her Church duties.

John's health had also been failing for some time, and he missed the kind words and loving actions of his beloved Ann. He recalled that they had shared many joys and sorrows together in their married life. Even when the time came for him to take a plural wife she freely gave her consent and did all in her power to promote peace and harmony in the home. By taking this course, the children in the two families lived happily and peacefully together. The children considered that they had two mothers, and while they were young they scarcely knew which was their real mother. Aunt Bella was equally kind and affectionate to all in the house. Although she was still there to attend to John's needs, he failed rapidly, and on the sixth day of May, 1910, he passed away. His funeral services were held in the stake tabernacle, and a large crowd was in attendance. Each speaker eulogized the patriarch for his noble character and the good he had done since coming to the valley in 1860. He had taken a prominent part in every enterprise that had been started for the good of the people. From the first log schoolhouse to the last public building erected, John had taken an active part and contributed liberally of his means. He had lived when the only light they had was from the tallow candle, and lived to see the coming of the electric light. He had also lived a few years to enjoy the comfort and benefits of hot and cold running water in the home. He was well known for his kindly interest in visiting the sick and afflicted and cheering, comforting and blessing them. He gave over 200 patriarchal blessings. He was respected for his wisdom, and when people were in trouble they often came to him for counsel and advice. He had the satisfaction of living to see his children become useful souls in the community and earnest workers in the Church. Several of his children were holding important Church offices before his death. Thomas and James had filled honorable missions. Joseph had also filled a short mission at Temple Square. John himself filled a short mission in Summit and Morgan counties during the winter of 1866. He had several sayings which are worth remembering and are as follows: "Although we cannot attain perfection in this life, we should be pointing that way." "The man that would make wealth from sheep must watch and pray while others sleep." He was told that a certain man used tobacco from boyhood and lived to be ninety years of age. "Well," said John, "you don't know how much longer he might have lived if he hadn't used it, do you?"

He loved the little valley of Heber and all of the people in it. He had prospered and was indeed blessed while living there. He was in his ninetieth year when he passed away. During his life he had been sorely tried and suffered many afflictions from hunger and poverty, yet he never wavered in his faith. He was buried by the side of his good wife Ann only six months after her death.

After John's death, Aunt Bella gave up the home and went to live with her daughter, Katie Hicken, where she could live more comfortably. John, knowing the laws of the land did not recognize Aunt Bella as his lawful wife, made ample provisions for her in his will. He also made provisions in his will that each of his children, by both wives, was to share alike in his property. His son Joseph A. was appointed administrator of his estate, and each of the children received about $900.00. There was no dissension or controversy in the settlement, as each felt the property had been fairly and equally divided.

Some may query in their minds as to whether a man could have the same love and affection for a plural wife as his first wife and whether she would have the same love for him. After John's death Aunt Bella was heard to say that if she could have the choice of all the men in the world, she would choose John Murray Murdoch, who had been such a true and faithful husband. Together John, Ann, and Isabella were a noble trio.

Isabella died six years after John on the tenth of April, 1916. All three are laid to rest in the Heber City Cemetery, Wasatch, Utah, until the day of their resurrection. May we all look forward to seeing them again and living forever as a family.

John Murray Murdoch

Ann Steel Murdoch

John Murray Murdoch and Ann Steel Murdoch and their nine children who lived to adulthood. Standing left to right: Millicent Sophia, David Steel, Jacobina W.O., Joseph A., Jannet Osborne, Sarah Jane, Thomas Todd; Seated left to right: Ann, John Murray Murdoch, Ann Steel Murdoch and Mary Murray

Five older daughters of John Murray Murdoch and Ann Steel. Back left to right: Mary Murray, Ann, Janett. Front left to right: Sarah Jane, Jacobina

In Our Home

In our home we lived together,
Father, mother, children too.
Half brothers and half sisters.
This we never knew.

Our father said, "Obey my will."
Our mother said, "Yes, do."
My mother said, "You must honor Muzz,
For she's your mother too."

We children never had a quarrel,
We were never known to fight.
Our mothers wise would stories tell
And soon set things aright.

They told of little Moses in bulrushes hid away.
And little Jesus in the manger on the hay.
They told of Daniel cast into the lion's den
And how God protected good, honest, righteous
    men.

The babies came close together.
Kate and Tom like twins seemed to be.
They both did nurse at mother's breast
And prayed at Muzz's knee.

We were very happy children until one day
Our father called us all together
And to us these words did say:
"I must obey the laws of the land,
And we must part for aye;
But to give up my wives and children
This I will never do.
I will go to the penitentiary
And serve a term or two,
But *that* I will never do."

My mother frail and sickly said,
"John I will set you free,
To send you forth to prison
Would be the death of me."

Muzz said, "Now dear Bella, this will never do.
We're going hairts an han's together,
And to me you've ere been true.
Now we'll continue onward
Though demons rage in hell."
Muzz stood and sweetly sang,
All is well, all is well."

My father went to prison,
Put on those stripes of shame;
But the angels looking down from heaven said,
"John, you're not to blame."

A term he served in Prison,
A fine he had to pay—
A hundred dollars down in cash
Before he could come away

Now we honor our dear parents
And the part they had to play,
Through trials and tribulations
Until our dying day.

Composed by Catherine Campbell Murdoch Hicken
August 16, 1921, for the Murdoch reunion.

"Muzz's Knee"; Ann Steel Murdoch

Isabella Crawford, John Murray Murdoch, Ann Steel

Ann Steel, John Murray Murdoch, Isabella Crawford

John Murray Murdoch's children and spouses. Picture taken at a reunion. Standing left to right: Brigham and Luann Murdoch, David and Emily Murdoch, Thomas and Sarah Murdoch, Martha and Joseph Murdoch, Isabella M. Nicol. Seated: David and Kate Hicken, Janett M. McMullin, and James and Sarah Murdoch

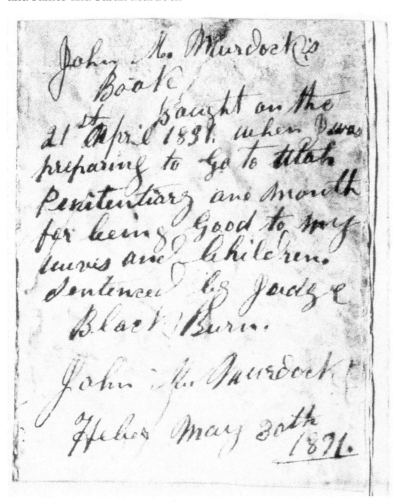

Written by John Murray Murdoch on the inside page of a Doctrine and Covenants now in the possession of Maybell McMullin Moulton

The Golden Wedding

In the town of fair Kirconnel
To the altar, Ann I led;
And she's been a true companion
Since the day that we were wed.

Though the way some times was stormy,
Other days were bright and fair;
Ann could always make me happy,
Haste away my every care.

Fifty years ago today, dear,
How they've quickly, swiftly fled.
And with them have gone some treasures—
Children, that we now call dead.

Ah, dear wife, the first that left us
Was our little son so fair,
And the day that he was taken
Seemed we not for life to care.

But a new hope seemed to cheer us,
As we traveled on our way;
Many babies came to love us,
Eight of them are here today.

Though they've grown to men and women
They were babies once, I said,
And we've rocked them, oh, so gently,
Pressed a kiss upon each head.

Prayed the little feet might travel,
Always in the path of right;
Till the Father called them home, dear,
To that mansion ever bright.

And the joys we've had were many,
All along these fifty years;
You are grandma, I am grandpa,
And great grandchildren appear.

Grandchildren, we now have fifty;
Children, living, we have eight;
There are seven in the heavens—
For our coming do they wait.

And we'll meet them some day, Ann dear,
For we both are growing old;
And the sunny side of youth, dear,

Like a story's long been told.

Yet, I love you just as dearly
As when first you were my bride,
And I brought you here to Utah,
O'er the ocean wild and wide.

Oh yes, John, we've lived together,
Having Bella with us too;
Plainly she is not forgotten,
John, you both of us did woo.

And you've been so kind and good, dear,
Treated us the very best,
That you have us both to love you
Set your heart at ease and rest.

Bella, come and sit beside us,
We will not put you aside;
What the Lord bath joined together
In the heavens will abide.

For we've worked for life eternal,
Tried to do our very best.
Praying God to ever guide us
Till our sun is in the West.

Oh my heart now beats with rapture,
As I view our children, dear,
And see the many kindred—
Our relations far and near;

Who have come this day together
With a word of love and cheer,
Saying, may you live together
Here on earth, while life is dear.

When your journey you've completed,
And to heaven you do hie;
May you meet us, may you greet us
Where the dear ones never die.

Written and read by Mrs. Jane Hatch Turner at John Murray and Ann Steel Murdoch's golden wedding celebration, Thursday, February 24, 1898. Fully 1,000 people participated in the ball honoring this occasion. Printed in Heber City Wasatch Wave.

John Murray Murdoch and Ann Steel Murdoch at their golden wedding celebration

John Murray Murdoch and Isabella Crawford at Ann Steel and John's golden wedding celebration

Mrs. Ann Murdock Passes Away.

Died 15 Dec 1909 — aged 82 years

Another Pioneer has Gone to Claim a Just Reward for the Labors of A Long and Useful Life.

At 1:00 a. m. Wednesday morning the spirit of "Aunt" Ann Murdock, peacefully and quietly took its flight from the tired, worn-out habitation in which it had labored for over eighty years. She had been failing for several years, sometimes she would have a very severe sick spell, then she would rally and feel better for a short time but she gradually grew more feeble as the machinery of life weakened and run down from the strain and burdens of years and the load of sorrows, cares, and troubles gathered during a long and active lifetime.

The last parting with our loved ones is always sad. To look upon the face of a dear relative or friend for the last time knaws at the very heart strings but in a case like this, where the life labors have been fully completed we would not call them back. "Aunt" Ann has laid her worn out body down to a well earned rest and her spirit has gone to claim a well earned reward. We will miss her pleasant, motherly smile, her wrinkled face and her gentle voice with its quaint Scotch accent, but we would not call her back to suffer pain, to endure sorrow nor to witness the suffering of others. The sorrow of all goes out to her lifelong companion, her aged husband, at whose side she has toiled, shoulder to shoulder, for almost sixty-two long years of married life. It is a hard ordeal for him but he would not call her back from that peaceful slumber.

Mrs. Ann Steel Murdock was born October 27, 1829, at Kirkconnel, Dumfrieshire, Scotland. She was a daughter of James and Elizabeth Hyslop Steel. She was married to John M. Murdock February 24, 1848, and joined the church of Jesus Christ of Latter-day Saints May. 29. 1850. She started

from Kirkconnel with her husband and two children for Salt Lake city January 1, 1852. After a long and tedious voyage the vessel went aground upon a sandbar near the mouth of the Mississippi river and they endured the riggors of hunger and thirst for two weeks before they were rescued. Here their babes contracted disease from which both died shortly after landing upon American soil. Their daughter Mary was born at Kansas city which was then the outfitting point for Utah.

After a trip of seventeen weeks in crossing the plains they reached Salt Lake city September 3rd. Eight years later, in 1860, they came as pioneers to Heber. She was the mother of fifteen children, eight of whom survive her. Besides these her posterity numbers 74 grand children and 61 great grand children.

She has always been an earnest worker in the church and took great interest in rendering assistance to others when in siekness or distress. She was president of the Relief Society for many years and held the same office in the Stake primary up to the time when her physical condition would not permit her to attend to the duties devolving upon her in that capacity. She also took a leading part in the Sunday school and mutual work; in fact she was always ready to respond to any call that was made upon her.

Funeral services were held in the stake tabernacle Thursday afternoon. The speakers were James C. Jensen, William Forman, Patriarch Thomas Hicken, Anna R. Duke president of the Stake Relief Society, William Lindsay, President Joseph R. Murdock, and Bishop Joseph A. Rasband. Each spoke in the highest terms of the saintly life and good works of the departed. Music was furnished by a chorus of mixed voices and a male quartette under the direction of Prof. D. A. Whitaker.

A large cortege of sorrowing relatives and friends followed the remains to the Heber cemetery where they were consigned to mother earth.

Isabella Crawford Murdoch

Isabella Crawford was born April 12, 1836 in Blantyre, Lanarkshire, Scotland. Her father was Andrew Crawford and mother Margaret McClure. When Isabella was six years old her father joined the British Army to go to war, went to Canada, and they never heard of him again until after his death a number of years later.

Her father's parents were Alexander Crawford and Ann Anthony and her mother's parents were Margaret Thom and George McClure. Isabella's mother is listed as having died on October 20, 1841, so Isabella would only have been five years old, and this would have been just before her father left with the army. Whom she lived with we don't know. It is said she was quite young when she went to work in the Blantyre Mills, where she learned the trade of weaver.

She was baptized into The Church of Jesus Christ of Latter-day Saints on August 16, 1855 in Scotland. It is said she was driven out of her home when she joined the Church. She emigrated to America, leaving all kindred, coming with four young girl companions, with whom she had labored at the Blantyre Mills. They were twelve weeks on the water sailing, and the ship was struck by lightning and eight sailors drowned.

These five girls, having to earn their living, found employment in the cotton mills in Holyoke, Massachusetts. Here they worked until they had saved enough to come to Utah. While working, Isabella became an expert weaver of fine linens. She had long black hair which she wore in two braids. One day a girl who worked beside her in the mill asked her why she didn't cut her hair off. Isabella replied she didn't want to. The girl said, "Well, it's too pretty," and with a pair of large scissors cut off one of the braids.

Isabella walked every step across the plains and arrived with her friends in Salt Lake City in 1858. They were taken to the public square with the other emigrants, where welcoming friends were in waiting to receive all of them except this lone girl, Isabella.

William Forman, having been engaged to marry one of the five girls, Catherine Campbell, was there to meet her, and he and Catherine asked Isabella to go with them to their home or to the home of the people where he was employed, which she did until she very soon found employment in Cottonwood and Salt Lake City.

In the meantime William Forman and Katie were married, and moved to Heber the same time as John M. Murdoch did. After laboring in Salt Lake City for some time Isabella came to Provo Valley to visit her friends, the Formans, and as the neighbors and friends lived close together and were all young people and very sociable, all soon became acquainted with this young girl. In the course of time she had many suitors for her hand in marriage.

John M. Murdoch and his wife Ann Steel were continually striving to keep the commandments of God, and the principle of plural marriage was taught and practiced in the Church. They made up their minds that if the way were opened up and the time became favorable they would obey this principle. John, in a patriarchal blessing he received in 1861, was told he would be blessed with wives and many children. So being close neighbors, they became well acquainted with each other and made known to all of them that this union was all right. With Ann Steel's full knowledge and consent John married Isabella Crawford on August 8, 1862 in the Endowment House in Salt Lake City, Utah.

Isabella, Ann, and John all lived together, each wife having her own area of their home. Isabella was the mother to four sons and three daughters as follows: Margaret Ann Murdoch Hawkes, Catherine Campbell Murdoch Hicken, James Crawford Murdoch, Brigham Murdoch, Robert Murdoch, John Murray Murdoch, Jr., and Isabella Crawford Murdoch. Robert died at age twenty-one of typhoid fever, and Margaret Ann also preceded her father and mother in death, leaving six motherless children. All of Isabella's children belonged to The Church of Jesus Christ of Latter-day Saints. Two of her sons, James and John Murray, filled honorable missions; Brigham was a bishop; and three of her grandsons took part in World War I in 1919.

Ann Steel had fifteen children in all, with nine growing to adulthood with Isabella's seven. Janett Osborne Murdoch McMullin, a daughter of Ann, said of them: "The two wives were true wives and true and loving mothers, sharing the burdens of rearing their families together. As I remember, at one time one child had the privilege of nursing both mothers, and did not know which was his own mother. Isabella was a true pioneer of this valley and state, assisting in many ways in the upbuilding of the community in which she lived. She was a knitter of beautiful fabrics and knit many useful articles. She went through the trials of pioneering and poverty without complaining and lived until they had comfortable homes with all the modern conveniences and even luxuries they desired."

Isabella's daughter, Isabella Crawford Murdoch Nicol, said, "I wonder if you liked to hear your mother laugh. We loved to hear Mother laugh. It had such a pleasant ring and was so cheering that we wanted to laugh with her. She was very determined, too, and when she said no we knew better than to ask her again. My mother had high ideals and a determination to carry on, which has ever been a guiding light to me. When Mother started school it was the custom for the children to give the teacher a curtsey every time they met. Her mother thought that once in the morning and again in the afternoon was enough and refused to do more. So after six days at school she was dismissed and sent home. That was all the schooling she ever had. Through her own efforts she became a good reader and an extra good Bible student. Many would come to her for a discussion of the scriptures. She was devoted to her church and held many responsible positions. She was blessed with the gift of speaking in tongues, and we children wondered if she were an angel from heaven as we listened to her one day in fast meeting."

"This is a testimony she bore to me and many others. She said, 'Nettie, (Janett Osborne Murdoch McMullin), what am I that God has been so good to me and brought me, a lone girl, to this favored land and given me all the blessings and privileges of the gospel; where I am surrounded with prophets of God and the holy priesthood and friends on every hand? And I have had the privilege of associating with men and women of God and had a patriarch of God to be the father of my children. So I say, "What am I?" And now this world has no charm for me. I am waiting to go, and your father and mother are coming every night to me and I am waiting to go with them.

Isabella Crawford Murdoch, better known as Aunt Bella, died at the home of her daughter, Mrs. David W. Hicken, Monday, April 10, 1916, of general debility, being eighty years old on Wednesday, the day of the funeral. Two of the funeral speakers said the following of her: "She was congenial and pleasant, always endeavoring to do good in the face of continued ill health." "Sister Murdoch had merited and would receive the blessings of the righteous." William Lindsay said he had known the departed more than fifty years and knew her to be a good woman. He testified that the family relations existing in the Murdoch family were of peace and pleasure. At the departure of her son John M. to fill a mission in New Zealand, she said that she might not live to see his return but rejoiced that he was going in the service of the Lord. She died before his return and was buried next to John and Ann.

I'm sure she would say the same today to her posterity as they continue to serve the Lord until we meet her, John, Ann, and all their children and become a forever family.

She Is Next to My Mother to Me

My memory turns back to my childhood days,
When with my father and mother to live,
A young bride she came,
And to us, Bella was her name.
She was beautiful, kind and joined in our glee.
Then I thought, "She is next to my Mother to me,"

When our fingers were mashed, and the slivers
    would pain;
We would all call for Bella, again and again.
If we cried with pain, some one would shout,
"Oh never mind, Bella will soon get it out."

In our tears, our sorrows, our joys and our mirth,
We would all gather round the old family hearth.
She would listen to our stories, and happy we'd be.
Then I said, "She is next to my Mother to me."

As to womanhood and manhood each were grown,
We'd leave the old homestead for homes of our
    own.
She would pray "That our lives could be happy and
    free."

Again I thought, "Yes, she is next to my Mother to
    me."

For eighty long years this lovely bride did live,
Her example to set, and wise council to give.
She had completed her labors on earth here below.
She said "I'm waiting your Father's call for me to
    go."

She told me one day, "Nettie, I'm left all alone.
Your Father and Mother, my companions, are gone,
But they are waiting and calling and coming for
    me."
Then I truly knew "She was next to my Mother to
    me."

In my vision I see that home over there,
Those beautiful crowns they have and do wear.
With loved ones, and honored ones their bright
    faces I see.
And still I know Bella is next to my mother to me.

Written in honor of Isabella Crawford Murdoch by her
step-daughter, Janett Murdoch McMullin

Isabella Crawford when she lived at the home of her daughter Catherine
Campbell Murdoch Hicken 1910–16.

Another Pioneer Called

Isabella Crawford Murdock, better known as "Aunt Bella", died at the home of her daughter Mrs. David W. Hicken, Monday, April 10, 1916, of general debility, being 80 years old on Wednesday, the day of the funeral.

Aunt Bella was one of the early pioneers of this valley, having come to Heber when a young woman and married John M. Murdock as a plural wife in 1862. To this union seven children were born and grew to manhood and womanhood in this community. They are Mrs. Margaret A. Hawks, who died in Idaho leaving a family of six children, Mrs. David W. Hicken of Heber, James C., a member of the high council, Brigham, bishop of Farnum, Idaho, Robert, who died of typhoid fever at the age of 21, John M., now on a mission in New Zealand, and Isabella C. wife of Hyrum Nicol of Duchesne.

Funeral services were held at the stake tabernacle Wednesday afternoon, April 12th, the services, which were well attended, being conducted by Bp. Crook of the Heber 3rd ward. The following songs: "Though Deepning Trials Throng Your Way," "Sister Thou Wert Mild and Lovely," and "Nearer My God to Thee" were sung by a mixed quartette consisting of Emd Murdock, Emma Carlile, Frank Epperson and Francis Carlile. Beautiful bouquets of flowers covered the casket, many coming from friends unable to attend the funeral.

The first speaker was Bishop Joseph A. Rasband of the Heber 2nd ward. He said that the departed sister had been a member of the 2nd ward ever since coming to Heber, until about a year ago when she was transferred to the 3rd ward. Said he had known Sister Murdock all his life. She was congenial and pleasant, always endeavoring to do good in the face of continued ill health. We have no occasion to mourn the departure of such as Sister Bella.

Henry L. McMullin said he knew the departed sister to be a righteous woman who has lived a righteous life. She joined the Church of Jesus Christ of Latter Day Saints when a girl of 17 years of age in her native land—Scotland, and left all relatives and friends who were near and dear to her and came to America for the gospel's sake. She worked in the factories of the eastern states for a number of years to earn money to come on to Utah. Spoke of the state of peace and rest for the righteous after death as told us by the Prophet Alma who said an angel had revealed these things unto him. Said that Sister Murdock had merited and would receive the blessings of the righteous.

Wm. Lindsay said he had known the departed sister for more than 50 years and knew her to be a good woman. Testified that the family relations existing in the Murdock family were of peace and pleasure, At the departure of her son John M. to fill a mission in New Zealand she said that she might not live to see his return, but rejoiced that he was going in the service of the Lord.

James C. Jensen of the stake presidency said he had been thinking ever since the opening song of the brevity of life which reminds him of the saying "Is Life Worth While." In the death of one such as Sister Murdock, the answer to this is "Yes." The posterity she has left, the fruits of her labors, all testify to the worth of such a life. What joy will be on the other side at meeting with her husband and companions who have gone before! All honor to such women! Her life is a testimony that life is worth living. The emaciated form lying before us will not always be the tabernacle of her spirit, but the spirit will attract to it until every particle will be restored to a perfect womanhood in the resurrection. The spirits of our ancestors are not far away. If Aunt Bella could give utterance to her greatest desire now, it would be that her posterity may remain faithful in the service of the Lord.

Bishop Crook said he had been intimately acquainted with the Murdock family, and wished to testify that the family of John M. Murdock had lived in peace and harmony notwithstanding there were two wives rearing families together. Admonished the children to emulate the good works of their parents. In behalf of the family, he thanked all who had assisted in any way during the sickness, death and burial of the deceased.

Interment was made in the Heber cemetery.

Helen July 19th 1873
Miss Maggie Murdoch
Linkieburn House
Muirkirk

My Dear Neice

Your very welcome and interesting Letter of June 18th came safe to hand July 15th: we ware all made glad to hear once more from our distant Friends; and more So; from they pen of a Young Lady whome none of us has ever seen in they flesh: yet they Spirit of your Letter throught Seemes So kind; So familiar: that I am constrained to Say; Maggie: I have Surley Seen you Some where Before; when I was about your age I had a Sweethert of your name that I Loved most affecanately; this perhaps is one reason why I find myself So familar with you: Be that ob it may; I asure you I am very hapy in having they pleasure of answering your very kind and intilligent Letter; fandely hoping that I may yet have many pleasing Opertunityes of they Same kind; we are hapy to heare that you are all well; and that mather Bears her affliction with So much petience I am hapy to know that She takes they Stars and Journal of discourses they are good companians and will help to comfort her and wiele away many a Lonley hour I am pleased to know you had a call from Elder Park; I have not seen Him in 15 years and was not awaire that He was in Scotland; those ather Elders whose

Mann you have Mentioned are all Strangers
to Me only I have Known there Characters
for Many years; I am happy to Know
that they Called on you; and more happy
that you Received them with Kindness for inso
doing you refreshed and Comforted the ffumble
Servents of God: who for the Sake of the
Gospile have Left there wives, there dear Little
Children, there Friends, and all the Comforts
of ffome; to travel amongst Strangers with
out purse or Scripe teling all who will
Listin, they may to Be Saived; those ffumble
men Leave there Blessings upon the ffouses an
Families of those who receive them. that the
future will disclose; therefore I Say as Paul
Saide Be Carefull to intertain Strangers for
Some thereby have intertamed Angles unaware
I am very happy to Learn that your father injoies
Good helth that Blessing which ffe So Much
Needs, in the midst of Many Cares and respon=
=sabilities; I much wonder how he Could find
time to go to Auchinleck twice and Still
think of Going to Edinbourough; teel ffim
not to do So; Let what ffe has already done
Sufice; he has proved ffis willingness. . . . . .
Besides if the Regester ant extendes only 50
years Back we can remember that Much —
My Brother James advises Me to Give this
Matter intirely up as ffe is Satisfied that
nothing Can be done; perhaps Nothing
More Can by done in this way; and if

So then we are Justified for God is Just and will not require of us that; that we can not perform: But I have other strings to pull upon Besides this one and if this will not work to our satisfaction we will try another God requires us to do our duty; and when we can do no more he will do the rest. But so sure as I write So sure will this thing be done some way or other. I will not Give up while Life Lasts and my Familey will take it up where I leave it; all the purposes of God are sure — we are all Much pleased with the Likness of Cousin James; I think Janett and Sarah have fallen in Love with Him already as I hear them Say they will compose a verse a pice and send to Him if they do I will enclose in this Letter we would Like Much to See Him here if he will pay us a visit we will make Him very welcome to our humble fare with a promice of plenty of it Such as it is. we are not rich in Money that is very scarce in this Countrey But we are blest with plenty to eat drink and more; I am not very well posted in buisness matters in Salt Lake City. we Live 40 — Miles from that place But there are many Railroads thraught the Teritory requiring many Engins; there are also Much Machinearey Being imparted in the Shape of woolen factory Steam Saw and grist Mills reapers and Mowers I think that a Good Steddy Machinist Might find Employmen. Wages of all

Kinds are higher here than they are any
where in they States; Living is almost as
cheap. we will be happy to form acquaintance
with David Sister Jannet yourself and all
Others who wish to favour us with a pew Lines
we are far away from Our Friends aur Kindred
and Old acquaintances; and when any favor
us with a pew Lines we feal much gratified
par as Cold water to a thursty Saul So
is Good news from a far Country
when you See any of our Kirkleannell
Friends pleas tell them to gin there
Adress and we wile write them a Lang
Letter Ann wishes Much to hear fram
them   pleas say to Father I thank Him
kindly far His attention to my Request and
pleas that in your next what expences is
due and Let Him trouble Himself no more
in this Matter untile I Shall further request
I am happy to Say that we are all well and all
Jain with Me in Kind Love to Father & Mother
David and James yourself and Sister Janet —
Sister Mary and Family are all well as also
all aur Friends hear! I have not Given you much
news this time. But in your next if you have any
question to ask upon any Subject whatever
with which I am acquainted; I will Be most
happy to Reply; Kind reguards to all inquiring
frends and Old acquaintances, Dear Maggie
I must Bid you adue at present, God Bliss you
farues. I am your affancate Uncle J. M. Murdock

Pioneer Memories

By Mrs. George F. Wells

My grandfather, Patriarch John M. Murdock was born in Gaswater in the year 1820. His youthful days were spent as a shepherd boy, roaming the green heathered hills of old Scotland.

He married Ann Steel and together they embraced the L. D. S. faith. They were convert- ed by the sincere testimony of her young brother James who had heard the strange religion preached in England.

Brigham Young had lashed that two shepherd boys with their Scotch collies be sent to Utah to herd his sheep. Franklin D. Richards, mission president, at once contacted grandfather and shortly thereafter with his wife, two children, a companion, and the dogs set sail on the Ken- nebc from Liverpool on Jan- uary 1, 1852. After nine weeks on the ocean they arrived in new Orleans where they char- tered a steamboat for the jour- ney up the Mississippi River. A ten day delay on a sand bar de- creased their food rations to a dangerously low level. James and Elizabeth, their sweet chil- dren, sickening on the oatmeal and blackish water began to waste away. Grandfather ask- ed a young man for some bread but was curtly refused. A burley stranger, seeing the chil- dren were starving, took the boy ashore and fed him, but he died that night. The little girl suc- cumed a few days later and was thought to have been buried at St. Louis, then an outfitting camp for the western trek. Grandfather said a stranger stepped up and after expressing sympathy, offered to send a wagon, free of charge to convey the child's coffin to the ceme- tery, but insisted that he and grandfather walk by way of a short cut so as to be there when the wagon arrived. The grave was dug and dedicated by grand- father, who then kindly thanked the stranger and with a heavy heart started back to camp.

Enroute to camp he noticed a large building and thought he would go inside. As he enter- ed, he saw a large vat of boiling water. To his surprise and hor- ror the head of his little girl, with her yellow curls came to the surface and disappeared. He later learned it was a dissecting establishment. The so-called friend had sold the child's body for medical science. This sor- row he kept to himself for over thirty years.

A month later his weary childless couple, were blessed with a baby girl. When the baby was eight days old, they mother walked and carried the babe the entire distance. Grand-

After joining the Abraham O. Smoot Co., grandfather was set apart to nurse and burry the dead, since cholera was taking the lives of many. On one oc- casion he covered his Scotch plaidy over the bodies of nine in one grave.

After many Indian scares, the journey was terminated when they reached the valley on Sep- tember 3. Brigham Young, ac- companied by Pitts brass band, personally gave the weary trav- elers a hearty welcome and gave them permission to stay in the Fort until their refuge could be built.

The shepherd boys with their dogs, the first in the valley, were doomed for more disappoint- ment. Brigham's sheep that he had purchased from emigrants enroute to Oregon had been nearly all devoured by we...'s and coyotes. The remainder had rented to his brother Lo- renzo.

John M. and Ann Steele Murdock on Their Golden Wedding Day.

Grandfather was given a job digging by hand, an acre and a half of potatoes, and he felt it was indeed a privilege to be em- ployed by a prophet of God.

He and his good wife saved means to bring his widowed mother, her brother James and his good wife and two sons to Utah. They started with the illfated Martin handcart com- pany, and Wee Granny, as she was called at the age of 74 pulled her cart to the foot of Chimney Rock, where through sheer exhaustion she laid down and died. Her last words were, 'Tell John I died with my face toward Zion.' James, a strong young man also succumbed and was buried at Bitter creek.

Undaunted courage led my grandfather and his family on After eight years in Salt Lake they loaded all their possessions in a wagon and with their four daughters moved to upper Provo Valley to what is now Heber City.

A large fort, three blocks long by two blocks wide, was build and under grandfather's super vision a log hall was erected, to serve as a church, school and for other gatherings.

He built a dugout in which to house his family until logs could be cut. Canals were dug; sage brush grubbed, rocks hauled, and crops planted. Altho the seasons were short and winters severe they pioneered and pros pered as few have ever done.

In 1862 he married as a plural wife a young scotch lassie named Isabel Crawford.

He with his wives and chil- dren took up a ranch 10 miles north of Heber and started in the sheep industry. He took a prominent part in every enter- prise from the first log cabin to the last public building; and in these efforts he donated both time and means.

The blessing Brigham Young gave him, that he would pros- per, have houses, and herds was literally fulfilled. A father of twenty-two children he lived long and well and at the age of ninety he passed away, beloved and honored.

For the past twenty-five years his posterity, numbering several hundred souls, have met in beautiful Provo Canyon, in a three day encampment where with song and pageantry they commemorate his memory.

He endured many trials, and knew the pangs of want. He also knew the joys of prosperity, but through it all he never wan- dered in his faith in God. He sleeps in lovely Wasatch Valley. Beside him lie his two faithful wives, who with him were courageous pioneers.

a true Story written by Malicieute Wells Feb. 14 - 1947 printed in the Green GeneraLin

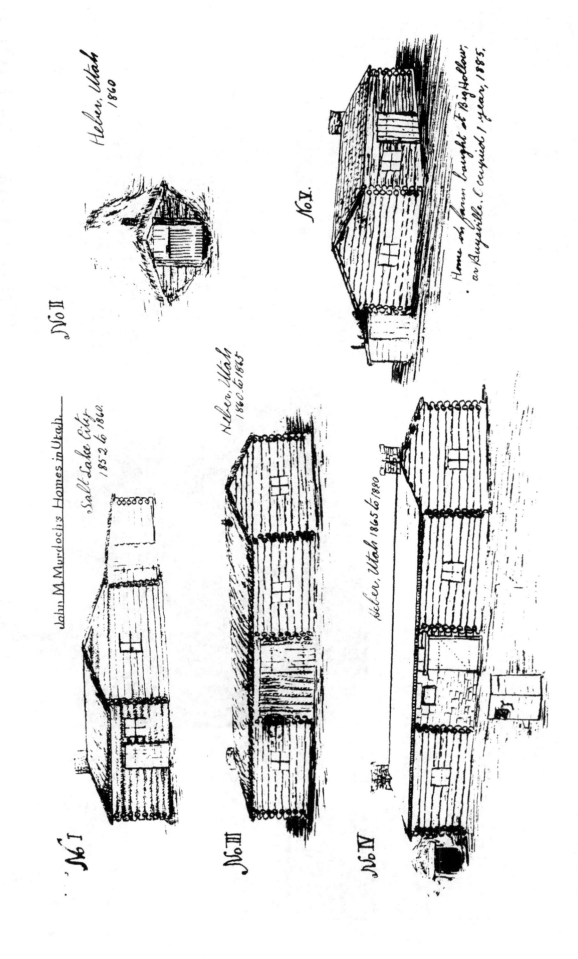

John M. Murdoch's Homes in Utah.

No. I
Salt Lake City
1852 to 1860.

No II
Heber, Utah
1860

No. III
Heber, Utah
1860 to 1865

No IV
Heber, Utah 1865 to 1880

No. V.
Home and farm bought at Big Hollow,
or Bugsville. C. acquired 1 year, 1885.

THESE DRAWINGS WERE
MADE FROM MEMORY BY
JOSEPH A. MURDOCK IN
THE 1930's .

1976

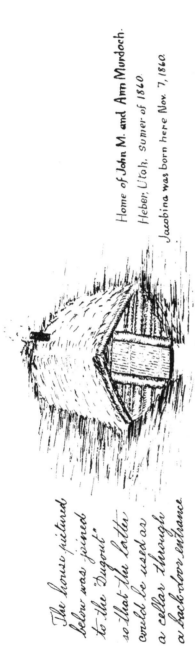

Home of *John M. and Ann Murdoch.*

Heber, Utah. Sumer of 1860.

Jacobina was born here Nov. 7, 1860.

The house pictured below was joined to the "Dugout" so that the latter could be used as a cellar through a back door entrance.

Home of John M. Murdoch and Ann and Isabella. 1860-65.

South

Bella's children born here: ↗

Margaret Ann born 19 May 1863
Catherine C. " 15 Nov. 1864

north

Ann's Children
born here:

John James 4 July 1863
Isabella " 21 April 1864
John William " 21 April 1864.

Representing the house built by John R. Murdoch in 1865.
on the spot where the large frame house stands which he
built in 1880, now owned by John J. Cummings, Heber, Utah.

Children born in this house were:

Isabella's children:

James C.   Born 11 Feb. 1869.
Brigham   "   2 Nov. 1870.
Robert   "   12 Sept. 1872
John Murray   "   1 May 1874.

Ann's children:

Thomas T.   Born 4 Mar. 1866.
Lucy Veronica   "   25 Nov. 1867.
Joseph A.   "   11 Mar. 1870
David S.   "   31 May 1872.
Millicent S.   "   21 Aug. 1874.

John Murray Murdoch home on ranch north of Heber City, Utah. Thought to be Uncle Jock (John Murray Murdoch, Jr.) standing in front.

John Murray Murdoch home west end of Heber City, Utah. Built in 1880.

John Murray Murdoch home by the Heber City, Utah depot. Ann Steel lived here. It was built after they were required by law to have separate households, about 1891.

John Murray Murdoch home of Grandma Bella and Grandma Ann. Each wife had own kitchen and bedroom and they shared a modern bathroom. Ann and John M. died here. Built about 1900 or later. 1st North and 1st West Heber City, Utah.

I Want To Go Over To Grandmother's

BRIGHAM MURDOCH

JOSEPH A. MURDOCH

I want to go over to Grand-ma's, She's always so good and so kind;
He tells me some won-der-ful stor-ies, Of herd-ing his dear daddy's sheep,

She just lets me run, jump and hol-ler, And tells me that she doesn't mind.
And roam-ing the high moun-tains over, Along with his broth-er called Pete.

She gave me a hand-ful of rais-ins, Some nuts and a big candy bar,
On dark storm-y nights with-out shel-ter, they lay in their damp, lonely bed;

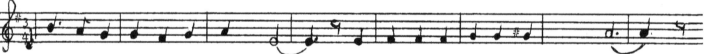

And said if I ever got hun-gry, To get me a cookie from her jar.
When roused by the howl of some prowl-er, They pulled the quilts over their heads.

I'd like you to meet dear old Grand-pa, He's old but he's big, strong and good;
Yes, I want to go over to Grand-ma's, And hope that I always will;

He lets me help him feed the chickens And bring in the kindling and wood.
And when I am old and they've left us, They'll live in my mem-ory still.

Nicknames

Ruth Schulz asked Maybell McMullin Moulton, the oldest living descendant of John Murray, and his granddaughter, to think of all the nicknames that John Murray Murdoch, wives, children, and grandchildren went by so we fourth, fifth, sixth, seventh, eighth, etc., generations will know who the older people are talking about. They are as follows:

Wives:
Ann Steel Murdoch—Muzz
Isabella Crawford Murdoch—Bella

Children:
Janett Osborne Murdoch McMullin—Net or Nettie
Jacobina Wells O. Murdoch Clegg—Jake
Millicent Sophia Murdoch Murdock—Gentie
Margaret Ann Murdoch—Mag
Catherine Campbell Murdoch Hicken—Kate
Robert Murdoch—Boot
John Murray Murdoch, Jr.—Jock
Isabella Crawford Murdoch Nicol—Tressa or Tressie

Grandchildren:
Jonathan Murdoch Duke—Dick
Mary Ann Duke—Doll
Jennett Duke—Nettie
James Monroe—Roe
Mary Isabell McMullin Moulton—Maybell
Emily Isabella Rasband—Embell
Janetta J. Clegg—Nettie
Lecia Murdoch—Lisa
Anna Isabella—Anabell

HUSBAND John Murray MURDOCH
Birth   28 Dec 1820
Place   Gaswater, Ayrshire, Scotland
Chr.   21 Jan 1821 Auchinleck Parish Church, Ayr., Scot.
Married 25 Feb 1848
Place   Kirkconnell, Dumfriesshire, Scotland
Death   6 May 1910 Heber, Wasatch, Utah
Burial   8 May 1910 Heber, Wasatch, Utah
Father   James MURDOCH
Mother   Mary MURRAY
Other wife (2) Isabella CRAWFORD (8 Aug 1862)

WIFE   (1) Ann STEEL
Birth   27 Oct 1829
Place   Kirkconnell, Dumfriesshire, Scotland
Chr.
Death   15 Dec 1909 Heber, Wasatch, Utah
Burial   16 Dec 1909 Heber, Wasatch, Utah
Father   James STEEL
Mother   Elizabeth KERR
Where was information obtained The James Murdoch Family
Organization Records

11TH CHILD Thomas Todd MURDOCH
Birth   4 Mar 1866 Heber, Wasatch, Utah
Married Sarah Ingeborg HANSEN 15 Jul 1915
Place   Salt Lake City, Salt Lake, Utah
Death   21 Oct 1953 Idaho Falls,Bonneville,Ida.
Burial   24 Oct 1953 Ashton, Fremont, Idaho

13TH CHILD Joseph A. MURDOCH
Birth   11 Mar 1870 Heber, Wasatch, Utah
Married Martha Ellen FORTIE 20 May 1891
Place   Logan, Cache, Utah
Death   27 Aug 1943 Vineyard, Utah, Utah
Burial   31 Aug 1943 Heber, Wasatch, Utah

14TH CHILD David Steele MURDOCH
Birth   31 May 1872 Heber, Wasatch, Utah
Married Mary Emily VAN WAGENEN 21 Oct 1891
Place   Midway, Wasatch, Utah
Death   1 Oct 1950 Provo, Utah, Utah
Burial   4 Oct 1950 Provo, Utah, Utah

15TH CHILD Millicent Sophia MURDOCH
Birth   21 Aug 1874 Heber, Wasatch, Utah
Married Edward Teancum MURDOCK 9 Dec 1891
Place   Heber, Wasatch, Utah
Death   7 Feb 1916 Heber, Wasatch, Utah
Burial   10 Feb 1916 Heber, Wasatch, Utah

3RD CHILD Mary Murray MURDOCH
Birth   20 May 1852 near Kansas City, Kansas
Married James DUKE 3 Oct 1868
Place   Salt Lake City, Salt Lake, Utah
Death   20 Dec 1917 Heber, Wasatch, Utah
Burial   Heber, Wasatch, Utah

4TH CHILD Ann MURDOCH
Birth   14 Sep 1854 SaltLakeCity,Salt L.Utah
Married William M. GILES 5 Jun 1871
Place   Salt Lake City, Salt Lake, Utah
Death   2 Jan 1890 Heber, Wasatch, Utah
Burial   5 Jan 1890 Heber, Wasatch, Utah

5TH CHILD Janett Osborne MURDOCH
Birth   20 Dec 1856 SaltLakeCity,Salt L.,Utah
Married Henry Lufkin McMULLIN 6 Dec 1875
Place   Salt Lake City, Salt Lake, Utah
Death   12 Jun 1949 Heber, Wasatch, Utah
Burial   15 Jun 1949 Heber, Wasatch, Utah

6TH CHILD Sarah Jane MURDOCH
Birth   15 Jan 1859 SaltLakeCity,Salt L.,Utah
Married Thomas Heber RASBAND 28 Nov 1878
Place   Salt Lake City, Salt Lake, Utah
Death   16 Jan 1933 SaltLakeCity,Salt L.,Utah
Burial   20 Jan 1933 Heber, Wasatch, Utah

7TH CHILD Jacobina Wells Osborne MURDOCH
Birth   7 Nov 1860 Heber, Wasatch, Utah
Married William Jonathan CLEGG 2 Dec 1880
Place   Salt Lake City, Salt Lake, Utah
Death   18 Oct 1933 Vineyard, Utah, Utah
Burial   Provo, Utah, Utah

DIED IN CHILDHOOD

	BORN	DIED
1ST CHILD Elizabeth MURDOCH	21 Nov 1848 Scotland	4 Apr 1852 St.Louis
2ND CHILD James MURDOCH	Jun 1850 Scotland	20 Mar 1852 Columbia
8TH CHILD John Murray MURDOCH JR.	4 Jan 1863 Heber,Utah	4 Feb 1863 H.Utah
9TH CHILD Isabella Lovina MURDOCH	21 Apr 1864 Heber,Utah	17 Jun 1870 H.Utah
10TH CHILD John William MURDOCH	21 Apr 1864 Heber,Utah	29 Aug 1864 H.Utah
12TH CHILD Lucy Veronica MURDOCH	25 Nov 1867 Heber,Utah	6 Jan 1873 H.Utah

JOHN MURRAY & ANN STEEL   MURDOCH
(Three Generations)

DESCENDANTS

M-Married
C-Had Children
D-Died as Child

JOHN MURRAY MURDOCH
Born 28 Dec 1820
Where Gaswater,Ayr.,Scot.
Died 6 May 1910
Where Heber, Wasatch, Utah

Married 25 Feb 1848
Where Kirkconnell,Dumf.Scot

ANN STEEL
Born 27 Oct 1829
Where Kirkconnell,Dumf.Scot
Died 15 Dec 1909
Where Heber, Wasatch, Utah

ELIZABETH MURDOCH
Nov 21 1848-Apr 4 1852

JAMES MURDOCH
Jun ? 1850-Mar 20 1852

MARY MURRAY MURDOCH
May 20 1852-Dec 20 1917
Married 3 Oct 1868
James Duke
Dec 21 1829-May 20 1892
Married 12 Jun 1906
William Ryan
Oct 2 1848-Aug 29 1936

ANN MURDOCH
Sep 14 1854-Jan 2 1890
Married 5 Jun 1871
William M. Giles
Sep 3 1846-Apr 30 1926
Married 29 Mar 1893
Rachel Howarth Fortie
Apr 19 1850-Jan 5 1943

JANETT OSBORNE MURDOCH
Dec 20 1856-Jun 12 1949
Married 6 Dec 1875
Henry Lufkin McMullin
Sep 4 1852-Dec 20 1932

SARAH JANE MURDOCH
Jan 15 1859-Jan 16 1933
Married 28 Nov 1878
Thomas Heber Rasband
Jan 15 1859-Jul 2 1899
Married 6 Sep 1918
William Lindsay
Feb 11 1847-May 14 1932

JACOBINA WELLS O. MURDOCH
Nov 7 1860-Oct 18 1933
Married 2 Dec 1880
William Jonathan Clegg
May 6 1859-Sep 15 1927

JOHN MURRAY MURDOCH JR.
Jan 4 1863-Feb 4 1863

ISABELLA LOVINA MURDOCH
Apr 21 1864-Jun 17 1870

JOHN WILLIAM MURDOCH
Apr 21 1864-Aug 29 1864

THOMAS TODD MURDOCH
Mar 4 1866-Oct 21 1953
Married 15 Jul 1915
Sarah Ingeborg Hansen
May 2 1895

LUCY VERONICA MURDOCH
Nov 25 1867-Jan 6 1873

JOSEPH A. MURDOCH
Mar 11 1870-Aug 27 1943
Married 20 May 1891
Martha Ellen Fortie
Jan 19 1871- Oct 7 1943

DAVID STEELE MURDOCH
May 31 1872-Oct 1 1950
Married 21 Oct 1891
Mary Emily Van Wagenen
Feb 19 1871-Mar 31 1943

MILLICENT SOPHIA MURDOCH
Aug 21 1874-Feb 7 1916
Married 9 Dec 1891
Edward Teancum Murdock
Jun 25 1872-Mar 12 1937
Married 25 Jun 1924
Bertha Mayho Jeffs
Jun 13 1885

	BORN	DIED
DUKE		
Jonathan Murdoch	Sep 9 1869	Oct 4 1942MC
Mary Ann	Sep 14 1871	Dec 20 1914MC
Janett	Mar 26 1873	Nov 11 1940MC
Lillie Isabella	Mar 21 1875	Feb 23 1940MC
John Murray	Jan 9 1877	Nov 14 1878D
Archibald Kerr	Oct 25 1878	Nov 6 1880D
James Monroe	Jul 2 1881	Jun 27 1907MC
Thomas T.	Dec 13 1883	Nov 6 1884D
GILES		
John Thomas	Sep 22 1872	Mar 6 1962MC
Mariah	May 4 1874	Dec 8 1876D
William Jr.	Oct 24 1875	Oct 15 1930
Jane Ann	Mar 13 1877	Oct 7 1966MC
George David	Jan 11 1879	Mar 21 1946MC
Sarah Elizabeth	Sep 30 1880	Dec 2 1915MC
Joseph Fielding	Jan 6 1882	Jul 10 1960MC
Orson Edward	Sep 25 1883	Jun 17 1956MC
James Alvin	Apr 18 1885	Feb 15 1970MC
Henry Alexander	Feb 15 1887	Jun 16 1930 MC
Charles Andrew	Mar 15 1888	Oct 17 1976 MC
MCMULLIN		
Sarah Jane	Aug 12 1876	Oct 20 1880D
Henry Pierce	Sep 20 1878	Mar 9 1919MC
John Edwin	May 3 1881	Oct 26 1971MC
Gladys Jacobina	Apr 18 1884	Dec 27 1931MC
Mary Isabell	Sep 10 1887	MC
Annie Janett	Jan 11 1891	MC
Thomas Heber	Oct 8 1893	MC
RASBAND		
Ann Elizabeth	Oct 20 1879	Aug 7 1928MC
Heber Raymond	Mar 28 1882	Mar 23 1948MC
Emily Isabella	Jan 6 1886	Jul 2 1967MC
Jennie Hyslop	Sep 19 1889	Sep 3 1904D
CLEGG		
Tillie	Sep 25 1881	Jun 13 1900D
Anna Isabella	May 20 1883	Mar 20 1916MC
Jacobina	Nov 13 1884	Nov 10 1975C
Janetta Juventa	Oct 27 1886	Aug 13 1977MC
William Francis	Nov 20 1888	Dec 17 1959MC
John Wallace	Nov 20 1888	Jun 28 1971MC
Malicent	Sep 18 1890	Feb 21 1982 MC
Lewis	Feb 11 1892	Jul 20 1968MC
Joy Osborne	Jan 9 1894	Dec 13 1969MC
Elinora	Jan 6 1396	MC
Henry Murray	Sep 3 1897	Sep 3 1897D
Brigham Otis	Jul 7 1899	Sep 29 1899D
Mary Verona	Jul 7 1899	MC
Joseph Heber	Jun 15 1901	MC
Thomas Edwin	Sep 27 1903	Sep 27 1903D
MURDOCH		
Thomas Todd	Nov 23 1916	Sep 17 1928D
LaVaughn	Aug 24 1918	M
Della Ann	Mar 22 1921	MC
Clara Marie	May 1 1923	Apr 28 1953M
Betty Mae	Mar 28 1925	MC
Gilbert Dean	May 10 1927	MC
Lynn Ray	Jan 17 1930	MC
MURDOCH		
Lecia	Sep 10 1892	Nov 21 1918D
Dona	Oct 27 1894	Mar 2 1966MC
Murray Alexander	Sep 13 1896	Jan 2 1952MC
Orpha May	Apr 3 1899	Jan 13 1902D
Martha Blanch	Apr 14 1901	Sep 18 1911D
Harold Joseph	May 1 1903	Oct 13 1975MC
Vida	Aug 27 1905	MC
Mary Gladys	Aug 14 1908	MC
Elroy	Dec 11 1910	MC
Cuthbert Fortie	Apr 11 1912	MC
Phyllis Rachel	Aug 21 1914	MC
Joan	Mar 11 1917	MC
MURDOCH		
Annie Pearle	Apr 14 1892	Apr 15 1892D
David Ellis	Apr 7 1893	Jul 15 1896D
Lilliard	Jun 10 1896	Apr 14 1900D
Emily Aritha	Jan 14 1898	MC
Ervan	Dec 29 1899	Jan 10 1953MC
Minnie LaPreal	Mar 26 1902	Oct 13 1930MC
Eva May	Jan 9 1904	MC
Lillie	Oct 24 1905	Sep 18 1978MC
Atha LeIsle	Apr 17 1907	MC
Chloe	Sep 9 1908	MC
Ray	Jul 26 1910	Feb 14 1975MC
Hattie	Dec 17 1911	Dec 20 1911D
Ethel Lucile	Jun 17 1913	MC
Velda	Nov 17 1914	MC
Emmitt	Apr 16 1916	MC
MURDOCK		
Murray Stacy	Jun 24 1892	Stillborn D
Edward Phares	Apr 11 1894	Jun 26 1961MC
Artnur	Jun 7 1897	Mar 1 1978M
Clarence	Jan 1 1900	Jan 20 1980MC
Prenetta	Dec 18 1901	Sep 7 1954MC
Annabell	Apr 18 1904	Oct 23 1947MC
Joseph Stacy	Jul 27 1906	MC
John Murray	Feb 17 1909	MC
Alma Robert	Feb 28 1912	M
Barney	Jul 13 1914	Apr 12 1929D
Edward Thomas	Oct 10 1925	MC
Bert	Nov 14 1929	M

HUSBAND John Murray MURDOCH

Birth	28 Dec 1820
Place	Caswater, Ayrshire, Scotland
Chr.	21 Jan 1821 Auchinleck Parish, Ayrshire, Scotland
Married	9 Aug 1862
Place	End. House, Salt Lake City, Salt Lake, Utah
Death	6 May 1910 Heber, Wasatch, Utah
Burial	8 May 1910 Heber, Wasatch, Utah
Father	James MURRAY
Mother	Mary MURRAY
Other Wives (if any):	(1) 24 Feb 1848 Ann STEEL

WIFE (2) Isabella CRAWFORD

Birth	12 Apr 1836
Place	Blantyre, Lanarkshire, Scotland
Chr.	
Death	10 Apr 1916 Heber, Wasatch, Utah
Burial	12 Apr 1916 Heber, Wasatch, Utah
Father	Andrew CRAWFORD
Mother	Margaret McCLURE
Other Wives (if any):	

Where was information obtained? Tressa Garrett & Guy Murdoch.

*List complete maiden name for all females.

1st Child Margaret Ann MURDOCH

Birth	19 May 1863 Died 11 Mar 1904
Place	Heber, Wasatch, Utah
Married to	Lewis Joshua Hawkes
Married	7 Nov 1889
Place	Logan, Cache, Utah

2nd Child Catherine Campbell MURDOCH

Birth	15 Nov 1864 Died 6 Mar 1945
Place	Heber, Wasatch, Utah
Married to	David William HICKEN
Married	21 July 1886
Place	Logan, Cache, Utah

3rd Child James Crawford MURDOCH

Birth	11 Feb 1869 Died 14 Aug 1959
Place	Heber, Wasatch, Utah
Married to	Sarah Elizabeth GILES
Married	27 Nov 1901
Place	Salt Lake City, Salt Lake, Utah

4th Child Brigham MURDOCH

Birth	2 Nov 1870 Died 13 May 1947
Place	Heber, Wasatch, Utah
Married to	(1) Mary Blanche ALEXANDER
Married	16 Dec 1891
Place	Logan, Cache, Utah

4th Child Brigham MURDOCH

Birth	2 Nov 1870 Died 13 May 1947
Place	Heber, Wasatch, Utah
Married to	(2) Martha Louannie HARMON
Married	8 Apr 1903
Place	Salt Lake City, Salt Lake, Utah

5th Child Robert MURDOCH

Birth	12 Sep 1872
Place	Heber, Wasatch, Utah
Married to	unmarried
Died	3 Sep 1891
Place	Heber, Wasatch Co., Utah

6th Child John Murray MURDOCH

Birth	1 May 1874 Died 26 Apr 1928
Place	Heber, Wasatch, Utah
Married to	(1) Minnie Marie MILLER
Married	30 Jan 1904
Place	Salt Lake City, Salt Lake, Utah

6th Child John Murray MURDOCH

Birth	1 May 1874 Died 26 Apr 1928
Place	Heber, Wasatch, Utah
Married to	(2) Cora Leona VAIL Bigler
Married	5 Jan 1921
Place	Salt Lake City, Salt Lake, Utah

7th Child Isabella Crawford MURDOCH

Birth	8 Jan 1876 Died 1 Dec 1940
Place	Heber, Wasatch, Utah
Married to	Hyrum Chase NICOL
Married	23 Sep 1903
Place	Salt Lake City, Salt Lake, Utah

10th Child

Birth	
Place	
Married to	
Married	
Place	

Place Picture of Child in Left Blank — Place Picture of Wife or Husband in Right Blank

Or Wedding Picture To Cover Both Blanks

JOHN MURRAY & ISABELLA CRAWFORD MURDOCH
(Three Generations)

DESCENDANTS

	BORN	DIED
HAWKES		
Lewis	Aug 2 1890	Aug 19 1974
Hazen Araho	Jul 20 1893	Apr 8 1976MC
Isabella Priscilla	Apr 7 1896	MC
Golden Murray	Apr 8 1898	Aug 29 1898D
Robert Joshua	Nov 16 1899	MC
Mary Deon	Mar 18 1902	M
Margaret Ann	Mar 5 1904	MC
Girl ?		D
Arthur E.	Jul 3 1914	??

MARGARET ANN MURDOCH
May 19 1863-Mar 11 1904
Married 7 Nov 1889
Lewis Joshua Hawkes
Jul 22 1867-Apr 23 1943

Married ? 1910 (Div)
Emily (Povey) Jay H.E.
Jan 4 1877-Jul 13 1954

Married 4 Aug 1925
Martha Easterling D.D.K.

HICKEN		
Zoa	Jun 26 1888	Jun 26 1968MC
Zola	Jun 26 1888	Aug 15 1970MC
David Rodney	Oct 20 1889	May 9 1929MC
Mary	Sep 11 1892	Stillborn D
John Murray	May 16 1893	Jun 3 1893D
Thomas Rollo	Jun 8 1895	Jan 6 1920MC
Dora Isabella	Jun 24 1901	MC
Ward M.	Jul 5 1904	MC
Jennie Ann	Nov 13 1909	MC

CATHERINE CAMPBELL MURDOCH
Nov 15 1864-Mar 6 1945
Married 21 Jul 1886
David William Hicken
Aug 8 1861-Oct 31 1953

MURDOCH		
Mary Althora	Jan 25 1903	M
Sarah Laraine	Jul 1 1904	Dec 25 1964MC
James Ruelof	Sep 18 1906	MC
George Merrol	Dec 16 1908	MC
John Bard	Sep 4 1910	MC
Grant Brigham	Mar 29 1913	
Ruby Isabell	May 7 1915	MC
Thomas Verd	Feb 5 1918	MC

JAMES CRAWFORD MURDOCH
Feb 11 1869-Aug 14 1959
Married 27 Nov 1901
Sarah Elizabeth Giles
Dec 4 1878-Aug 2 1961

JOHN MURRAY MURDOCH
Born 28 Dec 1820
Where Gaswater,Ayr.,Scot.
Died 6 May 1910
Where Heber,Wasatch,Utah

Married 9 Aug 1862
Where Salt Lake City,Utah

ISABELLA CRAWFORD
Born 12 Apr 1836
Where Blantyre,Lanarkshire
Died 10 Apr 1916   Scot.
Where Heber,Wasatch,Utah

MURDOCH		
Robert Rue	Nov 16 1892	Sep 19 1929MC
Blanche Priscilla	Feb 7 1904	MC
Brigham Dallas	Jun 4 1907	MC
Reed Chase	Nov 17 1909	MC
Thomas Hammon	Mar 16 1912	MC
Laura Jean	Jun 25 1914	MC
Tressa Isabell	Jan 5 1918	MC
Martha Lucile	Oct 3 1919	MC
James Howard	Mar 8 1922	MC
Wallace Pierce	Oct 23 1924	MC
Katherine Mearl	Aug 5 1926	MC

BRIGHAM MURDOCH
Nov 2 1870-May 13 1947
Married 16 Dec 1891
Mary Blanche Alexander
Feb 16 1873-Jun 22 1893

Married 8 Apr 1903
Martha Louannie Hammon
Oct 11 1885-Jun 30 1962

ROBERT MURDOCH
Sep 12 1872-Sep 3 1893

M-Married
C-Had Children
D-Died as Child

MURDOCH		
Minnie	? 1905	Stillborn D
Annabell	Sep 10 1907	Sep 14 1907D
Bessie	Feb 26 1909	Feb 12 1980MC
Raymond Nelson	Nov 18 1911	Oct 30 1975MC
BIGLER		
Frieda Jessie	Apr 10 1918	MC
Wanda Leona	Aug 25 1916	MC
MURDOCH		
Phyllis Beth	Aug 17 1926	MC
WALL		
Earl Vail	Jul 26 1930	MC

JOHN MURRAY MURDOCH JR.
May 1 1874-Apr 26 1928
Married 30 Jan 1904
Minnie Marie Miller
Oct 13 1878-Dec 19 1911

Married 5 Jan 1921
Cora Leona Vail
Mar 12 1894-Sep 10 1970
Married 4 Nov 1915
Jesse Bigler (1)(Died)
Married 7 Mar 1929
James Earl Wall (Div)
Married 23 May 1953
Jack Esmond McKnight

NICOL		
Thomas Murdoch	Aug 26 1904	MC
Hyrum Chase Jr.	Mar 19 1906	MC
Kenneth Crawford	Jul 11 1908	MC
John Murray	Jun 20 1912	MC
Alma Victor	Mar 6 1916	MC
Alva Moroni	Mar 6 1916	MC
Brigham Rue	Jun 27 1919	Nov 19 1963MC
Donnavieve	Jul 12 1923	MC

ISABELLA CRAWFORD MURDOCH
Jan 8 1876-Dec 1 1940
Married 23 Sep 1903
Hyrum Chase Nicol
Feb 9 1876-May 20 1945

Mary Murray Murdoch, James Duke, and William Ryan

Mary Murray Murdoch was born May 20, 1852, on the bank of a small ditch or creek at a wood camp nine miles from Kansas City, Missouri. Her father, John Murray Murdoch, said the following concerning the event in a letter written to Mary, who was working in Salt Lake City:

Entirely forgot to post until today. Please excuse my neglect and write soon.

Heber May 30th, 1896
My Dear Daughter Mary,

We got your loving little letter wrote on your 44th birthday all right, while scanning it over many reflections came to our minds of the past. I thought of the first time that I looked at your pleasant little face. It was in a very small tent put up in a hurry for the occasion, your mother being already in hard labour. You very soon made your first appearance to us in the midst of the most terrific thunder storm I have witnessed either before or since. The couch on which you and your Mother still lay was yet on the floor, and hail and rain had fallen all over camp to the depth of six inches or more and beginning to come into the tent. But the camp being nearby some growing timber, I soon got some sticks and soon had you and Mother and a bedspread high and dry above the slush and mud.

Camp laid over a day or two until the storm was over and the roads dried up a little. During this time I was doctor, nurse and cook, washer-woman and general superintendent. Your Mother had provided some tea, a bottle of wine and a few crackers. Aside from this we had flour and bacon. I fed your mother on fried donuts and bacon.

She did much better all along with you than any of the rest, either before or afterwards. I suppose as the old saying is, the back is made for the burden that it has to carry. Your mother carried you in her arms over the plains more than 1000 miles, and was healthy and strong. But ever since then I have pained to see your sweet little innocent lips stained with the juice of wild roots for want of any other food. And altho in your early life you suffered much privation and passed through many hardships, I am happy to know that you had faith to endure all with patience and womanly fortitude. And thank heaven better days have come to us all.

I am happy to tell you that those who were sick when you left are all well. Stella, Cliff Hickens death was very sudden, of which you no doubt have heard. Mary Ann and all the rest of your family except Dick were over and paid us a visit. They are all well. I expect you have seen the program for decoration day but the storm and floods prevented it. Is expected tomorrow (Monday) if the weather will permit. It is still raining and the waters are very high. All is well here at present. Some of us may be in about the fourth if all is well, if so we will surely see you. Mother sends kind love to your self David and Lizzie and all inquiring friends. Not forgetting your precious jewel the baby. Please excuse this awful handwriting, it is the very best my old cramped fingers will allow.

From your loving father, J.M. Murdock

Her mother, Ann Steel Murdoch, said that while she was in the agony of labor, she would reach out and get water with her hand and to relieve her discomfort would bathe her face and hands. The cholera had broken out in the camp and many people were dying. The guard on duty that night heard her crying and went to the tent to inquire who had cholera there, but he learned that a little baby girl had just been born to this poor couple, they having recently buried their two children on the trip down the Mississippi River as they were traveling toward their goal of Zion (Utah). Sister Elizabeth, the oldest, was three years eight months and brother James was one year eight months old at death. What a joy and comfort it must have been to John and Ann to have a new baby. They named her Mary Murray Murdoch after her paternal grandmother, "Wee Granny," who was just four feet seven inches tall and weighed a little over ninety pounds. Mary was the third child in this family out of fifteen children to be born, six brothers and nine sisters.

It was nine months from the time Mary's parents, John and Ann, had left Scotland until they arrived in Salt Lake City September 3, 1852. Mary's father, John Murray Murdoch, after joining The Church of Jesus Christ of Latter-day Saints in 1850 in Scotland, was called by the prophet of the Church, Brigham Young, to come to Zion to herd his sheep. Upon arriving and receiving a kindly welcome from Brigham Young after being introduced as the Scotch sheepherder, he was told the wolves had eaten many of the sheep and Brigham's brother was tending the rest. However, Brigham gave him some good advice and helped him to find employment. John worked some for him digging his potatoes and doing odd jobs. John had quite a struggle the next few years, as did most of the pioneers, to get food and shelter for his family. Ann with her little daughter Mary would go out in the hills and dig sego and thistle roots and eat them to appease their hunger. During this time three more daughters were born to them: Ann, Janett Osborne, and Sarah Jane. Mary was the big sister and she assumed a lot of responsibility for one so young by taking care of her little sisters and helping her mother in many ways.

In a story of Mary's life written by her sister, Janett O.M. McMullin, she writes: "Mary grew to be a nice little girl and was such a comfort to her parents after losing their two oldest children. Her life was made up of pioneering even when she was a very young child. When Ann was born in 1854, they grew up as twins and helped to make their home a happy one. Mary helped with the chores and when her father went into the chicken and wild duck business, she helped her mother pluck out feathers, then she would be so proud to dress up and go with her mother to deliver the nicely prepared ducks and chickens to the home of Brigham Young and the apostles.

"She also helped her mother make pillows and feather beds by stuffing the feathers in them. Mother (Ann) at this time was young and spry and went to market neatly dressed with a smiling face—and the whole family would accompany her and put their best foot forward rejoicing and being so happy to be able to work for the prophet Brigham Young and his apostles.

"One of the apostles gave father a beautiful book with a large picture of Brigham Young on the front of it. It was one of our prized possessions. One day when mother had gone to the market, Mary took the beautiful book down off the shelf and all the children were so delighted to kiss the picture of Brigham Young that they rubbed the nose off the picture. We all had to learn by degrees."

When the grasshoppers came and devoured their crops, and food was scarce, many of the Saints had to live on roots dug from the ground. There was one whole week that Mary never tasted bread. She would say, "Keep the bread for the babies and I will eat some roots with a little milk."

Mary's family lived in Salt Lake City for eight years. Then her father, John, sold their home, and with his wife and daughters moved to a new settlement in Heber City, Utah. They arrived in this new settlement on Mary's eighth birthday, the twentieth day of May, 1860. It took three days with oxen team to drive from Salt Lake City to Heber City, and all the way the little girls sang, "The twentieth day of May is Mary's birthday."

John and Ann lived the rest of their lives in Heber City. Soon after they arrived they secured some land and also a place in the fort, where John made a dugout for his family to live in until he could put in his crops. He also supervised the building of the first schoolhouse built, which was constructed of logs and stood in the old fort. This building served for schools, meetings, dances, and other public gatherings for about five years. Mary attended school and church in this building.

As the settlement of Heber City grew Mary attended other schools, and her father was able to provide bigger, better homes for his family. Sister Janett says of this time, "Mary did enjoy the conveniences in their new home and the schools she attended. She loved all the frivolities of school life—coasting, snowballing and skating on the frozen ponds of ice, also riding in the long sleds in the winter time with the oxen pulling the sled. She loved to make candles to light log rooms for their little plays and dances.

"Mary was our older sister and was a leader and helper to all of us during our childhood days and a comfort and guide to us in our married lives. She always helped father with all the work, as our boys in the family were too small. She made money picking and drying hops and selling them to dealers. She also made money by picking currants. She was a lovely vision to all of us in the family."

Mary loved to sing and dance and appear in amateur plays. She was young, slim, pretty, and full of life, and while acting in the amateur plays she became acquainted with James Duke, a very popular man with a great personality. He was president of the Dramatic Society Association. He acted in and directed the first plays produced in Heber City. He was instrumental in building the first playhouse, or theater hall, as it was called. He also played the fiddle for the dances and was well liked by everyone. For many years he arranged the amusements for the early pioneers of Heber City.

Mary and James fell in love, and he asked her to be his plural wife. He had been married to his first wife, Almira Moore, since 1851, and they had seven children at this time. Mary had been going with a fine young man who was single, and he also asked her to marry him, but she turned him down to become the plural wife of James Duke. So on October 3, 1868, in the Salt Lake City Endowment House, Mary at age sixteen and James Duke at age thirty-nine became married.

Zoe Johnson, Mary's granddaughter, asked her Aunt Christina Duke, the wife of Mary's oldest son (Jonathan or "Dick") how in the world great grandfather and grandmother Murdoch (John and Ann) could consent for their oldest child, who had been such a comfort and help to them, to marry a man twenty-three years older than she, especially when he had a wife and such a large family. She said they tried very hard to persuade her to marry her single young man, but she had fallen in love with the popular Mr. Duke and was bound and determined to marry him. Zoe goes on to say, "I have wondered many times if she hadn't regretted this decision. She loved her eight children and was always loyal to her husband although, at times, her life was a bitter struggle to survive.

Mary was a firm believer in the gospel and all the principles taught by The Church of Jesus Christ of Latter-day Saints, including polygamy, taught at that particular time. In fact, she had seen the principle of polygamy demonstrated with great harmony in her own family. Her father, John Murray Murdoch, had been married for fourteen years to Ann Steel and had seven children by her, five living, when he took a second wife, Isabella Crawford. She was a pretty, dark-haired young woman who had joined the Church in Scotland and had come to Zion to live. They were married when Mary was ten years old and for six years before her own marriage she had witnessed a plural marriage that had been most successful. During those

six years six new babies were born into her family, so she must have had to help a lot since she was the oldest child.

"Grandma Ann and Grandma Bella, as they were called, were not only polygamous wives but they were dear friends and helped each other raise their children as if they were their own. I have heard my mother (Janet Duke Hansen) and grandmother (Mary M. Duke) say that there had never been a quarrel or harsh word between them. I remember when I was visiting my Grandmother Duke when I was very young in Heber City, I saw two darling little ladies arm-in-arm coming up the walk smiling. They were both dressed in black with long full skirts, black silk blouses with high necks over their shoulders, and small black beaded capes. On their head they wore little black bonnets with brims on them, tied under their chins in a bow. They patted my head and said, 'You must be Nettie's little blonde girl.' They were so noble and quaint I have never forgotten them. At the same time I remember visiting the duplex with my Grandmother Duke. She explained to me that each wife had her own side of the home."

Mary Murdoch Duke was married to James Duke for twenty-four years. He died in Wallsburg, at the home of his first wife, when he was sixty-three years old, leaving Mary a widow at age forty. But in all her married life she had the responsibility of supporting and taking care of her large family. In the first thirteen years of her marriage she had eight children. She lived all of her married life to James Duke on the corner now known as Second East in a dirt-roof house. There were not many who suffered more hardships than she did. She was a wonderful, hard-working woman, making her own living washing, ironing, nursing, and dressmaking while taking care of her eight children.

Her mother had taught her how to sew as her mother's mother had taught her how to do it in Scotland. Her Grandmother Steel had been commissioned to sew and decorate a lovely dress for Queen Victoria. Under her mother's tutelage Ann became so skilled in embroidering that she was allowed to embroider flowers on this beautiful dress for Queen Victoria. Thus, Mary, with this skill, and with the knitting taught to her by her father, John, helped to support her family. Her reputation as a fine seamstress spread, and she made many beautiful dresses for the women of Heber City. One was a beautiful wedding dress for Aunt Teen Duke (Christina), her oldest son "Dick's" wife. It was made of white organdy with ruffles all around the bottom and a petticoat about five yards around. Annie Rasband, Mary's niece said, "Janet (Duke Hansen) used to come to Heber City from Park City when she was a young girl with the most beautiful stylish clothes made by her mother, Mary, who was working in Park City at the time. She would let me try them and I was so impressed. She was the envy of the young ladies of Heber City."

Shortly after Mary was married, James bought some land for a farm in Wallsburg and built a home for his first wife and her family that grew to a total of eleven children in all. He evidently spent most of his time on the farm trying to feed his large families. He must have helped Mary some, but most of the diaries and journals tell how Mary had to work and struggle and suffered while raising her family, but many pioneer women at that time did. Between farming seasons James Duke worked as a mason. His father, Jonathan O. Duke, was bound out as an apprentice to learn the mason trade for ten years in England, and he taught James, who in turn taught Johnathan, Mary's oldest son, this trade. When they built the stake house he and Johnathan plastered the whole building. Aunt Teen (Christina) Duke, Johnathan's wife, said, "I don't know how Mary ever made it because Grandpa Duke did very little for her."

When Mary was seventeen, after four days and nights of suffering, her son Johnathan Murdoch Duke was born. You could almost say mother and son grew up together. She always said he was one of the pioneers. At ten years of age he was doing a man's work, helping to support the family. Johnathan Murdoch's history in "How Beautiful Upon the Mountains" says, "Each child had to do his share to help with the living." Dick herded their four cows and as many more as he could get. He took them to the foothills above the cemetery. He did this until he was older and could do more work. He worked one summer for Henry McMullin's mother, who was building a hotel where Ashton's store now stands. For this work he added a room with two small rooms upstairs to their one-room home. His mother was made very happy. He next worked for Will Clegg for lumber and added a room on the back of the house. They thought they were in heaven to have a house that the rain didn't come in.

Grandma Duke, Mary's mother-in-law, gave Mary ten acres of hay land which young Dick had to work half the summer to get the hay up so they would have some to sell and to feed their animals.

In their little two-room house Mary's eight children were born: Johnathan Murdoch Duke, 1869; Mary Ann 1871; Janet, 1873; Lillie Isabell, 1875; John Mur-

ray, 1877; Archibald Kerr, 1878; James Monroe, 1881; and Thomas T., 1883. When Mary was twenty-five years old her fifth child, John Murray, fifteen months old, died of summer complaint (called commonly diarrhea). In 1880 when Mary was twenty-eight years old, she and three of her children came down with the dreaded diphtheria. The children were Dick, Lillie, and Archie Kerr. It was a heartrending time for this little mother. Archie died of this terrible disease November 6. Dick was on the point of death for many days and recovered after a long illness. Mary and her daughter Lillie were very ill but finally recovered also. The only medicine Mary had to doctor her children with was alcohol. She would dip a cracker in alcohol and feed it to the children. Dick said, "It was terrible." Her oldest little daughters, Doll (Mary Ann) and Net (Janet), ages nine and seven, were banished to the back lot and stayed in an old buggy. They were not allowed in the house for fear they would get this very contagious disease.

Four years later, little baby Thomas, one year old, died of summer complaint. He was Mary's eighth and last child. So by age thirty-two she had given birth to eight children and lost three of them to illness. As her family began to grow up they were able to work and help Mary with the food and clothing for the family. The little girls would go out and do housework and take care of children.

Between 1891 and 1893 three of Mary's children were married and James Duke died. Dick (Johnathan) married Christina Lindsay, Mary Ann (Doll) married Robert Simpson, and Lillie married Archie Shanks. Mary had the opportunity to live with the family of Dr. Lindsay and take care of his son Crawford. She remained there one year. At this time she had only one child at home, James Monroe (Roe), who was about eleven or twelve years old. He went to live with his brother Dick and wife Christina. He remained with them until he married. Nettie (Janet), Mary's other daughter, was working in Park City. During one of Mary's visits there she met the Keith family. Mr. Keith had struck it rich in a silver mine in Park City and had become a millionaire. Their son, David, was five months old and they wanted a nurse for him. So Mary was employed for this work. She lived in the beautiful mansion the Keiths had built on Brigham Street (South Temple) in Salt Lake City, Utah. The Keiths became very fond of Mary, and she was always treated as a member of the family. They spent most of their winters in California, New York, and Florida. One year they toured Europe. Mary visited many interesting places.

In Italy they visited Naples and climbed to the crater of Mount Vesuvius and looked down into it. They visited the Blue Grotto in Capri, also the ruins of Herculim and Pompei in Naples, Italy.

But the greatest thrill of her trip to Europe was her visit to Scotland and the old home of her ancestors in the towns of Gaswater and Kirkconnel. Her mother and father were born and married in Scotland. She visited some of her mother's sisters and one brother. She took young David with her and when she got off the train there were many people waiting at the depot, but she had no trouble locating her mother's sisters. The family resemblance was so great she walked right up to them. They were all delighted to see her and graciously gave her many tea parties so she could meet the family and their friends.

When Mary returned to Utah she brought back some beautiful Scotch plaid shawls for her mother, daughters, and daughters-in-law. When she came home to Heber City, the entire Murdoch clan, including grandparents, parents, children, grandchildren, and great grandchildren, eagerly gathered to hear Mary tell them all about their dear family they had left behind when they had joined the Church about forty-five years before. Annie Rasband told Zoe Hansen Johnson the following about the occasion- "There was great excitement because Mary was the first member of the family to visit Scotland since 1.852: She said Mary was beautifully dressed and had a lovely figure. She seemed quite sophisticated to us. Mary was delighted to be with her family again and felt very thankful to her Heavenly Father that she had the opportunity to visit the homeland and make this wonderful trip.

When David Keith was five years old it was necessary for him to have a governess instead of a nurse. So Mary came back to Heber City. She had had a marvelous experience living in luxury in the beautiful Keith Mansion for five years. She remained friends with the Keiths, especially David, and visited them often. At her funeral a huge blanket of pink roses with the word "Nanny" written on it was sent by young David, Jr.

Mary was glad to return to her home in Heber City and enjoy the beauty of the mountains and lovely green valley. She said the mountains reminded her of the Alps in Switzerland, although they were not quite so high.

After resting awhile she went to live in Park City in the home of her cousin, James "D" Murdoch, whose wife, Lizzy Lindsay, had passed away in December, 1896, leaving four little children, the oldest being thirteen. She was a devoted mother to these children and loved them like they were her own. At one of the Murdoch reunions a daughter of James "D," Ruby Hooper, told how much they had loved Mary and how she made their home a happy, beautiful place when they so needed her love and understanding. James "D" remarried in November, 1898, so Mary went back to Heber City.

In 1900 her daughter Janet (Nettie) married Arthur Emmanuel Hansen. She lived in Park City and had five daughters and one son.

On June 12, 1906, Mary married William M. Ryan, a widower. He had been a childhood sweetheart. They lived eleven very happy years together. Granddaughter Zoe Hansen Johnson writes the following about this part of Mary's life: "He built her a beautiful little bungalow on the side of a stream in Heber City. They were very happy together and really enjoyed life, and the next eleven years were probably the happiest of her life. This is the period that I knew my grandmother and grandfather. They were Grandma and Grandpa Ryan. We all loved Grandpa Ryan; he was cheerful and was always doing nice things for us when we visited in Heber City. It was a great event when they both visited us in Park City. He always had nickels to give to the kids and spent time playing with us.

"I remember my Grandma Ryan as being blonde, small, and slim. She was always neatly dressed. She was a talented seamstress and her clothes were all beautifully made and fitted well.

"The most exciting time of my life as a little girl was the one-week vacation each summer spent with Grandma and Grandpa Ryan in their new bungalow in Heber City. We lived in Park City, and four of my sisters and my one brother were invited to spend a week with them, one at a time. Grandma always acted as though it was a great pleasure to have us visit her and planned many events during the week. (Now that I am a grandmother I marvel at her patience—spending five weeks of her summer entertaining noisy little kids.)

"I loved the first step into her little bungalow: it smelled like new lumber and sweet peas. A large clock hanging on the wall seemed to have the loudest tick in the world. I would sit in a rocking chair and listen to that clock tick, and at night, sleeping in the big guest room on a feather bed, I was almost afraid. Everything was so quiet except the tick of that big clock in the middle of the night. I missed sleeping with my sisters and was just a bit homesick.

"One of the special things that Grandma planned was breakfast in the summer house. Sloping down from the main house was an incline, and through this incline a small swift creek ran through their yard.

"Down from the bungalow, a summer house was built over the creek, consequently, the summer house was always cool. In the summer house of one room was a stove, a breakfast table, and a cupboard. I loved to sit with Grandma and have breakfast there and listen to the sound of the creek rushing by. Grandma put up all her fruit and vegetables in the summer house because it was cool there.

"Grandma always planted beautiful flowers along the creek. At the side of the summer house was a trellis covered with beautiful sweet peas. It was so much fun to sit and play beside the creek, to throw rocks into it, to lie back on the sloping lawn and look for four-leaf clovers.

"At the back of the yard was a barn where she kept her pretty white horse and buggy. She also had chickens, and she always let us gather the eggs. This was an exciting event to us kids from Park City. Occasionally she would give two or three eggs to take to Uncle Dave Murdoch's grocery store, where we would buy penny candy. This was really a great adventure! One time when my sister Mary and I were staying with Grandmother we decided to take two of the eggs we had gathered to the store without telling Grandma. Mary hid them in her blouse. We had just told Grandma there were no more eggs that day when Mary turned suddenly and the two eggs fell to the floor and crushed. Grandma just smiled and told us quietly to clean up the mess. It was a good lesson for us; we were terribly embarrassed and humiliated.

"Grandma had her own pretty white horse and one-seated buggy with fringe around the top. She would go out in the barn all dressed up, looking so stylish, and talk softly to her horse while she hitched it to the buggy in a few minutes.

"I remember one summer my mother was also visiting my grandmother. That day Heber City was celebrating an anniversary of the Black Hawk War and they were having a band concert and big celebration downtown. We all dressed in our best clothes. I remember long white skirts with many petticoats underneath. They both had on big summer hats trimmed with flowers and feathers. "I sat in the back with my legs hanging out over a shiny box-like seat. I had on my new Mary Janes and my Fourth of July dress. I felt so proud to be riding along in this new buggy with two lovely ladies to attend this celebration.

"We still visited Aunt Teen Duke and Lillie Shanks in Heber City after my grandmother's death, but it was never the same happy time. My cousin and good friend, Lola Bell Shanks, and I used to walk by the bungalow and look longingly at the creek and the summer house. It belonged to someone else now and we felt sad."

Mary Murray Murdoch Duke Ryan passed away December 20, 1917, at the age of sixty-three. She died of cancer and was laid to rest in the Heber City Cemetery.

Five of Mary's children preceded her in death—the, three babies previously mentioned, and James Monroe Duke died six months after his marriage to Mary Alice (May) Pinnock. Seven months after his death a baby son was born. The mother named him after his father, James Monroe. May was a wonderful mother to their child. She taught school to provide for him. Later she married Robert Simpson, who had been the husband of Doll (Mary Ann), and they had three girls and two boys.

Doll, wife of Robert Simpson, died at the age of forty-three of childbirth; her child was never born. She was the mother of four girls and two sons. She is buried in Logan Cemetery.

Lillie, who married Archie Shanks, was the mother of eight children. She died in 1940.

Nettie married Arthur Hansen in the Salt Lake Temple. She died of a stroke at the home of her daughter Mary in 1940. She had six children.

In 1942, Dick, Mary's eldest, wandered away and was lost eight days and nights before his body was found. He had six children.

So, Mary Murray Murdoch Duke had twenty-seven grandchildren and many descendants who today can be thankful for the sacrifices she made in their behalf during her lifetime.

Sources:

Histories written by:
Zoe Hansen Johnson (Grand-daughter)
Christina Lindsay Duke (Daughter-in-law)
Janett O.M. McMullin (Sister)

History on Microfilm at the Genealogical Library, film # 247,886.
"How Beautiful Upon the Mountains," by the Wasatch D.U.P.
John Murray Murdoch letter submitted by Virginia Hansen Davis.
Family Group Sheets Genealogical Library and James Murdoch family records.

James Duke

James Duke was the oldest child of Jonathan Oldham Duke and Mary Stone. He was born in Albany, New York on December 21, 1829.

He came with his parents to Nauvoo in 1840 and as a boy of eleven years of age, saw and heard Joseph and Hyrum Smith preach many times. He and his brothers, John and Robert, used to relate how that on the day they were murdered in Carthage Jail, these boys were playing in a creek near Nauvoo and they said the water turned red, almost like blood. They were also in the grove at Nauvoo when Brigham Young was transformed so that he looked and talked just like Joseph Smith. He remembered many of the sufferings and persecutions of the Mormon people in and around Nauvoo and after they were driven from their homes in Nauvoo and forced across the Missouri River, sick and without shelter. The mobs sent their cannon balls all around them but their lives were preserved. They bore testimony to the fact that while the Saints as a body were living in a destitute condition after being driven away from their homes, that a very large flock of quail came into the camp and perched on their tents and wagons, so that even the sick could stretch forth their hands and take them.

In their coming to Utah in 1850, James seemed to have been the teamster and hunter, but we learn from his father's journal that one day, just returning from a buffalo hunt, he was taken down by mountain fever and was so bad they had to lay over a few days. They stopped near the Chimney Rock on the Sweetwater River. He improved and was able to go on and catch up with the train.

They lived in the Twelfth Ward in Salt Lake City for a year.

In the spring of 1851, they went to Provo, obtained some land, and built a home. He worked with his father and helped build some of the first buildings in Provo.

On October 10, 1851 he married Almira Moore, who bore him eleven children. She was left a widow many years after his death.

Soon after going to Provo, a company of men on horseback, along with James, went to what was called White Mountain in southern Utah. There they found a very rich silver ore. They brought enough back to make a sacrament set for the tabernacle in Salt Lake City. Many tried to find the place where the ore was found, but never did.

He came to Heber in 1860 among the first settlers. He was president of the dramatic association for some years. He was a prominent actor in early days when people had to furnish their own amusements.

He was a drummer in the Territorial Militia during the Black Hawk War in 1866 and 1867. He sometimes acted as an Indian interpreter. He built the old Heber tithing office and President Hatch's first house in Heber. He was engaged most of the time in farming after coming to this valley.

In October 1868, he married Mary Murray Murdoch as a plural wife and she bore him eight children.

He later got some land in Wallsburg and built a home there for his first wife and her family, where he died May 20, 1892, leaving two widows and large families. (The youngest child would have been eleven at this time.)

James Duke was a very friendly man, a promoter of amusements. He was the chief fiddler at the dances for many years. He was a member of the high priest quorum and a firm believer in the gospel and that Joseph Smith was a prophet of God and was duly authorized to organize his church on the earth. To this he often bore his testimony.

Although he never accumulated much of this world's goods, he was rich in kind words and deeds and had the love and good will of his associates.

Mr. James Duke & Ladies

Your presence is specially requested

At The Heber Hall,

Friday Evening, January 19th, 1883,

A Ball will be given under the auspices of the

Y. M. M. I. Association. 50¢

— Alexander's Orchestra at 7 p. m. —

COMMITTEE OF ARRANGEMENTS.

JOHN M. MURDOCK,

J. H. McDONALD,

THOS. H. WATSON,

WM. BUYS,

THOS. S. WATSON.

Mary Murray Murdoch Duke and children

Back row: Lillie Duke, Johnathon Duke, Mary Ann Duke. Front row: Janet Duke, Mary Murray Murdoch Duke, James Monroe Duke.

Back row: Mary Ann Duke Simpson (Doll), Mary Murray Murdoch Duke Ryan (Mother), Lillie Isabell Duke Shanks, Janet Duke Hansen (Nettie). Front row: James Monroe Duke, Johnathan Murdoch Duke.

HUSBAND James DUKE
  Birth   21 Dec 1829
  Place   Albany, New York
  Married 3 Oct 1868
  Place   Salt Lake City, Salt Lake, Utah
  Death   20 May 1892
  Place   Walsburg, Wasatch, Utah
  Burial
  Place   Heber, Wasatch, Utah
  Mother   Mary STONE
  Father   Jonathan Oldham DUKE
  Other Wives (1) Almira MOORE M-10 Oct 1851
               (2) Margaret Jane DAVIS

WIFE (3) Mary Murray MURDOCH
  Birth   20 May 1852
  Place   Kansas City, Kansas
  Death   20 Dec 1917
  Place   Heber, Wasatch, Utah
  Burial
  Place   Heber, Wasatch, Utah
  Mother   Ann STEELE
  Father   John Murray MURDOCH
  Other Husbands (2) William Ryan M-12 Jun 1906
  Information from Genealogical Library Archives-Mrs Victor
     DUKE & Raymond Heber MOON Sheets Poss. Oscar Hunter

1ST CHILD Johnathan Murdoch DUKE
  Birth   4 Sep 1869 Heber, Wasatch, Utah
  Married Cristina Kennedy LINDSAY
  Date   24 Jul 1891
  Place   Center, Wasatch, Utah
  Death   4 Oct 1942 Heber, Wasatch, Utah
  Burial   11 Oct 1942 Heber, Wasatch, Utah

2ND CHILD Mary Ann DUKE
  Birth   14 Apr 1871 Heber, Wasatch, Utah
  Married Robert Mitchell SIMPSON
  Date   23 Feb 1892
  Place   Heber, Wasatch, Utah
  Death   20 Dec 1914 Logan, Cache, Utah
  Burial   22 Dec 1914 Logan, Cache, Utah

3RD CHILD Janet DUKE
  Birth   26 Mar 1873 Heber, Wasatch, Utah
  Married Arthur Emmanuel HANSEN
  Date   5 Sep 1900
  Place   Salt Lake City, Salt Lake, Utah
  Death   11 Nov 1940 Salt Lake City, Utah
  Burial   S.L.C. Cem, S-Lk, Utah

4TH CHILD Lillie Isabell DUKE
  Birth   21 Mar 1875 Heber, Wasatch, Utah
  Married Archibald SHANKS
  Date   24 Jul 1893
  Place   Heber, Wasatch, Utah
  Death   23 Feb 1940 Los Angeles, L.A. Cal.
  Burial   Forest Lawn Cem. L.A. Cal.

5TH CHILD John Murray DUKE
  Birth   9 Jan 1877 Heber, Wasatch, Utah
  Married
  Date
  Place
  Death   14 Nov 1878 Heber, Wasatch, Utah
  Burial   Heber, Wasatch, Utah

6TH CHILD Archibald Kerr DUKE
  Birth   25 Oct 1878 Heber, Wasatch, Utah
  Married
  Date
  Place
  Death   6 Nov 1880 Heber, Wasatch, Utah
  Burial   Heber, Wasatch, Utah

7TH CHILD James Monroe DUKE
  Birth   2 July 1881 Heber, Wasatch, Utah
  Married Mary Alice PINNOCK (May)
  Date   26 Jun 1906
  Place   Salt Lake City, Salt Lake, Utah
  Death   27 Jan 1907 Salt Lake City, Utah
  Burial   Heber, Wasatch, Utah

8TH CHILD Thomas T. DUKE
  Birth   13 Dec 1883 Heber, Wasatch, Utah
  Married
  Date
  Place
  Death   6 Nov 1884 Heber, Wasatch, Utah
  Burial   Heber, Wasatch, Utah

1 MURDOCH, James 1786-1831   2 MURDOCH, John Murray 1820-1910
1 MURDOCH, Mary MURRAY, Sp. 1782-1856   2 MURDOCH, Ann STEEL, Sp. 1829-1909

DESCENDANTS OF--------
3 MURDOCH, MARY MURRAY 1852-1917

3 DUKE, JAMES, SP. (1) 1829-1892

4 DUKE, Johnathan Murdoch B-9 Sep 1869 D-4 Oct 1942
4 DUKE, Christina Kennedy LINDSAY, Sp. B-5 Mar 1873 M-24 Jul 1891 D-30 May 1963

        5 WHITAKER, Minnie Burns DUKE B-25 Jan 1892 D-
        5 WHITAKER, Moses, Sp. B-1 Mar 1889 M-26 Nov 1913 D-2 Apr 1965

                6 WHITAKER, Fred Duke B-26 Sep 1914 D-   1974
                6 WHITAKER, Ruth MARTINEAU, Sp. B-5 Nov 1918 M-15 Jun 1936

                        7 McNEELY Carolyn Ruth WHITAKER B-9 Jul 1937
                        7 McNEELY, Harry Dennis, Sp. B-   M-13 Jun 1958

                                8 McNEELY, Teresa Lynn   B-

                                8 McNEELY, Lauren Gail   B-

                                8 McNEELY, Steven Duane   B-

                                8 McNEELY, Brent Jaren   B-

                                8 McNEELY, Randall Dennis   B-

                                8 McNEELY, Andra Carolyn   B-

                        7 WHITAKER, Sheldon Fred B-6 Apr 1940
                        7 WHITAKER, Karren Marie CARD, Sp. B-   M-12 Sep 1963

                                8 WHITAKER, Michael Lynn   B-

                                8 WHITAKER, Richard Mark   B-

                                8 WHITAKER, James Lowell   B-

                                8 WHITAKER, Marie Rachel   B-

                                8 WHITAKER, David Sheldon   B-

                        7 WHITAKER, Paul LaMont B-17 Mar 1944
                        7 WHITAKER, Carol Ann MORROW, Sp. B-   M-26 Nov 1964

                                8 WHITAKER, Kimberly Ann   B-

                                8 WHITAKER, Cari Lee   B-

                                8 WHITAKER, Kenneth   B-

                        7 WHITAKER, Ralph Johnathon B-21 Dec 1947
                        7 WHITAKER, Ramona OLSEN, Sp. B-   M-17 Dec 1970

                                8 WHITAKER, Alan Duke   B-

                                8 WHITAKER, Wendy   B-

                                8 WHITAKER, Neil   B-

                                8 WHITAKER, Bryan Ralph   B-

                        7 WHITAKER, Lindsay Moses B-16 Oct 1952
                        7 WHITAKER, Claudia RIGBY, Sp. B-   M-

                                8 WHITAKER, Fred Duke II   B-

                        7 WHITAKER, Ervan Scott B-28 Feb 1958

6 WHITAKER, Charles Adelbert B-10 May 1916
6 WHITAKER, Darlene LaVonne EARL, Sp. B-30 Nov 1916 M-21 May 1937

    7 WHITAKER, Ronald Charles B-26 Oct 1938
    7 WHITAKER, Joann Lucille JOHNSON, Sp. B-   M-16 Jun 1962

        8 WHITAKER, Patrice   B-

        8 WHITAKER, Helen Cathryn   B-

        8 WHITAKER, Clarise   B-

        8 WHITAKER, Derrick Charles B-

    7 PERKINS, LaVonne DeNece WHITAKER Bottomfield B-24 Apr 1941
    7 BOTTOMFIELD, Gordon, Sp. (1) B-   M-26 Dec 1958
    7 PERKINS, Ronald Graham, Sp. (2) B-   M-

        8 BOTTOMFIELD, Denece   B-

        8 BOTTOMFIELD, Lori   B-

        8 BOTTOMFIELD, Sutton   B-

        8 BOTTOMFIELD, Gordon Troy B-

        8 PERKINS, Royce Graham   B-

        8 PERKINS, Jennifer Kristin B-

    7 GARRISON, Charlene ReNee B-25 Jun 1943
    7 KNIGHT, John Anthony, Sp. (1) B-   M-2 Mar 1962
    7 JACK, Thomas, Sp. (2) B-   M-10 Jan 1979
    7 GARRISON, Gerald, Sp. B-   M-

        8 KNIGHT, John Anthony II   B-

        8 KNIGHT, Janae Angela   B-

6 PELTON, Mary Clarissa WHITAKER Pratt B-22 May 1918
6 PRATT, Parker Maroni, Sp. B-   M-26 Nov 1935
6 PELTON, Robert, Sp. (2) B-   M-

    7 WAGONER, Valerie PRATT B-
    7 WAGONER, William, Sp. B-   M-

        8 WAGONER, Jeffery   B-

        8 WAGONER, Julia   B-

        8 WAGONER, Douglas   B-

        8 WAGONER, Wendy   B-

    7 MILLER, Marcia PRATT B-
    7 MILLER, Robert, Sp. B-   M-

        8 MILLER, Tracy Lynn   B-

        8 MILLER, Eric Robert   B-

6 DINUBILO, Grace WHITAKER Reese B-17 Mar 1920
6 REESE, Joseph Glen, Sp. B-   M-4 May 1940
6 DINUBILO, Harry Joseph, Sp. B-   M-

    7 DINUBILO, Robert Glen B-
    7 DINUBILO, Yvonne Marie HARRISON B-   M-

        8 DINUBILO, Matthew Joseph B-

        8 DINUBILO, Alethea Marie B-

        8 DINUBILO, Aaron Richard B-

6 KARPOWITZ, Clara Louise WHITAKER B-17 Nov 1921
6 KARPOWITZ, Don Robert, Sp. B-   M-27 Feb 1941

      7 JONES, Kathryn KARPOWITZ B-
      7 JONES, Gary R. Sp. B-   M-

           8 JONES, Michael Gary   B-

           8 JONES, Robert Christian   B-

      7 PORTER, Shauna KARPOWITZ Wheeldon B-
      7 WHEELDON, G. Stephen, Sp. B-   M-
      7 PORTER, Bill, Sp. (2) B-   M-

           8 WHEELDON, Robert Sean   B-

           8 WHEELSON, Stephanie Christine B-

6 TAYLOR, Dora Jean WHITAKER B-22 Jan 1924
6 CHRISTENSEN, Harold Phillip, Sp. B-   M-22 Jan 1942
6 TAYLOR, Frank, Sp. (2) B-   M-

      7 WYCINOWSKI, Sandra CHRISTENSEN B-
      7 WYCINOWSKI, Roger, Sp. B-   M-

           8 WYCINOWSKI, Teresa Marie   B-

           8 WYCINOWSKI, Christine Elaine B-

      7 COONS, Linda CHRISTENSEN B-
      7 COONS, Donald, Sp. B-   M-

           8 COONS, Kevin Barry   B-

           8 COONS, Katie Anne   B-

           8 COONS,

      7 CHRISTENSEN, Phillip B-
      7 CHRISTENSEN, Beverly KITCHEN, Sp. B-   M-

6 VANDERHAVE, Jessie Christina WHITAKER Navasio B-15 Mar 1928
6 NAVASIO, Robert Melvin, Sp. B-25 Nov 1925 M-1 Jun 1945
6 VAN DER HAVE, Hendrikus, Sp. B-   M-

      7 HOSKINS, Joanne Valee NAVASIO B- 8 Jan 1947 D-   1976
      7 HOSKINS, Lee, Sp. B-   M-

      7 NOVASIO, David Charles B-22 Feb 1949
      7 NOVASIO, Mary Rose CHAPA, Sp. B-   M-

           8 NAVASIO, Richard Thomas   B-

           8 NAVASIO, Gina Clecaria   B-

           8 NAVASIO, Shriley   B-

      7 NOVASIO, John Robert B-21 Dec 1952
      7 NOVASIO, Orleen JOHNSON, Sp. B-   M-

           8 NOVASIO, Christa Gail   B-

           8 NOVASIO, Robert Steven   B-

      7 NOVASIO, Joyce Adele B-15 Nov 1954 D-18 Nov 1954

      7 NOVASIO, Michele Christine B-25 Oct 1956

      7 NOVASIO, James Thomas   B-26 Jul 1958

      7 NOVASIO, Stephen Douglas   B-

6 CUMMINS, Elizabeth JoAnne WHITAKER B-9 Sep 1929
6 CUMMINS, Lawrence Earl, Sp. B-   M-21 Sep 1950

      7 PETERSON, Deborah Anne CUMMINS B-
      7 PETERSON, Ralph Walter, Sp. B-   M-

          8 PETERSON, Mickelle   B-

          8 PETERSON, Robert Walter   B-

          8 PETERSON, Adam Kent   B-

      7 BEECHER, Lisa Christine CUMMINS B-
      7 BEECHER, Blake Rex, Sp. B-   M-

          8 BEECHER, Nicole   B-

          8 BEECHER, Andrea   B-

      7 CUMMINS, Timothy Charles   B-

      7 CUMMINS, Laura Colleen   B-

5 DUKE, James Victor B-23 Mar 1897 D-   1967
5 DUKE, Emma Jean JACOB, Sp. B-3 Nov 1901 M-13 Aug 1918

    6 SHARP, Isabelle Deana DUKE B-19 Apr 1919
    6 SHARP, Fenton LaMont, Sp. B-   M-5 Dec 1936

      7 SHARP, Vee J B-
      7 SHARP, Judy OVERHOLT, Sp. B-   M-

          8 SHARP, Kimberly   B-

          8 SHARP, Amanda Lynn   B-

          8 SHARP, Megan Marie   B-

      7 SHARP, Jerry LaMont B-
      7 SHARP, Amelia Graehl OVITT, Sp. B-   M-

          8 SHARP, Benjamin Drew   B-

          8 SHARP, Zachary Graehel   B-

          8 SHARP, Alexander Graehel   B-

      7 SHARP, Drew Alferd B-
      7 SHARP, Abby SHARP, Sp. B-   M-

          8 SHARP, Peter Drew   B-

          8 SHARP, Adriann   B-

      7 SHARP, Kelly Dean B-   1950 D-28 Apr 1979

      7 SUNDBERG, Kae Lynne SHARP B-
      7 SUNDBERG, James Andrus, Sp. B-   M-

      7 SHARP, Robert Duke   B-

      7 SHARP, James Clair   B-

    6 JONES, Doris Christina DUKE B-11 Jan 1922
    6 JONES, Ralph Lamar, Sp. B-29 Apr 1921 M-1 Dec 1939

      7 IVERSON, Vicki Ann Jones B-11 Sep 1940
      7 IVERSON, William James, Sp. B-   M-26 Sep 1957

          8 IVERSON, Jeri Lynn   B-

          8 IVERSON, Chad   B-

```
        7 JONES, Ralph LaMont B-8 Jan 1948
        7 JONES, Virginia ELLIOTT, Sp. B-            M-13 Mar 1972

            8 JONES, Leslie Ann            B-

            8 JONES, Jody Elliott          B-

        7 FIELD, Christine JONES B-9 Dec 1950
        7 FIELD, William, Sp. B-            M-9 Aug 1975

            8 FIELD, Zachary               B-

    6 DUKE, Victor Hal B- 15 Jan 1925
    6 DUKE, Shirley JOHNSON, Sp. B-20 Jul 1925 M-21 Dec 1949

        7 FISHER, Selma Jean DUKE B-31 Mar 1951
        7 FISHER, Edwin L., Sp. B-          M-

            8 FISHER, Michael Ian          B-

            8 FISHER, Jenna Colleen        B-

        7 DUKE, Jonathan Murdoch B-7 Nov 1952
        7 DUKE, Shauna LEVIE, Sp. B-        M-

            8 DUKE, Clinton Earl           B-

            8 DUKE, Carl Levie             B-

        7 DUKE, James Victor          B-3 Oct 1963

5 DUKE, Harold Steele B-20 Nov 1902 D-      1975
5 DUKE, Mary MONTGOMERY, Sp. B-2 Jan 1905 M-15 Sep 1924

    6 DUKE, Harold Mont  B-9 Dec 1925 D-3 Jan 1944

    6 SIMS, Phyllis Mary DUKE Morris Lythgoe B-6 May 1930
    6 MORRIS, Donald Bryan, Sp. B-          M-10 Sep 1951 Div.
    6 LYTHGOE, Ramond White, Sp. (2) B-         M-24 Apr 1965
    6 SIMS, John Byron, Sp. (3) B-          M-

        7 MORRIS, Todd Bryan          B-

        7 MORRIS, Claudia Joan        B-

    6 NELSON, Elaine DUKE B-26 Oct 1934
    6 NELSON, Donald Tracy, Sp. B-29 Sep 1934 M-18 Jun 1954

        7 NELSON, Tracy               B-29 Jan 1962

        7 NELSON, Mark D.             B- 1 Dec 1965

        7 NELSON, Daniel D.           B- 5 May 1970
                                                      twins
        7 NELSON, Christopher D.      B- 5 May 1970

    6 DUKE, Richard Kay B- 9 Dec 1938
    6 DUKE, FaNon DAVIS, Sp. B-            M-18 Sep 1959

        7 DUKE, Tori                  B-

        7 DUKE, Trent R.              B-

        7 DUKE, Mequette              B-

5 DUKE, Carl Muir B-29 Aug 1906 D-20 Jun 1958 M-15 Jan 1934
5 DUKE, Edith PROVOST, Sp. B-
  Hansen, Wallace, Sp. (2) B-            M-

    6 DUKE, Jay Carl B-6 Apr 1940
    6 DUKE, Sharlene GAGON, Sp. B-            M-
```

```
                7 DUKE, Jay Shane              B-

                7 DUKE, Jamie Lane             B-

                7 DUKE, Traci Marie            B-

    5 FISHER, Jeanne Hylton DUKE B-20 Aug 1912
    5 FISHER, Ford David, Sp. B-16 Jan 1911 M-25 Mar 1930 D-20 Feb 1966

            6 WEHR, Mary Ann FISHER B- 8 Apr 1934
            6 WEHR, William, Sp. B-28 Apr 1932 M-11 Jun 1953

                7 WEHR, Michael B-15 Jul 1954
                7 WEHR, Elaine CALABRESE, Sp. B-         M-16 Nov 1979

                7 WEHR, William W. Jr.         B-28 Sep 1957

                7 BURKHARD, Lina WEHR B-19 Jul 1959
                7 BURKHARD, Richard, Sp. B-             M-4 Aug 1978

                    8 BURKHARD, Donna Diane        B-

            6 FOSTER, Christina Jane FISHER B-5 Aug 1938
            6 FOSTER, Ronald Lynn, Sp. B-13 Feb 1938 M-6 Aug 1961

                7 FOSTER, David George         B-15 May 1962

                7 FOSTER, Jennifer             B-30 May 1974

            6 FISHER,David George B-4 Sep 1942
            6 FISHER, Patricia Lucille ALLEN, Sp. B-9 Jan 1942 M-17 Aug 1963

                7 FISHER, David Scott          B-22 Mar 1964

                7 FISHER, Kari Ann             B-27 Sep 1966

            6 WHITTLE, Marjorie Vilate FISHER B-16 Jun 1949
            6 WHITTLE, Norman Fred, Sp. B-             M-

                7 WHITTLE, Mary Anne           B-

            6 FISHER, Katherine B-11 Apr 1955

    5 MINER, Maybell DUKE B-1 May 1921
    5 MINER, Merrill LaVar, Sp. B-15 Sep 1908 M-11 Sep 1939

            6 HALES, Suzanne Mae MINER B-4 Apr 1942
            6 HALES, Hugh Bradley, Sp. B-              M-22 Aug 1963

                7 HALES, Holly Ann             B-

                7 HALES, Hugh Michel           B-

                7 HALES, Matthew Edward        B-

            6 MINER, Merrill Edward B-21 Apr 1945 D-10 Oct 1968

4 SIMPSON, Mary Ann DUKE B-14 Sep 1871 M-23 Feb 1892 (1) D-20 Dec 1914
4 SIMPSON, Robert Mitchell, Sp. B-6 Jun 1869 D-7 May 1932
  SIMPSON, Mary Alice PINNOCK, Sp. (2) B-28 Apr 1885 M-26 Jun 1906 D-014 Jan 1977

    5 SIMPSON, Ruth B-18 May 1895

    5 SMALL, Mary Avelda SIMPSON B-4 Nov 1896 D-13 Jan 1978
    5 SMALL, Samuel Turner, Sp. B-16 May 1885 M-5 Jul 1937 D-5 Feb 1945

    5 BATESON, Cleo SIMPSON B-11 Oct 1898 D-29 Jul 1974
    5 BATESON, Russell Bordrero, Sp. B-13 Feb 1898 M-16 Jun 1920 D-24 Jun 1974

            6 KRAUS, Donna Marie BATESON Scharman B-15 Dec 1921 D-     1977
            6 SCHARMAN,          , Sp. B-        M-
            6 KRAUS,             , Sp. (2) B-        M-

        7
```

```
        6 BURTON, Cleo Patricia BATESON Lewis B-20 May 1927
        6 LEWIS,            Sp. B-            M-
        6 BURTON, Ronald B., Sp. B-                M-

               7                              B-

5 SIMPSON, Robert Don B-1 Sep 1900
5 SIMPSON, Loda HANSEN, Sp. B-            M-22 Feb 1922 D-28 Nov 1978

        6 HOWE, Cathrine SIMPSON B-
        6 HOWE,            Sp. B-            M-

               7 FLINT, Kitty HOWE B-
               7 FLINT, Robert, Sp. B-                M-

               7 HOWE, Don                   B-

        6 BURCHFIELD, Ruth SIMPSON B-
        6 BURCHFIELD, Don, Sp. B-            M-

               7 BURCHFIELD, Donny            B-

               7 BURCHFIELD, David            B-

5 KUNZ, Ardelle SIMPSON B-7 Nov 1906
5 KUNZ, Wilford Howard, Sp. B-16 Aug 1907 M-21 Dec 1928

        6 KUNZ, Howard Robert B-23 Apr 1929 D-        1936

        6 KUNZ, Don Lee B-6 Aug 1932        D-        1977

        6 MOOREHEAD, Elenore Alison KUNZ B-14 Dec 1936
        6 MOOREHEAD, John, Sp. B-            M-

        6 KUNZ, Douglas Simpson B-28 Jan 1940
        6 KUNZ,            Sp. B-            M-

               7 KUNZ, Douglas               B-

5 SIMPSON, James Duke B-2 Aug 1908 D-3 Aug 1908

4 HANSEN, Janet  DUKE B-26 Mar 1873 D-11 Nov 1940
4 HANSEN, Arthur Emmanuel, Sp. B-23 Sep 1876 M-5 Sep 1900 D-6 Jan 1943

        5 BREINHOLT, May Duke HANSEN B-5 May 1901
        5 BREINHOLT, Verdi Gleave, Sp. B-8 Apr 1901 M-7 Sep 1928 D-26 Jan 1976

               6 BREINHOLT, Richard Verdi B-17 Mar 1931 D-        1943

               6 WORMALD, June Madelyn BREINHOLT B-10 Jun 1933
               6 WORMALD, Bruce,       Sp. B-            M-

                      7 WORMALD, Christopher            B-

               6 BREINHOLT, William Marcus B-15 Nov 1934
               6 BREINHOLT, Shauna Margaret KILPARTICk, Sp. B-            M-

                      7 BREINHOLT, Benny William        B-

                      7 BREINHOLT, Mark Verdi           B-

                      7 BREINHOLT, Tracy K.             B-

                      7 BREINHOLT, Daron John           B-

               6 BREINHOLT, Kenneth Arthur B-18 Mar 1945

        5 HANSEN, Arthur Duke B-1½ Nov 1902 D-29 Dec 1967
        5 HANSEN, Mary Alice PACE, Sp. B-31 Dec 1903 M-15 Sep 1930

        5 JOHNSON, Matilda Zoe HANSEN B-7 May 1904
        5 JOHNSON, George Wesley, Sp. B-4 Dec 1904 M-16 Jan 1929 D-
```

6 JOHNSON, George Wesley, Jr. B-28 Apr 1932
6 JOHNSON, Marion Ashby, Sp. B-   M-22 Dec 1960

      7 JOHNSON, Cynthia Cecille   B-

      7 JOHNSON, Karolyn Zoe   B-

      7 JOHNSON, George Wesley III   B-

      7 JOHNSON, Benjamin Ashby   B-

6 TIPTON, Janet Marcia JOHNSON B-31 May 1934
6 TIPTON, Gary Prior, Sp. B-   M-7 Sep 1962

      7 TIPTON, Richard Gary   B-

      7 TIPTON, Jonathan Jay   B-

      7 TIPTON, Scott Wesley   B-

      7 TIPTON, Tiffany Ann   B-

5 JOHNSON, June Madeline HANSEN B-10 Jun 1906 D-15 Oct 1967
5 JOHNSON, Willard, Sp. B-   M-14 Feb 1906

5 PERRY, Ruth Jeanette HANSEN Nuttall B-28 Feb 1908
5 NUTTALL, Ralph Herron, Sp. B- 6 Dec 1903 M-7 Sep 1928 D-1 Oct 1954
5 PERRY, Dick Cook, Sp. (2) B-   M-9 Jun 1955

     6 NUTTALL, Robert Ralph B-19 Jun 1929
     6 NUTTALL, Jane Graves, Sp. B-   M-

      7 MANART, Katherine Ann NUTTALL B-
      7 MANART, Frank, Sp. B-   M-

      7 NUTTALL, Marjory Ruth   B-

      7 NUTTALL, Robert Graves   B-

5 DAVIS, Virginia Lucile HANSEN B-21 Jan 1915
5 DAVIS, Marcus Laurance, Sp. B-8 Feb 1910 M-15 Jan 1934

     6 DAVIS, Richard Thomas B-9 Nov 1936
     6 DAVIS, Kathryn Ogura, Sp. B-   M- 4 Feb 1974

      7 DAVIS, Mayli Louisa   B-

      7 DAVIS, Michelle Linda   B-

      7 DAVIS, Jennifer Sachiko   B-

      7 DAVIS, Richard Raymond   B-

     6 DAVIS, Louis Evan B-13 Feb 1939
     6 DAVIS, Beverly May SHOWELL, Sp. B-   M-12 Jun 1962

      7 DAVIS, Kai Lynne   B-

      7 DAVIS, Mary Jayne   B-

      7 DAVIS, Lu Ann   B-

      7 DAVIS, Matthew Louis   B-

      7 DAVIS, Sandra   B-

      7 DAVIS, Marcus Wilford   B-

     6 DAVIS, Janet B-11 Aug 1941

4 SHANKS, Lillie Isabell DUKE B-21 Mar 1875 D-21 Feb 1940
4 SHANKS, Archibald, Sp. B-29 Mar 1873 M-24 Jul 1893

        5 DANIELS, Lyla SHANKS B-15 Jan 1894 D-about 1951
        5 DANIELS, Ernest Lee, Sp. B-   M-

                6 DANIELS, Larell B-

        5 EVANS, Alta SHANKS B-2 Sep 1895
        5 EVANS, Byron, Sp. B-   M-

                6 Thought to be 2 or 3 children

        5 SHANKS, James Sylvan B-25 Aug 1897
        5 SHANKS, Chloe A. Edwards, Sp. B-   M-23 Sep 1916

                6 SHANKS, Ednal B-19 Jan 1917

        5 SHANKS, Dellis W. B-18 May 1900 D-
        5 SHANKS,   Sp. B-   M-

        5 JORGENSEN, Lola Bell SHANKS B-30 Dec 1904 D-7 Jan 1969
        5 JORGENSEN, William, Sp. B-   M-

                6 JORGENSEN, Jerrie B-

                6 JORGENSEN, Cissie B-

        5 SHANKS, Archie Doyle B-2 Mar 1906 D-3 Apr 1906

        5 ROCK, Merle May SHANKS B-14 May 1908
        5 ROCK, Frank E., Sp. B-   M-

        5 SHANKS, Jonathon Monroe B-25 Dec 1910 D-

4 DUKE, John Murray B-9 Jan 1877 D-14 Nov 1878

4 DUKE, Archibald Kerr B-25 Oct 1878 D-6 Nov 1880

4 DUKE, James Monroe B-2 Jul 1881 D-27 Jan 1907 M-26 Jun 1906
4 SIMPSON, Mary Alice PINNOCK DUKE (May), Sp. B-28 Apr 1885 D-14 Jan 1977
4 SIMPSON, Robert Mitchell, Sp. (2) B-6 Jun 1869 M-14 Jun 1917 D-7 May 1932

        5 DUKE, James Monroe B-15 Aug 1907
        5 DUKE, Edna HARRIS, Sp. B-3 May 1909 M-3 Nov 1946
        King, Owen (1) Sp. B-   M-   Div.

        SIMPSON, Robert Pinnock B-19 Apr 1918 M-10 Feb 1950
        SIMPSON, Dorothy SADLEIR, Sp. B-

        SIMPSON, Harold Watson B-13 Aug 1920 M-23 Apr 1944
        SIMPSON, Adella Mary RUTKOWSKI, Sp. B-

        HAYWARD, Margaret Alison SIMPSON B-27 Aug 1922 M-7 Jun 1944
        HAYWARD, Harold Ira, Sp. B-

        GUTHRIE, Dorothy Lucile SIMPSON B-22 Aug 1925 M-7 Jun 1944
        GUTHRIE, James W. Sp. B-

        GRUWELL, Lenora Jean SIMPSON B-24 Jan 1929 M-26 May 1952
        GRUWELL, Robert Alan, Sp. B-

4 DUKE, Thomas B-13 Dec 1883 D-6 Nov 1884

Ann Murdoch, William M. Giles, and Rachel Howarth Fortie Giles

Ann Murdoch was the fourth child of John Murray and Ann Steel Murdoch. She was born September 14, 1854 in Salt Lake City, Utah. She was named Ann after her mother. Ann was born the year the grasshoppers were so destructive to the crops in Salt Lake.

She was born of goodly parents who left their all and joined The Church of Jesus Christ of Latter-day Saints in Scotland, experiencing many tribulations for the gospel's sake, and came to Utah. They arrived in 1852. After eight years of struggle and working in the Church and mingling with the Saints of God, they decided to move.

In 1860, Ann, with her parents and sisters, came to Provo Valley (now Heber City) in company with William Forman and family and others. The first home of the family was a dugout built at the old Heber Fort located in the northwest part of Heber. There was no stove, so meals had to be cooked in an open fireplace. There were bake skillets in which the bread was baked and there were a few pots and pans. Their soap was homemade and also their cloth for making clothes was homespun from wool. The women had to work and were kept as busy as the men. They also made candles for lights out of mutton tallow. There was a good family love in the Murdoch family.

As a child, Ann was very active. The school she attended had only one room with a mud roof and rough homemade benches. She was very energetic and became a very good student. Her education was fair for those times.

She loved music and used her beautiful voice all her life for the benefit of others, in school and so-cial activities. As children at home, the girls enjoyed singing for their father and mother. Many pleasant times were spent during the long winter evenings in family singing.

"I remember Mother playing the comb while we sat on the floor and sang in the evenings. My mother was very talented musically—she could play most any instrument and had a lovely singing voice. In fact, she used to sing in all the funerals in Wasatch county."

Ann was a grand games player with the children and in our youth we spent many happy hours in and among the wild flowers as there were no other flowers grown there. We gathered many wild flowers, and we, as community children, gathered many wild berries for our parents, such as choke cherries and service berries, to dry and use in the home. She, with her older sister, gathered cattails to make beds, as did other pioneer children. She was the daughter of pioneers and she was a true pioneer herself. Her parents passed through trials of poverty, mud-roofed houses, and Indian troubles. She was one of the family and never considered these hardships as trials but always lent a helping hand.

As she grew older she, with her sisters (there being no brothers in the family at this time), was taught to drive the team of oxen, to milk the cows, to tend the chickens, and to make butter and cheese. She was a good girl to help our father with our little farm, doing whatever she was asked to do. She had a motto she would repeat to us: "All that you do, do with your might; things done by halves are never done right.

In our childhood days, there came a family from Nottingham, England, in 1862, and settled across the street from our residence. Their names were Thomas and Mariah Kirkham Giles, Elizabeth, George M., and William M. Giles. William became one of our intimate childhood friends. As we grew older, we all were in our social crowd together. We all joined in going to socials, plays, meetings, and dances, and roaming over the green fields. We gathered the wild berries and joined in all the fun of the young folks.

Then as Ann grew older, William selected her as his best girl. Their parents lived just one block apart, so William and Ann became very well acquainted with each other, and, as young people, took a large part in building up this western country.

She was the daughter of a farmer and he was the son of a farmer, so they were very well suited for each other. William was an Indian fighter, and when, as a young man, he was called to go guard against the Indians young Ann would ask Heavenly Father to protect William Giles and to spare his life so he could return to her. This was very much to the amusement of the family.

In the spring of 1866, Robert T. Burton and David J. Ross came to Heber to organize the militia and to get all to enlist if possible. It was known that Blackhawk and his warriors intended to start killing the cattle and making raids on the settlements. Practically all men of proper age enlisted and bought guns and ammunition so they could defend themselves and their property.

The gun that was purchased by William M. Giles at this time was later put in the Fort Duchesne Museum by James A. Giles of Myton, the son of William M. Giles. The gun was purchased in 1865 and the name on it is the Spencer Repeating Rifle Company, Boston, Massachusetts, patented March 6, 1860.

William M. Giles enlisted in the cavalry and took part in a number of expeditions. He, in company with twenty-three others, under Major John Hamilton, went to the Indian reservation with supplies of bacon, flour, rice, sugar, and other supplies, intending to pacify and make friends with the Indians if possible, and stop the war. But they found only a few of the very old Indians and squaws who received the supplies, and the war went on. Another time, later on, the Indians made one of their several raids on this valley, and William M. Giles was called to follow them and try to get them to give back the horses, but in this he failed. The Indians drove the horses across the Provo River near William Bagley's and over into American Fork Canyon, expecting to get ahead of our men. Our men followed them into the cedars, but finally lost track of them.

Of the seven raids made on this valley, the Indians got away with the stock six times.

Those were stirring times, and men ran many risks of their lives. Seventy white people and many Indians were killed during that war. William M. was one of those who often risked his life trying to protect the lives of others. He was a good provider for his family and did his full share in helping to build up this country, especially Heber City.

On the fifth day of June, 1871, William M. and Ann Murdoch were married in the Endowment House in Salt Lake City. Their first home was built down in the field just west of the Heber ball park. Later, they built a nice two-story brick house at 191 West 100 South in Heber. The house still stands and is owned by William Sheets.

To them the following children were born: John Thomas (also know as John T.M.) September 22, 1872; Mariah, May 4, 1874; William, 24 October 1875; Jane Ann, March 13, 1877; George D., January 11, 1879; Sarah Elizabeth, September 30, 1880; Joseph Fielding, January 6, 1882; Orson Edwin, September 25, 1883; James Alvin, April 18, 1885; Henry Alexander, February 15, 1887; and Charles Andrew, March 15, 1888. All of these children were born in Heber City, Utah.

William and Ann were hard working people. William M. homesteaded 160 acres southwest of Heber, down close to the river, known as the Bill M. Homestead. They farmed, milked cows, raised pigs and chickens, and churned butter. When Ann churned the cream it was put in an old wooden churn. There was a dash that had to be worked up and down for several minutes before the butter would come. Then the buttermilk would have to be worked out with a wooden paddle before the butter could be used. Ann would leave large chunks of butter in the buttermilk, then give it to some of her sisters or neighbors so they would also have some butter. She was kind to everyone.

Ann was a good housekeeper, and she loved her children dearly. She was always a wonderful mother, making home a pleasant place for her family and for many, many others who would call. One young man told the writer that the happiest time of his life was when he visited the home of Annie Giles with her family and she would play the comb music and they would all dance. She was a grand Relief Society worker and gave a tender helping hand to the poor and the needy. As Ann was blessed with a comfortable living, never were those in need turned from her door nor neglected by her. Her dear friend, Mary Foreman, composed a poem about her, but this verse is all I can remember:

Annie was a Mormon,
A friend unto the poor,
And never did she turn away
The hungry from her door.

She had to do her washing in a tub, scrub the clothes on a washboard, and wring the water out of them by hand. When she ironed, she used flatirons heated on top of the stove. The floors were just boards and had to be scrubbed with a scrubbing brush. So her household chores were very hard and time consuming.

They were successful in raising their family in spite of the many, many problems they had to solve. Ann was a true daughter, a true sister, a true wife and mother. They were both true pioneers.

Ann's life was short. She contracted pneumonia and was expecting her twelfth child. The pneumonia was too much for her, and she died January 2, 1890, leaving ten living children. One daughter, Mariah, preceded her in death.

A tribute to Ann Giles was written by Verna Giles, her granddaughter, in 1927. She was the daughter of George David and Mary Elizabeth Mair Giles of Heber City, Utah. Verna was looking at her dear Grandmother Ann's picture which was hanging on the wall of her father and mother's home when these wonderful thoughts came to her mind:

Dear Grandmother of Mine

Although your face I've never seen,
Nor felt your tender caress,
Your photograph is so serene,
It seems you're near to bless.

Your eyes so mild, your mouth so kind
Tell of beauty and love.
Your patient soul, your gentle mind,
God gave as gifts from above.

The kindness you rendered to others
Is written right there on your face,
It says, "Among wonderful Mothers,
You hold a most wonderful place."

As I study that dear picture of a wonderful you,
It tells me again and again
That you were a true friend through and through
And a beautiful mother to men.

And so, dear grandmother of mine,
I'm thankful day by day
That your life shows, lovely, true, and fine,
In your picture tucked away.

William took care of his little flock, and through the blessings of the Lord and with faithful and diligent labor, managed to raise them all to man and womanhood. Sometime after Ann's death, William married Rachel Howarth Fortie, widow of Alexander Fortie. She was a faithful helpmate to him in helping him raise his family.

History compiled by Melva E. Giles Mitchell from the following sources:

1. William Giles—Ann Murdoch 2. "A Historical Sketch of Ann Murdoch Giles and William M. Giles" by Janett Murdoch McMullin. 3. History of James Alvin Giles as told to Sharon Giles in spring of 1963. 4. William M. Giles History 5. "Memories of Grandmother Ann Murdoch and Grandfather William M Giles" by Gladys Zella Giles Rowley. 6. "A Short History of Ann Murdoch Giles" by Ruth Giles Davis Sweat.

Rachel Howarth Fortie Giles

Left to right: Jane Ann Giles, William Giles, Ann Murdoch Giles, John Thomas Giles, and George David Giles (baby on lap).

Home of William M and Ann Murdoch Giles Heber City, Wasatch, Utah.

Rachel Howarth Fortie Giles was born April 19, 1850, in Boulton, Lancashire, England. She was the daughter of John Howarth and Ellen Monks Howarth. She married Alexander Fortie on December 31, 1868, in the old Endowment House in Salt Lake City, Utah. He contracted pneumonia and died April 23, 1890. In March, 1893, she married William M. Giles, a widower with a family of ten children, eight of whom lived at home. The youngest was only five years old.

At the age of eighteen, Rachel Howarth came to Utah from Lancashire, England, with her mother's family. She was but four years old when her father died, so that she grew to womanhood without the protecting care of a father.

Like the other members of the family, and at an early age, she had to go out to work to help her mother maintain the home. She was the tenth child in a family of twelve and had one sister and a brother younger than she. She was betrothed to Alexander Fortie in England, and he came to Utah a year before to earn money to send for her. She was a very beautiful and attractive young girl, with dark hair and sparkling black eyes, and always dressed in neat and becoming clothing. Mr. Fortie was employed on the railroad at Echo, Utah, and the Howarth family went to Wanship to reside. Rachel had many boy friends call to see her and was a favorite among the younger class. Upon hearing of this, Alexander left his work, and came to Wanship, and they were married December 31, 1868. Soon after, they moved to Heber City and established a home. Alexander found employment as a carpenter and made a comfortable living from then on.

Many of the substantial buildings in Heber City stand as monuments of his labor, particularly the Wasatch Stake Tabernacle, of which he was the architect. It was erected under his direction and supervision. He contracted pneumonia and died April 23, 1890, leaving Rachel a widow with her three children—two daughters and a son. The two daughters married, leaving Rachel and her son, John A., at home.

In March, 1893, she married William M. Giles He had eight children living at home at the time. This was a tremendous undertaking for her, but she tackled the job with a determination to make a comfortable home for her husband and his motherless children, which she accomplished very well. She and her husband provided for them until all of them had homes of their own. The flour bin and bread can were never empty. William died 30 April 1926.

Rachel Howarth Fortie Giles died in Heber City, Utah, January 5, 1943.

Girl, left: Sarah Elizabeth Giles. Standing, back: William Giles. Standing, front: James Alvin Giles. Father sitting: William M Giles. Baby on lap: Charles Andrew Giles. Next: Joseph Fielding Giles. Holding child: John Thomas Giles. Child on lap: Henry Alexander Giles. Boy, back: George David Giles. Girl, right: Jane Ann Giles. Boy, front right: Orson Edwin Giles. Portrait: Mother Ann Murdoch Giles.

Mary Giles Larson Rhodehouse, oldest in picture, is a daughter of James Alvin and Margaret Gibson Giles. James is a son of William and Ann Murdoch Giles. Mary is a fifth-generation Murdoch from James and Mary Murray Murdoch. The baby is a ninth-generation Murdoch.

Four Generations of Giles. Left to right: William M Giles, born 1846; William Elliot Giles, born 1893; John Thomas Giles, born 1872; Lawrence Elliot Giles (baby), born 1918.

Back: Orson Edwin, William, Jane Ann, Mother Ann Murdoch Giles, Sarah Elizabeth, George David, Joseph Fielding. Front: Charles Andrew, James Alvin, Father William M Giles, John Thomas, Henry Alexander.

HUSBAND   WILLIAM "M" GILES
    Birth   3 September 1846
    Place   Arnold, Nottingham, England
    Married 5 June 1871
    Place   Salt Lake City, S.L., Utah Endowment House
    Death   30 April 1926 Heber City, Wasatch, Utah
    Burial   2 May 1926 Heber City, Utah Cemetery
    Mother   Mariah KIRKHAM
    Father   Thomas GILES
    Other Wives Rachel HOWARTH Fortie M-29 March 1893

WIFE   ANN MURDOCH
    Birth   14 September 1854
    Place   Salt Lake City, Salt Lake, Utah
    Death   2 January 1890 Heber City, Wasatch, Utah
    Burial   5 January 1890 Heber City, Utah Cemetary
    Mother   Ann STEEL
    Father   John Murray MURDOCH
    Other Husbands
    Information From James & Mary Murray Murdoch Family
    Records & William "M" Giles Family Records

1ST CHILD   John Thomas GILES
    Birth   22 September 1872 Heber,Wasatch,Utah
    Married Elsie Jane DAYTON
    Date   20 February 1892
    Place   Heber City, Wasatch, Utah
    Death   6 March 1962 Provo, Utah, Utah
    Burial   9 March 1962 Heber,Wasatch,Utah Cem

2ND CHILD   Mariah GILES
    Birth   4 May 1874 Heber, Wasatch, Utah
    Death   8 December 1876 Heber, Utah Ceme.

3RD CHILD   William GILES
    Birth   24 October 1875 Heber,Wasatch,Utah
    Death   15 October 1930

4TH CHILD   Jane Ann GILES
    Birth   13 March 1877 Heber, Wasatch, Utah
    Married James SHARP
    Date   18 January 1893
    Place   Logan, Cache, Utah Logan Temple
    Death   7 October 1966 Ogden, Weber, Utah
    Burial   10 October 1966 Heber, Utah, Ceme.

5TH CHILD   George David GILES
    Birth   11 January 1879 Heber,Wasatch,Utah
    Married Mary Elizabeth MAIR
    Date   25 December 1899
    Place   Heber, Wasatch, Utah
    Death   21 March 1946 Heber, Wasatch, Utah
    Burial   25 March 1946 Heber, Utah Cemetery

6TH CHILD   Sarah Elizabeth GILES
    Birth   30 September 1880 Heber,Wasatch,Utah
    Married George Caldwell PYPER
    Date   12 June 1901
    Place   Salt Lake City,S.L. Utah Temple
    Death   2 December 1915 Heber,Wasatch,Utah
    Burial   6 December 1915 Heber,Utah,Cemetery

7TH CHILD   Joseph Fielding GILES
    Birth   6 January 1882 Heber,Wasatch,Utah
    Married Mary Ellen SWEAT
    Date   21 Aug 1906
    Place   Heber City, Wasatch, Utah
    Death   10 July 1960 Richfield,Lncln,Ida.
    Burial   13 July 1960 Richfield,Lncln,Ida.

8TH CHILD   Orson Edwin GILES
    Birth   25 September 1883 Heber,Wasatch,Ut
    Married Gladys Ethel TADD
    Date   27 March 1907
    Place   Spanish Fork, Utah Utah
    Death   17 June 1956 Springville,Ut.,Utah
    Burial   20 June 1956 Springville,Ut.,Utah

9TH CHILD   James Alvin GILES
    Birth   18 April 1885 Heber, Wasatch, Utah
    Married Margaret GIBSON
    Date   31 October 1905
    Place   Heber, Wasatch, Utah
    Death   15 February 1970 Othello, Washing.
    Burial   19 February 1970 Heber, Utah, Ceme.

10TH CHILD   Henry Alexander GILES
    Birth   15 February 1887 Heber, Wasatch,Ut.
    Married Flossie LAKE
    Date   16 August 1911
    Place   Park City, Summit, Utah
    Death   16 June 1930 Heber, Wasatch, Utah
    Burial   19 June 1930 Heber, Utah, Cemetery

11TH CHILD   Charles Andrew GILES
    Birth   15 March 1888 Heber,Wasatch,Utah
    Married LaVerne Grace PROVOST
    Date   8 July 1911
    Place
    Death   17 October 1976
    Burial

1 MURDOCH, James 1786-1831   2 MURDOCH, John Murray 1820-1910
1 MURDOCH, Mary MURRAY, Sp. 1782-1856   1 MURDOCH, Ann STEEL, Sp. 1829-1909

                              3 MURDOCH, ANN 1854-1890
        DESCENDANTS OF--------
                              3 GILES, WILLIAM M, SP, 1846-1926

4 GILES, John Thomas B-22 Sep 1872 M-20 Feb 1892 D-6 Mar 1962
4 GILES, Elsie Jane DAYTON, Sp. B-1 Apr 1877 D-2 Sep 1959

        5 GILES, Rolland Dayton, Sp. (2) B-12 Jun 1892 M-15 Aug 1927 D-27 Apr 1944
        5 GILES, Vivian Euphima ALLEN Flyglare, Sp. B-4 Aug 1894 D-2 Jun 1964
          Flyglare, Clarence Edward, Sp. (1) B-15 June 1894 M-16 Sep 1912 D-2 Apr 1927

               Flyglare, Clarence Edward B-16 Mar 1913 D-2 Jul 1928
               Flyglare, Elmo Eugene   B-28 Jan 1915 M-   M-   M-
               Flyglare, Russell (GILES) B-17 Sep 1916 M-   M-(2) 5 May 1943
               Flyglare, Herbert Grant   B-23 Nov 1918 M-25 Sep 1940
               Flyglare, Harold LeRoy   B-18 Mar 1921 M-   M-
               Thacker Norma Flyglare   B- 1 Feb 1923 M-
               Flyglare, John William   B-14 Mar 1925 M-6 Mar 1943

        6 MORRISON, Vivian Colleen GILES B-26 Apr 1928 M-14 Jan 1950
        6 MORRISON, Jesse Martell, Sp. B-1 Jul 1918
          Morrison, Margaret Louise SWIN, Sp. (1) B-   M-

               Morrison, Larry Martell B-16 Jul 1941 M-6 April 1963
               Mercer, Mary Louise MORRISON, B-12 Oct 1942 M-18 Jun 1960

            7 HANSEN, Rebecca Ellen MORRISON, B-17 Mar 1957 M-30 Oct 1975
            7 HANSEN, Steven Dale, Sp. B-9 Mar 1950

                  8 HANSEN, Kevin Edward B-22 Mar 1978

            7 WIGNALL, Cynthia Susan MORRISON, B-23 Aug 1958 M-15 Oct 1976 Div.
            7 WIGNALL, Allan Douglas B-15 Dec 1956

                  8 WIGNALL, Jason Douglas B-24 Mar 1977

        6 RIGBY, Muriel GILES Ludlow Munn B-7 May 1930
        6 LUDLOW, Ray Thadeus, Sp. (1) B-   M-15 Jan 1946 (Div)
        6 MUNN, Jimmy Dale, Sp. (2) B-22 Nov 1929 M-1 Jan 1948 (Div)
        6 RIGBY, Aaron Webster, Sp. (3) B-11 Jun 1932 M-23 Nov 1963

            7 MELGOZA, Margaret Ann LUDLOW Cantebury Jones Clark B-11 Dec 1946
            7 CANTEBURY, James P. Sp. B-   M-6 Aug 1965 D-
            7 JONES,   Sp. B-   M-
            7 CLARK,   Sp. B-   M-
            7 MELGOZA, Marillio, Sp. B-   M-18 Sep 1970 Div.
            7 HYDE, Joe, Sp. B-   M-4 May 1979
                  8 CANTEBURY, Mark   B-
                  8 JONES, Raymond   B-
                  8 CLARK, Tony   B-
                  8 MELGOZA, Maurilio B-
                  8 MELGOZA, Viesnta   B-
                  8 MELGOZA, Juan   B-

            7 TUCKSEN, Betty Jean MUNN Beckmon B-21 Nov 1949
            7 BECKMAN, David, Sp. B-   M-4 Nov 1966 Div.
            7 TUCKSEN, Eddie, Sp. (2) B-   M-1 Jun 1980
                  8 BECKMAN, Tina Lee   B-
                  8 BECKMAN, Glenda Lynn B-

            7 NYE, Barbara Joan MUNN Golding B-2 Nov 1950
            7 GOLDING, Allen, Sp. (1) B-   M-3 Jun 1966 Div.
            7 NYE, Ed, Sp. (2) B-   M-19 Jan 1980
                  8 GOLDING, Susan Marie B-
                  8 GOLDING, Candy Ann   B-
                  8 GOLDING, Christy Jo B-

            7 FRANKLIN, Myra Lee MUNN Thomas B-15 Jan 1951
            7 THOMAS, Lovell Tommy, Sp. (1) B-   M-   Div.
            7 FRANKLIN, Gene, Sp. (2) B-   M-7 Aug 1975

```
                8 THOMAS, Tammy        B-
                8 THOMAS, Myra Marie   B-
                8 THOMAS, Bobby Dale   B-


        7 RIGBY, Aaron Wayne B-9 Sep 1968

6 CLEMENTS, La Rue GILES B-18 Jun 1932 M-21 Nov 1952
6 CLEMENTS, Carl Savage, Sp. B-9 Jun 1929


        7 CLEMENTS, Michael G. B-15 Oct 1953  M-19 Nov 1976
        7 CLEMENTS, Dianna BEVERLY, Sp. B-


                8                      B-
                8                      B-


        7 CLEMENTS, Carl Guy B-23 Aug 1955   M-10 Oct 1975
        7 CLEMENTS, Cathy Lynn WHITTAKER, Sp. B-


                8 CLEMENTS, Cherish Ann  B-
                8 CLEMENTS, Carl         B-


        7 CLEMENTS, Phillip G. B-22 Jan 1957  M-
        7 CLEMENTS, Treresa Ann BAILY, Sp. B-21 Apr 1979




        7 CLEMENTS, Son (Stillborn)

6 DAVIS, Mary Jean GILES B-17 Jul 1935 M-7 Sep 1952
6 DAVIS, William Joseph, Sp. B-24 Feb 1933  (Billy Joe)


        7 WENTZ, Christine DAVIS B-6 Mar 1953 M-17 Jul 1971
        7 WENTZ, Douglas, Sp. B-


                8 WENTZ, Danny       B-
                8 WENTZ, Robert      B-
                8 WENTZ,             B-


        7 DAVIS, William Joseph B-5 Sep 1954   M-4 Aug 1963
        7 DAVIS, Dixie Lynn VAN AUSDAL, Sp. B-


                8 DAVIS, Jeremy      B-
                8 DAVIS, Jason       B-
                8 DAVIS, Jennifer    B-


        7 DAVIS, Robert Lee B-5 Dec 1955

        7 KELSEY, Dorothy Elizabeth DAVIS B-30 Mar 1957 M-11 Feb 1977
        7 KELSEY, Gary Lynn, Sp. B-


                8 KELSEY, Michael    B-

        7 SNOW, Jeanette DAVIS B-12 Jun 1958 M-10 Oct 1975
        7 SNOW, Craig, Sp. B-


                8 SNOW, Jamie        B-
                8 SNOW, Kimberly     B-


        7 DAVIS, Jerald Roland B-12 Jun 1958 M-12 Jan 1978
        7 DAVIS, Annette HOLMES, Sp. B-

        7 DAVIS, Douglas Ray B-27 Jul 1959

        7 DAVIS, Ronald Gene B-20 Nov 1960

        7 DAVIS, Richard Dale B-16 Apr 1962

        7 DAVIS, Brenda Sue  B-30 Apr 1963

        7 DAVIS, Jeffery Allen B-9 Nov 1964

        7 DAVIS, Steven John B-26 Dec 1970
```

6 SUMMERS, Rollynne Dorthea GILES B-23 Jan 1940 M-10 Oct 1956
6 SUMMERS, Silas Londell, Sp. B- 19 Jun 1932

      7 MALLOUF, Collette Clara SUMMER B-14 Jun 1957 M- 27 Jun 1975
      7 MALLOUF, Ralph Douglas, Sp. B-

         8 MALLOUF, Jeremy Wayne B-

      7 BATTERMAN, Collene E. SUMMERS B-14 Jun 1957   M- 28 Jun 1974
      7 BATTERMAN, George Kevin, Sp. B-

         8 BATTERMAN, George Richard B-
         8 BATTERMAN, David Duane   B-

      7 SUMMERS, Silas Londell Jr. B-30 Aug 1958   M- 23 Dec 1978
      7 SUMMERS, Debra Lynn HALL, Sp. B-

      7 SUMMERS, Rollen Dayton B- 25 Oct 1959

      7 HOLMSTEAD, Rollynne Dorthea B-6 Oct 1961 M-29 Dec 1979
      7 HOLMSTEAD, Michael D., Sp. B-

      7 SUMMERS, Frank James   B-12 May 1964

      7 SUMMERS, Shanon Matthew B- 21 Feb 1966

      7 SUMMERS, Daniel Isaiah   B- 1 Jan 1974

5 GILES, William Elliot B- 17 Dec 1893 M-20 Oct 1913 D-2 Dec 1946
5 GUEST, Sarah Viva CARLILE Giles Sweat, Sp. B-18 Jan 1895
5 SWEAT, Lee Franklin, Sp. (2) B-   M-
5 GUEST, John Earl Sp. (3) B-   M-3 Oct 1959

      6 GILES, Elda Carlile B-7 Feb 1914 D-8 Jan 1919

      6 GILES, Lawrence Elliott B-21 Jun 1818
      6 GILES, Lucille Alberta POAGE, Sp. (1) B-15 Sep 1920 M-29 Nov 1938
      6 GILES, Stella E. Risninger Rice, Sp. (2)B-   M-
      Pierson, Donald Sp. to Lucille

      7 BURNS, Joyce Lucille GILES Doering B- 16 Oct 1939
      7 DOERING, Alfred, Sp. (1) B-   M-14 Jun 1958
      7 BURNS, Robert E. Sp. (2) B-   M-

         8 BURNS, Kirkham   B-
         8 BURNS, William Donald B-
         8 BURNS, Michael   B-

      7 GILES, Edward Lynn B-24 Mar 1942 M-6 Aug 1966
      7 GILES, Sherrie Elizabeth SATHER, Sp. B-

         8 GILES, Layne Beth   B-
         8 GILES, Joey Lael   B-
         8 GILES, Jonathan Matthew B-

      6 GILES, William Doyle B- 6 Mar 1922 M-2 Oct 1946
      6 GILES, Marilyn Maude BROWN, Sp. B-2 Apr 1924

      7 FLETCHER, Roxann GILES Banks B-27 Sep 1949
      7 BANKS, Dennis R. Sp. (1) B-   M-15 Mar 1967
      7 FLETCHER, Stephen, Sp. (2) B-

         8 FLETCHER, John Michael B-

      7 GILES, Mark Brown B-18 Sep 1951 M-6 Feb 1976
      7 GILES, Vivian CARR, Sp. B-

         8 GILES, Alan Elliott   B-

      6 GILES, Alan Carlile B-22 Feb 1928 D-19 Apr 1950

5 MALLETTE, Iona Ann GILES B-1 Dec 1895 M-18 Sep 1919 D-16 Dec 1975
5 MALLETTE, Nelson, Sp. B-17 Jul 1892 D-18 Sep 1964

6 MALLETTE, Letta B-14 Apr 1920 D-23 Dec 1922

6 WHITE, Nada MALLETTE B-14 Aug 1926 M-3 Feb 1959
6 WHITE, Albert Richard, Sp. B-12 Mar 1918

    7 WHITE, Richard Lynn   B-21 Jan 1962
    7 WHITE, Anne   B-29 May 1964
    7 WHITE, Leisa   B- 6 Oct 1965
    7 WHITE, Tamara   B- 2 Sep 1966

6 SHELTON, Retta G MALLETTE B-18 Jun 1929 M-25 Aug 1950
6 SHELTON. Kay Edwin, Sp. B-19 Dec 1926

    7 GORTON, Stephanie Kaye SHELTON B-11 Sep 1952   M-
    7 GORTON, James William, Sp. B-19 Feb 1953

        8 GORTON, William James   B-20 May 1972
        8 GORTON, David Jay   B-23 Jul 1973
        8 GORTON, Michelle Marlene B- 6 May 1975
        8 GORTON, Nathan Kay   B-22 Aug 1977

    7 GILGEN, Rebecca Ann SHELTON B-2 Aug 1957   M-
    7 GILGEN, Richard Stephen, Sp. B-

        8 GILGEN, Benjamin Richard B-9 Mar 1979
        8 GILGEN, Joseph Barthalomew B-18 Mar 1980

    7 SHELTON, Marc Mallette B-21 Nov 1959

    7 SHELTON, Meretta Jene   B-10 Sep 1963

    7 SHELTON, Matthew Mallette B-11 Jul 1965

5 JOHNSON, Edna Almina GILES Clayburn B-11 Jun 1898 D-11 Mar 1977
5 CLAYBURN, David, Sp. (1) B-30 Nov 1887 M-4 Dec 1914 D-23 Jul 1953
5 JOHNSON, Oscar August, Sp. (2) B-   M-30 Oct 1956

    6 CLAYBURN, Elsie Lois B-23 April 1915 D-9 Aug 1931

    6 CLAYBURN, Lawrence Dee B-16 Jan 1917
    6 CLAYBURN, Barbra FONNESBECK, Sp. (1) B-   M-24 Mar 1942 (Div.)
    6 CLAYBURN, Myrtle Colman Asborne, Sp. (2) B-   M-

    6 JOHNSON, Enid CLAYBURN Mecham Bollinger Miller B-18 Feb 1919
    6 MECHAM, Dazel Alma, Sp. (1) B-   M-30 Sep 1937 Div.
    6 BOLLINGER, Merlin Gene, Sp. (2) B-   M-4 Oct 1956 Div.
    6 MILLER, Albert E. Sp. (3) B-   M-16 Dec 1960 Annulment
    6 JOHNSON, Merle, Sp. (4) B-   M-

        7 JOHNSON, Louise MECHAM Carlson Allen Minish B-
        7 CARLSON, Richard, Sp. (1) B-   M-
        7 ALLEN, Edward Eugene, Sp. (2) B-   M-
        7 MINISH, Donald L. Sp. (3) B-   M-
        7 JOHNSON, Tracy, Sp. (4) B-   M-

            8 SMITH, Dixie CARLSON Hanson B-   M-
            8 HANSON, Larry, Sp. (1) B-   M-
            8 SMITH, Fred, Sp. (2) B-   M-

                9 HANSON, Amy Louise B-   1973

            8 JOHNSON, Sandra CARLSON B-   M-
            8 JOHNSON, Carter, Sp. B-

                9 JOHNSON, Jessica   B-

            8 D. E. Ustachio, Julie Allen B-   M-
            8 D. E. USTACHIO, Steve, Sp. B-

            8 ALLEN, Debra   B-
            8

                    9 ALIRES, Angela   B-

            8 MINISH, Kimberly B-

7 MECHAM, LaVerl B-22 Nov 1939 M-26 Dec 1958
7 MECHAM, JoLene EDWARDS, Sp. B-30 June 1941

            8 LEAVITT, Brenda Lee MECHAM B-10 Aug 1959 M-11 May 1978
            8 LEAVITT, Lee, Sp. B-13 Sep

                    9 LEAVITT, Brandon Harlow B-24Nov1978 D-5Feb1979

            8 DAY, Jodi Larae MECHAM B-12 Jan 1961 M-12 Sep 1980
            8 DAY, David Lynn, Sp. B-

            8 MECHAM, Verl D.   B-5 Aug 1963
            8 MECHAM, Angela Marcie B-21 Oct 1977

7 WARNER, Barbara Mecham B-   M-
7 WARNER, Thomas L. Sp. B-

            8 WILLIAMS, Mindi WARNER B-   M-
            8 WILLIAMS, Richard, Sp. B-

            8 WARNER, Machelle   B-

6 WALL, Margaret CLAYBURN Street B-13 Jul 1920
6 STREET, Joseph Melvin, Sp. (1) B-12 Dec 1915 M-8 Apr 1936 D-27 Jan 1953
6 WALL, Lloyd, Sp. (2) B-9 Jan 1912 M-5 Apr 1956

    7 WATSON, Lois STREET B-31 Jul 1937 M-5 Jun 1953
    7 WATSON, Nymphas Coridon, Sp. B-

            8 WATSON, Allen Nymphas B-   M-
            8 WATSON, Penny Jo POULSEN, Sp. B-

                    9 WATSON, James Coridon B- 7 Nov 1976
                    9 WATSON, Megan   B-20 Nov 1980

            8 WATSON, Cindy   B-
            8 WATSON, Mark Melvin B-

            8 DYCHES, Sharon WATSON B-   M-
            8 DYCHES,   Sp. B-

                    9 DYCHES, Ryan Eugne   B-19 Oct 1977

            8 WATSON, Thomas   B-
            8 WATSON, Douglas   B-
            8 WATSON, Heather   B-

    7 HENDERSON, Helen Kay STREET B-17 Sep 1939 M-   Jun 1956
    7 HENDERSON, Paul Jay, Sp. B-

            8 HENDERSON, David Paul B-   M-
            8 HENDERSON, Michelle YATES, Sp. B-

                    9 HENDERSON, Michal   B-
                    9 HENDERSON, Kelli Ann   B-
                    9 HENDERSON, Benjamin Lloyd B-
                    9 HENDERSON, Brian Lee   B-
                    9 HENDERSON, Sandra Jean   B-
                    9 HENDERSON, Daniel Evan   B-
    7 STREET, Karl Melvin B-23 Feb 1943 M-20 Jul 1963
    7 STREET, Carole Anntonette ZACCARIA, Sp. B-

            8 STREET, Bret Karl   B-
            8 STREET, Bradley Steven   B-
            8 STREET, Bart Lloyd   B-

    7 FILLMORE, Margaret Ann STREET B-8 Aug 1948 M-14 Jun 1968
    7 FILLMORE, David Max, Sp. B-

```
                8 FILLMORE, Angela      B-
                8 FILLMORE, Garret David  B-
                8 FILLMORE, Garld       B-

6 CLAYBURN, Theo  Neldon B-8 Aug 1921 D-28 Aug 1962
6 CLAYBURN, Laurel HECRERT, Sp. (1) B-            M-              Div.
6 CLAYBURN, Ardelle Bodily Bowman, Sp. (2) B-              M-           Div.
6 CLAYBURN, Pauline FRANCIS, Sp. (3) B-          M-21 Jun 1950 Div.
6 CLAYBURN, Eilene BACK, Sp. (4) B-              M-   Dec 1960

6 CLAYBURN, Almina B-22 Nov 1922 D-10 Dec 1922

6 CLAYBURN, David Theron B-2 March 1924 M-6 Jul 1944
6 CLAYBURN, Cora HENLINE, Sp. B-

        7 CLAYBURN, Alan David B-            M-
        7 CLAYBURN, Retta Marie LIKES, Sp. (1) B-          M-        Div.
        7 CLAYBURN, Malynne BLAKE, Sp. (2) B-       M-

                8 CLAYBURN, Calista     B-

                8 CLAYBURN, Kimberli    B-
                8 CLAYBURN, Carl David  B-

        7 CLAYBURN, Paul Dean B-            M-
        7 CLAYBURN, Virginia      , Sp. B-

                8 CLAYBURN, Curtis Paul  B-
                8 CLAYBURN, Kevin Vance  B-

        7 McDONALD, Pamela CLAYBURN B-            M-
        7 McDONALD, Joe, Sp. B-

                8 McDONALD, Toni Jo      B-
                8 McDONALD, Kelli Ann    B-

        7 DAVIS, Linda CLAYBURN B-
        7 DAVIS, Joe, Sp. B-            M-          Div.

                8 DAVIS, Robert Lynn     B-

        7 CLAYBURN Scott H. B-

        7 CLAYBURN, Jane     B-

6 CLAYBURN, John Thomas B-28 Jun 1926 M-6 March 1944
6 CLAYBURN, Norine TAYLOR, Sp. B-

        7 BLAYLOCK, Connie Rae CLAYBURN B-
        7 BLAYLOCK, David Robert, Sp. (1) B-            M-          Div.

                8 BLAYLOCK, Jeffery David  B-
                8 BLAYLOCK, Derek Layne    B-
                8 BLAYLOCK, Damon Thomas   B-

        7 CLAYBURN, Robert T. B-            M-
        7 CLAYBURN, JoLynn UPWALL, Sp. B-
                8 CLAYBURN, Cherree Lynn   B-          (Adopted)
                8 CLAYBURN, Christopher    B-

        7 CLAYBURN, Thomas N. B-            M-          D-
        7 CLAYBURN, Mary E. WILSON, Sp. B-

        7 CLAYBURN, Lynn D. B-            M-
        7 CLAYBURN, Sandra Jean McQUILAN, Sp. B-

                8 CLAYBURN, Lyndie Jean   B-
                8 CLAYBURN, Garrett Kelly  B-
```

5 GILES, John Golden B-2 Oct 1901 M-30 Jul 1929 D-28 Jul 1941
5 CHIPMAN, Mary Louisa SHEPHERD Giles Healey, Sp. B-24 Sep 1911
5 HEALEY, John Samuel, Sp. (2) B-   M-19 Apr 1946 D-   1956
5 CHIPMAN, Oscar Kenneth, Sp. (3) B-12 Apr 1903 M-7 Aug 1958

        6 EGGERS, Elaine Giles Lemmon Collier B-13 Jun 1930
        6 LEMMON, Royal W. Sp. (1) B-   M-14 Jun 1946 Div.
        6 COLLIER, Elvis Clyde, Sp. (2) B-   M-12 May 1956 Div.
        6 EGGERS, John Wesley, Sp. (3) B-19 Oct 1935 M-18 Feb 1966 Div.

                7 MORTENSEN, Mary Janine B-23 Jun 1960
                7 MORTENSEN, Stewart Nels, Sp. B-   M-6 Oct 1978

                7 EGGERS, Anna Elaine   B-16 Jun 1968

        6 GILES, Charles Golden B-9 Dec 1931
        6 McCORY, Jeanette TARIN Giles Sp. (1) B-   M-20 Sep 1952 Div.
          McCory, James Ellis, Sp. (2) B-   M-
        6 GILES, Lynette Joyce PRISBREY, Sp. (2) B-21 Feb 1953 M-3 Apr 1971

                7 LEIGHTON, Debra Ann GILES B-20 Sep 1954 M-17 Sep 1976
                7 LEIGHTON, Christopher De, Sp. B-

                        8 LEIGHTON, Christopher Bernard B-17 Oct 1978
                        8 LEIGHTON, Thomas Anthony   B-17 Oct 1978

                7 LANDIG, Taryn Marie GILES B-25 Aug 1958
                7 LANDIG, John, Sp. B-9 Oct 1957 M-25 Oct 1980

                7 GILES, Edward Golden B-6 Oct 1971

                7 GILES, Michael Charles B-2 Mar 1975

        6 GILES, Dale Kirkham B-28 Mar 1933 M-1 Jan 1958
        6 GILES, Marva Rae RICE, Sp. B-28 Jul 1940

                7 CROSS, Brenda Rae GILES B-23 Jul 1958
                7 CROSS, Steven E., Sp. B-   M-16 Apr 1981

                        8 CROSS, Shaun Franklin   B-26 Jan 1982

                7 GILES, Ronald Dale   B-25 Aug 1958
                7 GILES, Tamara Kay   B- 2 Sep 1961

                7 PETERSON, Jillynn B-24 Oct 1962
                7 PETERSON, Harvey Joe, Sp. B-   M-24 Feb 1982

                7 GILES, Teresa Ann   B-18 Jan 1964
                7 GILES, Sherri Lee   B-11 Feb 1967
                7 GILES, Brent William   B-14 Aug 1970
                7 GILES, Curtis John   B- 2 Mar 1976
                7 GILES, Caryn Louisa   B-30 Aug 1977
                7 GILES, Cortney Dawn   B- 9 Nov 1981

        6 YOUNG, Annette GILES B-22 Dec 1934
        6 YOUNG, James Hilton, Sp. B-21 Aug 1930 M-24 Apr 1951 Div.

                7 YOUNG, James Ralph B-26 Sep 1951
                7 YOUNG, Rebecca Lynn RACKHAM, Sp. B-29 Aug 1962 M-13 May 1978

                        8 YOUNG, Jennifer Lynn   B- 1 Dec 1980

                7 FUGAL, Connie Jean YOUNG B-23 Mar 1954 M-24 Nov 1971
                7 FUGAL, Christian Arthur, Sp. B-

                        8 FUGAL, Angel Annette   B-13 Nov 1973
                        8 FUGAL, Adam Arthur   B- 2 Aug 1975
                        8 FUGAL, Merrill Lynn   B-27 Sep 1976
                        8 FUGAL, Danny Lee   B-15 May 1978
                        8 FUGAL, Misty Ann   B-26 Aug 1979
                        8 FUGAL, David Allen   B-18 Jan 1981

                7 YOUNG, Danny Lee B-29 Jun 1955 D-30 Oct 1955

```
        7 RASMUSSEN, Peggy Elaine YOUNG B-16 Aug 1956
        7 RASMUSSEN, Steven Craig, Sp. B-              M-30 Jun 1978

                8 RASMUSSEN, Craig James        B-10 Dec 1978
                8 RASMUSSEN, Justin Ray          B-16 Mar 1982

        7 YOUNG, Larry Dean B-1 Jul 1957
        7 YOUNG, Karen Sue CLAYTON, Sp. B-4 Feb 1963 M-22 Jun 1981

        7 YOUNG, Ramona Gay       B-12 Jun 1959

        7 HORROCKS, Ellen Louise YOUNG B-18 Mar 1961
        7 HORROCKS, Ronnie Neil, Sp. B-              M-25 Feb 1976

                8 HORROCKS, Jared Niel          B-22 Jul 1978
                8 HORROCKS, Shawn Colby         B-24 May 1980

        7 YOUNG, Julie Ann        B-22 Jan 1963

  6 TUTTLE, Florence Elsie GILES B-19 May 1936
  6 TUTTLE, Harold Strong, Sp. B-21 Mar 1930 M-13 Jul 1951

        7 TUTTLE, Jay Harold B-14 May 1952
        7 TUTTLE, Phyleene Wanda HOWARD, Sp. B-              M-2 Dec 1977

                8 TUTTLE, Michael Adam          B-23 Sep 1978
                8 TUTTLE, Nathania Collette      B-19 Aug 1980

        7 RUBI, Catherine Marie TUTTLE B-5 Oct 1954 M-8 Aug 1973
        7 RUBI, Gilbert Joseph, Sp. B-30 Apr 1950 D-28 Mar 1980

                8 RUBI, Emily Marie             B-26 Nov 1974
                8 RUBI, Kimberly Ann            B-11 Jan 1979

        7 BARNEY, Carol Ann TUTTLE B-17 Jan 1956 M-28 Mar 1975
        7 BARNEY, Jay Kelvin, Sp. B-13 Oct 1956

                8 BARNEY, Keturah Ann           B-14 Nov 1976
                8 BARNEY, Angela BreAnn         B-15 Nov 1978
                8 BARNEY, Charlene Marie        B-11 Mar 1980

        7 TUTTLE, Brent Lynn B-29 Sep 1959 M-20 Mar 1982
        7 TUTTLE, Michelle BURROWS, Sp. B-

        7 TUTTLE, John Byron       B- 4 Mar 1961

  6 GILES, Darrell J B-17 Jan 1938 M-17 Jun 1958
  6 GILES, Myrna Loy SIMONS, Sp. S-

        7 GILES, Timothy Jay       B-26 Jun 1959
        7 GILES, Loyann Elaine     B- 3 Aug 1962
        7 GILES, Terry Denise      B-15 Jun 1964
        7 GILES, John Carl         B- 6 Jul 1966
        7 GILES, Mary Louisa       B-29 Nov 1968
        7 GILES, Stephanie Collette B-6 Jun 1970
        7 GILES, Sandra Melissa    B-30 Jun 1972
        7 GILES, Patti Jolyn       B- 6 May 1974
        7 GILES, Bobbi Jo Melinda B-26 Aug 1975
        7 GILES, Darrell J.        B- 2 Oct 1980

5 DURTSCHI, Nellie Amanda Giles B-25 June 1905 M-27 Jun 1923 (2) D-30 Nov 1978
5 DURTSCHI, Ernest, Sp. B-10 Jan 1878 D-11 Feb 1947
5 DURTSCHI, Elise FISCHER, Sp.(1) B-              M-

  6 SPRIGGS, Wilma June DURTSCHI B-30 Jun 1924 M-21 Dec 1945
  6 SPRIGGS, Max A. B-16 Jul 1924

        7 VAUGHN, Maxine Spriggs B-13 May 1947 M-21 Nov 1967
        7 VAUGHN, Warren Clyde, Sp. B-2 Feb 1945

                8 VAUGHN, Sharyl Lee            B-28 Jun 1968
                8 VAUGHN, Shae Lynn             B-25 Sep 1968
                8 VAUGHN, Shelly Ann            B-13 Dec 1971
                8 VAUGHN, Shannon               B- 6 Mar 1976
                8 VAUGHN, Warren Tyler          B-22 Jun 1981
```

7 SPRIGGS, Randall Earnest B-24 Feb 1950
7 SPRIGGS, Virginia Lynn FLOOR, Sp. B-6 Apr 1951 M-18 Mar 1972

        8 SPRIGGS, Nicole Nanette B- 9 Oct 1972
        8 SPRIGGS, Calie Sharrie B-23 Mar 1976
        8 SPRIGGS, Ashlie Anne B- 2 Feb 1978
        8 SPRIGGS, Randall Phillip B-12 Oct 1981

7 WILLARD, Marianne SPRIGGS B-23 Apr 1952 M-24 Sep 1976
7 WILLARD, Calvin A. B-4 Jun 1939

7 CAHILL, Janelle SPRIGGS B-5 Jul 1956 M-4 Jun 1979
7 CAHILL, James Randall B-2 Mar 1950

        8 CAHILL, Christopher Max B-8 Apr 1980

6 MACBETH, Elsie Vera DURTSCHI B-6 Sep 1927   M-27 Jun 1946
6 MACBETH, Jay Weldon, Sp. B- 29 Dec 1923

    7 OLDROYD, Jaylynn MACBETH B-23 Jul 1947 M-15 Jul 1966
    7 OLDROYD, Thomas Barr, Sp. B- 19 Sep 1942

        8 OLDROYD, David Thomas B-10 Aug 1969
        8 OLDROYD, Jonathan Jay B-10 Jul 1973
        8 OLDROYD, Matthew Ivory B-2 Nov 1975

    7 MACBETH, Dennis Ray B-18 Nov 1948

    7 MACBETH, David Weldon B-20 Nov 1952 M-13 Jun 1974
    7 MACBETH, Nadine CARTER, Sp. B-13 Jul 1953

        8 MACBETH, Stephen Eric B-12 Jun 1978

    7 MACBETH, Daryl Jay B-19 Jul 1955 M-15 Sep 1977
    7 MACBETH, Linda Mae OMAN, Sp. B- 17 Oct 1954

        8 MACBETH, Heather Amanda   B-
5 DOYLE, Elsie LeOra Giles Bowman B-10 Feb 1908
5 BOWMAN, John James, Sp. (1) B-23 Apr 1904 M-28 Jul 1925
5 DOYLE, James, Sp. (2) B-   M-

    6 JACKSON, Ora   E BOWMAN B-21 Jul 1926 M-27 Aug 1945 D-29 Oct 1966
    6 JACKSON, Lester William, Sp. B-

        7 JACKSON, J William (Bill) B-   M-
        7 JACKSON,

            8 JACKSON, Denice   B-
            8 JACKSON, Andrea

        7 MILLETTE Shauna JACKSON B-   M-
        7 MILLETTE, Frank, Sp. B-

            8 MILLETTE, Scott   B-
            8 MILLETTE, Ora Lee B-

    6 BOWMAN, James Melvin B-7 Nov 1927 M-3 Aug 1948
    6 BOWMAN, Joy Mae SABEY, Sp. B-11 Oct 1930

        7 BOWMAN, Randy Melvin B-2 Nov 1949   M-
        7 BOWMAN,

            8 BOWMAN, Heather   B-

        7 BOWMAN, Brent Roland B-15 Mar 1952
        7 BOWMAN,

            8 BOWMAN, Matthew   B-
            8 BOWMAN, Rachel   B-

        7 BOWMAN, Linda Jo B-20 May 1957

7 BOWMAN, Sharon   B-21 Jan 1964

7 BOWMAN, Baby boy (Stillborn) B-19 May 1966

6 BOWMAN, Neldon J B-4 Oct 1929 M-15 Jul 1950
6 BOWMAN, Shirley Rae KIRK, Sp. B-

    7 BOWMAN, Michael B-   M-
    7 BOWMAN,   Sp. B-

        8 BOWMAN, Joshua B-

    7 BOWMAN, Goldie Rae B-

    7 BOWMAN, Karlene   B-

    7 BOWMAN, Nedra   B-

    7 BOWMAN, Audrey   B-

    7 BOWMAN, Shirley   B-

6 MANN, Marva BOWMAN B-   M-
6 MANN, Joseph William, Sp. B-

    7 STEELE, Carrie Lyn MANN B-   M-
    7 STEELE, Cleston, Sp.

        8 STEELE, Russell

    7 MANN, Cindy   B-

    7 MANN, Joseph Jr.   B-

6 ANDERSEN, Rhea BOWMAN B-14 May 1934 M-16 Aug 1952
6 ANDERSEN, Max Earl ANDERSEN, Sp. B-25 Feb 1933

    7 PERKINS, Rhonda Kay ANDERSEN B-5 Oct 1954 M-8 Aug 1975
    7 PERKINS, John Gregory, Sp. B-
    7 ANDERSEN, Brenda Sue B-29 Apr 1956

    7 ANDERSEN, Peggy Deann B- 7 Sep 1961

    7 ANDERSEN, Glenn Earl B-19 May 1970

6 JESSEN, Beatrice Marie BOWMAN Wootton B-11 Feb 1936
6 WOOTTON, John, Sp. (1) B-   M-   Div.
6 JESSEN, Darrel, Sp. (2) B-   M-

    7 JONES, Debra JESSEN B-   M-
    7 JONES, Evan, Sp. B-

    7 JESSEN, James Darrell B-

    7 JESSEN, Ryan Tanner   B-

    7 JESSEN, Kathryn   B-

6 SORENSEN, LoAnn BOWMAN B-26 Mar 1937 M-
6 SORENSEN, Elwood, Sp. B-

    7 SORENSON, Stephen   B-

    7 SORENSON, David   B-

    7 SORENSON, DON   B-

    7 SORENSON, Marvin   B-

6 PARKER, Loretta BOWMAN B-17 Jun 1939 M-31 May 1957
6 PARKER, Henry Allen, Sp. B-9 May 1933

```
              7 PARKER, Jeanette          B-22 Sep 1958

              7 PARKER, Nedra Ann         B-22 Jun 1960

              7 PARKER, James Steven    B-20 May 1962  D-15 Aug 1975

              7 PARKER, Judilyn           B-11 Sep 1965

              7 PARKER, Curtis Allen     B-24 Nov 1967

              7 PARKER, Jason Richard  B-25 Apr 1970

              7 PARKER, Shaun Patrick  B-13 Feb 1974

              7 PARKER, Adrienne          B- 1 Nov 1975

5 GILES, Forrest Grant B-29 Sep 1910 M-21 Apr 1934
5 GILES, Viola SWEAT, Sp. B-27 Mar 1919

         6 MITCHELL, Melva E GILES B-8 Jan 1936 M-27 Sep 1963
         6 MITCHELL, Glen R  Sp. B-2 Sep 1934

              7 MITCHELL, Nolan Glen    B-14 Dec 1964

              7 MITCHELL, Wade Giles    B-23 Jan 1968

         6 GILES, Curtis LaVerl B-6 May 1940 M-26 Jul 1963
         6 GILES, Ilene MICHIE, Sp. B-13 Jul 1943

              7 GILES, Lisa LaNae       B-19 Nov 1965
              7 GILES, Janine           B-26 Feb 1967
              7 GILES, Carla Esther     B-26 Nov 1969
              7 GILES, Bradley Curtis   B-16 Apr 1973
              7 GILES, Gregory Kenneth B-18 May 1976

         6 DILLINGHAM, Fay Lorene GILES B-31 Oct 1942
         6 GORDON, Glade Casper, Sp. (1) B-9 Jan 1939    M-15 Jan 1957  Div.
         6 DILLINGHAM, James, Sp. (2) B-           M-9 Oct 1974 Div.
         6 BOYD, Alvin, Sp. (3) B-              M-          1978 Annulled

              7 GORDON, Gerold Glade    B- 7 Apr 1959

              7 GORDON, Mark Adrian B-18 Jul 1960 M-14 Feb 1979
              7 GORDON, Diane WILLIAMS, Sp. B-
              7 GORDEN, James Grant     B-28 Jul 1962
              7 GORDEN, Wendy Kaye      B- 6 Jul 1964
              7 GORDEN, Lorie Faye      B-16 Apr 1968

         6 GILES, Paul B-11 Apr 1945 M-29 Oct 1964
         6 GILES, Dixie Ann PARCELL, Sp. B-26 Oct 1946

              7 GILES, Judy Ann         B- 5 Aug 1965
              7 GILES, LeRoy Paul       B-19 Oct 1971
              7 GILES, Nathan Harris    B-24 Dec 1977

         6 SMITH, Gaylen GILES, B-25 Apr 1949 M-1 Dec 1967
         6 SMITH, DeVar Ivan, Sp. B-26 Jan 1945

              7 SMITH, Jennie Kirsten   B-27 Apr 1970
              7 SMITH, Ryan Bennett     B-11 Jul 1972
              7 SMITH, Summer Alisa     B-17 May 1974
              7 SMITH, Melodee Ann      B- 2 Mar 1976
              7 SMITH, Kami Lee         B-10 Dec 1977

         6 PROVOST, Enid GILES B-18 May 1950 M-14 Jan 1966
         6 PROVOST, Michael, Sp. B-29 Dec

              7 PROVOST, Tonya Marie    B-25 Dec 1966
              7 PROVOST, Amanda Jo      B-27 Feb 1976

         6 GILES, Marty B-5 Jun 1956 M-25 Jun 1974
         6 GILES, Tamara BULKLEY, Sp. B-22 Oct 1953
```

5 GILES, Fay Kirkham B- 10 Jul 1913 D-23 Jul 1927

4 GILES, Mariah B-4 May 1874 D-8 Dec 1876

4 GILES, William B-24 Oct 1875 D-15 Oct 1930

4 SHARP, Jane Ann GILES B-13 Mar 1877 M-18 Jan 1893 D-7 Oct 1966
4 SHARP, James, Sp. B-

    5 GALLI, Hazel Ann SHARP B- 13 Nov 1893 M-19 Jun 1912
    5 GALLI, Joseph Clarence, Sp. B-   D-   1974

        6 ROBERTS, Norma GALLI Kingsford B-   M-
        6 KINGSFORD, Dick, Sp. (1) B-   M-
        6 ROBERTS, Frank D. Sp. (2) B-   M-

            7 ROBERTS, David R. Kingsford B-   M-
            7 ROBERTS, Sondra PETERSON, Sp. B-

                8 ROBERTS, Derek David   B-
                8 ROBERTS, John Bradley   B-

            7 ROBERTS, Kenneth Arthur Kingsford, B-   M-
            7 ROBERTS, Mary Gail HANSON, Sp. B-

                8 ROBERTS, Lisa Gaye   B-
                8 ROBERTS, Kenneth Michael B-
                8 ROBERTS, Mark Stephen   B-
                8 ROBERTS, Leslie Gail   B-
                8 ROBERTS, Brett David   B-
                8 ROBERTS, David Brian   B-
                8 ROBERTS,   B-

            7 ROBERTS, Dan G. B-   M-
            7 ROBERTS, Sheila Rae Condie, Sp. B-

                8 ROBERTS, Dan Scot   B-
                8 ROBERTS, George Ryan   B-
                8 ROBERTS, David Jason   B-
                8 ROBERTS, Angela   B-

            7 HYTE, Jane ROBERTS B-   M-
            7 HYTE, Robert Brent, Sp. B-

                8 HYTE, Laura Jane   B-
                8 HYTE, Michelle Ann   B-
                8 HYTE, Robert Sean   B-
                8 HYTE, Brian Frank   B-
                8 HYTE, Daren James   B-
                8 HYTE, Lanae?   B-

            7 COX, Ann ROBERTS B-   M- .
            7 COX, Jesse Lamont, Sp B-

                8 COX, Jennifer Ann   B-
                8 COX, Christi Lynn   B-

      6 GALLI, Clarence Joseph B-21 May 1918 M-4 Dec 1947
      6 GALLI, Evelyn REED Goon, Sp. B-4 Feb 1920
      Goon, Theodore John, Sp. (1) B-   M-11 Apr 1941 Div.-1945

          7 GALLI, Jeffrey Reed Goon B- 29 Apr 1944 M-4 Apr 1968   (Adopted)
          7 GALLI, Robin Louise REID, Sp. B- 19 Sep 1949

              8 GALLI, Guy Morgan   B-18 Jan 1970
              8 GALLI, Nathan Lyle   B-26 Aug 1972
              8 GALLI, Christopher Robin B-17 Dec 1974

          7 GALLI, Steven Lynn B-28 Aug 1949
          7 GALLI, Valarie CANNON, Sp. B-17 Jul 1949 M-9 Mar 1968   Div.1972

              8 GALLI, Adam Blue   B-31 Jul 1968
              8 GALLI, Aaron Joseph   B-25 Mar 1970

```
                7 GALLI, Dina Joe   B- 4 Feb 1958

                7 GALLI, James Lee   B-30 Nov 1961

        6 GALLI, Melvin James B-              M-
        6 GALLI, Mildred SESSIONS, Sp. B-

                7 GALLI, Melvin James Jr. B-
                7 GALLI, Bonnie        Sp. (1) B-           M-
                7 GALLI, Nancy         Sp. (2) B-           M-

                        8 GALLI, Timothy James      B-
                        8 GALLI,                    B-
                        8 GALLI,                    B-
                        8 GALLI,                    B-

5 DEAN, Sadie Sharp B-7 Aug 1896 M-12 Feb 1916 D-31 Jul 1975
5 DEAN, William, Sp. B-8 Feb 1893 D-20 Apr 1942

        6 DEAN, Gene William B-20 Mar 1917 M-21 Dec 1939 D-5 Feb 1965
        6 WILLIAMS, Marcia Ann HOUSLEY Dean, Sp. B-21 May 1920
          Williams, Cleo Doyle, Sp. (2&3) B-         M-

                7 DEAN, Arlene      B-15 Feb 1941

                7 DEAN, Darlene     B-15 Feb 1941

                7 CROCKETT, Marcia Gene DEAN B-3 Nov 1942 M-21 May 1962
                7 CROCKETT, William Clair, Sp. B-

                7 BUTTERFIELD, Sylvia DEAN B-11 Mar 1945 M-15 Dec 1966
                7 BUTTERFIELD, Fred Bowlden, Sp. B-

                7 DEAN, Rolf Jon B-24 May 1950 M-
                7 DEAN, Sherrie        Sp. B-

                7 DEAN, Garth James B-24 Dec 1954
                7 DEAN, Luann JONES, B-            M-19 Jan 1973
                7 DEAN, Debra          PETERSON, Sp. (2) B-        M-       1980

        6 DEAN, Glen James B-29 Jun 1918 D-29 Dec 1939

        6 DEAN, Claude Charles B-3 Jun 1921 M-3 Apr 1945
        6 DEAN, Bernice WATSON, Sp. B-9 May 1922

                7 DEAN, Child (Stillborn)   B-30 Jul 1946
                7 DEAN, Child (Stillborn)   B-27 Apr 1949
                7 DEAN, Val                 B-12 Feb 1950 D-13 Feb 1950

                7 DEAN, Darrell Jae  B-9 Dec 1953 M-23 Feb 1974
                7 DEAN, Kim HAIGHT,Sp. B-

                7 DEAN Marvin Kay B-4 Dec 1955

                7 BURCH, Valerie DEAN B-26 Sep 1957 M-5 Apr 1974 Div.
                7 BURCH, Donald Dean, Sp. B-

                7 DEAN, Lance Elden B-4 Jun 1964

        6 DEAN, Leo Arthur B-9 Nov 1923 M-12 Sep 1946
        6 DEAN, Twila Mae BOND, Sp. B-6 Apr 1926

                7 DEAN, Glen Royden B-10 Jun 1947 M-10 Jul 1970
                7 DEAN, Alison LANGFORD, Sp. B-

                7 BAER, Lynette DEAN B-2 Oct 1950 M-18 Aug 1972
                7 BAER, Ralph A. Sp. B-

                7 DEAN, Marlo Leslie B-6 Mar 1952 M-23 Aug 1974
                7 DEAN, Marcee Elizabeth STEVENSON, Sp. B-

                7 BUTLER, Shauna DEAN B-15 Jun 1956 M-5 Oct 1979
                7 BUTLER, Van LaMar, Sp. B-
```

6 DEAN, Don Murray B-29 Jan 1929 M-30 Nov 1946
6 DEAN, Julia Pearl HEALEY, Sp. B-1 Sep 1929

    7 JAY, Donna Marie DEAN B-13 Jul 1947 M-1 Jul 1966
    7 JAY, James Robert, Sp. B- 25 Sep 1945

        8 JAY, Teresa   B-27 Apr 1969
        8 JAY, Julianne   B-24 Feb 1974

    7 TANKERSLEY, Dianna DEAN B-18 Mar 1949 M-28 Jan 1967
    7 TANKERSLEY, Richard James, Sp. B-21 Mar 1944

        8 TANKERSLEY, Richelle Diane B-29 May 1969
        8 TANKERSLEY, Stephanie Liane B-27 Jan 1975
        8 TANKERSLEY, Richard James B- 6 Sep 1978
        8 TANKERSLEY, Jamie Ann   B- 4 Aug 1980

    7 DEAN, Murray William B-19 Jun 1950 M-8 Jul 1975
    7 DEAN, Wendy Leah POND, Sp. B-10 May 1954

        8 DEAN, Ryan Murray   B-19 Jul 1977
        8 DEAN, Tyson William   B-15 Jul 1978

    7 WEEDEN, Barbara DEAN B-10 Sep 1953 M-12 Aug 1977
    7 WEEDEN, John Paul, Sp. B-26 Sep 1946

        8 WEEDEN, Adam Michael   B-15 May 1978

    7 DEAN, Byron Jay B-11 Mar 1955 M-3 Sep 1976
    7 DEAN, Merilynn ROWAN, Sp. B-28 Jul 1955

        8 DEAN, Melanie Joy   B-19 Feb 1978
        8 DEAN, Shelly Renee   B-25 May 1979
5 SHARP, James MURRAY B-   M-
5 SHARP, Mary Edith BYRNE, Sp. B-

    6 HARRIS, Mary Josephine SHARP Storey Palmer B-
    6 STOREY, Print Edward, Sp. B-   M-
    6 PALMER, Edward Puffpaff, Sp. (2) B-   M-   D-1965
    6 HARRIS, Arvil A. Sp. (3) B-   M-
    Harris, Viva Johnson, Sp. (1) to Arvil B-   M-

        7 STOREY, Terrell Brent B-   1943 D-   1943

        7 WEIGHT, Tawna STOREY B-   M-
        7 WEIGHT,

            8 WEIGHT, Sean Roger   B-
            8 WEIGHT, Aimee   B-
            8 WEIGHT, Brandon James B-
            8 WEIGHT, Treavor Ross   B-

    6 ROBBINS, June Annie SHARP CHRISTENSEN B-26 Jun 1923
    6 CHRISTENSEN, Donald Alma, Sp. B-27 or 28 Sep 1922 M-31 Dec 1943 D-18 Apr1945
    6 ROBBINS, Archie Clayton, Sp. (2) B-2 May 1919 M-2 Apr 1949

        7 ROBBINS, Dennis J Christensen B-19 May 1945 M-19 Dec 1969
        7 ROBBINS, Malinda Lee HOGGE, Sp. B-15 Mar 1948

            8 ROBBINS, Christian D   B-24 Feb 1972
            8 ROBBINS, Emily Roxanne B-16 Mar 1975
            8 ROBBINS, Iam J   B-27 Sep 1978

        7 ROBBINS, Jennifer Anne B-29 Sep 1963

    6 SHARP, James Robert B-29 Jan 1925   M- 29 Jan 1949
    6 SHARP, Kathleen Lucille PAINTER, Sp. B- 3 Aug 1930

        7 McQUISTON, Randi Kae SHARP B- 9 Dec 1949   M- 18 Jan 1969
        7 McQUISTON, Harry II. Sp. B-8 Jul 1947

            8 McQUISTON, Marci Kae   B- 25 Sep 1969
            8 McQUISTON, Harry Jason B- 6 Apr 1971

```
                    8 McQUISTON, Jacob Cooper  B- 14 Mar 1973
                    8 McQUISTON, Jonathan Andrew B- 16 Oct 1979


            7 WILSON, April Ann SHARP B-30 Apr 1953    M-11 Dec 1971
            7 WILSON, Mark Loring, Sp. B-22 Aug 1952

                    8 WILSON, Charles Colby     B-10 Jun 1972
                    8 WILSON, Chadwick Loring   B-15 Aug 1973
                    8 WILSON, Mindy Jo          B-28 Oct 1974
                    8 WILSON, Matthew Ryan      B- 9 Aug 1976
                    8 WILSON, Megan Elizabeth   B- 8 Jun 1980


            7 COLLINS, Susan SHARP B- 23 Jul 1955    M-30 Aug 1973
            7 COLLINS, Gary Lee, Sp. B-17 Sep 1953

                    8 COLLINS, Cory Lee         B-14 Jun 1974
                    8 COLLINS, Kathleen         B-12 May 1976



            7 SHARP, James Murray B-20 May 1957    M- 18 Feb 1977
            7 SHARP, Mary Jane Spainhower, Sp. B- 31 Dec 1957

                    8 SHARP, Amanda Jane        B-14 Jun 1978
                    8 SHARP, James Robert       B-21 Mar 1980


5 BYRNE, Luella SHARP B-5 Oct 1901 M-7 Oct 1919
5 BYRNE, Walter Moses, Sp. B-15 Jan 1898 D-13 Jul 1970

        6 BYRNE, Francis Walter B-17 Sep 1920 M-27 Nov 1941
        6 BYRNE, Emma TINGEY, Sp. B-21 May 1920

            7 REYNOSO, Renee BYRNE B-11 May 1953 M-26 Aug 1978 Div.
            7 REYNOSO, Amado, Sp. B-


        6 CROMPTON, Hazel Fae BYRNE B-7 Jan 1926 M-23 Feb 1946
        6 CROMPTON, Clifford Don, Sp. B-13 Mar 1924

            7 CROMPTON, Clifford Brent B-13 Jan 1948 M-8 Dec 1967
            7 CROMPTON, Vickie Lynn TIMPSON, Sp. B-27 Jul 1948

                    8 CROMPTON, Tiffany Lynn     B- 8 Apr 1971
                    8 CROMPTON, Kimberlie Bree   B-17 Jun 1976


            7 CROMPTON, Craig Byrne B-21 Dec 1950 M-18 Dec 1970
            7 CROMPTON, Charlene ANDERSON, Sp. B-18 May 1951

                    8 CROMPTON, Christa Lee      B-17 Oct 1973
                    8 CROMPTON, Angie            B-28 Nov 1975
                    8 CROMPTON, Marci            B- 7 Jun 1978


            7 CROMPTON, Kevin Lynn B-1 Nov 1952 M-13 Dec 1975 Div.
            7 CROMPTON, Colleen HUSON Huntsman, Sp. B-

            7 CROMPTON, Corey Dean B-28 Dec 1956 M-13 Oct 1978
            7 CROMPTON, Elene' Suzanne TURNEY, Sp. B-15 Apr 1959

                    8 CROMPTON, Casey Jordan     B-15 Jun 1979


            7 CROMPTON, Daryl Lee B-4 Aug 1958 M-30 May 1980
            7 CROMPTON, Tamara Joanne DE LORA, Sp. B-28 Feb 1961

        6 LARSON, Donna Ann BYRNE B-22 Oct 1927 M-28 Aug 1946
        6 LARSON, Ralph Alfred, Sp. B-29 Apr 1924

            7 LARSON, Grant Ralph B-25 Mar 1947 M-20 Jun 1968
            7 LARSON, Sarah Anne WILBUR (Sally), Sp. B-26 Jan 1948

                    8 LARSON, Kathleen Sarah     B-30 Apr 1969
                    8 LARSON, Michael Grant      B-11 May 1970
                    8 LARSON, Adam Trent         B-20 Oct 1971
                    8 LARSON, John Ray           B- 4 Dec 1972
                    8 LARSON, Ruth Ann           B-29 Nov 1974
                    8 LARSON, Paul Arron         B-30 Sep 1976
```

```
                    8 LARSON, Daniel Nathan      B-24 Jan 1978
                    8 LARSON, Martha Marie        B-30 Sep 1979


            7 LARSON, David Walter B-17 Jul 1948
            7 LARSON, Linda BURNETT, Sp. B-9 Dec 1947


                    8 LARSON, Rebecca Ann         B-30 Mar 1968
                    8 LARSON, Richard David       B-26 Jul 1969
                    8 LARSON, Alisa Lorraine      B-25 Feb 1971
                    8 LARSON, Debrrah VaNeta      B-17 Apr 1972


            7 LARSON, Robert Alfred B-27 Aug 1951 M-29 May 1976
            7 LARSON, Loriann GWYNN, Sp. B-12 Oct 1955


                    8 LARSON, Matthew Ryan        B-20 Apr 1977
                    8 LARSON, Jason Scott         B-13 Jan 1979


            7 LARSON, Keith Don B-6 Apr 1959


      6 RASMUSSEN, Fawn La Rae BYRNE B-9 Oct 1934 M-28 Jul 1951
      6 RASMUSSEN, Ronald Lee, Sp. B- 23 Sept 1934


            7 RASMUSSEN, Ricky Lee B-11 Mar 1952 M-27 May 1972
            7 RASMUSSEN, Karla BUTTERFIELD, Sp. B-22 Dec 1951


                    8 RASMUSSEN, Erin Lynne       B- 8 Dec 1974
                    8 RASMUSSEN, Clay 'R'         B- 6 Dec 1976
                    8 RASMUSSEN, Joni             B-23 Jul 1980


            7 BUHRLEY, Karen La Rae RASMUSSEN B-5 Jul 1953
            7 BUHRLEY, Ronald William, Sp. B-5 Apr 1953


                    8 BUHRLEY, Stephanie Karen    B- 5 Jun 1976
                    8 BUHRLEY, Jennifer Jill      B-15 Jun 1978


            7 MYERS, Wendy Lou RASMUSSEN B-15 Nov 1954 M-1 Feb 1974
            7 MYERS, Danny L., Sp. B-12 Jul 1953


                    8 MYERS, Cozette Lee          B-12 Sep 1974
                    8 MYERS, Cole Dan             B-23 Mar 1978
                    8 MYERS, Cache Lynn           B- 9 May 1980


            7 RHEES, Shanna Lynne RASMUSSEN B-8 Nov 1957 M-16 Sep 1977
            7 RHEES, David Jay, Sp. B-5 Jan 1956


                    8 RHEES, Ashlee Lynne         B-24 Oct 1979


            7 RASMUSSEN, Dale Lane B-1 Dec 1959 M-16 Nov 1977
            7 RASMUSSEN, Lori Jo ROSE, Sp. B-4 Nov 1959


                    8 RASMUSSEN, Luke Dale        B-12 Jun 1978


5 SHARP, William GILES B-3 Sep 1904   M-18 Aug 1927
5 SHARP, Ora Maren CHRISTENSEN, Sp. B-9 Jan 1903


      6 SHARP, Garold William B-14 Jun 1928    M-24 Jun 1947
      6 SHARP, Audrey Lou KILPACK, Sp. B-4 Feb 1930


            7 CARY, Dianne SHARP B-15 Mar 1941 M-24 Jun 1966
            7 CARY, James Douglas, Sp. B-14 Jul 1947


                    8 CARY, Robyn                 B-12 Dec 1966
                    8 CARY, Allison               B-15 Jun 1969
                    8 CARY, Raymond James         B-13 Apr 1972
                    8 CARY, Aaron Paul            B-25 Nov 1978


            7 WYMAN, Denise SHARP B-6 Oct 1952    M- 15 Jul 1971
            7 WYMAN, David Hadley, Sp. B-25 Oct 1951


                    8 WYMAN, Jeromy David         B-27 Sep 1972
                    8 WYMAN, Georgette            B-13 Oct 1975
                    8 WYMAN, Natalie              B-29 Dec 1978
```

```
        7 SHARP, Paul William B-24 Mar 1955 M-3 Sep 1976
        7 SHARP, Bonnie Lavon HATCH, Sp. B-24 Sep 1954

              8 SHARP, Melanie Lynn        B-11 May 1979

  6 ALLEN, Deon SHARP B-30 Dec 1929  M-21 Feb 1951
  6 ALLEN, Carl Hunter, Sp. B-7 Nov 1926

        7 ALLEN, Carla              B-24 Aug 1952

        7 JENSEN, Lynda ALLEN     B-20 Jul 1958      M- 12 Aug 1976
        7 JENSEN, Paul  Lee, Sp. B-3 Jul 1957

              8 JENSEN, Nathan Paul      B-28 Jan 1980

  6 JACKMAN, Carolyn SHARP B-6 Apr 1934 M-25 Jul 1952
  6 JACKMAN, Noel Vincent, Sp. B-25 Jul 1934

        7 JACKMAN, Michael Noel B-7 Sep 1953 M-17 Jun 1972
        7 JACKMAN, Joan Elizabeth Cannon, Sp. B-6 Nov 1952

              8 JACKMAN, Michael Noel      B-17 Nov 1973
              8 JACKMAN, Jame Beth         B-11 Jun 1975
              8 JACKMAN, Christopher John  B-14 Apr 1980

        7 GOUDRIAAN, Connie JACKMAN B-26 Jul 1955  M- 24 Jun 1977
        7 GOUDRIAAN, Lawrence Michael, Sp. B- 12 June 1958

              8 GOUDRIAAN, Kimberly      B- 7 May 1979

        7 JACKMAN, Kenneth Vincent B-12 Sep 1960

  6 SHARP, Ralph C B-30 Apr 1937   M-24 Jun 1958
  6 SHARP, Joy Carol FLANIGAN, Sp. B-13 Nov 1936

        7 SHARP, Steven Ralph      B-23 May 1959

        7 CHILDS, Sandra Denise SHARP B-21 Feb 1961 M-9 Aug 1980
        7 CHILDS, Thomas C., Sp. B-

        7 SHARP, Scott Douglas     B-17 May 1963
        7 SHARP, Suzanne           B-27 Aug 1964
        7 SHARP, Stephanie         B-24 Oct 1968
        7 SHARP, Stacia Erin       B-29 Oct 1970
        7 SHARP, Spencer Patric    B-20 Jan 1975


  6 SHARP, Jonathan Lee B-30 Oct 1942   M-28 Sep 1963 D-31 Dec 1979
  6 SHARP, Dorothy Ann COLFLESH, Sp. B-12 Jan 1945

        7 SHARP, Deborah Ann       B-27 Jul 1964
        7 SHARP, Todd James        B-20 Mar 1967
        7 SHARP, Wade Lee          B- 7 Jul 1968

5 SHARP, Rueland B-28 Feb 1907 D-29 Nov 1909

5 STRINGER, Viola SHARP B-7 Jun 1912 M-1 Jun 1931
5 STRINGER, Willard James, Sp. B-23 October 1909

  6 STRINGER, James Willard B-3 Jun 1932 M-8 May 1956
  6 STRINGER, Eugenia May FOLK, Sp. B-10 Aug 1933

        7 STRINGER, Bradly James B-25 Sep 1959

        7 ALLEN, Sara Lee STRINGER B-28 Sep 1961 M-14 Feb 1980
        7 ALLEN, Michal Jay, Sp. B-21 Jan 1960

  6 STRINGER, Glade William B- 17 Oct 1935 M-17 May 1954 Div-29 Aug 1964
  6 STRINGER, Saundra Lee Diane COX, Sp. (1) B-8 Oct 1938 D-7 Jan 1976 Div.1964
  6 STRINGER, Eula Fay TITSWORTH, Sp. (2) B-7 Aug 1940 M-23 Apr 1965
     Moore, Robert Lee, Sp. (1) to Eula B-        M-7 Jun 1961 D-2 Dec 1961
           7 HIGLEY, Vickie Lee B-23 Mar 1955 M-10 Feb 1973
           7 HIGLEY, Dennis Ray, Sp. B-3 May 1951
```

```
                    8 HIGLEY, Shay Dennis      B- 3 Apr 1975
                    8 HIGLEY, Bryson Kirt       B-17 Jan 1977
                    8 HIGLEY, Jausha Glen       B- 2 Dec 1978


               7 STRINGER, Robert Lee Moore   B-28 Mar 1962 (Adopted by Glade 1965)

         6 MANDROS, Norma Jean STRINGER B-13 Mar 1939 M-25 Apr 1952
         6 MANDROS, Gus Duane, Sp. B-13 Jul 1939


               7 MANDROS, Scott Duane  B-20 Nov 1959

               7 MANDROS, Mark Allan B-25 Oct 1960 M-5 Oct 1978
               7 MANDROS, Kathie Sue GOMES, Sp. B-17 Jan 1963


                    8 MANDROS, Rebecca Jean     B-14 Sep 1978

               7 SWETT, Kathy Jean MANDROS B-25 Feb 1962 M-14 Aug 1978
               7 SWETT, William, Sp. B-8 Jul 1958


                    8 SWETT, Monica Ann        B-9 Nov 1979

       5 SHARP, Fern B-20 Jun 1918 D-21 Jun 1918

   4 GILES, George David B-11 Jan 1879 M-25 Dec 1899 D-21 Mar 1946
   4 GILES, Mary Elizabeth MAIR, Sp. B-15 Aug 1882 D-17 May 1961


         5 FORRER, Mary Ann GILES B-22 Dec 1900 M-20 Sep 1920 D-26 Jul 1973
         5 FORRER, Karl William, Sp. B-19 Jun 1899 D-17 Apr 1974


               6 PATTERSON, Phyllis Mary FORRER B-29 Dec 1922 M-28 Sep 1945 D-25 Jul 1951
               6 PATTERSON, Frank David, Sp. B-4 Jul 1922
               6 PATTERSON, Marie Krebs, Sp. (2) B-              M-


                    7 KELSEY, Carol PATTERSON B-15 Feb 1947 M-2 Jun 1972
                    7 KELSEY, William Martin, Sp. B-22 Aug 1949


                         8 KELSEY, Christopher Ryan B- 9 Sep 1973
                         8 KELSEY, Mary Katherine   B-16 Nov 1976
                         8 KELSEY, Kimball Franklin B-27 Mar 1979


                    7 BAKER, Cheryl PATTERSON B-15 Feb 1947 M-10 Aug 1973
                    7 BAKER, Timothy Alan, Sp. B-14 Feb 1946


                         8 BAKER, Amy Elizabeth     B-11 Sep 1975
                         8 BAKER, Amber Marie       B- 9 Mar 1977
                         8 BAKER, Joel Alan         B-15 Apr 1979


                    7 ADAMS, Cindy Ann PATTERSON B-22 Apr 1951 m-3 Mar 1972
                    7 ADAMS, Gregory Burnett, Sp. B-12 Nov 1949


                         8 ADAMS, Gregory           B-10 Nov 1972  D-12 Dec 1972
                         8 ADAMS, Melanie Ann        B- 5 Nov 1973
                         8 ADAMS, Melissa Anne       B- 5 Jun 1977


         6 PICO, Lois Ann FORRER Bronson Thorpe B-19 Oct 1924
         6 BRONSON, La Zelle, Sp. B-            M-15 Apr 1942 Div.
         6 THORPE, Peter Emil, Sp. (2) B-       M-19 Oct 1946 Div.
         6 PICO, Mervin Joseph, Sp. (3) B-            M-3 Dec 1951


               7 TRUJILLO, Lynda Ann BRONSON Rose B-
               7 ROSE, James Arnold, Sp. B-          M-
               7 TRUJILLO,         Sp. (2) B-          M-


                    8 ROSE, Mary Ann        B-
                    8 ROSE, James Arnold II  B-


               7 HUGHES, Barbara THORPE B-           M-
               7 HUGHES, George, Sp. B-


                    8 HUGHES, Debra Ralene     B-
                    8 HUGHES, Jeana Christina  B-
```

```
          7 EPPERSON, Sharon THORPE Grace B-                    M-
          7 GRACE, Robert, Sp. B-                    M-
          7 EPPERSON, Michael Irving, Sp. B-                    M-

                    8 GRACE, Stephen Robert      B-
                    8 GRACE, Michael Ivan        B-

          7 COPLIN, Karon THORPE B-               M-
          7 COPLIN, David, Sp. B-

                    8 COPLIN, Douglas Allen      B-
                    8 COPLIN, Latisha Renee      B-

     6 FORRER, Ada B-23 Dec 1927 D-11 Jan 1928

     6 FORRER, George Grant B-7 Aug 1933 M-2 Feb 1951
     6 FORRER, Diane STEWART, Sp. B-8 Mar 1936

          7 FORRER, Glen Grant B-24 Feb 1953
          7 FORRER, Linda BOWMAN, Sp. B-               M-               Div.

                    8 FORRER, Phillip            B-
                    8 FORRER, Kevin              B-

          7 FORRER, William Kay B-11 Jun 1954 M-
          7 FORRER, Joan DUNLAP, Sp. B-

          7 BROWN, Sandra Lynn FORRER Sabey B-8 Apr 1956
          7 SABEY, Lynn, Sp. B-               M-               Div.
          7 BROWN, Larry, Sp. (2) B-               M-

                    8 SABEY, Gregory             B-
                    8 BROWN, John Douglas        B-

          7 FORRER, Paul Alan       B-22 Nov 1957

          7 FORRER, Clyde Brent     B-29 Oct 1960
5 SWEAT, Ruth GILES Davis B-2 Mar 1903
5 DAVIS, Orval, Sp. B-26 Nov 1898 M-13 Apr 1925 D-23 Nov 1962
5 SWEAT, Orvel, Sp, (2) B-               M-23 Jul 1974

     6 HENRIE, Fay DAVIS B-26 Jan 1947 M-10 Jun 1943
     6 HENRIE, Thomas "A", Sp. B-6 Feb 1923

          7 HENRIE, Thomas Dale B-28 Jan 1947 M-25 Oct 1975 Div.
          7 HENRIE, Alicia Antonia MACIEL, Sp. B-15 Jan 1954

          7 HENSON, Myrna Joy HENRIE Warren B-29 Aug 1948
          7 WARREN, Paul W. Sp. B-               M-18 Oct 1968 Div. Jun 1975
          7 HENSEN, Donald Dale, Sp. (2) B-               M-

                    8 WARREN, Stephanie Kim      B-5 Jul 1972
                    8 HENSEN, Laurie             B-

          7 HENRIE, Robert "A" B-19 Mar 1951 M-26 Jun 1976
          7 HENRIE, Patricia HANSEN, Sp. B-17 Apr 1955

                    8 HENRIE, Kinsi Ann          B-10 Jul 1977

          7 SCOTT, Jane HENRIE B-11 Mar 1955 M-8 Aug 1975
          7 SCOTT, Lawrence Richard, Sp. B-25 Jan 1951

                    8 SCOTT, Julie Marie         B-29 May 1977

          7 ROBINSON, Janice HENRIE B-11 Mar 1955 M-2 Jan 1975
          7 ROBINSON, Gary Russell, Sp. B-10 Jan 1951

                    8 ROBINSON, Lisa Bree        B-29 Sep 1975
                    8 ROBINSON, David Thomas     B-27 May 1977
                    8 ROBINSON, LeAnn            B- 8 Jan 1979

          7 HENRIE, David William B-13 Sep 1957
```

5 GILES, Verna B-20 Feb 1910 D-21 Mar 1932

5 GILES, Ray B-1 Jul 1913 M-3 Dec 1936 D-13 Jan 1977
5 GILES, Therma Mae BALL, Sp. B-8 Apr 1917

      6 GILES, Garry William B-11 Feb 1938 M-30 Jul 1957
      6 GILES, Rava Annie CLARK, Sp. B-10 Jan 1939

7 GILES, Gary Ray	B-25 Sep 1959
7 GILES, Troy Albert	B-26 Oct 1960
7 GILES, Keyo Lynn	B-16 Aug 1963
7 GILES, Kirk Frank	B- 8 Nov 1973
7 GILES, Chilee Ann	B- 2 Jul 1975

      6 GILES, George David II B-25 Jul 1939 M-10 Aug 1964
      6 GILES, Nelinda Beatriz ZANOTTA, Sp. B-6 May 1941

7 GILES, Nellie Gaye	B-16 May 1966
7 GILES, Marcia Kay	B- 2 Jan 1969
7 GILES, Cindy Lou	B-22 Jun 1971
7 GILES, Shellie Ann	B-25 Jul 1973
7 GILES, Mary Elena	B- 3 Aug 1977

      6 SWENA, Velda Kaye GILES B-23 Aug 1941 M-11 May 1959
      6 SWENA, William Marvin, Sp. B-8 Jan 1938
       Swena, Colleen DAVIS Knecht, Sp. (1) B-   M-

7 SWENA, William Kay	B-14 Sep 1959
7 SWENA, Lloyd Brent	B-20 Sep 1960
7 SWENA, Mark G	B-31 Mar 1968

      6 JOHNSON, Ruth Lou Ann GILES B-19 Nov 1942 M-31 Aug 1962
      6 JOHNSON, Richard Charles, Sp. B-26 Apr 1940

7 JOHNSON, Elizabeth Gwen B-16 Jun 1963	
7 JOHNSON, Richard Blake B- 9 Jul 1964	
7 JOHNSON, Susan Rae	B-5 Nov 1965
7 JOHNSON, Heidi Ann	B-3 Oct 1970
7 JOHNSON, Dani Marie	B-4 Apr 1975

      6 NELSON, Mary Rae GILES B-12 Apr 1954 M-8 Oct 1971
      6 NELSON, Donald Gene, Sp. B-18 Dec 1950

7 NELSON, Donald Gene Jr. B-30 Dec 1972	
7 NELSON, David Ray	B-14 Jul 1975
7 NELSON, Matthew Giles	B-11 Aug 1976

5 GILES, Helen B-3 Jun 1919 D-4 Jun 1919

5 GILES, Phyllis B-26 Aug 1921 D-28 Aug 1921

4 PYPER, Sarah Elizabeth GILES B-30 Sep 1880 M-12 Jun 1901 D-2 Dec 1915
4 PYPER, George Caldwell, Sp. B-31 May 1880 D-17 Jan 1970

    5 FORMAN, Aletha Fontella PYPER B-20 Feb 1902 M-27 Dec 1920
    5 FORMAN, Leonard, Sp. B-30 Jun 1897 D-10 Dec 1978

      6 FORMAN, Don Melvin B-18 Oct 1920 D-13 Jul 1921

      6 FORMAN, Marvin Ray B-1 Jul 1922 M-3 Apr 1943
      6 FORMAN, Georgia Faye STEVENS, Sp. B- 10 Aug 1926 D-30 Jul 1977

        7 POWERS, LaRae FORMAN B-27 Apr 1944 M-16 Apr 1962
        7 POWERS, James Edward, Sp. B-10 Jun 1941

          8   , POWERS, Debra Rae B-2 Oct 1962
          8   ,   Sp. B-

            9   B-

        8 POWERS, Kevin James   B-19 Feb 1965
        8 POWERS, Lisa Dawn   B-16 Jun 1967

7 MAIR, Sherri Louise FORMAN REIERSON B-9 Jun 1956
7 REIERSON, Gary, Sp. (1) B-   M-18 Jan 1973 Div.
7 MAIR, Jessie, Sp. (2) B-   M-

          8 REIERSON,   B-
          8 MAIR   B-
          8 MAIR   B-

7 GUTIERREZ, Georgia Lee FORMAN B-7 Jul 1959 M-8 Jul 1977
7 GUTIERREZ, Ferrando, Sp. (1)

          8 GUTIERREZ   B-
          8 GUTIERREZ   B-

7 FORMAN, Randy   B-19 Mar 1964 D-20 Mar 1964

6 FORMAN, Dean Roy B-24 Mar 1924 M-10 Dec 1943
6 FORMAN, Laura LIMB, Sp. B-30 Jan 1924

     7 CAVES, DeeAnn FORMAN B-28 Jan 1945 M-20 Sep 1961
     7 CAVES, Charles Lee, Sp. B-

          8 CAVES, Richard Dean   B- 4 Jul 1961
          8 CAVES, Christina Julean B-23 May 1964
          8 CAVES, Robert Charles   B-28 Jun 1965 D-20 Oct 1974
          8 CAVES, Mark Allen   B-26 Nov 1966
          8 CAVES, Dean Cody   B-10 Aug 1971
          8 CAVES, Michael Lynn   B-30 Jun 1974
          8 CAVES, Jamie   B- 8 Aug 1977

     7 KILSDONK, Norma Jean FORMAN B-31 Oct 1946 M-28 May 1962 Div.
     7 KILSDONK, Rodney Henry, Sp. B-21 Jun 1942

          8 KILSDONK, Laurie Jean   B- 2 Mar 1963
          8 KILSDONK, Rodney Henry Jr B-22 Apr 1964
          8 KILSDONK, Dwayne   B-27 Jan 1966

     7 FORMAN, Jimmy B-11 Sep 1947 M-   1970
     7 FORMAN, Susanne KING, Sp. B-

     7 FORMAN, Carl Dean B-24 Sep 1948 M-2 Jul 1970
     7 FORMAN, Tressa TREVINO, Sp. B-

6 FORMAN, John Junior B-28 Nov 1925 D-6 Jan 1926

6 FORMAN, George DeVar B-23 Feb 1927 M-21 May 1947 D-4 Oct 1979
6 FORMAN, Loretta June WARNER, Sp. B-8 Jun 1930 D-22 May 1960

     7 FORMAN, Joe Leonard B-26 May 1948 M-   1968
     7 FORMAN, Karen FYANS, Sp. B-

          8 FORMAN, Joe Leonard   B-22 Oct 1969 D-   Jan 1972
          8 FORMAN, Toby Shane   B- 6 Jan 1978

     7 FORMAN, George Roy B-20 Dec 1949 D-13 Apr 1950

     7 GROSS, Annette FORMAN B-12 Jan 1953 M-25 Feb 1971
     7 GROSS, Russell, Sp. B-

          8 GROSS, Jennifer Louise   B-21 Sep 1971
          8 GROSS, Russell Alan   B-28 Apr 1977

     7 FORMAN, Robert D. B-13 Jan 1954 D-16 Jan 1954

     7 BLACK, Susan Louise FORMAN B-27 Jul 1957 M-   Aug 1975
     7 BLACK, Donny, Sp. B-

          8 BLACK, Cori Jean   B-18 Nov 1976
          8 BLACK,   B- 9 Sep 1979

6 FORMAN, Leonard Vergil B-12 Sep 1930 M-23 Jul 1956
6 FORMAN, Katherine Snow McKINNEY, Sp. B-8 Aug 1936

```
              7 FORMAN, Norma Lynn      B- 4 Feb 1962
              7 FORMAN, Dorothy Kay     B- 2 Nov 1963
              7 FORMAN, Cindy Lynn      B-16 Apr 1965
              7 FORMAN, Virgie Joyce    B-19 Jan 1968
              7 FORMAN, John Dean       B-16 Sep 1969
              7 FORMAN, Tina Marie      B-22 May 1972


        6 FORMAN, Lynn J. B-24 Sep 1944 M-21 Jun 1964 D-22 Jun 1976
        6 FORMAN, Ethel Marie HINSINGER, Sp. B-28 Jan 1945


              7 FORMAN, Marie DeLynn    B-18 Jun 1967 D-18 Jun 1967
              7 FORMAN, Aletha Marie    B-15 Jun 1968
              7 FORMAN, Sarah Elizabeth B-12 Aug 1971

5 HENDERSON, Erma Rose PYPER B-29 Sep 1903 M-27 Jan 1927
5 HENDERSON, John Woodland, Sp. B-26 Jun 1903 D-19 Apr 1975


      6 HENDERSON, John Floyd B-7 Nov 1927 D-19 Jul 1944


      6 HENDERSON, George Pyper B-20 Feb 1931
      6 HENDERSON, Eleanor Sue EVANS, Sp. B-11 Sep 1933 M-18 Nov 1955 Div.
      6 HENDERSON, Carolynn ESKELSON, Sp. (2) B-              M-3 Dec 1977
              7 HENDERSON, Rose Ann      B- 5 Sep 1956
              7 HENDERSON, Sue Eleanor   B-28 Mar 1958
              7 HENDERSON, John Edward   B-25 Mar 1960
              7 HENDERSON, Martin Evans  B-29 Oct 1961
              7 HENDERSON, Jane Pyper    B- 2 Apr 1965
              7 HENDERSON, Emily Gwen    B-26 Sep 1966
              7 HENDERSON, Nan Elizabeth B-25 Mar 1970


      6 LARSEN, Erma Marie HENDERSON B-1 Feb 1933 M-22 Aug 1952
      6 LARSEN, Robert Done, Sp. B-21 Apr 1932


              7 LARSEN, Kevin Robert B-14 May 1955 M-12 May 1978
              7 LARSEN, Kathy Stewart, Sp. B-


                    8 LARSEN, Corey Kevin      B-25 Feb 1979

              7 RUESCH, Janica Marie LARSEN B-14 Feb 1959 M-21 Jul 1978
              7 RUESCH, Martin Albert, Sp. B-


                    8 RUESCH, Corey Kevin      B-25 Feb 1979


              7 LARSEN, Mary Ellen     B- 2 Sep 1960
              7 LARSEN, Lence Michael  B-24 Sep 1961
              7 LARSEN, Lisa Melaine   B-20 Mar 1963
              7 LARSEN, Trina Dawn     B-28 May 1967

      6 MOYES, Sarah LaVon HENDERSON B-7 Jun 1934 M-27 Aug 1953
      6 MOYES, Keith Eugene, Sp. B-27 Jan 1934 D-30 May 1971


              7 MOYES, Keith Henderson B-7 Jun 1954

              7 GIBSON, KariAnn H. MOYES B-24 May 1956 M-8 Jun 1978
              7 GIBSON, Richard, Sp. B-


                    8 GIBSON, Carl Jay       B- 6 Dec 1978
                    8 GIBSON, Sarah Ann      B-27 May 1980

              7 MOYES, Kirt Miller     B-28 Dec 1957
              7 MOYES, Karole          B-10 Jan 1963
              7 MOYES, Kraig Pyper     B-29 Nov 1964

      6 STANDING, Laura Reve' HENDERSON B-21 Dec 1935 M-6 Jun 1958
      6 STANDING, Harry Mifflin, Sp. B-27 Sep 1936


              7 JONES, Jeanette STANDING B-14 Jul 1959 M-5 Jan 1980
              7 JONES, Timothy D. Sp. B-


              7 STANDING, Laura          B-20 Feb 1961
              7 STANDING, Karen          B- 8 Nov 1963
              7 STANDING, Brent Hendersen B-15 Nov 1964
```

6 RIDINGS, PollyAnn HENDERSON, B-7 Mar 1939 M-28 Apr 1961
6 RIDINGS, James Robert (J.R.) Sp. B-5 Sep 1937

    7 RIDINGS, James Brent   B-28 Feb 1962
    7 RIDINGS, Kenneth Wayne B- 2 Apr 1964
    7 RIDINGS, Marcia Jane   B-26 Nov 1965
    7 RIDINGS, Anita Jo   B-15 Sep 1969
    7 RIDINGS, Sheri Elizabeth B-8 Sep 1970
    7 RIDINGS, Amy Michelle B- 4 Dec 1971

5 MILLINER, LaVon Murdoch PYPER B-28 Dec 1904 M-2 Jul 1936
5 MILLINER, Thomas Lesslie, Sp. B-31 Dec 1902

6 MILLINER, John Thomas Pyper B-20 Dec 1938 M-13 Apr 1959
6 MILLINER, Judith KELLER, Sp. B- 23 Jul 1938

    7 MILLINER, Judith Kathleen   B-12 Dec 1959
    7 MILLINER, John David   B-24 Mar 1961
    7 MILLINER, Elizabeth Lorene   B-12 Jun 1962
    7 MILLINER, Paul Lawerence   B-18 Jul 1963
    7 MILLINER, Joseph Lesslie   B-10 Oct 1964
    7 MILLINER, George Andrew   B-28 Jan 1967
    7 MILLINER, Sharla Jane   B-13 Apr 1968
    7 MILLINER, Cheryl Ann   B-25 Aug 1969
    7 MILLINER, Marie Louise   B-14 Apr 1971
    7 MILLINER, Thomas LaMont   B-11 Sep 1972

6 LANGLEY, Lesslie Marlene MILLINER B-8 Nov 1941 M-22 Jul 1963 D-14 Dec 1975
6 LANGLEY, Charley Clifton Jr. Sp. B-4 Mar 1940
6 LANGLEY, Nancy Lu RICHARDSON, Sp. B-   M-29 Jan 1976

    7 LANGLEY, Lesslie Marlene   B-24 Feb 1967
    7 LANGLEY, Charley Clifton III B- 7 May 1968
    7 LANGLEY, Bruce Delbert   B-28 Sep 1972
    7 LANGLEY, Cleone LaVon   B-11 Jul 1975

5 PYPER, George Albert B-6 Nov 1906 M-13 Feb 1930
5 PYPER, Alta Belva SORENSON, Sp. B-28 Aug 1911

6 DAVIS, Sarah Bonnie PYPER Sessions Blood B-11 Feb 1931
6 SESSIONS, William Boyd, Sp. B-   M-8 Apr 1949 Div.-14 Apr 1950
6 BLOOD, Bert, Sp. (2) B-3 Oct 1930 M-1 Jun 1950 Div.
6 DAVIS, Lyle, Sp. (3) B-   M-   1965

    7 SESSIONS,Gayle P. B-2 Sep 1949 M-14 Mar 1969
    7 SESSIONS, Maria J. PIORKOSDKI, Sp. B-11 Feb 1951

        8 SESSIONS, Sean   B-31 Jul 1978

    7   Jeanne Marie BLOOD B-19 Jan 1958 M-   1974
    7 McNIEL, Todd, Sp. B
        8 McNIEL, Brandon   B-18 Feb 1975
    7 BLOOD, Jeffrey Bert B- 3 May 1961 D-   1979

    7 DAVIS, Kenny Lee B-24 Jul 1965

6 PYPER, George Edward B-26 May 1932 M-6 Nov 1959
6 PYPER, Valera JENSEN, Sp. B-

    7 PYPER, Julie Ellen   B-26 Aug 1960
    7 PYPER, Bruce Alan   B-15 May 1962
    7 PYPER, Janet Leigh   B-17 Jun 1963
    7 PYPER, Ben David   B-23 Apr 1969
    7 PYPER, Karen Joy   B- 2 May 1972
    7 PYPER, Shelly Kay   B- 2 May 1972
    7 PYPER, Brian Lee   B-29 Apr 1977

6 FORD, Belva Marie PYPER B-3 Oct 1933 M-31 May 1952
6 FORD, William Clark FORD, Sp. B-25 Jan 1931

    7 CHRISTENSEN, Brenda Marie FORD B-12 Nov 1954 M-29 Sep 1972
    7 CHRISTENSEN, Grant J., Sp. B-

```
                8 CHRISTENSEN, Grant Casey B-24 Apr 1973
                8 CHRISTENSEN, Terril     B-13 Sep 1974

        7 JAQUES,  Debra Ann FORD B-30 Nov 1955 M-8 Nov 1974
        7 JAQUES, Steve, Sp. B-

                8 JAQUES, Tony Ann        B-16 Sep 1975
        7 FORD, Karla             B-29 Aug 1958

        7 FORD, James Lee         B-11 Jun 1965


    6 PYPER, Theron Lyle B-28 Oct 1936 M-6 Sep 1958
    6 PYPER, Charlotte Louise RICHARDS, Sp. B-29 Mar 1942

            7 PYPER, Martin Caldwell B-21 Apr 1961
            7 PYPER, Randy Lynn      B-24 Sep 1962
            7 PYPER, Jason Howard    B- 7 Dec 1965
            7 PYPER, Laura Fern      B-10 Nov 1967
            7 PYPER, Bradley Wayne   B-12 Oct 1968
            7 PYPER, Spencer Lyle    B-

    6 WILKINS, Sandra Ila PYPER B-31 Jan 1944 M-24 Aug 1962
    6 WILKINS, Myron Homer, Sp. B-4 Dec 19

            7 WILKINS, Laurel Lee    B- 9 Aug 1963

            7 COMER, Jodi Ann WILKINS B-          M-
            7 COMER, Kent, Sp. B-

                8 COMER, Garrett         B-16 Mar 1980

            7 WILKINS, Michelle      B- 3 Mar 1967
            7 WILKINS, Jennifer      B-28 Apr 1969
            7 WILKINS, Krisann       B-30 Aug 1970

    6 PYPER, Ralph A. B-8 Dec 1947 D-17 Sep 1972
    6 PYPER, Gay SULSER, Sp. B-          M-23 Sep 1965 Div. Feb 1968
    6 PYPER, Patrica HATCH, Sp. (2) B-          M-14 May 1969

            7 PYPER, Ryan Dee        B-31 Jan 1966 (adopted by Stepfather Mottley)

5 SIZEMORE, Sarah Althora PYPER B-27 Jun 1908 M-19 Aug 1927
5 SIZEMORE, Devar, Sp. B-19 Dec 1905 D-26 Feb 1979

    6 SIZEMORE, Allen DeVar B-27 Mar 1929 M-29 May 1952
    6 SIZEMORE, Myrna Lee SYME, Sp. B-18 Aug 1934

        7 SIZEMORE, Larry Allen  B-14 Feb 1953

        7 SIZEMORE, Kenneth Lee B-22 Jun 1954 M-18 Dec 1975
        7 SIZEMORE, Barbara Lyn ZOLMAN, Sp. B-21 Mar 1957

                8 SIZEMORE, Audrey Lynn    B-26 Sep 1976
                8 SIZEMORE, Jacob Allen    B- 8 Sep 1978
                8 SIZEMORE, Sarah ElizabethB-25 May 1980

        7 LARSEN, Myrna Christine SIZEMORE B-17 May 1955 M-29 Sep 1973
        7 LARSEN, Fred R., Sp. B-7 Dec 1954

                8 LARSEN, Robert LaDean    B-20 Sep 1976

        7 JARVIS, Vera Ellen SIZEMORE B-31 Jul 1957 M-11 Jul 1975
        7 JARVIS, Paul Michael, Sp. B-28 Sep 1956

                8 JARVIS, James Paul      B- 3 Oct 1976 D-3 Oct 1976
                8 JARVIS, Heather Lynette B- 2 Dec 1977

        7 SIZEMORE, John Devar   B-12 Jan 1959  M-
        7 SIZEMORE, Carole, Sp. B-
    6 AUSTIN, Frances Marian SIZEMORE B-11 Mar 1933 M-20 Mar 1951
    6 AUSTIN, Eugene Worlton, Sp. B-1 Oct 1928

        7 MAUCHLEY, Diana Jean AUSTIN B-26 Jun 1952 M-5 Nov 1971
        7 MAUCHLEY, Gregory Vern, Sp. B-16 Sep 1949
```

```
                    8 MAUCHLEY, Stephen GregoryB-14 Aug 1973
                    8 MAUCHLEY, Adam Trent      B-14 Sep 1974
                    8 MAUCHLEY, Jared Austin    B-11 Oct 1975
                    8 MAUCHLEY, Rebekah Jael    B- 1 Feb 1977

            7 AUSTIN, Mark Steven B-24 Aug 1955 M-16 Mar 1978
            7 AUSTIN, Lori DOXEY, Sp. B-2 May 1957

                    8 AUSTIN, Benjamin Thomas  B-13 Dec 1979

                    8 AUSTIN, Bradley Eugene    B-13 Dec 1979

            7 MANN, Cheryl Lyn AUSTIN B-14 Apr 1958 M-9 Feb 1979
            7 MANN, Renald Duwaine, Sp. B-18 Aug 1951

                    8 MANN, Malinda Sue        B-4 Dec 1979

            7 AUSTIN, Carolyn        B-20 May 1959
            7 AUSTIN, Jeffrey Dale   B- 8 Dec 1961
            7 AUSTIN, Linda Lee      B-24 Jun 1965
            7 AUSTIN, Stephanie      B-10 Feb 1967

        6 SIZEMORE, Dick LeRoy B-6 Jun 1938 M-6 Mar 1959
        6 SIZEMORE, Connie Cameron, Sp. B-2 Aug 1942

            7 SIZEMORE, Clinton LeRoyB-14 Mar 1960

            7 HARRISON, Wendy Alane B-19 Feb 1962 M-27 Jun 1980
            7 HARRISON, Mark, Sp. B-

            7 SIZEMORE, Amy Jo       B- 7 Nov 1975
            7 SIZEMORE, Caleb CaldwellB-20 Feb 1978

5 PYPER, Glen Giles B-6 May 1910 M-31 May 1933
5 PYPER, Ora LaRue ROSE, Sp. B-3 Mar 1914

        6 MARSHALL, Carolyn Rose Pyper B-1 Dec 1934 M-8 Dec 1955
        6 MARSHALL, Ray Dean, Sp. B-19 Feb 1927

            7 MARSHALL, Steven Ray    B- 6 Apr 1958
            7 MARSHALL, David Glen    B-23 Sep 1963
            7 MARSHALL, James Pyper   B-11 Apr 1966
            7 MARSHALL, Richard ScottB-17 Jul 1971

        6 GEORGE, LuDean PYPER B-8 Jan 1936 M-14 Apr 1962
        6 GEORGE, William Seth (Bill), Sp. B-29 Jul 1936

                7 GEORGE, Jennifer        B- 7 Jun 1964
                7 GEORGE, Tresa Ann       B-17 Sep 1966
                7 GEORGE, Amy Elizabeth   B-17 Aug 1971
                7 GEORGE, Melissa Dian    B- 5 Feb 1980

        6 GILL, Linda Maurine PYPER B-16 Sep 1942 M-25 Aug 1961
        6 GILL, John "D", Sp. B-20 Jul 1940

                7 GILL, Vickie Lyn        B-23 Apr 1965
                7 GILL, John Brent        B- 8 Mar 1970

        6 DIXON, Sherry Lyn PYPER B-27 May 1949 M-26 Jun 1969
        6 DIXON, Richard S., Sp. B-

                7 DIXON, Darin Richard    B-22 Jan 1971
                7 DIXON, Ryan Glen        B-10 Jul 1973
                7 DIXON, Angie Lynn       B-30 May 1975
                7 DIXON, Kristen Ann      B-19 Feb 1979

5 BURGENER, Thelma Ann PYPER B-6 Apr 1912 M-28 Nov 1930
5 BURGENER, Elmer Ray, Sp. B-19 Feb 1910

        6 BURGENER, Bobby Ray B-24 May 1931 M-21 Aug 1951
        6 BURGENER, Shirley Louise FRANTZ, Sp. B-17 Nov 1932
```

7 BURGENER, Glen Dee B-22 Jun 1954 M-

7 BURGENER, Shanna Rae MILLER, Sp. B-

       8 BURGENER, Justin Glen   B-26 Jul 1974
       8 BURGENER, Jeffrey Ray   B-10 Sep 1977
       8 BURGENER, Jay Lynn   B- 8 Jun 1979

7 BURGENER, Gary Ray B-4 Mar 1956 M-10 Dec 1975

7 BURGENER, Debra Sue JUDD, Sp. B-

       8 BURGENER, Jason Ray   B-1 May 1978

7 BURGENER, Gene LeRoy B-21 Jun 1957 M-6 Apr 1974

7 BURGENER, Michelle GUSTUS, Sp. B-

       8 BURGENER, Rebecca Lynn   B-29 Aug 1974
       8 BURGNER, Brandy Marie   B- 7 Jul 1979
       8 BURGENER, William John   B- 7 Oct 1980

7 BURGENER, Robbyn Louise B-27 Feb 1971

6 BURGENER, Glen DeLoy B-5 Jan 1933 M-26 Oct 1957
6 BURCENER, ArLee LABRUM, Sp. B-7 May 1936
  Nerdin, Glen Sp. (1) B-   M-

7 YENGICH, Terry Nerdin BURGENER Hackwell B-29 Jun 1954 (Legally Adopt.)
7 HACKWELL, Albert Stanley, Sp. (1) B-   M-
7 YENGICH, Dick Sp. (2) B-   M-

       8 HACKWELL, Tara Shu Ree   B-23 Sep 1973

7 SHILLING, Jodi Lynn BURGENER B-5 Nov 1958 M-2 Feb 1980
7 SHILLING, Lynn, Sp. B-

7 BURNINGHAM, Korby Ann B-26 Oct 1960 M-8 Dec 1979
7 BURNINGHAM, Jay R. B-

7 BURGENER, Dennis DeLoy B-25 Apr 1964

6 BROADHEAD, Nancy Marie BURGENER B-14 Mar 1939 M-13 Oct 1957
6 BROADHEAD, Larry Tex, Sp. B-31 Dec 1939

7 BROADHEAD, Ray Lynn B-19 Dec 1958

7 MARTINEZ, Cindy Marie B-11 Mar 1961 M-
7 MARTINEZ, Vincent Clark, Sp. B-

       8 MARTINEZ, Elisha M   B-30 Jul 1979

7 WARD, Debby BROADHEAD, B-3 Apr 1962 M- Dec 1979
7 WARD, Robin, Sp. B-
       8 WARD, Kilby   B-15 Feb 1980

6 BURGENER, Judy Ann B-5 Sep 1943

5 PYPER, Dean Ronald B-22 Oct 1913 M-17 Apr 1939
5 PYPER, Naomi STEVENS, Sp. B-2 Oct 1917

6 NIELSON, Marsha LaRee PYPER Maxwell Jackson B-28 Dec 1941
6 MAXWELL, Richard, Sp. (1) B-   M-   Div.
6 JACKSON, Wilbert R. Sp. (2) B-23 Jan 1936 M-31 Jan   D-16 Feb 1975
6 NIELSON, Dean, Sp. (2) B-   M-11 May 1978

7 CAMERON, Lynnette Jackson B-3 Jun 1960 M-17 Jan 1978 Div.
7 CAMERON, Thayne D. Sp. B-

6 PYPER, George Ronald B-7 May 1946 M-28 Jul 1967
6 PYPER, Joyce ANDREASON, Sp. B-2 Nov 1946

7 PYPER, Vint Troy B-15 Dec 1970

6 PYPER, Steven Dean B-4 May 1961

5 PYPER, Ann B- 2 Dec 1915 (Stillborn)

4 GILES, Joseph FIELDING B-6 Jan 1882 M-21 Aug 1906 D-10 Jul 1960
4 GILES, Mary Ellen SWEAT, Sp. B-21 Aug 1888 D-14 May 1972

    5 GILES, Earnest Roy B-20 Jun 1907 M-27 Jul 1929
    5 GILES, Bertha Jane COATS, Sp. B-2 Mar 1912

        6 GLEESON, Ellen Lueen GILES B-5 Sep 1930 M-12 Feb 1954
        6 GLEESON, Francis Gearld, B-

        6 GILES, Robert Roy B-14 Nov 1931 M-26 Dec 1955
        6 GILES, Mary Lou Ola WEBB, Sp. B-

        6 GILES, Violet Jane B-6 Jun 1933 D-6 Jun 1933

        6 GILES, Vernon, Ray B-11 Oct 1934 M-12 Aug 1961
        6 GILES, Margret Helen BOYD, Sp. B-

        6 HALSTEAD, Margie May GILES B-12 Oct 1937 M-24 Dec 1955
        6 HALSTEAD, Frank Martin, Sp. B-

        6 PRUITT, Alice GILES B-21 Jun 1939 M-16 Nov 1956
        6 PRUITT, George Robert, Sp. B-

        6 GILES, David Alvin B-25 Apr 1950 M-9 Oct 1971
        6 GILES, Gloria Denice CASEWELL, Sp. B-

    5 EDEN, Ida Ellen GILES B-31 Mar 1909 M-30 Sep 1924
    5 EDEN, Joseph William Sr. Sp. B-17 Oct 1902

        6 EDEN, Joseph William Jr. B-17 Feb 1925 D-25 Sep 1970
        6 EDEN, MarJean Matilda BOWDEN, Sp. (1) B-4 May 1926 M-22 Mar 1942 Div.
        6 Dalley, Arthella BLACKBURN Jones Eden Sp. (2) B-22 Feb 1924 M-8 Dec 1946
        Jones, Arthur Paul, Sp. (1) B-
        Dalley, Oliver, Sp. (3) B-

            7 EDEN, William Rodney B-29 Nov 1942
            7 EDEN, Marilyn SHAW, Sp. (1) B-   M-14 Feb 1960 Div.
            7 EDEN, Barbara COVERT, Sp. (2) B-   M-

                8 EDEN, Penny   B-
                8 EDEN, William   B-
                8 EDEN, Pat   B-

            7 EDEN, Ronald Lee   B-5 Nov 1945 D-31 Dec 1945

            7 HILDRETH, Peggy Ann EDEN B-18 Jul 1947 M-17 Jul 1964
            7 HILDRETH, Michael Erni, Sp. B-

                8 HILDRETH,
                8 HILDRETH,
                8 HILDRETH,

            7 EDEN, Dennis Ray B-16 Feb 1949 M-7 Nov 1970
            7 EDEN, Mary Lou Jennifer MARTINEZ, Sp. B-

                8 EDEN,

            7 BATES, Sheradeen Ranay EDEN B-25 Jan 1950 M-5 Aug 1968
            7 BATES, Joseph Arnold, Sp. B-

                8 BATES,
                8 BATES,
                8 BATES,
                8 BATES,

            7 JORGENSON, Vickie Lynn EDEN B-16 Oct 1951 M-9 Mar 1968
            7 JORGENSON, Randy Walter, Sp. B-

                8 JORGENSON,
                8 JORGENSON,
                8 JORGENSON,
                8 JORGENSON,

            7 TERRIL, Darla Deloris EDEN B-16 Nov 1952 M-8 Mar 1969
            7 TERRIL, Robert William, Sp. B-

```
                        8 TERRIL,
                        8 TERRIL,
                        8 TERRIL,

            7 EDEN, Joseph Charles B-26 Jun 1955
            7 EDEN, Jerri Kay MADSEN, Sp. B-              M-5 Jan 1973
            7 EDEN,                    Sp. (2) B-         M-

            7 EDEN, Randall Roy B-7 Aug 1956

            7 DALLEY, Ida Janell EDEN B-24 Aug 1957 M-15 Jun 1973
            7 DALLEY, John Oliver, Sp. B-

                        8 DALLEY
                        8 DALLEY
                        8 DALLEY

      6 BROWN, Nelda Ellen EDEN B-20 Nov 1926 M-8 Oct 1942
      6 BROWN, Grant V., Sp, B-11 Mar 1924

            7 BROWN, Kenneth Grant  B-24 Dec 1943

            7 ALLEY, Sherry Lee BROWN B-21 Jul 1947 M-20 Nov 1965
            7 ALLEY, George Michael, Sp. B-

                        8 ALLEY, Brenda        B-
                        8 ALLEY, Amy           B-
                        8 ALLEY, Wendy         B-

            7 BROWN, David          B-11 Jan 1962

            7 BROWN, Desiree Candie B- 4 Sep 1963

      6 EDEN, LaWayne Russell B-20 Nov 1934 D-6 Jun 1935

      6 EDEN, Ronald Lavar    B-30 Jul 1936 D-8 Apr 1945

      6 RIGBY, Deloris Mae EDEN B-25 Aug 1938 M-1 Apr 1960
      6 RIGBY, Russell Dale, Sp. B-23 Aug 1936

            7 MURRI, Deborah Lee B-19 Nov 1960 M-28 Oct 1977
            7 MURRI, Martin Charles, Sp. B-
                        8 MURRI, Cody          B-
            7 RIGBY, Jerry Todd     B-18 May 1963

            7 RIGBY, Russell Troy   B-18 May 1965

            7 RIGBY, Tracy William  B- 1 Apr 1970

      6 EDEN, Jack Ray B-2 Jul 1941 M-5 Aug 1960
      6 EDEN, Peggy Jean CLARK, Sp. B-30 Dec 1941

            7 EDEN, Terri Jean       B-26 Apr 1961
            7 EDEN, Daniel Ray       B-27 Feb 1965
            7 EDEN, Gordon Russell   B- 9 Jun 1966 D-10 Jun 1966
            7 EDEN, Patricia Lynn    B-29 Aug 1969
            7 EDEN, Connie Jo        B-20 Feb 1974

5 GILES, Leland Ray B-2 May 1911             D-10 Jun 1972
5 GILES, Lovina May BROWN, Sp. (1) B-          M-22 Oct 1932 Div.
5 GILES, Beulah       Sp. (2) B-             M-

      6 BURRUP, Norma GILES B-              M-
      6 BURRUP, Ted. Sp. B-

      6 GILES, Verl B-                M-
      6 GILES, Gayle       Sp. B-

      6 GILES, Darwin B-              M-

      6      Shyla GILES B-               M-
      6          ,        Sp. B-

      6      Shauna GILES B-              M-
      6          ,        Sp. B-

      6 GILES, Lonny B-
```

5 BROWN, Ethel May B-14 Jun 1913 M-1 Jun 1931
5 BROWN, James Richard, Sp. B-20 Apr 1905 D-17 Aug 1977

      6 BROWN, James Merlin B-27 Oct 1932 M-6 Jan 1951
      6 BROWN, Alberta Dorothy GILL, Sp. B-

      6 BROWN, Joseph LaRae B-2 Nov 1934 M-11 Dec 1953
      6 BROWN, Mary Jane HECK, Sp. B-

      6 HOLLAND, Mary Nadine BROWN B-1 Apr 1937 M-1 May 1954
      6 HOLLAND, Jerry Claude, Sp. B-

      6 BROWN, Bonnie Mae B-11 Apr 1942 D-18 Apr 1942

      6 STIRTON, Ida Maxine BROWN B-4 May 1943 M-15 Aug 1962
      6 STIRTON, George Dwain, Sp. B-

      6 BROWN Neldon Lynn B-7 Aug 1946 D-7 Aug 1946

5 GILES Joseph Alvin B-9 Jul 1917 D-25 Aug 1933

5 PARK, Nellie GILES B-19 Feb 1920 M-28 Mar 1938
5 PARK, Gerald Wayne, Sp. B-

      6   , Linda PARK B-   M-   D-
      6   ,   Sp. B-

      6   , Vila PARK B-   M-
      6   ,   Sp. B-

      6   , Mryna PARK B-   M-
      6   ,   Sp. B-

      6   , Carol Ann PARK B-   M-
      6   ,   Sp. B-

      6   , Melody PARK B-   M-
      6   ,   Sp. B-

5 GILES, Neldon B-19 Feb 1920 M-30 Apr 1937
5 GILES, Ruth BROWN, Sp. B-

      6 WUEBBENHORST, Nona GILES B-   M-
      6 WUEBBENHORST,   Sp. B-

      6 GILES, Jack B-   M-
      6 GILES, Pamela   Sp. B-

5 GILES, Ruland J. B-5 May 1928 D-4 Apr 1929

4 GILES, Orson Edwin B-25 Sep 1883 M-27 Mar 1907 D-17 Jun 1956
4 GILES, Gladys Ethel TADD, Sp. B-10 Nov 1889 D-24 Jun 1969

      5 ROWLEY, Gladys Zella GILES Hamilton B-2 Apr 1908
      5 HAMILTON, George Layson, Sp. (1) B-   M-21 Oct 1925 Div.Civ-1930 Temple-1936
      5 ROWLEY, Nello James,Sp. (2) B-9 Sep 1906 M-28 Sep 1931
      6 THOMPSON, Doris ROWLEY B-8 Jan 1933 M-16 Mar 1951
      6 THOMPSON, Cyril Peter, Sp. B-26 May 1931

      7 THOMPSON, James Rowley B-14 Oct 1951

      7 THOMPSON, Allan Peter B-20 Nov 1953 M-20 Jun 1975
      7 THOMPSON, Valerie FACKRELL, Sp. B-4 Aug 1956

      8 THOMPSON, Adrienne   B-26 Mar 1976
      8 THOMPSON, Amber   B- 9 Jun 1977
      8 THOMPSON, Kelly Peter   B-16 Nov 1978

      7 PETERSON, Linda THOMPSON B-22 Nov 1955 M-15 Jun 1978
      7 PETERSON, Deeth Lee, Sp. B-

      7 HOBBS, Lynn Ann THOMPSON B-3 Oct 1956 M-2 Apr 1975
      7 HOBBS, Charles Thomas, Sp. B- 2 Jul 1955

      8 HOBBS, Sandra Ann   B-29 Jan 1976
      8 HOBBS, Charles David   B-29 Oct 1977
      8 HOBBS, Carey Ann   B- 3 Aug 1979

7 THOMPSON, Michael Earl B-7 Feb 1960

7 THOMPSON, Steven Rowley B-14 Jan 1966

7 THOMPSON, Jean   B-17 Oct 1967

6 ROWLEY, Don B-11 Sep 1934 D-9 Oct 1934

6 ROWLEY, Dee B-11 Sep 1934 D-18 Oct 1934

6 CONDIE, Darlene ROWLEY B-19 Dec 1935 M-9 Sep 1958
6 CONDIE, Arthur Packard, Sp. B-27 Nov 1934

    7 GRAFF, Terri Lee CONDIE B-22 Jun 1958 M-1 Sep 1978
    7 GRAFF, Brad Lee, Sp. B-

    7 CONDIE, Arthur Rowley   B-12 Apr 1961
    7 CONDIE, Nello Rowley   B-31 Aug 1963 D-13 Apr 1968
    7 CONDIE, Karen   B- 4 Mar 1966
    7 CONDIE, Don Rowley   B-27 Jun 1968
    7 CONDIE, Diane   B-12 Oct 1971
    7 CONDIE, Marie   B-23 Aug 1974
    7 CONDIE, Reed Rowley   B-25 Nov 1977

6 ROWLEY, Richard B-13 Mar 1940 D-17 Mar 1940

5 NOAKES, Olive Ethel GILES Olson B-20 Dec 1909
5 OLSON, Robert Edwin, Sp. (1) B-28 Jun 1903 M-5 Jul 1929 D-14 Sep 1934
5 NOAKES, Sterling George, Sp.B-5 Dec 1913 M-5 Jun 1943

6 OLSON, Edwin Robert B-17 May 1930 M-5 Apr 1952
6 OLSON, Theresa BRUNNER, Sp. B-8 Jul 1927

    7 HINCKLEY, Ingrid Gerda OLSON B-7 Oct 1946 M-11 Aug 1967
    7 HINCKLEY, Craig Bryce, Sp. B-9 Jul 1945

        8 HINCKLEY, Lori Dawn   B-2 Jan 1970
        8 HINCKLEY, Ryan Craig   B-2 May 1972

    7 OLSON, Robert Kim B-14 Dec 1954 M-7 Feb 1976
    7 OLSON, Bari Lyn CORMANI, Sp. B-27 Oct 1956
        8 OLSON, Landon Kim   B-30 Jun 1979
6 OLSON, Melvin Ray B-17 Apr 1934 M-28 Jan 1961
6 OLSON, Marlene Madge CLAYSON, Sp. B-1 Oct 1940

    7 OLSON, Michael Ray   B-28 Jun 1962
    7 OLSON, Steven C.   B-20 Jul 1964
    7 OLSON, Nancy Lee   B-26 Mar 1973

6 SABIN, Catherine Lona NOAKES B-2 Dec 1944 M-22 Jul 1967
6 SABIN, Kimball B., Sp. B-14 Jun 1944

    7 SABIN, Dianna Lynn   B-25 Nov 1968
    7 SABIN, William Edwin B-13 Jan 1970
    7 SABIN, Denice Ann   B- 6 Nov 1972
    7 SABIN, Donna Kay   B- 1 Jun 1974

6 NOAKES, Gary Niles B-19 Mar 1947 M-11 Apr 1970
6 NOAKES, Lily Del Carmen Logreyra DIAZ, Sp. B-10 Jul 1949

    7 NOAKES, Gayle Monica   B-12 Oct 1971
    7 NOAKES, John Gary   B-19 Nov 1972
    7 NOAKES, Cheryl Nadine   B- 5 Oct 1977
    7 NOAKES, Derek Jason   B-28 Dec 1979
6 KEYTE, Nila Dian NOAKES B-26 Sep 1948 M-16 Dec 1973
6 KEYTE, Michael Stanley, Sp. B-11 Jul 1947

    7 KEYTE, Michael Shane   B-23 Jul 1974
    7 KEYTE, Ryan Craig   B-30 Jan 1976
    7 KEYTE, Tyler Paul   B-30 Dec 1977

5 GILES, Edwin Tadd B-20 Oct 1912 M-5 Apr 1933 D-11 Jan 1975
5 GILES, Mildred BARKER, Sp. B-25 Dec 1913

    6 BLACKETT, Loretta GILES B-2 Feb 1934 M-4 Jun 1953
    6 BLACKETT, Jimmy Dale, Sp. B-7 Jun 1933

```
                    7 BLACKETT, Jimmy Tadd B-15 May 1954 M-10 Sep 1976
                    7 BLACKETT, Laurie Jean ROBERTS, Sp. B-20 Apr 1957

                            8 BLACKETT, Matthew Jim    B-4 Sep 1978

                    7 BLACKETT, Dale Lynn B-9 Jul 1958

                    7 EWING, Julia BLACKETT B-16 Aug 1959 M-25 Nov 1977
                    7 EWING, Steven Fletcher, Sp. B-24 May 1957

                            8 EWING, Amy     B-27 Mar 1979

                    7 MITCHELL, Laura BLACKETT B-4 Jan 1962 M-12 Jul 1979
                    7 MITCHELL, Danny Lee, Sp. B-
                            8 MITCHELL, Danny Lee     B-21 Mar 1980
                    7 BLACKETT, Mark Gregory B-18 Nov 1964

            6 RUFF, Ardith GILES B-8 Oct 1936 M-2 Jul 1954
            6 RUFF, Glen Verlon, Sp. B-1 Aug 1930

                    7 RUFF, David Edward      B-11 May 1956
                    7 RUFF, Wesley "L"        B- 1 Jan 1958
                    7 RUFF, Ann               B- 6 Aug 1959

            6 THORPE, Barbara GILES B-31 Aug 1939 M-7 Sep 1955
            6 THORPE, Taylor Lewis, Sp. B-16 Dec 1935

                    7 THORPE, Taylor Brad     B-24 Mar 1957
                    7 THORPE, Tadd Howard     B- 7 May 1962

5 GURR, Lottie "H" GILES B-22 May 1914 M-11 Feb 1933
5 GURR, Wallace Refuge, Sp. B-10 Aug 1912

            6 GURR, Wayne G. B-22 Jan 1934
            6 GURR, Janet INGLEFIELD, Sp. B-            M-5 Oct 1955  Div. 1956
            6 GURR, Dorthy NATHER, Sp. (2) B-        M-10 May 1958     Div. 1958
            6 GURR, Maurine Flora DRAGE, Sp. (3) B-27 Dec 1933 M-11 Dec 1959
            ARGYLE, Ronald Charles, Sp. (1) to Maurine B-           M-          Div.

                    7 JOHNSON, Pamela Jean GURR B-4 May 1954 M-3 Nov 1972
                    7 JOHNSON, Russell Dean, Sp. B-9 Jan 1949

                            8 JOHNSON, Jamie         B-22 Sep 1973
                            8 JOHNSON, Jennifer      B- 1 May 1976

                    7 MARSHALL, Diane Gurr B-12 Nov 1957 M-12 Nov 1975
                    7 MARSHALL, Rodger Glen, Sp. B-1 May 1953

                            8 MARSHALL, Joshua        B- 3 Dec 1976
                            8 MARSHALL, Jody Wayne     B-22 Feb 1979
                            8 MARSHALL, Mellissa Ann   B-13 May 1980

                    7 MARSHALL, Brenda Dawn B-14 Jun 1961 M-
                    7 MARSHALL, Steven, Sp. B-

                    7 GURR, Wayne Kevin       B-12 Aug 1964
                    7 GURR, Kelly Giles       B- 3 Jul 1967

            6 TASKER, Elaine GURR B-17 Jul 1935 M-14 Feb 1953
            6 TASKER, Fredrick Robert, Sp. B- 24 Apr 1934

                    7 TASKER, Fred W. B-27 Aug 1953 M-27 Jun 1975
                    7 TASKER, Nancy Jo THROCKMORTON, Sp. B-29 Sep 1954

                            8 TASKER, Travis Fred      B-27 Mar 1976
                            8 TASKER, Jody             B-27 Aug 1977
                            8 TASKER, Stacey           B-27 Aug 1979

                    7 TASKER, Michael Robert B-13 Nov 1954 M-18 Jul 1975
                    7 TASKER, Robyn Yvette BUCHANAN, Sp. B-29 Jan 1955

                            8 TASKER, Summer Leigh    B-26 Nov 1977

                    7 TASKER, Bill Dee        B-30 Dec 1959
                    7 TASKER, Jill            B-30 Dec 1959
                    7 TASKER, Lynn            B-27 Jun 1962
```

6 MAAG, Afton Gurr B-28 May 1937 M-9 Apr 1955
6 MAAG, Conrad Eldores, Sp. B-7 Oct 1932

      7 MAAG, Jeffery Conrad B-17 Dec 1955 M-20 Apr 1978
      7 MAAG, Terry DaNece VERNON, Sp. B-

            8 MAAG, Jedidiah Conrad   B-14 May 1979

      7 MAAG, Kathleen   B- 7 Jan 1957

      7 CRAGUM, Annette MAAG B-8 Oct 1958 M-13 Apr 1979
      7 CRAGUM, Eddie L. Sp. B-

            8 CRAGUM, Melannie MAAG   B-23 Jul 1977
            8 CRAGUM, Eddie Brandon   B-15 Jun 1980

      7 MAAG, Mary   B-28 Oct 1960
      7 MAAG, Margene   B-25 Nov 1963

6 THOMAS, LaNyle GURR B-22 Nov 1938 M-29 Jun 1956
6 THOMAS, Gerald Lynn, Sp. B-25 May 1932

      7 WILLIAMS, Christina THOMAS B-1 Feb 1957 M-13 May 1976
      7 WILLIAMS, Drew MacLean, Sp. B-18 Mar 1954

      7 THOMAS, John Gurr   B-14 Apr 1958
      7 THOMAS, Paul Alan   B-24 Mar 1960
      7 THOMAS, Elizabeth   B- 4 Dec 1961
      7 THOMAS, Katherine   B-25 Dec 1963

6 GURR, Wallace Randall B-16 Apr 1951 M-8 Jun 1973
6 GURR, Pauline BEST, Sp. B-21 Apr 1954

      7 GURR, Amy Jean   B- 2 Jun 1974
      7 GURR, Justin William   B- 1 Aug 1975
      7 GURR, Mathew Paul   B-24 May 1977
      7 GURR, Brett Giles   B- 9 May 1980

6 MARSHALL, Terry GURR B-6 Nov 1952 M-17 Oct 1972
6 MARSHALL, Stephen Richard, Sp. B-16 Oct 1954

      7 MARSHALL, Jan   B-25 Nov 1974
      7 MARSHALL, Richard Steven B-19 Feb 1977

5 NAYLOR, Ila "M" GILES B-13 Mar 1919 M-27 Feb 1937
5 NAYLOR, Marvin Laird, Sp. B-8 Jul 1917

      6 PEAY, Ila LaRene NAYLOR B-14 Sep 1937 M-4 Apr 1958
      6 PEAY, Jimmy Clark, Sp. B-15 Jul 1935

            7 PEAY, Craig "M"   B-29 Mar 1964
            7 PEAY, JoAnn   B-14 Aug 1966
            7 PEAY, Robert "N"   B- 4 Aug 1967
            7 PEAY, Julie Ann   B-26 Aug 1974

5 GURR, LaWanna GILES B-30 Aug 1922 M-7 Dec 1943
5 GURR, Eugene James, Sp. B-26 Dec 1916

      6 DENNISON, Virginia GURR B-19 Dec 1946 M-9 Aug 1972
      6 DENNISON, Ernest Darnell, Sp. B-27 Jul 1948

            7 DENISON, Bart Giles   B- 5 Jul 1973
            7 DENISON, Trent Marshall B-26 Jan 1975
            7 DENISON, Clay Wiatt   B-13 Feb 1976
            7 DENNISON, KimberLee   B- 5 Mar 1981

      6. GURR, Eugene James B-18 Nov 1950 M-2 Apr 1971
      6 GURR, Jill HAFEN, Sp. B-23 Jul 1952

            7 GURR, Jennifer   B-15 Oct 1972
            7 GURR, Brian James   B-19 Sep 1974
            7 GURR, Jonathan Dean B-13 Feb 1980
            7 GURR, Daniel Adam   B- 3 Aug 1981

      6 GURR, Sue Ann B-15 Jan 1953 D-15 Jan 1953

5 GILES, Milton Bernell B-16 Dec 1924 M-2 Jul 1946
5 GILES, Myrna Jane MEASOM, Sp. B-11 Feb 1925

    6 GILES, Milton Craig B-2 Aug 1947 M-17 Jul 1970
    6 GILES, Donna Diane MARLIN, Sp. B-25 Feb 1949

        7 GILES, Crystal Diane   B-24 Nov 1968
        7 GILES, Melyssa Kay   B- 7 Jun 1971
        7 GILES, Milton Bradley B-31 Jul 1975
        7 GILES, Ryan Craig   B- 8 Nov 1976

    6 LUCCHETTI, DeLauna GILES B-13 Jan 1949 M-9 Oct 1970
    6 LUCCHETTI, James Albert, Sp. B-24 Jan 1947

        7 LUCCHETTI, Pietro James B-23 Apr 1971
        7 LUCCHETTI, John Bryan B-14 Jan 1975
        7 LUCCHETTI, Lydia   B-20 Aug 1976
        7 LUCCHETTI, Lisa   B- 3 Jul 1978
        7 LUCCHETTI, Alan Paul   B-29 May 1980
    6 BROWN, Debra GILES B-13 Mar 1952 M-7 Jun 1974
    6 BROWN, Charles Eugene, Sp. B-29 Jan 1948

        7 BROWN, Conan Charles   B-27 Mar 1975
        7 BROWN, Scott Giles   B-12 Jan 1977
        7 BROWN, Shawn Barrett   B- 6 Sep 1979

    6 GILES, Roger Thomas B-14 Nov 1956

    6 GILES, Edwin Kent   B-26 Aug 1958

    6 GILES, Larry   B-21 Nov 1959 D-21 Nov 1959

    6 GILES, Melanie   B-27 Aug 1962

5 RICHES, Audrey LaRae B-12 Jun 1927 M-12 Dec 1944
5 RICHES, David Karl, Sp. B-28 Dec 1923

    6 JOHNSON, Sherry Lynne RICHES B-4 Apr 1946 M-15 Dec 1965
    6 JOHNSON, Paul Stanley, Sp. B-17 Sep 1943

        7 JOHNSON, Joseph Paul   B-23 Feb 1967
        7 JOHNSON, Edward Allen B- 9 Oct 1969 Twin
        7 JOHNSON, Eric William   B- 9 Oct 1969 Twin
        7 JOHNSON, Cynthia Lynne B-31 Dec 1973
        7 JOHNSON, Tamra Lynne   B-19 Jul 1975

    6 RICHES, David Brent B- 9 Dec 1949

    6 CROOK, Kathy La Rae RICHES B-29 Aug 1952 M-19 Feb 1971
    6 CROOK, Jimmy Walter, Sp. B-8 Jul 1949

        7 CROOK, Jason William   B- 9 Jan 1973
        7 CROOK, Shanalee   B- 6 Nov 1974
        7 CROOK, Lauree La Rae   B- 6 Jun 1978

4 GILES, James Alvin B-18 Apr 1885 M-31 Oct 1905 D-15 Feb 1970
4 GILES, Margaret GIBSON, Sp. B-28 Feb 1888 D-8 Mar 1956

    5 RHODEHOUSE, Mary GILES Larson B-2 Apr 1906
    5 LARSON, William Theadore, Sp. B-10 Jan 1903 M-20 Sep 1922 D-29 Jan 1938
    5 RHODEHOUSE, Charles Albert Sp. (2) B-   M-

    6 IVES, Mary Thea LARSON Brown B-27 Oct 1923
    6 BROWN, Stewart, Sp. (1) B-   M-25 Oct 1939
    6 IVES, Raymond William, Sp (2) B-   M-

        7 DAVIDSON, Mary Ann BROWN B-   M-
        7 DAVIDSON,   Sp. B-

        7 BRUMLEY, Carrie Irene BROWN B-   M-
        7 BRUMLEY,   Sp. B-

        7 BROWN, Dave Stewart B-   M- ?

```
                  7 IVES, Frank  B-

                  7 MECKLER, Trena IVES B-                      M-
                  7 MECKLER,          Sp. B-

                  7 IVES, Charles B-

          6 PETERSON, Vilda Ann LARSON Orgill B-
          6 ORGILL,           Sp. B-                   M-
          6 PETERSON, Elmo C., Sp. B-              M-

                  7 ORGILL, Ted E. B-              M-?

                  7 SESSIONS, Brenda Lisa ORGILL B-              M-
                  7 SESSIONS,         Sp. B-

          6 LARSON, MARION George B-            M-
          6 LARSON, Dorine HANSEN, Sp. B-              M-
          6 LARSON, Enith K ATWOOD, Sp. B-                  M-

                  7 LARSON, Michael B-          M- ?

                  7 TIMMONS, Pamela Jo LARSON  B-              M-
                  7 TIMMONS,          Sp. B-

                  7 LARSON, Todd G.          B-

                  7 LARSON, Tana K.          B-

                  7 LARSON, Michelle E.       B-

          6 LARSON, Edwin Lorenzo B-          M-
          6 LARSON, Myrna Dawn ORR, Sp. B-

                  7 LARSON, Jeffrey L.       B-
                  7 LARSON, Randall E.       B-

                  7 CRAPO, Patsy LARSON B-            M-
                  7 CRAPO,          Sp. B-

                  7 LARSON, Bryan Theadore    B-
                  7 LARSON, Shelly Dawn      B-
                  7 LARSON, Da Lea          B-
                  7 LARSON, Suzette         B-
                  7 LARSON, Debra           B-
                  7 LARSON, Jared E.        B-

          6 LARSON, Hal Theadore  B-       1935 D-        1963

          6 LARSON, Don Coy B-          M-
          6 LARSON, Gayle Tueller, Sp. B-

                  7 LARSON, Ronald Coy      B-
                  7 LARSON, Teresa Gayle    B-
                  7 LARSON, Lisa Ellen      B-
                  7 LARSON, Sheldon Don     B-
                  7 LARSON, Alvin Theadore  B-
                  7 LARSON, Trevor Don      B-
                  7 LARSON, Sharae         B-
                  7 LARSON, La Rae         B-
                  7 LARSON, Ra Nae         B-
                  7 LARSON, Gregory Coy     B-

5 GILES, James Don B-10 Nov 1907 D-      1967
5 GILES, Elizabeth PETERSON, Sp. (1) B-              M-14 Nov 1929
5 GILES, Ellen MANNING, Sp. (2) B-          M-9 Apr 1934

          6 GILES, Gerald B-

          6 BRIGHTON, Mary Ellen GILES B-              M-
          6 BRIGHTON,          Sp. B-

          6 GILES, Paul B-
```

5 GILES, Clifford Alvin, B-18 Sep 1909 M-30 Sep 1931 D-31 Mar 1973
5 GILES, Phoebe Helen HALE, Sp. B-18 Mar 1911

      6 GILES, Frank James B-19 Jan 1933 M-10 Oct 1956
      6 GILES, Beverley Jean MILLER, Sp. B-

            7 GILES, Michal William   B- 8 Sep 1957 D-17 Sep 1957
            7 GILES, Mark Steven   B-17 Oct 1959
            7 GILES, Lori Jo   B-17 Jan 1961
            7 GILES, Theresa Lynn   B-31 Jan 1964

      6 CHARTRAND, Helen Jean GILES B-20 Jun 1935 M-5 Apr 1951
      6 CHARTRAND, George L., Sp. B-

            7 CHARTRAND, Lewis   B-29 Aug 1952
            7 CHARTRAND, Kathalen Anne B-27 Nov 1954
            7 CHARTRAND, Kent Clifford   B-29 May 1956

      6 GILES, Fred Alvin B-15 Nov 1939 M-7 Jun 1959
      6 GILES, Sanya Kay LAUSING, Sp. B-

            7 GILES, Shelly   B-19 Jan 1960
            7 GILES, Fred John   B- 8 Mar 1965
            7 GILES, Saunya Kay   B-24 Feb 1969

      6 GILES, Ned Hale B-11 Dec 1941 M-19 May 1961
      6 GILES, Lorraine ROWLEY, Sp. B-

            7 GILES, Brain Ned   B-27 Mar 1962
            7 GILES, Deniese   B-27 Mar 1964
            7 GILES, Blair Loran   B- 7 Aug 1966
            7 GILES, Brad Michal   B-13 Jan 1969
            7 GILES, Brandee Nicole   B-10 Oct 1976

5 GILES, William Guy B-28 Jul 1911 M-14 Oct 1930 Div.
5 GILES, Zona Lapreele CARRELL, Sp. B-

      6 GILES, William B-14 May 1933 M-14 Oct 1930
      6 GILES, Zelma POWERS, Sp. B-

      6 GILES, Orson Guy B-13 Apr 1936 M-16 Jun 1964
      6 GILES, Shirley WILKINSON, Sp. B-

      6 GILES, Theadore L. B-30 Jul 1937 M-19 May 1962
      6 GILES, Sharon ROBERTS, Sp. B-

            7 GILES, Dean Robert   B-22 Jun 1963
            7 GILES, Molly Ann   B-29 Jan 1966
            7 GILES, Terry Sue   B-14 Apr 1967
            7 GILES, Brent Liddell   B-15 Dec 1973
            7 GILES, Brian Bliss   B-15 Dec 1973

      6 GILES, Margaret Louise B-15 Oct 1946 D-16 Feb 1947

      6 SPROUL, Linda Sue GILES B-21 Jun 1948
      6 GOODSELL, Bruce Lynn, Sp. (1) B-   M-2 Aug 1968
      6 SPROUL, Jerry, Sp. (2) B-   M-14 Nov 1974

5 NATION, Christina GILES Brundage Fitzgerald White B-2 Apr 1913
5 BRUNDAGE, William, Sp. B-   M-9 Jan 1930
5 FITZGERALD, Bruce, Sp. (2) B-   M-
5 WHITE, Archie, Sp. (3) B-   M-
5 NATION,   Sp. (4) B-   M-

      6 BEELER, Wilma BRUNDAGE B-   M-
      6 BEELER, Dan, Sp. B-

      6 BRUNDAGE, Kay B-   M-   D-
      6 BRUNDAGE, Sharon KEAL, Sp. B-

      6 MARX, Patsy FITZGERALD B-   M-
      6 MARX, David, Sp. B-

5 GILES, Thomas B-28 Oct 1915 D-28 Oct 1915

5 MARTIN, Rachel Ann GILES B-22 Nov 1916 M-25 Jul 1935
5 MARTIN, Charles Edward, Sp, B-4 Dec 1906 D-23 Feb 1968

      6 MARTIN, James Morgan B-31 Jul 1936 D-15 Mar 1971
      6 MARTIN, Miriam Verbena KIERSTEAD, Sp. B-4 Feb 19 M-26 Jun 1959
      6 MARTIN, Donna Clara MORRISEY Glover, Sp. (2) B-7 Apr 19 M-4 May 1964
      6 MARTIN, Karen V HANSEN, Sp. (3) B-12 Jan 19 M-

        7 MARTIN, Timothy Lynn   B- 4 Dec 1962

        7 MARTIN, Donna Ann   B- 8 Jun 1966

        7 MARTIN, Charles Leslie   B-23 Feb 1969

      6 MARTIN, Charles Edward B-24 Jan 1940 D-24 Jan 1940

      6 MARTIN, Wayne Jennings B-16 Feb 1941 M-2 Jul 1965
      6 MARTIN, Vicki BENSON, Sp. B-12 Nov 1944

        7 MARTIN, Vicki   B- 9 Apr 1966
        7 MARTIN, William Kay   B-15 Jul 1967
        7 MARTIN, Lloyd Dirk   B-11 Aug 1974
        7 MARTIN, Joan Rochelle   B-14 Sep 1977

      6 MARTIN, Frank John B-12 Jul 1944 M-19 Nov 1977
      6 MARTIN, Kathryn Marie ANDERSON Butler, Sp. B-

      6 MARTIN, Edward A. B-16 Aug 1946 M-10 Aug 1968
      6 MARTIN, Anita Louise ANTHES,Sp. B-27 Dec 1949

        7 MARTIN, Paul Edward   B-22 Apr 1969
        7 MARTIN, Mark Edward   B-23 Oct 1970
        7 MARTIN, Eric John   B-28 Jun 1972
        7 MARTIN, Alisha Louise   B- 6 Apr 1976

      6 CHRISTIANSEN, Barbara Ann MARTIN B-10 Sep 1948 M-19 Jul 1968
      6 CHRISTIANSEN, Frank W., Sp. B-16 Oct 1946

        7 CHRISTIANSEN, Steven Scott B- 5 May 1969
        7 CHRISTIANSEN, Shelley Ann B-19 Oct 1970
        7 CHRISTIANSEN, Samuel Max B- 8 Jul 1972
        7 CHRISTIANSEN, Cherie   B-30 Sep 1974
        7 CHRISTIANSEN, Christina B-19 Dec 1977

      6 THOMAS, Margaret Susan MARTIN B-4 Aug 1950 M-30 Jun 1972
      6 THOMAS, Ted William, Sp. B-20 Apr 1952

        7 THOMAS, William John Trevor B-7 Jul 1977

      6 MARTIN, Craig Giles B-26 Feb 1952 M-1 Nov 1974
      6 MARTIN, Sherylun NIXON, Sp. B-3 Sep 1954

        7 MARTIN, Jennifer   B-19 Jun 1975
        7 MARTIN, Craig Zeke   B- 4 Feb 1977
        7 MARTIN, Jessica   B-25 Jan 1978

      6 MARTIN, Charles Thomas B-15 Mar 1954 M-29 Oct 1975
      6 MARTIN, Rebecca LLOYD, Sp. B-3 Jun 1956

      6 MARTIN, David Deloy   B- 7 Apr 1956

      6 MARTIN, Racheal Christina B- 4 Oct 1959

      6 MARTIN, Don Brent   B-11 Feb 1961

      6 MARTIN, Bruce Allen   B-22 Apr 1963

      6 MARTIN, Mary Virginia   B-11 Aug 1964

5 GILES, Rex Angus B-7 Nov 1918
5 GILES, Prudence Adrienne PORRITT, Sp. (1) B-   M-
5 GILES, Agnes Geneva WINN, Sp. (2) B-29 Nov 1910 M-11 Aug 1948
  Wilson, John Golden, Sp. (1) to Agnes B-   M-

6 GILES, Ronald Lorenzo B-19 Dec 1941 M-   Feb 1963
6 GILES, Velma Roaine POTTER, Sp. B-29 Jan 1944

        7 GILES, Ronald Lorenzo Jr. B-20 Dec 1963
        7 GILES, Glenn Nephi   B-25 Jan 1965
        7 GILES, Cindy Lee   B- 1 Nov 1969
        7 GILES, Suzette   B- 5 Nov 1971
        7 GILES, Terry Ray   B-29 Jan 1976

6 THOMPSON, Adrienne Dherie GILES B-25 Feb 1943 M-18 Oct 1963
6 THOMPSON, James Willard, Sp. B-4 Mar 1936

        7 THOMPSON, Wanda Cherrie   B-17 Sep 1970
        7 THOMPSON, James Aley   B- 7 Dec 1971
        7 THOMPSON, Ramona Lynn   B-25 Oct 1974

6 KAREN, Charma Joyce GILES B-18 Apr 1945 M-13 Dec 1963
6 KAREN, Lee Ernest, Sp. B-7 Dec 1937

        7 KAREN, Danny Lee   B-10 Sep 1965
        7 KAREN, Melinda Sue   B-28 Mar 1967

6 DAVIS, La Rene GILES B-22 Apr 1949 M-
6 DAVIS, George Harvey III, Sp. B-

        7 DAVIS, Roby Ann   B-21 Jul 1980

6 JOHNSON, Cla Rene GILES B-22 Apr 1949 M-13 Mar 1970
6 JOHNSON, Robert Frank, Sp. B-9 Mar 1949

        7 JOHNSON, Alan Boyd   B-27 Jun 1971
        7 JOHNSON, Michael Brian   B-21 Jul 1972
        7 JOHNSON, Brenda   B- 9 Apr 1974
        7 JOHNSON, Becky   B-29 Jan 1976

6 LUCKART, Evelyn GILES, B-10 Dec 1952 M-24 Dec 1970
6 LUCKART, Elton, Sp. B-14 Feb 1952

        7 LUCKART, Cheryl Lee   B-24 Oct 1971
        7 LUCKART, Elton Shawn   B- 4 Mar 1974
        7 LUCKART, Eric Shane   B- 3 Apr 1975

5 GILES, John B (Jack) B-1 Oct 1924 M-24 Nov 1948
5 GILES, Margaret Mary HARRIS, Sp. B-7 Jul 1930

    6 GILES, Elwood Barry B-13 Dec 1950

    6 GEGAX, Lanna Kae GILES B-10 Dec 1952 M-
        7 GEGAX Ryan Philip   B-6 Jul 1971
    6 GILES, Joni Irene   B-9 Jan 1962

5 JENKINS, Betty Jean GILES B-12 Mar 1928 M-27 May 1944
5 JENKINS, Edward Jay, Sp. B-16 Apr 1926

    6 TAYLOR, Jaelee JENKINS B-10 Dec 1947 M-15 Mar 1967
    6 TAYLOR, John Delbert, Sp. B-31 Dec 1946

        7 TAYLOR, Jay Duane   B-11 Jul 1968
        7 TAYLOR, John Daniel   B- 5 Dec 1969
        7 TAYLOR, James Dee   B-11 Jan 1971
        7 TAYLOR, Jennifer Jo   B- 1 Nov 1977

    6 JENKINS, Edward Duane B-26 Feb 1951 D-1 Mar 1956

    6 ARTHURS, Charlene JENKINS B-4 Feb 1952 M-6 Mar 1972
    6 ARTHURS, William James, Sp. B-

        7 ARTHURS, Anna Jean   B-17 Jul 1972
        7 ARTHURS, Angela   B-22 Aug 1973

    6 JENKINS, John Watkins B-19 Apr 1955

    6 MOLLOTTE, Janice JENKINS B-4 Jan 1957 M-29 Mar 1976
    6 MOLLOTTE, Richard Samuel, Sp. B-11 Jun 1956

```
                7 MOLLOTTE, Richard Jay        B-25 Apr 1977
                7 MOLLOTTE, Rebecca Lee         B- 5 Jan 1979

4 GILES, Henry Alexander B-15 Feb 1887 M-16 Aug 1911 D-16 Jun 1930
4 GILES, Flossie Lake, Sp. B-31 Aug 1893 D-29 Jun 1975

        5 BOSTWICK, Elizabeth Ann GILES B-8 Aug 1912 M-19 Aug 1933
        5 BOSTWICK, Walter Orville, Sp. B-18 Aug 1910

                6 MILLER, Walda Ann BOSTWICK Sargetis B-22 Sep 1936
                6 SARGETIS, John, Sp. (1) B-         M-18 Jun 1955 Div. 9 Nov 1957
                6 MILLER, Donald Carl, Sp. (2) B-19 Jun 1936 M-31 Dec 1960 *(Div. & Remarried)
                  Miller, Georgia Jean STEIN, Sp (1) B-        M-6 Oct 1957 Div.1 Dec 1959

                        7 KENDALL, Cynthia Ann MILLER B-22 Feb 1957 M-30 Nov 1974 (Leg. Adopt
                        7 KENDALL, Bruce D., Sp. B-9 Dec 1954                    by MILLER)

                                8 KENDALL, Clayton D       B-29 Nov 1976

                        7 ANDERSON, Michelle Diane BOSTWICK B-25 Nov 1950 M-28 Jul 1975
                        7 ANDERSON, Stephen Brent, Sp. B-23 Apr 1948
                          ANDERSON, Christine BARTON, Sp. (1) B-         M-         Div.

        5 HORROCKS, Leah Luella GILES B-25 Oct 1914 M-29 May 1933
        5 HORROCKS, William Glen, Sp. B-12 Nov 1910

                6 AZLIN, Glenna HORROCKS B-23 Apr 1934 M-4 Aug 1954
                6 AZLIN, Bob Carl, Sp. B-

                        7 MOULTON, Kathleen AZLIN B-        M-
                        7 MOULTON, Kent L. Sp. B-

                        7 AZLIN, Carolyn Y       B-

                        7 AZLIN, Connie R        B-

                6 HORROCKS, Thomas H. B-               M-4 Jun 1958
                6 HORROCKS, Jean SWEAT, Sp. B-

                        7 HORROCKS, David       B-
                        7 HORROCKS, Patricia    B-
                        7 HORROCKS, Tamra       B-
                        7 HORROCKS, Valorie     B-
                        7 HORROCKS, Amy         B-

        5 GILES, Laura May B-26 Oct 1916 D-10 Nov 1916

        5 MOORMAN, Erma GILES B-1 Oct 1917 M-6 Apr 1940
        5 MOORMAN, Leslie Leo, Sp. B-30 Jun 1913

                6 BUCHANAN, Forence MOORMAN B-3 Sep 1942 M-15 Sep 1962
                6 BUCHANAN, Fred Gaylon, Sp. B-

                6 TAYLOR,   Shirley MOORMAN B- 20 Apr 1946
                6 CRANDELL, James Edward, Sp. (1) B-        M-24 Aug 1964
                6 TAYLOR, Clifford George, Sp. (2) B-       M-30 Aug 1975

                6 FORSMANN, Julie Ann MOORMAN B-21 Jan 1952 M-16 May 1970
                6 FORSMANN, Stanley Joseph, Sp. B-

        5 GILES, Sherman Alexander, B-26 Apr 1920 M-8 Sep 1943
        5 GILES, Kaye Burch, Sp. B-17 Feb 1922

                6 GILES, David Sherman B-15 Jun 1944 M-1 Jul 1966
                6 GILES, Tony WELLS, Sp. B-15 Apr 1947

                        7 GILES, Marie          B-24 May 1967
                        7 GILES, Mark David     B-14 Jan 1969
                        7 GILES, Lisa           B- 1 Nov 1970
                        7 GILES, KayLyn         B-19 Jan 1975
                        7 GILES, Andrew Sherman B-26 Jul 1966 Adopted Twin
                        7 GILES, James Wells    B-26 Jul 1966 Adopted Twin

                6 JARDINE, Kathleen GILES B-11 Oct 1948 M-26 Jun 1973
                6 JARDINE, William Ellis, Sp. B-8 Jun 1949
```

```
              7 JARDINE, Janalee        B- 4 May 1974
              7 JARDINE, Melissa        B-30 Dec 1975
              7 JARDINE, Ellis Burke    B-30 Mar 1978

      6 HENDERSON, Joyce GILES B-21 May 1951 M-19 Dec 1969
      6 HENDERSON, Sidney Richard, Sp. B-31 Mar 1947

              7 HENDERSON, Sidney Benson II B-22 Jan 1971
              7 HENDERSON, Nathan Alexander B-14 Feb 1972 Twin
              7 HENDERSON, Richard Louis    B-14 Feb 1972 Twin
              7 HENDERSON, Bonnie Kaye      B-12 Mar 1974

      6 GILES, Lynn Kent B-28 Jul 1954 M-1 Sep 1978
      6 GILES, Pearl Ute' MOWES, Sp B-4 Jun 1957

              7 GILES, Mindy Kay          B-14 Jun 1979

      6 RUEGSEGGER, Jeanine GILES B-24 Sep 1956 M-9 Apr 1976
      6 RUEGSEGGER, Leland, Sp. B-15 Dec 1954

              7 RUEGSEGGER, Joshua Lee B-15 Jan 1977
              7 RUEGSEGGER, Jared E    B-18 Feb 1978
              7 RUEGSEGGER, Jason S    B-16 Mar 1980

      6 GILES, Scott   B-22 Jan 1960

  5 FINDLEY, Jennie GILES B-1 Aug 1922 M-25 Feb 1944
  5 FINDLEY, Ralph Anderson, Sp. B-

  5 GILES, Calvin B-19 Mar 1925 M-19 Jun 1946
  5 GILES, Amberzine PARCELL, Sp. B-

  5 GILES, Glen B-26 Nov 1927 M-20 Oct 1948
  5 GILES, Carol June HOOVER, Sp. B-

  5 PRICE, Nadine GILES B-24 Apr 1930 M-15 Nov 1950
  5 PRICE, "J" Fred PRICE, Sp. B-28 May 1924

      6 PRICE, John "H" B-1 October 1951 M-5 Jun 1970
      6 PRICE, Brenda PROBST, Sp. B-25 Nov 1950

              7 PRICE, Gregory John      B-21 Apr 1971
              7 PRICE, Jeremy Kay        B-21 Mar 1973
              7 PRICE, Karalee           B-17 Mar 1975
              7 PRICE, Marci             B- 9 Apr 1977
              7 PRICE, Crystal           B-13 Oct 1979
              7 PRICE, Camille           B-13 Oct 1979

      6 RAIL, Laurel June B-11 Aug 1953 M-19 Apr 1973
      6 RAIL, Joseph Hoffman, Sp. B-

              7 RAIL, Rebecca            B-
              7 RAIL, Alan Joseph        B-17 Oct 1978

      6 PRICE, Jay Fred B-22 Feb 1956 M-5 Sep 1975
      6 PRICE, Rebbecca Lynn PROVOST, Sp. B-

              7 PRICE, Angela            B-
              7 PRICE, Jason F           B-

4 GILES, Charles Andrew B- 15 Mar 1888 M-3 Jul 1911  D-17 Oct 1976
4 GILES, LaVerne Grace PROVOST, Sp. B-
```

Janett Osborne Murdoch and Henry Lufkin McMullin

Such wonderful memories I have of my mother and of her parents, our pioneer ancestors, John M. and Ann Steel Murdoch. For this history I have drawn in part from a previous history written by me and my sister Annie J. Rasband.

John Murray and Ann Steel Murdoch with their infant daughter Mary arrived in the Salt Lake Valley in 1852. The baby had been born near what is now Kansas City while John and Ann were waiting for the immigrant train to assemble for the trek across the plains. How sadly their young lives had been touched with the tragedy accompanying their arrival in America. They had left Scotland with two small children only to have them both die, yet they wholeheartedly accepted this trial and pressed on to Zion to enjoy the blessings promised them when they joined The Church of Jesus Christ of Latter-day Saints.

In 1854 another little girl was born to John and Ann. This baby was named Ann for her mother. Two years later on December 20, a third little girl came into the home. She was given the name of Janett Osborne. About this time, the little family was anxiously looking forward to the arrival of an immigrant train, a handcart company, which would include John's mother, Mary Murray Murdoch ("Wee Granny") and Ann's brother James. We can visualize Ann standing in the doorway of their one-room cabin as John would arrive from town and sadly say to her, "They have given their lives for the gospel's sake." This, indeed, was a great and sad disappointment and that is why, as Janett was a small child, mother Ann would stroke her hair and say, "No wonder that you cry so easily and are so tenderhearted, my little girl, for six weeks before you were born, I cried every day and couldn't sleep at night for thinking of poor Wee Granny and Uncle James."

As time passed and the family grew, though he had arrived in the valley in very poor circumstances, John managed to secure a yoke of oxen and a wagon. Word was getting around among the settlers of a beautiful place known as Provo Valley, so it became the desire of the Murdochs to move on to this place where they could establish themselves with a farm and a more permanent home. Janett was four years old, and in later years she would recall in detail the rough trip through Provo Canyon. How dangerous it was to cross the Provo River, which then was a rushing stream and quite deep in places. Some soldiers in the canyon helped the family to safely ford the river. The family arrived in this valley now known as Heber Valley, in 1860 and established their first home in the Old Fort. This was a two-block tract of land fenced around with "dugouts" which served as homes and provided some protection from the Indians. A dugout consisted of one room with a dirt floor and roof, a fireplace, very little—if any—furniture but perhaps a bed on the floor. A combination school and meetinghouse was built in the center of the fort; the benches were of rough-hewn logs, and the children would sit around the fireplace to keep warm, learn their letters, and study their lessons.

Janett was doing extra well one day in school and said all the letters to "F," but could not think of the next one, "G." "Now think hard, Nettie," the teacher said trying to help her, "Think what your father says to his oxen." But in her excitement, Nettie could not think of the ox-team command "G," but said with her childish lisp, "thook Bud, thook Bud," to the delight of the other children.

As time passed, John and Ann built more permanent houses and added to their family, but as the little boys came along they were still too small or young to help with the farm work in the fields or with the stock. Thus the four little girls had to learn how to do this work, how to call the oxen and yoke them, how to milk the cows and feed the sheep.

This family loved to sing, a trait which they passed on to their own families; they loved to gather round in the evenings and sing songs and listen to the stories told by their parents of their native land, of their lives and loved ones, and about crossing the ocean and the plains. They were good neighbors and had good neighbors willing to help one another and to work hard in building the new settlements, for this would be their home, and they loved this beautiful valley. Janett was especially proud and always willing to help when it was the Murdoch family's turn to make the candles for the community parties or meetings. How happy they were when preparing food for the winter storage; berries and cherries had to be gathered and dried, wool corded and spun, and clothes made for school.

The principle of plural marriage was advocated by the LDS Church authorities at this time, and so in 1862 John M. Murdoch chose Isabella Crawford to be his plural wife. She was a lovely woman, and the two families lived under the same roof until, in compliance with the federal law, the families were required to live in separate homes. In later years when someone would question or criticize the principle of plural marriage, Janett would say, "Oh, my child, you just don't understand." She loved "Bella," and her half-brothers and sisters as fully as her own.

In 1861 Henry McMullin, his wife Mary Pierce, and their three small sons and two little daughters arrived in Heber Valley. They had left their home at Vinalhaven, an island off the coast of Maine, where Henry had been a prosperous ship's carpenter and sawyer. They moved into the fort as neighbors to the Murdoch family, and it was not long before the McMullin boys had erected a big swing and the children found a choice gathering-place for their play. Like the Murdochs, the McMullins took a very active part in the development of the community and did so throughout their lives.

Several years of pioneer life passed happily by; now the little children of the Old Fort became the young men and women with the new log and frame homes scattered throughout the growing community. One of the McMullin boys was Henry L., a tall young man of twenty-one who loved these mountains and canyons and forests. His experiences had toughened him into an excellent teamster bringing loads of logs from the canyons into the community. Janett was a pretty young lady of seventeen, and we remember her telling how she hoped Henry L. would invite her to the dance on the twenty-fourth of July. He did, and their romance blossomed.

Janett went to work in the home of Sister Lavina Witt. This was the home where President Brigham Young stayed when he visited Heber Valley. She remembered how he would dip water from the big barrel at the side of the house into a pan to wash his hands and face. Many times Janett would tell of the helpful things Sister Witt taught *her*, such as bread-making and how to correctly dress and carve a chicken. She received $20 for her work, with which she could purchase articles for her marriage; one of the items was her first pair of overshoes.

On December 6, 1875, Henry Lufkin McMullin and Janett Osborne Murdoch were married in the Endowment House in Salt Lake City. As it took three days by team and wagon to make the trip to Salt Lake City, Janett and Henry stayed in the home of Janett's aunt in American Fork. This lovely lady was the widow of James Steel, who lost his life crossing the plains. In keeping with the custom of the times after returning home, the newlyweds gave a big community dance. Uncle Jim Duke played his fiddle for the music.

Henry and Janett were welcomed into his parents' home to live briefly. The elder McMullins were building a new larger home (which served as a hotel in Heber City for many years). Soon the new home was ready, and the old house was moved onto the west corner of the same block. The site of this house was 1st North and 1st West. They lived in this house until after the birth of their fourth child. (I will note here for any who may be interested: this house was later moved to a location on the corner North of the Dick Duke home in Heber City and at this time is still in use.) After this house was moved, Henry L. and Janett built a four-room home in its place; it had two rooms upstairs and two on the ground level. As time passed, additions were made along with later remodeling, and the home is in excellent condition. It stands across the street north of the old Social Hall in Heber City. Henry and Janett also added three more children to their family. Six of the seven children grew to maturity and reared families who have been a credit to their progenitors. The children of Janett and Henry have always spoken with love and devotion of their parents as "Pa" and "Ma."

When the youngest child, Tommy, was eleven months old, a letter arrived for Henry from "Box B" in Salt Lake City. This was a Church mission call to serve in the Northern States Mission. It was with great humility and considerable sacrifice that Henry left his little family in the care of loved ones in the community and with the knowledge that Father in Heaven would watch over them.

He filled a grand mission, and when he was released he had the privilege of visiting his cousins in Maine and bearing his testimony to them of the mission of Jesus Christ and of His restored church.

In Henry's absence many trials came to test the family's faith—Henry's beloved mother passed away and Piercy, the eldest boy, was greatly afflicted with rheumatism. Many people thought Henry should come home, but Janett said, "No, not until his mission is completed and he is properly released by those in authority." This is the kind of faith that was taught in the home.

In 1908 the Wasatch Stake of the LDS Church was reorganized, with the two Heber Wards being divided into three. Janett had always served the Church and had been president of the Second Ward Primary, but was now called to be the president of the Stake Primary, a position previously held by her mother, Ann. Later she served in stake YLMIA. These activities called for transportation, and Henry was always ready with the horse and buggy. Henry, too, filled many Church responsibilities, such as member of the stake Sunday School presidency and counselor to Bishop Joseph A. Rasband and as a member of the stake high council, a position he held at the time of his death.

Janett became a charter member and chaplain of the Forget-Me-Not camp of the Daughters of the Utah Pioneers and was an honored daughter until her death.

Janett and Henry were often called into homes where sickness and death were present, Henry to aid in administering to the sick and Janett to care for their physical comfort. They would often go to aid in the birth of babies. Janett was present and assisted in the delivery of her sister Jacobina's fifteen children.

The following paragraph was taken from the Wasatch Wave, December 12, 1925.

In honor of the Golden Wedding of Mr. and Mrs. Henry Lufkin McMullin, 300 guest were entertained at the Heber Amusement Hall, Saturday evening December 6. The bride and groom, and Mr. & Mrs. Andrew Lindsay, were seated at the center table under a golden bell suspended from the ceiling. The table was lighted with white and gold candles. The evening's entertainment was a banquet and an appropriate program followed by visiting and dancing.

Some eight years later, December 20, 1932, Henry passed away at his home at the age of eighty years, ending a life of wonderful service to his family, church, and community. Pa and Ma had a love and devotion of their children and grandchildren.

After Henry's death, Janett was pleased LU live in her own home which remained a gathering place for her family and her nieces, nephews, and their families, and how she truly enjoyed their visits to Heber City. Through the efforts and abilities of her son Tommy, the house was remodeled into an apartment house with a lovely comfortable apartment for Ma. She was especially interested in the young people and particularly her own grandchildren, who in turn adored their grandmother. She would join in and was welcomed to their fun and often would be the last to go to bed; her heart and mind were full of pioneer stories that had been her life and yet she rarely seemed to think of herself as a pioneer. She would say, "I knew every man, woman, and child in this valley during those years," and often she would add, "Yes, and every chicken, cow, and oxen." One time, Tommy rushed off to school in the morning without feeding the pigs. When he came home at noon, Ma said, "Tommy, those pigs tell me they haven't had food this day." Tommy looked at Ma and said, "Well, Ma, you certainly understand pig language the best of anyone I ever knew."

We think today of so many little events of home life and know they cannot even be mentioned in this history, only to say that we had a most happy, happy home surrounded by loving parents, grandparents, uncles, aunts, cousins, and dear friends. They were hard times of sudden illness, death of loved ones, and of mothers being taken from large families, and yet those trials served to fortify our affection and love for one another.

It was Janett's custom, when a member of the Daughters of the Utah Pioneers passed away, to write a short poem to her memory. These poems were read in the camp meetings and made a part of their minutes and histories. When the State Camps were compiling a songbook, one of her original poems was chosen and set to music and today is the DUP official song. The appreciation she felt for the pioneers and the devotion she felt for their cause and that of The Church of Jesus Christ of Latter-day Saints were so genuine that she created an atmosphere of reverence to those in her presence. Children by groups would come to her home to hear the stories of her life as a little pioneer girl. She would tell them: "We often went to school barefooted. We didn't know what a match was; often the neighbors would borrow a start of fire."

We hardly ever saw money. Bread and molasses were really good." Then she always added, "But we were happy, happy children for we knew no other way." In 1947 she followed accounts in the newspapers and on radio of preparations for the centennial celebration of the first company of pioneers entering the Salt Lake Valley. She must have been thrilled and yet perhaps mystified by it all. She could not, for instance, understand paying $1,000 for one dress for the centennial queen; such extravagance was not representative of pioneer times nor of pioneer thrift. Then when she witnessed the centennial parade in Salt Lake City from a comfortable seat, she was awed with the grandeur and beauty; it was all so different than she had expected. There wasn't a covered wagon or any weary pioneers pulling handcarts; it was all represented in bronze statues, beautiful floats, and extravagant costumes. Then she figured it out this way: "The pioneers are past history; the parade and celebration were glorifying their trials and spirit and extolling their accomplishments." She belonged to that age and yet she was here, one of the few to witness fulfillment of the great prophecy, "And the desert shall blossom as the rose." She had seen it depicted in all its beauty, art, culture, music and refinement, agricultural and industrial accomplishments that had been within man's power to assemble in the parade. It was this same understanding that came to her when she beheld the centennial queen, this lovely sweet girl and her attendants in the Wasatch Stake tabernacle. The exquisite dress was beyond her imagination, and the cost of it never bothered her again.

Two honors of which she was proud came to her during the centennial. One was a certificate signed by Governor Herbert B. Maw, then governor of Utah, recognizing her as a Utah Pioneer. The other was her selection to be the Pioneer Mother for the Wasatch County celebration. She was invited to ride on a beautiful white float in the county parade, which in its own right was as lovely as the one in Salt Lake City. She really caught the spirit, for she said, "I want a nice white dress for the parade, and I am not worrying about what it will cost." At the DUP meeting when she was announced as Centennial Pioneer Mother, President Emma Wherrit paid her a lovely tribute and placed a beautiful corsage on her and said, "Our dear mother is always an inspiration to us all. For me, she always has a smile and a clasp of the hand. It is written, 'We reap as we sow.' Aunt Nettie has sown in a wonderful way, for now in the twilight of her life she is surrounded with loving sons and daughters, and grandchildren, and a community of friends who adore her."

The men and women who have pioneered and built our communities and churches have been people of high ideals and of great courage. The benefits we now enjoy are a result of the labors of people such as our parents whom we cherish and uphold.

The ninety-two years of Janett's life represent something bigger than her own life or her family. It is the lives and traditions of many families which have significance for this land. Janett has become a historical figure in the lives of her descendants and many others; her life is a symbol of pioneer life and values.

On June 12, 1949, Janett O. Murdoch McMullin peacefully closed her eyes in death at the home of her daughter and son-in-law, Annie and J. Sylvan Rasband in Heber City, Utah. She was laid to rest at the side of her beloved husband, Henry Lufkin McMullin, in the Heber City Cemetery.

Henry L. and Janett Murdoch McMullin were the parents of six children:

The first child Janie passed away when about four years old.

Henry Pierce (H.P. or "Piercy") has been described by his younger brothers and sisters as a wonderful big brother. He was a prominent young man in the community, a farmer, and a great lover of fine horses. He took an active part in civic and church affairs and, like most of this family, took much pleasure In music. Afflicted with malaria fever during his mission to the southern states, it was necessary for him to return home after eleven months, and he was honorably released. Piercy married Mary Bonner, and to them were born three children. Jeaneve, a girl, died in infancy. Piercy passed away in 1919 while in Salt Lake City, where he was to welcome home and greet his younger brother Tommy returning from World War I in France. Henry Clark was born in 1908; he was a handsome and talented young man of twenty-three when he passed away in 1932. Lucile was born in 1912 and was a pretty young lady of eighteen when taken from this home in death in 1930.

Mary continued to live in her home in Heber City working as a seamstress and as a deputy county recorder. She was a gallant lady who bore the sorrow of her very great loss with dignity. She had a particular closeness and love with her mother-in-law, Janett McMullin, and to all the family.

John Edwin McMullin was born May 3, 1881. As a young man he served a mission for the Church in the north central states. He married Edna Mae Dayton August 25, 1909, in the Salt Lake Temple. Eddie took a very active part in Heber City community affairs. In his earlier years he worked as a delivery boy for the Heber Mercantile, working his way into department manager and buyer. Later on he operated his own confectionary and grocery store.

He served as city clerk for several years, then on the city council, and served two terms as mayor of Heber City. While serving as mayor many long_ term improvements and development of the city utilities were made. He was instrumental in the development of the Memorial Hill in Heber Valley with a monument with the names of all soldiers from the county who had served in all the previous wars. The first fire engine and full scale volunteer fire department was organized. It was also during his term of office of mayor that the power utility poles were removed from the center of the streets, and many of the lovely trees lining the streets of Heber were planted. Eddie and Edna's home was blessed with two sons and a daughter: Curtis, Basil, and Barbara. Their home was one of culture and of music, as each of the children were taught to develop their talents. These children were also taught community pride, and their home, yard, and garden were neatly trimmed and weed free. Eddie loved horses and taught his children to love and care for animals. Eddie and Edna took care of their parents' needs in the last days of their illnesses. They each were always available to the needs of others in the community. Like his brothers and sisters, Eddie was, even in his advance years, much loved by young and old, and he always reciprocated their attentions with a hearty_ greeting and a kind word. The family moved to Salt Lake City in 1933 and Eddie was affiliated with the Utah State Land Board and later worked for the Utah State Liquor Commission.

Edna passed away in April, 1971, and Eddie on October 26 the same year.

Gladys was greatly loved in both Heber City and later in Salt Lake City. She was always willing to serve and gave much of her time in the service of others. As with other members of this family, she was blessed with a beautiful voice and gave much time to music service for others. While living in Heber City she was a counselor in the Heber Second Ward Primary and chorister of the Wasatch Stake Relief Society. In Salt Lake City she was president of the Highland Park Ward Primary. Gladys married Archibald Livingston Davis.

As an orphan, "Arch," as he became affectionately known, was confronted with some very heavy obstacles to overcome. By fortunate circumstances as a young lad he made his way to Heber City and was helped by the Elijah Cummings and J.H. Moulton families in particular. He was converted to the LDS faith and under the sponsorship of Piercy McMullin was called upon to fulfill a mission in the north central states. His obvious willingness to become a part of Heber Valley assisted 111IR 1n the mission field, for his peers were most helpful in keeping him there.

Upon return from the mission field, Arch's renewed acquaintance with Gladys McMullin flourished, and they were married in 1906.

Through his personal endeavor, her full-fledged support, and a strong desire for independence, they elected to better their family's future and made a move away from Heber City to Salt Lake City. Here the boys were led into higher education and competition, yet the closeness of the family was always maintained.

Gladys and Arch are the parents of six sons, one of whom passed away when a very small child. The Davis home was one where young people loved to gather to be with the Davis boys; it was a home where the boys were taught the values of independence and self-reliance and to seek for accomplishment. The success of Arch and Gladys was realized many times over as each of the boys attained recognition within their chosen fields. The influence of these parents remains strong, clear, and constant today. The Davis sons are Neil, Theron, Floyd, Victor, and Newell. Gladys was taken in death as a result of an auto accident on Christmas, 1931. Arch continued to be much loved by his McMullin nephews and nieces. He later married Jennie Tanner, who became a lovely aunt to us all. Arch passed away in 1962.

Mary Isabell (Maybell) followed her brothers and sister in singing, and many times she and Gladys or Annie were called on to sing together. One outstanding musical event occurred when Gladys and Maybell, with their cousin Dona Murdoch (Montgomery) and Lena Murray won first place in the All-Church Quartet Festival held in the Assembly Hall in Salt Lake City in June 1913. Uncle Joe Murdoch was their teacher. Maybell served as president of the Heber Second Ward Primary when just a young woman. She was the president of the Second Ward Relief Society, a position she filled enthusiastically for over ten *years.* She also served the Church as a counselor in the Thirty-third Ward Relief Society in Salt Lake City. Over the span of many years, Maybell, along with the late Frank Epperson, sang in funerals in many parts of the state. No count of the number of funerals has been kept; suffice it to say that it could be hundreds.

Maybell married T. Henry Moulton and became the loving mother of Henry's daughter Stella. She and Henry became the parents of six sons and a daughter; two of the sons, Henry and Robert, died in infancy.

Their living children are Asael, Heber, Boyd, Thomas, and Carol. These children, too, were taught values of educations and of industriousness as they assisted in the work of a small farm. Here was a home where all friends, and oftimes those in need of a bed or a meal, were made welcome. All her life Maybell has been a thoughtful, kind, and generous lady.

Henry was a schoolteacher and farmer; he was very involved in civic affairs and served on the city council of Heber City. He was very active in farmer welfare programs or programs which advanced the cause of the farmers in Wasatch County. Maybell was very supportive of Henry in these efforts. Henry fulfilled a mission to the central states and held many positions of responsibility in the ward and stake in Heber City. He received his education at the University of Utah when it was merely a cluster of buildings high on the east bench above Salt Lake City and was surrounded by fields and pastures. Henry passed away in 1966, and Maybell, now nearing ninety-three years of age, physically is able to maintain her own apartment and is independent of assistance. It is quite possible at this writing that she is the oldest living descendant of John Murray Murdoch.

Annie Janett is the youngest sister. She was a pretty young lady and very popular with all the young people of the community. She too loved to sing and took part in the chorus and choirs in the community. She was the actress in the family and took part in many plays. When six years old she received a prize for her story of the life of Jesus. Annie taught in the public schools and served many years as president of the Heber Second Ward Primary (a position held by her mother, Janett McMullin, and grandmother, Anne Murdoch).

Annie married J. Sylvan Rasband, and to them were born two sons and five daughters, J. Mack, Victora, Beverly, Janett, Dale, Karma, and Ann. Sylvan spent most of his working life as director of the Wasatch County Welfare Office. His compassionate and thoughtful manner was well suited for this position and was complementary to that of Annie. For many years they had herds of purebred Jersey cows that took top prizes at county and state fairs. From their home they sold the delicious milk and cream from these animals. It would be interesting to know how much milk they "sold" during the hard years of the depression for which then were never paid.

Their home was a place where people loved to gather, and has been the scene of many happy times. Annie and Sylvan continue to live in their home in Heber City, and now it continues to be a favorite gathering place for their grandchildren and friends.

Thomas Heber was the youngest of the family. Maybell has said, "Tommy was our sweet baby brother, the life of our home." In his advanced years he remains a most devoted brother to Maybell and Annie and a favorite of his nephews and nieces. Tommy was a gifted athlete. Following his graduation from high school he taught for one year, then enrolled at the Utah Agricultural College in Logan (now Utah State University). He served in France during World War I. Returning home and to his studies in March of 1919, it is believed he was the first man at Utah State to win four letters in basketball. Following graduation he became the coach at Bingham High School, where he enjoyed the success of taking many fine teams to the state basketball tournaments. He later became principal at Bingham and also at Jordan High School. Prominent in civic affairs, he served in the Utah State Senate.

Tommy married Zelma Wootton. They are the parents of two fine sons, Richard and Paul. These men are the youngest grandchildren of Henry L. and Janett McMullin. They have been taught lasting values in their home. Zelma was a lovely lady, who was modest and quiet and yet greatly complemented Tommy's outgoing and friendly nature. She was greatly loved by all the members of the McMullin family. Following a very brief and sudden illness, Aunt Zelma passed away in 1967. Tommy lives in Midvale, where he continues to maintain his home. Richard and Paul with their families also live in the general area.

The family and descendents of Henry L. and Janett Murdoch McMullin have always held a great love for their grandparents and parents. It has often been said that they scarcely knew who was their mother and who was an aunt, or a father or uncle either. It should be noted that these grandchildren have been taught to honor their commitment to God and country. Twelve grandsons and one granddaughter saw military service during World War II.

By Maybell McMullin Moulton assisted by Thomas O. Moulton The following are two of Janett's many poems:

Heber City, Utah, Nov. 6, 1941

"To My Grandsons"

'Tis to you, My Grandsons, I write today,
Hoping I might find the right words to say,
That I may express my love to you,

That is direct and true.
I have loved you boys since that day and time,
I took you in these arms of mine,
And kissed you on your little face,
With a grandmother's love and a grandmother's
    grace,
Then when your Dear Mother was called away,
I humbly to Father in Heaven did pray
That He would guide you tenderly
In His kind and loving care,
And the following is a comfort in answer to my
    prayer.

My Visualized Dream

I dreamed I opened a-wide a door,
To a place I never had seen before,
With a most beautiful building there,
And beautiful steps and stair,
And myriads of couples, as husbands and wives,
Going step by step on the stairs of life,
And as I carefully stepped inside,
There was Gladys, your mother,
Right by my side,
With a hallowed light and pleasing grace,
And a dear anxious smile on her beautiful face;
While in that sweet influence we gazed,
And as you boys passed by, she said:
"I am still watching over them." I said, "So am I";
Then I turned to see the others come; turned back,
And the light and your mother was gone,
But that influence and sacred visit,
And the message she left so true,
"Do right; be prudent; step carefully,
Your mother's watching o'er you."

And that wonderful vision, and the message she did
    impart.
Are for our mutual good, and are stamped
On your aged grandmother's heart,
And that message and influence stays with me yet,
It is so sweet to remember, I will never forget.

Your aged grandmother, (85 years of age)
Janett Murdoch McMullin

Dedicated to the sons of Archibald and Gladys Davis.

This poem was written by Janett Murdoch McMullin two weeks prior to her death and in her ninety-third year.

Memories

Oh, I love these sun-kissed mountains
and rugged canyons rare.
The snow-fed crystal fountains,
green valleys and pure, fresh air.
For the sacred childhood guidance
that blessed us all those years
For the parentage and heritage
of those noble pioneers.

Oh, I love the rocky hillsides
where the pioneer toilers brave
Subdued the snake and cactus,
saved a cemetery for the grave.
Where thousands of our sires
now rest in sweet repose
With God's blessings on their labors,
the desert now blossoms as the rose

A vision of the rustic church
lovingly comes to view
With their social meetings and greetings
Oh, they know the gospel is true.
I have joined their speech and singing
shared their prayers and tears
From the parentage and heritage
of those noble pioneers.

Oh, I see the mud-roofed cabins
with all the children playing round
With our hearthstone and tallow candles—
our carpet, the ground.
Now my aged heart swells with emotion
and loving tears
Visualizing the bended knee
of those noble pioneers.

"Home Sweet Home" Heber, Wasatch, Utah.

Maybell, Ellie and Annie

Pa's sleigh and horses. Left to right on sleigh: Maybell, friend Effie, and Annie.

Daughters, left to right: Annie, Gladys, and (Maybell) Mary Isabell.

Henry Piercy and Sarah Jane Mc-
Mullin.

Children, left to right: Maybell, Henry, John,
Gladys, Annie in chair.

Back row, left to right: John Edwin, Gladys Jacobina, Henry Pierce.
Front row, left to right: Mary Isabell (Maybell), Janett Osborne
Murdoch McMullin, Thomas Heber, Henry Lufkin McMullin, and
Annie Janett.

Henry L. and Janett M. McMullin family reunion in 1953.

Janett McMullin at age 80.

HUSBAND   Henry Lufkin McMULLIN
Birth   4 September 1852
Place   Rockport, Knox, Maine
Married   6 December 1875
Place   L.D.S. Endowment House,Salt Lake City, Utah
Death   20 December 1932
Place   Heber, Wasatch, Utah
Burial
Place   Heber, Wasatch, Utah
Mother   Mary PIERCE
Father   Henry McMULLIN
Other Wives

WIFE   Janett Osborne MURDOCH
Birth   20 December 1856
Place   Salt Lake City, Salt Lake, Utah
Death   12 June 1949
Place   Heber, Wasatch, Utah
Burial   15 June 1949
Place   Heber, Wasatch, Utah
Mother   Ann STEELE
Father   John Murray MURDOCH
Other Husbands
Information from James Murdoch Family Records

1ST CHILD Sarah Jane McMULLIN
Birth   12 Aug 1876 Heber,Wasatch,Utah
Married
Date
Place
Death   20 Oct 1880 Heber,Wasatch,Utah
Burial   Heber,Wasatch,Utah

2ND CHILD Henry Pierce McMULLIN
Birth   20 Sep 1878 Heber,Wasatch,Utah
Married   Mary Clark BONNER
Date   9 Jan 1907
Place   L.D.S. Temple Salt Lake City, Utah
Death   9 Mar 1919 Salt Lake City, Utah
Burial   12 Mar 1919 Heber,Wasatch,Utah

3RD CHILD John Edwin McMULLIN
Birth   3 May 1881 Heber,Wasatch,Utah
Married   Edna Mae DAYTON
Date   25 Aug 1909
Place   L.D.S. Temple Salt Lake City, Utah
Death   26 Oct 1971 Salt Lake City, Utah
Burial   30 Oct 1971 Salt Lake City, Utah

4TH CHILD Gladys Jacobina McMULLIN
Birth   18 Apr 1884 Heber,Wasatch,Utah
Married   Archibald Livingston DAVIS
Date   3 Oct 1906
Place   L.D.S. Temple Salt Lake City, Utah
Death   27 Dec 1931 Heber,Wasatch,Utah
Burial   30 Dec 1931 Heber,Wasatch,Utah

5TH CHILD Mary Isabell (Maybell) McMULLIN
Birth   10 Sep 1887 Heber,Wasatch,Utah
Married   Thomas Henry MOULTON
Date   3 Sep 1913
Place   L.D.S. Temple Salt Lake City,
Death
Burial

6TH CHILD Annie Janett McMULLIN
Birth   11 Jan 1891 Heber,Wasatch,Utah
Married   Joseph Sylvan RASBAND
Date   12 May 1915
Place   L.D.S. Temple Salt Lake City, Utah
Death
Burial

7TH CHILD Thomas Heber McMULLIN
Birth   8 Oct 1893 Heber, Wasatch, Utah
Married   Zelma WOOTTON
Date   5 Aug 1938
Place   Logan, Cache, Utah
Death
Burial

8TH CHILD
Birth
Married
Date
Place
Death
Burial

1 MURDOCH, James 1786-1831   2 MURDOCH, John Murray 1820-1910
1 MURDOCH, Mary MURRAY, Sp. 1782-1856   2 MURDOCH, Ann STEEL, Sp. 1829-1909

                                   3 MURDOCH, JANETT OSBORNE 1856-1949
DESCENDANTS OF---------
                                   3 McMULLIN, HENRY LUFKIN, SP. 1852-1875

4 MURDOCH, Sarah Jane B-12 Aug 1876 D-20 Oct 1880   B-Born
                                                              M-Marriage
4 McMULLIN, Henry Pierce B-20 Sep 1878 D-9 Mar 1919   D-Died
4 McMULLIN, Mary BONNER, Sp. B-6 Aug 1884 M-9 Jan 1907 D-19 Dec 1968 Sp.-Spouse
                                                              Div.-Divorced

        5 McMULLIN, Jenieve B-9 Jan 1908 D-18 Jan 1908

        5 McMULLIN, Henry Clark B-13 Dec 1909 D-25 Oct 1932

        5 McMULLIN, Rowena Lucille B-5 Feb 1912 D-21 Jul 1930

4 McMULLIN, John Edwin B-3 May 1881 D-26 Oct 1971
4 McMULLIN, Edna Mae DAYTON, Sp. B-19 Jun 1887 M-25 Aug 1909 D-10 Apr 1971

        5 McMULLIN, Edwin Curtis B-23 Jun 1910
        5 McMULLIN, Ruth FISHER, Sp. B-5 Sep 1916 M-25 Nov 1939

                6 PETERSON, Kathleen Ruth McMULLIN B-7 Aug 1946
                6 PETERSON, Kay LeRoy, Sp. B-   M-

                        7 PETERSON, Kristi   B-

                        7 PETERSON, Kimberli   B-

                        7 PETERSON, Kelli   B-

                6 McMULLIN Michael Curtis B-10 May 1950
                6 McMULLIN, Patricia BURDETT, Sp. B-   M-

                        7 McMULLIN, Michelle   B-

                        7 McMULLIN, Shannon   B-

                        7 McMULLIN, David Burdett   B-

        5 McMULLIN, Basil Dayton B-22 June 1915
        5 McMULLIN, Louise Beatrice MOENCH, Sp. B-20 Apr 1913 M-21 Jun 1940

                6 ROYLANCE, Linda Louise McMULLIN B-13 Feb 1947
                6 ROYLANCE, Paul Victor, Sp. B-   M-

                6 McMULLIN, James Patrick B-3 Feb 1950
                6 McMULLIN, Sherry PACE, Sp. B-   M-

        5 PATTERSON, Barbara McMULLIN B-17 Sep 1921
        5 PATTERSON, Robert Alexander, Sp. B-18 Jan 1919 M-2 Jun 1947

                6 SARGENT, Margaret Patterson B-6 Apr 1948
                6 SARGENT, William L. Sp. B-   M-

                        7 SARGENT, Catherine   B-   May 1980

                6 RICH, JoAnne PATTERSON B-26 Mar 1950
                6 RICH, James Allen, Sp. B-   M-

                        7 RICH, Jacob Patterson   B-15 Jul 1978

                        7 RICH, Benjamin Patterson   B-29 Oct 1980

                6 SONNENBERG, Janette PATTERSON B-13 Dec 1953
                6 SONNENBERG, Brent Cloyd, Sp. B-   M-

                        7 SONNENBERG, Renee   B-

                        7 SONNENBERG, Jennille   B-

```
                6 PATTERSON, Robert McMullin B-11 Mar 1956
                6 PATTERSON, Elizabeth POULSON, Sp. B-              M-7 May 1980

    4 DAVIS, Gladys Jacobina McMULLIN B-18 Apr 1884 D-27 Dec 1931
    4 DAVIS, Archibald Livingstone, Sp. B-22 Oct 1878 M-3 Oct 1906 D-25 Sep 1962

            5 DAVIS, Neil L B-6 Oct 1907
            5 DAVIS, Louise BOWRING, Sp. B-15 Dec 1906 M-28 Nov 1933

            5 DAVIS, Theran McMullin B-8 Jul 1909
            5 DAVIS , Jeannette BARRETT, Sp. B-3 May 1912 M-23 Dec 1932

                6 DAVIS, Phillip Theran B-22 Sep 1933
                6 DAVIS, Jacquiline MEIER, Sp. B-          M-          Div.

                    7 DAVIS, Courtney Grace        B-      1965

                    7 DAVIS, Clayton Meier         B-      1967

                6 DAVIS, Michael Berrett B-23 Apr 1940
                6 DAVIS, Andrea Lee HILDT, Sp. B-          M-

                    7 DAVIS, Theran Michael        B-      1969

                    7 DAVIS, John Michael          B-      1973

                    7 DAVIS, Annette Elizabeth     B-      1976

            5 DAVIS, Floyd A. B-24 Apr 1912
            5 DAVIS, Lucile Grace JENKINS, Sp. B-4 Oct 1916  M-12 Jan 1938

                6 DAVIS, Robert Floyd B-30 Nov 1942
                6 DAVIS, Deborah ROWLAND, Sp. B-          M-

                    7 DAVIS, Mathew                B-      1969

                    7 DAVIS, Brett                 B-      1971

                6 MOSELEY, Valerie Lee DAVIS B-4 Dec 1946
                6 MOSELEY,              Sp. B-          M-          Div.

                    7 MOSLEY, Rossi                B-      1967

            5 DAVIS, Victor Royal B-19 Nov 1917
            5 DAVIS, Enid Morgan DIXION, Sp B-7 Jul 1921 M-23 Mar 1945

                6 DAVIS, Laurel Jeannette B-23 May 1950

                6 SPARRS, Sherry DAVIS B-
                6 SPARRS, Dennis Lee, Sp. B-          M-

            5 DAVIS, Edwin Fay B-23 Feb 1916 D-21 Jan 1917

            5 DAVIS, Newell Pierce B-1 Jan 1921
            5 Davis, Adele SQUIRES, Sp. B-13 Aug 1919 M-  Nov 1941

                6 DAVIS, Randall Kent B-23 Jun 1945

                6 DAVIS, Richard Newell B-6 Jul 1948
                6 DAVIS, Penelope Ann WILSON, Sp. B-          M-

    4 DAVIS, Jennie Albertina ANDERSON Tanner, (2) Sp. B-24 Jun 1891 D-30 Jul 1969
      Tanner, Ebenezer, (1) Sp. B-          M-11 Jul 1933 D-

            5 MURDOCH, Faye TANNER B-4 Nov 1918
            5 MURDOCH, Guy GARRETT, Sp. B-5 Oct 1916 M-9 Apr 1938  (See Brigham Murdoch History)

    4 MOULTON, Mary Isabell (Maybell) McMULLIN B-17 Oct 1887 M-3 Sep 1913 (2)
    4 MOULTON, Thomas Henry, Sp. B-28 Jul 1881 D-1 Oct 1966
      MOULTON, Estella BODILY, Sp. (2) B-12 Oct 1885 M-13 Apr 1906 D-13 Mar 1907

            NIELSON, Estella Merle MOULTON B-2 Mar 1907 D-24 Jan 1971  (had 9 children)
            NIELSON, Milton Cory, Sp. B-27 Oct 1909 M-11 Nov 1928
```

5 MOULTON, Henry Dee B-29 Mar 1915 D-30 Mar 1915

5 MOULTON, Asael B-12 Oct 1916
5 MOULTON, Doraine HERBERT, Sp. B-15 Oct 1920 M-19 Nov 1942

      6 MOULTON, Steven Asael B-2 Feb 1946
      6 MOULTON, Janice Ann Williams, Sp. B-

            7 MOULTON, Bryce Aaron   B-

            7 MOULTON, Scot Adamson   B-

      6 GEARY, Mary Jane MOULTON B-14 Feb 1950
      6 GEARY, Steven, Sp. B-

            7 GEARY, Melissa Jane   B-

            7 GEARY, Kristen Elizabeth   B-

      6 MOULTON, David Richard B-26 Jan 1959

5 MOULTON, Robert L. B-5 Jun 1918 D-5 Jun 1918

5 MOULTON, James Heber B-21 Sep 1920
5 MOULTON, Genevieve ROMNEY, Sp. B-16 Sep 1921 M-16 Mar 1948

      6 HANSEN, Jennifer Ann MOULTON B-20 Dec 1949
      6 HANSEN, Eric George, Sp. B-6 Jan   M-17 Oct 1980

      6 MESERVY, Michele MOULTON B-2 Jun 1951
      6 MESERVY, Rayman David, Sp. B-30 Nov 1948 M-17 Aug 1972

            7 MESERVY, Melodie Joy   B-12 Dec 1973

            7 MESERVY, David Moulton   B-24 Jun 1975

            7 MESERVY, Lydia Ann   B-10 Jun 1976

            7 MESERVY, Thomas Oliver   B- 6 Jul 1977

            7 MESERVY, Joseph Rayman   B- 4 Nov 1978

            7 MESERVY, Charlene   B-19 Nov 1980

      6 MCBETH, Cheryl MOULTON B-6 Jan 1953
      6 MCBETH, Brent Hendrix, Sp. B-2 Mar 1951 M-6 Sep 1974

            7 MCBETH, Jeffery Brent   B-20 Aug 1976

            7 MCBETH, Alisa   B- 2 Apr 1979

            7 MCBETH, Christine   B- 6 Oct 1981

      6 MOULTON, Jolane B-2 Jun 1954

      6 MOULTON, James Romney B-9 Jul 1958
      6 MOULTON, Joanne Kathleen MICHALEK, Sp. B-12 Dec 1959 M-23 Aug 1980

            7 MOULTON, James Ryan   B- 8 Aug 1981

5 MOULTON, Boyd Lufkin B-13 Apr 1922
5 MOULTON, Marian Lavina DIAL, Sp. B-7 Mar 1926 M-9 Aug 1948

      6 PUTERBAUGH, Judy Lynne MOULTON Nemitz B-26 Apr 1949
      6 NEMITZ, Lawrence, Sp. (1) B-   M-12 Jun 1970 Div.
      6 PUTERBAUGH, Ronald Duane, Sp. (2) B-1 Dec 1948 M-22 Mar 1975

            7 NEMITZ, La Nea   B-19 Mar 1971

            7 NEMITZ, Jeffery Duane   B- 1 Feb 1972

```
        7 PUTERBAUGH, Michael John        B-19 Sep 1976

        7 PUTERBAUGH, Jaime Lee           B-12 Mar 1978

        7 PUTERBAUGH, Kristie Anne        B-15 Jul 1981

    6 NORVIEL, Sharon Sue MOULTON B-9 Mar 1951
    6 NORVIEL, Mark Stephen , Sp. B-10 Sep 1951 M-4 Feb 1974

        7 NORVIEL, Joshua Aaron           B-30 Mar 1975

        7 NORVIEL, Rachel Marie           B- 9 May 1976

        7 NORVIEL, Aaron Levi             B-31 Aug 1977

        7 NORVIEL, Caleb Ethan            B-25 Jul 1979

        7 NORVIEL, Matthew Adam           B-10 Dec 1980

    6 MOULTON, Kenneth Dee B-28 Oct 1952

    6 DOYLE, Debra Anne MOULTON Romney B-23 Mar 1955
    6 ROMNEY, Eldon, Sp. (1) B-          M-11 Jun 1974 Div.
    6 DOYLE, Dan, Sp. (2) B-        M-   Jun

        7 DOYLE, Dustin Aaron             B-9 May 1980

    6 RUSSELL, Becky La Nea B-11 Sep 1957
    6 RUSSELL, Jerry Wayne, Sp. B-3 Dec 1959 M-13 Feb 1982

    6 ROSENVAL, Reanna Lee MOULTON B-29 May 1959
    6 ROSENVAL, Blake Albert, Sp. B-7 Mar 1958 M-28 Mar 1980

    6 MOULTON, Robert Dane B-19 Apr 1961

    6 MOULTON, Neil Scott  B-

5 MOULTON, Thomas Denton B-13 Nov 1924
5 MOULTON, Evva Jean PEAY, Sp. B-27 Apr 1929 M-15 Mar 1950

    6 MOULTON, Thomas Dale B-17 Mar 1951
    6 MOULTON, MyrLynn HAWS, Sp. B-        M-

        7 MOULTON, Myndee                 B-20 Nov 1974

        7 MOULTON, Marci                  B- 3 Mar 1977

        7 MOULTON, Mari Jo                B- 6 Feb 1981

    6 ANDREWS, Mardyne MOULTON B-5 Jun 1953
    6 ANDREWS, Craig Richard, Sp. B- 11 Aug 1951 M-14 Jun 1971

        7 ANDREWS, Ryan Craig            B-26 Apr 1972

        7 ANDREWS, Gina Marie            B- 2 Jun 1974

        7 ANDREWS, Alysa                 B-21 Apr 1978

        7 ANDREWS, Holly                 B-24 Dec 1980

    6 PETERSON, Kathi MOULTON B-30 Mar 1957
    6 PETERSON, Corey Darrell, Sp. B-        M-

        7 PETERSEN, Justin Corey         B- 7 Nov 1978

        7 PETERSEN, Jodi                 B-25 Jul 1980

    6 CAMPBELL, Karen MOULTON B-30 Mar 1957
    6 CAMPBELL, Wayne, Sp. B-        M-

        7 CAMPBELL, Katie                B-26 May 1979
```

5 PETERSON, Gladys Carol MOULTON B-7 Aug 1930
5 PETERSON, Jack Olin, Sp. B-3 Sep 1927 M-26 Nov 1958

    6 PETERSON, Loriann   B- 7 Jul 1961

    6 PETERSON, Kyle William   B- 2 Jan 1964

4 RASBAND, Annie Janett B-11 Jan 1891
4 RASBAND, Joseph Sylvan, Sp. B-4 Nov 1891 M-12 May 1915

    5 RASBAND, Joseph Mack B-13 Feb 1916
    5 RASBAND, Marian PARRISH, Sp. B-27 Apr 1919 M-16 Sep 1939

        6 RASBAND, Wayne Sylvan B-15 Feb 1942

        6 RASBAND, Janett   B-16 Jul 1943 D-31 Jul 1956

        6 RASBAND, Joseph Stanley B-8 Apr 1946
        6 RASBAND, Mary Lu DAVIDSON, Sp. (1) B-   M-   Sep 1965 Div.
        6 RASBAND, Roberta McINNIS, Sp. (2) B-

            7 RASBAND, Craig Lee   B-30 Jul 1968

        6 RASBAND, Darrell Mack B-11 Nov 1949
        6 RASBAND, Roleen RAMSAY, Sp. B-   M-

            7 RASBAND, Andrina Marie   B- 4 Feb 1974

            7 RASBAND, Jacque Lynn   B- 2 Nov 1975

            7 RASBAND, Michael James   B-14 Oct 1976

            7 RASBAND, Jay Mack   B-24 Jul 1978

        6 RASBAND, Scott Alan B-28 Sep 1952
        6 RASBAND, Jeanett MONTOYA, Sp B-9 Feb 1956 M-

            7 RASBAND, Jan Amber   B- 6 May 1977

            7 RASBAND, Ronald Scott   B-12 Jul 1980

        6 RASBAND, David Ford B-29 Jul 1955
        6 RASBAND, Patsy GARRIS, Sp. B-25 May 1959 M-

            7 RASBAND, Naomi Susan   B-15 Dec 1975

            7 RASBAND, Tammy Lynn   B- 7 Dec 1978

        6 GARCIA, Mary Anne RASBAND B-22 Jan 1957
        6 GARCIA,   Sp. B-   M-   Div.

            7 GARCIA, Manuel Adrian   B-30 Apr 1974

        6 RASBAND, Donna B-30 Dec 1960

        6 RASBAND, Stewart Dale B-29 Sep 1965 D-   1973

    5 DIXON, Victoria RASBAND B-11 Nov 1917
    5 DIXON, Paul Schaerrer, Sp. B-14 Aug 1917 M-4 Aug 1943

        6 LOVELL, Jane DIXON B-1 Dec 1945
        6 LOVELL, Kay LAVORGE, Sp. B-   M-

            7 LOVELL, Debra   B-16 May 1968

            7 LOVELL, Cynthia   B-22 Apr 1970

            7 LOVELL, Tamara   B-27 Jul 1973

            7 LOVELL, Russell Kay   B-15 Apr 1977

            7 LOVELL, Edward   B-10 Jul 1980

6 DIXON, John Paul B-22 Nov 1947
6 DIXON, Patricia HUFF, Sp. B-   M-

    7 DIXON, Ryan   B-28 Dec 1972

    7 DIXON, Hilary   B-15 Mar 1974

    7 DIXON, Sarah   B-12 May 1977

6 LEFTWICH, Anne DIXON B-10 Jun 1949
6 LEFTWICH, Robert A., Sp. B-   M-

    7 LEFTWICH, Sandra Dawn   B-27 Sep 1967

    7 LEFTWICH, Alan   B- 3 Apr 1969

    7 LEFTWICH, Christie Anne   B-16 Feb 1973

    7 LEFTWICH, Shelly Lorraine   B-20 Aug 1977

6 DIXON, Brain J. B-22 Oct 1950
6 DIXON, Ellen Joy FOSTER, Sp. B-   M-

    7 DIXON, Jeremy Brian   B-27 Dec 1973

    7 DIXON, Spencer Michael   B- 7 Oct 1979

6 DIXON, Jay Christopher B-26 Aug 1952
6 DIXON, Bonnie Gay JANES, Sp. B-   M-

    7 DIXON, Jay Sylvan   B-28 Dec 1978

    7 DIXON, Andrew Simeon   B-11 Aug 1980

6 HUFF, Merrie DIXON B-12 Sep 1954
6 HUFF, Blain, Sp. B-   M-

    7 HUFF, Katie Nicole   B-15 Feb 1974

    7 HUFF, Erik Blain   B- 8 Nov 1976

    7 HUFF, Lindsey   B-30 Mar 1978

6 DIXON, Philip Henry B-24 Jul 1950
6 DIXON, Carolyn STEWART, Sp. B-   M-

    7 DIXON, Nathan Philip   B-29 Jun 1976

    7 DIXIN, Stewart Paul   B- 2 Aug 1978

6 DIXON, Mark Vee B-2 Sep 1961

5 DIXON, Beverly RASBAND B-6 Jun 1920
5 DIXON, Sheldon Schaerrer, Sp. B-2 Oct 1915 M-22 Jul 1946

6 MARSHALL, Eunice DIXON B-10 May 1947
6 MARSHALL, Jack Anthony, Sp. B-   M-

    7 MARSHALL, Mindy   B-18 Oct 1971

    7 MARSHALL, Jared Anthony   B- 7 May 1974

    7 MARSHALL, JaJece   B-15 Mar 1977

6 DIXON, Neil Sheldon B-21 Jun 1948
6 DIXON, Suzanne STEWART, Sp. B-   M-

    7 DIXON, Jason Neil   B-26 Jun 1975

    7 DIXON, Monica   B-28 Jun 1976

```
                7 DIXON, Justin Lynn            B-26 Jun 1979

                7 DIXON, Amy                    B- 5 Mar 1981 D-13 Mar 1981

        6 DIXON, Boyd Rasband B-24 May 1952

        6 DIXON, Ralph Sylvan B-10 Dec 1955

        6 DIXON, Lecia        B-19 Mar 1962

5 MERRELL, Eliza Janett RASBAND B-31 Dec 1922
5 MERRELL, Robert Winston, Sp. B-4 Jul 1924 M-20 Jun 1947

        6 MERRELL, Steven Robert B-22 Oct 1948
        6 MERRELL, Judith LISH, Sp. B-              M-

                7 MERRELL, Todd Sylvan          B- 2 Mar 1969

                7 MERRELL, Brandon Robert       B-23 Jun 1971

        6 MERRELL, Ronald James B-21 Jan 1951
        6 MERRELL, Penny Louise BOLIN, Sp. B-          M-

                7 MERRELL, Michael Winston      B- 8 Dec 1975

                7 MERRELL, David James          B-21 Jan 1978

                7 MERRELL, Brian Joseph         B-11 Sep 1979

                7 MERRELL, Christopher Paul     B-29 Dec 1980

        6 MERRELL, Melvin Clyde B-28 Mar 1953
        6 MERRELL, Dennise Marie NEWSOME, Sp. B-            M-

                7 MERRELL, Elaina Janett        B-17 Nov 1977

                7 MERRELL, Annie Don            B- 1 Nov 1979

        6 MERRELL, Kenneth Winston B-24 Nov 1957

        6 MERRELL, David Joseph     B-14 Feb 1961

5 RASBAND, Dale J. B-12 Feb 1927
5 RASBAND, Majene FOFMAN, Sp. B-13 Jul 1930 M-29 Oct 1949

        6 MCGREGOR, Marsha Loy RASBAND B-9 Apr 1952
        6 MCGREGOR, Kenneth, Sp. B-             M-

                7 MCGREGOR, Tavish              B-8 Sep 1979

        6 RASBAND, Thomas J. B-2 Oct 1955
        6 RASBAND, Peggy JOHNSON, Sp. B-            M-

        6 RASBAND, Jonathan D. B-2 Sep 1959

5 BESENDORFER, Karma Jean RASBAND B-1 Feb 1930
5 BESENDORFER, James Moroni, Sp. B-27 Jan 1928 M-27 Oct 1948

        6 BESENDORFER, James Moroni B-18 Sep 1953
        6 BESENDORFER, Lila STRINGHAM, Sp. B-          M-

        6 BESENDORFER, Jeffery R B-22 Dec 1957

        6 BESENDORFER, Laurie Jean B-1 Apr 1962

5 McDONALD, Annne Mauree RASBAND B-7 Sep 1931
5 McDONALD, Hiram Smith, Sp. B-27 Jan 1925 M-6 Mar 1952

        6 McDONALD, Eric Joseph B-7 Mar 1953 M-
        6 McDONALD, Ellen MALCOLM Horsley, Sp. B-
           Horsley,            Sp. (1) B-        M-           Div.
```

```
            7 HORSLEY, Kirsten                B-

      6 McDONALD, Bruce Hiram B-18 Dec 1954

      6 SORENSON, Shelley Anne McDONALD B-16 Oct 1957
      6 SORENSON, Robert J, Sp. B-                M-

            7 SORENSON, Shane Robert         B-

            7 SORENSON,                      B-
      6 McDONALD, Randall H B-9 Dec 1958 D-10 Dec 1958

      6 McDONALD, Von R         B-6 Aug 1960

      6 McDONALD, Jill          B-25 Jan 1963

      6 McDONALD, Janett        B- 1 Jun 1965

      6 McDONALD, Laurel        B-12 Sep 1967

      6 McDONALD, Diane         B- 4 Feb 1970

      6 McDONALD, David Sylvan  B-28 Jul 1972

4 MCMULLIN, Thomas Heber B- 8 Oct 1893
4 MCMULLIN, Zelma WOTTON, Sp. B-14 Jul 1903 M-5 Aug 1938 D-3 Sep 1967

      5 MCMULLIN, Thomas Richard B-3 Apr 1940
      5 MCMULLIN, Evah Mary VISSER, Sp. B-30 May 1939 M-21 Apr 1960

            6 MCMULLIN, Darin Richard B-19 Apr 1963

            6 MCMULLIN, Sharolyn      B- 6 Jul 1964

            6 MCMULLIN, Brandon       B- 3 Mar 1968

            6 MCMULLIN, Ryan          B-14 Jan 1973

      5 MCMULLIN, Henry Paul B-25 Apr 1943
      5 MCMULLIN, Barbara Ann BEERS, Sp. (1) B-10 Dec 1945 M-24 Aug 1965 Div.
      5 MCMULLIN, Jean Leslie HEATH Borg, Sp. (2) B-25 Oct 1945 M-5 Oct 1967
        Borg, James, Sp. (1) B-              M-

            6 MCMULLIN, Paul          B-27 Apr 1968 D-27 May 1968

            6 MCMULLIN, Jamie         B-13 Jul 1969

            6 MCMULLIN, Brent Borg    B-11 Jan 1964

            6 MCMULLIN, Kirk Borg     B-25 Jan 1965

            6 MCMULLIN, Michelle Borg B-24 Jun 1966
```

Sarah Jane Murdoch, Thomas Heber Rasband, and William Lindsay

My name is Sarah Jane Murdoch. I was born in Salt Lake City, Utah, on January 15, 1859. My parents are John M. Murdoch and Ann Steel Murdoch. They were converts to the Church of Jesus Christ of Latter-day Saints and came from their home in Scotland to Salt Lake City, Utah in 1852. When they left Scotland they had two children, a boy and a girl, but they became ill and died during the journey. My mother was pregnant and gave birth to a baby girl in Kansas. She is my oldest sister, Mary. When Mary was eight days old they started on their long journey across the plains to Salt Lake City with an ox-team. They had three more daughters in Salt Lake City and when I was a baby they moved to Heber Valley with thirty other families to make their home. This was in 1860 and we lived in a dugout where my next sister, Jacobina, was born.

We lived in the old fort and Porter Dawdell lived north and Thomas Todd lived on the south of us and we loved our neighbors as ourselves. When Sadie Davis moved away I suffered much and cried about it; it was the same when Margaret moved to a new home. We were dear friends and playmates.

As time went on, Father built two log rooms and we used the dugout as a cellar. We always had plenty to eat. I never remember of going hungry. My mother took pride in keeping our hair curled or braided neatly. She did her best to teach us to be honest and truthful and to be kind and thoughtful of each other and our playmates. One day there was a dance held for the

children in the log meeting house. I was there and the girls were told to choose the boys. I did not want to choose but my older sisters carried me over to where the boys were sitting in a row. One smiling boy said, "Come and take me." His name was Thomas Heber Rasband. So I did and we danced together. That was our first meeting.

William Forman, one of our neighbors, was quite fond of us children and would call us his boys. At dinner time Margaret Todd and I would stand near his door and he'd say, "Here are my boys; if you will stay here and be my boys you can have some dinner." And he would put us up to the table. We suffered afterwards planning how we could get away. Finally we would make a break and run home; more than once we did this.

My childhood was very happy. One time a show came to town and Sadie Davis wanted to go but did not have a suitable dress. I let her have my clothes and went to bed so she could go. About this time four more children had been born. Two for Bella, and my mother had twins, a boy and a girl. The little boy did not live long. He was born April 21, 1864 and died August 29, 1864. We children were happy when the children came but thought it was cruel when they were taken away and put in the ground.

Father built another house down in the field and he thatched the roof with straw so it would not leak and we moved down to the double log house. I was beginning to be useful to care for the babies and doing little chores around the home. I started to go to school and these were golden days for me. I had learned the letters of the alphabet by going to summer school; they taught us to sing songs and the Wilson Readers were then in use in the schools. I started in the first reader but I could only repeat the words after the teacher. This went on for some time and my teacher was very patient and all at once it came to me and I was able to read, and I was so glad and proud to read.

We all attended Sunday School, where we received

spiritual training. Our father and mother were teachers and when we all went to church, it seemed like heaven on earth to me.

I was eight years old on January 15 and on July 25 I was baptized by Daddy Thompson in Spring Creek and confirmed the same day by Thomas Todd. In those days there was one baptizing day each year, usually in July or August.

We had to carry our water from a little spring down in the field. One day I was taking the cow to pasture and felt tired so I tied my little bucket to the cow's tail. To my astonishment old Blackie started to run and didn't stop until she got to the big field gate, which happened to be shut or she wouldn't have stopped. When I got the bucket untied it was smashed flat. I took it home and my parents didn't scold me. Father got out the hammer and straightened it out, put a wooden bottom in it, and used it in the wheat bin to measure wheat. These were happy days spent in roaming in the fields and hunting the birds' nests.

In winter Father would bring a big log and put it in the fireplace to keep us warm and give us light to read by. It was then he taught me to knit stockings by the firelight. My father learned to knit as a very small boy, while herding sheep and cows on the bonnie heather hills in Scotland. He could keep us spellbound listening to the tales of his boyhood days. It was at this fire I used to toast long slices of good bread on a long wooden fork and put them on a server. This was in Bella's room. About this time one of her children was born (I think Jim). Mother would come and spread butter on the toast; she would also bring a bowl of gruel. I waited awhile and then went up to the bed thinking I would get a piece of toast, but it was all gone. I said, "I didn't understand how anyone could claim to be so sick when they could eat so much." They all had a good laugh.

One day my girl chum and I went into the school room and a little parcel was handed to us; it read "Dear Valentine." We opened it and there was a cedar pointer of beautiful workmanship and a stick of candy. Thomas Heber Rasband and John Carlisle were the givers. Our teachers required us to have pointers so we could keep the place in our reading class. If we missed a word, we had to go to the foot of the class. If we corrected a word and spelled it correctly we could go to the head of the class. One day our class was called up to read and I didn't have a pointer. Parley Murdock was standing next to me and he had a flat piece of wire. He nipped it in two and handed me a piece just as it came my turn to read. That just saved

my life. We took our lunch to school. Mary Lorintha Clyde would give me a slice of her salt rising bread. Oh! it was good. Our school days went on and we learned many valuable lessons in every way.

I was in my teens and John Crook, who was the choir leader, asked me to join the choir, which I did. My sister Janet was 18 years old and I was 16 when I went to work on ranches. I worked for Henry Cluff, William Moulton, William Davis and Nymphus Murdock. My father had taken up a ranch and Aunt Bella and her family were living on it. Father appointed me as governess to teach the children, as they were too far away to go to school. There were seven children in my class every day. Father got slates, books, and pencils and they all say they got a good start at that time.

The young folks from Moulton's came down in the evening to our ranch to spend the evening together. Heber Rasband was then working at Moulton's ranch. He had worked for my father two years before this time. While working for my father, he told me of some of the counsel his father had given him. One night he had been out quite late; when he came home he found his father waiting for him, and he said, "Heber, my boy, where have you been until this time in the morning? I want you to stop it. If you want to see the girls and get a good wife, why don't you go down to Brother Murdoch's. I know he has some girls that would make good wives. Now Heber, my boy, take my advice and do as I have told you." So he took his father's advice. He and I were exactly the same age, born on the same day, so he came and got my parents consent and we became engaged, and began to get ready to get married. We all liked him very much.

About this time I was chosen treasurer of the first Young Ladies Mutual Improvement Association in Heber. Annie Rasband Duke was the president.

Early in June, my father's brother, William, his son David, wife, & sister, Veronica came from Scotland. All were made welcome at my parents' home. My mother was so delighted at their coming, she notified the whole town of their arrival and everything possible was done to make them comfortable until they got settled down. They were quite well to do and brought a sum of money with them and soon got some land and a home of their own. David and his wife were both well educated. She understood music and was probably the first church organist in Heber. What a glorious summer we spent with our Scottish cousins, who very soon got acquainted with the Heber young people. John Adamson had an accordion and could play it well, and we had moonlight dances and many other little parties. Our cousins felt happy and glad to be with their friends in this beautiful little valley in Utah. Uncle William was a widower; his wife had died in Scotland just a few months before they came to Utah.

In the fall, Heber and I made preparations for getting married. We were married in the Endowment House in Salt Lake City on November 28, 1878. We were married for time and eternity by Daniel H. Wells. It was Thanksgiving Day and two other couples from this county were married the same day. They were Joseph Murdock and wife and John Carlisle and wife. The night we got home, the town was in an uproar. It was the custom to shivaree the young married couples and put them to bed. We slipped away over to a neighbors and they put out their lights and hid us. They went all over the town and could not find us. They went to Bishop Rasband's home (Heber's father). His brother Fred went into his mother's bed and started to pull them out of bed and discovered it was his mother and father. They kept up their racket until after midnight. David L. Murdoch was one of the ringleaders and when they couldn't find us they went home.

Aunt Bella was still at the ranch so we lived in Bella's room at Father's house until we could get another house of my father's called the Nelson house. Heber had been working and had saved some money and we bought some furniture, a stove, some chairs, a cupboard, a table, and a bed. Father and Mother gave me two nice flannel dresses, bought some bedding and 20 yards of rag carpet. Mother gave us two bed ticks and we soon had things fixed up in good shape. We lived in that house until Heber bought two lots west of J.W. Clydes. Then we went to the canyon and got logs and built a good log cabin with a lean-to. Our first child was born October 20 1879 and we named her Ann Elizabeth.

The next winter Brother Moulton and his families moved into a fine new home built on the ranch. They had a fine housewarming party and invited all who had worked for them in years gone by. Some of the Park City Mining people were there and of course Heber and I were there. We stayed all night and had a wonderful time.

The next spring Heber and his brothers went to John Turner's sawmill on Beaver Creek above Kamas to work. Heber by this time owned a yoke of oxen and a wagon. His father had sold some mining stock and received a good sum of money for it and he gave Heber a share of it. Heber bought a team and wagon,

as that was considered a needful outfit in those days. In the summer we all moved up to the saw mill and Heber worked for lumber to finish our new home, in which we lived the next winter.

It was quite a temptation for young men who wanted to work to go to Park City where they could get good wages. Heber went and soon had a job driving a team for Ezra Thompson, who had the contract to haul from the mine to the railroad cars. The longer he stayed the longer he wanted to stay. His father did not like him to be over there and asked me to use my influence to come home and stay in Heber even if he didn't make much money; but it was not to be that way.

The next summer my mother lived on Father's ranch. It was lonesome for her so she asked me to live with her and it would be closer to where Heber was working, so we took our cow and moved up to the ranch and lived there that summer. Then I came back to our own little home in Heber.

Soon Heber got a team of his own, a span of horses and an ore wagon and worked for himself. At this time I was living in our own cozy home in Heber and had plenty, but I did not enjoy being alone. My sister and her husband, Henry McMullin, asked me to come and stay at their home which I did for weeks at a time. There was a great rejoicing when Heber would come home from Park City and stay overnight, but he would have to go back to work the next day.

In February of 1882, Heber hired a man to drive his line. He came home and built some sheds and put a board fence around the corral and while he was home, our son, Heber Raymond, was born, March 28, 1882. A few days after the baby was born, Heber went back to his work in Park City and three months later he came home and moved me and the children over to Park City. We sure were happy that summer being all together and Heber could come home nights. It began to get cold weather so I moved back to my little house in Heber. I had met some of the grandest people I had ever known, but I had to leave them. I was glad I had a home to come to even if I was alone again.

In 1883, Heber bought some cattle and for about four years he looked after the cattle in summer and worked in Park City in the winter. The cattle wintered east toward Green River and during this time I was living in our little home in Heber. Another daughter was born to us January 6, 1886 and we named her Emily Isabella. My health was not good between 1882 and 1886. One night I was quite ill; my brother Joseph was staying with me, so I got him up and sent him to get the elders. He did not get them that night but the next night Bros. John Horrocks and George Harbour came. When they administered to me, Bro. Horrocks said I was about to receive a blessing from the hand of God and in about 10 months our beautiful little Emily Isabella was born, and we called her our blessing from heaven.

In about two years the three Rasband Brothers, Fred, Heber, and Jim, went into the butcher business in Park City. We moved to a new place in the lower end of Park City, which was later called the "slaughter house." Heber was the butcher and the cattle were killed and dressed here and taken to the shop for sale. The boys had turned everything into the business and they all worked hard; the business prospered for several years. But finally through giving credit and people failing to pay their bills, the business failed.

While living at the "slaughter house," another baby daughter was born September 19, 1888. She was very welcome indeed, and we were very pleased with our baby. Grandma Bella used to visit us. One time on the 4th of July, our boy had been given a bunch of firecrackers. He put them in his pocket and lit the one on the end and they kept going off and he kept going higher. Grandma Bella came to him and pulled his coat off, as it was all afire.

We moved up into Park City and I was wishing that a branch of the Church would be organized so that we could attend our meetings. In 1894 a branch was organized in answer to my prayers. Brother Thomas L. Allen was President and his counselors were Brother Adamson and Brother J. Glade. Edward Stromness was Supt. of the Sunday School. A good choir was also formed. The first meeting was held at our home and later at Roy's Hall, but it was decided we should build a meeting house and every member of the church worked willingly until it was finished. We all rejoiced in the splendid meeting and Sunday Schools. Heber and I were teachers in the Sunday School and the whole family was happy to attend. When the big fire came in 1898, our beautiful meeting house was burned along with the other buildings in that part of town, but we went ahead and rebuilt it and it is still being used.

When the Salt Lake Temple was dedicated in 1893, Heber and I went with many others from the Park City Branch.

After the failure of the butcher business, we left the slaughter house and moved into town. Heber was a policeman for a year, then he went to work in the Silver-King mine and later in the Anchor Mine. It was

then we built our nice new home in Park City. Our son, Ray, worked at Weeter's Lumber yard and got lumber to build our house. We were all well and happy. Annie had graduated from grade school and we sent her to the Brigham Young Academy at Provo, where she did very well. She came home at vacation time. Our social activities were grand. On the 24th of February 1898, our family and the Adamson's and all other Murdoch relations came to Heber to attend my parents' golden wedding which was indeed a fine occasion. They had a banquet in the daytime and a dance and program at night. The children and near relatives presented Father with a gold-headed cane and each of his two wives a diamond ring. James "D" Murdoch was the master of ceremonies and made the presentations. In June, Annie came home from the Academy and spring cleaning was almost done.

I had been asking Heber to quit the mine and he finally said he would. He also said we would go home on the 4th of July and have the time of our lives. I went to the tailor's and ordered a suit and I made dresses for myself and the girls. Heber said, "I will just quit and when Captain Dick comes along he will say 'Where can Rasband be?" and then he laughed heartily. It pleased me to hear that. He was a kind and loving husband and father and a true friend and neighbor and had many friends.

It was Sunday morning and fast day, July 2, 1899, Annie had prepared breakfast and put up her father's lunch. There was a dance the night before and I had taken care of some children so did not get to bed very early. I heard him get up to go to work. We all went to Sunday School and Fast Meeting right after, then came home to prepare dinner for Papa when he got off work at 3 P.M. All at once I heard someone crying outside. I went out and there were people running up to our house and I said "What is the matter?" Annie said, "There has been a terrible accident at the mine and Papa was in it." I said, "Come inside and we will kneel down and pray that there will be no lives lost." We heard no more until 3 o'clock and then James Rasband came in and said, "Sarah, it is Heber that is in the accident. He had fallen down the shaft 275 feet into a sump filled with water and they didn't know if they could ever get him out. You may as well know it now, it is true. My first thought was that I must go to the mine. I started up the little hill in front of our house and went blind and fell. They carried me_ back into the house and laid me on the bed and would not let me get up.

Heber had a faithful bird dog that would go with

him to the mine then come home and go to meet him when it was time to come home. The dog went but could not see the horse nor Heber. He came in the bedroom and looked at his clothes and made a terrible noise and went out again. By this time the house was full of people trying to console and comfort us and everything possible was being done at the mine. No human tongue can tell what I passed through at that time. What a terrible calamity had overtaken me to think that my dear companion was in such distress and that I would never see him alive again. Then to hear the pitiful cries of our dear children. Their cries were heartbreaking. I tried to make myself believe it was all a mistake and not true. Then I hoped, at least his body could be found and that he could have a Christian burial. At 8 P.M. word came that his body had been found and taken to the undertaker. This was little consolation in this terrible trying time. There were many people outside crying and praying for me. I was helped into the room when I got to look at that dear face and mangled body. There were no tears for me for I was past shedding tears. I knew I would meet him again. They led me back to my room, everything was so silent and still. A little while towards morning I slept a little and on wakening realized the truth and tears came to me. I thought of my unkind words that I might have said. Was I to blame in any way for the accident? A thousand thoughts ran through my mind. Oh! it was real sorrow and grief, more than I was able to bear.

Patriarch Hicken and his son, Thomas, had been visiting in Coalville and had heard of the accident and came to my home. When Patriarch Hicken saw the plight I was in he said, "Let us kneel around the bed and pray for the Comforter to come." What a beautiful prayer he offered. I shall never forget it, and the Comforter did come. I felt a sweet calm spirit come over me and it gave me strength. I arose from my bed and washed my face and never felt so bad again. I felt I was greatly blessed by the Lord in my severe trial. Sure enough, as Heber had said, Captain Dick Williamson did come and say "Where's Rasband?" We went to Heber for-the 4th, as my husband said we would, but it was to attend his funeral instead of having the time of our lives as he expected. After the tragic death of our beloved husband and father we returned to our home in Park City. Our son Ray was 17 years old and the mining company gave him a job in their blacksmith shop, and our daughter, Annie, worked for different families. At the time of Heber's death we only owed $10.00 and he had a check coming, so we were not bad

off. Our little girl, Jenny, remarked that it just looked like Papa was getting ready to leave us, building this new house and getting nice things in it. We went on with our church work and did the best we could.

Our daughter, Annie, was keeping company with a young man named Walter Phillips. They planned to be married in June and the Church called them on a mission to the Hawaiian Islands. They were married June 13, 1900 in the Salt Lake Temple, and left a few days later for their mission. The Park City Branch gave them a farewell party.

When they arrived in Hawaii, Annie was assigned to labor at the mission home and Walter was to go on the Island of Hawaii, about 200 miles away. He would return to the mission home every 6 months to conference. There was great rejoicing when the Elders met in their conferences. Annie was active in Relief Society and Sunday School at the branch headquarters. They both performed their duties well.

On the 4th of March, 1901, Annie gave birth to a baby girl. They named her Anna LeIsle. Bro. Phillips was allowed to come home at the time of the child's birth. Then he came home again in October. He wrote home to me and among other things he said, "Mother, I want to tell you, I have the sweetest wife and baby in all the world." He also said, "When I was sparking Annie, I thought you were a little over careful of Annie, but I don't think so now. I think you did just right."

Bro. Phillips through faith and prayer learned the language very soon and became very capable and could speak fluently the native tongue and was accomplishing a good work. He was greatly loved by the natives and had said he would like to live and die with these people.

In December Bro. Phillips took ill with pneumonia. His companion called a doctor and he pronounced it "catarrhal pneumonia" and said there was no apparent danger. However, he took a heavy chill and had a high fever and spit up some blood, then he started to ramble in his talk and asked for his wife and his mother. They noticed a strange expression on his face and his hands and feet were cold. They realized that he was dying. He took sick December 10th and passed away on December 14, 1901. Elder Bush was with him right to the end. They called an undertaker and he came from Hilo, a distance of 50 miles. He was put in an airtight casket and said he could be shipped home in it, but they found it was not airtight and they had to bury him. The Branch President had a burial lot on his property for his family, and he said there was a place for Bro. Phillips. He was buried at Waimea on the Island of Hawaii. Bro. Bush wrote one account of his sickness, death, and burial to the President of the Church. He said, "Bro. Phillips died the death of a hero in full performance of his duty. Sister Phillips is standing the ordeal as only a faithful Latter-day Saint could." Annie held up bravely and continued her missionary work until the next summer. She and LeIsle came home in June 1902 accompanied by Bro. Bush and received a hearty welcome by the members of the Park City Branch. They had a party and dance in honor of her safe return.

While Annie was gone on her mission, I got some work to do and with what Ray earned, we were able to support ourselves and send Annie what money she needed. Soon after Annie returned, she got work at Welch Driscoll and Buck Sore and worked there for 7 or 8 years until we moved to Heber in 1908. 1 took care of the home and Annie's baby and Annie resumed her work in the church. I was Relief Society President for a number of years. Our son, Ray, was married to Stella Brim September 19, 1903, in our home, by Bishop Fred Rasband. Our two daughters Embell and Jenny were graduating from grade school and we were preparing to take them to the Brigham Young Academy. Jenny was taken ill with typhoid fever. We had two doctors but she just couldn't seem to get well. Everything was done for her that loving hands and kind hearts could do but sweet Jenny's spirit took its flight on September 3, 1904, which caused us again deep grief and sorrow. She was within a few days of being 16 years old. She was the only child born in Park City.

I then took Embell and LeIsle to the Academy in Provo and stayed there all winter. LeIsle was 3 years old and she went to kindergarten at the Academy. At the end of the term we went home to Park City. During the summer one Sunday, we had come home from Sacrament Meeting, and Annie was talking with friends on the front porch and I had gone to bed and LeIsle had crawled in with me to wait for her mother. We had a large bathroom and we hung clothes in one end near the window. Embell went in to get her nightgown and struck a match to see. After she got in bed I called to her and said I could see a light flickering on the back porch through the window. She ran to the bathroom and the clothes on the wall were all ablaze. She grabbed them in her arms and ran to the back porch and threw them over the banister. LeIsle was so frightened she ran out the front door screaming. The neighbors all came to their doors and asked what was wrong and she screamed, "Our house is on fire."

In less than two minutes the house was full of people and they put out the fire and saved our house from burning to the ground. Some men climbed in the attic and it took eight buckets of water up there to put it out. Since the town had nearly burned down, we all had such a terrible fear of fire. Embell was burned but went to the Academy in the fall. When she came home she got work in a confectionary. The girls were both working and I was taking care of the home. As time went on my health began to fail and we decided to move back home to Heber. Then we decided to build a new home. We still had an extra lot next to our other home and with what money the girls and I had saved and some money I had received from my father, we got our new home finished. When we got ready to leave Park City, the ward gave us a nice party and we were all presented with a nice gift, as a token of appreciation for our faithful labors. I then gave my son Ray, the deed to my home in Park City. We left Park City where we had had many joys and sorrows and came to our nice new home in Heber.

Annie went to work at the Heber Mercantile and Embell worked in my brother David's store. I had a growth in my right breast and the doctor said I should have it removed, so I went to the L.D.S. Hospital in Salt Lake City and had my breast removed and felt much better afterward.

We were all very active in the Church. Annie was on the Stake Board of the Young Ladies M.I.A. I was a teacher in the Relief Society, and Embell, a teacher in the Sunday School. By this time my dear parents were both getting quite old and feeble. I spent much time with them visiting and trying to comfort them. Finally my dear old mother was called home to a well-earned rest on the 15th of December 1909. About this time Annie went to Salt Lake City to take a course in nursing. LeIsle was 8 years old and was baptized in Heber. In 1910 we moved to Salt Lake City. In May of 1910 my dear old father passed away. They both had been faithful members of the Church for fully 60 years. They had met many severe trials during that time and proved faithful and true to the end of their days and were naturally loved and respected by everyone. The same can be said of Aunt Bella who lived until April 10, 1916. They were a very worthy trio.

Embell was married to Victor Dee Cram on June 22, 1910. Victor was a hard working honest young man. We decided to buy a lot on Taylor Ave. (now 24th South). We all joined together and started to get a home of our own. We built a three-room house on the back of the lot to live in while our home was being built. We called it the "shack." While living in the shack, Embell gave birth to her first baby boy on May 9, 1911; his name, Dee Raymond Cram. He was a beautiful baby. Then in 1912, she had another baby boy on October 22, and named him Heber Rasband. Then we started to build our 10 room brick home in which Embell and Vic are still living. They had 10 children born to them at 155 East 24th South. In the rearing of these children, I took the Grandma's part and Annie took the nurse's part. We were living in the old Farmer's Ward, but soon it was divided and we were in the Burton Ward. We all had important church work to do and enjoyed it very much.

My sister Mary had been quite ill for some time and died in December 1917. We were notified of her death and attended her funeral in Heber City. About this time Annie was married to John T. Roberts and moved to Twin Falls, Idaho, where her husband was working. I went with them and visited for the winter. In March 1918, I came back to Salt Lake City. I went to visit my sister Nettie in Heber for a while and went back again for Decoration Day. Soon after this William Lindsay, who was married to my cousin and was a good friend of the family, wrote me a letter and asked if I would be his wife and share his home for life. His wife had passed away two years before. I wrote back accepting his offer. I later made arrangements for the marriage, which took place in the Salt Lake Temple, September 6, 1918, and we came to his home in Heber, September 9th, where I have been ever since. I have tried to fulfill my part of the bargain and so far I think we have gotten along very well.

My son had moved from Park City to California with his wife and family. Stella had a cancer on her face and a doctor in California was treating her for it. We were now all scattered. Annie rented our side of the home in Salt Lake City. LeIsle was going to high school in Twin Falls and was married to Lorin Rasmussen in 1921, and they came to Salt Lake to live.

In 1927 Annie became ill and came to Salt Lake for medical attention. The doctor said it was cancer, the fast growing kind and not much can be done. It had gone too far. She went to the hospital and had radium treatments, which the doctor said prolonged her life about a year. We knew it would be a long hard battle ahead and she could not go back to Idaho and be alone, so she moved into the Salt Lake home once more. LeIsle lived in Salt Lake City, and with my husband's consent, I went to Salt Lake to help care for her. In January 1928, she was bedfast and for nine long months, Embell, LeIsle and I took care of her. We had a good doctor attending her and all was done that skill and loving hands could do, but to no avail. She passed away from this world of trouble and trials on August 7, 1928. We love her and still miss her very much. Since I came to William Lindsay's home, I have been treated kindly. We have a comfortable home and all we need to supply our wants and some to spare to help others. Our son's wife, Stella, passed away in California, July 24, 1931. She also had cancer. Ray was left with five children. We buried Annie in Heber with her father and Jenny.

Note: William Lindsay passed away in Heber in 1932; leaving Grandmother a widow once more. She moved back to her home in Salt Lake City and spent the rest of her life with Embell and her family. She passed away quietly one day after her 74th birthday, January 16, 1933. I have always said that my Mother Annie, and Grandmother Sarah, really lived their religion. They were true Latter-day Saints all their lives. I loved them dearly, and I still miss them very much.

Submitted by LeIsle Phillips Rasmussen

Jennie Hyslop and Emily Isabella Rasband

Sarah Jane Murdoch and Grandchilren
Ray, Heber, Lorna, and Rea Cram

Butcher Shop-Park City   Charles Rasband and Fred Rasband

Missionaries Who Have Died While in the Mission Field

LeIsle Phillips

Walter F. Phillips   Mrs. Walter F. Phillips

Walter F. Phillips was born Oct. 16, 1877. He arrived in the Hawaiian Islands Aug. 1, 1900, where he took up the labors of a missionary. After serving for one year, 4 months and 13 days, he contracted pneumonia and died Dec. 14, 1901, at Maliu, Kona, Hawaii. It was not possible to ship his body back to the states, so he was buried at Kamuela, Hawaii. His wife and small child later returned to the mainland.

John Murray Murdoch
Sarah Jane Murdoch Rasband
Ann Elizabeth Rasband Phillips
LeIsle Phillips Rasmussen

Sarah Jane Murdoch Rasband
Ann Elizabeth Rasband Phillips
LeIsle Phillips Rasmussen
Virginia Rasmussen Zobrist

HUSBAND   THOMAS HEBER RASBAND

Born   15 January 1859
Place   Provo, Utah, Utah
Chr:
Married   28 November 1878
Place   Salt Lake City, Salt Lake, Utah
Death: 2 Jul 1899 Park City, Summit, Utah
Burial   4 Jul 1899 Heber, Wasatch, Utah
Father   Thomas RASBAND
Mother*   Elizabeth GILES
Other Wives
(if any)

WIFE   SARAH JANE MURDOCH

Birth   15 January 1859
Place   Salt Lake City, Salt Lake, Utah
Chr:
Death: 16 Jan 1933 Salt Lake City, Salt Lake, Utah
Burial   20 Jan 1933   Heber, Wasatch, Utah
Father   John Murray MURDOCH
Mother*   Ann STEEL
Other Husbands   (2) William LINDSAY M-6 September 1918
(if any)
*Where was information obtained? Rasband family

*List complete maiden name for all females.

	1st Child	Ann Elizabeth RASBAND
	Birth:	20 October 1879
	Place:	Heber, Wasatch, Utah
	Married to	(1) Walter Freeman PHILLIPS
	Married	13 June 1900 Temple
	Place	Salt Lake City, Salt Lake, Utah
	Died	7 August 1928 Salt Lake City, Utah

	2nd Child	Heber Raymond RASBAND
	Birth	28 March 1882
	Place	Heber, Wasatch, Utah
	Married to	Estella BRIM
	Married	19 Sep 1903
	Place	Park City, Summit, Utah
	Died	24 March 1948

	3rd Child	Emily Isabella RASBAND
	Birth	6 January 1886
	Place	Heber, Wasatch, Utah
	Married to	Victor Dee CRAM
	Married	22 June 1910 Temple
	Place	Salt Lake City, Salt Lake, Utah
	Died	2 July 1967 Salt Lake City, Utah

	4th Child	Jennie Hyslop RASBAND
	Birth	19 Sep 1888
	Place	Park City, Summit, Utah
	Sealed to	Victor Dee CRAM
	Sealed	22 June 1910 Temple
	Place	Salt Lake City, Salt Lake, Utah
	Died	3 September 1904

Heber

Raymond

Rasband

Old Home at 155 West 24th South

Salt Lake City, Utah

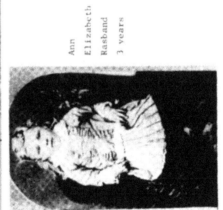

Ann

Elizabeth

Rasband

3 years

Heber Utah Sept. 6th 1927.
To William & Jacobina Clegg.
Dear Brother & Sister we
received your kind letter a few days ago & though glad to
hear from you we were very sorry, indeed to learn that
Brother Will's health was no better. But as you said we all
have our troubles & trials to bear in this life & it is for us
to do the best we can under the circumstances & conditions we find, our selves placed in. But still let
us hope for the best. Because it is often said as long
as there is life there is hope in the human heart.
We often speak of you & earnestly wish we could help
you in your time of serious sickness especially when
Jacobina's own health & condition is also very poorly
We are told that we should help bear each others burdens
which is surely very good advice. But often conditions
arise where it is very little we can do to help each other
especially when we live so far apart, And of course we
know you have your own Dear Sons & Daughters near by
who love you both & will do everything in their power to
aid you & lighten your burdens in every possible way
And we earnestly pray that God may be merciful to you
& cheer & comfort your hearts & ease your pains & cause
everything to work together for your best good.

Of course Aunt Nettie would tell you of Uncle Henry's condition. We went down to see him Sunday evening & he thinks he is feeling better & stronger. Aunt Mary Dukes funeral services were held here Sunday & many good things were said of her & the good deeds she had done she was 87 years of age & had lived a long & useful life.

Of course we found the $5.00 enclosed in your letter for which I thank you. But really I tried to have you understand that I wanted to do that much for you as a friend & without any pay especially when Will was sick. But I see you too have that Scotch independent spirit which is a good thing if not carried too far.

I might say that this is the ninth anniversary of our marriage and I feel taking everything into consideration that we have got along very nicely. And I am pleased to say we are both wonderfully blessed with good health & our prospects for the future are still good if we only do our part well.

Well Dear Brother & Sister may God bless you all with every blessing necessary for you at this time is the desire & prayer of your Brother & Sister

William & Sarah R. Lindsay

Letter written by Sarah Jane Murdoch Rasband
Lindsay to Jacobina Murdoch Clegg

Heber Mar 5th 1929

Dear Sister and family

So glad you started to write I have
been going to for along time but it
Seams I did not do it. glad to hear that
the boys are getting better and a lady
told me you were looking better than
She had seen you for years was glad
to hear that. that same lady said
you and your nice boys were at the
Party and she told you I was looking a
little better I saw her at Millies
at a meeting of the Daughters of the
Pioneers central Co. of which I am
the Treasurer, they served a grand
lunch, on my way out there I
stoped at Kates She is better but
still in bed but since then I hear
she is up said she had been
in bed for 6 weeks, to bad sure,

you say you haven,t heard from Joe
and Betty for a long time I hope they are
all right, but one cant help feeling
ancious about them, same thing with
My Folks did not hear from Ray
and Stella but LeRsle said in her last
letter Verginia Rays Married
girl had written to her said
her Mothers face no better and
that they got the nice Christmas
Box that we all joined together and
Sent them, said the rest were well.
LeRsle said her family were well
now but they have been quarantined
and have had sickness all winter, so
has Erubell but they are getting
better to. yes the Radio has been
quite a cheer up for me it sure is
wonderful. Wm has gone to meeting and I turned to Calf. S. A. and have
been listning to the grandest music
and singing it sure is charming
wish you were here to enjoy it with me

I did not go down to Mc Mullins
for 5 weeks when it was so cold
but since then I have been several
times I found them looking pretty
good, our sister likes to ask some
one who comes in to sing for her then
she sings. likes the old songs we
used to sing, we sang Mother kissed
Me in my dream, then Uncle Henry
sings some of his old songs and they
are good. so you see that is better
than to be gloomy all the time.
John H. Murdock and Uncle War or Uncle
Orson hicken are the mane singers
I think Uncle orsen is looking over
the nest again so come up, Ha' Ha'
I know you can take a joke by this
time when you know what your
humble servant stood from all of
you. Jock murdock even picked out

Millie Mc. Gill for me. Ha! Ha! you
are supposed to laugh now, I was the
other night thinking over some of my
Engage-ments to a bout 5 W.H's you can
guess who they were, and I landed one of
them at last of course it was just
in fun, mostly, last sunday night
as I listened to the chorus that sings
for Bro Talmages Lecture over the
Radio, the announcer said he would
give the names of the singers and
Moroni Thomas was there, and I
heard that beautiful sound in his
voice that charmed us on the Ranch
fifty years ago, sure did. well guess
this is all, hopping this will find you
all well and happy. Mae is going to
write and you will enjoy that
        much love to all,
            your loving sister
            Sarah S. M. R. Lindsay

```
1 MURDOCH, James 1786-1831                    2 MURDOCH, John Murray 1820-1910
1 MURDOCH, Mary MURRAY, Sp. 1782-1856         2 MURDOCH, Ann STEEL    Sp. 1829-1909
```

DESCENDANTS OF--------3 MURDOCH SARAH JANE 1859-1933
3 RASBAND, THOMAS HEBER, SP. 1859-1899

```
                                                          Div.-Divorced
                                                          Sp.-Spouse
                                                          B-Birth
                                                          M-Married
4 ROBERTS, Ann Elizabeth RASBAND Phillips B-20 Oct 1879 D-7 Aug 1928   D-Death
4 PHILLIPS, Walter Freeman, Sp. (1) B-16 Oct 1876 M-13 Jun 1900 D-14 Dec 1901
4 ROBERTS, John Thomas, Sp. (2) B-            M-30 Nov 1917

    5 RASMUSSEN, Anna LeIsle PHILLIPS B-4 Mar 1901
    5 RASMUSSEN, Lorin Neils, Sp. B-11 Jun 1901 M-22 Mar 1921 D-9 Apr 1971

        6 ZOBRIST, Virginia Ann RASMUSSEN B-7 Jan 1922 M-25 Feb 1939
        6 ZOBRIST, Herman Arthur, Sp. B-12 Feb 1920

            7 ZOBRIST, Kendall Arthur B-7 Oct 1939 M-27 Jan 1958
            7 ZOBRIST, Ivalee LLEWELYN, Sp. B-1 Jan 1940

                8 ZOBRIST, Kendall Arthur Jr.   B-21 May 1958
                8 ZOBRIST, Julie Anne           B- 7 Sep 1959
                8 ZOBRIST, James Duane          B- 6 Nov 1960
                8 ZOBRIST, Jennifer Lee         B-12 Dec 1961
                8 ZOBRIST, Gretchen Anna        B-12 Oct 1965
                8 ZOBRIST, Mina Fay             B-  Mar 1969


            7 ZOBRIST, Duane Herman B-11 Sep 1940 M-26 Jun 1964
            7 ZOBRIST, Sharon Ann JONES, Sp. B-5 Jan 1944

                8 ZOBRIST, Duane Herman II      B-23 Apr 1967
                8 ZOBRIST, Melinda             B-14 Jan 1970
                8 ZOBRIST, Darren Neils         B- Apr 1971
                8 ZOBRIST, Brooke              B-18 Dec 1974
                8 ZOBRIST, Lindsay             B-  Apr 1977

            7 FORSTON, Anne LeIsle ZOBRIST B-20 Jan 1942 M-8 Aug 1962
            7 FORSTON, Robert Francis, Sp. B-17 Oct 1940

                8 FORSTON, Melanie Marguerite   B- 2 Aug 1966
                8 FORSTON, R Scott              B- 6 May 1968
                8 FORSTON, Jenny LeIsle         B-21 Mar 1973

            7 ZOBRIST, Ray Phillip B-5 Aug 1946 M-27 May 1964
            7 ZOBRIST, Janet Marie KNOTTS, Sp. B-22 Jan 1948

                8 ZOBRIST, Madonna LaRae        B-17 Jan 1965
                8 ZOBRIST, Katherine Dawnae     B-14 Jan 1967
                8 ZOBRIST, Robert Phillip       B-31 Oct 1968
                8 ZOBRIST, Anna Janae           B-30 Jan 1973
                8 ZOBRIST, Michael Lorin        B-11 Jan 1976
                8 ZOBRIST, Jared Ray            B- 3 Jan 1979

            7 ZOBRIST, Gerry R B-22 Jul 1949 M-12 Jul 1968
            7 ZOBRIST, Jolin GOODRICH, Sp. B-17 Dec 1949

                8 ZOBRIST, Gerry G              B-20 Nov 1969
                8 ZOBRIST, Mitchell Ryan        B-10 Sep 1971
                8 ZOBRIST, Brandon Tyler        B-16 Aug 1975
                8 ZOBRIST, Kristin             B-  Aug 1977
                8 ZOBRIST, Stacy Ann            B-  Jun 1979

            7 SNYDER, Ginnie Lynn B-22 Jul 1949 M-19 Jun 1970
            7 SNYDER, Paul A. Sp. B-24 Apr 1946

                8 SNYDER, Daniel Steven         B-27 Oct 1971
                8 SNYDER, Angelynn              B-27 Nov 1973
                8 SNYDER, Spencer Brian         B-30 Sep 1975
                8 SNYDER, Heather Ann           B- 7 Dec 1978
        6 RASMUSSEN, Raymond Phillip B-27 May 1925 M-22 May 1947
        6 RASMUSSEN, Donna Irene MULCOCK, Sp. B-7 Jul 1927

            7 CURTIS, Annette RASMUSSEN B-3 Jan 1948 M-12 Jun 1969
            7 CURTIS, Richard Lindsay, Sp. B-18 Dec 1947
```

```
        8 CURTIS, Jennifer            B-28 Mar 1970
        8 CURTIS, Rachael            B-24 Feb 1972  D-24 Feb 1972
        8 CURTIS, Rebecca            B-24 Feb 1972  D-24 Feb 1972
        8 CURTIS, Stacie             B-27 Sep 1974
        8 CURTIS, Heather            B- 8 Feb 1977
        8 CURTIS, Emily              B- 3 Mar 1978

    7 BUIE, Cynthia RASMUSSEN B-5 May 1953 M-25 Aug 1978
    7 BUIE, Randal Thomas, Sp. B-18 Oct 1950

    7 HOWARD, Susan M RASMUSSEN B-13 Aug 1960 (Adopted) M-21 Feb 1979
    7 HOWARD, Rock, Sp. B-4 Mar 1958

    7 RASMUSSEN, Ray Phillip B-22 Nov 1962 (Adopted)

6 GRAEHL, Marilyn RASMUSSEN B-17 Oct 1927 M-8 Jul 1946
6 GRAEHL, Alvin Paul, Sp. B-5 Sep 1925

    7 GRAEHL, Thomas Paul B-27 Dec 1947 M-3 Oct 1972
    7 GRAEHL, Marie PRATT, Sp. B-16 Feb 1954

        8 GRAEHL, Lisa Marie         B-30 Jun 1973
        8 GRAEHL, Elizabeth          B-20 May 1977

    7 GRAEHL, Lorin Mark      B-8 Jul 1950

    7 THOMAS, Sally Anne GRAEHL B-12 Nov 1951 M-22 Aug 1975
    7 THOMAS, Reed Mason, Sp. B-13 Nov 1952

        8 THOMAS, Anthony Evans       B-30 Mar 1979

    7 GRAEHL, David William B-22 Apr 1954

    7 GRAEHL, Elizabeth      B-29 Aug 1956

    7 GRAEHL, Karen Alice    B-25 Apr 1958

    7 GRAEHL, James Alvin B-20 Nov 1959
    7 GRAEHL, Jodi Lynn ANDERSON, Sp. B-1 Mar 1960  M-26 Jun 1978 Div.

        8 GRAEHL, Joshua James         B-27 Nov 1979

6 BULLOCK, Dona LeIsle RASMUSSEN B-13 Dec 1929 M-19 Aug 1948
6 BULLOCK, Oriville Lynn, Sp. B-15 Mar 1929

    7 BULLOCK, Donald Lynn B-13 Aug 1951 M-27 Dec 1973  Div.
    7 BULLOCK, Karen JONES, Sp. B-

        8 BULLOCK, Pamela Jane         B-
        8 BULLOCK, Wendy Lynn          B-
        8 BULLOCK, David Donald        B-

    7 RYVER, Linda LeIsle BULLOCK B-26 Jun 1953 M-1 Mar 1972
    7 RYVER, Kevin Don, Sp. B-

        8 RYVER, Kristine LeIsle        B- 1 Aug 1972
        8 RYVER, Jeremy Shane          B-25 Jun 1977

    7 BULLOCK, Bradley Rasmussen B-31 Mar 1955 M-
    7 BULLOCK, Pattie GREENWOOD, Sp. B-

        8 BULLOCK, Adam                B-

    7 ARRINGTON, Julie Anne BULLOCK B-11 Sep 1956 M-23 Apr 1972
    7 ARRINGTON, Jeffrey Brian, Sp. B-

        8 ARRINGTON, Jeffery Brian      B-25 Jun 1972
        8 ARRINGTON, Jodi Anne          B-11 Sep 1974
        8 ARRINGTON, Jimmy John  (Twin) B-12 Aug 1977
        8 ARRINGTON, Jessie John (Twin) B-12 Aug 1977 D-14 Aug 1977

    7 BULLOCK, Jeffrey Nathan B-21 Sep 1957 M-
    7 BULLOCK, Debbie MARTINEZ, Sp. B-
```

                8 BULLOCK, Erik   B- Sep 1979

            7 BULLOCK, Todd Harold B-15 Feb 1961 M-
            7 BULLOCK, Patty SPRAGUE, Sp. B-

        6 RASMUSSEN, Lorin Neil B-22 Nov 1931 M-10 Apr 1953
        6 RASMUSSEN, Sally Ann ANDERSON, Sp. B-10 Mar 1933

            7 RASMUSSEN, Scott Neil B-28 Apr 1956 M-17 Aug 1979
            7 RASMUSSEN, Mary Ann HANSEN, Sp. B-23 Apr 1956

            7 RASMUSSEN, Howard Anton B-14 Aug 1958 M-14 Sep 1979
            7 RASMUSSEN, Elizabeth Rae CHILD, Sp. B-

                8 SCOTT, David   B-   Jun 1980

            7 RASMUSSEN, Bruce Charles   B- 6 Aug 1959
            7 RASMUSSEN, Lorraine   B-11 Jun 1962
            7 RASMUSSEN, Clark Joseph   B-27 May 1964
            7 RASMUSSEN, Dwight Ephraim   B-29 Apr 1974
            7 RASMUSSEN, Jessica Ann   B-13 Jan 1976

    4 RASBAND, Heber Raymond B-28 Mar 1882 M-19 Sep 1903 D-17 Mar 1948
    4 RASBAND, Estella Alene BRIM, B-26 Mar 1880 D-24 Jul 1931

        5 RASBAND, Merrill Brim B-26 Mar 1904 M-   1961
        5 RASBAND, Patricia BOND, Sp. B-

            6 RASBAND, Karen,   B-

        5 RASBAND, Wayne B-

        5 KIRKWOOD, Virginia RASBAND B-10 Nov 1911 or 12 M-
        5 KIRKWOOD, John A C, Sp. B-

            6 KIRKWOOD, Jack   B-

            6 KIRKWOOD, JoAlene B-

        5 TRUESDALE, Jennie B RASBAND Murray B-
        5 MURRAY,   Sp. (1) B-   M-
        5 TRUESDALE, Hugh Hillis, Sp. (2) B-   M-

            6 GILBERT, Luanne MURRAY B-   M-
            6 GILBERT,   Sp. B-

            6 WHITACRE, Patricia Rae MURRAY B-   M-
            6 WHITACRE,   Sp. B-

            6 MURRAY, Michael Edward B-   M-   ?

        5 WHITE, Anna Leone RASBAND B-7 Oct 1922 M-
        5 WHITE,   Sp. B-

    4 CRAM, Emily Isabella RASBAND B-6 Jan 1886 M-22 Jun 1910 D-2 Jul 1967
    4 CRAM, Victor Dee, Sp. B-6 Oct 1880 D-23 Jan 1964

        5 CRAM, Dee Raymond B-9 May 1911 D-22 Apr 1970
        5 CRAM, Jessie Edna OGZEWALLA, Sp. (1) B-11 Jul 1910 M-6 Jul 1929 D-20 Jul 1931
        5 CRAM, Eva Alberta LEWIS, Sp. (2) B-4 Jul 1912 M-22 Dec 1934 D-4 Mar 1960
        5 CRAM, Bonnie Deloris DENHAM, Sp. (3) B-13 Nov 1934 M-11 Dec 1960 Div.

            6 LARSON, Carmen Rayola CRAM B-20 Feb 1930 M-16 Mar 1950
            6 LARSON, Don, Sp. B-27 Oct 1927

                7 LARSON, Randall Cram B-21 Jan 1951 M-8 Nov 1974
                7 LARSON, Kimberly Ann HANSEN, Sp. B-

                7 HUNT, Kerri Turia LARSON B-5 Apr 1960 (Adopted) M-30 Aug 1977
                7 HUNT, Mitchell Lyman, Sp. B-15 May 1959

                    8 HUNT, Benjamin Layne   B-10 Apr 1978

```
                7 LARSON, Donald Todd    B-24 Sep 1961
                7 LARSON, Tania Dee      B- 8 Apr 1968 (Adopted)
                7 LARSON, Mereana Kim    B-18 Sep 1968
                7 LARSON, Derek Ray      B-16 Sep 1970

    5 CRAM, Heber Rasband B-22 Oct 1912 D-7 Aug 1934

    5 CRAM, Lois B-6 Nov 1914 D-19 Nov 1914

    5 McFarland, Lorna Ruth B-2 Nov 1915 M-18 Oct 1932
    5 McFarland, Archie Paul, Sp. B-24 Jun 1914 D-18 Jan 1980

        6 McFARLAND, Archie Ray B-17 May 1933 M-20 Jan 1951
        6 McFARLAND, Leah Rae Green, Sp. B-11 Apr 1934

            7 McFARLAND, Archie Paul B-29 Aug 1951 M-24 Aug 1975
            7 McFARLAND, Georgia JONES, Sp. B-6 May 1952

                8 McFARLAND, William Paul    B- 9 Jul 1977
                8 McFARLAND, Britta Lyn      B-16 May 1979

            7 McFARLAND, Thomas Dale B-4 Oct 1952

            7 CHAVEZ, Kaye Anne McFARLAND B-6 Apr 1956 M-5 Mar 1973
            7 CHAVEZ, Patric Dee, Sp. B-5 Oct 1950

                8 CHAVEZ, Daniel Dee      B-30 Dec 1973
                8 CHAVEZ, David Dee       B-17 Sep 1975
                8 CHAVEZ, Benjamin Dee    B- 4 Jan 1978

            7 GREEN, Leslie Lynn McFARLAND B-17 Jul 1959 M-7 Nov 1975
            7 GREEN, Robert Alan, Sp. B-15 Sep 1956

                8 GREEN, Aubria Ann         B-15 Jun 1976
                8 GREEN, Tina Mishone       B-15 Dec 1977
                8 GREEN, Robert Alan Jr.    B- 1 Oct 1979

            7 McFARLAND, DeAnne B-19 Sep 1964

        6 McFARLAND, Victor Dee B-1 Jan 1937
        6 McFARLAND, Sylvia SMITH, Sp. (1) B-21 Dec 1937 M-26 Apr 1956 Div.
        6 McFARLAND, JoAnne FREEZE, Sp. (2) B-          M-
        Hancock, Larry, Sp. (2) to Sylvia Smith  M-          1963

            7 McFARLAND, Victor Cory  B-2 Dec 1956

            7 ZIMMERMAN, Kim Michele McFARLAND B-19 Dec 1957 M-
            7 ZIMMERMAN,          Sp. B-

            7 McFARLAND, Roger Todd B-26 Mar 1959
            7 McFARLAND Lane        B-


            7 McFARLAND, Jo Lyn     B-3 Nov 1963    (JoAnne F. by Prev. Marriage)

            7 McFARLAND, Jeff      B-6 Aug 1964
            7 McFARLAND, Jo Dee    B-13 Sep 1967

        6 McFARLAND, Gary Paul B-24 Nov 1938
        6 McFARLAND, Sandra Helen IBA, Sp. (1) B-4 Sep 1941 M-24 Feb 1956 Div.
        6 McFARLAND, Anita SANCHEZ Worthen, Sp. (2) B-          M-    Dec 1962
        Taylor, Gary, Sp. (2) to Sandra
        Worthen, Gary, Sp. (1) to Anita

            7 LEWIS, Debra Lyn McFARLAND B-17 Sep 1956 M-
            7 LEWIS, William, Sp. B-

                8 LEWIS, Clinton          B-
                8 Lewis, (Boy)            B-

            7 KELLY, Susan McFARLAND B-28 Jan 1958 M-
            7 KELLY, Shaun, Sp. B-
```

```
            7 McFARLAND, Gary Stephen B-4 Jul 1959 M-
            7 McFARLAND, Cynthia          Sp. B-

                 8 McFARLAND, Tiffany              B-

            7 McFARLAND, Kevin            B-22 Oct 1960

            7        ,Cordelia WORTHEN McFARLAND (Sealed) B-9 Jan      M-
            7        ,              Sp. B-

            7 McFARLAND, Christina Paulette B-12 Sept
            7 McFARLAND, Jon Paul          B-16 Jun 1965
            7 McFARLAND, Justin            B-30 Dec 1974

    6 BUTTERFIELD, Lorna Christina McFARLAND B-16 Feb 1945 M-8 Oct 1964
    6 BUTTERFIELD, Robert L. Sp. B-21 May 1945

            7 BUTTERFIELD, Michelle        B-11 Nov 1966
            7 BUTTERFIELD, Kimberlee       B-21 Nov 1969
            7 BUTTERFIELD, Angie           B-22 Jun 1973

5 STEFFENSEN, Rea Ann CRAM B-17 Dec 1917 M-9 Jul 1937
5 STEFFENSEN, Wesley Lamar, Sp. B-24 Jul 1914

    6 GRAHAM, Sonia STEFFENSEN B-21 Jul 1938 M-25 Jun 1971 Div.
    6 GRAHAM, David Brooks, Sp. B-

            7 GRAHAM, David Lamar          B-3 Jul 1972

    6 STEFFENSEN, Carol B-29 Apr 1941

    6 ROSS, Linda STEFFENSEN B-24 Feb 1945 M-26 Feb 1971
    6 ROSS, Thomas Edward, Sp. B-27 July

            7 ROSS, Tamara                 B-18 May 1972
            7 ROSS, Krist                  B-18 May 1974
            7 ROSS, Nicole                 B- 3 May 1976
            7 ROSS, Amanda                 B-24 May 1977

    6 SIMONS, Nancy STEFFENSEN B-28 Apr 1950 M-22 Jul 1969
    6 SIMONS, Jarold Martell, Sp. B-7 Jul 1946

            7 SIMONS, Stephen              B-9 Jul 1971
            7 SIMONS, Brian                B-9 Mar 1974
            7 SIMONS, Stephanie            B-5 Jun 1975
            7 SIMONS, Michael              B-3 Jun 1977

    6 STEFFENSEN, Scott Cram    B-23 Feb 1954

    6 STEFFENSEN, Kathy         B- 1 Jun 1958

5 CRAM, Victor James B-1 May 1920 D-2 May 1920

5 CRAM, Mark Rasband B-22 May 1921 M-20 Jul 1943
5 CRAM, Melba Marie NIELSEN, Sp. B-24 Feb 1925

    6 GOECKERITZ, Constance CRAM B-27 May 1949 M-2 Jun 1967
    6 GOECKERITZ, Klaus Jochen, Sp. B-25 Jun 1941

            7 GOECKERITZ, Amy              B-10 Aug 1969
            7 GOECKERITZ, Quinn Klaus      B- 6 Mar 1972
            7 GOECKERITZ, Lafe Klaus       B-30 May 1974
            7 GOECKERITZ, Toby Mark        B-26 Nov 1977

    6 CRAM, Vickie          B-12 Nov 1950

    6 OGZEWALLA, Janene CRAM B-21 Aug 1954 M-1 Aug 1974
    6 OGZEWALLA, Roger Lane, Sp. B-30 Mar 1952

            7 OGZEWALLA, Courtney Ann      B-21 Mar 1976
            7 OGZEWALLA, Megan             B-13 May 1978
```

```
        6 CRAM, Mark Nielson B-19 Jun 1956 M-29 Jul 1977
        6 CRAM, Robyn CRUMP, Sp. B-30 Mar 1958

                7 CRAM, Jamie Lynne            B-25 Jun 1978

        6 CRAM, Reed Nielson B-28 May 1958 M-18 Sep 1979
        6 CRAM, Tina Christine DUNN, Sp. B-

        6 CRAM, Kent Nielson B-4 Aug 1959 M-1 Jun 1979
        6 CRAM, Deanne Esther AUBREY, Sp. B-

5 POST, Sarah LeIsle CRAM B-3 Aug 1923 M-28 May 1941
5 POST, William Allsworth, Sp. B-4 Mar 1911

        6 LINDQUIST, Sara Emily POST B-3 Dec 1943 M-28 May 1941
        6 LINDQUIST, James Edward, Sp. B-

                7 LINDQUIST, Robert  Kenneth    B-31 Dec 1965
                7 LINDQUIST, KarylAnne          B-27 May 1968
                7 LINDQUIST, Bethanie           B-31 May 1978
                7 LINDQUIST, Meridyth           B- 2 Feb 1980

        6 POST, Harry Lewis II B-11 Jul 1945 M-
        6 POST, Maxine Sydney LARSEN, Sp. B-

                7 POST, Joshua Wesley           B- 2 Jun 1974
                7 POST, Jamie                   B-30 Oct 1977

        6 POST, William Allsworth Jr. B-19 Jun 1949 M-
        6 POST, Priscilla Ann COYLE, Sp. B-

                7 POST, Leslie Paula            B- 7 May 1976
                7 POST, Lindsay Sara            B-   Oct 1979

        6 POST, Robert Cram B-19 Jul 1952 M-
        6 POST, Helen WITTWER, Sp. B-

                7 POST, Ann Marie               B- 9 Aug 1976

        6 POST, Thomas Cram B-19 Feb 1954 M-
        6 POST, Heidi HILTON, Sp. B-

                7 POST, Thomas Jacob            B- 5 May 1973
                7 POST, John Nathan             B-16 Sep 1975
                7 POST, Nicolas Alsworth        B-24 Dec 1977

        6 POST, John Cram B-21 Jul 1955 M-22 Sep 1977 D-25 May 1980
        6 POST, Jane PERKINS, Sp. B-

                7 POST, John Adam               B-   Nov 1979

        6 POST, Cinda LeIsle       B- 3 Jun 1958

        6 POST, Joseph Cram        B-22 Apr 1963

5 CRAM, Joy Rasband B- 29 Sep 1925 M-18 Jul 1945
5 CRAM, Gertrude Barbara Elizabeth BURGARD, Sp. B-23 Apr 1924

        6 CRAM, Michael Dale B-14 Feb 1947 M-            Div.
        6 CRAM, Leann QUICK, Sp. B-

                7 CRAM, Ekim                    B-

        6 CRAM, Richard Dee B-24 Jul 1950 M-
        6 CRAM, Linda        Sp. B-

                7       Aaron                   B-          (Previous Marriage of Linda)
                7 CRAM, Aja                     B-

        6 CRAM, Victor Joy B-12 Mar 1955
```

```
6 EINBUND, Stacy Kay CRAM B-9 Aug 1959 M-
6 EINBUND, John Sp. B-

        7 EINBUND, Amy Sue                B-

6        , Trudy Ann CRAM B-9 Aug 1959 M-
6        , Ron    Sp. B-

        7            , Daniel             B-

5 CRAM, Thomas Dale B-6 May 1928
5 CRAM, Carolyn Ruth HUTCHINSON, Sp. (1) B-21 Jan 1935 M-7 Oct 1948 Div.
5 CRAM, Helen Catherine Theresa GUERRA, Sp. (2) B-26 Apr 1935 M-29 May 1954

        6        , Carolyn Stephanie CRAM B-29 Jan 1950 M-
        6        ,           Sp. B-

                7        , Boy             B-

6 CRAM, Ronald James B-14 May 1956 M-23 Feb 1978
6 CRAM, Rosann WHITEHEAD, Sp. B-11 Jan 1959

        7 CRAM, Rena                B-27 Dec 1978
        7 CRAM, ReAnne Maurielle        B-18 May 1981
6 HOLMES, Kathryn Elaine CRAM B-2 Jun 1958 M-23 Sep 1976
6 HOLMES, Henry R., Sp. B-22 Sep 1954

        7 HOLMES, Heather Ann        B-    Oct 1978
        7 HOLMES, Heath              B-    May 1979

6 CRAM, Jean Lorraine     B-26 Dec 1959

6 CRAM, Jay Bryan         B-19 Feb 1961

6 CRAM, Thomas Dale II    B-27 Mar 1967

6 CRAM, Tanna Lynne       B- 1 Nov 1970

6 CRAM, Shannon Joy       B-14 Dec 1973

6 CRAM, Justin Lamont     B-14 Apr 1975

6 CRAM, Dalen Jared       B-12 Aug 1976

4 RASBAND, Jennie Hyslop B-19 Sep 1889 D-3 Sep 1904 (Sealed 22 Jun 1910 to Victor Dee CRAM)
```

Jacobina Wells Osborne Murdoch and William Jonathan Clegg

On May 6, 1859, in the sparsely settled village of Springville, Utah, Father was born; the second son to Henry and Ann Lewis Clegg. At thirteen years of age he moved with his parents and Henry Clegg's plural wife, Margaret Ann, and his nine brothers and sisters to Heber Valley, Wasatch County, Utah.

The Clegg family homesteaded a tract of land in southeast Heber Valley and pioneered as few have ever done. Father didn't have the opportunity of attending school more than a few terms. He had to work to help support their large family. He hauled timber from the canyons, helped farm land covered with rocks and sagebrush, and worked in the Clegg sawmill and in the Clegg rock quarry. Many of the red sandstone buildings in Heber still standing today were built with rock from their quarry east of Heber City in Center Creek.

At nineteen years of age Father started to court a pretty young girl by the name of Jacobina Osborne Wells Murdoch, whom he had known from childhood. She, as well as Father, was a native Utah pioneer, born before the railroad came to Utah. She was born in a dugout in the old Indian fort, November 7, 1860, one of the first white children born in the valley. At that time it was called Upper Provo Valley instead of Heber Valley. Father and Mother had sweet voices, often singing together. They attended the dances, dancing barefoot. Father played the drum and violin, which afforded him great pleasure all his life.

Their courtship ended with a happy marriage on December 2, 1880, in the old Endowment House in Salt Lake City, Utah. Apostle Daniel H. Wells performed the ceremony. They were accompanied to Salt Lake by three other couples who were to be married. They traveled in a bobsleigh with quilts and hot rocks to keep them warm. When they returned to Heber, receptions and parties feted the newlywed couples. For a whole week the entire town celebrated.

Their first home was a small log house located in southwest Heber Valley near Mother's parents, John M. and Ann Steel Murdoch. It was there that Tillie and Anabel were born. In 1883, Father built a house on the east side of Main Street, and they moved there. Bina was the first to be born in that home, which still stands at 511 Main Street, Heber. They lived there twelve years. Nettie, the twins (William and Wallace), Malicent, Lewis, and Joy O. were all born in that house. Those were happy childhood days for all of us. We lived near the school and the meetinghouse. Although we had many Indian scares, we had happy times, especially with our numerous cousins who all lived near us.

In 1895 Father purchased a farm in southeast Heber Valley and moved his family there. Father was truly a great pioneer builder, and it was not long until he had a good home and one of the finest barns in Heber, with corrals and sheds. We children had a busy time clearing rocks off the land. Father was a good provider, and we had plenty of milk, eggs, cheese, meat, and potatoes. Fruit wasn't available, but we enjoyed the wild berries that we gathered from the nearby mountains.

We lived on that farm four years. Nora, Henry Murray (who died at birth), and the second set of twins, Verona and Brigham Otis, were born there. Brigham died when three months old.

Father disliked the cold winters and short growing seasons, and when his corn was frozen on August 18, 1899, he was convinced that he should take the advice of his close friend, William Blake, to move to Utah County. Brother Blake had moved to Utah County in 1898 after living in Center Creek near Heber. He came to Heber often to help Father and had told him many times of the advantages of living in Utah County, and also that there was a farm near his for sale. Father came to Vineyard (at that time the boundaries were different and it was called Lake View) and purchased the 160-acre farm from Phil Margaretts, a businessman from Salt Lake.

On November 13, 1899, the family moved to Vineyard. What a move that was! Eleven children, horses, cows, dogs, chickens, furniture—all loaded in wagons. It was hard to leave all our relatives, but we were an excited family.

Baby Verona, Nora, Mother, and I rode down on the train, and what a thrill that was—our first train ride! It had only been two months before that the train had first entered Heber City. I recall very well the celebrations that were staged.

Our house consisted of two rooms and a shanty on the east. It had a dirt floor. Tillie came down a week before we were ready to move to get the house in readiness. The two rooms were an adobe construction and the house wasn't too inviting for such a large family. The lower part of our farm was covered with swamps and alkali beds, and what a job father faced to subdue and drain the desolate, unproductive ground. But that winter was mild and such a change from the cold winters we had lived through in Heber. We lived in the Lake View Ward, Utah Stake, and soon won friends. Tillie and Anabel with their sweet voices were very popular. We all started school at the Vineyard school and I was in the fourth reader. Such a happy winter we had!

But summer came, and there was an epidemic of typhoid fever. That summer brought sorrow, sickness, and death. Our relatives in Heber thought we had made a great mistake in moving there. Dear Tillie contracted typhoid and died June 13, 1900, at the age of nineteen. What a shock! And how our dear parents and all of us did grieve over her passing. Anabel, Wallace, Nora, Joy, and Lewis were all stricken with typhoid. Wallace and Nora had fever for fifty-six days. Such hot days, with little shade on that tin-roofed house, made the fever even worse, I am sure. Nettie, Bina, and Will went to Heber and stayed with Grandpa Murdoch for three months. I helped father and mother nurse the sick, as I had had typhoid in Heber when I was six years old.

On June 15, 1901, Joseph, the eleventh child, was born in Heber at Aunt Nettie McMullin's home. Mother, Nettie, Nora, and Verona stayed up there for two months until the blessed event had taken place. How we all loved Joseph and still do! Anabel took over the housekeeping while mother was gone, and we all helped out. That year father planted two rows of silver-leafed poplar trees in front of his place, and we children carried water to keep them alive. They stood as a landmark for over forty years. It wasn't long until we had a fine orchard and raspberry patch. Fruit was such a treat, as we had never been able to get our fill

in Heber Valley. We children loved our surroundings. The Powell Slough was such an attraction with its abundance of wildlife. Our Heber cousins visited us often, and we did have good times.

Anabel was the first to marry and leave home, but as the years went by, each of us married and started families and homes of our own. We celebrated father's birthday each year, and his loved ones from Heber came and joined us. The lilacs were in bloom and our early garden was such a treat. Our home was the gathering place for old and young. We spent many happy evenings singing—mother with her sweet alto voice and father singing tenor. He often brought out his violin, and we girls would chord on the organ. Those evenings are such pleasant memories now.

Our farm, with its many acres of beets, afforded work for all. We children didn't always get started when school started, nor did we get to stay until it ended for the year. But I think we appreciated school all the more, as we did study hard to pass our grades. Father saw to it that each of us had at least one term at BYU.

During our growing-up period we were stricken with smallpox and were under strict quarantine regulations. We also had scarlet fever and other children's diseases along with the toothaches, earaches, and growing pains. I often wonder how our dear parents survived such ordeals.

Father loved good horses and always had fine teams. We sported a cutter sleigh in Heber and brought the bobsleigh down here but didn't get much use out of it. However, Joy used it many times in later years to give the school children a ride. What a treat for them!

Those were the days of hand plowing, scraping, and harrowing—a far cry from the modern machinery we use today. We did get a disk, Sulky plow, and a Fresno scraper, but the fertilizing was generally spread by manpower—yes, and sometimes girl power! (Anyone who has never spread manure can hardly appreciate this.)

Father took ill in the late fall of 1926 and after nine months of suffering with cancer passed away September 15, 1927. We all missed his wise counsel, and mother dear was so lonely after he left us. She lived six years; then on October 18, 1933, she died of a heart attack. The world seemed so empty without them, but we children can be thankful that we were born of goodly parents. Father's patriarchal blessing said that his posterity would love and honor his memory and hand down his honorable name to generations yet unborn.

We want to make our parents proud of all of us and to be proud of ourselves. I am sure their love extends to everyone who has married into the family and made our name more honorable. As the years go by let us meet the many challenges and problems we are called to face with courage and fortitude, for we know our heritage is of the greatest. Our dear parents will smile their approval on all our good deeds, and I'm sure their desire would be for us to be "firm as the mountains around us" and to "Carry on! Carry on! Carry on!"

Malicent C. Wells

Jacobina Murdoch, age 18.

Pictured from left to right: front row: Mary Verona, William Francis, Jacobina Osborne Wells Murdoch (Mother), William Johnathan Clegg (Father), Anna Isabella Elnora; middle: Joseph Heber; back row: Joy Osborne, Janette Juventa, Lewis, Jacobina, John Wallace, Malicent.

Not Pictured (deceased): Tillie, Henry Murray, Brigham Otis, Thomas Edwin

The four living children of William Johnathan and Jacobina Osborne Wells Murdoch Clegg are: Malicent Wells, 89; Nora Harding, 83; Verona Winter, 80; Joseph H. Clegg, 78.

Other known living descendants include: 49 grandchildren, 226 great grandchildren 3 great, great, great grandchildren, 138 in-laws.

There are 657 total living descendants with 42 deceased. 66 direct line descendants have served missions for the church. (Statistics compiled by Merlene Wells Bailey, August 1979.)

Pictures of Jacobina Murdoch Clegg   taken from a scrapbook

1921

The spring of 1931

1921

Prizes awarded to
Jacobina M. Clegg,
Sarah and Velda
Murdoch for best
Indians at the
Murdoch reunion
August 1924

Taken

March 4, 1924

HUSBAND WILLIAM JONATHAN CLEGG
Birth: 6 May 1859
Place: Springville, Utah, Utah
Chr:
Married: 2 December 1880
Place: Salt Lake City, Salt Lake, Utah
Death: 15 September 1927 Vineyard, Utah, Utah
Burial: 18 September 1927 Provo Cemetery, Utah, Utah
Father: Henry CLEGG
Mother: Ann LEWIS
Other Wives:

WIFE JACOBINA OSBORNE WELLS MURDOCH
Birth: 7 November 1860
Place: Heber, Wasatch, Utah
Chr:
Death: 18 October 1933 Vineyard, Utah, Utah
Burial: 22 October 1933 Provo Cemetery, Utah, Utah
Father: John Murray MURDOCH
Mother: Ann STEEL

Where was information obtained? Marlene W. Bailey & family Records
*List complete maiden name for all females.

1st Child Tillie CLEGG
Birth: 25 September 1881
Place: Heber, Wasatch, Utah
Married to:
Married:
Place:
Died: 13 Jun 1900

2nd Child Anna Isabella CLEGG
Birth: 20 May 1883
Place: Heber, Wasatch, Utah
Married to: Albert Arthur HOLDAWAY
Married: 3 December 1902
Place: Salt Lake City(Temple) Salt Lake, Utah
Died: 20 March 1916 Provo, Utah, Utah

3rd Child Jacobina CLEGG
Birth: 13 November 1884
Place: Heber, Wasatch Utah
Married to:
Married:
Place:
Died: 10 November 1975

4th Child Janette Juventa CLEGG
Birth: 27 October 1886
Place: Heber, Wasatch, Utah
Married to: Joseph William McDONALD Clement DALLEY
Married: 28 June 1909   18 Oct 1940
Place: Midway, Wasatch, Utah Salt Lake Temple
Died: 13 Aug 1977

5th Child William Francis CLEGG (twin)
Birth: 20 November 1888
Place: Heber, Wasatch, Utah *Note: two more -
Married to: Geneva Ann ASTON wives - over
Married: 29 Jun 1908
Place: Salt Lake City(Temple) Salt Lake, Utah
Died: 17 December 1939 Provo, Utah, Utah

6th Child John Wallace CLEGG (twin)
Birth: 20 November 1888
Place: Heber, Wasatch, Utah
Married to: Mary Ellen WADLEY
Married: 21 August 1918
Place: Salt Lake City(Temple) Salt Lake, Utah.
Died: 28 June 1971

7th Child Malicent CLEGG
Birth: 18 September 1890
Place: Heber, Wasatch, Utah
Married to: George Franklin WELLS
Married: 15 December 1915
Died: Salt Lake City(Temple) Salt Lake, Utah.

8th Child Lewis CLEGG
Birth: 11 February 1892
Place: Heber Wasatch, Utah
Married to: Reva Jane STEWART Lena YOUNG Pearson.
Married: 15 January 1925   15 Jan 1946
Place: Salt Lake Temple
Died: 20 July 1968 Provo, Utah, Utah.

9th Child Joy Osborne CLEGG
Birth: 9 January 1894
Place: Heber, Wasatch, Utah
Married to: Oriel Janet GRIFFIN
Married: 10 February 1926
Place: Salt Lake City(Temple) Salt Lake, Utah
Died: 13 December 1969 American Fork, Utah

10th Child Elnora CLEGG
Birth: 6 January 1896
Place: Heber, Wasatch, Utah
Married to: Roland J HARDING
Married: 24 November 1915
Place: Salt Lake City(Temple) Salt Lake, Utah.
Died:

		11th**Child**	Henry Murray CLEGG
		Birth	3 September 1897
		Place	Heber, Wasatch, Utah
		Married to	
		Married	
		Place	
		Died	8 September 1897

		12th**Child**	Brigham Otis CLEGG (twin)
		Birth	7 July 1899
		Place	Heber, Wasatch, Utah
		Married to	
		Married	
		Place	
		Died	29 September 1899

		13th**Child**	Mary Verona CLEGG (twin)
		Birth	7 July 1899
		Place	Heber, Wasatch, Utah
		Married to	Arthur Cyrel WINTERS
		Married	28 June 1927
		Place	Salt Lake City, Salt Lake, Utah
		Died	

		14th**Child**	Joseph Heber CLEGG
		Birth	15 June 1901
		Place	Heber, Wasatch, Utah
		Married to	Ruth SCORUP
		Married	10 February 1931
		Place	Salt Lake City(Temple) Salt Lake, Utah
		Died	

		15th**Child**	Thomas Edwin CLEGG
		Birth	27 September 1903
		Place	Vineyard, Utah, Utah
		Married to	
		Married	
		Place	
		Died	27 September 1903 Vineyard, Utah

		Married to	(2) Mary Malinda MOULTON
		Married	14 May 1913
		Place	Salt Lake City(Temple)Salt Lake, Utah
		Married to	(3) Ida Grace FERGUSON Baum Peay
		Married	29 January 1952
		Place	Provo, Utah, Utah

* 2 & 3 wives of William Francis CLEGG

1 MURDOCH, James 1786-1831
1 MURDOCH, Mary MURRAY, Sp. 1782-1856

2 MURDOCH, John Murray 1820-1910
2 MURDOCH, Ann STEEL Sp. 1829-1909

DESCENDANTS OF-------3 MURDOCH, Jacobina Osborne Wells 1860-1933
3 CLEGG, William Jonathan 1859-1927

B-Birth
M-Married
D-Death
Sp.-Spouse
Div.-Divorced

4 CLEGG, Tillie B-25 Sep 1881 D-13 Jun 1900

4 HOLDAWAY, Anna Isabella B-20 May 1883 M-3 Dec 1902 D-20 Mar 1916
4 HOLDAWAY, Albert Arthur, Sp. B-5 Jun 1881 D-26 Aug 1968

    5 HARDING, Zelda Leora B-17 Jan 1904 M-24 Mar 1926
    5 HARDING, Owen Scott, Sp. B-29 Jan 1905

        6 ANDERSON, Cherie Anabel B-11 Apr 1943
        6 ANDERSON, Niles Odean, Sp. B-25 Sep 1944 M-16 Sep 1966 Div.

            7 ANDERSON, Michelle   B-

        6 HARDING, Robert Owen B-5 Oct 1945 M-
        6 HARDING, Cynthia THOMPSON, Sp. B-

            7 HARDING, Jenifer   B-
            7 HARDING, Christiane   B-
            7 HARDING, Joshua   B-
            7 HARDING, Natalie   B-
            7 HARDING, Stacey Lyn   B-
            7 HARDING, Andrew Scott   B-

    5 HOLDAWAY, Ellis Dee B-17 Jun 1905 M-4 Jun 1931
    5 HOLDAWAY, Clista BECK, Sp. B-8 May 1907

        6 JOHNSON, Lorna Dee HOLDAWAY B-16 June 1932
        6 JOHNSON, De Monte, Sp. B-4 Jun 1925 M-2 Mar 1953 D-12 Jun 1960
        6 BEVAN, R.M. Sp. (2) B-   M-   Div.

            7 JOHNSON, Jeffrey Dee   B- 6 Oct 1953
            7 JOHNSON, Colleen   B- 3 Sep 1954
            7 JOHNSON, James T.   B- 7 Dec 1955 D-7 Dec 1955

            7 JORGENSEN, Rebecca Kay JOHNSON B-19 Dec 1957 M-
            7 JORGENSEN, Jeffery, Sp. B-

                8 JORGENSEN, Kelly   B-

            7 JOHNSON, Gina   B-23 Aug 1960

        6 HOLDAWAY, Marion Kay B-7 Nov 1934
        6 HOLDAWAY, Elaine STOTT, Sp. B-7 Aug 1940 M-31 Jul 1959 Div.

            7 HOLDAWAY, Kraig E   B-12 May 1960
            7 HOLDAWAY, Kris G   B-12 May 1960

        6 HOLDAWAY, Kay MOORE, Sp (2) B-   M-

            7 HOLDAWAY, Brian   B-
            7 HOLDAWAY, Tina (adopted) B-

        6 HOLDAWAY, Sherman Elwin B-3 Jul 1939 M-25 Oct 1958
        6 HOLDAWAY, Kathleen MARSHALL, Sp. B-28 Nov 1938

            7 SUNQUIST, Jill HOLDAWAY B-12 Oct 1960 M-
            7 SUNQUIST, Alan, Sp. B-

            7 HOLDAWAY, Frank Sherman B-15 Nov 1962
            7 HOLDAWAY, Kerri Lynn   B-23 Apr 1968
            7 HOLDAWAY, Jo Anna   B-

        6 HOLDAWAY, Ellis Paul B-3 June 1942
        6 HOLDAWAY, Roberta Wynn BOSWELL, Sp. B-4 Oct 1942 M-15 Feb 1960 Div.

            7 HOLDAWAY, Mark Damon   B-16 Sep 1960
            7 HOLDAWAY, Gregory Paul   B-15 May 1962

        6 HOLDAWAY,   Sp. (2) B-   M-

            7 HOLDAWAY, Derek   B-

6 LEATHAM, Marilyn HOLDAWAY B-2 Aug 1944 M-6 Jun 1962
6 LEATHAM, Kenneth LeRoy, Sp. B-14 May 1939

      7 LEATHAM, Christine   B- 7 Jan 1963

      7 LEATHAM, Kenneth Michael B-29 Apr 1964 M-
      7 LEATHAM, Susan ASHTON, Sp. B-

         8 LEATHAM, John Michael   B-

      7 LEATHAM, Kiberley   B-

6 HOLDAWAY, Nan B-19 Feb 1947

6 HOLDAWAY, Ned B-19 Feb 1947 M-
6 HOLDAWAY,   Sp. B-

      7   B-

5 HOLDAWAY, Alvas LaVar B-24 Aug 1908 M-
5 HOLDAWAY, Alvira Mae BENNETT, Sp. B-10 Aug 1908

      6 PIPKIN, Donna Vee HOLDAWAY B-4 Jan 1937 M-18 Mar 1960
      6 PIPKIN, James Whitney, Sp. B-5 May 1935

        7 PIPKIN, Kaye Re Nell   B-29 Dec 1960
        7 PIPKIN, Lynae   B-17 Nov 1962
        7 PIPKIN, Jill   B- 4 Dec 1965
        7 PIPKIN, Cindy   B-

      6 STEWART, Valene HOLDAWAY B-13 Aug 1938 M-25 Jun 1957
      6 STEWART, Evan Smith, Sp. B-6 Aug 1937

        7 STEWART, Vicky Lynn   B-13 Jul 1958
        7 STEWART, Shyrleen   B-27 Jun 1960
        7 STEWART, Janice   B- 6 May 1962
        7 STEWART, Sheri   B-
        7 STEWART, Mark Evan   B-
        7 STEWART, Michael Evan   B-

      6 BRIDGES, Bonnie HOLDAWAY B-25 Dec 1944 M-18 Oct 1962
      6 BRIDGES, Sheldon Lloyd, Sp. B-25 Sept 1942

        7 BRIDGES, Guy Lloyd   B-24 May 1963
        7 BRIDGES, Lynn LaVar   B- 2 May 1965
        7 BRIDGES, Scott   B-
        7 BRIDGES, Wade   B-

5 HOLDAWAY, Randall Bert B-30 Apr 1910 M-29 Nov 1933 D-12 Apr 1977
5 HOLDAWAY, Ida Marie WAGSTAFF, Sp. B-2 Mar 1911

      6 WILLIAMS, Rita Ann HOLDAWAY B-11 May 1934 M-31 Aug 1956
      6 WILLIAMS, Arlen Cayle, Sp. B-31 Mar 1931

      7 WILLIAMS, Lisa Ann B-23 Oct 1958
      7

         8 WILLIAMS, Charmin   B-

        7 WILLIAMS, James Michael   B-15 Dec 1960
        7 WILLIAMS, Mark Kale   B- 9 Mar 1962
        7 WILLIAMS, Shauna Maria   B- 9 Sep 1965
        7 WILLIAMS, Michael Steven   B- 3 Mar 1968

      6 HOLDAWAY, Klin Morvel B-B-13 Feb 1938 M-4 Mar 1959 D-   1977
      6 HOLDAWAY, Linda GREY, Sp. B-24 Nov 1940
      6   Sp. (2 to wife) B-   M-

        7 HOLDAWAY, Bradley   B-1 Aug 1960
        7 HOLDAWAY, Delayne   B-4 Dec 1961
        7 HOLDAWAY, Shaun Randall   B-4 Sep 1965
        7 HOLDAWAY, Melinda   B-20 Apr 1972

      6 HOLDAWAY, Dennis Lane B-13 Jun 1939 M-21 Aug 1963 Div.
      6 HOLDAWAY, Sherry Avon SKELLY, Sp. B-28 Jul 1942

```
                    7 HOLDAWAY, Travis L          B-14 Oct 1964
                    7 HOLDAWAY, Camille           B-28 Mar 1968

              6 HOLDAWAY, Blaine Randall B-30 Jul 1943
              6 HOLDAWAY, Joyce JENSEN, Sp. B-          M-          Div.
              6 HOLDAWAY, Denise        Sp. (2) B-          M-

              6 MASTERSON, Anabel HOLDAWAY B-31 Jul 1947 M-25 Mar 1966
              6 MASTERSON, Royce Arasmus, Sp. B-31 Jul 1941

                    7 MASTERSON, Troy A.          B-29 Jan 1968
                    7 MASTERSON, Don Royce        B-21 Aug 1971
                    7 MASTERSON, Jerry Reed       B- 1 Mar 1974
                    7 MASTERSON, Amy Marie        B-20 Feb 1977

         5 BRETZ, Inez HOLDAWAY B-11 Nov 1911
         5 HICKS, Val Dunn, Sp. (1) B-22 Jul 1910 M-14 Nov 1930 Div. D-27 Apr 1958
           Winwood, Betty, Sp. (2) to Val B-          M-27 Oct 1954
         5 BRETZ, Frederick Lewis, Sp. (2) B-25 May 1903 M-3 Jun 1944

              6 HICKS, Jo Ann B-19 Aug 1931

              6 HICKS, Val J B-6 Feb 1933
              6 HICKS, Lorna June Frendt, Sp. (1) B-27 Apr 1931 M-22 Jul 1965 Div.
              6 HICKS, Joann REECE Olsen, Sp. (2) B-          M-4 Jul 1972
                Olsen, Larry Sp. (1) B-          M-          Div.

                    RICHEY, Vickie OLSEN B-7 Apr 1958 M-
                    RICHEY, Brent, Sp. B-

                         Richey, Melanie Ann          B-17 Apr 1979

                    OLSEN, Steve             B-16 Jul 1961
                    OLSEN, Valerie           B-27 Jul 1966
                    7 HICKS, Jennifer Allana  B-24 Jun 1974

              6 WARNICK, EuDonne HICKS B-30 Aug 1935 M-15 May 1959
              6 WARNICK, Ray Richard, Sp. B-14 Sep 1934

                    7 WARNICK, Douglas Ray      B-25 Mar 1960
                    7 WARNICK, Susan Kay        B-28 Aug 1962
                    7 WARNICK, Bret Randy       B-29 Nov 1972

              6 HICKS, Gary Lee B-4 Jun 1942 M-9 Jun 1967
              6 HICKS, Robin OLSON Nemelka, Sp. B-22 Oct 1944
                Nemelka, Mark Stephen, Sp. (1) B-          M-          D-          1965

                    NEMELKA, Jeffery          B-29 Jun 1964
                    NEMELKA, Mark             B-14 Apr 1966
                    7 HICKS, Mindy Louise     B-29 Mar 1968
                    7 HICKS, Russell          B-23 May 1970
                    7 HICKS, Joseph Jordan    B- 9 Jun 1975
                    7 HICKS, Judith Elaine    B-18 Mar 1979

              6 CHERRY, Katherine BRETZ Dobbs B-22 Apr 1945
              6 DOBBS, John, Sp. (1) B-30 Sep 1942  M-10 Sep 1965 Div.
              6 CHERRY, Gregory, Sp. (2) B-15 Aug 1948 M-24 Aug 1979
                Cherry, Marien Kaye McKee, Sp. (1) B-          M-15 Apr 1948 Div.-13 Mar 1979

                    7 DOBBS, Hollie Ann        B-1 May 1968
                    7 DOBBS, Heather Marie     B-2 Mar 1970
                    7 DOBBS, John Frederick    B-8 Apr 1973
                    CHERRY, Jamie Craig        B-2 Dec 1969
                    CHERRY, Rachelle           B-27 Apr 1975
                    CHERRY, Michelle           B-30 Oct 1972

   4 CLEGG, Jacobina B-13 Nov 1884 D-10 Nov 1975

         5 HOLLAND, Jena V CLEGG B-24 Apr 1904 M-1 Oct 1930
         5 HOLLAND, William LeGrand, Sp. B-6 Oct 1906 M-1 Oct 1930

              6 HOLLAND, William Hal B-10 Jun 1934 M-5 Oct 1956
              6 HOLLAND, Betty Jeane GIBB, Sp. B-10 Jun 1934

                    7 HOLLAND, Bradley Gibb     B-28 Mar 1958
                    7 HOLLAND, Steven Craig     B-14 Aug 1960
```

```
              7 HOLLAND, Sue Lyn          B- 5 Jul 1965
              7 HOLLAND, Dan Paul         B- 1 Sep 1967
              7 HOLLAND, Kristi           B- 9 Feb 1971


          6 HOLLAND, John Lee B-30 Oct 1940 M-25 May 1967
          6 HOLLAND, Rosemary Siedenhiedel, Sp. B-1 Jul 1943


              7 HOLLAND, Valerie Ann      B- 8 Jan 1969
              7 HOLLAND, Anthony LeGrande B-14 Oct 1972
              7 HOLLAND, Heidie Marie     B-12 Sep 1975

4 DALLEY, Janetta Juventa CLEGG McDonald B-27 Oct 1886 D-13 Aug 1977
4 McDonald, Joseph William, B-24 Aug 1882 M-28 Jun 1909 Div. D-18 May 1955
4 DALLEY, Clement Thomas, B-8 Aug 1896 M-18 Oct 1940 D-
  Dalley, Maria Heida, Sp. (1) B-           M-


        5 McDONALD, Alvin Glen B-12 Jul 1910
        5 McDONALD, Goldie Viola BELCH, (1) B-2 Jul 1910    M-          Div. 15 Sep 1938
        5 McDONALD, Helen STEVENS Stowers, Sp. (2) B-28 Nov 1911 M-14 Jun 1942
          Stowers, Alvin A, Sp. (1) B-           M-14 Jun 1944 Div.


            STOWERS, Beverly Jo  B-31 Dec 1930
            STOWERS, Alvin Rex    B-27 Aug 1932
            STOWERS, Douglas J.   B- 9 Aug 1934


4 CLEGG, William Francis B-20 Nov 1888 D-17 Dec 1959
4 CLEGG, Geneva Ann ASTON, Sp, B-4 Mar 1888 M-29 Jun 1908 D-25 Apr 1912
4 CLEGG, Mary Malinda Moulton, Sp. (2) B-5 Jul 1885 M-14 May 1913 D-25 Jun 1946
4 CLEGG, Ida Malinda Grace FERGUSON Baum Peay, Sp. (3) B-4 Oct 1886 M-29 Jan 1952 D-24 Jan 1958
  Baum, William A. Sp. (1) B-           M-12 Dec 1906
  Peay, William R. Sp. (2) B-           M-2 Apr 1922


        5 CLEGG, Weldon Durwood B-23 Jun 1909 M-30 May 1929 D-29 Mar 1936 Div.
        5 McCARTY, Wanda BARNES Clegg, Sp. (1) B-12 Nov 1908
          Mc Carty, Roy William, Sp. (2) B-           M-14 Oct 1933


            6 DILL, Gail Geneva CLEGG Roberts Casto B-15 Jun 1930
            6 ROBERTS, Ralph Garr, Sp. (1) B-           M-29 Apr 1949 Div.
            6 CASTO, John Desmond, Sp. (2) B- 23 Oct 1927 M-   Oct 1954
            6 DILL, James, Sp. (3) B-           M-3 Mar 1963


                7 ROBERTS, Scott Ralph     B-15 Oct 1950
                7 CASTO, Adrienne          B-      1955
                7 CASTO, Christopher       B-10 Jan 1957

        5 STARLEY, Murl Ann CLEGG B-19 Mar 1911 M-11 Jan 1930
        5 STARLEY, Lynn A, B-4 Sep 1907


            6 STARLEY, Merlyn Clegg B-29 Aug 1930

            6 STARLEY, Ted Dion B-19 Jan 1933 M-7 Apr 1953
            6 STARLEY, Janice Maria Fullmer, Sp. B-21 Dec 1933


                7 STARLEY, Robert Lynn     B- 6 Jan 1954
                7 STARLEY, Fulmer Brent    B-24 Dec 1955
                7 STARLEY, Steven Kyle     B-11 Sep 1964

            6 STARLEY, John Weldon B-21 Oct 1939 M-10 Sep 1962
            6 STARLEY, Judith Rae COCHRAN, Sp. B-10 May 1940


                7 STARLEY, John Todd       B-11 Jul 1963
                7 STARLEY, Amy Lynn        B-30 Apr 1966

        5 LOGAN, Velda CLEGG B-6 Oct1914
        5 LOGAN, John, Sp. B-15 Mar 1914 M-18 Sep 1935 Div. Mar 1960


            6 LOGAN, Richard William B-18 Jun 1940 M-23 Apr 1963
            6 LOGAN, Eileen Marie ALBRECHT, Sp. B-7 Oct 1942


                7 LOGAN, Shannan Lee       B-22 Jun 1968

        5 THOMAS, Zelma Fern CLEGG B-2 Aug 1916 M-11 Oct 1935
        5 THOMAS, George Daniel, Sp. B-3 Apr 1914


            6 THOMAS, Michael Daniel B-4 Jun 1940 M-
            6 THOMAS, Adrienne Alder St. Pierre, Sp. B-


                7 THOMAS, Michael Daniel    B-13 Mar 1964

            6 THOMAS, Malinda Kaye B-9 Aug 1953
```

5 CLEGG, Verlin Moulton B-24 May 1919 M-21 Nov 1938
5 CLEGG, Laberta Dean, Sp. B-20 Jan 1920

    6 *GORNICHEC, De Ann CLEGG* B-27 Jun 1939 M-16 Nov 1960
    6 GORNICHEC, Richard Forsyth, Sp. B-21 Dec 1940

        7 GORNICHEC, Terri Lynne   B-17 Aug 1961
        7 GORNICHEC, Brian Richard B-17 Apr 1965
        7 GORNICHEC, Angela   B-

    6 CLEGG, Larry Verlin B-2 Jun 1942 M-4 Jun 1965
    6 CLEGG, Mary Janette BROWN, Sp. B-19 Sep 1943

        7 *CLEGG, Lesa*   B-
        7 CLEGG, Malinda   B-
        7 CLEGG, Bert Lee   B-
        7 CLEGG, Larry Charles   B-

    6 CLEGG, James Dean B-8 Sep 1945 M-25 Aug 1967
    6 CLEGG, Mary McARTHUR, Sp. B-

        7 CLEGG, Robert Verlin   B-13 Aug 1968
        7 CLEGG, Suzette   B-
        7 *CLEGG, Scott Ross*   B-
        7 CLEGG, Kristine   B-
        7 CLEGG, Mary Ann   B-

5 CLEGG, Murice Alvin B-19 Oct 1922 D-17 Dec 1922

    6 CHAPPELL, Nila Mary CLEGG B-13 Oct 1948 M-
    6 CHAPPELL, Nathan Rex Sp. B-

        7 CHAPPELL, Ryan Christopher B-
        7 *CHAPPELL, Jenifer Marie*   B-

    6 CLEGG, Leland William B-7 Jun 1952 M-
    6 CLEGG, Debra ORTON, Sp. B-

        7 CLEGG, Timothy Leland   B-

    6 CLEGG, Allan Weldon B-8 Sep 1955

    6 CLEGG, Ronald Moulton B-15 Sep 1960

    6 CLEGG, Keith Leon B-14 Mar 1921 M-4 Nov 1947
    6 CLEGG, Fay Lois BRAILSFORD, Sp. B-4 Nov 1930

        7 *CLEGG, Arland K*   B-24 Jan 1949
        7 *CLEGG, Rayanna*   B-17 Oct 1951
        7 CLEGG, Laura Ranae   B- 4 Mar 1959
        7 CLEGG, Jay Lynn   B- 7 Mar 1962

4 CLEGG, John Wallace B-20 Nov 1888 M-21 Aug 1918 D-28 Jun 1971
4 CLEGG, Mary Ellen WADLEY, Sp. B-18 Nov 1897

    5 CLEGG, Wallace Eugene B-13 Dec 1919

    5 CLEGG, La Vere Wadley B-2 Dec 1921 D-28 Aug 1943

    5 MINER, Helen CLEGG B-17 Jun 1924 M-5 Jul 1944
    5 MINER, Richard Keith, Sp. B-9 Jul 1924

        6 MINER, Richard La Vere B-27 Nov 1946 M-20 Mar 1971
        6 MINER, Rhea ROBERTS, Sp. B-

            7 MINER, Steven Richard   B-6 May 1972
            7 *MINER, Stephanie*   B-21 Sep 1973
            7 MINER, Susan   B-26 May 1976
            7 MINER, Sara Ann   B-26 Apr 1978
            7 *MINER, Shane*   B-24 Nov 1979

        6 MINER, Alan Clegg B-1 Nov 1948 M-3 Sep 1970
        6 MINER, Barbara Ann DEDRICKSON, Sp. B-

```
            7 MINER, Michael Alan        B- 8 Dec 1971
            7 MINER, Paul Ray            B-14 Sep 1973
            7 MINER, Bradley  D          B-10 Mar 1976
            7 MINER, Alison Christine    B-25 Aug 1977


        6 MINER, Jane B-6 Apr 1951


        6 CHERRINGTON, Mary MINER B-25 Aug 1953 M-26 Apr 1974
        6 CHERRINGTON, Thomas Merrill, Sp. B-


            7 CHERRINGTON, Jill          B- 6 Aug 1976
            7 CHERRINGTON, Laura         B-23 Jun 1978


        6 MINER, Ann B-15 Aug 1957


        6 MINER, Gary Lynn B-27 May 1959


    5 CLEGG, Howard Daniel B-18 Sep 1926 M-25 Oct 1950
    5 CLEGG, Inez Ann JOLLEY, B-12 Aug 1929


        6 BLEWETT, Patricia Ann CLEGG B-5 Jun 1951 M-14 Feb 1974
        6 BLEWETT, Preston, Sp. B-


        6 MARTIN, Lisa CLEGG B-13 Mar 1954 M-8 Dec 1973
        6 MARTIN, Robert, Sp. B-


            7 MARTIN, Robert Wade        B-27 Jul 1974
            7 MARTIN, Tyler Daniel       B-19 Apr 1976
            7 MARTIN, Becky Ann          B- 9 Nov 1978


        6 JONES, Carrie Dawn CLEGG B-20 Dec 1958 M-6 Apr 1979
        6 JONES, Kirk Paul, Sp. B-


        6 CLEGG, Russell Howard B-30 Jan 1964


    5 CLEGG, Don Ray B-19 May 1929 M-19 Dec 1954
    5 CLEGG, Sophia Alba PANTIN, Sp. B-14 Oct 1935


        6 BERTOLA, Carmen Diane CLEGG B-6 Sep 1957 M-3 Oct 1975
        6 BERTOLA, Edmond Jules, Sp. B-


            7 BERTOLA, Lisa Marie        B-30 Sep 1976
            7 BERTOLA, Wendy Lynn        B-11 Feb 1979
            7 BERTOLA, Melanie Ann       B-11 Feb 1979


        6 CLEGG, Don Wallace     B- 2 Jan 1959
        6 CLEGG, Steven Brian    B-28 Feb 1961
        6 CLEGG, Christine Maria B-11 Oct 1962
        6 CLEGG, Barbara Ivone   B- 6 Jul 1967
        6 CLEGG, Robert Glenn    B- 7 Jul 1968


    5 HYER, Marilyn Gale CLEGG B-6 Dec 1932 M-12 Mar 1958
    5 HYER, Howard Joseph, Sp. B-4 Oct 1930


        6 HYER, Mark Howard      B-23 Dec 1958
        6 HYER, Eric Lee         B-21 Jun 1960
        6 HYER, Reed Joseph      B- 6 Jan 1963
        6 HYER, Collin Robert    B-14 Jul 1966
        6 HYER, Jeffrey Clegg    B-26 Jun 1970


4 WELLS, Malicent CLEGG B-18 Sep 1890 M-15 Dec 1915 D-21 Feb 1982
4 WELLS, George Franklin, Sp. B-22 Mar 1890


    5 BAILEY, Tillie Merlene B-3 Jul 1917 M-15 Feb 1939
    5 BAILEY, Harold, Sp. B-3 Jan 1911


        6 JACKSON, Constance BAILEY B-30 Apr 1940 M-17 Nov 1961
        6 JACKSON, Russel Henry, Sp. B-10 Feb 1938


            7 JACKSON, Jeanne           B-14 Feb 1964
            7 JACKSON, Quinn Bailey     B-
            7 JACKSON, Chad Henry       B-
            7 JACKSON, Drew Russell     B-


        6 BAILEY, Grant B-18 Dec 1941 D-10 Mar 1959
```

6 BAILEY, David Harold B-14 Aug 1948 M-
6 BAILEY, Linda Mary Johnson, Sp B-

    7 BAILEY, Cynthia Louise   B-

6 PRESTON, Cheryl Merlene B-23 Nov 1952 M-
6 PRESTON, Stanley Joseph, Sp. B-

    7 PRESTON, Laura Merlene   B-

5 WELLS, Lewis Franklin B-6 Aug 1920 M-15 Jun 1942
5 WELLS, Helen Mary HENDRICKSEN, Sp. B-24 May 1923

    6 RICE, Lorna Faye WELLS B-18 Mar 1943 M-17 Jun 1964
    6 RICE, Carl James, Sp. B-29 Apr 1939

        7 RICE, Karen Christine   B- 3 Oct 1969
        7 RICE, Mark Arnold   B-20 Jan 1971
        7 RICE, Curtis James   B- 4 Jul 1972

    6 ROYLE, Mary Lou WELLS B-27 Sep 1946 M-8 Jun 1966
    6 ROYLE, Kenneth Mack, Sp. B-7 May 1943

        7 ROYLE, Matthew Todd   B-16 Apr 1971
        7 ROYLE, Brian La Mar   B-11 Mar 1974
        7 ROYLE, Bret Andrew   B- 6 Aug 1979

    6 WELLS, Lewis Franklin Jr. B-11 Mar 1949 M-14 Sep 1973
    6 WELLS, Kimberly Ann GIAQUE, Sp. B-6 Sep 1955

        7 WELLS, Jaycum La Mar   B- 4 Dec 1974
        7 WELLS, Brandon Arnold   B-15 Nov 1975
        7 WELLS, Samantha Dawn   B-17 May 1977

    6 WELLS, George La Mar B-5 Nov 1952 D-21 May 1973

    6 SLYVESTER, Mabel Ann WELLS B-19 Sep 1954 M-   Div.
    6 SLYVESTER, Lewis, Sp. B-

    6 WELLS, John Hendricksen   B-23 Mar 1956
    6 WELLS, Paul Arnold   B- 2 Jul 1958
    6 WELLS, Steven Keith   B-14 Jul 1960
    6 WELLS, Cora Janette   B- 1 Jan 1963

5 WELLS, Leland Joy B-4 Aug 1922 M-27 Mar 1943
5 WELLS, Mary Lorraine WADLEY, Sp. B-6 Oct 1924

    6 OLIVER, Edith Ann WELLS B-5 Jan 1944 M-8 Aug 1964
    6 OLIVER, Rodney Isaac, Sp. B- 23 May 1943

        7 OLIVER, Jedlund Isaac   B-28 Aug 1966
        7 OLIVER, Angie Oliver   B-15 May 1968 D-18 May 1968
        7 OLIVER, Jason Wells   B-12 Oct 1974
        7 OLIVER, Kristie Ann   B- 9 Jun 1976

    6 ANDERSON, Sharon Malicent WELLS B-16 Sep 1946 M-
    6 ANDERSON, Bryant Ford, Sp. B-

        7 ANDERSON, Melinda Joy   B- Feb
        7 ANDERSON, Alisha Noel   B-
        7 ANDERSON, Tyler Ford   B-
        7 ANDERSON, Spencer Wells   B-
        7 ANDERSON, Jared Bryant   B-

    6 GURR, Lynette WELLS B-22 May 1948 M-   Jun
    6 GURR, Cecil F. Sp. B-

        7 GURR, Dax B   B-   1974
        7 GURR, Shalon Lynette   B-   1977
        7 GURR, Slade C   B-   1979

    6 PUGMIRE, Laurel WELLS B-17 Jan 1951 M-
    6 PUGMIRE, Mark Dee, Sp. B-

```
                7 PUGMIRE, Jill Laurel      B-
                7 PUGMIRE, Cheryl Lorraine  B-
                7 PUGMIRE, Mark Glenn       B-
                7 PUGMIRE, Brent Leland     B-


        6 BULLOCK, Mary Lee WELLS B-26 Mar 1954 M-
        6 BULLOCK, Carl Scoville, Sp. B-


                7 BULLOCK, Angela Marie     B-        1974
                7 BULLOCK, Christina Joy    B-
                7 BULLOCK, Benjamin Carl    B-


        6 WELLS, George Leland B-23 Feb 1958
        6 WELLS, Sheryl Lynn MATHWIG, Sp. B-


        6 WELLS, Daniel Wadley    B-15 Jan 1964

5 WELLS, William Thomas B-6 Aug 1927
5 WELLS, Phyllis Marion FOUTZ Farnsworth, Sp. (1) B-13 Jan 1929 M-2 Feb 1949 Div.1960
  FARNSWORTH, James Lee, Sp. (1) B-            M-
5 WELLS, Colene GOODRICH Mahoney, Sp. (2) B-18 Oct 1934 M-31 May 1962
  MAHONEY, A. J. Sp. (1) B-


        FARNSWORTH, Antoinette B-2 Oct 1947


        6 TAYLOR, Rebecca WELLS B-13 Oct 1949 M-
        6 TAYLOR, Terry Lee, Sp. B-


                7 TAYLOR, Brian Kieth       B-
                7 TAYLOR, Terry Lee         B-
                7 TAYLOR, James Wesley      B-


        6 RODGERS, Shauna WELLS B-8 Aug 1951 M-
        6 RODGERS, Edgar Doyle, Sp. B-


                7 RODGERS, Ryan Chase       B-
                7 RODGERS, William Keegan   B-


        6 UNDERWOOD, Angelique WELLS      B-21 Oct 1953 M-
        6 UNDERWOOD, Robert Don, Sp. B-


                7 UNDERWOOD, Robert Don Jr. B-
                7 UNDERWOOD, Carissa        B-
                7 UNDERWOOD, Lacey Janice   B-


        6 WELLS, Kevin Thomas B-8 Apr 1957 M-
        6 WELLS, Laurie Jean MELCHER, Sp. B-


        6 TANNER, Andra Jean Mahoney WELLS (adopted) B-18 Dec 1959 M-
        6 TANNER, Kenard, Sp. B-


                7 TANNER, Ian Kinard        B-


        6 WELLS, Dianna Lee     B-14 Sep 1963
        6 WELLS, Grant William  B-17 Dec 1966
        6 WELLS, Kimberly Kay   B- 7 Dec  ?

5 LARSON, Wilda WELLS B-6 Aug 1927 M-4 Jun 1947
5 LARSON, Desmond Orin, Sp. B-17 Feb 1922


        6 LARSON, Dennis Orin B-19 May 1948 M-
        6 LARSON, Marjorie Carol BRIDGE, Sp. B-


                7 LARSON, Darrin Dennis     B-
                7 LARSON, Leslie            B-
                7 LARSON, Brady Marc        B-


        6 LARSON, Kaye Ellen B-6 Feb 1951


        6 LARSON, Brian Wells B-9 Jun 1952 M-
        6 LARSON, Susan Melissa STROUSE B-


                7 LARSON, Sara Catherine    B-
                7 LARSON, Amy Melissa       B-
```

6 LARSON, Gary William B-17 Dec 1955 M-
6 LARSON, Joni JACKSON, Sp. B-

    7 LARSON, Christian William B-

6 LARSON, Lisa Ann   B-21 Feb 1958

6 LARSON, Layne Desmond B-6 Feb 1963

4 CLEGG, Lewis B-11 Feb 1892 D-20 Jul 1968
4 CLEGG, Reva Jane STEWART, Sp. (1) B-24 Apr 1899 M-15 Jan 1925 D-13 Jul 1942
4 CLEGG, Lena YOUNG Pearson, Sp. (2) B-22 Apr 1899 M-15 Jan 1946 D-13 Oct 1958
  Pearson, Ernest Allen, Sp. (1) B-3 Aug 1898 M-11 Aug 1923 D-15 Feb 1949

5 CLEGG, Floyd Wallace B-25 Dec 1925 M-25 Jan 1950
5 CLEGG, Nina STRATTON, B- 2 Oct 1928

6 CLEGG, Irving Floyd B-5 Feb 1951 D-31 Mar 1956

6 BOWEN, Reva Louise CLEGG B-14 Sep 1952 M-
6 BOWEN, Lon, Sp. B-

    7 BOWEN, Mathew Lewis   B-
    7 BOWEN, Bradley James   B-
    7 BOWEN, Nina Rachelle   B-

6 CLEGG, Ralph Lewis B-3 Jun 1955
6 CLEGG, Diane Helen BROWN, Sp. B-

6 CLEGG, Julie Nina   B-31 Jan 1959

5 CLEGG, Darrel Lewis B-12 Jul 1927 M-12 Dec 1961
5 CLEGG, Beth WARDELL Olson, Sp. B-28 Jul 1935
  Olson,   Sp. (1) B-   M-

6 CLEGG, Darren Lewis B-19 Oct 1962
6 CLEGG, Elayna   B- 1 Sep 1964
6 CLEGG, Jaynann   B-27 Mar 1966
6 CLEGG, Larayn   B- 8 May 1968
6 CLEGG, Dayna   B-
6 CLEGG, Dallin Wardell B- 3 Dec 1974

5 CLEGG, George Udell B-19 Sep 1928 M-6 Nov 1964
5 CLEGG, Phyllis June CULBERT Phister, Sp. B-21 Jun 1931
  Phister, Everet Milton, Sp. (1) B-   M-   Div. 11 Dec 1963

6 CLEGG, Tammy   B-19 Jul 1966
6 CLEGG, Julie Ann   B-17 Aug 1967

5 FRESH, Reva Luana CLEGG B-26 Nov 1930 M-7 Aug 1951
5 FRESH, William Albert, Sp. B-15 Oct 1928

6 FRESH, Stephen William B-30 Mar 1953 M-26 Jul 1975
6 FRESH, Arnella Greco, Sp. B-7 Mar 1953

    7 FRESH, Arianna Polly   B-24 Jul 1976

6 FRESH, Allyn Clegg B-23 Aug 1956 M-28 Dec 1978
6 FRESH, Deborah Lee JENSEN, Sp. B-21 Nov 1958

    7 FRESH, Sherry Luana   B-25 Nov 1980

6 LITTLEFORD, Linda Marie FRESH B-27 Jul 1959 M-15 May 1981
6 LITTLEFORD, Joel Don, Sp. B-

6 FRESH, Lisa Ann   B-23 Jan 1966

5 JENSEN, Norma LuRee CLEGG B-21 Jun 1935 M-29 May 1956
5 JENSEN, Darrell LeGrande, Sp. B-10 Sep 1935

6 JENSEN, Ronald Darrel B-16 Mar 1957
6 JENSEN, Janese   B- 1 Mar 1959
6 JENSEN, Douglas Kay B-17 Aug 1962
6 JENSEN, Kurt James B-12 Oct 1966
6 JENSEN, Andrea   B- 1 May 1971

5 SAVAGE, Anabel CLEGG B-30 May 1937 M-1 Jul 1960
5 SAVAGE, Don Hansen, Sp. B-23 May 1935

```
               6 SAVAGE, Jo Anne        B-30 Apr 1962
               6 SAVAGE, Don Ray        B-19 Nov 1964
               6 SAVAGE, REBECCA        B-19 Nov 1964
               6 SAVAGE, Rhonda         B-10 May 1966
               6 SAVAGE, Rodney Clegg   B-18 Feb 1974
```

4 CLEGG, Joy Osborne B-9 Jan 1894 M-10 Feb 1926 D-13 Dec 1969
4 CLEGG, Oriel Janet GRIFFIN, Sp. B-5 Sep 1900 D-20 Jun 1970

```
        5 SUNDBLOM, Janet Ruth CLEGG B-3 Jun 1927 M-1 Apr 1948 Div. 25 Jun 1948 D-22 Mar 1957
        5 SUNDBLOM, J Charles, Sp. B-

                6 JENSEN, Lauralee SUNDBLOM B-1 Jun 1948 M-22 Nov 1967
                6 JENSEN, Gert Sommer, Sp. B-9 Sep 1940

                        7 JENSEN, Fin Sommer      B-
                        7 JENSEN, Jeni Sommer     B-
                        7 JENSEN, Sara Sommer     B-
                        7 JENSEN, Katie           B-29 Aug 1979

        5 WEBSTER, Margaret Jean CLEGG B-8 Oct 1928 M-12 Sep 1949
        5 WEBSTER, Nelson Junior, Sp. B-24 Feb 1925

                6 WEBSTER, Samuel Joy  B-30 Dec 1951  D-30 Dec 1951

                6 WEBSTER, Jenell CLEGG B-19 Jun 1952

                6 WEBSTER, William Nelson B-11 May 1954

                6 WEBSTER, Janet        B-14 Jan 1956

                6 NIELSON, JoAnn WEBSTER B-29 Apr 1957 M-2 Mar 1978
                6 NIELSON, Mike, Sp. B-

                6 DUNN, Judy WEBSTER B-18 Jun 1960 M-          Div.
                6 DUNN, Rick, Sp. B-

                        7 DUNN, Brandon Wade       B-16 Mar 1979

                6 WEBSTER, Jillene      B-22 Apr 1963

                6 WEBSTER, Joyce        B- 17 Mar 1965  D-17 Mar 1965

        5 CLEGG, Val Joy B-20 Jun 1930 D-5 Jul 1932

        5 CLEGG, Vaughn Thomas B-20 Jun 1930 M-20 Nov 1953
        5 CLEGG, Lola Joyce BOWDEN, Sp. B-10 May 1933

                6 CLEGG, Kerry J  B-9 Sep 1954 M-
                6 CLEGG, Gina JOHNSTON, Sp B-

                        7 CLEGG, Brittany Lane     B-17 Oct 1978

                6 CLEGG, Karl B        B- 7 Dec 1959
                6 CLEGG, Kyle V        B-12 Jan 1962
                6 CLEGG, Kenneth       B-30 Sep 1966
                6 CLEGG, Korene        B-19 Aug 1968
                6 CLEGG, Karen         B-

        5 CLEGG, Morris Griffin B-17 Oct 1933 M-
        5 CLEGG, Patricia BROWN Holdaway, Sp. B-
          Holdaway, LeRoy, Sp. (1) B-

                6 CLEGG, Jonathan Morris B-
                6 CLEGG, Juliane        B-20 Jul 1978

        5 CLEGG, William Ballard B-15 Apr 1937 M-
        5 CLEGG, Carol Kay MILCZAREK, Sp. B-

                6 CLEGG, Steven Todd    B-
                6 CLEGG, Kevin J        B-
                6 CLEGG, Kimberley      B-
                6 CLEGG, Sandi Kay      B-
                6 CLEGG, Randy Brandon  B-
                6 CLEGG, Brian W.       B-11 Sep 1979
```

5 LYSAGER, Emily Ann CLEGG B-27 Jun 1941 M-
5 LYSAGER, Howard, Sp. B-

      6 LYSAGER, Lincoln   B-
      6 LYSAGER, Jefferson   B-
      6 LYSAGER, Tyler   B-
      6 LYSAGER, Holly Ann   B-21 Apr 1978

4 HARDING, Elnora CLEGG B-6 Jan 1896 M-24 Nov 1915
4 HARDING, Roland J, Sp. B-23 Jul 1893 D- Jan 1975

    5 HARDING, Vernile B-4 Apr 1917 D-21 Feb 1920

    5 ROWLEY, Leah Nora HARDING B-14 Sep 1918 M-14 Sep 1936
    5 ROWLEY, John Reed, Sp. B- 12 Jan 1918

      6 PAGE, Betty Lou ROWLEY B-13 Jan 1938 M-28 Jun 1956
      6 PAGE, William H, Sp. B- 30 Oct 1937

        7 PAGE, Robert Joseph B-27 Mar 1957 M-20 Apr 1979
        7 PAGE, Joy GYLLENSKOG, Sp. B-

        7 PAGE, Lori Ann   B-20 Jun 1960
        7 PAGE, Carie Lyn   B-20 Jun 1965

      6 ROWLEY, Jerry Reed B-25 Oct 1942
      6 ROWLEY, Judy Ann DAVIS, Sp. B-18 Apr 1942 M-18 Mar 1960 Div.
      6 ROWLEY, Delores O'CONNEL, Sp. (2) B-21 Nov 1943 M-3 Jun 1972 Div.
      6 ROWLEY, Linda HAWKINS, Sp. (3) B-30 Jan 1943 M-24 Jun 1977 (2 Children Prev.
                                                                       Marriage)

        7 ROWLEY, Trina Dee   B- 6 Aug 1960
        7 ROWLEY, Debra Ann   B-29 Jan 1962
        7 ROWLEY, Troy Reed   B-24 Dec 1962
        7 ROWLEY, James Scott   B-19 Jan 1964

        7 ROWLEY, Jay Reed   B- 6 Jan 1974
        7 ROWLEY, Shelby   B 30 Jan 1976

      6 HEGSTED, Dianne ROWLEY B-14 May 1945 M-24 Sep 1964
      6 HEGSTED, John Glen, Sp. B-13 Oct 1944

        7 HEGSTED, Wyndy   B-29 Sep 1967
        7 HEGSTED, Dezerene   B-
        7 HEGSTED, David Glen   B-   1976

      6 PETERSON, Delone ROWLEY B-15 Aug 1949 M-
      6 PETERSON, James E., Sp. B-

      6 ROWLEY, Calvin Ricky B-6 Jan 1953 M-
      6 ROWLEY, Barbara BRIMHALL, Sp.

      6 ROWLEY, Ronald K B-6 Sep 1955 D-19 Sep 1955

    5 LOVELESS, Verna V HARDING B- 22 Jun 1921 M-15 Jul 1943
    5 LOVELESS, Gail C, Sp. B-5 Aug 1921

      6 LOVELESS, Eric Gail B-25 Apr 1946 M-
      6

      6 SUTHERLAND, Nican LOVELESS B-16 Feb 1949 M-
      6 SUTHERLAND, Brent, Sp. B-

      6 LOVELESS, Rayland B-14 Oct 1956 M-
      6 LOVELESS, Linda   Sp. B-

    5 HARDING, Eldon Roland B- 19 May 1923
    5 HARDING, Golda Norlyene OHRAN, Sp. B-13 Nov 1926 M-26 Jun 1946 Div.

      6 HARDING, Eldon Randy B-11 Oct 1947 M- Apr 1979
      6 HARDING, Susan CHAPMAN, Sp. B-

      6 HARDING, Roland Duane B-2 Aug 1949 M-20 Jan 1972
      6 HARDING, Vivian KITCHEN, Sp. B-27 Aug 1951

```
          7 HARDING, Benjamin Roland   B-18 Dec 1972
          7 HARDING, Virginia Anne     B-15 Jun 1974
          7 HARDING, Kristine          B-25 Aug 1976


     6 HARDING, Carl Lance   B-14 Dec 1951

     6 HARDING, Gary Mark    B-29 Mar 1955

     6 THOMAS, Debra Kay HARDING B-15 Oct 1956 M-    Aug 1976
     6 THOMAS, Nicholas, Sp. B-

          7 THOMAS, Nikki Ann          B-      1977
          7 THOMAS, Shannan Marie      B-      1979

5 HARDING, Alvin Clegg B-10 Apr 1925 M-18 Aug 1945
5 HARDING, Marjorie Bernice STUBBS, Sp. B-4 Aug 1927

     6 HARDING, Sharlene     B-14 Nov 1945

     6 WILDE, Linda HARDING B-19 Jun 1947 M-15 Jul 1967
     6 WILDE, Norman Fred, Sp. B-12 Dec 1942

          7 WILDE, Jennifer            B-
          7 WILDE, Jared               B-

5 HAWKINS, Mary Louise HARDING B-27 May 1927
5 HAWKINS, Douglas Ray, Sp. B- 27 Apr 1927 M-2 Sep 1944 Div.   Dec 1952
5 LARSEN, Udell, Sp.(2) B-              M-

     6 HAWKINS, Douglas Craig B-5 Apr 1945 M-
     6 HAWKINS, Karen Jean DODGEN, Sp. B-

          7 HAWKINS, Desiree Autumn    B-
          7 HAWKINS, Donielle Brooke   B-
          7 HAWKINS, Dusty Lynn        B-

     6 HAWKINS, Michael Ray B-3 Oct 1946
     6 HAWKINS, Shauna FRAMPTON, Sp. B          M          Div.

          7 HAWKINS, Benjamin Cory     B-

     6 HAWKINS, Roland Jeffrey B- 17 Jul 1951
     6 HAWKINS, Connie LARSEN, Sp. (1) B-       M-         Div.
     6 HAWKINS, Patti WRIGHT, Sp. (2) B-        M-

          7 HAWKINS, Michael Craig     B-
          7 HAWKINS, Laura Lee         B-        (Mother-Patti Wright)

5 HARDING, Dale J B-27 Jun 1929
5 HARDING, Joyce LaRue FARNSWORTH, Sp. (1) B-15 Sep 1929 M-19 Jul 1948 Div.
5 HARDING, Sylvia         Sp. (2) B-          M-

     6 BROWN, Stephanie HARDING B-4 Jun 1949 M-     1967
     6 BROWN, Daniel, Sp. B-

     6 HARDING, James Dale B-19 Jul 1950  D-9 Aug 1950

     6          Susan HARDING B-4 Sep 1951 M-
     6          ,        Sp. B-

     6 HARDING, Dee J B-26 Oct 1952

     6          , Julie HARDING B-1 Apr 1955 M-
     6          ,        Sp. B-

     6 HARDING, Rondo        B- 5 Feb 1961
     6 HARDING, Robbie       B-20 Oct 1962

     6 HARDING,              B-
     6 HARDING,              B-
```

4 CLEGG, Henry B-3 Sep 1897 D-3 Or 8 Sep 1897

4 CLEGG, Brigham Otis B-7 Jul 1899 D-29 Sep 1899

4 WINTERS, Mary Verona CLEGG B-7 Jul 1899 M-28 Jun 1927
4 WINTERS, Arthur Cyril, Sp. B-28 Sep 1894 D-7 Mar 1973

     5 WINTERS, Arthur Wayne B-26 Aug 1929 M-16 Nov 1957
     5 WINTERS, Marva TOONE, Sp. B-20 Jan 1936

          6 WINTERS, Donna   B- 1 Oct 1961
          6 WINTERS, David Wayne B- 1 Nov 1963
          6 WINTERS, Kent Lee   B- 6 Sep 1967
          6 WINTERS, Colleen   B-25 Aug 1969
          6 WINTERS, Linda   B- 3 Jun 1972

     5 JONES, Litha Verlene WINTERS B-26 Dec 1931 M-19 Jul 1960
     5 JONES, Dale Wayne, Sp. B-21 Aug 1934

          6 JONES, Rebecca Ann B-21 Mar 1962
          6 JONES, LaMar Dale   B-20 May 1964
          6 JONES, Perry Lynn   B- 9 Apr 1967
          6 JONES, Joel Wayne   B-17 Apr 1969

     5 WINTERS, Arlene B-26 Dec 1931 D-28 Dec 1931

     5 WINTERS, Weston Derl B-29 Mar 1933 M-29 Nov 1957
     5 WINTERS, Carol Sue TRIMBLE, Sp. B-21 Oct 1936

          6 WINTERS, Wendi Sue   B-15 Dec 1959
          6 WINTERS, Cari Lou   B-14 Jun 1963
          6 WINTERS, Noel Weston B-30 Aug 1967

     5 MOOY, Mary Wanda WINTERS B-19 Apr 1935 M-19 Sep 1955
     5 MOOY, William Frederick, Sp. B-19 Mar 1932

          6 MOOY, William Arthur B-22 Jun 1956
          6 MOOY, Mary Analeen   B-29 Mar 1958
          6 MOOY, Starla J   B- 4 Jun 1962
          6 MOOY, Daniel Fredrick B-25 May 1968

     5 WINTERS, Garry Orlan B-5 Aug 1938
     5 WINTERS, Carole Jean FOSTER, Sp. (1) B-12 Dec 1939 M-1 Apr 1959 Div.
     5 WINTERS, Brenda Jeanne COLLINGS Roberts B-3 Nov 1939 M-
       Roberts,   Sp. (1) B-

          6 WINTERS, Shelly Dee   B- 2 Mar 1960
          6 WINTERS, Gary Douglas B-11 Jan 1964

          Roberts, Larry Gene   B-   M-
          Roberts, Terrie JENKINS, Sp.

          Norton, Carolyn ROBERTS B-   M-
          Norton, Kevin, Sp. B-

     5 WINTERS, Cyril Arnell B-28 Jul 1939
     5 WINTERS, Patricia BLAKENSHIP Friess, Sp. B-4 Dec 1946 M-26 Nov 1971 (seal-28 Aug 1975)
       Friess, Mark, Sp. (1) B-   M-   Div.

          6 WINTERS, Richard Michael Friess B-26 Apr 1967
          6 WINTERS, Kimberly Richele Friess B-14 Oct 1969
          6 WINTERS, Darren Christopher   B-24 Dec 1972

4 CLEGG, Joseph Heber B-15 Jun 1901 M-10 Feb 1931
4 CLEGG, Ruth SCORUP, Sp. B-9 Jun 1908

     5 PETERSON, Ruth Jolene CLEGG Crane B-6 Feb 1932
     5 CRANE, Raymon Doyle, Sp. (1) B-29 Jan 1932 M-15 Jun 1957 Div. 14 Jun 1959
     5 PETERSON, Clayton Reed, Sp. (2) B-19 Jul 1932 M-12 Jun 1962

          6 CRANE, Raylyn   B- 5 May 1958
          6 PETERSON, Reed C   B-28 May 1966
          6 PETERSON, Ron J   B-

     5 RUSHTON, Ora LeAnn CLEGG B-14 Sep 1934 M-9 Jun 1953
     5 RUSHTON, Darrel Young, Sp. B-20 Nov 1930

```
        6 RUSHTON, Stephen Darrel B-15 Apr 1954 M-
        6 RUSHTON, Mabel Deborah BURKE, Sp. B-

        6 RUSHTON, David Mark B-   Oct 1955 M-
        6 RUSHTON, Geraldine SMITH, Sp. B-

                7 RUSHTON, Emily Elizabeth   B-
                7 RUSHTON, Christopher David B-

        6 CAMERON, Julie Ann RUSHTON B-15 May 1957 M-
        6 CAMERON, Joseph Rod, Sp. B-

                7 CAMERON, Carrie Lisa      B-
                7 CAMERON, Darrel Brodie    B-

        6 RUSHTON, Jeffery Lynn B-4 Sep 1958

        6 RUSHTON, Hal Jay  B-7 Dec 1959 M-
        6 RUSHTON, Sandra Lee JOHNSON, Sp. B-

        6 RUSHTON, Kent Shaun   B-29 Apr 1965

        6 RUSHTON, Jay Nathan   B-              (Adopted)

    5 CLEGG, Arla B-18 Jan 1936

    5 CLEGG, Joseph Halvor B-23 Jul 1937 M-13 Jun 1962
    5 CLEGG, Miriam WEBB, B-22 Apr 1943

        6 CLEGG, Ruth          B- 1 Jun 1966
        6 CLEGG, Maren         B-17 Jan 1969
        6 CLEGG, Jens Halvor    B-17 Feb 1971
        6 CLEGG, Michael Joseph B-12 Feb 1974
        6 CLEGG, Joshua Webb    B-10 Sep 1975
        6 CLEGG, Christian Thomas B-14 Oct 1978

    5 CLEGG, Wildon Jonathan B-17 Nov 1940 M-27 Jan 1964
    5 CLEGG, Alive LaRae SHAFFER, Sp. B-9 Aug 1944

        6 CLEGG, Alice Gabrielle  B-2 Nov 1965
        6 CLEGG, Kerri Jeannine   B-
        6 CLEGG, Jonathan Daniel  B-
        6 CLEGG, Jennifer Lynn    B-
        6 CLEGG, Blaine William   B-
        6 CLEGG, Mitchell Adam    B-

    5 JAMES, Edith DaLee CLEGG B-23 May 1944 M-
    5 JAMES, David H., Sp. B-

        6 JAMES, Jennifer        B-
        6 JAMES, Rebecca Elena    B-
        6 James, Daniel Vance     B-

4 CLEGG, Thomas Edwin B-27 Sep 1903 D-17 Sep 1903
```

Thomas Todd Murdoch and Sarah Ingeborg Hansen

It has now been fourteen years since John and Ann Murdoch have left their home amid the beautiful heathered hills in Scotland to come and settle with the Saints in Utah. Hardship, heartache, and lots of hard work and faith have been their lot, and desiring to be true pioneers, they had, in 1860, come to settle in the beautiful Heber City, Utah, among the Wasatch hills, John, having taken a plural wife, Isabella Crawford, in 1862, built a large and comfortable home for his large family.

It was under these pleasant circumstances that Thomas Todd Murdoch was born on March 4, 1866. A beautiful Scotch lad, with many adoring sisters, his childhood was very pleasant and he said he never really knew which of the women was his mother until his long blond ringlets had to be cut when he was six years old and his mother, Ann, cried. Thomas was the eldest of six brothers that were born during the next eight years, and the boys were taken to the field at an early age by their father to learn how to till, sow, and harvest the crops. They also learned how to care for the sheep and cattle with their father, as he kept a nice flock of sheep that went to the southern mountains in the summer to range. School was a must, and Thomas was an apt student. He learned to love good books and quoted often some of the poems and quotes of famous authors. He was very strong in his arms and being small in stature, amazed many with his ability as a wrestler. His youth was spent pleasantly in the community where he grew up, and he was then privileged to attend the BYU Academy for two years.

Late in the 1890s, Tom and his brother, Brigham, made a trip to Idaho to look over the vast prairie of tall grass, clear streams, and rich sagebrush land surrounded by the majestic mountains as it had been described to them. They were not disappointed by what they saw, and in 1901 they decided to come to this area of the Snake River Valley and take up their homesteads in the small community called Farnum.

They arrived in Rexburg, Idaho, where the railroad ended at that time, with their livestock and machinery in March, just as winter was having its last fling. A severe blizzard greeted them, and it was with difficulty that they found hay and shelter until they could push on some thirty miles to the northeast to their land. They worked hard to develop their land, using their hand plows and horses to break up the prairie and soon had much of their 160 acres under cultivation. They were busy with other men in the community surveying and building canals and ditches so they could water. In 1903, Brigham married Luann Hammon, a beautiful girl from Wilford, Idaho. Dad continued to spend summers with them, returning to Heber City and the vicinity to spend part of the winters. Luann used to chide him for remaining a bachelor, to which he answered, "I will yet live to hold my grandchildren on my knee."

In December of 1907, Thomas received a call to serve a mission to the central states, headquartered in Texas. He gladly answered the call and was set apart in Salt Lake City. As all other missionaries of that time, he traveled without purse or scrip, and had many wonderful and valuable experiences. He returned in December of 1909, in time to attend his mother's funeral.

He resumed his farming and noted that the community was growing. They now had a post office and store. A church house had been built and dedicated, and a rock schoolhouse built. The land was all taken up, and it was a thriving Mormon community. Dad fiddled at the dances while Uncle Brig chorded on the piano accompanied by a neighbor who played banjo and guitar along with another who played the harmonica and the accordion. The years passed pleasantly, and Thomas was called to go on a second short-term mission in 1914, with headquarters in St. Louis, Missouri. Again he accepted and went to do the Lord's work.

During the summer of 1911, a lovely young girl, Sarah Hansen, had spent the summer at the home of an uncle, Hans Nielsen, whose farm adjoined the

Murdoch brothers' farms, and she had enjoyed many evenings with Thomas and a nephew, Piercy McMullin, as Thomas played the violin and they sang and danced. During this time they tried to teach Sarah the gospel, but being sixteen, and not having heard much about the Mormons, she was unimpressed. During the years of 1914–15, she met Piercy McMullin in Salt Lake City. He was delighted to see her and shared a letter with her that he had just received from Thomas. It said in part, "I am still looking for the future Mrs. Murdoch, but she will have to be an LDS woman." Piercy asked Sarah to write to Thomas, which she did. She was living with and working for the Warren Snow family, who were very good LDS people. She had accompanied them to Church and now confided in Mrs. Snow concerning Thomas. When Thomas returned in June, their friendship quickly turned to love and after three dates they decided to be married. Sarah was baptized July 13, 1915, and they were married at the Warren Snow home July 15, 1915. They returned to Salt Lake for October Conference, and at this time they were sealed in the Salt Lake Temple for time and eternity.

They returned to Farnum to the modest home that Thomas had built for them and settled into the community life of Farnum, both being active in the Farnum Ward.

During the next few years two sons, Thomas Todd and LaVaughn Hansen, were born to them, and life was good. World War I was just ending, and the war clouds cleared away. Thomas and Brigham decided they would rent their farms, and moved across the state to Rupert, Idaho, where the winters were not so harsh and they could grow more diverse crops. While they were living there their first daughter, Della Ann, was born. Hard times came upon them, and in 1923 they decided to move back to Farnum and resume their occupation there. Soon two more daughters, Clara Marie and Betty Mae, blessed their home. Thomas was a kind and loving father who truly enjoyed his children, and many happy hours were spent teaching his children to sing and dance and enjoy life. In 1927, another son joined the family and was given the name of Gilbert Dean.

Thomas was busy in his Church duties and was a religion class teacher in the grade school. Walking was a way of life, because Thomas had no car and the horses needed their rest on Sunday. He would walk six miles to town to catch the train to ride the fifteen miles to St. Anthony to stake meetings and stake conference, and if the weather permitted, he sometimes started on foot to St. Anthony. He walked behind the plow and the harrow as he prepared the ground for planting, and was always seen in the summer with a shovel over his shoulder as he "tended" the water on his farm. No matter how tired he was, he always brought out his violin and stood in the door of his home in the summer or in the house in the winter and played beautiful music for us. He truly loved that violin.

Our prayers were said at his knee, and he would scratch our backs as we prayed (sometimes very long prayers were said). Then when we were all in bed, we always expected an interesting story from him about his boyhood days, encounters with the Indians, lonely nights in the mountains as he herded sheep, or fun times he had in his family. Ours was truly a happy home!

In 1928 tragedy struck the home—Thomas's oldest son, Todd, died of Diphtheria: This tugged at the tender heart of Thomas, his wife, and his family. Much love and consideration came to us at this time; also a call for Thomas to be the bishop of the Farnum Ward. His feelings are best expressed in this letter that was written to his sister, Janett McMullin, at this time.

Father's Birthday (John Murray)
Drummond, Idaho
December 28, 1928
Mr. and Mrs. H.L. McMullin
Dear Folks. How I would like to see you and visit with you this Christmas time. This has been a wonderful Christmas in many ways. I think the spirit of peace on earth, good will to man, is more in evidence this year than any time in my history.

I am trying to bear my burden alone and not stir up feelings of others, but oh, how I miss my poor boy. I have been touched at the death of loved ones and have tried to share some of the sorrow, but this has been the greatest trial that has ever come to me.

We are all well and have spent a splendid Christmas visiting and feasting and working, and with all we have much to be thankful for. We have plenty to eat and wear and a house to shelter us, so there is nothing to complain of after all. We received a very valuable present from Bro. William Lindsay. A record of our Fathers and Mothers and sisters and brothers, and it has certainly caused many things to pass thru my mind. My relatives mean a great deal to me and as time goes on I think of our parents what they sacrificed in order that we might enjoy the great blessings of being privileged to live in this wonderful land blessed above all other lands, also that we might enjoy the blessings of the Gospel which gives us the assurance that we shall meet our loved ones again, and not only meet them but love them and go on unto perfection.

I feel that I should try and say some-thing to encourage you although not given to poetry my-self I ran across a few lines in a book which brought many happy thoughts to my mind and caused me to think of you folks in your home. I will try and write a few lines and trust it will cause a few old time thoughts.

"They are left alone in the dear old home
After so many years.
When the house was so full of frolic and fun,
Of childish laughter and tears.

They are left alone, they two once more
Beginning life over again.
Just as they did in the days of yore
Before they were nine and ten.

And the table is set for two these days
The children went one by one
Away from home on their separate ways
When the childhood days were done.

How healthily hungry they used to be!
What romping they used to do!
And Mother—for weeping—can hardly see
To set the table for two.

They used to gather around the fire
While someone would read aloud
But whether at study or work or play
'Twas a loving and merry crowd

And now they are two that gather there
At evening to read or sew.
And it seems almost too much to bear
When they think of the long ago.

Ah well—all well 'tis the way of the world,
Children stay but a little while.
And then into other scenes are whirled
Where other homes beguile.

But it matters not how far they roam
Their hearts are fond and true,

And there's never a home like the dear old home
Where the table is set for two."

Jan. 2, 1929

Since writing the foregoing we have been hurled into another year. Our cold weather has turned warmer and we are getting a little more snow. We are all at home tonight, the children are playing hide and seek, Sarah is singing the baby to sleep, and I am trying to finish my letter to you. Bro. Brig has been here all day looking over the family record and helping to complete the year's report on the ward books. I have lately been appointed Bishop of the Farnum Ward. Lester C. Hendrickson, first and George Kidd, second counselors, Brigham Murdoch, ward clerk. We are to be set apart at our quarterly conference which convenes at St. Anthony Jan. 12th and 13th. I wish to relate a little history. When Brig and I were getting ready to move to Idaho, Father said, "Boys, I would like to give you a patriarchal blessing before you go." I will not attempt to write all of the blessing at this Lime, but he said among other things, "Brother Thomas, the Lord has had his eye over you. Your life has been preserved for a wise purpose. A great work lies before you which you were ordained in the eternal world. Therefore prepare thine heart to receive the revelations of the spirit of God that shall come upon you. Therefore seek diligently to understand the whisperings of the spirit for a great work is before you, and great blessings await you, all which shall be fulfilled in the due time to the Lord."

I have often wondered why so much responsibility has come to me all unsot on my part, and wonder if I will be able to measure up to the great responsibility of Bishop of this ward. I hope you folks are improving in health and that you are receiving the kind treatment to which you are entitled from family, kindred and friends, and I feel assured that you will never lack for anything that loving hands can do, or willing hearts can accomplish. We received words of simpathy, and comfort from far and near during our hour of sorrow, and we appriciate the same. We long to hear from all of you. Brig's folks are all well and we are all well. Lizzabell, Uncle Willie's daughter, was here to visit us the other day. Aunt Mary is feeling fairly good. Georgeinnia is in very poor health; has been under a very serious operation.

Uncle Lew Hawkes and family are well. We all join in sending love and best wishes for a Happy New Year, and would be pleased to get a good long letter soon.

Asking God's blessings upon you all

T.T. Murdoch & Family

Drummond, Idaho

Dad was a good bishop, walking two miles to the church. The custodian job was also part of being bishop, and since one large heating stove was all the heat they had, he had to be there early to get it warm for everyone as well as keeping the building clean. He was very compassionate and a good counselor for those in need.

In 1930, his youngest son, Lynn Ray, joined the family. By now we were in the throes of a depression, and just to make a living was a big task. Dad rode a work horse six miles every day and in the cold of winter just to work to buy a few commodities for his family. Our parents were good managers, and we were never in want for a warm home, good food, and clean clothing. The winter wood was hauled from the mountains by team and wagon, then sawed and chopped for our fuel. We had no electricity or modern conveniences in our small, four-room home.

In 1936, Dad and Mom decided to leave the farm and move to Idaho Falls, some fifty miles south, where there would be more opportunities for the family to find work. It was with some sadness that they said good-bye to their family, friends, and way of life in Farnum.

The Lord had a work for them to do in Idaho Falls, and they were immediately involved in the small branch in their vicinity. Dad was called to be a stake missionary and Mom was called to be the Relief Society president. Their home began to be the gathering place for young and old, and they knew they had made a good move.

On July 15, 1940, Dad and Mom celebrated their silver anniversary with all their children and many of their relatives celebrating with them. It was a good time in their lives. They were very comfortable in their home, and the yard and garden blossomed under their care. In November of this year, their first grandchild was born, and Thomas fulfilled his prophecy that he would yet live to hold his grandchildren on his knee. He blessed this baby and gave his name, then eight years later confirmed him a member of the Church. He had the privilege of holding five grandchildren on his knee and enjoyed them very much.

During the 1940s, four more of his children married, and now Tom and Sarah were back to just the two of them, since their youngest son, Lynn, was in the Army. In all these years the family never failed to be together on Dad's birthday; it was a just cause for a good family get-together. Betty and her husband lived in the East and were not always able to be there after her marriage in 1946, and we surely missed them.

Family reunions were still the big event of the year, and Bessie Dawson was very good to help get Dad and Mom to Utah to enjoy them. Thomas reflected much on the goodness of his parents, brothers, and sisters, most of whom were gone by now, and he began to long for the day when he would be able to be with them once more.

In April of 1953, his daughter, Clara Marie, passed away suddenly and was buried on her thirtieth birthday. The snow was falling softly in the open grave, and Aunt Luann said, "This means another member of the family will go within six months." And thus it was that Thomas Todd Murdoch passed away on October 21, 1953. Another of God's chosen sons had finished so well his mission on this earth, having endured to the end.

Mere words cannot express the greatness, the goodness, and the effect of his life here on earth. The hardships, the joys, and the sorrows of this life were a true test of his faith. We follow a noble father!

Thomas's wife, Sarah, continued to guide the family and care for their home as she had cared for our father and looked after him so patiently for the thirty-eight years they had together. She recognized what a great and good man Thomas was and taught us all to have a great love and respect for him. She honored his priesthood and knew of its power. Sarah now lives with her daughter and husband, Della and Joe, and enjoys the companionship of her children, grandchildren, and great-grandchildren. She is an example to all of us, and we love her for her sacrifices and the hard work she did to bring about this family. This is the song that Thomas loved and sang so often to Sarah, and it holds dear memories for all of us:

Dear Heart, I find we're growing old, the years so
  quickly pass away,
Since first we met have left their trace upon us both
  in threads of gray.
The rose has faded from your cheeks, but never has
  your heart grown cold
Nor do we love each other less, Dear Heart,
  because we're growing old.

To me you're fairer than you were the day I won
you for my bride,
And held you fondly in my arms, unconscious of all
else beside
Your faded cheeks and whitened hair have yet for
me some charms untold,
That only strengthens with each year, Dear Heart,
now we are growing old.

Full forty years have passed since then, years filled
with only purest joy.
No cloud has ever crossed our path, our bliss has
been without alloy.
And when we reach that golden shore, and pearly
gates for us unfold,

God grant that both may enter in, Dear Heart, and
never more grow old.

Chorus:
Dear Heart and never more grow old,
Dear Heart, and never more grow old.
God grant that both may enter in and never more
grow old.

It is great to be a part of this great heritage we have
in the Murdoch family!

Della Ann Murdoch Davis Perry and Sarah I. Hansen
Murdoch

Tom and Sarah's family in 1942. Left to right, back row: Betty Mae, Clara Marie, Della Ann, LaVaughn Hansen. Front row: Lynn Ray, Thomas Todd Murdoch, Sarah Ingeborg Hansen Murdoch, Gilbert Dean.

The home Thomas had built for his bride in 1915, Farnum, Idaho.

Tom and Sarah's home in Idaho Falls, Idaho

Sarah Hansen Murdoch
as a young girl

HUSBAND   THOMAS TODD MURDOCH
Birth   4 March 1866
Place   Heber City, Wasatch, Utah
Married   15 July 1915
Place   Salt Lake City, Salt Lake, Utah
Death   21 October 1953
Place   Idaho Falls, Bonneville, Idaho
Burial   24 Oct 1953
Place   Ashton, Fremont, Idaho (Pineview Cemetery)
Mother   Ann STEEL
Father   John Murray MURDOCH
Other Wives

WIFE   SARAH INGEBORG HANSEN
Birth   2 May 1895
Place   Odense, Funen, Denmark
Death
Place
Burial
Place
Mother   Anna Mette ANDERSON
Father   Hans Peter HANSEN
Other Husbands
Information from James & Mary Murray Murdoch Family
Thomas Todd & Sarah I. Hansen Murdoch Family Records

1ST CHILD   Thomas Todd MURDOCH
Birth   23 November 1916   Farnum,Fre.,Idaho
Married
Date
Place
Death   17 September 1928 Farnum,Fre.,Idaho
Burial   Ashton,Fre.Idaho

2ND CHILD   LaVaughn Hansen MURDOCH
Birth   24 August 1918   Farnum,Fre.,Idaho
Married   Beth HOLBROOK
Date   26 August 1945
Place   Ashton, Fremont, Idaho
Death
Burial

3RD CHILD   Della Ann MURDOCH
Birth   22 March 1921 Rupert,Minidoka,Idaho
Married   Stephen Reese DAVIS Joseph F. PEREY
Date   8 November 1939   5 November 1976
Place   Salt Lake Temple   Ashton, Idaho
Death
Burial

4TH CHILD   Clara Marie MURDOCH
Birth   1 May 1923 Farnum,Fremont, Idaho
Married   Blane Wilkes HOLBROOK
Date   9 September 1945
Place   Idaho Falls, Bonneville, Idaho
Death   28 April 1953 IdahoFalls,Bonn.,Idaho
Burial   1 May 1953   Ashton, Fremont, Idaho

5TH CHILD   Betty Mae MURDOCH
Birth   28 Mar 1925   Farnum,Fremont, Idaho
Married   Richard T. MARQUISE
Date   16 November 1946
Place   Durham, Durham, North Carolina
Death
Burial

6TH CHILD   Gilbert Dean MURDOCH
Birth   10 May 1927   Farnum,Fremont, Idaho
Married   Zelma Darlene JOHNSON
Date   20 August 1952
Place   Idaho Falls, Bonneville, Idaho (Temple)
Death
Burial

7TH CHILD   Lynn Ray MURDOCH
Birth   17 January 1930 Farnum,Fremont,Idaho
Married   Beverly May RODGERS
Date   18 August 1958
Place   Idaho Falls, Bonneville, Idaho
Death
Burial

8TH CHILD
Birth
Married
Date
Place
Death
Burial

1 MURDOCH, James 1786-1831   2 MURDOCH, John Murray 1820-1910
1 MURDOCH, Mary Murray, Sp. 1782-1856   2 MURDOCH, Ann STEEL, Sp. 1829-1909

DESCENDANTS OF------3 MURDOCH, Thomas Todd 1866-1953
                    3 HANSEN, Sarah Ingeborg 1895-

4 MURDOCH, Thomas Todd Jr. B-23 Nov 1916 D-17 Sep 1928

4 MURDOCH, LaVaughn Hansen B-24 Aug 1918 M-26 Aug 1945
4 MURDOCH, Beth HOLBROOK, Sp. B-26 Sep 1926

4 PERRY, Della Ann MURDOCH Davis B-22 Mar 1921
4 DAVIS, Stephen Reese, Sp. (1) B-1 Jan 1915 M-8 Nov 1939 D-4 Jul 1975
4 PERRY, Joseph Francis, Sp. (2) B-29 Mar 1910 M-5 Nov 1976

        5 DAVIS, Reece Junior B-3 Nov 1940 M-21 Jun 1963
        5 DAVIS, Mary Lou BLOOM, Sp. B-8 Sep 1945

                6 DAVIS, Sherry LaRae   B-16 Nov 1963
                6 DAVIS, Reeca Marie   B- 5 Aug 1965

        5 BOLLAND, Linda Kay DAVIS B-13 Aug 1944 M-28 Dec 1962
        5 BOLLAND, Herbert Leroy, Sp. B-17 Feb 1940

                6 BOLLAND, Stephen Leroy   B- 1 Nov 1963
                6 BOLLAND, Tammy Ilene   B-21 Aug 1965
                6 BOLLAND, Lori Diane   B-27 Dec 1968
                6 BOLLAND, Sharon Ann   B-27 Mar 1972

        5 DAVIS, Nancy Dawn B-21 Aug 1948 D-21 Aug 1948

4 HOLBROOK, Clara Marie MURDOCH B-1 May 1923 M-9 Sep 1945 D-28 Apr 1953
4 HOLBROOK, Blane Wilkes Sp. B-4 Jan 1920
4 HOLBROOK, Hazel STEELE Mickelsen, Sp. (2) B-

        MICKELSEN, Kay   B-
        MICKELSEN, Gregory   B-

4 MARQUISE, Betty Mae MURDOCH B-28 Mar 1925 M- 9 Nov 1946
4 MARQUISE, Richard T. Sp. B-11 Jun 1923

        5 MARQUISE, Richard Anthony B-6 Aug 1947 M-20 Dec 1969
        5 MARQUISE, PATRICIA BARSALU, Sp. B-26 Oct 1948

                6 MARQUISE, Ian Mark   B-13 Oct 1970
                6 MARQUISE, Christian Erick B- 5 Dec 1972
                6 MARQUISE, Jonathan Richard B-16 Sep 1976

        5 MARQUISE, Gregory Thomas B-3 May 1949 M-6 Jan 1973
        5 MARQUISE, Susan DEMERS, Sp. B-17 Jan 1954

                6 MARQUISE, Dustin Andrew   B-19 Jun 1973
                6 MARQUISE, Derek Matthew   B-22 Sep 1976
                6 MARQUISE, Damien Michael   B-24 Mar 1980

        5 MARQUISE, Dennis Geoffrey B- 4 Jan 1952

        5 MARQUISE, Sheila Marie   B-14 Mar 1956

        5 MARQUISE, Michael Albert B- 1 Oct 1964

4 MURDOCH, Gilbert Dean B-10 May 1927 M-20 Aug 1952
4 MURDOCH, Zelma Darlene JOHNSON, Sp. B-14 Jul 1935

        5 MURDOCH, Gilbert Fritz B-31 May 1953 M-13 Jun 1973
        5 MURDOCH, Patti Sue NEIBAUR, Sp. B-20 Sep 1953

                6 MURDOCH, Jenni Anne   B-12 Mar 1974
                6 MURDOCH, Megan Marie   B-28 Jul 1975
                6 MURDOCH, Thomas Fritz   B-27 Mar 1978

5 WEBB, Merrilee MURDOCH B-5 Apr 1955 M-20 Aug 1975
5 WEBB, Alan Jay, Sp. B-11 Feb 1955

      6 WEBB, Anthony James   B-29 Jun 1976
      6 WEBB, Sarah Marie   B-19 Mar 1978
      6 WEBB, Jory Russell   B-26 Nov 1979

5 MURDOCH, Hal "J"   B- 8 Apr 1957

5 WALKER, Barbara Janene MURDOCH B-1 Sep 1958 M-2 Jun 1977
5 WALKER, Mikel "D", Sp. B-14 Dec 1956

      6 WALKER, Aimee Michelle   B-16 Jun 1978
      6 WALDER, Mikel Ty   B-30 Dec 1979

5 MURDOCH, Donna   B-28 May 1962

5 MURDOCH, Juan Trinidad B- 8 Nov 1966

5 MURDOCH, Thomas David   B-22 Apr 1969

5 MURDOCH, Manuel Travis B- 7 Dec 1971

5 MURDOCH, Alicia Ann   B-14 Jan 1975

5 MURDOCH, Daniel Ray   B-15 Apr 1977

4 MURDOCH, Lynn Ray B-17 Jan 1930 M-18 Aug 1958
4 MURDOCH, Beverly May RODGERS, Sp. B-13 May 1941

5 SMITH, Cindee Maree Rodgers MURDOCH Coles B-26 Nov 1956 (adopted by Lynn Murdoch 1959)
5 COLES, Jerry Lee, Sp. (1) B-   M-27 Mar 1972
5 SMITH, Stephen Franklin, Sp. (2) B-7 May 1952 M-7 Apr 1979

      6 COLES, Brandee Maree   B-18 Oct 1972
      6 COLES, Jeremy Lee   B-26 Apr 1975
      6 SMITH, Stephanie Lynn   B-11 Nov 1980

5 MURDOCH, Gregory Lynn B-18 Apr 1959 M-26 Nov 1976
5 MURDOCH, Tona Marie WEST, Sp. B-9 Apr 1959

      6 MURDOCH, Fawn Marie   B- 7 May 1977 D- 8 May 1979
      6 MURDOCH, Shilo Lee   B-28 Dec 1979

5 MURDOCH, Todd "R"   B-11 Feb 1961 D-11 May 1967

5 MURDOCH, Michael Vaughn B-17 Nov 1965

5 MURDOCH, Bryan Russell B- 8 Aug 1967

Joseph "A" Murdoch and Martha Ellen Fortie

This is the history of Joseph A Murdoch and Martha Ellen Fortie Murdoch, early residents of Heber, Utah. Joseph A was born on March 11, 1870, in Heber, to John Murray and Ann Steel Murdoch, the thirteenth child. Martha was born to Alexander and Rachel Howarth Fortie on January 19, 1871, in Heber City. She was the second child of three.

They were reared in Heber. Martha was tall, with black eyes and black hair. She attended school, which at the time was very limited. Her mother was widowed early and Martha began working at an early age to help support the family. In her youth she was a good horse rider and dancer. She remained a beautiful woman all her life, and had long, black hair, with very little gray in it at the time of her death.

Joseph A was blond, with blue eyes, not too large in stature. He attended all the schools in Heber at this time and on May 21, 1891, he and Martha were married in the Logan Temple. They lived in Heber and became the parents of twelve children. The were all born in the same home.

Their home was busy with so many children, but always open to friends for visits and practices. Martha was a good cook and housekeeper and spent most of her time in the home. The children were taught right from wrong and the standards of the LDS Church. Joseph A became very active in the community. He worked for the Wasatch Wave, publishers, as a typesetter. He was called on a short-term mission for the Church to Salt Lake as a Temple Square guide from 1904–1905. He also studied music at the Evan Stephens School of Music. He attended the University of Deseret and Brigham Young Academy, as well as the Wasatch Stake Academy in Heber. Mr. Murdoch became a music teacher in Heber Valley, traveling from school to school by horse and buggy. Many students were taught music by note for the first time. He started a successful stake choir in 1900, as well as leading the old Second Ward choir. He played baritone horn in the Heber brass band. From 1906 to 1916, Joseph A was the Heber City recorder. He was an excellent penman and took much pride in his writing.

In 1920, after having suffered through the flu epidemic, which took their oldest daughter Lecia's life, they moved to Vineyard, Utah, to a farm. This home was one mile south of the big Geneva Steel Plant. Here they reared most of their younger children. They were active in both the Church and community. This couple were mild, kind people, and at the age of seventy-two and seventy-three respectively, they died within five weeks of each other, being buried in the Heber City Cemetery.

Their children: Lecia, Dona, Murray, Orpha May, Martha Blanch, Harold Joseph, Vida, Mary Gladys, Elroy, Cuthbert Fortie (Bert), Phyllis Rachel, and Joan.

This sketch is taken from the book *How Beautiful Upon the Mountains,* published by the Daughters of the Pioneers, found on pages 446–447.

Following is a brief biography of the life of Joseph A Murdoch, written by Malicent Clegg Wells and read at his funeral services by Oriel G. Clegg.

Joseph A Murdoch passed away August 27, 1943, at his home in Vineyard. When word was received of the sudden passing of dear Uncle Joe, we were all so shocked. We hadn't thought about him leaving us so soon. It just seems he would always be with us to counsel and cheer us. But though we bow our heads in grief, in our hearts is a peaceful feeling that all is well with him.

Born of goodly parents, his seventy-three years have been full to the brim in service to his fellow men. He was the thirteenth child of a family of 15 children born to Patriarch John M. and Ann Steel Murdoch. His early boyhood days were happy ones roaming the hills in Heber Valley, helping herd the sheep and cattle. Indian scares were plentiful, but his home surroundings were the best that pioneer life offered in those days. He attended school and was always an apt student. He acquired a good education. He was musically inclined and was a member of the first brass band in Heber, also sang in the ward choir. He was the Stake chorister and hundreds of boys and girls have learned the beautiful songs of Zion under his able leadership.

When 21 years of age he married a beautiful dark-eyed girl named Martha Ellen Fortie, who has been a devoted companion for more than 52 years. Heber City was their home for 28 years, where their 12 children were born. They, with their family, were leaders in the community in every way.

He held many positions of trust, both in civic and church affairs. His journey through life has been a steady climb, no wavering or turning back. Improvement and progression has marked his every step. Their home was one of comfort and cleanliness, filled with love, music, and prayer. In such a fine background their lovely family grew up. His children were loved, and were cared for by kind parents whose every act was exemplary.

In 1919, they purchased their present home in Vineyard and moved here for the better of Aunt Martha's health, but their hearts were always with the fine people of Wasatch Valley. They have returned many times to attend funerals, for visits to loved ones, also attended weddings and Stake Conferences and other important events. Decoration Day was always a must for a visit to Heber. Since coming to Vineyard, he has been an ardent worker in the Church.

Among other assignments he served as counselor to Bishop Victor Anderson for 5 years, and has been an energetic genealogy and temple worker. He has kept the records of the James and Mary Murray Murdoch family in a very efficient manner. He served as secretary-treasurer of the building committee during the erection of our ward chapel. Uncle Joe loved life. No one enjoyed a good laugh more than he did. He was a real sport, always taking part in the games for old and young. He spent many hours in playing horseshoes, a game he mastered with skill.

He was always neat and clean in his dress and habits.

His kind personality made for him a host of friends. He and his good wife have visited the homes of the sick, lending a helping hand and leaving a blessing of comfort and cheer. The Savior said, "Blessed are the meek for they shall inherit the earth." His trials and sorrows he faced with courage, for he had an abiding faith in the teachings of the gospel; he loved every principle and lived so exemplary that no one could question his sincerity. He rejoiced in teaching the youth of Zion. In addition to serving as a missionary at Temple Square, he also served 2 years as a missionary in the Sharon Stake. A gifted musician, composer and poet, he has gladdened many hearts with his music and verse. He was a lover of good books and was well versed in the scriptures. How he enjoyed having his family around him to sing with him, his face fairly beamed with happiness as he listened to their sweet voices. Old and young found a place on his knee, his arms were always outstretched to comfort those in need. We shall miss his sweet smile and kindly face. There is a joyous welcome awaiting him in the world of spirits where hundreds of loved ones will welcome him home.

He was truly one of Gods chosen servants . . .
We shall meet . . . , but we shall miss him.
There will be a vacant chair. We will linger to caress him
When we breathe our evening prayer.

Martha Ellen Fortie Murdoch

Martha Ellen Fortie was born in a three-roomed log house on January 19, 1871. Her parents were Rachel Howarth and Alexander Fortie. She was blessed May 7, 1871, by Alex Fortie, or J. Murdoch.

Her early life was spent as any youngster would spend her time. Doing a little work here and there and playing the rest of the time. At the age of nine, she was baptized August 12 1880, by John McDonald or Joseph Moulton. She was confirmed August 12, 1880 by John Jordon or John Duke.

At seven or eight she started school in an old rock building near the John Witt residence. She also attended school in the courthouse. Her education was limited because her father died when she was sixteen. For four years before he had been ill and she had to help support the family because her brother wasn't old enough to work.

From sixteen until she married, she worked out to help keep the family. Her first job brought fifty cents a week, and white top apron, hair in place, and ready to meet the situations of the day.

She was quiet and reserved, but she had a heart filled with empathy, especially for hungry children. No person was ever turned away from her door. Her home-made bread won the hearts of young and old. A slice—no three or four—with her home-made butter was a fitting meal for a king. Lecia, Evan and any other young children of the neighborhood loved grandma's cookies or jam sandwiches. She only asked two things, clean face and hands, and polite ways. If these were forgotten, the sandwich or cookie was placed back on the pantry shelf until her rules were obeyed. She never turned away a hobo from the nearby railroad tracks. She always fed them in return for someone taking care of her sons if they were ever unfortunate enough to find themselves in similar circumstances.

The only time that I ever saw grandma lose her reserve was when Elroy sent Evan in with some baby mice in his cap to show to her. The next instant she was standing on the table ordering in no uncertain terms, "—get them out—get them out!" I wasn't so brave myself but I wasn't so fast either.

Grandma missed grandpa so very much after he passed away so suddenly on August 27, 1943. She was such a homebody, not inclined to go visiting with friends or relatives.

Elroy never missed checking on her in the morning before he left for school. Again in the afternoon as he came home, he, knowing her loneliness, called in again to tell her about his day.

On the last Thursday in September, she was not feeling very well. She went down very quickly the next two days. On Sunday morning, she called me in to give her a bath, fix her face and hair, put on her new garments and her nicest gown.

I knew that something was bothering her. She had never let me do these things even when I asked her—I had begged her to let me help. She was so independent and did not want to be a burden on anyone. This was the last day that she really was herself. By that night, she had drifted off into a deep sleep. On Thursday, October 7, 1943, she was still sleeping. Dr. Anderson had told us to get the family there. All, but Dona, had arrived, and she could not make it because of army restrictions. The family all gathered around her bed that morning with Elroy as mouthpiece to dedicate his mother to the Lord, if that was His will and her desire. Within minutes, her breathing became slower and slower, until it ceased and the lines of pain and care left her face. She looked calm and peaceful and a smile came to her lips. All that stood around her bed

knew that her desire had been fulfilled. The birth that we call death had come to grandma.

She would tend the baby and do all the dishes every day. This was at the age of eleven. She then began working out to several places. She did the chores, such as milking cows as well as the inside work, including cooking.

She then went to Park City where she worked for about six to seven years. She then came back to Heber and worked for Lacy Hatch. While working here, she married Joseph A Murdoch, 20 May 1891, at the Logan Temple, Logan, Utah. Their honeymoon was spent traveling in the caboose of a train to reach Heber.

The couple lived in Heber for thirty years and reared their family of eight girls and four boys. They then moved to Provo in 1921, and later to Vineyard, where they lived till taken by death.

She was a good mother and wife. She was always willing to sacrifice for the sake of her children.

Memories with Grandpa Joseph "A" and Grandma Martha Ellen Murdoch May 18, 1980, by Jennie W. Murdoch

As Elroy and I lived with grandpa and grandma Murdoch in a front apartment that we had built on their home, we had more opportunity to be near them and to feel of their love for one another and for us and our children.

Grandpa never missed a morning that he did not come in to play with Lecia. She was nearly four years old, really a little conversationalist with her grandpa. He would sit on the piano stool and sing to her, and Richard who was not quite a year yet, also understood the "Pony Ride Song." I can hear them now laughing as grandpa tossed them up high with his foot. Many times Evan would hear the music and come to join in the fun.

Grandpa always made the grandchildren feel special because he paid *attention* to them—he noticed their sparkling eyes, their hair neatly combed, their clean clothes, and their voices that sounded like happy singing birds. He even gave Lecia a ride before she could walk on a big white pig that lived in the field next to the lawn. How precious these memories are to them, for they were both gone so early in the children's lives. Grandpa passed away suddenly, and Grandma six weeks later.

The loss was very keen to them. Lecia asked me many times, "Where Gumpa? Where Gumpa?" Richard knew his face, and when he lay in his casket, he nearly jumped out of my arms bending down over him to give him a big love. It surprised me so. I had not expected this response from the baby, but he really knew him.

Grandma Murdoch was a beautiful stately woman with hair as black as coal. She seemed to have everything under control in her home. Her home was her castle and she kept it immaculate, but everyone was welcome anytime.

Poems by Joseph "A" Murdoch

I Want to Go Over to Grandma's

I want to go over to Grandmas,
She's not very busy today,
She asked me last night to come over
And help her put things away.

I left my red truck on her table,
My wagon and gun by the door;
And mud on my boots in the parlor
And blocks scattered round on the floor.

I'll ask her to make me a sandwich
And I'll be as quiet as can be,
While she makes a pan full of cookies
Because I want to taste one you see.

Written November 26, 1938

My Pony

I have a dandy pony.
As gentle as can be,
I never need a saddle
Or bridle you can see.

He can be the fastest,
Come and race with me;
Gid-di up, Gid-di up, see me go,
On my daddy's knee.

Written 1940. Joseph "A" Murdoch used to say this poem as he swung his grandchildren on his knee.

Home in Heber, Wasatch, Utah

Home in Vineyard, Utah

Joseph "A" and Martha E. Murdoch
April 1938

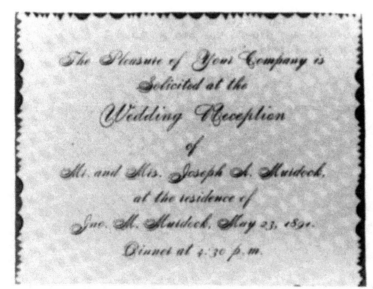

Marriage invitation

Wedding Picture 1891

Top L to R Dona #2, Elroy #9 Joseph A, Martha E.,
Bert #10 Lecia #1, Bottom Row L to R, Harold #6,
Gladys #8, Murray #3, Vida #7. Across the bottom,
Orpha #4, Blanch #5, Phyllis #11, Joan #12. All
born in the same home in Heber, Wasatch, Utah.

HUSBAND   Joseph "A" MURDOCH
Birth   11 March 1870
Place   Heber, Wasatch, Utah
Chr
Married   20 May 1891
Place   Logan Temple, Logan, Cache, Utah
Death   27 August 1943 Vineyard, Utah, Utah
Burial   31 August 1943 Heber Cemetery, Heber, Utah
Father   John Murray MURDOCH
Mother*   Ann STEEL
Other Wives
(if any)

WIFE   Martha Ellen FORTIE
Birth   19 January 1871
Place   Heber, Wasatch, Utah
Chr   7 May 1871
Death   7 October 1943 Vineyard, Utah, Utah
Burial   10 October Heber Cemetery, Heber, Utah
Father   Alexander FORTIE
Mother*   Rachel HOWARTH
Other Hus
(if any)

*Where was information obtained? James and Joseph "A" Murdoch family records.
*List complete maiden name for all females.

1st Child	Lecia MURDOCH	
Birth	10 September 1892	
Place	Heber, Wasatch, Utah	
Married to	Unmarried	
Married		
Place		
Died	21 Nov 1918 Heber, Utah	
2nd Child	Dona MURDOCH	
Birth	27 October 1894	
Place	Heber, Wasatch, Utah	
Married to	Francis Clayton MONTGOMERY	
Married	19 December 1917	
Place	Salt Lake City, Salt Lake, Utah	
Died	2 March 1966 Heber, Wasatch, Utah	
3rd Child	Murray Alexander MURDOCH	
Birth	13 September 1896	
Place	Heber, Wasatch, Utah	
Married to	Priscilla PULLEY	
Married	15 January 1925	
Place	Salt Lake City, Salt Lake, Utah, Utah	
Died	2 Jan 1952 American Fork, Utah, Utah	
4th Child	Orpha May MURDOCH	
Birth	3 April 1899	
Place	Heber, Wasatch, Utah	
Married to		
Married		
Place		
Died	13 Jan 1902 Heber, Wasatch, Utah	
5th Child	Martha Blanch MURDOCH	
Birth	14 April 1901	
Place	Heber, Wasatch, Utah	
Married to		
Married		
Place		
Died	18 Sep 1911 Heber, Utah	

6th Child	Harold Joseph MURDOCH
Birth	1 May 1903
Place	Heber, Wasatch, Utah
Married to	1Clara Mae MORSE 2Bettie Fae FARQUHARSON
Married	14 Mar 1933 28 Jul 1962
Place	Heber,Wasatch,Utah Elko,Humbolt,Nevada
Died	13 Oct 1975 Vineyard, Utah, Utah
7th Child	Vida MURDOCH
Birth	27 August 1905
Place	Heber, Wasatch, Utah
Married to	Edgar Glenn FILLMORE
Married	14 August 1926
Place	Heber, Wasatch, Utah
Died	
8th Child	Mary Gladys MURDOCH
Birth	14 August 1908
Place	Heber, Wasatch, Utah
Married to	Grant William TURNER
Married	19 June 1930
Place	Nephi, Juab, Utah
Died	
9th Child	Elroy MURDOCH
Birth	11 December 1910
Place	Heber, Wasatch, Utah
Married to	Jennie WALKER
Married	30 September 1938
Place	Salt Lake City, Salt Lake Utah
Died	
10th Child	Cuthbert Fortie MURDOCH
Birth	11 April 1912
Place	Heber, Wasatch, Utah
Married to	1Jean V PRESTWICH 2Lora Chloe ROSE
Married	19 May 1939 14 June 1955
Place	Salt Lake City, Salt Lake, Utah (both)
Died	

11th Child	Phyllis Rachel MURDOCH
Birth	11 August 1914
Place	Heber, Wasatch, Utah
Married to	Paul Halma VAN WAGONER
Married	19 September 1935
Place	Salt Lake City, Salt Lake, Utah
Died	

12th Child	Joan MURDOCH
Birth	11 March 1917
Place	Heber, Wasatch, Utah
Married to	Glen MAXWELL
Married	2 July 1937
Place	Salt Lake City, Salt Lake, Utah
Died	

1 MURDOCH, James 1786-1831   2 MURDOCH, John Murray 1820-1910
1 MURDOCH, Mary MURRAY, Sp. 1782-1856   2 MURDOCH, Ann STEEL, Sp. B-1829-1909

                              3 MURDOCH, JOSEPH "A" 1870-1943
DESCENDANTS OF---------
                              3 MURDOCH, MARTHA ELLEN FORTIE, SP, 1871-1943

4 MURDOCH, Lecia B-10 Sep 1892 D-21 Nov 1918   B-BIRTH
                                                                 M-MARRIAGE
4 MONTGOMERY, Dona MURDOCH B-27 Oct 1894 M-19 Dec 1917 D-2 Mar 1966   D-DEATH
4 MONTGOMERY, Francis Clayton, Sp. B-7 Jul 1892 D-5 Aug 1967   Sp-SPOUSE
                                                                 Div-DIVORCE

        5 JENSEN, Lecia Elaine MONGOMERY B-26 Oct 1918 M-20 Jun 1941
        5 JENSEN, Kenneth Denmark, Sp. B-14 Nov 1918

                6 SORENSON, Marcia Jean JENSEN B-3 Apr 1944 M-7 Sep 1965
                6 SORENSON, Robert Earl, Sp. B-24 Dec 1942

                        7 SORENSON, Scott Robert   B-10 Dec 1967

                        7 SORENSON, Lecia Marie   B-17 Aug 1969

                        7 SORENSON, Kenneth Earl   B-17 Sep 1973

                6 JENSEN, Robert Wayne B-8 June 1947 M-6 Sep 1969
                6 JENSEN, Sandra Kay BEHRMANN, Sp. B-9 Dec 1949

                        7 JENSEN, Sean Robert   B-17 Mar 1971

                        7 JENSEN, Heidi Colleen   B- 8 Mar 1973

                        7 JENSEN, Kimberly Kay   B-28 Jan 1978

        5 CANNON, Frances MONTGOMERY B-14 Feb 1921 M-7 Dec 1945
        5 CANNON, Judson Glen, Sp. B-

                6 SPRING, Colette CANNON B-12 Aug 1950 M-19 Dec 1970
                6 SPRING, Arthur Emmett, Sp. B-

                        7 SPRING, Kimberly   B-12 Aug 1976

                        7 SPRING,   B-
                                    Twins
                        7 SPRING,   B-

        5 MONTGOMERY, Jay Clayton B-27 Feb 1925 M-18 Feb 1956 D-20 May 1964
        5 MONTGOMERY, Betty TEASER, Sp. (2) B-

                6 MONTGOMERY, Jay   B-26 Jan 1959

        5 MACK, Monta MONTGOMERY B-3 Apr 1927 M-11 Mar 1951 D-12 Sep 1952
        5 MACK, Lee, Sp. B-

        5 BOURNE, Alice Annette MONTGOMERY B-9 June 1931 M-21 June 1953 D-22 Feb 1964
        5 BOURNE, Hal "H", Sp. B-

                6 BOURNE, Stephanie   B- 3 Dec 1974

                6 BOURNE, Michael   B-18 Apr 1956

                6 BOURNE, Robert Bryan   B- 2 May 1958

                6 BOURNE, Susan   B-12 Mar 1961

        5 MONTGOMERY, Steve B-29 Aug 1934 M-8 Feb 1963
        5 MONTGOMERY, Beverly WATKINS, Sp. B-26 Sep 1941

                6 MONTGOMERY, Elizabeth Annette B-11 Sep 1964

                6 MONTGOMERY, William Clayton   B-28 Jul 1967

                6 MONTGOMERY, Thomas Palani   B- 1 Jun 1967

4 MURDOCH, Murray Alexander B-13 Sep 1896 M-15 Jan 1925 D-2 Jan 1952
4 MURDOCH, Priscilla PULLEY, Sp. B-6 Feb 1895

    5 MURDOCH, Ralph Alexander (Abe) B-18 Oct 1925 M-4 Aug 1950
    5 MURDOCH, Glenda RICHINS, Sp. B-4 June 1929

        6 MURDOCH, Murray "R" B-31 Dec 1951 M-8 Mar 1974
        6 MURDOCH, Kathy THOMAS, Sp. B-27 Aug 1952

            7 MURDOCH, Lori Ann   B-28 Jun 1974

            7 MURDOCH, Glen Murray   B- 8 Aug 1976

            7 MURDOCH, Jeff Thomas   B- 4 Oct 1980

        6 THOMPSON, Debra MURDOCH B-10 May 1953 M-18 May 1973
        6 THOMPSON, Mark Shelley, Sp. B-11 Aug 1952

            7 THOMPSON, Reed Murdoch   B-22 Aug 1974

            7 THOMPSON, Thad Mark   B- 1 Nov 1975

            7 THOMPSON, Trenton Brett   B- 9 Nov 1976

        6 WALKER, Susan MURDOCH B-30 Oct 1954 M-24 Nov 1972
        6 WALKER, David Russell, Sp. B-25 May 1954

            7 WALKER, Brandon David   B-13 Oct 1975

            7 WALKER, Tyson "R"   B- 1 Sep 1976

            7 WALKER, Trenton Brett   B-14 Apr 1981

        6 VARNEY, Jone MURDOCH B-17 Dec 1957 M-24 Nov 1972
        6 VARNEY, Jon Merrill, Sp. B-19 Mar 1955

            7 VARNEY, Heather Jo   B-17 May 1978

            7 VARNEY, Trevor Jon   B-28 Oct 1979

        6 LAYCOCK, Sharon MURDOCH B-8 June 1962 M-1 July 1981
        6 LAYCOCK, Jon David, Sp. B-11 Dec 1959

    5 MURDOCH, Francis Lynn (Fin) B-30 June 1927 M-5 June 1952
    5 MURDOCH, Carol McMILLAN, Sp. B-6 Dec 1931

        6 BECK, Marsha Lynn MURDOCH B-28 Mar 1953 M-26 Jan 1973
        6 BECK, Dennis L, Sp. B-16 Nov 1951

            7 Beck, Russell "D"   B-20 Dec 1978

        6 MURDOCH, Jay "M" B-7 June 1955 M-21 Nov 1975
        6 MURDOCH, Cindy GALLEGOS, Sp. B-13 July 1960

            7 MURDOCH, Cassie Jo   B-22 Mar 1976

            7 MURDOCH, Christina Micol B-21 Jan 1977

            7 MURDOCH, Bridget Lynn   B-26 Jun 1978

        6 MURDOCH, Allen "M"   B-7 Jun 1955 D-9 Jun 1955

        6 MAYNE, Lorna Kay MURDOCH B-18 June 1958 M-16 May 1974
        6 MAYNE, George L. Sp. B-21 June 1955

            7 MAYNE, Michelle   B-20 Jan 1975

            7 MAYNE, Jason Finn   B-24 Dec 1975

            7 MAYNE, Carla Marie   B-18 Mar 1977

            7 MAYNE, Rebecca Josephine B-21 Aug 1980

        6 MURDOCH, Joe "M"   B-16 Feb 1962

5 MURDOCH, Elmo Gene (MO) B-28 May 1929 M-9 Dec 1954
5 MURDOCH, Betty Jeanne THORNE, Sp. (Nielsen, Div.) B-4 Jul 1927

    6 OLSEN, Linda Jeanne MURDOCH B-28 June 1947 M-8 Sep 1967
    6 OLSEN, William Anthon, Sp. (Tony) B-5 Nov 1946

        7 OLSEN, Cory Anthon   B- 7 Apr 1968

        7 OLSEN, Micol Ann   B-16 Jun 1970

        7 OLSEN, Jeana Elizabeth   B- 5 Aug 1973

        7 OLSEN, Kelly Dawn   B-19 Mar 1976

    6 MURDOCH, Max Thorne B-19 Dec 1956

    6 YEARGIN, Holly Ann MURDOCH B-21 July 1960 M-12 Dec 1980
    6 YEARGIN, Harry Alvin Jr., Sp. B-14 Oct 1958

    6 MURDOCH, Nancy Lee   B- 6 Aug 1961

    6 MURDOCH, Reed Howard   B-17 Jan 1963

4 MURDOCH, Orpha May   B- 3 Apr 1899 D-13 Jan 1902

4 MURDOCH, Martha Blanche B-14 Apr 1901 D-18 Sep 1911

4 MURDOCH, Harold Joseph B-1 May 1903 D-13 Oct 1975
4 MURDOCH, Clara Mae MORSE, Sp. B-19 May 1914 M-14 Mar 1933 Div.
4 MURDOCH, Bettie Faye FARQUHARSON, Sp. (2) B-18 Feb 1925 M-28 Jul 1962

    5 MURDOCH, Evan Carlos B-26 Sep 1934 M-1 Jun 1954
    5 MURDOCH, Barbara SHEFFIELD/TAYLOR Sp. B-4 Sep 1936

        6 PYNE, Kathleen MURDOCH B-19 Feb 1955 M-20 Jul 1974
        6 PYNE, Kim Gerald, Sp. B-14 Aug 1952

            7 PYNE, Travis Cory   B- 7 Apr 1976

            7 PYNE, Jesse Kim   B-30 Jan 1978

            7 PYNE, Jennifer Jill   B- 5 Apr 1980

        6 SQUIRES, Joni MURDOCH B-25 Sep 1957 M-18 Mar 1977
        6 SQUIRES, Alan David, Sp. B-22 Feb 1956

            7 SQUIRES, Cheryl   B-22 Feb 1980

        6 MURDOCH, Brenda   B-14 May 1959

        6 MURDOCH, Lori Kay   B-20 Aug 1964

        6 MURDOCH, Joe Evan   B-12 Sep 1974

    5 MURDOCH, Neil Joseph B-10 Mar 1940 M-30 Mar 1965
    5 MURDOCH, Ingrid Hildi LICHENBERGER, Sp. B-24 Oct 1947

        6 MURDOCH, Christine B-5 Apr 1966

    5 HICKEN, Linda MURDOCH B-29 Aug 1941 M-9 Jun 1959
    5 HICKEN, Philip Pratt, Sp. B-27 Aug 1939

        6 CURTIS, Ilene HICKEN B-21 May 1960 M-28 Sep 1979
        6 CURTIS, Randal Jay, Sp. B-24 May 1963

        6 HICKEN, Keith Pratt B-12 Oct 1961

        6 FENN, Diane HICKEN B-22 Oct 1963 M-12 Dec 1981
        6 FENN, Grant R, Sp. B-13 Sep 1963

        6 HICKEN, Kenneth Harold   B-21 Aug 1965

        6 HICKEN, Douglas Philip   B-10 Jun 1971

5 MURDOCH, George "C" B-13 Aug 1943 M-5 Jul 1963 Div.
5 MURDOCH, Patricia Leigh HARPER, Sp. B-26 Dec 1943

    6 MURDOCH, Joel   B-16 Jul 1970

    6 MURDOCH, Tara   B-27 Sep 1971

4 FILLMORE, Vida MURDOCH B-27 Aug 1905 M-14 Aug 1926
4 FILLMORE, Edgar Glenn, Sp. B-7 Oct 1902

    5 DEANNE, Glenna FILLMORE B-7 Oct 1927
    5 JONES,   Sp. (1) Annulled
    5 LOVELACE,   Sp. (2) Divorced
    5 DEANNE, Jarvis W, Sp. (3) B-4 May 1918 M-22 Jul 1977

        6 CASTLE, Sheri Lyn JONES B-22 Jul 1942 M-15 Jan 1966
        6 CASTLE, Donald William, Sp. B-22 Jul 1942

            7 CASTLE, Heather Dawn   B-11 May 1970

            7 CASTLE, Donald William Jr.   B-23 Aug 1972

        6 LOVELACE, Phillip Glenn B-26 Oct 1948 M-24 Oct 1971
        6 LOVELANCE, Dyane G. SILVA, Sp. B-2 Mar 1951

            7 LOVELACE, Audra Marie   M- 6 Mar 1973

            7 LOVELACE, Adam Glenn   M-21 Feb 1974

        6 LOVELACE, Charles Evan Jr.   B-10 Nov 1950

        6 LOVELACE, Sandra   B- 4 Apr 1951

        6 LOVELACE, Scott Fillmore   B-25 Sep 1951

        6 SMAGACZ, Martha Ellen LOVELACE B-5 Nov 1954 M-19 Aug 1978
        6 SMAGACZ, Gale, Sp. B-19 Oct 1954

    5 FILLMORE, Edgar Joseph B-1 Mar 1930 M-20 Dec 1952 Div.
    5 FILLMORE, Laura Ann VAN WAGONER, Sp. B-23 Aug 1935

        6 FILLMORE, Edgar Joel B-19 Nov 1954 M-18 Oct 1974 Div.
        6 FILLMORE, Cheri Ann MILLRING, Sp. B-

            7 FILLMORE, Melanie Ann   B-29 Apr 1975

            7 FILLMORE, Edgar Joel   B-27 Jul 1977

            7 FILLMORE, Brandee   B-24 Jul 1981

        6 HARVEY, Jenette FILLMORE B-22 May 1956 M-1 Jun 1973
        6 HARVEY, Jerry D, Sp. B-1 Dec 1955

            7 HARVEY, Jake   B-16 Feb 1976

            7 HARVEY, Jason   B-30 Nov 1976

            7 HARVEY, Jodi Ann   B-19 Feb 1979

        6 ROBINSON, Julie FILLMORE B-20 Aug 1959 M-20 Jan 1978
        6 ROBINSON, Jay, Sp. B-

            7 ROBINSON, Mick Jay   B-20 Jun 1978

        6 FILLMORE, Jill Ann   B-14 Sep 1961

        6 FILLMORE, Jolene   B-27 Sep 1964

        6 FILLMORE, Jamie   B- 8 Oct 1968

    5 FILLMORE, Bob Kenneth B-9 Dec 1933 M-11 Oct 1957
    5 FILLMORE, Madeline Yvonne NORDHOFF, Sp. B-30 Aug 1935

```
        6 FILLMORE, Lori Elizabeth        B-21 Jul 1959

        6 FILLMORE, Bob William           B- 1 Feb 1963

        6 FILLMORE, Edwin John            B-16 Jun 1965

        6 FILLMORE, Michele Yvonne        B-17 Mar 1967

        6 FILLMORE, Debra Gwen            B-10 Mar 1969

4 TURNER, Mary Gladys MURDOCH B-14 Aug 1908 M-19 Jun 1930
4 TURNER, Grant William, Sp. B-24 Oct 1909

    5 SCOTT, Patricia Ann TURNER B-29 Sep 1933 M-29 Dec 1952
    5 SCOTT, Mark Christian Jr., Sp. B-12 Feb 1931

        6 OWENS, Stefanie Jo SCOTT B-15 Mar 1955 M-19 Aug 1977
        6 OWENS, Christopher James, Sp. B-16 Jun 1954

            7 OWENS, Chelsea Leigh        B-15 Feb 1979

        6 SCOTT, Mary Lisa                B-29 Apr 1957

        6 PROBERT, Ann Kathleen SCOTT B-18 Jan 1960 M-23 Apr 1981
        6 PROBERT, Dudley Leslie, Sp. B-

        6 SCOTT, Karen Kristen            B-17 Feb 1963

        6 SCOTT, Bonnie Rae               B- 8 Jun 1968

    5 TURNER, Joseph Grant B-22 May 1937 M-31 May 1962
    5 TURNER, Sherri Lee BIDDULPH, Sp. B-26 Jun 1941

        6 TURNER, Jeffery Joseph          B-21 Mar 1966

        6 TURNER, Cory Reed               B-18 Aug 1967

        6 TURNER, Sheia Lynn              B-21 Feb 1969

        6 TURNER, Mark Alan               B-30 May 1972

        6 TURNER, Mary Shereece           B-26 Jun 1974

        6 TURNER, Ruth Ann                B-19 Sep 1977

    5 BASTIEN, Judith Ann TURNER B-25 Feb 1948 M-29 Mar 1969
    5 BASTIEN, Stephen Ray, Sp. B-23 Sep 1949

        6 BASTIEN, Jacob                  B-27 Jun 1971

    5 NICOLSON, Joyce Diane TURNER Fry Brown B-23 May 1949
    5 FRY, George Edward, Sp. (1) B-          M-          Div. (George Edward Butler)
    5 BROWN, Leslie Rand, Sp. (2) B-          M-          Div.
    5 NICOLSON, Scott Trevor, Sp. (3) B-          M-13 Jul 1973

        6 FRY, Kimberly Jean              B-29 Apr 1969

        6 FRY, Eric Rembrandt             B- 9 Jun 1970

4 MURDOCH, Elroy B-11 Dec 1910 M-30 Sep 1938
4 MURDOCH, Jennie WALKER, Sp. B-23 Jan 1913

    5 GILBERT, Lecia Rae MURDOCH B-6 Sep 1940 M-3 Jun 1966
    5 GILBERT, Don Jesse, Sp. B-8 Dec 1943

        6 GILBERT, Danielle              B-22 Jul 1969

        6 GILBERT, Byron Jesse           B-29 Nov 1971

        6 GILBERT, Amy Lea               B-11 Nov 1973

        6 GILBERT, Kyle Elroy            B-14 Jun 1980
```

5 MURDOCH, Richard Kent B-7 Nov 1942 M-30 Sep 1965
5 MURDOCH, Ann ROBERTSON, Sp. B-3 Jan 1947

    6 MURDOCH, Nancy   B- 4 Jul 1966

    6 MURDOCH, Kenneth R   B- 3 Dec 1967

    6 MURDOCH, Leslie   B-5 Jan 1969

    6 MURDOCH, Gina   B- 9 Aug 1971

    6 MURDOCH, Joseph "A"   B-22 Aug 1974

    6 MURDOCH, Kent Elroy   B-19 Feb 1977

5 MURDOCH, Robert E B-21 Jan 1944 M-16 Aug 1968
5 MURDOCH, Susan PLUMMER, Sp. B-28 Nov 1948

    6 MURDOCH, Desarie   B- 9 Sep 1969

    6 MURDOCH, Anthony Robert   B-19 Nov 1971

    6 MURDOCH, Mica Murray   B-11 Jul 1978

    6 MURDOCH, Patrick Perry   B- 5 Jan 1980

5 MURDOCH, Reece Elroy B-18 Mar 1947 M-4 Aug 1971
5 MURDOCH, Launa Ann CRONQUIST, Sp. B-29 Mar 1952

    6 MURDOCH, Rebecca Ann   B-29 Oct 1973

    6 MURDOCH, Scott Layne   B- 7 Jul 1975

    6 MURDOCH, Blake Reece   B-10 Aug 1977

    6 MURDOCH, Rachel Marie   B- 1 Jan 1980

    6 MURDOCH, Janelle   B-22 Jan 1982

5 MURDOCH, Lee R B-16 Sep 1949 M-11 Oct 1973
5 MURDOCH, Alice Ann WINEGAR, Sp. B-18 Jun 1955

    6 MURDOCH, Grant Lee   B- 7 Nov 1974

    6 MURDOCH, Cody J   B-13 Sep 1977

    7 MURDOCH, Robert "E"   B-24 Jan 1981

5 MURDOCH, Layne B-13 Dec 1951 M-11 Jul 1975
5 MURDOCH, Deborah Ann KEETCH, Sp. B-25 Feb 1955

    6 MURDOCH, William Reece   B- 6 May 1976

    6 MURDOCH, Lance Elroy   B-11 Jul 1977

    6 MURDOCH, Jami Lynn   B-25 Feb 1979

    6 MURDOCH, Buc Robert   B- 2 Sep 1980

4 MURDOCH, Cuthbert Fortie (Bert) B-11 April 1912
4 MURDOCH, Jean V. PRESTWICH, Sp. (1) B-18 Jul 1915 M-19 May 1939 D-23 Jul 1953
4 MURDOCH, Lora Chloe ROSE (Dahle, Div.), Sp. (2) B-14 Jan 1908 M-14 Jun 1955

    5 SHROCK, Joyce MURDOCH B-26 Aug 1947 M-15 Feb 1969
    5 SHROCK, Robert Michael, Sp. B- 2 Aug 1944

        6 SHROCK, Christie Lenee   B- 8 Mar 1970

        6 SHROCK, Allyson Rae   B-14 Jul 1972

        6 SHROCK, Kami Joe   B-21 Mar 1974

        6 SHROCK, Amy Jean   B-13 Apr 1976

6 SHROCK, Robert Joseph   B-28 Apr 1978

6 SHROCK, Shelli Rose   B- 9 Apr 1980

5 STAM, Muriel   MURDOCH B-18 Feb 1929 M-10 Feb 1948
5 STAM, Richard Vaughn, Sp. B-26 Dec 1925

   6 HANSON, Loralee STAM B-26 Aug 1949 M-30 Jun 1969
   6 HANSON, Jimmy Paul, Sp. B-1 Apr 1947

      7 HANSON, Trenton James   B- 2 Mar 1971

      7 HANSON, Troy Paul   B-13 Oct 1972

      7 HANSON, Kamylee   B- 5 Dec 1977

      7 HANSON, Kalisa   B- 8 Mar 1981

   6 STAM, Lon Richard B-6 Mar 1951
   6 STAM, Claudia HOLSTEIN, Sp. (1) B-   M-19 Jun 1970 Div.
   6 STAM, Pamela Ruth REED, Sp. (2) B-24 Mar 1952 M-6 Jan 1979

      7 STAM, Jeremy   B-20 Nov 1970

      7 STAM, Melinda   B-20 Sep 1974

      7 STAM, Corbin Richard   B-10 Dec 1979

   6 JENSEN, Jillyn STAM B-20 Feb 1955 M-6 Jan 1975
   6 JENSEN, Don "W", Sp. B-30 Jan 1952

      7 JENSEN, Jamilynn   B-25 Sep 1977

      7 JENSEN, Janelle   B- 3 Feb 1979

      7 JENSEN, Juliadon   B-30 Jan 1981

   6 STAM, Darren Vaughn   B- 9 Mar 1957

   6 STAM, Renee   B-23 Mar 1967

4 VAN WAGONER, Phyllis Rachel MURDOCH B-21 Aug 1914 M-19 Sep 1935
4 VAN WAGONER, Paul Halma, Sp. B-9 Jan 1909

   5 VAN WAGONER, Philip B-5 Aug 1937
   5 VAN WAGONER, Marva MONTGOMERY Kohler, Sp. (1) B-9 Aug 1937 M-3 Nov 1955 Div.
     Kohler, Doyle, Sp. (1) B-   M-   Div.
   5 VAN WAGONER, Gail HOPWOOD, Sp. (2) B-   M-5 Aug 1972 Div.

      6 KOHLER, Steven   B- 2 Jul 1953

      6 LUPER, Suan VAN WAGONER B-29 Dec 1955 M-3 Aug 1973
      6 LUPER, Rodney, Sp. B-2 Feb 1954

         7 LUPER, Michelle   B-17 Mar 1974

         7 LUPER, Michael Scott   B- 6 May 1975

         7 LUPER, Matthew Adam   B-12 Apr 1978

         7 LUPER, Mark Charles   B-10 Mar 1981

      6 VAN WAGONER, Philip Lynn B-25 Apr 1957 D-25 Apr 1957

      6 JOHNSON, Julie Ann VAN WAGONER B-4 Apr 1958 M-19 Nov 1976
      6 JOHNSON, Russell Joseph, Sp. B-22 Oct 1952

         7 JOHNSON, Amanda Kay   B-13 Sep 1977

         7 JOHNSON, Jodi Ann   B- 5 Oct 1979

      6 VAN WAGONER, Brent B-6 Aug 1959 M-14 Feb 1981
      6 VAN WAGONER, Lorraine THOMSON, Sp. B-9 May 1958

```
              7 VAN WAGONER, Paige              B-11 Nov 1981

        6 VAN WAGONER, Sean              B- 5 Nov 1961

        6 VAN WAGONER, Jeffery Scott     B- 8 May 1964

    5 KOHLER, Paula Nan VAN WAGONER B-22 Aug 1945 M-21 Jun 1963
    5 KOHLER, Norman, Sp. B-30 May 1939

            6 KOHLER, Lynette            B-6 Jun 1965

            6 KOHLER, Scott Alan         B-18 Sep 1968

            6 KOHLER, Shelly Dawn        B-27 Sep 1969

            6 KOHLER, Craig Norman       B- 6 Sep 1972

            6 KOHLER, Kirt               B- 3 Oct 1975

            6 KOHLER, Katy Sue           B- 7 Mar 1977

            6 KOHLER, Derek Bill         B-16 Feb 1978

            6 KOHLER, Matthew Quinn      B-26 Mar 1979

    5 THACKER, Peggy VAN WAGONER B-22 May 1949 M-19 Sep 1969
    5 THACKER, Floyd Edwin, Sp. B-30 Mar 1948

            6 THACKER, Darin Edwin       B-26 Aug 1970

            6 THACKER, Denise            B- 7 Aug 1974

            6 THACKER, Tammy             B-18 Sep 1975

            6 THACKER, Alison            B-10 Feb 1977

    5 REMUND, Martha VAN WAGONER B-20 Aug 1952 M-6 Sep 1974
    5 REMUND, Roy Shumway, Sp. B-29 Aug 1952

            6 REMUND, Jessica            B-11 Aug 1975

            6 REMUND, Brett "J"          B- 5 Mar 1978

    5 VAN WAGONER, Paul Murdoch B-18 Sep 1954 M-23 Mar 1979
    5 VAN WAGONER, Debora L EGBERT, Sp. B-16 Jul 1957

            6 VAN WAGONER, Skyler Paul   B- 2 Oct 1979

            6 VAN WAGONER, Seth          B-24 Mar 1981

4 MAXWELL, Joan MURDOCH B-11 Mar 1917 M-2 Jul 1937
4 MAXWELL, Glen, Sp. B-21 Mar 1914

    5 LADLE, Mary Ellen MAXWELL B-27 Oct 1938 M-14 Aug 1959
    5 LADLE, John Noel, Sp. B-24 Jan 1936

        6 LADLE, Michael Kay B-8 Jun 1960 M-30 Dec 1981
        6 LADLE, Annette NIELSEN, Sp. B-3 Oct 1960

        6 GOLDHARDT, Janel Diane LADLE B-28 Jan 1962 M-7 May 1981
        6 GOLDHARDT, David Kunz, Sp. B-20 Dec 1958

        6 LADLE, Lori Ann            B-14 Jan 1964 D-16 Jan 1964

        6 LADLE, Wendy Elizabeth      B- 5 Jul 1965

        6 LADLE, Devin Eugene         B-22 Jun 1968

        6 LADLE, Trent Glenn          B-24 Aug 1970

        6 LADLE, Kathryn Ruth         B- 4 Jul 1973

    5 MAXWELL, James "B" B-16 Apr 1941 M-10 Jul 1963
    5 MAXWELL, Donna Deone POULSEN, Sp. B-7 Sep 1943
```

```
        6 MAXWELL, Garry Troy          B- 6 Oct 1967

        6 MAXWELL, Sherrie Ann         B- 1 Mar 1970

        6 MAXWELL, Scott James         B-14 Aug 1976

5 ZUNDEL, Judith Ann MAXWELL B-8 Oct 1945 M-23 Jul 1965
5 ZUNDEL, Steven William, Sp. B-27 Jul 1941

        6 ZUNDEL, Teresa Ann           B-29 Sep 1966

        6 ZUNDEL, Kathy Sue (Susie)    B-27 Apr 1968

        6 ZUNDEL, Robert Steven        B-27 Jul 1969

        6 ZUNDEL, Jonathan Maxwell     B-14 Oct 1972

        6 ZUNDEL, Steffany JoAnn       B- 3 Jul 1975

        6 ZUNDEL, Andrea Ellen         B-19 May 1978

        6 ZUNDEL, Judith Errin         B- 2 Jun 1980

5 ALLEN, Barbara Joy MAXWELL B-14 Aug 1949 M-11 Jul 1969
5 ALLEN, Kerry Lynn, Sp. B-14 Apr 1947

        6 ALLEN, Katrina "W"           B-13 Jun 1970
```

David Steel Murdoch and Mary Emily Van Wagenen

David Steel Murdoch was born May 31, 1872, in Heber, Utah. He was the fourteenth child and the youngest son in the family of fifteen children of John Murray and Ann Steel Murdoch. John and Ann and their parents came to Utah with the Mormon pioneers.

His Early Life

David's adult life reflected the rich experience of his early boyhood and young manhood. His earliest days in a loving family gave him a sensitive appreciation and affection for people. He loved and was loved by others, and soon learned that he was among people who wanted him. This gave him a feeling of confidence in the goodness of life and an understanding and appreciation of others. He spent most of his childhood on a ranch north of Heber City in an area now known as Keetley. David's father had a co-op sheep herd so took care of other farmers herds part of the time.

Being the youngest son, he enjoyed some uncommon privileges, and on occasion was chided as being a favorite child. He loved to be constantly with his parents, and through ingenious ways found methods of being with them, especially on trips or journeys of any kind. He had such love for his mother; many times he would follow her when she would go as a midwife, night or day, and stay on the porch until she would go home.

By sharing the common experiences of his family and neighbors, he learned to feel at home on the farm and stock ranch. There was plenty of work for him to do. Without shoes, he herded sheep over the fields and hills, for shoes for children in those days were mostly a Sunday affair. During his early days he developed a love for good horses and later owned teams and racers that were the pride of him and his family. In pursuing useful work, his mind and body developed without major tension and stress. This helped him to place important things first and to keep his mind uncluttered with minor problems and frustrations. Throughout his life, his children and their children could feel a steadiness coming from his stability and serenity. He was lovingly known as "Papa" to all of us.

David was an attractive man, a typical Scotch type, short of stature, happy, sociable, and friendly. As he matured and sought independent work, his interests were in the fields of construction, livestock, and mining. One of the buildings on which he worked that is still standing is the white brick hotel at the Homestead Resort at Midway. He also built the first home of his own, a red brick structure that is still standing.

In his boyhood he learned to play as well as to work. He took special interest in baseball, fishing, and hunting. The love of these sports stayed with him throughout his life and was transmitted to his sons, who shared with him many happy hours in the mountains and streams of Utah.

Courtship and Marriage

Myth and reality are hard to separate in stories and David's courtship and marriage. There seems to have been no scarcity of girl friends. From bobsleigh riding, dancing, and other parties he found recreation and associations which led him from everyday affection to love and marriage. Finally the apple of his eye became Emily Van Wagenen, a dark-eyed community beauty and musician who soon took his entire interest and attention. After a courtship (not to be discussed in this document), they were happily married on October 21, 1891. The marriage ceremony was performed by

Bishop John H. Van Wagenen, father of the bride, and was later solemnized in the Salt Lake Endowment house in 1894. His selection of a wife proved to be his wisest decision of his life. Throughout her married life Emily was an outstanding wife and mother. Her sterling quality made her an appropriate teammate in the high achievements that were to come in their family life.

To this new family unit happiness was to be born from the early sorrow occasioned by the loss of their first three children. In those days it must have been difficult to see the joy that was to follow as eleven additional sons and daughters were to come and bless their home.

During their early married life David and Emily found both pleasures and sobriety in flavoring their vocational lives with church and community recreation and music. At first David took up mining, becoming mine superintendent over a period of years. Then he returned to merchandising in which he operated general merchandising stores first in Midway and then in Heber during the period 1900 to 1914.

Their lives were not completely channeled in their occupations, but were richly flavored with music and church activities and recreation. They knew how to enjoy life in their family and community. As musicians in demand, they organized and managed the Murdoch Orchestra. This orchestra was well known in the Wasatch and Provo valleys in the succeeding forty years. Emily played the piano and David the violin. Highly active in their wards and stakes, David and Emily freely furnished orchestra music for benefit dances and entertainments. Through his priesthood activities he became a high priest in the Church, holding many important positions.

Papa played the guitar and sang. After he and Mother were married she taught him the fingering scale of the violin, which was the beginning of a real career in the music world. He had a wonderful ear for music and was able to play the violin by ear for over forty-five years in their fine orchestra. Mother played the piano and was sometimes assisted by Minnie and Atha and other members of the family. Ray played the saxophone. The Murdoch Orchestra was a very popular band. This was where we all acquired the desire to play and sing. These times were a wonderful part of our lives as a family. Many happy times were spent in our home at 188 North and Third West in Provo. Dancing, singing, and eating were the main events. Many people would pass by and stop to enjoy the music and the fun times we were having. Papa and Mama were always happiest when we were all having fun together.

Provo Period 1914–1950

November, 1914, when the family moved to Provo, opened a significant chapter in the David Murdoch family history. To be anticipated was the earning of a livelihood for a family of eleven with two more to follow. In Provo, David took up the distribution of produce and poultry and supplemented that income with the earnings from the orchestra. During the thirty-three year period 1917–1950, the family home was on the corner of 188 North and Third West in Provo. By this time the family was complete with the two youngest children added. The days and years were filled with satisfaction and the daily fortunes of family life. The eleven children in the family were: Aritha, Ervan, Minnie, Eva, Lillie, Atha, Chloe, Ray, Ethel, Velda, and Emmitt. In this home there were no dull moments; every member had his part to play and some overplayed their parts.

By the time each son and daughter had found his life's companion, the procession of grandchildren had started—each one as welcome as the first. The family home seemed to bulge at the seams. There were very few days when some married branch of the family had not returned for a visit. There were family programs with each branch competing in talent shows; there was jovial conversation, music, and with the close of the day's work, each evening there was a family reunion.

Among all the rolls played by David and Emily Murdoch none exceeded in joy and satisfaction that of grandparents. In this they found sheer delight; deeply in love with all members, they never evidenced any partiality. Throughout their lives the family spirit was "all for one and one for all."

David's later life was saddened by the long illness and passing of his loved companion on March 31, 1943. David passed away eight years later on October 1, 1950. Their posterity at the date of this writing numbers 328, May 31, 1980.

David Steele and Mary Emily Van Wagenen Murdoch and Daughters
Back Row: Chloe, Lillie, Ethel, Eva, and Aritha
Front Row: Velda, David S., Mary Emily V., and Atha

David S. Murdoch family home
188 N. 300 W. Provo, Utah

David S. Murdoch and brother
Thomas Todd Murdoch

David Steele Murdoch   Mary Emily Van Wagenen

David S. and Mary Emily W. Murdoch   David Steele Murdoch and Son - Emmitt
August 1938

HUSBAND DAVID STEELE MURDOCH
Birth 31 May 1872
Place Heber, Wasatch, Utah
Married 21 October 1891
Place Midway, Wasatch, Utah
Death 1 October 1950 Provo, Utah, Utah
Burial 4 October 1950 Provo, Utah, Utah
Mother Ann STEEL
Father John MURRAY MURDOCH
Other Wives

WIFE MARY EMILY VAN WAGENEN
Birth 19 February 1871
Place Heber, Wasatch, Utah
Death 31 March 1943 Provo, Utah, Utah
Burial 7 April 1943 Provo, Utah, Utah
Mother Julie Ann PROVOST
Father David VAN WAGENEN
Other Husbands
Information From David & James Murdoch Family Records

1ST CHILD Anne Pearle MURDOCH
Birth 14 April 1892
Place Midway, Wasatch, Utah
Married
Death 15 April 1892
Place Midway, Wasatch, Utah
Burial Midway Midway, Wasatch, Utah

2ND CHILD David Ellis MURDOCH
Birth 7 April 1893
Place Midway, Wasatch, Utah
Married
Death 15 July 1896
Place Midway, Wasatch, Utah
Burial Midway Midway, Wasatch, Utah

3RD CHILD Lilliard MURDOCH
Birth 10 June 1896
Place Midway, Wasatch, Utah
Married
Death 14 April 1900
Place Midway, Wasatch, Utah
Burial Midway Midway, Wasatch, Utah

4TH CHILD Emily Aritha MURDOCH
Birth 14 January 1898
Place Midway, Wasatch, Utah
Married Earl Gunnel LLOYD
Date 2 April 1919
Place Salt Lake City, Utah
Death

5TH CHILD Ervan MURDOCH
Birth 29 December 1899
Place Midway, Wasatch, Utah
Married Zora FLEMING
Date 10 July 1919
Place Provo, Utah, Utah
Death 10 January 1953

6TH CHILD Minnie Preal MURDOCH
Birth 26 March 1902
Place Midway, Wasatch, Utah
Married Bliss A. CLUFF
Date 28 July 1919
Place Provo, Utah, Utah
Death 13 October 1930

7TH CHILD Eva May MURDOCH
Birth 9 January 1904
Place Midway, Wasatch, Utah
Married Bliss LeRoi BUSHMAN
Date 20 January 1921
Place Salt Lake City, Utah
Death

8TH CHILD Lillie MURDOCH
Birth 24 October 1905
Place Midway, Wasatch, Utah
Married Wesely P. LLOYD
Date 30 December 1926
Place Provo, Utah, Utah
Death 18 September 1978

9TH CHILD Atha Le Isle MURDOCH
Birth 17 April 1907
Place Midway, Wasatch, Utah
Married George Earl STEWART
Date 13 December 1927
Place Salt Lake City, Utah
Death

10TH CHILD Chloe MURDOCH
Birth 9 September 1908
Place Midway, Wasatch, Utah
Married Paul SALISBURY
Date 10 September 1928
Place Provo, Utah, Utah
Death

11TH CHILD Ray MURDOCH
Birth 26 July 1910
Place Heber, Wasatch, Utah
Married (1)Mignon HOWE (2)Neva C. PICKERING
Date 17 Oct 1933 22 June 1962
Place Salt Lake Temple Salt Lake Temple
Death 14 Feb 1975

12TH CHILD Hattie MURDOCH
Birth 17 December 1911
Place Heber, Wasatch, Utah
Married
Death 20 December 1911
Place Heber, Wasatch, Utah
Burial Midway Midway, Wasatch, Utah

13TH CHILD Ethel Lucile MURDOCH
Birth 17 June 1913
Place Heber, Wasatch, Utah
Married William W. WILSON
Date 11 September 1933
Place Salt Lake City, Utah
Death

14TH CHILD Velda MURDOCH
Birth 17 November 1914
Place Provo, Utah, Utah
Married W. Marston DE POISTER
Date 27 September 1936
Place Chica 3, Cook, Illinois
Death

15TH CHILD Emmitt MURDOCH
Birth 16 April 1916
Place Provo, Utah, Utah
Married Emma G. HINDLEY
Date 3 April 1936
Place Salt Lake City, Utah
Death

```
1 MURDOCH, James 1786-1831                    2 MURDOCH, John Murray 1820-1910
1 MURDOCH, Mary MURRAY, Sp. 1782-1856          2 MURDOCH, Ann STEEL , Sp. 1829-1909

                            3 MURDOCH, David Steele 1872-1950
   DESCENDANTS OF--------
                            3 VAN WAGENEN, Mary Emily, Sp. 1871-1943

   4 MURDOCH, Annie Pearl B-14 Apr 1892 D-15 Apr 1892        B-Birth
                                                             M-Married
   4 MURDOCH, David Ellis B- 7 Apr 1893 D-15 Jul 1896        D-Death
                                                             Sp.-Spouse
   4 MURDOCH, Lilliard    B-10 Jun 1896 D-14 Apr 1900        Div.-Divorced
                                                             Numbers-Generation
   4 LLOYD, Emily Aritha MURDOCH B-14 Jan 1898 M-2 Apr 1919
   4 LLOYD, Earl Gunnell, Sp. B-24 May 1896 D-21 Mar 1970

         5 CUILLARD, Mary Maxine LLOYD B-1 Apr 1920 M-15 Nov 1938
         5 CUILLARD, Russel Thomas, Sp. B-19 Oct 1903

              6 CUILLARD, David Russel B-29 Apr 1942 M-3 Jan 1969
              6 CUILLARD, Elizabeth Jeanne ZIRENBERG, Sp. B-25 Jul 1943

                   7 CUILLARD, Keith Russel      B-20 Dec 1969

                   7 CUILLARD, Kevin David       B-15 May 1972

                   7 CUILLARD, Kimberly Marie    B-12 Mar 1976

                   7 CUILLARD, Kelly Wayne       B- 9 Aug 1977

              6 NUTTALL, Mary Jean CUILLARD,B-2 Feb 1945 M-10 Jun 1964
              6 NUTTALL, David Eugene, Sp. B-5 Jul 1940

                   7 NUTTALL, David Eric         B-27 May 1966

                   7 NUTTALL, Gary Eugene        B-24 Jul 1968

                   7 NUTTALL, Alicja             B-22 Feb 1973

                   7 NUTTALL, Michael Jay        B-10 Apr 1974

                   7 NUTTALL, Michelle           B-21 May 1978

                   7 NUTTALL, Jill               B-14 May 1979

              6 CUILLARD, Thomas Earl B-31 Mar 1949 M-26 Jan 1968
              6 CUILLARD, Donna Lou DEBEVEC, Sp. B-13 Nov 1947

                   7 CUILLARD, Steven Thomas     B- 1 Jul 1968

                   7 CUILLARD, Craig Michael     B-17 Jan 1971

                   7 CUILLARD, Scott Russel      B-22 Aug 1972

                   7 CUILLARD, Robert Todd       B-25 Feb 1975

                   7 CUILLARD, Nancy Michelle    B- 9 May 1977

                   7 CUILLARD, James David       B-01 Nov 1980

              6 COWDEN, Tiena Juanita VAUGHN B-7 Sep 1956 (Sealed)
              6 COWDEN, Christopher Marc, Sp. B-14 Mar 1957 M-27 Mar 1976

                   7 COWDEN, Joe Francis         B-22 May 1977

                   7 COWDEN, Jason Thomas        B-10 Mar 1979

              6 SAMFORD, Alice Virginia MOOSMAN B-23 May 1958 (Sealed)
              6 SAMFORD, Randall Frank, Sp. B-18 Jul 1958 M-6 May 1977

                   7 SAMFORD, Adam Frank         B-22 Dec 1977

                   7 SAMFORD, James Alma         B-24 Jun 1979
```

        6 SMITH, Linda "B" CUILLARD B-8 Jan 1959 (Adopted & Sealed)
        6 SMITH, Ricky Lynn, Sp. B-7 Aug 1956 M-11 Apr 1980

        6 CUILLARD, Richard Barney B-17 Apr 1960 (Adopted & Sealed)

5 LLOYD, Joseph Earl B-1 Aug 1921
5 LLOYD, Glenna MAHONEY, Sp. B-16 Aug 1927 M-8 Oct 1948

        6 LLOYD, Joseph Ross B-18 Feb 1950
        6 LLOYD, Sharon Foy, Sp. B-31 Dec 1948 M-21 Nov 1970

                7 LLOYD, Joseph Ryan   B-10 Oct 1973

                7 LLOYD, Jennifer   B- 1 Oct 1975

                7 LLOYD, Griffin R   B-19 Feb 1979

        6 LLOYD, Mark Kay B-20 Apr 1952
        6 LLOYD, Phylis CARLSON, Sp. B-12 Oct 1953 M-10 Jun 1972

                7 LLOYD, Larie   B- 3 Jun 1974

                7 LLOYD, Brett M   B- 1 Sep 1975

                7 LLOYD, Marci   B-23 Oct 1979

        6 LLOYD, Kelly Earl B-12 Sep 1955
        6 LLOYD, Beverly BROWN, Sp. B-29 Apr 1956 M-13 Jun 1975

                7 LLOYD, Melissa   B-12 Apr 1977

        6 LLOYD, Leann B-19 May 1957

        6 GRIGGS, Kristine LLOYD B-22 Dec 1961
        6 GRIGGS, Daniel Wardell, Sp. B-16 Sep 1953 M-8 Dec 1979

5 LLOYD, David Kenneth B-28 May 1923
5 LLOYD, Cleo COOK, Sp. (1) B-16 Mar 1931 M-3 Mar 1947 Div.
5 LLOYD, Connie CARPENTER, Sp. (2) B-   M-1 Aug 1970

        6 HOHMAN, Peggy Ann LLOYD B-7 Oct 1947
        6 HOHMAN, Ron, Sp. B-   M-5 Feb 1967

        6 LLOYD, Larry Kenneth B-7 Feb 1949
        6 LLOYD, Shelia   , Sp. B-   M-

        6 LLOYD, Robert Earl B-29 Jun 1950
        6 LLOYD, Rinnette TISCHNER, Sp. B-   M-2 Aug 1975

        6 LLOYD, Kathleen B-12 Aug 1952

        6 LLOYD, Daniel Boon B-9 Nov 1953
        6 LLOYD, Vicki   , Sp. B-   M-

5 AIKIN, Martha Nadine LLOYD B-25 Nov 1924
5 AIKIN, Chester Dale, Sp. B-22 Sep 1922 M-13 Feb 1943

        6 SCHMITZ, Suzan Nadine AIKIN B-4 Oct 1944
        6 SCHMITZ, Joseph Henry, Sp. B-19 Apr 1938 M-13 Sep 1974

                7 SCHMITZ, Joseph Christopher B-25 Mar 1976

                7 SCHMITZ, Alysha Dawn   B-18 May 1978

        6 HUGHES, Sherry Dee AIKEN B-9 May 1946
        6 STEIN, Richard, Sp. (1) B-   M-
        6 HUGHES, Gerald Phillip, Sp. (2) B-29 Sep 1948 M-23 Nov 1973

                7 STEIN, Andrea   B- 9 Apr 1965

                7 STEIN, Richard Barton   B- 7 Jan 1969

                7 HUGHES, Gerald Bret   B- 5 Sep 1974

                7 HUGHES, Tori   B-23 Jun 1976

6 AIKEN, Paulette B-13 Nov 1951

5 BALLIGER, Aritha Deaun B-23 Jan 1926
5 BALLIGER, John Ronald, Sp. B-28 Jan 1930 M-25 Aug 1956

    6 BALLIGER, Sheila Denise B-28 May 1957

    6 BALLIGER, Stephen Ronald B- 6 Jun 1959

5 CLYDE, Cleo Earlene LLOYD   B-18 Oct 1928
5 CLYDE, James W, Sp. B-4 Sep 1927 M-19 May 1948

    6 CLYDE, Richard Don B-25 Nov 1948
    6 CLYDE, Eunice FARNSWORTH, Sp. B- 10 Feb 1949

        7 CLYDE, Richard Zachary   B-23 Jul 1975

        7 CLYDE, Jamie Sunshine   B- 6 May 1977

    6 CLYDE, James L.   B-12 Jan 1954

    6 CLYDE, Matthew L. B- 6 Mar 1958

5 LLOYD, Franklin B-5 Sep 1930 D-6 Sep 1930

5 LLOYD, Orson Ray B-25 Nov 1932
5 LLOYD, Sharlene SCHEAR, Sp. B-8 May 1934 M-22 Aug 1952

    6 LLOYD, Steven Ray B-13 May 1953

    6 GERTSCH, Suzanne LLOYD B-2 Sep 1955
    6 GERTSCH, Keith Reed, Sp. B-13 Jan 1953 M-2 Sep 1972

        7 GERTSCH, Sunny Lynn   B-22 May 1974

        7 GERTSCH, Stefannie Ann   B-25 May 1975

    6 LLOYD, Jeffery Dee B-5 Mar 1957
    6 LLOYD, Annette COLLINS, Sp. B-18 Jul 1963 M-18 Aug 1979

        7 LLOYD, Tiffany Ann   B- 3 Feb 1980

    6 LLOYD, Johnni B-16 Jul 1958 D-16 Jul 1958 Stillborn

    6 LLOYD, Douglas B-16 Mar 1961 D-16 Mar 1961 Stillborn

5 FITZGERALD, Ruth LaNae LLOYD B-5 Nov 1934
5 FITZGERALD, Mont B, Sp. B-4 Feb 1932 M-22 Jun 1951

    6 FITZGERALD, Rodney M B-29 Dec 1951
    6 FITZGERALD, Rhonda MARCHANT, Sp. B-3 Apr 1953 M-10 Sep 1971

        7 FITZGERALD, Rowdy R   B-16 Apr 1972

        7 FITZGERALD, Kasey M   B-14 Mar 1975

        7 FITZGERALD, Lacy   B-30 Jan 1979

    6 FITZGERALD, Kay L B-11 Jul 1954
    6 FITZGERALD, Janette RUTLEDGE, Sp. B- 8 Mar 1958 M-28 Jun 1980

    6 PROVOST, Brenda FITZGERALD B-28 Sep 1955
    6 PROVOST, Clair Luke, Sp. B-16 Feb 1956 M-14 Jul 1977

        7 PROVOST, Jason Luke   B- 3 Jun 1978

    6 JONES, Jan FITZGERALD B-29 Sep 1959
    6 JONES, Jeffery Dee, Sp. B-30 Jul 1957 M-19 Nov 1976

        7 JONES, Jamie Dee   B-25 Jun 1977

        7 JONES, Jodie Lynn   B-28 Dec 1978

5 LLOYD, John Wayne B-29 Mar 1937
5 LLOYD, Joyce JACOBSON, Sp. B-20 May 1941 M-1 Nov 1957

      6 LLOYD, De Anna   B-29 Nov 1958

      6 LLOYD, Debra   B-24 Sep 1961

      6 LLOYD, Teri   B- 1 Mar 1964

      6 LLOYD, Shonna   B-13 Feb 1970

4 MURDOCH, Ervan B-29 Dec 1899 D-10 Jan 1953
4 MURDOCH, Zora FLEMING, Sp. B-30 Jan 1898 M-10 Jul 1919

      5 MURDOCH, Richard Dean B-22 Dec 1919
      5 MURDOCH, Charlene Winifred CROSS, Sp. (1) B-20 Feb 1921 M-30 Jul 1942 Div.
      5 MURDOCH, Sarah S., Sp. (2) B-   M-   D-16 Aug 1979
      5 MURDOCH, Margie Maxine   Sp. (3) B-   M-

          6 MURDOCH, Stephen Richard B- 25 Feb 1944
          6 MURDOCH, Collette THOMAS, Sp. B-   M-

              7 MURDOCH, Stephanie Ruth   B-

              7 MURDOCH. Robert Stephen B-

              7 MURDOCH, Mark Charles   B-

              7 MURDOCH, Nicholas Thomas B-

          6 BELL, Julie MURDOCH B-2 Jan 1946
          6 BELL, Richard, Sp. B-   M-

              7 BELL, David   B-

              7 BELL, Daniel Brian   B-

              7 BELL, Carolyn

          6 MURDOCH, William Cross B-20 Jun 1950
          6 MURDOCH, Wendy   , Sp. B-   M-

              7 MURDOCH, Melissa Deanne B-

              7 MURDOCH, Annalee   B-

              7 MURDOCH, Matthew James   B-

          6 HEPWORTH, Dixene MURDOCH B-28 May 1954
          6 HEPWORTH, Jeffrey, Sp. B-   M-

              7 HEPWORTH, Jenifer   B-

      5 MURDOCH, Vivian B-30 Mar 1921 D-22 Feb 1932

      5 BROWN, Dorothy MURDOCH B-12 Feb 1923
      5 BROWN, Zack Darrell, Sp. B-12 Mar 1922 M-11 Jun 1942

          6 BURNS, Dorothy Linda BROWN B-6 Apr 1943
          6 BURNS, Richard Bennett, Sp. B-   M-25 Jun 1964

              7 BURNS, Darrell   B-31 Mar 1965

              7 BURNS, David   B- 1 May 1967

              7 BURNS, Sterling   B-

              7 BURNS, Douglas   B-

          6 STEWART, Beverly BROWN B-23 Oct 1946
          6 STEWART, Bryce Burton, Sp. B-26 Oct 1942 M-9 Sep 1965

```
        7 STEWART, Michael        B-28 Nov 1966

        7 STEWART, Gregory        B-

        7 STEWART, Robert         B-

        7 STEWART, Christopher    B-

    6 BROWN, Roger Darrell B-14 Apr 1949
    6 BROWN, Susan Green, Sp. B-          M-9 Jul 1971

        7 BROWN, Zack Roger       B-

        7 BROWN, Spencer James    B-

        7 BROWN, Brian David      B-

    6 BURTON, Janet BROWN B-28 Jul 1953
    6 BURTON, Mark Harker, Sp. B-         M-18 Aug 1972

        7 BURTON, Steven          B-

        7 BURTON, Jennifer        B-

5 MURDOCH, Donald Dean B-3 Jan 1927
5 MURDOCH, Betty Jean GEREN, Sp. B-12 May 1929 M-23 Dec 1949 D-      1961

    6 MURDOCH, Scott Ervan  B-14 Mar 1951
    6 MURDOCH, Janet CASCIO, Sp. B-        M-

    6 MURDOCH, Clifford Dean  B-7 Jul 1952

    6 HILLWIG, Patricia Dayle MURDOCH B-9 Nov 1953
    6 HILLWIG, Ronald, Sp. B-

5 CORAY, Betty MURDOCH B-2 Dec 1928
5 CORAY, John Louis, Sp. B-31 Jan 1928 M-1 Sep 1948

    6 MURPHY, Kathleen CORAY B-19 Sep 1950
    6 MURPHY, Gary W. Sp. B-              M-

        7 MURPHY, Justin Wayne    B-

        7 MURPHY, Kristen         B-

    6 CORAY, John Brent B-2 Sep 1954
    6 CORAY, Deborah        , Sp. B-            M-

    6 RILEY, Christine CORAY B-1 Sep 1957
    6 RILEY, Kevin L., Sp. B-

        7 RILEY, Elizabeth        B-

        7 RILEY, Stephanie        B-

    6 BROWN, Coleen CORAY B-16 Jan 1959
    6 BROWN, William K., Sp. B-           M-

        7 BROWN, Jessie           B-

    6 CORAY, Robert Lewis  B-16 Sep 1964

5 FRANKLIN, Elaine MURDOCH B-26 Apr 1933
5 FRANKLIN, John Robert, Sp. B-          M-18 Aug 1953

    6 NATION, Annette FRANKLIN Breedlove B-11 Feb 1955
    6 BREEDLOVE, William Payton, Sp. (1) B-        M-          Div.
    6 NATION, Richard A., Sp. (2) B-          M-

        7 BREEDLOVE, Natalie      B-

    6 BECK, Marie FRANKLIN B-25 Mar 1956
    6 BECK, Russell D., Sp. B-
```

                7 BECK, Patrick   B-

                7 BECK, Phillip Andrew   B-

                7 BECK, Christine Nicole   B-

                7 BECK, Grant   B-

        6 DUNCAN, Susan FRANKLIN B-9 Nov 1957
        6 DUNCAN, Kevin C., Sp. B-   M-

        6 FRANKLIN, John Robert Jr. B-28 Aug 1959

        6 FRANKLIN, Richard Douglas B-17 Jul 1961

4 CLUFF, Minnie LaPreal MURDOCH B-26 Mar 1902 D-13 Oct 1930
4 CLUFF, Bliss Adelbert, Sp. B-14 Mar 1898 M-28 Jul 1919

      5 RICHEY, Ruth CLUFF B-4 Feb 1920
      5 RICHEY, Frank Stanley, Sp. B-9 May 1918 M-17 Apr 1940

          6 ROBERTS, Linda Jean RICHEY B-19 Feb 1952
          6 ROBERTS, Alan G., Sp. B-   M-

          6 RICHEY, Kevin Bruce B-27 Aug 1954
          6 RICHEY, Ruth Ann SPENCER, Sp. B-   M-

          6 RICHEY, Craig Stanley B-8 Sep 1955

      5 CLUFF, Jerry B-29 Nov 1921 D-   Jan 1922

      5 ROLLIN, June CLUFF B-21 Jun 1923
      5 ROLLIN, Carl Bernard, Sp. B-26 Sep 1919 M-3 Jan 1942

          6 ROLLINS, Carl Boyd Jr. B-21 Jan 1943
          6 ROLLINS, Joanne Grace BORISOF, Sp. B-10 Mar 1944 M-7 Apr 1967

                7 ROLLIN, Cathleen Jennifer B-26 Aug 1968

                7 ROLLIN, Caryn Elizabeth   B-17 Dec 1971

                7 ROLLIN, Michael Carl   B- 4 Sep 1976

          6 ROLLIN, Bruce Bliss B-7 Oct 1944
          6 ROLLIN, Susan Kay PARTRIDGE, Sp. B-22 May 1952 M-23 Sep 1972

                7 ROLLIN, Brian Bliss   B-19 Apr 1974

                7 ROLLIN, Keith Allen   B-26 Jun 1975

          6 FEUDNER, Sandra Joan ROLLIN B-20 Sep 1946
          6 FEUDNER, Daniel Arthur, Sp. B-3 Sep 1942   M-29 Oct 1964

                7 Feudner, Tracy Lyn   B- 7 Dec 1969

          6 ROLLIN, Gary Joseph B-8 Mar 1948
          6 ROLLIN, Karen Kay COLSON, Sp. B-28 Dec 1953 M-10 Apr 1976

                7 ROLLIN, Jenny Marie   B-21 Aug 1977

          6 ROLLIN, James Neil B-7 Oct 1949
          6 ROLLIN, Jill Marie MASTERS, Sp. B-29 Nov 1952 M-15 Oct 1971

                7 ROLLIN, Jeanie Marie   B- 9 Jan 1973

                7 ROLLIN, Janet Lee   B-20 Jun 1976

          6 ROLLIN, Ronald Michael B-8 Apr 1952
          6 ROLLIN, Laurie June LED, Sp. B-3 Jan 1954 M-6 Apr 19

          6 KURPIESKI, Terry Lynn ROLLIN B-11 Nov 1956
          6 KURPIESKI, Walter John, Sp. B-19 Oct 1954 M-17 Sep 1977

5 CLUFF, Robert Bliss B-10 Dec 1925
5 CLUFF, Rula HUFF, Sp. B-16 Feb 1929 M-23 Sep 1948

     6 CLUFF, Robert Alma B-14 Jul 1950 D-   1951

     6 CLUFF, John Arthur B-19 Dec 1951
     6 CLUFF, Julie CAZIMERO, Sp. B-   M-

          7 CLUFF, Nathan Kalani   B-

     6 CLUFF, Alice Ruth B-31 Dec 1953

     6 CLUFF, David Jerry B-31 May 1957

5 HALKYARD, Atha Jean CLUFF B-1 Nov 1927
5 HALKYARD, Edward Uriah, Sp. B-   M- Apr 1945

     6 CURRIN, Susan Ruth HALKYARD B-6 Feb 1946
     6 CURRIN, Pete, Sp. B-   M-

          7 CURRIN, Charlyene   B-

          7 CURRIN, Tammy Sue

     6 BEALL, Genny Carol HALKYARD B-16 Dec 1949
     6 BEALL, Robert, Sp. B-   M-

          6 BEALL, Terry Jason   B-

          6 BEALL, Toby John   B-

          6 BEALL, Michael   B-

     6 HALKYARD, Edward Robert B-22 Aug 1952
     6 HALKYARD, Carol Ruth JOHNSTON, Sp. B-   M-

     6 HALKYARD, James Stanley B-13 Sep 1959

     6 HALKYARD, Jerry Thomas   B-27 Jun 1956

4 BUSHMAN, Eva May MURDOCH B-9 Jan 1904
4 BUSHMAN, Bliss LeRoi, Sp. B-9 Jul 1899 M-20 Jan 1921

     5 BARTON, Eva Nadine BUSHMAN B-15 Nov 1921
     5 BARTON, James Richard, Sp. B-21 Jul 1917 M-6 Jan 1943

          6 CLARK, Marilee BARTON B-6 Sep 1944
          6 CLARK, Joseph William, Sp. B-7 Oct 1943 M-27 Jun 1969

               7 CLARK, Bryan Joseph   B- 9 Jul 1970

               7 CLARK, Thayne Harold Glen B- 3 Oct 1971

               7 CLARK, Jordon   B-17 Mar 1973

               7 CLARK, Kimball James   B-5 May 1975

               7 CLARK, Ashley   B- 6 Feb 1979

               7 CLARK, Nathan Driggs   B- 3 Apr 1981

               7 CLARK, Nathan Driggs   B-17 Mar 1973

          6 BARTON, Richards B-25 Sep 1947 D-Stillborn

          6 BARTON, James Bushman B-10 Aug 1949
          6 BARTON, Becky Bea GUNN, Sp. B-16 Oct 1934 M-12 Feb 1976

               7 BARTON, Emily Nadine   B-21 Nov 1976

               7 BARTON, James   B- 6 Sep 1978

               7 BARTON, Stephanie Kaye   B- 8 Feb 1980

               7 BARTON, Jermey Bushman   B-16 Nov 1981

6 GLAZIER, Beverly Kay BARTON B-31 Dec 1951
6 GLAZIER, David Lewis, Sp. B-8 Mar 1955 M-18 Jun 1977

      7 GLAZIER, Bryon Richards   B- 3 May 1978

      7 GLAZIER, Rebecca   B- 9 Sep 1980

6 CALL, Jayne BARTON B-1 Aug 1954
6 CALL, Thomas Flandro, Sp. B-   M-20 May 1978

      7 CALL, Richars Barton   B- 7 Dec 1978

      7 CALL, Tiffany   B- 6 Jul 1980

      7 CALL, Brian Thomas   B- 6 Nov 1981

6 BARTON, Steven Robert B-7 Mar 1958

5 BUSHMAN, Bliss Murdoch B-26 Nov 1924
5 BUSHMAN, Mary Jean GALLACHER, Sp. B-11 Apr 1926 M-27 Jan 1956

    6 BUSHMAN, Debra Jean B-9 Mar 1962

    6 BUSHMAN, Becky Lee   B-7 Sep 1963

5 LEMMON, Colleen BUSHMAN B-14 Jul 1927
5 LEMMON, George Van, Sp. B-10 Sep 1924 M-16 Jun 1945

    6 LEMMON, Celia Susanne B-20 Jun 1948 D-5 Sep 1952

    6 DAVIS, Janeane LEMMON B-27 Nov 1949
    6 DAVIS, Roy Howard Jr., Sp. B-3 Oct 1945 M-12 Aug 1968

      7 DAVIS, Brian Gant   B-27 Sep 1969

      7 DAVIS, Lance Howard   B-23 Sep 1970

      7 DAVIS, Jason Colby   B-30 Sep 1971

      7 DAVIS, Eric Lael   B-27 Jun 1975

      7 DAVIS, Scott Kyle   B-25 Oct 1976

    6 LEMMON, Roger Dale B-22 Oct 1954
    6 LEMMON, Joni Lynn STUART, Sp. B-12 Aug 1957   M-10 Aug 1979

      7 LEMMON, Tracie Lynn   B-24 Feb 1981

    6 LEMMON, Thomas William B-14 Nov 1955
    6 LEMMON, Michele Kay CHRISTENSEN, Sp. B-22 Nov 1957 M-18 Feb 1981

5 McCUNE, Beverly BUSHMAN Young B-22 Oct 1930
5 YOUNG, Gaylen Snow Jr, Sp. (1) B-   M-4 Aug 1950 Div.
5 McCUNE, Keath, Sp. (2) B-   M-27 Dec 1979

    6 YOUNG, Gaylen Bushman B-11 May 1951
    6 YOUNG, Lori SMITH, Sp. B-27 May 1954 M-31 Jul 1975

      7 YOUNG, Jessica   B- 6 Oct 1976

      7 YOUNG, James Gaylen   B-28 Nov 1980

    6 BIRD, Julie YOUNG B-4 Aug 1952
    6 BIRD, Clark, Sp. B-18 Jun 1950 M-12 Feb 1970

      7 BIRD, Angela Alihilani   B-16 Jul 1970

      7 BIRD, Chad   B-15 Jan 1972

      7 BIRD, Matthew   B- 2 Oct 1974

```
            7 BIRD, Sean Michael              B-27 Jul 1977

            7 BIRD, Melissa                   B-26 Oct 1980

      6 KEPLER, Susan YOUNG B-18 Apr 1955
      6 KEPLER, Darrell, Sp. B-18 Jun 1956 M-28 Jul 1977

      6 McFARLAND, Beverly Jane YOUNG B-31 Oct 1956
      6 McFARLAND, Steven James, Sp. B-3 May 1956 M-7 Oct 1977

            7 McFARLAND, Daniel Young         B-6 Dec 1979

      6 FAIRBANKS, Colleen YOUNG B-23 Apr 1958
      6 FAIRBANKS, Mark, Sp. B-   Mar 1958 M-21 Oct 1978

            7 FAIRBANKS, Dillon Murdoch       B-29 Jul 1981

      6 YOUNG, Mary Lou  B-27 Apr 1962

  5 DOXEY, Joanne BUSHMAN B-17 Apr 1932
  5 DOXEY, David Watson, Sp. B-26 Apr 1931 M-7 Jun 1954

      6 DOXEY, David Bushman B-3 Mar 1955
      6 DOXEY, Merle Marie WICKER, Sp. B-              M-4 May 1979

            7 DOXEY, Tiffany Marie            B- 3 Apr 1980

      6 DOXEY, Gary Bushman    B-16 Apr 1956

      6 DOXEY, Stephen Bushman B- 7 Aug 1957

      6 DOXEY, James Bliss     B-14 Sep 1958

      6 DOXEY, Jospeh Bushman  B- 1 Mar 1960 D-27 May 1960

      6 DOXEY, Debbie Lyn      B- 6 Aug 1962

      6 DOXEY, Cynthia         B- 7 Dec 1964

      6 DOXEY, Christie Joanne B-29 Dec 1966

4 LLOYD, Lillie MURDOCH B-24 Oct 1905 D-18 Sep 1978
4 LLOYD, Wesley Parkinson, Sp. B-15 Jun 1904 M-30 Dec 1926 D- 7 Mar 1977

    5 LLOYD, Wesley MURDOCH B-30 May 1928 D-27 Nov 1928

    5 LLOYD, Kent Murdoch B-5 Mar 1931
    5 LLOYD, Eleanor FOERSTL, Sp. (1) B-28 Feb 1936 M-4 Jun 1954
    5 LLOYD, Diane Louise RAMSEY McFerson, Sp. (2) B-           M-15 Sep 1973
      McFerson, Richard, Sp. (1) B-            M-

        6 ERIKSON, Lorie LLOYD B-4 Jun 1956
        6 ERIKSON, Glenn R. Sp. B-           M-30 Aug 1977

        6 LLOYD, Jeralie        B-27 Feb 1958

        6 LLOYD, Kathie         B-26 Dec 1961

        6 LLOYD, Susan Diane    B-13 May 1961  (adopted & sealed)

        6 LLOYD, Leslie         B-31 Jan 1963

        6 LLOYD, Donna Jean     B-22 May 1963  (adopted & sealed)

        6 LLOYD, Kellie         B-12 Feb 1969  (adopted & sealed)

    5 LLOYD, Gary Murdoch B-17 Sep 1934
    5 LLOYD, Carolyn Eleanor PROVAN, Sp. B-25 Feb 1936 M-25 Sep 1958

        6 LLOYD, James Wesley   B-20 Jan 1960

        6 LLOYD, Jeffery Provan B-20 Oct 1961

        6 LLOYD, Michael Gary   B- 6 Apr 1963
```

            6 LLOYD, Scott Charles   B- 6 Dec 1967

            6 LLOYD, Jon William   B-

4 STEWART, Atha Le Isle MURDOCH B-17 Apr 1907
4 STEWART, George Earl, Sp. B-5 Jul 1907 M-13 Dec 1927 D-21 Sep 1960

        5 STEWART, George Keith B-12 Aug 1928
        5 STEWART, Nancy TAYLOR, Sp. B-15 Nov 1927 M-26 Jun 1952

            6 STEWART, Brent Taylor   B- 6 Mar 1954
            6 STEWART, Karen GARDNER, Sp. B-24 Dec 1954 M-18 Dec 1976

            6 STEWART, Kim Taylor B-
            6 STEWART,   , Sp. B-   M-

            6 STEWART, Jan   B- 9 Mar 1960

            6 STEWART, Jon Taylor   B-25 Dec 1965

        5 STEWART, David Murdoch B-28 Mar 1935
        5 STEWART, Jo Ann HARDING, Sp. B-21 Jan 1936 M-30 Jun 1955

            6 STEWART, Randy David B-19 Dec 1956
            6 STEWART, Julie ROBINS, Sp. B- 6 May 1957 M-15 Apr 1977

                7 STEWART, Nicole   B- 8 Oct 1978

            6 STEWART, Larry Kyle   B- 1 Jun 1958

            6 STEWART, Brenda Lee   B-10 Oct 1959

            6 STEWART, Michael Allen B-20 Oct 1961

            6 STEWART, Jolynn   B-10 Apr 1963

            6 STEWART, Marsha Ann ˙ B-27 Mar 1966

4 PEAY, Chloe MURDOCH Salisbury B-9 Sep 1908
4 SALISBURY, Paul, Sp. (1) B-21 Nov 1903 M-10 Sep 1928 D-6 Mar 1973
4 PEAY, Ellis York, Sp. (2) B-24 May 1907 M-11 Jun 1976
   Peay,   Veda Anderson, Sp. (1) B-   M-

        5 KELLY, Geraldine SALISBURY B-21 Jan 1930
        5 KELLY, John Karl, Sp. B-3 Feb 1930 M-24 Feb 1949

            6 KELLY, Karl Stuart B-6 May 1952
            6 KELLY, Karla VAWDREY, Sp. B-   M-21 Jun 1975

            6 KELLY, Kendall Salisbury B-28 Feb 1956

            6 KELLY, Kris Salisbury B-14 Dec 1958
            6 KELLY, Patricia LARSEN, Sp. B-   M-14 Dec 1977

        5 SALISBURY, Paul Murdoch B-14 Sep 1931
        5 SALISBURY, Marilyn VINCENT, Sp. B-26 Mar 1937 M-8 Feb 1958

            6 SALISBURY, Craig Paul B-1 Sep 1959

            6 SALISBURY, Brian Vincent B-25 Apr 1964

            6 SALISBURY, Andrea   B-20 Sep 1970

4 MURDOCH, Ray B-26 Jul 1910 D-14 Feb 1975
4 MURDOCH, Mignon HOWE, Sp. B-22 Aug 1912 M-17 Oct 1933 D-30 Aug 1961
4 MURDOCH, Neva Catherine PICKERING Ford, Sp. (2) B-25 Jun 1912 M-22 Jun 1962
   Ford, Harvey, Sp. (1) B-18 Jul 1907 M-6 May 1931 D-20 May 1954

        5 MURDOCH, Gordon Ray B-8 Aug 1936
        5 MURDOCH, Joanne Lea HOOVER, Sp. (1) B-   M-5 Jun 1959 Div. - 1 Nov 1964
        5 MURDOCH, Sandra VAN VLEET, Sp. (2) B-   M-22 Aug 1965 Div.
        5 MURDOCH, Lee SMITH, Sp. (3) B-2 Jan 1940 M-17 Mar 1978

```
        6 MURDOCH, Julene           B-15 Nov 1960

        6 MURDOCH, Jacqueline       B-21 Jul 1962

        6 MURDOCH, Kathy Lyn        B-

   5 MURDOCH, John William B-10 Feb 1942
   5 MURDOCH, Barbara Joanne STRINGHAM, Sp. (1) B-12 Aug 1942 M-23 May 1959 Div.
   5 MURDOCH, Sue          , Sp. (2) B-              M-

        6 MURDOCH, Natalie Ann   B-24 Dec 1959

        6 MURDOCH, John William  B-15 Nov 1960

        6 MURDOCH, Angela        B-21 Jul 1967

   5 STULCE, Sharlene MURDOCH B-10 May 1946
   5 STULCE, Louis Gene, Sp. B-20 Oct 1943

        6 STULCE, Elizabeth Mignon  B-19 Aug 1963

        6 STULCE, Jeffery Louis     B-15 Feb 1966

        6 STULCE, Craig MURDOCH     B- 8 Feb 1968

        6 STULCE, Cory Ray          B-

   5 MURDOCH, Robert Howe B-23 Mar 1951
   5 MURDOCH, Sherilyn Denise BLACK, Sp. B              M-5 Jul 1973

4 MURDOCH, Hattie B-17 Dec 1911 D-20 Dec 1911


4 WILSON, Ethel Lucile MURDOCH B-17 Jun 1913
4 WILSON, William (Bill) Woodrow, Sp. B-4 Mar 1913 M-11 Sep 1933

   5 ANDERSON, Shirley Anne WILSON B-25 May 1934
   5 ANDERSON, John Burton, Sp. B-17 May 1930 M-4 Sep 1953

        6 WHITE, Julie ANDERSON B-24 Sep 1954
        6 WHITE, Craig Allen, Sp. B-          M-11 Oct 1974

            7 WHITE, Ember Anderson       B-25 Oct 1975

            7 WHITE, Jace Aaron Anderson B-28 Dec 1977

            7 WHITE, Jonathan Craig       B-20 Dec 1979

        6 PEARSON, Denece ANDERSON B- 4 Jun 1956
        6 PEARSON, Jace David, Sp. B-          M-15 Sep 1978

            7 PEARSON, Michael Jace       B-8 May 1980

        6 OLSEN, Karilee ANDERSON  B-21 Nov 1958
        6 OLSEN, Kevin Victor, Sp. B-          M-8 Oct 1977

            7 OLSEN, Beckee               B-25 Jan 1979

        6 ANDERSON, Laurie         B- 7 Jul 1963

        6 ANDERSON, John Douglas   B- 4 Jun 1966

        6 ANDERSON, Amy            B- 1 Apr 1974

   5 WILSON, William Douglas B-17 Dec 1946
   5 WILSON, Jeannette THOMPSON, Sp. B-12 Nov 1949

        6 WILSON, Emily            B- 3 Jun 1972

        6 WILSON, Jennifer         B- 4 Jul 1973

        6 WILSON, Stefanie         B- 7 Apr 1976
```

```
              6 WILSON, Cynthia          B- 2 Sep 1977

4 PIRTLE, Velda MURDOCH De Poister B-17 Nov 1914
4 DE POISTER, W. Marshon, Sp. B-12 Jul 1912 M-27 Sep 1936
4 PIRTLE,Arthur, Sp. (2) B-          M-

        5 DE POISTER, David Marshon B-9 Apr 1942

        5 FISHER, De Anne DE POISTER B-4 Aug 1944
        5 FISHER, George Melvin, Sp. B-          M-17 Mar 1966

        5 DE POISTER, Douglas MURDOCH  B-18 Apr 1952
        5 DE POISTER, Maria SANTOS, Sp. B-          M-24 Aug 1974

4 MURDOCH, Emmitt B-16 Apr 1916
4 MURDOCH, Emma Genieve HINDLEY, Sp. B-26 Jul 1917 M-3 Apr 1936

        5 WRATHALL, Carol Ann MURDOCH B-20 Mar 1938
        5 WRATHALL, Taft Wallace, Sp. B- 15 Jan 1937 M-17 Aug 1956 Div. 7 Dec 1970
           Wrathall, Carol Peek WILMSHURST, Sp. (2) B-          M-10 Dec 1970

              6 WRATHALL,Brenda        B- 9 Aug 1958

              6 WRATHALL, Scott Murdoch B-23 Feb 1960

              6 WRATHALL, Douglas Murdoch B-2 Aug 1963

        5 MURDOCH, David Emmit B-31 May 1942
        5 MURDOCH, Charlane OLIVER, Sp. (1) B-11 Sep 1943 M-28 Dec 1960
        5 MURDOCH, Eileen OLSON, Sp. (2) B-15 Jul 1945 M-12 May 1970

              6 MURDOCH, Shelly Ann     B-15 Jul 1961

              6 MURDOCH, Tera Leigh     B-30 Jul 1971

              6 MURDOCH, David Shane    B-23 Jul 1976

                 DAVIS, Trent          B-10 Jun 1963
```

Millicent Sophia Murdoch and Edward Teancum Murdock

Millicent Sophia Murdoch (Gentie) was born August 21, 1874, to John Murray and Ann Steel Murdoch. She was their fifteenth and last child. She may have received her nickname because of her complexion, or because she was a "gentle" woman.

Gentie was a happy, delightful child, blessed with the gift of singing. The gospel was very dear to her and strengthened her throughout her life. She often bore her testimony through song.

Edward Teancum Murdock was born June 26, 1872, in Heber City, the fourth child of Bishop Joseph Stacy and Pernetta Murdock. Bishop Murdock's first wife, Eunice was childless. He bought two Indian children through Porter Rockwell to save their lives. Eunice raised these two children, a boy, Pickett, and a girl, Pernetta. When Pernetta grew to womanhood Bishop Murdock and Eunice became very concerned over her welfare and future and sought Brigham Young's counsel. He told Bishop Murdock to marry the Indian girl, Pernetta, as a plural wife. Five children were born to this couple, Benjamin Sweet, Betsy Eunice, Albert Alma, Edward Teancum, and Franklin Judson.

As a boy Edward was not husky and strong. His father would say to him, "Now, Teddy, it iss time to take your tar and milk." He and his brother Frank played the accordion on many occasions. Edward played the guitar and violin and was an excellent singer.

Through their musical abilities and willingness to perform, Edward and Gentie were drawn together and on December 9, 1891, they were married in Heber City. Although their two surnames are pronounced the same, there has been no genealogical relationship found.

Edward and Gentie lived in a small home one block from her parents so she could help her mother. Their first child, Murray Stacy, was stillborn. Nine other children were born to this couple: Edward Phares, April 11, 1894; Arthur. June 7, 1897; Clarence, January 1, 1900—the first baby born in the state of Utah both for the New Year and the century; Pernetta (Nettie), December 18, 1901; Annabell (Ann), April 18, 1904; Joseph Stacy, July 27, 1906; John Murray, February 17, 1909; Alma Robert, February 28, 1912; and Barney, July 13, 1914.

The family home was always filled with music. Gentie kept a clean and organized home but she always took time to sing and play with Ed and the children.

Arthur, the second son, records in his diary, "Our home had an organ. Father would play the fiddle and guitar. Everyone in the family could play well and we would make the rafters of the old house raise up after supper about every evening. Those were the best days of our family life."

Alma, the second youngest son, says, "My dad ran our family with the fiddle bow. He sat by the window while playing the fiddle so he could keep an eye on us kids. When he would see us getting out of line, he would rap on the window with the bow. That was a signal to us that we were doing wrong. My dad was a quiet man, he did not tolerate violence. His eyes were sharp; he missed nothing. He never whipped us, he didn't have to. We knew when things were going well and when they weren't by the way he played the fiddle."

Arthur continues, "As the family grew from three or four to nine it got past a joke. We really became crowded. The older boys had to make an extra bedroom outside in a tent. It would get quite cold in the winter but we enjoyed it all.

"My mother was a wonder. It will always be a mystery to me how she could make ends meet. How it was possible to set a full table for a big family day in and day out. My mother had the faith of Job. She would always say, 'Everything will be all right, just do the best you can.' As younger children the neighbor kids would call us half-breeds, we would run home and tell mother. Just tell them, 'sticks and stones will break your bones but names will never hurt me.' She was continually telling the older boys to be honest and always tell the truth. When I would tease the younger children, mother would give me some good raps with a dish cloth, or anything she had in her hand, that would quiet me down. When my father was home every child was quiet and stayed in his place. He always had good order in the home but I never saw him lay a hand on one of the children in my life."

Alma says, "I do not remember my mother but Aunt Net (Nettie McMullin) told me she was a pretty little woman, a good singer, and she could imitate people. My sister, Nettie, told me that my mother was sandy complected and she was small in stature. She had blue eyes and that my brother Joseph looked more like my mother than any in the family. Clarence said that she was very religious and that she led the singing in church. When she was younger, she would lift her skirts and run foot races with the kids and they had to go some to beat her. Aunt Betsy told me that my mother nursed one of her babies because she (Aunt Betsy) couldn't. To me she was one of the best women on this earth."

Art tells of his dad, "I never did hear him tell much about his younger years. As I became older I went with him several times to the reservation. I was always tickled to go with him. I never did know what my dad did for a living. I know he used to deal in wild horses—he would bring bands of horses in from the reservation, ship them out in carloads, or sell or trade them around the valley. He loved horses. He always had good horses—buggy, riding, and a few pretty good running horses.

"My father always liked to see his boys in athletics. He was a good country ball player in his day. I have seen him pitch some nice ball. He liked to watch his boys play ball. No matter how good or how bad you played, he never said anything about it, just took it for what it was."

Alma writes, "My dad was a patient man. When I was small, he would throw the ball to me back and forth until I learned how to throw and catch a ball. 'Never drop the ball if you can help it.' 'Throw straight and never take your eye off the ball.' He told me once if you can't say good things about people say nothing. My father was a good-looking man, a clean man, a musical man, a good athlete, a proud man, a family man and one of the best checker players in Wasatch County. He was a deep thinker. He loved to train horses and race them."

Clarence says, "We always had a camp of Indians by our place. They didn't bother anyone, but my dad always visited with them. He was always gone somewhere trading horses with the Indians and anyone who wanted to trade. He worked quite a bit in the blacksmith shop with his brother, Frank. He was a good fixer, painter, and horse shoer. I used to go with him and help."

On February 7, 1916, Millicent Sophia died. Clarence records, "One night it seemed like a dream, my mother just took sick and Net, Ann, and I went in her little bedroom and she went to sleep. But I know since that she had a bad hemorrhage and died." The death certificate gives cause of death as cerebral apoplexy. Gentie had been attended by Dr. Wherrett since the birth of her last child, Barney, eighteen months previous.

Of this time Arthur writes, "It was a brand new era. Life changed for every member of the family. The father tried to hold the family together for some time and he did quite well—but you could feel it breaking slowly apart. The older boys had to get out more or less on their own. I didn't get to finish my last year of high school. I got a job making fence. I would give a little to the family, but not like I should. Clarence and Phares were the main providers. Then Phares got married. The bulk of taking care of the children was left almost solely on Clarence. He did a good job."

On March 1, 1916, Edward took the children to the Salt Lake Temple with Mary D. Ryan acting as proxy for Millicent, and they were sealed to each other and the children to their parents.

Barney, the youngest child, eighteen months old, went to live with Frank and Stella Murdock, Ed's brother and wife. He was a fine singer. At the age of fourteen he was in a bus accident and bumped his head behind the ear. This eventually caused his death on April 12, 1929, of a brain abscess.

Alma, the next youngest child, was taken by Aunt Betsy Blackly, Ed's sister, and her husband Tom. They lived on the east side of Heber and made a good home for Alma. However, he would get lonely and run away from them going back down to the old house to play with Joe, John M. and the neighbor kids. Clarence,

Joe, John A., Nettie, and Ann lived at the old home. Art says, "The little girls were good cooks, clean housekeepers. I have seen as many as twenty shirts on the line. Those little girls scrubbed them out on the washboard by hand, and they were done first class."

Joe tells that things were not easy for the family. One winter he and John M. lived on bread made by the neighbor lady with lard spread on it like butter. (Ann and Net were both away working and in school and Clarence was attending the agricultural college at Logan.) John M. had shoes to wear but they were both for the same foot. Things were tough for them so they slipped up to Aunt Betsy's while she was in southern Utah and raided her larder for something to eat.

On June 25, 1924, Edward Murdock married again to Bertha Mayho. She was born in Blackburn, Lancashire, England, June 13,1885, to Henry and Elizabeth Howsan Mayho. She had previously been married to William Gothern Jeffs on July 6, 1904. They had five children: Mark Mayho, Theora, Mardene, Harry Mayho, and Helen. They were living in Provo, and during the flu epidemic of 1918 William Gothern Jeffs died November 12, leaving Bertha a widow with five small children.

The following is from *Forever Ours,* the personal family history of Bertha Mayho Jeffs Murdock.

"In 1920, I became acquainted with Edward Teancum Murdock. I sometimes waited on Ed when he came to shop at the Mercantile. I soon discovered he was a widower with nine children. Ed was a very talented musician. He could take any instrument and in no time have it mastered. He played the violin, piano, and banjo in a band that he and a few of his friends had formed which played for many of the dances and doings in the Valley. Ed and I dated for about two years before he asked me to be his wife. There was a large range between his children's ages. Some were quite young and some were planning to be married before we were.

"We arranged to be married June 25, 1924, in the Salt Lake Temple without the sealing ordinance as part of the ceremony. Somehow the officiator misunderstood that I had been sealed to my first husband and should therefore not be sealed to Ed. He proceeded with the wedding ceremony and without a pause sealed me to Ed.

"After my marriage to Ed, I quit work at the Mercantile. I stayed home with the children and worked our one quarter acre. We raised a large garden and ate or canned all of the food we grew. We had two hundred and fifty laying hens that provided us with eggs for our family as well as eggs to sell for cash. Our Jersey cow provided our family with milk and lots of rich cream. There was always extra cream which we sold. Ed worked at many odd jobs such as working in the welfare department or as a farmer or musician in the band. On October 10, 1925, our son Edward Thomas Murdock was born.

"Through my marriage to Ed I became friends with many wonderful Indians. With Ed, I was allowed to go to their hunting grounds. A good friend of Ed's was old Chief Johnie Dunken. He would come to Heber from the reservation to get supplies and visit. Ed's land on the White Rock Reservation and the land of Chief J. Dunken joined together. They had spring water on their lands and could irrigate anytime they wanted.

"In 1929 the stock market crashed and threw the entire country into a depression. The 13th of November 1929, our son Bert Murdock was born.

"Every fall the Indians came to Heber to get supplies. Old Ephraim Panavitch and his wife Susan, and Johnny Dunken and his son Willie would always come and stay at our place. We tried and tried to get them to sleep in the house because there was plenty of room. They always refused. Old Ephraim finally confessed that they were afraid of falling off the bed!

"In the early part of 1937, Bert, our son became ill with scarlet fever. With such a contagious disease we had to be so careful to scrub everything that he came in contact with. Ed and I decided to open up all the windows; scrub the walls and floors; wash the drapes and rugs; really clean. We had worked for several days when Ed took sick. He climbed up on the chair to hang the drapes. Right now he said, 'I feel very ill. I must have something to eat to get my strength back.' After eating things became worse. He went straight to bed. That Friday night he could not hold anything down. By 5 A.M. he was in the Heber hospital. On Saturday the doctor said he could do nothing for him and referred us to a specialist in Salt Lake City. We left for the city that afternoon. Ed lived in agony for the next four days. About Tuesday morning the doctors decided to operate. They found that one foot of the large intestine was gangrenous. They removed that section hoping his condition would improve. Ed slumped into a coma and passed away the 12th of March 1937. He was buried in Heber Cemetery."

Edward Teancum Murdock   Bertha Maho Jeffs Murdock

Left to Right: Nettie, Joseph S., Millicent, Annabelle,
Edward T. Murdoch, Clarence and Arthur

Millicent - Ann Steel Murdoch
and Phares

Back Row: Barney, Alma, Clarence, Arthur and Joe.
Kneeling: Edward Teancum Murdock with Edward Thomas
             on his knee. Taken in 1926

Edward Teancum Murdock – second from left

Front Row: Clarence, John M., Bert, Edward.
Back Row: Joseph, Arthur, Alma, Phares and Uncle Frank

Arthur, Nettie, Clarence and Phares

Alma, Nettie and Joe
1922

Edward T. Murdock
1903
Heber Baseball Team

HUSBAND EDWARD TEANCUM MURDOCK

Birth	25 June 1872
Place	Heber City, Wasatch, Utah
Chr	
Married	9 December 1891 (Sealed 1 March 1916 SLT)
Place	Heber City, Wasatch, Utah
Death	12 March 1937 Salt Lake City, Wasatch, Utah
Burial	14 March 1937 Heber City, Wasatch, Utah
Father	Joseph Stacy MURDOCK
Mother*	Pernetta SWEET
Other Wives (if any)	(2)Bertha MAYHO Jeffs 25 June 1924 (Temple)

WIFE MILLICENT SOPHIA MURDOCH

Birth	21 August 1874
Place	Heber City, Wasatch, Utah
Chr	
Death	7 February 1916 Heber City, Wasatch, Utah
Burial	10 February 1916 Heber City, Wasatch, Utah
Father	John Murray MURDOCH
Mother*	Ann STEEL
Other Hus. (if any)	
Where was information obtained?	Sara Lec Ann M. Sorensen

*List complete maiden name for all females.

1st Child MURRAY STACY MURDOCK

Birth	24 June 1892 (Stillborn)
Place	Heber City, Wasatch, Utah
Married to	
Place	
Death	24 June 1892 Heber, Wasatch, Utah

2nd Child EDWARD PHARES MURDOCK

Birth	11 April 1894
Place	Heber City, Wasatch, Utah
Married to	(1) Nora JONES (2) Ora PIKE
Married	4 October 1916 16 December 1938
Place	Salt Lake City, Salt Lake, Utah
Death	26 June 1961 Salt Lake City, Utah

3rd Child ARTHUR MURDOCK

Birth	7 June 1897
Place	Heber City, Wasatch, Utah
Married to	Laura Dean FREEMAN
Married	27 May 1922 Provo, Utah, Utah
Place	
Death	1 March 1978 Salt Lake City, Utah

4th Child CLARENCE MURDOCK

Birth	1 January 1900
Place	Heber City, Wasatch, Utah
Married to	(1)Sarah McALISTER(2)Alice CHRISTENSEN
Married	3 June 1931 22 November 1969
Place	Logan, Utah Idaho Falls, Idaho
Death	20 January 1980 Hooper, Weber, Utah

5th Child PERNETTA (NETTIE) MURDOCK

Birth	18 December 1901
Place	Heber City, Wasatch, Utah
Married to	Thomas Bertell BONNER
Married	25 September 1926
Place	Salt Lake City, Salt Lake, Utah
Death	7 Sep 1954 Midway, Wasatch, Utah

6th Child ANNABELL (ANN) MURDOCK

Birth	18 April 1904
Place	Heber City, Wasatch, Utah
Married to	Ralph Edmond STRUB
Married	11 June 1924
Place	Salt Lake City, Salt Lake, Utah
Death	23 Oct 1947 Pocatelo, Bannock, Idaho

7th Child JOSEPH STACY MURDOCK

Birth	27 July 1906
Place	Heber City, Wasatch, Utah
Married to	Melba Estella (Midge) HOLMES
Married	6 August 1930
Place	
Death	

8th Child JOHN MURRAY MURDOCK

Birth	17 February 1909
Place	Heber City, Wasatch, Utah
Married to	Amy TEASDALE
Married	5 May 1948 (Temple)
Place	Salt Lake City, Salt Lake, Utah
Death	

9th Child ALMA ROBERT MURDOCK

Birth	28 February 1912
Place	Heber City, Wasatch, Utah
Married to	(1)Eunice HARRIS (2) Helen POOLE
Married	September 1934 12 November 1944
Place	
Death	

10th Child BARNEY MURDOCK

Birth	13 July 1914
Place	Heber City, Wasatch, Utah
Married to	
Married	
Place	
Death	12 April 1929

Place Picture of Wife or Husband in Right Blank

Picture To Cover Blanks

LC. (Wilson form)

```
1 MURDOCH, James 1786-1831              2 MURDOCH, John Murray 1820-1910
1 MURDOCH, Mary MURRAY, Sp. 1782-1856   2 MURDOCH, Ann STEELE, Sp. 1829-1909

                        3 MURDOCH, MILLICENT SOPHIA 1874-1916 (1)
   DESCENDANTS OF------
                        3 MURDOCK, TEANCUM EDWARD, SP. 1872-1937  Sp-Spouse
                                                                  B-Born
 4 MURDOCK, Murray Stacy  B-24 June 1892 (Stillborn)              M-Married
                                                                  D-Died
 4 MURDOCK, Edward Phares B-11 Apr 1894                           Div.-Divorced
 4 MURDOCK, Nora JONES, Sp. (1) B-2 May 1895 M-4 Oct 1916 Div. D-18 May 1970
 4 MURDOCK, Ora PIKE, Sp. (2) B-         M-16 Dec 1938

        5 MURDOCK, Dora "J" B-6 Apr 1918  D-12 Jun 1918

        5 MURDOCK, Lowell   B-27 Sep 1920 D-16 Dec 1920

        5 MURDOCK, Roy      B-2 Feb 1921

        5 MURDOCK, Duane    B-9 July 1947 (Adopted)

 4 MURDOCK, Arthur  B-7 Jun 1897 M-27 May 1922 D-1 Mar1978
 4 MURDOCK, Laura Dean Freeman, Sp. B-2 Feb 1895 D-28 Jun 1976

 4 MURDOCK, Clarence B-1 Jan 1900 D-20 Jan 1980 M- 3 June 1931
 4 MURDOCK, Sara McALISTER, Sp. (1) B-22 Oct 1905 D-8 Jan 1969
 4 MURDOCK, Alice Loretta CHRISTENSEN Rowe Hansen, Sp. (2) B-         M-22 Nov 1969

        5 HOOPER, Melicent Clarissa (Clixie) MURDOCK B-10 Mar 1932 M-26 Mar 1954
        5 HOOPER, Donald Harvey, Sp. B-21 Nov 1930

                6 HOOPER, Donald HarveyJr. B-7 Jul 1955
                6 HOOPER, Clair Michelle MASON, Sp. B-         M-11 Jan 1975 Div.

                6 HOOPER, Sara Diane      B-26 Sep 1958

                6 HOOPER, Lisa Kaye       B- 1 Aug 1968

        5 SORENSON, Sara Lee Ann MURDOCK B-17 Apr 1934 M-17 Sep 1954
        5 SORENSON, David Walter, Sp. B-22 Nov 1931

                6 ESSIG, Mary Ann SORENSON B-14 Feb 1956 M-16 Mar 1978
                6 ESSIG, Fred Delmar, Sp. B-14 Dec 1955

                        7 ESSIG, Joan Esther       B-25 Apr 1979

                        7 ESSIG, Mary Rebecca      B-28 Aug 1980

                6 SORENSON, James David (twin) B-18 Dec 1956 M-11 May 1979
                6 SORENSON, Dana Lynn CARLISLE, Sp. B-6 Jun 1959

                        7 SORENSON, Joni Lynn       B-14 May 1980

                6 SORENSON, Robert Clarence (twin) B-18 Dec 1956 M-29 Jun 1979
                6 SORENSON, Heather Ann, Sp. B-27 Jun 1980

                6 SORENSON, Sue            B-20 May 1959

                6 SORENSON, Peggy Lee      B- 4 Jun 1961

        5 MURDOCK, Clarence McAlister (Mac) B-31 Aug 1938 M-5 Aug 1959
        5 MURDOCK, Deanna Evelyn BERGER, Sp. B-18 Oct 1939

                6 MURDOCK, Jann            B-29 Aug 1965

                6 MURDOCK, Jill            B- 2 Feb 1967

                6 MURDOCK, Jeff Clarence   B-26 May 1969

                6 MURDOCK, Edward Berger   B- 3 Dec 1970

                6 MURDOCK, Brett George    B-12 Jan 1975
```

5 MURDOCK, Ralph Edward B-4 Aug 1943
5 MURDOCK, Phyllis LaRae HIGBEE, Sp. (1) B-31 Jan 1962 M-11 Aug 1961 Div.
5 MURDOCK, Varlane TAYLOR, Sp. (2) B-   M-18 Aug 1971

      6 MURDOCK, Patricia Rae   B-31 Jan 1962

      6 MURDOCK, Shanda Cherece B-25 May 1973

      6 MURDOCK, Meisha Danielle B- 5 Dec 1974

      6 MURDOCK, Ressha Michelle B-28 Feb 1976

      6 MURDOCK, Triska Paulette B- 7 Jul 1977

      6 MURDOCK, Edward Ralph   B-11 Oct 1978

      6 MURDOCK, Damon Ralph   B- 2 May 1980

5 PRINSTER, Betsy Jayne MURDOCK (twin) B-19 Feb 1947 M-14 Aug 1970
5 PRINSTER, Timothy Craig, Sp. B-

      6 PRINSTER, Michael Timothy B-17 Jul 1971

      6 PRINSTER, Steven Craig   B- 7 May 1973

      6 PRINSTER, Kris Ann   B-16 Sep 1975

      6 PRINSTER, Kari Jillian   B-29 Dec 1977

      6 PRINSTER, Joel Paul   B-22 Apr 1980

5 MURDOCK, Robert Wayne (twin) B-19 Feb 1947 M-3 Jun 1969
5 MURDOCK, Linda Lee HENDRIX, Sp. B-

      6 MURDOCK, Saralee   B-21 Sep 1970

      6 MURDOCK, Robert Stacy   B-27 Jun 1972

      6 MURDOCK, Benjamin Wayne B-10 Jan 1974

      6 MURDOCK, Jessica   B-26 Dec 1975

      6 MURDOCK, Mark Ervin   B- 5 Jul 1978

      6 MURDOCK, Richard Murray B-18 May 1980

4 BONNER, Pernetta (Nettie) MURDOCK B-18 Dec 1901 M-25 Sep 1926 D-7 Sep 1954
4 BONNER, Thomas Bertell, Sp. B-10 Sep 1895 D-13 Jul 1948

    5 BONNER, Bertell Murdock B-6 Mar 1931 M-11 Aug 1959
    5 BONNER, Barbara Lee LOERTSCHER, Sp. B-

      6 BONNER, Chris   B-30 Sep 1960

4 STRUB, Annabell (Ann) MURDOCK B-18 Apr 1904 M-11 Jun 1924 D-23 Oct 1947
4 STRUB, Ralph Edmond, Sp. B-2 Nov 1897 D-3 Nov 1977
4 STRUB, Geraldene Ramona SAMSEL Anderson, Sp. (2) B-   M-30 Jun 1949
  Anderson, Douglas, Sp. (1) B-   M-   Div.

    5 GREAVES, Ralphine STRUB B-19 Jan 1925 M-14 Jun 1945
    5 GREAVES, Harley C., Sp. B-20 Oct 1922

      6 GREAVES, Craig B-18 Jan 1947 M-
      6 GREAVES, Deborah RAYMOND, Sp. B-

         7 GREAVES, Victoria Ashley   B-

      6 GREAVES, Terry Scott B-   M-
      6 GREAVES, Rindy CLAYBAUGH, Sp. B-

4 MURDOCK, Joseph Stacy B-27 Jul 1906 M-6 Aug 1930
4 MURDOCK, Melba Estella HOLMES, Sp. B-13 Mar 1913

      5 BURGENER, Darsa MURDOCK B-4 May 1931 M-13 Sep 1947 D-21 Jun 1980
      5 BURGENER, Ted C., Sp. B-

            6 BURGENER, Lynn Ted   B-19 Nov 1948

            6 BURGENER, Susan   B-23 Aug 1951

            6 BURGENER, Don J.   B-20 Aug 1954

            6 BURGENER, Jan   B-

      5 MURDOCK, Barney B-28 Jun 1932 M-
      5 MURDOCK, Louise McDONALD, Sp. B-

      5 EDLER, Joan MURDOCK McKnight B-8 Sep 1933
      5 McKNIGHT, Ray, Sp. (1) B-   M-   Div.
      5 EDLER, Loren, Sp. (2) B-   M-

            6 McKNIGHT, Mickey Ray   B-

            6 McKNIGHT, Marcy Jo   B-

            6 EDLER, Carey L.   B-

      5 ELDER, Marily MURDOCK B-8 Aug 1935 M-19 Apr 1952 D-27 Jul 1978
      5 ELDER, Claybourne Lavell, Sp. B-16 Mar 1933

            6 ELDER, Cray Lavell   B-24 Sep 1952

            6 ELDER, Randy   B-24 Nov 1953

            6 ELDER, Wayne Joe   B-16 Dec 1955

4 MURDOCK, John Murray B-17 Feb 1909 M-5 May 1948
4 MURDOCK, Amy TEASDALE, Sp. B-7 Jul 1916

      5 SHELL, Amy Deanne MURDOCK Gammon B-26 Feb 1950
      5 GAMMON, James Raymond, Sp. (1) B-   M-11 Apr 1970   Div.
      5 SHELL, Billy, Sp. (2) B-   M-

            6 GAMMON, Tonya   B-

            6 SHELL, Stoney S.   B-

      5 HOHREIN, Charlene Anne MURDOCK B-23 May 1952 M-
      5 HOHREIN, Errol Dennis, Sp. B-

            6 HOHREIN, Soothie Anne   B-

            6 HOHREIN, Talin Yulentrun B-

            6 HOHREIN, Armin Trenton   B-

4 MURDOCK, Alma Robert B-28 Feb 1912
4 MURDOCK, Eunice Merle HARRIS, Sp. (1) B-   M- Sep 1934
4 MURDOCK, Helen Jamie POOLE, Sp. (2) B-9 Aug 1919 M-12 Nov 1944

4 MURDOCK, Barney B-13 Jul 1914 D-12 Apr 1929

DESCENDANTS OF------- MURDOCK, Teancum Edward 1872-1937

JEFFS, Bertha MAYO, Sp. (2) B-13 Jun 1885 M-25 Jun 1924

JEFFS, William Gothern, Sp. (1) B-   M-6 Jul 1904
D-12 Nov 1918

JEFFS, Mark Mayho

JEFFS, Theora

JEFFS, Mardene

JEFFS, Harry Mayho

JEFFS, Helen

MURDOCK, Edward Thomas B-10 Oct 1925 M-17 Mar 1948
MURDOCK, Gloria PALFREYMAN, Sp. B-

      MURDOCK, Steven Edward   B-13 Apr 1949

      MURDOCK, Nancy Gloria   B-28 Oct 1953

      MURDOCK, Patricia Ann   B- 5 Jun 1955

      MURDOCK, Richard Dean   B-10 Jun 1963

MURDOCK, Bert B-14 Nov 1929 M-
MURDOCK, Elsie Marie JORGENSON, Sp. (1) B-   M-23 Jun 1950 Div.
MURDOCK, Phyllis SALMON, Sp. (2) B-   M-23 Nov 1962

Margaret Ann Murdoch and Lewis Joshua Hawkes

On May 19, 1863, a baby girl arrived at the home of John Murray and Isabella Crawford Murdoch in Heber City, Utah. The grandparents were James and Mary Murdoch and Andrew and Margaret Crawford. The name given to this lovely baby with black hair and dark brown eyes was Margaret Ann. As time went on, she was called Maggie.

The Murdochs were very industrious. Maggie was an active, healthy child, and always did her share of the work. At an early age, Maggie was taught to do housework, knit, crochet, embroider, and sew.

Maggie was the oldest of her mother's children. Her sisters and brothers were Catherine Campbell, James Crawford, Brigham, Robert (Boot), John Murray, and Isabella Crawford (Tressa). As the children became older and could carry on with the work, Maggie went to Salt Lake City, where she worked for several wealthy families. With her talents in housekeeping, cooking, and sewing, and with her pleasing personality, she won the friendship of the people for whom she worked.

At about this time, Maggie was introduced by her half-sister, Jacobina, to a handsome young man by the name of Lewis J. Hawkes. To his friends he was known as "Lew." It was love at first sight. Oh, how Lew and Maggie could dance! They were an attractive, graceful couple on the dance floor. After a very short courtship, Lewis J. Hawkes took Margaret Ann Murdoch to the Logan Temple, where they were married on November 7, 1889, for time and all eternity. None of us were there, but I have an idea there was a wedding supper or whatever else could be crowded into a short time, because just before their marriage, Lew had accepted a call to fill a mission in New Zealand for the LDS Church. On November 13, 1889, Lew bid farewell to his new bride, family, and friends at the railroad depot in Ogden, Utah.

From now on, I shall refer to Lew as Father and to Maggie as Mother, as in time we became their children.

Mother went to Heber City to live with Grandpa and Grandma Murdoch, while Father was on his mission.

After the Thanksgiving and Christmas holidays were over, the Murdoch home became a very busy place. Out came the knitting needles, crochet hooks, large hairpins to do hairpin lace on, thread, and yards and yards of white material. Grandma and Mother were as busy as hard-working beavers. Maybe Grandpa did some of the knitting too, for he knew how.

On August 4, 1890, a baby boy was born to Father and Mother. The baby was given the name Lewis Murdoch Hawkes. While Lewis was still a baby, he was stricken with meningitis, but with prayers, fasting, faith, and loving care, Lewis recovered. One morning, Mother was bathing Lewis, when a voice said, "I am home Maggie." Mother turned, saw Father standing in the doorway, and fainted, falling to the floor. Had Grandma not been standing nearby, Lewis would have fallen with his mother. When conditions got partly back to normal, Father explained why he had been released early from his mission. I will give some of the details in Father's part of the history. After his return, Father worked for a number of years for the railroad and in the mines at Park City, Utah.

On July 20, 1893, a son, Hazen Araho, was born at Franklin, Idaho, where Father's parents lived.

On April 7, 1896, a daughter was born at Heber City, Utah. She was named Isabella Priscilla.

Golden Murdoch Hawkes was born April 8, 1898 at Heber City, Utah. Golden didn't stay long with his family. On August 29, 1898, our Heavenly Father called Golden home. Golden had completed his mission on earth.

Robert Joshua "M" Hawkes was born November 16, 1899. Our parents were living at Heber City, Utah then.

In spring of 1899, Father and Mother took up a farm in Teton, Fremont County, Idaho. Only those who were there could know of the hours of hard work. At times, with no modern equipment, the work seemed to be of no use. The winters were cold and long. During those cold winters our parents would live at Franklin, Idaho, or Heber City, Utah.

Mother's health was beginning to cause her to slow down with her work. There were never any complaints, but her beautiful black hair was turning prematurely gray, her steps were slower, and she had to rest more often. Father, by now, had built a small house on the land at Teton. There were two rooms and a small storage room. With Mother's talent, these rooms became a home.

On March 18, 1902, Mary Deon "M" Hawkes was born at Teton, Idaho. Mother's health was poor, but she kept on doing her work regardless of how she felt.

On March 5, 1904, another baby girl was born at Teton, Idaho. On March 11, 1904, the baby was given a name and a blessing by her Uncle James Murdoch. Her name was Margaret Ann Murdoch Hawkes.

Mother wasn't recovering from the birth of her baby. She asked to have her "babies" brought to her. Mary Deon was laid on one of Mother's arms, and Margaret Ann on the other. Our sweet darling mother knew her time was short. Calling Hazen to her bedside before he left for school, she had Hazen promise her that he would not gamble or play cards. The last time I talked to Hazen, he told me of this promise. With a struggle to control his voice, he said, "I have kept that promise to my mother." Our sweet, kind, loving Mother was called home by our Heavenly Father on March 14, 1904. In two months, she would have been forty-one years of age. It is very hard to think and accept the knowledge that there is greater work for a mother than taking care of her six children and her husband. Father was quite sure that Mrs. Hansen would take care of the baby. That care didn't last long, because Mrs. Hansen became ill. With promises that her daughter Irene would help with me, Aunt Mary Wickham took me. Everything went fine until Aunt Mary Ann became ill and Irene got married. The rest of the children were now in different homes. Isabella and Bob were at Uncle Dave and Aunt Kate Hicken's home in Heber City, Utah. Deon, Hazen, and Lewis were with Father's folks in Franklin, Idaho. Once again the question was asked, "Where is Margaret Ann going?" Someway, somehow, Margaret went to live with Aunt Sarah Ann Hawkes, who was Grandfather Hawkes's second wife in plural marriage. From here I was taken to the home of Robert James and Hannah O. Kerr in Wellsville, Utah. My Grandfather and Grandmother Hawkes had lived in Wellsville for several years before moving to Franklin and Preston, Idaho.

I lived for some time with the Kerr family before adoption papers were signed. Father signed the papers on February 5, 1916. R.J. and Hannah O. Kerr signed them February 11, 1916. An event that is interesting to me as I look back upon it occurred when I was in about the second grade. I came home from school, and there sat a man with blue eyes, black hair, and a nose that I thought was too big. I didn't like "that man" because everyone insisted that I sit on his knee. I was there no longer than necessary. Ma called him "Lew." He called her "Hannah." When Pa came in it was "Lew and Jim." After some supper, for some reason Lew was looking at my teeth. Clamp, went my teeth on "the man's" fingers. He jerked his fingers from my mouth, exclaiming, "She bit me!" When Ma asked why I would do such a thing, I answered, "I don't want his dirty fingers in my mouth." I ran to Pa and up on his knee. It seemed that his arm drew me closer to him and his whiskers were close to my face. Pa had a mustache and neatly trimmed beard. The "man" was my father, Lew Hawkes. Later as we talked about this experience Father said he would liked to have given me a spanking, but when he saw how close Pa and I were to each other, that feeling left, and a feeling of security for me took its place. I had a lovely home with the Kerr family. I was, and still am, loved by all of my foster relatives; never once did I have a feeling of not being one of the family. For the help I received with this history of our Mother, I give special thanks to my father, Lewis J. Hawkes; to my brother, Hazen Hawkes; to Uncle Brig Murdoch and his wife, Aunt Louannie, and to Uncle Tom Murdoch. Records at the St. Anthony, Idaho, courthouse and Father's genealogy sheets and his mission diary were of great help too. With more than thanks, I express love and appreciation to my sister, Isabell, and her husband, Francis (Frank) Bratt. Without their help, very few of the dates recorded here would have been available.

Lewis Joshua Hawkes

Lewis Joshua Hawkes was born July 23, 1867, at Willard, Box Elder County, Utah. His parents were Joshua Alvard and Mary Lewis. He was baptized a member of the LDS Church in June, 1877. With his family, Father moved to Wellsville, Utah, some time between 1871 and 1873. In 1873, the family moved from Wellsville to Franklin, Oneida County, Idaho. While living in Franklin, Father and Grandfather Hawkes hauled rocks by ox team to help build the temple in Logan, Utah.

The farm proved too small to support the family, so Father found work at other places. One of his jobs was working for the railroad, which took him to various places in Idaho, Utah, and Montana. During this time, Father went to visit some friends and relatives in Heber City. While there, he was introduced to a pretty young lady named Margaret Ann (Maggie) Murdoch by Maggie's half-sister, Jacobina, with whom Father was "keeping company." The events related to their courtship and subsequent marriage in the Logan Temple on November 7, 1889, are described in Mother's part of the history.

Following are some of the highlights recorded in Father's missionary diary:

12 Nov. 1889—Set apart to go on a mission in New Zealand by Elder John Henry Smith.

13 Nov. 1889—Bid farewell to his bride of one week, and relations and friends at the Ogden depot, and departed for San Francisco, California.

16 Nov. 1889—Left California for New Zealand on the steamship *Mariposa*.

24 Nov. 1889—Visited the Hawaiian Mission.

7 Dec. 1889—Arrived at Auckland, New Zealand.

Father's diary indicated that he enjoyed his work and had a deep love for the people. Additional events are:

3 Sept. 1892—Received a telegram from the mission president, requesting him to be in Auckland by Sept. 10 to accompany the body of Elder Waltho Chipman home. (Father was the next elder scheduled to be released, and this explains his early and unexpected arrival in Heber City, which so surprised and shocked our mother.)

5 Sept. 1892—Bid farewell to Watangi and the Saints and friends there.

Following his return, he worked again for the railroad, and with some of the Murdochs and other friends, he also worked in the mines at Park City, Utah. There was talk of rich, fertile land available in Idaho for homesteading. After careful study, Father and Mother filed for land in Teton, Fremont County, Idaho in September, 1899. The significant events from this date until 1904 are described in Mother's part of the history. Father told me once that the Hawkes kids brought the whooping cough from Utah to Idaho. At night, Mother would insist that Father put the wagon in a big irrigation ditch, so the moist air would help the children to sleep better. To be sure they wouldn't fall out, a rope was tied to their waists, with the other end tied to the wagon.

During 1903, the family stayed at Teton and worked the land. At the same time, Father was building a new home at Lillian (now Drummond), which was a few miles northeast of Teton. Their plans were to move into the new home after I was born and the weather became more like spring than winter.

Mr. and Mrs. William Baird had a home just west of where Father was building. The Baird and the Hawkes families had been close friends in Heber City, and Mother dreamed of and looked forward to living near her dear friend. These plans and dreams were never realized, because Mother passed away March 11, 1904, at Teton, Idaho.

I have explained earlier how we children were living with different families. It was Father's aim to have us all back with him again as soon as possible. In June, 1910, he married Emily Povey in the Logan Temple. To this union a son, Arthur, was born. Things did not work out as planned, and their marriage was dissolved in 1920 with a Church and civil divorce.

In 1925, Father married Martha Dewyer. Martha was especially good to Lewis. In 1.936 they moved to St. Anthony, Idaho. Father loved to fish and do some hunting. During his later years, he was a high priest, active in Church work, and was working on genealogy records. After about one week's illness, Father passed away on April 23, 1943, at St. Anthony, Idaho. He was buried on April 27 beside his loving Maggie in the beautiful, quiet Teton Cemetery, which seems to rest in the shadows of the Teton Peaks. Again, I express real appreciation to all who have helped gather and provide this information.

To round out this brief history of Margaret Ann Murdoch and her husband Lewis Joshua Hawkes, we think it is important to include a few pertinent and personal notes related to the lives of their seven children.

Lewis Murdoch Hawkes was born August 4, 1890, in Heber City. Lewis was never married. All reports indicate that he was a lovable, pleasant person to be with. Lewis spent most of his life in Fremont County, Idaho. However, he did live in California for about eighteen years. Lewis expressed a wish to be buried in Grass Valley with his California friends. He died 19 August 1974 at the age of 84 years.

Hazen Araho Hawkes was born July 20, 1893, in Franklin, Idaho. He attended school in Teton, Idaho, and Heber City, Utah. He served in the military during World War I. On November 23, 1917, he married Helen Gray Emery in Albion, Idaho. Hazen and Helen are the parents of four children: Hazen Emery, who gave his life while serving as a B-17 tail gunner during World War II; Lewis Eugene; Mrs. Lawrence (Margaret) Lindsley; and Mrs. Lloyd (Alta) Van Sickle. Hazen worked and retired as a U.S. postal and Forest Service employee. He loved to be outdoors, and hunting and fishing were included in his hobbies. Hazen and Helen celebrated their fortieth wedding anniversary at their daughter Margaret's home on November 29, 1957. Hazen died at the age of eighty-two years at Overton Beach, Nevada. He is remembered as being friendly, soft-spoken, even-tempered, and enjoyable to be with. Hazen was buried in the Pineview Cemetery at Ashton, Idaho.

Isabella Priscilla was born April 7, 1896, at Heber City, Utah. When her mother died, Isabell went back to Heber to live with her Aunt Kate and Uncle Dave Hicken until her father remarried. Isabell married Francis (Frank) Bratt on January 24, 1920. Isabell and Frank are the parents of a son, Harold Bratt. They celebrated their fifty-first wedding anniversary January 24, 1971, at their son Harold's home. We remember Frank as always being neatly dressed and a talented musician. Isabell is presently living in her home at Drummond, Idaho.

Golden Murray Hawkes was born April 8, 1898 He was only permitted to live a few months. He died August 29, 1898 one of those special spirits who are assured a place in the celestial kingdom.

Robert Joshua Hawkes was born November 16, 1899, at Heber City, Utah. He, with his sister, Isabella, went back from Teton to live with Uncle Dave and Aunt Kate in Heber City. When the United States became involved in World War I, Robert ran away to Twin Falls, Idaho, to "sign up." He was too young to enlist, so he "fibbed" about his age, put rocks in his pocket to help meet the weight requirement, and joined the Marines. We understand that Robert was wounded only a few minutes before the Armistice was signed on November 11, 1918, and "celebrated" his eighteenth birthday in a military hospital in France. He married his lovely wife, Miriam, on July 5, 1930. They are the parents of three children. Bob and "Nettie" celebrated their golden wedding anniversary in Carson City, Nevada, June 30, 1979. They now live in Mill City, Oregon.

Mary Deon Hawkes was born March 18, 1902, at Teton, Idaho. She was just two years old when her mother passed away. After her mother's death, she lived with her Hawkes grandparents and then with her Aunt Lucy Hopkins in Buhl, Idaho. Her sister, Margaret, has a picture taken with Deon in the summer of 1926. Both girls were in their early twenties, and this was the first time they had been together since they were babies. Margaret said, "We enjoyed that week beyond words!" Deon is married to Lamond Bowler. They live in St. George, Utah. Her health isn't the best, but she doesn't complain. Her letters indicate that Lamond and the people in her ward are very good to her.

Margaret Ann Hawkes (Kerr) was born March 5, 1904, at Teton, Idaho. When she was six days old, her mother, Margaret Ann, died. Events leading up to her adoption by the R.J. Kerr family are described in preceding parts of this history. She was much loved and well cared for in that family. Margaret attended school and graduated from Wellsville Jr. High, South Cache High School, and Brigham Young College at Logan. Following graduation, she taught school, a profession that she enjoyed very much. On May 29, 1929, Margaret married Junius Bailey Murray in the Logan Temple. They are the parents of eight children: Amanda Lee, who died when still a baby; R. Jay Murray; Mrs. Virgil (Mary) Carter; Blaine Murray; Mrs. Thurman (LaRae) Babbitt; Byron Murray; Mrs. Homer (Carolyn) Leong; and Mrs. Jay (Isabell) Sudweeks. Margaret and Junius celebrated their golden wedding anniversary on May 20, 1979, in Idaho Falls, Idaho. Margaret's church activities have included leadership and teaching positions in religion class, Primary, Sunday School, MIA, and Relief Society, and as a genealogy instructor. For the past three years, Margaret has served as the family representative of the Margaret Ann Murdoch Hawkes branch of the John Murray and Isabella Crawford family.

Compiled by Margaret Hawkes Murray, youngest child of Lewis Joshua and Margaret Ann Murdoch Hawkes.

Margaret Ann Murdoch Hawkes and oldest son
Lewis Murdoch Hawkes

Lewis Murdoch Hawkes as a baby in about 1890

Lewis Murdoch Hawkes about 1921

Frank and Isbella P. Hawkes Bratt

Margaret Ann Hawkes Kerr
and Mary Deon Hawkes

Robert Joshua Hawkes

Margaret Ann Hawkes Kerr Murray as a baby

Margaret Ann Hawkes Kerr Murray
as a young girl

Robert James Kerr   Hannah O. Kerr

The Kerr's adopted and raised
Margaret Ann Hawkes Kerr

Margaret Ann Hawkes Kerr Murray
November 1923 in Junior High

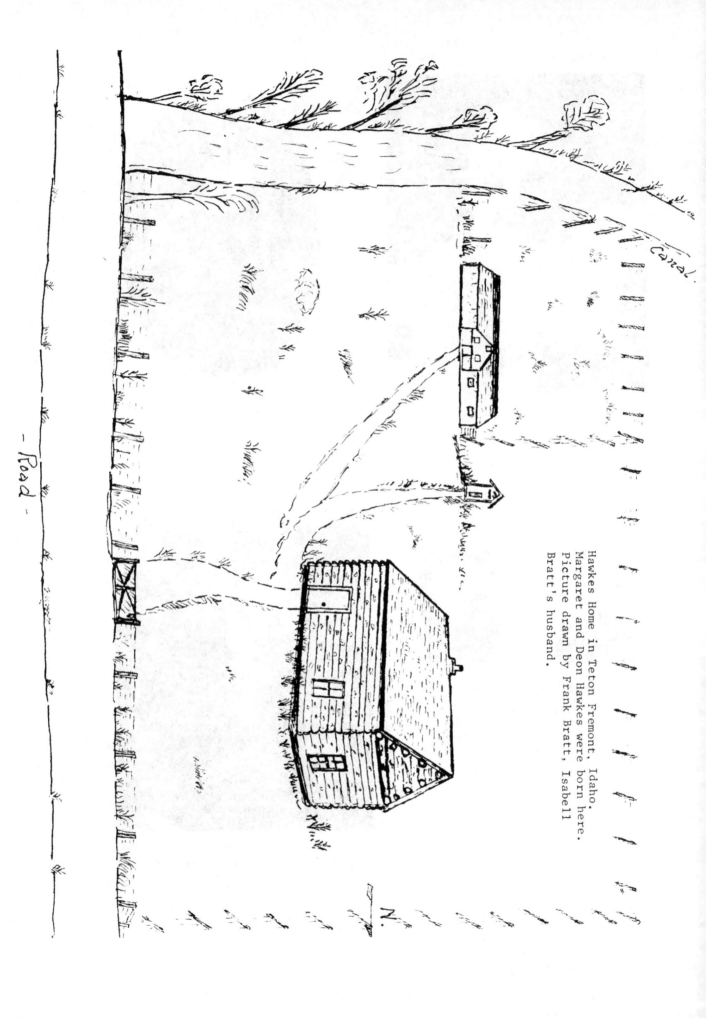

Hawkes Home in Teton Fremont, Idaho.
Margaret and Deon Hawkes were born here.
Picture drawn by Frank Bratt, Isabell
Bratt's husband.

Canal.

- Road -

N.

HUSBAND   LEWIS JOSHUA HAWKES
    Birth   22 July 1867
    Place   Willard, Box Elder, Utah
    Married   7 November 1889
    Place   Logan, Cache, Utah (Logan Temple)
    Death   23 April 1943
    Place   St. Anthony Fremont, Idaho
    Burial   27 April 1943
    Place   Teton, Fremont, Idaho
    Mother   Mary LEWIS
    Father   Joshua Alvard HAWKES
    Other Wives (2) Emily POWEY Jay Jun 1910 (3) Martha E.
                 DEWYER Davidson Kadoo 4 Aug 1925

WIFE   MARGARET ANN MURDOCH
    Birth   19 May 1863
    Place   Heber, Wasatch, Utah
    Death   11 March 1904
    Place   Teton, Fremont, Idaho
    Burial   14 March 1904
    Place   Teton, Fremont, Idaho
    Mother   Isabella CRAWFORD
    Father   John Murray MURDOCH
    Other Husbands
    Information From

1ST CHILD   Lewis Murdoch HAWKES
    Birth   4 August 1890 Heber, Wasatch, Utah
    Married
    Date
    Place   19 August 1974 Grass Valley, California
    Death   19 August 1974 Grass Valley, California
    Burial   21 August 1974 Grass Valley, California

2ND CHILD   Hazen Araho HAWKES
    Birth   20 July 1893 Franklin, Franklin, Idaho
    Married   Helen Grey EMERY
    Date   23 November 1917
    Place   Albion, Cassia, Idaho
    Death   8 April 1976 Overton, Beach Nevada
    Burial   14 April 1976 Ashton, Fremont, Idaho

3RD CHILD   Isabella Priscilla HAWKES
    Birth   7 April 1896 Heber, Wasatch, Utah
    Married   Francis BRATT
    Date   24 January 1920
    Place   Idaho Falls, Bonneville, Idaho
    Death
    Burial

4TH CHILD   Golden Murray HAWKES
    Birth   8 April 1898   Heber, Wasatch, Utah
    Married
    Date
    Place
    Death   29 August 1898
    Burial

5TH CHILD   Robert Joshua HAWKES
    Birth   16 November 1899 Heber, Wasatch, Utah
    Married (1)Lois LERWELL (2)Miriam A. BLANCHARD D.
    Date   Div.   5 July 1930 S-25Jun1942
    Place   Weiser, Wash., Idaho
    Death
    Burial

6TH CHILD   Mary Deon HAWKES
    Birth   18 March 1902 Teton, Fremont, Idaho
    Married Harry Lamond BOWLER (5)
    Date   22 March 1949 (sealed 25 Jan 1950
    Place   Las Vegas,Clark,Nevada St.George,Ut.
    Death
    Burial

7TH CHILD   Margaret Ann HAWKES
    Birth   5 March 1904 Teton, Fremont, Idaho
    Married Junius Bailey MURRAY
    Date   29 May 1929
    Place   Logan, Cache, Utah (Temple)
    Death
    Burial

8TH CHILD
    Birth
    Married
    Date
    Place
    Death
    Burial

1 MURDOCH, James 1786-1831
1 MURDOCH, Mary MURRAY, Sp. 1782-1856

2 MURDOCH, John Murray 1820-1910
2 MURDOCH, Isabella CRAWFORD, Sp. 1836-1916

DESCENDANTS OF-------
3 MURDOCH, Margaret Ann 1863-1904
3 HAWKES, Lewis Joshua, Sp. 1867-1942

4 HAWKES, Lewis Murdoch B-4 Aug 1890 D-19 Aug 1974

B-Born
M-Married
D-Died
Sp-Spouse
Div.-Divorced

4 HAWKES, Hazen Araho B-20 Jul 1893 M-23 Nov 1917 D-8 Apr 1976
4 HAWKES, Helen Grey EMERY, Sp. B-6 Mar 1896

    5 LINDSLEY, Margaret Estella HAWKES B-9 Jan 1919 M-30 Jul 1938
    5 LINDSLEY, Lawrence Brainerd, Sp. B-

        6 McMULLIN, Helen Diane LINDSLEY B-26 Dec 1943 M-18 Apr 1975
        6 McMULLIN, Jerry, Sp. B-12 May 1927

    5 VANSICKLE, Alta Marie HAWKES B-8 Mar 1922 M-13 Jun 1938
    5 VANSICKLE, Lloyd, Sp. B-7 Jun 1918

        6 VANSICKLE, Karen Thula B-15 Mar 1940 D-15 Mar 1940 Stillborn

        6 VANSICKLE, Clinton Lloyd B-8 Aug 1941 D-8 Aug 1941

        6 BRYAN, Sandra Marie VAN SICKLE Ballard B-17 Mar 1943
        6 BALLARD, Gorden, Sp. (1) B-   M-   1964 Div.
        6 BRYAN, J.C. Sp. (2) B-   M- Jul 1972

           7 BALLARD, Bart   B-20 Jan 1966

        6 DEXTER, Sara Annette B-8 Nov 1946
        6 WHITE, John, Sp. (1) B-   M- Dec 1966 Div.
        6 DEXTER, Jim, Sp. (2) B- Aug   M-

           7 WHITE John Emery   B-3 Jan 1968

        6 VAN SICKLE, Steven Emery B-16 Oct 1947
        6 VAN SICKLE, Sherri BLANN, Sp. (1) B- Jul M-   Div.
        6 VAN SICKLE, Linda   , Sp. (2) B-   M-

    5 HAWKES, Hazen Emery B-12 Feb 1925 D-7 Mar 1944 (World War II)

    5 HAWKES, Lewis Eugene B-3 Feb 1927 M-28 Dec 1951
    5 HAWKES, Janice Mortensen HARDY, Sp. (1) B- Apr M-   Div.
    5 HAWKES, Bernie ALLRED, Sp. (2) B-   M-

        6 HAWKES, Marcus, B-4 Jul 1956
        6 HAWKES, Jovita   , Sp. B-   M-2 Jul 1977

        6 HAWKES, Valerie B- Oct   (Adopted)

4 BRATT, Isabella Priscilla B-7 Apr 1896 M-24 Jan 1920
4 BRATT, Francis, Sp. B-23 Jun 1895 D-13 Feb 1981

    5 BRATT, Harold Francis B-13 Apr 1923 M-24 Jun 1946
    5 BRATT, Monna Beth HOWARD, Sp. B-27 Oct 1928

        6 BOGGETTI, Linda Jean BRATT B-8 Jan 1949 M-17 May 1980
        6 BOGGETTI, Jack William, Sp. B-

    5 BRATT, Lawrence Henry B-9 Jun 1928 D-9 Jun 1929 Stillborn

4 HAWKES, Golden Murray B-10 Oct 1898 D-4 Aug 1899

4 HAWKES, Robert Joshua B-16 Nov 1899
4 HAWKES, Lois LERWILL, Sp. (1) B-   M-   Div.
4 HAWKES, Mirriam Annette BLANCHARD DeHart, Sp. (2) B-17 May 1910 M-5 Jul 1930 S-25 Jun 1942
  De Hart, Lloyd Sp. (1) B-   M-

    5 CARLSON, Roberta Lois HAWKES B-23 Jul 1925
    5 CARLSON, John M. Sp. B-   M-

```
        6 CARLSON, Terry        B- 3 Jun 1948

        6 CARLSON, John         B-21 May 1951

        6 CARLSON, Ricky        B-11 May 1953

        6 CARLSON, Susie        B-      1958

   5 DE HART, Floyd Charles B-8 Aug 1928 D-       1928 (sealed Robert J. Hawkes 1942)

   5 ROWE, Agnes Annette HAWKES Pedrolli B-10 Oct 1930
   5 PEDROLLI,       , Sp. (1) B-         M-          Div.
   5 ROWE, Alan, Sp. (2) B-               M-

        6 PEDROLLI, Robert B-           1950
        6 PEDROLLI, Rosie, Sp. B-          M-           Div.

            7 PEDROLLI, Shane           B-

            7 PEDROLLI, Jimmy           B-

   5 AVERY, Isabella Beatrice HAWKES Deyoe B-9 Jul 1933
   5 DEYOE, Harold, Sp. (1) B-            M-          Div.
   5 AVERY, Roger, Sp. (2) B-             M-

        6 DEYOE, Donald B-21 May 1951 (2) Sp.
        6 DEYOE, Connie, Sp. B-           M-

            7 DEYOE, Marcel             B-          ( Adopted by Donald)

            7 DEYOE, Tenia              B-          ( Adopted by Donald)

        6 AVERY, Brenda  B-

   5 MIHERIN, Barbara Joyce HAWKES Tippet B-26 Sep 1936
   5 TIPPIT, Bill, Sp. (1) B-             M-            Div.
   5 MIHERIN, Mike, Sp. (2) B-            M-

        6 COY, Mary TIPPIT B-13 Jun 1952
        6 COY, Guy, Sp. B-         Sp. B-    M-        M-

            7 COY, Marsha               B-

            7 COY, Milo                 B-

        6 TIPPIT, Bill B-6 Nov 1956 (twin)
        6 TIPPIT, Elaine        Sp. B-            M-

            7 TIPPIT, Jody              B-

        6 TIPPIT, Bob B-6 Nov 1956 (twin)
        6 TIPPIT, Heidi        Sp. B-            M-

            7 TIPPIT,                   B-

        6 MIHERIN, Michael   B-

        6 MIHERIN, Barbara   B-

        6 MIHERIN, Marine    B-

        6 MIHERIN, Mark      B-

4 BOWLER, Mary Deon HAWKES Lane Sundquist Lang Shrider B-18 Mar 1902
4 LANE, William Robert, Sp. (1) B-          M-22 Jul 1927 Div.-Oct 1933
4 SUNDQUIST, Floyd Walter, Sp., (2) B-          M-19 Apr 1934 Div.-1938
4 LANG, Carlos Steven, Sp. (3) B-          M-22 Apr 1939 Civ-Div 1942 Temple Div-1948
4 SHRIDER, John Stanley, Sp., (4) B-          M-22 Jul 1945 D-20 Aug 1947
4 BOWLER, Harvey Lamond, Sp., (5) B-14 Dec 1907  M-22 Mar 1949
  Fullmer, Harriet Elizabeth BARNUM Bowler, Sp. (1) B-27 Dec 1915  M-1 Jun 1933 Div.

        Bowler, James L.      B-24 Oct 1934
        Bowler, Ferris Elmo   B-10 Nov 1936 D-11 Aug 1955   (Not Murdoch's)
        Bowler, Jennie Lynn   B-25 Dec 1940
```

4 MURRAY, Margaret Ann HAWKES Kerr B-5 Mar 1904 M-29 May 1929
4 MURRAY, Junius Bailey, Sp. B-20 Sep 1897

    5 MURRAY, R Jay B-30 Jun 1930

    5 CARTER, Mary Murray B-7 Nov 1932 M-8 Jul 1953
    5 CARTER, Virgil Ray, Sp. B-17 Mar 1932

        6 CARTER, Craig Allen   B-23 Mar 1957

        6 CARTER, Leslee Gayle B-31 May 1960

    5 MURRAY, Amanda Lee B-12 May 1935 D-17 Jun 1936

    5 MURRAY, Junius Blaine B-5 Oct 1936 M-12 Aug 1961 Div.
    5 MURRAY, Ann Stuart MUFFITT, Sp. B-

        6 MURRAY, Lexie Catherine B-

        6 MURRAY, Michael Blaine B-

        6 MURRAY, Melisa Ann   B-

    5 BABBITT, Margaret LaRae MURRAY B-18 Oct 1938 M-24 Apr 1959 Div.
    5 BABBITT, Thurman, Sp. B-10 Jun 1933

        6 BABBITT, Harold Kevin   B-19 Jul 1969 Adopted

    5 MURRAY, Byron Kerr B-14 Jul 1940 M-27 May 1967
    5 MURRAY, Ilene Kay PORTIE, Sp. B-3 May 1945

        6 MURRAY, Ryan McKay   B-27 Oct 1969 D-28 Apr 1971

        6 MURRAY, Blake McKay   B-28 Feb 1972

        6 MURRAY, Dawn Camille   B- 9 Mar 1973

        6 MURRAY, Randall Kerr   B-20 May 1976

        6 MURRAY, Booke Michell   B-22 Apr 1978

        6 MURRAY, Dena Christine B-25 Jun 1980

    5 LEONG, Carolyn MURRAY B-16 May 1942 M-27 Apr 1969
    5 LEONG, Homer Combs, Sp. B-19 Jan 1938

        6 LEONG, Marcus Murray   B-19 Mar 1972

        6 LEONG, Nicole Natale   B-13 Nov 1976

    5 SUDWEEKS, Isabell MURRAY B-27 May 1943 M-25 Feb 1966
    5 SUDWEEKS, Jay Dean, Sp. B-

        6 SUDWEEKS, Jay Dean Jr. B- 4 Mar 1967

        6 SUDWEEKS, Justin Derek B-23 May 1968

        6 SUDWEEKS, Jeremy Don   B-9 Jan 1973

        6 SUDWEEKS, Jennifer Dee B-2 Dec 1973

        6 SUDWEEKS, Judy Dena   B-30 Oct 1980

DESCENDANTS OF----------HAWKES, Lewis Joshua 1867-1942

POVEY, Emily, Sp. (2)   B-4 Jan 1877 M-   1910 Div. 1920
                        D-1 Apr 1954

Other Husbands
(1)William George JAY B-   M-
(2)Axel ERICKSON   B-   M-

Other Wives
(1)Margaret Ann MURDOCH B-19 May 1863 M-7 Nov 1889 D-11 Mar 1904
(3)Martha Easterling DEWYER Davidson Kadoo B-
                                           M-4 Aug 1925
                                           D-

HAWKES, (little girl) died

HAWKES, Arthur E. B-3 Jul 1914

Catherine Campbell Murdoch and David William Hicken

Few people are born into the world with the qualities of spirit that came with Catherine Campbell Murdoch, always called Kate, born on November 15, 1864, in Heber City, Utah. She was the second child of John Murray Murdoch and Isabella Crawford, John M.'s second wife. Kate, named Catherine Campbell after her mother's best friend, was eighteen months younger than her sister Maggie (Margaret Ann), and the love between the two sisters endured beyond Maggie's death in 1904 until Kate's death on March 6, 1945.

Kate was a family person. The members of her own family were always seen by her through heavy veils of love, and they could do little or no wrong in her eyes. And she had room in her heart to love many, many people.

It was Maggie to whom Kate spoke in the days before her death. "Who am I talking to? Where are your eyes, girl? Aunt Mag is sitting right there in that chair beside you!"

But Maggie was probably no dearer to her than Jock (John Murray Murdoch—the sixth child; or Brig; or Jim; or Tressa (Isabella Crawford Murdoch—the seventh child); or any of the others. A visit from Thomas Murdoch, Uncle Tom, was a delight she looked forward to for days. Tom was a child of Ann Steel Murdoch, John M.'s first wife. He was two years younger than Kate. She said once that she didn't know until she was "a girl grown that Tom was a half-brother." And perhaps he was favored even a bit over those boys born of her own mother.

A visit from any of her relatives was an occasion for cleaning and baking and hoping for a long stay if the relative was from out of town, and if a family member who lived in town came for less than a day-long visit, she would see them out the door with regret. Kate had been reared in the Mormon way—people provided the main entertainment and amusement for themselves in the mountain-bound communities like Heber City, where Kate was to live all of her life. What others did, how they did it, and who said what, were all fascinating subjects for conversation—not exactly gossip, for there was always compassion and understanding and humor in the talk. And if the individual's behavior was questionable, as it could often be in that strict moral climate of Mormon Utah, the subject was given the benefit of the doubt. "Give him the benefit of the doubt," Kate would say. "You weren't there. You don't really know what happened. And if you had been there, you'd have probably done the very same thing. People mostly do what they have to do."

Kate was a gently mischievous child, too loving to hurt anyone with her mischief, but full of life, wanting to sing and dance and play games and charades. Even in her late years, she was willing to allow her precious basques and skirts of yesteryear to be used in the "plays" her children and grandchildren presented, and while she felt bad about the rents and tears we put into them, she never scolded. "What's done is done."

Small-boned and delicately made, with dark hair and beautiful brown, almond eyes, Kate must have teased her husband-to-be beyond bearing, because David William Hicken once grabbed Aunt Tressa's pet kitten and bobbed its tail when his light-of-love went to a dance with another young man. Years later such frustration had long disappeared from David's character, and the story shocked his children when they were told of it.

But Kate did marry David on July 21, 1886, in the Logan Temple, and the love between them has been an example of marital rapport for their children, grandchildren, and great-grandchildren, and perhaps for many others.

Then Kate and Dave became Mama and Papa. Children were very special to them. Not only their own children, but all children. And once in a moment of rapture, love, and selflessness, Mama cried, "Oh, I hope this house is never empty of children." And it never was, during her lifetime. Mama and Papa Hicken had nine children. One of them died in early infancy, one was still-born, and the other seven lived to adulthood. Their second son, Rollo, was killed in a mine accident when he was twenty-five, leaving his young wife seven months pregnant. Their first son, Rodney, died of Bright's disease in 1929, leaving his wife to face the hard depression years with four children, one of them a year-old baby.

In 1901, with five children, one of them a baby of six months, Papa was called on a mission to the Southern States, and he went without "purse or scrip." Mama sewed; the twins, Zoa and Zola, worked as housemaids, ran errands, and literally "sang for their suppers." Young Rodney ran the farm as best he could with Mama's help, and even four-year-old Rollo sold pins to provide himself with a new suit and his mother with an occasional twenty-five cents. Dora Isabella, the baby, provided the family with entertainment. Papa came home from his mission to find the family only five dollars in debt—the last payment on the sewing machine that had supported the family while he was on his mission. However, Mama's and Papa's brothers and sisters had helped the family, too, when they could, and many a pinched penny went out of their pockets into the mission field.

While Mama's family was growing, Mama's sister Maggie died, leaving her family, and the Hicken's took two of the children into their home. They wanted all of them, but considered themselves "privileged" to be able to take two of them, Isabella and Robert. Then Mama's brother Jock's wife, Minnie, died from complications of childbirth, leaving a month-old baby boy, Raymond Nelson, and a three-year-old doll of a daughter, Bessie. Jock brought the children to his sister, Kate, and went on a mission to the South Seas. Mama moved her two-year-old daughter, Jenny Ann, out of the parental bed, and put the ailing baby in Ann's place.

For weeks the family walked the floor with Ray. Some sort of a glandular trouble in his throat threatened to choke him if he was not kept upright. However, such was the love and cooperation in this household that there was no jealousy, no fear that one child would get more in the way of attention or material things than another. As both Kate and Dave had been reared in polygamous families where all were equally loved brothers and sisters, it made no difference now which children were born of whom. They were children of the family, and they were all loved. If little Jenny Ann was perhaps a bit overzealous in the care of the new little brother, preparing his bottles and substituting him for her not nearly-as-responsive doll, her efforts were appreciated. It was Ann who weaned Raymond

from his bottle by mistakenly pouring his milk into a similar bottle that had once held turpentine. One mouthful of the turpentine-flavored milk, and Ray drank from a cup—the easiest weaning Mama had ever known.

Aunt Maggie's husband remarried and came for the Hawkes' children, to Mama's distress, and later, when Bessie was about fourteen, Uncle Jock remarried, and Bessie went to live with her father for a while and later with her mother's brother in Shelley, Idaho. The childless couple adored their lovely little niece. But Raymond had known only Mama and Papa as parents, and he refused to stay home, to his foster parents' great relief.

In 1927, Mama and Papa adopted their granddaughter, Rodello, the daughter of their son, Rollo, who had been killed, and they reared this child to young womanhood. By this time, they were getting on in years, and a life of giving had not left them with any appreciable amount of material wealth, but they felt wealthy. They owned their own home and their land and never knew debt. Papa's gardens fed his family, and there were wagon loads of produce to share with the "sick and afflicted, the poor and the needy, the widow and the orphan," who were included in the daily family prayers.

The story of Catherine Campbell Murdoch Hicken is a family story. She and her adored husband, David, were the pivots around which the family revolved, for they were incredibly strong people. They taught their children by example. Honesty was stressed, and when dishonesty appeared in others, it was a shocking thing. Loving, getting along with one another, appreciation, and making do with what one had without bitterness or envy were the cornerstones of their family life. Mama's budget shortcuts and saving ways have carried over into the lives of her daughters, who still remember her saying, "Watch the pennies, the dollars will take care of themselves."

Mama was a mystery in many ways, a mystery that deepens as the years pass and we become more appreciative of the woman she was. For instance, she quoted Shakespeare frequently and fluently, but she never said she was quoting from Shakespeare, so it was years later that study made us realize the source of so many of the familiar aphorisms common to our home life. Where did Mama learn Shakespeare? We had a *Complete Works* in the small library in the parlor, but when did Mama read it? Did she read it at night? Hardly, when she went to bed at dark to keep the light bills down and her strength up. "Down at dark, up at dawn!" Had she been exposed to Shakespeare in the Murdoch home or in the school years when she had shared the same school benches that Papa sat on? But that is unlikely. Papa knew nothing of Shakespeare. He was a scripture reader. He told us once that he had read only one piece of fiction in his life and "never read another because the last page was torn away and Id just wasted my time!"

Mama was also familiar with Robert Burns, whom she often quoted: "Oh wad some power the giftie gie us/To see oursels as others see us! It wad frae monie a blunder free us,/An foolish notion." She had read Keats, Shelley, and Brownings, and it is only recently some of us have learned that she wrote poetry, quite passable verse. Most likely, she kept this to herself, for she was in awe of some of her elder sister's gifts along this line, and Mama was much too modest. While she told her children that they were "not to hide their lights under a bushel," she very carefully hid her own most of the time. Mama had read Hawthorne's books and Poe's and most of the early well-known English and American writers. Did she pick these things up from her children as they grew and went through the Wasatch County Schools? She knew much more than we realized she knew until we had lived long enough to learn some of it.

She avidly read the novels of Kathleen Norris (published in *The Deseret News* in serial form) and Temple Bailey and Faith Baldwin. She never missed a column by Dorothy Dix. She read the women's Church magazines assiduously. She loved the poetry and short stories and the articles in *The Young Woman's Journal* and in *The Relief Society Magazine* (oh, how she looked forward to that magazine!) and the *Era*. But she may have been of two minds about the *Exponent*. For if ever a woman looked to her husband for leadership, it was Mama. To a point. The house was Mama's domain and she ran it. But it was run for Papa's convenience and comfort, and if Papa was late for dinner, all of us waited for him. Mama could often soften a decision he had made, but the softening was done in private and then Papa would come to us with, "Well, I've been thinking this over, and hasty judgment is not always good judgment. Why don't we talk over what you want to do again?" But we learned that when this happened, it was because sometime between night and morning, Mama had said something like this: "You can't hold love in a closed fist, you squeeze it right out. Love only stays in an open hand."

Papa led and Mama followed serenely, except for the times when Papa wasn't there, and then Mama could put her size-five feet into his big boots and march ahead without faltering. Their lives revolved around the Church and the Church activities, and even after Mama was far along in years, she looked forward to "doing her best" (going Relief Society teaching). She enjoyed the activities of the Relief Society and especially enjoyed being a Daughter of the Utah Pioneers.

Mama loved plays and later the movies, although she couldn't afford to go very often. Twenty-five cents was always an expenditure to "look at twice." Most of all, she loved the Murdoch reunions and the singing and laughter, parades, and general family love and enjoyment she found in them. She would save and plan for a year and then cook for a week to be able to attend one of the marvelous clan gatherings that were quite often held in Vivian Park in Provo Canyon. And if Papa couldn't leave, Mama would pack up the cookies, cakes, and kids, and hitch up the wagon and drive the team down herself.

She adored surprises, especially people surprises. Aunt Tressa surprised her about once a year. When Mama opened the front door, the two of them would stare solemnly at each other with no word of greeting. Then Mama would open the door an inch at a time, and Aunt Tressa would push her way in. And they would smile a little, and when Aunt Tressa was finally in all the way, they would smile a lot. Then as the families (because they were never alone) watched in amazement, Mama would get down behind a chair and peek through the slats in the back and giggle, and Aunt Tressa would squeeze behind the overstuffed chair and peek out and giggle, and before long their laughter would fill the room and engulf us all. And we never knew what they were laughing at—these grown and dignified women—in their sixties—who had never really grown up!

After the laughter had finally calmed to chuckles, and tears of joy were wiped away, and Aunt Tressa had gone out into the garden to make herself a lettuce and sugar sandwich, there were the days of visiting and "catching up." We would slip as unobtrusively as possible into the rooms where they were talking, to hear, if we could, all the perfectly marvelous things they talked about—the marriages, births, illnesses, interesting diseases, bankruptcies, and deaths, and their opinions of all of these. The opinions were gentle. We thought we must have very good people in our family, because we didn't know of one dishonest person, although we heard of a few that were "close" (tight-fisted) or who "had to get married." (But they were not discussed.) We realize now that the people in our family (uncles, aunts, cousins, etc.) weren't so much "good" as they were surrounded by love and guidance, and as Mama said often enough, "Children must be given the *iron* rod to grasp." When we asked her about that iron rod, she explained that it was the word of God. Then there was the Golden Rule. We didn't hear so much about the Golden Rule—we saw it lived, and lived, and lived.

Mama played the jews harp, and she could twang out anything you wanted. She could also play the harmonica. She told marvelous, detailed stories about the family past, the Indians, the days of polygamy, and life with her parents. She was a poet and a writer without a pen. When we asked her what she thought of polygamy, she would say that their own family was close and loving, and the names Mother and Muz were always spoken in the same breath; but then she would shake her head and say, "But I'm glad that's in the past; polygamy is not for me!" Once in a while, usually after a visit with her half-sisters, she would shake her head and murmur, "Being a child of the second wife is always down on the stick, no matter how it's whittled!" or "To my way of thinking, it was the first wife who is the 'tony' one." And after the Manifesto, her feeling about the differences in plural wives strengthened, but they were never strong enough nor bitter enough to lessen her brother-sister relationships.

Mama was a fine seamstress, and she quilted beautifully and shook her head in dismay if one of us sewed a crooked stitch. She was also an excellent cook, although there was never a cookbook in our house, but she was an implacable teacher. Her idea of teaching us to do something was to say, "You are ten years old; you've watched me mix the bread hundreds of times; now it's your turn. I'm going visiting. You mix the bread while I'm gone." There was never anything but praise for the grayish, hard-textured, unrisen loaves turned out, except from Papa: "Just as one of them learns how to make good bread, you start another one out!" But the next time Mama mixed bread, you watched, and the next time it was your turn the bread looked more nearly like the luscious white loaves that Mama made.

Mama made an occasion of everything. If a child sang a song for the family or bore testimony in fast meeting, it was an excuse for celebration. She must have baked thousands of celebration cakes in her lifetime. She would work for hours to be repaid by a child's smile of pleasure, and each Christmas was months of careful stitching, because her gifts were made with very little money and a lot of skill and imagination.

Mama's pride was her family. The picture of the U.S.S. *Kidder,* rope-framed, hung on her living room wall. That was Ward's ship, and Ward, the youngest son, had made the Navy his life. She never knew that her fondest dream was fulfilled when he married and moved back to Heber for several years. Rodney's boyhood drawing of a bear hung on another wall, and in Mama's eyes it had all the excellence of the oil paintings that Papa had so carefully carried back from the mission field. Her daughters were loving and thoughtful and constantly brightened her life with letters, gifts, and, as frequently as possible, visits.

Mama "set a store by good breeding," and that included giving the best you had to company—your bed, while you slept on the floor; your dessert, if necessary; and anything else you had that someone needed more than you did. It was keeping a pleasant face and a welcoming voice when someone came to visit that you would rather had stayed at home. It was "minding your manners," speaking when spoken to, being seen and not heard, and always doing what you said you would do. It was keeping your word. I learned the word "noblesse oblige" from Mama. Where did Mama learn it?

Good breeding was keeping your skirts down and your knees together, and sitting properly on the chair. It was keeping your hair brushed, and wearing clean underclothes. Mama had a great admiration for "tony" people—people who entertained with originality and flare, who dressed neatly but elegantly, and who spoke softly. "A voice, gentle, soft, and low—an excellent thing in a woman!" Mama never raised her voice except to call Raymond home from play, and it was an effort that made it very interesting. "Ray"—the name would start out softly and would rise—"moond." But it carried. When Ray heard "moond" he started for home. When asked why she didn't get a whistle, Mama said, "You whistle for a dog!"

Mama had the gift of second sight. Mostly she dreamed things that would happen, and sometimes they happened and sometimes they didn't, if she could convince Papa to take steps to prevent them. It was Mama's gift of second sight that sent Papa out in the night to rescue a son with a broken leg; his horse had fallen on him while crossing a creek. It was this gift that sent Papa to Salt Lake City to find the grandchild, Rodello, whose mother had dropped from sight, taking the child with her.

Well-bred people took what came and made the

best of it and did not complain, Mama thought. Mama didn't complain. She had rheumatism and arthritis and a bout with cancer; and in her later years, dangerously low blood pressure caused her to black out at times, and she had broken bones and terrible burns from falling on the stove, but she bore them without more than a small moan. She was a delicately made woman, and was heir to all the discomforts of such women, but she welcomed every pregnancy and accepted gladly the dangers of childbirth in those pioneer times. After she caught her arm in the wringer of her new washing machine, only the look in her eyes as she stared at the scars and the twisted fingers of her damaged hand let us know that she suffered. Her stoicism as she lay a year with a broken hip was amazing, but it was indicative of her life. If she couldn't smile about what happened, she said very little.

So it was with her grieving. She had much to grieve about: the deaths of loved parents and brothers and sisters; the tragedies of her sons' deaths; the loss of her babies, not only the children she had borne, but those like Isabella and Robert and Bessie who were taken away from her after they had settled in her heart. But she did not mourn or cry as many women do; she made the dead come alive with her remembering, and she spoke so frequently and lovingly of the living that when we younger ones met them, we knew them as well as those whom we saw daily. If Mama cried, she did it when she was alone. And when was she ever alone?

Aloud, she counted herself a happy woman with children who grew to be law-abiding, God-fearing, productive people. And she was always sheltered by the strong arms and character of the man she loved. If she worried about the depression years, her worries were confined to seeing enough food on the table and beds for the homeless wanderers who mysteriously found their way to her home. At least, those were the only worries she allowed us to see. It is quite likely that she did not fear at all, because she had complete faith in God and in his goodness, and in Papa's abilities to take care of everything. Or perhaps again, it was because well-bred people "do not complain; they take what they have and make something good come of it." She did this.

Mama disliked vanity in others, and she made sure that her daughters had none of it. Sometimes her tongue could be exceedingly sharp, and she would say, if we stood at the mirror a whit too long, "You're pretty enough, and looking at yourself won't make you prettier!" and "Pretty is as pretty does!" Yet Mama had her own small vanities. She was proud of her truly beautiful legs and feet—slender ankles and wrists were a mark of breeding, she pointed out. Even when she was in her late seventies, she wore girlish pumps and buckles, and she loved silk stockings.

She thought that daintiness was the essence of womanhood, and she admired women who could get through a pregnancy with as few people knowing as possible. "You'd never know that Helen (Rodney's wife) was in a family way right up to the day she delivered, unless she told you!" Helen wore pretty front aprons, and Mama loved lacy aprons, embroidered linens, pieced quilts, and silk dresses. But her main passion was fine china, especially blue and white patterns. She loved flowers and growing things, birds and animals. And her quick eye and sense of humor allowed her to see daily the priceless little things with which she made her life and the lives of others rich— for instance, a cat teaching a kitten to wash its face and impatiently cuffing it if the kitten proved inept. Mama empathized with that cat. She expected her kitten to learn in one lesson, and Mama expected her children to learn just as quickly. It was justification from the animal world for her way of thinking. Not that Mama was harsh; far from that, she was more than gentle, except when driven to a willow switch, which the offender had to go out and cut for himself, and it took a while to learn that the smaller the switch, the more it stung.

The Hicken house was always full as long as Mama was alive. She had long visits from relatives with their large families, and no matter how many people came, the walls and the tables stretched to accommodate them. Grandma Murdoch, Mama's mother, lived for several years in the front room, and her gentle spirit was still there for the youngest of us as we grew up. Mama's wish that her home would always have children in it was fulfilled. Rodney's baby daughter, Rhea Jean, was to grow up at the other end of the Hicken block, and long after the other children had grown and gone, Rhea Jean would spend her days playing at Mama's feet, or when Mama's eyes were dulled by old age and ill health, her arms were ready to hold a child with an earache or a heartache.

On her deathbed, two of her small great granddaughters were visiting, and while the granddaughter took a turn caring for Mama, she heard the little voices in the kitchen and asked, "Whose children are they? Bring them in here." "But we thought they might disturb you." "Never, never. It is always so good to hear the young ones play. Please don't keep them from me."

To Mama, life was a gift filled with people she loved, worked for, gave to, protected, and encouraged—most of all encouraged. If you were a relative or friend of Catherine Campbell Murdoch Hicken's, you were wonderful, accomplished, beloved, and welcomed. And because of this, Mama Kate didn't really die in 1945 at the age of eighty. She just slipped into another room, from where she calls out to us, "Oh, my, you are doing just fine. I'm so proud of you, and I can hardly wait until you can find the time to come and stay awhile with me. Our door is never locked; if we're not here when you come, just come right in and make yourself at home. I've just gone out to chop that rooster's head off so we can have chicken and dumplings for dinner!"

This profile of Catherine Campbell Murdoch Hicken was written by her granddaughter, Rodello Hicken Hunter Calkins. Copyright 1979 by Rodello Hunter.

"House of Many Rooms." Hicken home, Heber, Utah.

HICKEN FAMILY— A turn-of-the century photo of Kate Hicken and children. Twins, Zoa and Zola, elder son, Rodney, younger son Rollo, and holding baby daughter, Dora.

This is a picture of Kate Hicken and family while David W. Hicken was on his mission in the Southern States Mission, 1902-1903. Ward and Ann were born after he came home.

Gathering at the golden wedding anniversary of Kate and David W. Hicken:
left to right: Harry Christenson; Grandma Park (Billys mother), Dora
Larson holding Linda Ann Larson, infant of Dora; Ann Dawson, behind Dora;
Kathryn Park; Zoa Christenson; Kate Hicken; David W. Hicken; in front,
Vivian Christenson; Ladorna Larson; Rodello Hicken, behind Bessie Dawson;
LuRae Frkovich; boy in front, Tony Larson; behind Tony, someone from
California with Larsons—likely a relative of Lloyds; Ann Hicken; Lloyd
Larson; Zola Park; Ray Park; Billie Park; Dee Christenson. Insert: Ward
Hicken, who was away in the Navy when the anniversary picture was taken.

Catherine C. Murdoch Hicken and David W. Hicken at their golden
wedding anniversary, July 1936, surrounded by flowers at their home.

Mr. and Mrs. David W. Hicken

request the pleasure of your company at the

Fiftieth Anniversary of their Marriage

Tuesday, July twenty-first, Nineteen thirty-six

at seven-thirty o'clock in the evening

Annex Social Hall   Heber, Utah

No Presents

1886   1936

David W. Hicken   Catherine C. Murdoch

HUSBAND   David William HICKEN
Birth   8 August 1861
Place   Heber, Wasatch, Utah
Chr
Married   21 July 1886
Place   Logan Temple, Logan, Cache, Utah
Death   31 October 1953 Salt Lake City, Salt Lake, Utah
Burial   4 November 1953 Heber, Wasatch, Utah
Father   Thomas HICKEN
Mother   Catherine FEWKES
Other Wives
(if any)

WIFE   Catherine Campbell MURDOCH
Birth   15 November 1864
Place   Heber, Wasatch, Utah
Chr
Death   6 March 1945 Heber, Wasatch, Utah
Burial   9 March 1945 Heber, Wasatch, Utah
Father   John Murray MURDOCH
Mother   Isabella CRAWFORD
Other Wives
(if any)
Where was information obtained? Ward M. Hicken
*List complete maiden name for all females.

1st Child	Zoa HICKEN
Birth	26 June 1888
Place	Heber, Wasatch, Utah
Married to	Harry CHRISTENSON
Married	27 April 1920
Place	Salt Lake City, Salt Lake, Utah
Died	26 June 1968 Salt Lake City, Utah

2nd Child	Zola HICKEN
Birth	26 June 1888
Place	Heber, Wasatch, Utah
Married to	William Duncan DuFosee PARK
Married	17 November 1920
Place	Salt Lake City, Salt Lake, Utah
Died	15 August 1970

3rd Child	David Rodney HICKEN
Birth	20 October 1889
Place	Heber, Wasatch, Utah
Married to	Helen COLEMAN
Married	16 November 1910
Place	Salt Lake City, Salt Lake, Utah
Died	9 May 1929 Heber, Wasatch, Utah

4th Child	Mary HICKEN
Birth	11 Sep 1892 (Stillborn)
Place	Heber, Wasatch, Utah
Married to	
Married	
Place	
Died	11 Sep 1892 Heber, Wasatch, Utah

5th Child	John Murray HICKEN
Birth	16 May 1893
Place	Heber, Wasatch, Utah
Married to	
Married	
Place	
Died	3 June 1893 Heber Wasatch, Utah

6th Child	Thomas Rollo HICKEN
Birth	8 June 1895
Place	Heber, Wasatch, Utah
Married to	Venus Deon HARRIS
Married	29 March 1919
Place	Provo, Utah, Utah
Died	6 Jan 1920 Provo, Utah, Utah

7th Child	Dora Isabella HICKEN
Birth	24 June 1901
Place	Heber, Wasatch, Utah
Married to	Lloyd Anthone LARSON
Married	10 October 1922
Place	Heber, Wasatch, Utah
Died	

8th Child	Ward "M" HICKEN
Birth	5 July 1904
Place	Heber, Wasatch, Utah
Married to	Lois BAIRD
Married	8 March 1945
Place	Providence, Rhode Island
Died	

9th Child	Jennie Ann HICKEN
Birth	13 November 1909
Place	Heber, Wasatch, Utah
Married to	
Married	
Place	
Died	

10th Child	Thora Rodello HICKEN (Adopted)
Birth	23 March 1920
Place	Provo, Utah, Utah
Married to	(1) Ross Hunter (2) James Calkin
Married	27 Jan 1939 7 Sep 1965
Place	Holden, Utah
Died	

Benefactl No. SLC (Wagner Form)

1 MURDOCH, James 1786-1831   2 MURDOCH, John Murray 1820-1910
1 MURDOCH, Mary MURRAY, Sp. 1782-1856   2 MURDOCH, Isabella CRAWFORD, Sp. 1836-1916

DESCENDANTS OF--------- 3 MURDOCH, Catherine Campbell 1864-1945
                        3 HICKEN, David William, Sp. 1861-1953

                                                             B-Born
4 CHRISTENSEN, Zoa HICKEN B-26 Jun 1888 D-26 Jun 1968   M-Married
4 CHRISTENSEN, Harry, Sp. B-25 Jan 1893 M-27 Apr 1920 D-19 May 1943   D-Died
                                                             Sp.-Spouse
    5 CHRISTENSEN, Harry David B-24 Jan 1922   Div.-Divorced
    5 CHRISTENSEN, Ethel Mary VAN CORLOR, Sp. (1) B-14 Sep 1922 M-15 Sep 1942
    5 CHRISTENSEN, Betty Nadean BOLTON Wycherly, Sp. (2) B-   M-

        6 McQUILLAN, Linda CHRISTENSEN B-8 Apr 1947
        6 McQUILLAN, Dale Ray, Sp. B-   M-6 Apr 1968

            7 McQUILLAN, Todd Dale   B-30 Nov 1968

            7 McQUILLAN, Cody Ray   B-19 Jul 1973

            7 McQUILLAN, David Casey   B-23 Oct 1975

        6 HILL, Vicky Lynn CHRISTENSEN B-4 Jun 1948
        6 HILL, John Kenton, Sp. B-16 Jul 1948 M- 7 Apr 1967

            7 HILL, Chad Kenton   B- 1 Mar 1969

    5 CHRISTENSEN, Florence Maren B-22 June 1924 D-19 Nov 1924 (child)

    5 TUCKETT, Vivian Irene CHRISTENSEN B-23 Mar 1926
    5 TUCKETT, William Holden, Sp. B-18 May 1925 M-25 Aug 1947 D-25 May 1971

        6 KNUTSON, Leslee Ann TUCKETT B-8 Jan 1949
        6 KNUTSON, James Albert, Sp. B-9 Jun 1948 M-12 Aug 1970

            7 KNUTSON, Melisa   B-29 Mar 1976

            7 KNUTSON, Suzanne   B-20 Mar 1978

        6 BARTON, Michele Lee TUCKETT B-29 Sep 1953
        6 BARTON, Randall Jay, Sp. B-30 Dec 1952 M-25 Dec 1972

            7 BARTON, Tobie   B-20 Sep 1977

        6 TUCKETT, Gregory William B-19 Jul 1956
        6 TUCKETT, Linda PERKINS, Sp. B-   M-20 Aug 1978

        6 TUCKETT, Rick Holdon   B-30 May 1958

        6 TUDKETT, Brett Christopher   B-30 Jan 1962

    5 CHRISTENSEN, Vern Murray B-3 Jun 1933
    5 CHRISTENSEN, Vania THOMSON, Sp. B-18 Sep 1935 M-17 Feb 1955

        6 ANDERSON, Julie CHRISTENSON B-28 Nov 1955
        6 ANDERSON, Scot Evan, Sp. B-16 May 1955 M-15 Aug 1975

            7 ANDERSON, Anthony Evan   B-28 Jul 1978

        6 WARNER, Valicia CHRISTENSEN B-27 May 1958
        6 WARNER, Larry Glen, Sp. B-9 Feb 1957 M-23 Sep 1978

        6 CHRISTENSON, Janae   B-18 Sep 1959

4 PARK, Zola HICKEN B-26 Jun 1888 D-15 Aug 1970
4 PARK, William Duncan DuFosee, Sp. B-2 Jul 1892 M-17 Nov 1920 D-10 Jun 1968

    5 STENSRUD, Kathryn Alice PARK B-25 Aug 1921
    5 STENSRUD, David Norman, Sp. B-26 Jun 1921 M-24 Oct 1945

        6 STENSRUD, Cherilyn Signy   B-27 Aug 1946

6 STENSRUD, David William B-26 Jan 1949
6 STENSRUD, Shiela Louise PICKENS, Sp. B-21 Sep 1948 M-11 Sep 1971

    7 STENSRUD, David Wayne   B-28 Oct 1974

    7 STENSRUD, Jamie Bree   B-28 Mar 1977

6 GARDNER, Diane Kay STENSRUD B-23 Feb 1952
6 GARDNER, Robert Chad, Sp. B-31 Dec 1951 M-4 Jun 1971

    7 GARDNER, Christopher Chad   B-17 Dec 1974

    7 GARDNER, Collette Kathryn   B-18 Feb 1977

6 HOWICK, Laurie Ann STENSRUD B-26 May 1957
6 HOWICK, Scott Douglas, Sp. B-21 Aug 1955 M-5 Sep 1975

    7 HOWICK, Brock Scott   B-5 Mar 1976

5 PARK, William Finley (Ray) B-10 Mar 1924
5 PARK, Paula Mae Moon, Sp. B-1 Oct 1925 M-22 Feb 1955

    6 KNUDSEN, Claudia Rae PARK B-20 Jul 1955
    6 KNUDSEN, James Edward, Sp. B-   M-6 Dec 1974

        7 KNUDSEN, Jamie Rae   B- Jun 1977

    6 PARK, William David Craig   B-11 Nov 1959

4 HICKEN, David Rodney B-20 Oct 1889 D-9 May 1929
4 HICKEN, Helen COLEMAN, Sp. B-1 Mar 1892 M-16 Nov 1910 D-9 Jan 1971

5 FRKOVICH, LuRae HICKEN B-7 May 1912
5 FRKOVICH, John Louis, Sp. B-5 Apr 1908 M-18 Jul 1931

    6 FRKOVICH, Michael B-12 Jan 1932 D-12 Jan 1932

    6 FRKOVICH, Baby boy B-18 May 1934 D-18 May 1934

    6 ALVEY, Joan LuRae FRKOVICH B-21 Oct 1935
    6 ALVEY, Donald, Sp. B-31 Mar 1933 M-16 May 1953

        7 ALVEY, Don Jay B-20 Mar 1954
        7 ALVEY, Detta Ingrid REFOS, Sp. B-15 Oct 1952 M-4 Aug 1975

            8 ALVEY, Cindy June   B-26 Jul 1973

            8 ALVEY, Tiffany Felice   B-17 Apr 1976

            8 ALVEY, Pamela   B- 9 Jun 1977

        7 ALVEY, Fay Marie   B- 6 Nov 1956

        7 ALVEY, Michael Kent   B-29 Sep 1959

        7 ALVEY, Cameron   B-23 Aug 1962

    6 STAHLE, Joyce Marie FRKOVICH B-2 Sep 1937
    6 STAHLE, Elmer George, Sp. B-13 Oct 1920 M-24 Jun 1960
      STAHLE,   Sp. B-   M-

    6 FRKOVICH, John B-3 Sep 1939 D-6 Sep 1939

    6 GROSE, Carolyn Anne FRKOVICH B-6 Aug 1940
    6 GROSE, Dee LaMAR, Sp. B-27 Apr 1936 M-29 Apr 1960

        7 GROSE, Laurie   B-25 Oct 1963

        7 GROSE, Trent Dee   B- 3 Apr 1966

        7 GROSE, Joel Kent   B-26 Jan 1972

    6 FRKOVICH, John Jerry   B-14 Nov 1943

5 COHN, Helen Eva HICKEN Naglich B-28 Nov 1914
5 NAGLICH, Nikolas Lucas, Sp. (1) B-4 Dec 1904 M-25 Jul 1931 D-20 Jun 1969
5 COHN, Hartley Saul, Sp. (2) B-   M-19 Jul 1972

     6 NAGLICH, Jay Louis B-29 Nov 1932
     6 NAGLICH, Claudette THOMPSON, Sp. B-17 Apr 1934 M-28 Jun 1952

          7 MEREL, Lanette NAGLICH House B-28 Apr 1953
          7 HOUSE, Franklin Michael, Sp. B-28 Jan 1953 M-31 Oct 1971 Div.
          7 MEREL, Kevin, Sp. B-5 May 1956 M-10 Feb 1979

               8 HOUSE, Tauri Ann   B-26 Apr 1971

          7 NAGLICH, Stephen Louis B-21 Jan 1955
          7 NAGLICH, Eve Ann FOSTER, Sp. B-24 Dec 1957 M-14 Feb 1976 Div.

          7 KOHLENBERG, Nickie Lee NAGLICH B-31 Jul 1956
          7 KOHLENBERG, Wayne Thomas, Sp. B-23 Aug 1954 M-25 Jul 1976

               8 KOHLENBERG, Christopher Wayne B-14 Dec 1976

               8 KOHLENBERG, Kimberly Ann   B- 5 Jan 1978

               8 KOHLENBERG, Kathryn Lee   B-27 Sep 1979

          7 COUTURIER, Jalynn NAGLICH B-26 Nov 1957
          7 COUTURIER, Clare Richard, Sp. B-22 Nov 1954 M-30 Nov 1974

               8 COUTURIER, Cher   B- 6 Jun 1975

               8 COUTURIER, Clare Justin   B-17 Aug 1978

          7 NAGLICH, Gregory   B- 6 May 1960

     6 MURRAY, Helen Eva NAGLICH B-2 Jun 1936
     6 MURRAY, Allen Glen, Sp. B-24 Sep 1934 M-19 Nov 1955 D-3 Mar 1976

          7 GILES, Glenna Marie MURRAY B-9 Sep 1956
          7 GILES, William Thomas, Sp. B-22 May 1952 M-13 Jun 1977

          7 JONAS, Tracy Ann MURRAY B-18 Nov 1957
          7 JONAS, Mark Lee, Sp. B-19 May 1957 M-29 Mar 1977

               8 Jonas, Mark Allen   B-30 Oct 1977

          7 MURRAY, Kevin Allen   B-29 Jan 1961

          7 MURRAY, Lois Allison   B-19 Feb 1967

5 HICKEN, William Russell B-25 Jul 1918
5 HICKEN, Ruby Lucille BURGAN, Sp. B-28 Sep 1924 M-12 May 1945

     6 HICKEN, Wayne Russel B-23 Apr 1947 D-11 Aug 1957

     6 CHRISTENSEN, Nancy Ann HICKEN B-13 Jul 1948
     6 CHRISTENSEN, Evan Dykes Jr. Sp. B-11 Apr 1938 M-9 Apr 1971

          7 CHRISTENSEN, Nathan Dykes   B-20 Nov 1974

          7 CHRISTENSEN, Emily Denise   B-20 Aug 1977

          7 CHRISTENSEN, Thomas Wayne   B-19 May 1980

     6 HICKEN, William Rodney B-17 Jun 1952
     6 HICKEN, Sharon Neilson, Sp. B-6 May 1953 M-11 Sep 1975

          7 HICKEN, Jennifer Ann   B-17 May 1977

5 JOHNSON, Rhea Jean HICKEN B-30 May 1928
5 JOHNSON, Alvin Ferris, Sp. B-5 Jan 1922 M-6 Nov 1946

6 JOHNSON, Alvin Dale B-26 Jun 1947
6 JOHNSON, Diana Marie JANSEN, Sp. B-14 Mar 1947 M-8 Nov 1969
6 JOHNSON, Linda Lorraine BECK, Sp. B-9 Jun 1949 M-29 Sep 1979

    7 JOHNSON, Dean Ferris   B-17 Feb 1972

    7 JOHNSON, Dawn Marie   B-24 Jul 1977

6 JOHNSON, Alan Gene B-29 Jun 1948
6 JOHNSON, Deborah Eileen SEAYRS, Sp. (1) B-   M-27 Feb 1970 Div.
6 JOHNSON, Frieda Aielene HENSENBARGER, Sp. (2) B-19 Jun 1945 M-3 Jun 1976

6 REEVES, Lorea Johnson Mann B-23 Oct 1952
6 MANN, David Jeffrey, Sp. (1) B-24 Sep 1951 M-25 Sep 1971 Div.
6 REEVES, Stephen Gale, Sp. (2) B-24 Apr 1949 M-3 Feb 1980

    7 MANN, Jeffrey Lee   B- 9 May 1972

    7 MANN, Tiffany Dawn   B-27 Apr 1975

    7 MANN, Tonya Ann   B- 6 Sep 1977

    7 MANN, Brian Karl   B-17 Jul 1979

6 JOHNSON, Robert Ferris B-12 Oct 1953
6 JOHNSON, Cynthia Kay HANKS, Sp. (1) B-18 Apr 1954 M-10 Nov 1972
6 JOHNSON, Esther Ana LOPATIN, Sp. (2) B-11 Nov 1955 M-27 Jun 1979

    7 JOHNSON, Robert Michael   B-21 Aug 1973

    7 JOHNSON, Christa Marie   B-22 Jun 1975

6 JOHNSON, William Brent B-16 Jun 1956
6 JOHNSON, Patricia Lynn SWINEHEART, Sp. B-5 May 1959 M-7 Jul 1979

4 HICKEN, Mary B-11 Sep 1892 (Stillborn)

4 HICKEN, John Murray B-16 May 1893 D-3 Jun 1893

4 HICKEN, Thomas Rolo B-8 Jun 1895 D-6 Jan 1920
4 HICKEN, Venus Deon HARRIS, Sp. B-17 Mar 1900 M-29 Mar 1919 D- Nov 1976

    5 CALKINS, Thora Rodello HICKEN Hunter B-23 Mar 1920
    5 HUNTER, Ross, Sp. (1) B-2 May 1909 M-27 Jan 1939 Div.-17 Feb 1965
    5 CALKINS, James Frank, Sp. (2) B-   M-7 Sep 1965 Div.

        6 SEARLE, Sally HUNTER Heller B-3 Nov 1939
        6 HELLER, Bruce Wayne, Sp. (1) B-   M-18 Feb 1959
        6 SEARLE, LeRoy, Sp. (2) B-16 Jun 1941 M-6 Mar 1965

            7 HELLER, Terry Todd   B-31 Aug 1960

            7 SEARLE, Holly   B- 3 Mar 1966

        6 HUNTER, Ann   B-27 Mar 1942

        6 BAILEY, Barbara HUNTER B-5 Mar 1948
        6 BAILEY, James Stephen, Sp. B-   M-6 Jun 1970

            7 BAILEY, Johanna   B-17 Jun 1975

            7 BAILEY, Jacob James   B-16 Mar 1978

4 LARSON, Dora Isabella HICKEN B-24 Jun 1901
4 LARSON, Lloyd Anthone, Sp. B-28 Jun 1900 M-10 Oct 1922

    5 EICHENBERG, LaDorna Ellison LARSON Perine B-12 Sep 1923
    5 PERINE, Robert Heath, Sp. (1) B-30 Nov 1922 M-14 Mar 1947
    5 EICHENBERG, Robert Jr., Sp. (2) B-12 Oct 1922 M-28 Feb 1975

        6 ROBINSON, Jorli PERINE B-12 Mar 1948
        6 ROBINSON, David Beverly, Sp. B-12 Feb 1950 M-7 May 1977

            7 ROBINSON, Damon   B-23 Mar 1977

6 HIGHBERG, Lisa PERINE B-18 Aug 1949
6 HIGHBERG, Gregory Paul, Sp. B-7 Nov 1949 M-28 Feb 1970

      7 HIGHBERG, Kristin   B- 1 Oct 1970

      7 HIGHBERG, Erin Gregory   B-26 Dec 1975

6 PERINE, Terri Anna B-8 Aug 1952 D-30 May 1973

5 LARSON, Lloyd Anthony B-21 Jan 1929
5 LARSON, Marilyn ASHTON, Sp. B-14 Sep 1935 M-19 Dec 1956

    6 LARSON, William Ty   B-25 Sep 1957

    6 LARSON, Wayne Ashton   B- 3 Jun 1959

    6 LARSON, Todd Anthone   B-21 Jul 1961

    6 LARSON, Scott Lloyd   B- 6 Jul 1965

    6 LARSON, Sharilyn   B-24 Sep 1967

    6 LARSON, Marc Reed   B-15 Jun 1973

    6 LARSON, Sara   B-12 May 1978

5 McBRIDE, Linda Ann LARSON B-28 Aug 1935
5 McBRIDE, Darvil David, Sp. B-8 Jan 1935 M-27 Dec 1958

    6 RENFELDT, Deborah Annette (Norris) McBRIDE B-1 Apr 1955 (Adopted)
    6 RENFELDT, Robert B., Sp. B-11 Feb 1953 M-21 Jun 1975

      7 RENFELDT, Trina Rachelle   B-29 Apr 1976

      7 RENFELDT, Nadine Kaycee   B-21 Jun 1977

      7 RENFELDT, Kari Lanae   B-21 Apr 1979

      7 RENFELDT, Pennie Leann   B-26 Aug 1980

    6 McBRIDE, Darvil Anthone   B-11 Feb 1960

    6 McBRIDE, Michael Jon   B-27 Jan 1962

    6 McBRIDE, Rachel Lee   B- 5 Dec 1963

    6 McBRIDE, David Paul   B- 3 Dec 1964

    6 McBRIDE, Jonah Steven   B- 5 Sep 1969

    6 McBRIDE, Joshua Jared   B- 5 Jun 1973

    6 McBRIDE, Jo Linda   B- 4 Nov 1976

5 LARSON, Delbert LaClead B-13 Feb 1941
5 LARSON, Vicki Lee HEARD, Sp. B-24 Feb 1945 M-5 Sep 1966

    6 LARSON, Jeffrey LaClede   B-19 Dec 1967

    6 LARSON, Travis Lee   B- 3 Aug 1969

    6 LARSON, Chandra Lynn   B-19 Jun 1973

4 HICKEN, Ward "M" B-5 Jul 1904
4 HICKEN, June MARTIN, Sp. (1) B-   M-
4 HICKEN, Louis BAIRD Barber Bond, Sp. (2) B-11 Jun 1914 M-8 Mar 1945
  Barber, Alvin, Sp. (1) B-   M-
  Bond, Alfred Clift, Sp. (2) B-   M-

    5 BOND, Farrel Dee B-1 Feb 1935 (sealed to Ward "M" Hicken)
    5 BOND, Elosie WINTERTON, Sp. B-6 Nov 1937 M-15 Jun 1955

```
                6 BOND, Melanie              B- 9 Jul 1956

                6 BOND, Cindy               B- 1 Jan 1958

                6 BOND, Lynn Alan           B-22 May 1959

                6 BOND, Steven Alfred       B- 4 Aug 1960

                6 BOND, Geraldine           B-29 Sep 1962

        5 HICKEN, David Kent B-14 Feb 1946
        5 HICKEN, Diedre Louise SANBORN, Sp. B-9 Aug 1948 M-26 May 1970

                6 HICKEN, Adrianne Colleen Joy  B-14 Jul 1977

        5 HICKEN, Colleen Joy B-29 Dec 1947 D-29 Jun 1948

        5 HICKEN, Blaine Ward B-20 Mar 1950 D-28 May 1952

    4 HICKEN, Jennie Ann B-13 Nov 1909
```

James Crawford Murdoch and Sarah Elizabeth Giles

James Crawford Murdoch was the third child of John M. and Isabella Crawford Murdoch. He was born February 11, 1869, in Heber City, Utah, where he lived out his remaining life. He was known by people of his own age and older as "Skinny Jim." This was due to there being another man named James S. Murdock living in Heber who was a much larger man than James Crawford and who was known as "Big Jim."

James Crawford's boyhood days were spent very much like those of other pioneer children, herding cows, gathering wood, going fishing, and swimming in the swimming holes and streams near his home. As he grew older, he played on the Heber baseball team and also played a bass horn in the city band.

James grew up in the Mormon Church and was a very active member throughout his life, having served on two missions and serving on the high council of the Wasatch Stake for twenty-five years. In February, 1898, he was called on a mission to serve as a traveling elder in the Wisconsin Conference of the Northern States Mission and was released from the mission on March 15, 1900. During his mission, the missionaries traveled without purse or scrip and depended upon the Saints in the area for room and board.

After completing his mission and returning to his home in Heber City, Utah, James married Sarah Elizabeth Giles on November 27, 1901, in the Salt Lake Temple. To this union eight children were born, three girls and five boys: Mary Althora Sackett, Sarah Laraine Giles, James Ruelof, George Merrol, John Bard, Grant Brigham, Ruby Isabel Jasperson, and Thomas Verd.

Shortly after their marriage, James was called on another mission for eighteen months to Mesa, Arizona. While on this mission, his eldest child, Mary Althora, was born. His wife and baby lived with Sarah's father and mother until his return in 1903, then they moved into a small log house located on the corner of 200 West and 400 South in Heber City, Utah. This home and lot was a wedding present given to them by Sarah's parents.

James, Sarah, and family lived in this house until 1913, when they moved into their new home, which they had built by John Bond. The new home is located at the same address, still stands today, and is owned by their son Grant. The older home was sold to Wilford Howarth and his wife and was moved to where it stands today at 217 North and 100 West in Heber City, Utah. Basically, James Crawford's occupation was that of a freighter and farmer. As a freighter, he would haul supplies from Wasatch County to Duchesne County and on the return trips would haul wool for the sheep men and other supplies back to Heber. While farming, he also raised cattle and horses. He had some well-bred draft horses that were generally sold to a Mr. Spalding out of Salt Lake City, Utah. Sugar beets and, later, peas for the canning company were the main cash crops raised. James also took on many other various jobs to support his wife and growing family. During the winter months he worked in the mines at Park City, worked as a night watchman for the Woods Cross Canning Company, and was a member of the threshing crew during harvest time, going from farm to farm threshing grain. He did everything possible to keep his family warm, clothed, and fed. Each fall, he would go into the hills and get enough wood for winter, and the same with coal, by driving a team and wagon to Coalville to get the winter's supply of coal.

He would take grain to Johnson's grist mill, located in Midway, and have the grain ground into flour. A trip would be made by team and wagon to Provo, with his wife, Sarah, or one of the children accompanying him. This trip was to get enough fruit to can and bottle for the winter, with generally a trip later to Provo for a load of apples. These supplies, together with a five-gallon can of honey from Duchesne and items raised on the farm, including meat, potatoes, eggs, and milk, gave the family ample supplies for winter. Also to be noted is that James and Sarah had their own cheese press to make cheese for the family and a smokehouse to smoke meat, such as hams and bacon from hogs raised on the farm.

Early in his married life, James was stricken with arthritis from which he suffered greatly and eventually became an invalid. All chores and farm work were turned over to his wife and sons. He would ride to the fields in the buggy or wagon and show his sons what and how things were to be done. This included plowing and tilling the soil, planting, irrigating, and harvesting. His wife, Sarah, would also help out in the fields as much as she could, especially in harvesting the sugar beets and picking potatoes. James would also hire William and Nancy Thompson, their neighbors, to help with the sugar beet harvesting.

In the fall of 1922, after all the hay was in the barn and two stacks erected outside and the threshing was done, fire wiped out the barn, sheds, and all the hay and straw. The grain in the granary and the home were saved, although paint on the house was badly blistered and some windows were cracked. James had been kind to people in need of help all through his married life. He would have his sons deliver a load of hay to this widow or that widow so she could feed her cows. When butchering for the family, meat would be sent to various neighbors. At Thanksgiving and Christmas time it was always a sack of flour, potatoes, and meat to be sent to Auntie Mayoh, his wife's aunt, and others. People remembered what James had done and after the fire, donations of all kinds came to him, and the neighbors gathered together and built a new barn for his stock. Others helped by bringing a load of hay to feed the stock. This help was never forgotten by either James or Sarah.

In the fall of 1924, fire struck again, burning two stacks of wild hay in the north fields. The cause of this fire was never determined, but was another setback in the lives of James and Sarah.

James continued to have health problems. In 1935, he had cataracts removed from both of his eyes. Af-ter the operation, he could see fairly well out of one eye, but the other still had blurred vision. In 1937, he started suffering from excruciating pains above the good eye. He was taken to Salt Lake City for treatment. He had an examination by an eye specialist, Dr. Palmer, who found an abscess in back of the eye, leaving him with only the one with the blurred vision. He had been an avid reader all his life, reading mostly scriptures. From this time on, his faithful wife, Sarah, would read news items, letters, and scriptures to him.

James was a devoted Church member and served to the best of his ability. Even after it was hard for him to get around, he would carry a cushion to church to sit on. He was also called upon to administer to the ill time after time It has been said by those with authority that James had been blessed with the powers for healing. He taught his children the truths of the gospel and what prayer and the priesthood meant to each of them. The priesthood was always in his and Sarah's home. All of his children, except one, who is not married, have been married in the temple. As of this writing, he has had two sons, five grandsons, and nine great-grandsons serve on missions. His sons have held Church positions as bishops and counselors, stake presidents and counselors, ward clerks and temple workers.

James liked to be with his children and entertain them whenever he could. He would take the older boys, together with their friends, swimming, fishing to Current Creek, to the circus in Provo, or to Salt Lake by way of Provo by train to the State Fair. The neighbor boys, as well as his own sons, would look forward to these trips. At the age of eighty-two, James went hunting with his son, Merrol, Noah Giles, and Noah's son, Elvin, and others, and stayed in the hills until they had killed their deer. James didn't do any hunting, nor did he carry a gun, but went along to enjoy the outing with them.

James was strict but fair with his children. All chores had to be done before play. Animals had to be taken care of before the family meals. At mealtime, everyone was expected to be at home. Once each day, generally at the evening meal, family prayers were held. On Sunday morning, every child was required to have his chores done and be ready in time for Sunday School and the same for Sacrament meeting. James always kept his machinery and wagons painted and under sheds when not in use. Each spring, the harnesses had to be disassembled, washed, dried, and soaked in Neatsfoot oil and painted. After James became ill and couldn't do these things, he tried to impress upon his sons the importance of the maintenance of tools and equipment.

In November 1951, James Crawford and his wife, Sarah, celebrated their golden wedding anniversary with all of their children present.

James always looked forward to the Murdoch family reunion, where he could visit with his brothers and sisters and other members of the family.

James Crawford Murdoch passed away August 14, 1959, at the age of ninety. He had been the oldest living person in Wasatch County at that time. On the date of this writing, he has a living posterity of 118.

Written by Grant B. Murdoch (son), with contributions from other family members May 1980.

Marriage picture, 1902. James Crawford Murdoch and Sarah Elizabeth Giles.

James Crawford Murdoch-Age 18   James Crawford Murdoch-Age 32
                                                Wedding Picture

Sarah Elizabeth Giles At   Sarah Elizabeth Giles At
        Age 15   Age 18

Sarah Elizabeth Giles Murdoch

Sarah Elizabeth Giles, the daughter of George M. and Mary Elizabeth Mayoh Giles, was born in Heber City, Utah, on December 4, 1878.

Sarah spent her childhood on the James Davis ranch, where her father moved his family when she was eight years old. The ranch was seven miles north of Heber City and was known at that time as Elkhorn. Later, they returned to their home in Heber, which is located on the corner of 100 South and Main. The large sandstone home still stands, although it has changed hands many times. It has been used as living quarters, barbershop, doctor's office, floral shop, and is presently being occupied and used as a ceramic shop.

Sarah's father hauled freight between Heber City and Park City for the A.C. Hatch Company. In order to supplement the family income, Sarah would follow along behind her father driving another team and wagon loaded with freight.

Sarah attended the old Sleepy Hollow School, which was located on the corner of 200 West and 300 South in Heber City. She later attended and graduated from the Wasatch Stake Academy. She was always a faithful Church worker until her health and age prevented her from serving. She taught in the Primary for a number of years, was first counselor in the stake MIA, was a Relief Society visiting teacher, and also served as assistant secretary in the ward Relief Society. She also was a member of the Sunday School choir in 1896.

In addition to taking care of her home and family, Sarah was also a midwife for a number of years, working with Dr. W.R. Wherritt and Dr. T.A. Dannanberg. After her husband became ill and unable to work, you could see Sarah helping out in any way that she could in the fields and at home, milking cows, cutting wood, feeding the animals, and working in the garden.

Sarah loved people, especially the children, and the children showed their love for her by being in her home daily. As they grew older, the James and Sarah Murdoch yard was a playground for all the neighborhood children.

In 1937, Sarah had a close call with her life, being involved in an automobile accident. Sarah, her son, Merrol, and his daughter Merilyn, had been to the LDS Hospital in Salt Lake City to get James, her husband, who had been recovering from an eye operation. Shortly after leaving the hospital, they were involved in a two-car accident. James, Merrol, and Merilyn were badly shaken up and frightened, but without injury.

Sarah was thrown through the windshield. Her scalp was cut and peeled back from just above the eyes to just above the ears. This being such a severe wound, Sarah had to remain in the hospital. It was not known for weeks whether she would recover. Dr. Karl Nielson, the family doctor from Heber, by chance was at the hospital when Sarah was admitted. He performed the necessary surgery and also treated her after she was released.

In 1952, once again Sarah had a narrow escape with her life. This time, a severe stroke disabled her. Dr. Nielson had given her from six to twenty-four hours to live and suggested to the family members present that they notify the other members of the family of her condition. Once again, Sarah became well enough to care for her husband and home. She often stated that it was through the prayers of administering elders and the family that she remained alive.

If medals were given to people for love, kindness, and devotion, Sarah E. Giles Murdoch would have accumulated many. The kindness and love she showed to all she met, both young and old, and the devotion she had for her church, husband, and family was exemplary. She nursed and waited on her husband for many years, often having to bathe and dress him. She also had to tie his shoes, as he had arthritis in his hands and could not do it for himself. Often Sarah remarked to her family that she hoped and prayed she could remain on earth long enough to see James put to rest and given a proper burial. This was accomplished, as her husband, James, preceded her in death. Sarah passed away August 2, 1961, and was buried beside her husband August 5, 1961, in the Heber Cemetery.

Written by Grant B. Murdoch, with contributions from other members of the family, May 1980.

James C. and Sarah E. Giles Murdoch home prior to 1973.

Mary Althora, James Ruelof And Sarah Laraine Murdoch

James C. And Sarah E. Giles Murdoch at a
Murdoch Family Reunion

James Crawford Murdoch Age 18 Years

James Crawford Murdoch on Porch
In front of his home

James Crawford and Sarah E. Giles Murdoch Family: Back row L to R:
George Merrol, John Bard, Grant Brigham, James Ruelof. Front Row
L to R: Mary Althora, Sarah E., Ruby Isabell, James C, Thomas Verd,
Sarah Laraine. (taken 1920)

James C. and Sarah E. Giles Murdoch on their
Golden Wedding Anniversary November 27, 1951

James C. And Sarah E. G. Murdoch
1945

Sarah Elizabeth Giles Murdoch 1945

Sarah Elizabeth Giles in center
of picture with graduating class

Home previously owned by James Crawford Murdoch 1981

James C. and Sarah E. Giles Murdoch with their sons and daughters and their spouses New Years Day of 1946

(Him)   James Crawford Murdoch and Missionaries 1898-1900

HUSBAND   JAMES CRAWFORD MURDOCH
Birth   11 February 1869
Place   Heber City, Wasatch, Utah
Married   27 November 1901   Salt Lake Temple
Place   Salt Lake City, Salt Lake, Utah
Death   14 August 1959
Place   Heber, Wasatch, Utah
Burial   17 August 1959
Place   Heber, Wasatch, Utah
Mother   Isabella CRAWFORD
Father   John Murray MURDOCH
Other Wives

WIFE   SARAH ELIZABETH GILES
Birth   4 December 1878
Place   Heber City, Wasatch, Utah
Death   2 August 1961
Place   Heber City, Wasatch, Utah
Burial   5 August 1961
Place   Heber City, Wasatch, Utah
Mother   Mary Elizabeth MAYOH
Father   George M. GILES
Other Husbands
Information from Family Records - Grant B. Murdoch

5TH CHILD   John Bard MURDOCH
Birth   4 September 1910 Heber City,Wasatch,Utah
Married   Jennie Lois SIMPSON
Date   10 June 1935   (Salt Lake Temple)
Place   Salt Lake City, Salt Lake, Utah
Death
Burial

6TH CHILD   Grant Brigham MURDOCH
Birth   29 March 1913 Heber City, Wasatch, Utah
Married
Date
Place
Death
Burial

7TH CHILD   Ruby Isabell MURDOCH
Birth   7 May 1915 Heber City,Wasatch,Utah
Married   William Theodore JASPERSON
Date   1 December 1938   28 October 1970
Place   Salt Lake City, Utah Salt Lake Temple
Death
Burial

8TH CHILD   Thomas Verd MURDOCH
Birth   5 February 1918 Heber City,Wasatch,Utah
Married   Margaret BARTON
Date   2 June 1943   (Salt Lake Temple)
Place   Salt Lake City, Salt Lake, Utah
Death
Burial

1ST CHILD   Mary Althora MURDOCH
Birth   25 January 1903 Heber City,Wasatch,Ut
Married   Ervin Alfred SACKETT
Date   27 May 1926   24 June 1967
Place   Preston, Idaho   Salt Lake Temple
Death
Burial

2ND CHILD   Sarah Laraine MURDOCH
Birth   1 July 1904 Heber City,Wasatch,Utah
Married   William Montell GILES
Date   18 August 1926   (Salt Lake Temple)
Place   Salt Lake City, Salt Lake, Utah
Death   25 December 1964 Heber City, Utah
Burial   28 December 1964 Heber City, Utah

3RD CHILD   James Ruelof MURDOCH
Birth   18 September 1906 Heber City,Wa.,Utah
Married   Rhea Vivian STEWART
Date   12 May 1927   14 July 1977
Place   Salt Lake City, Utah Ogden Temple
Death
Burial

4TH CHILD   George Merrol MURDOCH
Birth   16 December 1908 Heber City, Wa..Utah
Married   Rhea Mae JOHNSON
Date   6 September 1932   15 September 1933
Place   Farmington, Utah   Salt Lake Temple
Death
Burial

1 MURDOCH, James 1786-1831   2 MURDOCH, John Murray 1820-1910
1 MURDOCH, Mary MURRAY, Sp. 1782-1856 2 MURDOCH, Isabella CRAWFORD, Sp. 1836-1916

DESCENDANTS OF------- 3 MURDOCH, JAMES CRAWFORD 1869-1959

        3 MURDOCH, SARAH ELIZABETH GILES, SP. 1878-1961

4 SACKETT, Mary Althora MURDOCH B-25 Jan 1903   B-Birth
4 SACKETT, Ervin Alfred, Sp. B-10 Aug 1900 M-27 May 1926 D-24 Nov 1970 M-Marriage
                      D-Death
4 GILES, Sarah LaRaine MURDOCH B-1 Jul 1904 D-25 Dec 1964 Sp-Spouse
4 GILES, William Montell, Sp. B-11 Oct 1901 M-18 Aug 1926 D-23 Jun 1980 Div-Divorced

  5 SHELTON, Connie Renee GILES B-3 Sep 1928
  5 SHELTON, Charles Junior, Sp. B-26 Dec 1924 M-3 Sep 1947

    6 SHELTON, Kenneth Mont B-11 Jul 1948
    6 SHELTON, Katherine Melba LEAVITT, Sp. B-15 Nov 1950 M-13 Aug 1970

      7 SHELTON, Stephanie   B- 6 Sep 1972

      7 SHELTON, David Kenneth B-12 Nov 1976

      7 SHELTON, Mandy Fawn   B-12 Sep 1979

    6 SHELTON, Lynn Charles B-1 Jan 1952 Div.-2 Oct 1978
    6 SHELTON, Isabel Rubela MENDIOLA, Sp. B-29 Dec 1950 M-12 Apr 1973

      7 SHELTON, Carmen Loraine B-21 Jul 1974

      7 SHELTON, Jesse Lynn   B-17 Nov 1976

  5 WALQUIST, LuAnn GILES B-4 Jul 1934
  5 WALQUIST, Lynn Aaron, Sp. B-9 May 1941 M-9 Apr 1972 Div.-30 Oct 1972

4 MURDOCH, James Ruelof B-18 Sep 1906
4 MURDOCH, Rhea Vivian STEWART, Sp. B-12 Sep 1909 M-12 May 1927

  5 MURDOCH, Kent B-13 Aug 1927
  5 MURDOCH, Shirley Jean OLSEN, Sp. B-11 Jun 1928 M-14 Aug 1948

    6 GUNTHER, Margo MURDOCH B-29 Jul 1949
    6 GUNTHER, David Lee, Sp. B-13 Feb 1947 M-17 Sep 1969

      7 GUNTHER, David Ryan   B- 1 Mar 1971

      7 GUNTHER, Kristopher Kent B-16 Jun 1972

      7 GUNTHER, Patrick Lloyd B- 6 Apr 1974

      7 GUNTHER, Andrew Paul   B-26 Mar 1976

      7 GUNTHER, Mauri Jean   B- 3 May 1978

    6 MURDOCH, Kent Olsen B-20 Jan 1951
    6 MURDOCH, Tonya Lee DAHL, Sp. B-12 Apr 1952 M-17 Aug 1973

      7 MURDOCH, Tyson Kent   B-18 Oct 1976

      7 MURDOCH, Kelli Jo   B-11 Jan 1979

    6 LIGHTHALL, Nan MURDOCH B-19 Dec 1952
    6 LIGHTHALL, Jay Thomas, Sp. B-6 Dec 1952 M-16 May 1975

      7 LIGHTHALL, Brady Jay   B- 2 Oct 1976

      7 LIGHTHALL, Dirk Murdoch B- 8 Mar 1979

    6 MURDOCH, "J" Blake B-4 Jan 1955
    6 MURDOCH, Julie WEAVER, Sp. B-8 Feb 1955 M-21 Jun 1979

      7 MURDOCH, "K" Blake   B-18 Mar 1980

    6 MURDOCH, Tammy Jean   B-20 Oct 1966

5 MURDOCH, Annette B-5 Mar 1933 D-11 Mar 1933

5 MURDOCH, Stewart R. B-17 May 1936
5 MURDOCH, Connie PORTER, Sp. B-11 Mar 1938 M-21 Feb 1957

      6 MURDOCH, Cortney Stewart   B-21 Jan 1962

      6 MURDOCH, Lynette   B-20 Jun 1963

      6 MURDOCH, Shannon   B-13 Aug 1970

5 MURDOCH, James Lowell B-22 Jul 1945
5 MURDOCH, Christine THACKERAY, Sp. B-16 Feb 1948 M-5 Aug 1965

      6 MURDOCH, James Darin   B-17 Feb 1966

      6 MURDOCH, Wade T.   B-11 May 1969

      6 MURDOCH, Nathan Deane   B- 5 Oct 1973

      6 MURDOCH, Amber   B- 7 Aug 1977

4 MURDOCH, George Merrol B-16 Dec 1908
4 MURDOCH, Rhea Mae JOHNSON, Sp. B-20 May 1911 M-6 Sep 1932

5 BARRUTIA, Merilyn MURDOCH B-5 Nov 1932
5 BARRUTIA, Albert, Sp. B-3 Jun 1924 M-31 Jan 1961

      6 BARRUTIA, Karma   B- 4 Aug 1962

      6 BARRUTIA, Steve Murdoch   B-25 Oct 1963 D-26 Oct 1963

      6 BARRUTIA, Marci   B- 6 Dec 1968

5 DEAN, Margie MURDOCH B-19 Apr 1938
5 DEAN, Nowlan Kelly, Sp. B-28 Dec 1935 M-27 Mar 1949

      6 DEAN, Kelly MURDOCH   B-19 Jan 1960

      6 DEAN, Lyn M.   B-15 Jun 1963

      6 DEAN, Eric N.   B- 9 Feb 1965

      6 DEAN, Dixie   B-24 Aug 1966

      6 DEAN, Dana   B-16 Feb 1969

      6 DEAN, David   B-29 Apr 1970

5 MURDOCH, Richard J. B-8 Dec 1939
5 MURDOCH, Elaine GORDON, Sp. B-17 Nov 1941 M-5 Nov 1959

      6 MURDOCH, Richard G.   B- 8 Jun 1960

      6 MURDOCH, Brian George   B- 2 Dec 1961 D- 2 Dec 1961

      6 MURDOCH, Gordon J.   B-20 Jul 1963

      6 MURDOCH, Emily   B-10 Aug 1965

      6 MURDOCH, Carol Anne   B-28 Dec 1968

      6 MURDOCH, Marie   B-20 Feb 1976

      6 MURDOCH, Mark   B- 2 Sep 1978

      6 MURDOCH, Mary Michelle   B-24 Feb 1981

4 MURDOCH, John Bard B-4 Sep 1910
4 MURDOCH, Jennie Lois SIMPSON, Sp. B-3 Sep 1912 M-10 Jun 1935

5 PETERSEN, Joanna MURDOCH B-2 Aug 1936
5 PETERSEN, Richard Diamond, Sp. B-10 Feb 1933 M-22 Jul 1953

     6 PETERSEN, Richard Diamond, Jr. B-14 Sep 1953
     6 PETERSEN, Doretta Gay GILL, Sp. B-12 Mar 1955 M-6 Jun 1975

          7 PETERSEN, Jason Curtis   B-18 Jun 1976

          7 PETERSEN, Christopher Jay   B- 5 Nov 1977

     6 PETERSEN, John Raymond B-14 Oct 1954
     6 PETERSEN, Rebecca DAYTON, Sp. B-18 Jan 1955 M-20 Aug 1976

          7 PETERSEN, Jauna Omera   B- 7 Dec 1977

          7 PETERSEN, John Jordan   B-24 Nov 1980

     6 PETERSEN, Michael Reed B-26 Sep 1956
     6 PETERSEN, Gwen TURNER, Sp. B-4 Feb 1956 M-23 Mar 1979

          7 PETERSEN, Stephanie   B-27 Dec 1980

     6 PETERSEN, Brent Wayne B-25 Oct 1957
     6 PETERSEN, Bernadine LYTLE, Sp. B-8 Mar 1961 M-19 Apr 1980

          7 PETERSEN, Ryan Wayne   B-13 Mar 1981

     6 PETERSEN, Mark David B-28 Aug 1959
     6 PETERSEN, Kathleen EGBERT, Sp. B-22 Oct 1961 M-28 Mar 1980

          7 PETERSEN, Jeremy Guy   B- 2 Feb 1978

          7 PETERSEN, Terri Nicole   B- 5 Jan 1981

     6 PETERSEN, Kent Douglas B-12 Sep 1960
     6 PETERSEN, Judith Lynn STOCKS, Sp. B-18 Dec 1962 M-27 Jun 1980

     6 PETERSEN, Robert Scott   B-21 Feb 1966

     6 PETERSEN, Jeffrey Allen   B- 3 Jul 1970

5 COMPTON, Sara Joyce MURDOCH B-20 Feb 1938
5 COMPTON, John Hilary, Sp. B-3 Dec 1929 M- 29 Aug 1958

     6 COMPTON, Colleen   B-30 Jun 1959

     6 CARLOS, Annette COMPTON B-5 Jan 1961
     6 CARLOS, Martin Christopher, Sp. B-   M-25 Mar 1977

          7 CARLOS, Angela   B-30 Jul 1977

     6 COMPTON, Stewart Dee   B-18 Nov 1962

5 THOMPSON, Norene MURDOCH B-4 May 1939
5 THOMPSON, Stanley Gene, Sp. B-24 Aug 1937 M-30 Jul 1955 D-9 Apr 1974

     6 THOMPSON, Stanley Gene, Jr. B-21 Sep 1955
     6 THOMPSON, Betty Jo BUCKLEY, Sp. B-14 Mar 1958 M-18 Sep 1976

          7 THOMPSON, Michael Gene   B-10 Jun 1977

          7 THOMPSON, Meaghan Jo   B-17 Oct 1978

          7 THOMPSON, Stanely James   B- 9 Apr 1980

5 THOMPSON, William T. B-8 May 1957
5 THOMPSON, Ellen DAVIES, Sp. B-20 Aug 1961 M-7 Aug 1980

5 THOMPSON, Don Mark B-26 May 1958
5 THOMPSON, Cheryl Dawn HURD, Sp. B-15 Dec 1962 M-25 Oct 1980

```
        6 BANCROFT, Carole Ann THOMPSON B-5 May 1960
        6 BANCROFT, Douglas Raymond, Sp. B-13 Dec 1957 M-9 Sep 1978 Div.-25 Oct 1980

            7 BANCROFT, John William        B- 4 May 1979

    5 LLOYD, Judith Kay MURDOCH B-25 May 1944
    5 LLOYD, Lonnie Carl, Sp. B-15 Oct 1941 M-7 May 1965

            6 LLOYD, Jennifer            B-10 Jun 1966

            6 LLOYD, Gordon Jay          B- 7 Jul 1967

            6 LLOYD, Shane Bennett       B- 5 Jul 1972

    5 MURDOCH, John David B-8 Oct 1947
    5 MURDOCH, Beverlee Ann LUNSFORD, Sp. B-15 Apr 1944 M-11 Dec 1970

            6 MURDOCH, Melissa Ann       B-14 Jul 1971

            6 MURDOCH, Jennie Michelle   B-28 Feb 1973

            6 MURDOCH, Lori Kae          B-31 Aug 1974 D-19 Apr 1975

            6 MURDOCH, John Levi         B-13 Feb 1978

            6 MURDOCH, Emily Sue         B- 5 Sep 1979

4 MURDOCH, Grant Brigham B-29 Mar 1913

4 JASPERSON, Ruby Isabell MURDOCH B-7 May 1915
4 JASPERSON, William Theodore, Sp. B-19 Mar 1914 M-1 Dec 1938 D-23 Jul 1958

    5 JASPERSON, Paul William B-31 Aug 1955
    5 JASPERSON, Marilyn JACOBS, Sp. B-26 Oct 1954 M-16 Jul 1977

            6 SCHMITT, Bryan Ross        B-27 Jun 1972

            6 JASPERSON, Sarah Anne      B-19 Jun 1979

4 MURDOCH, Thomas Verd B-5 Feb 1918
4 MURDOCH, Margaret BARTON, Sp. B-2 Oct 1919 M-2 Jun 1943

    5 PARKE, Margaret Dianne MURDOCH B-14 Apr 1944
    5 PARKE, Darwin Morgan, Sp. B-18 Dec 1938 M-28 Aug 1963

            6 PARKE, Daniel Lee          B- 3 Jan 1966

            6 PARKE, Denise Diane.       B- 7 Dec 1967

            6 PARKE, David Morgan        B- 6 Jan 1970

            6 PARKE, Darin Douglas       B-19 Feb 1973

            6 PARKE, Derrick Crawford    B- 8 Nov 1976

    5 HANSEN, Mary MURDOCH B-7 Jan 1948
    5 HANSEN, Jon Duane, Sp. B-6 Feb 1943 M-27 Nov 1968

            6 HANSEN, Jennifer Diane     B- 3 Oct 1970

            6 HANSEN, Jon Barrett        B-30 Mar 1973

            6 HANSEN, Jordan Murdoch     B- 4 Mar 1976

            6 HANSEN, Julie Ann          B-20 Feb 1979

    5 MURDOCH, James Verd B-1 Dec 1949
    5 MURDOCH, Denise FRANCOM, Sp. B-3 Sep 1952 M-3 Feb 1972

            6 MURDOCH, Todd Eric         B-14 Dec 1978
```

5 MURDOCH, Gary Lynn B-2 Oct 1951
5 MURDOCH, Linda Jean SANCHEZ, Sp. B-12 Jan 1954 M-12 Apr 1974

      6 MURDOCH, Laura Adelia   B-11 Feb 1975

      6 MURDOCH, Kelby   B-11 Sep 1976

      6 MURDOCH, Casey   B-15 Oct 1977

      6 MURDOCH, Brett Andrew   B-22 Sep 1979

5 MURDOCH, Barton Ray B-28 Mar 1953
5 MURDOCH, Karen Anne PERKINS, Sp. B-2 Aug 1955 M-6 Jun 1980

      6 MURDOCH, Tyson Lee   B-6 Mar 1981

5 MERRELL, Peggy MURDOCH B-26 Dec 1954
5 MERRELL, Dean Brimley, Sp. B-9 Jul 1955 M-1 Apr 1977

      6 MERRELL, Erin Dean   B-29 Jan 1978

      6 MERRELL, Lisa Ann   B-19 Oct 1979

5 BENNION, Cindy Lee MURDOCH B-13 Feb 1957
5 BENNION, Douglas Baird, Sp. B-9 Sep 1955 M-27 Dec 1977

      6 BENNION, Kara Ann   B-28 Sep 1978

      6 BENNION, Krista Lynn   B-17 Aug 1980

5 MURDOCH, Jolene   B-1 Jun 1959

Brigham Murdoch, Blanche Alexander, and Louannie Hammon

Brigham Murdoch was born November 2, 1870, in Heber City, Utah. He was the second son of a family of seven, four boys and three girls, born to John Murray and Isabella Crawford Murdoch.

Brig's childhood was spent with loving parents; brothers, and sisters who were taught the principles of the gospel by example. The children were taught to work, to respect and love each other. They were accustomed to hardship and inconveniences (by today's standards) but they were never lacking for food, clothing, shelter and love. They were taught to say their prayers the blessing on the food and to attend church regularly.

In the summer they worked on the farm with the crops and livestock, feeding pigs and chickens and milking cows. They maintained a "home herd" of about one hundred ewes in the summer, which was merged with the range flock to go south in the winter because of the long winters in Heber Valley. While in their teens, Brig and his next-older brother, James, herded the two thousand head of sheep on the summer range in the mountains.

Brig attended Primary and was baptized August 28,1881.

In due time, he was ordained a deacon and was chosen as first counselor to assist Frederick Crook, president of the deacons quorum. Fred later became bishop of Heber First Ward. They became lifelong friends. While a deacon, Brig was privileged to pass the sacrament during a conference presided over by President Wilford Woodruff. Brig was very impressed with President Woodruff and thought he looked much like his own father.

The children attended schools in Heber. Brig studied for one term at a branch of the Brigham Young Academy, also in Heber. He was active in the Young Men's Mutual Association and participated in plays presented by the thespians group in most of the communities in the valley.

Social activities for young people also included dances and singing groups. Most of Brig's brothers and sisters loved music and could play musical instruments and all of them loved to sing. They were taught sewing, knitting weaving, and poetry to add to the beauty of their home life.

During Brig's later school days, he met a girl he thought to be the most beautiful girl in the world. She was Mary Blanche Alexander, a popular girl and a talented piano player. She played for dances with various musical groups in the Heber Valley. Brig played the guitar and they had many good times together. In Brig's own words, "Our good feelings about each other were mutual and our courtship was pleasant and happy." Blanche's parents were Charles Marsteller Alexander and Lovisa Comstock Snyder. Her mother was a fine seamstress and was also the first telephone operator in Heber City. Blanche was born February 16, 1873, in Midway, Wasatch County, Utah. She was baptized in August, 1883. Brig was ordained an elder in the

Melchizedek Priesthood on December 14, 1891, and they were married in the Logan Temple on December 16, 1891. They lived in Heber City during the winter. In the spring, they moved to Park City, where Brig had worked in the mines previous to their marriage. They were very happy. Brig was working for good wages, and they were getting ahead. The future looked bright as he worked through summer and the expectation of the arrival of their first child became assured.

They planned for Blanche to return to her mother's home, prior to the arrival of the baby, so she could have good care for herself and the baby. Robert Rue was born November 16, 1892. He was named and given a blessing also by his grandfather, John Murray Murdoch, who was, at this time, a stake patriarch.

Living with Brig and Blanche in Park City was Brig's brother, Robert (Boot), who also worked in the mines. Blanche's sister, Luella, was a frequent visitor in their home, and a strong friendship developed between Boot and Luella.

Shortly after Robert Rue was born, Brig contracted typhoid fever. He recovered in due time, but was unable to return to work for the remainder of the winter. As Brig recovered and gained sufficient strength, they moved into a part of their old home in Heber City, where there would be more room. They were comfortable and happy again. The baby was strong and healthy. When spring came, Brig was ready to go back to work at Park City at the same place. Blanche and Rue came in a few days. Springtime was beautiful, and they were so happy to be back together in their little home again.

They had been settled in their home only a short time when Brig came off the night shift to find his wife had been very ill all night. He could see that fever was developing. At times she would seem to get temporarily better and then get worse. As the fever continued to recur, they decided it would be better for her to go back to her parents in Heber, where she could be near her mother and receive better care. After returning to Heber, she gradually grew worse, and Brig was sent for. When he arrived, she did not recognize him. She would beg for her baby and would hug him so hard the family was afraid she might hurt him. Someone gave her a large rag doll to hold. She was so ill she did not know the difference.

On June 22, 1893, Blanche passed away, leaving a loving husband and a seven-month-old son. She was buried in the Heber cemetery.

Robert (Boot) and Luella also contracted the disease and failed to recover. Within a period of three months,

Brig had lost three people very near and dear to him. In Brig's words, "We can overcome our emotions, but it is hard to forget. Our baby who was seven months old also contracted the fever but with more skillful treatment he recovered. From that time, and through the rest of my life, it seemed as if some unseen power was my guest."

The baby, Rue, remained in the home of Blanche's parents where he was given all the love and kindness that only sorrowing grandparents can give. This was to be his home for several years in his early life.

Brig returned to the mine in Park City where he pondered his future. He was doing well there but, as the years went by, a restlessness continued to grow. He recalled his father's experiences and hardships in the mines of Scotland. He was told of his Grandfather James Murdoch's early death in the gas-filled mineshaft, which left his grandmother, Wee Granny, a poor widow with seven children.

During the winter of 1899 and spring of 1900, the Church secured a tract of land in the Big Horn Basin in Wyoming and was encouraging Church members to colonize it. Brig and Thomas, his brother, became interested and decided to take a look at it. Bishop Thomas Hicken and a neighbor, Robert Giles, were also going. All preparations were made to leave June 15, 1900.

At this time, their father, who was the stake patriarch, told them that as they were going on a long journey, he was impressed to give each of them a patriarchal blessing. He placed his hands on each of their heads and gave them a blessing. The brothers then bade their folks goodbye and started their journey. They did not take a copy of their blessing with them. Brig was now thirty and Tom was thirty-four. They arrived at the colony about June 25. There were a large number of wagons camped along the Grey Bull River. A canal had been started. The project was under the supervision of Apostle Owen Woodruff. Meetings were held and instructions and advice were given. It was announced there would be a dance held on a certain night. Since Brig had a guitar and Tom a violin, they were asked to play for the dance. The dance was in the open. As there was not a building or floor to dance on, they danced on the ground. Elder Woodruff joined in the dance and enjoyed it as much as anyone.

After looking over the land for two days, the Heberites decided not to locate there. The bishop remarked that there was nothing that looked pleasing to the eye. After the horses had rested for three days, they started their journey back to Heber, arriving in time to celebrate the Fourth of July.

Brig had taken a leave from his mining job in Park City and now returned to work. He was more restless than before. Something kept urging him to get out and get some land. That thought was on his mind most of the time. Brig's sister, Margaret Ann, had married Lewis J. Hawkes on November 7, 1889. Later they had acquired a farm in southern Idaho in an area called Horseshoe Flat, about three miles west of Drummond. They had first lived at Franklin, Idaho, Lewis' father, Joshua Hawkes, in company with a group from Franklin, Idaho, located in the Drummond area about 1896. There was still land available for homesteading, but it was being settled rapidly. Canals had to be made and water brought to the land before it could be "proved upon."

Brig continued working at Park City. He had a good paying job and liked the boss he was working with. In late October, the urge to change prompted him to write his brother, Tom, suggesting another trip, this time to Idaho. Tom answered that he was ready to go any time. A date was set, Brig took some time off, and they started for Idaho. They had a buckboard (heavy buggy), a team of horses, a camping outfit, and bedding. They had a good trip and arrived at their sister Margaret Ann's house a few days before election day. They liked the looks of the area much better than the Big Horn Basin they had visited earlier in the summer. They had a good visit with Margaret and Lewis.

They located land they could acquire and returned to Utah. During the winter of 1900–1901 they made preparations for returning to Idaho and setting up their homesteads.

The Oregon Short Line Railroad was completed as far as Rexburg, Idaho. On April 1 Brig and Tom arrived in Rexburg with two cars of livestock and farming equipment. En route to their land, they were caught in a snowstorm that lasted for several days. Their livestock were scattered and it took them several more days to gather them up again.

At that time, most of Idaho's land was open to homesteading under the Homestead Act or the Carey Act, which permitted individuals to file on 160 acres of land and improve it with fences, buildings, by cropping and bringing irrigation water to the land within five years. Consequently, most of the Snake River Valley was being claimed by farmers, ranchers, business people, and speculators.

The land Brig and Tom acquired was in the Farnum district, south of the Fall River, about five or six miles south of what is now Ashton, Idaho, and about five miles west of Drummond.

Brig acquired the interests of a homesteader on 107 acres bordered on the north by the Fall River. It had a one-room log house. Tom homesteaded 160 acres, joining Brig on the south and Hans Nielson, a Danish emigrant, on the west. These three bachelors were to spend many years together as neighbors and community builders.

Brig's one-room log house became headquarters for the three as they proceeded to improve their farms. Tom's homestead was open prairie with no buildings or water on it. Brig's home was about seventy-five yards from Fall River, which provided domestic water but no irrigation. Hans' buildings were developed near the river downstream half a mile from Brig's.

The first concern as a community was to build a canal to irrigate the farm as a final step to "proving up" on the homestead to qualify for ownership of the land. In 1896, a group of settlers from Franklin had located in Horseshoe Flat, a fairly level area with good soil. Surveys conducted by this group showed that water could be taken from Conant Creek by a long hillside canal to irrigate a large area, including the land Brig and Tom acquired. They filed on the water that year, and work was started on the canal.

As few homes were available on the new land, the settlers would return to Franklin in the winter and return in the spring to continue improving their land and working on the canal. Some homesteaders gave up and sold or traded their interests in the land to other settlers.

The work on the canal was paid for by issuing stock ownership in the canal. The wages were $1.50 a day for a man and $2.50 for a man with a team, for a ten-hour day. The canal was dug with plows and slip scrapers pulled by a team of horses. It was nine miles from the head of the canal to the terminal, where lateral ditches were extended to carry the water to the various farms. No water was taken out for irrigation above the terminal. The entire nine miles of main canal was on a steep hillside covered with bushes, trees, and rocks.

When Brig and Tom arrived in April 1901, the canal was underway with much yet to be done. Each settler had to build a home to live in first, together with corrals and some fences when they had livestock. The waist-high natural grasses provided summer feed for livestock and winter feed where it could be harvested for hay. Little farming could be done without irrigation water.

Martha Louannie Hammon Murdoch

Martha Louannie Hammon Murdoch was born October 11, 1885 in Hooper, Davis County, Utah. Her parents were Heber Chase Hammon and Martha Priscilla Christensen. She was the fourth of nine children, six boys and three girls. One girl and two boys died in infancy.

Her father, Heber Chase Hammon, was born March 18, 1854, in Uintah, Weber County, Utah, the eighth of fourteen children born to Levi Hammon and Polly Chapman Bybee. There were ten girls and four boys. Two boys were stillborn and two girls died in early childhood.

Louannie's mother was born February 28, 1858, in Ogden, Weber County, Utah. She was the oldest of nine children born to Rasmus Christensen, who came from Denmark, and Priscilla Victoria Mitchell, who came from England. They were both converts to the L. D. S. Church and crossed the plains to Utah.

Louannie's parents were married January 28, 1877 at Hooper. During the next eight years, four children were born. When Louannie was one year old the family moved to Wilford, Idaho, with several other families. Some were close relatives of Heber and Martha. This area was open to homesteading and was being settled by people from various places, especially from Utah. Many of them were members of the Church. The closeness of the community through the ward and strong family ties provided a strong bond of security and trust. The depth of this friendship and love was tested often through sickness, accidents, deaths, storms and discouragement.

The children were taught to love and respect each other and their parents and to honor their church leaders. As they became old enough, each child shared the household duties and helped with outside chores and on the farms. The Church was the central interest in the community. School was held, when possible, for three months in the winter and three months in the summer. As time went on schools were improved and established with regular terms.

The Hammon's home progressed from one room in an Uncle's home to a large one room log home and then a four room home built by Heber and his relatives. To be self sufficient in a pioneer community it was necessary to have a large garden with fruits, berries, vegetables and flowers. The children helped with the preparation and planting and developed a love for growing things. Louannie's love for flowers developed when she was small and continued to grow throughout her life.

In 1893 Heber homesteaded a farm in Hog Hollow or East Wilford, about one half mile from the Teton River. Another home and buildings were built and another cycle of clearing off brush, building fences, planting a garden, trees, shrubs, flowers and lawn. The growing family all helped and in due time were reestablished. They enjoyed friendly neighbors and were active in the ward activities.

Louannie was baptized August 2, 1894, in the old Wilford Canal by Elder George Pincock, who was later bishop of the ward. She was confirmed by a Brother Moore. The children drove to East Wilford School for about six months of the year until full terms were established.

On August 3, 1895, Heber was fishing with his brother-in-law, Joe Phillips, in Buckman's Bottom on the Teton River where there was some deep pools. They were fishing on horseback when Heber's fishing line got tangled up with his horse's legs and both horse and Heber were plunged into the current where Heber drowned.

It was about 10 o'clock in the morning when he drowned and his body was recovered about 3 o'clock in the afternoon. Martha was not notified until his body was found. Martha was in poor health and expecting a baby in early October. Louannie's sister Laura was fifteen years old and sick with St. Vitus dance. The day Heber drowned he received a call to go on a foreign mission for the Church. It was a poor time to lose a dear husband and father. He was a Seventy in the Priesthood.

Louannie's brother Heber Levi was now seventeen, Laura, fifteen; Daniel, twelve; Martha Louannie, ten; Delbert, six; Marion Byrum was born October 2, 1895 two months after Heber's death. With the help of relatives, friends and Heber Jr.'s hard work the family was able to get along. Martha learned how to weave carpets and was an accomplished seamstress. She was often called upon to help with the sick. She always put her Church work first. She was a strict tithe payer and helped regularly with the missionary fund. She was warm and very loving to her children and set a good example for them. She was firm in the discipline in her home.

Laura married Melvin Allred April 27, 1898. Heber Levi married Sarah Ann Waters, June 12, 1902. As these brothers and sisters lived near the Hammons the families socialized with each other from time to time. As Louannie matured into a young woman she was often teased about the boys. Once while visiting at Laura's home a couple of bachelor boarders there told her she should get acquainted with the Murdoch brothers who lived in Farnum and played for dances throughout the area. They told her how nice Brig was and that his wife had died and left him with a little boy.

Finally, Louannie saw the Murdoch brothers, Brig and Tom, at Teton City on the twenty-fourth of July, when they played for a dance. While she did not meet them, she was attracted to Brig and wondered what kind of a fellow he was. In late August Louannie was again visiting with her sister Laura. The Brown brothers, the boarders, were being visited by the Murdoch brothers. Louannie was introduced to them. She was impressed with Brig. He was of medium height, with dark brown hair and eyes. The brothers sang songs for them. She thought he was a swell fellow, but considered herself too young for him.

As the summer passed Louannie dated other young men at dances, parties, buggy rides and at home. At Thanksgiving time their ward had a dance the Murdoch brothers played for so they met again. Brig danced with her several times and took her home from the dance. He told her about his wife and little son Rue. It made her like and respect him even more. He continued to come to their home to visit and showed her Rue's picture. Louannie loved the little fellow from the start.

At Christmas time Brig returned to Heber to be with Rue and his family for the holidays and return to Park City to work until spring, when he would come back to the farm at Farnum. Before he left for Heber, he and Louannie decided they would be married in the Salt Lake Temple before he returned to Farnum in the spring.

For Louannie it was a long lonesome winter in some ways. She was busy helping her mother, making quilt blocks and sewing her clothes. Late in the winter Brig wrote a nice letter to Martha telling of their plans to be married and asking her consent to marry Louannie. This made Martha very happy, especially since they would be married in the temple. On April 2, 1903, Louannie and her mother boarded the afternoon train at St. Anthony. It was Louannie's first train ride since she was a small girl. They enjoyed the ride to Kaysville, Utah where they stayed overnight with Martha's sister, Aunt Libby Lewis. The next day they went to Salt Lake City, where Brig met the train. They spent the day attending general conference. The following morning they joined Brig on the train to go with him to Heber where they would visit his family.

At the depot in Heber, they were met by Tom and

their sister Tressie. She had visited the brothers in Idaho and had met Louannie then. Others were on the platform too, but the first one Louannie saw was an excited ten-year-old boy who had been anxiously waiting for them to get off the train. Rue jumped and threw his arms around her, and she knew they would always love each other and get along beautifully as mother and son.

Brig's mother, Isabella, had been very sick that winter, and it took a special effort for her to be able to sit up in her chair and receive Brig's girl. As they entered the home, a strange feeling came over Louannie. There was Brig's father, John Murray Murdoch, his first wife, Anne (Muz), and Brig's mother, Isabella (Bella), sitting there waiting for them. Here were three special people who had given up so much, endured great hardships, sickness, and death in return for their membership in the Church of Jesus Christ of Latter-day Saints and hope for an eternal family.

After the introductions, Louannie felt at ease. She described Isabella as a sweet, gracious lady every one could love. They were received very warmly by all of Brig's family as they came in a few at a time during the two-day visit.

John Murray was Wasatch Stake Patriarch and he asked Louannie if he could give her a patriarchal blessing. She was very happy to receive it. It was a beautiful blessing and was a source of strength and comfort to her throughout her life. As Brig and Louannie prepared to return to Salt Lake to be married, a deep sense of sadness came over the family. Tom was going with them. The family realized that now the boys were leaving Heber for good, the family link would be broken again. They would join their sister Margaret Ann Hawkes in eastern Idaho.

Wednesday morning, April 8 was beautiful as Brig and Louannie went to the courthouse for their marriage license.

Tom helped Louannie's mother to the temple with their suitcases and then went on to Idaho to get their cattle out on the range.

Martha's cousin, Margaret Cain, was a temple worker.

She helped them get ready and then came back at three o'clock to see them married. After the newlyweds and Martha went to Margaret's home for a party with Martha's relatives who had gathered to wish them well. The next day they visited around Kaysville, Layton, Hooper and Clearfield, where many of Martha's relatives lived.

They returned to Wilford on April 15. After visiting

with sister Margaret Hawkes at Teton, a few miles to the south and getting Louannie's things ready to move, they loaded their belongings on the wagon and started for their new home on April 21, 1903. The full impact of the exciting events of the previous nineteen days came upon Louannie as she and Brig left her mother's home to travel to their own home at Farnum. Again there was sadness with the separation from her mother, brothers and sisters. The agony and the ecstasy of the separation from their families and the fulfillment of their marriage in the holy temple for time and eternity deeply touched the emotions of Louannie, as she was the first of her mother's family to be married in the temple.

As they traveled from Martha's to their home they went through a rain storm but were protected by a large slicker big enough for both of them. Tom had a nice dinner ready when they arrived. After dinner the storm was over and they moved all the furniture out of their one room log house. After thoroughly cleaning it the furniture was moved back in. Brig helped around the house two or three days to get things organized. They sewed factory (light cloth) together and attached it to the log walls and ceiling. They thought they had a fine home for beginners.

It was a beautiful time of the year with green grass and the wild flowers in bloom. Louannie planted shrubs, fruit bushes and flowers she had brought from her mother's place. They planted a garden. The grain was planted and doing well, when a late frost set it back. About this time a wedding dance was held, and the newlyweds were happy to see their neighbors, friends, and Louannie's folks present.

When the crops were in, the settlers turned their attention to working on the Conant Creek Canal, which reached an important phase that year (1903). The main canal was completed to the terminal where the lateral ditches to the various farms took off.

Brig and Louannie, together with other homesteaders, camped near where the canal work was going on. Louannie and the other wives cooked for the men and helped out where ever possible. Evenings were spent socializing, singing, visiting and planning their community. Brig and Tom were often the entertainment with their guitar and violin.

Despite the late frost the crops and gardens turned out well. The grain was cut with a binder and the bundles were hauled and stacked under the hill near the buildings and corral, to wait for the threshing machine. Because of the steep road leading down to the stacks, no thresher owner would move their machines down the hill, fearing they would tip over. Finally on December 2, Cutler's threshing machine from Vernon (west of Ashton) crossed the Fall River from the west and threshed their grain. Normally there would have been deep snow on the ground, but that year the weather was warm and dry and farmers were able to plow in December.

Tom continued to live with Brig and Louannie, and Hans Nielsen, the deaf Danish man, continued to eat with them frequently. Louannie did their cooking, washing, and mending. Each man worked on his own farm, but often worked together exchanging work. So, their official family consisted of four individuals. This was increased to five when Rue came to live with them on September 15. Thirty-eight years later Louannie commented that she and Brig had never spent a night alone in their home, "That someone has always been with us." At Christmas time Brig, Louannie and Rue had a good time to themselves. Tom was spending the winter in Utah. On Christmas day Louannie's mother, sister Laura, and husband Melvin had dinner with them. Louannie was expecting their first child and was not feeling well. It was decided that she would return with Martha and stay there until the baby was born. Occasionally Brig and Rue would visit with her. She was homesick for them.

Blanche Priscilla was born February 7, 1904, at Wilford. Her name was decided before she was born. She was named after Blanche Alexander, Brig's first wife, and Louannie's mother. Her arrival brought joy to everyone, especially Rue who was delighted to have a baby sister. Louannie was sick for several weeks, but was well enough to move back to their home on April 21, a year to the day since they had arrived after their marriage.

On March 11, Brig's sister, Margaret Ann Hawkes, died leaving a baby girl three days old and five older children. They were still living in Teton. Brig's sister Nettie and brothers Jim and Jock came from Heber to attend the funeral. They visited Louannie at her mothers home and then went to the farm with Brig and Tom for a visit. They all slept in one long bed.

In 1904 Brig was elected a director of the Conant Creek Canal Company. At various times he was also secretary or president until 1937. In 1905 he was called to be first counselor to James W. Green, president of the Conant Branch, later called the Farnum Branch of the Church. The meetings were held in a log building also used as a school. It was built about 1899. Louannie was called as second counselor in the Relief Society.

The Murdoch home located "under the hill" was nearly one half mile off the county road when it was established. They decided to build a new home, barn and corrals near the road upon the hill. Louannie sold the milk cow her mother had given her as a wedding present, and bought lumber for the house. It was a two room frame house with an attic and a shingled roof. It was the first house Louannie had lived in that did not have a dirt roof. No more shoveling dirt upon the roof during a rainstorm to keep it from leaking.

New fences, corrals and sheds had to be built in the new location, and trees, shrubs, and a garden planted. Brig and Tom were still breaking up more sod to bring more land into production. Drinking water had to be hauled from the river when water was not in the canal. The new home was one and a quarter miles to school, two and a quarter miles to church and three quarters of a mile to the store and post office.

On June 4, 1907 their first son, Brigham Dallas, was born with Dr. E. L. Hargis attending Louannie in their home.

He was a healthy, happy baby and was given lots of love and attention.

On October 31, 1909 a very severe blizzard struck. During the blizzard Brig rode out to the stack yard to drive away some stray horses from his grain piled in the yard. A horse kicked him breaking his leg. With much difficulty he got to the house. Louannie luckily intercepted the Doctor who was in the area to see a sick neighbor, Will Cazier. Dr. Hargis set the bones and after put on a cast so Brig could get around with crutches. Delbert, Louannie's younger brother, came and took care of the chores until Rue could come home from Heber where he was going to Nigh School. The snow melted and Rue was able to plow while Brig was recuperating.

November 17, 1909, Reed Chase, was born. Following his birth Louannie got the flu and was sick for a long time. Her mother came up to take care of her. In 1907 Tom had received a call to the Central States Mission at Dallas, Texas. He accepted the call. He traveled without purse or script and had many faith promoting experiences. After two years he was released in time to attend his mother's funeral in Heber, in December 1909. He returned to Farnum in time to help Brig administer to Louannie. That night she had the first good night's sleep she had had for a long time. She began to feel better. They were happy Tom could be with them again.

In 1909 a one room brick school house was built to replace the original log building that had been used for both a school and a church. The same year a new church was built, costing around seven thousand dollars. At the same time the ward was helping to pay for the Yellowstone Stake Tabernacle in St. Anthony and the Ricks Academy in Rexburg.

To meet these obligations, the ward rented land from three land owners. The members and nonmembers alike turned out to prepare and plant the crops and also to harvest it. At times there were as many as forty horse-drawn outfits in the fields at one time. The crops were good and so were the prices, enabling the ward to pay off the obligations and still have a surplus. Brig was a member of the bishopric at this time. This project did much to strengthen the community and make it proud of its success.

Brig was trustee, secretary or chairman of the school board throughout the years they lived in Farnum. He enjoyed his positions in the church and school and the other services he was asked to perform. He was very conscientious about meeting his responsibilities.

On May 6, 1910, the Murdoch family was again saddened with the death of their beloved father and patriarch, John Murray Murdoch. John would have been ninety years old on December 28. His first wife, Anne Steel had passed away the previous December. Now mother Isabella was in failing health and went to live with her daughter Catherine Hicken. There she received much love and good care for six more years.

As their farms were improved and more crops could be grown, Brig and Tom were able to add to their buildings, equipment, livestock, and complete their fencing. They also brought more of their land under irrigation. Brig bought eighty acres that joined his homestead on the east. The canal ran through the entire length of it. The north half was watered and the south half was dry-farmed. Rue helped in the summers between high school terms at Heber City. Louannie's brother Marion also worked for Brig.

It became necessary to add to the house to accommodate the growing family. A lean-to of two rooms was built on the north side, with a front and back door. Stairs were built on the outside west wall up to the attic where two more bedrooms were finished. The new rooms were very welcome as there were Tom and three children besides Rue and Marion in the summer. In the fall of 1911 while the threshing crew was at the Murdoch's farm, Brig's new log barn was set on fire. The fire was started when four and half year old Dallas climbed up in the loft where the hired hands slept and tried to make and light a cigarette he found in their belongings. A dropped lighted match ignited the straw in the loft and soon it was in flames. Dallas climbed down to the ground and stood with two and half year old Reed in the doorway of the barn oblivious to the roaring flames above them. Louannie, hearing the roar of the flames, looked out of the kitchen door, then rushed out to hustle the boys away from the burning barn. The threshing crew hurried out of the field to help put out the fire by carrying water from the ditch and throwing it on the fire. The barn was too far gone to save so the water was thrown on the other buildings which were saved. The water wagon from the threshing machine was finally brought in and water was pumped on the roof of the house and it was saved.

The entire barn, the big haystack, derrick, corrals and some chickens were destroyed. Horses in the barn had to be blindfolded before they could be led out. Some calves and pigs were also burned. This was quite a financial blow to Brig and Louannie, and a memorable lesson to young Dallas.

A third son was born on March 16, 1912. He was named Thomas Hammon after Uncle Tom. When he was three weeks old he caught Whopping Cough. All the other children had it too. During a bishop's meeting held in their home, Tom was blessed by Alfred Woodland, one of the bishopric. He had also blessed Dallas and Reed. The family feared that the baby might not live until a regular fast meeting was held.

With the harvest of 1912 safely put away, the family settled down for a long winter. At this point, Brig and Louannie were reminded that their children had never seen their grandparents. With Grandmother Bella the only one left, they decided to visit her for Christmas at Heber. They went by train and were accompanied by Isabella Hawkes, their cousin. Rue stayed home to do the chores while they were gone. It was Louannie's first visit back to Heber since their marriage. The train trip was very cold in below-zero weather, and the train was late getting into Salt Lake City. But the children took it in stride, being very excited about it all.

Grandmother Bella was delighted to see them, and they were warmly welcomed by the Murdoch Clan. The children got acquainted with uncles, aunts, and cousins they had never seen. They had a delightful Christmas and enjoyed several parties and visits with the numerous Murdoch families in Heber.

In November 1913, Brig was called to be Bishop of the Farnum Ward. He was set apart as bishop on February 1, 1914 by Apostle Hyrum G. Smith. He had been counselor to Bishop Smith since January 22, 1911. His counselors were Iver Hendrickson and Dan Gibson.

On December 24, 1913, Rue married Mearl Garrett, a very lovely girl, whose family lived across the Fall River from home. They lived in the upstairs of the Murdoch home the first winter. Laura Jean was born to Brig and Louannie June 25, 1914. She had dark hair and eyes. This brought the family up to three boys and two girls. Jean was a joy to the family, always pleasant and sweet.

During 1914, Uncle Tom was called on a short-term mission to Kansas City, Missouri, the mission headquarters. He returned to the farm and continued to live with Brig and Louannie. She would tease him about being an old bachelor. He would reply, "I will yet live to hold my grandchildren on my knee."

On July 4, 1915, Louannie's mother passed away after several years of failing health. She had sold their farm and moved to St. Anthony several years before. At the time of her death she was Relief Society president. The funeral was held in the Yellowstone Stake Tabernacle. She was fifty-seven.

Uncle Tom was Farnum's most eligible bachelor. While older than most unmarried girls in the area, he was popular with them. He was always pleasant to be with. He was humble and set a good example to young and old alike. He had a well matched driving team with light harness and a flashy one-seated buggy. His driving outfit would compare with the sports car of today.

On July 15, 1915, Tom and Sarah Hansen were married in the Salt Lake Temple for time and eternity. She was twenty years old; he was forty-seven. They had met two years earlier when she had come to Farnum and spent the summer with her Uncle Hans Nielsen, a close friend and neighbor to the Murdochs. She had come from Denmark as a child, and her parents had settled in Utah. She was a pretty girl—ambitious, full of fun, and a source of joy and strength to the Murdoch family.

Uncle Tom had moved the two-room frame granary from his lower forty to a location up on the hill about a quarter of a mile from the Farnum School on the main road. He added a two room lean-to, making it an attractive, comfortable home. He built straw sheds and corrals, dug a cistern, and had things well organized for operating his 160 acre farm.

The two families were very close and harmonious in all their activities. They worked together, socialized together, and worshiped together. They often ate together, had family evenings together, and were usually together at Thanksgiving, Christmas, and many other occasions.

On April 10, 1916, Brig's mother died. Brig and Tom went to the funeral in Heber City. She was buried in the Heber Cemetery beside her husband, John Murray, and his first wife, Ann Steel. John had provided well for Bella, although she was not recognized as his legal wife. He had also provided for the equal distribution of his estate, which gave each of his living children about nine hundred dollars, a substantial amount at that time.

Brig was very busy during the war years. The ward was growing and took lots of his time as a bishop. He conducted many funerals and some marriages. During 1918 the Spanish Influenza swept through the country. Many people were sick, and deaths were very common. Emergency law banned gatherings such as schools, church meetings, and shows. A person had to wear a face mask to enter a store to buy supplies. Funerals could not be held indoors, and Brig conducted graveside services for those who died in the ward. One good neighbor, Simeon Saunders, lost his wife and four children in less than a year.

All of the family contracted the disease at different times. It was difficult to have enough healthy ones to take care of the sick ones. The neighbors helped each other, and many sought the. Lord for recovery of their loved ones. It was a time of great humility for members of the ward and people throughout the country.

Until about 1914, the livestock were watered at the ditch that ran in front of the house and down over the hill. In the winter, there were springs below the barns the animals could drink from. It was a long, steep climb back up the hill. For house use, water had to be hauled from Fall River in wood barrels in a wagon or sleigh. Uncle Tom dug a cistern that could be filled from the ditch in the fall. If it got empty in the winter, water was hauled from the river. In the winter, snow was brought in a large copper boiler or metal tub and placed on the cook stove to melt overnight. More snow was added as it melted. Louannie washed the family's clothes with a tub, washboard, and wringer turned by child power. It was lovely water to bathe in or wash hair in, as it was soft. The babies were bathed first, then the next oldest, all in the same water. Then it was used to mop the floor.

About 1914, Brig had a well drilled 120 feet deep, mostly through solid lava rock. It was a great thrill to have water in our own backyard. The thrill wore off for the children, as they had to pump the water by hand for the cattle, horses, and pigs, and carry it in for the house. When the kids were in school, Brig pumped the water himself. No electricity was available then, and gasoline engines were expensive and not too reliable.

On January 7, a third daughter, Tressa Isabella, was born. The weather was mild and farmers were plowing. Within twenty-four hours a raging blizzard moved in, and winter had come again.

The year of 1919 was very dry. Brig had bought a good number of hogs to feed out, and although wheat was three dollars a bushel, he made good money on them. However, the crops were poor. In fact, a wagon box full of grain was all that was harvested and that did not equal the seed planted.

Brig had bought a new Ford car in 1918, his first. He and his brother Tom took a trip to the Rupert, Idaho, country and looked it over as they had the Farnum country nineteen years before. They located established farms they could buy, and returned to Farnum, discussed their ideas with their wives, and decided to move to Rupert.

Brig sold the east eighty acres for eight thousand dollars to Asa Hawkes, whose farm cornered on the eighty. Brig and Tom held an auction sale and the accumulation of nineteen years was sold. The sale of the good horses was the most painful, especially the beautiful big stallion, Pedro. The furniture and household articles were shipped by freight car. The farms they bought were equipped and included the horses and cows they would need. Dan and May Gibson also bought land near them. Dan was one of Brig's counselors in the bishopric. Brig was released from the bishopric, resigned from the school board, and resigned as president of the Conant Creek Canal Company. Louannie was released from the Relief Society presidency. It was painful to leave when so much faith, labor, and love had been shared with so many wonderful pioneer people.

A surprise party was held at their home by the community, and a beautiful wall clock was presented to Brig and Louannie as a going-away gift. Many farewell tears were shed that evening among young and old alike.

The move to Rupert was made early in November. The Murdochs had nice homes on well-leveled farms. Brig had forty acres; Tom had ten acres. They had rented their farms in Farnum, Brig to the Sparkman brothers and Tom to the Brothertons.

The children got settled in school and enjoyed the luxury of riding to school in a horse-drawn school wagon. It was a little awesome to go to school with several rooms in it. Dallas made it through the first two weeks before getting in a fight. He lost, but gained a close friend.

On October 3, another daughter, Martha Lucile, was born. Louannie had the responsibility of a new baby on top of the preparations for moving. Blanche was now fifteen and Dallas was twelve. They were helpful in many ways.

The crops the first year were good, but the prices fell to seven dollars a ton for hay and less than a dollar a hundred weight for potatoes. Store prices were still high, however. Coal was very scarce, as transportation difficulties had many things out of order. The brothers had hoped to sell their farms at Farnum to finish paying for their farms in Rupert. Since the depression was settling in, it was not possible to sell their farms. Brig traded his equity in his farm on a smaller thirteen-acre farm called Green Acres. It was about three quarters of a mile southwest of Rupert along the railroad tracks. He also got possession of a garage building in Rupert that was rented out.

In the spring of 1921 the family moved to Green Acres, keeping their livestock and equipment. Brig worked outside the farm, and older children worked out thinning beets and onions. Dallas worked for a farmer named Simms.

The Depression deepened, and it became evident that they could not pay for their farms even though they had a lot invested in them. So they made plans to move back to their old homesteads they had taken up twenty-one years before.

While in Rupert, the Murdochs were active in the branch, which was in the Blaine Idaho Stake. Brig was called to serve in the Sunday School presidency in July 1920. On August 15, 1921 he was called to the stake high council.

On March 8, 1922, another son was born. He was named James Howard. The Howard was for Howard Hewitt, Dallas's friend that had beat him up in the first fight Dallas had at Rupert. On April 21, 1922 the Murdochs left Rupert to return to Farnum. Louannie, with the four girls and baby Howard, went to Burley to visit Aunt Libby Lewis before returning to Farnum by train. Brig took Reed and son Tom in the car with him. Aunt Sarah and their children were also going by train. Uncle Tom and Dallas went on a freight car with the livestock and furniture.

It took two days and nights for the freight car to reach the siding at Ashton. As the train pulled up there was a long string of teams and wagons and sleighs lined up waiting for the car to be set. The large group of drivers waiting there looked familiar. They were those wonderful neighbors there to welcome the Murdoch's back two and a half years after that memorable farewell. The outfits were soon loaded with the belongings and they formed a caravan creeping through the mud and the snow to the old homestead where Brig and Louannie had gone exactly nineteen years before.

What Uncle Tom and Dallas didn't know was that Brig and the boys had a car accident on the way, near Pocatello, that had put them all in the Linn Brothers Hospital with broken collar bones. Brig also had some broken ribs. They had very poor care in the Hospital. No bones were set until the Hospital could verify they would be paid. They took the car for payment.

Later in the day Louannie and the girls arrived at the farm from the train. There was hardly a full pane of glass in the house. They went on to Uncle Tom's home, where Aunt Sarah and the Relief Society had a warm supper. The Relief Society came and cleaned up the house. They brought food and made the family as comfortable as possible.

Brig and Reed were released from the Hospital a few days later, little Tommy was kept two more weeks before being released. It was a great feeling to have all the family together again, although bruised, broken and discouraged.

Brig was unable to work for several weeks. The farming season was at hand. They had only three horses and limited equipment so the plowing went slowly. One day several of the neighbors turned out with their farming equipment and had the entire farm prepared and planted that day.

This outpouring of help and love from the neighbors was very encouraging and reassuring to Brig and Louannie, who were back where they started from, but now with eight children and broken health. The many favors and help the couple had extended to others through the years were now being returned.

Back in familiar surroundings, things gradually fit into place. The river, the flat, the bushy hillsides, the old neighbors and the old friends all helped to bring back a continuity of purpose. Brig was soon back on the Board of Directors of the Conant Creek Canal Company, back on the School Board, back in the bishopric as ward clerk. Louannie was back in the Relief Society and the Primary. The children returned to the Farnum Grade School. Family unity was stronger than ever. Blanche and Joseph Reiman were married on Christmas day, 1922, ten years after Rue and Mearl were married in the same room. Joe was a farmer from Green Timber, a very steady, reliable fellow of good habits. He was very considerate of all Blanche's family, especially her parents.

As each of the children graduated from the eighth grade of the Farnum School they attended Ashton High School. It was five miles to Ashton and the parents of neighboring children shared the responsibility of transportation to high school. The children were good students and active in school activities within the limits of their transportation facilities.

By the spring of 1923 Brig had recovered to where he was able to take over most of the work on the farm with the help of his growing family. He had brought some excellent Jersey cows from Rupert and gradually enlarged the number of cows. They were the principal source of income for the family. The milk was separated and the cream made into butter by Louannie and the children. She sold the butter to the Ashton stores which reserved it for special customers.

On October 23, 1924, Wallace Pierce was born, becoming the fifth son. The next few years were fairly stable. The financial picture was improving gradually. Brig's health was slightly impaired from an inward goiter. He took medication to slow it's development. He was advised to have it removed, but he did not have the money for an operation. His right arm was still slightly stiff from the car accident.

Katherine Mearl was born August 5, 1926 becoming the fifth daughter and tenth child. She had lots of people to give her much love and attention as there were now five boys and five girls, all living at home. During the bad part of the winter the high school students boarded in Ashton, returning home on week ends, and when the weather moderated in the spring.

In February 1928 Dallas had inflammatory rheumatism that kept him bed for several weeks. Dallas was called home from his work in the timber in mid-March to help take care of his Dad and the chores, as the younger boys were in high school. He helped with the planting and farm work during the summer and prepared to enter the University of Idaho in September. Brig gradually recovered and by early summer was able to return to most of his usual work.

Dallas completed his first year at the University and returned home, Reed attended the University the first semester the next year. When Reed came home, Dallas returned to school for the second semester. Reed went to work for Charles Burrell in his store. On November 3, 1931 Reed and Ruth Grover were married. She was a very lovely, talented girl from St. Anthony.

Thomas Hammon graduated from high school, farmed with Brig one year, and married his high school sweetheart, Alta Hillam, in the Salt Lake Temple, October 5, 1932. Her father was Abraham Hillam, stake patriarch. Tom went to work in the City Market in Ashton. He became manager and eventually bought the store. Laura Jean was married January 11, 1933 in the Salt Lake Temple to Angus Blanchard, a returned missionary. They settled in his parents' home in Chester and bought the home and farm, where they lived throughout their married life.

During the winter of 1931–32 Brig was very sick. He worried about the operation of the farm the coming season. The older boys were married and had jobs, the younger boys were in school and too young to do the farming. Dallas was a junior at the University. He got permission to leave school six weeks early and arrive home about the first of May 1932.

Brig gradually recovered so that he could do some of his work. His goiter was enlarging and overtaxing his heart. Finally, Dr. H. Ray Hatch, a boyhood friend, then in Idaho Falls told him he might not survive an operation and that he wouldn't survive without it. On June 12, 1933, he was operated on in the Idaho Falls L.D.S. Hospital. The faith and prayers and fasting of the family and friends were rewarded and Dad was on his way to a slow but gradual recovery. Dallas graduated from the University the same time Dad was operated on. He received a B. S. degree in Agricultural Education.

For several years during the depression farm prices were very low. In addition to that a frost, hail, wind, or drought occurred each summer to destroy the crops and sap the spirit. The dairy cows provided the family with food and bare necessities. The children worked on the farm and got other jobs when they could. There was no money for missions or college. Regardless of how small the amount of money coming in, tithing came out first. This principle was taught to all the children as they earned money.

Through all the years of hard work, crop failures, depression, and sickness Louannie took each challenge in stride, never complaining, always attentive to Brig's and the children's needs. She loved her flowers and despite the competition from kids, chickens, pigs, horses and weather, she always had some nice flowers inside the house and out. She helped Brig with his work as ward clerk. She was constantly teaching the principles of the gospel by example and word.

Dallas was married to Winona Lee June 6, 1934, in the Salt Lake Temple. They were accompanied by Tom and Alta. Tressa and Martha lived with Dallas and Winona for the next two years, attending high schools where Dallas was teaching Vocational Agriculture. This arrangement relieved Brig and Louannie of the worry of getting the girls to Ashton High because of the rough winters.

On September 5, 1936, Martha married Ralph Godfrey, whom she had met while going to school in Emmet. The fall of 1938 Brig and Louannie sold the farm to Angus and Jean. They bought a house with three lots and a barn across the street from their son Tom's home in Ashton. The milk cows were then moved into the new place.

The rich Jersey milk was sold whole to the stores and restaurants. A good business was soon established that was easier to operate and manage than running the farm. Tressa married Clyde Garrett on January 4, 1938 in the Salt Lake Temple. Wallace married Pauline Clements May 11, 1946. Howard married Grace Hillam June 4 in the Idaho Falls Temple. Katie married Glade Lyon December 1, 1946. While the boys were in the service, Brig could no longer manage the cows and sold them. That relieved Louannie of considerable work and she had more time to care for Brig, as his health continued to worsen.

Brig died the evening of May 13, 1947 at the age of seventy-six. His passing brought sadness to many people, but gladness to know that his mortal suffering had ended. All ten of their sons and daughters and spouses and children were present at the funeral. A telephone strike was on and many relatives could not be contacted. It was the largest funeral ever held in Ashton. It was held in the new Ashton Ward Chapel. Brig's son Tom was the bishop during the planning and building of the church.

Brig was buried in the Pineview Cemetery at Ashton, where Uncle Tom, Hans Nielson, and other pioneer friends would rest nearby.

Louannie missed Brig. She was grateful for their many years together. She always honored him as her husband, a father, a priesthood bearer, and a servant of the Lord. She had always supported his decisions and helped him in his various callings. She was always busy. Even when sitting and visiting, her hands were busy crocheting and embroidering. She liked to read and was well grounded in the scriptures. All during the year she would be working on Christmas presents for each child and grandchild. She now had time for her flowers, both inside and outside the house in spring and summer.

Louannie spent many hours on genealogy work for both the Murdoch and Hammon families. One of her happiest times of the year was the family reunions.

Every third year the Murdoch Reunion was held in Idaho near Ashton. The next two years it was held in Utah near Heber. Louannie, Aunt Sarah, and cousin Bessie Dawson were the regulars from Idaho, usually accompanied by other members of their families.

Her home was always the gathering place for her children and grandchildren, especially on Mother's Day and any holiday or Sunday.

In December 1952, Louannie had a gall bladder operation, which improved her health for a time. She was able to attend church services and Relief Society meetings, which she had done so faithfully throughout her life. When the children were small she used to walk to Primary with them if the horses were working in the field. It was four and a half miles round trip.

As the children grew up, Louannie and Brig were very appreciative of their response to the teachings of the gospel. It was lived in the home and taught by example. During some periods of time, some of the children seemed to stray as they reached adulthood. However, the folks never lost faith that each child would be worthy to be married in the temple. As this record is brought to a close (1982) all but one of the ten children have received their endowments. All ten children are still living. Louannie was very independent and would rather help than be helped. Despite her poor health and suffering, she kept smiling. Finally, when she could no longer care for herself, she went to Blanche's home, where she received the warm love and care that Blanche is special for. The other sons and daughters were also very close to Mother and were available when needed.

Louannie passed away June 30, 1962, after being in and out of the Ashton Memorial Hospital with a severe illness. She had a lovely funeral, attended by all her children and many relatives and friends in the Ashton Ward. She had been alone for fifteen years: patient, uncomplaining, always striving to make others happy. She was buried beside Brig in the Ashton Pineview Cemetery. The following poem written by Winifred Kirkham, a dear friend, was read by Della Davis, a niece who read Mother's obituary. It was written on the morning Mother passed away.

"Aunt Luannie, when I heard of your passing, I walked out into my flower garden; somehow you seemed to be very near, for all around me were blooms from the starts of flowers you have given me. I looked at the forget-me-nots, with their tiny blooms facing toward the sun, and I thought of Proverbs 31:31: 'Give her of the fruit of her hands; and let her own works praise her in the gates.'

"I came in the house and wrote this verse especially for you:

Aunt Luannie:

I know that heaven has a garden now,
Because you would not stay
If there weren't tulip bulbs to plant
And tend and give away.

The yard around your little house
Ran golden in the sun,
And there you labored in your garden
From early morn 'til day was done.

Your hollyhock's fluffed crimson skirts
Against your house's gray
And the beauty and fragrance of your lilies
Were talked of blocks away.

You've raised your children as your flowers,
To grow and face the sun
And to choose their path of life

To be the righteous one.

Now as I tend and watch my flowers bloom
Which to me will be second to none,
I'll feel you are walking beside me
To see how it is done.

As the family and friends have visited the Ashton Cemetery each Memorial Day, it has been easy to locate Brig's and Louannie's graves from a distance by the numerous bouquets and floral offerings placed around the graves—a loving tribute to a wonderful couple who had served so many so well. Lack of space and time make it necessary to omit many items that would be of interest to Brig's and his wives' posterity. I hope this history will become the thread that will be used by all the family to help weave the final pattern we desire as we all move into eternity.

Written by Brigham Dallas Murdoch, son, from the personal histories of Brigham and Luann Murdoch, and from genealogy records compiled by Tressa Murdoch Garrett and Ruby Murdoch Hooper.

Brig and Louannie's second home

Brigham Murdoch home in Ashton, Idaho

Mearl Garrett Murdoch

Blanche Alexander Murdoch About 1890

Brigham Murdoch
Age 14

Rue and Blanche Murdoch

Back: Robert Rue Murdoch   Middle: Brigham and
Louannie Hammon Murdoch Front: Blanche Priscilla Murdoch

Brigham Murdoch

Louannie Hammon
Age 16

Rue Murdoch and Earl Garrett
Kansas City 1916

Robert Rue Murdoch

Brigham Murdoch

Brigham Dallas and Blanche Murdoch

Back: Louannie, Brigham and Brigham Dallas Murdoch
Middle: Howard, Reed, and Tom Murdoch
Front: Martha, Tressa, and Jean Murdoch

Back Row Left to Right: Tressa, Reed, Howard, Dallas, Tom, Wallace, Blanche. Front Row Left to Right: Jean, Martha, Brigham, Louannie (Hammon), and Katie Murdoch. Taken about 1943.

Reed, Tom, and Jean Murdoch

Howard, Wallace and Katherine Murdoch

Tressa and Martha Murdoch

Back - Tressa, Blanche and Jean Murdoch
Front - Martha Murdoch

Bishopric

Brigham Murdoch
and horse-Pedro

Left to Right: Iver Hendrickson, Bishop Brigham Murdoch
and Daniel Gibson

Brigham Murdoch on mower

Brigham Murdoch family and friends hauling hay

Back Row Left to Right: Brigham Dallas Murdoch, Reed Chase Murdoch,
Thomas Hammon Murdoch, James Howard Murdoch, and Wallace Pierce
Murdoch. Front Row Left to Right: Blanche Priscilla M. Reiman,
Laura Jean M. Blanchard, Tressa Isabell M. Garrett, Martha Lucille M.
Godfrey Reed, Katherine Mearl M. Lyon.

Back Row Left to Right: B. Dallas and Agnes S. Murdoch, Ruth G. and
Reed C. Murdoch, Alta H. and Thomas H. Murdoch, J. Howard and L. Grace
H. Murdoch, Pauline C. and Wallace P. Murdoch. Front Row Left to Right:
Clyde R. and Tressa M. Garrett, C. Angus and L. Jean M. Blanchard, Blanche
M. Reiman, Martha M. Reed, Katherine (Katie) M. and Glade Lyon.

FAMILY PORTRAIT

HUSBAND Brigham MURDOCH
Birth   2 November 1870
Place   Heber City, Wasatch, Utah
Married   16 December 1891
Place   Logan, Cache, Utah Temple
Death   13 May 1947
Place   Ashton, Fremont, Idaho
Burial   16 May 1947
Place   Ashton, Fremont, Idaho
Father   John Murray MURDOCH
Mother   Isabella CRAWFORD
Other Wives 2-Martha L. HAMMON

WIFE Mary Blanche ALEXANDER
Birth   16 Febuary 1873
Place   Midway, Wasatch, Utah
Death   22 June 1893
Place   Heber, Wasatch, Utah
Burial   25 June 1893
Place   Heber, Wasatch, Utah
Father   Charles Marsteller ALEXANDER
Mother   Lovisa Comstock SNYDER
Other Husbands
Information From Guy G. MURDOCH

1st Child Robert Rue MURDOCH
Birth   16 November 1892   Heber, Wasatch, Utah
Married   Mearl GARRETT
Date   25 December 1913 (Temple-9 May 1930-SL)
Place   Ashton, Fremont, Idaho
Death   19 September 1929 Ashton, Fremont, Idaho
Burial   23 September 1929 Ashton, Fremont, Idaho

1 MURDOCH, James 1786-1831   2 MURDOCH, John Murray 1820-1910
1 MURDOCH, MARY MURRAY, Sp. 1782-1856   2 MURDOCH, Isabella CRAWFORD, Sp. 1836-1916

DESCENDANTS OF--------
3 MURDOCH, Brigham 1870-1947
3 ALEXANDER, Mary Blanche, Sp. (1) 1873-1893

4 MURDOCH, Robert Rue B-16 Nov 1892 M-25 Dec 1913 D-19 Sep 1929
4 SMITH, Mearl GARRETT Murdoch Smith, Sp. B-2 Mar 1896
  SMITH, Samuel H. Sp. (2) B-13 Jan 1895 M-28 Dec 1935 D-6 Oct 1960
  SMITH, James Albert, Sp. (3) B-29 Apr 1898 M-25 Feb 1978 D-   1981

    5 LONG, Ellen Elaine MURDOCH Lee B-8 Oct 1914
    5 LEE, Claude Lester, Sp. (1) B-6 Feb 1908 M-29 Sep 1931 Div.-2 Sep 1938
    5 LONG, Raymond, Sp. (2) B-   M-28 Oct 1950

        6 LEE, Robert Rue B-28 Feb 1932 M-19 Aug 1960
        6 LEE, Gwen JENSEN, Sp. B-23 Sep 1938

            7 LEE, Robert Jensen   B-26 Jan 1962

            7 LEE, Kevin Murdoch   B-19 Sep 1963

            7 LEE, Jennifer   B-25 Mar 1966

            7 LEE, Vanessa   B-12 Mar 1970

            7 LEE, Bryan DeMott   B-10 Jun 1973

            7 LEE, Richard Garrett   B- 8 Jun 1975

            7 LEE, Jared Thomas   B-14 Apr 1977

        6 KIDD, Marilyn Mearl LEE B-12 Jul 1934 M-29 Aug 1952
        6 KIDD, Clark Jackson, Sp. B-11 Oct 1929

            7 OLSEN, Teresa Ann KIDD B-11 Feb 1954 M-13 Jul 1973
            7 OLSEN, Phillip K. Sp. B-2 Feb 1951

                8 OLSEN, Kaehla Marie   B-30 May 1980

            7 KIDD, Clark Bruce B-6 May 1955 M-13 Mar 1980
            7 KIDD, Elaine JORGENSEN, Sp. B-15 Jul 1956

            7 KIDD, Robert Lee B-8 Jul 1957 M-8 May 1981
            7 KIDD, Marilyn J. WALKER, Sp. B-30 Nov 1959

            7 KIDD, Michael Lee   B-30 Apr 1960

            7 KIDD, George Curtis   B-29 Mar 1968

7 KIDD, Allen   B-25 Apr 1970

6 NATRESS, Claudia Kay LEE Taylor B-1 Oct 1936
6 TAYLOR, Robert Lee, Sp. (1) B-14 Feb 1935 M-25 Mar 1954 Div.
6 NATRESS, Robert, Sp. (2) B-1 Aug 1925 M-18 Jul 1968 Div.

        7 TAYLOR, Stephen Neal B-10 Oct 1955 M-19 May 1976
        7 TAYLOR, Robyn WILDEN, Sp. B-10 Feb 1959

                8 TAYLOR, Stacie Marie B-10 Dec 1977 D-5 Mar 1978

                8 TAYLOR, Amanda Nicole   B-15 Jul 1979

                8 TAYLOR, Rebecca Dawn   B-16 Sep 1981

        7 TAYLOR, Kenneth Claude B-29 Jun 1958 M-5 Aug 1980
        7 TAYLOR, Colleen Diana HACKETT, Sp. B-29 Mar 1957

        7 DAMRON, Laura Lee TAYLOR B-30 Nov 1960 M-   1979
        7 DAMRON, Clark, Sp. B-10 Jan 1960

        7 TAYLOR, John Charles   B- 9 Apr 1963

        7 NATRESS, Alethia Ann   B-24 Jul 1969

        7 NATRESS, Mary Felicia   B-17 Feb 1973
5 MURDOCH, Guy GARRETT B-5 Oct 1916 M-9 Apr 1938
5 MURDOCH, Faye TANNER, Sp. B-4 Nov 1918

        6 MAY, Faye Diane MURDOCH B-31 Jan 1945 M-3 Jun 1966
        6 MAY, Bruce Earl, Sp. B-21 Jul 1945

                7 MAY, Bret Earl   B- 3 Jul 1967

                7 MAY, Clint Bruce   B-10 May 1970

                7 MAY, Robert Bart   B-30 Jan 1974

                7 MAY, Jeffery Dirk   B-21 Apr 1976

                7 MAY, Danette   B-13 Dec 1977

        6 VAUGHN, Pamela Jeanne MURDOCH B-6 Jul 1947 M-29 Jan 1971
        6 VAUGHN, David Brent, Sp. B-15 Mar 1952

                7 VAUGHN, Cecily Paige   B-24 Feb 1976

                7 VAUGHN, Jordan Diane   B-11 May 1978

                7 VAUGHN, Reagan   B-18 Nov 1980

        6 MURDOCH, Robert Guy B-14 May 1949 M-30 Dec 1970
        6 MURDOCH, Linda Susan ALEXANDER, Sp. B-22 May 1949

                7 MURDOCH, Jennifer Lynn   B-23 Apr 1972

                7 MURDOCH, Heather Sue   B-10 Aug 1974

                7 MURDOCH, Robyn Michell   B-23 Mar 1976

        6 MURDOCH, Paul Michael B-7 Nov 1955 M-17 May 1978 (2)
        6 MURDOCH, Rebecca V. ACOSTA Kusman, Sp. B-30 Jan 1953
           Kusman,   Sp. (1) B-   M-   Div.

                7 MURDOCH, Joshua Kusman   B-24 Oct 1974

                7 MURDOCH, Brooke Lynne   B-16 Jun 1980

        6 MURDOCH, Richard Kent B-15 Jul 1959 M-22 May 1981
        6 MURDOCH, Kathy CROWELL, Sp. B-24 Jul 1959

        6 MURDOCH, Michael Alan   B-28 Oct 1961

5 MURDOCH, Robert Murray B-25 Oct 1918   Div.-5 Nov 1947
5 TIBBETTS, Arvena Ruth SMITH Hammond Murdoch, Sp. (1) B-18 Aug 1915 M-26 Oct 1939
5 MURDOCH, Zelta Lillian CROFTS Glover, Sp. (2) B-4 Apr 1922 M-15 Jan 1957

HUSBAND   BRIGHAM MURDOCH
Birth   2 November 1870
Place   Heber City, Wasatch, Utah
Chr
Married   8 April 1903
Place   Salt Lake City, Salt Lake, Utah (Temple)
Death   13 May 1947 Ashton, Fremont, Idaho
Burial   16 May 1947 Ashton, Fremont, Idaho
Father   John Murray MURDOCH
Mother*   Isabella CRAWFORD
Other Wives Blanche ALEXANDER (1) 16 December 1891
(if any)

WIFE   MARTHA LOUANNIE HAMMON
Birth   11 October 1885
Place   Hooper, Weber, Utah
Chr
Death
Burial   30 June 1962 Ashton, Fremont, Idaho
             2 July 1962 Ashton, Fremont, Idaho
Father   Heber Chase HAMMON
Mother*   Martha Priscilla CHRISTENSEN
Other Wives
(if any)
Where was information obtained Tressa I. Murdoch Garrett

*List complete maiden name for all females.

1st Child   BLANCHE PRISCILLA MURDOCH
Birth   7 February 1904
Place   Twin Groves, Fremont, Idaho
Married to   Joseph Theadore REIMAN
Married   25 December 1922
Place   Farnum, Fremont, Idaho
Death

2nd Child   BRIGHAM DALLAS MURDOCH
Birth   4 June 1907
Place   Farnum, Fremont, Idaho
Married to   (1)Winona LEE   (2)Agnes SIMONSEN
Married   6 June 1934   6 January 1956
Place   Idaho Falls-Temple-Idaho Falls, Ida
Death

3rd Child   REED CHASE MURDOCH
Birth   17 November 1909
Place   Farnum, Fremont, Idaho
Married to   Ruth GROVER
Married   3 November 1931
Place   St. Anothony, Fremont, Idaho
Death

4th Child   THOMAS HAMMON MURDOCH
Birth   16 March 1912
Place   Farnum, Fremont, Idaho
Married to   Alta Blanche HILLAM
Married   5 October 1932
Place   Logan, Cache, Utah
Death

5th Child   LAURA JEAN MURDOCH
Birth   25 June 1914
Place   Farnum, Fremont, Idaho
Married to   Charles Angus BLANCHARD
Married   11 January 1933
Place   Salt Lake City, Salt Lake, Utah

6th Child   TRESSA ISABELL MURDOCH
Birth   5 January 1918
Place   Farnum, Fremont, Idaho
Married to   Clyde Raymond GARRETT
Married   4 January 1938
Place   Salt Lake City, Salt Lake, Utah
Death

7th Child   MARTHA LUCILE MURDOCH
Birth   3 October 1919
Place   Farnum, Fremont, Idaho
Married to   (1)Ralph Edmund GODFREY (2)Marion REED
Married   5 Sep 1936 (Divorced)   29 Dec. 1962
Place   Emmett, Gem, Idaho
Death

8th Child   JAMES HOWARD MURDOCH
Birth   8 March 1922
Place   Rupert, Minadoka, Idaho
Married to   Lauretta Grace HILLAM
Married   4 June 1946
Place   Idaho Falls, Bonneville, Idaho
Death

9th Child   WALLACE PIERCE MURDOCH
Birth   23 October 1924
Place   Farnum, Fremont, Idaho
Married to   Pauline CLEMENTS
Married   11 May 1946
Place   Tyler, Texas
Death

10th Child   KATHERINE MEARL MURDOCH
Birth   5 August 1926
Place   Farnum, Fremont, Idaho
Married to   Glade Marvin LYON
Married   1 December 1946
Place   Ashton, Fremont, Idaho

1 MURDOCH, James 1786-1831   2 MURDOCH, John Murray 1820-1910
1 MURDOCH, Mary MURRAY, Sp. 1782-1856   2 MURDOCH, Isabella CRAWFORD, Sp. 1836-1916

DESCENDANTS OF------3 MURDOCH, BRIGHAM 1870-1947
                    3 HAMMON, MARTHA LOUANNIE, SP. 1885-1962

4 REIMAN, Blanche Priscilla MURDOCH B-7 Feb 1904 M-25 Dec 1922
4 REIMAN, Joseph Theadore, Sp. B-6 Mar 1897 D-4 Apr 1973

     5 TIGHE, Blanche Jean REIMAN B-26 Oct 1923 M-26 Jul 1944
     5 TIGHE, Marvin Eugene, Sp. B-28 Jun 1921

          6 MOWER, Kay Lynn TIGHE B-13 Jun 1947 M-10 Dec 1965
          6 MOWER, Lynden, Sp. B-12 Jun 1946

               7 MOWER, Lynden Brett   B-24 Jun 1966

               7 MOWER, Bart Joseph   B- 2 Apr 1968

               7 MOWER, Kevin DeLayne   B- 1 Jul 1974

               7 MOWER, KELLY Jay   B-10 Apr 1976

               7 MOWER, Jeremy James   B- 8 Mar 1979
               7 MOWER, Jamey   B- 8 Jul 1981
          6 KIDD, Marva Annette TIGHE B-7 Aug 1951 M-30 Jun 1967 (Div)
          6 KIDD, Dennis Jackson, Sp. B-9 Jul 1948

               7 KIDD, Lisa Michelle   B-13 Nov 1967

          6 TIGHE, Vincent Robert B-14 Dec 1953 M-3 Nov 1978
          6 TIGHE, Kandy Lee BROWER, Sp. B-27 Aug 1957
               7 TIGHE, Amanda   B-21 Jul 1981
          6 TIGHE, Marvin Brent B-24 April 1955 M-28 Jul 1978
          6 TIGHE, Kristine CONGER, Sp. B-26 Feb 1959

               7 TIGHE, Brandon Robert   B-24 Mar 1980

          6 CROUCH, Jolene Uywan TIGHE B-29 Jun 1957 M-27 Jul 1973
          6 CROUCH, Bryce Ray, Sp. B-26 May 1953

               7 CROUCH, Sonya Heather   B-18 Feb 1974

               7 CROUCH, Devani Uywan   B- 5 Feb 1978
               7 CROUCH, Hilary Ray   B-21 Nov 1981
     5 MARSDEN, Helen Marian REIMAN B-9 Nov 1924 M-10 Dec 1946
     5 MARSDEN, John Curtis, Sp. B-13 Sep 1920

          6 JENKINS, Bonnie Jean MARSDEN B-29 May 1947 M-29 Oct 1968
          6 JENKINS, Kim V, Sp. B-4 Feb 1946

               7 JENKINS, Chad M   B-17 May 1969

               7 JENKINS, Christina   B-18 Oct 1970

               7 JENKINS, Mark William   B-23 Apr 1978

          6 MARSDEN, Gary John B-5 Jun 1951 M-20 Aug 1971
          6 MARSDEN, Susan Ann MAROTZ, Sp. B-22 Jun 1951

               7 MARSDEN, Dustin Curtis   B-20 May 1974

               7 MARSDEN, Megan Sue   B-16 Jun 1976

               7 MARSDEN, Jordan Graham   B- 1 Mar 1981

          6 MARSDEN, Steven R B-2 Feb 1955 M-5 May 1978
          6 MARSDEN, Mary Lynn TAYLOR, Sp. B-11 Aug 1957

               7 MARSDEN, Gichin Steve   B-30 May 1980

6 DAWSEY, Mary Lee MARSDEN B-29 Oct 1957 M-7 Oct 1977
6 DAWSEY, Charles Lee, Sp. B-20 Sep 1953

       7 DAWSEY, Kolin John   B-2 Apr 1977

       7 DAWSEY, Sunny   B-12 Jul 1979

   6 MARSDEN, Dee Ann B-19 Jan 1960

5 REIMAN, Lynn Theodore B-8 Dec 1925
5 REIMAN, Anola Jewel BIRD, Sp. (1) B-27 Jul 1929 M-30 Jun 1946 Div.
5 REIMAN, Lucile Mildred WARD,Neitzel, Sp. (2) B-6 Jun 1922 M-18 Aug 1966
  Neitzel, James Morris, Sp. (1) B-   M-   Div.

   6 REIMAN, Teryl Lynn B-14 Dec 1947 M-
   6 REIMAN, Pam   B-15 Jul 1951

       7   , Steven   B- 3 Nov   Pam's children from
                                          previous marriage.
       7   , Sonja   B- 6 Aug

       7   , Kristi   B-30 Sep

   6 PETERSON, Paula Maud REIMAN B-29 Jan 1950 M-25 Nov 1966
   6 PETERSON, David, Sp. B-20 Jan 1949

       7 PETERSON, David Shane   B-22 May 1967

   6 REIMAN, Joel Scott B-22 Jun 1951

   6 SMITH, Lori Ann REIMAN B-13 Jan 1954 M-5 May 1978
   6 SMITH, Gary, Sp. B-14 Mar 1953

   6 REIMAN, Douglas Craig B-25 Apr 1955 M-
   6 REIMAN,

       7 REIMAN, boy   B-

   6 BORUP, Darla Janae' REIMAN, B-11 Mar 1960 M-24 Aug 1979
   6 BORUP, David, Sp. B-13 Apr 1957
       7 BORUP, Bryan Rov   B-18 Dec 1981
   6 SHARP, Karla Sue REIMAN B-30 Jun 1961 Twin
   6 SHARP, Mark, Sp. B-   M-6 Jun 1981
   6 REIMAN, Philip   B-30 Jun 1961 Twin

   6 NEITZEL, James Ward B-7 Apr 1947 M-19 Aug 1972
   6 NEITZEL, Claudia Jean WEBSTER, Sp. B-

       7 NEITZEL, Janea' Patrice   B-30 May 1973

       7 NEITZEL, Jason Morris   B-17 Apr 1975

       7 NEITZEL, Joy Lynn   B-28 Feb 1977

       7 NEITZEL, Jeffery Claude B-23 Mar 1980

   6 NEITZEL, Dennis Kay B-29 Sep 1948 M-12 Jan 1968
   6 NEITZEL, Brenda Paulette JONES, Sp. B-10 May 1947

       7 NEITZEL, Michelle Denise B-4 Jan 1969

       7 NEITZEL, Branden Dennis B-15 Dec 1970

       7 NEITZEL, Matthew Paul   B-12 May 1974

       7 NEITZEL, Alisa Carey   B-27 Dec 1975

       7 NEITZEL, Jarom   B- 5 Jun 1979

   6 FULMER, Joyce NEITZEL Maher B-8 Nov 1949
   6 MAHER, Thomas Francis, Sp. (1) B-9 Jul 1947 M-10 Feb 1968 (Div.) D-Mar 1973
   6 FULMER, Jerry Wallace, Sp. (2) B-4 Oct 1950 M-26 Jun 1972

```
        7 MAHER, Shelisa Michele       B- 2 Sep 1968

        7 MAHER, Ahtanya Lanee'        B- 2 Feb 1972

        7 FULMER, Jarod Wyatt          B- 3 Oct 1973

        7 FULMER, Tobin Bartley        B-17 Nov 1974

    6 NEITZEL, Gerald Lynn B-8 Jul 1953 M-8 Nov 1973
    6 NEITZEL, Carol Lynne HAMMON, Sp. B-

        7 NEITZEL, Julene Marie        B-11 Aug 1974

        7 NEITZEL, Daniel Wayne        B-30 Jun 1978

        7 NEITZEL, Jacob Levi          B-12 Dec 1980

    6 NEITZEL, David Ray B-2 Jun 1959

5 REIMAN, Kay Murdoch B-8 May 1927 M-10 May 1948
5 REIMAN, Althea MarJean HARRIS, Sp. B-11 May 1926

    6 CUMMINGS, Althea Denise REIMAN Whitmore B-31 Aug 1950
    6 WHITMORE, David Lawrence, Sp. (1) B-21 Feb 1947 M-          Div.
    6 CUMMINGS, David E, Sp. (2) B-19 Feb 1955 M-6 Oct 1979

        7 WHITMORE, Corbett Lyle       B- 3 Oct 1967

        7 WHITMORE, Ricky Lance        B- 7 Oct 1970

        7 CUMMINGS, Nicholas Aaron     B-26 Dec 1980

    6 MAUGHAN, Yvonne REIMAN B-1 Nov 1955 M-25 Sep 1976
    6 MAUGHAN, Randall G., Sp. B-31 Dec 1948

        7 MAUGHAN, Kara Lee Reiman     B- 2 Jul 1975

        7 MAUGHAN, Greer Reiman        B- 8 Jun 1978

    6 REIMAN, Lyle Kay B-3 Dec 1956 M-26 May 1979
    6 REIMAN, Marcia Jane BUTTARS, Sp. B-19 Jan 1959

        7 REIMAN, Joshua Ben           B-18 Aug 1980

4 MURDOCH, Brigham Dallas B-4 Jun 1907
4 MURDOCH, Winona LEE, Sp. (1) B-14 Aug 1910 M-6 Jun 1934 D-22 Mar 1953
4 MURDOCH, Agnes SIMONSEN, Sp. (2) B-7 Jul 1920 M-6 Jan 1956

    5 MURDOCH, Ronald Lee B-23 Apr 1935 D-10 Nov 1938

    5 HALL, Helen Winona MURDOCH B-31 Aug 1936 M-22 Aug 1958
    5 HALL, Ronald Earl, Sp. B-22 Aug 1935

        6 HALL, Stephanie Ann    B-21 Jun 1959

        6 HALL, Stewart Douglas B-16 May 1960

        6 HALL, Gregory Alan     B-24 May 1961

        6 HALL, Natalie Kay      B- 2 Sep 1962

        6 HALL, Kimberly Jean    B-14 Jan 1964

        6 HALL, Bradley Clayton B-16 Apr 1965

        6 HALL, Lorilee          B-19 May 1967

        6 HALL, Lisa Marie       B-28 Apr 1969

        6 HALL, Marsha Lynn      B- 9 Jun 1970

        6 HALL, Brent Richard    B- 7 Jan 1972

        6 HALL, Steven Michael   B- 9 Mar 1974

        6 HALL, Brian Curtis     B-19 Dec 1975
```

5 MURDOCH, Dallas Earl B-23 Oct 1937 M-10 Dec 1959
5 MURDOCH, Joan HALE, Sp. B-18 Mar 1937

    6 MURDOCH, Kathleen   B-11 Mar 1961

    6 MURDOCH, James Dallas B-23 Nov 1962

    6 MURDOCH, Karen   B- 9 May 1968 Adopted

    6 MURDOCH, David Clayton B-22 Mar 1972 Adopted

    6 REDSTONE, Sheydene Lee B-24 Apr 1975 Foster

5 MURDOCH, Thomas Ray B-6 Jul 1940 M-10 Sep 1965
5 MURDOCH, Sharon Lee WELLS, Sp. B-15 **Aug** 1944

    6 MURDOCH, Ray Dallas   B-23 Aug 1967

    6 MURDOCH, Rachelle Lee B-19 Aug 1969

    6 MURDOCH, Ryan Kent   B-27 Mar 1972

    6 MURDOCH, Roger Thomas B-23 May 1975

    6 MURDOCH, Royce John   B-15 Aug 1976

    6 MURDOCH, Rod Tyler   B-29 Mar 1980

5 MATESEN, Ann Marie MURDOCH B-24 Dec 1941 M-15 Jun 1962
5 MATESEN, Allan Evan, Sp. B-6 Oct 1933 D-23 Apr 1971

    6 SHAW, Michelle Marie MATESEN B-5 May 1963 M-21 Mar 1981
    6 SHAW, David Vern, Sp. B-23 May 1962

        7 SHAW, Peter David   B-17 Apr 1981

    6 MATESEN, Thomas Allan B-5 Nov 1966

5 SCHULZ, Ruth Lorraine MURDOCH B-7 May 1945 M-13 Jun 1968
5 SCHULZ, Alan Edward, Sp. B-2 Dec 1942

    6 SCHULZ, Rebecca Lynn B-10 Mar 1971

    6 SCHULZ, Mark Alan   B-28 Feb 1979 Adopted

5 MURDOCH, John Brigham B-14 Jan 1950 M-11 May 1972
5 MURDOCH, Marie BRADY, Sp. B-8 Jun 1953

    6 MURDOCH, Laura   B-19 Apr 1973

    6 MURDOCH, John Brady   B-31 May 1974

    6 MURDOCH, Amy   B- 3 Aug 1975

    6 MURDOCH, Donna Lee   B-14 Dec 1977

    6 MURDOCH, Julie   B- 5 Oct 1979

5 VERSEY, Mary Lou MURDOCH B-15 Nov 1956 M-10 Oct 1980
5 VERSEY, Wayne Robert, Sp. B-15 Jun 1955

    6 VERSEY, Sara Lou   B-28 Oct 1981

5 DODDS, Luann Agnes MURDOCH B-14 May 1959 M-7 Aug 1981
5 DODDS, Ross William, Sp. B-17 Nov 1954

4 MURDOCH, Reed Chase B-17 Nov 1909 M-3 Nov 1931
4 MURDOCH, Ruth GROVER, Sp. B-8 Apr 1913

    5 MURDOCH, Reed DeLynn B-31 May 1933 M-25 Jun 1952
    5 MURDOCH, Joyce Marie HOUSLEY, Sp. B-14 Feb 1933

        6 MURDOCH, Steven DeLynn B-1 Jan 1954 M-4 Sep 1975
        6 MURDOCH, Latona HUDSON, B-26 Aug 1956

```
                    7 MURDOCH, Steven Lynn Jr.      B-19 Jan 1977

                    7 MURDOCH, Andrea Danielle      B-19 Apr 1978

                    7 MURDOCH, Jennifer Leigh       B- 6 Jan 1980

            6 MURDOCH, Micheal Duane B-1 Jan 1956 M-9 Apr 1976
            6 MURDOCH, Deneice DAHN, Sp. B-9 Jul 1951

                    7 MURDOCH, Bonnie Leigh         B- 6 Sep 1976

                    7 MURDOCH, Micheal Sean         B-27 Feb 1979
                    7 MURDOCH, Sarah Ann            B-16 Jan 1982
            6 MURDOCH, Kenneth D B-20 Dec 1956

            6 MURDOCH, James D B-30 Apr 1958 M-21 Aug 1980
            6 MURDOCH, Tamara Lee STOLP, Sp. B-17 Sep 1960
                    7 MURDOCH, Haunz                B-15 Oct 1981
            6 KAWANO, Jolin MURDOCH B-13 May 1960 M-19 Aug 1978
            6 KAWANO, Gary Frank B-25 Mar 1954

                    7 KAWANO, Baby boy              B-       1980 (Stillborn)
                    7 KAWANO, Tina Lee              B- 9 Oct 1981
    5 BERGER, Sharon Jean MURDOCH B-7 Apr 1936 M-13 Feb 1959
    5 BERGER, Gene Raymond, Sp. B-16 Mar 1938

            6 HAMBLIN, Sandra Lynne BERGER B-8 Jan 1960 M-19 Dec 1980
            6 HAMBLIN, Garth Mangum, Sp. B-19 Nov 1958
                    7 HAMBLIN, Ashley               B-
            6 BELL, Kim Rae BERGER B-16 Mar 1961 M-19 Feb 1979
            6 BELL, Brian, Sp. B-27 Jul 1956

                    7 BELL, Kirk Brian              B- 1 Oct 1980

            6 BERGER, Jeannie Evelyn    B- 1 Jan 1964

            6 BERGER, Jacqueline Lee    B- 2 Nov 1966

            6 BERGER, William Reed      B-20 Aug 1971

    5 MURDOCH, Thomas Albert B-28 Sep 1942 M-15 Oct 1964 D-20 Jul 1967
    5 MURDOCH, Sandra Lee CHRISTIANSEN, Sp. B-5 May 1947

            6 MURDOCH, Chase J.         B-20 Apr 1965

    5 MISKIN, Gerriane MURDOCH B-23 Feb 1953 M-5 May 1972
    5 MISKIN, Kaylen, Sp. B-28 Nov 1949

            6 MISKIN, Ladonalee         B- 9 Feb 1973

            6 MISKIN, Garen Cordell     B-26 Apr 1974

            6 MISKIN, Corbet R'tel      B-20 Apr 1975

            6 MISKIN, Troyce Brandon    B- 9 May 1977

            6 MISKIN, Darien Dayn       B- 9 Jun 1978

            6 MISKIN, Aliena            B- 4 Oct 1979

            6 MISKIN, Adrina            B-21 Apr 1981

4 MURDOCH, Thomas Hammon B-16 Mar 1912 M-5 Oct 1932
4 MURDOCH, Alta Blanch  HILLAM, Sp. B-25 Feb 1913

        5 MURDOCH, Ronald Thomas  B-3 Nov 1933 D-5 Nov 1933

        5 MURDOCH, Darrell Dean B-2 May 1935 M-16 Oct 1957
        5 MURDOCH, Marva Lynn ANGLESSEY, Sp. B-9 Feb 1938

            6 MURDOCH, Dena Lynn        B-12 Nov 1961

            6 MURDOCH, Christy Jo       B-25 Jul 1963
```

6 MURDOCH, Debra Lee   B-14 Nov 1964

6 MURDOCH, James Scott   B- 8 Jul 1968

6 MURDOCH, Bruce Cameron   B- 2 Jan 1970

6 MURDOCH, Kurt Thomas   B- 2 Oct 1973

6 MURDOCH, Connie Gay   B-19 Jan 1976

6 MURDOCH, Marcia Jean   B- 2 Dec 1977

5 REYNOLDS, Mary MURDOCH B-15 Jun 1937 M-12 Mar 1971
5 REYNOLDS, Shirley WELDON, Sp. B-19 Sep 1938

6 REYNOLDS, Dawn Mary   B- 4 Sep 1976 Adopted

6 REYNOLDS, Ladd Weldon   B-27 Feb 1979 Adopted

5 HEMMING, Judith Ann MURDOCH Atchley B-23 Jun 1942
5 ATCHLEY, William Junior, Sp. (1) B-7 May 1942 M-5 Mar 1959 Div.
5 HEMMING, Eugene Alfred, Sp. (2) B- 8 Nov 1925 M-25 Apr 1975 D-14 Nov 1977

6 STRONKS, Jan ATCHLEY B-24 Sep 1959 M-9 Mar 1979
6 STRONKS, Todd Harold, Sp. B-11 Oct 1955

7 STRONKS, Mary Frances   B-23 Jul 1980

6 ATCHLEY, Thomas William B-13 Apr 1962 M-25 Apr 1980
6 ATCHLEY, Tara Ann LARSON, B-7 Feb 1962

7 ATCHLEY, Thomas William   B-9 Sep 1980

6 ATCHLEY, Julie   B-19 Jan 1966

6 ATCHELY, Patti Ruth   B- 2 Aug 1969

6 ATCHELY, Dori Ann   B-13 Apr 1971

6 HEMMING, Suzanne Ruth B-3 Aug 1967 (Eugene's child previous marriage
                                       adopted by Judy after his death)
5 CIKAITOGA, Tamra MURDOCH B-15 May 1951 M-6 Mar 1975
5 CIKAITOGA, Samuela Koroi, Sp. B-16 Feb 1948

6 CIKAITOGA, Maikeli Koroi B-17 Nov 1976

6 CIKAITOGA, Amelia Kate   B-24 Apr 1980 Adopted

6 CIKAITOGA, Brooke KeAloha B-6 Feb 1981 Adopted

4 BLANCHARD, Laura Jean MURDOCH B-25 Jun 1914 M-11 Jan 1933
4 BLANCHARD, Charles Angus, Sp. B-12 Apr 1905

5 BLANCHARD, Dale Robert B-3 Oct 1933 M-18 Dec 1955
5 BLANCHARD, Rulene PARKINSON, Sp. B-23 Aug 1937

6 BLANCHARD, Robert Noel   B-28 Mar 1957

6 BLANCHARD, Brent Alan   B- 1 Mar 1960

6 BLANCHARD, Boyd Angus   B- 2 Oct 1964
                                          twins
6 BLANCHARD, Brian Royal   B- 2 Oct 1964

5 BATEMAN, Barbara Joyce BLANCHARD B-2 Mar 1936 M-19 Aug 1960
5 BATEMAN, Charles Richard, Sp. B-4 May 1936

6 BATEMAN, Don R. B-17 Sep 1961 M-3 Apr 1981
6 BATEMAN, Deide WILLIAMS, Sp. B-5 Jul 1962

6 BATEMAN, Cindy Lou   B-13 Feb 1965

6 BATEMAN, Heidi Jo   B-30 Nov 1970

```
          5 BLANCHARD, Don Lee B-18 Jan 1939 M-18 Dec 1967
          5 BLANCHARD, Linda Lee WOOLARD, Sp. B-18 Jan 1947

                    6 BLANCHARD, David Lee      B-19 Dec 1971

                    6 BLANCHARD, Duane Lee      B-16 Feb 1974

                    6 BLANCHARD, Lee Ann        B-20 Jul 1977

                    6 BLANCHARD, Darin Lee      B-25 Sep 1978

          5 SMITH, Virginia KAYE BLANCHARD Jones B-3 Oct 1940
          5 JONES, Samuel Douglas, Sp. (1) B-25 May 1940   M-10 May 1963 D-10 Nov 1963
          5 SMITH, Stanley Parley, Sp. (2) B-3 Sep 1941 M-22 Dec 1964

                    6 SMITH, Brittany Lynn      B- 4 Dec 1967

                    6 SMITH, Christopher Yuri B-13 Nov 1968

          5 GARDNER, JoAnne BLANCHARD B-16 Sep 1943 M-2 Mar 1974
          5 GARDNER, Randell Ferron, Sp. B-2 Feb 1947

                    6 GARDNER, Lindsey Chante   B- 9 Sep 1976

                    6 GARDNER, Justin Randell B-20 Nov 1977

          5 FLOYD, Marlene BLANCHARD B-17 Oct 1948
          5 PETERSON, Lennie D. B-16 May 1948 M-23 Dec 1968 Div.-20 Sep 1977
          5 FLOYD, Glen C., Sp. (2) B-7 Sep 1942 M-3 Jul 1981

                    6 PETERSON, Joy Lynn     B-10 Sep 1974 Adopted

4 GARRETT, Tressa Isabell MURDOCH B-5 Jan 1918 M-4 Jan 1938
4 GARRETT, Clyde Raymond, Sp. B-15 Apr 1917

          5 MERRILL, Geraldine GARRETT B-21 Nov 1938 M-10 Mar 1956
          5 MERRILL, Wendell Lamoine, Sp. B-1 Nov 1936

                    6 IVERS, Tammera Kay MERRILL B-13 Dec 1957 M-4 Aug 1979
                    6 IVERS, Gary, Sp. B-20 Sep 1956

                            7 IVERS, Jennifer Nichole     B-10 Jan 1981

                    6 MERRILL, Michael Lamoine B-27 Feb 1959 M-20 Dec 1980
                    6 MERRILL, Lisa Kay DIXON, Sp. B-2 Jul 1961

                    6 MERRILL, Terry Kent     B-23 Jul 1960

                    6 MERRILL, Bruce Evan      B-18 Jul 1961

                    6 MERRILL, Todd           B-16 Jun 1966

          5 WOMACK, Tressa Clydene GARRETT B-22 Feb 1940 M-7 Oct 1958
          5 WOMACK, Dennis Lee, Sp. B-11 Jul 1938

                    6 WOMACK, Jerry           B-22 Mar 1960

                    6 WOMACK, Kathy           B- 1 May 1963

                    6 WOMACK, Carol Ann       B- 5 Jun 1965

          5 SCHMITT, Sandra Jean GARRETT B-15 Sep 1943 M-21 Jun 1963
          5 SCHMITT, Irvin, Sp. B-31 Jan 1943

                    6 SCHMITT, Stephanie Joann B-27 Mar 1964

                    6 SCHMITT, Ida Suzanne    B-31 Mar 1965

                    6 SCHMITT, Karl Raymond   B-20 Dec 1969

                    6 SCHMITT, Theresa Ruth   B-26 Aug 1972

                    6 SCHMITT, Scott Irvin    B-19 Oct 1978
```

5 WINKLE, Pamela GARRETT B-28 Sep 1948 M-25 Sep 1969
5 WINKLE, James Anthony, Sp. B-13 Jun 1949

    6 WINKLE, Desiree   B- 4 Jan 1971

    6 WINKLE, Marie Rachael   B-26 Apr 1973

    6 WINKLE, Mari'e AnJannette B-11 Mar 1975

5 NEBEKER, Ivana GARRETT B-18 Apr 1950 M-17 Mar 1973
5 NEBEKER, Leland Wyllie, Sp. B-14 Jun 1947
    6 NEBEKER, Brian Lee   B-18 Oct 1975

    6 NEBEKER, Kurt Austin   B- 2 Sep 1977

    6 NEBEKER, Jill   B-17 Oct 1978
    6 NEBEKER, Bruce Trent   B-13 Feb 1982
5 GARRETT, Brigham Earl B-21 Feb 1959 M-9 Mar 1978 Div.
5 GARRETT, Melanie Rae BROWER, Sp. B-11 Jul 1960

    6 GARRETT, Brandon Earl   B-23 Mar 1979

4 REED, Martha Lucile MURDOCH Godfrey B-3 Oct 1919
4 GODFREY, Ralph Edmund, Sp. (1) B-10 Feb 1917 M-5 Sep 1936 Div.
4 REED, Marion, Sp. (2) B-19 Oct 1916 M-29 Dec 1962

    5 GODFREY, Ralph Orvile B-7 Aug 1946 M- Jan 1970
    5 GODFREY, Sharon Joann WHITAKER, Sp. B-29 Mar 1945

        6 GODFREY, Criag Douglas B-19 Aug 1970

        6 GODFREY, Christopher Lee B- 3 Nov 1973

    5 GODFREY, John Edmund   B-24 Jan 1950

    5 GODFREY, James Murdoch B- 3 Jan 1952

4 MURDOCH, James Howard B-8 Mar 1922 M-4 Jun 1946
4 MURDOCH, Lauretta Grace HILLAM, Sp. B-3 Apr 1925

  . 5 FREEMAN, Lauretta Gwen MURDOCH B-12 Sep 1947 M-1 Aug 1968
    5 FREEMAN, Fred Stanley, Sp. B-29 Sep 1946

        6 FREEMAN, Angela   B-10 Jun 1970

        6 FREEMAN, Curtis Wayne   B-14 Sep 1972

        6 FREEMAN, Christopher James B-15 Jan 1974

        6 FREEMAN, Wendy Marie   B-14 Feb 1976

    5 WODSCOW, Patricia MURDOCH B-13 May 1949 M-8 May 1969
    5 WODSCOW, Ronnie Sutton, Sp B-13 Apr 1945

        6 WODSCOW, Ronette   B-18 Feb 1970

        6 WODSCOW, Kimberly   B- 7 Nov 1971

        6 WODSCOW, Chad Murdoch B-18 Jul 1973

        6 WODSCOW, Saralee   B-15 May 1975

        6 WODSCOW, Alison   B- 5 Mar 1977

        6 WODSCOW, Scott Sutton B-21 Jan 1979

    5 MURDOCH, Bryan Howard B-18 May 1953 M-4 Aug 1976
    5 MURDOCH, Deborah STOLWORTHY, Sp. B- 5 Jul 1957

        6 MURDOCH, Brett Howard B- 8 Jun 1977

        6 MURDOCH, Brandon Gerald B-26 Apr 1979

        6 MURDOCH, Brittney Ann B-23 Dec 1980

5 COOK, Molly MURDOCH B-25 Mar 1955 M-12 Aug 1976
5 COOK, Karl Thurman, Sp. B-9 Dec 1954

      6 COOK, Jeffrey Murdoch   B-28 Jul 1977

      6 COOK, Kevin Thomas   B-14 Nov 1978

      6 COOK, Kali   B-23 Feb 1980

      6 COOK, Todd Charles   B- 5 Jul 1981

5 MURDOCH, Richard B-3 Feb 1959 M-5 Jun 1981
5 MURDOCH, Lori Ann CORDOZA, Sp. B-17 Feb 1962

5 MACKAY, LaRae MURDOCH B-9 Jan 1961 M-22 Oct 1980
5 MACKAY, Gary Wayne, Sp. B-9 Oct 1961

5 MURDOCH, Marilyn   B-24 Mar 1963

5 MURDOCH, Bradley Kay B-24 Feb 1969

4 MURDOCH, Wallace Pierce B-23 Oct 1924 M-11 May 1946
4 MURDOCH, Pauline CLEMENTS, Sp. B-8 Jul 1925

      5 MURDOCH, Wallace Pierce Jr. B-25 Nov 1948 M-9 Nov 1974
      5 MURDOCH, Sandra Kimiko SAITO, Sp. B-31 Jan 1948

      5 MURDOCH, Robert Alan B-18 May 1952 M-
      5 MURODCH, Debbi COPPERSMITH, Sp. B-

      5 MURDOCH, Jon Paul   B-23 Nov 1956

      5 MURDOCH, Kenneth Scott B-26 Mar 1959

4 LYON, Katherine Mearl MURDOCH B-5 Aug 1926 M-1 Dec 1946
4 LYON, Glade Marvin, Sp. B-2 Sep 1923

      5 LYON, Jack M. B-10 Jun 1951 M-29 Sep 1972
      5 LYON, Cecilia Anne WILLIAMS, Sp. B-25 Nov 1951

      6 LYON, Rebeka Anne   B-14 Sep 1973

      6 LYON, John Aubery   B-30 Sep 1974

      6 LYON, Mathew Williams   B-28 Mar 1978

      6 LYON, Rachel Alynn   B-12 May 1980

5 HAMILTON, Suzanne LYON B-24 Jul 1953 M-24 Oct 1975
5 HAMILTON, Larry Grant, Sp. B-20 Mar 1951

      6 HAMILTON, Ryan Taylor   B-13 May 1976

      6 HAMILTON, Aaron Lyon   B-12 May 1979

      6 HAMILTON, Emily Wren   B-26 Jul 1981

5 MILLER, Robin LYON B-2 Apr 1957
5 MILLER, Verl Ralph, Sp. B-10 Jan 1952 M-18 Jul 1973 Div. 1982

      6 MILLER, Cody Verl   B-14 Jan 1976

      6 MILLER, Scott Lyon   B-18 Aug 1977

5 LYON, Kathy   B-3 Oct 1961

Robert Murdoch

Robert Murdoch, the fifth child of John Murray and Isabella Crawford Murdoch, was born in Heber City, Utah, on September 12, 1872. His grandparents were James and Mary Murray Murdoch and Andrew and Margaret McClure Crawford. His brother Brigham, who was two years older, recalled that Robert, nicknamed "Boot," was a happy and much-loved brother. He was closely surrounded and looked after by three sisters, three brothers, and many other loved ones, who made sure that his preschool and childhood days were happy ones. As he reached young adulthood, Robert actively participated in the dances and plays that provided much of the entertainment in Heber City and other towns in the valley. Robert and Brigham were both employed at the mines in Park City. When Brigham married Blanche Alexander in December of 1891, they invited "Boot" to live with them in Park City, where they would be close to their work. Blanche's younger sister, Luella Alexander, also spent considerable time with them.

Blanche was a talented pianist, and she and Brig were in great demand to play music for dances in nearby communities. Robert shared these fun times with them. Blanche, Boot, and Luella all became seriously ill with the fever. Within a period of less than three months, Robert, Blanche, and Luella died of typhoid fever. The loss of these fine young people was deeply felt and remembered by their families and friends.

Robert died on September 3, 1893, and was buried in the Heber Cemetery. He would have been twenty-one years old on September 12. Maybell Moulton remembered the funeral procession. She also recalled that Florinda Cummings, one of Robert's friends, planted a lilac bush on his grave, and that many of the young ladies in Heber thought this was a special and long-lasting tribute.

Church records indicate that Robert was baptized by John McDonald on the third of September, 1882, confirmed by Thomas R. Hicken, and that on October 9, 1900, his brother James C. Murdoch served as proxy for his temple endowment work. We look forward to a time when we will know and love firsthand this special member of our "forever family."

John Murray Murdoch Jr., Minnie Marie Miller, and Cora Leona Vail Bigler

John Murray Murdoch, Jr., was born May 1, 1874, in Heber City, Wasatch County, Utah. He was the sixth of seven children born to Isabella Crawford and John Murray Murdoch. Isabella was John's plural wife. There were twenty-two children in the family, and though there were two different mothers, the children interacted as though it was one big happy family, which indeed it was, until plural marriage became unlawful and the families had to be separated.

John M., Jr., was only about seventeen years old when his father was arrested for living in polygamy. John, Sr., asked the federal officials if he could go home and get a change of clothing; he promised that he would present himself at the penitentiary to serve a one-month sentence. He was given permission to go home. He gathered the articles he needed and presented himself at the penitentiary for imprisonment. The prison officials had no entry papers for him but he insisted on serving his sentence. This determination to keep his word must have greatly impressed his namesake. John Murray, Jr., was heard to say many

times, "A man is only as good as his word," and "My word is my bond." These phrases have been passed down to his sons and daughters and grandchildren.

John grew up in the beautiful valley surrounding Heber City, Utah. He loved the serenity and calm of the valley surrounded by ranges of towering mountains.

Jock, as he was called by most who knew him, was a tall, handsome young man with soft, brown, wavy hair. He was, according to those who knew him, shy but nevertheless popular with the pretty girls of Heber, Midway, and Park City.

He was able, however, to elude any girls who had designs on him until he was almost thirty years old. Then, never dreaming that heartache would soon after enter his life, he married Minnie Miller. Minnie was the second child of Nelson Miller and Annie Michelson.

Minnie's mother had died when Minnie was ten years old, and her father when she was twenty-one. As the oldest daughter she had assumed a great deal of responsibility for the care and raising of the younger children. As she grew older she moved to Salt Lake City, where she worked in the homes of several families. One of her employers was Emeline Wells, whom she considered difficult to work for.

John and Minnie were married on January 30, 1904, and later, on October 31, 1907, were sealed in the Salt Lake Temple. Their first home was in Deer Valley, a part of Park City. Very little is known of their life together, other than that they shared sorrow at the loss of their two infant daughters, Minnie and Annabelle. It is little wonder, then, that Bessie, who was born February 26, 1909, was a great joy in their lives. Minnie was an excellent seamstress, and always had Bessie dressed beautifully with her hair brushed and curled. On November 28, 1911, another child blessed their home. Minnie had little opportunity to enjoy this baby boy. After just nine short years of marriage, just one month to the day after the birth of her first son, Raymond, John's beloved Minnie passed away, leaving him with two very young children. John had fervently hoped that Minnie could get better, and had pled with her not to leave him with the two babies to raise. He knew that he and they both desperately needed her. His pleading, however, was in vain. Finally, the doctor who was attending Minnie told him that she was so ill he must let her go, and so, to his great sorrow, she passed to the other side on December 19, 1911.

It must have been very cold that winter because John froze his toes when he was accompanying Minnie's body from Park City to Heber City for burial. The snow was so deep that the horses would not go unless they were led, so John walked in front of them all the way. He did not get the benefit of the warm bricks and blankets brought for those who rode in the sleigh.

After Minnie's death, her brother and sister-in-law, Nels and Etta Miller, asked permission to have Bessie return to Idaho with them. John was anxious to have the two children together and so would not let her go. Instead, he had the children remain with his sister, Kate Hicken, who had come to take them when Minnie died.

There, with the Hickens, Ray and Bessie grew up together in the warmth of a loving family where "borrowed" children were well loved and cared for. Kathryn and her husband, David, became Papa and Mama to Bessie and Ray. The children were warmly accepted into the family and shared a close, warm relationship with the Hicken children that lasted all their lives.

With the children well cared for at the Hicken home, John returned to the mines at Park City and, undoubtedly, to a lonely existence. He visited the children as often as he could. They were always excited to see this handsome man. One of Bessie's favorite activities was combing his hair, and John, with great patience, was always willing to let her do it.

John was remembered by his children and his stepchildren as being a loving and patient person who consistently tried to teach them good principles.

His self-control was exemplary, and his strongest words were said by his children to be "my word." When he was really disgruntled, he always said MY WORD in capital letters. When the children misbehaved, a "Scotch blessing" was in order.

One bright summer day Ann Hicken, Ray, and Bessie and some neighborhood friends were wading on the lawn on watering day. Papa watered from the ditch, and it was great fun to go wading. Bessie said a bad word that started with S. John heard her and invited her to go for a walk with him. She enjoyed being with him, so was thrilled to follow along. They sat on the cool, shady porch on the north of the Hicken home, and John said to her, "Bessie, I heard a dirty word come from your mouth today. Can you remember what it was?" She said, "No, daddy." "Think hard," he said, and told her what she was doing when she said it. She thought and thought and finally said, "Oh, now I know it. I said s——." "Yes," he said. "Now I want to tell you something. Never let anything come out of your mouth that you wouldn't put in it." This was a great lesson that Bessie always remembered.

Jock used to say of himself, "I am a man of few words, but very eloquent." Cora Vail Bigler, his second wife, would say of him, "Jock is a shy, and quiet man, and he doesn't speak lightly. But when he does speak, his words are carefully thought out and are, indeed, eloquent. One waits for Jock to speak; his dignity and bearing give added weight to his spoken word."

Jock continued to work in the mines of Park City, visiting his children whenever he could. Time passed, and he was asked to serve a mission for the LDS Church in New Zealand. This was a difficult time for Jock. He was already separated from his children most of the time, and this would mean a total separation for several years. But he accepted the call, and when he was ready to leave, the whole Hicken family, including his mother, Isabella Crawford Murdoch, who was living with the Hickens, walked to the depot to see him leave on the Heber Creeper.

His children sorely missed him, as his visits had been a delight to them, but theirs was a background of being taught to serve the Lord as asked, and so they waited patiently for his return. There was great excitement when his all-too-infrequent letters arrived from the far-away land where he labored on his mission. He rode the train to San Francisco, where he and several other missionaries caught a boat for New Zealand. One of those missionaries was Matthew Cowley, who was later called to be an Apostle. Matthew was just seventeen and Jock Murdoch was over forty, but they developed a real love for one another. They spoke often of one another after their return.

They traveled seventeen or eighteen days by boat and landed in Wellington, where they were met by mission personnel and traveled on to Aukland, where the mission headquarters were. The first night in Aukland, the new missionaries met for prayer, and Brother Miller, the elder in charge, called on Jock to pray. Silence greeted the group as nothing happened. Jock soon said that he could not pray and left the group. In a later conversation with Brother Miller, it came to light that Jock had not been particularly close to the Church during the years just before his mission and felt uncomfortable giving a public prayer at that time. It was thought by Brother Miller that Jock was very lonely, and that either he or his bishop had been inspired to have him serve a mission to help him grow closer to the Lord and learn to cope with his great grief and loneliness at the loss of his wife. (Elder Miller, now over ninety years old, resides in Idaho Falls, Idaho, and was interviewed by John Murray's granddaughter, Ann D. Bingham, in May 1980.)

Jock was assigned to the South Island near Christchurch. It was a difficult assignment, since just a few years before that time a Mormon elder had been killed there, and there was great animosity toward the Church.

Although he was busy with the business of his mission, Jock's diary gives evidence that Minnie was still in his thoughts. On the first page, dated August 13, 1915, the following poem is written:

Thoughts of My Wife

But now she sleeps where the daisies nod
And the clover hangs its head.
Where the wild birds come
And the wild bees hum
Above her lonely bed.

She fought the fight.
She kept the faith.
Her fame shines bright and clear.
And her memory lives in my heart,
Which will ever hold her dear.

By the time Jock had been on his mission six months, he had truly caught the vision of the missionary work, and was described by Brother Miller as a humble, faithful, dedicated missionary. Many reports were received that he was doing good work. Although he was shy at the beginning of his mission, his shyness seemed to disappear as he became involved in the missionary work.

His diary shows that much time was devoted to study and reading. The general pace of life seemed to be leisurely The missionaries traveled either by horse or bicycle most of the time. When the distance was long, they went by train or boat. Most of their long-distance communication was by wire.

Learning the language was difficult. John recorded in his missionary diary that his first preaching in the Maori language was done on January 22, 1916. Life

was not always pleasant and easy. The missionaries were tormented by fleas and mosquitoes on some occasions so badly that they could not sleep. Typhoid fever was a frequent problem.

Jock's diary tells of the common tasks of the missionaries in that time and place. Catching the horses, milking the cows, fixing the fences, and traveling were common to them. They spent much time with the Maori people, and many Maori words slip into the writing of the diary.

Horses, the main mode of travel for Jock and his companion, were also occasionally a source of grief. In his diary on May 31, 1916, he wrote:

Arose early, held prayer, tried to get Elder Schofield up, too sleepy. Got my horse. Trying to catch them, I slipped and fell down the hill on the wet grass. After breakfast I started for TeHoro to carige horses the road was wet and muddy. Arrived at TeHoro about 12 noon. Went to our paddock, chased the horses, lost my bag of books, my horse got away, chased him around through the boxsiers. *I was thinking of getting mad.*

This entry provides a good example, of Jock's extraordinary patience and forbearance.

Priesthood meetings were held monthly, often at the home of a member. Jock tells of one conference held in a large tent. One shilling was solicited from each person for food. They came by train and horseback and on boats to attend the conference. There were many people there.

Jock's willingness to continue to serve the Lord is recorded in his diary on his birthday, May 1, 1916, when he reflected on being there for the second birthday and hoped that there would be another and perhaps more if he were asked to stay.

Jock's children, however, were glad that Jock did not stay an extra-long time on his mission. It was a joyful day when he returned and was reunited with his children. It was a nice summer day, and the children were playing outside barefooted on the grass when a surrey with fringe on top drove up and John got out with his trunks and bags. At first the children didn't know him, but they recognized his hair, which was still wavy. He had grown a mustache. When the children realized their father had returned, they jumped for joy.

To add to their excitement, he had brought trinkets and treasures from New Zealand, not only for his children, but for the nieces, nephews, and other family members. Maori beads and lap robes made of sheepskin were among the gifts he brought.

Jock had many missionary companions, but spoke most often upon his return of Matthew Cowley, predicting that he would hold a high position in the Church, which he later did.

Brother Cowley also talked of Jock. Many relatives reported hearing mention made of Jock in Brother Cowley's conference talks throughout the Church. On one occasion, while in Idaho Falls, Idaho, Bessie was in the audience to hear one of these talks and after introduced herself to Elder Cowley as Jock's daughter. The apostle gave her a warm welcome and told her of his great love for her father. He spoke of what a good man he was and how he was very lonely when his wife passed away and how he had missed Ray and Bessie while on his mission. Jock, he said, was most grateful for his dear sister Kate and her husband Dave and how good they were to the children. After his return from his mission, Jock returned to work in the mines in Park City as shift boss, and again would visit his children on weekends when the weather permitted. He was known as one of the "Park City Bunch" and numbered among his friends some of the prominent mining investors of Park City. Jock had a reputation for integrity with these men.

Jock loved fishing and baseball. He didn't live too far from the Provo River and this was his favorite spot to fish. Jock also had great love for his family, brothers and sisters, parents, and his children. Indeed, he had a great love for everyone, especially little children. He was always asking them what their pretty name was, and if they had a cold, he wiped their noses.

Jock loved music and played several instruments. He had a steel guitar and a violin, which he played often. He, Bessie, and Ray would play together with Jock playing the violin, Ray the mouth organ, and Bessie chording on the piano.

After his mission he would often play his violin and sing Maori songs to his own children and his nieces and nephews, often teaching them the words. Bessie, Ray, and Ann would often sing them in Primary. While Ray and Bessie were living near, the three of them continued to sing the songs together when they met.

Another of Jock's great loves was attending Murdoch reunions. He delighted in dressing up and marching in the parade. The whole family enjoyed meeting all their kinfolk, and each reunion became a fond memory. Jock's daughter, Bessie, kept up the tradition, and truly enjoyed being the life of the Murdoch reunion party. Some time after Jock's return home to

Heber, a young widow, Cora Vail Bigler, became the postmistress of Midway, Utah. Her husband had been tragically killed by lightning, leaving her with two small daughters to raise. Cora, the daughter of John Riley Vail and Alice White, had grown up in Midway and knew of Jock's mission to New Zealand and of the loss of his wife. One day he just walked into the Midway post office, and they began to chat. In time they began to keep company. Cora was aware of Jock's still-deep sorrow over his wife's early death Jock was aware of Cora's still being shattered by the death of her twenty-six-year-old husband. They knew that each had two children. Jock had a pre-teen daughter and a young son. Cora had two daughters ages three and one and a half.

Despite the challenges they saw, Jock and Cora married on January 3, 1921. They were married in the Salt Lake Temple for time only, knowing they cared for each other, but differently than the love they each felt for their first spouses. There were step-children to be loved and adjusted to, and new parents for the children to learn to love.

For a time all lived in the nice home with running water, which Ray and Bessie thought quite special since in Heber they still used an outside privy and coal stove, as many others did in those days. Corals two daughters, Freida and Wanda, were very young, and found John to be an extraordinary father. He provided a good home and was, all in all, patient and loving. Each day they would run two blocks to Jacobsen's Store to meet him and walk back home with him holding his hands.

Things did not go so happily for Bessie and Ray, who were older at the time of the marriage and had more difficulty adjusting. Ray soon returned to the only parents he had ever really known, Mama and Papa Hicken. Bessie lived with Jock and Cora long enough to graduate from Park City High School and then left to live first with friends in Park City and then with her mother's brother and his wife in Idaho.

John enjoyed surprises. On one occasion John, Cora, and Corals sister and her husband, Elsie and Orville, went for a horseback ride. They started up where the Wasatch State Park is now. John wouldn't tell them where they were going. He wanted to surprise them, he said. They rode up, up, and up the mountain until either on purpose or accidentally they got lost. They wandered up the very steep mountaintop. A terrible rainstorm came and really drenched them. They wandered some more and came upon a sheepherder's wagon. They broke in and made some coffee to warm them up. The storm went on for a long time. The sheepherder came back to his wagon and found his uninvited guests. He cooked them a good hot meal and had to escort them down the face of the mountain. John would never admit whether he got lost or whether it really was a "special" horseback ride. The "new route" over Brighton today is still a scary, rocky road, and goes to Brighton from Park City. From that time on he was to be almost constantly in and out of the hospital.

On August 17, 1926, during one of his many hospital stays, a baby girl, Phyllis Beth, was born to John and Cora. She was adored and cherished by her older half brother and sisters. But once again Jock's time with a child would be cut short, this time by his own death.

During Jock's stays in the hospital, Matthew Cowley visited him almost daily. Also, his mission president, President Lambert, was superintendent of the hospital, and saw that he had very good care. He even brought him to Park City to see the family just after Phyllis Beth was born.

John still had the home he and Minnie had occupied in Heber City, where he had stored many of his things in the upstairs while renting out the first floor. The home was close to his parents' home in the northwest end of Heber. He said he wanted to live and die in Heber, so during the illness he and Cora moved back to Heber. Cora, knowing that she would need a way to make a living, went to Salt Lake City to learn the barber and beauty trade.

While Bessie was in nurse's training in Idaho, John often wrote her, instructing her to better herself, to write often, and to write to Ray and to Mama and Papa Hicken, to be a good girl and make all of them proud of her, and to remember to go to church and pay her tithing and remember her prayers, and Heavenly Father would bless her.

Jock seemed to know when his time on earth was growing short, and he was sad about leaving his family. He would hold Phyllis on his knee and say, "If I could live to help raise this baby." He had left Bessie and Ray as young children to fill his mission, and now seemed to know that he would again have to leave a child in the care of others.

John died on April 26, 1928, in Heber. He was very ill for a long time, and his last days were far from pleasant as he suffered from osteomyelitis, for which there was then no cure. He was buried next to Minnie in the Heber City Cemetery.

Before John's death, Bessie had moved to Idaho. In May 1930, she graduated with an R.N. degree. During her training she met her future husband, Oliver P. Dawson. They were married May 29, 1930, just after her graduation. At that time Oliver was the manager of the Boise Payette Lumber Company in Shelley. That same year they built a new home in Shelley, where they lived until November 1949, when they moved to Idaho Falls. Bessie lived in Idaho Falls the rest of her life. Although Oliver did not share her religious beliefs, she remained active and faithful in the Church throughout her life. She served as a stake missionary and as a Relief Society president, as well as in other Church post ions.

Bessie and Oliver had three children: Oliver Murray, who resides in Cody, Wyoming; Ann Bingham, who lived in Idaho Falls, Idaho; and James Murdoch (J.M.), who lives in Kaysville, Utah. Oliver had a daughter, Betty Jean, who was six years old when they married, and she lived with them until she completed high school. Betty lives in Sunnyvale, California.

Bessie passed away on February 12, 1980. In her history, which was written by her husband, Oliver, he said, "Her entire life was devoted first to myself and her family and gave us full support and love. Never once did she fail to give any of us her full knowledge obtained in her earlier training. With her love and training she had brought all of us love and life to this day. Second on her list was the Church which she believed in sincerely and supported."

Bessie will be sorely missed by her family and the countless friends she made wherever she was.

Ray grew up in Heber. He was active in Scouting and received the first Eagle badge to be awarded in Wasatch County. He was active in drama, sports, speech, and music. He was drum major for the Wasatch High School Band.

In 1932 he won a music scholarship to Weber College. While attending Weber he met Shirley Dickson, and after their graduation from Weber they were married June 27, 1934, in the Salt Lake Temple. In the fall of that year they moved to Logan, where Ray attended U.S.U. He worked for twenty-five cents an hour on the experiment farm, while Shirley babysat for a dollar a day. In 1937 Ray graduated from the Agricultural College, and they moved to Blanding, where he was hired as an Ag teacher.

After living in Blanding for three years, they moved to Princeton, California, where Ray taught school. He got interested in bees, and soon had so many hives he decided to give up teaching and buy a farm. In December, 1949, Ray and Shirley moved to Yuba City,

California. Here they had prunes, peaches, almonds, cattle, and bees. The flood of 1955 took all the bees, so after that they just farmed.

Ray always took an active part in the Church and community affairs. He was a good teacher, scout leader, stake Sunday School superintendent, and ward teacher supervisor. He sang in the ward choir for many years.

He was president of the Bee Breeders Association, high school board, and vice president of the Tax Payers Association.

Ray and Shirley have three children: RaShirl J., who is a teacher at Chico, California; Larry E., who is supervisor for the Oakland Sector FAA; and a daughter, Eulene, whose husband is chief master sergeant in the USAF There are three grandchildren, Bert E. Murdoch, David Morgan, and Mindy Morgan.

Ray passed away, from cancer, October 30, 1975. He was a good husband and a good father, and his family miss him very much, but know they will be with him again.

Following John Murray Murdoch Jr's death, his wife Cora was once again a widow with three young daughters to raise. Frieda and Wanda Bigler from her first marriage and Phyllis Murdoch, the daughter of John Murray Murdoch Jr.

Cora married one year later to a James Earl Wall on January 22, 1929. He had three children from a pervious marriage that lived with them also. A son, Earl Vail Wall, was born to Cora and James on July 26, 1930. Cora and James were eventually divorced in 1943. James died on March 22, 1961.

Cora worked as a beautician in Park City to help support her family for many years. She went through many trials in her life with two husbands dying after only a short time of being married to each of them. In later years she married for the fourth time to Jack Esmond McKnight on May 23, 1953. He however died also in a few years on August 24, 1947.

Cora served two missions for the Church of Jesus Christ of Latter Day Saints. One to the Southern States and the other to Florida. She passed away on September 10, 1970 in Salt Lake City, Utah, and was buried in Midway, Wasatch, Utah.

John and Cora's daughter, Phyllis Murdoch Giolas, writes the following:

Phyllis Murdoch Giolas was born August 17, 1926 in Park City, Summit County, Utah. Her place of birth was a humble home located on 1015 Park Avenue. Her parents were Cora Loemma (Leona)

Vail Bigler and John Murray Murdoch Jr., both of Heber City and Midway, Wasatch County, Utah. Her young years were spent in simple pleasures, unaware of the heartaches and sorrows of others.

Phyllis completed her primary and secondary schooling in Midway and Park City, Utah, graduating with honors from Park City High School in May 1944. She had completed two years of college when illness forced her to discontinue her studies. Phyllis made her life full of fun and church activities. Her mother encouraged her in the cultural arts and Phyllis was fortunate in being able to sing and play the flute, guitar and piano. She played roles in plays, musicals and operettas. She loved her life and busy schedule.

The world at war in 1944 provided Phyllis the opportunity to learn a trade when she was employed as an aircraft mechanic at Hill Air Force Base, Ogden, Utah. She also worked for the Genealogical Society of Utah. She received further technical training when she was employed by Mountain States Telephone Company.

Phyllis married James "J" Giolas, son of James Peter and Annie Haines Shepherd Giolas on 6 June 1947 in the Salt Lake Temple. Phillis and James were blessed with three Children: James Richard Giolas, born 21 January 1950. Rick enjoyed his church and scout activities. He earned his Duty to God and Eagle Scout awards. He graduated from Skyline High School, Salt Lake City, Utah in 1968.

He progressed from a Safeway bag boy to Safeway Incorporated Management. He inherited the shy quiet dignity of his grandfather, John Murray Murdoch Jr. He loved to sing in groups and madrigals. He enjoyed work and play with the youth of his ward. Rick Married Gay Lynne Martin, daughter of Gary Martin and Janice Chadwick Martin, both of American Fork and Salt Lake City, Utah, in the Salt Lake Temple on 30 June 1970.

John Murdoch Giolas, born 29 July 1960. He was a long-awaited adopted baby. He was sealed to his parents in the Salt Lake Temple on 15 August 1961. He graduated from Skyline High School, Salt Lake City, Utah in 1978. He attended the University of Utah and became employed by Pameco-Aire Inc. of Salt Lake City, Utah. John too, developed the sweet reserved manner of his grandfather John Murray Murdoch Jr.

Lisa Ann Giolas, born 3 August 1962, also a loved adopted baby, was sealed to her parents in the Salt Lake Temple on 15 June 1964. She graduated with honors from Skyline High School, Salt Lake City, Utah in 1980. Her plans include attendance at the University of Utah in 1980. Lisa has developed the Murdoch talents to make life for herself and others full and happy.

Phyllis was blessed with three grandchildren born to James Richard and Gay Lynne Martin Giolas, Andrea Giolas, James Martin Giolas, and Amanda Giolas.

Phyllis fulfilled a stake mission. She served as a Primary and Relief Society president. She served in many stake and ward positions. She also was privileged to serve as secretary for her Vail-White Family Organization.

Phyllis, proud of her Scottish Murdoch, and her Vail-White English-Irish heritage, has found that the combination of her bloodlines give her many blessings. The gift of discernment sometimes told ahead of events to take place. She sews, sings, enjoys church activities, and genealogy work. She loves fun, happy times. Her life evolves around her family and her church

She has a knowledge of the truthfulness of the gospel. She knows God does live and that as long as she heeds his word and obeys his will, that he will pour His blessings and love upon her. She knows too, that if she but listens to that "still small voice" (she sometimes has to yell to be heard.) that she can be strong and able to help her family through trials and hardships that have and will yet come to them. This would be in fulfillment of her patriarchal blessing."

John Murray Murdoch Jr.
and
Minnie Marie Miller Murdoch

Bessie Murdoch

Back Left to Right: Beverly S. Dawson, Darold L. and Ann Dawson
                       Bingham, Betty Dawson and Dick Kamarath,
                       Goldie M. Dawson.
Middle Left to Right: James M. Dawson, Bessie Murdoch Dawson,
                       Oliver P. Dawson, Oliver M. Dawson.
Front Left to Right: Jeri J. Dawson, Rick Kamarath, Cynthia
                       M. Dawson, Nancy Dawson, Gary Kamarath,
                       Ted M. Dawson.

Shirley D. Murdoch, Raymond Murdoch
and Bessie Murdoch Dawson

Larry D. Murdoch   RaShirl J. Murdoch   Eulene Murdoch Morgan

Front Left to Right: John Murdoch Giolas, Lisa Ann Giolas
Back Left to Right: James J. Giolas, James Richard Giolas
                       Phyllis Murdoch Giolas

Left to Right: Gaylynn Martin Giolas, James Martin Giolas
James Richard Giolas, Lisa Ann Giolas, John Murdoch Giolas
Andrea Giolas

HUSBAND John Murray MURDOCH
Birth 1 May 1874
Place Heber, Wasatch, Utah
Married 30 January 1904
Place Salt Lake Temple, Utah
Death 26 April 1928
Place Heber, Wasatch, Utah
Burial 29 April 1928
Place Heber, Wasatch, Utah
Father John Murray MURDOCH
Mother Isabella CRAWFORD
Other Wives (2) Cora Leona VAIL

WIFE Minnie Marie MILLER (1)
Birth 13 October 1878
Place Near Heber, Wasatch, Utah
Death 19 December 1911
Place Park City, Summit, Utah
Burial
Place Heber, Wasatch, Utah
Father Rasmus Nelson MILLER
Mother Anna Maria MIKKELSEN
Other Husbands
Information From James Murdoch
  & John Murray Murdoch records

1ST CHILD Minnie MURDOCH
Birth 1905 (Stillborn)
Married
Date
Place
Death
Burial

2ND CHILD Annabell MURDOCH
Birth 10 September 1907 Park City, Summit, Utah
Married
Date
Place
Death 14 September 1906 Park City, Summitt, Utah
Burial

3RD CHILD Bessie MURDOCH
Birth 26 February 1909 Park City, Summit, Utah
Married Oliver Painter DAWSON
Date 29 May 1930
Place Brigham, Box Elder, Utah
Death 12 February 1980 Idaho Falls, Bonneville, Idaho
Burial 16 February 1980 Idaho Falls, Bonneville, Idaho

4TH CHILD Raymond Nelson MURDOCH
Birth 18 November 1911 Park City, Summit, Utah
Married Shirley Maude DICKSON
Date 27 June 1934
Place Salt Lake City, Salt Lake, Utah (Temple)
Death 30 October 1975   California
Burial   California

HUSBAND John Murray MURDOCH
Birth 1 May 1874
Place Heber, Wasatch, Utah
Married 5 January 1921
Place Salt Lake City, Utah
Death 26 Aprirl 1928
Place Heber, Wasatch, Utah
Burial 29 April 1928
Place Heber, Wasatch, Utah
Father John Murray MURDOCH
Mother Isabella CRAWFORD
Other Wives 1-Minnie Marie MILLER

WIFE Cora Leona VAIL (2)
Birth 12 March 1894
Place Chapin, Fremont, Idaho
Death 10 September 1970
Place Salt Lake City, Utah
Burial 14 September 1970
Place Midway, Wastach, Utah
Father John Riley VAIL
Mother Alice WHITE
Other Husbands 1-Jesse BIGLER
  3-James Earl WALL 4-Jack McKNIGHT
Information From Family Records

1ST CHILD Phyllis MURDOCH
Birth 17 August 1926
Married James "J" GIOLAS
Date 6 June 1947
Place Salt Lake City, Salt Lake , Utah (Temple)
Death
Burial

1 MURDOCH, James 1786-1831
1 MURDOCH, Mary MURRAY, Sp. 1782-1856

2 MURDOCH, John Murray 1820-1910
2 MURDOCH, Isabella CRAWFORD, Sp. 1836-1916

DESCENDANTS OF------

3 MURDOCH, John Murray Jr. 1874-1928
3 MILLER, Minnie Marie, Sp. 1878-1911

4 MURDOCH, Minnie B-   1905 (Stillborn)

4 MURDOCH, Annabell B-26 Feb 1906 D- 10 Sep 1907

4 DAWSON, Bessie MURDOCH B-26 Feb 1909 M-29 May 1930 D-12 Feb 1980
4 DAWSON, Oliver Painter, Sp. B-14 Sep 1899 D-28 Jan 1981
   DAWSON, Mary WOOD, Sp. (1) B-   M-   D-·

         Kamarath, Betty Jean DAWSON B-   M-
         Kamarath, Arthur, Sp. B-
      5 DAWSON, Oliver Murray B-23 Apr 1931 M-7 Aug 1955
      5 DAWSON, Goldie MEHAS, Sp. B-2 Aug 1931

            6 DAWSON, Cynthia Marie   B-18 May 1956

            6 DAWSON, Ted Murray   B-19 Apr 1959

      5 BINGHAM, Ann DAWSON B-18 Apr 1932 M-9 Sep 1957
      5 BINGHAM, Darold Leroy, Sp B-1 May 1933

            6 BINGHAM, Tod Dawson   B-16 Jul 1961 (Adopted)

            6 BINGHAM, Lisa Ann   B-15 Aug 1964 (Adopted)

      5 DAWSON, James Murdoch B-8 May 1938 M-4 Jun 1958
      5 DAWSON, Beverly SWENSON, Sp. B-11 Apr 1935

            6 DAWSON, Jeri Jean   B-22 Sep 1960

            6 DAWSON, Diane   B- 7 Dec 1962

            6 DAWSON, Bryan James   B-12 Aug 1968

            6 DAWSON, Suzanne   B-15 Jul 1972

4 MURDOCH, Raymond Nelson B-18 Nov 1911 M-27 Jun 1934 D-30 Oct 1975
4 MURDOCH, Shirley Maude DICKSON, Sp. B- 18 Nov 1911

      5 MURDOCH, RaShirl J. B-12 Apr 1937

      5 MURDOCH, Larry D.   B-29 Sep 1938 M-10 Jun 1960
      5 MURDOCH, Alice Umfress, Sp. B-13 Aug 1941

            6 MURDOCH, Bert D.   B- 8 Jul 1961

      5 MORGAN, Eulene MURDOCH B-21 Dec 1944 M-14 Jan 1966
      5 MORGAN, David William, Sp. B-6 Dec 1942

            6 MORGAN, David William   B-13 Aug 1967

            6 MORGAN, Mindy Elaine   B-27 Aug

                         3 MURDOCH, John Murray Jr. 1874-1928
DESCENDANTS OF------
                         3 VAIL, Cora Leona, Sp (2) 1895-1970
                            BIGLER, Jesse, Sp (1) B-9 Apr 1888 M-4 Nov 1915 D-5 Sep 1917
                            WALL, James Earl, Sp. (3) B-22 Jan 1891 M-3 Mar 1929 D-22 Mar 1961
                            McKNIGHT, Jack Esmond, Sp (4) B-20 Aug 1886 M-23 May 1953
                                                                     D-24 Aug 1957

4 GIOLAS, Phyllis MURDOCH B-17 Aug 1926 M-6 Jun 1947
4 GIOLAS, James "J", Sp. B-11 Nov 1923

          5 GIOLAS, James Richard B-21 Jan 1950 M-30 June 1970
          5 GIOLAS, Gaylynne MARTIN, Sp. B-26 May 1950

                 6 GIOLAS, Andrea   B-11 Jul 1974

                 6 GIOLAS, James Martin   B- 5 Jun 1978

                 6 GIOLAS, Amanda   B-29 Jan 1981

          5 GIOLAS, John Murdoch B-29 Jul 1960 (Adopted)

          5 GIOLAS, Lisa Ann   B- 3 Aug 1962 (Adopted)

OTHER CHILDREN OF Coral Leona VAIL Bigler Murdoch Wall McKnight

WORTLEY, Frieda Jessie BIGLER B-25 Aug 1916 M-9 Jul 1934
WORTLEY, John Edwin, Sp. B-

GARDNER, Wanda Leona BIGLER B-10 Apr 1918 M-25 May 1953
GARDNER, Roy, Sp. (3) B-

WALL, Earl Vail B-26 Jul 1930 M-
WALL, June   Sp. B-

Isabella Crawford Murdoch and Hyrum Chase Nicol

As a family the time has arrived when we must do what we have wanted to do for a very long time. To satisfy our feelings, we desire to express ourselves as to how we all feel about our mother; and, of course, Mother's story could not be complete without our father being included in many of Mother's experiences. Father was always affectionately concerned in supporting our mother, and likewise Mother to Father.

As a result of the Lord's working through Joseph Smith, The Church of Jesus Christ was once again established on the earth. Our grandparents on both our Mother's and Father's sides accepted the Church, joined it, and came to Utah, where they settled in the beautiful Heber Valley. Our Grandfather Murdoch married into polygamy; our mother was the last child of Grandfather's second wife, Isabella Crawford. From these grandparents was born our mother, Isabella Crawford Murdoch, on January 8, 1876. Our father, Hyrum Chase Nicol, was born February 9, 1876.

Both of these families prospered well while living in Heber City. Our parents knew each other before they could crawl, and it was said that perhaps they were wheeled around in the same baby carriage.

Because of her beautiful long hair, which flowed from the crown of her head down her back to her knees, Mother became known as Tressa. She had brown eyes and a wasp-like waist.

In Mother's school days she took part in many school activities and was popular with the young people. Since school in Heber did not extend beyond the eighth grade, Mother attended only that far. Mother, as a young lady, learned to cook and sew and take care of her small nieces and nephews.

Although Tress was courted by many young men, she saved her love for a young missionary who was soon to return from a mission to New Zealand. She and our father were married in the Salt Lake Temple for time and all eternity on September 23, 1903. From this marriage were born seven sons and one beautiful daughter, the youngest of the family The birth of a

daughter was a great event in our family. Mother often told us, "At last you have a sister." We brothers felt this too, and we could not have personally picked a more perfect sister. Donnavieve was and is wonderful. Her brothers are Thomas Murdoch, Hyrum Chase, Kenneth Crawford, John Murray, Alva Moroni and Alma Victor (twins), and Brigham Rue. After Father's return from his mission, he told us how much he had enjoyed going to the Murdoch home to see his girlfriend Tress. He told us that they would sing songs way into the evening and how enjoyable it was.

Our parents lived under the influence and light of the gospel in their own parents' homes and continued under this gospel light all their lives. As a result of this, our family was trained under this light. Family prayers were practiced and blessings were given through the priesthood for healing the sick and for giving comfort when needed.

As very young children we were taught by our mother, with our heads in her lap, to pray and to love each other. One statement we all remember saying in our prayers was taught by Mother: "Bless me to be a good boy," and to Donnavieve: "Bless me to be a good girl." We were also taught to be thankful for all our blessings—health, strength, and opportunities for development.

Our training around the home by our parents was very good for us. We always felt that we were loved and wanted because of the expressions of affection and communication expressed by their personal examples for us. This way of life, radiating from our parents to us, was a motivating force that helped us all feel like living a clean good life—no smoking, no drinking of alcohol or even tea or coffee. Swearing was a no-no. We were taught that "please," "thank you," "excuse me," "you're welcome," and so on, were magic words that if developed into a habit would lead us to become more refined and beautiful people.

The early married life of Mother and Father was

spent in the beautiful Heber Valley, where they prayer-fully planned and dreamed about their future together.

Preparatory to the opening of the Uinta Reservation for homesteading, Father and Mother made trips to Duchesne to locate homesteading property. Duchesne town was selected as home and a sawed log house was built on a town site lot. Duchesne was made the county seat, and church, school, shops, and stores were built. From this location homesteading began. Mother and Father, with other adventuresome young people, homesteaded a ranch in a settlement named Midview, which is approximately ten miles downriver east of Duchesne. This was a dry, fertile valley with fine prospects for a ranch. This property is now part of the Indian reservation and is covered with a reservoir of water. This was the beginning of hard times, especially for the women, who had to live in wagons and tents, raise children, haul water, wash by hand, sew clothes, mend, patch, darn socks, live by lantern light, and serve the men who built houses, fences, canals, and irrigation systems to bring water to the lands home-steaded. This took three to four years of very trying times. After success seemed sure, and because there was no drainage for the water, the ground became a swampland. This meant leaving the land and going back to the town of Duchesne, where there was a school which Mother insisted the boys must attend. After the failure in Midview, Mother and Father did not give up their hopes and dreams. Father became the manager of a newly developed stage and transporta-tion company. Mother again set her dreams high, and they were on their way to prosperity. This lasted four to five years. Then the automobile became available. The transportation company changed management and replaced the horse and stage coach with cars and buses. This left Mother and Father again to try pioneer-ing, and this time they settled on a ranch in Sowers Canyon, a very hot, lonesome, dry area approximately fifteen miles south of Duchesne. We lived in a log cabin with dirt floors and a dirt roof that leaked when it rained. We still had our home in Duchesne town, but it meant moving to the ranch in the summer and to Duchesne in the winter so the boys could go to school. Also it meant weekly trips with horse and wagon to attend church on Sunday. This lasted three to four years. These continuing hardships were taking their toll on Mother's health.

Father could not see Mother enduring these hard-ships any longer. So, after prayerful consideration, they disposed of the ranch in Sowers Canyon and purchased the Indian farm of approximately 248 acres,

two and a half to three miles up the Duchesne river north of Duchesne. This meant going into heavy debt and selling our Duchesne home. The Indian ranch had good possibilities and was convenient to church and school. Mother and Father's hopes and dreams had grown high again.

In their dreams and plans, they could not foresee the severe winter that would cause failure in this new venture. The snow came early in the fall, the win-ter lasted long, and it was severely cold—as much as forty degrees below zero. Food for the livestock was used up. Cattle were turned out on the range to find food for themselves, and they starved. Oth-ers huddled in washes to keep warm, and sometimes froze to death, so close together that you could walk across the washes on their frozen bodies. Debts to buy food for the livestock left on the ranch were increased. Many of the farmers and ranchers were going broke.

Father still had a home in Heber City which he had inherited from his father. This was sold to cover some of the debts incurred due to the severe winter and for interest on mortgage loans. Father had written checks to cover the debts and interest and had deposited the money received from the sale of his home in Heber in the Duchesne bank.

The following morning he was informed that the bank had closed because they could not pay off loaned money. Therefore, the check Father had written could not be honored at the bank. This caused foreclosure on all mortgaged properties. Father was broke. This was enough to break the body and soul of any ordi-nary person. However, pride still existed in Mother and Father, and they still held hope that through faith and prayer they would be able to see that somehow their children would have the opportunity to achieve the goals they had previously set for themselves after they were married. After considering all objectives and options, they decided to leave the reservation and move to Provo, where their children would have an opportunity to gain an education to enrich their lives.

With a team and wagon and some belongings, in-cluding a cage full of chickens, they headed with their children once again toward Heber City to Mother's and Father's relatives. Needless to say, this was not so happy a trip!

On arriving at Heber the decision was made to move to Provo. Life was much different in Provo after having so much in material things in Duchesne. This meant, for Father, getting a job here and there for years to come.

Then came the great depression in 1929. It was then

root hog or die, and the whole world was filled with this great depression. Our mother and father knew not where the next meal would come from or the home they would live in the next month. It was then that the family must have moved ten times. At one time we lived in tents salvaged from our Duchesne escapade. It was at this time Father mortgaged our Duchesne piano, which we were never able to recover. Mother and Father felt very bad over this loss because it deprived the children of a special musical opportunity to play the piano.

It was during these times we learned to eat oatmeal and flour mush daily. Potatoes and gravy with lots of bread and pink-eye beans were our main source of meals.

Money to pay for work performed was very scarce, and we boys learned the value of hard work and to walk, walk, and walk—from Provo to Vineyard, where Uncle Willie and Aunt Jacobina Murdoch Clegg, Mother's sister, lived. They gave us food and shelter and farm products in return for our work. We would also walk out to Orem, pick fruit, and then walk back to our rented home in Provo; then early the next day we would, arise to walk out to Orem again. This would be repeated all summer. Mother would put up fruit for the winter by cooking over a hot coal-burning stove. Under her direction we peeled and bottled, scrubbed floors, scrubbed clothes on a washing board, and did the ironing. Father's little income for his work paid the rent and utilities.

Mixed in with all this were the Sunday activities. Again we walked to church and took part. We were always so proud when Father would speak in sacrament meeting or Mother would sing or take part in drama activities.

What sleepless nights must have been Mother's and Father's, thinking of seven hungry boys and one lovely daughter to feed and clothe and to make happy. This was the time Mother used the phrase "F.H.B.," meaning "family hold back," whenever we had guests to eat with us.

We had lived in the Provo-Orem area for some time when Mother became very ill from the many trials and struggles and emotional concerns engendered by the process of life's adventures. A serious health problem occurred, and Mother needed attention all the time. The older boys had left and found work away from home. The younger boys and Donnavieve were at home. John remained out of school for one year to help care for Mother's needs.

Mother never fully recovered from this illness, and later in the twilight years of her life, Father, Alva and Brigham along with Donnavieve, were at home. Father went to work while the three children remained home with Mother. These were the last days of Mother's life.

Donnavieve relates this: "Just before Mother's death she motioned for us—Alva, Brigham, and I—toward her. We could tell she was passing on. On our knees at her bedside we prayed to the Lord for help. But Mother had passed away. As I looked up for a moment from praying I saw the spiritual image of Mother rise from her body, hover there shortly, and leave. Mother had gone to Heaven."

Our mother, Isabella Crawford Murdoch Nicol, wrote this tribute to her mother on Mother's Day, Sunday, May 14, 1939:

Mother—it seems
That in the far distant past,
I knew you in another land,
Where there were many mothers
And children.
Then one day you went away.
It was a long time,
And I missed you.

Then I was sent to find you.
I did not know you at first.
I was so small and helpless,
But you were so kind and
Loved me so much.
I soon learned to
Call you "Mother."

We spent many happy years
In this new land,
Then you went away again.
This time I seemed
To understand.
But the corner where you sat
Seemed so lonely—And your chair, I moved to
     another place—To ease the ache in my heart.

But after a while I will be called
To find you again.
I will go to a new
And beautiful world
Where there will be no more partings;
Where there will be
Many mothers and children.
There I will find you
And know you are my mother.

The following is a song written by Mother for the Murdoch Reunion, August 11, 12, 13, 1939. It follows the tune "Auld Lang Syne."

The word's gone out, the time is set,
For the meetin' o' the clan.
So pass the news frae ye to yours
To be there every man.

Frae Aug. 11th to Sunday noon
We'll talk and feast and sing
When the Murdoch's meet at Upper Falls
We'll make the welkin ring.

The trees will gee us shade by day
We'll to oor tents by night
We'll spread oor lunches on the green
And make the campfires bright.

Surrounded by grand mountains high,
Wi moon and stars above
The river runnin' gently by
Twill fill our souls wi love.

Mother passed from this life to the next on December 1, 1940, at her home in Grandview Ward, Provo, Utah. After the lovely service in the chapel, Mother was escorted for the last time up Provo Canyon to the Heber City cemetery, where her own mother and father were laid to rest.

Mother's seven sons were her pallbearers. At the gravesite the casket was opened for the last time, and Father and the children placed their rose boutonnieres around Mother's neck in necklace form as a last loving tribute to a wonderful angel Mother.

In addition to the description of the lives of Mother and Father Nicol, the following interesting stories and anecdotes are related by their children:

Mother and Father were proud people. They felt the need to lift their family to a higher destination than to be just ordinary. They both expressed through faith and good works that they could overcome all the obstacles that they had to face in the support of their family.

While living in Duchesne we would often have some of the General Authorities of the Church stay overnight at our home. Whenever we would have a meal, the food would be prepared for eating and we little kids, with our mouths watering, would be told to go outside and play, and after the adults had eaten we would be called back into the house for our turn to eat. This we did, but we never felt very good about this arrangement.

Some fifteen years later some of us were working in California, and our mother and father came down to visit. This was after the depression. While on this visit, Mother took us aside and told us she wanted to talk to us. She said, "I want to apologize to you." One of us interrupted and told Mother, "You don't have to apologize to us for anything." But Mother said, "Well, I want to tell you how I have felt for a long time." We said, "Okay." Mother said, "Do you remember out in Duchesne how, when the General Authorities came to our home and I would have you boys wait until we had eaten and you boys would come in and eat?" Someone told Mother yes, and Mother said, "I am sorry for that. Will you forgive me?" We said we would and we remember how you would stay at the table serving us until we were finished eating. We hugged each other and all was straight after so long a time.

Later Mother sent each of her children the following letter:

May 14th, 1939
Dear Son,
Sunday is Mother's Day. I will be thinking of you and they will be something like this. Son, you are bound to me by the ties of love, should you be tempted, think of me my boy and turn your thoughts to God. He will strengthen you amid all fears and temptations. Where ever you may be my love will follow you to the last and your memory will go with me where ever I may be called.
Love, Mother

Mother was strong and very defiant in the defense of her children and their actions. During our late teens and early twenties, when someone would tell Mother one of us boys was not living up to her teachings of righteous conduct, Mother would stand firm and say, "My boys know what is right and I don't believe you." We boys knew when we were wrong in our actions, and we were always impressed with Mother's defense of us, and we were made better because of this trust and love.

One special blessing was given to Mother before John was born, which she related many times. She told it this way: "I was very sick and the doctors told me that there was almost no chance at all for my child to be born alive and that there was also a big chance that I might also lose my own life. It was Stake Conference time and I knew President William Smart would be visiting. It was a Sunday morning and I felt the need for a special blessing. I told Hyrum and he said he would go to town and get President Smart. I told him not to go because President Smart would come of his free will. The day wore on and the rain was coming down. Still President Smart did not come and I was getting very ill. As the day was ending and the time was nearing 2:00 A.M. on Monday I had almost given up hope when a knock came on the door and when Hyrum opened the door there stood President Smart. He said he had started for his home in Heber City when he had an impression to return to Duchesne and come to our place. He said that at one time someone in his family had received a blessing from my father, John M. Murdoch, and that he wanted to return that blessing upon the head of one of my children. As I came into the room, President Smart was walking the floor and weeping. The tears were as large as huge raindrops. Hyrum asked him if he could not help give me the blessing I needed so much. President Smart told him that this was to be given by his hands by the prompting of the spirit. He then proceeded to give me the blessing with the following promise. He promised me 'full health and that I would live to have this child and many more.' He said that the child I was carrying would be a boy and that his name should be John Murray. He also said that he would be a counselor to bishops and would do a great work with young people." (This blessing literally came to pass, as John has been a counselor in two bishoprics and has worked successfully with young people in the Church and as a principal in the public school system.) For many years after the blessing Mother did have good health and also had four more children.

Mother loved to read the scriptures. She always taught that the scriptures held the answers to her every problem. She always had some interesting questions for any of the General Authorities who came to our home to visit. She knew the teachings of many of the Church leaders, and it was her belief that they were true, and she supported them in each of their special callings, and taught her children to do the same.

Mother really had a special way with young people; they really liked to be around her. Donnavieve recalls that when her boyfriends would come to the house, they would inform her that they had come to take her mother for a ride or an afternoon of fishing in Spring Creek. When Mother thought any of the children were parked too long outside the house, she would flip on the porch light for a warning and five minutes later would bring out a plate of cookies or some other goodie. That stopped the parking until the friends became hungry for more cookies.

Mother and Father's example and teachings have impressed us and have influenced our lives for whatever good we have done. We truly love them.

During the early years of living in Duchesne we had the "horn of plenty." Father was the leader in all church, social, and community activities. We had a spotless home, even though it was a crude frontier home. Mother scrubbed it on her hands and knees. Our home was open to all—we were the preferred on the list of all dignitaries or bums. Our table was spread with food for the body and soul, and everyone partook. At conference time the beds were spread in every room. There were music, laughter, and spontaneous skits. Mother was a riot. She had a beautiful singing voice and served home-made ice cream and delicious lemon pie or chocolate layer cake, which became the snack before going to bed. Mother was always out of homemade bread, as it was the best in Duchesne County, and was eaten with compliments and pleasure, with plenty of milk to go along with it.

On the Indian ranch there was always plenty of work, and Mother did her share in making clothing and forever patching and darning. She also fed the livestock, made soup, put up fruit, and grew vegetables, as well as the housework.

Mother and Father would plan all year for the annual trip to Heber City to see our relatives. This was a great adventure for us boys. We would get up early in the morning, harness up the horses, hook them to the wagon, and take the two-day journey. We would spend days making flippers or slingshots, and gather and select the best rocks for our ammunition. While we traveled, the rocks would be in a pile in the middle of the wagon, and we would fire away at prairie dogs or other objects.

We would always stay out overnight, camping and sleeping under the stars. If it was raining, we would sleep in the wagon or tent. It was a great feeling to gather around the campfire and hear the stories Mother and Father would tell of the pioneers and their many hardships. We would listen to their plans and anticipations for all the family. We always had our family prayers while we knelt around the campfire. To listen to those prayers by Father and Mother, it seemed like Heavenly Father was really there with us while they talked to him and asked for his Spirit to be with us.

On our arrival at Heber City we greeted all the relatives, with seven boys following along. Mother would announce, "ZCMI," meaning "Zion's Children Must Increase."

For two weeks Mother's joy and enthusiasm were boundless, as she visited all her relatives, and we kids were always getting hugged and kissed. We never went for want of food to eat. Mother, along with her sisters, would put up fruit and vegetables, which we brought back to Duchesne to last until our next round trip.

Mother always made a special effort to attend the Murdoch family reunions. She attended the first one to be held at Vivian Park in Provo Canyon. Father had made arrangements for her to ride to the reunion with a man by the name of Jake Croupe in the first car she had ever ridden in. When she arrived at Vivian Park and the relatives saw Mother, they literally dragged her from the car through the window. It was exciting to say the least. Because of the excitement, Mother forgot to pay the driver; however, she left her expensive hat in the car, which should have taken care of the bill. It was at this reunion that we learned how close brothers and sisters could become. Most of them had set up a large tent, and beds were made on the floor, where we all slept. Everyone talked all night. When we were not talking, we were giggling. We loved the feeling of togetherness, and the campfire programs were great. We loved to sing the song our great-grandfather John Murdoch had composed, "Oh Scotland My Country, My Dear Native Land." On many occasions the family would dance far into the night. It was great to be a Murdoch.

At the end of World War I Mother joined with the other folks in Duchesne to celebrate. As Mother was one of the best singing mothers in the group, she would often lend her voice to help others enjoy the activities. It was one of our delights to hear her above all others as her beautiful voice would ring out singing the good news. Whenever Mother was around, there was always music. Even on her deathbed she would sing many of the songs she had learned as a child. On one occasion while we were visiting with her she began to sing, and we listened to a song she and her sister Millicent Sophia M. (Genty) had sung before she passed away. Sometime after this we asked Mother about this event. This was her story. She said that she had gone to heaven and had met Genty and they were playing in their backyard; while then swinging together they began to sing. She said that her spirit had left her body and everything was beautiful where she was. While she was visiting with Genty, Mother said she heard Father call to her to come back. The call was so powerful that, although she didn't want to,

she heeded the call, and her spirit again entered her body. To the day of her death she insisted it was not a dream but that her visit with Genty was a reality.

Mother was always proud of her children and tried to accept each of us as individuals. She was happy when we were successful and although she attempted not to show it, she felt bad when we did not do so well. Mother was very devoted to her family and she was also very proud. Her tears would often flow when one of her "fine boys" gave a talk in church or made an advancement in the priesthood or the Boy Scout program. She thought her daughter Donnavieve was the greatest thing in the world, and they were the best of companions up until the time of Mother's death. She would tell us that if we would spend our time doing good things for someone else that it would become a habit that we would carry on throughout our lives. One of her mottoes was to be of service to each other, to the family, to the Church, and to our fellowman. She was a devoted wife and mother; she loved Father more than anything else in the world.

Throughout their lives Mother and Father were sweethearts. There was never a time when Father didn't want to buy or give something to Mother that would make her happy. One day while walking down the streets of Provo, Father saw a beautiful dress in one of the stores. He thought it would look good on Mother. He didn't have money enough to buy the dress at that time, so he asked the clerk to save it for him until he could get the money. When he went back for the dress it had been sold. Father felt disappointed, but Mother, being the kind of wife she was, told him that the thought was worth more than the dress. A very valuable lesson was taught to us at this time.

Even to the day of her death Mother was always cheerful. Though she suffered intolerable pain, and had for many years, she would never complain. In her closing hours she would sit or lie on the bed and guide her family in preparation of things around the house. When she would get so terribly ill she would always ask for the elders to come and give her a blessing. Because of her severe pain and the burden she felt she was putting on the family, Mother desired to die. On more than one occasion she asked that Father, through the Priesthood, would let her die. Father loved Mother so much that, though it deprived him of his lifelong companion, he finally consented to her plea. The last blessing he gave her was one of sadness and sorrow when he said, "I give her unto you, Lord, and your care and keeping until we shall meet again." That night Mother passed away. She was faithful to her family and the gospel unto the very end.

Mother was one of those choice spirits who came to this earth to bear her testimony to the divinity and truthfulness of the gospel. Our home was a home of faith and prayer, and she always knew that God was near to give aid when it was needed. Through the faith and prayers of Mother, several of her children have been saved from serious accidents or severe health problems. She knew that man had to do the work for the Lord but that the Lord gave the directions. One such occasion occurred when Chase, along with some of his friends, failed to come home from town on time. As the hours dragged by from early evening to early morning she became increasingly worried as to his welfare. She knelt in prayer and asked the Lord to guide them in what they should do. Upon arising from her knees she told Father that Chase was on top of the steel girders which spanned the Duchesne River and he could not get down. It was high water time and the water was raging. Father knew Mother so well that he was willing to accept her direction from the Lord. He went to the river, found Chase and his companions, and returned them safely to their homes.

When John was a young boy, living in Provo, he became very ill with "quinzy." Day after day Mother would take care of his needs. Even though he was a freshman at Provo High School, he weighed less than one hundred pounds. Mother and Father prayed for him, and Father gave him several blessings. Mother, day and night, would spend her time bathing his face with cool water to help reduce the fever. Still Mother never lost faith that he would become well. Mother would often go with him to the doctor to have his tonsils lanced. Finally she and Dad had Chase take him to the doctor to have his tonsils lanced for the sixth time. On this visit the doctor decided to remove his tonsils. He could only remove one of them by freezing it, and the other one could not be frozen so he took it out without any kind of deadening. Because John was so very sick after this, Father and Mother took him to get a blessing from Mother's brother, Uncle Joseph A. Murdoch. After Uncle Joe and Father gave him that blessing, he began to recover. We will ever be grateful to Mother that she never lost faith in the priesthood.

When Mother made soap it seemed she would burn wood for days on end to get enough ashes for the required recipe, and while Father and the older boys would cut the wood, it was the job of those younger boys to haul it in. We remember the threshers and the good food Mother would prepare and serve to all who

came. On some hot summer days Mother and Father would take us out to pick bullberries and blackberries. They grew wild and were in abundance. While Father took care of the ranch and the cattle, Mother taught the children how to unroll a large canvas, spread it under a bullberry bush, and then shake the bush to get the berries to fall onto the canvas. Sometimes instead of picking bullberries, we would pick wild blackberries, from which Mother would make the most delicious jam ever tasted.

Some of the experiences of the boys in living a particular type of lifestyle in a new western settlement would try the very sanity of any mother, let alone the rigors of a hostile country.

To mention a few, starting with the oldest sons: Tom, fourteen, and Chase, twelve, left on horseback to round up some loose cattle. Tom always liked guns, so he carried his pistol. Stopping at one of the ranches to inquire about the lost cattle, a friend of theirs entered into a conversation, asking about Tom's gun and wanting to take a look at it. In the hand-to-hand exchange the gun accidentally discharged. The bullet entered the front of the man's neck and came out the back of his neck.

Tom immediately left for his home. Chase remained to give what help he could. When Tom arrived home all excited, he announced simply to Mother and the rest of us, "I by accident just shot Len Nielson!" What a shock! Mother collapsed to the ground. At this time we all gathered around on the grass and offered a prayer for his recovery. It wasn't known until later in the day that the victim was alive because of Chase's handkerchief stuffed in both ends of the holes in his neck and his remaining there until help came. Len is alive today and occasionally sees Tom and Chase.

Then there was Kenneth, who would leave on horseback to do a sheep herding job for one of the ranchers. This would take him many miles away. Communications in those days were by yelling one to another or going on foot or horseback. One time a horseman came to Mother and gave her a message from Kenneth written with a lead bullet on a wrapping from a coffee can. The message was a cheerful greeting that Ken was well. Mother was glad to receive the welcome note. John, Alva, and Alma were riding triple on a bareback horse, all of us holding on to each other. John was a good rider but one of the twins slipped when the horse shied from something, and the three of us fell from the horse. John broke his arm in two places, more concern for Mother in the struggle for survival.

Then Alva claims that his nose holes were put there

because of a shotgun blast over the top of his head which made a hole in the corner of the room about the size of a basketball. It all happened while we kids were sitting around the kitchen table watching Tom clean a shotgun when it accidentally discharged. More woes for Mother.

Alva and Alma for their entertainment went out to the horse corral to play with the horses. They each cut themselves a willow stick and began to chase Old Burt, a work horse, around the hay stack, hitting him on the heels as they ran behind him. About the third time around, Old Burt let fly with a backward kick, striking Alma in the forehead. Down went Alma, and Alva ran for the house. Mother and Father were in town at a meeting. Ken jumped on a horse and headed for the town meeting. His brothers ran to the corral. Ken burst through the door at the meeting and yelled, "Alma has been kicked in the head by Old Burt." Again Mother had to hang on. Well, Alma survived and so did Mother.

Brigham being just a baby in the walking stage, we brothers would take him outside to play. Sometimes he would be missing and we would run to tell Mother. The first thing Mother would say was, "Go look for him around the pig pens. The old sow with her litter is loose and may eat him. And some of you go to the river; he just might have fallen." More worries for Mother, even though Brig was always found safe.

Tom, out hunting with some of his friends, came home one day in the afternoon being helped into the house and dragging his leg. A gun accident had happened (again) and Tom was shot through the leg. Mother was getting used to things now and took it in stride. Tom's leg healed well under Mother's loving care.

When Donnavieve was born things seemed to calm down, and Mother was thankful. We had all come through with our bodies still together and all well.

One of Ken's favorite stories follows: "One time I remember when I came home from the herd. I hadn't had a shave or haircut and I guess I looked pretty ratty. I tried hard to fool Mother; I knocked on the front door. She was out sweeping the back porch. She came to the door and said, "Yes?" I asked her if she had a little handout for a hungry man. She took one look at me and said (and it was the first and only time I ever heard Mother swear), 'Kenneth, damn you to hell, where have you been?' She took one swat at me with the broom, and down the street I ran. I was laughing so hard and she was laughing so hard she was crying. I had been gone a long time. As I turned around in the street, she threw her broom down, our arms went around each other, and one of the grandest, emotional lovings I ever got from my mother was that day. Then she said, 'Oh, goodness, what will the people say? What will the neighbors think of us out here like this?' So we went home. I spent a few days with the family. But time began to hang heavy so I went back to the herd."

Whenever one of us kids had any problems, whether great or small, she was always willing to listen, sit down, and talk and tell us what she thought.

But there is one thing we'll never forget. When we had the stomach ache or headache or whatever it was, out popped the castor oil bottle. It cured all ills, even to the extent that if we were on the offish side, such as little things like pushing little biddies in the ditch, out came the castor oil bottle.

Mother and Father

They say that time will heal the wounds of the soul,
But "Oh," how I long for you because I miss you so.
As a young lad I thought that I knew everything
And never had a thought for you.
At times if I could only hear you speak,
And see your tender faces,
I could tell you how I long for you and give my
    thanks
For all your graces.
But for me dear parents the road is long and wide.
If only I could live to be like you,
Then we will meet on the other side.

Brigham Rue Nicol

Mother and Father often had hilarious and fun times. We will never forget the time, so the story goes, that Mother and Father, while attending a dance in Duchesne, had their baby switched. As they left the dance they took with them someone else's baby. It was not until they reached home that the differences were noticed. At first they were angry, but when they got their own children back they found the situation quite humorous.

On another occasion while living in Provo, we had dug a large hole in our backyard which we were planning to use as a root cellar. Mother wanted to learn how to ride a bicycle so she took one of the bicycles and proceeded to try. We can hear her laugh now when someone accused her of falling from the bicycle and creating the hole in the backyard.

Mother was never one to hold bad feelings against anyone. She would often tell a humorous story, mostly about herself. We remember when she and Esther Boulton, a lifelong friend, bought a bag of candy and attended a movie. They ate all they could and then on the way home hid the rest under a culvert. The next day they sent one of the boys down to the culvert to get the candy. When he got there all he could find was the empty sack. They often laughed about hiding an empty bag and accused each other of eating the last piece.

Another interesting story is told of Mother lifting a fifteen-hundred-pound horse out of a ditch. One morning as we were beginning the day's work, we found that one of the work horses had fallen into the irrigation ditch and in her efforts to get out she had rolled onto her back. We tried as best we could to get her out but failed. Mother, hearing the commotion, came from the house and, seeing our frustration, took charge. She had us get a long pole from the fence, which she inserted under the horse and on the edge of the ditch bank. Mother at this time weighed about 130 pounds. As she walked out toward the end of the pole we saw the horse being literally lifted from the ditch. She often told the story and made the point that "there is nothing impossible if we have the desire and fortitude to accomplish the seemingly impossible."

Mother was always good to her family and supported us in all the things we wanted to do, as long as they were in harmony with the teachings of the Church. She and Father together were a good team. Their thoughts and actions were always commendable and they always set a good example for the rest of us

to follow. It seemed that they always made a special time to give council and to teach their children a better way of life. They had a deep and abiding testimony of the gospel of Jesus Christ. It was their testimony that they knew that we have a living Mother and Father in Heaven and that the truth has once more been restored to the earth. They Were sure that Joseph Smith was a true prophet and that through him the gospel had been restored. They were also sure and taught that since the time of the Restoration that every President of the Church was and is a true prophet of the living God.

As Mother and Father grew older and Mother became quite ill, Father always stayed close by. He and Mother had great faith, and they would often kneel together and pray for the things they needed most. Mother would often ask Father to get someone to administer to her, and many times after the blessing she would say, "I feel much better now."

There is a beauty among the senses that expresses the feelings of love and devotion that defy description, but our parents had this very special way about them. Mother, we remember you in this solemn hour. Our Dear Mother, we remember the days when you did dwell on earth, and your tender love watched over us like a guardian angel. You have gone from us, but the bond which unites our souls can never be severed. Your image lives within our hearts. May our merciful Father in Heaven reward you for the faithfulness and kindness you have ever shown us. May he lift up the light of his countenance upon you and grant you eternal peace. Amen.

Isabella Crawford Murdoch Nicol

Hyrum Chase Nicol Sr.-----about 1903

Isabella Crawford Murdoch Nicol

Primary Officers & Teacher Grandview Ward 1938
Isabella M. Nicol President-back row third from
left. I. Donnavieve Nicol third person second
row. Margaret Nicol fourth on second row.

Hyrum Chase & Isabella Crawford Murdoch Nicol Family

July 1940

Written on the back of the this picture is the following:
"This is the Childrens play tent they have a good time.
Tom is always making something. I wish you could see it.
The boy standing by Tom with his hat on one side, the little girl and the boy by her are neighbors children also the
one just back of John with the paper in his hand. The rest
are mine. Can you tell them by their looks? All well hope
you are. Don't think that house is ours. Ours is a little
bigger than that. I wish I could see you all but don't know
when that will be."   Love to all
                                 Tressa

Descendants of Hyrum Chase & Isabella Crawford Murdoch Nicol 1951

Left to Right: Thomas, Mother-Isabella
Hyrum Chase Jr., Dad-Hyrum, Kenneth.
Log Cabin where family lived on ranch
in Midview near Duchesne about 1909

Hyrum C. & Isabella M. Nicol Home in
Duchesne, Utah

Hyrum C. & Isabella M. Nicol Home on
"Indian Ranch" in Duchesne, Utah.

Thomas Murdoch Nicol
and
Hyrum Chase Nicol Jr.

Second from left on back row:
Isabella Crawford Murdoch Nicol
President of the Relief Society

HUSBAND   HYRUM CHASE NICOL, SR.
  Birth   9 February 1876
  Place   Heber City, Wasatch, Utah
  Married 23 September 1903
  Place   Salt Lake City, Salt Lake, Utah (Temple)
  Death   20 May 1945
  Place   Provo, Utah, Utah
  Burial   24 May 1945
  Place   Heber City, Wasatch, Utah
  Mother   (2) Johanna Christina Michalena HANDBERG
  Father   Thomas NICOL
  Other Wives

WIFE   ISABELLA CRAWFORD MURDOCH
  Birth   8 January 1876
  Place   Heber City, Wasatch, Utah
  Death   1 December 1940
  Place   Provo, Utah, Utah
  Burial   4 December 1940
  Place   Heber City, Wasatch, Utah
  Mother   Isabella CRAWFORD
  Father   John Murray MURDOCH
  Other Husbands
  Information from   Hyrum Chase Nicol Family Records

1ST CHILD   Thomas Murdoch NICOL
  Birth   26 August 1904 Heber, Wasatch, Utah
  Married Ellis Delours BETHERS
  Date   24 November 1929
  Place   Evanston, Wyoming
  Death
  Burial

2ND CHILD   Hyrum Chase NICOL Jr.
  Birth   19 March 1906 Heber, Wasatch, Utah
  Married Anne Bonnie BUSSIO
  Date   24 November 1935   T.M. 17 May 1980
  Place   Berkeley, California Washington Temp.
  Death
  Burial

3RD CHILD   Kenneth Crawford NICOL
  Birth   11 July 1908 Heber, Wasatch, Utah
  Married Charlotte LAMPMAN
  Date   12 December 1941
  Place   Pittsburg, California
  Death
  Burial

4TH CHILD   John Murray NICOL
  Birth   20 June 1912 Duchesne, Duchesne, Utah
  Married Margaret Alice NUTTALL
  Date   26 June 1936
  Place   Salt Lake City, Salt Lake, Utah Temple
  Death
  Burial

5TH CHILD   Alva Moroni NICOL
  Birth   6 March 1916 Duchesne, Duchesne, Utah
  Married Mary Martha GAYLOR
  Date   19 January 1946   T.M. 17 Feb. 1954
  Place   Provo, Utah, Utah   Manti Temple
  Death
  Burial

6TH CHILD   Alma Victor NICOL
  Birth   6 March 1916 Duchesne, Duchesne, Utah
  Married Olga ALLRED
  Date   18 August 1950
  Place   Manti, Sanpete, Utah Manti Temple
  Death
  Burial

7TH CHILD   Brigham Rue NICOL
  Birth   27 June 1919 Duchesne, Duchesne, Utah
  Married Ruby PHILLIPS
  Date   11 December 1942
  Place   Salt Lake City, Salt Lake, Utah Temple
  Death   19 November 1963   Orem, Utah, Utah
  Burial   Orem, Utah, Utah

8TH CHILD   I. Donnavieve NICOL
  Birth   12 July 1923 Provo, Utah, Utah
  Married Roy Blackburn SMITH
  Date   29 September 1949 T.M. 29 Sept. 1958
  Place   Provo, Utah, Utah   S.L.C. Temple
  Death
  Burial

1 MURDOCH, James 1781-1831
1 MURDOCH, Mary MURRAY, Sp. 1782-1856

2 MURDOCH, John Murray 1820-1910
2 MURDOCH, Isabella CRAWFORD, Sp. 1836-1916

DESCENDANTS OF------------3 NICOL, Isabella Crawford MURDOCH (Tressa) 1876-1940
3 NICOL, Hyrum Chase Sr. Sp. 1876-1945

B-Born
M-Married
T.M.-Temple Marriage
D-Died
Sp-spouse

4 NICOL, Thomas Murdoch B-26 Aug 1904 M-4 Nov 1929
4 NICOL, E Delours BETHERS, Sp. B-30 Aug 1905 D-17 Dec 1975

5 NICOL, Thomas Keith B-4 Apr 1931 M-18 Jul 1951 T.M. 18 Jul 1979
5 NICOL, Coe Arlene PENROD, Sp. B-11 Jun 1933

6 MURRAY, Kerreen De NICOL, B-11 Sep 1953 M-5 Mar 1972 T.M. 27 Jul 1978
6 MURRAY, Robert Thayne, Sp. B-19 Dec 1953

7 MURRAY, Christopher Shane B-1 Jul 1974
7 MURRAY, Thomas Clayton, B-11 Dec 1975
7 MURRAY, Angie De   B-20 Oct 1977
7 MURRAY, Breena Melissa B-27 Nov 1979

6 STRATTON, Pamela Kay NICOL B-3 Apr 1955 M-16 Oct 1974
6 STRATTON, Vern Alma, Sp. B-

7 STRATTON, Ryan Keith   B-16 Apr 1975
7 STRATTON, Vern "A"   B-10 Sep 1979

6 NICOL, Lisa Anne B-4 Aug 1961

5 CARTER, Mary Jean NICOL B-11 Jun 1933
5 CARTER, Clifford John, Sp. B-20 Oct 1919 M-
5 SATTERFIELD, Marvin, Sp. (2) B-   M-
6 CARTER, Bradford Alan B-18 Aug 1950 M-
6 CARTER, Sherry HURST, Sp. B-

7 CARTER, Cody   B-6 Dec 1976
7 CARTER, Shane,   B-

6 RADAMACHER, Cathy Jean Carter Peterson B-16-Sep 1953
6 PETERSON, Keith, Sp. (1) B-   M-
6 RADAMACHER, Don, Sp. (2) B-

7 RADAMACHER, Jason   B-
7 RADAMACHER, Melanie   B-

6 SATTERFIELD, Nicole B-3 Nov 1973

5 NEWTON, Carol De NICOL Straw B-26 Jan 1935
5 STRAW, Reéd C. Sp. (1) B-13 Sep 1932 M-4 Apr 1952
5 NEWTON, Rodney Sp. (2) B-25 Aug 1933 M-13 Dec 1968

6 STRAW, Laurie Lee   B-10 Nov 1953
6 STRAW, Randy Craig   B-
6 STRAW, Todd   B-19 Aug 1961

5 NICOL, Paul Lavar B-13 Jun 1936 M- Sep 1962
5 NICOL, Diane LOVELESS, Sp. B-22 Feb

6 NICOL, Thomas Paul   B-16 Jul 1964
6 NICOL, Steven Troy   B-22 Apr 1967

5 DRAPER, Betty Gay NICOL Christensen B-8 Jul 1938
5 CHRISTENSEN, Scott J. Sp. (1) B-23 Jun 1931 M-5 Feb 1955
5 DRAPER, Wendell, Sp. (2) B-20 Jun 1942 M-1 Sep 1978

6 ESKELSON, Terry CHRISTENSEN B-30 Aug 1956 M-1 Sep 1979
6 ESKELSON, Gene, Sp. B-

7 ESKELSON, Tiona   B-29 Jan 1978

6 CHRISTENSEN, Scott David B-27 Oct 1962
6 CHRISTENSEN, Darren John B-14 Oct 1965

4 NICOL. Hyrum Chase Jr. B-19 Mar 1906 CM-24 Nov 1935 TM-17 May 1980
4 NICOL, Bonnie Anne BUSSIO, Sp. B-5 Jul 1914

     5 HOOPER, Karen Anne NICOL B-6 June 1939 TM-23   1960
     5 HOOPER, Gerald Ray, Sp. B-27 Aug 1937

          6 HOOPER, Laurie Anne B- 3 Oct 1961
          6 HOOPER, Gary   B-   Jan 1964 D-   Jan 1964
          6 HOOPER, Boyd Claude B-25 May 1966 Twin
          6 HOOPER, Michael Chase B-25 May 1966 Twin

     5 NICOL, Alan Chase B-30 Mar 1943 CM-8 Jun 1968 TM-9 Sep 1969
     5 NICOL, Vivian Marcia MAC Kenzi, Sp., B-11 Jan 1945

          6 NICOL, Kimberly Anne B-12 May 1970
          6 NICOL, Laurel Lee   B-14 May 1971
          6 NICOL, Cristie Laurie B-18 Apr 1972
          6 NICOL, Loran Alan   B-19 Mar 1974
          6 NICOL, Bonnie Lynn B- 5 Oct 1975
          6 NICOL, Sunny Jean   B- 3 Jul 1977
          6 NICOL, Glen Cory   B-14 Nov 1979

4 NICOL, Kenneth Crawford Sr. B-11 Jul 1908 M-12 Dec 1941
4 NICOL, Charlotte LAMPMAN, Sp. B-25 Nov 1922

     5 NICOL, Cheryl M B-15 Apr 1940

     5 WHITLOCK, Donna Kay NICOL, B-6 Oct 1942 M-23 Mar 1968
     5 WHITLOCK, Charles M. Sp. B-7 Jan 1942

     5 NICOL, Kenneth Crawford Jr. B-30 Jul 1943 M-
     5 NICOL, Linda KALEBAUGH, Sp. B-26 Apr 1950

          6 NICOL, Rachel K   B-30 Dec 1968
          6 NICOL, K.C.   B- 7 Sep 1970

4 NICOL, John Murray Sr. B-20 Jun 1912 TM-26 Jun 1936
4 NICOL, Margaret Alice NUTTALL,Sp. B-30 Oct 1917

     5 NICOL, John Murray Jr. B-1 May 1937
     5 NICOL, Beverly Joan McCLURE, Sp.(1) B-5 Aug 1937 M-24 Mar 1956
     5 NICOL, Brenda DAMICO, Nuttall, Sp. (2) B-22 Dec 1941 M-11 Feb 1967

          6 RAY, Cindy NICOL B-21 Oct 1956 M-23 Aug 1980
          6 RAY, Rickey Curtis, Sp. B-2 Oct 1956

          6 NICOL, Kenneth Rex   B-16 Oct 1959
          6 NICOL, John Russell B-12 Nov 1960
          6 NICOL, Richard Mark B-11 Aug 1962
          6 NICOL, Shelly   B-20 Jul 1963
          6 NICOL, Michael Joe   B- 8 Jul 1966

          6 Nuttall, Cristie Dee B- 6 May 1962
          6 Nuttall, Nick Layne B-13 May 1963
          6 NICOL, Daman Anthony B- 8 Jun 1972

     5 NICOL, Robert Rue B-10 Mar 1941
     5 NICOL, Judy Ann BARTHOLOMEW, Sp. (1) B-2 Oct 1944 M-5 Sep 1962
     5 NICOL, Filipa Marie NARANJO Montag, Sp. (2) B-20 Oct 1946 M-6 Jul 1974

          6 NICOL, Patricia   B- 7 Mar 1964
          6 NICOL, Sandra   B- 2 Nov 1966

          6 Montag, Tony Lynn   B- 3 Jan 1967
          6 Montag, Anna Marie B-19 Apr 1968

     5 NICOL, Grant Chase B-7 Mar 1943 M-2 Sep 1961
     5 NICOL, Helen Mae FRANCE, Sp. B-10 Jan 1943

          6 NICOL, Jeffrey Grant B-20 Dec 1962
          6 NICOL, Lori Jane   B-15 Apr 1965

5 NICOL, William Wayne B-17 Nov 1944 M-16 Jul 1970
5 NICOL, Janice Lorraine HATCH, Sp. (1) B-30 Sep 1946 M-16 Jul 1970
5 NICOL, Glenda Sue DIXON Climer, Sp. (2) B-4 Jan 1954 M-5 Oct 1973

      6 NICOL, Suana   B-31 Jan 1971

      6 Climer, Michelle Kay B-23 Feb 1972
      6 NICOL, Chad Wayne   B-24 Aug 1974

5 NICOL, Daved Lee B-2 Jun 1948 TM-16 Apr 1968
5 NICOL, Diana Lynn NIELSEN, Sp. B-20 Jan 1948

      6 NICOL, Jilynn   B- 7 Feb 1974
      6 NICOL, Amie   B- 1 Aug 1976
      6 NICOL, Gregory Douglas B-23 Sep 1978

5 NICOL, Lynn James B-5 Jun 1956 M-12 Jun 1976
5 NICOL, Marsha Lynn ZAELIT, Sp. B-2 Jun 1957

      6 NICOL, Curtis James B-14 Oct 1977
      6 NICOL, Stacy Marie   B-14 Mar 1980

4 NICOL, Alva Moroni B-6 Mar 1916 CM-19 Jan 1946 TM-17 Feb 1954
4 NICOL, Mary Martha GAYLOR, Sp. B-20 Mar 1925

   5 NICOL, Richard Allen B-11 Oct 1946
   5 NICOL, Mary Jane EBY, Sp. B-1 Jun 1956 M-

      6 NICOL, Justin   B-28 Nov 1975

   5 CARPENTER, Janet NICOL B-13 APR 1949 M-14 Oct 1966 TM
   5 CARPENTER, Robert John, Sp. B-14 Sep 1948

      6 CARPENTER, Richard John B-12 Oct 1967
      6 CARPENTER, Eric David   B-15 Feb 1971

   5 NICOL, Steven Ted B-8 Jul 1950
   5 NICOL, Elaine BIGELOW, Sp. B-   M-20 Sep 1968

      6 NICOL, Stephanie   B- Jul 1969
      6 NICOL, Jalayne   B-   Jul 1970

   5 VAN RIJ, Tressa NICOL B-15 Apr 1952 M-11 Sep 1970
   5 VAN RIJ, Francis Paul, Sp. B-

      6 VAN RIJ, Heather   B-23 May 1975

   5 CHAMBERLAIN, Shauna NICOL B-18 May 1954 M-29 Dec 1979
   5 CHAMBERLAIN, Spencer, Sp. B-22 Nov 1950

   5 NICOL, Gayle B-16 Oct 1959

   5 NICOL, Scott Brady B-6 May 1963

      6 Katrina   B-11 Jun 1980

4 NICOL, Alma Victor B-6 Mar 1916 (Twin) TM-18 Aug 1950
4 NICOL, Olga ALLRED, Sp. B-16 Apr 1920

   5 CARTER, Sandra Kay NICOL B-25 Feb 1955 TM-19 Aug 1977
   5 CARTER, Roger, Sp. B-12 Jun

      6 CARTER, Jared William B-14 Jul 1978
      6 CARTER, David Alma   B-14 May 1980

   5 NICOL, Lynda Gayle B-27 May 1956

   5 MECHAM, Tanya Marie NICOL B-13 Dec 1957 M-3 Jul 1976
   5 MECHAM, Terry Lee, Sp. B-

      6 MECHAM, Casey   B- 5 Jul 1977
      6 MECHAM, Jill   B-31 Oct 1979

   5 NICOL, Diana B-8 Dec 1960

4 NICOL, Brigham Rue   B-27 Jun 1919 TM-11 Dec 1942 D-19 Nov 1963
4 NICOL, Ruby PHILLIPS, Sp.   B-6 June 1923

    5 NICOL, Michael Rue   B-2 Dec 1943 TM-18 Aug 1967
    5 NICOL, Marsha Rae MARLEY, Sp. B-1 May 1944

        6 NICOL, Holly Ann   B-18 Feb 1969
        6 NICOL, Natalie Dawn   B-23 Dec 1970
        6 NICOL, Christie Michelle B-29 Oct 1973
        6 NICOL, Marchel Susanne   B- 7 Jul 1975
        6 NICOL, Rachael Diane   B-28 May 1978

    5 NICOL, Phillip Kent   B-21 Mar 1947 TM-21 Aug 1976
    5 NICOL, Marilyn MIGNON, Bagley, Sp. B-4 Mar 1953

        6 NICOL, Courtney   B- 4 Oct 1979

    5 NICOL, Hyrum Dale B-22 Feb 1949

    5 NICOL, Kevin Rex   B-27 Aug 1953 TM-4 Jun 1976
    5 NICOL, Jolene BROWN, Sp. B-19 Sep 1954

        6 NICOL, Mark Robert   B- 4 Jan 1978

    5 ROWLEY, Kathryne NICOL   B-14 May 1957 TM-23 Mar 1979
    5 ROWLEY, Robert Lewis, Sp.   B-11 Jul 1957

        6 ROWLEY, Rogan Robert   B-22 Dec 1979

4 SMITH, I Donnavieve NICOL   B-12 Jul 1923 CM-29 Sep 1949 TM-29 Sep 1958
4 SMITH, Roy Blackburn, Sp. B-9 May 1917

    5 SMITH, Carol Lynn B-22 Sep 1938 D-11 Jan 1964

    5 SMITH, Roy Burdell B-2 Oct 1943 TM-14 Jul 1967
    5 SMITH, Carolyn Kirkman, Sp. B-16 Jul 1945

        6 SMITH, Cory Burdell   B-14 Jun 1969
        6 SMITH, Christina Carolyn B-28 Feb 1973
        6 SMITH, Donald Roy   B- 8 Sep 1974
        6 SMITH, Chad Tyler   B- 6 Nov 1977
        6 SMITH, Belinda Sue   B-10 Feb 1980

    5 SMITH, Garyl Duane B-22 May 1946 TM-13 Jan 1967
    5 SMITH, Jacquelynn JOHNS, Sp. B-30 Jan 1946

        6 SMITH, Alissa Danette   B- 8 Dec 1967
        6 SMITH, Heidi Lynn   B-30 Apr 1974
        6 SMITH, Garyl Juane Jr.   B-28 Oct 1976
        6 SMITH, Gregory Tobias   B-20 May 1978

    5 RICHARDS, Tressa Colleen SMITH B-2 Apr 1952 TM-10 Sep 1971
    5 RICHARDS, Arlyn Bingham, Sp. B-9 Dec 1949

        6 RICHARDS, Darren Clark   B-24 Apr 1974
        6 RICHARDS, Philip Lloyd   B-22 Jun 1976
        6 RICHARDS, Kenneth Roy   B-10 May 1979

    5 SMITH, Travis B. B-5 May 1956 TM-8 Sep 1978
    5 SMITH, Jayne THOMPSON, Sp. B-28 Apr 1959

William Murdoch, Janet Lennox, and Mary Reid Lindsay

William P. Murdoch was the eighth child and youngest son of James and Mary Murray Murdoch. He was born at Gaswater, Ayrshire, Scotland, July 3, 1825. He was christened July 24, 1825, in the Parish Church at Auchinleck. His parents were Presbyterians. His early history is one of hardship and trial. He was only six years of age when his father died, October 20, 1831, leaving his mother in very humble circumstances. The father lost his life trying to rescue a young man by the name of George Baird of Dalford, who had gone down into a mine shaft and was overcome by "black damp." They both died.

Just as soon as he was old enough to herd a few sheep on the bonnie heathered hills close by, he was hired out to do that kind of work, to earn a little to help provide for himself and assist his widowed mother. She saw to it that he had a little schooling during the winter months. He was provided with yarn by his thrifty mother, and he learned to knit stockings for himself and others. Very shortly before his death, he knitted a pair of stockings for each of his children. When nearly twenty years of age, William went to work in the coal mines. Wages for farm work were very low and he wanted to earn more money so he could someday marry and have a home of his own.

He soon found in the person of a very choice young woman who lived nearby named Janet or "Jessie" Lennox, a suitable mate, and they were married June 23, 1846, at Old Cumnock, Ayrshire, Scotland. Janet Lennox and William Murdoch's first child was a girl whom they named Elizabeth after her grandmother. She was born to them while they were living in Gaswater, Ayrshire, Scotland in 1847. Next to be born were two sons. James "D," in 1850, was named after William's father, and David Lennox, in 1852, was named after Janet's father. Both boys were born in a place called Cronberry, Ayrshire, Scotland. Then came a daughter in 1854 whom they named Mary after her grandmother Mary Murray Murdoch. However, to their sorrow she lived only eleven days and then was interred in Auchinleck Churchyard. Their third daughter was born in 1855 and was named Janet after her mother. Both Mary and Janet had been born in Gaswater also. The sixth and last child, Margaret, was born in 1858 in Ponesk, Ayrshire, Scotland. They again had cause to sorrow when their oldest daughter, Elizabeth, passed away in her seventeenth year in 1864. She was buried in Muirkirk, Ayrshire, Scotland where they were living, and her mother was placed beside her in 1877.

A few years after William's marriage, his brother John, sister Mary, and his mother joined The Church of Jesus Christ of Latter-day Saints, and shortly afterwards his wife Janet became convinced that it was the true church and was baptized October 8, 1853, by James Gallacher. William at this time could see no need of his making a change. He was already a member of the good old Church of Scotland that his forefathers had lived and died members of. They were all good, honest, religious people, and he felt sure they were safe in heaven, so why should he make a change? He was highly respected in the community and it was considered a disgrace to join the despised Mormons. His wife, though, fully convinced of the truth, went about her daily tasks quietly so as to keep peace and love in the home. She cherished the hope that at some future time her husband would come to see the truth and beauty of the gospel. She wanted also to teach it to her children, and ultimately go to Zion and make her home among the Saints in Utah.

Uncle Willie, as he was usually called, was a very steady, sober man, very dependable, trustworthy, and a willing worker. He did well in a temporal way and in time became underground manager in one of the coal pits owned by the Eglinton Coal and Iron Company. He lived in the village of Muirkirk, Ayrshire, Scotland where he was considered one of the most prominent men in the village. Getting better pay than the common miners, he was able to and did send his two sons, James "D" and David L., to some of the best schools in the country after they graduated from the village school. They both received a very good education and they became prominent young men in the community where they lived.

Uncle Willie, knowing the faith and hope his dear wife had cherished for so many years and seeing her health failing day by day, came to the conclusion that he had not really taken the interest he should have taken in his dear wife's ideas regarding religion. Now that she seemed likely to be taken by death in a very short time, he began to investigate the doctrines of the Latter-day Saints. In a short time he and his daughters Janet and Margaret were baptized October 8, 1877, by Elder David Milne, just two months before his dear Jessie, as he called her, passed away.

Before Jessie passed away she had the blessed assurance that as soon as convenient her husband and the family would make their home among the Saints in Utah. She died in Kilmarnock, Ayrshire, Scotland, on December 20, 1877. She was an exceptional woman in more ways than one. In death she rejoiced in seeing her fond hopes realized and could lay her weary, wasted body calmly down to rest in peace in the Kirkyard at Muirkirk, where their daughter Elizabeth had been buried some years before. Having performed the sad task of laying the body of his dear Jessie in the silent grave, William and his daughters continued to live in Gilmour Street, Kilmarnock, until they had all arrangements made for going to Utah. About the first of May 1878, they left Kilmarnock and went by train to Glasgow, where they joined David and his young wife. John Adamson, a young man who was engaged to marry his daughter, Margaret, was with them. From Glasgow they went to Liverpool where they joined a company of Mormon emigrants on board a steamship in which they crossed the Atlantic Ocean in about ten days. They left May 24, 1878, on the steamship Nevada. Very different was this voyage from the nine weeks spent by Uncle John on the sailing ship in 1852 with poor accommodations and very little food to eat. Accommodations on the steamship were very good and the food good and plentiful, so they missed most of the trying experiences of early-day travel on their journey to Utah. The journey by train from New York was finished in three days, so that it was only two weeks from Kilmarnock to Salt Lake City.

Letters had been received stating the date of their leaving Liverpool and their probable arrival in Utah. Uncle John, William M. Giles, and William Lindsay met them in Salt Lake City with two teams of horses and wagons. They prepared to take them to Uncle John's home in Heber.

The trip from Salt Lake to Heber took just one long day. They all arrived safely in Heber the next day and the brothers and sisters met, having been separated many years. It was a joyful meeting. At last they were all reunited in this blessed land and all were now members of the true church. They had left their homes and native land to cast their lot with the Saints in Utah's peaceful valleys.

Much credit is due to Uncle Willie. After he did become convinced of the truth, he gave up a good position where he was respected in his community, and in his old age came to a new country, among strangers, to make a new home. However, they all seemed contented and went to work at any little job they could find.

On June 29, 1882, in the Endowment House in Salt Lake City, Utah, William married again to a woman named Christina Graham. She was also born in Scotland and had been baptized earlier when about twelve years old. This marriage wasn't entirely satisfactory and they later divorced. They had no children.

Uncle Willie bought a land claim up on Lake Creek, four miles east of Heber, and also a team of horses. With the help of his son-in-law John Adamson, they built houses, stables, sheds, and fences. Soon they had one of the best farms on Lake Creek. Of course they had to hire help until they learned how to irrigate the crops and many other things, but they had the money to do so. Uncle Willie's experience on the farm as a young boy with cattle and sheep and horses was a valuable asset to him now. In order to irrigate part of his land it was necessary to make a new irrigation ditch in which about twelve other farmers were interested further down the ditch. They all agreed to help put the ditch clear through so all could get the use of the water. Some of them seemed to have no further interest in it after it reached their land, but Uncle Willie, although his land was at the head of the ditch, helped through to the lower end, so all could benefit. John Adamson, Margaret's husband, helped him considerably the first five or six years. He stayed with him until the farm was fenced and under cultivation.

William Murdoch became an American citizen March 18, 1884. He received his temple endowment June 29, 1882. About 1887, he married Mary Reid Lindsay, the widow of Samuel Lindsay, who had four children, the oldest being fourteen at the time of their marriage. William and Mary had three children: a son named William Louis and two daughters, Mary

Murray and Lizziebell. Uncle Willie was quite robust, even in his old age, and a very industrious man. He was sixty-nine years old at the birth of his last child.

When about seventy-five years of age he sold his farm and bought a house and lot in Heber, where he lived some twelve or thirteen years. He was cautious in making transactions, but once made, he would stand by them regardless of the consequences. He was honest and honorable in his dealings with his fellow men. Being very industrious himself, he despised laziness and shiftlessness in others.

He held the office of a high priest in The Church of Jesus Christ of Latter-day Saints for some years before his death, which took place on March 12, 1913.

Uncle Willie was a highly respected member of the community and left a splendid record behind him as a true friend, a good neighbor, and a respectable citizen. He set a good example in every way for his children and grandchildren to follow. He had a total of nine children and thirty-eight grandchildren. Many good things were said of him at his funeral services. He had filled a long life of usefulness, being eighty-eight years of age at the time of his death. He was buried in the Heber City Cemetery.

From writings of William Lindsay

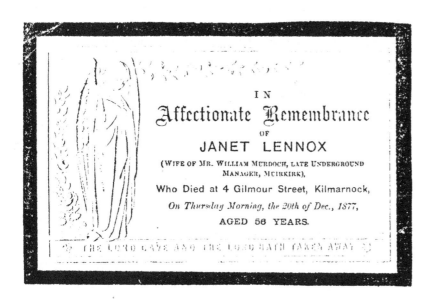

Mary Reid Lindsay Murdoch

Mary Reid was born October 23, 1851, in Glasgow, Ayrshire, Scotland, to James and Elizabeth Cummings Reid. She was the third child in a family of nine. Her parents and four children left Scotland for America in 1856, enduring many hardships and suffering from exposure. Mary, a child of five years, walked all the way. She was in the same company as "Wee Granny" (Mary Murray Murdoch), the ill-fated Martin-Willey Company.

They moved to Heber Valley in the fall of 1862 and later were called to help settle Cache Valley. Mary returned to Heber and worked for various people, doing general housework.

Samuel Lindsay and Mary Reid were married December 31, 1871, in Heber. Samuel Lindsay was born March 4, 1851, in Lanarkshire, Scotland, to William

and Christina Howie Lindsay. He was the fifth in a family of nine. His father was killed in a mine accident in 1861.

In the spring of 1862 his widowed mother and family of eight made plans to come to Utah. They left Kilmarnock on April 19 1862, and sailed from Liverpool April 22, landing in New York on June 4. They traveled on to Florence, Nebraska, where they waited for ox teams to take them to Utah, arriving in Heber on September 21, 1862.

Samuel and Mary Reid Lindsay had the following children: William C., James Reid, Margaret, and Georgiana. They homesteaded a plot in Center Creek. Samuel worked part-time in the mines in Park City to earn the necessary means to provide for his family, and while there, in 1880, he contracted an illness which caused his sudden death on July 27, 1880.

The same pioneer faith and determination that

helped them cross the plains made it possible for Mary to carry on now in her time of grief. With the help of her children, she made a brave struggle, with no complaint and with a grateful heart for any kindness shown her by friends and relatives.

In 1887 she was married to William Murdoch, a widower, who had arrived from Scotland in 1878 and had located in Lake Creek. His family, two sons and two daughters, were all married. They were: James "D," David L., Margaret Adamson, and Janet Baird. William and Mary had three children, namely: William Louis, Mary Murray, and Lizziebell.

They sold their Lake Creek property and moved to Heber, where they lived many years. William Murdoch passed away in March, 1913, and was buried in the city cemetery in Heber, Utah.

Mary was again called to mourn the loss of loved ones with the death of her daughter Margaret Lindsay Burt, in January, 1916, and again in the death of her daughter Mary in November, 1918. After this sorrow, she felt it best to sell her home and move to Idaho to be near her children living there and her two sisters and a brother at Lorenzo, Idaho. She passed away there June 22, 1929, and was brought to Heber City for burial beside her first husband, Samuel Lindsay. She had led a long and useful life.

Parents and Family of
Mary Reid Lindsay Murdoch

James Reid was born on January 12, 1816, in Iuch, Wigton, Scotland, to John and Mary Murray Reid. His father was a seaman and died at sea when James was a very small boy His mother later married John Muir.

Elizabeth was born July 8, 1824, at Monkton, Ayr, Scotland, to Louis and Elizabeth Wilson Cummings.

They were married about 1841 and lived in Glasgow, Scotland. James was a leather worker and made and repaired shoes most of his life. Elizabeth was a skilled needle worker and did eyelet embroidery by contract for the royalty of Scotland. They were blessed with a family of nine children, five born in Scotland. They were: Elizabeth Reid Smith, William G. Reid, Mary Reid Lindsay Murdoch, James, John, Margaret Ann Nelson, Isabell Muir, and Robert.

They joined the LDS Church in Scotland and immediately made plans to come to the valleys of the mountains. They left their native land March 17, 1856, crossed the ocean in a small and poorly equipped sailing vessel, and were eight weeks reaching New York. Finally they reached Florence, Nebraska, and made plans to travel with the James Willie Handcart company across the plains to Zion. They, along with all others, endured great hardships and suffering. A near tragedy came to them one night when their daughter Lizzie fell through the ice while attempting to get a bucket of water from the stream nearby. They worked with her all night, taking turns warming blankets over the campfire to keep her alive and as comfortable as possible. When morning came and they were packed and ready to start on the day's journey they found that the father's fingers and mother's feet were frozen. On they trudged each day, paying no attention to their own ailments. The mother's toes rotted off before they reached their destination. Due to these injuries they were not able to work at their trades for many months. They were taken care of by his mother and stepfather, James and Mary Murray Muir, who had arrived in 1853 with the Appleton Harmon Company. They settled in Heber Valley in the fall of 1862 and lived in the fort for some time. Later they built a home on a lot now located about Second West and Center. They also tried to prove up on a claim in Daniels Creek, but because of Indian troubles were advised to give it up. James Reid was a member of the Wasatch Militia.

A few years later they were called to help settle Cache Valley, and spent their remaining years in Smithfield. James continued his work there, in charge of the shoe repairs in the U & I Shoe Shop for many years. He passed away January 12, 1886. He was buried in Smithfield City Cemetery, Utah. Elizabeth passed away August 1, 1910, at the home of a daughter in Lorenzo, Idaho. She was laid to rest beside her husband in Smithfield.

(Taken from "How Beautiful Upon the Mountains," by Wasatch County Daughters of Utah Pioneers.)

William Murdoch's Home in Heber City, Utah

William Murdoch

Picture taken by David L. Murdoch
Muirkirk, Ayrshire, Scotland

Four generations, oldest to youngest: William
Murdoch, David Lennox, William, and David Lennox Jr.

William Murdoch, Margaret,   Janet Lennox Murdoch   Janet, James "D", Elizabeth,
Janet, and Janet L. Murdoch   Margaret, and David Lennox

I went to Stellenbosch in
1857

was paid at the rate
of 9/6 per her shift for
about 18 months
then got the onset
of Heidenbank Pit
by contract
then became Manager

Manager in 1860
and was stein by the surface
the rates being as under
common coal 1/6 per 100 tons

gross

this amounted to about

=8 per month for about
for about 8 years

about 1865 I got
1/ added to the .
Gas coal rate which
maid my pay snuch
like £2 or 3 per month
more the Gas coal output
being large owing to a new
plate and in 1872

I got an advance which
maid my pay £16 per week

this seems very small
only about £1.30 per year
and I thought it was
the dirt as I can come
looking back over the work
then 6 pits sunk and the
work done in the mine down
though the Coy Book (out of sight
was made by myself with the lift
of the other money too.

HUSBAND William MURDOCH
Birth   3 July 1825
Place   Gaswater, Ayrshire, Scotland
Chr.   24 July 1825 Auchinleck,Ayr,Scot
Death   12 Mar 1913 Heber, Wasatch, Utah
Burial   14 Mar 1913 Heber, Wasatch, Utah
Father   James MURDOCH
Mother   Mary MURRAY
Other Wives (2)Christina GRAHAM 29 Jun 1882
              (Divorced - no children)
Information From Ruby E. Murdoch Hooper

WIVES (1) Janet LENNOX   (3) Mary (REID) LINDSAY
Birth   24 Sep 1821   23 Oct 1851
Place   Moor,Old Cumnock,Ayr,Sctl   Glasglow,Lanark,Scotland
Chr.   21 Oct 1821,Old Cumnock,Ayr,Sctl.
Married   23 June 1846   26 Nov 1887
Place   Farm of Mulr, Cumnock,Ayr,Sctl Heber, Wasatch, Utah
Death   20 Dec 1877 Kilmarnock,Ayr,Sctl 22Jun1929 Lorenzo, Idaho
Burial   Muirkirk, Ayr, Scotland   Heber, Wasatch, Utah
Father   David LENNOX   James REID
Mother   Elisabeth TEMPLETON   Elizabeth CUMMING
Other Husbands   (1)Samuel LINDSAY 31 Dec 1871

1ST CHILD Elizabeth MURDOCH
Birth   18 Apr 1847 Gaswater, Ayr, Scotland
Death   24 Mar 1864 (Age 17 years)
Burial   Mulrkirk, Ayr, Scotland

2ND CHILD James "D" MURDOCH
Birth   3 Jan 1850 Cronberry, Ayr, Scotland
Married   (1) Lizzie LINDSAY (2) Eliza THACKERAY
Date   1 Jan 1883   14 Nov 1898
Place   ParkCity, Summit, Utah Croydon,Morgan, Utah
Death   2 Dec 1924 Salt Lake City, Salt Lake, Utah
Burial   4 Dec 1924 Salt Lake City, Utah Mt. Olivet Cem

3RD CHILD David Lennox MURDOCH
Birth   13 Jan 1852 Cronberry, Ayr, Scotland
Married   Elizabeth Pinkerton THYNE
Date   18 Apr 1878
Place   Glasglow, Lamark, Scotland
Death   24 Apr 1928 Salt Lake City, Utah
Burial   27 Apr 1928 Salt Lake City, Utah

4TH CHILD Mary MURDOCH
Birth   9 Sep 1854 Gaswater, Ayr, Scotland
Death   20 Sep 1854 (Age 11 Days)
Burial   Auchinleck Churchyard, Scotland

5TH CHILD Janet MURDOCH
Birth   18 Oct 1855 Gaswater, Ayr, Scotland
Married   William BAIRD
Date   5 Feb 1880
Place   Salt Lake City, Salt Lake, Utah
Death   23 Sep 1898 Carey, Blaine, Idaho
Burial   Sep 1898 Carey, Blaine, Idaho

6TH CHILD Margaret MURDOCH
Birth   27 Aug 1858 Ponesk, Ayr, Scotland
Married   John ADAMSON
Date   16 Jan 1879
Place   Salt Lake City, Salt Lake, Utah
Death   29 Oct 1915 Carey, Blaine, Idaho
Burial   2 Nov 1915 Carey, Blaine, Idaho

NOTE: Children 1,2,3,4,5, & 6 have Janet LENNOX
       as their mother.

NOTE: Children 7,8, & 9 have Mary Reid LINDSAY
       as their mother.

7TH CHILD William Louis MURDOCH
Birth   4 Apr 1888 Heber, Wasatch, Utah
Married   Elizabeth IVIE
Date   1 Oct 1913
Place   Provo, Utah, Utah
Death   6 Dec 1937 Idaho Falls, Bonneville, Idaho
Burial   9 Dec 1937 Archer Madison,Idaho Sutton Cem

8TH CHILD Mary Murray MURDOCH
Birth   26 Feb 1891 Heber, Wasatch, Utah
Death   9 Nov 1918 (Age 27 years)
Burial   Heber, Wasatch, Utah

9TH CHILD Lizziebell MURDOCH
Birth   25 Jan 1894 Heber, Wasatch, Utah
Married   Hugh "J" DAVIS
Date   26 Oct 1912
Place   Provo, Utah, Utah
Death
Burial

WILLIAM MURDOCH

&

WIVES

(THREE GENERATIONS)

DESCENDANTS

ELIZABETH MURDOCH
18 Apr 1847-24 Mar 1864

		BIRTH	DEATH

JAMES "D" MURDOCH
3 Jan 1850-2 Dec 1924
Married 1 Jan 1883
Lizzie Lindsay (1)
6 Jun 1858-4 Dec 1896

MURDOCH

	BIRTH	DEATH
William Wallace	30 Oct 1883	19 Jul 1954MC
Effie Lisle	24 Jun 1886	24 Oct 1969MC
Robert Bruce	29 Sep 1889	20 Jan 1905D
Ruby Estella	9 Dec 1892	26 Feb 1976MC

Married 14 Nov 1898
Eliza Thackeray (2)
21 Feb 1870 27 Nov 1938

	BIRTH	DEATH
James Douglas	26 Sep 1899	14 Jan 1934MC
Helen Janet	17 Nov 1902	15 Oct 1969MC
Gwendolyn Thackeray	6 Jan 1904	3 Oct 1981MC
Margaret Eliza	1 Jul 1908	8 Dec 1956MC

WILLIAM MURDOCH
Born 3 Jul 1825
Where Gaswater,Ayr,Sctl
Died 12 Mar 1913
Where Heber,Wastch,Utah

Married 23 Jun 1846
Where Farm of Muir
  Cumnock,Ayrshire,Sctl

JANET LENNOX (1)
Born 24 Sep 1821
Where Moor,OldCumnock
   Ayrshire,Sctl
Died 20 Dec 1877
Where Kilmarnock,Ayr,
   Sctl

Married 29 Jun 1882-Div
Where Salt Lake City,Ut.
CHRISTINA GRAHAM (2)
Born Apr 1835
Where Perth,Perth,Sctl
Died ?
  (No Children)

Married 26 Nov 1887
Where Heber,Wastch,Utah
MARY REID LINDSAY (3)
Born 23 Oct 1851
Where Glasgow,Lanark
   Sctl
Died 22 Jun 1929
Where Lorenzo, Idaho

DAVID LENNOX MURDOCH
13 Jan 1852-24 Apr 1928
Married 18 Apr 1878
Elizabeth Pinkerton Thyne
12 Nov 1851-16 Apr 1927

MURDOCH

	BIRTH	DEATH
William	15 Sep 1878	8 Oct 1940MC
Elizabeth P. T.	17 Mar 1880	19 Jun 1882D
James Thyne	19 Jun 1881	11 Aug 1881D
Janet Lennox	7 Aug 1884	24 Apr 1953M
Veronica	3 Jul 1886	5 Apr 1896D
Nora Thyne	7 Feb 1890	9 May 1959MC
Mary Murray	23 Jul 1891	
Afton Lennox	2 Jun 1894	MC
Stillborn-Twin Girls Before Oct 1882		

MARY MURDOCH
9 Sep 1854-20 Sep 1854

JANET MURDOCH (1)
18 Oct 1855-23 Sep 1898
Married 5 Feb 1880
William Baird
3 Nov 1849-28 Jun 1946

Married 29 Jan 1902
Isabelle Sneddon (2)
3 Mar 1868-15 Mar 1938

BAIRD

	BIRTH	DEATH
John "D"	15 Mar 1881	8 Nov 1960MC
Jessie Lennox	15 Aug 1882	15 Apr 1964MC
William	6 Oct 1884	13 Jul 1956MC
Elizabeth Marshall	25 Mar 1887	5 Jul 1901D
Ernest Wallace	17 Apr 1889	19 Jul 1975MC
James Alexander	26 Feb 1891	12 Aug 1956MC
David	23 Dec 1892	MC
Bruce	6 Apr 1896	24 Dec 1972MC
Margaret	20 Sep 1898	25 Oct 1898D
Thomas Sneddon	8 Nov 1903	29 Jul 1962MC

MARGARET MURDOCH
27 Aug 1858-29 Oct 1915
Married 16 Jan 1879
John Adamson
22 May 1849-29 Oct 1915

ADAMSON

	BIRTH	DEATH
John Robert	25 Nov 1879	7 Jul 1920MC
William Lennox	11 Feb 1882	19 May 1967MC
Isabelle	1 Jan 1885	29 Oct 1915MC
James Murray	13 Jun 1887	29 Oct 1915D
David Edwin	9 May 1891	3 Mar 1975MC
Edith Mary	6 Jun 1893	6 Jul 1977MC

WILLIAM LOUIS MURDOCH
4 Apr 1888-6 Dec 1937
Married 1 Oct 1913
Elizabeth Ivie
21 Aug 1892-19 Aug 1960

MURDOCH

	BIRTH	DEATH
Marie	22 Jun 1914	9 May 1980MC
Margaret Ellen	5 Jun 1915	M
Jennett	9 Aug 1920	MC
Lennox Merl	9 Jan 1923	MC
Mary Ivie	25 Jan 1929	10 Dec 1968
David Louis	16 Jul 1931	MC

MARY MURRAY MURDOCH
26 Feb 1891-9 Nov 1918

LIZZIEBELL MURDOCH
25 Jan 1894-
Married 26 Oct 1912
Hugh "J" Davis
22 Sep 1890-15 Sep 1957

DAVIS

	BIRTH	DEATH
William Murdoch	9 Apr 1913	MC

Married 31 Dec 1871
(1)SAMUEL LINDSAY
4 Mar 1851-27 July 1880

*

M-Married
C-Had Children
D-Died Young

LINDSAY

	BIRTH	DEATH
William C. Lindsay	3 Jan 1873	6 Dec 1945
Unmarried		
James Reid Lindsay	4 Jun 1875	30 Nov 1955
Married 1 Mar 1893 to Annette Olsen		
Margaret Lindsay	12 Jan 1878	9 Jan 1917
Married 16 Nov 1897 to Peter Burt		
Georgiana Lindsay	9 Jan 1881	6 Dec 1933
Married 11 Jun 1902 to Thomas Walker		

(Information from families and Ruby E. Murdoch Hooper records)

603

Elizabeth Murdoch

Elizabeth Murdoch was born April 18, 1847, the oldest child of Janet Lennox and William Murdoch. Her parents lived in Gaswater, Ayrshire, Scotland at the time of her birth. Two brothers, James "D" and David Lennox, and three sisters, Mary, Janet, and Margaret were born into the family in the next eleven years. Sister Mary died shortly after her birth and was buried in Auchinleck Churchyard, Ayrshire, Scotland.

Elizabeth probably was depended upon by her mother to help tend her younger brother and sisters and with household duties. She attended school also. (Janet Gill has a book she used before James "D" used it in school.)

Elizabeth's father worked as an agricultural laborer and in the mines. He eventually became the underground manager of the Eglinton Coal and Iron Works in Muirkirk, Ayrshire, Scotland. They lived in the Linkieburn House, and because her father was better paid than the common miner, the family enjoyed a better standard of living.

Elizabeth was growing into a pretty young lady when she died, at just age seventeen, on March 24, 1864. She was buried in Muirkirk, Ayrshire, Scotland. Her mother was buried beside her thirteen years later. The rest of her family immigrated to America.

James "D" Murdoch, Lizzie Lindsay, and Eliza Thackeray

James "D" Murdoch was born January 3, 1850, in the small village of Cronberry in the Parish of Auchinleck, Ayrshire, Scotland. His parents were William Murdoch and Janet Lennox Murdoch. James was the second child in the family. His sister Elizabeth was older and his brother David Lennox and sisters Mary, Janet, and Margaret were younger. Elizabeth died at age seventeen and Mary shortly after her birth.

James's father worked as an agricultural laborer and eventually went to work in the mines where more money could be earned to support his growing family. They lived in William's boyhood town of Gaswater. James's grandmother "Wee Granny" (Mary Murray Murdoch), a widow, lived there also. She, along with her son John Murray and daughters Mary M. Mair, Veronica M. Caldow, and James's mother, Janet Lennox Murdoch, had all been baptized into The Church of Jesus Christ of Latter-day Saints when the American Mormon missionaries came teaching the restored gospel in their area. In 1856 "Wee Granny" left Gaswater to emigrate to Utah to join John, who had gone there in 1852. She died on her way to Zion at Chimney Rock in the Martin Handcart Company. James's father, William, belonged to the Free Church and could see

no need for changing his religious beliefs at that time. But twenty-four years later he also was baptized into the LDS Church.

The family lived in Cronberry when James and David were born, then moved back to Gaswater. They left there to go to Cumnock, James's mother's childhood town, about the time "Wee Granny" left for America. Brother David L. writes, "My father and family moved from the Grasswater row to Cumnock where we were located for some two years or so and then again moving to Muirkirk for reasons of Father's employment there." James's grandfather David Lennox died in January, 1857, in Old Cumnock. His grandmother Elisabeth Templeton Lennox had died when James's mother was a young girl. The information written by William Murdoch (*Murdoch Messenger* edition 6 page 8) states that he went to Muirkirk in 1857. Here he became underground manager of the Eglinton Coal and Iron Works. James would have been seven years old at this time, and his family lived in the Linkieburn House.

At an early age James began to work in the mines also, but not with his father's approval. William wanted James to spend his time and energy securing the best education possible. In an effort to encourage his son in this direction, William, as underground manager, gave the order that James was not to be allowed to ride the train that transported the miners from their homes to the mine and back. James insisted on walking the few miles to work and the few miles back home, exhibiting the perseverance that helped to bring him success later. However, James too recognized the value of a good education and was anxious to gain one, so he attended night school.

James gained his education at the Muirkirk Iron Works School and in 1867, at age seventeen, he attended the Glasgow Mechanics Institution at Glasgow, Scotland. Here he served a two-year apprenticeship, being "found out" as was the custom in those days in

Scotland. He received $1.75 per week for a sixty-hour work week.

James needed to spend every minute possible on his studies, but he also needed to spend time to knit his stockings. He resolved this conflict by wearing long pants and short stockings instead of knickers and over-the-knee stockings usually worn by boys at that time. He chose a long-range goal of education over a short-range goal of dressing like his peers, even though he was an excellent knitter. Later at the beginning of World War I, he taught his wife a better way to turn the toes and heels of stockings, and she in turn showed the Red Cross ladies how to do so. This was to aid the Red Cross in providing hand-knitted stockings for men in the armed services. James called the stitches "rig and furrin" (ridge and furrow) instead of knit and purl.

James had trained to be a marine engineer. Boulton and Watt, having built a ship at the mouth of the Clyde River, hired him to be the boatswain to take the ship to Birmingham, England. Because there was such motion in the water at the mouth of the Clyde, people who came aboard to visit the ship were often overtaken by seasickness. One such person had been sick at the wheel, and when the captain told James that his first duty would be to clean up the wheel, he answered, "I wouldn't clean it up if you'd give me the ship," and walked off the ship in disgust and indignation. This was his first and last experience working on a ship.

Soon after the ship episode in 1870 James decided to leave his native land. He remembered the stories the Mormon missionaries had told him about the wonders of America when they visited at his parents' home when he was a small boy, so he resolved to go there and see if these tales were true. When he informed his parents he intended to go as a steerage-class passenger, his mother said in indignation, "No son of mine is going to travel steerage—that's for animals," and made him buy a second-class ticket. As further evidence of her concern, his mother quilted gold coins into James's vest, which he wore constantly. Each coin could be removed independently as needed and until then was kept safely hidden. She also told him, "I'm going to give you nine months to return. Read the Bible, and keep out of debt."

In May, 1870, he went to Pittsburgh, Pennsylvania, where he worked as a machinist at the Water Works. When the financial panic of 1873 struck, he returned to Scotland for a visit of eighteen months, then went back to Pittsburgh in 1874. He helped to install the new waterworks there after his return from Scotland.

His family had planned to leave Scotland in January 1878 to join him, but his mother died in December,1877, so their plans were delayed. His father, together with his brother David Lennox, David's wife Elizabeth, and his two sisters Margaret (Maggie) and Janet (Jennie), arrived in New York in June 1878. James met them on the boat at Ellis Island and was quarantined with the passengers overnight because of some minor disease that had broken out during the crossing. The following day he took his loved ones to Pittsburgh and showed them the sights of the "Smoky City." The same day his family entrained for the West, but he remained at his job in Pittsburgh for the time being. On March 22, 1879, James received a certificate of declaration of intention of becoming a citizen of the United States of America in Allegheny County, Commonwealth of Pennsylvania.

In 1879 James decided to visit other parts of these great United States, and came to Salt Lake City. After visiting his relatives, he intended going to San Francisco to apply for a position with the waterworks in that city. He stayed in Salt Lake City at the Walker House, which was located on the west side of Main Street between 200 South and 300 South where the first Keith O'Brien store was later located. As he walked around Salt Lake City, he met an old friend, Mr. Ben Morgan, who had been his boss in the installation of the new Pittsburgh waterworks. Mr. Morgan suggested to him that his talents were needed in the mining town of Park City, in Summit County, Utah, where Mr. Morgan was operating the Lady of the Lake Mine, located in McHenry's Gulch. McHenry's Gulch led down from Lake Flat toward Heber City. Mr. Morgan was in charge of the pumps that had been installed to drain the water from the lower levels of the mine. He had just that day hired a man to work on the pumps, of whose ability he was very dubious. Later this man proved to be very undependable, so James got the job.

After he had visited his family and other relatives who resided in Heber City, James went to Park City. He was not much impressed at first with the town and said so to an acquaintance: "If I ever get one paycheck out of Park City, it will be the last." Nevertheless, he stayed there twenty-one years and became a very valuable employee and investor in several of the great mines in that locality, especially the Silver King and the Daly West. He assisted Ben Morgan in building a hoisting works at the Lady of the Lake Mine and continued working in the mechanical department of that mine for some time. This mine later became known as the Park Utah.

In the early 1880's James began working as a machinist at the Ontario Mining Company Mill. His rise was rapid, as his knowledge of the technical as well as the practical end of the mining industry made him a valuable man to have around. On October 6, 1885, James received a certificate of citizenship of the United States of America from the Third Judicial District Court of the Territory of Utah. In 1888 he began a twelve-year period as master mechanic and chief engineer *for* the Ontario and Daly Mining Companies and did much to help those properties become known the world over. In 1890 he was loaned to a mining company in Anaconda, Montana, to solve a pumping difficulty and soon after that went to Pioche, Nevada, on a similar mission.

In 1893 he was elected to be a councilman for Park City and served along with Ezra Thompson, with whom he later became associated in business enterprises in Salt Lake City. He numbered among his friends in Park City many prominent men of the community and was sent in 1894 with David Keith and Thomas Kearns to Salt Lake City as a delegate from Summit County to help write the constitution for the state of Utah. They were all three pledged to vote for women's suffrage, but James was the only one of the three who kept his promise. This issue was the most contentious one of the convention.

While working at the mine James lived at the boardinghouse owned by Marion Brown Johnson and her husband. There he met a young lady named Lizzie Lindsay who was working for the Johnson Family. Lizzie was a daughter of Samuel and Euphemia Wright Lindsay of Midway, Utah. On January 1, 1883, in Park City, Utah, James and Lizzie were married. Four children were born to this union:

William Wallace, born October 30, 1883 in Park City, died July 19, 1954.

Effie Lisle, born June 24, 1886 in Park City, died October 24, 1969.

Robert Bruce, born September 29, 1889 in Park City, died January 20, 1905.

Ruby Estella, born December 9, 1892 in Park City, died February 26, 1976.

Lizzie's health failed and she suffered for several years with dropsy and tuberculosis. James had moved her and the children to Salt Lake City about 1894 so that she could have the attention of the best physicians available, but their skill could not stay the ravages of the disease. She died December 4, 1896, and was buried December 7, in Alt. Olivet Cemetery. The beautiful house that had been in the process of building would have been ready for occupancy on New Year's Day, 1897, but Lizzie's death brought a great change in the lives of her husband and children. The oldest child was thirteen and the youngest just four years old at her death.

The four children were taken into the home of David T. Murdoch and his beloved wife, Elizabeth, where they were welcomed into the family and kindly cared for until August, 1897. Then James took his family back to Park City, where his sister, Margaret, and her husband, John Adamson, opened their home to them. By the time these dear people moved to Idaho in the spring of 1898, a cousin of James, Mary Murdoch Duke, had returned from Europe, where she had gone as a governess for David Keith Jr. when his parents went to the British Isles and the Continent. "Aunt Mary," as the children called her, became housekeeper for James.

In the meantime James had moved his furniture from the small home in Salt Lake City where Lizzie had died to a house in Park City next door to the home the family had formerly occupied near the mouth of the Ontario Canyon. This home was near the house of Lizzie's mother, Euphemia Wright Lindsay.

"Aunt Mary" Duke kept James's home until late in the year of 1898, when on November 14, he married Eliza (Lyde) Thackeray of Croyden, Utah, the daughter of George and Helen Condie Thackeray. James had met Eliza in Park City when she went there to visit her sister and brother-in-law, Margaret Ann (Nan) Thackeray Paradise and Reuben Paradise, who were living there.

To James and Eliza were born four children:

James Douglas, born September 26, 1899 in Park City, died January 14, 1834.

Helen Janet, born November 17, 1902 in Salt Lake City, died October 15, 1969.

Gwendolyn Thackeray, born January 6, 1904 in Salt Lake City.

Margaret Eliza, born July 1, 1908 in Salt Lake City, died December 8, 1956.

By 1900 James decided he had worked in the mines long enough, so he moved again to Salt Lake City in September and established Eliza and the children in the beautiful house he had built at 541 South Main Street. During the period of time between the completion of the house (January, 1897) and the occupation of it by the family (September, 1900), the house was rented by George Sutherland. Mr. Sutherland was an attorney and a senator in the Utah State Legislature who later became a representative and senator to the

Congress of the United States, president of the American Bar Association, and an associate justice of the Supreme Court of the United States.

James became a partner with Ezra Thompson, former operator of the Silver King Mine and Daly-West Mining interests, in the ownership and management of the Thompson-Murdoch Investment Company, owners of the Newhouse Office Building and other valuable business properties in Salt Lake City. He was made secretary-treasurer of the company on its organization and later became president upon the death of Mr. Thompson. He was also president of Commercial Warehouse Company, secretary-treasurer of Cardiff Mining and Milling Company, treasurer of Kennebec Consolidated Mining Company, and treasurer of Peerless Coal Company.

Since he had displayed such good judgment in his own business affairs, he was chosen to become a director in Utah-Idaho Sugar Company, Zion's Savings Bank and Trust Company, Utah State National Bank, Beneficial Life Insurance Company, and Home Benefit and Building Society. In these positions he contributed much to the stability and security of each institution. He had always refused to hire men who were known to be drinkers when employing workers for the mines. In his youth in Scotland he had signed a temperance union pledge to never use intoxicating liquor and to peaceably fight the liquor interests. During the years in Park City he attended a small gathering of friends, and when each chose his beverage, James elected buttermilk. He was immediately given the nickname "Buttermilk Jim," which persisted for years in spite of the fact most people addressed him as "Mr. Murdoch."

After James's death, President Heber J. Grant told Eliza, his widow, that whenever a director's meeting was held at the bank and liquor interests were seeking loans, James voted against the deals every time, despite the fact they were willing to pay much higher interest rates. Later President Grant stated in a four-page, handwritten letter to Eliza, "I rejoice with you that your beloved husband accepted the Gospel of our Redeemer before passing away. I have, as you know, been associated with him for many years in a business way, and I found him to be a man of the highest integrity and one with not only high ideals but with the moral courage to stand solidly for the right as he saw the right. His sense of right was high."

Ezra Thompson, James's partner, was elected for the second time as mayor of Salt Lake City, and in 1907 James was elected to serve under him as a member of the city council for two years. He was extremely interested in every project that increased the welfare and progress of the community, and he always gave full cooperation to such efforts. He was a candidate in 1909 for mayor of Salt Lake City on the Republican ticket, opposing John S. Bransford, who headed the American Party. James was not interested in politics, however, and he failed to campaign, so of course Mr. Bransford won the election. In 1909 he again became a member of the city council and also a member of the Commercial Club, serving well in both capacities. After serving two terms as councilman, he was appointed to serve as Salt Lake County commissioner, and it was during those years that the Salt Lake County Hospital was built at State Street and 2100 South. He also held many important civic positions in Salt Lake City, being known as a successful and "canny" Scotsman.

With the exception of a period in 1898 when he was Grand Master of the Masonic order for the state of Utah, James spent little time in social affairs, but loved home life. He spent much time in reading and improving his mind and became a well-educated citizen. He set the finest of examples for his children, friends, and the community at large.

He was a close personal associate of President Heber J. Grant and often remarked that if he ever joined the Church it would be because of the example of this esteemed friend. Even though James was not a member of the Church, when a drive was begun to collect funds for the construction of the Salt Lake Eighth Ward building, Eliza went to the bishop with a $50 donation which she had saved from her housekeeping money. She asked that he not tell James she had made the gift. The bishop didn't know how to react to the situation—whether he ought to accept the money without James's knowledge or whether he ought to refuse it and deny Eliza the blessings to which she would be entitled. He went to President Grant to seek counsel. President Grant's answer was, "Go to the husband and ask him for a donation." As the bishop was leaving, President Grant asked, "Who is this family? Who is the husband?" When the bishop replied, "James 'D' Murdoch," President Grant added, "I'll match anything you get from him." President Grant had long known of James's frugality.

The bishop, who was also aware of James's ability to preserve his financial resources, went to James and made a request for a gift to the building fund. James replied, I've been wondering when you were going to come to see me," and gave the bishop $500. The bishop then took James's money, went back to see President Grant, and collected another $500. The Eighth

Ward building was constructed; it was and still is a beautiful edifice.

James was baptized in the Salt Lake Tabernacle font by Elder Francis L. Dent on August 2, 1924, and was confirmed a member of the Church on the next day by Elder Louis E. Iverson On August 6 he was stricken with a fever of 107 degrees which prevailed for several days, necessitating that he be packed in ice bags. For the second time in his life he was plagued with hiccups that would not allow him to eat or sleep. Several doctors in attendance could not diagnose his trouble. Carbonated water was all he could tolerate, and a machine to produce this was set up in the basement.

However, on Sunday, August 10, he was ordained an elder by Hugh J. Cannon, president of the Eighth Quorum of Elders and former president of Liberty Stake. From then on his health improved rapidly for one main reason: Eliza, Effie Lisle, and Ruby Estella were praying and had been praying for many years that he would live to go to the temple and have his wives and children sealed to him. He received his endowment September 19, 1924, and some of the sealings were performed the same day by President George F. Richards. Others have followed in the years since. Thus were dreams fulfilled and prayers answered.

Early on the morning of December 2, 1924, James "D" Murdoch passed away following a heart attack. Funeral services were held in the Eighth Ward chapel and burial took place in Mt. Olivet Cemetery on December 4, 1924.

James and Eliza had talked for several hours the night before he died, he giving her advice about many financial problems. Helen and Gwendolyn had been out to a dancing party until about midnight. Being tired, they soon went to sleep and were filled with surprise and sorrow when their mother awakened them about 6:00 A.M. to tell them their father had passed away in his sleep. Doctors who were called said his heart had just stopped beating. Eliza passed away on November 27, 1938, and was buried on November 30, 1933, in bit. Olivet Cemetery. (Written by Ruby Estella Murdoch Hooper and Janet Oberg Gill.)

JAMES D. MURDOCH.

IT was a great shock to the many friends and business associates of James D. Murdoch to learn of his death Tuesday morning at the family residence in this city. Mr. Murdoch had been somewhat indisposed for several months but when the final summons came he was regarded as having passed the crucial stage of his illness and was feeling better than he had done for some time. His sudden passing, therefore, was entirely unlooked for and was a great blow to his family and friends.

In the death of James D. Murdoch a good citizen and sterling character goes to his reward. Born in Scotland he came to America as a young man and by dint of perseverance and hard work soon made his presence felt in the communities in which he lived. For many years he was closely associated with the mining industry in Utah and did much to open up and develop some of the best mines in the state. He was a striking type of the "canny" Scotchman and possessed many of the virtues of that sturdy race—frugal, industrious, conservative and above all else scrupulously honest in his dealings with his fellow men. As a county commissioner serving the people of this community, he gave close attention to every detail and not a dollar was expended with his approval until he had first satisfied himself that the outlay was fully justified and actually required. His business judgment was regarded by his associates as thoroughly reliable.

Though affiliated with the Republican party politically Mr. Murdoch was far from being a politician. To him certain phases of political life were altogether distasteful and had it not been for his aversion to public office he might have received greater honors politically than were accorded him. To intimate friends he loved to speak of his boyhood days in Scotland, his native land, and of his achievements as a young man struggling for a livelihood independent of his father's home. He was successful in a business way because he early in life adopted business principles and applied himself in an intelligent manner to business pursuits. He was a pillar of strength to the institutions with which he was connected and could always be depended upon to meet every appointment and discharge faithfully and well every duty required of him. Greatly devoted to his family, his absence from the home circle will be keenly felt. To those who are immediately deprived of the wise guidance and loving counsel of husband and father, the sincere sympathy of the community will be extended.

Lizzie Lindsay Murdoch

My Mother, Lizzie Lindsay, was born in Springfield, Sangamon County, Illinois on June 6, 1858. Her parents had stayed there since the late summer of 1856 after disembarking from the sailing vessel, "Wellfleet," at Boston, Massachusetts. They had come to America in this ship from Scotland.

Her father was Samuel Lindsay and her mother was Euphemia Wright. Both had joined the Church in Scotland about 1850, when the first missionaries were sent to that country. They had married about that time also on 25 March 1850. Their first child, Janet Pryde Lindsay, was born in Wanlockhead, Dumfries, Scotland, and was about four years old when her little sister Lizzie was born in their new home in Illinois.

Lizzie's father, Samuel, was the fifth child and fourth son of Robert Mc Queen Lindsay. Samuel's oldest brother, William Lindsay (who married Christina Howie) had a son, William, who married Mary Mair. As a result, all of Lizzie Lindsay Murdoch's descendants are "double cousins" to all of William and Mary Mair Lindsay's numerous posterity.

A beautiful love for each other existed between these two sisters, and for most of their young lives they were inseparable companions. Even after marriage they were privileged to live near each other most of the time, and between their deaths only four years intervened. Both died when thirty-eight years of age and each was the mother of four children. Their mother had five children. The second, Euphemia, was born at Kilmarnock, Ayrshire, Scotland on 24 January 1855. She lived only three days and died on 27 January. Robert W. Lindsay was born at Springfield on 4 June 1860. The fifth child, Maggie C., was born in Utah on 18 April 1866.

When Lizzie Lindsay was three years old, her parents decided to continue their journey to Utah. They had accumulated enough means while in Springfield to travel in whatever meager comfort they could obtain, so they came across the plains either in a stage-coach or a well-equipped wagon outfit.

We have no definite record, but we know that for as long as he lived, Samuel Lindsay secured for his wife and family the best of everything that was available, and left them well-provided for at his death. They did not know or suffer many of the hardships on their journey across the plains that pioneers had endured a few years earlier because, by 1861, trading posts and forts had been established along the route of travel. However, even then the long journey had its hazards. We read in church history that bands of savage Indians often wreaked vengeance upon those who passed through their hunting grounds, and the stagecoaches were frequently held up by renegade white men who relieved the passengers of their possessions and rifled the mail bags.

Our people came through safely as far as we know, and were made welcome by their friends when they arrived in Salt Lake City. They visited there and in Heber and Park City with friends and relatives for some time while the father investigated ways of obtaining a livelihood. He had been a miner in his native land, and now his interest in mining enterprises led him farther west to Virginia City, Nevada. He took his wife and family with him, so again they had a long journey behind horses, over drier and hotter trails than on their way to Utah. They went to Nevada in 1862, but stayed only two years before returning to Utah in 1864.

When Lizzie returned from this trip, she saw for the first time her grandfather, Robert McQueen Lindsay, and her grandmother, Elizabeth Geddes Lindsay, who had recently come from Scotland. The elderly couple rejoiced to have their son bring his family back to Utah, so they could live near each other. Her parents established a home in Park City, and there Lizzie received her schooling.

She grew to womanhood, skilled in domestic arts and homemaking. She was well known for her ability in cooking and needlework. She knitted, crocheted, and did many kinds of beautiful embroidery. One unfinished embroidered flounce for a petticoat gives mute testimony to her descendants that she spent little time in idleness. The quaint appliquéd quilts she made would, if they had been preserved, be models of skill and beauty, even today.

Lizzie loved to dance, and no partner was more proud to escort her than her brother, Robert. He was unmarried, and lavished his affection and gifts upon his sisters. At one time, he presented Lizzie with a gold watch and chain. She was a favorite with all of her associates. Just recently, I learned from the daughter of an old friend of Mother, that she had two other suitors besides my father.

James "D" Murdoch won her favor over his two rivals, and their marriage took place on New Year's Day 1883, in Park City, Summit County, Utah.

The first ten years of their married life together were spent happily in Park City. Their four children: William Wallace, Effie Lisle, Robert Bruce, and Ruby Estella were born in a cabin perched on a steep hill on one side of Ontario Canyon. (This cabin was swept down in the canyon by a snow slide just a short time after we moved out of it.)

Lizzie Murdoch was an expert horse-woman and spent many happy hours at the side of her husband, riding gracefully in her side-saddle, with her long, flowing riding skirt always managed skillfully. There were many beautiful scenes within riding distance of Park City, and to these beauty spots the young married couples would go for exercise and recreation. Brighton and the Hot Pots near Heber City were two of their favorite gathering places.

Soon after I was born, these happy associations came to an end as my mother's health began to fail. Her illness was diagnosed as dropsy. The last few years of her life, she was confined to her bed, and her daughter, Effie Lisle, would kneel by the side of her mother's bed so Lizzie could brush and braid Effie's long flowing tresses.

With thought only for our mother's comfort and wellbeing, Father moved her and us children to Salt Lake City, where the altitude was much lower and expert medical care more quickly available. He hired a housekeeper for us and provided for every future need, and then had to return to his work as master mechanic at the famous Ontario mine, near where we had lived.

At times our mother's health seemed to improve considerably, giving rise to Father's hopes that she would eventually recover her health. As a result of these hopes, he had a beautiful home built for her

next to the cottage where we lived. Every convenience known at that time was installed and the very best of materials were ordered throughout. I pause now to pay humble tribute to the architect who built it. With only occasional supervision by the owner, he could very easily have substituted inferior materials, but instead, he even added to the specifications. Be it said of architect Headlund that he builded well and honorably.

We all watched patiently the progress of the building operations until the new home was nearly completed, and we were anticipating with pleasure, moving into it for the new year, 1897.

Lizzie died of consumption on 4 December 1896, just five days before her youngest daughter turned four. Our mother departed this life sorrowful at the thought of leaving her mother, her husband, and children, but resigned to the fate that had been decreed for her. Her father, two sisters and her only brother had preceded her in death, and were no doubt waiting to welcome her to an abode on high, more beautiful than the one that had been provided for her here.

Written By Ruby Hooper and Oscar Hunter

Eliza Thackeray Murdoch

Eliza Thackeray Murdoch was born February 21, 1870 in Croydon, Morgan County, Utah. She was the seventh of ten children descended from George and Helen Condie Thackeray. Her parents had moved from Salt Lake City to Croydon in 1863 to help colonize and settle that area. They suffered the hardships incident to living in a new place. Their first home was dug in the side of a mountain until logs were cut and hauled for a one-room house with straw on the floor and a dirt roof over tree limbs. They had little meat but kept healthy on coarse grains, pigweeds, sego lily bulbs and other greens. Of the twenty families who lived there, in eight years there were no deaths. The Indians were many and treacherous and caused them much trouble. Sometimes they had to flee for their lives.

In 1878 diphtheria raged in the town of Croydon, and there were many deaths. They held special fast and prayer meetings and the disease abated. In 1880 many cattle died of starvation as the grasshoppers were so numerous that they ate everything that was green. They hauled hay from Kaysville, many miles distant, and paid $25 a ton for it.

Eliza's father was a rancher and farmer. He had

come from York, England, to Salt Lake City when he was seventeen years old, the only one of a family of eight to join the Church of Jesus Christ of Latter-day Saints. His parents were Robert Thackeray and Elizabeth Jackson.

Eliza's mother was the third of twelve children born to Thomas and Helen Sharp Condie. The family had come from Clackmannan, Scotland, to Salt Lake City after a difficult journey of almost four years, which cost the lives of three of the children and nearly claimed the mother. When she was 15 years old Helen (Thackeray) had come west in the Isaac Russell Company, driving a team most of the way. Her parents had come in the Howell Company.

Helen Thackeray became Croydon's first Relief Society President on October 14, 1875 and held that position for thirty-three years. In 1887 Helen began the study of medicine and obstetrics. Eliza received a certificate of recommendation from Dr. Ellis R. Shipp's School of Obstetrics on March 14, 1890. She attended the Agriculture College at Logan, Utah, in 1890 and 1891. On April 6, 1893 Helen and Eliza were each issued a certificate licensing them to practice obstetrics in the Territory of Utah. Helen became the doctor and midwife for Croydon and the surrounding communities. Because of her family's history of dedication to and sacrifice for the L.D.S. Church, Eliza felt a need for counsel in making her decision when James Murdoch, who was not a member of that Church, asked her to marry him. She received a blessing in which she was promised that if she married him and lived righteously the time would come that he would join the L. D. S. Church. This same promise was repeated in later blessings and did come true shortly before his death. Eliza also received a Patriarchal Blessing by John Murray Murdoch October 8, 1902 that appears to be recorded in the handwriting of James "D" Murdoch.

Eliza and James were married November 14, 1898. She instantly became the stepmother to four children by James' previous marriage. This is never an easy task for any woman. Eliza and James had four children that she was the mother to also. She did many things with her hands, painting china and pictures, beadwork, crochet work, and knitting. She was plagued by ill health caused by a goiter and heart condition. Therefore, her home was mainly the center of her activities. In about 1901 she and James did however visit Scotland. Her own children were married in 1922, 1927, 1929, and 1933. She lived as a widow for fourteen years after her husbands death. Eliza died November 27, 1938 and was buried in the Mount Olivet Cemetery.

Written by Janet Oberg Gill and Ruth Murdoch Schulz.

James "D" Murdoch home, 541 South Main Street, Salt Lake City, Utah

IT IS CONTRACTED, AGREED, and ENDED, among the Parties following, viz.: SMITH, BROTHERS & Co., *Engineers, Millwrights, and Machine Makers in Park Street, near Paisley Road, Glasgow,* and HUGH SMITH, JAMES SMITH, and OSBOURNE SMITH, *Engineers, Millwrights, and Machine Makers* there, the individual partners of said Company, ON THE ONE PART, and *James Murdoch Ninety five Crosshill street Crosshill Glasgow* with the special advice and consent of *the said William Murdoch, undersigned Manager and the said William Murdoch, his father* as Cautioner, Surety, and full Obligant, and taking burden upon him for and with the said *James Murdoch* ON THE OTHER PART in manner following: that is to say, the said *James Murdoch* with consent foresaid, hereby becomes bound, and binds and obliges himself as an Apprentice to the said SMITH, BROTHERS, & Co., and their Successors carrying on business under the said Firm, in the *Fitting* branch of their business, whether to be carried on in the works presently occupied by them, in Park Street, near Paisley Road, Glasgow, or in any other works to be occupied by them from time to time, situated in or within three miles of Glasgow, or to be carried on outwith their works, and within the United Kingdom of Great Britain and Ireland, and that for the space of *five* years from and after his entry thereto, which is hereby declared to have begun and commenced on the *Third* day of *July* One Thousand Eight Hundred and *Sixty Seven* years, notwithstanding the date hereof, during which space the said *James Murdoch* as Principal with consent foresaid, and the said *William Murdoch* as Cautioner, bind and oblige themselves, jointly and severally, their respective Heirs, Executors, and Successors, whomsoever, that the said Apprentice shall at no time be absent, or divert himself from his said Masters' Service, without leave asked and obtained; or, otherwise, he shall pay FIVE SHILLINGS STERLING, for each day's absence, and in proportion for each part of a day; or, in the option of the Masters, shall serve two days for each day's absence at the expiry hereof; declaring that, in the case of absence from sickness, when such sickness shall not have been caused directly by the Apprentice's misconduct, he shall only be bound to work an equal quantity of days corresponding to the number he shall have been so absent, such days of absence to be ascertained by a writing under the hand of any one of the Partners of the said Firm; or, in the option of the Masters, by the oath of their Manager, Foreman, or Time-keeper at the Work, without further evidence, and it is declared that the whole absent time of the Apprentice, whether arising from sickness or from other causes, shall be made up immediately upon expiry of the said period of *five* years, by the Apprentice then serving two days, or one day, as the case may be, for each day's absence, and that at the respective rates of wages applicable to the years during which the days of absence shall have occurred. That he shall not associate with idle or improper company, and by no means reveal or discover to any person or persons any of his Masters' Secrets or Transactions that he may come to know or be instructed in, relative to any branch or branches of their Business; that he shall not be privy to or know of anything that may tend to the hurt and prejudice of the said Masters, without giving the earliest notice thereof, and endeavouring to prevent the same; and that he shall faithfully, honestly, and diligently serve and obey his said Masters by Night and by Day, as the exigencies of their business may require, in the aforesaid branch of their Business, or in any other branch connected therewith, or any other lawful Work that may be required of him, appertaining to, or connected with, the Business of the said Masters, and that though not relating to the said branch of their Business. And, further, the said Apprentice binds and obliges himself to conform to any Rules made, or which may be made by the said Masters for the Regulation of their Workshops. In consideration of all which, and on the other part, the said SMITH, BROTHERS & Co., and Partners thereof, bind and oblige themselves, and the said Copartnery Firm and its Successors, that they shall teach and instruct, or cause to be instructed, the said Apprentice in the *Fitting* branch of Business aforesaid, at which the said Apprentice may be set to Work, as aforesaid, and that in so far as the said Masters know themselves, or the said Apprentice's capacity can reach, and shall use their best endeavours to render the said Apprentice expert and skilled therein, and pay him the following Sums in name of Wages, viz.:— *Seven shillings per week, for each week of the first year; and eight shillings per week for each week of the second and last year of* this Indenture; it being hereby declared that all Wages due prior to the date of this Indenture have been paid and discharged, and that a Week shall be held to consist of Sixty Working Hours, and should the Apprentice work a greater number of Hours in any one week than Sixty, such overtime shall be paid for at the respective rate of Wages above specified; and on the other hand, should he work a less number of hours, whether through absence from Sickness, or arising from any other cause whatever, his Wages shall be subject to a corresponding deduction, and that without prejudice to the obligation to make up absent time as aforesaid. And when the said Masters shall have occasion to send the said Apprentice from home, to any part of the United Kingdom of Great Britain and Ireland, in the exercise of their business, they shall pay him an additional sum of Six Shillings Weekly, over and above his Weekly Wages; but if the said Master shall provide the said Apprentice with Lodgings and Victuals on any of these occasions, which they shall have the option of doing, then they shall only be bound to make payment to the said Apprentice of the one half of his usual Weekly Wages; but, in either case, they shall pay the Apprentice's Travelling Expenses. And it is hereby mutually agreed by and between the whole parties hereto, that in all actions, diligence, and procedure arising out of or to follow on these presents, at the instance of any of the parties against the others, whether at Common Law, or under the Act Fourth George the Fourth, caput thirty-four, or "The Summary Procedure Act 1864," or other Statutes applicable to such actions, diligence, and procedure, the same shall be competent in the Courts of the Sheriff of Lanarkshire, or of any of his Substitutes, at Glasgow, or before the Court at Glasgow of the Justices of the Peace for the Lower Ward of Lanarkshire, the jurisdiction of the said Sheriff of Lanarkshire, and of his Substitutes at Glasgow, and of the said Justices of the Peace, being hereby prorogated to that end and effect by the whole parties hereto, who renounce all objections to the contrary. And both parties bind and oblige themselves, and their foresaids, to fulfil and perform their respective parts of the premises to each other, under the penalty of FIFTEEN POUNDS, to be paid by the party failing to the party observing, or willing to observe, besides performance ; and they consent to the Registration hereof in the Books of Council and Session, or other Judges' Books competent for preservation, and execution on a six days' charge, in form as effeirs, and thereto constitute

Procurators. ☙ witness whereof, these presents (so far as not printed) written on Paper duly Stamped by *David Munn Scoular, Clerk to the said Smith Brothers Company, are subscribed by the said Smith Brothers and Company, (the signatures of the said Company being adhibited by the said William Smith) and by the said Hugh Smith, James Smith and Osbourne Smith and by the said James Murdoch, all at Glasgow, the twenty third day of December, eighteen hundred and sixty seven years; before these witnesses, John Crow, apprentice dresser to the said Smith Brothers and Company; and the said David Munn Scoular, above designed; and by the said William Murdoch, before these witnesses, George Ford, pithead contractor, and Alexander Christie Brusher, all at Newkirk, the twenty third day of January eighteen hundred and sixty eight years.*

John Crow Witness
David Munn Scoular Witness
George Ford Witness
Alexander Christie Witness

Smith Brothers
Osbourne Smith
James Smith
Hugh Smith
James Murdoch
William Murdoch

Office of Hartupee, McGill & Burke,

Manufacturers of

Marine and Stationary Engines,

Also,

Hartupee's Patent Compound Engine and Grate Bar.

Nos. 33 and 34 Water Street,

Pittsburgh, June 10th 1879

To whom it may concern!

This is to certify that Mr James Murdock the bearer is a machinist of uncommon ability & judgement. He has been in my employ for the past four years and during that time has been employed on various kinds of work where skill and ability were required, and in every case he has given entire satisfaction. In an experience of thirty years in the Engine Business it has never been my fortune to employ a more skillful, conscientious or industrious workman. He is sober and to be relied upon, and in recommending him I feel certain that any position he undertakes to fulfil, he will discharge his duties faithfully and to the satisfaction of his employer.

Respectfully

A. Hartupee
Engine Builder

WIFE (1) lizzie LINDSAY
Birth 6 Jun 1858
Place Springfield, Sngm., Illn.
Married 1 Jan 1883
Place Park City, Summit, Utah
Death 4 Dec 1896
Place Salt Lake City, S-Lk., Ut.
Burial 7 Dec 1896
Place Mt. Olivet Cem. S-Lk, Ut.
Mother Euphesia WRIGHT
Father Samuel LINDSAY

HUSBAND James "D" MURDOCH
Birth 3 Jan 1850
Place Cronberry, Ayr., Scotland
Death 2 Dec 1924
Place Salt Lake City, S-Lk., Ut.
Burial 4 Dec 1924
Place Mt. Olivet Cem. S-Lk., Ut.
Mother Janet LENNOX
Father William MURDOCH
Information from Ruby M. Hooper, Oscar M. Hunter, Janet O. Gill

WIFE (2) Eliza THACKERAY
Birth 21 Feb 1870
Place Croyden, Morgan, Utah
Married 14 Nov 1898
Place Croyden, Morgan, Utah
Death 27 Nov 1938
Place Salt Lake City, S-Lk., Ut.
Burial 30 Nov 1938
Place Mt. Olivet Cem. S-Lk., Ut.
Mother Helen CONDIE
Father George THACKERAY

CHILDREN OF (1) WIFE

1ST CHILD William Wallace MURDOCH
Birth 30 Oct 1383 Park City, Summit, Utah
Married Myrtle Hardwick CARTWRIGH
Date 20 Oct 1910
Place Salt Lake City, Salt Lake Utah
Death 19 July 1954 Salt Lake City, Utah
Burial 22 July 1954 City Cem. S.L.C., Utah

2ND CHILD Effie Lisle MURDOCH
Birth 24 Jun 1386 Park City, Summit, Utah
Married Oscar Chipman HUNTER
Date 16 Nov 1910
Place Salt Lake City, Salt Lake Utah
Death 24 Oct 1969 Salt Lake Cit, S-Lk., Ut.
Burial 28 Oct 1969 Mt. Olivet Cem. S.L.C., Ut.

3RD CHILD Robert Bruce MURDOCH
Birth 29 Sep 1889
Place Park City, Summit, Utah
Death 20 Jan 1905
Place Salt Lake City, S-lk, Utah
Burial
Place Mt. Olivet Cem. S.L.C. Ut

4TH CHILD Ruby Estella MURDOCH
Birth 9 Dec 1892 Park City, Su lt, Ut
Married John Albert HOOPER
Date 12 Jun 1919
Place Manti, Sanpete, Utah
Death 26 Feb 1976 Ogden, Weber Utah
Burial 2 Mar 1976 Mt. Olivet Cem S.L.C., Ut.

CHILDREN OF (2) WIFE

5TH CHILD James Douglas MURDOCH
Birth 26 Sep 1899 Park City, Summit, Utah
Married Marguerite McMILLAN
Date 17 Jan 1922
Place Salt Lake City, Salt Lake, Utah
Death 14 Jan 1934 Salt lake City, Utah
Burial 17 Jan 1934 Mt. Ol vet Cem. S.L.C. Ut.

6TH CHILD Helen Janet MURDOCH
Birth 17 Nov 1902 Salt Lake City, S-Lk, Ut.
Married Seth Michael OBERG
Date 15 May 1929
Place Salt Lake City, Salt Lake, Utah
Death 15 Oct 1969 Salt Lake City, S-Lk., Ut.
Burial 18 Oct 1969 Mt. Ol vet Cem. S.L.C, Ut.

7TH CHILD Gwendolyn Thackery MURDOCH
Birth 6 Jan 19__ Salt Lake City, S-Lk., Ut.
Married (1) Kuno DO__ Jr. Q Gerald FITZGERALD
Date 19 Aug 1__3 ? Apr 1942
Place Salt Lake Cit, Utah Lirst, Torrant, Texas
Death 3 Oct 19 Salt Lake City, S.L, Utah
Place 7 Oct 19 Mt. Olivet Cem. S.L.C.,Utah

8TH CHILD Margaret Eliza MURDOCH
Birth 1 July 19_8 Salt Lake City, S-Lk., Ut.
Married Raymond __ hello HARVEY
Date 1 Feb 19
Place Santa Mo ca, Los Angeles, California
Death 8 Dec 1 San Mar no, Los Angeles, Cal.
Burial 13 Dec __6 Forest Lawn Cem L.A. Cal.

1 MURDOCH, James 1786-1831   2 MURDOCH, William 1825-1913
1 MURDOCH, Mary MURRAY, Sp. 1782-1856   2 MURDOCH, Janet LENNOX, Sp. 1821-1877

                          3 MURDOCH, JAMES "D" 1850-1924
DESCENDANTS OF--------
                          3 MURDOCH, LIZZIE LINDSAY, (1) SP. 1858-1896

4 MURDOCH, William Wallace B-30 Oct 1883 D-19 Jul 1954
4 MURDOCH, Myrtle Hardwick CARTWRIGHT, Sp. B- 10 Oct 1882 M-20 Oct 1910 D- 6 Apr 1955

        5 RUSSELL, Lucile Ann MURDOCH B- 6 Aug 1911
        5 RUSSELL, Walker Lee, Sp. B-6 May 1894 M-28 Jul 1961 D-26 Oct 1971

        5 MURDOCH, William Wallace Jr. B-19 Sep 1913
        5 MURDOCH, Eileen Louise MURPHY, Sp. B-2 Jan 1923 M-12 Sep 1944

                6 MURDOCH, Alyn B-1 Jan 1946
                6 MURDOCH, Barbara Jean MANOWN, Sp. B-4 Nov 1941 M-3 Jan 1973

                        7 MURDOCH, April Elizabeth   B-24 Sep 1974

                        7 MURDOCH, Bryan Anthony   B-19 Jul 1978

                6 MURDOCH, Baby Boy (Stillborn) B-13 Dec 1949

                6 MURDOCH, James Wallace B-23 Aug 1951
                6 MURDOCH, Shirley Rae BRUMMELL, Sp. B-15 Jan 1950 M-6 Sep 1969

                        7 MURDOCH, Brook Rochelle   B-18 Oct 1971

                        7 MURDOCH, Kimberly Dawn   B-28 Jul 1974

                        7 MURDOCH, Ryan Travis   B-23 May 1977

        5 FACER, Virginia MURDOCH B-12 May 1917
        5 FACER, Keith Holbrook, Sp. B-5 Dec 1916 M-24 Jun 1942

                6 HUGHES, Jeanne FACER B-26 May 1944
                6 HUGHES, Ernest Allen, Sp. B-24 Jan 1940 M-24 Jun 1964

                        7 HUGHES, Shellie   B-17 Jul 1967

                        7 HUGHES, Baby Boy   B-   1969 D-   1969

                        7 HUGHES, Scott Allen   B-3 Jan 1973

                6 PARKIN, Suzanne FACER B-8 Oct 1946
                6 PARKIN, Earl LeGrande, Sp. B-31 Aug 1944 M-24 Aug 1967

                        7 PARKIN, Blake Lee   B-14 Mar 1969

                        7 PARKIN, Julie   B-28 Sep 1971

                        7 PARKIN, Steven Jeffrey   B-21 May 1974

                        7 PARKIN, Kimberly   B- 4 Aug 1977

                        7 PARKIN, David Lonie   B-21 Dec 1978

                6 PETERSON, Laraine FACER B-15 Oct 1948
                6 PETERSON, Bruce Lynn, Sp. B-6 Apr 1947 M-26 Nov 1969

                        7 PETERSON, Jennifer   B-10 Apr 1971

                        7 PETERSON, Douglas Lynn   B-10 May 1973

                        7 PETERSON, Bryan David   B-30 Mar 1976

                        7 PETERSON, Tyler Jeffrey   B-23 Aug 1977

                6 FACER, David Murdoch   B-17 Aug 1951

5 GOWANS, Grace MURDOCH B-18 May 1922
5 GOWANS, Albert Sherman, Sp. B-27 Oct 1917 M-14 Mar 1942

 6 GOWANS, Richard Sherman B-17 Feb 1943
 6 GOWANS, Judy Ann CLIFT, Sp. B-2 Jul 1945 M-12 Sep 1968

  7 GOWANS, Baby Girl   B-16 Nov 1969 D- 1969

  7 GOWANS, Daniel Sherman B- 9 Nov 1972

  7 GOWANS, Tiffany

  7 GOWANS, Benjamin Matthew B-18 Apr 1978

 6 KIRKHAM, Roger Leslie, Sp. B-23 Apr 1944 M-9 Jun 1967

  7 KIRKHAM, Nathan Roger B-12 Nov 1968

  7 KIRKHAM, Heather   B-10 Sep 1970

  7 KIRKHAM, Ryan Grand   B-26 Jul 1972

  7 KIRKHAM, Darin Gowans

  7 KIRKHAM, Kellie   B- 3 Oct 1977

 6 AAMODT, Marilyn GOWANS B-3 Oct 1947
 6 AAMODT, John Rice, Sp. B-5 Sep 1942 M-6 Sep 1967

  7 AAMODT, David Sherman B-29 Jun 1968

  7 AAMODT, Amy Lynn   B-25 Aug 1971

  7 AAMODT, Angela Kristine B- 9 Nov 1974

 6 WEST, Connie GOWANS B-12 Aug 1952
 6 WEST, Doran Arthur, Sp. B-4 May 1950 M-5 Jun 1973

  7 WEST, Amber   B-14 Apr 1974

  7 WEST, Joshua Doran   B-28 Feb 1976 D-25 Jun 1976

  7 WEST, Heidi   B-28 Dec 1977

  7 WEST, Rachel   B-25 Oct 1981

 6 GOWANS, Ronald Blaine B-3 Apr 1954
 6 GOWANS, Michele CREYER, Sp. B-17 Oct 1956 M-29 Oct 1976

 6 GOWANS, Alan Dean   B-21 Jun 1959

5 MURDOCH, Grant Robert B-10 Mar 1924
5 MURDOCH, Vera Dolores REEVE, Sp. B-25 Apr 1924 M-12 May 1945

 6 MURDOCH, Robert Steven B-21 Aug 1947

 6 LAURITZEN, Vera Kathleen MURDOCH B-26 Mar 1949
 6 LAURITZEN, Terry Lynn, Sp. B-12 Dec 1946 M-18 Mar 1969

  7 LAURITZEN, Benjamin Grant B-13 Feb 1976

  7 LAURITZEN, Joshua Steven B- 1 May 1979

 6 JENSEN, Linda Susan MURDOCH B-5 Aug 1951
 6 JENSEN, Flemming, Sp. B-23 Apr 1949 M-13 Jun 1975

 6 MURDOCH, Gary Reeve B-19 Apr 1954
 6 MURDOCH, Lynn GREGG, Sp. B-16 Oct 1955 M-2 Aug 1975 Div.

  7 MURDOCH, Heather Gene B-24 Sep 1976

  7 MURDOCH, Marlo Carolyn B-22 Sep 1978

```
        6 BIRDSLEY, Charlene Dolores MURDOCH B-1 Aug 1956
        6 BIRDSLEY, Robert, Sp. B-14 Jan 1954 M-14 Feb 1976

4 HUNTER, Effie Lisle MURDOCH B-24 Jun 1886 D-24 Oct 1969
4 HUNTER, Oscar Chipman, Sp. B-21 Jun 1882 M-16 Nov 1910 D-2 Dec 1918

      5 REYNOLDS, Elizabeth Mindwell HUNTER B-31 Jul 1913
      5 REYNOLDS, Luther Smith, Sp. B-9 Feb 1905 M-8 Feb 1940

           6 REYNOLDS, James Murdoch B-14 Dec 1942
           6 REYNOLDS, Carol Lolita RICHARDSON, Sp. B-2 Mar 1945 M-19 Dec 1967

                7 REYNOLDS, Marybeth Carol      B- 2 Oct 1970

                7 REYNOLDS, Rebecca Alice       B-27 Dec 1971

                7 REYNOLDS, Nathan Luther       B-23 Mar 1976

                7 REYNOLDS, Jacqueline Kay      B- 7 Oct 1978

                7 REYNOLDS, Lisa Katherine      B-28 Jun 1981 D-2 Jul 1981

           6 JONES, Mary Elizabeth REYNOLDS 10 Apr 1946
           6 JONES, Brent "M", Sp. B-22 Jan 1946 M-20 Dec 1968

                7 JONES, Robert Brent           B- 3 Nov 1969

                7 JONES, Loren McKay            B-13 Sep 1971

                7 JONES, Annette Elizabeth      B-31 Oct 1973

                7 JONES, Steven Reynolds        B-29 Oct 1974

                7 JONES, Clinton Frank          B-21 May 1981

      5 HUNTER, Oscar MURDOCH B-6 May 1915
      5 HUNTER, Orpha LaFrance YORK, Sp. B-3 Sep 1920 M-6 Mar 1940

           6 SEARBY, Suzanne HUNTER B-5 Feb 1943
           6 SEARBY, Edward Porter, Sp. B-16 Nov 1935 M-31 Dec 1971 Div.

           6 HUNTER, Edward Oscar B-14 Mar 1947 M-1 May 1970
           6 HUNTER, Kathleen Clawson JEPPERSEN, Sp. B-27 Jun 1948

                7 HUNTER, Cambria Lynn          B-10 Jul 1971

                7 HUNTER, Brandon Jeppersen     B-28 Jun 1972

                7 HUNTER, Justin Lee            B-20 Nov 1975

                7 HUNTER, Paul Romney           B-30 Jun 1978

           6 BLYLE, Elizabeth HUNTER Talbot B-18 Jun 1949 D- 9 Jun 1981
           6 TALBOT, Terry Eugene, Sp. B-3 Dec 1945  M-18 Nov 1969 Div.
           6 BLYLE, Fontaine Eugene, Sp. (3) B-18 Feb 1938 M-9 Dec 1980

                7 TALBOT, Jennifer              B-31 Mar 1970

           6 HUNTER, Robert Blaine      B- 1 Apr 1955

           6 HUNTER, Rosemary           B- 4 May 1957

      5 HUNTER, James Murdoch B-31 Jan 1918
      5 HUNTER, Mildred Annie Moore, Sp. B-24 Nov 1918 M-15 Feb 1941

           6 HUNTER, Jill Annette       B-21 Aug 1944

           6 COSBY, Karen Louise HUNTER B-17 Jul 1946
           6 COSBY, Joseph Michael, Sp. B-15 May 1945 M-27 May 1963
```

```
            7 COSBY, Christine Marie        B- 9 Dec 1963

            7 COSBY, Joseph Michael II      B- 3 Jul 1966

            7 COSBY, James Richard          B-31 May 1969

            7 COSBY, Jason Robert           B- 4 Aug 1971

            7 COSBY, Kelli Ann              B-21 Mar 1977

            7 COSBY, Justin Todd            B-23 Jan 1980

        6 HUNTER, James David B-8 Aug 1952
        6 HUNTER, Peggy HIRSCHI, Sp. B-28 May 1952 M-15 Aug 1975

            7 HUNTER, Andrea                B- 2 Oct 1978

            7 HUNTER, David Cody            B-20 Sep 1981

        6 HUNTER, John Stephen B-16 Feb 1955
        6 HUNTER, Christelle Marie MARCHANT, Sp. B-24 Feb 1957 M-19 Jun 1980

            7 HUNTER, Cory John             B-8 Jul 1981

        6 HUNTER, Mark Alan B-25 Feb 1957
        6 HUNTER, Cindi Lynne TRIMBLE, Sp. B-28 Dec 1958 M-16 Jun 1981

4 MURDOCH, Robert Bruce B-

4 HOOPER, Ruby Estella MURDOCH B-9 Dec 1892 D-26 Feb 1976
4 HOOPER, John Albert, Sp. B-15 Sep 1894 M-12 Jun 1919 D-6 Jul 1961

    5 GAUCHAY, Catherine HOOPER B-8 Apr 1920
    5 GAUCHAY, Philip Spafford, Sp. B-23 Apr 1915 M-15 Sep 1942 D-1 Mar 1963

        6 LOVELAND, Ann Marie CAUCHAY B-18 Jun 1943
        6 LOVELAND, Alan See, Sp. B-20 Sep 1944 M-27 Jan 1967

            7 LOVELAND, Catherine Michele   B-13 Feb 1969

            7 LOVELAND, Rebecca Ann          B-24 Jun 1970

            7 LOVELAND, Kimberly Rae         B-13 Sep 1973

            7 LOVELAND, Sarah Elaine         B-11 Jan 1977

        6 RHOADES, Janet GAUCHAY B-19 Oct 1946
        6 RHOADES, Fred Arnold II, Sp. B-20 Sep 1944 M-1 Jun 1966

            7 RHOADES, Fred Arnold III      B-11 May 1967

            7 RHOADES, Bret Philip          B-25 Nov 1968
            7 RHOADES, Cory Robert          B-26 Jan 1970
            7 RHOADES, Aaron Michael        D-30 Aug 1971

            7 RHOADES, Jeremy Benjamin      B-10 Dec 1973

            7 RHOADES, Matthew Jonathan     B-19 Jul 1

        6 HERZOG, Alice LaPrele GAUCHAY Weaver  B-25 Jan 1950
        6 WEAVER, Howard Cecil, Sp. B-15 Oct 1950 M-17 Jul 1970 Div.
        6 HERZOG, Edward Eric, Sp. B-4 Dec 1944 M-26 Aug 1974

            7 HERZOG, Rachel Cory           B-16 May 1976

            7 HERZOG, Erich Philip          B-15 Nov 1977

            7 HERZOG, Samuel Edward         B- 3 Sep 1979

    5 HOOPER, John Bruce B-19 Apr 1922
    5 HOOPER, Norma Delilah ANDERTON, Sp. (1) B-17 Apr 1922 M-10 Aug 1942 D-25 Dec 1944
    5 HOOPER, Vay Anna PRICE, Sp. (2) B-13 Apr 1930 M-17 Apr 1957 D-12 Jun 1980
```

6 HOOPER, Douglas Bruce B-25 Dec 1944
6 HOOPER, Barbara Ann JOHNSTON, Sp. (1) B-6 Jan 1947 M-9 Feb 1967 Div.
6 HOOPER, Priscilla Jan PINKHAM, Sp. (2) B-4 Jan 1947 M-   Div.
6 HOOPER, Deborah Vivian GANT, Sp. (3) B-22 Mar 1955 M-26 Nov 1975
    Rice, Herbert L., Sp. (2)(to Barbara) B-   M-

        7 RICE, Corrina June Johnston   B-12 Jun 1965

        7 RICE, Janene Collette Hooper   B-26 Sep 1967

        7 RICE, Robert Jay Hooper   B-30 Nov 1970

        7 HOOPER, Crystal Ann   B-30 Aug 1971

        7 HOOPER, Jamison Douglas   B-20 Dec 1972

        7 HOOPER, Heather Lee   B-25 Mar 1975

        7 HOOPER, Sean Douglas   B-19 Aug 1976

6 HOOPER, John Calvin B-30 Apr 1958
6 HOOPER, Nannette Therese LAMP, Sp. B-30 Aug 1957 M-23 Aug 1980

        7 HOOPER, Raina Kristine   B-14 Jan 1981

6 HOOPER, Ronald Lloyd   B- 8 Jul 1959

6 HOOPER, David Lee   B- 5 Feb 1961

6 HOOPER, Vay Anna   B-14 Apr 1963

6 HOOPER, Cheryl Dene   B- 7 Mar 1965

6 HOOPER, Marilee   B-30 Jul 1967

5 HOOPER, David James B-25 Nov 1929
5 HOOPER, Juanita PATTERSON, Sp. B-25 Oct 1935 M-14 Aug 1954

    6 HOOPER, Dennis James B-30 Jun 1955
    6 HOOPER, Sandra Kay OSTLER, Sp. B-15 Jun 1958 M- 3 Nov 1977

        7 HOOPER, Brandon James   B- 1 Aug 1978

        7 HOOPER, Juston Royal   B-16 Feb 1980

    6 HAWKES, Jamie Denise B-10 Apr 1957
    6 HAWKES, Jeffery Edgley, Sp. B-10 Aug 1959 M-2 Jan 1981

    6 WEEKES, Leann HOOPER B-2 Feb 1959
    6 WEEKES, Harold Mark, Sp. B-13 Oct 1956 M-15 Sep 1978

        7 WEEKES, Weston Shay   B-28 Jun 1979

        7 WEEKES, Dallon James   B- 4 May 1981

DESCENDANTS OF--------   ### 3 MURDOCH, James "D" 1850-1924
                         ### 3 MURDOCH, Eliza THACKERAY, Sp. (2) 1870-1938

4 MURDOCH, James Douglas B-26 Sep 1899 D-14 Jan 1934
4 McCORMICK, Marguerite McMILLAN Murdoch Sp. B-18 Nov 1901 M-17 Jan 1922 D-19 Mar 1937
    McCormick, E. B., Sp. (2) B-   M-
        5 THORESON, Dorothy Eliza MURDOCH B-11 Nov 1922
        5 THORESON, Ole Thorold Eldon, Sp. B-6 Jul 1916 M-30 Apr 1944

            6 THORESON, Girl (Stillborn)   B-28 Mar 1945

            6 HILBUS, Gwendolyn Ann THORESON B-13 Jun 1948
            6 HILBUS, Essley Christopher, Sp. B-18 Jan 1945 M-20 Jul 1968

```
              7 HILBUS, Traci Leilani            B-14 Nov 1969

              7 HILBUS, Lindsey Kahuanani       B- 8 Dec 1978

              7 HILBUS, Kimberly Haunani        B-21 Aug 1981

      6 MORZELEWSKI, Barbara Lee THORESON B-10 Dec 1953
      6 MORZELEWSKI, David Frazier, Sp. B-11 Oct 1950 M-8 Dec 1973

              7 MORZELEWSKI, Dawn Lynn          B-29 Jul 1974

              7 MORZELEWSKI, Todd David         B-14 May 1976

              7 MORZELEWSKI, Eric Thoreson      B-15 Dec 1977

              7 MORZELEWSKI, Erin Ann           B-13 Oct 1979

4 OBERG, Helen Janet MURDOCH B-17 Nov 1902 D-15 Oct 1969
4 OBERG, Seth Michael, Sp. B-19 Oct 1902 M-15 May 1929 D-9 Jan 1970
  Oberg, Faye KEMPTON, (1) Sp. B-            M-
  Oberg, Ellen PRITCHARD, (3) Sp. B-        M-
  Oberg, Frances McCORMICK Hall, (4) Sp. B-          M-

      5 GILL, Janet OBERG B-16 Oct 1930
      5 GILL, Gordon Lee, Sp. B-10 Aug 1926 M-16 Oct 1957

              6 WARE, Lauralee GILL B-30 Jul 1958
              6 WARE, Kevin Reed, Sp. B-8 Jul 1958 M-6 Jun 1980

                      7 WARE, Andrea Marie          B-14 Nov 1980

              6 GILL, Jennifer              B- 5 May 1960

              6 McNABB, Veronica GILL B-3 Sep 1962
              6 McNABB, Richard Scott, Sp. B-18 Apr 1958 M-12 Jan 1982

              6 GILL, Carolyn              B-16 May 1965

              6 GILL, Natalie             B-13 Dec 1968

              6 GILL, George Michael       B-13 Mar 1972

      5 OBERG, Seth Michael Jr. B-16 Apr 1932
      5 OBERG, Julia Elaine MICHELSEN, Sp. B-1 Nov 1937 M-20 Jul 1957

              6 OBERG, Julie Marie         B-31 May 1958

              6 OBERG, Elizabeth Ann       B-16 Apr 1960

              6 OBERG, Boy (Stillborn)     B-31 Aug 1964

              6 OBERG, Eric Murdoch        B-11 May 1966

      5 SLY, Marian Jean OBERG B-31 Dec 1933
      5 SLY, Donald Henry, Sp. B-5 Jan 1928 M-12 Apr 1956

              6 SLY, Stephanie Jean        B-12 Jul 1957
              6 SLY, Girl (Stillborn)      B-27 Dec 1958
              6 SLY, Holly Marie           B- 3 Jan 1960

              6 SLY, Corbin Matthew        B- 8 Sep 1961

      5 OBERG, Lawrence Murdoch B-26 Mar 1935 M-unmarried D-17 Nov 1957

      5 OBERG, James Douglas B-1 Apr 1938
      5 OBERG, Marilyn Eileen BOYDSTUN, Sp. B-30 Aug 1937 M-20 Apr 1960

              6 OBERG, Mark Boydstun B-29 Nov 1961
              6 OBERG, Rebecca Naomi BARRACLOUGH, Sp. B-21 Jan 1962 M-10 Jan 1981

                      7 OBERG, Hilary Anne          B- 2 Aug 1981
```

        6 OBERG, Allison Marie   B-29 Jun 1964

        6 OBERG, Leslie Janette   B-29 May 1967

        6 OBERG, Timothy Andrew   B-30 Nov 1968

4 FITZGERALD, Gwendolyn Thackeray MURDOCH Doerr B-6 Jan 1904 D- 3 Oct 1981
4 DOERR, Kuno Jr. Sp. B-3 May 1904 M-19 Aug 1933 D-13 Oct 1960
4 FITZGERALD, Gerald, Sp. (2) B-22 Jan 1897 M-24 Apr 1962 D-23 Feb 1981
  Fitzgerald, Geraldine SAEGER (1) Sp.
  Fitzgerald, Elizabeth MOYLE (2) Sp.

       5 DOERR, Kuno III B-19 Aug 1935
       5 DOERR, Elsie June SIMPSON, Sp. B-3 Mar 1938 M-25 May 1957

            6 DOERR, Deborah   B-22 Jan 1960

            6 DOERR, Kimberly   B- 5 Oct 1962

       5 DOERR, Suzanne B-14 May 1938 D-20 Dec 1938

       5 TOTTEN, Jane Elizabeth DOERR B-28 Jan 1940
       5 TOTTEN, Richard Norman, Sp. B-14 Dec 1933 M-18 Apr 1960

            6 TOTTEN, Richard Doerr   B-18 Apr 1961

            6 TOTTEN, Roberta Gay   B-20 Jun 1963

            6 TOTTEN, Rebecca Joy   B-23 Jul 1965

4 HARVEY, Margaret Eliza MURDOCH B-1 Jul 1908 D-8 Dec 1956
4 HARVEY, Raymond Othello, Sp. B-18 Apr 1903 M-1 Feb 1927
  Harvey, Violette Christine Victoria Alvina HANSON Boylan, Sp. (2) B-12 Dec 1904 M-29 Dec 1958
  Boylan,   Sp. (1) B-   M-

       5 HARVEY, James Raymond B-26 Nov 1928
       5 HARVEY, Doris Adelle FRISBY Brandel, Sp. (1) B-15 Feb 1926 M-18 Jul 1952 D-4 Apr1968
         Brandel,   Sp. (1) B-   M-   Div.
       5 HARVEY, Sarah Sue STERIN, Sp. (2) B-19 Oct 1926 M-26 May 1972

            6 HARVEY, Philip Arnold   B- 6 Nov 1954

            6 HAYWARD, Brenda Gail HARVEY B-8 Mar 1960
            6 HAYWARD, James, Sp. B-27 Nov   M-23 Feb 1980

                 7 HAYWARD, James Alan   B-21 Jul 1980

            6 HARVEY, Karen Leigh   B- 2 Jun 1961

       BOYLAN, Daniel Henry B-18 Apr 1946

David Lennox Murdoch and Elizabeth Pinkerton Thyne

"A good heart, benevolent feelings and a balanced mind, lie at the foundation of character. Other things may be deemed fortuitous; they may come and go; but character is that which lives and abides and is admired long after its possessor has left the earth."—John Todd

So it was that Father's life impressed family. He possessed a heart of gold, a goodly share of benevolent feelings, and certainly a well-ordered, balanced mind. He was kind, yet stern; generous, yet intolerant with extravagance and waste; very sympathetic, yet not given to overindulgence. His life portrayed a keen intellect, an orderly mind, and a disciplined soul.

How futile words seem in attempting to pay tribute to him. He lived so abundantly. His ever-thoughtful consideration for others, his sincerity of purpose, his dignity and poise, and his profound humility were shining examples of a true Christian citizen.

Father lived daily the pattern he wanted his children to follow, and that pattern daily directed us to no uncertain paths. He definitely impressed upon our minds our obligation to face life honorably, truthfully, and humbly. We were all healthy, mischievous youngsters, and I dare say Father's task was not an easy one—but thanks for all the "spankings" and corrections he saw fit to administer—they are greatly appreciated now.

We enjoyed a glorious privilege in having a father who definitely defined a course he considered proper for us to follow. There was never a half-way point we might cling to—right was right and wrong was wrong. He pointed the way, led the way forcefully, and clearly emphasized the requirements necessary for successful living. There were two requisites he particularly wanted his children to possess. He wanted them to acquire the true spirit of obedience, and to reap the fullness of honest endeavor. Early in life we were taught the maxim, "Obedience is Heaven's first law, and order is its result; this a lesson good to learn for child and for adult." Also, "Honesty is the best policy." These principles, so strongly implanted in our lives, are now priceless, and frequently we remind ourselves of the debt we owe our parents. Their constant, fine tutelage taught us many of the deep things of life—faith, spirituality, duty, honor, truth, courage, love of home, love for one another, obedience, devotion, simplicity, patience, and perseverance, self-denial, kindness, and helpfulness—all those human elements that go into the building of substantial, worthwhile characters.

Father was the third child of William and Janet Lennox Murdoch, and was born in Cronberry, County of Ayr, Scotland, on the thirteenth day of January, 1852.

William Murdoch had few opportunities for the type of education he was anxious to acquire; however, he obtained sufficient schooling and understanding to become socially prominent in the community in which he lived. He rose to be underground manager of the Muirkirk Iron and Coal Works, a position he held until coming to America. The home he occupied still stands. It was maintained for the use of the underground manager. On its front wall is a plaque stating: "Linkienburn Place, Home of William Murdoch, Underground Manager of the Muirkirk Iron and Coal Works."

Grandmother Janet Lennox Murdoch was the first of her immediate family to join the Church. Father states in his diary that he often heard his mother singing: "Redeemer of Israel our only delight, On whom for a blessing we call. Our shadow by day and our pillar by night, Our King, our Deliv'rer our all."

In his youth, he did not sense the impact of it, but

in the intervening years it recurred to him many, many times, and he often wondered if his mother sang it purposely, in order to make an impression upon him.

Father's education was quite limited. However, he was an apt student and eager to acquire all the schooling possible. When fourteen years of age, he left home to become associated with the Whitelaw family as office boy. Later, by constant study and application to his work, he became secretary to Mr. William Whitelaw, a member of Parliament for the City of Glasgow. He served in that capacity for over four years, and lived all during that period of time with the Whitelaw family, part-time in London and part-time in Glasgow. It was interesting to hear Father tell of the style and ceremony of such a position. He invariably dressed for breakfast, luncheon, and dinner, and oftentimes strictly formally for evening affairs; but that type of life appealed to him. It was fascinating, elevating, and held for him a particular charm. He became accustomed to and enjoyed it.

It is most amusing to read in his diary how upsetting it was to him when he decided to notify Mr. Whitelaw of his intention to marry and go to America. He says, "I always was a kind of tender-hearted chap and this occasion and occurrence could not take place without my shedding tears. However, I was greatly relieved when it was over."

Father married Mother in Glasgow and sailed early in May 1878 for the United States. They were eleven days on the Atlantic. Their party consisted of William Murdoch; Mother and Father; Father's sisters, Janet and Margaret; Aunt Veronica; and John Adamson from Muirkirk.

Upon arrival in Salt Lake City, they were sealed in the old Endowment House and then traveled to Heber City by four horse teams—there was not a railroad operating at that time between Salt Lake and Heber.

In view of the fact that Father had no particular work to go to, he spent the summer months working in the fields, haying and so on. This type of work was such a departure from the fine position he had occupied that his hands became very sore, and many blisters formed. In the winter months he taught school in Heber City. His first son, William, was born there.

Later he moved to Salt Lake City and became an employee of ZCMI, where he remained for many years as chief accountant and credit man.

It was his great pleasure to return to his native land and have the opportunity of preaching the gospel that was so dear to his heart. The entire period of his mission was spent in Scotland, where he served as mission president, and where some of the happiest experiences of his life were recorded. To be able to return to his native land, the place of his birth, and to renew his old friendships and live over again the simple, yet wholesome pleasures of his youth, brought indescribable joy to him, and as an outlet to his emotions, he penned on the fifteenth of September, 1906, the following verses:

The Place Where I Was Born

In the upland, near the moss, where grows the
    bonny heather,
'Twas yesterday, I hied away in lovely autumn
    weather
To Gaswater and old Cronberry, the place where I
    was born
Some fifty years and more ago, upon a January
    morn.

Ensconced within a grove of trees, I found the little
    cot
Where first I saw the light of day, a pure and
    hallowed spot,
'Twas there a mother tenderly around me did
    entwine
Her arms of loving kindness about that little form
    of mine.

'Twas here I learned to creep and walk and play
    about the door,
And share the little ills of life which all mortals
    have in store,
No matter where I wander now or wherever I may
    be,
I'll cherish always fondly the dearest thoughts of
    thee.

Time's ravages so plainly show what changes you
    have seen
And from the bonny sheltered nook that looked
    upon the green
No sound of human life we hear, all, all is quiet and
    still
As we gaze upon the ruins of the house upon the
    hill.

That dear old place, I love it yet, tho' shattered are
    its walls,
And crumbling down to mother earth as rock and
    mortar falls,

I see its form as there I stand and gaze upon its face
A few more years and then, alas, no remnant we
    can trace.

In the upland, near the moorland, let me wander
    once again,
And hear the lark prolong its notes through the
    sunshine and the rain,
Let me see the cot beside the wood, the place
    where I was born
Which sheltered me in infancy upon that winter
    morn.

Mother and I left Salt Lake early in June, 1907, to join Father in Scotland, tour about some, and then return home with him. What a delight to visit such interesting places with them—what a great opportunity to again live with them their experiences of the past, and what a privilege to have Father escort us to all the historic spots of England and Scotland that were so dear and familiar to him.

Upon his return home, he and his son, William, established the Murdoch Grocery, purchasing property and erecting a building to house such an establishment. By January 1, 1908, the store was completed, fully stocked and ready for business. However, before the building was completed, Father joined the office staff at ZCMI and remained there until two and one-half months before his death.

All his life, Father enjoyed excellent health. His robust constitution fortified him to weather any illness he might have developed. In his married life he never spent one day in bed because of illness. I remember upon one occasion remarking to my brother, "Well, I hope when I reach Father's age (he was then seventy-five), I'll have the mentality he has." My brother jokingly replied, "Well, I hope I'll have his stomach." He was never too old to go coasting or bobsleighing. He was a great lover of the outdoors and thoroughly enjoyed canyon picnics. He was particularly fond of hiking and could outdistance many of the younger boys and girls.

One day over twenty years ago, he chanced to meet an old friend on the street who had met with reverses. In the course of conversation this person persuaded Father to loan him two or three hundred dollars on some property in Lamb's Canyon. Father knew nothing of the place, had never seen it, but he did not question his friend's word, and immediately gave him the money. Eventually the property fell into Father's possession. Later on he decided to visit the property

and investigate the situation. Certainly this small act of kindness richly rewarded Father—he discovered he owned one of the choicest lots on the Forest Home property in Lamb's Canyon. Negotiations were immediately made to construct a summer home, and since that time many, many happy summers have been spent there.

Father would roam all over the hills surrounding the Forest Home property. On reaching one of the highest peaks (probably 11,000 feet high) in that vicinity, he decided it would be a fine thing to make yearly excursions to it, and took pride in guiding visitors there. He made it a point to see that everyone who made the trip contributed to the "rock pile." This he called the Cairn. He christened this peak Mount Murdoch—today it has its place on geography maps and is known as Mount Murdoch.

Father's sister, Janet, married William Baird of Heber City. They and their family moved from Heber to Carey, Idaho, where they purchased extensive land interests and followed ranching and cattle raising as a vocation. They became quite independent and prospered in their ventures. Several members of the family are now located there.

Another sister, Margaret, married John Adamson, one of those who accompanied Grandfather William Murdoch's party to America. Uncle John and Aunt Maggie, as we called her, became very prominent in Church work, both in Park City and in Carey, Idaho. Uncle Billie and Uncle John (Father's brothers-in-law) were splendid, energetic, reliable, dependable men, and accumulated considerable means in the ranching business, at one time owning extensive land interests and the Hot Springs near Carey. Uncle John's boys branched out into the mercantile business and at present are engaged in this business as well as the sheep industry.

Uncle James (Father's brother) came to America before his family, and located in the East. After the family came to Utah, Uncle Jimmie followed them and located in Park City, where he became very prominent and wealthy through his connections with the mining industry. He was very active in Masonry, having served as a past Grand Master of that order. Consequently, he did not join the Church until very late in life. He was greatly respected in the community for his honest dealings, yet he was considered a "close" Scotsman.

In reflecting upon the past, I am sure Father's family today would say, "How well Father used what money he had." Well do I remember one evening when he came home from business quite upset. He was a director in a certain building society, and in one of their meetings that particular day, it was decided that the stockholders were to be paid a certain amount for every meeting they attended. Father was much grieved over this decision. He had made a motion at that meeting that instead of the stockholders being paid for attendance at the director's meetings, the money be used for helping widows and other struggling women depositors to carry their load. His motion did not carry, and for some days he was quite perturbed over the affair.

He enjoyed fine business connections, and although he did not acquire much of this world's goods, he did maintain a large home and was a splendid provider. There was an abundance of everything about the home. Father's independent nature saw to it that there was plenty for the family. There was plenty for those less fortunate and plenty to hold him secure in his declining years. He was always quite proud of the fact that it was his privilege to be one of the owners of the first paper mill erected in Utah. It was located at the mouth of Cottonwood canyon, and burned down before operations began.

Again, I hope I shall be pardoned for quoting some of the sentiments expressed when Father passed on, April 24, 1928. Brother Orson Romney said: "The home-life of Brother Murdoch was most admirable; his business life most honorable; his faithfulness to Church duties was untiring. We love to think of his home—we appreciate our long acquaintance with him."

Brother William Romney, a close business associate said, "It is in business where you come to know men and know their true worth. I was always inspired by his fidelity, his honesty, and his ability. He was one of the best office men I have ever had the pleasure of meeting. He was punctual and thorough, and during many years of close association I learned to love his many good qualities. He was a man to be trusted; his word was his bond. As a young man I used to look up to him as an exemplar along those lines, and as years advanced, that respect for him grew into ripened knowledge of his intrinsic value. As a member of the Church, Brother Murdoch was consistent and thorough. He was one of those who did not take everything for granted. When he was not quite sure of a thing, through study and research he endeavored to convince himself as to the truth or falsity of things, and having been convinced that he was right, stood up manfully for his convictions. He believed thoroughly

to carry out in his every thought and conversation the principles of the meek and lowly Nazarene."

James H. Moyle said: "Brother Murdoch was the same solid, substantial, stalwart, courageous character always independent, completely intelligent, but above all, courageous and true to his convictions. A true friend—there was no favor that he ever could do for one that he did not grant. He never asked anything much of anybody. He stands out as one of the outstanding and upstanding characters of my business life. He has lived a noble life and was ever an example well worthy of emulation."

An expression from Nephi L. Morris: "In all his official acts I can certify to his unquestioned integrity and his honesty of purpose and his sound business judgment. David L. Murdoch was a trained businessman, technically trained. He had a principle in business, he knew what ought to be, and yet he had a heart. Often there was a conflict between his heart and his judgment as to what should be done, for there is nothing more pathetic than to see a human being in distress when he needs help, and I suppose nearly all of us have been that person at some time in life. I have often seen the exacting demands of business practice speak "No," and then I have seen David L. Murdoch come and plead for a new decision, and when it could not be given I have seen him pledge his own name and his own credit to help a brother who was in need. David L. Murdoch was of a literary trend, in addition to his business training. He wrote poetry, he was highly spiritual minded, and a very intelligent man, always giving personal attention to the question of religion. I congratulate his family on having had so noble a sire, one of such assertive independence as to deny or defy the demands of conformity, for if you wish to succeed, just conform; but some stalwart people have succeeded in spite of their nonconformity, and he defied the traditions and the orthodoxies of his homeland, his native land, and the traditions of the time, and took his place manfully with the people of his adoption. He came to this country, has made a name—he has won distinction and honor." George Albert Smith made this statement: "It was a little difficult for me to get acquainted with Brother Murdoch when I was a child; in fact I rather felt that he was cold and distant, but as the years went by and I discovered his real worth and the tenderness of his heart, I learned to love him, and I am grateful to my Heavenly Father to have had the companionship of such a man. The only favors he ever asked of me that I can recall were in the interest of somebody else—a desire to please someone who needed encouragement."

Father passed away very suddenly—he had just picked up his pen to write a check when death called him. There has always been consolation in the words of Brother Nephi L. Morris; he said, "You had better let the vibrating string of the violin snap while vibrating with sweet harmony, with vitality and life, than to die out gradually and see a decline of power and influence and ability to produce."

But in the living of such an honorable life, may I dare say, he was deserving of all the blessings he enjoyed. His whole life was dedicated to the service of others. His motto, "Service before self," and his favorite quotation, "Oh why should the spirit of mortal be proud," gave impetus to a rich and noble life. In conferring gifts or favors, or in dispensing or sharing his material belongings, Father was very particular to see that his right hand knew not what his left hand did. His modesty in such matters was one of his charms.

It has been my desire not to write so much of his business or occupations in life, but to give some idea as to how well he lived. If this short biography can inspire others to emulate his philosophy of life, I shall be happy indeed.

Written by Janet Murdoch Thompson, a daughter June 5, 1938

Elizabeth Pinkerton Thyne Murdoch

My wish:
To keep a green point growing within myself
Whatever winds be blowing
To put out blossoms one or two
And when my leaves are thin and few
To have some fruit worth showing.

The above verse is so attuned to the life Mother lived, so typical of her ideals, ambitions, and desires, and so in harmony with her accomplishments, it seems most fitting and appropriate that I should commence this short biography by quoting it.

From my earliest recollections, Mother always kept a green point growing within herself, a green point growing within her home and garden, and a green point growing within her community. Countless blossoms she shared, bounteous fruits she harvested.

Mother's exemplary life, enriched by years of abso- lutely unselfish devotion and endeavor, has given to her posterity a heritage it should not fail to be worthy of.

At the present time Mother has only one surviving close relative—cousin James P. Gilmour of London, England. A short time ago I wrote to him asking for in- formation regarding Mother's people. It has been quite a regrettable situation that we did not press Mother into telling us more of her early life and her family. She was most modest in relating any of her personal affairs and we, in our youthful and thoughtless years, neglected to learn more about her.

Cousin James has graciously sent the following, and I shall quote him before going into Mother's life as we have known her. Referring to Mother he says, "Cousin Elizabeth Thyne bore considerable resemblance to her mother, but on a smaller scale. As I knew her, she was a comely lass, high-spirited, with a vibrant, ex- pressive personality. Self-reliant and adaptable, she efficiently and faithfully performed the duty nearest at hand and earned the respect and affection of all in any circle in which she moved. Her interests and activities extended far beyond the limits of home and found scope in church work, especially as a Sunday School teacher. A pianist of more than average talent, I was touched when on her visit to us in Glasgow, over forty years ago, she played for me my mother's favorite air. Cousin Lizzie, attractive as she was in form and feature, and even in greater measure for her mental and moral merits, did not encourage philanderers, and altho she had not nearly reached the old-maidenish age, we had somehow come to think of her as vowed for the single life. It was therefore a great surprise when David Lennox Murdoch, then private secretary to William Whitelaw, a Scottish member of Parliament, who was a fine, upstanding handsome young man with charming manners, was introduced to us as her accepted lover. When he came courting her, and the parlor was "verboten" to us, we used to vie with one another as to who would carry in the cups of coffee which were served to the wooer and his "lady fair" towards the close of the long evenings of their fore- gathering. It was a still greater and more perturbing surprise when, leaving all to follow the man of her choice, Cousin Lizzie married David and they almost forthwith set sail for the United States.

"It is difficult for us who have not lived through those narrower and harder times into the wider life and more liberal and humane thought and feeling of the present day, far as it still is from complete eman- cipation of the mind from the bonds of tradition and prejudice, to realize the virulence of the odium theologicum sixty years ago, when even the mildest heresy was looked upon with abhorrence, and its exponent treated almost as an outlaw. Mormonism in particular was held in evil repute, simply because of the gross misrepresentation of the doctrines of the Church of the Latter-day Saints, and the wicked fabrications as to the moral character of its members. I have sorrowfully to record that in our household, from Grandfather downwards, Cousin Lizzie was judged to have yoked herself to the ungodly and to have gone off to worship false gods. But none of us, and least of all we youngsters, could banish from our minds the thought of her goodness and kindness of heart, so that secretly we felt sure that, even were she a strayer from the fold, a place would be found for her at last in whatever heaven was reserved for us, and this mightily comforted us."

In speaking of religion, Cousin James writes, "Altho Grandfather, Uncle William, and my father were in substantial agreement theologically, there were minor points of doctrine upon which they did not see eye to eye and in discussing them more *heat* than light was apt to be generated. Once only did I venture to put in my oar. This was reproved as an act of presumption, but the head and front of my offending was the use of the word 'Sunday.' I think, even now, that I hear Uncle William thundering, "Never let me hear ye say that word again. I tell ye it's a pawgin word. Sawbath is God's word for the first day o' the week."

I am, indeed, grateful to Cousin James for his consideration, thoughtfulness, and helpfulness in forwarding this material to me.

Mother was born November 12, 1851, in Glasgow, Scotland. Her parents were James Thyne and Elizabeth Barr Gilmour Thyne. Grandfather passed on during Mother's childhood days, and Grandmother Thyne moved to her father's estate in Kelvin Grove, Great Grandfather Gilmour being a prominent and influential nurseryman. Mother was reared in her grandfather's home and remained there until her marriage to Father.

As I have already intimated, Mother was not much given to speaking of herself or of her relatives, but from occasional conversations, we gathered a few facts we have always been grateful for.

From facts obtained from Cousin James, we know Mother was a clever individual in her younger days, and we children knew Mother as a real executive in the home—most original, ingenious in mind, and active in body. In her enthusiasm to have her children amount to something, she occasionally referred to the things she had accomplished in her younger years. When I was nine years of age Mother taught me to crochet, and one of the first things I made was a silk tie for my father. I remember taking it to school and showing it to my teacher. The teacher seemed to think it quite incredible that I could crochet as well as the tie indicated. When I returned home and told Mother the attitude the teacher had taken, she said, "Well, you just tell your teacher that I crocheted my grandfather one when I was *six* years of age." One can well believe that to be true, for Mother's indomitable will to succeed was predominantly conspicuous.

Grandmother Thyne and her father saw to it that Mother's education was carefully planned. Every opportunity was afforded her, and her alert, keen mind fashioned for her early in life abundant resources upon which she could draw.

Mother was educated at Dollar Academy near Glasgow, and was given the best schooling available at that time in music. Also, she was given practical training in sewing and homemaking.

Cousin James has often told us Mother was the life of the Gilmour household. Her cheerful, willing disposition to be of service seemed to ever prevail, and she achieved wide popularity because of her radiant personality and spirit of helpfulness.

Mother belonged to the Glasgow Choral Society for years. She was thoroughly acquainted with the music and words of the masters. She was also familiar with the best operas and could without hesitation repeat phrase after phrase of different oratorios and operas when occasion presented itself.

Needless to say, immediately upon her arrival in Salt Lake, she sought affiliation with the different musical organizations, being a member of the old Salt Lake Oratorio Society, also the Tabernacle Choir. She was the first organist in Heber City, Utah, and after returning to Salt Lake to reside permanently, became organist in the Twentieth Ward.

Ten children were born to Father and Mother, eight girls and two boys. However, only five lived to maturity, one boy and four girls, all of whom are at present living. They are William Murdoch, city commissioner of finance; Janet M. Thompson, a member of the General Board of the Relief Society; Norah T. Clark, at present hostess for the Twin States Light and Gas Company, Rochester, New Hampshire; Mary Murdoch, cashier of the Murdoch Grocery Company; and Afton M. Warner of Midvale, Utah. If space would permit, many interesting stories might be told regarding Mother's active life. She radiated life itself in every word and deed, and saw to it that all those with whom it was her good fortune to mingle radiated the best they possessed.

Mother was an expert with needlework and dress-making, doing all the sewing for her family, even to making coats and hats. And oh, for the beautiful underwear she designed and made! It was not an uncommon thing for her daughters to wear panties and petticoats with yards and yards of insertion and lace or embroidery. Our wash days, always on Mondays, were quite an event, and seemed to consume most of the day. We took turns at turning the handle of the washer. At present, there are three old relics of washers painted up in our backyard. They are now used for flower stands and surely have considerable value.

Mother was not a very active Church worker. She maintained that her first duty was at home, and I guess her vociferous family pretty much saw to it that she magnified her first duty. However, she was generous with her contributions, always willing to give of her time, talents, and money for the interest of the Church or the community. Well do I remember, when a certain ward bazaar was held, how determined she was that the Relief Society should dispose of all the aprons Mother could make. If I recall correctly, she made approximately one hundred aprons. Although not an active member, she was imbued with the spirit of Relief Society, and her Scottish determination saw to it that that organization excelled in sales at that particular affair. Never once did she question Father's pocketbook, and never once did Father question her wisdom in spending. Both by nature were very generous.

Mother followed her father's inclinations for gardening, and her house plants and garden plants were always things of beauty. Everything seemed to bloom so prolifically—perhaps because she so generously shared the beauty of it with those about her. Every spring she and Father spent hours searching the flower catalogs for rare and beautiful plants. How insistent Mother was that each plant should be placed in a definite spot in her garden—and Father invariably acceded to her wishes. How often have I heard Mother correct Father for the way he watered the garden. In her garden, as with everything else, there was a systematic way of doing things, and the entire family was the victim of that system. But I dare say, we are deeply grateful for the system Mother attempted to inculcate.

In looking back on Mother's life, one is impressed with the splendid sense of balance she possessed. When we were small children we always had help in the home, but Mother and Father saw to it that no member of the family was slighted in having sufficient work to do to keep us "out of mischief" as Mother said. Each one was allotted a portion, and each one met his or her portion without question. None of our excuses ever worked. We usually enjoyed about two picnics a summer out to some resort. We were given a certain amount to spend—our parents never questioned what we spent it for—but we were never permitted to ask for more—it was definitely understood before leaving home what our obligations would be.

Another outstanding characteristic was Mother's sympathy and understanding for animals. When horses were so popular, she delighted in seeing they were not abused. Often we children were embarrassed when Mother would severely reprimand some teamster for the manner in which he handled the "poor dumb brutes," as she called them.

Our home was one of genuine hospitality; friends were always welcome. In fact, Mother insisted that we bring them home and entertain them; then she knew what we were up to. Frequently after school, half a dozen or more of our playmates would return with us, and we'd go into the laundry, where Mother had a stove for laundry work. We would light a fire, fry potatoes, bake apples, and devour the cookies concealed in the basement. It was Mother's delight to plan parties for us. Especially I remember one time she planned a beautiful party for the entire eighth grade. This party was held on the second of December, and many of the mothers thought our mother extravagant for having such a party so close to the holiday season. Mother also saw to it that the larder was filled every Saturday with pies and cakes and fruit for the boys and girls who might drop in. It is refreshing after all these years to hear some of these same boys and girls reminisce about the experiences they enjoyed at our house.

In reflecting over the happenings of past years, and analyzing the mission performed by Mother, we are not unmindful of the many sacrifices she made for the sake of the gospel and for the sake of her family. Mother left all that was dear to her in her native land, and embraced the gospel regardless of all protests of the family. She came to Utah, where she knew no one, and where few cultural things could be offered at that time and where few luxuries such as she had been accustomed to could be found. But Mother was fearless, she had implicit faith in the gospel. She knew that "in the way of righteousness is life; and in the pathway thereof there is no death."

One of Mother's friends said, "When I think back upon the life and the association that we have had with

Sister Murdoch, I can think of nothing but goodness in her life. She was a lover of all that was beautiful in the home and outside of the home. Pass their house anytime, and you will be impressed with the beautiful surroundings, beautiful flowers, and the well-kept garden—everything suggestive of that high nature."

We shall ever cherish Mother's devotion to her family—everyday in our home was children's day, and the spirit of friendliness, joy, and happiness that persistently radiated from our parents will ever endear them to their family and those they befriended. Surely, Mother was in every sense of the word a skilled homemaker. Her love for the gospel, for her family and friends, for flowers and music, confirms the fact that in every deed, thought, and action, she kept a green point growing—that the blooms she produced have born fruit. Such an exemplary life will ever serve as a beacon to her family and will always be worthy of emulation.

Mother passed away on the sixteenth of April, 1927, just one year to the month before Father's passing. We shall ever remember her independent spirit and her absolute determination that she should never be a burden to anyone. She succeeded nobly. She seemed to understand that her mission was completed and just slept peacefully on until the summons came.

Janet Murdoch Thompson, June 5, 1938.

Journal of a Voyage

By David Lennox Murdoch Liverpool, England to Heber City, Utah

Friday—May 24, 1878

Busy getting luggage on board. "Neveda" steam tender lying at No. L Bridge landing stage for "Neveda." Goodby company (over 300) of Danes, Norwegians, English, Scotch, Irish, all busy looking after their luggage and beds. Great many strangers looking on and evidently wondering at so many going to "Utah," which was printed on most of the boxes. Left landing stage at 7:00 o'clock P.M. for Neveda barywell in mid river. Arrived at Neveda in a few minutes and commenced pulling women, children on board, then the luggage which was strung on board in big bundles and pretty roughlike handled some of it was. Only hope it may reach its destination in something like safety. Waited by to see all our luggage strung on. Afterwards

went and had tea in Ladies Saloon—slept first night on board in cabin—our own bunk not being made up.

Saturday—May 25, 1878

Got up at 6:00 o'clock and visited Father Aird and the steerage. Some up and some getting up, some washing. Men, women and children all huddled together and apparently quite happy. Father Aird not very well. Got a little better after breakfast. He told us that a number of those in steerage had never been in bed, but had been singing and dancing and playing musical instruments. Father Aird not feeling very well felt annoyed at the noise and said there was no fools like those of latter days. He also said the Scotch saints were the best. Got breakfast shortly after 8 o'clock which consisted of Irish stew and roasted steak and coffee. Between breakfast and dinner a number of Immigrants came on board. Dinner at 12:00 o'clock, broth, roast beef and potatoes was our dinner. We all enjoyed dinner very well. 2:13 from the steam tender which brought few other passengers has just left. Anchor being weighed we sailed at 2:20 from nearly opposite the Victoria Dock Liverpool. Weather very fine and warm slight and everyone seems in first rate spirits and quite glad to leave their native land. Have not seen anyone grieved like. Would almost have been impossible to have left under more auspicious weather. 6:00 P.M. Sailing continues fine, have just had tea and cold meat to it. Feel first rate. Got on top coat and up to deck again. Meeting held at 9:00 P.M. when the arrangements were announced for the voyage as regards worship namely one half past 7 in the morning and 8:00 o'clock at night. Thomas Judd as president on Captain with elders Neve and Howell as Councilors. Elder Ball as Chaplain. Elder Clawson as secretary and other elders and brethren to assist all in their power.

Sunday—May 26, 1878

Got up about 6:00 o'clock having slept well and passed a nice night. Got on deck and found a good many there already Off the coast of Ireland a few drops of rain falling occasionally but think it will keep up and be fine throughout the day. Prayers at 7:30 by Elder Neve, it was announced that for the future the hour of morning prayer would be 7:00 instead of 7:30. Signalled the sister ship Wyoming 7:45 which takes a number of elders to England. 11:45 A.M. entered Cook Harbor leading up to Queenstown where about

30 passengers were taken on board, 3 went ashore. The harbor of Cook is very beautifully situated. Has works and erections of defense placed at the mouth entering into Queenstowne Bay. Much indebted to brother John Allan for use of field glass which brings Queenstown and surrounding scenery quite near to us. 11:45 A.M. Leave Queenstown Bay. Shortly will have one last look of land for a few days. Dinner at 12:00, broth, roast beef, potatoes and plum pudding. Have just come on deck from our dinner. Sun shines bright slight lead moved, with the exception of part of coast of Ireland we now see nothing but the great expanse of the mighty deep as far as the eye can reach. Just visited the steerage, they are coming up from their dinner and a number are busy washing their dishes. Brother Aird is busy washing his with cold water. He has never done the like of this all his days, he says and can't get on with the cold water. I advise him to rub them well but he says that cold water will not rub off *Greesh!* Went down to steerage at 2:30 to meeting. Brother Ball spoke very plainly to the saints as to using their soap keeping themselves cleanly and I am sure his words were much needed. More Latter Day Saints than those on board the Neveda require the same preaching. Had tea at 5:00. Boat heaving a little several had to rise from the tea table. Janet could not come to tea. Maggie had to rise from it. Good deal of sickness aboard this Sunday afternoon. Janet gone to her bed wishing she was landed. Maggie also in bed. Lizzie vomited and a little better afterwards. Just going out of sight of land 8:40 P.M. Very many of our company sick and vomiting sorely this afternoon and evening.

Monday—May 27, 1878

Got up shortly after 6:00 o'clock—boat heaving a good deal. Vomitis on nothing up could not take breakfast. Got cup of tea and small piece of bread, threw it up sometime after. Could not go to dinner. Great amount of sickness on board vessel dipping at stem and shipping seas. Lizzie not up today. Janet and Maggie the same. Father and Aunt never been sick at all. Two or three hail showers today, wind pretty high and cold. Have seen nothing in the shape of vessel outward or home bound. Nothing would stay on my stomach at all today. I got a little brandy at bedtime which made me sleep and feel better.

Tuesday—May 28, 1878

Got up about 8 and dressed. Got on deck and found it literally covered with passengers. Morning beautiful and fine, wind slightly changed to southwest. Sea so smooth that no white seen at all. Most passengers great deal better this morning. I could not go to breakfast but got some oat cakes, pickles and red herring and enjoyed it fine. Made me thirsty and drink a great deal. Went down to dinner and got pea soup and corned beef and potatoes. Feel nearly alright today. Lizzie went to breakfast and also to dinner today. Jennie and Maggie great deal better also and all on deck. Ladies all retired early except Lizzie and all feel sickly again, sea little rougher. Retired shortly after 8:00 o'clock. Slept very little, heaving considerably.

Wednesday—May 29, 1878

Got up about 8:00 o'clock. Boat still rocking a good deal, had a little tea and bread to breakfast. Then went on deck. Good number there already notwithstanding a drizzling rain accompanied by a mist which enshrouds everything at a distance of about 200 yards. Informed we passed the "Idaho" this morning about 4:00 o'clock. On her homeward bound voyage. Ladies all in bed this morning and taking very little. Lizzie up laughing and vomiting alternately, back to bed again, went to dinner today—had broth, currie rice and potatoes. 4:00 P.M. Rained all day, up til now. Clearing up somewhat. Passed a brigantine outward bound. Lizzie managed on deck a short time, had tea at usual time. Weather rather unsettled like wind pretty much ahead. Went to bed about 7 or little after. Not feeling quite well.

Thursday—May 30, 1878

Awoke before 5 and found we were standing still. Get up about 6 and got on deck. Good many there and working away at engines. Got a start made about 7. Strong head winds. Was told by man in cabin that some of the brasses round one of the cylinders were getting too much heated and were melting. Was told by 2nd mate that a rat had got its tail into the safety valve and so had stopped the engines and that the rat was so anxious to get its tail out as they were to have it out. Surly looking day. Got breakfast of dryhash and cold water. Lizzie, Jenny and Maggie all in bed and getting some breakfast. They all seem pretty well but won't get up, all that we can do. Lizzie got up a little before and went to dinner. I had for dinner today, soup, halicot, potatoes, and plum pudding. Day keep dry but very gusty. Birth on board this morning, a boy—a dane or rather an oceanic boon in the steerage of the steamship Neveda on Thursday morning about 8 o'clock. The boy was blessed this afternoon and named Neveda Atlantic.

Friday—May 31, 1878

Got up this morning before 6 o'clock. Not having rested very well and feeling as if I would like to vomit. Got on deck and very stormy morning and very few there. Out of 342 saints and about a one hundred of a crew. Vomited shortly after getting on deck and felt much better afterwards. Before going down to breakfast at 8 o'clock we sight a Barque outward bound she was battling with the strong breeze as well as she could but seas laboring good deal. Had salt fish and tea for breakfast. Felt better afterwards. Lizzie up this morning—Jenny and Maggie for the first time for 3 days. Saw a bottle nosed whale this morning a short distance off, blowing the water in the air. Strong head wind still blowing, keeping us back considerably. Had dinner of pea soup, hotch potch potatoes. Did not enjoy it very much. Got disgusted this afternoon at so many dirty devils of Mormon boys and men smoking and spitting all around. Felt so bad that quite out of sorts and like to vomit. It's quite evident that a good number of people on board are carrying all their old pernicious habits with them. Had tea with a little pie, but still suffering from an ill temper caused by the selfishness of some dirty fellows smoking and blowing away like a furnace even beside women and young children. Took a little brandy—retired to bed about half past 6. Slept well at intervals.

Saturday—June 1, 1878

Got up about 7 and got on deck. Few there, morning cold and strong north west wind blowing went down to breakfast shortly after 8. None of our ladies up this morning except Aunt. (Veronica Murdoch Caldow) Was told we were on the "Bank of Newfoundland." Water seems green this morning instead of blue as heretofore. Had curried beef—rice to dinner, cold wind still blows. Into last thousand miles. Passed two Barques today, one outward, other homeward bound. Had tea as usual got on deck again, still blowing strong and very cold. Sighted few more Newfoundland fishing boats, passed one quite close by and waved to them they waved to us.

Sunday—June 2, 1878

Got up this morning about 7 o'clock and got on deck. Lovely morning, slight head wind, nearly everybody on deck even our ladies have all got dressed and got on deck. Had breakfast at 8—hot bacon and tea. Enjoyed this meal better than any yet on board. The bacon was really first rate. Sun shines bright this morning and everyone seems cheery and in good spirits. This is our 2nd Sunday at sea, the day is so fine, the ship going so steadily that one quite forgets all the sickness and unpleasantness of a sea voyage. Had dinner of Kidney soup, stewed rabbit and plum duff, appetite gets keener and enjoyed it well. Present at meeting this morning about 11:00 o'clock in the cabin when the Captain went through the English church service form of worship. The cabin was quite filled—was present also at meeting in the steerage at 2:00 o'clock when brothers Ball, Morton spoke. Had tea at 5 with some pie. Was at meeting for prayers in steerage at 8 o'clock and retired shortly afterwards.

Monday—June 3, 1878

Got up on deck this morning about 5 o'clock—about half a dozen there. Sun just breaking through. Water calmer this morning than any day since beginning our voyage. Fog came on about 6 o'clock and has been very dense all day. Fog whistle blowing nearly all day and one to 10 at night. Had breakfast of Irish stew and tea, dinner of soup, boiled pig, cabbage and potatoes. Tea at 5 o'clock again. Went down to meeting in the steerage at half past 6 o'clock when directions were given as to how we were to proceed at New York with luggage by tickets etc.

Tuesday—June 4, 1878

Got up at half past 5. Got on deck and found a few there. Dense fog still prevails and we seem to steer very slowly. Sailors busy washing and cleaning, so as to appear as clean as possible. Had breakfast of potatoes, soup and tea. Some people think they smell land this morning, had dinner at 12 of pea soup, stewed rabbits and potatoes. Shortly after noon the mist cleared quite away and the sun shone out bright and warm. Had tea at 5 with cold meat. Great preparations going on this afternoon for a concert which is to take place for the delectation of those invites in the cabin. Myself and wife were not invited and so did not attend. Mist still comes at intervals and goes off again. Passed quite close by an American fishing boat with a good number of hands on board. The men waved their hats and bonnets towards us and a number of our company did the same.

Wednesday—June 5, 1878

Got up at 5 o'clock and got on board. Few there, morning finer, mist quite cleared away. Was told we took pilot on board at z past 12 at night. Sighting a good many smacks etc this morning. Went down to breakfast at 8 and had a red herring and some Irish stew. Steerage passengers throwing their beds and mear utensils overboard 10 A.P. land not yet seen but all gages on the outlook for it. 11 A.P.T. approaching land, sun gets warmer, everybody on deck. Who all seem glad our sea journey is at an end. Steaming up the Hudson River and are waiting for doctor. Doctor ultimately comes on board and we all pass before him. Being all in good health and in sickness. We then proceed to the Guron landing place where a few of cabin passengers get ashore. Steam out again to the Guron pier, where Brother James met us. (James "D" Murdoch) We had a busy time getting baggage out of hold and putting it on a tender. We got through it, very smartly and well. Everything was in ship shape fashion and there was no trouble. Got into Castle Gardens about half past 5. Stayed overnight at Stevens Hotel, which is on the European plan. In Broadway we were informed this morning that the "Idaho" one of the Guron lines which we passed on Wednesday 29th of May had struck on a rock off the Irish coast and gone down in 20 minutes. All hands saved.

Thursday—June 6, 1878

Got up this morning, had breakfast and took a walk up Broadway and then to Central Park. Saw the menagerie there and were much pleased with the exhibition of so many animals, birds etc. Had ice cream and some fancy bread. This treat is immensely thoughtful. We being all a little tired and hot, it was so cooling. Came back to hotel, had dinner and then took ourselves off again to the Castle Gardens. We got into steam tender again and crossed over to the Jersey side where we got onto the railroad cars. We got started on our railway journey about 7 P.M. We got away very slowly within numerable stopovers.

Friday—June 7, 1878

We are all awake at day break. Few of us slept much. Some none at all but all seemed pretty well and before

6 o'clock we had a little singing pioneering—beautiful. Then about 6 o'clock we began to go along the "Banks of the Susquehanna," we continue to run alongside a considerable way. It is a beautiful broad but shallow river, the scenery at some parts is very fine particularly at the Susquehanna. Quite a bridge moving it up and down the river. Preceeding on towards the Allegheney Mts., which is following a river most of the way. The scenery is very beautiful, perhaps a little sameness about it. The horseshoe bend was pointed out to us as being a very quick drive. Got into Pittsburgh about 9, where we had to change cars. This movement was encountered with the utmost confusion and disorder. It was understood by those in charge of companies that we should all take up the relative positions in the new cars as we held on the old. This was not carried out at all. The Scotch and a number of English got all muddled up together in the first carriage. The English would not move and the Scotch thinking they were in the right place stood firm, so we stood this for sometime in the utmost confusion, at length those of the Scotch and English who could not get accomodations in the first car had all to move themselves and their luggage through 7 or 8 cars right at the end of the train. In the center of the train as made up at Pittsburgh were placed the Russian Immigrants, 2 carloads so that in moving we had to leave through the Russian ranks. The odors and smells arising from those people together with the wild ghastly appearances they had as they lay. Men, women and children separated up on the floors of the carriage on seats and every inch of vantage grounds was sickening and when the journey had to be made more than worse it became doubly so, however as the darkest night has always its dawn so our little troubles will come to an end. At length we got arranged as well as we could and got to sleep. We all slept better this night than the previous ones from the fact I suppose of being all more tired.

Saturday—June 8, 1878

Awoke about 4 o'clock. Morning wet. People soon begin to stir, some to eat, some to wash. Was told this morning that the cars with the Russians had been moved to the back of the train. After leaving Pittsburgh this rectified matters very much, as our people were as before—in continuous and succeeding cars. We had frequent stops today of short duration but long enough to permit of many of our company stepping out to pluck flowers. Arrived at Chicago about 9 o'clock, changed onto the Chicago and North Western

Railway. At Chicago and for many miles around the ground soaked with wet, in some places flooded. The ground here abouts is as level as the floor of a house and of course this will account for the dampness.

Sunday—June 9, 1878

Did not sleep much during the past night. Awake at intervals and hearing the rain falling heaveily. Got up, washed about 6 o'clock. Morning continues dull til about noon, when it cleared up fine and warm. Stopped at several places today a short time which gave us time to take runs out for water, flower etc. At the larger of those stations at which we stopped today the residents thronged down to see us I suppose they knew by wire about the time we would arrive because they were in considerable numbers. Some of them were very curious to see us all and forced their way down through the cars, some of them were very forward and gave evidence of malicious feelings, others were quite pleasant to talk to and seemed very anxious to make into conversation. Crossed over the Missouri by a very large bridge as we entered into Omaha The darkness of the night prevented us from getting a very good view. Got into Omaha about 10 o'clock where we changed into Union Pacific Railroad cars. This change was for the worse as regard to the accomodations in the cars. The cars themselves were old and dirty and rattled as if we were riding slickers instead of upon rails. The luggage also had to be changed into UPRR cars which took up a little time. This was the fist change the luggage undergone since leaving New York. Got started somewhere about midnight. Traveling very slowly our train load being pretty heavy. It consists of three baggage cars in front, followed by 3 carloads of Immigrants (American) for California. They again were followed by car loads of our company.

Monday—June 10, 1878

Got properly awaked this morning about 6 o'clock having slept badly during the last night. Morning cold but soon got very warm. Still traveling nicely but rather slowly along. Stopping today as yesterday at good many stations for water etc. Got out, sometimes for a run and to pull a flower or two. Grasshoppers this morning. First real natives we had seen. Got out several of us, got out in the afternoon and amused ourselves by high leaping and running. There was a concert in our carriage in the evening when several fine songs were sung by members of our company.

Tuesday—June 11, 1878

Got up this morning at half past 5 having slept well. Dark morning, cold but grew warm as it approaches noon. Moving along at miserably slow pace with frequent stoppages Many taking runs out today to pluck flowers and to look at any object having any interest at all attached to it. Arrived at Cheyenne about 4 o'clock shortly before there was a thunderstorm passed over us. The rain which fell cooled the atmosphere nicely. At Cheyenne we saw several bars of silver for New York Market. Reached summit of Rocky Mountains about 8 o'clock. Shortly after leaving here we passed through a good many snow sheds.

Wednesday—June 12, 1878

Got up about 6 o'clock. Stopped a short time at Carbon where one or two of the old country people came in and talked a short time with some of our company with whom they were acquainted. Morning very warm. 377 miles to Ogden from this station. This is our 18 day from Liverpool. After breakfast my wife and self got bad with sickness vomiting and diarrhea. The vomiting and retching was very painful. Got some brandy loaned and took it which helped us very much. One curious thing about this illness was that we both got bad at same time and both seemed to get better about same time.

Thursday—June 13, 1878

Got up about 6 o'clock feeling much better after yesterdays illness. Fine bright morning and much cooler and pleasanter than some mornings past. Traveling very slow and don't understand why. It seems as if the journey from Omaha to Ogden was more tiresome and wearisome than the rest of the whole journey put together. The cars still rock and vacillate very much and when starting or stopping the shock is like to tear one in pieces. Stopped at Evanston a short time. A few people there recognized some amongst our company and chatted a little. Passing down the Echo Canyon the scenery becomes at once wild and grand. The rocks tower way above us many hundred feet. Arrived at Echo station, the greeting that some of our people received from friends and relations and acquaintances was quite enthusiastic and warm. Our car was quite besieged for a short time, passing on from there we shortly pass the Devil's Slide. We next pass through Weber and the Valley seems rich and fertile, while the surrounding mountains are clad with snow. Passing along the Devil's Gate is pointed out to us which is a large projecting rock contracting the channel of the water to a narrow pass. The water rushing down through at a very rapid pace. A road passes round the ledge of the road just the breadth of the wheels and no more. This continues for a considerable distance and should two vehicles meet one or other must give way and turn back before they can pass. The scenery at the Devil's gate is of that wild and grand character portrayed above. We reached Ogden about 6 P.M. Confusion prevailed here for a short time so soon as we had stopped, just so soon were our cars beseiged by people looking for their friends and the talk and the changing of cars and personal luggage and the meeting of friends occupied about an hour. We then got off for Salt Lake City which we reached some where near 9 o'clock. Of course our first outlook was for mule pack but no mule pack was there. We having arrived a day or two earlier than was expected. We shortly found H.G. Park who kindly took us to the Bailey House where we remained over night. Then down at the station next morning I found Uncle John on horseback who then took charge of us and conveyed us to his home in Heber in wagons where we found many friends ready and willing to minister with our wants. It was quite like returning home after a long absence. So many friends around us hardly left us time to think on the old country. Our Journey up to Salt Lake City was performed in 19 days, 11 days by sea, 1 day and night in New York and 7 days by rail across vast continent, America, (the distance was at sea 3100 miles and rail 2475). It is now past and gone as a dream. It returneth not any more. At times it seemed wearisome and we felt like as if we never would undertake another such, but after a little rest and after so much kindness from friends we seem to quite forget our little hardships and troubles and think no more of them. Our luggage turned out all right and nothing so far as known lost. Our Captain of Company, Thomas Judd deserves a word of praise for his kind and patient and impartial attention to all. Like a good Captain having a great responsibility upon him, he was always at hand late and early looking after the comfort and welfare of his charge. His mind must have been greatly relieved if it was possible to have been embarrassed when he got released of his charge at Salt Lake City. His company did well under him and turned out one more on arrival at destination than what we commenced with. The cleverest man amongst our company and another man rumor says, got left at Chicago. I presume they would come on soon after. (Taken from "History of David Lennox Murdoch" compiled by his daughter Afton Warner 1974)

THE MURDOCH STAVE.

FEW of the present generation may ever have heard of the Murdoch Stave, or know anything concerning it. It is principally associated with the Parish of Auchinleck. That Parish seems to have been the home of many Murdochs. There were in the last two centuries, Murdochs in "Commondyke," Murdochs in the "Common," Murdochs in the "Orchard," Murdochs in the "Raw," Murdochs in Auchinleck, Murdochs in "Skerrington Mill," and Murdochs in "Bellowmill." In addition to these there were Murdochs in New Cumnock "Ashmark," and Old Cumnock, and also in Muirkirk. Besides all these there were Murodchs in other parts of Scotland, so that they must have formed altogether quite a numerous family. The question has often been asked, were those Murdochs located in the Parish of Auchinleck and adjoining parishes related to each other? At the present day it is somewhat difficult to determine whether they were or not; and if they were what that relationship was. The genealogy of the Bellowmill Murdochs has been traced out somewhat clearly on account, no doubt, of the early associations of that place with William Murdoch, the inventor of gas, etc., his life covering a period of some 85 years, 1754-1839. The inventor's father was John Murdoch of Bellowmill, who would be born somewhere about 1720, his six children ranging from 1748 till 1765. John Murdoch's father was William Murdoch of Skerrington Mill, which is as far back as we can go at the present. The maker and donor of the Murdoch Stave is supposed to have been John Murdoch of Bellowmill, father of the inventor, who was "miller, farmer, and millwright, a man of considerable mechanical skill, inventor of toothed circular irongearing," whose ancestors are said to have resided in the district for centuries. Having long had a strong desire to see this stave, and availing myself of the opportunity while in my native land after an absence of thirty years, I journeyed to Auchinleck and made inquiry as to its whereabouts. I was not long in locating it, and examining it I found that it is a manufactured article, and not a native grown cut stick, but is made out of some smooth even-grained wood of foreign growth. It is a strong, well-made stave, with the head or handle projecting about half-way on either side of it. In other words the handle is fastened somewhat in the relative position that a handle is to a hammer. At the head of the stave is a wide brass ferrule containing the following original inscription, which is here given just as it appears on the brass ferrule:—

THIS STAVE I LEAVE
IN LEAGSIE TO THE
OLDEST MURDOCH
AFTER ME
IN AUCHINLECK. 1743.

The date is some eleven years prior to the time of the inventor's birth. The stave is now 163 years old, and is in a well-preserved condition, all things considered. It has now passed through many hands, some of whom have cared well for it, others, it is regretted, have not shown that interest in the relic that might have been, and ought to be, expected of them. Let us hope that in the years to come it may be more highly esteemed and prized as a most interesting memento of by-gone days. The stave is in the possession, for the time being, of John Girvan, whose mother, Mrs Girvan, Jean Murdoch, was the last custodian of the stave. It descended to Mrs Girvan from Mrs Terras, Dalsalloch, who was also a Jean Murdoch. Mrs Terras inherited it from David Murdoch, gardener to the Marquis of Bute, who is said to have cared well for it and put the ferrule on it at the end of the stick. David Murdoch inherited it from one John Murdoch, Coalroad, Auchinleck, who is said to have "ripeit the ribs" with it, evidence of which is not altogether lacking. This John Murdoch is said to have inherited it from a Mrs Rankine, Lugar. This is as far as I can trace it at the present time. Perhaps this may catch the eye of some one who can throw some further light upon it. The whiter of this is a descendant of Robert Murdoch of Commondyke whose wife's name I

should like very much to learn. They were married in 1737. He died in 1792. The stave, then, is intimately associated with the Parish of Auchinleck, and is destined to so remain for all coming time. Mr Matthew M'Turk, whose demise occurred a few years ago, and whose knowledge and information, especially of matters pertaining to the parish, were unexcelled by any, took a great interest in the Murdoch family, and saw to it that the stave was always handed to the next "oldest" in the parish. His son, Matthew also by name, appears to be peculiarly adapted to succeed his father in this interesting work.

While upon this subject, the idea suggests itself to the writer that, as the Murdochs have now become a very numerous clan, being found in every country on earth, that it might be deemed advisable to have a federation of all bearing that name; that their history might be kept and their genealogy preserved, and that the clan might be like others of purely Scottish origin, designated by a tartan which should become emblematic of them.

DAVID L. MURDOCH.

David L. Murdoch holding the stave.

This article was written about 1906. Mrs. Terras was Agnes Murdoch, daughter of David of Dalsalloch, according to "The Murdochs". Robert Murdoch of Commondyke was married to Margaret Wyllie.
                                    --Ruby Hooper

An Appreciation

Lord keep us, Leck,[1] what's this you've sent
In carton big, well tied wi' hemp
And stamps galore, tae bring it through
By parcel post, addressed by you.

Fish, fowl, or duck or deer, Na! Na!
'Tis something else as guid and braw.
A great big cabbage new unfolds its face
Solid and sweet, the biggest in the place.

Fair fa this jewel o' the Scotch broth pot
Man, Leck, I'll sup them when they're hot
And smack my lips o'er ev'ry dish—
Nae greater treat could I e'er wish.

Fit specimen fra the Hot Springs Ranch
Near Carey, up the Hailey Branch,
A great resort, too little known
But time its greatness yet will own.

Friend Condie is the owner there

Of honest toil he has his share
The fruits of which are plainly seen
Hay stacks and stock on pastures green.

Long may he reap big bumper crops
Of hay and grain and horned stocks
That bring returns of honest gain
Filched from the soil by brawn and brain.

Carey, my dear, I love you well
There oft I think I'd like to dwell
'Tis there I've spent some happy hours
Wood River's banks and shady bowers.

There yet I hope some time to bide
And wily tempt the finny tribe
Fresh caught and cooked—oh, what a treat!—
On rivers' banks so clean and neat.

David Lennox Murdoch, October 19, 1917

---

1. Nickname for William Lennox Adamson, to whom this poem is addressed.

David Lennox Murdoch's
home at 73 G Street
Salt Lake City, Utah

Children of David L. Murdoch

Back row, left to right:
William Murdoch
Norah Thyne Murdoch
Mary Murray Murdoch

Front row, left to right:
Janet Lennox Murdoch
Afton Lennox Murdoch

Camp Murdoch
in
Lamb's Canyon

Mary Murray Murdoch
Afton Lennox Murdoch
Elizabeth Pinkerton Thyne Murdoch
    (Mother)
Jerrold Elvirus Thompson
David Lennox Murdoch (Father)
Janet Lennox Murdoch Thompson

June 1916

Veronica Murdoch, William Murdoch,
and Janet Lennox Murdoch

William Murdoch, David L. Murdoch,
Jerrold Elvirus Thompson, and fish

David L. Murdoch and Elizabeth
with Elizabeth's show flowers

David L. Murdoch's descendants after the burial of Norah Thyne Murdoch Clark
May 1959

HUSBAND   DAVID LENNOX MURDOCH

Birth   13 January 1852
Place   Cronberry, Ayrshire, Scotland
Chr
Married   18 April 1878
Place   Glasgow, Lanark, Scotland
Death   24 April 1928   Salt Lake City, Salt Lake, Utah
Burial   27 April 1928   Salt Lake City Cemetery, Utah
Father   William MURDOCH
Mother*   Janet LENNOX
Other Wives,
if any

WIFE   ELIZABETH PINKERTON THYNE

Birth   12 November 1851
Place   Glasgow, Lanark, Scotland
Chr
Death   16 April 1927   Salt Lake City, Salt Lake, Utah
Burial   19 April 1927   Salt Lake City Cemetery, Utah
Father   James Service THYNE
Mother*   Elizabeth Barr GILMOUR
Other Wives,
if any

Where was information obtained Afton Warner-David L. Murdochs
                                                 papers & letters

*List complete maiden name for all females.

1st Child   William MURDOCH
   Birth   15 September 1878
   Place   Heber City, Wasatch, Utah
   Married to Jeannette Cousins SMITH
   Married   19 September 1900
   Place   Salt Lake City, Salt Lake, Utah(Temple)
   Died   8 October 1940 Salt Lake City, Utah

2nd Child   Elizabeth Pinkerton Thyne MURDOCH
   Birth   17 March 1880
   Place   Heber City, Wasatch, Utah
   Married to
   Married
   Place
   Died   19 June 1882 Salt Lake City, Utah

3rd Child   James Thyne MURDOCH
   Birth   19 June 1881
   Place   Heber City, Wasatch, Utah
   Married to
   Married
   Place
   Died   11 August 1881 Salt Lake City, Utah

4th Child   Baby Girl MURDOCH (Twin)
   Birth   Stillborn   before 18 Oct 1882
   Place   Salt Lake City, Salt Lake, Utah
   Married to
   Married
   Place

5th Child   Baby Girl MURDOCH (Twin)
   Birth   Stillborn   before 18 Oct 1882
   Place   Salt Lake City, Salt Lake, Utah
   Married to
   Married
   Place

6th Child   JANET Lennox MURDOCH
   Birth   7 August 1884
   Place   Salt Lake City, Salt Lake, Utah
   Married to Jerrold Elvirus THOMPSON
   Married   29 September 1909
   Place   Salt Lake City, Salt Lake, Utah (Temple)
   Died   24 April 1953 Salt Lake City, Utah

7th Child   Veronica MURDOCH
   Birth   3 July 1886
   Place   Salt Lake City, Salt Lake, Utah
   Married to
   Married
   Place
   Died   5 Apr 1896 Salt Lake City, Utah

8th Child (2)Norah Thyne MURDOCH
   Birth   7 February 1890
   Place   Salt Lake City, Salt Lake, Utah
   Married to Herman Everette CLARK
   Married   17 July 1912
   Place   Salt Lake City, Salt Lake, Utah
   Died   9 May 1959 Concord, Merrimack, N.H.

9th Child   Mary Murray MURDOCH
   Birth   23 July 1891
   Place   Salt Lake City, Salt Lake, Utah
   Married to
   Married
   Place
   Died

10th Child   Afton Lennox MURDOCH
   Birth   2 June 1894
   Place   Salt Lake City, Salt Lake, Utah
   Married to Joseph Moroni WARNER
   Married   24 September 1919
   Place   Salt Lake City, Salt Lake, Utah(Temple)
   Died

Bookcraft Inc. S.L.C. (W-100 Form)

1 MURDOCH, James 1786-1831   2 MURDOCH, William 1825-1913
1 MURDOCH, Mary MURRAY, Sp. 1782-1856   2 MURDOCH, Janet LENNOX, Sp. 1821-1877

DESCENDANTS OF-----------3 MURDOCH, DAVID LENNOX 1852-1928
                         3 MURDOCH, ELIZABETH PINKERTON THYNE, Sp. 1851-1927

4 MURDOCH, William B-15 Sep 1878 M-19 Sep 1900 D-8 Oct 1940   B-Birth
4 MURDOCH, Jeannette Cousins SMITH,Sp. B-14 Feb 1879 D-28 Feb 1945   M-Marriage
                                                                    D-Death
     5 MURDOCH, David Lennox B-29 Jun 1901 M-3 Jun 1930 D-20 Nov 1978 Sp-Spouse
     5 MURDOCH, Ora Maureen CLARK, Sp. B-19 Jul 1909   Div-Divorced
                                                                    Numbers-Generation

          6 MURDOCH, William Richard B-19 Oct 1931 M-11 Jun 1953
          6 MURDOCH, Arthell WILKINS, Sp. B-12 Aug 1931

               7 WINEGAR, Deborah MURDOCH B-13 May 1957 M-14 Apr 1978
               7 WINEGAR, Drew LeMar, Sp. B-4 Feb 1957

                    8 WINEGAR, Andrew James   B-2 Aug 1979

               7 MURDOCH, Alison   B-4 Feb 1960
               7 MURDOCH, Rosemary   B-11 Oct 1968
               7 MURDOCH, William Matthew B-10 Jan 1970

          6 MURDOCH, Michael Clark B-28 Feb 1936 M-12 Aug 1960
          6 MURDOCH, Connie Lou RILEY, Sp. B-11 Aug 1941

               7 MURDOCH, Janthia Ann   B-11 May 1961
               7 MURDOCH, Kathryn Ilene   B- 4 Oct 1963
               7 MURDOCH, David Lennox   B-11 May 1966
               7 MURDOCH, Michael Clark   B-13 Aug 1969

          6 WILSON, Janet Lennox MURDOCH B-18 Jun 1945 M-12 Jul 1968
          6 WILSON, Charles Allan, Sp. B-2 Nov 1944

               7 WILSON, Michelle Diane   B- 6 Oct 1969
               7 WILSON, Margo Ann   B-17 Oct 1972
               7 WILSON, Meg Elizabeth   B-20 May 1977

     5 WEGGELAND, Mary Smith MURDOCH B-10 Aug 1903 M-5 May 1927
     5 WEGGELAND, Gordon LeRoy, Sp. B-15 Jul 1903

          6 SMITH, Mary Barbara WEGGELAND B-10 May 1929 M-31 Jul 1950 Div.
          6 SMITH, Wallace Burbidge, Sp. B-25 May 1929

               7 STONEBROOK, Martha Gay SMITH B-18 Mar 1953 M-   1979
               7 STONEBROOK, Charles, Sp. B-

               7 SMITH, Sandra   B-16 Mar 1956
               7 SMITH, Mary Jane   B-28 Nov 1961
          6 WEGGELAND, Gordon Gail B-6 Jul 1930 M-19 Jun 1953
          6 WEGGELAND, Flora Ann, Sp. B-12 Sep 1931

               7 WEGGELAND, Mark Cannon B-17 Dec 1955 M-21 Nov 1978
               7 WEGGELAND, Lisa HANCOCK, Sp. B-

               7 WEGGELAND, Mary Lynn   B-15 May 1957
               7 WEGGELAND, Leslie Ann   B-12 Jun 1962

          6 WEGGELAND, John B-24 May 1932 D-28 May 1932

          6 WEGGELAND, Jeannette B-24 May 1932 D-28 May 1932

          6 WEGGELAND, Warren Murdoch B-17 Jan 1935
          6 WEGGELAND, Barbara Marie RAY, Sp. (1) B-19 Mar 1937 M-24 Apr 1956 Div.

               7 WEGGELAND, Steven Rav B-23 Nov 1956 M-   July 1978
               7 WEGGELAND, Jenny   ,Sp. B-
                    8 WEGGELAND Courtney   B- Aug 1979
               7 HALE, Karen Jeanne B-24 Jun 1958 M-1 Jun 1979
               7 HALE, John, Sp. B-

          6 WEGGELAND, Mary Susan OSTLER, Sp. (2) B-   M-21 Jul 1965 Div.

```
              7 WEGGELAND, Heidi          B-17 May 1966
              7 WEGGELAND, Amy            B-10 May 1971


  5 MURDOCH, John Thyne B-7 Sep 1905 M-3 Apr 1933  D-12 Jun 1974
  5 MURDOCH, Ruth Streeper, Sp. B-17 Nov 1905


         6 MURDOCH, John Streeper B-22 Apr 1935 M-26 May 1956 D-3 Apr 1957
         6 MURDOCH, Martha Jane BROWN, Sp. B-10 Sep 1936
           Isaacson, Lyle Edward, Sp. (2) B-2 Mar 1927 M-1 Jan 1959


                 7 WHITLOCK, Jahn Streeper  B- 2 Oct 1957 M-28 Dec 1978
                 7 WHITLOCK, Warren, Sp. B-

                    Isaacson, Lizabeth       B-13 Apr 1960
                    Isaacson, Susan          B- 9 Dec 1961
                    Isaacson, John Steven    B- 3 May 1964


         6 MURDOCH, Thyne Streeper B-26 Jun 1938 M-       1960
         6 MURDOCH, Teresa Jane Conner, Sp. B-12 Jul 1941

                 7 MURDOCH, Shannon        B- 9 Apr 1961
                 7 MURDOCH, Melinda        B-29 Jun 1963
                 7 MURDOCH, Brandy         B-10 Mar 1972


         6 MURDOCH, Charles Stephen B-20 Sep 1941 M-15 Apr 1967
         6 MURDOCH, Ann TROXELL, Sp. B-28 Dec 1942

         6 MURDOCH, James Philip B-16 Jun 1945

         6 MURDOCH, Richard Bruce B-19 Mar 1949 M-          Div.
         6 MURDOCH, Beverly EVANS, Sp. B-

                 7 MURDOCH, Johnathan Zan   B-21 Nov 1974
                 7 MURDOCH, Syndey Brooke   B-11 Mar 1977

  5 HATCH, Elizabeth MURDOCH Ross B-26 Dec 1908
  5 ROSS, George John II, Sp. (1) B-17 Apr 1906 M-3 Jun 1931 D-28 Mar 1944
  5 HATCH, LeMoyne Lyerla, Sp. (2) B-26 Nov 1903 M-20 Jan 1954
    Hatch, Esther Alleen FAGG, Sp. (1) B-6 Sep 1908 M-7 Sep 1929 D-10 Jun 1953


         6 ROSS, William Murdoch B-3 May 1932

         6 ROSS, George John III, B-17 Oct 1937 M-26 Dec 1958
         6 ROSS, Diane Rosella MILLER, Sp. B-29 Jan 1939

                 7 ROSS, Kimberly        B-17 Oct 1961
                 7 ROSS, Stephanie       B-21 Nov 1962
                 7 ROSS, Stacie          B-29 Jun 1965
                 7 ROSS, Bradley John    B-11 May 1968


         6 HULTQUIST, Carolyn ROSS B-6 Apr 1942 M-24 Aug 1964
         6 HULTQUIST, Richard Arthur, Sp. B-19 Mar 1940

                 7 HULTQUIST, Richard Allen B-28 Jan 1967
                 7 HULTQUIST, Sarah        B-23 Nov 1969
                 7 HULTQUIST, Cari         B- 4 May 1972 D-4 May 1972
                 7 HULTQUIST, Ashley       B-16 Oct 1973


            TRONIER, Marilyn HATCH B-21 Jan 1933  M-5 Sep 1953 (Mother-Esther Fagg)
            TRONIER, Ronald Bruin, Sp. B-

                    TRONIER, Tamaralyn       B-19 Jun 1954


  5 ROMNEY, Jeannette MURDOCH B-14 Jan 1911 M-15 Jul 1935
  5 ROMNEY, Wendall Bitner, Sp. B-5 Mar 1906


         6 HULL, Janet ROMNEY B-19 Jun 1941 M-30 Dec 1964
         6 HULL, Clyde L , Sp. B-1 Jan

                 7 HULL, Scott Romney     B-28 Feb 1966
                 7 HULL, Mark Steven      B-16 Oct 1967
                 7 HULL, Allyson          B-12 Apr 1970
```

6 WILLIAMS, Nan Murdoch ROMNEY B-12 Jul 1945 M-1 Sep 1967
6 WILLIAMS, Dwight Bradley, Sp. B-27 Oct 1943

      7 WILLIAMS, Dwight Bradley III B-3 Dec 1970
      7 WILLIAMS, Wendell Romney   B-3 Jul 1972
      7 WILLIAMS, Ann Marie   B-29 Dec 1976
      7 WILLIAMS, Elisabeth   B-12 Apr 1978

5 MURDOCH, William Jr. B-15 Jan 1911 M-7 Oct 1936
5 MURDOCH, Lucy Deanne Parkinson NIBLEY, Sp. B-6 Mar 1914

    6 McQUEEN, Anne Nibley MURDOCH B-31 Jan 1939 M-7 Jun 1963
    6 McQUEEN, Craig Hugh, Sp. B-14 Mar 1939

      7 McQUEEN, Melissa Anne   B-24 Aug 1966
      7 McQUEEN, Heather Jane   B-13 Apr 1968
      7 McQUEEN, Rebecca Susan   B-11 Feb 1970
      7 McQUEEN, Jennifer Jill   B-25 Aug 1977

    6 BRIGGS, Susan Nibley MURDOCH B-31 Jan 1939 M-20 Mar 1969
    6 BRIGGS, John Frank, Sp. B-6 Feb 1942

      7 BRIGGS, Jason Scott   B-21 Feb 1970
      7 BRIGGS, Jennifer Susan   B- 8 Sep 1971
      7 BRIGGS, Jaron Sean   B-24 Dec 1974

    6 GARDNER, Jane Nibley MURDOCH B-23 Jun 1948 M-13 Dec 1968
    6 GARDNER, Martin Ralph, Sp. B-   Nov

      7 GARDNER, Joshua   B- 2 Jan 1970
      7 GARDNER, Erin Michelle   B-13 Aug 1971
      7 GARDNER, Bryn Elizabeth B-30 Jan 1976
      7 GARDNER, Lynsey Jill   B- 4 Jul 1979

5 BUCKWALTER, Ellen Jean MURDOCH B-2 Oct 1918 M-21 Sep 1940
5 BUCKWALTER, David Jesse, Sp. B-

    6 BUCKWALTER, David B-18 Sep 1947 M-
    6 BUCKWALTER,   Sp. B-

      7 BUCKWALTER, Ashley   B-

5 MURDOCH, Robert Gail B-10 Jun 1921
5 MURDOCH, Betty Lou MATTHEWS, Sp. B-28 Sep 1922 M-30 Mar 1944 Div.

    6 BOYD, Janice MURDOCH B-22 Apr 1947 M-
    6 BOYD, Charles Wilbur, Sp. B-

      7 BOYD, Eric   B-
      7 BOYD, Lance Robert   B-
      7 BOYD, Charles   B-

    6 CHRISTENSEN, Betty Ann MURDOCH B-17 Oct 1949   M- 4 Jun 1971
    6 CHRISTENSEN, Randall Wynn, Sp. B-4 Apr 1949

      7 CHRISTENSEN, Jennifer   B- 8 Apr 1972
      7 CHRISTENSEN, Ryan Wade   B-16 Apr 1974
      7 CHRISTENSEN, Richard Warren B-28 Oct 1976
      7 CHRISTENSEN, Reed Willaim B-30 Jun 1978
    6 PORTER, Heather Sheri MURDOCH B-19 Feb 1952   M- 18 Apr 1974
    6 PORTER, David Preston, Sp. B-28 Jan 1951

      7 PORTER, Ami   B-12 Feb 1975
      7 PORTER, Chad David   B-15 Jun 1976
      7 PORTER, Michael John   B- 9 Oct 1977

5 LEONARD, La Vonne MURDOCH B-13 Aug 1923 M-19 Sep 1950
5 LEONARD, John Granville, Sp. B-20 Aug 1921

    6 LEONARD, John Granville III B-6 Apr 1952

6 GOGGIN, Patricia Ann LEONARD (Penny) B-13 Sep 1953 M-
6 GOGGIN,   Sp. B-

6 LEONARD, Bonnie Jane B-10 Aug 1958

4 MURDOCH, Elizabeth Pinkerton Thyne B-17 Mar 1880 D-19 Jun 1882

4 MURDOCH, James Thyne B-19 Jun 1881 D-11 Aug 1881

4 MURDOCH, Baby girl (Stillborn) before Oct 1882

4 MURDOCH, Baby girl (Stillborn) before Oct 1882

4 THOMPSON, Janet Lennox MURDOCH B-7 Aug 1884 M-29 Sep 1909 D-24 Apr 1953
4 THOMPSON, Jerrold Elvirus, So. B-2 Jun 1881 D-28 Mar 1942

4 MURDOCH, Veronica B-3 Jul 1886 D-5 Apr 1896

4 CLARK, Norah Thyne MURDOCH (2) B-7 Feb 1890 M-17 Jul 1912 Div. D-9 May 1959
4 CLARK, Herman Everette, B-26 Aug 1877 D-25 Aug 1955
  Clark, Katherine R. Rich, Sp. (1) B-   M-31 Dec 1903   .
  Clark, Mattie   ?   , Sp. (3) B-   M-

     5 WADMAN, Elizabeth Thyne CLARK, (2) B-10 May 1913 M-1 Jun 1941 D   1979
     5 WADMAN, Grosvenor, Sp. B-2 Sep 1903 D-25 Dec 1963
       Wadman, Dorothy Smith, Sp. (1) B-   M-   Div.
       Campbell, David, Sp. (2) to Dorothy B-   M-

              WADMAN, Bill   B-
              WADMAN, Timothy B-
     5 CLARK, Charles Everette B-4 Feb 1917 M-10 Oct 1945
     5 CLARK, Nancy KERN, Sp. B-10 Nov 1923

          6 CLARK, David Lennox B-30 Apr 1947

          6 CLARK, Constance B-7 Sep 1949 D-30 Nov 1949

          6 CLARK, Jeanne B-5 Feb 1955

     5 GEYER, Georgia Varney CLARK B- 12 Mar 1920 M-10 Jan 1942
     5 GEYER, Abbott Winfield, Sp. B-24 Jun 1918

          6 EHLERS, Gay GEYER B-31 Oct 1945 M-24 Sep 1966
          6 EHLERS, Dwayne, Sp. B-

                  7 EHLERS,

     5 CLARK, Janet B-12 Mar 1920

     5 CORSON, Martha Varney CLARK B-4 Aug 1924 M-22 Apr 1943
     5 CORSON, Bernard Whitehorn, Sp. B-16 Jun 1920

          6 CORSON, Clark (2) B-20 Oct 1944 M-
          6 CORSON,   Sp. B-
                  ,   Sp. (1)B-   M-   (1 Child by Sp. (1)

          6 CORSON, Craig Bartlett B-21 Mar 1949

4 MURDOCH, Mary Murray B-23 July 1891

4 WARNER, Afton Lennox MURDOCH B-2 Jun 1894 M-24 Sep 1919
4 WARNER, Joseph Moroni, B-15 Jan 1893 D-13 Jul 1969

     5 OMO, Thyne WARNER B-9 Dec 1920 M-11 Jun 1941
     5 OMO, Stonewall Jackson, Sp. B-12 Feb 1910

          6 MURASKO, Michelle OMO Bush B-6 May 1947
          6 BUSH, Gary Lee, Sp. (1) B-20 Oct 1944 M-23 May 1965 Div.
          6 MURASKO, Michael Vincent, Sp. (2) B-5 Feb 1940 M-31 Dec 1976
            Murasko,   Sp. (1) B-   M-   Div.

```
              7 BUSH, Shane Scott        B-14 Oct 1965
              7 BUSH, Shawn Michael      B-19 Jul 1968

                MURASKO, Michael         B-16 Dec 1963
                MURASKO, Brad            B-10 Apr 1966
                MURASKO, Don             B- 3 Oct 1967

5 WARNER, Joseph Murdoch B-7 Nov 1923 D-24 Nov 1970

5 WARNER, David Lennox B-16 May 1925 M-3 Apr 1957
5 WARNER, Mildred Boscovich, Sp. B-18 Aug 1934

      6 WARNER, David Lennox III   B- 7 Nov 1958
      6 WARNER, Frederic LaMont    B-26 Jul 1961
```

Janet Murdoch and William Baird

William Baird, Sr., was born November 3, 1849, at Rutherglen, Lanarkshire, Scotland. His parents were John Baird, Sr., and Elizabeth Marshall. His grandparents were Robert Baird and Agnes McGowan, and William Marshall and Ann Willey.

William Baird was known by many as Billy Baird. His parents had invited the Mormon missionaries into their home and had attended cottage meetings in other homes when living in Rutherglen, and he was baptized October 18, 1859, along with his neighbors and acquaintances. He was always full of life and adventure as a young man. At the early age of nine he left school and went to work. His experiences took him from the shipyards to a tailor shop, where he was bound as an apprentice for seven years at a half crown per week with a raise of about twenty-five cents per year. Because he was a few minutes late one morning his employer abused him and choked him, so he ran away to Glasgow. Penniless, he walked the streets for some time, and finally got a job with another tailor.

His parents, unknown to him, were visiting relatives in Glasgow on their way to port for sailing to America. They were en route to Salt Lake City with seven hundred other Mormons. He accidentally met them on the street and sailed with them to America on the ship Bellwood. It was a vessel propelled only by the wind, and their journey took them seven weeks. Many a night he awoke and listened to the captain instruct the crew as they pumped water to keep them afloat. On the ship's return trip to Liverpool, it sank in mid-ocean. Their food during the trip was salt pork and hard tack, and it was rationed out each day to make sure they had enough to feed them during the trip.

The Baird family stayed on the east coast just long enough to provide themselves with a covered wagon and supplies for them to cross the plains. Young William, a boy of about seventeen years, left his family and went as a driver of a freight wagon for a shipping company. After driving for some time, he and four other boys could not stand the cruelty of their employer and left him. They took their bedrolls on their backs and a little flour and bacon. They walked across the plains. The only protection they had was a gun, and it had no ammunition. When they arrived at Green River, Wyoming, they were almost starved, but soon found friends and got a job driving wagons to Salt Lake City. When they arrived in Salt Lake City, they found the Baird family once more. William was much surprised, for while he was walking across the plains, he found a buffalo skull upon which was written the account of his family being killed during an Indian raid. It was the custom of the pioneers to leave messages written on buffalo skulls for the companies that followed. Shortly after arriving in Salt Lake Valley, the family moved to Heber. Here his youngest sister was born. She is Mrs. Jane Phillips. The night she was born, he spent the night holding milk pans over his mother's bed to keep her dry as the water ran through the dirt roof.

Billy met and courted Janet Murdoch in Heber. They were married February 5, 1880, in the old Endowment House in Salt Lake City, Utah. They had nine children. They had a farm adjoining his father's farm in Lake Creek. In April of 1898 they moved to Carey, Idaho, and bought the Hot Springs Ranch. This ranch contained more than one thousand acres, along which was located a group of hot springs giving it its name. Through the claim flowed the waters of Fish Creek, which fed the lake. This ranch was off the highway, and they grubbed sagebrush off it. It had plenty of water, and the farm flourished.

On September 20, 1898, his wife, Jennie, gave birth to a baby girl, and three days later she passed away with complications due to childbirth. This was a frightening experience for the family. She was a very close companion to William, and he was lonely. His eldest daughter, Jessie, was sixteen years of age and did her best to help her father take care of the family and keep up the home for three years. At the age of nineteen she was married.

January 29, 1902, Billy married Isabelle Sneddon in the Salt Lake Temple. She was called Belle by most people. He had a large house built for her closer to town in Carey. One by one the boys were on their own herding sheep, breaking horses, farming, and so on. As the boys grew older, they bought land from their father and were successful farmers and livestock men. He soon found the large home too much for the two of them, and built a smaller one next to it. Belle was very devoted to him. They sang beautifully together. They had one son, Thomas. As they grew older they spent many winters in St. George and California. He loved to tell stories about his bonnie Scotland, and he loved Carey and the people there. He was a very temperate man in everything he did. He loved to go fishing, and raised a garden up to the time he was ninety-five years of age.

Isabelle died at the age of seventy, March 15, 1938. She was a very quiet, uncomplaining person. She was very thin, and wasn't very well for several years, but was up and taking care of Billy and their home. Their son Thomas was married, and they had three grandchildren, a girl and two boys.

Billy's daughter, Jessie, was left a widow, and in later years lived with her father; this helped his loneliness. As promised in his patriarchal blessing, his posterity praise him and his companion, and he always had plenty of the bounties of the earth. He was always alert and active in knowing what was going on around him. Although his boys were all away from home at an early age making their own livelihood, they had a strong bond of love and duty for one another throughout their lives.

An outstanding virtue of Billy and his sons was that of honesty. He worked hard as a young man, and taught his sons this virtue. He was a very good manager, was always clean, and kept his surroundings clean. He was a man blessed abundantly with good health. He remarked once, "I cannot remember when I have ever been ill or in pain." He had a skin cancer on his face close to his eye, and the last year of his life it started to grow so much that it impaired his vision. He passed away at the age of ninety-six, June 27, 1946. He is buried in the cemetery at Carey, Idaho.

Janet Lennox Murdoch was born October 18, 1855, at Gaswater, Ayr, Scotland. She was the daughter of William and Janet Lennox Murdoch. Her grandparents were James and Mary Murdoch, and David Lennox and Elisabeth Templeton. She was the fifth child of six children born to them. William also had another wife,

Mary Reid Lindsay, and three children were born to them.

Her father and mother were hard-working people, and she followed in their footsteps. She grew up in a family with close family ties. They learned to work together and were happy together. Her oldest sister was Elizabeth; then came James "D." David Lennox, and in 1854 a baby sister, Mary, who lived only eleven days. Janet was born in 1855 and was named after her mother. The last child in the family was born in 1858; her name was Margaret.

Janet was known to all as Jennie. She lived in several towns in Scotland in her early years, Gaswater, Ponesk, Muirkirk, and Kilmarnock. When she was nine years old, her sister Elizabeth, just seventeen years of age, passed away, and when Janet was twenty-two years of age, in 1877, her mother was also laid to rest by the side of her daughter Elizabeth in Muirkirk.

Janet's parents were members of the Church of Scotland. She had aunts and uncles who joined The Church of Jesus Christ of Latter-day Saints, and her mother also joined October 8, 1853. Her father, William, could see no need for making a change until several years later, October 8, 1877. Her parents were good, honest, religious people, and were well respected in the communities wherever they lived. Her mother went quietly about her duties in her home, where there was love and peace, but she was waiting for her desire to have her children and husband join the Church and come to Zion.

Her schooling commenced in Muirkirk. She had a fair education and was always an outstanding student in her class.

At the age of twenty-one, October 8, 1877, Janet was baptized along with her father and sister Margaret. At this time they were living on Gilmore St. Kilmarnock. She was baptized by David Milne and confirmed by James Houston, John Aird, and David Milne. This was a dream come true for her mother, Jessie (as she was called). Her mother died December 20, 1877, and Janet continued to live with her father and sister Margaret.

In May, 1878, she, with her father and other family members, left Kilmarnock, Ayrshire, Scotland, and went by train to Glasgow, where they joined her brother David and his young wife. John Adamson, a young man who was engaged to marry her sister, Margaret, was with them. In the same party was her father's sister, Veronica. From Glasgow they went to Liverpool, where they joined a company of Mormon emigrants. They left May 24, 1878, on the steamship

Nevada. They crossed the Atlantic Ocean in about ten days. Accommodations on the steamship were good, and they had plenty of food. From New York they went by train (three days) to Salt Lake City, Utah. It only took two weeks from Scotland to Utah. They were met in Salt Lake City by Uncle John, William Giles, and William Lindsay with two teams of horses and wagons, and they went to Uncle John's in Heber City. She was happy to be here, and thought of how elated her mother would have been. She and Margaret lived with her father on a farm in Lake Creek, four miles east of Heber. Her sister, Margaret (or Maggie, as she was called), was married in 1879.

William Baird was living with his parents and family on a homestead adjoining the Murdochs. There was a little hill between the two places. The Bairds sold milk to the Murdochs and William used to take the milk over the hill, and Janet would meet him and take the milk home. Thus started the courtship of William and Janet. At the age of twenty-five, she and William were married in the old Endowment House in Salt Lake City, Utah, on February 5, 1880.

William, or Billy, as he was called, took up a farm adjoining his father's farm, and they lived there until 1898. They had eight children, six sons and two daughters, all born at Lake Creek. The eldest, John, was born in 1881, and the youngest, Bruce, was born in 1896. Jennie was a devoted wife and mother and shared many of the tribulations of the early pioneers in a new country and community. She was a dressmaker by trade, and an excellent seamstress. She made all of their clothes, and as she had no equipment, they were all made by hand. She was especially interested in teaching her children the principles and doctrines of The Church of Jesus Christ of Latter-day Saints.

She was a small woman, being 5 feet 2 inches tall, and her weight was 105 pounds. Her eyes were gray and she had fine-textured brown hair. She had good health, and many have noted that she had a wonderful disposition and never complained. Billy loved to tease, and they had lots of fun and love in their home. Jennie was very reserved and modest. She liked a quiet life.

Her sister, Maggie, and brother-in-law, John Adam-son, lived in Park City, where John worked in the Daly Mine. The mine closed due to an economic depression. They talked to Billy and Jennie about making a move to Idaho. Billy was anxious to find land where he could get more water than was available near Heber. John Adamson and his brother-in-law, James "D" Murdoch, went by train to look at land in the Upper Snake River Valley, but while on the train they read an advertisement about the Hot Spring Ranch in Carey being for sale. They went right to Carey, liked what they saw, and bought it. The Hot Spring Ranch had unlimited water for irrigation and many acres of wild hay, and grass grew in abundance. Billy was excited about owning part of the ranch. He and Jennie were concerned about making a move at this time, as she was expecting her ninth child. After much thought and planning, they packed their belongings and moved to Carey, Idaho, in April, 1898. No doubt Billy was anxious to be there and take care of the farm work in the spring of the year.

A baby girl was born September 20, 1898, five months after their arrival in Carey. Three days later, September 23, 1898, Jennie passed away from complications of childbirth. It was necessary for someone to go by horseback to Hailey, Idaho, for a doctor, but by the time he arrived in his buggy it was too late to save her life. The baby was named Margaret, and Billy gave her to Maggie to raise. She did all that was possible to save the baby, but the baby passed away one month later, October 25, 1898.

Even though Jennie had passed on, the family felt a closeness to her, and in times of sickness and other trouble they felt their mother was aware of them and brought comfort to them.

Her children have all been baptized members of The Church of Jesus Christ of Latter-day Saints, and have been honest, hard-working people.

Her children are: John "D" Jessie Lennox, William Murdoch, Elizabeth Marshall, Ernest Wallace, James Alexander, David, Bruce, and Margaret. She is the grandmother of seventeen boys and sixteen girls. She was laid to rest in the old Carey Cemetery.

HUSBAND WILLIAM BAIRD

Birth 3 November 1849
Place Rutherglen,Lanark,Scotland
Chr
Married 5 February 1880 (E.H.)
Place Salt Lake City, S.L. Utah
Death 27 June 1946 Carey,Blaine,Idaho
Burial 30 June 1946 Carey,Blaine,Idaho
Father John BAIRD
Mother Elizabeth MARSHALL
Other Wives (2) Isabelle SNEDDON M-29Jan1902
(if any)

WIFE (1) JANET MURDOCH

Birth 18 October 1855
Place Gaswater,Ayrshire,Scotland
Chr
Death 23 Sep 1898 Carey,Blaine,Idaho
Burial Carey,Blaine,Idaho
Father William MURDOCH
Mother Janet LENNOX
Other Wives (if any)

*List complete maiden name for all females.

ISABELLE SNEDDON (2)

3 March 1868
Clackmannan, Scotland

15 March 1938 Carey,Blaine,Idaho
16 March 1938 Carey,Blaine,Idaho
Thomas SNEDDON

Note: is mother of child #10
married Salt Lake Temple

Information from Ada Halford

1st Child John "D" BAIRD
Birth 15 March 1881
Place Lake Creek, Wasatch, Utah
Married to Nora Ella PHIPPEN
Married 11 October 1905 Temple
Place Salt Lake City, Salt Lake, Utah
Died 8 Nov 1960 LosAngeles,California

2nd Child Jessie Lennox BAIRD
Birth 15 August 1882
Place Lake Creek, Wasatch, Utah
Married to Parke George KELLEY (1st)
Married 5 December 1901
Place Hailey, Blaine, Idaho
Died 15 April 1964 Eugene, Lane, Oregon

3rd Child William Murdoch BAIRD
Birth 6 October 1884
Place Lake Creek, Wasatch, Utah
Married to Allison Watson SIMPSON
Married 10 Nov 1909
Place Heber, Wasatch, Utah
Died 13 Jul 1956 Carey,Blaine, Idaho

4th Child Elizabeth Marshall BAIRD
Birth 25 March 1887
Place Lake Creek, Wasatch, Utah
Married to
Married
Place
Died 5 July 1901

5th Child Ernest Wallace BAIRD
Birth 17 April 1889
Place Lake Creek, Wasatch, Utah
Married to Florence Edith HARRIS Pace
Married 3 August 1922
Place Hailey, Blaine, Idaho
Died 19 July 1975

6th Child James Alexander BAIRD
Birth 26 February 1891
Place Lake Creek, Wasatch, Utah
Married to Ada "B" CONDIE
Married 10 Jan 1917 Temple
Place Salt Lake City, Salt Lake, Utah
Died 12 Aug 1956 Stevensville, Montana

7th Child David BAIRD
Birth 23 December 1892
Place Lake Creek, Wasatch, Utah
Married to Lida Laurine RALLS
Married 5 December 1923
Place Hailey, Blaine, Idaho
Died

8th Child Bruce BAIRD
Birth 6 April 1896
Place Lake Creek, Wasatch, Utah
Married to Erma Enola SMALLWOOD
Married 10 Oct 1917
Place Hailey, Blaine, Idaho
Died 24 December 1972

9th Child Margaret BAIRD
Birth 20 September 1898
Place Carey, Blaine, Idaho
Married to
Married
Place
Died 25 Oct 1898

10th Child Thomas Sneddon BAIRD
Birth 8 Nov 1903
Place Salt Lake City, Salt Lake, Utah
Married to Agnes LaVaun TOLMAN
Married 13 February 1929
Place Shoshone, Lincoln, Idaho
Died 29 July 1962 Boise, Ada, Idaho

```
1 MURDOCH, James 1786-1831              2 MURDOCH, William 1825-1913
1 MURDOCH, Mary MURRAY, Sp. 1782-1856   2 MURDOCH, Janet LENNOX, Sp. 1821-1877

                       3 MURDOCH, JANET 1855-1898
      DESCENDANTS OF------
                       3 BAIRD, WILLIAM, SP. 1849-1946
                                                           B-Birth
4 BAIRD, John D. B-15 Mar 1881 M-11 Oct 1905 D-8 Nov 1960  M-Married
4 BAIRD, Nora Ella PHIPPEN, Sp. B-20 Jan 1888              D-Death
                                                           Div.-Divorced
      5 BAIRD, Melvin John B-10 Oct 1907 M-8 May 1937 D-19 Jun 1981  Sp.-Spouse
      5 BAIRD, Ruth Alicia LITTLE, Sp. B-21 Apr 1911

            6 BAIRD, John Melvin B-27 Feb 1946 M-19 Apr 1967
            6 BAIRD, Jill Elaine HAGER, Sp. B-26 Mar 1949

                  7 BAIRD, Amy Ruth        B-29 Oct 1968
                  7 BAIRD, Elizabeth Jean  B- 4 May 1971
                  7 BAIRD, Alison Jill     B-20 Jun 1974

      5 SHERMAN, Retta Geneva BAIRD B-8 Sep 1911 M-1 Oct 1936
      5 SHERMAN, Stanely Stepehn, Sp. B-30 Sep 1903 D-1 Oct 1936

            6 SHERMAN, John Edward B-3 Jun 1945 D-

4 FATOR, Jessie Lennox BAIRD Kelley B-15 Aug 1882 D-15 Apr 1964
4 KELLEY, Parke George, Sp.(1) B-23 Nov '881 M-5 Dec 1901 D-23 Apr 1926
4 FATOR, Frederick William, Sp. (2) B-          M-24 Dec 1940 Div.

      5 PICKETT, Eva Jean KELLEY B-12 Apr 1908 M-20 Sep 1930
      5 PICKETT, Carole Eldon, Sp. B-20 Jul 1911

            6 PICKETT, Wayne Erwin B-14 Sep 1931
            6 PICKETT, Carolyn HARRIS, Sp. (1) B-          M-25 Jun 1950
            6 PICKETT, Melva June MUNSELL, Sp. (2) B-2 Jun 1930 M-16 Dec 19

                  7 PICKETT, James Michael   B- 2 Jun 1953

                  7 PICKETT, David Alan      B-26 Oct 1959
                  7 PICKETT, Susan Rene      B-31 Aug 1961

            6 COOK, Margaret Louise PICKETT B-23 Aug 1934 M-24 Dec 1949 D-
            6 COOK, Earl Lee, Sp. B-18 Dec 1929

                  7 COOK, Wayne Leo          B-3 Mar 1951

      5 HELENIAH, Margaret Julie KELLEY B-13 Jun 1911
      5 FIZZIE, Thomas Raymond, Sp. (1) B-          M-          Div.
      5 HELENIAH, John H, Sp. (2) B-20 Jan 1898 M-26 Oct 1936 D-16 Jan 1956

            6 RICHARDS, Fay Earl KELLEY B-1 Sep 1930

            6 HELENIAH, Donald Lee  B-10 Mar 1937

4 BAIRD, William Murdoch B-6 Oct 1884 M-10 Nov 1909 D-13 Jul 1956
4 BAIRD, Allison Watson SIMPSON, Sp. B-25 Nov 1887 D-30 Aug 1955

      5 BAIRD, Wallace William B-5 Oct 1910 D-28 Mar 1925

      5 BAIRD, Leonard  John B-27 Mar 1912 M-5 Oct 1935 D- 8 May 1969
      5 BAIRD, Alta Alice RALLS, Sp. B-16 Apr 1914

            6 DAVIS, Winnifred Jean BAIRD Groverson B-10 Mar 1939
            6 GROVERSON,          Sp. B-          M-
            6 DAVIS,              Sp. (2) B-          M-

                  7 ROONEY, Wendy GROVERSON B-      1957
                  7 ROONEY,              Sp. B-      M-

                        8 ROONEY, Heather        B-      1974
                        8 ROONEY, Amy Marie      B-      1975

                  7 GROVERSON, Raymond B-      1958
```

```
         6 BAIRD, Wallace Mitchel B-15 Apr 1941 D-15 Apr 1941

         6 HAAS, Betty Leonor BAIRD B-28 May 1942 M-
         6 HAAS, Marvin, Sp. B-

                7 HAAS, Brian              B-       1964
                7 HAAS, Kelli Jean         B-       1965

         6 BAIRD, Leonard Scott B-10 Dec 1943 D-17 Nov 1980
         6 BAIRD, Malinda       Sp. (1) B-         M-          Div.
         6 BAIRD, Faye BRITT, Sp. (2) B-           M-
         6 BAIRD, Thelma Ann BROCK, Sp.(3)
                7 BAIRD, Bryce             B-       1965
                7 BAIRD, Pamela            B-       1968
                7 BAIRD, Britt Marie       B-   May 1974

         6 BAIRD, Lennox Dixie B-12 Aug 1949

                7 BAIRD, Leonard John      B-   Nov 1970

         6 BAIRD, Melanie Marie B-13 May 1958

   5 BAIRD, Morris Todd B-30 Dec 1913 D-8 Nov 1934

   5 BAIRD, Robert Dean B-8 Dec 1915 M-23 Nov 1936
   5 BAIRD, Annie SHELLEY, Sp. B-1 Dec 1915

         6 BAIRD, Robert Shelley B-29 Oct 1937
         6 BAIRD, Janice LEONHARDT, Sp. B-10 Jul 1937 M- 23 Dec 1960
         6 BAIRD, Wanda Williamson.Sp. (2) B-          M-1 Apr 1972

                7 BAIRD, Bart Elwood       B-10 Sep 1961

         6 BAIRD, Wilbur Dean B-28 Dec 1938
         6 BAIRD, Karen TAYLOR, Sp. (1) B-14 Oct 1942 M-8 Nov 1958 D-25 Nov 1979
         6 BAIRD, Jelene McCOY Clements, Sp. (1) B-          M-1 May 1981

                7 HANSON, Bonnie Ray BAIRD B-14 Jan 1961
                7 HANSON, Tony, Sp. B-               M- 27 Jun 1981

                7 BAIRD, Gerald B-18 Mar 1962
                7 BAIRD, Sandra BURCH, Sp. B-              M-20 Mar 1982

                7 BAIRD, William Larry     B-14 Jul 1964

         6 WHITE, Sharon Annette BAIRD B-16 Nov 1940 M-11 Jul 1959
         6 WHITE, Delmar Leone, Sp. B-8 Aug

                7 WHITE, Brenda LeAnne      B-19 Aug 1963
                7 WHITE, Trudy Alison       B-14 Feb 1965
                7 WHITE, Melissa            B-
                7 WHITE, Bradley            B-28 Jun 1968
                7 WHITE, Elizabeth Karen    B- 2 Apr 1978
   5 SPARKS, Janet Arta BAIRD B-19 Jan 1918 M-30 Apr 1936
   5 SPARKS, Merrill Sterling, Sp. B-29 Oct 1905

         6 SPARKS, Larry B-6 Nov 1937
         6 SPARKS, Patricia PETERSON, Sp. B-              M-

                7 SPARKS, Hovey            B-

         6 SPARKS, Michael B-1 Feb 1941
         6 SPARKS, Millie       Sp. B-              M-

   5 BAIRD, Richard Earl B-15 Mar 1920 M-10 Nov 1943
   5 BAIRD, Ireta Earline GREEN, Sp. B-20 Oct 1927
   5 BAIRD, Carole STAGG, Sp. (2) B-          M-1 Dec 1964

         6 KAES, Patricia Mae BAIRD B-7 Jun 1946 M-18 Feb 1968
         6 KAES, Richard, Sp. B-
```

```
                7 KAES, Kristy Lynn          B-
                7 KAES, Angela Dawn          B-
                7 KAES, Scott William        B-

        6 RAY, Connie Joe BAIRD B-11 Nov 1947
        6 RAY, Earnest Lee Jr. Sp. B-              M-    Apr 1969

                7 RAY, Richard Lee           B-
                7 RAY, Maurine Lucille       B-
                7 RAY, Randy Eugene          B-
                7 RAY, Spencer Lyle          B-
                7 RAY, Michael               B-
                7 RAY, George                B-

        6 BAIRD, Leonard William B-18 Apr 1952 D-   Apr 1952

        6 BAIRD, Kenneth Earl B-18 Apr 1952
        6 BAIRD, St. Jane     Sp. B-                M-

                7 BAIRD, Amanda Nicole       B-

        6 BAIRD, Loma Ruth B-        1967

    5 BAIRD, Edwin Simpson B-17 Apr 1922 M-1 Apr 1944 or 5
    5 BAIRD, Rollie Evelyn YOUNG, Sp. B-20 Feb 1928 D-31 Oct 1977

        6 DUTCHER, Caroline Evelyn BAIRD B-11 Feb 1947
        6 DUTCHER, John, Sp. B-               M-

                7 DUTCHER, Jason             B-
                7 DUTCHER, Ian               B-

        6 BAIRD, Wallace Edwin B-26 Sep 1950
        6 BAIRD, Mala      Sp. B-                M-
        6 BAIRD, Virgina       Sp. (2) B-              M-

                7 BAIRD, daughter            B-

    5 BAIRD, baby boy B-26 May 1928 (Stillborn)

4 BAIRD, Elizabeth Marshall B-25 Mar 1887 D-5 Jul 1901

4 BAIRD, Ernest Wallace B-17 Apr 1889 M-3 Aug 1922 D-19 Jul 1975
4 BAIRD, Florence Edith HARRIS Pace, Sp. B-16 Dec 1894 D-10 Mar 1969
Pace, Doyle, Sp. (1) B-           M-

        BENTON, Iris June PACE B-11 Sep 1917 M-4 Nov 1947
        BENTON, Lansing M. Sp. B-16 Sep 1902

        Patterson, Norma Frances PACE B-13 Apr 1919 M-23 Dec 1940
        Patterson, Elmo Ray, Sp. B-12 Nov 1911

    5 BAIRD, Ernest Russell B-16 Jan 1924

    5 BAIRD, Owen Linford B-23 Jun 1925
    5 BAIRD, Betty GREER, Sp. B-              M-3 Jan 1952 Div.
    5 BAIRD, Mary B.      Sp. B-              M-

        6 BAIRD, Scott B-

        6 BAIRD, Monte B-

        6 BAIRD, Chris B-

    5 BARFUSS, Barbara Mary BAIRD B-27 Oct 1926 M-17 Jul 1951
    5 BARFUSS, Victor Roland, Sp. B-24 Feb 1923

        6 BARFUSS, Victor Robert B-19 May 1952
        6 BARFUSS, Lee Anna HATCH, Sp. B-              M-

                7 BARFUSS, Julie             B-
                7 BARFUSS, Jason             B-
                7 BARFUSS, Lisa              B-
```

        6 CHRISTENSEN, LaDawn BARFUSS B-15 Jun 1953
        6 CHRISTENSEN, Robert, Sp. B-   M-

                7 CHRISTENSEN, Wendy   B-
                7 CHRISTENSEN, Vonn   B-

        6 MONSON, April BARFUSS B-17 Apr 1955
        6 MONSON, Scott, Sp. B-   M-

                7 MONSON, Lori Ann   B-

        6 RASMUSSEN, Dree BARFUSS B-22 Jul 1956
        6 RASMUSSEN, Todd, Sp. B-   M-

                7 RASMUSSEN, Ander   B-
                7 RASMUSSEN, Kimberly   B-
                7 RASMUSSEN, Mitchell   B-

        6 BARFUSS, "J" Brock B-27 Nov 1958
        6 BARFUSS, Natlie WILLIAMS, Sp. B-   M-

        6 BARFUSS, Scott Baird B-21 Sep 1963

        6 BARFUSS, David John   B-16 Sep 1965

    5 BAIRD, George Donald B-8 May 1928 M-8 May 1948
    5 BAIRD, Nettie Luella SMITH, Sp. B-18 Nov 1931

        6 WOOD, Barbara Ileen BAIRD B-22 Jan 1951 M-
        6 WOOD, Sid, Sp. B-

                7
                7
                7
                7

        6 BAIRD, Russell Gorden B-16 Mar 1953
        6 BAIRD, Carolyn   Sp. B-   M-

                7 BAIRD, Ryan   B-
    5 BAIRD, Iona B-24 Jul 1929 D- 24 Jul 1929

    5 ARRINGTON, Vella Cleone BAIRD B-23 Jan 1933 M-19 Sep 1952
    5 ARRINGTON, Donald Charles, Sp. B-25 Jul 1929

        6 ARRINGTON, Douglas Reed   B-20 Oct 1954

        6 ARRINGTON, Donna Lou   B-17 May 1956

        6 ARRINGTON, John   B-

4 BAIRD, James Alexander B-26 Feb 1891 M-10 Jan 1917 D-12 Aug 1956
4 BAIRD, Ada B CONDIE, Sp. B-6 April 1894 D-4 May 1965

    5 TOLLEY, Elizabeth Condie BAIRD Patterson B-2 Apr 1918 D-28 Sep 1980
    5 PATTERSON, Wilford Measome, Sp. B-10 Mar 1916 M-5 Jun 1940 Div.
    5 TOLLEY, Eldon Delbert, Sp. (2) B-6 Apr 1916 M-24 Jun 1958
      Tolley, Mary Berniece DRAPER, Sp. (1) B-   M-31 Oct 1942

        6 TAYLOR, Emily Elizabeth PATTERSON B-15 Apr 1944 M-13 Sep 1969
        6 TAYLOR, Dennis Leon, Sp. B-22 May 1945

                7 TAYLOR, Vaughn Dennis   B-27 Jan 1977
                7 TAYLOR, Vincent Leon   B-20 Mar 1978
                7 TAYLOR, Jennifer Elizabeth B-4 Jan 1981

        6 PATTERSON, James Wilford B-18 Jan 1947 M-17 Nov 1967
        6 PATTERSON, Donna Lee MASSEY, Sp. B-18 Dec 1947

                7 PATTERSON, Thomas James   B-16 Oct 1968
                7 PATTERSON, Samuel Mark   B-10 Dec 1971

5 TOLLEY, Edith Condie BAIRD B-17 Jul 1920 M-21 Apr 1946
5 BARTLETT, Delwin Erwin, Sp. (1) B-10 Oct 1914 D-3 May 1960
5 TOLLEY, Eldon Delbert, Sp. (2) B-6 Apr 1916 M-7 Feb 1981

5 POPP, Margaret Condie BAIRD B-14 Jul 1922 M-23 Dec 1942 D-1 May 1974
5 POPP, Wilbur Eldred, Sp. B-31 Jan 1920 D-8 Aug 1964

    6 POPP, William James B-14 Sep 1944 M-29 May 1967
    6 POPP, Caroline Irene FULLER, Sp. B-

        7 POPP, Cindy Lynn   B- 4 May 1968
        7 POPP, David   B-   May 1970
        7 POPP, Jeanna Kaye   B-24 Aug 1971
        7 POPP, Kimberley Ann   B-16 May 1975
        7 POPP, Jennifer Ada   B-29 Jul 1980

    6 WITTWER, Kaye Halene POPP B-29 Nov 1946 M-6 Jun 1968
    6 WITTWER, Richard Wayne, Sp. B-29 Aug 1947

        7 WITTWER, Richard Konstanty B-31 Dec 1971
        7 WITTWER, Hala Kaye   B-26 Sep 1973
        7 WITTWER, Jonathan Wayne B-21 Jan 1976
        7 WITTWER, James Thomas   B-24 May 1981

    6 SIMMONS, Sandra Ruth POPP B-14 Jun 1950 M-20 Dec 1973
    6 SIMMONS, Donald Wayne, Sp. B-27 Sep 1944

        7 SIMMONS, Michael Phillip B-17 Oct 1974
        7 SIMMONS, Stefanie Joy   B-11 Oct 1975
        7 SIMMONS, Susan Fern   B-12 Oct 1976

    6 POPP, Richard Louis B-14 Feb 1957

5 HALFORD, Ada Condie BAIRD B-6 Feb 1925 M-29 Sep 1955
5 HALFORD, Woodrow Norman, Sp. B-15 Feb 1919

    6 HALFORD, Gayla B-9 May 1958

    6 LONGSHAW, Julianne HALFORD B-17 Jul 1959
    6 LONGSHAW, Richard, Sp. B-   M-   Div. 1 Mar 1979

5 BAIRD, James Condie B-10 May 1927 M-18 Feb 1953
5 BAIRD, Evelyn Mae WHITING, Sp. B-

    6 HOLYOAK, Lennox Whiting BAIRD B-5 Apr 1954 M-
    6 HOLYOAK, Lenn Merrill, Sp. B-16 Jan 1954

        7 HOLYOAK, Maren Lenae   B-24 Mar 1977
        7 HOLYOAK, Lyle Eugene   B-29 Mar 1978
        7 HOLYOAK, Lyman Merrill B-21 Sep 1980

    6 BAIRD, Dave Whiting B-2 Jul 1955 M-29 Nov 1975
    6 BAIRD, Diana Gay EVERTZ, Sp. B-11 Apr 1952

        7 BAIRD, James John   B-19 Aug 1976
        7 BAIRD, Dave William   B- 1 Sep 1977

    6 BAIRD, James Whiting B-14 Apr 1957

    6 BAIRD, Murray Whiting B-10 Jul 1960

    6 BAIRD, Robert Whiting B-31 Oct 1962

    6 BAIRD, Mary Whiting B-23 Jun 1965

5 SNOW, Helen Condie BAIRD B-18 Mar 1929 M-25 Nov 1947
5 SNOW, Richard Lindsay, Sp. B-15 May 1926

    6 SNOW, Douglas Richard B-13 May 1952 M-24 May 1978
    6 SNOW, Maura Kathleen Crow, Sp. B-9 Apr 1959

```
                    7 SNOW, Brian              B- 2 Aug 1979
                    7 SNOW, Kevin Richard      B-26 Jul 1981

              6 SNOW, John William    B-11 Dec 1957

              6 SNOW, Laurel Ann      B-30 Apr 1968

4 BAIRD, David B-23 Dec 1892 M-5 Dec 1923
4 BAIRD, Lida Laurine RALLS, Sp. B-27 Sep 1903 D-5 Jun 1973

        5 BAIRD, Raymond David B-17 Oct 1924 M-28 Mar 1948
        5 BAIRD, Carley Jean VANSANT, Sp. B-7 Mar 1929

              6 BAIRD, David Lee B-4 Feb 1949
              6 BAIRD,          Sp. (1) B-          M-
              6 BAIRD, Linda Rae SOLES, Sp. (2) B-12 Feb 1948 M-22 Jun 1974

                    7 BAIRD, Darcy             B-26 Jul 1971
                    7 BAIRD, Dawn Marie        B- 2 Oct 1972

              6 BAIRD, Richard Ray B-20 Jul 1950 M-6 May 1972
              6 BAIRD, Diane CANNON, Sp. B-25 Apr 1948

                    7 BAIRD, Neil Patrick      B-29 Mar 1976
                    7 BAIRD, Eric Scott        B- 2 Aug 1978

              6 BAIRD, Gary Gene      B-20 Jun 1952

              6 BAIRD, Jack William   B- 6 Sep 1955

              6 BAIRD, Brock Allen    B-19 Jan 1958

              6 BAIRD, Randy Kim       B-15 Sep 1960
              6 BAIRD, Cindy JUSTESEN, Sp. B-24 May 1960 M-   Sep 1979

                    7 BAIRD, Jennifer          B-24 Apr 1980

                    7 BAIRD, Ammanda Jo        B-29 Jan 1982

        5 BAIRD, Earl William B-20 May 1926 M-18 Oct 1950
        5 BAIRD, Phyllis Nadine Wilderman, Sp. B-25 Jul 1926 D-   Jan 1982

              6 BAIRD, Laura Laurine B-15 Dec 1952

              6 BAIRD, Melinda Marie B-13 Apr 1956 D-14 Dec 1962

              6 BAIRD, Dennis Dave    B-21 Jul 1957

        5 JONES, Janis Mary BAIRD Randall B- 14 Mar 1937
        5 RANDALL, Norman K, Sp. (1) B-               M-2 Feb 1957
        5 JONES, Reese E. Sp.(2) B-4 Jan 1925       M-          Div

              6 RANDALL, Rodney K     B-12 Oct 1957

4 BAIRD, Bruce B-6 Apr 1896 M-10 Oct 1917 D-24 Dec 1972
4 BAIRD, Erma Enola SMALLWOOD, Sp. B-1 Dec 1896

        5 BAIRD, Harold Bruce B-7 Sep 1918 M-23 Jul 1938
        5 BAIRD, Verlyne Arden KELLY, Sp. B-14 Nov 1920

              6 CRAFT, Bonetta Verlyne BAIRD B-24 Apr 1939 M-
              6 CRAFT, Tom, Sp. B-

                    7 CRAFT, Dannie           B-
                    7 CRAFT, Denia            B-

              6 HAZZARD, Coleen B BAIRD B-9 Nov 1942 M-
              6 HAZZARD, Tom, Sp. B-

                    7 HAZZARD, Cassie         B-
                    7 HAZZARD, Lori           B-
```

5 KELLY, Marjorie Maurine BAIRD Deckard B-29 Aug 1920
5 DECKARD, Oral Wesley, Sp. (1) B-10 Oct 1915 M-30 Dec 1936 Div.
5 KELLY, Henry Thompson, Sp. (2) B-11 Dec 1913 M-25 Jun 1941 D-   1970

      6 MARTIN, Carroll Maurine DECKARD B-23 Oct 1937
      6 MARTIN,   Sp. B-   M-

      6 ROBINS, Jean Elaine DECKARD B-28 May 1940
      6 ROBINS,   Sp. B-   M-

      6 TUTTLE, Marie Eloise KELLY B-7 Jul 1942
      6 TUTTLE,   Sp. B-   M-

      6 RODERICK, Estella Faye KELLY B-
      6 RODERICK,   Sp. B-   M-
5 BAIRD, Reid Robert B-26 Dec 1923
5 BAIRD, Rosemary ANDERSON, Sp. B-   M-
5 BAIRD, Alma McDONALD, Sp. (2) B-   M-13 Sep 1969

      6 BAIRD, Miles   B-11 May 1956
      6 BAIRD, L J   B- 2 Nov 1957

5 DAUGHERTY, FAYE Erma BAIRD B-26 Jan 1927 M-12 Oct 1946
5 DAUGHERTY, Virgil Lavern, Sp. B-29 May 1927

      6 ROBINETT, Judy Faye DAUGHERTY B-27 Feb 1949 M-17 Sep 1965
      6 ROBINETT, Oliver, Sp. B-

        7 ROBINETT, Ted Oliver   B-
        7 ROBINETT, Rocky Allen   B-

      6 DAUGHERTY, Lee Lavern B-9 Oct 1952 M-29 Jun 1974
      6 DAUGHERTY, Jennifer Shawley, Sp. B-

      6 DAUGHERTY, June Elaine   B-20 Feb 1962

5 BAIRD, Darol Dean B-25 May 1929 M-15 Sep 1952
5 BAIRD, Helen ALMA, Sp. (1) B-   M-15 Sep 1952 D-21 Jan 1979
5 BAIRD, Loen SMITH, Sp. (2) B-   M- Feb 1980

      6 ELLIS, Connie Faye BAIRD B-11 Nov 1953
      6 ELLIS,   Sp. B-   M-

      6 BAIRD, Robert Darol   B-2 Sep 1955

      6 BAIRD, Wayne Francis   B-9 Apr 1957

      6 BAIRD, William Joseph   B-10 Dec 1958

      6 BAIRD, Lyle James   B-15 Jul 1960

      6 BAIRD, Deloris Alma   B-26 Jul 1962

      6 BAIRD, Glen Virgil   B-26 Dec 1964

      6 BAIRD, Neil Patrick   B- 1 May 1968 D-21 Jan 1979

      6 BAIRD, Lesa Marie   B-16 Jan 1971 D-21 Jan 1979

4 BAIRD, Margaret B-20 Sep 1898 D-25 Oct 1898

DESCENDANTS OF ‑‑‑‑‑‑‑‑3 BAIRD, WILLIAM 1849-1946
3 SNEDDON, ISABELLE 1868-1938 (2ND) SPOUSE.

4 BAIRD, Thomas Sneddon B-8 Nov 1903 M-13 Feb 1929 Div. Oct 1941 D-29 Jul 1962
4 BAIRD, Agnes LaVaun TOLMAN, Sp. B-29 Dec 1911

        TURNER, Belva Maxine B-27 Dec 1929 M-   Jun 1951
        TURNER, Calvin, Sp. B-

        BAIRD, Norman Thomas B-3 Jul 1933 D-7 Feb 1934

        BAIRD, DelRay   B-23 Jun 1936

Margaret Murdoch and John Adamson

Margaret Murdoch Adamson was called Maggie by her family and friends. She was the sixth and youngest child of William Murdoch and Janet Lennox. Her father, William, was the youngest child of James Murdoch and Mary Murray. Maggie was born August 27, 1858, in Ponesk, Ayr, Scotland. She joined the Mormon Church October 8, 1877, just two months before the death of her invalid mother.

Her mother, Janet Lennox Murdoch, had a crippling disease, which must have been arthritis. She was confined to a wheelchair for many years before her death. Her children thought she was a very stern, demanding woman. She was very particular about the cleanliness of her person, her clothing, and her home. Her meals had to be served on a highly polished tray covered with a fresh linen napkin and laid with her best china and silverware. She required her girls to iron the linens with neat, square corners and with no sign of a wrinkle. This must have been one of her ways of teaching her daughters how to keep house after she was unable to do it herself.

Maggie's father, William Murdoch, was a kind and gentle man. He was very patient with his invalid wife and his young daughters, who were always striving to please their mother in carrying out their many household responsibilities. Many of William's descendants have inherited his kindly, twinkling, smiling eyes, that seemed to close completely when he laughed.

Maggie was nineteen years old when her mother died shortly before Christmas in 1877. Soon after the death of her mother, William and the remaining members of the family decided to migrate to America. James, the oldest son, was already in America. He had written them about the opportunities to be found there. It had long been the wish of their mother that they join the Mormon Church and go to Utah. The Church at that time encouraged new members to migrate to Utah. They began to make preparations to go.

By May of 1878 they were ready to leave Scotland. Their immediate party consisted of William; his sister, Veronica Caldow; his son David L.; David's new wife, Elizabeth Thyne; daughters Janet (Jennie) and Margaret (Maggie); and John Adamson, to whom Maggie was betrothed. They joined the company of Mormon emigrants in Liverpool and sailed for America May 24, 1878 on the S.S. *Nevada*. David L. in his journal wrote that Jennie and Maggie were seasick for the first three days at sea. However, they were able to get out of bed on the fourth day. Then David L. became sick. He and Lizzie traveled first class. It was their honeymoon trip.

The others had steerage accommodations. They had to prepare their own food and wash their own dishes without the benefit of hot water.

The crossing took twelve days. They arrived in New York June 5. When their ship docked in New York Harbor, James "D" was there to meet them. He was working in Pittsburgh, Pennsylvania, at that time. They engaged rooms at the Steven's Hotel on Broadway, did a little sightseeing, then went to Castle Garden to see a show that night. The next day they went to "Jersey" to catch the west-bound train. James "D" rode with them as far as Pittsburgh, where they changed cars. Here the English and Scottish companies were separated by two cars of "bad smelling" Russians. Next morning the Russian cars were moved to the end of the train. At every large stop, crowds of curious people pushed their way through the train to look at the immigrants.

They changed trains in Chicago and again in Omaha. The new accommodations at Omaha were on the Union Pacific. The cars were very dirty. All baggage was loaded tightly into three baggage cars. There were twelve passenger cars. Besides the nine cars for Utah, there were three for California. The most tiresome part of their journey was from Omaha to Salt Lake City in those dirty cars. They arrived in Salt Lake at 9 P.M. on Thursday, June 13, 1878, twenty days from Liverpool, and only seven days from New York City.

When William's party arrived in Salt Lake City, there was no one at the station to meet them. They had arrived two days earlier than they were expected. So they stayed overnight at a nearby hotel called "Valley House." Early the next morning William went back to the train station where he found his brother, John, with teams and wagons enough to transport them and all their luggage to Heber City. That trip took one long day.

A short time after their arrival in Heber, they rented a small one-room house from Thomas Giles. All seven of them lived in that little house until David L. and Lizzie were able to find a house for themselves. That still left five adults living in one small room. Inasmuch as it was the summer season, they very likely made good use of the front porch and the lawn for sleeping as well as eating areas.

William soon obtained land four miles up Lake Creek. John Adamson helped him build a house, a stable, sheds, and fences. Some of the land had to be cleared, and irrigation ditches had to be dug. They helped to dig the irrigation ditch to all the farmers who lived below them, while some of the men dug only till the ditch reached their individual property. William was fifty-eight years old at this time; John was twenty-eight.

John Adamson was born in Muirkirk, Ayr, Scotland. He was born May 22, 1849. He was nine years old when Maggie was born. She must have known him all her life. She was born nearly two years after Wee Granny died. Wee Granny was paternal grandmother. John was the eighth child of ten children. His father was Robert Adamson (1807–1863). His mother was Margaret Millar Murdoch. John was fourteen when his father died. He worked for farmers who lived nearby. Later he went to work in a coal mine. He apparently received a good schooling, as he had nice penmanship, was quick and accurate with figures, and read considerably as an adult. He was gifted in music, and may have had some training in that line.

Just recently we have received a copy of a letter written to John Adamson by Janet Lennox Murdoch, Maggie's mother, advising him of the arrival of a guest in her home and inviting him to call on them the following day. We know that John's mother was bitterly opposed to the Mormons and had forbidden John to meet with them. We think that Mr. Macfarlane, who is

mentioned in the letter, was a Mormon missionary, and that Maggie's mother was being very cautious about letting John know that a missionary had arrived and a cottage meeting was planned at her home.

John Adamson joined the Mormon Church on April 28, 1878, against the wishes of his widowed mother, whereupon she immediately disowned him. As soon as John got a job in America, he began to send money to her. This seemed to appease her displeasure to some extent.

John and Maggie were married on January 16, 1879, in the old Endowment House, in Salt Lake City, seven months after their arrival in America. They continued living with Maggie's father for some time, helping him to get well established with his farming. Then they moved into town. Four children were born to them in Heber, three boys and one girl: John Robert (Bert), William Lennox (Leek), Isabelle, and James Murray (Jim).

In 1890, John went to work in Park City as engineer for the Daly Mine. He moved his family to Park City, where life was considerably different than it had been in the farming community of Heber. There were no big yards or wide meadows where the children could run and play, no cows to milk, no eggs to gather, no horses to ride. The boys missed their grandfather's horses more than anything else.

The Adamson home was built on a steep hillside, as were most homes in Park City at that time. The small dooryard slanted down the hill at very nearly a forty-five degree angle. Adjacent to their small yard was a long wooden stairway that gave them access to the street above and the street below their house. A new red brick schoolhouse was not far away on the street below. The schoolyard added to their play area, They had a male teacher who disciplined his pupils with a ruler on their knuckles and a leather strap across their backs when he caught the one responsible for the outlandish tricks they played.

Brother Thomas L. Allen was the presiding elder in charge of the LDS branch of the Church in Park City at that time. He came from Coalville every weekend to conduct church meetings. John Adamson and George Curtis were his counselors. Brother Allen always stayed overnight, so John built an extra room on his house to accommodate Brother Allen. To this day when we grandchildren go to Park City, we drive past that old house and point out Brother Allen's room to *our* grandchildren. We take pictures and walk up and down that long flight of stairs. The old house is still in fairly good condition and is still occupied, ninety years later. Its present address is 206 Woodside Street. (See picture on next page.)

Two more children were born to the Adamsons while they lived in Park City, David Edwin, who was called Dick, and Edith Mary, who was later called Edu (pronounced Eedoo) which was begun by a small niece and nephew who could not say her name.

In 1897 the mines in Park City stopped operating because of an economic depression. So John Adamson was out of work. He and Maggie had long been aware of the fact that their boys would soon be old enough to work in the mines if they remained in Park City. This seemed to be a good time to get the boys away from that possibility.

The Adamson home in Park City

William (Billy) Baird, who had married Maggie's sister Jennie, wanted some land with more irrigation water than he could get in Heber where they were living; so he was ready for a move, too.

After much investigation, consideration, and advice, and with some financial assistance from Maggie's and Jennie's brother James "D" John and Billy Baird bought the Hot Springs Ranch in Carey, Idaho. John was now nearly forty-nine years old; Maggie was forty. Their oldest child, Bert, was eighteen, their youngest, Edith, was five. The Bairds had eight children, approximately the same age as the Adamson children.

It was April of 1898 when they left Utah. In addition to their personal belongings and household furnishings, each family took tools, farming equipment, a farm wagon, a two—seated buggy, a team of horses, a saddle horse, a saddle, harness for the team, and innumerable other items. The horses became family pets. The Adamson's team, "Dick and Milly," and the saddle horse, "Penny," were remembered and talked about by the Adamson children all the rest of their lives.

The trip to Idaho was made by train. Their belongings were loaded into two freight cars. The men rode in the one carrying the horses. The women and children had seats in a passenger car. At Shoshone, Idaho, the freight cars were switched to the branch line that ran to Ketchum, Idaho, via Hailey. The family members changed trains, and the journey continued to a small loading station called Tikura. There the freight cars were left on a siding, the horses were unloaded, the wagons were assembled, and the two families with their belongings were hauled to their new homes on the Hot Springs Ranch, a distance of fifteen miles. They made many trips over a period of several days before the freight cars were emptied.

Little Wood River, which runs through Carey Valley, split into two channels at that time, both of which crossed the main road through town. There were no bridges across those streams. It was spring and the water was high. Both streams had to be forded. Every time they drove through the streams, the water flooded into their wagons, so there was much drying-out to be done of both clothing and furniture. There were two log houses with sod roofs on the ranch. One house had four rooms; the other had two. The Adamsons got the four-room house because they had the most furniture (and because Jennie insisted.) John and Billy divided the property; the Adamsons took the north part and the Bairds took the south. The present road was the dividing line.

Immediately upon arrival the children explored their surroundings. There was not a tree in sight. Several hot springs bubbled out of the ground near one of the houses. The largest one made a deep pool with the others running into it. All of them seemed to be filled with moss that grew on the bottom, up the sides, and in a thick layer all around the edges. A stream of hot water ran from the big pool through a rather deep ditch three or four feet wide. The ditch went across the yard, down a gentle slope, and emptied into a nearby lake surrounded by a forest of cattails. Dick, who was seven years old, tried to jump the ditch, and fell into the hot water. Luckily he was not burned, but the incident was the beginning of his dislike of his new home.

He would not drink the water from the hot springs, even after it had been cooled. He made himself and everyone else miserable by constantly demanding a drink of cold water. The nearest cold water came from a spring a quarter of a mile away. So drinking water had to be hauled from that spring.

The old Oregon Trail lay at the foot of the hills, less than a mile to the north of their home. The six-horse teams pulling the big freight wagons raised continuous clouds of dust all that summer. The children counted as many as one hundred wagons that passed each day.

John soon acquired some adjoining land through the U.S. government's Homestead Act, and began to develop it. Much of the Hot Springs property was for cattle grazing and raising wild hay. The new land gave room for other crops. It was also closer to the cold-water springs. John built a new house and moved his family out of the sod-roofed log house.

The years they lived on the ranch must have been difficult for Maggie Adamson. She was afraid of horses, and disliked the long ride to church each Sunday in the white-topped two-seated buggy. Teams of horses were easily spooked in those days, and would often run away, sometimes causing the buggy or wagon they were pulling to tip over. Maggie preferred riding in the small one-seated buggy with her son, Lennox, doing the driving. She thought he handled the horses better than John or the other boys.

Another disturbing thing for Maggie was the fact that the Indians would often come to the area to dig camas roots. She was distrustful of them, although they were not as threatening as the ones who had bothered them in Utah. It was still a worry having them so near. Then only five months after their arrival in Idaho, her sister, Jennie, died from complications of childbirth. The premature baby girl was given to Maggie, who spent day and night trying to keep it alive. The baby lived for one month. These weren't the only deaths in the Baird family. Less than three years after Jennie's death her second daughter, Elizabeth, who was fourteen, died. This left Jessie, the only other girl in the Baird family, to keep house for her father and six brothers.

Wild hay grew profusely on the ranch. It was harvested and stacked for winter feeding. Meadow grass grew thick and tall adjacent to the fields of wild hay. One day a fire sprang up suddenly in the dry grass. It spread so quickly that Maggie and the younger children ran to the nearest hill for safety. The men and older boys fought the fire. They saved the houses, the barns, and the livestock, but lost all the hay and grass and some of the sheds.

The following winter was a hard one. They had to buy feed for their animals. Money was scarce and food was scarce. Maggie was grateful for their milk cows and their chickens; also for the wild sage hens that were their main source of meat for some time. There were no near neighbors; no other women to visit or to give help if needed.

In 1902, possibly to make life easier for Maggie, John arranged to sell his share of the ranch to Billy. He bought a house and some land in town; then, in partnership with several other men, bought the only general store in the valley. They erected a new building with an adjoining office area that was used as the post office. They named the store Blaine Co-op.

Post Office and Co-op in 1906. Men in front of store are: William F. Rawson, Lennox Adamson, Bert Adamson, D. H. Hollingsworth, Cyrus J. Stanford, Edward Davis, and John Adamson. The store proved to be a successful business enterprise and became one of the largest general mercantile establishments in the county. They sold groceries, dry goods, ready-to-wear, hardware, building materials, and farm equipment. Later this store was destroyed by fire. The Adamson family rebuilt the business and renamed it, calling it Carey Mercantile Company. A soda fountain and a fresh meat counter were added. At one time a lending library was a popular service at the store. At the present time they are doing business in a new, larger building that was recently completed. The name has been changed again. It is now Adamsons. They have added frozen foods, electrical equipment, and some appliances. They have a repair department for servicing farm equipment, motorcycles, and snowmobiles. In conjunction with the store, they operate Texaco service stations and tire shops in Carey, Hailey, Arco, and Ketchum. The business is now owned by stockholders who work in some department of the business operation. It is managed by Robert D. Adamson, who is a great-grandson of John and Maggie Adamson.

John Adamson organized and directed the first ward choir in Carey. His daughter, Isabelle, was the organist. The Adamsons owned the only piano in the valley at that time. It was moved from place to place for socials and dances. John encouraged his children to learn to play a musical instrument. They each spent lengthy visits to Salt Lake for lessons on their chosen instruments. Then with the help of a friend, John Bush, who played violin, they organized a family dance band and were soon playing for dances throughout the valley and in neighboring communities. This group was the nucleus of a larger town band that played for celebrations, band concerts, and parades throughout the county.

Adamson family orchestra. Front, left to right: Lennox, Robert (Bert), Edwin (Dick), James. Back, left to right: Edith, John Bush, Isabelle.

John became a counselor in the second bishopric in Carey. William F. Rawson was the new bishop and Cyrus J. Stanford was the other counselor. The ward was called the Blaine Ward until it was added to the newly formed Boise Stake in 1913. It was changed to the Carey Ward and the Adamson's second son, William Lennox (Leck), was made bishop.

Second Bishopric in Carey Ward, then known as Blaine Ward. Standing, Bishop William F. Rawson; seated, Counselors Cyrus J. Stanford, and John Adamson.

Maggie was active in the auxiliary organizations of the Church. She was considered to be the best Sunday School teacher in the ward because she could manage the boys. She also had the reputation of being one of the best cooks in town.

John always raised a large vegetable garden. He also had an orchard with pear, plum, and apple trees. Adjoining the orchard was a raspberry patch and a row of currant bushes. After the apples had been picked, or while they were still on the trees, we grandchildren were allowed to help ourselves as often as we liked. But during the summer we liked to pick fresh peas from his garden. Grandfather would scold us and tell us to stay out of the garden.

Recreation in those days consisted of baseball in the summer, basketball in the winter, dances, stage plays, a taffy pull, a song Pest. The billiard games at the pool hall held a strong interest for the young men in town. So to keep their boys from playing pool at the pool hall, Maggie and John bought a pool table and installed it in their parlor. It filled up the entire room, so the sofa and most of the easy chairs were moved into their dining room, which became the family room in the Adamson home. This attraction made the Adamson home very popular with the young people. Maggie could always supply them with good food, and occasionally John would treat them to a glass of his homemade root beer.

A favorite pastime of the Adamson family was camping and fishing. There were beautiful camping areas nearby, and fishing was always good. An overnight fishing trip was a delightful experience, and became a favorite way to entertain visitors.

Their sons went on missions. When they returned, they married and moved into nearby homes of their own. With the help of his sons, John built a tall water tank. He connected a gasoline engine to the well pump, which then pumped water into the tank, thus supplying running water to his home and the homes of the married sons.

Ever since the death of his mother, in October of 1886, John had nurtured a desire to return to Scotland to see the remaining members of his family. He had two brothers who were still living there. He wanted to teach them the gospel. On May 28, 1910, he left for a mission to Scotland. His brothers were glad to see him and gave him a joyful welcome, but they did not join the Church as he had hoped. They both died, about a year apart, while John was still in Scotland. He was able to attend both funeral services.

During John's absence, Maggie supported herself by taking the lady schoolteachers into her home to room and board. The family dance band assisted financially toward their father's missionary expenses.

After returning from his mission, John and Maggie went to Salt Lake, where they spent the winter doing temple work for deceased members of John's family. He had collected the names and dates needed for this work while he was in Scotland.

Both John and Maggie Adamson died in 1915. They were loved and admired by all who knew them. They had always been industrious, hard-working people. They were remembered for their faithfulness to the Church, their kindness to friends and neighbors, their good humor in spite of many trials and tribulations, and their honesty in all their dealings. Their children were all honorable citizens and good Church members with strong testimonies of the truthfulness of the gospel, for *which* their father gave up his birthright.

None of their six children are living now. At present count there are 174 direct descendants, including 18 grandchildren, 49 great-grandchildren, 99 great-great-grandchildren, and 2 great-great-great-grandchildren.

Compiled by Lexie C. Sutton, granddaughter of John Adamson and Margaret Murdoch.

John Adamson home in Carey, Idaho

Margaret Murdoch Adamson & John Adamson about
1914

Left to right: William Lennox (Leck), Isabelle, and
John Robert (Bert), Adamson children.

Left to right: James Murray (Jim), Edith, and David
Edwin (Dick), Adamson children.

HUSBAND   JOHN ADAMSON
  Birth   22 May 1849
  Place   Muirkirk, Ayrshire, Scotland
  Married   16 January 1879
  Place   Salt Lake City, Salt Lake, Utah--EndowmentHouse
  Death   29 October 1915
  Place   Carey, Blaine, Idaho
  Burial   2 November 1915
  Place   Carey, Blaine, Idaho
  Mother   Margaret Millar MURDOCH
  Father   Robert ADAMSON
  Other Wives

WIFE   MARGARET MURDOCH
  Birth   27 August 1858
  Place   Muirkirk, Ayrshire, Scotland
  Death   29 October 1915
  Place   Carey, Blaine, Idaho
  Burial   2 November 1915
  Place   Carey, Blaine, Idaho
  Mother   Janet LENOX
  Father   William MURDOCH
  Other Husbands
  Information from James & Mary Murray Murdoch Family
            Records & John Adamson Family Records

1ST CHILD   John Robert ADAMSON
  Birth   25 November 1879 Heber,Wasatch,Utah
  Married   Elna Pearl STANFORD
  Date   5 October 1904
  Place   Salt Lake City, Utah (Temple)
  Death   7 July 1920 Carey, Blaine, Idaho
  Burial   9 July 1920 Carey, Blaine, Idaho

2ND CHILD   William Lennox ADAMSON
  Birth   11 February 1882 Heber,Wasatch,Utah
  Married   Laura Jane RAWSON
  Date   3 January 1912
  Place   Salt Lake City, Utah (Temple)
  Death   19 May 1967 Salt Lake City, Utah
  Burial   22 May 1967 S.L.C.,Utah, City,Cemet.

3RD CHILD   Isabelle ADAMSON
  Birth   1 January 1885 Heber,Wasatch,Utah
  Married   William Henry CAMERON
  Date   27 Dec 1905
  Place   Hailey, Blaine, Idaho
  Death   29 October 1915 Carey,Blaine,Idaho
  Burial   2 November 1915 Carey,Blaine,Idaho

4TH CHILD   James Murray ADAMSON
  Birth   13 Jun 1887 Heber,Wasatch,Utah
  Married   Not
  Date
  Place
  Death   29 October 1915 Carey,Blaine, Idaho
  Burial   2 November 1915 Carey,Blaine, Idaho

5TH CHILD   David Edwin ADAMSON
  Birth   9 May 1891 Park City, Summit, Utah
  Married   Rebecca Ann RAWSON (1)
  Date   8 October 1914
  Place   Salt Lake City, Utah (Temple)
  Death   3 March 1975   Carey, Blaine, Idaho
  Burial   Carey, Blaine, Idaho

            (wives of David)
  Married   Viola Pearl CRITCHFIELD (2)
  Date   June 1921
  Place   Salt Lake City, Utah (Temple)

  Married   Eva RICE Robbins (3)
  Date   12 March 1940
  Place

6TH CHILD   Edith Mary ADAMSON
  Birth   6 June 1893 Park City, Summit, Utah
  Married   Edward Cheney RAWSON
  Date   4 October 1916
  Place   Salt Lake City, Utah (Temple)
  Death   6 July 1977   Orem, Utah, Utah
  Burial   9 July 1977 SLC,Utah Sunset Lawn Ceme.

8TH CHILD
  Birth
  Married
  Date
  Place
  Death
  Burial

1 MURDOCH, James 1786-1831   2 MURDOCH, William 1825-1913
1 MURDOCH, Mary MURRAY 1782-1856   2 MURDOCH, Janet LENNOX, Sp. 1821-1877

DESCENDANTS OF_____ 3 ADAMSON, Margaret MURDOCH 1858-1915
                    3 ADAMSON, John, Sp. 1849-1915

4 ADAMSON, John Robert B-25 Nov 1879 M-5 Oct 1904 D-7 Jul 1920
4 ADAMSON, Elna Pearl STANFORD, Sp. B-10 Dec 1882 D-21 Mar 1946

    5 ADAMSON, Robert Eldon B-27 Aug 1905 M-5 Jun 1929 D-8 Nov 1955
    5 ADAMSON, Vera Agnes PATTERSON, Sp. B-12 Sep 1910

        6 ADAMSON, Robert Don B-23 Mar 1931 M-30 Dec 1952
        6 ADAMSON, Erma Bonita PECK, Sp. B-24 Nov 1933

            7 ADAMSON, Robert Kay B-27 Mar 1955 M-31 Jul 1976
            7 ADAMSON, Deanna Somsen, Sp. B-18 Sep 1950

                8 ADAMSON, Robert Jeremy   B-5 Apr 1978
                8 ADAMSON, Kaydee Lynn   B-26 Mar 1979

            7 ADAMSON, Craig Lee B-20 Sep 1958 M- 1 Apr 1982
            7 ADAMSON, Betty Jean HIATT, Sp. B-17 Oct 1960

            7 ADAMSON, Jed Eldon B- 8 Oct 1959 M-21 Aug 1981
            7 ADAMSON, Anita Irene TREE, Sp. B- 1 Sep 1960

            7 ADAMSON, Brent Richard   B- 3 Apr 1961
            7 ADAMSON, Jill   B-23 Apr 1963
            7 ADAMSON, Jan   B- 8 Dec 1964

        6 ADAMSON, John Thomas B-25 Nov 1935 M-31 Oct 1975
        6 ADAMSON, Twila MECHAM Shaffer, Sp. B-14 Oct 1931

            7 SHAFFER, Larry B.   B- 3 Nov 1954 M- 3 Jul 1981
            7 SHAFFER, Karla Kay HYDER, Sp. B-14 Sep 1952

            7 SHAFFER, Gary R.   B-10 Jul 1956 M-17 Sep 1981
            7 SHAFFER, Sarah Ann WOOLF, Sp. B-12 Feb 1962

            7 PETERSON, Rosemary SHAFFER   B-17 Dec 1957 M-18 Jan 1975
            7 PETERSON, Richard Eldon, Sp. B-16 May 1955

                8 PETERSON, Becky Ann   B-30 Mar 1975
                8 PETERSON, Brandy Lynn B-16 Dec 1976
                8 PETERSON, Lacy   B-28 Nov 1978

            7 DEEDE, Lori SHAFFER   B-10 Oct 1960 M- 14 Feb 1981
            7 DEEDE, Brian, Sp.   B-

            7 SHAFFER, Susan   B- 2 May 1963
            7 SHAFFER, Michael V.   B-24 Aug 1965

    5 ADAMSON, Lynden Stanford B-28 Jun 1907 M-1 Apr 1938
    5 ADAMSON, Elizabeth COLTRIN, Sp. B-18 Mar 1917

        6 DELLOS, Karen Elizabeth ADAMSON B-1 Dec 1938 M-9 May 1957
        6 DELLOS, William Herman, Sp. B-12 May 1937

            7 DELLOS, Scott   B- 4 Dec 1962
            7 DELLOS, Lynette   B- 2 Feb 1965
            7 DELLOS, Steven William   B-17 Feb 1971

        6 ADAMSON, Lyn Stanford B-4 Feb 1940 M-22 Feb 1969
        6 ADAMSON, Susan Yvonne ROBERTSON, Sp. B-19 Jun 1945

            7 ADAMSON, Nathaniel Scott B-10 Aug 1973
            7 ADAMSON, Travis Garrett   B-29 Dec 1974
            7 ADAMSON, Jenteal Elaine   B-20 May 1977
            7 ADAMSON, Marcie Lynn   B-27 Mar 1979

        6 LARSON, June ADAMSON Wolf B-14 Jun 1941
        6 WOLF, Wendell Corry, Sp. (1) B-2 Oct 1937 M-8 Dec 1961 D-17 Jan 1972
        6 LARSON, Orlo, Sp. (2) B-1 May 1930 M-15 Jun 1974

```
                    7 LARSON, Randall C. Wolf      B-18 Sep 1962
                    7 LARSON, Rhonda Lyn Wolf       B-17 Dec 1964
                    7 LARSON, Richard Louis Wolf B-30 Jan 1969
                    7 LARSON, Oralie June          B-16 Aug 1975
                    7 LARSON, Karalie MaryBeth     B-16 Nov 1976


    6 ADAMSON, Phillip Richard B-25 Sep 1947 M-10 Jun 1969
    6 ADAMSON, Barbara Jane ROBINSON, Sp. B-13 Jan 1949


                    7 ADAMSON, Larissa Toinette    B-6 Feb 1970
                    7 ADAMSON, Carissa Annette     B-6 Feb 1970
                    7 ADAMSON, John Phillip        B-31 Oct 1972
                    7 ADAMSON, Monica Lynne        B-27 Feb 1974
                    7 ADAMSON, Michael Blaine      B- 9 Sep 1975
                    7 ADAMSON, Melinda Kaye        B-31 Mar 1977
                    7 ADAMSON, Russell Jay         B-26 Jan 1979


    6 MENGELKOCK, Jeanne Pearl ADAMSON Giles B-2 Feb 1950
    6 GILES, Fred, Sp. (1) B-            M-6 Jun 1969 Div.
    6 MENGELKOCK, Paul, Sp (2) B-10 Feb 1950 M-28 Dec 1973


                    7 MENGELKOCK, Andrea Rae GILES B-14 Dec 1971


    6 LANCASTER, Joanne Ocea ADAMSON B-2 Feb 1950 M-31 Jul 1969
    6 LANCASTER, Gary Lorraine, Sp. B-29 Oct 1949


                    7 LANCASTER, Lorrie Anne       B-24 Jul 1970
                    7 LANCASTER, Jeri Lee          B-15 Jul 1972
                    7 LANCASTER, Gary Brandt       B-16 Jul 1974
                    7 LANCASTER, Jamie Retta       B-11 Mar 1977
                    7 LANCASTER, Tonia Rae         B-18 Jan 1980


    6 ADAMSON, James Robert B-6 Oct 1953 M-17 Jan 1976
    6 ADAMSON, Nina Kay NORBERG, Sp. B-16 Jun 1954


                    7 ADAMSON, Shelley Lynn        B-11 Nov 1976
                    7 ADAMSON, Brian Scott         B-23 Apr 1979

5 OLSON, Delsa Pearl ADAMSON, B-22 Jul 1913 M-28 Jul 1939
5 OLSON, Ralph Dallas, Sp. B-1 Jun 1908


    6 OLSON, Dallas Stanford B-28 Jun 1942
    6 OLSON, Alice Irene ALLEN, Sp. (1) B-4 Jun 1943 M-23 Aug 1966 Div. 1968
    6 OLSON, Barbara Joan WAGONER, Sp. (2) B-30 Jun 1947 M-29 Aug 1970


                    7 OLSON, Dallas Stanford Jr. B-13 Nov 1972
                    7 OLSON, Rebecca Marie         B- 9 Mar 1974
                    7 OLSON, Andrew Edward         B-21 Jan 1979


    6 OLSON, Ralph Blair B-30 Jun 1944 M-28 May 1970
    6 OLSON, Shirley Rae SMITH, Sp. B-31 Jul 1948


                    7 OLSON, Dale Blair            B-20 Aug 1973
                    7 OLSON, Scott Ralph           B- 7 May 1975
                    7 OLSON, Ann Marie             B- 4 Jan 1977
                    7 OLSON, Darla Rae             B-28 Feb 1979


    6 SCOVILLE, Candis OLSON B-17 Sep 1948 M-17 Jun 1972
    6 SCOVILLE, Winston Ousley Jr., Sp. B-14 Jun 1948


                    7 SCOVILLE, Christine          B-21 Jun 1973
                    7 SCOVILLE, Shon Winston       B-13 Oct 1975
                    7 SCOVILLE, Derek Randy        B-30 Apr 1980


    6 OLSON, Kim Dorcus B-31 Mar 1952 M-30 Apr 1976
    6 OLSON, Sylvia Ann von NIEDERHAUSERN, Sp. B-22 Apr 1954


                    7 OLSON, Ryan Kim              B-19 May 1977
                    7 OLSON, Lori Ann              B-11 Jun 1979
                    7 OLSON, Joni Lyn              B- 2 Dec 1980
```

5 CHURCHILL, Lorna Lodema ADAMSON Adams B-29 Jun 1918
5 ADAMS, Hugh Liljenquist, Sp. (1) B-24 Dec 1912 M-24 Nov 1938 Div.-22 Mar 1941
5 CHURCHILL, Lyman Edward, Sp. (2) B-3 Apr 1917 M-13 Apr 1942

     6 VEGOS, Tamara Kay ADAMS CHURCHILL B-14 Feb 1940 M-13 Sep 1963
     6 VEGOS, Charles John, Sp. B-16 Aug 1931

          7 VEGOS, Kelly Dee   B-
          7 VEGOS, Matthew Gregory   B-12 Mar 1964

     6 JOHNSON, Sandra Lee CHURCHILL Harris B-13 Aug 1943
     6 HARRIS, Phil Mose, Sp. (1) B-22 Apr 1940 M-28 Jun 1963
     6 JOHNSON, Kurt Dwain, Sp. (2) B-27 Mar 1940 M-6 Dec 1975

          7 JOHNSON, Chrisann (Harris) B- 5 Mar 1968
          7 JOHNSON, Kurt   B-

     6 CHURCHILL, Gordon Edward B-12 Nov 1945 M-16 Dec 1966
     6 CHURCHILL, Arlene HANSEN, Sp. B-24 Mar 1948

          7 CHURCHILL, Kimberly   B-17 May 1970
          7 CHURCHILL, April   B- 4 Nov 1975
          7 CHURCHILL, Danielle   B-21 Jan 1979

     6 LAPRAY, Janice CHURCHILL B-8 Aug 1947 M-22 Aug 1969
     6 LAPRAY, Brent Jensen, Sp. B-16 Jun 1943 D-20 Jan 1977

     6 KIRK, Terrilyn CHURCHILL B- 1 Jun 1961 M-11 Jun 1981
     6 KIRK, David Vance, Sp. B- 5 Jun 1959

4 ADAMSON, William Lennox B-11 Feb 1882 M-3 Jan 1912 D-19 May 1967
4 ADAMSON, Laura Jane RAWSON, Sp. B-18 Aug 1888 D-18 Sep 1957

    5 WILLETT, Isa Mary ADAMSON Burke B-30 Nov 1912
    5 BURKE, Frederick Richard, Sp. B-5 May 1912 M-1 Jan 1936 D-14 Oct 1962
    5 WILLETT, James F. Sp. B-   M-2 Oct 1964

     6 BURKE, Frederick William B-1 Nov 1941 M- 21 Dec 1965
     6 BURKE, Susan Hill BARTLETT, Sp. B-

          7 BURKE, William Willett   B-14 Oct 1967
          7 BURKE, Taylor Lee   B-25 Aug 1973

     6 BURKE, Richard Lennox B-1 Nov 1941 M-13 Jun 1964
     6 BURKE, Judith Ann COAKLEY, Sp. B-

          7 BURKE, Patrick Lennox   B-24 Mar 1965
          7 BURKE, Anne   B-14 Oct 1969

    5 ADAMSON, Jack Hale B-21 Apr 1918 M-5 Sep 1941 D-9 Sep 1975
    5 ADAMSON, Margaret BOYLE, Sp. B-17 Jul 1921

     6 ADAMSON, Hugh Douglas B-30 Sep 1944 M-29 Dec 1969
     6 ADAMSON, Alice LEETH, Sp. B-10 Dec 1945

          7 ADAMSON, Marie Donnell   B-23 Dec 1977
          7 ADAMSON, Katherine Boyle B- 4 Aug 1981

     6 WILSON, Martha Jane ADAMSON B-3 Oct 1947 M-10 Jun 1968
     6 WILSON, Edward Brimhall, Sp. B-16 Feb 1946

          7 WILSON, Laura Jane   B- 4 Apr 1970
          7 WILSON, Anne Marie   B-12 Sep 1971
          7 WILSON, Edward Glen   B- 5 Mar 1974
          7 WILSON, Sarah Margaret B-10 Mar 1976

     6 ADAMSON, John Lennox B-8 Feb 1951 M-30 Oct 1976
     6 ADAMSON, Janet Moe, Sp. B-

     6 ADAMSON, David McLaren B-28 Nov 1956

5 HIXSON, Rebecca Jean ADAMSON B-20 Aug 1923 M-5 Jun 1948
5 HIXSON, Robert Edward, Sp. B-22 Apr 1925

5 LARSON, Janet Lennox ADAMSON B-18 Nov 1926 M-16 Sep 1948
5 LARSON, Reed Parkinson, Sp. B-7 Jan 1920

      6 LARSON, William Reed B-30 Jan 1951 M-10 Sep 1974
      6 LARSON, Robin RIRIE, Sp. B-6 Sep 1954

         7 LARSON, Russell William B-26 May 1977
         7 LARSON, Scott Andrew   B-29 Dec 1978
         7 LARSON, Katharine   B-18 Feb 1982

      6 LARSON, Brent Adamson B-17 Jun 1952 M-1 Aug 1975
      6 LARSON, Mary NEBEKER, Sp. B-9 Feb 1955

         7 LARSON, Matthew Brent B-25 Sep 1979
         7 LARSON, Michael Nebeker B-23 Nov 1981

      6 DEMILL, Lennox Ann LARSON B-12 Nov 1954 M-22 Mar 1977
      6 DEMILL, Donald Edwin, Sp. B-22 Jun 1954

         7 DEMILL, Adam Donald   B-27 Aug 1980

      6 LARSON, Eric Adam B-10 May 1968

4 CAMERON, Isabelle ADAMSON B-1 Jan 1885 M-27 Dec 1905 D-29 Oct 1915
4 CAMERON, William Henry, Sp. B-27 Sep 1879 D-31 Oct 1915

   5 SUTTON, Lexie Mayme CAMERON B-29 Sep 1906 M-18 Jun 1936
   5 SUTTON, George Levis, Sp. B-13 Aug 1903 D- 4 Aug 1974

      6 SUTTON, David Levis B-20 Aug 1938 M-24 Aug 1968
      6 SUTTON, Christina Louise MORTENSEN, Sp. B-16 Dec 1942

         7 SUTTON, Patricia Louise B-21 Feb 1974
         7 SUTTON, John David   B-28 Dec 1977
         7 SUTTON, Sara Christina   B-27 Feb 1980
      6 SUTTON, James Michael B-19 Jun 1944 M-10 Aug 1967
      6 SUTTON, Catherine Ann JOHNSTON, Sp. B-19 Jun 1947

         7 SUTTON, Amy Lyn   B- 6 Jul 1970
         7 SUTTON, Allison Janel B-13 Oct 1971
         7 SUTTON, James Lennox B- 1 Oct 1973
         7 SUTTON, Erin Elizabeth B-12 Jul 1977
         7 SUTTON, Leslie Ann   B-13 Jul 1979
   5 CAMERON, Berle William B-9 Mar 1909 M-10 Jun 1936 D-28 Jul 1967
   5 CAMERON, Verna Joyce PYRAH, Sp. B-4 Dec 1913 D-14 Oct 1969

      6 CAMERON, Steven Berle B-23 Apr 1938 M-9 Jun 1961
      6 CAMERON, Peggy JoAnn PAYNE, Sp. B-2 Apr 1939

         7 CAMERON, Gary Walter   B-14 May 1962
         7 CAMERON, Lisa   B- 1 Nov 1964
         7 CAMERON, Michael Lee   B-21 Jan 1967
         7 CAMERON, Susan   B- 9 Aug 1968
         7 CAMERON, Jenifer Ann   B-26 Dec 1971
         7 CAMERON, Richard Steven B-18 Jun 1973
         7 CAMERON, Becky   B-30 Oct 1976

      6 RASMUSSEN, Rose Marie CAMERON B-16 Feb 1943 M-31 Jul 1964
      6 RASMUSSEN, Bruce Owen, Sp. B-24 Sep 1939

         7 RASMUSSEN, Kristine   B- 1 Feb 1968 Twin
         7 RASMUSSEN, Kathryn   B- 1 Feb 1968 Twin D 1 Feb 1968
         7 RASMUSSEN, Robert Bruce B-23 Feb 1969 Twin
         7 RASMUSSEN, Anne Marie B-23 Feb 1969 Twin

      6 CAMERON, Dale William B-6 Apr 1945 M-30 Jan 1969
      6 CAMERON, Ruth KAITSCHUCK, Sp. B- 6 Jan 1948

```
                7 CAMERON, Trina          B-17 Sep 1969
                7 CAMERON, Kerry          B-29 Dec 1970
                7 CAMERON, Jacob William B-30 Oct 1972
                7 CAMERON, Benjamin Dale B-16 Apr 1976

        5 BURGGRAAF, Margaret Violet CAMERON Condie B-11 Oct 1911
        5 CONDIE, Gibson Adlai, Sp. (1) B-19 May 1910 M-24 May 1935 D-11 Jun 1942
        5 BURGGRAAF, Maxwell Vernon, Sp. (2) B-17 Jul 1918 M-3 Mar 1949

                6 BURGGRAAF, Samuel Ernest B-11 Apr 1943
                6 BURGGRAAF, Rebecca        B-19 May 1944
                6 BURGGRAAF, Susan          B- 2 Apr 1947

        5 CAMERON, Elesta June B-14 May 1914 D-29 Oct 1915

4 ADAMSON, James Murray B-13 Jun 1887 D-29 Oct 1915

4 ADAMSON, David Edwin B-9 May 1891 D-3 Mar 1975
4 ADAMSON, Rebecca Ann RAWSON, Sp. B-23 Sep 1892 M-8 Oct 1914 D-3 Feb 1920
4 ADAMSON, Viola Pearl CRITCHFIELD, Sp. (2) B-12 Dec 1889 M-  Jun 1921 D-11 Mar 1958
4 ADAMSON, Eva RICE Robbins, Sp. (3) B-29 Jan 1912    M-12 Mar 1940

        5 McDEVITT, Margaret ADAMSON B-8 Mar 1917 M-25 Apr 1941
        5 McDEVITT, Charles LeRoy, Sp. B-18 Aug 1915

                6 McDEVITT, Marian B-20 Jul 1948

                6 McDEVITT, Baby Girl B-13 Apr 1956 D-13 Apr 1956

        5 ADAMSON, Robert Kay B-26 May 1923 M-20 Sep 1945
        5 ADAMSON, Dorothy Ellen MERRILL, Sp. B-28 Aug 1923

        5 SANCHEZ, Diane ROBBINS ADAMSON B-16 Dec 1934 M-3 Sep 1957  (sealed to David E. Adamson)
        5 SANCHEZ, Frank Gamboa, Sp. B-24 Jul 1929

                6 MURDOCK, Linda Jean SANCHEZ B-12 Jan 1954 (adopted) M-12 Apr 1974
                6 MURDOCK, Gary Lynn, Sp. B-2 Oct 1951

                        7 MURDOCK, Laura Adelia    B-11 Feb 1975
                        7 MURDOCK, Kelby           B-11 Sep 1976
                        7 MURDOCK, Casey           B-15 Oct 1977
                        7 MURDOCK, Brett Andrew    B-22 Sep 1979

                6 LEMONS, Mary Diane SANCHEZ B-14 Feb 1958 M-4 May 1978
                6 LEMONS, Kelly Don, Sp. B-19 Sep 1956

                        7 LEMONS, Stephen Richard   B-22 Mar 1979

                6 CAZIER, Carol Ann SANCHEZ B-6 Apr 1960 M-16 Jun 1979
                6 CAZIER, Mark Snow, Sp. B-12 Mar 1957

                6 SANCHEZ, Joseph Richard (Twin)   B-18 Sep 1963
                6 SANCHEZ, Laura Jean (Twin)       B-18 Sep 1963

4 RAWSON, Edith Mary ADAMSON B-6 Jun 1893 M-4 Oct 1916 D-6 Jul 1977
4 RAWSON, Edward Cheney, Sp. B-5 Mar 1894 D-19 Nov 1970

        5 RAWSON, James Murray B-10 Jul 1918 M-26 Mar 1943
        5 RAWSON, Anna GURR, Sp. B-1 Aug 1918

                6 RAWSON, James Murray Jr. B-7 Jul 1944 M-2 Dec 1963
                6 RAWSON, Afton Carol CHIPMAN, Sp. B-11 Sep 1944

                        7 RAWSON, Gregory Chipman B-25 Jul 1964
                        7 RAWSON, Jennifer Lynne  B-16 Dec 1965
                        7 RAWSON, Geoffrey Scott  B- 1 Dec 1967
                        7 RAWSON, Kimberly Ann     B-24 Feb 1971
                        7 RAWSON, Suzanne Michelle B-24 Mar 1975

                6 SIMPSON, Rebecca Ann RAWSON B-15 Aug 1946 M-1 Dec 1966
                6 SIMPSON, Stewart E. Sp. B-1 Jul 1946
```

7 SIMPSON, Stewart Andrew B-29 Jul 1971

6 FILLMORE, Edith Mary RAWSON B-22 Jun 1949 M-13 Sep 1973
6 FILLMORE, William L. Sp. B-9 Oct 1947

       7 FILLMORE, Joshua   B-25 Sep 1974
       7 FILLMORE, Benjamin   B-27 Dec 1975
       7 FILLMORE, Jeremiah   B-25 Mar 1977
       7 FILLMORE, James Spencer B-22 Mar 1979

6 RAWSON, Richard Gurr B-5 Aug 1952 M-19 Dec 1975
6 RAWSON, Carol HUISH, Sp. B-23 Nov 1953

       7 RAWSON, Richard Huish   B- 1 Nov 1976
       7 RAWSON, Taylor Huish   B-23 Jan 1979

5 RAWSON, Reed Edward B-13 Jan 1921
5 RAWSON, Marjorie May KEEFER, Sp. B-10 May 1922 M-6 Feb 1942 Div. 14 Aug 1947
5 RAWSON, Betty Gene GILMORE, Sp. (2) B-18 Nov 1927 M-1 Apr 1948
  Davison,   Sp. (2) to Marjorie B-   M-
      6 DAVISON, Jeffrey Edward RAWSON B-11 Aug 1945 M-1 July 1967
      6 DAVISON, Judith Kay McCLELLAN, Sp. B-5 Jul 1944

       7 DAVISON, Shelly Lynn   B- 6 Mar 1970
       7 DAVISON, Jeffrey Ross   B-11 Jun 1973
       7 DAVISON, Mitchell Ralph B- 5 Oct 1976

6 RAWSON, Cheryl Linda B-16 Aug 1949

6 AIKEN, Jill Valerie RAWSON B-28 Jun 1951 M-21 Aug 1972
6 AIKEN, Terry Gray, Sp. B-21 Jan 1948

       7 AIKEN, Ryan Daniel   B-30 Oct 1974
       7 AIKEN, Taryn Renee   B- 7 Jun 1976
       7 AIKEN, Mandy Gene   B-30 Aug 1977
       7 AIKEN, Lisa Caroline   B-28 Dec 1979

6 ROBERT, Terry Lynn RAWSON B-9 Sep 1955 M-12 Jun 1975
6 ROBERT, Lance Peter, Sp. B-21 Nov 1950

       7 ROBERT, Erin Michelle   B- 5 Nov 1976

5 LINDSAY, Janet RAWSON B-24 Mar 1928 M-7 Aug 1951
5 LINDSAY, Lionel Ronald, Sp. B-25 Apr 1921 D-5 Sep 1980

      6 LINDSAY, Gary Rawson B-19 May 1952

      6 LINDSAY, Mark David B-29 Sep 1954 M-29 Apr 1978
      6 LINDSAY, Debra HENINGER, Sp. B-11 Mar 1957

       7 LINDSAY, Bradley Douglas   B-23 Jan 1979

      6 LINDSAY, Scott Douglas B-16 Aug 1957

      6 LINDSAY, Karen   B- 1 Apr 1965

5 RAWSON, William Franklin B-5 Oct 1932 M-20 Mar 1959
5 RAWSON, Billie Jo KIMBALL, Sp. B-18 Nov 1933

      6 RAWSON, Kelly   B-31 May 1964

      6 RAWSON, Laurie   B-22 Jun 1966

      6 RAWSON, Jennifer   B-12 Nov 1969

William Louis Murdoch and Elizabeth Ivie

William Louis Murdoch was born April 4, 1888 to William Murdoch and Mary Reid Lindsay, at Heber City, Utah. William Louis' father William was born in Gaswater, Ayrshire, Scotland July 3, 1825. He married Janet Lennox June 23, 1846, at old Cumnock, Ayrshire, Scotland. Their children were: Elizabeth, James' D,' David Lennox, Mary, Janet, and Margaret. All of these children were born in Scotland. Janet Lennox Murdoch died December 20, 1877 in Scotland and in 1878 William Murdoch came to Utah.

He married Mary Reid Lindsay in 1887 at Heber City, Utah. She was the widow of Samuel Lindsay and had four children by him as follows; William C., James Reid, Margaret, and Georgiana Lindsay.

William Murdoch and Mary Reid Lindsay had three children: William Louis Murdoch, Mary Murray and Lizziebell Murdoch Davis Mary Murray Murdoch died of the flu on November 9, 1918. William Murdoch was quite robust even in his old age, and a very industrious man. He was 69 years old at the birth of Lizziebell, his last child. He died March 12, 1913 at Heber City, Utah. His wife Mary died June 22, 1929 at Lorenzo, Idaho, and was buried in Heber City, Utah, also.

William Louis Murdoch attended the Heber City schools and at an early age began working in the mines at Park City, Utah, during the winter months and doing general farm work during the farming season. While in Heber City he met and married Elizabeth Ivie of Center Creek on October 1,1913 at Provo, Utah. They lived in Heber City. While there, two children were born, Marie Murdoch and Margaret Ellen Murdoch.

In 1916 they moved to Idaho, making their home at Thornton. Here they purchased a forty-acre farm in the Independence Ward and to them four more children were born: Jennett, Lennox Merl, Mary Ivie, and David Louis Murdoch.

Louis was an honest, energetic man and a kind and loving father and a good neighbor. He was always willing to be of assistance to anyone in need. He, like all of us, was proud of his Scottish ancestry and he tried to live up to the teachings of his parents.

Louis, as he was always called, died December 6, 1937 at the age of 49 after a long illness with cancer, leaving his wife Lizzie, as she was always called, with the small family to care for in hard times and without much money. Their son David was only six and Mary eight at the time of his death. After Mary's graduation from high school she went to Idaho Falls, Idaho, and got a job.

Later Lizzie sold the farm and moved to Idaho Falls to live with Mary as the rest of the family were all married: Marie to Lowell A. Safford, Margaret to Andrew J. Young, Jennett to Craig A. Hooper, Lennox to Joseph Wayne Case, and David Louis to Uvon Mortensen. Lizzie died August 19, 1960 at the age of 68. Two of their children are deceased, Mary Ivie Murdoch December 10, 1968 and Marie Murdoch Safford May 9, 1980.

Louis and Lizzie had eleven grandchildren (See Descendant Chart) and 7 great grandchildren by 1980. We are proud today to pay tribute to our dear Murdoch "Kin." Let us who are left appreciate the heritage they have left us.

Written by Margaret Murdoch Young, a daughter

Home of William Louis & Elizabeth Ivie Murdoch
Thornton, Idaho

Elizabeth & Mary Ivie
Murdoch home in Idaho
Falls, Idaho

Howard Wayne Case   Ruth Lennox Case Lybbert   Reid Louis Case

Steven L. Murdoch

Warren Albert Safford

Mitzi Murdoch

Mary & David Murdoch at
Thornton, Idaho home

WIFE   ELIZABETH IVIE
    Birth   21 August 1892
    Place   Center Creek, Wasatch, Utah
    Death   19 August 1960
    Place   Idaho Falls, Bonneville, Idaho
    Burial   22 August 1960
    Place   Archer, Madison, Idaho
    Mother   Margaret Alice BROADHEAD
    Father   David Martin IVIE
    Other Husbands
    Information From Family records-personal knowledge of
                     Margaret E. Murdoch Young.

HUSBAND   WILLIAM LOUIS MURDOCH
    Birth   4 April 1888
    Place   Lake Creek, Wasatch, Utah
    Married   1 October 1913
    Place   Provo, Utah, Utah
    Death   6 December 1937
    Place   Idaho Falls, Bonneville, Idaho
    Burial   9 December 1937
    Place   Archer, Madison, Idaho
    Mother   Mary REID
    Father   William MURDOCH
    Other Wives

1ST CHILD   Marie MURDOCH
    Birth   22 June 1914 Heber City,Wasatch,Utah
    Married   Lowell Albert SAFFORD
    Date   28 May 1946   (Temple)
    Place   Idaho Falls, Bonneville, Idaho
    Death   9 May 1980 Idaho Falls,Bonn., Idaho
    Burial   13 May 1980 Archer, Madison, Idaho

2ND CHILD   Margaret Ellen MURDOCH
    Birth   5 June 1915 Heber City,Wasatch,Utah
    Married   ANDREW Josias YOUNG
    Date   17 July 1948
    Place   Thornton, Madison, Idaho
    Death
    Burial

3RD CHILD   Jennett MURDOCH
    Birth   9 August 1920 Thornton,Madison,Idaho
    Married   Craig Arvine HOOPER
    Date   26 May 1948   (Sealed in Temple)
    Place   Thornton, Madison, Idaho
    Death
    Burial

4TH CHILD   Lennox Merl MURDOCH
    Birth   9 January 1923 Thornton,Madison,Ida.
    Married   Joseph Wayne CASE
    Date   16 April 1945
    Place   Logan, Cache, Utah. (Temple)
    Death
    Burial

5TH CHILD   Mary Ivie MURDOCH
    Birth   25 January 1929 Thornton,Madison,Ida
    Married
    Date
    Place
    Death   10 December 1968 Idaho Falls, Idaho
    Burial   14 December 1968 Archer, Md. Idaho

6TH CHILD   David Louis MURDOCH
    Birth   16 July 1931 Thornton,Madison,Idaho
    Married   Uvon Marie MORTENSEN
    Date   25 May 1951   (Temple)
    Place   Idaho Falls, Bonneville, Idaho
    Death
    Burial

```
1 MURDOCH, James 1786-1831                    2 MURDOCH, William 1825-1913
1 MURDOCH, Mary MURRAY, Sp. 1782-1856          2 MURDOCH, Mary REID Lindsay, Sp. 1851-1929
```

DESCENDANTS OF------- 3 MURDOCH, William Louis 1888-1937
3 IVIE, Elizabeth, Sp. 1892-1960

```
4 SAFFORD, Marie MURDOCH B-22 Jun 1914 M-28 May 1946 D-9 May 1980
4 SAFFORD, Lowell Albert, Sp. B-20 Nov 1913

        5 SAFFORD, Warren Albert B-16 Nov 1948
        5 SAFFORD, Kay Berniece FREEMAN, Sp. (1) B-12 Nov 1948 M-30 Sep 1967 Div.-   Oct 1972
        5 SAFFORD, Kristena HERRERA, Sp. (2) B-24 Dec 1947 M-

                6 SAFFORD, Tate Lowell      B-31 Mar 1968

4.YOUNG, Margaret Ellen B-5 Jun 1915 M-17 Jul 1948
4 YOUNG, Andrew Josias, Sp. B-28 Feb 1908 D-18 Jun 1980

4 HOOPER, Jennett MURDOCH B-9 Aug 1920 M-26 May 1948
4 HOOPER, Craig Arvine, Sp. B-2 Aug 1922

        5 HOOPER, Lloyd Craig B-6 Sep 1952 M-5 Oct 1972
        5 HOOPER, Gloria Jean HENINIGER, Sp. B-11 Aug 1952

                6 HOOPER, Craig Werner      B-26 Mar 1974

                6 HOOPER, Jeanette Yvonne   B-23 Feb 1976

                6 HOOPER, Chad Lloyd        B-29 Sep 1979

                6 HOOPER, Sarah Helen       B- 4 Aug 1981

        5 HOOPER, Bruce Gary B-19 Nov 1956 M-14 Sep 1979
        5 HOOPER, Marjorie Helen WEST, Sp. B-23 Jan 1962

                6 HOOPER, Andrea Helen      B- 5 Mar 1981

4 CASE, Lennox Merl MURDOCH B-9 Jan 1923 M-16 Apr 1945
4 CASE, Joseph Wayne, Sp. B-19 March 1912

        5 CASE, Howard Wayne B-31 Mar 1946 M-1 Aug 1977
        5 CASE, Marla Ellen LeCheminant, Sp. B-29 May 1952

        5 CASE, Reid Louis B-13 Oct 1947
        5 CASE, Judy ANDERSEN,  Sp. B-          M-            Div.-

        5 LYBBERT, Ruth Lennox CASE B-13 Oct 1947 M-5 May 1967
        5 LYBBERT, Danny Ogden, Sp. B-29 Nov 1947

                6 LYBBERT, Tate Ogden       B- 7 Jul 1970

                6 LYBBERT, Jeremy Dan       B-11 Sep 1975

                6 LYBBERT, Camille Ruth     B-17 Oct 1977

4 MURDOCH, Mary Ivie  B-25 Jan 1929 D-10 Dec 1968

4 MURDOCH, David Louis B-16 Jul 1931 M-25 May 1951
4 MURDOCH, Uvon Marie MORTENSEN, Sp. B-13 Apr 1933

        5 MURDOCH, Steven L. B- 3 Mar 1953

        5 MURDOCH, Dan E.    B- 7 Nov 1955

        5 MURDOCH, Lori      B- 9 Jun 1958  D-10 Aug 1959

        5 SAVAGE, Mitzi MURDOCH B-19 Feb 1961 M-30 Jul 1980
        5 SAVAGE, Richard Neal, Sp. B-11 Nov 1959

                6 SAVAGE, Maegan       B-28 Jul 1981

        5 MURDOCH, Vernon Clay B-11 Apr 1964
```

Mary Murray Murdoch

Mary Murray Murdoch was born in Heber City, Wasatch, Utah, on February 26, 1891. She was the daughter of William Murdoch and Mary Reid Lindsay Murdoch. She was named for her father's mother Mary Murray and also for her mother's grandmother Mary Murray Reid Muir. She was their second child and had one brother, William Louis Murdoch, and one sister, Lizziebell Murdoch Davis. They spent their childhood in Heber in the family home on Third North and First West. She attended Heber City schools and churches.

Both of her parents were born in Scotland. They both had families by previous marriages. Her father, William, had married Janet Lennox in 1846 in Scotland. To them were born six children: Elizabeth, James "D," David Lennox, Mary, Janet, and Margaret. Elizabeth died at age sixteen and Mary as a baby in Scotland. Shortly before and after the mother, Janet Lennox, died William and his children David L., Janet, and Margaret were baptized members of The Church of Jesus Christ of Latter-day Saints. They then immigrated to Utah in 1878 to be with the other Saints and William's brother John Murray Murdoch and sister Mary Murdoch Mair McMillan and their families.

When William came to Utah, he married Christina Graham, but they were soon divorced. He then married a widow, Mary Reid Lindsay, in 1887. Mary had come to Utah in 1856, at age five, with her family in the James Willie Handcart Company. Her first husband, Samuel Lindsay, contracted an illness that caused his sudden death in 1880. Mary had had four children by her marriage to Samuel Lindsay, as follows: William C. Lindsay, James Reid Lindsay, Margaret Lindsay Burt,

and Georgiana Lindsay Walker. Georgiana was six years old at the time of their mother's marriage to William Murdoch.

William was about sixty-six years old when Mary Murray was born, and all of his children by his first marriage to Janet Lennox were all married with children of their own that Mary Murray could play with when they went to visit. She often visited in the home of David Lennox, his two living daughters, Mary Murray Murdoch and Afton Lennox Murdoch Warner, recall. They were about the same age and spent many good times together. As a teenager she also lived each summer with Mary's and Afton's brother, Salt Lake City Commissioner William Murdoch, and his wife, Jeanette Cousins Smith, to help with their growing family. Their twins, Jeannette and William, were born in 1911 when Mary was twenty years old. She was loved and respected by the children and sometimes brought the three older ones to Heber for their vacation. There were several Marys in the family, so she was called Heber Mary.

She suffered a back injury while on a coasting party with school friends and for the rest of her life she suffered great pain and had to wear a heavy brace. She was blessed with a disposition to accept trials as they came and to radiate sunshine at all times. She busied herself with sewing and embroidery and was able to sell all she could make. Some of her work is among Heber friends today.

Mary was eager to assist others who had misfortunes. She visited the sick and home-bound and always left them laughing over some of her nonsense. She was a kind friend to Corey Hanks, who had lost both eyes and hands. She read to Corey for hours at a time to help him prepare his lectures. Corey visited at Mary's mother's home often and called her mother "Aunt Mary."

Ruby Hooper told a story of Mary's kindness. While in Salt Lake City one time she invited Ruby and Corey Hanks to go with her to visit a friend, Tom Baxter. Tom was bedfast with a broken back, Corey Hanks blind and without hands, Mary incased in a heavy cast at that time. Ruby was the only one with complete health. She says the visit was an inspiration to her. Not a word of complaint was heard, just an hour of happiness, joking, and laughter, but with complete understanding of each other's trials. That was Mary's way of life doing good to all mankind.

Her last vacation, June, July, and August of 1918 was at the home of Lizziebell Murdoch Davis in Lorenzo, Idaho. Mary and her mother brought Reid and Margurite Burt with them. These children had been left in their care when their mother, Margaret Lindsay Burt, died in January of 1917. Margaret was a half-sister to Lizziebell and Mary.

Mary was stricken with Influenza during the epidemic of 1918 and passed away on November 9. Graveside services were held and burial was in the family plot in the Heber City Cemetery beside her father.

(Compiled from William Murdoch family records, Lizziebell Murdoch Davis, Mary Murray Murdoch, and Afton Lennox Murdoch Warner. James Murdoch Hunter submitted this and Ruth Murdoch Schulz added to it.)

This is the only picture we could locate of Mary Murray Murdoch. She is seated on the running board of the car. David Lennox Murdoch, Afton Lennox Murdoch, and Elizabeth Pinkerton Thyne Murdoch are in the front seat. Mary had gone up to their cabin, Camp Murdoch, in Lamb's Canyon, Utah. The other ladies and man are friends of the family.

Lizziebell Murdoch and Hugh J. Davis

Lizziebell Murdoch Davis was born January 25, 1894, in Heber City, Wasatch, Utah. She is the daughter of William Murdoch and Mary Reid Lindsay Murdoch and was the third and last child born to them. She was born in their home on Third North and First West.

Both of her parents were born in Scotland and both had families by previous marriages. Her father William had married Janet Lennox in 1821 in Scotland. To them were born six children: Elizabeth, James "D", David Lennox, Mary, Janet, and Margaret. Elizabeth died at the age of seventeen and Mary died as a baby; both died while living in Scotland. Before the death of Janet Lennox, William and his children David L., Janet, and Margaret were baptized members of The Church of Jesus Christ of Latter-day Saints. They then immigrated to Utah in 1878 to be with the other Saints and William's brother John Murray Murdoch, and sister Mary Murdoch Mair McMillan and their families.

When William came to Utah, he married Christina Graham, but they were soon divorced. He then married a widow, Mary Reid Lindsay, in 1887. Mary had come to Utah in 1856, at the age of five, with her family in the James Willie handcart company. Her first husband, Samuel Lindsay, contracted an illness that caused his sudden death in 1880. Mary had had four children by her marriage to Samuel Lindsay, William C. Lindsay, James Reid Lindsay, Margaret Lindsay Burt, and Georgiana Lindsay Walker. Georgiana was six years old and William was fourteen years of age at the time of their mother's marriage to William Murdoch.

William's children by his first marriage were all grown and married with children of their own by the time Lizziebell was born. Her father was sixty-nine at this time and later, because of his age, she often accompanied her father to help care and look after him when he would go to Salt Lake City to visit his older children. She was the same age as many of her nieces and nephews she played with. Lizziebell always told many stories she heard as a child as she went with her parents to visit their Scottish friends. It was important to her that her grandchildren learn the customs, stories, and bits of that Scottish heritage that she knew.

Lizziebell spent her childhood in Heber attending grade school there at the Central School on Third South and plain. She then had one year of high school. She remembers attending Primary in the back room of the tabernacle on Heber's Main Street. Her half sister, Georgiana Lindsay, took her and she stood on the bench beside and sang "Sweet Alice Ben Bollta" while the rest of the children sang Primary songs.

She later attended church in the old amusement hall, next to Buell's store. She remembered being taken to a Primary Christmas party in the hall above the store. Santa Claus came with gifts, candy, and nuts for each one. At that time there were two wards in Heber. One was on the east of Main Street, and the other ward was on the west side. It wasn't long before there were three wards there. Lizziebell's family lived in the Second Ward, northwest of the tabernacle. They attended church in the old hall until the new chapel on West Center Street was built.

She had many friends and enjoyed various activities. The new amusement hall brought young people from the outlying communities. It was a real pleasure to dance on the spring floor, something great for those days.

Lizziebell played the piano, and for two years she played for the silent movies in the William Wootton Show House The slides would be tried out on the screen in the late afternoon, and she would watch them and pick suitable music for them. She said, "I was glad to get the small amount of pay and to have the opportunity."

She met Hugh J. Davis through his cousin and Lizziebell's dear friend, Ruby Wall. On October 26, 1912, Lizziebell, at eighteen years of age, and Hugh were married in the courthouse in Provo, Utah. Judge Booth performed the marriage Her sister Mary and Hugh's brother-in-law, Wade Cummings, witnessed the wedding. They had a wedding dinner at the home of James R. Lindsay, Lizziebell's brother. Then Lizziebell and Hugh left by train for Eureka.

Hugh worked in the mines that winter. In the spring he sheared sheep south of Eureka. Their only child, a son, William Murdoch Davis, was born to them while they lived at Eureka. Then they moved back to Heber where Hugh sheared sheep. They then went to Strawberry Valley to work at the Charles Thacker Sawmill. They lived in a tent with a board floor and cooked over a camp stove. Then they moved to Wallsburg. Lizziebell played the piano with others playing violin and cornet for dances each Friday. This helped with the groceries, etc.

Lizziebell's Aunt Maggie Nelson died. She was her mother's sister. Maggie's son, Samuel, came to attend the funeral. He talked Hugh into going to Idaho with him to look over property there. Hugh was a good barber, but had not been to barber school. At that time Idaho did not require a graduate license, so they moved to Lorenzo, Idaho, where Hugh barbered.

They loved Idaho and made new friends and enjoyed relatives. They lived in Lorenzo one year then Hugh went to Thornton, three miles north, to barber.

While they were in Lorenzo, Hugh became acquainted with Bishop Albert Beazer. He came with his two little boys to get their hair cut. Lizziebell and Hugh bought Mr. Beazer's store and had living quarters in the back rooms. They added two rooms to the south and had a nice comfortable home for several years.

Mr. Beazer often spoke at funerals far and near. He was often asked to bring musical numbers, so Lizziebell would go along to provide the music and she also provided the transportation because Mr. Beazer didn't drive. It was a service needed and she appreciated the chance to serve in time of need.

Hugh and Lizziebell gained much through knowing Mr. Beazer. They sought his advice many times. He was like a father to them. After his death, the daughters Jessie and Ella took care of the post office. When they decided to give up the job, Lizziebell took the exams and was made the postmistress.

Then Hugh and Lizziebell sold their store to Del Blanchard and took over his ranch in Chester, Idaho. This was a great undertaking for them. Lizziebell knew nothing of ranch life and Hugh had little training. They had a lot to learn what with fifteen cows to milk, milk to be separated and the cream shipped to Salt Lake City twice a week. They had a few pigs, sheep and chickens. It was a continual job to keep the fences mended around their land. Lizziebell loved the ranch life even with the hard work. She worked alongside her husband, helping where she could, be it driving horses on the hay rake or milking cows.

They had lots of visitors. People they had known and loved while they were in Lorenzo would come for a few days at a time. Their Murdoch relatives living in Ashton and Farnum came to visit them often and Hugh and Lizziebell would go to visit them. Two cousins, Brigham and Thomas Murdoch, and a second cousin, Isabelle Hawkes Bratt and her husband Frank, arranged to have a Murdoch reunion and sent invitations to all their Utah relatives.

Among the relatives who came from Utah were Arch and Gladys McMullin Davis. They came to the ranch with their two boys Victor and Newell. The boys enjoyed riding horses and taking a plunge in the stream nearby. It was July and they went to St. Anthony to see a parade. Arch did some barbering at a shop there and helped with gasoline expenses.

Gladys was a good help with the ranch work and cooking. She made delicious cream cake. We had large juicy ever-bearing strawberries, so we had strawberry cake and pie.

Sadness came when cousin Rue Murdoch, son of Brigham Murdoch, was killed in an auto accident when he was on his way to repair machines on a dry farm near Ashton. He had mentioned many times to his father and wife that he would like to be buried in Heber, where he had lived for many years. A good neighbor who had a new Buick car insisted that Hugh take it to Heber to take Rue's family back for the funeral and burial.

At this time, in 1929, they felt the urge to return to Utah. Lizziebell's mother, Mary Reid Lindsay Murdoch, had died in June at Lorenzo. Her father had died about six months after she had married. Hugh talked about his desires to Joseph A. Murdoch and was told of a general merchandise store in Vineyard that was for sale. After talking to Hyrum Larsen and his wife (owners of the store) he agreed to make the deal.

They were very rushed to sell the ranch and had an auction to sell all equipment, furniture, etc. It was time for their son Billy to enter high school. They took him to Ashton to catch the night train to Salt Lake City. He lived with Joseph A. Murdoch and family and enrolled in high school.

Lizziebell and Hugh enjoyed the years they were in Vineyard until Hugh's health began to fail. His heart was not strong, so he thought a lighter job would be better. They took a Raleigh Products route in north Logan, Utah. After one year Hugh had not improved, so they decided to move back to Vineyard among friends and relatives. Here he rested and it helped him to get well enough to work again. A dear friend, Ariel Larsen, got Hugh started at buying raw furs and it worked well for him. He was out in the fresh air a lot, and it was not strenuous work. This business afforded the opportunity to travel in nearly every state in the union and Lizziebell always accompanied him. After a time Hugh did produce trucking and also fur buying. He carried on with this until they moved to Provo and bought two homes at 970 and 978 West, 100 North.

After their retirement, Hugh and Lizziebell spent their winters in California. They would spend Christmas with their family in Utah and then the next three or four months were spent on the coast.

Sorrow came to Lizziebell and family when Hugh's heart gave way. It was a terrible shock, even though specialists in Salt Lake City had told them about his condition. He passed away at their home in Provo, September 15, 1957 and was buried in Heber City, Utah.

Since Hugh's death Lizziebell has continued to live at 978 West 100 North in Provo, near her son and five grandchildren and great grandchildren. She became a victim of arthritis and for the last twenty-five to thirty years of her life she has used crutches and a wheel chair to assist her in getting around.

In her more active years she had a special talent in handwork, knitting, crocheting and embroidery. Her family and friends were recipients of many articles created by her hands. She joyed in giving to others.

She worked in the Daughters of the Utah Pioneers, church work, sharing her talents in Relief Society, M.I.A., and giving compassionate service to many. She played piano for all ward and stake dance practices in preparation for the M.I.A. dance festivals held each year at Salt Air. She traveled so much to share her talents and be of assistance for funerals.

She especially enjoyed the friendship and good times with her Murdoch relatives. She was a loyal promoter and supporter of the Murdoch family reunions as long as her health permitted her to do so.

At age eighty-three, in 1.977, she said, "I just bide time and take each day as it comes. I have love for all people. My family and dear friends and neighbors are all more than choice. All are so kind and thoughtful of me."

As of this writing Lizziebell Murdoch Davis still lives with her only child, Billy, and family who faithfully meet her needs each day. She is the only grandchild of James and Mary Murray Murdoch that is still living.

Hugh J Davis & Lizziebell Murdoch 1948   Lizziebell Murdoch & Hugh J Davis 1950

Provo, Utah home about 1938

Left to Right:
Lizziebell Murdoch Davis
Hugh J Davis
Faye Ross

Afton Murdoch Warner, Lizziebell
Murdoch Davis, and Mary Jean Davis
in a Murdoch Reunion dress-up parade
at Vivian Park, Utah

Lizziebell Murdoch & Hugh J Davis, Aspen Grove
June 1954

HUSBAND HUGH J DAVIS
Birth 22 September 1890
Place Wallsburg, Wst., Utah
Married 26 October 1912
Place Provo, Utah, Utah
Death 15 September 1957
Burial 18 Sep 1957 Heber, Ut
Father William Luce DAVIS
Mother Rosalie WALL
Other Wives

WIFE LIZZIEBELL MURDOCH
Birth 25 January 1894
Place Heber, Wasatch, Utah
Death
Burial
Father William MURDOCH
Mother Mary REID Lindsay
Other Husbands
Information From

1ST CHILD William Murdoch DAVIS
Birth 9 April 1913 Eureka, Juab, Utah
Married Kathryn BAIRD
Date 7 September 1939
Place Salt Lake City, Salt Lake, Utah
Death
Burial

HUSBAND WILLIAM MURDOCH DAVIS
Birth 9 April 1913
Place Eureka, Juab, Utah
Married 7 September 1939
Place Salt Lake City, Utah
Death
Burial
Father Hugh "J" DAVIS
Mother Lizziebell MURDOCH
Other Wives

WIFE KATHRYN BAIRD
Birth 7 September 1916
Place Metropolis, Elko, Nevada
Death
Burial
Father Henry BAIRD
Mother Elizabeth Ann RASBAND
Other Husbands
Information From

1ST CHILD Doyle J. DAVIS
Birth 1 January 1942 Provo, Utah, Utah
Married Carolyn GLENN
Date 9 July 1965
Place Logan, Cache, Utah
Death
Burial

2ND CHILD Mary Jean DAVIS
Birth 28 January 1944 Provo, Utah Utah
Married Larry Wayne DRAPER
Date 29 March 1979
Place Salt Lake City, Salt Lake, Utah
Death
Burial

3RD CHILD Kathleen DAVIS
Birth 1 June 1949 Provo, Utah, Utah
Married Arnold Julian GILCHRIST
Date 28 Jan 1971
Place Salt Lake City, Salt Lake, Utah
Death
Burial

4TH CHILD Donita DAVIS
Birth 14 July 1952 Provo, Utah, Utah
Married Rodney Kent POLSON
Date 6 August 1976
Place Provo, Utah, Utah
Death
Burial

5TH CHILD William Lyle DAVIS
Birth 16 May 1956 Provo, Utah, Utah
Married
Date
Place
Death
Burial

```
1 MURDOCH, James  1786-1831                    2 MURDOCH, William 1825-1913
1 MURDOCH, Mary MURRAY, Sp. 1782-1856          2 MURDOCH, Mary REID Lindsay, Sp. 1851-1929

                              3 MURDOCH, LIZZIEBELL 1894-
           DESCENDANTS OF--------
                              3 DAVIS, HUGH J, SP. 1890-1957

4 DAVIS, William Murdoch  B-9 Apr 1913 M-7 Sep 1939
4 DAVIS, Kathryn BAIRD, Sp. B-7 Sep 1916

       5 DAVIS, Doyle "J"  B-1 Jan 1942 M-9 Jul 1965
       5 DAVIS, Carolyn GLENN, Sp. B-7 Mar 1942

              6 DAVIS, Michael "J"        B-25 Nov 1967

              6 DAVIS, Todd Jeffery       B-23 Jun 1969

              6 DAVIS, Stephanie          B-14 Feb 1972

              6 DAVIS, Kyle "J"           B-21 Aug 1973

              6 DAVIS, Kevin "J"          B-30 Oct 1976

              6 DAVIS, Matthew "J"        B- 5 Apr 1979

              6 DAVIS, Scott Jared        B- 5 Oct 1980

       5 DRAPER, Mary Jean DAVIS  B-28 Jan 1944 M-29 Mar 1979
       5 DRAPER, Larry Wayne, Sp. B-27 Aug 1951

       5 GILCHRIST, Kathleen DAVIS  B-1 Jun 1949 M-28 Jan 1971
       5 GILCHRIST, Arnold Julian, Sp. B-13 Oct 1947

              6 GILCHRIST, Aaron Davis    B- 2 Dec 1972

              6 GILCHRIST, Marcelen       B-17 Aug 1974

              6 GILCHRIST, Nathan Hugh    B- 2 Jun 1978

              6 GILCHRIST, Lindsey        B-20 Nov 1980

       5 POLSON, Donita DAVIS  B-14 Jul 1952 M-6 Aug 1976
       5 POLSON, Rodney Kent, Sp. B-31 Aug 1954

              6 POLSON, Natalie           B-29 Oct 1978

              6 POLSON, Jason Kent        B-13 May 1980

       5 DAVIS, William Lyle  B-16 May 1956
```

Writings Of David Lennox Murdoch on the James Murdoch Family

Introductory

I have been asked repeatedly to write something about our ancestors,[2] where they hailed from—what were their avocations, where they resided etc. I fully realize unless this is at least attempted soon, the generation of people to which I belong will soon all have passed away and the succeeding generation will be left without much information pertaining to those times, circumstances and events. With these thoughts then, and with a desire to comply with the request so made, I will attempt to put in writing what little I know of the past of our ancestors on the Murdoch side and others also, associated with them, by marriage and otherwise.

In writing this narrative, I feel that from our point of view on this far western land of America, the subject of the cause of our gathering here demands first consideration—the primal consideration was the restored gospel through the means of the Prophet, Seer, and Revelator, Joseph Smith. The gospel was restored and I take it every Latter-day Saint is familiar with this most wonderful event. The Church of Jesus Christ of Latter-day Saints was organized on April 6th, 1830 with some six members.

The gospel was carried to England by Heber C. Kimball, Willard Richards, Joseph Fielding and John Goodson in the late summer of 1837. These brethren arrived there, so Heber C. Kimball's life story by Orson F. Whitney advises us, without any means to prosecute their labors in a strange land. Heber C. was absolutely penniless. With wonderful humility and faith and reliance upon the Lord they were led to go to Preston, Lancashire where the way was immediately opened up. Friends were raised up and it seems that the people were eagerly waiting for and ready to receive the message then delivered to them. The wonderful, it might

be truly said the marvelous success these Elders met with is most interestingly narrated in Whitney's Life of Heber C. Kimball. The reader should own a copy of this book and read it. Heber C. Kimball then, with these other brethren, were the Fathers and Founders of the British Mission! They spread out in the surrounding country and established many branches. This work was greatly augmented and further established over a large part of England in 1840. When Heber C. Kimball, Brigham Young, Wilford Woodruff, Parley P. and Orson Pratt, John Taylor and others went over there at that time and added upon and developed that which had already been accomplished some two or three years previously.

The Introduction of the Gospel to Scotland

In 1839, Elders Samuel Mulliner and Alexander Wright carried the gospel to Scotland, their native land and were instrumental in opening up and establishing branches at Paisley, Johnstone, Bridge of Wur, and Thornlybank. In 1840 Scotland was visited by Apostle Orson Pratt who established the Edinburgh Branch. Thus was the gospel carried to Scotland and shortly afterwards Glasgow was included with the above mentioned places, and with the news filtering through from England where it was introduced some three years earlier, and its establishment in Scotland it spread out into Ayrshire, and sometime before 1852 it had reached Grasswater, Kirkconnel, etc. It was here that Uncle John received his first impressions at the hands of Aunt Ann's brother, James Steel while on a visit from England where he was then located. James Steel received it from a young lady who had received it and been a member of the church for some years. This young lady became Mrs. James Steel and these two with their two children, James E. and George im-

---

2. Editors note: This material was taken from a journal written by David Lennox Murdoch after his return from a mission to Scotland in 1905–07. Since he had been born in Scotland, grew up with an acquaintance of places and family members of that time period, immigrated to Utah, returned to Scotland in his later life, and then recorded his remembrances of that early period of time in Murdoch family history, it is felt that this record should be included in this book.

migrated in the year 1856 on the good ship "Horizon." On that ship in their company was Mary Murdoch of Grasswater, about two miles from Lugar and six or seven from Muirkirk. Mary Murdoch was known in her day as "Wee Grannie." Being as I have heard it stated many times by my Mother and others, quite short in stature but strongly and I presume stockily built. But of this we shall have more to say further on. According to our genealogical records James Murdoch of Grasswater was born about 1786 and Mary Murray of Glencairn was born October 13, 1782. They were married January 10, 1811 at Glencairn. They had children—Janet, born December 8, 1812, died June 28, 1866, Mary born June 16, 1813—died in infancy, James born July 29, 1814—died September 12, 1884, Veronica born June 16, 1816—died October 4, 1908, Mary born October 13, 1818—died December 5, 1900, John M. born December 28, 1820—died May 6, 1910, Margaret born December 30, 1822—died in infancy, William born July 3, 1825—died March 12, 1913 in Heber City.

Their family then consisted of eight children, two of whom died in infancy. The conditions then of life and existence were somewhat poor. The period was before the days of railways. The iron and coal industry was in its infancy. Manufactures were few and about the only employment or work obtainable by these growing children was by hiring out to farmers in the surrounding neighborhood. Grandfather and grandmother could not afford to keep them at home because his wages would be very small and the great wonder is how they managed to get along at all, frugal to a degree they must have been. The very strictest economy must have been of necessity, their constant thought and care. Their home was Grasswater where the family was all raised. Grasswater is some 6 or 7 miles west of Muirkirk—2 miles from Lugar and about 4 miles from the town of old Cumnock, all in the county of Ayr. Their pleasures and enjoyments were very few and only such as are or were incidental to a "farming" life in that rural district at this early age.

A sorrowful event happened to this contented little family on the 20th of October, 1831. The father, James Murdoch, was employed at some of the pits sought to be established at this period not far from his happy little home and family. The son of a farmer at a place called Dalfad happened around and his curiosity or something of that nature produced a desire within him to be lowered into a new shaft which had been lately sunk. The pits at this early date in this neighborhood were all sunk on the out croppings of the mineral field—not deep, but on the contrary very shallow and operated by a windlass. The boy went down and was overcome by foul air or choke damp which had accumulated at the bottom and he fell helplessly out of the bucket or whatever it was. The alarm was given and Grandfather was lowered down to his rescue but he also was overcome in a similar manner. By the time that efforts were made to disperse the damp and foul air and bring the bodies to the surface, life, in both instances was gone—and thus the lives of two had been snuffed out in a few minutes. The father, the provider of this little family was thus taken and we can imagine what a sad and sorrowful little home it was. My father was but five years of age. Uncle John was 10 or 11. Granny was very brave. Her elder children had to go out and work. Uncle John was almost old enough to herd cows at some nearby or neighboring farm. My Father before he was seven years of age was doing the same and from those early years in their lives they never knew anything else but work and then for a mere pittance, but they got some kind of board, chiefly oatmeal. Tea they got once a year at New Years Day and that was then considered wonderful. Time went on, the opportunities for education were of the most meager nature. Very, very little they got. And in thinking it all over and reflecting upon the times then, their impoverished condition, the hardships they had to endure and the struggles of life and existence, it appears really marvelous and wonderful that men like Uncle John and Father could ever come to maturity and keep level or on a par with others far more favorably raised and situated. It is almost unbelievable that Uncle John could ever be expected to attain to the learning and understanding that he acquired during his life and to the high social standing he held in the community in which he so long resided. It is equally the same with my Father. He rose to be underground manager at the Muirkirk Iron and Coal Works, a position he held for quite a number of years before immigrating to America. I always loved Aunt Mary. She was always so good and kind and considerate. Aunt Veronica was another member of that family from Grasswater. The mother of a large family by her husband George Caldow in Scotland, she saw hard times, trials and difficulties and poverty. Being a widow alone, her family having all married but one, and he was old enough to be almost a grandfather, she was immigrated and came with us in 1878. Thus four out of the six embraced the gospel and left their native land for the gospels sake. Aunt Jennie, the oldest, married Alex Smith, and lived at Birnickucewe about three miles from Grasswater. She had quite a family and was rather in poor circumstances the most of her life. Her husband, a good man but rather delicate and asthmatical. A son, William whom I knew in Glasgow, immigrated to the state Washington some number of years after we came. He and his wife are now gone but they have left up there several sons and at least one daughter. There remains but one more to mention and that was James. He married Margaret McCall. The had a large family and lived in Glasgow. I think they all must be gone now as I could get no trace of any of them while over there 1905–6–76 altho I even advertised in the paper for them. A son, William, came here and lived for a time in Heber City and Park City. He died in this city and was buried in the City Cemetery.

I felt as if I must take space enough to say what I have about the Grasswater Murdochs. Notwithstanding their humble station in life, they got along wonderfully well, overcame many obstacles that would have made the stoutest hearts quail. They succeeded admirably in life's battle and came through as much respected and loved as the great majority of mankind.

Uncle John tells us in his journal or record which he wrote with his own hand at a very advanced age, some eighty or thereabouts, that after attaining manhood he boarded with his Mother at Grasswater. When about 28 years of age he married Ann Steel in 1848 whose home was at Kirkconnel. They lived for awhile there and here it was that he got his first impressions of Mormonism from James Steel, brother of Aunt Ann who was residing then somewhere in England. The gospel had now been preached in England for some eleven years. James Steel was keeping company with a young lady there who had been a Mormon for years. And their close intimacy led to his conversion. Uncle John narrates that James Steel from being very indifferent had now become thoroughly familiar with the scriptures and could easily overcome any arguments or statements that Uncle John could put forth. This was a wonderful surprise to Uncle John. He felt that James Steel had acquired a wonderful knowledge of the scriptures and things spiritual.

In 1850 James Steel visited them at Kirkconnel and it was at this time that Uncle John began to seriously investigate. He states that his business called him back to England and that Uncle John never saw him again. Very shortly after this Thomas Todd, for many years a resident of Heber City, and then a native of Langechar was baptised. Some two weeks later Sister Todd was baptised and also Uncle John and Aunt Ann, The first fruits of the gospel in this dispensation in that part of Scotland. "All from the planting of James Steel." His records proceeds. In the spring of 1851 I moved my family to Birnickucewe around there, were a few scattered saints and a little branch was established. "We soon baptised a few more—my Mother and my sister Mary being amongst the number." By this time they were being visited by the Elders by whom they were encouraged and comforted. Meetings were held at Uncle John's house—perhaps the only place where the little branch and the few saints could meet, hold their little meetings, and rejoice in each other's society. Meetings were also held at "Wee Grannies" house at Grasswater and here it was that my mother had the opportunity of attending them and becoming familiar with the gospel. My Father then belonged to a church in Cumnoch and I believe it was while he would be away there that the meetings were held at "Wee Grannies."

Shortly after this Uncle John moved to Garallan, near Cumnoch, which was the last place he lived before immigrating to America. His home here was the meeting place also for the saints and Elders but not for long. President Brigham Young sent to Franklin D. Richards then presiding in Liverpool, for two Scotch Shepherds and their dogs. Uncle John was one of those selected. Preparations were made to depart. Farewell parties were held at Garallan and at Kirkconnel immediately prior to their departure and on the morning of January 1, 1852 they took the train at Kirkconnel for Glasgow en route thus far. From Glasgow they proceeded to Liverpool staying there eight or ten days for the vessel to get her cargo in. At length on the 10 day of January 1852, the "Kennebec" sailed for America.

Just before leaving his native land Uncle John composed and sung the following song to the tune of "Afton Water." The time seems very appropriate for near there, Kirkconnel, where Aunt Ann spent their last night in Scotland the "Afton" flows quietly along amongst its green braes and joins the "Nich" lower down.

Oh Scotland, my country, my dear native home
Thou land of the brave and the home of my song
Oh why should I leave thee and cross the deep sea
To far distant lands lovely Scotland from thee?

How pleasant to view are thy mountains and hills
The sweet blooming heather and farfamed
   blue-bells

The haunts of my childhood where oft I have
    strayed
With my faithful companions—my dog, crook and
    plaid.

Oh Scotland, my country and land of my birth
In fondness I'll ever remember thy worth
For wrapt in thy bosom my forefathers sleep
Oh why should I leave thee and cross the wide
    deep?

But why should I linger or wish for to stay?
The voice of the Prophet is haste, flee away Lest
    judgments o'ertake you and lay Scotland low
To the faithful in Zion oh then let me go.

Farewell then loved Scotland, my home and my all
When duty requires it we bow to the call.
We brave every danger, we conquer each foe
To the voice of the prophet oh then let me go.

Farewell then dear kindred, one last fond adieu
Farewell my dear brethren, so faithful and true
May angels watch o'er you till warfares are o'er
And in safety we all meet on Zion's fair shore.

A very creditable composition and worthy of repro-
duction in his memoirs. It might be mentioned, that
wherever the gospel has been introduced the spirit
of poesy takes possession of the people affiliating as
Latter Day saints. In every number or volume of the
"Millennial Star" poetic effusions are there found, ex-
pressive of joy, gratitude, affection and love. The same
spirit prevailed in this land. Our hymn book is full of
many choice pieces by early members and prominent
members of the Church. It is needless to mention a
few names, both male and female, of the authors. The
hymn book, I presume, is in the home of every member
of the church and forms very interesting and instruc-
tive reading. I hope that some day, the history of every
composition in the hymn book will be published, and
the authors suitably mentioned and honored.

From the Millennial Star, volume 14 the sailing of
the Kennebec is noted as follows: "This large, new
and commodious ship of ten hundred and seventy
tons register, went out of the Bramly-mine dock on
the morning of the tenth instant-loth January 1852—
having been detained two days by adverse winds,
which blew a heavy gale outside. She had three hundred and thirty three souls of the saints on board. We
had chartered the ship Devonshire, but being a little

disappointed in her qualifications for sea, we also blew
a head wind and secured the Kennebec, which is an
unusually spacious and commodious vessel. After getting their luggage put to rights, the saints seemed very
cheerful and gave out to their feelings in songs and
praise as the noble ship passed out upon the bosom
of the sea and left the shore fading in the distance.
Included in this company were Elders John L. Higbee,
John Spiers, Thomas Smith and W. C. Dunbar, each
presidents of conferences, faithful in their callings and
going up to the Zion of the Lord. Having done a great
and good work in this land, many thousands, who
will have obtained the gift of "Eternal Life" thru the
instrumentality of these faithful men will rejoice with
them in the Kingdom of God. We have pleasure also
in announcing the departure of Elder John Pack of the
French Mission with about a dozen saints from the
Channel Islands. How joyous to witness the departure
of saints of the different tongues and families of the
earth from their native lands to mingle with God's
people in establishing his purposes on the earth. Elder
Higbee was appointed President of the company and
the several Elders above named were called to be his
counsellors, under whose excellent superintendence
the saints will doubtless enjoy much of the spirit of
God during their passage on the waters."

I have not been able to find much about the voyage
of the "Kennebec" in Vol. 14 of the Millennial Star.
From Uncle John' record, we find they were some
nine weeks at sea which was an unusually longtime.
It seems provisions were very scarce and water also
for the steerage passengers and this caused much discomfort and sickness especially amongst the children.
Uncle John speaks of oatmeal, which was, as I would
take it their principal food. Having no money and no
other means of subsistence the children suffered and
pined during this period and by the time they got
on the Mississippi they were in a very reduced and
sickened condition. It must have been distressing and
heartrending to see their two little ones pine away and
cry for bread which could not be got for them. Nine
weeks at sea would bring us to about March 15. They
were detained at the mouth of the river eight or ten
days on a sand bar. It would therefore be now about
March 25. The river boat was very crowded and with
the sick children we can well imagine what a terrible
trying time it was for Uncle John and Aunt Ann and
all the rest of them. The little boy, James by name,
died on March 20—age one year and eight months
and was buried in a wood yard on the banks of the
Mississippi river 12 miles from Columbia. It will be

seen that there is apparently some discrepancy about dates here. The journal proceeds "we landed at St. Louis" and were then in the care of A.O. Smoot from Salt Lake City, who was in charge of the immigration that year. Uncle John says "Our little girl, Elizabeth by name, had now become very weak and although everything that willing hands and kind hearts could do for her she passed away April 4—age three years and eight months and was buried in a strange land amongst strangers. The people were very kind to us. We remained in St. Louis about one month waiting a ship load of saints that left Liverpool after us. We then went up the Missouri River to Kansas City where we got our outfits for crossing the plains." Cholera now broke out and quite a few died and were buried there about nine miles out on the plains.

On May the 20th a little girl was born to them in a small tent in the midst of a terrible thunderstorm. She was blessed and named Mary Murray Murdoch. This was cousin Mary Duke and later Mary Ryan. Aunt Ann was able to walk and carry her baby almost every foot of the way from the time her baby was eight days old. On the way Captain Smoot was taken sick with the cholera and the train was held up some to allow him needed rest. Uncle John was his day nurse. Later on, while in the Black Hills country, Uncle John was taken sick with the mountain fever and was in turn nursed by Captain Smoot.

On Sept 3, Captain Smoot landed his large company of weary pilgrims in Salt Lake City after a long and tedious journey of 17 weeks on the plains. This was the first company that came by the Perpetual Emigration Fund. Captain Smoot introduced Uncle John to President Young as one of his shepherds with their dogs and gave him a very good recommend. President Young informed them that he had rented what few sheep he had left to his brother, Lorenzo, for five years and would not need them at present for that purpose. He said all needed rest and to remain at camp and the brethren would find them something to eat and the way would be opened up for him to get work. Before the evening of the second day there was not a soul left in camp but the two shepherds, their wives, the two children, and the two dogs. A man by the name of Dalton from Farmington came to camp and hired us to work for him one month. He took us home and was very kind to us. My companions foot was still getting worse and became unable to work and was anxious to return to Salt Lake. Uncle John finished his month, got his pay and considered himself rich enough to divide with his companion. He then was hired to dig potatoes

for President Young. He says he had much joy in his labours altho the work was hard, thinking that he was working for the prophet of the Lord and the greatest man on earth.

Uncle John located in the Third Ward in Salt Lake City and became second counselor to Bishop Jacob Miller. On the removal from the ward of the first counselor, he was made first counselor in which capacity he acted until the time of the "move" caused by Johnson's army coming here. With others he then moved to Provo Valley, now and for long known as Heber City. This was in 1860. Their first home was a dug out and others had similar places to live in. This was a new start in life again. They all obtained land and proceeded to subdue it, plant crops and do everything requisite and necessary in a new and virgin country. With industry, perseverance, and a faith that knew no faltering they gradually grew up in their new settlement and with the blessings of the Lord they patiently toiled on and overcame all hindrances, obstacles, privations and suffering until life became more tolerable and prosperity and comparative comfort came to them in their little domicile there. None of the present generation, none but those who actually came through such times and days and years of toil and labor and striving can ever know how much they are indebted to the pioneers, yes the grand and noble fathers, mothers, sons and daughters of the most worthy people that ever lived. Firm and undaunted in their faith, they pursued their course and kept right along in the way mapped out for the children of our Heavenly Father in these latter-days in building the Zion of our God in the valleys of the mountains.

The blessings of the Lord were with them and chief amongst these, was the blessing of health and strength to enable them to overcome all hardships and privations incidental to the establishing themselves in this new country. Another great blessing they enjoyed was the gift of a large and helpful family. Mary they brought with them, a babe in arms. Elizabeth and James, as has already been stated, died on the way. Ann, Janet Osborne and Sarah Jane have the Third Ward, Salt Lake City, for their birth-place. Jacobina Wells Osborne was born in Heber City as were also John, Isabella, Lovina, John William who died in infancy, Thomas Todd, Lucy Veronica also died in infancy, Joseph A., David Steel and Millicant Sophia. Some fifteen in all—Glory Hallelujah! Praise the Lord. Altho the first portion of the family were all girls, they were not only a comfort and blessing to their parents but were also a real aid and assistance to their father and mother in the days of hardships and toil.

In those days polygamy was practiced by the Latter Day Saints. Uncle John and Aunt Ann were just as much impressed with the importance and necessity of observing that principal of the gospel then as any other, and when the proper time and person should come along it was understood that Uncle John should observe it. In the course of events, Isabella Crawford from Blantyre, Scotland, immigrated to Holyoake, Massachusetts, in company with others and was engaged there in a cotton mill. Some five years passed—they saved their earnings and were enabled to purchase a yoke of oxen and a wagon in which they came to Utah. One of the scotch lassies with whom Isabella Crawford immigrated was named Catherine Campbell who married William Foreman who was later one of the Bishops in Heber City. Isabella Crawford was visiting her friend there and in this way an acquaintance was formed which ripened into friendship and a little later led to a visit to the Salt Lake Temple where Uncle John and Isabella Crawford were married the eighth day of August 1862. From this union the following were issue: Margaret Ann, Catherine Campbell, James C. Brigham, Robert, John Murray Jr., and Isabella Crawford. Twenty two children altogether—fifteen of whom lived to manhood and womanhood. At a Murdoch reunion held at Vivian Park 17, 18, 19, August 1921 commemorating the one hundreth anniversary of Uncle John's birth, the following statistics were given.

In the late eighties, the raid was on and it was hot, hateful, vindictive and in many cases bitterly, ruthlessly and heartlessly cruel and severe. Judge Charles T. Lane was on the bench and tried many of the cases. Feeling was pretty high while it lasted. The leaders of the Church were in exile, hiding up from the officers of the law who were using every device and stratagem that the devil could inspire them with to harrass, annoy, and imprison. To the great credit of most of those arrested, tried and convicted for disobeying the Edmunds—Tucker Act, they paid the fine and went to the penitentiary to suffer the term of imprisonment inflicted like men. Uncle John was getting along in life. He had lived in Heber City a long time, everybody knew him, and he was one of those who were caught, tried and convicted and sentenced by Judge Lane to a term in the penitentiary. He asked the judge for the privilege of going home to Heber City from Provo where the trial was held for the purpose of getting the necessary change of underwear while in the pen. This was granted. He returned home, got the necessary

clothing and left home of his own free will and option to go to Salt bake to serve the time imposed upon him to satisfy the laws demand. In due time he presented himself at the penitentiary, told them his name, where he hailed from and that he had come to suffer imprisonment according to the sentence passed upon him. It appears that no commitment papers had been sent the marshall or warden—they knew nothing about him or the papers and could not receive him. Uncle left and came up to our place and told his tale. "They won't have me," he said. And he seemed very much put out about it. Any other ordinary man would have rejoiced at the reception he got and might have and most likely would have thought at least, if he had not said it, "Well you can go to the devil. I will go home and when you really want me bad enough, you can come for me." Not so with honest to goodness Uncle John, he explained the whole matter to them and they told him to come back again at a certain time when they would have the papers and receive him and give him a zebra-striped suit which all prisoners then wore. Can you imagine of a more honorable, honest, guileless soul than his. He returned to the pen, was admitted and served his term. He might have gone to California or Timbuktu if he had wanted to. This incident is a wonderful illustration of his honesty, reliability and dependability and keen sense of right and trust. "They won't have me." I could occupy much more space in writing and commenting upon the lives of these good people, but I realize that Uncle John himself has made a history of his life, brief at that, also Nettie, Sarah and Kate with the assistance of William Lindsay who has written much for them, have also written many particulars and incidents in the lives of their parents and these all in greater detail which will be more interesting to the families directly concerned and affected, and as considerable is said and was printed in the papers at the time of their demise, I will copy that herein and finish this portion of my narrative and succeeding that, proceed to give a brief account of the gathering of Aunt Mary and her family of three, Mary, Andrew and Aleck in 1866. And following that a brief account of the gathering of Father, myself and wife and sisters Janet and Margaret and Aunt Veronica and John Adamson in 1878.

The following by Mrs. Janet McMullin written for the Daughters of the Pioneers is will worthy of a place here and quite appropriately follows what has preceded it.

1. Let us turn our memories back far along that
   dreary track

there's a band of pilgrims filled with hopes and
fears
they had left their home, their all, gathered here at
Father's call,
and now are known as Utah's pioneers.

Chorus
Then all honor to their name who have given us
this fame.
It was earned with love and toil and faith and
prayers.
As we meet from day to day, we feel it in our hearts
to say
We are children of those grand old Pioneers.

2. When they reached this promised land mid those
mountain vales so grand
they were earnest serving God, who brought them
through,
nice log houses they did build with large families
they were filled
oh! they truly builded better than they knew.

3. They were invited in their ways and their flocks
and herds did raise
they did card and spin and weave and make our
clothes,
with their faithful honest toil they did cultivate the
soil
and made the desert blossom as the rose.

4. As their children when we meet in those vales so
calm and sweet
we prize their lives of service more than gold,
and love them more and more as we read their
history old
yet the half of this grand story not's been told.

The spirit of gathering very quickly takes possession of the church members after baptism as a rule.
Their associations with friends and neighbors, becomes often-times strained and unpleasant. Those
who are not impressed with the truth and will not
join the church are frequently somewhat hostile in
their feelings and bitter in their denunciation of it—
and it has not at all been unusual for the saints to be
ostracized and persecuted. This condition, no doubt
increases their desire to gather and get away from
amongst them.

Mary Murdoch at Grasswater (Wee Grannie) and
Mary Murdoch Mair, at the stables, about a mile or

so distant, and mother (Janet Lennox Murdoch) at
the Grasswater Rows were left behind. Little meetings
continued to be held at Grannies and with an occasional visit from the Elders in Ayrshire, the fire within
kept flickering and burning and in the case of each
one of them, it never dimmed nor became extinct as
long as life lasted. Time went on—some four years
had now passed since the departure of Uncle John and
Aunt Ann on the "Kennebec." Uncle John was by this
time able to send for James Steel and wife and his
two children and his mother, Mary Murdoch. I can just
remember the day "Wee Grannie" came down to our
house to bid us good bye, on her way to Liverpool. My
recollection is not clear however. I can just remember
the occasion. Twelve days after Uncle John left his
native land, I was born, so that by 1856 when Grannie
and the others left, I was but four years of age.

In the eighteenth volume of the Millennial Star, we
find that the ship Horizon, Captain Reed sailed from
Liverpool for Boston May 25, 1856 with 856 souls of
the Saints on board, under the presidency of Elders
Edward Martin, Jesse Haven and Geo P. Waugh.

"The following Elders who have held responsible
positions in this country, also sailed on this ship: Elders T. B. Broderick and John Toone from Utah—The
latter retires from his labors on account of ill health.
John Jaques, Robert Hold, Thomas Ord, James Stones,
Henry Squires and Robert Evans were Presidents of
Conferences. Elder Martin has labored in the ministry
in Britain over three years, and during most of the
present seasons immigration, has been engaged with
us in the immigration department of the office. His
labors have been of that faithful and efficient character
which commend themselves."

The following piece is taken from the "Star" May
5, 1856, and is very fitting for this and every other
company leaving Europe's shores:

I'm away, I'm away, o'er the wide spreading sea
To the land of the brave, to the land of the free,
To the land of the light, to the land of the truth
To the land of our Joseph, a prophet in youth
To the land where the gospel first dawned on our
day
Ship, spread out thy canvas and bear me away.

I'm away, I'm away, for to see and to know
The things which our prophets have told us below
To build up the Temple, that now is begun
High up in the mountain, for father and son
Who died without hearing the truth of the day

Ship spread out thy canvas and bear me away.

I'm away, I'm away, where the husband and wife
Unite to be one for the regions of life
Where the love and the joy of the life giving rain
Can only be known by the just who are there
Where the Lord in his mercy, his wisdom displays
Ship, spread out thy canvas and bear me away.

I'm away, I'm away where the sire and the son
In the cause of their God, have unitedly run
Where the priest and the prophet, the matron and
    maid
For the sake of religion, the ransom have paid,
To where they departed from temples of clay
Ship, spread out thy canvas and bear me away.

I'm away, I'm away and I bid you adieu
Oh elders of Israel be faithful and true
And pluck not the daisies that grow o'er the green
Full fresh in my country and blossom unseen
And for your deliverance for ever I'll pray
Ship, spread out thy canvas and bring them away.

Crooked Stick from the Mountains

The eighteenth volume of the Millennial Star contains a number of choice poetical effusions from some
on board the Horizon, and others, contemplating leaving their native land about this time. To my mind, they
are full of beautiful sentiment and thought, and so
much do I admire their poetic style and beauty that
I now reproduce some of them, nearly seventy years
after their first publication.

"The Hour of Prayer"
On the ship Horizon, May 23, 1856

List to that sound, soft, floating through the air
It is the hymn of praise, the voice of prayer.
From gathered hundreds upon yon proud ship
Where bursts the chorus from each joyous lip
In loud hosannahs praising him on high
Who rules o'er earth and heaven eternally
Now hushed the strains while silence still and deep
Reigns o'er all, e'en nature seems asleep
A meek petition follows—raised above
To seek the aid divine, the ransomed love
Of him, the lofty one, to Israel dear
Whom Saints delight to praise, and sinners fear

To ask for blessings on that chosen land
Taking a farewell of their native land
To seek in mountain wilds repose and joy
Where sin is not and peace knows no alloy.
Blest of their God, confiding in his care
They know no sense of danger, fear no snare
They have obeyed his laws, fulfilled his will
And life or death for them can bring no ill
Proud of their calling, cheered with hopes of bliss
In other worlds—pain turns to joy in this
From every lip repeated o'er again
The prayer concluded, comes the deep "amen"
E'en strangers seem to feel the spell's control
And simple prayer to steal away the soul
Its peaceful influence calms all minds to rest
And gentiles feel midst Saints supremely blest.

K. J. R.
London

"Farewell to Thee England"

Farewell to thee England—bright home of my sires
Thou pride of the freeman, and boast of the brave.
I have loved thee—and never till being expires
Can I learn to forget thee, thou star of the wave.

Farewell to thee England, a long, long farewell
To every dear scene of my infancy's hours
Ne'er more shall I roam through each moss covered
    dell
Nor pluck the sweet gems of thy blossomy flowers.

Farewell to thee England and farewell to all
Whose love hath yet hallowed my pathway below
Though sadly I leave thee, I would not recall
One hour of the past, for the present to know.

Though sorrow may cast its deep shade oe'r my
    soul
When memory recalls one dear form to my mind
And anguish of spirit which passeth control
May crush the lone heart where that form is
    enshrined.

I wish not to linger thy beauties among
I dare not be false to the God I adore
Hence forward my lyre to his praises is strung
And to him I relinquish those memories of yore.

Yes England, I love thee, all dear though thou art
A country more precious lies over the wave
With hope for thee Albion, I turn to depart
God guard thee my country, protect thee and save.

The rose of thy beauty may fade from thy brow
The day of thy glory in darkness decline
But a halo of splendour overrides thee now
Which in regions immortal more highly shall shine.

There are hearts on thy bosom shall hallow thee yet
There are spirits too noble and feelings too pure
There are creatures too worthy for God to forget
whose love like his goodness will ever endure.

His blessing be on thee—thou land of my sires
Thou pride of the freeman and boast of the brave
I have loved thee, and never till being expires
Can I learn to forget thee—thou star of the wave.

S. C. R.

Composed on the deck of the Horizon May 24, 1856

From the foregoing we have traced the sailing of the "Horizon" from Liverpool which contained some 856 souls of the saints, and from all accounts written by passengers, it was an excellent company in every respect, exceptionally well behaved and gave no trouble at all to the ships captain and crew. In fact it is related that so well behaved were they that when singing the well known song "I'll marry none but Mormons" as a pastime and for amusement while on the sea, the captain said "And if I can have my way I'll carry none but Mormons." Their troubles began on their long, tedious and tiresome journey across the plains. Travel stained, weary, worn out, foot-sore, faint, fatigued and ready to drop, they trudged along, day after day, week after week, month after month, suffering much from a most unfortunate late start and becoming very much belated on arriving at their journeys end on November 30, 1856, in considerable snow and severely cold weather during the last portion of the journey.

Many fell by the way overcome by fatigue and the very severe trials and ordeals and exposure incident to such a prolonged journey. Young, middle aged and elderly people succumbed and were laid away by the road-side as well as they could under the circumstances, which at the best were poor, meager and heart rending to relatives and survivors accompanying.

One by one at first they were gathered in. Latterly they died in such numbers that decent internment was scarcely possible. What does the present generation know about the faith, endurance, hardships, privations, sufferings of the early pioneers, who left all for the gospels sake? And who made this desert and wilderness a fit, habitable and delightful country to live in.

From people who have come over the trail or highway in these early days, yet living, it is learned that the road-way or highway then was about three or four miles from Chimney Rock. So that as near as we know, or are ever likely to learn, Mary Murdoch, who would then be nearly seventy four years of age, died at or near Chimney Rock, October 3, 1856. This is the date that Martin's Hand Cart Company is said to have passed that historic spot. There—nature gave out. We believe she walked most of the way, waded streams, etc. Her heart was set on Zion, the valley, the valley her son John and his wife and Aunt Ann who proceeded her some four years. It is related of her, and we believe it is absolutely correct, that, when she was stricken and realized that her most cherished hopes, desires and ambition could not be accomplished, she said to those in whose company she came, "Tell John that I died with my face to the valley." Brave little woman! Wee Grannie was truly a heroine, and her name will be remembered and spoken of as long as a Murdoch from her loins is found in the land.

James Steel, in whose care she came, died at Bitter Creek, Wyoming, farther on in the journey.

Some eleven years ago, the ZCMI calendar was Chimney Rock from a painting by Alfred Lambourne. It proved so popular amongst the institutions friends and patrons, that a second supply had to be procured to meet the demands for it. This picture appealed also to many who had either come that way, or whose relatives had, myself amongst the number—and I wrote the following lines, not claiming for them any merit whatever, but offering them merely as a token of love and appreciation to the memory of that true, devoted soul who gave her life for the gospels sake. The picture was entitled: "SUNRISE AT CHIMNEY ROCK," and shows that well known land mark, with an immense lot of caravans, or covered wagons on the trail westward to the valley.

What solemn thoughts pervade the soul
As on this scene we meditate
This resting place for wearied saints
Tired, travel stained and desolate.

This scene portrays in vivid ways
A spot made dear on journey drear
By hand cart means in early days
A halfway place on journey here.

Impelled by faith and filled with hope
That soon they'd reach the appointed place Inured
    to toil with trials cope
To Utah's vales they set their face.

But some along this dreary road
Worn out and faint, oft fell asleep
Ere they could reach the cherished spot
The valley dear and friends to greet.

Brave honest souls at early morn
As pilgrims in a holy cause
Who dared to face a world of scorn
To obey Gods call and keep his laws.

Somewhere around the stopping place
As years go by—tis fifty seven
Wee Grannie died—there is no trace
Of earth's abode—her soul's in heaven.

Tell John she said as she laid down
Her worn out frame in this lone place
That I died here, but with my face
Turned Zionwards, the cherished place.

Blest be their names with fondest love
We'll cherish aye their mem'ries dear
Soon we may meet with them above
And greet them in their higher sphere.

December 24, 1913
David L. Murdoch

With wonderful faith the early saints, the first fruits of the gospel in their native lands, embraced the gospel giving a willing and ready ear to its glad sound and identifying themselves in small branches, studying, reading, seeking for truth and this too in neighborhoods, villages and towns that were exceedingly hostile and bitter in their attitude towards them. They kept on—faithful and true—hoping and praying that some day deliverance would come to them and that they too would be privileged to gather to the valleys, to Zion, and mingle and associate with their kindred, friends and acquaintances who had already got there.

Like a beacon light, these thoughts were ever uppermost in their minds—their hearts were fixed, their minds were family set and quietly they prepared for the time and the opportunity to get away. It took time—and patience, much care and anxiety to accomplish this object so dear to their hearts. The trials, tribulations and sorrowful and terrible experiences of the past daunted them not. With marvelous faith, and relying upon the commands of the Lord, "Come out of her o ye my people that ye be not partakers of her sins and calamities that shall come upon her." Their chief purpose was, ever prepare to get away. The gospel light kept burning steadily in the bosoms of those left behind and who had identified themselves with the Church prior to Wee Grannies departure in 1856. Aunt Mary, still residing at the Stables, at Grasswater, as before mentioned and having raised a large and very fine family, was handicapped very seriously by her husband Alan Mair, who could not see or accept the gospel as had his wife. The did not see alike on this vital point and none but those who have had experience either personal, or by observation can fully comprehend what a serious thing it becomes in families. Aunt Mary was loving and kind and bore her cross for years without murmur or complaint. She had now no neighbors to confide in or talk to and give comfort and consolation to and receive same in return, as my Father and our family moved from the Grasswater Row to Cumnock where we were located for some two years or so and then again moving to Muirkirk for reason of Fathers employment there. Thus Aunt Mary and my mother, who joined the Church, being baptised by James Gallacher in 1853, were separated by some eight miles or so, and as both were still having families, their opportunities for meeting and talking over matters were very few. I remember upon one occasion, my mother took me to Cumnock with her, ostensibly to visit some friends there and get some merchandise. I think we went by train, but walked all the way back. How it happened that we met Aunt Mary at Grasswater, I do not know, but Mother and Aunt Mary were engaged in a long conversation as we walked along. Neither do I know what they were talking about, but I do remember very distinctly and it has remained with me all my life, that Mother kept urging me to go on a little faster and not be in the way. I was then about *10* years of age or so. I did not know and I did not then think much about it, but from what has happened since then, I am firmly convinced they were having a real heart to heart talk about conditions as affecting them each in their different situations as pertaining to their position as relating to the gospel and the difficulties they had with husbands that could not then see as they did. They certainly did not want me to hear their conversation. Time went on. Often as I would come home from school or come into the house after being out for a while, especially if Mother was alone, I would find her attending to her household duties and humming away at something which then I did not know what, but as time went on I became familiar with the tune which later I discovered to be "Redeemer of Israel, our only delight, on whom for a blessing we call, our shadow by day and our pillar by night, our King, our deliverer, our all."

Time and again I heard this. I can see now that when alone she was contemplating the things she had learned at Wee Grannies in the little cottage meetings which they held previous to Grannies departure for the valley on the "Horizon" May 1856. This is one of the things I never forgot. Many, many times it has recurred to me all through the intervening years. I presume that most people have had similar experiences, there are things that happen in our youthful years that seem to make a lasting impression. I never heard her sing or hum it when other members of the family were present and I have wondered often times if it was purposely done for my benefit. By the year 1866 in the month of January I got a job as cashier at the Lugar Iron Works Cooperative Store, about two and a half or three miles from the stables at Grasswater where Aunt Mary lived. When there I would walk home to Muirkirk on Sunday mornings to get my weekly change of clothing and walk back to Lugar again in the afternoon. The distance was about eight miles. One Saturday afternoon, I think it was in June or the last of May, cousin Mary came into the Lugar store and said her mother was outside the door and wished to see me a minute. I went out and had a short interview with them. I was but a boy fourteen years of age and I did not fully sense what was said or what it really meant. I understood however that they were off. They had very quickly slipped away making some excuse of their making a visit to some relatives a bit away from home. Aunt Mary had with her Mary, Andrew and Aleck. The real facts were that after years of preparation, much thought and planning, they were saying goodbye to home and country and were going to Liverpool to sail for America. The Millennial Star Vol. 27 tells us that on the sixth day of June 1866 "the fine packed ship Saint Mark" cleared from Liverpool for New York carrying several hundred immigrants. The second cabin was occupied by 5 American adult passengers, members of

the Church of Latter-day Saints. Elder Alfred Stevens, an English sea captain was appointed President and unanimously sustained by the vote of the saints. The saints were instructed in relation to the voyage and were promised a safe passage on condition of due diligence to all their duties. William Lindsay of Heber City writes on the date of December 13, 1924 as follows— "I find from Jensen's Chronology that the sailing ship Saint Mark, the one on which Aunt Mary and her family crossed the Atlantic sailed from Liverpool with 104 saints under the direction of A. Stevens on the sixth day of June, 1866. She came across the plains in Captain Scotts company. They left Iowa on the Missouri River August 8th with 49 wagons and about 300 immigrants and landed in Salt Lake City October 8th, 1866, and soon after arrived in Heber at Uncle John's. Now while you may think that Aunt Mary acted rather rashly in leaving her husband as she did, and it surely was a most unheard of undertaking, I perhaps received as great a benefit from it as *ariy* other person. If it had not been done, I never could have got the faithful, loving wife that I did get. I can hardly think that any other woman could have filled her place so completely to my joy and satisfaction, so kind, so loving and so unselfish through all our married life.

We had 11 children, 46 grandchildren and 16 great grandchildren. Two of our sons have filled missions and one grandson. All our children have been to the Temple and I do feel so thankful that I got such a wife as a Mother to my children." I do not deem it wise or necessary to enter into details or particulars of this occurrence. Those who know and understand all the reasons for it will I am sure not feel to censure Aunt Mary for her course. I may add that when Uncle Alan discovered that they had gone he was very much worked up about it. I understand that he went to Liverpool to obtain his children at least but he was too late. The ship had sailed. His next step was to try and intercept them at New York and he had his two sons, John and James, who had previously emigrated to America, go to New York City to have them returned but nothing came of it and as we have already learned they came on and went to Heber City. It was a bold strategy and successfully carried out. Looking at it from our standpoint and view, it was not a matter for censure or even criticism. It was eminently successful and I believe better for all concerned. It created quite a commotion at the time and even forty years afterwards when on my mission in Scotland in 1906 and 1907 I encountered it at New Mills where a lady told me about it when tracting at her door.

I fully agree with what William Lindsay has said about his wife, my cousin. She was all that he says, she had a wonderful personality, was very kind and devoted to her husband and family and was a true Latter Day Saint, peace to her ashes. Her name and memory will no doubt be cherished and revered by generations yet unborn. She died in Heber City, date June 16, 1916. Aunt Mary's act was a great coup. It goes to show what can be done when there is the will and the determination to do it. The following, taken from the Millennial Star Vol. 28, tersely puts it:

"Where there's a will there's a way"

There's an adage that no one should ever forget
as he travels through life's ragged road,
and encumbered with care, looks around him for a
    hand to help on with his load,
let him never despond, let him never despair
far aside from the path never stray.
Let him buckle his armour and gird up his strength,
singing "Where there's a will there's a way."

If the world should look on with a cynical sneer
and the worldly efforts despise,
if a scoff or a jest from a friend that he loves
wrings a tear from his sorrowful eyes,
let him never be daunted, but still persevere.
And his strength shall suffice for his day,
so that cheer'd and refreshed he may still struggle
    on,
singing "Where there's a will there's a way."

There are foes to be conquered and feuds to be
    fought.
There are traitors without and within,
and the toil may be hard, and the battle,
but the one who endureth shall win,
for the good is at hand and the clouds shall
    disperse
When he least looketh out for the day,
to that looking and hoping still let him press on,
singing, "Where there's a will there's a will there's a
way."

My mother now was alone, the last left of the Grasswater saints. Uncle John and wife immigrated in 1852—Grannie, Mary Murdoch in 1856. Aunt Mary and her children Mary, Andrew and Aleck came in 1866. Mother therefore was left. No other members of the Murdoch family of Grasswater had up 'til now

joined the church. My Father was under ground manager at the Muirkirk Iron Works. The fire kindled in Mothers bosom kept burning and patiently she kept on. Father was an Elder in the Free Church. Mother never would attend any church. The reason why, us youngsters did not know and understand then. But she had joined the Church of Jesus Christ of Latter-day Saints in 1853 and had remained faithful ever afterwards. She is the only one of her family, the Lennox's of the Moor Farm, Old Cumnock, that has ever joined. Alone she kept on, biding her time. For many years no communications came from across the great deep. Occasionally a traveling Elder would make a brief call. It was kept quiet. Bye and bye Uncle John opened up a correspondence which resulted in communications between us on either side of the Atlantic. Father gradually was led to consider and ponder over matters and at length Mother got him persuaded to make up his mind and quit his employment and move to the town of Kilmarnock preparatory to him immigrating to America to come to the Valley. The Elders now had a fine home to come to and they were not slow to avail themselves of their hospitality. Father soon got baptised. Janet and Margaret were also baptised at the same time. Shortly after this Mother, who had long been afflicted with rheumatism took worse and passed away December—1877 and was buried in Muirkirk Church yard beside my sister Elizabeth who died at Muirkirk. About this time I was giving serious thought myself to the situation that I would be placed in. They were all going and I would be left behind. I was meeting the Elders at Fathers and elsewhere occasionally and was in what might be said in some what close touch with them. I concluded that I would tell Mr. Whitelaw, a member of Parliament for the City of Glasgow to whom I had been his private secretary for the past four years, that I proposed leaving him, getting married and going to America. I remember the occasion very distinctly. I always was a kind of tender-hearted chap and this occasion and occurrence could not take place without my shedding tears, however I was greatly relieved when it was over. Mr. Whitelaw was very kind to me. When at Liverpool prior to our sailing, I mailed him from the Liverpool offices all the church works I could get and this brought forth from him a very fine letter wishing me all manner of success and enclosing his check for fifty pounds sterling. I corresponded some with him after coming to this country. That same year or the following at most he died and was buried in old Monkland Church yard and when over there went with Mr. Alexander

Park, his Father, to the cemetery and placed a wreath upon his grave.

We sailed away from Liverpool on the steamship "Nevada" in the beginning of May, 1878 and landed in New York eleven days afterwards and were met there by my brother, James. He had emigrated to America and was then working in Pittsburg. Our party consisted of Father, myself and wife, Janet and Margaret, my sisters, and Veronica and John Adamson from Muirkirk, who after arriving here some little time married my sister, Maggie and first took up their abode in Heber City. On arriving in Salt Lake City towards the end of May, 1878, we were met by Uncle John, William Lindsay, and William M. Giles who came into the city to meet us and take—is to Heber City. They had three or four horse teams as there was then no railway nearer than Salt Lake City and Provo. William Lindsay as has already been stated was married to my cousin, Mary Mair. William M. Giles was married to my cousin Annie Murdoch. It is now nearly forty seven years since and many changes have occurred since then. In preparing this little history of the Murdoch immigration and gathering here, I have interviewed many people and sought diligently to get data particularly about Wee Grannie's demise but so far and I think I have exhausted nearly every avenue of information that I can think of—without getting what I was most anxious to obtain. "The Journal of John Jaques" typewritten in the historians office does not afford a word about Mary Murdoch. James G. Bleak's journal as used by Josiah Rogerson in his story of the Martin Hand Cart Company and published in the then "Salt Lake Herald" in the fall of 1907 makes no mention of it. Edward Martin, Captain of the company in which Grannie came, made a complete journal I understand. I sought out his family to see if I could obtain it. After getting in touch with several members of his family I had an appointment with his daughter, Martha to visit her. Great were my expectations and hopes that at last I had run it down, but when I got to see and peruse what they called his journal, it was only a journal of his missionary work and labors in Scotland and England, all prior to 1856. To that it was of no use whatever to me for the purpose to which I wanted it. It is very questionable if Edward Martin's journal of the Martin Hand Cart Co. of 1856 has been saved and preserved. What with intervening time, the somewhat indifference as to its real worth and value, the moving of households from time to time, it may have been discarded, thrown out amongst papers not considered of any particular value and thus lost. The pity is that the Church's Historians Office did not procure it and save it for record and use. I am still following the matter up in the hope that I may yet find some mention of the death of Wee Grannie.

The Handcart Song

After much inquiry and search I obtained a copy of this song from Mrs. Westenholme, a daughter of William Clayton, a very early convert to the Church from Penwortham, England, and author of "Come, Come ye Saints" and "When first the Glorious Light of Truth."

Ye Saints who dwell on Europe's shore
Prepare yourselves with many more,
To leave behind your native land
For sure God's judgments are at hand.
For you must cross the raging main
Before the promised land you gain
And with the faithful make a start
To cross the plains with your handcart.

CHORUS
For some must push and some must pull
As we go marching up the hill;
So merrily on the way we go
Until we reach the Valley-o.

The lands that boast of modern light
We know are all as dark as night
Where poor men toil and want for bread,
And rich men's dogs are better fed.
This land that boasts of liberty
We ne'er again desire to see
When we from it have made a start
To cross the plains with our handcart.

But some would say, that is too bad
The Saints upon the foot to pad
And more than that to pull a load
As they go marching on the road
But this we know it is the plan
To gather up the best of man,
And women too, for none but they
Would ever gather in this way.

As on the road the carts were pulled
It very much surprised the world
To see the old and feeble dame
Lending her hand to pull the same
Young maidens, they did dance and sing

Young men more happy than a king
And children they did laugh and play
Their strength increasing day by day.

And long before the Valley's gained,
We shall be met upon the plain
With music sweet and friends so dear
And fresh supplies our hearts to cheer.
And then with music and with song
How cheerfully we'll march along
And thank the day we made a start
To cross the plains with our handcart.

When you get there among the rest
Obedient be and you'll be blest.
And in your chambers be shut in
While judgements cleanse the earth from sin
For we do know it will be so,
God's servants spoke it long ago
And so be glad you made a start
To cross the plains with your handcart.

Now to the Murdochs, their numerous relatives and friends in America and everywhere the little story has been told. The Pilgrim Fathers sought a "Faith's Pure Shrine" and they found it in New England. Their descendants are scattered over much of America, and they have found and made a wonderful influence upon the character of early American pioneers and citizens. 'Twas a holy cause that brought them here, freedom to worship god. That influence has unquestionably permeated the generations succeeding them through the succeeding years and centuries. The Murdochs, like hundreds of thousands more, came here for the gospel's sake. The restored gospel through the instrumentality of Joseph Smith, the prophet, was the shrine that impelled them to leave father and mother, houses and lands, lucrative positions, and much prospective advancement commercially and socially in their native land, and gather here where the "House of the Lord" is established in the top of the mountains. These thoughts undoubtedly inspired President Penrose to write and thousands upon thousands to sing "O ye mountains High."

While upon my mission to Scotland, 1905–07, I visited Grasswater where the Murdoch family of this generation was born and raised, James Murdoch and Mary Murdoch and their eight children. Their memory like the upland-Mooreland place in which their youthful married days were spent raising their family in toil and hardship with but little of this worlds goods around them, is sweet and dear to me. I saw the ruins of Grannies wee house. I visited Foulds Mair and wife who resided near there and spent a few pleasant hours with my cousin Foulds. He inherited his Mother's kindly disposition to a marked extent. He showed me where Grandfather lost his life trying to rescue and save that young man from Dalfad who was so anxious to see and go down a pit. I also saw what was Wee grannies cupboard, preserved remarkable well by him all these years. When made it must have been a very fine and pretentious piece of furniture and with what pride Grannie must have prized it in her day. I also made the acquaintance of Mrs. Moffatt living at Grasswater, a daughter of cousin Foulds. She had very much the same expression and countenance of cousin Mary Mair Lindsay and I doubt not very much the same kindly disposition. So much did the resemblance strike me that I could even see it in the teeth being just a little separated in the front. Many sisters did not look so much alike, I am sure, as did this niece and aunt. Being right in the midst of what to the Murdochs is historic ground, I could not leave without visiting the place where I was born, January 13, 1852, in fact it was one of the principal reasons of my going there.

Editors note: This material was originally copied from the journal of David Lennox Murdoch by his daughter Afton Warner. The above material was taken from the original journal and the copy by Afton Warner and was edited by Dallas E. Murdoch.

The Passing of the Pot

Sarah Murdoch

As far back as Farnum,
As memories may go,
One household vessel greets me
That wasn't made for show.
Beneath the bed 'twas anchored,
Where only few could see,
But served the entire family
With equal privacy.
Some called the critter "Fanny,"
And some the "thundermug,"
A few called it the "Johnny,"
But I called it the "jug."
The special one for company
Was decorated swell,
But just the same it rendered
The old familiar smell.
One was enormous
And would accommodate
A watermelon party
Composed of six or eight.
To bring it in at evening
Was bad enough no doubt,
But heaven help the party
Who had to take it out.
At times when things were pressing
And business extra good,
Each took his turn at waiting,
Or did the best he could.
And sometimes in the darkness
Without benefit of flame,
We fumbled in the darkness
And slightly missed our aim.
Now today this modernism
Relieves me a lot,
And only in my visions
Do I see the family pot.

Biographical Sketches of Current Officers of the James and Mary Murray Murdoch Family Organization

Dallas Earl Murdoch

Dallas Earl Murdoch was born on October 23, 1937, at Rigby, Idaho, the son of Brigham Dallas Murdoch and Winona Lee. His grandparents are Brigham Murdoch and Luann Hammon. Brigham is the son of John Murray Murdoch and Isabella Crawford.

Dallas lived his early life at Ucon, Idaho; Lima, Montana; and Grant, Idaho. He graduated from Rigby High School, attended Ricks College for two years, and served a mission in the Northern California Mission from 1957 to 1959. Following his mission, he married Joan Hale, daughter of Clayton and Clara Hale of Pocatello, Idaho. He attended Brigham Young University and the University of Washington, where he graduated in 1964 with a degree in dentistry. Following graduation, Dallas moved his family to Grace, Idaho, where he established his practice. Later, he moved his practice to the nearby town of Soda Springs. Dallas and Joan are the parents of five children: Kathleen, age twenty-one; James age nineteen; Karen, age fourteen; David, age ten; and Sheydene, age seven.

Dallas has held many positions in the Church, including elders quorum president, and stake mission president. He is currently a member of the Grace Idaho stake high council. He has served on the school board of Grace school district 148 for five years and is presently vice-chairman.

His activities for the James and Mary Murdoch Family Organization include having been chairman of the Idaho reunion in 1972 and 1975. He became a member of the executive committee of the family organization at the annual reunion in August of 1974, serving as second vice-president to President R. Philip Rasmussen. At the annual reunion of 1976, he was designated as president-elect and at the reunion on August 13, 1977, he was sustained as president of the family organization.

Jeanette Smith Boggan

Margaret Jeanette Smith was born June 9, 1915, at Endicott, Washington. She was the third child in a family of five born to Alexander Smith and his wife Margaret Boyd Scott Smith. Her father was the youngest child of Alexander and Janet Murdoch Smith. Janet Murdoch Smith was the oldest child of James and Mary Murray Murdoch.

Her parents were living on a sheep ranch in Whitman County, Washington, when she was born, but sold the ranch the following year and moved to Clarkston, where they built a home and lived for the next five years. They then moved to a wheat ranch at Anatone, Washington, when she was six years old. After two years of ranching, her father sold the ranch due to failing eyesight and hearing, and the family moved into the small town of Anatone, where the children all attended school and grew up.

Jeanette married Carroll Boggan, who also grew up in Anatone, and they lived on a wheat and cattle ranch, where they raised their family of four children—two sons and two daughters. Jerry Carroll Boggan of Bellevue, Washington; Clyde Boggan of Anatone, Washington; Janice Boggan Botts of Anatone, and Toni Boggan Runquist of Spokane, Washington.

Jeanette's father died in Anatone on November 1936, and her mother passed away in Clarkston on December 6, 1964. Both are buried at Endicott, Washington. When her husband became ill and needed constant care, they moved to Clarkston, Washington, in 1976, where he passed away May 5, 1978. Jeanette has five grandchildren, and her son Clyde and son-in-law Dwight Botts run the family ranch, which is about twenty-five miles from Clarkston, Washington, where Jeanette still resides.

Jeanette and her sister Pauline Smith McDonald Mercer attended their first Murdoch reunion in August 1977. They were surprised to find out they had so many relatives, and we were so pleased to meet them. Jeanette was promptly put to work in our family organization as the Smith Family board of directors representative. We are very grateful to her for the information she has supplied for this book regarding the descendants of Janet Murdoch and Alexander Smith.

William Dale Mair

William Dale Mair (Bill) was born October 15, 1934, at Park City, Utah, the son of John B. Mair and Nina Sessions. His grandparents were William Allen Mair and Isabella McIntosh Burt. William Allen Mair was the son of Andrew Mair and Mary Ann Thompson, and Andrew was the son of Allan Mair and Mary Murdoch, who was the daughter of James and Mary Murray Murdoch.

Bill, with his parents, moved to Heber City at age five. He attended elementary and high school in Heber City, and graduated from Wasatch High School in 1952.

He served two years in the Army during the Korean conflict. He later attended Utah State University and gained a B.S. in Civil Engineering in 1960. He then became employed with the Bureau of Reclamation at the Central Utah Projects office in Provo, Utah. In August 1966, he transferred his employment to the Tooele Army Depot, where he was head of the Facilities Engineering Branch. During his employment at the Army depot, he was sent to Frankfurt, Germany for three years (April 1973 to April 1976). He served as the facilities engineer at the Pueblo Army Depot Activity in Pueblo, Colorado, for a brief period, and is presently the assistant facilities engineer at the defense depot in Ogden, Utah. Bill and his family reside in Ogden, Utah.

On March 1, 1963, he married Susann Huntsman of Shelley, Idaho, in the Idaho Falls Temple. They have four children, Beverly, seventeen; Brent, fourteen; James, eleven; and Paul, nine.

He has held several Church positions, including elders quorum presidency, bishop's counselor, ward executive secretary, high councilor, scoutmaster, high priests group leader, and Sunday School president. He is currently blazer scout leader in the Ogden sixty-second Ward.

His hobbies include coin collecting and camping with his family. His activities with the James Murdoch Family Organization include chairman of the 1977 annual reunion and director of the Mary Murdoch Mair family. Bill has recently been nominated as president-elect of the family organization, and will be sustained at the annual meeting in December 1981 as president. The family is fortunate to have someone of Bill's caliber as president, and under his leadership great things will be accomplished.

Mark Rasband Cram

Mark Rasband Cram was born in Salt Lake City, Utah, on May 22, 1921, to Isabella Rasband and Victor Dee Cram. His grandparents are Sarah Jane Murdoch and Thomas Heber Rasband. His great-grandparents are Ann Steel and John Murray Murdoch. Thus, his great-great-grandparents are Mary Murray and James Murdoch.

After graduation from high school, Mark attended the University of Utah during 1939–41, where he was active in sports, mainly football. Then from 1941–43, he served in the California Mission. Upon returning, he was in the United States Air Force during World War II from 1943–1946.

Mark married Melba Nielson in the Logan Temple on July 20, 1943. They are the parents of three girls and three boys: Constance C. Goenckenritzi, Vicki Cram, Janene C. Ogzewalla, Mark N. Cram, Reid N. Cram, and Kent N. Cram. Mark also is a grandfather to seven grandchildren. He has been in sales management and sales since coming out of the service in 1946. He is presently working in the investment field. He and his family reside at 7646 Dell Road in Salt Lake City, Utah. His hobbies are hunting, fishing, and water-skiing.

His community service and activities have included the following: member of the South Salt Lake Planning and Zoning, member of Cottonwood Heights Community Council, and county and state delegate to political conventions.

Mark's LDS Church callings have involved him in the following ways: bishop's counselor, bishop of two wards (South Ward, 1950–55, and Butler Third Ward, 1957–63), high council Butler Stake, Sunday School teacher, high priests quorum group assistant, scoutmaster, and MIA president. He is presently a stake missionary and host at the visitors' centers on the Salt Lake Temple grounds.

Mark serves as board of directors member from the Ann Steel and John Hurray Murdoch family in the James and Mary Murray Murdoch Family Organization. He is responsible for helping the nine representatives from that family to carry out the James Murdoch family goals and better organize their own family lines. Previously, Mark spearheaded the collection and the organizing of the computer list of all the names and addresses of all the descendants of James and Mary Murray Murdoch. (Oscar Hunter is now in charge of this assignment.) As a family, we owe a great debt of gratitude to Mark for his many hours of work for our family. Mark says: "I have a firm testimony of the gospel. I know that God lives and Jesus is the Christ, and am appreciative of the great heritage of the Murdoch family."

Guy G. Murdoch

Guy Garrett Murdoch was born October 5, 1916, at Farnum, Fremont County, Idaho, the son of Robert Rue Murdoch and Mearl Garrett. His grandparents on the Murdoch side of the family are Brigham Murdoch and Mary Blanche Alexander. Brigham is the second son of John Murray Murdoch and Isabella Crawford. John Murray Murdoch was the son of James and Mary Murray Murdoch.

Guy has a sister, Elaine, who lives in Provo. His mother and brother, Murray, live in Salt Lake City, Utah. During their early years, their father, Rue, worked for the U.S. Reclamation Service. Consequently, the family moved several times as new irrigation and power plant projects were started and completed. For short periods of time, they lived at King Hill, Idaho, Emmett, Idaho, and Rimrock, Washington, before returning to the Farnum and Ashton area in Idaho.

Guy graduated from South High School in Salt Lake City and attended the University of Idaho South in Pocatello, Idaho. On April 9, 1938, he married Faye Tanner.

They are the parents of six children: Diane, Pamela, Robert, Paul, Kent, and Michael. They also have thirteen grandchildren. Following their marriage, Guy and Faye lived for two years in Boise. In February, 1942, he accepted employment at Hill Air Force Base near Ogden, Utah, which extended into more than thirty years of challenging and satisfying work as a logistics officer and plans and management analyst. He retired from government service several years ago.

His activity in the Church has included positions as general secretary, priest advisor, scout leader, counselor in the bishopric, bishop, high priests group instructor, Sunday School president, high councilor, and stake executive secretary. Civic activities have involved him as a member of a city recreation and planning committee and a Lions Club board of directors. He became a member of the executive committee of the Murdoch Family Organization in August, 1977, and has served as the board of directors member for the John Murray Murdoch and Isabella Crawford family.

He and his wife, Faye, and son Michael, moved in August, 1979, from Layton, Utah, to their present home in Hyrum, Utah. There he hopes to continue activity in the Church, genealogy and temple work, fishing, hunting, and enjoying his children and grandchildren. He has a special love and appreciation for the members of this great Murdoch family organization, and is deeply grateful to all who have helped so generously to make the *Murdoch Messenger* and the James and Mary Murdoch history book become first a possibility and then a reality.

James C. Baird

James C. Baird was born May 10, 1927, at Carey, Blaine, Idaho, joining five sisters as children of James A. Baird and Ada Condie. Paternal grandparents are William Baird and Janet Murdoch, daughter of William Murdoch, son of James and Mary M. Murdoch, and Janet Lennox.

Jim spent his boyhood years in Carey, and after high school graduation and World War II military service entered into partnership with his father to farm. This led them to Bitterroot Valley in Montana, where he met Evelyn Whiting, whom he married after a mission to western Canada.

Following his father's death, the farm was sold, and he returned to college, graduating from Montana State University with B.S and M.S. degrees. He taught in the Billings, Montana, high school one year, and joined the USDA soil conservation Service in 1960, which has taken his family to Sidney and Big Sandy, Montana; Idaho Falls, American Falls, and Rigby, Idaho.

Jim and Evelyn are parents of six children: Lennox (now Mrs. Lenn Holyoak, with a daughter, Maren Lenae), Dave (married Diana Evertz; two sons—James John and William), James W., Murray, Robert, and Mary. Diana Bruce from Minneapolis has been with them three years now on the Indian placement program.

His Church service includes Sunday School superintendency, branch, ward, and district MIA superintendent; service in four branch presidencies, including four years as president of the Sidney Branch; two district councils; seventies group leader; stake high councilor; and high priest group leader.

His hobbies are gardening, reading, and stamp collecting, all of which have been badly neglected the past few years. We are fortunate to have Jim serving as the William Murdoch family representative to the James and Mary Murray Murdoch Organization. James was released in 1978 but continues as the Janet Murdoch Baird third generation family representative.

James Murdoch Hunter

James Murdoch Hunter was born in Salt Lake City, Utah, on January 31, 1918, the son of Oscar Chipman Hunter and Effie Lisle Murdoch. His Murdoch grandparents were James "D" Murdoch and Lizzie Lindsay. James "D"" Murdoch was the son of William Murdoch and Janet Lennox, and William was the youngest son of James Murdoch and Mary Murray or "Wee Granny."

After graduation from East High School, James at-tended the University of Utah from 1935–37 and 1938–39. Then, during the fall of 1939, he joined the Army Air Corps as a flying cadet and graduated as a second lieutenant military pilot in the Army Reserves in 1940. Active duty started immediately, and he served one and a half years before World War II started.

James married Mildred Annie Moore on February 15, 1941, in Reno, Nevada. On October 11, 1943, they were sealed in the Salt Lake Temple. They are the parents of five children: Jill Annette, American Fork Training School; Karen Louise Cosby, Ogden, Utah; James David, Salt Lake City; John Stephen, Bountiful; Mark Alan, still at home in Bountiful. All three boys served foreign missions. James and Mildred have seven grandchildren. Two more are due this year.

James had duty in several parts of the United States training pilots in combat flying. He helped train the first black pilots who saw action in Europe. He spent sixteen months in Iceland and his last duty station was Hill Field.

He separated from active duty December, 1946, as a lieutenant colonel.

James opened the Hunter Ice Cream Store in 1947 in Bountiful, Utah. It was great to be able to take ice cream to the family reunions. He made ice cream for twenty-three years, and also catered to parties and weddings.

He served as MIA superintendent in the Bountiful Sixth Ward and was called to organize and pilot a multi-regional handicapped mutual.

James is presently serving as a family representative on the board of directors for the William Murdoch and Janet Lennox family.

Virginia H. Davis

Virginia Lucile Hansen Davis was born in Park City, Utah, on January 31, 1915, to Arthur E. Hansen and Nettie Duke Hansen, who was the daughter of Mary Murray Murdoch Duke, the oldest child of John Murray Murdoch and Ann Steel Murdoch.

Virginia was the sixth child in her family of one brother and four sisters, namely: Mary H. Breinholt, Arthur Duke Hansen (deceased), Zoe H. Johnson, June H. Johnson (deceased), and Ruth H. Nuttall Perry.

When Virginia was three years old, her family moved from Park City, where her father had been in the grocery business, to Provo, Utah. She went to school there until 1930, when the family moved to Salt Lake. She graduated from high school in 1933.

In 1934 she married Marcus L. Davis, who had lived all his life in Salt Lake City and who started working for the Union Pacific Railroad about this time. They have raised three children: Richard T. Davis, who is a physician and surgeon in Tempe, Arizona; Louis E. Davis, who is a mechanical engineer in Thousand Oaks, California; and Janet Davis, who is the executive director for the Utah Academy of Family Physicians in Salt Lake City. Virginia and Marcus have ten grandchildren.

Virginia never worked outside her home until her sons were called on missions to Hong Kong at the same time. She then worked as a dental assistant and receptionist for about seven years, where she learned to appreciate working mothers.

She worked seventeen years in the Primary, three of them as president, and has been MIA president, Junior Sunday School coordinator, and has served in three Relief Society presidencies. She also served on a genealogy mission from 1964 to 1966 and at the present time is chairman of the compassionate service committee in the Thirty-third Ward, where her husband is the ward membership clerk.

She remembers well going to the Murdoch reunions at Vivian Park in Provo Canyon as a child and the wonderful times she had there. She also remembers taking her own children to Murdoch reunions and attending many since then, always with fond memories of wonderful, friendly people with beautiful voices.

One of the greatest highlights in Virginia's life was a trip to the Holy Land in April, 1980. It was the thrill of a lifetime to walk where Jesus walked and to see where he taught and performed miracles.

Virginia has served as secretary for the James M. Murdoch Association since March, 1978, and has caught the vision and spirit of this wonderful organization and feels it an honor and a pleasure to have been asked to do so. She feels the Lord has blessed all who have served in helping to get the James and Mary Murray Murdoch book published.

Mary Ellen Maxwell Ladle

Mary Ellen Maxwell Ladle was born October 27, 1938, at Elko, Nevada. She is the daughter of Glen and Joan Murdoch Maxwell. Her grandparents are Joseph "A" and Martha Ellen Fortie. Joseph "A" Murdoch is the son of John Murray Murdoch and Ann Steel.

Mary Ellen attended elementary schools in Utah, and secondary schools in Utah and Idaho, graduating in 1956 from Madison High School, Rexburg, Idaho. She attended Ricks College for two years, and was graduated from Brigham Young University in 1960 with her degree in Business Education.

In 1959, Mary Ellen and J. Noel Ladle (son of J. Eldon and Shirley Ladle) were married. They are the parents of six children: Michael(married to Annette Nielsen), Janel (Mrs. David K.) Goldhardt, Wendy, Devin, Trent, and Kathryn.

She has held several Church positions. Among these are Primary teacher and presidency and Relief Society presidency—ward and stake—and teacher. Her hobbies include sewing, crafts, and sports.

Mary Ellen has served as treasurer of the family organization since August of 1977 and has been responsible for keeping the family finances in order. In this she has done an outstanding job and deserves the thanks and appreciation of each member of the family.

Oscar Murdoch Hunter

Oscar Murdoch Hunter was born in Salt Lake City, Utah, on May 6, 1915, the son of Oscar Chipman Hunter and Effie Lisle Murdoch. His Murdoch grandparents were James "D" Murdoch and Lizzie Lindsay. James I'D" Murdoch was the son of William Murdoch and Mary Murray, more endearingly called "Wee Granny."

Oscar graduated from East High School in Salt Lake City and attended Henegar Business College. On March 6, 1940, he married Orpha York in the Salt Lake Temple. They are the parents of five children: Suzanne H. Searby, San Francisco, California; Edward O. Hunter, Troy, Michigan (near Detroit); Elizabeth H. Bleyl, (deceased) Robert B. Hunter, Denver, Colorado, and Rosemary Hunter, who just served in the England Coventry Mission. Oscar and Orpha have five grandchildren.

After serving as a chaplains' assistant in the Army during World War II, Oscar directed a fireside every Sunday night for eleven years, which was attended by young people from all over the Salt Lake Valley. Aside from teaching positions, his jobs in the Church include counselor in the ward MIA superintendency, counselor in the Bonneville Stake Mission Presidency, one of the seven presidents of two different seventies quorums, president of the ward MIA and he is presently serving as second counselor in the Bonneville First Ward bishopric.

In 1958, he and a partner established their own brokerage firm, founded Bonneville Life Insurance Company, and sold two million dollars worth of stock to initially launch the insurance company. This has proven to be the largest amount ever raised in the state of Utah (up to 1981) to capitalize a new insurance company.

Oscar is now the descendant genealogist for the James Murdoch Family Organization. This entails keeping addresses, births, marriages, and deaths as current as possible with the help of all the Murdoch descendants. This is a huge job, and Oscar has spent untold hours working on it, for which we all owe him much thanks. Some of Oscar's choicest memories stem from Murdoch reunions, reaching back through the years to the 1920s in Vivian Park. Everyone looks forward to seeing how Oscar will dress up for the Murdoch parades.

Oscar is extremely grateful for the new generation of dedicated and talented Murdochs who are carrying on our great traditions, creating a record like the *Murdoch Messenger,* and publishing a book that will be cherished by future generations and will extol the virtues of our great Murdoch ancestors who left us such a priceless heritage.

Janet Oberg Gill

Janet Oberg Gill was born October 16, 1930, in Salt Lake City, Utah, the oldest of five children of Seth Michael Oberg and Helen Janet Murdoch. Her maternal grandparents were Eliza Thackeray and James RD" Murdoch, the son of William Murdoch and Janet Lennox. Janet grew up in Salt Lake City, graduated from East High School in 1948, and attended the University of Utah for three years. She served in the West Central Stakes Mission during 1954 and 1955. Following her return she again attended the U of U and graduated in elementary education in 1958.

On October 16, 1957, Janet was married to Gordon Lee Gill in the Salt Lake Temple, and they moved to Centerville, Utah, where they have lived ever since.

They are the parents of six children: Lauralee (Mrs. Kevin R. Ware), twenty-three; Jennifer, twenty-one; Veronica, eighteen; Carolyn, sixteen; Natalie, twelve; and Michael, nine. They also have one granddaughter.

She has served in the LDS Church as a teacher in Sunday School, Primary, Cub Scouts, Relief Society, MIA, and also as a counselor and president of MIA. She has worked in the community for the PTA, Soccer Association, American Diabetes Association—Utah affiliate as a member of the board of directors—and currently is president of the Educational Foundation of Right to Life of Utah.

Janet has been ancestral genealogist for the Murdoch family since 1976, and during that time has developed a keen appreciation for the effort that has been made by many other members of the family in the past to secure information about our ancestors. She is grateful for this opportunity to serve the Murdoch Family Organization and for all she has learned in the process.

Over the years there has been a great expenditure of time and energy to collect the genealogy of the Murdoch family. Many prayers have been said asking for guidance, and much help has been received. For their sacrifices, deep gratitude is expressed to David Lennox Murdoch, Joseph A. Murdoch, and Ruby Murdoch Hooper, the family genealogists, and to the many other members of the family who have labored faithfully to aid the progress of this necessary and sacred work. Also, the support and cooperation from members of their families is recognized. Finally, we wish humbly to thank the Lord for his inspiration and kind, persistent encouragement through all these efforts.

Ruth L. Murdoch Schulz

Ruth Lorraine Murdoch Schulz is the daughter of Winona Lee and Brigham Dallas Murdoch. (Winona Lee is deceased, and her other mother is Agnes Simonsen Murdoch.) She was born as World War II was coming to a close on May 7, 1945, in Idaho Falls, Idaho. Her grandparents are Martha Luann Hammon and Brigham Murdoch, who is the son of Isabella Crawford and John Murray Murdoch, who is the son of Mary Murray and James Murdoch.

Ruth is the sixth child in her family and has four brothers and four sisters, namely: Ronald Lee Murdoch, (deceased), Helen Winona Hall, Dallas Earl Murdoch, Thomas Ray Murdoch, Ann Marie Matesen, John Brigham Murdoch, Mary Lou M. Versey, and Luann Agnes M. Dodds.

Ruth attended grade school in Lima, Montana, and Lewisville, Idaho, and junior and senior high school at Roberts, Idaho. She then studied nursing at Ricks College and after graduating there went on to the University of Utah and received her bachelor's degree in nursing in 1968.

While attending the University of Utah, she met Alan Edward Schulz. He had just recently moved to Utah from Chicago, Illinois, and was converted to The Church of Jesus Christ of Latter-day Saints. They were married on June 13, 1968, in the Idaho Falls Temple. They are the parents of three children, Rebecca Lynn (age eleven), Elsie Ann Begay (Indian foster daughter—age eleven), and Mark Alan (three years). Alan teaches at the Rose Park Elementary School and serves on the Salt Lake Stake High Council at present. They reside in Salt Lake City, Utah.

Ruth worked at the University Hospital during the three years she attended school there. Then she worked three years at the Salt Lake Community Nursing Service. She quit to assume her duties as a mother. She has served in various callings in the Church, such as: Sunday School secretary, librarian, editor of Sunday bulletin, sports director, drama director, activity counselor MIA, visiting teacher, homemaking counselor, and president of ward Relief Society, Relief Society stake education counselor, and presently as the stake Primary president in the Salt Lake City Stake. She also has served on the Washington Elementary School Council and as a district chairman for the Cancer and Pennies by the Inch fund drives.

Ruth serves the James Murdoch family as the editor of the *Murdoch Messenger*. The first edition came out in April, 1977. During the many hours spent typing the family histories, she has become well acquainted with and come to love those who have passed on in the Murdoch family who did so much for us who are presently living.

Cuthbert Fortie Murdoch

Cuthbert (Bert) Fortie Murdoch, was born April 11, 1912 at Heber, Wasatch, Utah. He is the tenth child of twelve born to Joseph A and Martha Ellen Fortie Murdoch. Joseph A was a son of John Murray Murdoch and Ann Steel.

Bert attended the old Central School in Heber then the family moved to Provo for six months then settled in Vineyard, Utah. Here he finished his elementary schooling and then graduated from the Lincoln High School in Orem, Utah. He then attended Brigham Young University for a short time.

During the depression years he worked at various jobs around the country going as far as Canada to find employment. In 1939 he resided in Salt Lake City, Utah and went to work for the Mountain States Telephone Company as a construction worker. He continued to work for this company for thirty-six years and saw the telephone go from manual to dial to electronic. From 1956 to 1964 he lived in Denver, Colorado in the telephone company's general offices as a supervisor in the training department.

On May 20, 1939, in the Salt Lake Temple, he married Jean V. Prestwich. She passed away with cancer July 23, 1953. They have one daughter Joyce Murdoch Shrock and she has six children. On June 14, 1955, in the Salt Lake Temple, Bert married Lora Chloe Rose. She had one daughter, Muriel Murdoch Stam, and they have five more grandchildren and ten great grandchildren.

Bert has been active in the Church of Jesus Christ of Latter Day Saints all his life. He has served as a teacher in various auxiliaries and president and Superintendent in Sunday School and MIA in the stake and ward. Also as a High Councilman.

Bert and his wife served as temple officiators for six years in the Salt Lake Temple. He retired from the phone company in 1974 and they then served a mission to the Oklahoma Mission.

His hobbies include lapidary, walking, gardening and genealogy work.

Bert has served as the Bulk Mailing Chairman to see that the *Murdoch Messengers* got sorted and sent to the right addresses for the James Murdoch Family Organization.

Raymond Phillip (Bud) Rasmussen

Phil was born May 25, 1925, in Magna, Utah, to Lorin N. and LeIsle Phillips Rasmussen. The family moved to Salt Lake City shortly afterwards, and he has resided there since The second of five children, he attended elementary and junior high school and graduated from South High in 1943. He entered the armed forces in 1944 and was assigned to the Navy, serving six months in Virginia and Mississippi and then two years in the South Pacific theatre of operations, specifically in the Russell Islands of the Solomon Islands group.

Upon discharge from the armed forces, he was the cofounder of the Salt Lake Venetian Blind Company in 1946. In 1949 he founded the Kool Breeze Awning Company. In 1968 he divested himself from Kool Breeze and pursued the wholesale distribution of his products through Amsco, of which he is president and chairman of the board. He is also chairman of the board of Sun Control Supply, a wholesale awning and patio manufacturer.

In 1947, he married Donna Mulcock of Salt Lake City in the Salt Lake Temple. They are the parents of four children, three daughters and one son. All of the daughters are married, and five living granddaughters add much joy to their lives. The family enjoy being together, and spend time at their home in the mountains and enjoy boating and water sports at their Bear Lake home.

In 1977, he was elected to the board of directors of the Sealed Insulating Glass Manufacturers Association, a national and international association of manufacturers and suppliers in the insulating glass industry. He was named a vice-president later that year, and in 1978 was elected president for a two-year term. He is currently serving as immediate past president of that organization.

In 1980, he was elected to the board of directors of Utah Bancorporation, a holding company of the Valley Bank and Trust organization. He serves in several civic clubs and organizations.

He is currently serving in the LDS Church as a high councilor in the Olympus Stake and also as a sealer in the Salt Lake Temple. He has served as a bishop of the Highland View West and Highland View Second Wards, and as a high councilor in the Canyon Rim and University Second Stakes. He also served five years as a counselor in the University Second Stake Presidency.

Phil has served as immediate past president of the James Murdoch Family Organization and is at present in charge of fundraising for this book.

Phil has recently been called to be Mission President of the Ohio Cleveland Mission and will be leaving on July 1, 1982.

John Murray Nicol and Margaret Alice Nuttall Nicol

John Murray Nicol was born June 20, 1912, at Duchesne, Utah, the son of Hyrum Chase Nicol and Isabella Crawford Murdoch. His grandparents were John Murray Murdoch and Isabella Crawford, and Isabella was the daughter of James and Mary Murray Murdoch.

John spent his early youth at Duchesne, where his parents were homesteading on the old Indian Ranch. They later moved to Provo. He attended Franklin Elementary School and graduated from Provo High School and Provo Seminary, where he was chosen as valedictorian.

After graduation, he served in the Civilian Conservation Corps from 1932 to 1933. He was employed at Pacific States Cast Iron Pipe Company and later at Geneva Steel. In 1947, the opportunity came for John to attend Brigham Young University and fulfill a lifetime dream to teach. He gained a bachelor of science degree in 1949 and his master of educational administration degree in 1965. John began his teaching career at Union Elementary School in Vineyard in Alpine School District. He was appointed as a principal in 1955 and enjoyed serving the children and patrons of the area until his retirement in June 1977.

As a young man, John developed a keen interest in scouting activities. He earned the Eagle Scout award and also the Master "M" Men award. His callings in the Church have included counselor in two bishoprics, stake Sunday School president, elders quorum presidency, president of YMMIA, ward clerk, Scoutmaster, Scout commissioner, and ward Scouting coordinator. He has also been a Sunday school teacher.

On June 26, 1936, he married Margaret A. Nuttall of Provo in the Salt Lake Temple. Her parents are William Albert Nuttall and Margaret Grace Greer. They had seven children, John Murray, Jr., Robert Rue, Grant Chase, William Wayne, David Lee, Mary (deceased), and Lynn James.

Margaret also has been busily engaged in Church and community activities. She graduated from Lincoln High School in 1935 and attended BYU. She is a golden gleaner and has served as MIA president, Primary counselor, Relief Society secretary, teacher, music director, dance director, and stake Primary and YWMIA teacher. Margaret was district registration agent and election judge in Orem for several years and served as an officer of the Orem City PTA council.

From December 3, 1977 to July 3, 1979, John and Margaret served as missionaries in the Florida Tallahassee Mission and are now temple workers at the Provo Temple. John is presently serving as Bishop of his ward.

The Nicol family feels a deep love and pride in their Murdoch heritage and have attended and become involved in the great family reunions over the past forty-five years. John has served as chairman of the reunion several times and vice-president of the Murdoch Family Organization. He is presently the Managing Editor of *The James and Mary Murray Murdoch Family History* book.

Jack and Anne Lyon

Jack M. Lyon, son of Glade Marvin Lyon and Katherine Mearl Murdoch, was born June 10, 1951, in Ashton, Idaho. He married Cecilia Anne Williams in 1972. In 1974, he received a bachelor's degree in English from Brigham Young University, after which he taught high school for two years in North Robinson, Ohio. In 1976, he again attended BYU, taking business classes and working as an accountant, and in 1978 became proofreading coordinator at BYU Press. Later in 1978 became proofreading coordinator at BYU Press. Later that year he accepted a position as assistant editor with the editing section of the Church of Jesus Christ of Latter-day Saints. In 1980, he became associate editor with Deseret Book Company. Jack has served in various positions in the Church, including as a member of an elders quorum presidency, an APYW director, a Sunday School teacher, a ward music chairman, and a ward clerk.

Cecilia Anne Lyon, daughter of Harold Wayne Williams and Allie Rae Setterington, was born November 25, 1951, in Hays, Kansas. Because of her father's employment, Anne has lived in many states, including Texas, New Mexico, Kentucky, and Ohio. She and her family joined the Church in 1967, and Anne met Jack while they were both attending BYU.

Anne has served in the Church as a Primary teacher, a visiting teacher, a ward typist, a Primary counselor, a secretary in the MIA and in the Primary, a nursery coordinator, and a Junior Sunday school chorister.

Anne is an excellent wife and mother, always working hard to make life better and happier for her family and for others.

Jack and Anne have spent many hours editing, typing, and proofreading this book, and are grateful they have had this opportunity.

Joan Murdoch Maxwell

Joan Murdoch Maxwell was born in Heber City, Utah, on March 11, 1917. She was the daughter of Joseph "A" Murdoch and Martha Ellen Fortie. Her Murdoch grandparents were John Murray Murdoch and Ann Steel. John Murray was the son of James Murdoch and Mary Murray Murdoch, often called "Wee Granny." Joan was named for her father and Grandmother Murdoch.

Home delivery was the only way babies entered this world, at the time she was born. In fact, on that Sunday night in March a number of years ago during her grand entrance, the doctor didn't even get to the home before she did. She arrived on her father's birthday, and Aunt Net McMullin was the very first person to hold her in her arms. Could it have been possible that in all the excitement of her arrival, concerns of weight and length in inches were not even considered, or the color of her hair, if she had any? It was possible that child number twelve was just another little daughter, and gratitude that she was hale and hearty and that all was well with the mother were the most important things. Grandma Giles (Rachel Fortie Giles) was also there, and the cries of the baby were the first inkling she had of the arrival, because the new mother-to-be had earlier left the small gathering around the dining-room table with the excuse that she had to go get the clothes separated for the Monday morning wash.

Of course, older sister Lecia and Dona (Montgomery) giggled and nudged each other with knowing winks when their father, who was the ward chorister, left sacrament meeting early without leading the closing song. The next morning when Papa went upstairs to ask the younger children to guess what they had downstairs that was new, Elroy said he knew they had a new calf because he had heard it bawl. The excitement of Joan's arrival must have marked her ever after, because her life has been full and exciting.

Being reared in a happy home and having a lot of consideration and encouragement from loving parents, Joan always looked forward to and enjoyed school. Her growing-up years were full of happy, exciting events and a lot of activity, as anyone being reared on a farm can testify. Growing up during the great depression was of no great concern. The worrisome problems of our parents never reached the surface, as they still made life happy and full for us. We always had food and shelter on the farm. Clothing was always limited.

In 1937 Joan met and married Glen Maxwell. The ceremony was performed by David O. McKay in the Salt Lake Temple. They now have four children: Mary Ellen Ladle, of Salt Lake City, Utah; James "B" of Carmel, California (a missionary to Scotland); Judith Ann Zundel (Judy) of St. Anthony, Idaho; Barbara Joy Allen of Anniston, Alabama. They also have eighteen grandchildren.

Her Church activities have been constant. She has served in presidencies and teaching positions in the MIA, Primary, and Relief Society. Just as Grandma Ann was the first Relief Society president in Heber Valley, it was a happy blessing for Joan to be chosen as the first Relief Society president of the Ricks College Third Ward, Ricks College Stake.

Joan has gained closer insight into the lives of our ancestors and a great feeling of pride and respect and love for them, and a greater appreciation for membership in The Church of Jesus Christ of Latter-day Saints, after learning of the sacrifices our ancestors made in our behalf. She feels it has been a privilege to help with the Murdoch Organization and the James and Mary Murray Murdoch book. She has served as Historian.

Message from the Family Ancestral Genealogist

Since 1976, I have been ancestral genealogist for the Murdoch family and during that time have developed a keen appreciation for the effort that has been made by many other members of the family in the past to secure information about our ancestors. I am grateful for this opportunity to serve the family organization and for all I have learned in the process.

Insofar as possible I have searched for and found documentation for Ruby Murdoch Hooper's genealogical records of the Murdoch and Murray ancestors. This has been for the purpose of ensuring the most accuracy and completeness in preparation for printing the information in this book.

When we have been unable to verify records or find information sometimes it has been because the registration for a given locality during a certain period of time does not exist or is illegible. At other times we have been unable to find documentation because some ancestors did not choose to have entries made of their births, marriages, and deaths. Very probably some items have not been found because we have not yet looked in the right places.

Whenever documentation has been found on a microfilm of original sources in the Genealogical Library of the Church of Jesus Christ of Latter-day Saints, the number of that film has been entered on the family group sheet next to the item it verifies.

On the family group record sheets, the "X" in front of the name of one child in the family indicates that that person is the direct-line ancestor of James or Mary Murray Murdoch. When more proof is found, additional sheets will be prepared and distributed.

On the third-generation descendant sheets the numbers in front of the names represent the generation to which those persons belong. The numbering starts with "1" for James and Mary Murray Murdoch, goes to "2" for their children, and then proceeds to later generations. In some families there are now nine generations.

Many prayers have been said asking for guidance and much help has been received. For their sacrifices deep gratitude is expressed to David Lennox Murdoch, Joseph A Murdoch, and Ruby Murdoch Hooper, the family genealogists, and to many other members of the family who have labored faithfully to aid the progress of this necessary and sacred work. Also the support and cooperation from members of their families is recognized. Finally, we wish humbly to thank the Lord for his inspiration and kind, persistent encouragement through all these efforts.

Janet Oberg Gill

HUSBAND James MURDOCH

Born	abt 1786	Place Commondyke, Ayrshire, Scotland
Chr.		Place
Mar	10 Jan 1811 1	Place Auchinleck, Ayrshire, Scotland
Died	20 Oct 1831 2	Place Gaswater, Ayrshire, Scotland
Bur.	Oct 1831	Place

HUSBAND'S FATHER James MURDOCH   HUSBAND'S MOTHER Janet OSBORNE

HUSBAND'S OTHER WIVES

WIFE Mary MURRAY

Born	13 Oct 1782	Place Glencairn, Dumfriesshire, Scotland
Chr.		Place
Died	3 Oct 1856 3	Place Chimney Rock, Scottsbluff, Nebraska
Bur.		Place

WIFE'S FATHER John MURRAY   WIFE'S MOTHER Margaret MC CALL

WIFE'S OTHER HUSBANDS

Husband James MURDOCH   Wife Mary MURRAY

Ward   Examiners: 1.   2.

Stake or Mission

SEX M F	CHILDREN List each child (whether living or dead) in order of birth. Given Names	SURNAME		WHEN BORN DAY	MONTH	YEAR	WHERE BORN TOWN	COUNTY	STATE OR COUNTRY	DATE OF FIRST MARRIAGE TO WHOM	WHEN DIED DAY	MONTH	YEAR
1 F	Janet MURDOCH		chr	29 Dec 1811		102812	Boghead	Ayr	Sctl	20 Dec 1833 Alexander SMITH	28 Jun 1866		350912 102812
2 F	Mary MURDOCH		chr	27 Jun 1813		102812	Birth: 16 Jun 1813 Boghead	Ayr	Sctl				
3 M	James MURDOCH		chr	10 Aug 1814		102812	Gaswater	Ayr	Sctl	24 Nov 1841 Margaret MC CALL	12 Sep 1884		1 102812
4 F	Veronica MURDOCH		chr	30 Jun 1816		102812	Gaswater	Ayr	Sctl	15 Feb 1839 (1) George CALDOW	4 Oct 1908		26030 102853
5 F	Mary MURDOCH		chr	8 Nov 1818		102856	Gaswater	Ayr	Sctl	4 Jun 1841 (1) Allan MAIR	5 Dec 1900		483507 102812
6 M	John "Murray" MURDOCH		chr	21 Jan 1821		102812	Gaswater	Ayr	Sctl	25 Feb 1848 (1) Ann STEEL	6 May 1910		26030 102322
7 F	Margaret MURDOCH			30 Dec 1822		102812	Gaswater	Ayr	Sctl	23 Jun 1846 (1) Janet LENNOX	12 Mar 1913		26988 102812
8 M	William MURDOCH			3 Jul 1825		102812	Gaswater	Ayr	Sctl				
9													
10													
11													

SOURCES OF INFORMATION
102812 Auchinleck Parish Register, 102853 Muirkirk Parish Register, 102856 Old Cumnock Parish Register, 102322 Kirkconnel Parish Register,
1 David Lennox Murdoch's Family and Temple Record Book
2 William Murdoch's record book (compiled 1878)
3 Martin Handcart Company Record of J. G. Bleak, Salt Lake Herald 13 Oct 1907

OTHER MARRIAGES
#4 md (2) 3 Jul 1879 Thomas GILES
#5 md (2) 1 Dec 1866 Thomas TODD, (div)
#5 md (3) 26 Jun 1871 Daniel MC MILLAN
#6 md (2) 9 Aug 1862 Isabella CRAWFORD
#8 md (2) 29 Jun 1882 Christina GRAHAM, (div)
#8 md (3) 26 Nov 1887 Mary REID Lindsay

HUSBAND Alexander SMITH

Born	abt 1808	Place	of Birnieknowe, Auchinleck, Ayrshire, Scotland
Chr.		Place	
Marr.	20 Dec 1833	102812	Place Auchinleck, Ayrshire, Scotland
Died	1876	Place	Glasgow, Lanarkshire, Scotland
Bur.		Place	

HUSBAND'S FATHER
HUSBAND'S MOTHER
HUSBAND'S OTHER WIVES

WIFE Janet MURDOCH

Born	8 Dec 1811	Place	Boghead, Auchinleck, Ayrshire, Scotland
Chr.	29 Dec 1811	102812	Place Auchinleck, Ayrshire, Scotland
Died	28 Jun 1866	350912	Place Commondyke, Auchinleck, Ayrshire, Scotland
Bur.		Place	

WIFE'S FATHER James MURDOCH
WIFE'S MOTHER Mary MURRAY
WIFE'S OTHER HUSBANDS

Husband Alexander SMITH
Wife Janet MURDOCH

Ward 1
Examiners: 2
Stake or Mission

SEX M F	CHILDREN List each child (whether living or dead) in order of birth Given Names / SURNAME	WHEN BORN DAY MONTH YEAR	WHERE BORN TOWN	COUNTY	STATE OR COUNTRY	DATE OF FIRST MARRIAGE TO WHOM	WHEN DIED DAY MONTH YEAR
M	James SMITH	102812 17 May 1834	Auchinleck	Ayr	Sctl		
2 M	William SMITH	102812 23 Sep 1836	Auchinleck	Ayr	Sctl	Jane Farquhar GRAY	23 Oct 1905
3 M	John SMITH	102812 29 Aug 1838	Auchinleck	Ayr	Sctl		
4 M	Robert SMITH	102812 28 Sep 1840	Auchinleck	Ayr	Sctl	Catherine SMITH	28 Jan 1871 224615
5 M	James SMITH	102812 3 Nov 1842	Auchinleck	Ayr	Sctl		16 Apr 1865 330135
6 M	John SMITH	102812 2 Feb 1845	Auchinleck	Ayr	Sctl		11 Oct 1863 294765
7 F	Mary SMITH	102812 24 May 1846	Auchinleck	Ayr	Sctl		17 Jun 1864 323680
8 M	Stewart SMITH	102812 30 Mar 1848	Auchinleck	Ayr	Sctl		
9 M	Stewart SMITH	102812 19 May 1850	Birnieknow	Ayr	Sctl		1877
10 F	Agnes SMITH	1852	Birnieknow	Ayr	Sctl	James JOHNSTON	abt 1890
11 F	Janet Osborne SMITH	1854	Birnieknowe	Ayr	Sctl		5 Feb 1859 280389
12 M	Alexander SMITH	256485 24 Jan 1856	Birnieknowe	Ayr	Sctl	13 Apr 1902 Margaret Boyd SCOTT	5 Nov 1936

SOURCES OF INFORMATION
102812 Auchinleck Parish Register
256485
350912
History of Alexander Smith written by Jeanette SMITH Boggan

330135
294765
323680
280389
224615

HUSBAND James MURDOCH

Born	29 Jul 1814	Place	Gaswater, Ayrshire, Scotland
Chr.	10 Aug 1814 102812	Place	Auchinleck, Ayrshire, Scotland
Marr.	24 Nov 1841 102812	Place	Leadhills, Lanarkshire, Scotland
Died	12 Sep 1884	Place	Glasgow, Lanarkshire, Scotland
Bur.		Place	

HUSBAND'S FATHER James MURDOCH   HUSBAND'S MOTHER Mary MURRAY

HUSBAND'S OTHER WIVES

WIFE Margaret MC CALL

Born	abt 1820	Place	Leadhills, Lanarkshire, Scotland
Chr.		Place	
Died	abt 1880	Place	Scotland
Bur.		Place	

WIFE'S FATHER   WIFE'S MOTHER

WIFE'S OTHER HUSBANDS

Husband	James MURDOCH
Wife	Margaret MC CALL
Ward	1.
Examiners	2.
Stake or Mission	

SEX M F	CHILDREN List each child (whether living or dead) in order of birth SURNAME Given Names	WHEN BORN DAY MONTH YEAR	WHERE BORN TOWN	COUNTY	STATE OR COUNTRY	DATE OF FIRST MARRIAGE TO WHOM	WHEN DIED DAY MONTH YEAR
1 M	James MURDOCH	102898 26 Jul 1841	Leadhills	Lanark	Sctl		
2 M	Alexander MURDOCH	30 May 1843	Gaswater	Ayr	Sctl		3 Sep 1861 224449
3 M	John MURDOCH	11 Feb 1846	Cumnock	Ayr	Sctl		
4 M	William MURDOCH	1 Jul 1848	Auchinleck	Ayr	Sctl		26 Aug 1854
5 M	Robert MURDOCH	15 May 1851	Auchinleck	Ayr	Sctl		28 Jun 1873 300395
6 M	Thomas MURDOCH	7 Nov 1853	Glasgow	Lanark	Sctl		25 Oct 1879 103422
7 M	William MURDOCH	256493 5 Apr 1856	Anderston, Glasgow	Lanark	Sctl		2 Nov 1899 026554
8 M	George MURDOCH	280584 30 Jan 1859	Hutchesontown,Glasgow	Lanark	Sctl		
9 M	Andrew MURDOCH	224133 25 Jan 1861	Hutchesontown,Glasgow	Lanark	Sctl		6 Oct 1862 292894
10							
11							

SOURCES OF INFORMATION

102812 Auchinleck Parish Register
102898 Crawford (Leadhills) Parish Register
256493
280584
224133

224449
300395
103422
026554
292894

HUSBAND (1) George CALDOW (limestone Miner)

Born	abt 1812	Place	Commondyke, Ayrshire, Scotland
Chr.	102853	Place	
Marr	15 Feb 1839 102812/	Place	Muirkirk, Ayrshire, Scotland
Died	pre-1855* 103510	Place	
Bur.		Place	

HUSBAND'S FATHER _____ HUSBAND'S MOTHER _____

HUSBAND'S OTHER WIVES

WIFE (1) Veronica MURDOCH

Born	16 Jun 1816	Place	Gaswater, Ayrshire, Scotland
Chr.	30 Jun 1816 102812	Place	Auchinleck, Ayrshire, Scotland
Died	4 Oct 1908 26030	Place	Heber City, Wasatch, Utah
Bur.		Place	Heber City, Wasatch, Utah

WIFE'S FATHER James MURDOCH   WIFE'S MOTHER Mary MURRAY

WIFE'S OTHER (2) 3 Jul 1879 Thomas GILES
HUSBANDS

		Husband	George CALDOW
		Wife	Veronica MURDOCH
		Ward	1
		Examiners:	2
		Stake or Mission	

CHILDREN

SEX M F	Given Names / SURNAME	WHEN BORN DAY MONTH YEAR	WHERE BORN TOWN	COUNTY	STATE OR COUNTRY	DATE OF FIRST MARRIAGE TO WHOM	WHEN DIED DAY MONTH YEAR
1 F	Mary CALDOW	102853 28 Jul 1839	Muirkirk	Ayr	Sctl	BAIRD	
2 M	George CALDOW	102853	Muirkirk	Ayr	Sctl		
3 M	James CALDOW	17 Jun 1841 304671 7 Jan 1844	Muirkirk	Ayr	Sctl		
4 M	John CALDOW	abt 1847**	Muirkirk	Ayr	Sctl		
5 M	Alexander CALDOW		Muirkirk	Ayr	Sctl		
6 M	William CALDOW	abt 1852*	Muirkirk	Ayr	Sctl		1 Aug 1855 103510
7 M	Thomas CALDOW		Muirkirk	Ayr	Sctl		
8 M	Joseph CALDOW		Muirkirk	Ayr	Sctl		
9 M	David CALDOW		Muirkirk	Ayr	Sctl		
10 M	Brigham CALDOW		Muirkirk	Ayr	Sctl		
11 M	Nephi CALDOW		Muirkirk	Ayr	Sctl		

SOURCES OF INFORMATION
102853 Muirkirk Parish Register
102812 Auchinleck Parish Register
26030 Heber City Records/LDS
304671 Muirkirk Free Church Register
103510 Scottish register of deaths, 1855, Ayrshire

* #6 death record shows his age as three years, and shows his father as deceased
** Scottish Census of 1851 shows #4 as 4 years of age

HUSBAND (2) Thomas GILES						Husband Thomas GILES

HUSBAND (2) Thomas GILES

Born 5 Oct 1804 — Place Lowdam, Nottinghamshire, England
Chr. — Place
Marr. 3 Jul 1879 — Place Salt Lake City, Salt Lake, Utah
Died 1 Jul 1887 — Place Heber City, Wasatch, Utah
Bur. — Place

HUSBAND'S FATHER   HUSBAND'S MOTHER Elizabeth GILES
HUSBAND'S OTHER WIVES (1) 30 May 1832 Maria Kirkham

WIFE (2) Veronica MURDOCH

Born 16 Jun 1816 — Place Gaswater, Ayrshire, Scotland
Chr. 30 Jun 1816 102812 — Place Auchinleck, Ayrshire, Scotland
Died 4 Oct 1908 026030 — Place Heber City, Wasatch, Utah
Bur. — Place Heber City, Wasatch, Utah

WIFE'S FATHER James MURDOCH   WIFE'S MOTHER Mary MURRAY
WIFE'S OTHER HUSBANDS (1) 15 Feb 1839 George CALDOW

Husband Thomas GILES
Wife Veronica MURDOCH
Ward 1.
Examiners: 2.
Stake or Mission

SEX M F	CHILDREN List each child (whether living or dead) in order of birth Given Names SURNAME	WHEN BORN DAY	MONTH	YEAR	WHERE BORN TOWN	COUNTY	STATE OR COUNTRY	DATE OF FIRST MARRIAGE TO WHOM	WHEN DIED DAY	MONTH	YEAR
1 M	Alexander Caldow GILES				Muirkirk	Ayr	Sctl				
2 M	William Caldow GILES			abt 1852*	Muirkirk	Ayr	Sctl		1 Aug	1855	103510
3 M	Thomas Caldow GILES				Muirkirk	Ayr	Sctl				
4 M	Joseph Caldow GILES				Muirkirk	Ayr	Sctl				
5 M	David Caldow GILES				Muirkirk	Ayr	Sctl				
6 M	Brigham Caldow GILES				Muirkirk	Ayr	Sctl				
7 M	Nephi Caldow GILES				Muirkirk	Ayr	Sctl				
8											
9											
10											
11											

* #2 death record shows his age as three years

SOURCES OF INFORMATION
102812 Auchinleck Parish Register
26030 Heber City Records/LDS
103510 Scottish register of deaths, 1855, Ayrshire

HUSBAND Allan MAIR

			Husband Allan MAIR	
			Wife Mary MURDOCH	
Born	23 Apr 1815	102849	Place	Killoch, Mauchline, Ayrshire, Scotland
Chr.	7 May 1815		Place	Mauchline, Ayrshire, Scotland
Marr.	4 Jun 1841	102812	Place	Cronberry, Ayrshire, Scotland
Died	2 May 1897	103431 1	Place	Lugar, Ayrshire, Scotland
Bur.			Place	Auchinleck Cemetery, Auchinleck, Ayrshire, Scotland

Ward _____
Examiners: 1. ___ 2. ___
Stake or Mission _____

HUSBAND'S FATHER John MAIR
HUSBAND'S MOTHER Mary FOULDS

WIFE (1) Mary MURDOCH

Born	3 Oct 1818	102856	Place	Gaswater, Ayrshire, Scotland
Chr.	8 Nov 1818	102856	Place	Old Cumnock, Ayrshire, Scotland
Died	5 Dec 1900	483507	Place	Heber City, Wasatch, Utah
Bur.			Place	Heber City, Wasatch, Utah

WIFE'S FATHER James MURDOCH
WIFE'S MOTHER Mary MURRAY
WIFE'S OTHER HUSBANDS (2) 1 Dec 1866 Thomas TODD (div); (3) 26 Jun 1871 Daniel MC MILLAN

SEX M/F	CHILDREN Given Names SURNAME	WHEN BORN DAY MONTH YEAR	WHERE BORN TOWN	COUNTY	STATE OR COUNTRY	DATE OF FIRST MARRIAGE TO WHOM	WHEN DIED DAY MONTH YEAR
1 M	John MAIR	102812 6 Sep 1841	Carbellow	Ayr	Sctl	1867 Catherine CONNOLY	27 May 1872
2 M	James MAIR	102812 17 Dec 1843	Carbellow	Ayr	Sctl	4 Oct 1868 Mary Ann PENGELLY	27 Apr 1915
3 M	Allan Fowls (Foulds) MAIR	102812 25 Dec 1845	Carbellow	Ayr	Sctl	10 Jun 1870 Jane RONALD 363160	14 Jun 1907
4 M	Matthew MAIR	102812 17 Jan 1848	Cartellow	Ayr	Sctl		child
5 M	William MAIR	102812 3 May 1850	Cartellow	Ayr	Sctl		child
6 F	Mary MAIR	102812 1 Aug 1852	Carbellow	Ayr	Sctl	15 Dec 1868 William LINDSAY	3 Jun 1916
7 F	Janet MAIR	256485 4 Nov 1854	Carbellow, Auchinleck	Ayr	Sctl	24 Jul 1879 Mary Ann THOMPSON	17 Mar 1855 103508
8 M	Andrew MAIR	17 Feb 1856	Carbellow, Auchinleck (Stables)	Ayr	Sctl	24 Jul 1879 Mary Ann THOMPSON	6 Jul 1924
9 M	Alexander MAIR	280572 18 Feb 1959	Gaswater, Auchinleck	Ayr	Sctl	15 Feb 1883 Eliza THOMPSON	11 Apr 1936
10							
11							

SOURCES OF INFORMATION

102849 Mauchline Parish Register
102812 Auchinleck Parish Register
103431
102856
483507
1 Picture of Tombstone of Alan Mair (found in this book)

103508
256485
280572
363160

#3 listed in birth entry as "Allan Fowls", but used "Allan Foulds" during life. "Foulds" is surname of paternal grandmother.

HUSBAND John "Murray" MURDOCH

Born	28 Dec 1820	Place	Gaswater, Ayrshire, Scotland
Chr.	21 Jan 1821	102812	Place Auchinleck, Ayrshire, Scotland
Marr.	25 Feb 1848	102322	Place Kirkconnell, Dumfriesshire, Scotland
Died	6 May 1910	026030	Place Heber City, Wasatch, Utah
Bur.	8 May 1910		Place Heber City, Wasatch, Utah

HUSBAND'S FATHER James MURDOCH HUSBAND'S MOTHER Mary MURRAY

HUSBAND'S OTHER WIVES (2) 9 Aug 1862 Isabella CRAWFORD

WIFE (1) Ann STEEL

Born	27 Oct 1829	102322	Place Kirkconnell, Dumfriesshire, Scotland
Chr.			Place
Died	15 Dec 1909	1	Place Heber City, Wasatch, Utah
Bur.	16 Dec 1909		Place Heber City, Wasatch, Utah

WIFE'S FATHER James STEEL WIFE'S MOTHER Elizabeth KERR

WIFE'S OTHER HUSBANDS

Husband	John Murray MURDOCH
Wife	Ann STEEL
Ward	
Examiners:	1. 2.
Stake or Mission	

SEX M F	CHILDREN List each child (whether living or dead) in order of birth Given Names SURNAME	WHEN BORN DAY MONTH YEAR	WHERE BORN TOWN	COUNTY	STATE OR COUNTRY	DATE OF FIRST MARRIAGE TO WHOM	WHEN DIED DAY MONTH YEAR
1 F	Elizabeth MURDOCH	21 Nov 1848	Kirkconnell	Dmfr	Sctl		4 Apr 1852
2 M	James MURDOCH	Jun 1850	Kirkconnell	Dmfr	Sctl		20 Mar 1852
3 F	Mary Murray MURDOCH	20 May 1852	near Kansas City	Wyndt	Kans	3 Oct 1868 (1) James DUKE	20 Dec 1917
4 F	Ann MURDOCH	14 Sep 1854	Salt Lake City	S. L.	Utah	5 Jun 1871 William M. GILES	2 Jan 1890
5 F	Janett Osborne MURDOCH	20 Dec 1856	Salt Lake City	S. L.	Utah	6 Dec 1875 Henry Lufkin MC MULLIN	12 Jun 1949
6 F	Sarah Jane MURDOCH	15 Jan 1859	Salt Lake City	S. L.	Utah	28 Nov 1878 (1) Thomas Heber RASBAND	16 Jan 1933
7 F	Jacobina Wells Osborne MURDOCH	7 Nov 1860	Heber City	Wstch	Utah	2 Dec 1880 William Jonathan CLEGG	18 Oct 1933
8 M	John Murray MURDOCH	4 Jan 1863	Heber City	Wstch	Utah		4 Feb 1863
9 F	Isabella Lovina MURDOCH (twin)	21 Apr 1864	Heber City	Wstch	Utah		17 Jun 1870
10 M	John William MURDOCH (twin)	21 Apr 1864	Heber City	Wstch	Utah		29 Aug 1864
11 M	Thomas Todd MURDOCH	4 Mar 1866	Heber City	Wstch	Utah	15 Jul 1915 Sarah Ingeborg HANSEN	21 Oct 1953

OTHER MARRIAGES
#3 md (2) 12 Jun 1906 William RYAN
#6 md (2) 6 Sep 1918 William LINDSAY

SOURCES OF INFORMATION
102812 Auchinleck Parish Register
102322 Kirkconnell Parish Register
26030 Heber City Records/LDS
Joseph A Murdoch records in possession of Elroy Murdoch,
RFD Santaquin (Genola), Utah
1 Obituary Heber City "Wasatch Wave"

HUSBAND John "Murray" MURDOCH

Born	28 Dec 1820	Place Gaswater, Ayrshire, Scotland
Chr.	21 Jan 1821 102812	Place Auchinleck, Ayrshire, Scotland
Marr.	25 Feb 1848 102322	Place Kirkconnell, Dumfriesshire, Scotland
Died	6 May 1910 26030	Place Heber City, Wasatch, Utah
Bur.	8 May 1910	Place Heber City, Wasatch, Utah

HUSBAND'S FATHER James MURDOCH HUSBAND'S MOTHER Mary MURRAY

HUSBAND'S OTHER WIVES (2) 9 Aug 1862 Isabella CRAWFORD

WIFE (1) Ann STEEL

Born	27 Oct 1829 102322	Place Kirkconnell, Dumfriesshire, Scotland
Chr.		Place
Died	15 Dec 1909	Place Heber City, Wasatch, Utah
Bur.	16 Dec 1909	Place Heber City, Wasatch, Utah

WIFE'S FATHER James STEEL WIFE'S MOTHER Elizabeth KERR

WIFE'S OTHER HUSBANDS

Husband John Murray MURDOCH
Wife Ann STEEL
Ward 1.
Examiners 2.
Stake or Mission

SEX	CHILDREN List each child (whether living or dead) in order of birth Given Names	SURNAME	WHEN BORN DAY MONTH YEAR	WHERE BORN TOWN	COUNTY	STATE OR COUNTRY	DATE OF FIRST MARRIAGE TO WHOM	WHEN DIED DAY MONTH YEAR
12 F	Lucy Veronica	MURDOCH	25 Nov 1867	Heber City	Wstch	Utah		6 Jan 1873
13 M	Joseph A	MURDOCH	11 Mar 1870	Heber City	Wstch	Utah	20 May 1891 Martha Ellen FORTIE	27 Aug 1943
14 M	David Steele	MURDOCH	31 May 1872	Heber City	Wstch	Utah	21 Oct 1891 Mary Emily VAN WAGENEN	1 Oct 1950
15 F	Millicent Sophia	MURDOCH	21 Aug 1874	Heber City	Wstch	Utah	9 Dec 1891 Edward Teancum MURDOCK	7 Feb 1916

OTHER MARRIAGES

SOURCES OF INFORMATION
102812 Auchinleck Parish Register
102322 Kirkconnell Parish Register
26030 Heber City Records/LDS
Joseph A Murdoch records in possession of Elroy Murdoch
RFD Santaquin (Genola), Utah

HUSBAND John "Murray" MURDOCH

Born	28 Dec 1820	Place	Gaswater, Ayrshire, Scotland
Chr.	21 Jan 1821	102812	Place Auchinleck, Ayrshire, Scotland
Marr.	9 Aug 1862	183395	Place Salt Lake City, Salt Lake, Utah
Died	6 May 1910	026030	Place Heber City, Wasatch, Utah
Bur.	8 May 1910		Place Heber City, Wasatch, Utah

HUSBAND'S FATHER James MURDOCH   HUSBAND'S MOTHER Mary MURRAY

HUSBAND'S OTHER WIVES (1) 25 Feb 1848 Ann STEEL

WIFE (2) Isabella CRAWFORD

Born	12 Apr 1836		Place Blantyre, Lanarkshire, Scotland
Chr.			Place
Died	10 Apr 1916	026028	Place Heber City, Wasatch, Utah
Bur.	12 Apr 1916		Place Heber City, Wasatch, Utah

WIFE'S FATHER Andrew CRAWFORD   WIFE'S MOTHER Margaret MC CLURE

WIFE'S OTHER HUSBANDS

Husband John Murray MURDOCH
Wife Isabella CRAWFORD
Ward 1.
Examiners: 2.
Stake or Mission

SEX M/F	CHILDREN List each child (whether living or dead) in order of birth Given Names SURNAME	WHEN BORN DAY	MONTH	YEAR	WHERE BORN TOWN	COUNTY	STATE OR COUNTRY	DATE OF FIRST MARRIAGE TO WHOM	WHEN DIED DAY MONTH	YEAR
1 F	Margaret Ann MURDOCH	19	May	1863	Heber City	Wstch	Utah	7 Nov 1889 Lewis Joshua HAWKES	11 Mar	1904
2 F	Catherine Campbell MURDOCH	15	Nov	1864	Heber City	Wstch	Utah	21 Jul 1886 David William HICKEN	6 Mar	1945
3 M	James Crawford MURDOCH	11	Feb	1869	Heber City	Wstch	Utah	27 Nov 1901 Sarah Elizabeth GILES	14 Aug	1959
4 M	Brigham MURDOCH	2	Nov	1870	Heber City	Wstch	Utah	16 Dec 1891 (1) Mary Blanche ALEXANDER	13 May	1947
5 M	Robert MURDOCH	12	Sep	1872	Heber City	Wstch	Utah	unmarried	3 Sep	1893
6 M	John Murray MURDOCH	1	May	1874	Heber City	Wstch	Utah	30 Jan 1904 (1) Minnie Maria MILLER	26 Apr	1928
7 F	Isabella Crawford MURDOCH	8	Jan	1876	Heber City	Wstch	Utah	23 Sep 1903 Hyrum Chase NICOL	1 Dec	1940
8										
9										
10										
11										

SOURCES OF INFORMATION

102812 Auchinleck Parish Register
26030, 26028 Heber City Records/LDS
102322 Kirkconnell Parish Register
183395

Murdoch family records in possession of Tressa M. Garrett, St. Anthony, Idaho

OTHER MARRIAGES

#4 md (2) 8 Apr 1903 Martha Louannie HAMMON
#6 md (2) 5 Jan 1921 Cora Leona (Loemma) VAIL Bigler

HUSBAND William MURDOCH

Born	3 Jul 1825	102812	Place	Gaswater, Ayrshire, Scotland
Chr.	21 Jul 1825	102812	Place	Auchinleck, Ayrshire, Scotland
Marr.	23 Jun 1846	102812	Place	Old Cumnock, Avrshire, Scotland
Died	12 Mar 1913	026988	Place	Heber City, Wasatch, Utah
Bur.	14 Mar 1913		Place	Heber City, Wasatch, Utah

HUSBAND'S FATHER James MURDOCH   HUSBAND'S MOTHER Mary MURRAY

HUSBAND'S OTHER WIVES (2) 29 Jun 1882 Christina GRAHAM (div) ; (3) 26 Nov 1887 Mary REID Lindsay

WIFE (1) Janet LENNOX

Born	24 Sep 1821	102857	Place	Moor, Old Cumnock, Ayrshire, Scotland
Chr.	21 Oct 1821	102857	Place	Old Cumnock, Ayrshire, Scotland
Died	20 Dec 1877	103421	1 Place	Kilmarnock, Ayrshire, Scotland
Bur.	Dec 1877	1	Place	Muirkirk, Ayrshire, Scotland

WIFE'S FATHER David LENNOX   WIFE'S MOTHER Elisabeth TEMPLETON

WIFE'S OTHER HUSBANDS

Husband William MURDOCH
Wife Janet LENNOX
Ward
Examiners: 1.
2.
Stake or Mission

SEX M F	CHILDREN List each child (whether living or dead) in order of birth Given Names	SURNAME	WHEN BORN DAY MONTH YEAR	WHERE BORN TOWN	COUNTY	STATE OR COUNTRY	DATE OF FIRST MARRIAGE TO WHOM	WHEN DIED DAY MONTH YEAR
1 F	Elizabeth	MURDOCH 103805	18 Apr 1847	Gaswater	Ayr	Sctl		24 Mar 1864 323681
2 M	James "D"	MURDOCH 103805	3 Jan 1850	Cronberry	Ayr	Sctl	1 Jan 1883 (1) Lizzie LINDSAY 3	2 Dec 1924
3 M	David Lennox	MURDOCH 103805	13 Jan 1852	Cronberry	Ayr	Sctl	18 Apr 1878 Elizabeth Pinkerton Thyne 4	24 Apr 1928
4 F	Mary	MURDOCH 103805	9 Sep 1854 103368	Gaswater	Ayr	Sctl		20 Sep 1854 2
5 F	Janet	MURDOCH 103805	18 Oct 1855 280513	Gaswater	Ayr	Sctl	5 Feb 1880 William BAIRD 183402	23 Sep 1898
6 F	Margaret	MURDOCH 103805	27 Aug 1858	Ponesk	Ayr	Sctl	16 Jan 1879 John ADAMSON 183402	29 Oct 1915
7								
8								
9								
10								
11								

OTHER MARRIAGES #2 md (2) 14 Nov 1898 Eliza Thackeray 5

SOURCES OF INFORMATION 183402
102812 Auchinleck Parish Register, 102357 Old Cumnock Parish Register
103421 Female Deaths Scotland 1377, 26988 Deseret News 13 Mar 1913
1 letter in posession of Janet O. Gill
2 David Lennox Murdoch's records (compiled 1903-1928), and tombstone
3,4,5, Marriage certificates in possession of Janet O. Gill
103805 1861 Census, Muirkirk, Scotland

HUSBAND (2) William MURDOCH

Born	3 Jul 1825	102812	Place Gaswater, Ayrshire, Scotland
Chr.	21 Jul 1825	102812	Place Auchinleck, Ayrshire, Scotland
Marr.	26 Nov 1887	1	Place Heber City, Wasatch, Utah
Died	12 Mar 1913	026988	Place Heber City, Wasatch, Utah
Bur.	14 Mar 1913		Place Heber City, Wasatch, Utah

HUSBAND'S FATHER James MURDOCH   HUSBAND'S MOTHER Mary MURRAY

HUSBAND'S OTHER WIVES (1) 23 Jun 1846 Janet LENNOX, (2) 29 Jun 1882 Christina GRAHAM (div)

WIFE (3) Mary REID

Born	23 Oct 1851		Place Glasgow, Lanarkshire, Scotland
Chr.			Place
Died	22 Jun 1929		Place Lorenzo, Jefferson, Idaho
Bur.	25 Jun 1929		Place Heber City, Wasatch, Utah

WIFE'S FATHER James REID   WIFE'S MOTHER Elizabeth Cummings

WIFE'S OTHER HUSBANDS (1) 31 Dec 1871 Samuel LINDSAY

SEX M-F	CHILDREN — List each child (whether living or dead) in order of birth. Given Names / SURNAME	WHEN BORN DAY MONTH YEAR	WHERE BORN TOWN	COUNTY	STATE OR COUNTRY	DATE OF FIRST MARRIAGE TO WHOM	WHEN DIED DAY MONTH YEAR
1 M	William Louis MURDOCH	4 Apr 1888 026029	Heber City	Wstch	Utah	1 Oct 1913 Elizabeth IVIE	6 Dec 1937 488402
2 F	Mary Murray MURDOCH	26 Feb 1891 026029	Heber City	Wstch	Utah		9 Nov 1918
3 F	Lizziebell MURDOCH	25 Jan 1894	Heber City	Wstch	Utah	26 Oct 1912 Hugh "J" DAVIS	488401
4							
5							
6							
7							
8							
9							
10							
11							

OTHER MARRIAGES

SOURCES OF INFORMATION

102812 Auchinleck Parish Register, 026029
1 marriage license
26988 Deseret News 13 Mar 1913
488401 Utah County marriage licenses
488402 Utah County marriage licenses

Husband William MURDOCH

Wife	Mary REID
Ward	1
Examiners	2
Stake or Mission	

PEDIGREE CHART

James MURDOCH
BORN abt 1786
WHERE Commondyke,Ayr,Sctl
WHEN MARRIED 10 Jan 1811
DIED 20 Oct 1831
WHERE Gaswater, Ayr, Sctl
Mary MURRAY
NAME OF HUSBAND OR WIFE

James MURDOCH
BORN abt 1752
WHERE Commondyke, Ayr, Sctl
WHEN MARRIED 8 Feb 1781
DIED abt 1846
WHERE

Robert MURDOCH
BORN 14 Mar 1712
WHERE Murdoch's town, Ayr
WHEN MARRIED 2 Jun 1737
DIED 9 Nov 1792
WHERE Commondyke, Ayr, Sctl

John MURDOCH
BORN abt 1676
WHERE of Auchinleck, Ayr
WHEN MARRIED
DIED
WHERE

BORN
WHERE
DIED
WHERE

Margaret WYLLIE
BORN 23 Dec 1716
WHERE Kilmarnock, Ayr, Sctl
WHEN MARRIED 27 Nov 1781
DIED
WHERE Commondyke, Ayr, Sctl

Andrew WYLLIE
BORN abt 1684
WHERE Kilmarnock, Ayr, Sctl
WHEN MARRIED 24 Dec 1701
DIED
WHERE

Jean MUCKLE
BORN abt 1688
WHERE Kilmarnock, Ayr, Sctl
DIED
WHERE Commondyke, Ayr, Sctl

Janet OSBORNE
BORN chr. 21 Apr 1756
WHERE Fogston,Ochiltree,Ayr
    Sctl
DIED
WHERE

James OSBORNE
BORN chr. 15 Mar 1730
WHERE Boxtown,Ochiltree,Ayr,
    Sctl
WHEN MARRIED
DIED
WHERE

Allan OSBORNE
BORN abt 1693
WHERE Ochiltree, Ayr, Sctl
WHEN MARRIED
DIED
WHERE

Robert OSBORNE
BORN chr. 22 May 1671
WHERE of Stair, Ayr, Sctl
WHEN MARRIED 29 Nov 1691
DIED
WHERE

Margaret OSBORNE
chr. 23 Jun 1672
of Ochiltree, Ayr

BORN
WHERE
WHEN MARRIED
DIED
WHERE

BORN
WHERE
WHEN MARRIED
DIED
WHERE

BORN
WHERE
WHEN MARRIED
DIED
WHERE

BORN
WHERE
DIED
WHERE

Lawrence OSBORNE
BORN abt 1645
WHERE of Ochiltree, Ayr,Sctl
WHEN MARRIED 16 Aug 1670
DIED
WHERE

Jean WATSON
BORN abt 1649
WHERE of Ochiltree, Ayr,Sctl
DIED
WHERE

HUSBAND James MURDOCH

Born	abt 1752	Place Commondyke, Ayrshire, Scotland
Chr.		Place
Marr.	8 Feb 1781 102812	Place Auchinleck, Ayrshire, Scotland
Died	1846	Place
Bur.		Place

HUSBAND'S FATHER Robert MURDOCH   HUSBAND'S MOTHER Margaret WYLLIE

HUSBAND'S OTHER WIVES (2) 18 Jun 1802 Veronica KIRKLAND

WIFE (1) Janet OSBORNE

Born		Place Fogston, Ochiltree, Ayrshire, Scotland
Chr.	21 Apr 1756 102855	Place Ochiltree, Ayrshire, Scotland
Died		Place
Bur.		Place

WIFE'S FATHER James OSBORNE   WIFE'S MOTHER

WIFE'S OTHER HUSBANDS

SEX M/F	CHILDREN Given Names SURNAME	WHEN BORN DAY	MONTH	YEAR	WHERE BORN TOWN	COUNTY	STATE OR COUNTRY	DATE OF FIRST MARRIAGE TO WHOM	WHEN DIED DAY	MONTH	YEAR
1 M	Robert MURDOCH			abt 1784	Commondyke	Ayr	Sctl	Agnes AITKEN			
2X M	James MURDOCH			abt 1786	Commondyke	Ayr	Sctl	10 Jan 1811 Mary MURRAY		20 Oct 1831	
3 M	William MURDOCH			abt 1788	Commondyke	Ayr	Sctl	unmarried		6 Jul 1815	
4 F	Margaret MURDOCH			abt 1790	Commondyke	Ayr	Sctl	Andrew MC TURK		31 May 1862	
5											
6											
7											
8											
9											
10											
11											

SOURCES OF INFORMATION

James Murdoch Family Organization Records
102812 Auchinleck Parish Register
102855 Ochiltree Parish Register
William Murdoch's Record Book (compiled 1878)

Husband James MURDOCH
Wife Janet OSBORNE
Ward
Examiners: 1.
2.
Stake or Mission

OTHER MARRIAGES

HUSBAND James MURDOCH

Born	abt 1752	Place Commondyke, Ayrshire, Scotland
Chr.		Place
Marr.	18 Jun 1802 102812	Place Auchinleck, Ayrshire, Scotland
Died	1846	Place
Bur.		Place

HUSBAND'S FATHER Robert MURDOCH   HUSBAND'S MOTHER Margaret WYLLIE

HUSBAND'S OTHER WIVES (1) 8 Feb 1781 Janet OSBORNE

WIFE (2) Veronica KIRKLAND

Born		Place
Chr.		Place
Died		Place
Bur.		Place

WIFE'S FATHER   WIFE'S MOTHER

WIFE'S OTHER HUSBANDS

Husband James MURDOCH
Wife Veronica Kirkland

Ward
Examiners: 1.
2.
Stake or Mission

SEX M F	CHILDREN List each child (whether living or dead) in order of birth Given Names SURNAME	WHEN BORN DAY MONTH YEAR	WHERE BORN TOWN COUNTY STATE OR COUNTRY	DATE OF FIRST MARRIAGE TO WHOM	WHEN DIED DAY MONTH YEAR
1 F	Mary MURDOCH	1807		John LIDDELL 1	28 Nov 1869 1
2 F	Janet MURDOCH	abt 1809		John KERR 2	
3					
4					
5					
6					
7					
8					
9					
10					
11					

OTHER MARRIAGES

SOURCES OF INFORMATION
1 **William Murdoch's record book** (compiled 1878)
2 **David Lennox Murdoch's** Family and Temple Record Book (compiled 1878)
102812 Auchinleck Parish Register

HUSBAND	Robert MURDOCH			Husband Robert MURDOCH	
Born	14 Mar 1712	102812	Place Murdoch's town, Ayrshire, Scotland	Wife Margaret WYLLIE	
Chr.			Place	Ward	1.
Mar	2 Jun 1737	102812	Place Auchinleck, Ayrshire, Scotland	Examiners:	2.
Died	9 Nov 1792 1 3		Place Commondyke, Ayrshire, Scotland	Stake or Mission	
Bur.	12 Nov 1792 1 3		Place Auchinleck Parish Cemetery		

HUSBAND'S FATHER John MURDOCH   HUSBAND'S MOTHER _____

HUSBAND'S OTHER WIVES _____

WIFE	Margaret WYLLIE		
Born	23 Dec 1716	102837	Place Kilmarnock, Ayrshire, Scotland
Chr.			Place
Died	27 Nov 1781	102812	Place Commondyke, Ayrshire, Scotland
Bur.	Nov 1781		Place Auchinleck Parish Cemetery

WIFE'S FATHER Andrew WYLLIE   WIFE'S MOTHER Jean MUCKLE

WIFE'S OTHER HUSBANDS _____

SEX M F	CHILDREN List each child (whether living or dead) in order of birth. Given Names	SURNAME		WHEN BORN DAY MONTH YEAR	WHERE BORN TOWN	COUNTY	STATE OR COUNTRY	DATE OF FIRST MARRIAGE TO WHOM	WHEN DIED DAY MONTH YEAR
1 F	Janet MURDOCH		chr	22 Apr 1738 102812	Commondyke	Ayr	Sctl		
2 F	Jane MURDOCH		chr	26 Nov 1744 102812	Commondyke	Ayr	Sctl	William HOWAT	
3 F	Ann MURDOCH			abt 1746	Commondyke	Ayr	Sctl	John LOGAN	
4 M	John MURDOCH			abt 1748	Commondyke	Ayr	Sctl	(1) Isabella SHARP	
5 M	Robert MURDOCH			abt 1750	Commondyke	Ayr	Sctl	Grizzle BRAIDFOOT 8 Feb 1781	
6 X M	James MURDOCH			abt 1752	Commondyke	Ayr	Sctl	(1) Janet OSBORNE 102812	
7									
8									
9									
10									
11	Euphemia, born 2 Nov 1757 to another Robert Murdoch and his wife, Jane Brekenridge, is no longer listed as a child of Robert Murdoch and Margaret Wyllie.(3) 102812								

OTHER MARRIAGES   #6 md (2) 18 Jun 1802 Veronica KIRKLAND

SOURCES OF INFORMATION
102812 Auchinleck Parish Register
102837 Kilmarnock Parish Register
1   letter in posession of Janet O. Gill tells of death, funeral, and burial
2   William Murdoch's record book (compiled 1878)
3   David Lennox Murdoch's Family and Temple Record Book (compiled 1903-1928)

| HUSBAND | John MURDOCH | | | | (page 1 of 2) | Husband | John MURDOCH |

HUSBAND John MURDOCH

Born	abt 1676	Place of Auchinleck, Ayrshire, Scotland
Chr.		Place
Marr.		Place
Died		Place
Bur.		Place

HUSBAND'S FATHER _____ HUSBAND'S MOTHER _____
HUSBAND'S OTHER WIVES

WIFE Mrs. John MURDOCH

Born	abt 1678	Place of Auchinleck, Ayrshire, Scotland
Chr.		Place
Died		Place
Bur.		Place

WIFE'S FATHER _____ WIFE'S MOTHER _____
WIFE'S OTHER HUSBANDS

SEX M/F	CHILDREN List each child (whether living or dead) in order of birth Given Names SURNAME	WHEN BORN DAY MONTH YEAR	WHERE BORN TOWN	COUNTY	STATE OR COUNTRY	DATE OF FIRST MARRIAGE TO WHOM	WHEN DIED DAY MONTH YEAR
1		102812 2 Dec 1694					
2		102812 6 Jan 1695					
3 F	Ana MURDOCH	102812 30 Jun 1695					
4 F	Janet MURDOCH	102812 1 Dec 1696	Ra, Auchinleck	Ayr	Sctl		
5 F	Agnes MURDOCH	102812 19 Dec 1697	Webster, Auchinleck	Ayr	Sctl		
6		102812 24 Apr 1698	Auchinleck Mill	Ayr	Sctl		
7 M	John MURDOCH	102812 7 Jan 1700	Tompland, Auchinleck	Ayr	Sctl		
8 F	Isbell MURDOCH	102812 25 May 1701	Mill, Auchinleck	Ayr	Sctl		
9 F	Marion MURDOCH chr	102812 4 Nov 1701	Creckstown, Auchinleck	Ayr	Sctl		
10 M	John MURDOCH chr	102812 22 Nov 1702	Ra, Auchinleck	Ayr	Sctl		
11 M	Hugh MURDOCH chr	102812 18 Mar 1705	Ra, Auchinleck	Ayr	Sctl		

OTHER MARRIAGES

SOURCES OF INFORMATION

James Murdoch Family Organization Records
102812 Auchinleck Parish Register
1 Letter in posession of Janet O. Gill tells of death, funeral, and burial.
2 David Lennox Murdoch's Family and Temple Record Book
   (compiled 1903-1928)

Husband John MURDOCH
Wife Mrs. John MURDOCH

Ward
Examiners 1. ___ 2. ___
Stake or Mission

HUSBAND John MURDOCH

Born	abt 1676	Place of Auchinleck, Ayrshire, Scotland
Chr.		Place
Marr.		Place
Died		Place
Bur.		Place

HUSBAND'S FATHER _____ HUSBAND'S MOTHER _____

HUSBAND'S OTHER WIVES

WIFE Mrs. John MURDOCH

Born	abt 1678	Place of Auchinleck, Ayrshire, Scotland
Chr.		Place
Died		Place
Bur.		Place

WIFE'S FATHER _____ WIFE'S MOTHER _____

WIFE'S OTHER HUSBANDS

Husband	John MURDOCH
Wife	Mrs. John MURDOCH
Ward	Examiners 1. 2.
Stake or Mission	

SEX M/F	CHILDREN — List each child (whether living or dead) in order of birth — Given Names — SURNAME		WHEN BORN DAY MONTH YEAR	WHERE BORN TOWN	COUNTY	STATE OR COUNTRY	DATE OF FIRST MARRIAGE — TO WHOM	WHEN DIED DAY MONTH YEAR
1	F	Elizabeth MURDOCH	chr	102812 8 Feb 1708	Auchinleck/ Ballancholm	Ayr	Sctl		
2 X	M	Robert MURDOCH	chr	102812 14 Mar 1712	Auchinleck/ Murdoch'stown	Ayr	Sctl	2 Jun 1737 Margaret WYLLIE	9 Nov 1792 1, 2 102812
3	F	Mary MURDOCH	chr	102812 6 Apr 1712	Auchinleck/ Ballancholm	Ayr	Sctl		
4									
5									
6									
7									
8									
9									
10									
11	At least two John Murdochs were having children in the Auchinleck area at the same time. Since it is not known which children belong to each John Murdoch, all of the children are listed here.			OTHER MARRIAGES				

SOURCES OF INFORMATION

James Murdoch Family Organization Records
102812 Auchinleck Parish Register
1 Letter in posession of Janet O. Gill tells of death, funeral, and burial.
2 David Lennox Murdoch's Family and Temple Record Book

Husband	James OSBORNE	
Wife	Mrs. James OSBORNE	
Ward		1.
Examiners:		2.
Stake or Mission		

Husband James OSBORNE

Born abt 1728   Place Boxtown, Ochiltree, Ayrshire, Scotland
Chr. 15 Mar 1730   102855   Place Ochiltree, Ayrshire, Scotland
Mar.   Place
Died   Place
Bur.   Place

HUSBAND'S FATHER   Allan OSBORNE   HUSBAND'S MOTHER

HUSBAND'S OTHER WIVES

WIFE   Mrs. James OSBORNE

Born abt 1732   Place of Ochiltree, Ayrshire, Scotland
Chr.   Place
Died   Place
Bur.   Place

WIFE'S FATHER   WIFE'S MOTHER

WIFE'S OTHER HUSBANDS

SEX M/F	CHILDREN List each child (whether living or dead) in order of birth. Given Names SURNAME		WHEN BORN DAY MONTH YEAR	WHERE BORN TOWN	COUNTY	STATE OR COUNTRY	DATE OF FIRST MARRIAGE TO WHOM	WHEN DIED DAY MONTH YEAR
1 M	Allan OSBORNE	chr	8 Dec 1754 102855	Fogston, Ochiltree	Ayr	Sctl		
2 X F	Janet OSBORNE	chr	21 Apr 1756 102855	Fogston, Ochiltree	Ayr	Sctl	8 Feb 1781 James MURDOCH 102812	
3 M	William OSBORNE	chr	25 Feb 1759 102855	Tarbeg, Ochiltree	Ayr	Sctl		
4 M	Robert OSBORNE	chr	22 Feb 1761 102855	Tarbeg, Ochiltree	Ayr	Sctl		
5 F	Elizabeth OSBORNE	chr	15 May 1763 102855	Tarbeg, Ochiltree	Ayr	Sctl		
6 F	Jean OSBORNE	chr	28 Aug 1765 102855	Tarbeg, Ochiltree	Ayr	Sctl		
7 M	James OSBORNE	chr	17 Apr 1768 102855	Tarbeg, Ochiltree	Ayr	Sctl		
8 M	John OSBORNE	chr	5 Aug 1770	Tarbeg, Ochiltree	Ayr	Sctl		
9								
10								
11								

OTHER MARRIAGES

SOURCES OF INFORMATION
102855 Ochiltree Parish Register
102812 Auchinleck Parish Register

HUSBAND   Allan OSBORNE (weaver)

Born	abt 1693	Place	of Ochiltree, Ayrshire, Scotland
Chr.		Place	
Marr.		Place	
Died		Place	
Bur.		Place	

HUSBAND'S FATHER   Robert OSBORNE   HUSBAND'S MOTHER   Margaret OSBORNE

HUSBAND'S OTHER WIVES

WIFE   Mrs. Allan OSBORNE

Born	abt 1697	Place	of Ochiltree, Ayrshire, Scotland
Chr.		Place	
Died		Place	
Bur.		Place	

WIFE'S FATHER   WIFE'S MOTHER

WIFE'S OTHER HUSBANDS

SEX M/F	CHILDREN List each child (whether living or dead) in order of birth Given Names SURNAME		WHEN BORN DAY MONTH YEAR	WHERE BORN TOWN	COUNTY	STATE OR COUNTRY	DATE OF FIRST MARRIAGE TO WHOM	WHEN DIED DAY MONTH YEAR
1 F	Jean OSBORNE	chr	102855 3 May 1719	Ochiltree	Ayr	Sctl		
2 F	Helen OSBORNE	chr	102855 14 May 1721	Boxtown, Ochiltree	Ayr	Sctl		
3 M	William OSBORNE	chr	102855 24 Apr 1726	Boogstown, Ochiltree	Ayr	Sctl		
4 X M	James OSBORNE	chr	102855 15 Mar 1730	Boxtown, Ochiltree	Ayr	Sctl		
5								
6								
7								
8								
9								
10								
11								

Husband Allan OSBORNE
Wife   Mrs. Allan OSBORNE

Ward
Examiners: 1.
            2.
Stake or
Mission

OTHER MARRIAGES

SOURCES OF INFORMATION
102855 Ochiltree Parish Register

HUSBAND Robert OSBORNE

Born	22 May 1671	102855	Place of Stair, Ayrshire, Scotland
Chr.			Place Ochiltree, Ayrshire, Scotland
Marr.	29 Nov 1691	102855	Place Ochiltree, Ayrshire, Scotland
Died			Place
Bur.			Place

HUSBAND'S FATHER Lawrence OSBORNE   HUSBAND'S MOTHER Jean WATSON

HUSBAND'S OTHER WIVES

WIFE Margaret OSBORNE

Born	23 Jun 1672	102855	Place of Ochiltree, Ayrshire, Scotland
Chr.			Place Ochiltree, Ayrshire, Scotland
Died			Place
Bur.			Place

WIFE'S FATHER   WIFE'S MOTHER

WIFE'S OTHER HUSBANDS

	CHILDREN		WHEN BORN			WHERE BORN			DATE OF FIRST MARRIAGE	WHEN DIED	
SEX M F	List each child (whether living or dead) in order of birth Given Names SURNAME		DAY	MONTH	YEAR	TOWN	COUNTY	STATE OR COUNTRY	TO WHOM	DAY MONTH	YEAR
1 X M	Allan OSBORNE				abt 1693	of Ochiltree	Ayr	Sctl			
2 M	Robert OSBORNE	chr	23 Jun	1695	102855	Ochiltree	Ayr	Sctl			
3 F	Janet OSBORNE	chr	1 May	1698	102855	Chalmerston	Ayr	Sctl			
4											
5											
6											
7											
8											
9											
10											
11											

OTHER MARRIAGES

Husband Robert OSBORNE
Wife Margaret OSBORNE
Ward 1
Examiners 2
Stake or Mission

SOURCES OF INFORMATION

102855 Ochiltree Parish Register

HUSBAND Lawrence OSBORNE

Born	abt 1645	Place of Ochiltree, Ayrshire, Scotland
Chr.		Place
Marr.	16 Aug 1670 102855	Place Ochiltree, Ayrshire, Scotland
Died		Place
Bur.		Place

HUSBAND'S FATHER _____ HUSBAND'S MOTHER _____
HUSBAND'S OTHER WIVES

WIFE Jean WATSON

Born	abt 1649	Place of Ochiltree, Ayrshire, Scotland
Chr.		Place
Died		Place
Bur.		Place

WIFE'S FATHER _____ WIFE'S MOTHER _____
WIFE'S OTHER HUSBANDS

SEX M F	CHILDREN List each child (whether living or dead) in order of birth Given Names	SURNAME		WHEN BORN DAY MONTH YEAR	WHERE BORN TOWN	COUNTY	STATE OR COUNTRY	DATE OF FIRST MARRIAGE TO WHOM	WHEN DIED DAY MONTH YEAR
1 X M	Robert OSBORNE		chr	102855 22 May 1671	Ochiltree	Ayr	Sctl	29 Nov 1691 Margaret OSBORNE 102855	
2 M	James OSBORNE		chr	102855 7 Oct 1677	Ochiltree	Ayr	Sctl		
3 F	Janet OSBORNE		chr	102855 4 Jul 1680	Ochiltree	Ayr	Sctl		
4 M	Alexander OSBORNE		chr	102855 18 Feb 1683	Ochiltree	Ayr	Sctl		
5									
6									
7									
8									
9									
10									
11									

OTHER MARRIAGES

SOURCES OF INFORMATION
102855 Ochiltree Parish Register

Husband Lawrence OSBORNE

Wife	Jean WATSON
Ward	1.
Examiners:	2.
Stake or Mission	

Husband **Andrew WYLLIE**
Wife **Jean MUCKLE**
Ward 1.
Examiners 2
Stake or Mission

Born	abt 1684	Place of Kilmarnock, Ayrshire, Scotland
Chr.		Place
Marr.	24 Dec 1701 102838	Place Kilmarnock, Ayrshire, Scotland
Died		Place
Bur.		Place

HUSBAND'S FATHER
HUSBAND'S MOTHER
HUSBAND'S OTHER WIVES

WIFE   Jean MUCKLE

Born	abt 1688	Place of Kilmarnock, Ayrshire, Scotland
Chr.		Place
Died		Place
Bur.		Place

WIFE'S FATHER
WIFE'S MOTHER
WIFE'S OTHER HUSBANDS

SEX M/F	CHILDREN — List each child (whether living or dead) in order of birth — Given Names — SURNAME	WHEN BORN DAY MONTH YEAR	WHERE BORN TOWN	COUNTY	STATE OR COUNTRY	DATE OF FIRST MARRIAGE — TO WHOM	WHEN DIED DAY MONTH YEAR
1 F	Jean WYLLIE	102837 / 31 May 1703	Kilmarnock	Ayr	Sctl		
2 F	Janet WYLLIE	102837 / 6 Jun 1705	Kilmarnock	Ayr	Sctl		
3 F	Agnes WYLLIE	102837 / 6 Feb 1707	Kilmarnock	Ayr	Sctl		
4 F	Mary WYLLIE	102837 / 4 Oct 1708	Kilmarnock	Ayr	Sctl		
5 M	Andrew WYLLIE	102837 / 27 Aug 1710	Kilmarnock	Ayr	Sctl		
6 F	Janet WYLLIE	102837 / 14 Nov 1714	Kilmarnock	Ayr	Sctl		
7							
8 X F	Margaret WYLLIE	102837 / 23 Dec 1716	Kilmarnock	Ayr	Scot	2 Jun 1737 — Robert MURDOCH	27 Nov 1781 102812
9 M	William WYLLIE	102837 / 29 Jul 1719	Kilmarnock	Ayr	Sctl		102812
10							
11						OTHER MARRIAGES	

SOURCES OF INFORMATION
Kilmarnock Parish Register   102837, 102838
Auchinleck Parish Register   102812

PEDIGREE CHART

William MURRAY
BORN abt 1722
WHERE of Kirkconnell, Dmfrs, Sctl
WHEN MARRIED
DIED
WHERE

BORN
WHERE
WHEN MARRIED
DIED
WHERE

BORN
WHERE
DIED
WHERE

Mrs. Grizzel MURRAY
BORN abt 1726
WHERE of Kirkconnell, Dmfrs, Sctl
DIED
WHERE

BORN
WHERE
WHEN MARRIED
DIED
WHERE

BORN
WHERE
DIED
WHERE

Thomas MC CALL
BORN abt 1727
WHERE of Cloughfoot, Kirkcon- nell, Dmfrs, Sctl
WHEN MARRIED
DIED
WHERE

BORN
WHERE
WHEN MARRIED
DIED
WHERE

BORN
WHERE
DIED
WHERE

Mrs. Jane MC CALL
BORN abt 1731
WHERE of Cloughfoot, Kirkcon- nell, Dmfrs, Sctl
DIED
WHERE

BORN
WHERE
WHEN MARRIED
DIED
WHERE

BORN
WHERE
DIED
WHERE

John MURRAY
BORN abt 1755
WHERE Ayrshire, Scotland
WHEN MARRIED 8 Jan 1779
DIED 21 Jul 1812
WHERE Scotland

Margaret MC CALL
BORN abt 1759
WHERE of Dmfrs, Sctl
DIED 13 Nov 1821
WHERE Scotland

Mary MURRAY
BORN 13 Oct 1782
WHERE Glencairn, Dmfrs,
WHEN MARRIED 10 Jan 1811
DIED 3 Oct 1856
WHERE Chimney Rock, Sctsb, Nbrsk
James MURDOCH

NAME OF HUSBAND OR WIFE

(page 1 of 2)

HUSBAND	John MURRAY		
Born	abt 1755	Place	Ayrshire, Scotland
Chr.		Place	
Mar	8 Jan 1779	Place	Scotland
Died	21 Jul 1812 170385	Place	Scotland
Bur.		Place	

HUSBAND'S FATHER William MURRAY   HUSBAND'S MOTHER Grizzel

HUSBAND'S OTHER WIVES

WIFE	Margaret MC CALL		
Born	abt 1759	Place	Dumfriesshire, Scotland
Chr.		Place	
Died	13 Nov 1821 170385	Place	Scotland
Bur.		Place	

WIFE'S FATHER Thomas MC CALL   WIFE'S MOTHER Jane

WIFE'S OTHER HUSBANDS

Husband	John MURRAY
Wife	Margaret MC CALL
Ward	Examiners: 1.
Stake or Mission	2.

SEX M/F	CHILDREN List each child (whether living or dead) in order of birth. Given Names SURNAME	WHEN BORN DAY MONTH YEAR	WHERE BORN TOWN	COUNTY	STATE OR COUNTRY	DATE OF FIRST MARRIAGE TO WHOM	WHEN DIED DAY MONTH YEAR
1 M	Thomas MURRAY	14 Feb 1780	Glencairn	Dmfrs	Sctl		
2 M	John MURRAY	14 Feb 1780	Glencairn	Dmfrs	Sctl		
3X F	Mary MURRAY	13 Oct 1782	Glencairn	Dmfrs	Sctl	10 Jan 1811 James MURDOCH	3 Oct 1856 1
4 M	William MURRAY	16 Jun 1784	Dumfries	Dmfrs	Sctl		6 Sep 1804
5 M	Adam Goldie MURRAY	15 Mar 1786	Wanlockhead	Dmfrs	Sctl	28 Feb 1812 Janet KEIR	
6 M	John MURRAY	11 Jul 1788	Sanquhar	Dmfrs	Sctl		
7 F	Grizzel MURRAY	25 Jul 1790	Muirkirk	Ayr	Sctl	30 Jul 1819 James THOMPSON	
8 M	Campbell MURRAY	20 Jul 1792	Muirkirk	Ayr	Sctl	12 Feb 1815 Margaret KYLE	15 May 1848 170385
9 M	Hugh MURRAY	1 May 1794	Muirkirk	Ayr	Sctl		19 Dec 1811
10 M	George MURRAY	28 Apr 1796	Wilsontown	Lanark	Sctl		19 Jul 1807
11 F	Jane MURRAY	5 Jan 1798	Wilsontown	Lanark	Sctl	Robert CHAPMAN	5 Mar 1856 170385

OTHER MARRIAGES

SOURCES OF INFORMATION

James Murdoch Family Organization Records   13 Oct 1907

170385

1 Martin Handcart Company Record of J. G. Bleak, Salt Lake Herald.

David Lennox Murdoch's Family and Temple Record Book
(compiled 1903-1928)

HUSBAND	John MURRAY		
Born	abt 1755	Place	Ayrshire, Scotland
Chr.		Place	
Mar	8 Jan 1779	Place	Scotland
Died	21 Jul 1812	Place	Scotland
Bur.		Place	

HUSBAND'S FATHER William MURRAY   HUSBAND'S MOTHER Grizzel

HUSBAND'S OTHER WIVES

WIFE	Margaret MC CALL		
Born	abt 1759	Place	Dumfriesshire, Scotland
Chr.		Place	
Died	13 Nov 1821	Place	Scotland
Bur.		Place	

WIFE'S FATHER Thomas MC CALL   WIFE'S MOTHER Jane

WIFE'S OTHER HUSBANDS

Husband	John MURRAY
Wife	Margaret MC CALL
Ward	1.
Examiners:	2.
Stake or Mission	

SEX M F	CHILDREN List each child (whether living or dead) in order of birth. Given Names SURNAME	WHEN BORN DAY MONTH YEAR	WHERE BORN TOWN	COUNTY	STATE OR COUNTRY	DATE OF FIRST MARRIAGE TO WHOM	WHEN DIED DAY MONTH YEAR
F 12	Margaret MURRAY	28 May 1800	Wilsontown	Lanark	Sctl		
M 13	Thomas MURRAY	abt 1802	Wilsontown	Lanark	Sctl	Janet FERGUSON	23 May 1829 170385
M 14	William MURRAY	28 Jul 1805	Muirkirk	Ayr	Sctl		

OTHER MARRIAGES

SOURCES OF INFORMATION

James Murdoch Family Organization Records
170385

Husband   William MURRAY

Born   abt 1722   Place   of Kirkconnel, Dumfriesshire. Scotland
Chr.   Place
Mar.   Place
Died   Place
Bur.   Place

HUSBAND'S FATHER   HUSBAND'S
HUSBAND'S   MOTHER
OTHER WIVES

WIFE   Mrs. Grizzel MURRAY

Born   abt 1726   Place   of Kirkconnel, Dumfriesshire, Scotland
Chr.   Place
Died   Place
Bur.   Place

WIFE'S FATHER   WIFE'S
WIFE'S OTHER   MOTHER
HUSBANDS

SEX M F	CHILDREN List each child (whether living or dead) in order of birth. SURNAME Given Names	WHEN BORN			WHERE BORN			DATE OF FIRST MARRIAGE TO WHOM	WHEN DIED		
		DAY	MONTH	YEAR	TOWN	COUNTY	STATE OR COUNTRY		DAY	MONTH	YEAR
1X M	John MURRAY			abt 1755	of Kirkconnel	Dmfrs	Sctl	8 Jan 1779 Margaret MC CALL		21 Jul 1812	
2											
3											
4											
5											
6											
7											
8											
9											
10											
11											

SOURCES OF INFORMATION
family record of emigrant ancestor

Wife   Mrs. Grizzel   MURRAY

Ward   1.
Examiners: 2.

Stake or
Mission

OTHER MARRIAGES

HUSBAND	Thomas MC CALL		Husband	Thomas MC CALL

HUSBAND Thomas MC CALL

Born abt 1727   Place of Cloughfoot, Kirkconnel, Dumfriesshire, Scotland

Chr.   Place

Mar   Place

Died   Place

Bur.   Place

HUSBAND'S FATHER   HUSBAND'S MOTHER

HUSBAND'S OTHER WIVES

WIFE Mrs. Jane MC CALL

Born abt 1731   Place of Cloughfoot, Kirkconnel, Dumfriesshire, Scotland

Chr.   Place

Died   Place

Bur.   Place

WIFE'S FATHER   WIFE'S MOTHER

WIFE'S OTHER HUSBANDS

Husband	Thomas MC CALL
Wife	Mrs. Jane MC CALL
Ward	Examiners: 1.
	2.
Stake or Mission	

SEX M/F	CHILDREN List each child (whether living or dead) in order of birth. Given Names SURNAME	WHEN BORN DAY MONTH YEAR	WHERE BORN TOWN	COUNTY	STATE OR COUNTRY	DATE OF FIRST MARRIAGE TO WHOM	WHEN DIED DAY MONTH YEAR
1 M	Robert MC CALL	102322 16 Sep 1753	Cloughfoot, Kirkconnel	Dmfrs	Sctl		
2 X F	Margaret MC CALL	abt 1759*	of Cloughfoot, Kirkconnel	Dmfrs	Sctl	8 Jan 1779 John MURRAY	13 Nov 1821
3							
4							
5							
6							
7							
8							
9							
10							
11							

SOURCES OF INFORMATION

102322 Kirkconnel Parish Register

David Lennox Murdoch's Record Book

*102322 Unnamed daughter born Jan 1755, may be Margaret (#2)

Bibliography

A History of the James Murdoch and Mary Murray Murdoch Family and Their Children Who Came to America, Compiled by R. Phillip Rasmussen from histories read at reunions in 1952, 1955, 1956, 1958.

Wasatch County Daughters of Utah Pioneers, *How Beautiful Upon the Mountains,* Compiled and Edited by Wm. James Mortimer, 1963, Dessert News Press.

David Lennox Murdoch, *Missionary Journal to Scotland 1905–1906, Journal of Voyage to America 1978, Writings on James Murdoch Family, Book of Genealogy of John Murray Murdoch* (copied by David L. Murdoch).

William Murdoch, *Genealogical Data,* handwritten in 1878.

Joseph A. Murdoch, *Microfilm 247,886,* Genealogical Library, Church of Jesus Christ of Latter Day Saints, Salt Lake City, Utah. 1944.

Maybell Moulton, *Microfilm 000,156,* Genealogical Library, Church of Jesus Christ of Latter Day Saints, Salt Lake City, Utah. 1963.

James Murdoch Family Records, Compiled by Joseph A Murdoch, Ruby Murdoch Hooper, and Oscar Hunter in the possession of Oscar Hunter and Janet Gill.

James Murdoch Family Computer Printout, Compiled by Mark Cram, and Oscar Hunter, 1977–1981.

Editors Note: Credit for the histories written in this book are in most cases where known given at the end of the individual histories. Many, many people have contributed to this book whom we have not given credit. To them we also say thanks for helping make this marvelous history available for the descendants of James and Mary Murray Murdoch.

CPSIA information can be obtained
at www.ICGtesting.com
Printed in the USA
BVHW011620290520
580482BV00010B/304